Reviewers

author and publisher wish to thank the following industry and teaching professionals for their valuable
[in]put into the development of *Child and Youth Development*.

[A]guna Anasuri
[Ass]ociate Professor/Tenured Faculty
[Ala]bama A&M University
[No]rmal, Alabama

[Te]ri Anders
[Ear]ly Childhood Education Instructor
[Eas]t Central Community College
[De]catur, Mississippi

[K]ari Andrews-Stiglich
[E]CED instructor
[Ivy] Tech Community College
[Ga]ry, Indiana

[Ro]xanne Atterholt
[As]sistant Teaching Professor
[Pen]nsylvania State University—Shenango
[Sh]aron, Pennsylvania

[D]erek Bardell
[Pr]ofessor
[De]lgado Community College
[Ne]w Orleans, Louisiana

[Gl]en Breeding
[A]djunct Professor
[Pa]lomar College
[Sa]n Marcos, California

[T]eresa Bridger
[Fu]ll Professor
[Pr]ince George's Community College
[L]argo, Maryland

[M]arianne Brown
[C]entral New Mexico Community College
[A]lbuquerque, New Mexico

Shannon Burghart
Associate Professor
Guilford Technical Community College
Jamestown, North Carolina

Andrea Bush
Talent Connection Manager/Adjunct
    Instructor
Ivy Tech Community College
Sellersburg, Indiana

Sulema Caballero
Professor
Coastalbend College
Beeville, Texas

Toni Cacace-Beshears
Adjunct Professor
Tidewater Community College
Portsmouth, Virginia

Linda M. Carlson
Instructor
Aims Community College
Greeley, Colorado

Thomas Chiaromonte
Professor, Child Development & Educational
    Studies
Fullerton College
Fullerton, California

Dawn Cross
Associate Professor, Early Childhood program
    Coordinator
Florida Gateway College
Lake City, Florida

Child and Youth Development

Sharleen L. Kato, EdD, CFCS-HDFS
Emerita Professor of Family and Consumer Sciences
Seattle Pacific University
Seattle, Washington

Publisher
The Goodheart-Willcox Company, Inc.
Tinley Park, IL
www.g-w.com

Library of Congress Control Number: 2022944378

ISBN 978-1-63776-728-3

1 2 3 4 5 6 7 8 9 – 24 – 26 25 24 23 22

Preface

Child and Youth Development is designed to help students understand human growth and development from birth to emerging adulthood. As you consider a career in early childhood care or education, this text informs you about the developing child—how they change physically, intellectually, and socio-emotionally as they grow and mature. Understanding these dramatic changes in growth and development are key factors in learning how to support and guide children into thriving adulthood. In *Child and Youth Development*, Unit 1 lays the groundwork through domains of development, foundational theories, genetics, and pregnancy and birth. Units 2 through 5 progress through the childhood ages and stages, from the developing brain and nervous system of the neonate to the growing independence of the emerging adult by age 18.

Child and Youth Development explores issues and trends in child development, encompassing family and work-related issues such as parenting, teen employment, balancing work and family, and family and career transitions. This text stands apart in its sensitivity to promoting, initiating, and sustaining diversity, equity, and inclusion throughout. The text supports constructive dialogue about complex issues such as antibias education and does so with intellectual humility and compassion.

Each chapter offers multiple points to reflect on learning and respond to application questions to help students gauge their understanding of the material. An abundance of study aids—such as learning outcomes matched to key chapter summary content—and application and assessment opportunities increase students' ability to succeed in this rewarding course.

About the Author

Sharleen L. Kato loves teaching as well as learning. She is a professor emerita at Seattle Pacific University, where she encourages students to become creative problem-solvers and to make a positive impact in their communities. Dr. Kato has taught undergraduate students for over 25 years, and currently serves as the Family and Consumer Sciences Department Director. She holds a Doctorate in Education, a Master's in Human Ecology, and an undergraduate degree in Home Economics. Dr. Kato has served on the Bellevue Christian School's Education Committee and Board of Directors, Hilltop Children's Center Board of Directors, the Health and Wellness Advisory Committee for Seattle Public Schools, and education committees and task forces for Washington State Public Schools. Dr. Kato has published many books and articles and has presented papers in the education field. She travels extensively, spending at least two weeks each year serving in an orphanage, school, teen home, and prenatal clinic in the Philippines. Dr. Kato is passionate about inspiring others to take on the challenge of improving the quality of life of those around them.

Julia Heberle
Associate Professor
Albright College
Reading, Pennsylvania

Regina Herbertson
Adjunct Faculty
Riverside City College
Riverside, California

Jane Hildenbrand
Former Early Childhood and Education Program
    Chair and Current Adjunct
Ivy Tech Community College
Indianapolis, Indiana

Lisa Hill
Dean of Arts and Sciences
Beaufort County Community College
Washington, North Carolina

Susan Hill
Community College Instructor and Early
    Childhood Consultant
Arapahoe Community College/Hill-Kleespie LLC
Littleton, Colorado/Centennial Colorado

Valerie Hill
Professor and Undergraduate Program Director,
    Department of Psychology
Lewis University
Romeoville, Illinois

Sharon Hirschy
Professor Emeritus
Collin College
Plano, Texas

Jeanne Hopkins
Department Chair and Associate Professor
Tidewater Community College
Portsmouth, Virginia

Caryn Huss
School Psychologist/Adjunct Instructor
Psych Manhattanville College
Purchase, New York

Maria James
Associate Professor
South Carolina State University
Orangeburg, South Carolina

Jody Johnson
Associate Professor
Santiago Canyon College
Orange, California

Tara Kaser
Education Department Chair
Ivy Tech Community College, Kokomo Service
    Area
Kokomo, Indiana

Marika Koch
Associate Professor, Education
Eastern Florida State College
Melbourne, Florida

Dawn Kriebel
Professor and Program Director, Undergraduate
    Psychology
Immaculata University
Immaculata, Pennsylvania

Carol LaLiberte
Early Childhood Education Coordinator,
    Professor
Asnuntuck Community College
Enfield, Connecticut

Laura J. Lamb Atchley
Associate Professor
Southeastern Oklahoma State University
Durant, Oklahoma

Laura Lamper
Department Chairperson/Online Manager
Central Texas College
Killeen, Texas

Debra Lawrence
Assistant Professor
Delaware County Community College
Media, Pennsylvania

Rebecca Lorentz
Adjunct Faculty, College of Education
Marquette University
Milwaukee, Wisconsin

Rose Maina
Chair of Business Civic Engagement and Professor
   of Child Dev/ECE
Los Angeles Trade Technical College
Los Angeles, California

Amarilis Marques Iscold
Lecturer
Cuesta College & Cal Poly State University
San Luis Obispo, California

Anita McDonald
Professor Teacher Education
North Central Texas College
Gainesville, Texas

Patricia Mendez
Professor
Oxnard College
Oxnard, California

Jennifer Mischel
Visiting Assistant Professor of Psychology
Oxford College of Emory University
Oxford, Georgia

Nanci Monaco
Associate Professor and Licensed Psychologist
SUNY Buffalo State
Buffalo, New York

Donna Nasso
Instructor
Southwest Tennessee Community College
Memphis, Tennessee

Philip Nelson
Associate Professor
Oral Roberts University
Tulsa, Oklahoma

Ross Nunamaker
Adjunct Faculty, Teacher Education &
   Graduate School
Wright State University
Dayton, Ohio

Koryn Parker
Adjunct Professor
BIOLA University
La Mirada, California

Rena Pate
Instructor
Danville Area Community College
Danville, Illinois

Catherine Phillips
Assistant Professor
Northwest Vista College
San Antonio, Texas

Kristen Pickering
Program Chair Early Childhood
   Education
Ivy Tech Community College
Terre Haute, Indiana

Lily Pimentel-Stratton
Faculty
Bakersfield College
Bakersfield, California

Maureen Powers
Adjunct Faculty/Course Developer:
   Early Childhood and Human
   Development
Rio Salado College
Tempe, Arizona

Diana Reece
Assistant Professor/Program Director
Assistant Professor
Central Ohio Technical College
Newark, Ohio

Features of the Textbook

The instructional design of this textbook includes student-focused learning tools to help you succeed. This visual guide highlights these features.

Chapter Opening Materials

Each chapter opener contains a list of learning outcomes, a list of key terms, and an introduction. The **Learning Outcomes** clearly identify the knowledge and skills to be gained when the chapter is completed. **Key Terms** lists the key words to be learned in the chapter. The **Introduction** provides an overview and preview of the chapter content.

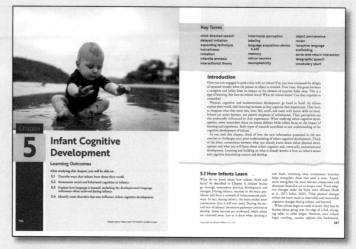

AJ_Watt/E+ via Getty Images; SDI Productions/E+ via Getty Images

Figure 5.16 Reading to infants has many benefits, including supporting language acquisition. What are some benefits of daily reading with infants?

☑ **CHECKPOINT**

☐ When do infants show signs of understanding receptive language?

☐ Describe the general timeline of infant language development, using specific terminology when possible.

☐ Compare the nativist, environmental, and interactionist theories of language development.

☐ What is meant by the terms babbling and vocabulary spurt? When do these actions typically appear and what role do they play in language acquisition?

☐ How might you counsel a parent who is concerned that their child will become confused if their partner uses two languages at home?

☐ Given the opportunity, would you support or oppose the use of baby signing in a childcare setting? Why?

Apply Here!

What languages are typically spoken in your community? Do you speak multiple languages? If so, when were these languages learned? What do you consider to be your primary or first language? If possible, interview the parent of a bilingual child. Ask them about the challenges and rewards of raising a child bilingually. Did the child experience a speech delay? Was the delay temporary? Then, interview a person who was raised bilingually. Compare the interviews with the parent and the individual raised bilingually. As an alternative to conducting an interview, write a newsletter for parents of infants in your care. How might you describe good practices for promoting language development in infants? Would you encourage or discourage bilingualism? Why or why not?

5.4 Infants with Disorders or Delays Related to Cognitive Development

Common milestones in cognitive development can be observed as infants reach certain ages within the first 2 years of life (see Table 5.4). By age 3 months, most infants coo to show their enjoyment, respond to sounds, and move their arms in circles in response to an interaction. Between ages four and seven months, most infants know their names and can distinguish between two similar languages. Other milestones, as discussed earlier, also become apparent. But what if those milestones are unmet? What if the infant does not babble or seem to understand simple requests? Measuring infant cognitive abilities may be done through simple observation. Although anyone can make observations, valid and credible assessments should be made by trained professionals (Mackin et al., 2017).

Assessing Cognitive Abilities

Primary caregivers and healthcare professionals often need and rely on accurate assessments to make good care decisions for infants. However, determining an infant's cognitive abilities when their language and motor skills are limited and developing can be challenging. Infants cannot answer surveys, offer opinions, express their reasoning, or share memories.

Additional Features

Additional features are used throughout the body of each chapter to further learning and knowledge. **Checkpoints** support reflection and knowledge after major chapter sections. **Apply Here!** provides reflective prompts and critical thinking questions to stimulate application of concepts to classroom situations. **Global Perspectives** support critical thinking and deeper consideration of developmental topics from a national and international point of view. **Practical Issues and Implications** support discussion and reflection on current topics and evolving trends in child development.

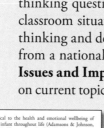

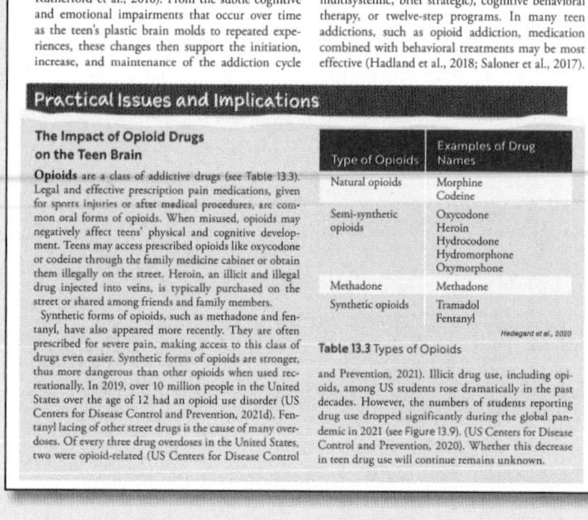

[partial text]
increase for single parents. For example, financial and social support may be inadequate if only one parent can provide for the family. According to the Annie E. Casey Foundation, in 2016 about 32% of single-parent families lived in poverty versus just 7% of two-parent families (2018). Being overwhelmed with responsibilities combined with feelings of insecurity can make bonding difficult.

Even when fathers do not live in the household, their involvement with the new family member is

critical to the health and emotional wellbeing of the infant throughout life (Adamsons & Johnson, 2013). The quality of a father's relationship with their infant is associated with infant cognitive development. The more quality indicators reported—such as time spent together and interactions through basic care, such as feeding, diapering, comforting, and playing—the higher infant cognitive achievement as well as parental mental health (Rolle et al., 2019; Sethna et al., 2017; Shorey & Ang, 2019).

Global Perspectives

Global Infant Caregiver Diversity and Antibias Early Childhood Programs

It is essential for infant caregivers to have an awareness and respect for diverse global infant caretaking practices. The National Association for the Education of Young Children (2020) recommends that all early childhood caregivers develop trusting, respectful, culturally responsive, and affirming partnerships with the children and families that they serve. These practices that actively respect and honor children and their families are an integral part of **antibias early childhood programs** (Derman-Sparks & Leekeenan, 2015; Nimmo, 2015). Antibias early childhood programs help caregivers better understand the specific needs of infants in their care (Kaiser & Rasminsky, 2019). They also strengthen the relationship with an infant's family while building trust and support between the infant and caregiver (Ray, 2015; US Department of Health and Human Services, 2020).

There are many similarities between infant caregiving practices worldwide, primarily related to keeping infants alive and thriving. However, many differences exist in daily cultural practices (see Figure 6.4). Some differences center on beliefs about verbal interactions, approaches to sleeping arrangements, and practices and general ideas about what infants need (LeVine & LeVine, 2016; Pause, 2020; Trawick-Smith, 2018). For example, many agrarian (farming) societies, such as in rural Senegal, focus less on intense interactions between an infant and a caregiver and more on exposing an infant to language that is naturally occurring all around them (Weber at al., 2017). Other cultural differences may include whether to give indirect or direct instruction to toddlers and varying expectations related to an infant or child's response and compliance. In China, giving instructions to a toddler may be direct and nonnegotiable. Most of the world practices infant-parent co-sleeping, so those who do are puzzled by the those who choose to sleep separately. A naturalistic approach to sleep

and body rhythms is practiced and preferred over scheduled naps or bedtimes in many parts of the world. One of the most significant differences in infant caregiving practices is the ideology behind and preference for stimulating versus soothing infant interactions. For example, in many African cultures and in Mexico, infant caregivers express the importance of soothing care. Interaction occurs casually as a matter of daily activities with many family members who wear or hold infants close to the body. Infants tend to be integrated into the daily happenings of family life rather than family life focusing on the infant (Gross-Loh, 2013; LeVine & LeVine, 2016).

In the United States, caregivers tend to provide stimulating environments for infants because they believe this will best aid their development. Caregivers stress the importance of verbal interaction with an infant. This interaction is ideally face-to-face, direct, engaging, and often stimulates a conversation, even before the infant can respond verbally. Facial expressions become a part of the dialogue as caregivers react to all an infant's cues. This interaction is often considered crucially important during experiences. Toys and other stimulating experiences, along with conversational interactions between caregivers and their infants, are often prized and encouraged. Parents often place infants in strollers rather than carry them or use floor play sets, sit-up chairs, and swings to entertain them.

In the United States, training a child to sleep alone is based on the idea that it is safer and promotes infant independence (Gross-Loh, 2013). The American Academy of Pediatrics recommends co-sleeping in the same room or nearby (Moon et al., 2016). Caregivers often schedule an infant's sleep, including specified nap- and bedtimes. Bedtime routines that involve taking a warm bath, wearing pajamas, bedtimes stories, and other sometimes elaborate behaviors are often a part of infant sleep routines. Training an infant to self-soothe or cry it
(Continued)

to chronic or prolonged stress. Chronic or prolonged stress may cause fluctuating neural or endocrine responses, often referred to as *allostatic load*. Over time, a heightened allostatic load negatively affects physical and mental health (Ersig et al., 2021; Whelan et al., 2021). This may illuminate why some mental disorders such as anxiety, depression, schizophrenia, and possibly even eating disorders develop during adolescence (National Institutes of Health, 2020).

Because the developing teen brain is highly malleable, teens may be particularly vulnerable to the effect of drugs on their cognitive functioning (Fuhrmann et al., 2015). (This will be discussed further in Chapter 14.) A teen's prefrontal cortex, the part of the brain that exerts behavioral control, is slower in developing than other parts of the brain. This can result in more impulsive behaviors and makes teens more prone to developing addictions (Potenza, 2013; Rutherford et al., 2010). From the subtle cognitive and emotional impairments that occur over time as the teen's plastic brain molds to repeated experiences, these changes then support the initiation, increase, and maintenance of the addiction cycle

(Argyriou et al., 2018). Other neurological changes that contribute to addiction may include socioemotional processing difficulties, working memory disruptions, increased anxiety, and a heightened risk for addiction in adulthood (Salmanzadeh et al., 2020).

Teens may be addicted to many things, such as video games, pornography, alcohol, food, or smartphone use. Addiction treatment is complex because the problem likely consists of multiple overlapping factors. Potential causes might include adverse childhood experiences (ACEs), quality of caregiver attachment, social environmental factors, sleep patterns, genetics, and individual brain functioning and development (Logan et al., 2018; Singh & Gupta, 2017; Strathearn et al., 2019). Therapies that treat the underlying behaviors that may be causing the addiction may be effective for some adolescents. Examples include family therapy (multidimensional, multisystemic, brief strategic), cognitive behavioral therapy, or twelve-step programs. In many teen addictions, such as opioid addiction, medication combined with behavioral treatments may be most effective (Hadland et al., 2018; Saloner et al., 2017).

Practical Issues and Implications

The Impact of Opioid Drugs on the Teen Brain

Opioids are a class of addictive drugs (see Table 13.3). Legal and effective prescription pain medications, given for severe injuries or after medical procedures, are common oral forms of opioids. When misused, opioids may negatively affect teens' physical and cognitive development. Teens may access prescribed opioids like oxycodone or codeine through the family medicine cabinet or obtain them illegally on the street. Heroin, an illicit and illegal drug injected into veins, is typically purchased on the street or shared among friends and family members.

Synthetic forms of opioids, such as methadone and fentanyl, have also appeared more recently. They are often prescribed for severe pain, making access to this class of drugs even easier. Synthetic forms of opioids are stronger, thus more dangerous than other opioids when used recreationally. In 2019, over 10 million people in the United States over the age of 12 had an opioid use disorder (US Centers for Disease Control and Prevention, 2021d). Fentanyl lacing of other street drugs is the cause of many overdoses. Of every three drug overdoses in the United States, two were opioid-related (US Centers for Disease Control

Type of Opioids	Examples of Drug Names
Natural opioids	Morphine
	Codeine
Semi-synthetic opioids	Oxycodone
	Heroin
	Hydrocodone
	Hydromorphone
	Oxymorphone
Methadone	Methadone
Synthetic opioids	Tramadol
	Fentanyl

Hedegaard et al., 2020

Table 13.3 Types of Opioids

and Prevention, 2021). Illicit drug use, including opioids, among US students rose dramatically in the past decades. However, the numbers of students reporting drug use dropped significantly during the global pandemic in 2021 (see Figure 13.9). (US Centers for Disease Control and Prevention, 2020). Whether this decrease in teen drug use will continue remains unknown.

Illustrations

Illustrations have been designed to communicate the specific topic clearly and simply. Photographic images have been selected to reflect the diversity of children, families, communities, and classrooms of students and early childhood teachers.

Expanding Your Learning

Apply Here! and **Checkpoint** questions extend learning and develop students' abilities to use learned material in new situations and from diverse perspectives. **To Think About** critical thinking questions appear within features to develop higher-order thinking and problem solving and personal, classroom, and workplace skills.

End-of-Chapter Content

End-of-chapter material provides an opportunity for review and application of concepts. A concise **Summary** provides an additional review tool and reinforces key learning outcomes. An expanded summary matches content to the learning outcome for section-by-section review. This helps students focus on important concepts presented in the text. **Chapter Review** questions enable students to demonstrate knowledge and comprehension of chapter material.

Summary

During the first year of infancy, neurons in the brain grow and sprout branches, and the brain makes more connections than it will ever need. The neuron pathways continue to develop during the second year of infancy. While some are reinforced, others are trimmed away. This physical change results in observable and measurable cognitive changes during nfants integrate nitive develop- erception, the from multiple

Chapter Review

1. Describe how neonates, babies, and toddlers learn about their world.

2. Do an online search and find an image (chart, infographic, figure, or photo) that visually portrays an aspect of infant cognitive development that was described in this chapter.

3. How would you describe the ability to remember experiences during infancy and toddlerhood to the parent of a newborn?

TOOLS FOR STUDENT AND INSTRUCTOR SUCCESS

Student Tools

Student Text

Child and Youth Development provides an overview of human lifespan development from infancy through adolescence using a student-friendly writing style that makes moving theory into application easier to understand. The text builds a holistic view of child development, beginning with major child development theories and social determinants of health and emotional well-being. Adding real-world subject matter, features focus on practical global topics as well as issues relating to diversity, inclusion, and equity to enhance student interest and involvement.

G-W Digital Companion

E-flash cards and vocabulary exercises allow interaction with content to create opportunities to increase achievement.

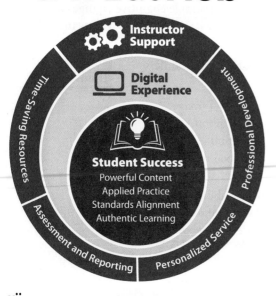

Instructor Tools

LMS Integration

Integrate Goodheart-Willcox content within your Learning Management System for a seamless user experience for both you and your students. EduHub® LMS–ready content in Common Cartridge® format facilitates single sign-on integration and gives you control of student enrollment and data. With a Common Cartridge integration, you can access the LMS features and tools you are accustomed to using and G-W course resources in one convenient location—your LMS.

G-W Common Cartridge provides a complete learning package for you and your students. The included digital resources help your students remain engaged and learn effectively:

- **Digital Textbook**
- **Drill and Practice** vocabulary activities

When you incorporate G-W content into your courses via Common Cartridge, you have the flexibility to customize and structure the content to meet the educational needs of your students. You may also choose to add your own content to the course.

For instructors, the Common Cartridge includes the Online Instructor Resources. QTI® question banks are available within the Online Instructor Resources for import into your LMS. These prebuilt assessments help you measure student knowledge and track results in your LMS gradebook. Questions and tests can be customized to meet your assessment needs.

Online Instructor Resources (OIR)

- The **Instructor Resources** provide instructors with time-saving preparation tools such as answer keys, editable lesson plans, and other teaching aids.
- **Instructor's Presentations for PowerPoint®** are fully customizable, richly illustrated slides that help you teach and visually reinforce the key concepts from each chapter.
- Administer and manage assessments to meet your classroom needs using **Assessment Software with Question Banks**, which include a wide variety of questions to assess student knowledge of the content in each chapter.

See https://www.g-w.com/child-youth-development-2024 for a list of all available resources.

Professional Development

- Expert content specialists
- Research-based pedagogy and instructional practices
- Options for virtual and in-person Professional Development

Brief Contents

Contents

UNIT 3

Early Childhood (Ages 2–6). 191

Chapter 9
Early Childhood: Socioemotional
Development. 250

UNIT 4

Middle Childhood (Ages 6–11). . . .277

UNIT 5

Feature Contents

Introduction

Child and Youth Development is a book about children—about how children grow physically, emotionally, and cognitively from infancy through adolescence and emerging adulthood. In this book you will learn about the types of development that occur throughout childhood as we grow and learn. In the first five years of life alone, babies learn to roll, crawl, stand, walk, run, hop, and skip. They learn to laugh, talk, and sing. They learn to trust and to interact with others though words and gestures. Children learn to spell, to jump, and to tell a joke. They learn to build friendships and care for others. They become industrious and learn self-control. Sometimes, there are tantrums and meltdowns. Later as teens, they learn independence. Their minds process more complex ideas and as a result, teens shift from concrete thinking to abstract thinking. They have a greater ability to express their feelings and often embrace moral or political issues with conviction. You will find that the span of human development is truly amazing, even just within the first eighteen years of life.

In this book, you will learn strategies that provide for the individual needs of the developing child that will support them through their lifetime. As the stages of human growth and development are explored, you will learn about foundational developmental theories including psychoanalytic, cognitive, behavioral and social cognitive, and ecological approaches. Further foundational learning will cover the evolutionary perspectives, genetics, and stages of prenatal development. These theories will help you understand how and why people develop and learn throughout each stage of child and youth development. The more you understand child and youth development, the better you will understand the needs, capabilities, motivations, and expectations of those you care for or work with in professional settings.

This text stands apart from others in its sensitivity toward initiating and sustaining diversity, inclusion, and equity. It embraces constructive dialogue about complex issues such as antibias education and does so with intellectual humility and compassion. Specific social issues that affect students, teachers, and society as a whole include poverty, abuse, and neglect. Racism, prejudice, and bullying are others. You will share in the wonder of the differences and uniqueness of children. As teachers, parents, and caregivers you have a role in socializing young students to become productive members of society, shaping the values and attitudes needed to be successful in the world.

Sharleen Kato

Unit 1

Foundations of Human Development

1

Ways of Discovery

Learning Outcomes

After studying this chapter, you will be able to:

1.1 Describe several contemporary issues that can influence child and adolescent growth and development.

1.2 Discuss how cultural expectations about children's education have changed over time.

1.3 Explain how a deepening knowledge of child and adolescent development can aid personal relationships and professional care.

1.4 Summarize the three interrelated domains within which children and teens grow and change during different ages and stages of life.

1.5 Describe how empirical research methods can be used to expand knowledge about child and adolescent growth and development.

Key Terms

adverse childhood experience (ACE)
big data
case studies
chronological age
cognition
cognitive development
cohort group
correlational studies
cross-sectional studies
dependent variable
descriptive data

descriptive studies
development
developmentally appropriate practice (DAP)
ethics
experimental research
growth
human development
independent variable
lifespan development
longitudinal studies

mixed data collection methods
motor skills
nature versus nurture debate
physical development
physiological measures
qualitative data
quantitative data
social age
socioemotional development
standardized tests

Introduction

How far back can you remember when you think back over your life? Do you feel like the same person you were when you were younger, just older and wiser, or have you significantly changed? What did you like to do, and with whom did you like to play? Which people or experiences most influenced you during childhood and adolescence, and how did they help shape who you are today?

From conception to burgeoning adulthood, a lot happens in the lives of children and teenagers as they grow from infancy to childhood and through adolescence. Each child is an individual with unique characteristics, traits, personalities, and abilities. Throughout the process of **human development**, children grow and mature, learn, and form relationships in predictable ways, but they follow their own time schedules. They encounter risks and use protective reflexes that enhance their *resiliency*, the process of adapting to change or adversity. Knowledgeable educators and care and service providers create contexts for children and adolescents to learn and grow. They also minimize any risks and enhance protective factors, such as the nurturing from caregivers that helps them thrive.

As you read this chapter, think about the challenges you will face when working with children and teens. Have you ever been confused about the best way to handle a situation when interacting with children or teens? How will you know if learning materials and activities are appropriate to address a learner's needs? How can you create an educational setting to form positive relationships and more effectively address the diverse needs of children? The place to start is by learning how children and teens grow and develop over time.

1.1 The Context of Human Development

The most basic debate about what influences human development is the comparative importance of heredity versus environment. Consider two peers sitting in class waiting for their turns to read aloud. André is shy and reserved. He is nervous about reading in front of the class. On the other hand, his classmate Bryson is bursting with energy and can hardly wait for his turn to read. When Bryson's turn comes, he speaks loudly and confidently, even when he stumbles over words. André, in contrast, is hesitant to speak his mind, even when he is articulate in expressing opinions and insights. Were André and Bryson born shy or outgoing? Did André's parents teach him to be shy, or is shyness a natural part of who he is? If André was born with a tendency to be shy, would he have been more outgoing if he had been raised in Bryson's family rather than his own?

This question has been debated continually. Is it nature (heredity) or nurture (environment)? This is known as the **nature versus nurture debate** (see Figure 1.1). In other words, are a person's personality traits, abilities, skills, and tastes a result of genetics (what they were born with) or their environment (their surroundings and the people in it)? Most researchers today will answer "both." It is not a matter of which, but how large a part each factor plays. How much did heredity affect André's shyness or Bryson's outgoingness? How much did the influences of the people around affect their personalities? How much did individual personal experiences affect each child?

The challenge for researchers is that heredity and the environment interact in complex ways. The genes a person has at birth have far-reaching influence. They carry a person's biological inheritance that determines basics such as hair and eye color. Genes also impact intellectual potential, a predisposition for certain disorders and conditions, and much more. Genetic predisposition even influences the kind of environment a person seeks. For example,

Bryson is sociable and outgoing. He is energized by and enjoys being with people. He makes friends quickly. In short, children's experiences in any environment are a personal response between their genetic makeup and that environment. A shy child, however, can become a more outgoing person. No single gene determines a particular behavior. Like all complex traits, behaviors involve multiple genes that are affected by various environmental factors. Genes do influence human development, but they are just part of the story. Just because a person has the genetic makeup to have a particular trait does not necessarily mean that a specific trait will develop.

How does the environment influence development? A person is shaped by both genes and individual and group experiences. We assume that the environment affects social and emotional traits, but physical characteristics and cognitive abilities are also affected. For example, infants who are held and cared for develop more connections between brain cells (neural connections). Frequent interaction, communication, and stimulation prompt a child's neural connections to form and strengthen, resulting in more efficient problem-solving and processing speed over time. That formation is critical for future growth and development. The same is true of children who grow up in an environment that offers them new and diverse stimulations and opportunities for exploration. Some aspects of the environment influence development more than others do. Researchers today recognize that the interaction between biology and environment is complex and that human responses are quite diverse (Ellis & Solms, 2018; Hosken, 2019; Tabery, 2014).

Environmental Factors that Shape Development

Experiences, social relationships, and the surrounding physical environment greatly impact children's growth and development. Examples of environmental influences include family and peer relationships, socioeconomic status, availability of socioeconomic resources, quality of play, educational opportunities, and adverse experiences.

The Effect of Family and Peers on Development

A family is a social unit consisting of parents or guardians and the children for whom they provide

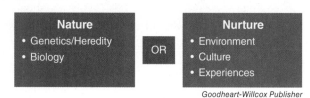

Goodheart-Willcox Publisher

Figure 1.1 Components of Nature Versus Nurture

fizkes/Shutterstock.com; Davide Zanin Photography/
Shutterstock.com; Mladen Zivkovic/Shutterstock.com

Figure 1.2 Family units come in many different configurations, such as nuclear, same-sex, and single-parent, to name a few examples.
Are there other family configurations you might add?

brain architecture in young children. In families, infants gain their first experiences with the world through the care and attention they receive. The bond between primary caregiver and child is the most basic. When a primary caregiver consistently responds to an infant's needs, a lifelong attachment and a trusting relationship develop (Sullivan et al., 2011). Infants become more attuned to others, as seen in harmonized and responsive facial expressions, body movements and positions, and vocalizations (Legerstee et al., 2013; Lerner et al., 2013). As infants become toddlers around age one, their prosocial behaviors begin to develop further as they rely less on actions from others and begin to understand the emotions of others (Moore et al., 2015; Vaish, 2018). Prosocial behaviors include positive, helpful, and relationship-enhancing actions, such as comforting a parent by rubbing their back.

Most children learn how to interact with others within the family. Primary caregivers, grandparents, aunts and uncles, cousins, siblings, and other family members all play a part in the socialization of young children (Harter, 2006). Not surprisingly, research studies suggest that the quality of the home environment is essential to children's development and that these influences are complex. For example, self-esteem is greatly influenced by a child's immediate caregivers; but as children grow, outside influences become more critical to their development. (Hosogi et al., 2012; Kostelnik et al., 2015).

Primary caregivers impact all aspects of a child's development—physical, cognitive, social, and emotional. Parents also guide children's moral development. Families share social and cultural traditions, language, and communication styles. Researchers continue to study how and why families affect various aspects of development. Sibling relationships, the impact of being an only child, birth order, and a home's emotional climate are a few areas of study for researchers. Siblings can profoundly affect a young child's social and emotional development (Dunn, 1983; McHale et al., 2012). When sibling conflict is high over an extended period, negative consequences can result, such as increased aggressive behavior between siblings and peers, and even showing up later in adolescents' substance use (Criss & Shaw, 2005; Fagan & Najman, 2005).

Families have the most significant social influence on children's early development. Primary caregivers

care and socialization (see Figure 1.2). Typically, a family shares physical resources, including food and shelter, and emotional resources, such as providing nurturing and a sense of safety. Families have a tremendous effect on human development. According to the Center on the Developing Child at Harvard University (2017a), responsive family relationships are the most critical factor in building robust

remain the main source of attachment during middle childhood; and even as children approach adolescence, they prefer their parents over their peers for support (Seibert & Kerns, 2009; Bosmans & Kerns, 2015). The trusting relationship between parents and children continues to be important when children and teens are navigating social relationships and learning new skills (Raikes & Edwards, 2009).

Peers have a growing influence on the socialization of children, and their power grows during later childhood and adolescence when many children spend more time outside of the home. Children often adopt new social behaviors, language, and other norms as peer influence grows. The ability to make and maintain friendships and attain social power and status, acceptance, and belonging all affect aspects of development.

The Effect of Socioeconomics on Development

Socioeconomics is the interaction of social and economic factors that affect available resources and opportunities, such as the quality of available childcare and schools. Although quality care and nurturing relationships between primary caregivers and young children can exist at any socioeconomic level, the availability of sufficient economic resources aids in providing for basic needs such as adequate nutrition, housing, and additional resources for optimal development. Everyone needs nutritious food and enough exercise for normal physical growth, development, and functioning, especially children and teens. Lack of proper nutrition affects cognitive development, limiting learning and productivity. Children who lack nutritional needs may experience stunted growth and delayed puberty. Poor nutrition and lack of exercise can also negatively affect social and emotional development and physical and cognitive growth and health (Bradley, 2019; Solimon et al., 2014; Truesdale et al., 2019).

Higher-level socioeconomic communities offer more stimulating opportunities than lower-level socioeconomic communities can. Such communities may have more parks and outdoor activities, libraries, cultural engagements, and sporting events to attract children and teens. Neighborhood communities also play a role in children's development. Playgrounds, open spaces, community pools, beaches, and other ways of accessing outdoor activities and

participating in outdoor play can reduce the stress and anxiety that sometimes comes from learning (Ginsburg, 2007). Some neighborhoods and communities are safer than other neighborhoods, and crime rates play a large part in keeping children safe and optimizing their growth and development.

Experiencing violence is a type of **adverse childhood experience (ACE)**, the term for a traumatic event that can negatively affect a child's growth and development. Violence can affect how a child thinks, acts, and feels, and it may impact mental and physical health during childhood and throughout life (US Department of Justice, 2017). In the forms of abuse and neglect, violence takes place against children in many settings—homes, schools, communities, religious organizations, and among family and friends (UNICEF, 2020). The violence directed toward girls is a significant health concern, especially in low- and middle-income countries (UNICEF, 2014). More than half of child deaths from unintentional injuries happen in lower-income countries (Alonge & Hyder, 2014). ACEs are explored in more detail a little later in this chapter.

Schools are a part of communities. A school's culture—which includes academic and behavioral expectations, available educational resources, a record of academic achievement, and emotional climate—has a positive or negative effect on student growth and development. Schools in poor or lower socioeconomic communities may lack adequate resources such as public-school funding to foster students' cognitive, physical, and emotional development (Berkowitz et al., 2017; Bradley, 2019; Rosen et al., 2018). For example, multiple studies have shown that when children have playgrounds for active recess play during the school day, they are physically healthier, have enhanced peer social skills, and have improved emotional regulation and attentiveness, making them subsequently more productive in the elementary school classroom (Barros et al., 2009; Sibley & Etnier, 2003).

The availability of health care can also influence development. When children receive regular checkups, developmental problems are more likely to be discovered and addressed with interventions. This precaution often reduces the impact of potential complications from ongoing health issues. Socioeconomic status also affects family health and lifestyle choices, which influence children's growth and development. For example, children who live in poverty are more likely to experience delays in physical, cognitive, and socioemotional development. Inadequate socioeconomic resources disadvantage a child throughout life, including leading to poorer health outcomes (McCoy et al., 2016; Minh et al., 2017; Sun et al., 2017). Some diseases and illnesses, such as asthma or diabetes, may interrupt a child's normal development because they miss more days from school and have difficulty with schoolwork.

Neighborhoods and the availability of socioeconomic resources do matter because a lack of community and family socioeconomic resources affects the optimal growth and development of children and teens. Younger children are particularly impacted by a lack of socioeconomic resources as poverty has a lifelong impact on their learning, health, behavior, and general well-being (Hertzman & Boyce, 2010). Even brain and cognitive growth and development are negatively affected by poverty, especially when poverty is experienced in the first three years of life (Hanson et al., 2013; Lee & Jackson, 2017). As research moves from studying individuals to utilizing linkages between population-level databases and child and teen development outcomes, deepening knowledge may be helpful in shaping community and governmental public policy (Farah, 2018; Guhn et al., 2016).

☑ CHECKPOINT

☐ How do responsive family relationships affect children?

☐ What is the nature versus nurture debate?

☐ What are some examples of the components that make up a child's environment?

☐ Name several ways socioeconomics influences optimal growth and development in children and teens. Name three other influences on child growth and development.

The Effect of Race and Ethnicity on Development

Culture encompasses shared values, beliefs, language, other forms of communication, and lifestyle practices. The relationship between ethnic identity and culture and children's growth and development is complex; understanding its complexities requires sorting out the concepts of race, ethnicity,

and even immigration status. Socioeconomic variables, inequalities, and racism complicate the matter. How do ethnic identity and culture impact childhood growth and development? It depends on many factors. *Race* is the categorization of people based on the geographic location of ancestry. Ethnicity includes cultural practices, specific attitudes, and beliefs shared by a group. Life stressors, ethnic-racial discrimination, and acculturation or assimilation level can impact identity formation, emotional and social development, and overall mental health (Pauker et al., 2015). When ethnic and racial identity is explored and affirmed, the physiological benefits for children and teens include optimal physical and cognitive health (Borrero & Yeh, 2011; Zeiders et al., 2018).

Ethnic identity refers to a person's sense of belonging or membership in a particular ethnic group. When families provide a strong personal ethnic identity reinforced within the larger community, children and teens benefit as they grow and develop. Ethnic identity and perception of others affect the child directly. As early as infancy, children can distinguish between given racial or ethnic groups. By ages 4 to 5, a child may already be socialized to show preference to some groups over others (Perszyk et al., 2019; Vogel et al., 2012; Xiao et al., 2018). The child's primary caregivers influence their children and teens in both overt and subtle ways. For example, values, beliefs, and expected roles can influence experiences and behaviors, which, in turn, affect growth and development (White et al., 2018). For example, if a family values academic achievement, it influences a child or teen's academic achievement (Miller-Cotto & Byrnes, 2016).

When biases exist against racial or ethnic groups, they can have a detrimental effect on growth and development (Causadias et al., 2018; White et al., 2018). Sometimes cultural and generational differences may cause conflicts between parents and grandparents and extended family caregivers, including aunts, uncles, and cousins, laying a foundation for social, cognitive, and emotional development (Lee & Brann, 2015; McHale, 2007; McHale et al., 2014). Cultural values held by primary caregivers seem to be strongly connected to the specific ways in which they socialize their children, such as emphasizing individualism by offering choices and communicating expectations of responsibility for self and possessions, caring for others, or demonstrating a strong work ethic when completing tasks (Gartstein & Putnam, 2019; LeVine & LeVine, 2016).

The effect of structural-level or large-scale economics (macroeconomics), health care, and other policies has contributed to disproportionately higher maternal morbidity and mortality rates. *Maternal mortality* refers to the number of deaths of mothers before, during, or after giving birth; and *maternal morbidity* refers to the prevalence or incidence rates of unhealthy conditions associated with motherhood and birth. The United States currently ranks last of all developed countries in access to community services like prenatal care, childcare, housing, and other resources. This is despite evidence that links increases in public health spending to a decline in inequitable treatment, preventable pregnancy and childbirth, other adverse outcomes, or death. As discussed further in Chapter 3, Black mothers are disproportionately affected. There is no evidence that complications in pregnancy or childbirth are a result of genetic differences (Freedman & Kruk, 2014; Lemke & Brown, 2020; Mays, 2011). Adverse outcomes extend into adolescence; and for many teens in the United States, ethnic identity and race become a matter of safety. Black and Hispanic teens are much more likely to be exposed to violence in their communities than White teens due to inequities in resources and less safety, which has a profound negative impact on the wellness and health of all members of the community (Galovski et al., 2016; Paradies et al., 2015; Slopen et al., 2016; Wildeman & Wang, 2017).

The Effect of Adverse Childhood Experiences on Development

When children ages 0 to 17 experience potentially traumatic events in their lives, these occurrences are often referred to as adverse childhood experiences (ACEs), as mentioned previously. The term ACE originated with a longitudinal study conducted in the early 2000s that reported on the negative long-term effect of adverse experiences on the health and well-being of adults (Felitti, 2002). The US Centers for Disease Control and Prevention (CDC) describes ACEs as any potentially painful experiences, such as abuse, neglect, violence, family member substance abuse, exposure to smoking and other pollutants, physical or mental health issues, homelessness,

joblessness, poverty, and toxic stress. ACEs can be both experienced and observed. The CDC (2021) reported that over two-thirds of American adults had experienced ACEs, with 16% having experienced four or more episodes (see Figure 1.3). Women and certain groups are even more likely to have had an adverse childhood experience.

Much medical research explores the effect of ACEs on children and teens. Many studies have found that, although the negative effects on children are immediate, ACEs also have a lifetime effect on the health and well-being of individuals and families (CDC, 2021; Karr-Morse & Wiley, 2012). These detrimental effects may include later alcohol and drug abuse, mental health issues, certain cancers, heart disease, and unhealthy body weight, including obesity (Godoy et al., 2020; Holman et al., 2016; Merrick et al., 2018).

The brain development of young children who are neglected or have nonresponsive primary caregivers is negatively affected. Likewise, young children who experience chronic (ongoing) stress may have lifelong altered brain architecture (Harvard University Center on the Developing Child, 2007). Chronic stress is not situational but long-term. For instance, a primary caregiver who is severely depressed may repeatedly neglect their child, perpetuating the child's stress. A child who lives in conditions of extreme poverty experiences constant stress.

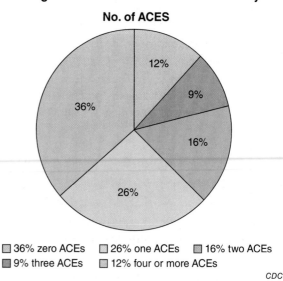

ADVERSE CHILDHOOD EXPERIENCES
Looking at how ACEs affect our lives & society

No. of ACES

□ 36% zero ACEs   □ 26% one ACEs   □ 16% two ACEs
□ 9% three ACEs   □ 12% four or more ACEs

CDC

Figure 1.3 Adverse Childhood Experiences

Preventing Child Abuse and Neglect

Strategy	Approach
Strengthen economic supports to families	• Strengthening household financial security • Family-friendly work policies
Change social norms to support parents and positive parenting	• Public engagement and education campaigns • Legislative approaches to reduce corporal punishment
Provide quality care and education early in life	• Preschool enrichment with family engagement • Improved quality of child care through licensing and accreditation
Enhance parenting skills to promote healthy child development	• Early childhood home visitation • Parenting skill and family relationship approaches
Intervene to lessen harms and prevent future risk	• Enhanced primary care • Behavioral parent training programs • Treatment to lessen harms of abuse and neglect exposure • Treatment to prevent problem behavior and later involvement in violence

Fortson, B. L.; Klevens, J.; Merrick, M. T.; Gilbert, L. K.; & Alexander, S. P. (2016). Preventing child abuse and neglect: A technical package for policy, norm, and programmatic activities. *Atlanta, GA: National Center for Injury Prevention and Control, Centers for Disease Control and Prevention.*

Figure 1.4 What Can Be Done About Adverse Childhood Experiences?

How should caregivers respond? When the caregiver is a parent, education, support, and resources may help them break the cycle created by ACEs. For educators and other care providers, the American Academy of Pediatrics (2020) along with the US Department of Health and Human Services (2020) offer important guidelines for properly caring for children who experience trauma. The guidelines include trauma education, recognizing ACEs, listening tips, avoiding triggers (reminders), and developing trust. Most importantly, educators and caregivers should take care not to add more trauma when addressing children's needs. In addition, social policies and community educational programs that support families, accessible and affordable quality childcare, and community intervention services contribute to reducing the impact of adverse childhood experiences (see Figure 1.4).

☑ CHECKPOINT

☐ How are race and ethnicity different? How would you describe a person's ethnic identity?

☐ How do stress and ethnic-racial discrimination negatively affect growth and development?

☐ Define, give examples of, and discuss the effect of adverse childhood experiences on growth and development throughout life.

Apply Here!

Think about your local community, city, or town. What are the potential ACEs you are witnessing or hearing reported? What impact might these experiences have on children and teens growing up today?

1.2 Historical and Cultural Perspectives on the Education of Children in America

During every era, historical events and changes in American life affect expectations of the educational system and the public's perception of it. In every period, society, history, and government shape the availability and quality of education. The education children receive also affects society. Historical events and social trends significantly affect children's socialization and education.

The Early Years

Although many Indigenous people lived on the land we call the United States, this section will cover the American Early National Period and the American Common School Period. These periods cover the years between 1776 and 1880.

Global Perspectives

Applying Research to Foster Global Understanding

How did the COVID-19 global pandemic personally affect you and your community? Around the world, the pandemic profoundly affected the lives of children and teens due to the isolation caused by contact restrictions, health concerns, interruptions in formal schooling, and loss of family members and livelihoods. This was despite the potential for increased family cohesion (see Figure 1.5). Parental stress may have caused child maltreatment, and children who were already at risk may have experienced profound peril. The long-term effects of the global pandemic on children and teens will be the topic of research studies for years to come (Fegert et al., 2020).

Hananeko_Studio/Shutterstock.com

Figure 1.5 During the COVID-19 pandemic, children worldwide experienced social isolation as many schools closed and moved to remote learning through a variety of platforms, including online instruction.
How did the pandemic affect your educational experience?

Many developmental researchers recognize the importance of understanding global issues and how they affect children's optimal growth and development. For example, global food supply chains control children's and adolescents' diets and food accessibility and, subsequently, their overall health and wellness (Nordhagen, 2020). Maternal and infant health and wellness profoundly affect children's overall growth and development. Today, about 90% of children and teens worldwide live in poverty (Tomlinson et al., 2019). Understanding the effect of extreme poverty on children's and teens' developing minds and bodies can sharpen public policy and guide research agendas around the world. It can be a more cost-effective way to provide

equitable opportunities for their growth and development (Banati & Lansford, 2018; Dua et al., 2016).

Applying research to global migration patterns can lend insight. Although most people around the world live in the country where they were born, about 3.5% of the world's population has migrated to live in a country other than their country of birth. Migration has increased significantly since the 1970s, and most immigrants are of working and childbearing age (International Organization for Migration, 2017; United Nations, 2019). According to the Pew Research Center, nearly 14% of the US population are immigrants born in another country (Budiman, 2020). Sometimes, families with children migrate as they seek new opportunities, and occasionally they relocate as refugees (see Figure 1.6). *Refugees* are people who have been forced to leave their country to escape oppression or persecution, war, or

A

B

David Peinado Romero/Shutterstock.com; Nelson Antoine/Shutterstock.com

Figure 1.6 Families migrate to other countries for a variety of reasons. This Honduran family (A) is requesting political asylum in the United States, while this Haitian family (B) seeks refuge in Mexico following a devastating earthquake in 2021.

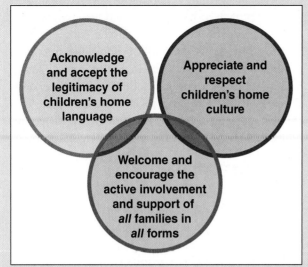

Figure 1.7 Core Components of Culturally Competent Early Childhood Education Programs

natural disaster. Refugees are often characterized by their sense of hope. It may be hope for physical or emotional safety, more prosperity, new opportunities, or expanding social relationships.

Throughout this book, you will be exposed to global concerns that affect children's optimal growth and development. Why? Educators and care providers should be aware of cultural and societal shifts in their communities and worldwide. Culturally competent educators are committed to learning about the lives of the children and teens they serve and must be diligent when creating environments that promote optimal growth and development in all three domains—physical, cognitive, and socioemotional—free of stereotyping, prejudice, favoritism, or racism. It takes personal commitment, time and energy, knowledge of developmental growth and abilities, and reliance on objective theoretical foundations and empirical research. The National Association for the Education of Young Children, or NAEYC (2020), identifies teacher cultural competency as the primary element of high-quality early childhood education programs (see Figure 1.7).

To Think About:

- How did the COVID-19 global pandemic affect the lives of children and teens in your schools and community? Will there be long-term impacts?
- Are there other global issues affecting the health and well-being of children in your care?
- Do you have recent immigrant communities in your local area? If so, where are they from? Why have they congregated as a community? How can you learn more about their cultural practices?

The American Early National Period (1776–1840)

In the American Early National Period (1776–1840), most children lived on farms or in small towns, and they expected their adult lives to be much like their parents' lives. Young children were cared for at home. Educational changes began in cities where populations were more diverse, and people freely shared and discussed new ideas before eventually moving on to rural areas. During this time, educators believed that schools could be a vehicle for making a better society. Growing communities focused on teaching skills to help children prepare to enter fields such as agriculture, business, and shipping (Spring, 2018; Urban & Wagoner, 2014).

Benjamin Franklin and Thomas Jefferson were two influential political leaders of the time. Benjamin Franklin worked to expand educational opportunities by offering education to anyone who could pay the tuition, regardless of religious beliefs. Thomas Jefferson argued that education was critical to the success of the newly formed democracy. If ordinary people were well educated, they could participate in democratic government, and it would thrive (Addis, 2003; Fraser, 2014).

The American Common School Period (1840–1880)

The American Common School Period (1840–1880) marked events that significantly altered the American way of life. The expansive West inspired many people to find their fortune and start new lives for their families. For some, labor-saving devices like sewing and washing machines freed up more time for other interests and pursuits. Throughout the 1850s, the United States experienced internal strife leading up to the Civil War (1860–1865) as some Americans realized the injustice of slavery and worked actively to end it. Ultimately, the freeing of slaves altered American life (Good & National Society for the Study of Education, 2000; Nasaw, 1979).

Around 1840, most American children received minimal schooling, if they received any at all. By 1880, education—including free public education for many—was much more widely available. However, laws in some places within the South prevented Black Americans from obtaining an education because Whites feared that education would lead to rebellion. Very few enslaved Black Americans learned to read or write; most who learned did so in secret. Formerly enslaved people in northern states also faced tremendous educational obstacles, both social and economic. Black Americans, as a group, usually struggled with very low wages, so children often found work as soon as they were old enough to do so, often as young as 6 or 7 (Guthrie, 2003; Mondale et al., 2001; Urban & Wagoner, 2014).

Friedrich Froebel (1782–1852), a German educator, developed the idea of kindergarten. He believed that young children learned best through play (see Figure 1.8). The goal of the first kindergarten classes established in America was to help poor

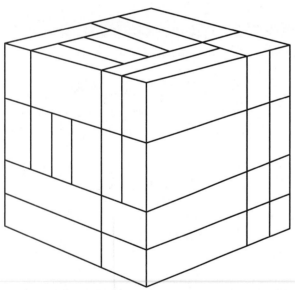

Morphart Creation/Shutterstock.com

Figure 1.8 As part of his theory of play, Friedrich Froebel developed hands-on games and activities he called "Gifts and Occupations" to facilitate a young child's learning about nature and physical relationships. This illustration of a divided cube is an example of Froebel's "Gift Three."
How might a child play with a divided cube toy such as this? How do children typically play with blocks?

children succeed in school. Froebel's creative and social approach to learning worked well with young children, and educators noticed the success of his methods. In the 1870s, public schools began to offer kindergarten programs. Before this time, young children did not attend school until they were about 7 years of age. Play and social interaction are still the foundation for educational programs for young children (Allen, 2017; Hinitz & Miller, 2013).

☑CHECKPOINT

☐ How did national views on education change between the American Early National Period and the American Common School Period?

☐ What effect did Benjamin Franklin and Thomas Jefferson have on how society viewed school and children?

☐ How did the American Common School Period change lives for children in the United States? Who was excluded?

☐ Where did kindergarten originate, whom did it serve, and what did it uniquely offer?

The Latter Nineteenth and Early Twentieth Centuries

The period from the late nineteenth and early twentieth centuries included the American Progressive Period and two world wars, covering 1880–1960.

The American Progressive Period (1880–1920)

During this period, the United States had endured the First World War and women were gaining more political and social rights. Millions of European immigrants sought work in the nation's cities, and American citizens began abandoning farming, relocating to towns and cities to find work. Urban areas quickly became overcrowded. Many new city dwellers lacked education, practical skills, and financial resources. Poverty and disease became widespread. Those who did find work in factories found their lives profoundly changed during that time. Work hours were long, and working conditions were often hazardous. Many children worked alongside their parents, limiting their educational opportunities (see Figure 1.9). Urban schools quickly became overcrowded, and conditions in the schools were poor. Early childhood education was not available to the children of most working parents, and orphanages

National Child Labor Committee Lewis Hine photographs

Figure 1.9 Young children often juggled school and work during the 1900s. The children in this photo spent seven hours a day shucking oysters for a canning company in South Carolina, attending school for a few hours in between work.

were sometimes the answer to those who had no extended family to help take care of children (Pastorello, 2014; Ramey, 2012).

Progressives, or those in power who desired to make the world a more democratic place, passed laws to limit the number of hours children could work in factories. John Dewey, an educational philosopher, was a leading voice for progressive education during this time (Urban & Wagoner, 2014). By 1920, all states had laws requiring children to attend elementary school. However, schools during this period were still highly segregated. Black children attended separate public schools that received less public funding and had insufficient or outdated books and other educational materials, often the castoffs from the White schools.

Maria Montessori, Italy's first female doctor, tried to find ways to help children who had difficulty learning. She believed that young children were capable of great discovery and that sensory experiences should come before learning to read and write. She pioneered an educational method that considers all a child's needs, not just intellectual needs. Montessori classrooms are stimulating environments with many opportunities for motor development and sensory exploration, including language, science, art, geography, and math. Children direct their learning with teachers as their partners (Debs, 2019; Follari, 2019).

The 1920s and the Great Depression Era (1921–1940)

The economic prosperity of the 1920s increased the size of the middle class. Available early childhood education programs included family childcare homes, religious and benevolent childcare programs, employer-sponsored childcare, and public-school prekindergarten programs (Hinitz & Miller, 2013; Lascarides & Hinitz, 2011). However, things changed dramatically in 1929 with the New York Stock Market crash that led to Great Depression.

During the Great Depression of the 1930s, public schools struggled financially. Some districts made the school year shorter while others permanently closed. Decreases in or the elimination of teacher pay were common, and course offerings were cut back to basic subjects. Many families lacked the money for books and school supplies. Some children were unable to attend school, and those who were able to work often helped supplement the family income (see Figure 1.10). Eventually, the federal government stepped in to help. Schools began offering free hot lunches for children (Fraser, 2014; Spring, 2018).

The 1940s and 1950s

World War II dominated the first half of the 1940s. Thousands of young men left each month to fight the war overseas. At the end of the war, the troops

*Marion Post Walcott, photographer. US Farm Security Administration/
Office of War Information Black & White Photographs*

Figure 1.10 The children in this photo from 1938 are attending school at the Mileston Plantation in Mississippi. Because they were needed to pick cotton, their school year did not begin until late in the year, and many children did not attend school at all.

flooded back into civilian life. Young people married in record numbers. The result was a baby boom, a surge in the birth rate over the following years. As factories stopped producing products for the war effort, consumer goods became more available. There were new options in housing, home technology, fashion, and even food. Industries grew, jobs were available, and Americans were hopeful. The education of children was not immune to this era of change. The children of the baby boom began to enter the public school system, and their sheer numbers created a need for more schools and teachers (Samuel, 2012).

When the Soviet Union launched the first satellite in 1957, the US government feared that the Soviets' emphasis on teaching math and science in their schools gave them a technological advantage that could later translate into a military advantage. Congress made money available to improve scientific equipment for public and private schools and encouraged US schools to strengthen their math, science, and foreign language instruction. Homework requirements increased and expanded children's school days into the evening hours (Fraser, 2014; Spring, 2018).

Many schools were still racially segregated based on "separate but equal" policies, yet, Black schools still were not equal in funding. Educational materials were inferior and usually outdated. Black teachers could only instruct Black children, and they received significantly lower pay than White teachers. With the *Brown v. Board of Education* ruling in 1954, the Supreme Court confirmed that the racial segregation of schools violated the Constitution because segregated schools were, by nature, unequal. As a result, public schools were ordered to desegregate. Some districts did so (see Figure 1.11). Others used delaying tactics. The push to integrate schools was the most radical—and potentially influential—aspect of desegregation, affecting the lives of many children and their families (Sherry & Powell, 2021).

The Latter 20th Century

The latter twentieth century spanned the time after World War II, from the 1960s through the new millennium in 1999.

The 1960s and 1970s

The 1960s were a time of change and a decade of contrasts. The decade began with the optimism of

Thomas O'Halloran, photographer. Library of Congress Prints and Photographs Division, Washington, D.C. 20540 USA

Figure 1.11 This photo from 1955 shows an example of an integrated school located in Washington, DC.

a newly elected John F. Kennedy as president and later witnessed the first person to walk on the moon in 1969. However, the 1960s also included America's involvement in the Vietnam War and the assassinations of John F. Kennedy, Dr. Martin Luther King Jr., and Robert F. Kennedy. The civil rights movement was especially active during this period, and children worldwide heard Dr. Martin Luther King Jr.'s famous "I Have a Dream" speech. The civil rights movement spurred other groups to work for their equality, including women, Hispanic Americans, Native Americans, and people with disabilities (Rielly, 2003; Samuel, 2012). The most significant changes affected children who were disadvantaged economically or educationally (see Table 1.1).

During the 1970s, America had many foreign and domestic preoccupations. The divorce rate rose, and the number of single parents increased. Overall, significantly more women were in the workforce in a broader range of jobs, making the availability of early childhood care and education critical. As unemployment rates increased, people had less disposable income, and they became less willing to spend resources on children and education. Many schools suffered from inadequate funding (Sagert, 2007; Samuel, 2012).

The Civil Rights Movement continued to push for equality. Desegregation at the school level had not solved unequal education. By choice or lack of opportunity, neighborhoods tended to be divided by race. That meant that schools often had little racial

Federal Programs to Aid Disadvantaged Children	Description
The Civil Rights Act of 1964	• The act formally outlawed segregation in United States public schools and public places. • School districts were ordered to end segregation and "undo the harm" segregation had caused by racially balancing schools. • Federal guidelines were issued; however, some school districts continued to stall, and problems remained.
The Elementary and Secondary Education Act of 1965	• The "War on Poverty" and "Great Society" programs sought to improve the schools most in need. • Federal dollars were given to school districts based on the number of poor children enrolled to help equalize educational opportunities.
Project Head Start of 1965	• This program was designed to help preschool children from low-income families develop the skills they needed for success in school. • It was based on the idea that young children who begin with a good start in school are less likely to experience academic problems later. • Head Start programs provide a positive, high-quality environment for preschool children.

Kato

Table 1.1 Significant Changes Affecting Economically or Educationally Disadvantaged Children in the United States During the 1960s

diversity, and those with primarily Black and Brown populations often had inadequate facilities and lacked sufficient, up-to-date educational materials. School districts were mandated to desegregate at the larger district level, leading to forced integration that included bussing children to schools outside of their neighborhoods. This plan was not without controversy, however. Many families objected to forcing children to take long bus rides to schools (Rymsza-Pawlowska, 2017).

The Civil Rights Act affected education in several ways. It spurred on a variety of subsequent laws that provided equal opportunities for other groups. Title IX, or the Equal Opportunity in Education Act, prohibited discrimination based on gender in all programs and activities. The Supreme Court ruled that language was a barrier to equal education, and they ordered schools to provide basic English language classes for children who had limited English skills. Congress passed the Education for All Handicapped Children Act (1975), now the Individuals with Disabilities Education Act (1990), that guaranteed free public education for children with disabilities in the least restrictive environment, involving parents in decisions about their child's placement (Franciosi, 2004; Fraser, 2014).

The 1980s and 1990s

Despite growth and prosperity for some people, the gap between rich and poor widened. Consumerism was at an all-time high. Buying on credit was a way of life for many. The families of Baby Boomers, on average, had fewer children, so children had few or no siblings. There were more single-parent families as the divorce rate continued to rise. In addition, two-income families were more common than in previous decades as women gained more career opportunities (Samuel, 2012).

A Nation at Risk, a report published by the United States National Commission on Excellence in Education, asserted that America's competitive edge was at risk, stating that the United States was falling behind other countries in business, science, and technology. There were calls for school reform. Many Americans believed that schools again needed to emphasize reading, writing, and math, while critics of the movement felt that students needed more than those basic skills to succeed in a complex world (Heath & Oxford Analytica, 1986; Rury, 2005).

The 1990s were about technology. The internet began changing how people communicated, received information, shopped, and conducted business. The ability to use computers skillfully soon became an essential career skill. Today, education and information are readily available via computer and other digital media, making learning available at a time and place convenient to the student.

The federal government established guidelines for achieving excellence in education. Individual states complied by setting specific standards and objectives, then evaluating both students and schools to determine whether the criteria were being met. **Standardized tests** were designed to measure students' performance compared with that of a large number of other students. For example, they would measure the reading comprehension skills of third-grade students across the country (Fraser, 2014; Spring, 2018).

The Early 21st Century and Beyond

The 2000s brought new challenges. After the terrorist attacks on September 11, 2001, the United States went to war in Afghanistan and Iraq. At home, the economy seemed strong, with rising real estate values and high consumer spending, much of it on credit, until a financial crisis in 2008 plunged the country into uncertainty. Some financial institutions failed. People lost their jobs as consumer spending slowed. Many children were living in poverty, and some faced homelessness.

The No Child Left Behind Act (NCLB) of 2001 was passed to improve the performance of US schools. Its essential components included increased accountability for teachers and schools, more choices for parents when choosing schools for their children, and an increased focus on reading. The NCLB's underlying premise was the belief that high expectations and goals would result in success for all students. One of its most controversial features was the expectation that every child should meet state standards in reading, math, and science. One method of measuring achievement was using standardized tests at specific grade levels. Receiving federal educational funds was tied to school performance; schools demonstrating success in meeting high standards would receive more money than schools with lower scores. NCLB also allowed parents to move their children from low-achieving schools to higher-achieving schools (Fife, 2013; Finn & Rebarber, 1992; McGuinn, 2006).

In 2015, the Every Student Succeeds Act (ESSA)—less prescriptive legislation than NCLB—gave individual states more flexibility and a commitment included from the federal government to equal opportunity for all students regardless of race, geographic location, disability, or socioeconomic level. After its enactment and implementation, national high school graduation rates rose, dropout rates fell, and the number of high school graduates attending college increased (Fraser, 2014; Spring, 2018).

As the decade ended, people around the world experienced a global pandemic. COVID-19 shut down many early childhood, elementary, and secondary schools. Many young children received remote learning from their homes. The country became divided socially, economically, and politically over many issues. Due to a plethora of reasons, many children fell behind in their education. Understanding the impact of these experiences became a major focus of educators who rely on their understanding of human growth and development to provide optimal resources and support for children and teens.

☑CHECKPOINT

- ☐ How did children's education change during the 1950s to 1970s?
- ☐ In the 1980s to 1990s, the federal government established guidelines for achieving excellence in education. Name two.
- ☐ What are three influences on the lives and education of children during the 2000s and onward?

Apply Here!

Choose someone you know, age 50 or older, and interview them about their educational experiences during childhood and adolescence. Through the process of interviewing the person, create an oral history by summarizing their answers to 10 or more of the following questions. Create a summary of your reflections to share on your interview interactions and learning.

- Where were you born?
- Where did you grow up? What was it like?
- How many siblings did you have?
- Where did you go to school? What was it like?
- What subjects were you good at in school?

- Who were your favorite teachers? Why?
- What is your best memory of elementary school? Middle school? High school?
- What is the bravest thing you ever did related to being in school?
- What is something you accomplished/experienced related to school that makes you most proud?
- If you could be any grade in school again, which would you choose? Why?
- What role did school play in preparing you for your life today?
- How do you personally contribute to making this world a better place? Was this something that was encouraged in your early schooling?

1.3 Why It Matters: Understanding Growth and Development

All humans start as a single cell that biologically transforms into a fetus, then into an infant, child, adolescent, and finally, through continued transformation, an adult. The blueprint from that single cell is carried in all our cells throughout our lives. **Growth** refers to physical changes in size, such as gains in height and weight. Most growth occurs during the first 19 years of life, although growth continues into adulthood (Hargreaves et al., 2015; Salam et al., 2016a). **Development** is the gradual increase in skills and abilities over a lifetime. Development relates to growth and includes changes that affect our emotions, health and wellness, ways of thinking and processing, and methods of connecting socially.

Throughout their lives, individuals develop and change in the process of maturation and growth known as *human development*. Human development is an amazing, gradual process in which people grow and change from birth to death. This expansive, lifelong view is **lifespan development**. This book focuses on the foundational stages of life—human growth and development from pre-conception through the end of adolescence at about age 19. People go through similar stages of development, especially during childhood and adolescence (Barrouillet, 2015; Erikson, 1982; Morra, 2008; Kenny, 2013; Salkind & Rasmussen, 2008).

Both childhood and adolescence are particularly intriguing and vital stages of development. During just the first two years of life, brain processing speed increases at the most rapid pace of any life stage (Barkovich & Raybaud, 2019; Diamond et al., 2011; Gross, 2019). Much of the foundation is laid for optimal health, wellness, and learning within the childhood and teen years. For example, fetuses begin learning in utero and start adapting to their new environment right after birth as newborns (Mennella et al., 2001). Newborns learn by combining reflexes with motor skills. Their thinking is organized through simple concepts that gradually change to become more complex as the brain matures and experiences increase over time (Mandler, 2004). Lifestyle choices in childhood and adolescence can influence health and wellness in adulthood, even biologically altering outcomes (Salam et al., 2016b). For example, overeating can lead to the onset of type 2 diabetes mellitus, which changes the biological or health condition of the body.

While each person progresses individually, the stages of development, or how humans grow and change throughout life's ages and phases, are similar for almost everyone. When newborns have low birth weights, most of these infants still show normal growth and development, although others have exceptionalities that will require specialized care (Bremner & Wachs, 2010; Brink, 2013; Gross, 2019). Likewise, two 4-year-olds share some common traits, but a 6-year-old is very different from a 13-year-old in typical ways. All are different from an infant, a 20-year-old, or an older adult. Why? Human growth patterns are determined biologically and impacted by the environment (National Institutes of Health, 2019; Steinberg, 2014).

There is no shortage of information available, both factual and anecdotal, about how children or adolescents (teenagers) develop, grow, and mature. Some information is non-factual and based on feelings and opinions, passed down between family members or friends. You are likely aware that babies learn to roll, crawl, stand, walk, run, hop, and skip in the first 5 years of life alone. They learn to laugh, talk, joke, and sing. They learn to feed themselves. They learn to trust and to interact with others through words and gestures. Children learn to count, spell, and write. They learn to build friendships and care for others. They become industrious and learn self-control. They learn to organize their activities (American Academy of Pediatrics, 2014; Davies & Troy, 2020). Later, as teens, they learn independence. Their minds process ideas that are more complex. As teens continue to transition, they take on more responsibility for themselves and others, preparing them for adulthood (Hagan et al., 2017).

The focus of this book will be on factual knowledge derived from research, theories, and science. Some information will come from experienced care and service providers, including educators and medical care providers. Knowing that children grow and develop in a typical fashion can be helpful for educators and care and service providers. Children and teens usually do things for a reason. Figuring out those reasons can help primary caregivers and professionals who work with children support children's optimal growth and development while minimizing risk factors and maximizing protective factors. This awareness can also help educators create more effective programming and activities that support primary caregivers and families. Ultimately, understanding human development can help educators create a vision for current and future programs, even shaping public policy and resources that affect children and teens domestically and globally (McCoy et al., 2016; Sharma et al., 2017; United Nations, 2018).

Principles of Development Help Determine Age Milestones

In most cultures, the date of a child's birth is known, sometimes even down to the exact hour. From that point on, age is counted in days, months, and years. Projections are made about what an infant or child should be able to do or know at any given age. A child's physical growth is often charted, and the child is assessed against shared norms or standards. **Chronological age** is the term for recognizing age in this manner, and it carries certain expectations that, when not met, can be a cause of worry, especially for primary caregivers. Most projections are made with ranges in mind. For example, although the average age for an infant to take their first steps is about twelve months, two siblings may present very differently. One child may begin walking at age 10 months, whereas the sibling, raised in the same

environment, begins walking at 14 months. Both siblings may be running by age 2, and by age 3 they may demonstrate no differences in their abilities. Does it matter? It depends.

Whether or not a young child is walking at 10 months may be less important to the child's overall growth and development but more a matter of convenience to both the child and the primary caretaker. Is the child frustrated or content with continuing to crawl? Is it a matter of convenience to the caretaker that the child is not yet mobile, requiring more oversight? Is any concern more a matter of expectations? Expectations about how and when a child should be able to perform are based on ideas about appropriate **social age**. In many cultures, a given age is valued as a measure of whether an infant, child, or teen is meeting growth and development expectations. Caregivers often have strong opinions about childhood and teen behaviors and skill attainments, such as when a child begins toilet learning, starts kindergarten, stays home unsupervised, drives a car, or graduates from high school. Often, expectations of social age are based on people's opinions or culture rather than on empirical research.

By building and deepening knowledge about child and adolescent development, educators and care providers can cultivate realistic, flexible, and individualized expectations of the children and teens in their care. Understanding human development ages and stages gives more insight into what is age-appropriate for children and what might be cause for concern. It can also offer insight into ways that stimulating environments, relationships, or activities might promote growth and development (Davies & Troy, 2020; Oster, 2019; Payne & Isaacs, 2016).

Principles of Human Development Guide Expectations

It is human nature to try to figure things out. Observations about human development go back to the beginning of recorded history, and research on development continues to this day. There are some basic shared principles that explain what is already known about human development (see Figure 1.12).

Development occurs in a predictable and orderly manner—a sequence of steps that consistently follows one after another. Children learn sounds,

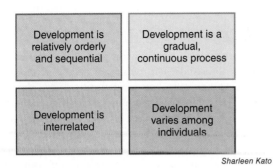

Development is relatively orderly and sequential	Development is a gradual, continuous process
Development is interrelated	Development varies among individuals

Sharleen Kato

Figure 1.12 Shared Principles of Human Development

then words. Eventually, they learn the letters of the alphabet, and they learn that these can be combined to represent words. Each of these steps must occur before children can read. Teachers use their knowledge of how development progresses to design effective learning strategies appropriate to the ages of their students.

Most developmental changes happen gradually and are apparent over time. A 3-year-old may learn to ride a tricycle while a 6-year-old masters the more difficult skills needed to ride a bicycle. A teen refines these skills and uses them, along with additional knowledge and judgment, to learn to drive a car. An adult driver typically has fewer accidents than a teen because years of practice and experience have improved their skills.

Most development is not solely in one realm, as acquiring new skills typically requires gains in several of these areas. Think about what it takes to become a skilled basketball player. You need physical stamina, coordination, and endless practice to be able to shoot the ball precisely into the hoop from any angle on the court. It also takes cognitive development to learn plays and figure out those of your opponents. You must be able to judge the potential success of a shot. Socially, teamwork is required, as is the ability to read the intent of the player you are guarding. You will note the body language and expressions of other players. Emotionally, you must have confidence, decisiveness, and perseverance. It takes all aspects of development, and more, to play basketball well.

Although development is orderly and predictable, everyone's progress is unique. That is because so many factors affect development. No two people—even twins raised together—have the same experiences (Boomsma et al., 2002; Segal, 2012, 2017). Each individual faces life-changing experiences and responds to them based on their personality, knowledge, and prior experiences. Everyone grows and changes at a different rate and on a slightly different schedule. Whether learning to build a play fort from blankets, brush one's teeth, solve a math problem, or play basketball, growth and development are complex and involve several domains, or areas, of development.

Principles of Development Inform Practice

A deepening understanding of child and youth growth and development can give educators insight into what to expect—what is predictable, normal, or typical, even despite individual differences. Knowledge of these typical growth and development patterns at specific ages and stages can help inform best practices in classroom settings, play and learning activities, socialization opportunities, and methods of communication. Possible signs of concern or trouble become easier to identify when typical childhood and adolescent development ages and stages are better understood (Center on the Developing Child at Harvard University, 2017b).

A deepening understanding of child and youth growth and development can also help inform educators of best practices to facilitate optimal growth and development of children and teens. It can aid outcomes such as building resiliency, especially for at-risk children and youth (Center on the Developing Child at Harvard University, 2017a; National Commission on Social, Emotional, and Academic Development, 2019). It can also add to an understanding of cultural diversity and the implications for policy, pedagogy, and practice (Reid et al., 2017). Understanding the stages of growth and development at typical ages can even reduce health consequences and promote best practices in nutritional, medical, and dental care (Sharma et al., 2017; Shonkoff et al., 2009; Shonkoff, 2016;).

The National Association for the Education of Young Children (NAEYC, 2020) offers nine guidelines and recommendations for developmentally appropriate practices for early childhood teachers and caregivers. These include recognizing and acknowledging the following concepts:

1. Children actively learn from birth through social relationships and their environment.

2. Development is a dynamic process between biology and the environment. Each affects and shapes the other in an ongoing way.

3. All domains of human development are interrelated and develop simultaneously. Each domain is important and shapes the others in an ongoing way. Growth in one domain may influence growth and learning in another domain.

4. Play is critical to development, especially for children ages 0–8, because it fosters self-regulation, cognitive abilities, language skills, and social relationships.

5. Cultural expectations and practices affect a child's development and learning.

6. When children feel a sense of belonging, purpose, and agency, they are more motivated to learn. Teachers and caregivers can create these environments and relationships.

7. Children learn in a multidisciplinary fashion, not subject by subject.

8. Development and learning are enhanced for young children who are given the opportunity to learn something just beyond their current skill level and who have a chance to reflect on their learning.

9. Interactive technology can support childhood development and learning when used responsibly and intentionally.

☑CHECKPOINT

☐ Define chronological age and social age. Name how each way of looking at age might be used to understand growth and development.

☐ How do the principles of human development guide educators and caregivers' expectations of a child's behavior and abilities?

☐ How might principles of development inform teacher and caregiver practices?

Apply Here!

Imagine that your school plans to do a fundraiser that involves the children in preschool through 6th grade. The planning group has decided on a "Jog-a-thon" in which the children solicit sponsors to pledge money for each lap a child runs, walks, or rides around the school track. You are concerned about the wide range of developmental abilities across this age range. Your school administrator has asked you to submit questions that will help guide the planning committee in using appropriate recommendations for children's involvement in the activity at all developmental levels.

- Make a list of questions or issues that the planning committee might consider in implementing developmentally appropriate practices for the Jog-a-thon.

- Do you have any recommendations for specific practices? If so, list and describe them.

1.4 The Domains of Development

The field of human development is a science. It is multidisciplinary, drawing from many fields, including anthropology, biology, chemistry, psychology, sociology, and education. If the interaction between biology and environment in human growth and development is complex and human responses are diverse, how might learning be organized to better reflect the complexity of development? With an understanding that human development is too multifaceted and individualistic to separate into distinct categories, it is nevertheless helpful to approach the study of children and teens with the idea that intersecting and interrelated domains coexist. These include the physical, cognitive (or intellectual), and socioemotional development domains. Social and emotional development are intertwined and thus will be approached together as socioemotional development. All three domains—physical, cognitive, and socioemotional—are codependent. When a child learns to use a crayon to color, this skill likely includes a level of development in all three areas—the physical ability to hold and manipulate a crayon with fingers, the cognitive understanding of the crayon's function, and the socioemotional will, self-regulation, and social modeling to perform the

Practical Issues and Implications

Applying Research to Foster Developmentally Appropriate Practices

When empirical, science-based research is used to guide best practices for providing care and resources for children and teens, it results in their optimal growth and development (Black et al., 2017; Dua et al., 2016; Lake & Chan, 2014). The National Association for the Education of Young Children (NAEYC) terms the use of empirical research to guide practices **Developmentally Appropriate Practices** (DAP), based on the work that was first proposed by Dr. Sue Bredekamp (1987, 2005) in the late 1980s (Dunn et al., 1997). The NAEYC (2021) identifies and promotes ten essential developmentally appropriate teaching practices for educating young children (see Figure 1.13). Educators should consider both Developmentally Appropriate Practices (DAP) and Developmentally Inappropriate Practices (DIP) when working with children of all ages, especially young children (see Table 1.2).

In older childhood and adolescence, different age-appropriate practices continue to positively affect learning and relationships with others (Gerde et al., 2013; Good, 2008; Willingham, D., 2009). For example, providing more equity in resource availability to children and teens plays a significant part in delivering developmentally appropriate experiences and opportunities (Sanders & Farago, 2018). Alford et al. (2016) found that when US primary school teachers were trained in and subsequently used DAP, their students were more likely to stay on learning tasks and not become distracted. The students were also more likely to engage in teacher-led discussions, engage in learning exploration, and participate in kinesthetic (hands-on manipulation) learning.

Following DAP with teens is important, too (Meschke et al., 2012). DAP can provide optimal opportunities for children and teens who have experienced ACEs to become more resilient (Ungar, 2015). Using DAP is especially important for those who care for and serve children and teens in the child welfare system, foster care, or juvenile justice system (Haight et al., 2014; Lamb, 2015; Vries et al., 2015). Studies show that when multiple systems are involved in caring for children and teens, evidence-based empirical practices are most effective. When working with children and teens, healthcare providers play a distinct role by using DAP in patient education (Morsa et al., 2020).

Culturally competent educators and primary caregivers are dedicated to continuing self-assessment, staying up-to-date with developmental research, and using DAP. DAP skills must be learned and developed for most teachers and care providers as empirical knowledge grows and changes.

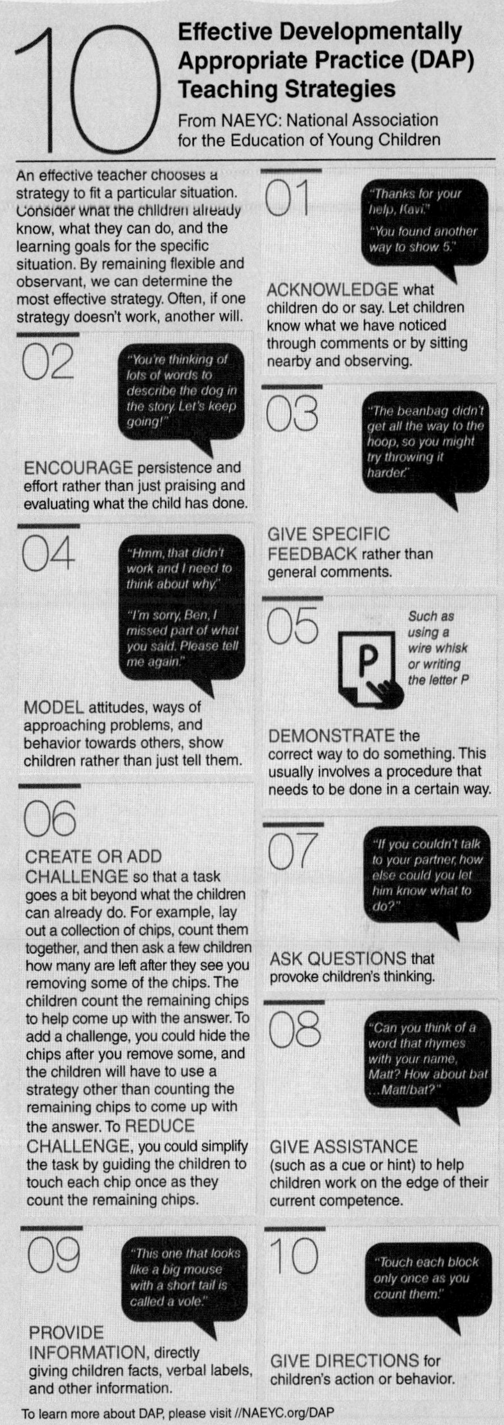

Effective Developmentally Appropriate Practice (DAP) Teaching Strategies

From NAEYC: National Association for the Education of Young Children

An effective teacher chooses a strategy to fit a particular situation. Consider what the children already know, what they can do, and the learning goals for the specific situation. By remaining flexible and observant, we can determine the most effective strategy. Often, if one strategy doesn't work, another will.

01 *"Thanks for your help, Ravi." "You found another way to show 5."*

ACKNOWLEDGE what children do or say. Let children know what we have noticed through comments or by sitting nearby and observing.

02 *"You're thinking of lots of words to describe the dog in the story. Let's keep going!"*

ENCOURAGE persistence and effort rather than just praising and evaluating what the child has done.

03 *"The beanbag didn't get all the way to the hoop, so you might try throwing it harder."*

GIVE SPECIFIC FEEDBACK rather than general comments.

04 *"Hmm, that didn't work and I need to think about why." "I'm sorry, Ben, I missed part of what you said. Please tell me again."*

MODEL attitudes, ways of approaching problems, and behavior towards others, show children rather than just tell them.

05 Such as using a wire whisk or writing the letter P

DEMONSTRATE the correct way to do something. This usually involves a procedure that needs to be done in a certain way.

06 CREATE OR ADD CHALLENGE so that a task goes a bit beyond what the children can already do. For example, lay out a collection of chips, count them together, and then ask a few children how many are left after they see you removing some of the chips. The children count the remaining chips to help come up with the answer. To add a challenge, you could hide the chips after you remove some, and the children will have to use a strategy other than counting the remaining chips to come up with the answer. To REDUCE CHALLENGE, you could simplify the task by guiding the children to touch each chip once as they count the remaining chips.

07 *"If you couldn't talk to your partner, how else could you let him know what to do?"*

ASK QUESTIONS that provoke children's thinking.

08 *"Can you think of a word that rhymes with your name, Matt? How about bat ...Matt/bat?"*

GIVE ASSISTANCE (such as a cue or hint) to help children work on the edge of their current competence.

09 *"This one that looks like a big mouse with a short tail is called a vole."*

PROVIDE INFORMATION, directly giving children facts, verbal labels, and other information.

10 *"Touch each block only once as you count them."*

GIVE DIRECTIONS for children's action or behavior.

To learn more about DAP, please visit //NAEYC.org/DAP

© National Association for the Education of Young Children (Note: This infographic was created from Developmentally Appropriate Practice, 3rd edition, 2020. Please refer to the fourth edition of DAP for the latest information and updates on DAP.)

Figure 1.13 NAEYC Developmentally Appropriate Teaching Strategies

(Continued)

DAPs Versus DIPs		
Age	**Examples of DAPs**	**Examples of DIPs**
Infants	• Encouraging guided movement activities, such as "patty cake" or "walking" • Scheduling tummy time for young infants • Encouraging the safe exploration of a room by crawling, scooting, or walking • Reading sturdy picture books with few words and lots of pictures • Providing clean, colorful toys that can be safely handled and mouthed • Holding, rocking, and cuddling by a caregiver • Playing and singing music that encourages motion	• Leaving child alone or with little caregiver interaction • Limiting physical exploration • Containing infants in small or limited space • Reading fragile books with more words and complex pictures • Providing toys with small parts or sharp edges and toxic finishes • Giving inadequate physical contact • Providing an unstimulating sensory environment
Toddlers	• Using flexible schedules • Providing child-size furniture • Providing moveable toy containers, such as baskets or carts • Creating play areas that promote gross-motor development • Encouraging sensory experiences, such as rice tables, soft toys, or toys that can be shaken, hammered, or wheeled	• Maintaining rigid schedules • Providing restrictive environments that minimize motor activity • Providing toys with small pieces • Using a time-out chair • Providing toys with just one specific use
Preschoolers	• Promoting child-directed art activities • Encouraging dramatic play areas with props • Providing building materials, such as blocks • Preparing outdoor areas for exploration • Maintaining flexibility in schedules • Providing play opportunities that utilize tools used in real life, such as in cooking or cleaning	• Providing only teacher-directed activities • Closely monitoring activities, such as with the use of worksheets and coloring pages • Providing games and toys that can only be manipulated one way • Maintaining rigidity in schedules • Enforcing compliance with adult choices

Kato; Goodheart-Willcox Publisher

Table 1.2 Examples of Developmentally Appropriate Practices (DAP) and Developmentally Inappropriate (DIP) Practices When Working with Young Children

To Think About:

• Have you observed teachers or caregivers using developmentally appropriate practices when working with children? Give a specific example of adapting an activity to the appropriate developmental level of a child.

• What do you feel you still need to learn about using Developmentally Appropriate Practices in creating equitable learning environments for children and teens?

task of coloring. When a child exhibits disordered eating such as bulimia or binge eating, physical, cognitive, and socioemotional factors contribute to this condition, and the child's development in all three domains is affected (Jaffa & McDermott, 2007). Child and teen obesity are likewise complex issues involving all three domains of development (Burniat, 2002). However, for simplicity and organization,

Physical	Cognitive	Socioemotional
• Height changes • Weight changes • Brain development • Teeth • Motor skills • Health and wellness • Puberty	• Brain development • Cognitive processing • Perception • Language • Memory • Information processing • Problem solving	• Emotions • Social relationships • Personality • Identity • Self-regulation • Prosocial behaviors • Self-confidence and self-esteem

Sharleen Kato

Figure 1.14 Major Components of Human Development with Examples

each domain will be discussed separately for each life stage in the upcoming chapters of this book (see Figure 1.14).

The Physical Development Domain

Physical development encompasses all growth and bodily changes that occur as an individual matures. This includes all dimensions of physical change, such as the development of eyesight over the first year, the growth and loss of teeth, brain growth and change, puberty, physical skills, and changes in body size, muscles, and fat tissue. The rapid physical growth in the first years of life is astonishing as infants often triple their body weight and double their length in just a year's time (Bremner & Wachs, 2010; Brink, 2013; Gross, 2019). Both the brain and nervous system continue to develop rapidly during infancy (Diamond et al., 2011). However, physical development involves more than just physical growth; it also manifests in advances in physical abilities. A newborn cannot change body position, but a 2-year-old can run. Many individual developmental steps make this progression possible. The newborn's random arm and leg movements build muscle strength until the infant eventually becomes strong enough to roll over. Crawling follows. Next, the baby learns to stand upright and finally takes a few steps. It takes months of walking practice for steadiness and coordination to improve, and then running is possible. Physical development also involves cognitive abilities and socioemotional development. These developmental milestones come from biological programming and social achievement through interactions with primary caregivers and the environment. Knowing this, primary caregivers and educators provide infants and young children with safe environments while at the same time encouraging active exploration as much as possible (Haibach-Beach et al., 2018; Payne & Isaacs, 2016).

Part of physical development is the increasing ability of the body to perform tasks such as running, skipping, or hitting a baseball. Holding a bottle, writing one's name, playing a video game, or building a model are parts of physical development, too. These abilities are referred to as **motor skills** since they depend on increasing the strength and coordination of muscles. Large or gross motor skills, such as walking and throwing, depend on the development of the large muscles, including those in the body core, arms, legs, back, and shoulders (see Figure 1.15). Fine motor skills, such as picking up objects and eating with a spoon, depend on the development of the small muscles such as those in the hands and wrists.

ziggy_mars/Shutterstock.com

Figure 1.15 The ability to balance is a gross motor skill that develops between 18 months and 2 years and continues to improve as children mature.

Beyond infancy, physical development continues, but the skills and abilities become more complex. As a child learns new physical feats such as hopping or climbing, playing the piano, or learning dance choreography, these new skills lead to better physical coordination and cognitive problem solving (Lubans et al., 2010). In middle childhood, or from ages 6 to 11, motor skills increase as children become faster, more adept, and stronger. This continues through adolescence and into young adulthood, when motor skills begin to increase in speed and agility (Leverson et al., 2012). Once again, the three domains of development are intertwined. Even the use of technology not only requires motor and cognitive skills but also affects the physical development of a child or teen's brain (Bergen et al., 2016).

The Cognitive Development Domain

Cognitive development refers to neurological and psychological development that includes information processing, perception, memory, language, and adaptive learning, or the ability to build on previous experiences and knowledge. Humans can think, sense, memorize, and organize their ideas, thoughts, and actions. These and other mental processes involving thought and knowledge are termed **cognition**. The way people change and improve in their ability to think and learn throughout life is *cognitive development*, or *intellectual development*.

Like physical skills, cognitive abilities increase gradually. Cognitive development is interrelated with physical and socioemotional development. Primary caregivers, educators, and medical professionals have long known that children, even infants, are affected by their physical and social surroundings (Calkins, 2015). Research has shown that negative experiences can affect the development of the brain during infancy (Legerstee et al., 2013). Even very young children play an active role in their learning, including deciding what will capture their attention and hold it and what the response will be based on their motivation, maturation, and experiences (Lerner et al., 2013; Xu, 2019; Wells, 2020). Thus, primary caregivers and educators can provide an environment that encourages optimal brain development during a child's first years. Language is a fascinating area of cognitive development that connects with physical and socioemotional development. An infant goes from babbling to understanding that words can have more than one meaning and can mean different things to different people (Wang, 2014).

Consider how math skills differ between a first grader, an eighth grader, and a high school senior (see Figure 1.16). Cognitive skills may improve dramatically over that time span. As a result, the way children and teens receive instruction in math

Anna Kraynova/Shutterstock.com; Aedka Studio/Shutterstock.com; Rido/Shutterstock.com

Figure 1.16 Cognitive skills improve dramatically as children mature, as shown in the differing abilities of a toddler, middle schooler, and high schooler.

changes, too; and as time progresses, they understand more complex concepts. Because formal schooling generally begins during the middle childhood years, there are opportunities to meld social relationships and the child's cognitive development to facilitate learning (Cozby & Bates, 2020). Social relationships and the surrounding environment have a tremendous effect on cognitive development and learning in adolescence (Gray & MacBlain, 2015; Pritchard, 2008; Schunk, 2012).

With an increasing understanding of how the brain develops and works, scientists provide new insights into cognitive development. The development of connections between nerve cells in the brain is a crucial component to cognitive development at all stages of life. Brain connections grow and strengthen with new experiences and the repetition of familiar ones. Thanks to advances in medical equipment, advanced brain imaging has revealed that the teenage brain has much more maturing to do, specifically the prefrontal cortex area of the brain, which is responsible for the ability to organize, plan, demonstrate self-control, problem-solve, judge, and be self-aware (Casey et al., 2008; Choudhury, 2010; Geidd, 2004).

The Socioemotional Development Domain

Besides their physical and cognitive growth and development, children and teens are also developing their personalities, acquiring social skills and attitudes, and learning how to care about others. They must develop both self-confidence and self-esteem. **Socioemotional development** includes growth and maturation in identity, social relationships, emotions, and feelings. For example, learning self-control is an essential socioemotional skill for kindergarteners that relies on physical and cognitive development. Students learn to wait their turn, form a line, and listen when the teacher gives instructions.

Socioemotional development occurs throughout childhood and adolescence and is critical to optimal physical and cognitive development. Physical and cognitive development are essential to socioemotional development as well (Legerstee et al., 2013; Lerner et al., 2013). Primary caregiver and infant social interactions, such as playing together, cuddling or rocking, and the volleying of verbal and nonverbal interactions, affect all three domains of growth and development. These caregiver and infant social interactions have positive physical effects. For example, there is a calming effect on the infant's heart rate and breathing regulating while the infant and the caregiver are building reciprocal cognitive understanding and socioemotional sensitivity and responsiveness (Davies & Troy, 2020; Oster, 2019). The opposite is also true, as infants with lower levels of interpersonal contact show more distress seen in fussiness or crying. It may also result in a molecular or biochemical cell profile for their age, indicating potential health issues (Moore et al., 2017). When a primary caregiver consistently responds to an infant's needs, a secure, lifelong attachment and a trusting relationship develops (Sullivan et al., 2011; van IJzendoorn & Bakermans-Kranenburg, 2008).

Infants learn how to interact socially from their caregivers. Young children learn about the people, relationships, and cultural life around them. As they develop, they learn how and where they fit in, how to form close relationships with adults, siblings, and peers, and how to express and regulate emotions in socially and culturally appropriate ways. Both observation and social interactions contribute to developing a sense of identity in the context of family, community, and culture (see Figure 1.17) (Bilmes, 2012; Robinson, 2008; Yates et al., 2008). Socioemotional development affects a young child's overall well-being as it sets the stage for all relationships and social interactions, including later school readiness and success, relationships with others, positive or

Figure 1.17 Children develop a positive sense of cultural identity through their participation in family traditions. In this photo, a mother helps her daughter place a small oil lamp on the family altar to celebrate Diwali.

Rawpixel.com/Shutterstock.com

Figure 1.18 Relationships with peers become increasingly important to adolescents, providing them with a sense of belonging and teaching them social and emotional skills.

deviant social behaviors, and mental health throughout life (Blair & Raver, 2015; Darling-Churchill & Lippman, 2016; Williams & Lerner, 2019).

Successfully learning new socioemotional development skills can provide children with a sense of confidence that they can master a situation that will yield favorable results. However, if these skills are not learned, the child may develop a sense of inferiority (McCormick & Scherer, 2018). Primary caregivers and educators can offer reassurance and demonstrate trust that helps children and teens develop a sense of competence and confidence in their ability to work toward achieving new skills (Gonzalez-DeHass & Willems, 2013; Gonzalez-DeHass, 2020). Peer relationships can either influence children positively by teaching social skills and enforcing social relationship expectations, or negatively if rejection or unhealthy relationships occur (see Figure 1.18) (Holder & Coleman, 2015; Maunder & Monks, 2019; Shin et al., 2016). At each stage of development, children and teens must learn new skills to deal with increasing independence, such as in social situations and as emotional or psychological issues become more complex. How well individuals meet those challenges depends on the skills they develop early in life and how well they can adapt those skills to new situations.

☑CHECKPOINT

- ☐ What are the three domains of human growth and development?

- ☐ How are the three domains interrelated? Give an example.
- ☐ Name and describe the domain that includes emotional and social development.

Apply Here!

As young children learn new skills such as riding a tricycle or writing and forming letters of the alphabet, it involves all three domains of development. Choose an activity or skill to teach a young child of a specific age. Select an activity that would be unfamiliar to a child of this age, such as how to play a specific card or board game. As part of your planning, consider the following:

- Is the game developmentally appropriate for a child of this age? What criteria did you use to assess a potential match for the activity and child?
- For each developmental domain, what skills or cognitive understanding are necessary?
- If you have access to a young child, teach the child that skill.
- To take this activity further, consider developing a guide for the puzzles, games, or toys that the children in your care can access. Besides the recommended age that the manufacturer provides, what additional developmentally appropriate skills or cognitive abilities might you add?

1.5 Methods of Expanding Knowledge

A basic understanding of common research methods will help you evaluate the plausibility of the many facts or studies conducted about human development. Many unverified stories are reported by news sources or shared on social media. For example, are children programmed by genetics to become obese? Does online learning reduce bullying?

Sometimes, questions about human development can be answered through research in the *natural sciences* (Brownson et al., 2018). You can review experiments that were involved in the study of the physical world and its phenomena, including in the fields of biology, chemistry, and physics. Such research would explore questions such as: how does sugar intake affects a child's heart rate? Does taking folic acid reduce the number of infants born with nervous system disorders? Do childhood vaccinations cause learning challenges? The natural sciences are precise, deterministic, and independent of the researcher.

Questions about human development may also be answered by studying the *applied sciences*, which focus research on practical goals, or the *social sciences*, which study human behavior within a cultural perspective (McClure, 2020; Scholtz et al., 2020; Skinner et al., 2019). This includes research in psychology, sociology, nutrition, family studies, and education. Social science research would explore questions such as whether classroom buddy (mentoring) programs decrease classroom bullying behaviors. Are infants who are frequently held better able to self-regulate emotions? Are there relationships between the racism and violence exhibited in a community and school performance in teens? There is a higher degree of measurement error in the social sciences, more uncertainty, and less agreement on how social science findings should affect policy decisions. For example, if the maternal mortality rate is higher in the United States for Black women than for White women, how should policies change? The problem can be acknowledged, but unraveling its causation can be complex.

Most often, human development research is a combination of natural, social, and applied science. For example, consider the questions: "What effect does an ACE during the preschool years have on a person's future diagnoses of anxiety, depression, heart disease, or cancer? Are any noted relationships causal or correlated?" All three approaches could be pursued. Researchers might use the natural science to conduct **physiological measures** or bodily changes, the social sciences to measure changes and influences of the family and neighborhood, and the applied sciences to measure the effect of intervention programs.

Those who care for children and teens often observe and wonder about the particularities of development. Why does that behavior follow a particular action? How do two or more factors influence growth and development? Caregivers make observations and sometimes come to conclusions based on limited data or limited personal knowledge, prejudices, or the influence of those who claim expertise or power. This type of anecdotal observation provides limited credibility or repeatable information. So, what do human development researchers do? They utilize the scientific method.

The Scientific Method

Modern science is complex, but so are humans. Making it further complicated, each human is an individual with different physical traits, environmental factors, and both socially learned and genetically programmed abilities and reactions. Then, social relationships, each with one or more individuals, increase the complexity. Even so, the scientific method helps researchers pursue their goals, increase understanding, and formulate questions for future research and exploration. The classic scientific method consists of making an observation, asking a question or forming a hypothesis, testing the hypothesis by collecting data, analyzing the results of the data collected, and making conclusions (see Table 1.3). Researchers are careful not to make broad generalizations from results or assume that the results would be the same for all populations or samples.

Data Collection Methods

There are many ways to collect data to further understand human development. **Quantitative data** collection methods are most often used in human development research (Demuth, 2015; Scholtz et al., 2020). These methods emphasize objective mathematical or numerical measurements that are statistically analyzed. Surveys, questionnaires, polls, or other numerical data sources work well in quantitative data collection. Data can include huge data sets such as data mined from websites, collected in large census surveys, or obtained from online analytic tools. Known as **big data**, the large-scale collection of quantitative data is used increasingly in developmental research. This is because it lends itself to a greater understanding of the complexities of social factors such as socioeconomic demographics and other public policy concerns affecting children and teens (Davis-Kean & Jager, 2017; Lovasi et al., 2021; Woo et al., 2020).

Qualitative data describes qualities or characteristics of people, things, experiences, or behaviors. Qualitative data collection methods are helpful in identifying behaviors of children and teens and recognizing patterns of thinking, historical experiences, reactions, and situations. These methods can also aid in understanding the complexities of social relationships, customs, and social norms. Traditionally, qualitative data did not include mathematical

The Scientific Method Steps	Description	Example
Make an Observation	• Observe and ask questions about what is intriguing or perplexing regarding some aspect of a child or adolescent development. • Read and study what other researchers have thought or concluded about this topic. • Evaluate the quality of the research, the subjects (participants), and their specific traits, ask questions, and look for gaps in knowledge.	As an early childhood classroom teacher, you notice that primary caregivers of young children who are early walkers (before age one) often say that their child is "extremely bright" or mature beyond their peers, using the early walking as evidence.
Ask a Question	• Formulate a hypothesis during or even after completing the observation stage. • Remember that a measurable hypothesis includes two or more variables. • You will need to test your hypothesis about what might be an expected outcome from conducting this research. • State the hypothesis so that it can be supported or unsupported.	Children who walked before age one demonstrate no significant differences in cognitive problem-solving skills at age three when compared to their peers who begin walking after age one.
Collect Data to Test the Hypothesis	• Collect information through a chosen, measurable data collection means. • Measure with accuracy and efficiency.	Methods of collecting data may include • surveys, • interviews, • observation, and • cognitive tests.
Examine the Results and Draw Conclusions	• Perform data analysis and decipher if results were achieved by chance or if they were statistically or numerically significant. • Summarize the data, analyze the results, and draw conclusions based on the evidence.	You conclude that walking before age one had no correlation with increased cognitive ability at age three among the children attending the given school.

Kato

Table 1.3 Steps in the Scientific Method, Descriptions, and Examples

or numerical measurements. However, most current qualitative research now consists of an objective scoring or measurement system that helps researchers lower the risk of overt subjectivity. For example, when observing a young child at play, a researcher might use a scoring sheet that includes numerical rankings that will be compiled, calculated, and analyzed. Of course, subjectivity is not eliminated, but it is decreased, giving more credibility to the conclusions (Demuth, 2015; Gough & Lyons, 2016; Levitt et al., 2017).

Mixed data collection methods, which combine both quantitative and qualitative methods, are also commonly used to provide a deeper and more complex picture. For example, an extensive survey that includes socioeconomic variables, health statistics, and genetic or biological profiles might provide quantitative data combined with qualitative interviews of individual subjects that delve into their personal experiences. Because the opportunities for vast amounts of data are possible, work continues on how to reliably analyze mixed data (Gunasekare, 2015; Ivankova et al., 2016). Methods of collecting data, descriptions of these methods, their uses and benefits, and their limitations are described in Table 1.4.

Depending on the desired outcome(s), there are different ways of conducting research. **Experimental research** methods explore cause-and-effect

Method of Data Collection	Description	Uses/Benefits	Limitations
Observation	• Watching subjects systematically and objectively while coding and recording data • May include what subjects do or say or their reactions to controlled variables • May include a controlled laboratory or naturalistic (home, classroom) environment	• Helps discern the behaviors, actions, and emotions of subjects	• Researchers' subjectivity makes complete objectivity difficult to achieve. • Observation is time-consuming and labor-intensive to implement. For example, observing young children can take vast amounts of time and energy. • The observer has less control over both the environment and external factors that may influence responses. • The subject may be aware of the researcher's presence, influencing responses.
Surveys and interviews	• Asking subjects for answers or responses to specific questions • May be administered verbally, electronically, or in written format	• Allows for comparison between hundreds or thousands of other people • Collects large amounts of data, especially when administered electronically • Provides greater accuracy in data analysis • Less likely to be biased as scoring is procedural • Records emotional and physical responses in person-to-person interviews	• Surveyor's biases or perceptions cannot be separated entirely from subjects' responses. • They must be developmentally appropriate for the subject. • Respondents may try to guess the "right" or "acceptable" response rather than giving honest answers. For example, a survey that asks teens about their sexually intimate relationships may not be highly accurate due to sample bias or misperceptions. • They may not ask all pertinent questions, leading to skewed data results. • Respondents who are not good test-takers may not accurately reflect their performance. • The environment may influence test performance.
Case studies	• Look at a single individual's life experience • Evaluate the individual's response within the scenario	• Delve deeply in personal stories, life histories, medical and mental health conditions, and culture • Provide technical information that may otherwise be unavailable	• Because case studies are so multidimensional and personal, it is difficult not to inject bias when rendering data outcomes. • Typically, case studies cannot be replicated and are used when the subject's life experiences are unique.
Standardized tests	• Used to measure differences, abilities, attitudes, or other factors across large swaths of people	• Best known for their use in schools to test academic achievement, aptitude, or understanding	• Run the risk of trying to be "one size fits all." • May not be culturally sensitive or relevant.

(Continued)

Kato

Table 1.4 Methods of Collecting Data, Uses, Benefits, and Limitations

Method of Data Collection	Description	Uses/Benefits	Limitations
Physiological measures	• Evaluate bodily functions or changes • Include blood tests, magnetic resonance imaging (MRI), hearing tests, and many other medical measuring procedures	• Have been especially significant in understanding brain growth and development, mental health issues, and genetic influences	• People are complex, and sometimes factors that can only be measured through social science research can shed light on the complexity of human growth and development.

Kato

Table 1.4 Continued

relationships. Did *this* factor cause *that* outcome? Variables are established to determine the cause. An **independent variable** represents the cause or reason for an outcome. **Dependent variables** are *dependent* on the independent variable. As the independent variable is manipulated, researchers observe and record changes in the dependent variable. In short, independent variables are methodically manipulated to measure their effect on the dependent variable. **Correlational studies** determine relationships between variables. They are sometimes used to measure the strength of variable relationships, too. Instead of manipulating variables, descriptive research describes human growth and development through observations, case studies, or surveys (Baker & Charvat, 2008; Cozby & Bates, 2020; Jones et al., 2020; Scholtz et al., 2020).

Limitations of and Issues in Child and Adolescent Research

Conducting research on child and adolescent growth and development can be tricky. First, the progressive and rapid changes in stages of growth and development sometimes make it challenging to fit studies into a stable period. Second, children and adolescents may lack the cognitive ability, vocabulary, or emotional maturity to provide meaningful feedback or accurately respond to prompts. These first two challenges fall under the category of childhood ages and stages. Third, the subjects are all under-age minors, which requires special sensitivity toward causing no harm and permission from primary caregivers. These challenges fall under the category of ethical concerns (Dickson-Swift et al., 2008; Scholtz et al., 2020).

Ages and Stages

Children vary vastly as they change from age to age and pass through life stages. Sometimes researchers want to know whether data change over time. There are many ways to collect data to test a hypothesis. Examples include the following:

- **Descriptive studies** use information (**descriptive data**) that depicts people and situations and then tabulates the different responses. For example, how many 11-year-olds versus 18-year-olds expect to receive an allowance from their parents? How many teen boys were texting while involved in a car accident?

- **Longitudinal studies** observe the same individuals over a period of time. For example, a researcher may ask a child their opinion on an allowance as a teen, and then again as an adult. By following the same individual over time, the researcher can begin to understand variables that cause change.

- **Cross-sectional studies** compare groups of various ages at the same time. For example, they may ask primary caregivers from a cross-section of socioeconomic populations to share their opinions about giving allowances to teens.

People are born into a certain generation or **cohort group** that shares common historical experiences and ideologies. Humans are heavily influenced by their cohort groups (Pew Research Center, 2015). Table 1.5 presents the names and typical characteristics of cohort groups from the last five generations, roughly from 1940 to 2010. Children born after 2010 are commonly referred to as Generation Alpha. The subsequent generation may be

Generation Cohort Name	Years of Birth	Common Characteristics
Baby Boomers	1944–1963	• Dual-career families • Working primary caregivers • Upwardly mobile • Socioeconomic divide
Generation X	1964–1979	• 40% from single-parent families ("latchkey kids") • Half live at home while going to college or establishing a career • Later marrying • College educated • Delay childbirth
Generation Y	1980–1995	• Digital natives (tech-savvy) • Value collaboration • Family relationships are important • Highly educated • Millennials
Generation Z	1996–2010	• More racially and ethnically diverse • May be the best-educated generation • Desire an activist government

Kato; Pew Foundation

Table 1.5 Generational Cohorts, Years of Birth, and Common Characteristics

termed Generation Beta, each having its own distinct cohort experiences and characteristics (Pinsker, 2020).

Studies in human development are affected by the cohort group within which a child is a member. Although some common things can be expected as a cohort ages, such as when older cohorts demand more accessible and affordable housing and care services and younger generations demand more from school systems, each cohort has its own unique shared experience that binds and shapes them (Pew Research Center, 2015). For example, Gen Xers may remember watching the explosion of the Space Shuttle Challenger, while Gen Yers were students during the 9/11 attacks on the United States. Younger members of Generation Z share the common experience of being in school during a global pandemic. Children born within the next decade will someday say about the COVID-19 global pandemic, "that happened before I was born."

Many Baby Boomers and Gen Xers are now grandparents. Especially during the global COVID-19 pandemic, many grandparent-child-grandchild relationships were altered by either interacting less often and more remotely or becoming more intense as grandparents filled in gaps in accessible childcare when education became remote. For many families, the global pandemic resulted in the loss of family members, especially those who were older.

Ethical Concerns

Researchers must follow ethical standards to ensure research subjects are safe and not harmed during an experiment or afterward. Information gathered must be kept confidential. The research must be considered moral. *Moral* refers to personal standards of behavior or beliefs concerning what is and is not acceptable. Subjects must grant permission, or, in the case of minors, legal guardians must grant permission. Studies involving children must be extra diligent in making sure they follow ethical standards and cause no harm. The scientific method demands truthfulness and diligence in seeking to further people's understanding.

Ethics, or the conduct of activity guided by moral principles, should be integral to conducting research experiments. When research involves people, the rights of experiment participants are relevant and necessary. Universities, hospitals, and research laboratories often have ethics committees to evaluate the legitimacy of proposed experiments. Ethics committees will review the overall purpose of the experiment and means of gathering information to determine if the research will be properly and ethically conducted. Criteria that ethics committees apply during the investigation, as well as the rights of the research participant, include the following:

- Participants must be informed of the purpose of the experiment and consent or agree to participate in the study. They must also be informed of their right to exit the research participation at any point during the experiment.
- If information about the experiment is withheld to prevent influencing the participant's responses, the researcher must inform or debrief the participant of the entirety of the experiment upon the experiment's conclusion.
- The researcher must protect the physical and mental well-being of the patient. This includes appropriate behavior from the researcher.
- Information about the participant must remain confidential and anonymous, unless agreed upon otherwise (American Psychological Association, 2017).

Research to Theory

Research gives valuable insights into how children and teens grow, develop, change, emote, behave, think, learn, and relate to self and others. In traditional research, as described in this chapter, the researcher focuses on others with the motivation to improve understanding. For example, an early childhood care provider may focus research on improving her classroom practices to create the best environment for her students. Care must be taken not to be biased when potential results affect

personal involvement and engagement (Skinner et al., 2019; Hilton et al., 2020).

At the same time, massive studies involving thousands or even millions of subjects are becoming more common as technology lends itself to efficiently and accurately collecting large pools of data and analyzing them (Woo et al., 2020). According to the Pew Research Center, younger generations, those with higher education, and Generations Y and Z are more likely to participate in citizen science, which includes crowdsourcing data collection and clinical or medical research studies, or to give financial support to medical or science research (Thigpen & Funk, 2020).

☑ CHECKPOINT

- ☐ What are the steps in the scientific method?
- ☐ Compare and contrast quantitative versus qualitative data collection techniques.
- ☐ Define *big data* and describe a good reason for using it as a data collection measure.
- ☐ How are dependent and independent variables used when conducting research?
- ☐ Why are ethics critical in research that involves children and adolescents?

Apply Here!

Think of a child or adolescent issue that confounds you. It may involve a specific observed behavior, such as a child biting peers despite being guided away from the practice or a teen having difficulty with social transitions. How might you gain some insight into the matter using theory and research rather than folklore or opinions? Are you noticing any trends?

Summary

There are numerous ways to learn about child and adolescent growth and development. Customs, habits, myths, and traditions offer subjective insight. The scientific method provides more objective data to draw from, although it is still imperfect because humans are complex. Understanding growth and development in children and teens is an ongoing endeavor, one that will likely continue as long as there are new generations with individual traits and shared experiences. In any piece of research, it is typical to start with the theoretical framework that we base our research on. In the next chapter, you will learn about foundational theories of child and adolescent growth and development, along with a growing understanding of heredity and the influence of genetics.

Learning Outcomes and Key Concepts

1.1 Describe several contemporary issues that can influence child and adolescent growth and development.

- Responsive family relationships build social bonds and robust brain architecture in young children.
- Having adequate resources and quality care and nurturing relationships aids optimal growth and development.
- Stress and ethnic-racial discrimination can affect identity formation, emotional and social development, and overall mental health.
- When ethnic and racial identity is affirmed, it contributes to optimal physical and cognitive health.
- ACEs (adverse childhood experiences) may cause negative effects on lifelong health and well-being.

1.2 Discuss how cultural expectations about children's education have changed over time.

- In the Early Years (1776 to 1880), schools were primarily focused on the elementary grades, but many believed that schools could be a vehicle for making a better society.
- By the end of the early period, free public education for many was much more widely available.

- In the American Progressive Period (1880-1920), many children worked alongside their parents, and urban schools quickly became overcrowded.
- After World War II, there was a push to strengthen math, science, and foreign language instruction in schools.
- Mid-20th-century schools were racially segregated based on "separate but equal" policies, but they still were not equal in funding.
- In the latter 20th century, the federal government established guidelines for achieving excellence in education, and standardized tests were used to measure students' performance.
- The No Child Left Behind Act focused on school performance and equal opportunity for all students regardless of race, geographic location, disability, or socioeconomic level.

1.3 Explain how a deepening knowledge of child and adolescent development can aid personal relationships and professional care.

- Growth refers to physical changes in size, with most growth occurring during the first 19 years of life.
- Development is the gradual increase in skills and abilities over a lifetime.
- Chronological age is determined by time lived, social age by expectations.
- Development occurs in a continuous, gradual, predictable, and orderly manner.
- Understanding development gives insight into what is predictable and typical, informing best practices.

1.4 Summarize the three interrelated domains within which children and teens grow and change during different ages and stages of life.

- Human growth and development include three interrelated domains.
- Physical development includes all growth and bodily changes that occur as a child grows and matures.
- Cognitive development includes neurological and psychological development that includes learning.
- Socioemotional development includes maturation in identity, social relationships, emotions, and feelings.

1.5 Describe how empirical research methods can be used to expand knowledge about child and adolescent growth and development.

- The scientific method consists of forming a hypothesis, collecting data, and making conclusions.
- Quantitative data collection uses objective numerical measurements that are statistically analyzed.
- Big data lends itself to better understanding the complexities of social factors and public policy.
- Qualitative data aids in understanding the complexities of social relationships and norms.
- Experiments use dependent and independent variables to determine variable relationships.
- Descriptive research describes human growth and development.
- Studies involving children must follow ethical standards and cause no harm.

Chapter Review

1. If you were writing a blog about how responsive family relationships build social bonds and robust brain architecture in young children, what would be your main points?

2. If you were assigned to lead a workshop for new teachers at an early childhood learning center about how stress and ethnic-racial discrimination can affect identity formation, emotional and social development, and overall mental health, what types of learning activities would you include?

3. How do ACEs negatively affect lifelong health and well-being? Be as specific as possible.

4. Define and contrast the terms *growth* and *development*. How does the concept of age affect one's views of growth and development?

5. Write a position statement that supports furthering understanding of human growth and development. Why is it important, and what does it offer teachers and care providers?

6. Name and describe the developmental domains in human growth and development, including a visual that shows the relationships between the domains.

7. Create an infographic that defines the scientific method and lists its component parts.

8. Define and differentiate between quantitative and qualitative data collection. Give an example of a current issue in your personal or work setting that could be studied with one of these types of data collection. What specific type of data-gathering instrument might you use?

9. Name and describe an issue in your community (university, town, city, state) that could be explored using *big data* to better understand the complexities of social factors and to possibly be used to affect future public policy.

10. Locate an empirical research study that focuses on one aspect of the growth and development of children or teens. Read the study and locate the dependent and independent variables.

11. Describe how descriptive research might enhance understanding of human growth and development in a particular care setting.

12. Why must studies involving children make sure to follow ethical standards and cause no harm? Create an ethics checklist to be used as a reference guide in a classroom or care setting.

13. Think about an issue in child or adolescent growth and development that intrigues you. Write a hypothesis. Consider taking the issue further by collecting and analyzing data and drawing a conclusion. How might this process offer more insight than only relying on intuition or experience?

Matching

Match the following terms with the correct definitions.

A. applied sciences   **E. correlational studies**

B. big data   **F. longitudinal studies**

C. case studies   **G. mixed data**

D. cohort group   **collection methods**

1. People born to a certain generation who share common historical experiences and ideologies.

2. Research studies used to determine relationships between variables.

3. Research studies that use the same individuals over time.

4. Science fields that focus research on practical goals.

5. Large-scale collection of quantitative data used in developmental research that lends itself to better understanding the complexities of social factors such as socioeconomic demographics.

6. Collection methods that combine both quantitative and qualitative methods to lend a deeper and more complex picture.

7. Collection methods that look at a single life experience and evaluate the subject's response within the scenario.

2

Developmental Theories and Genetics

Learning Outcomes

After studying this chapter, you will be able to:

2.1 Describe the four foundational theories in human development.

2.2 Identify some major theories related to the evolutionary perspective on human development.

2.3 Explain how genetics influences human growth and development.

2.4 Analyze the interaction between nature and nurture in human growth and development.

Key Terms

accommodation
adaptive behavior
assimilation
autosome
behavioral genetics
behaviorism
cell
cell nucleus
cognitive development theory
cognitive theory
conservation
developmental theories
dizygotic
DNA
dominant traits
ecological theory

enactive learning
epigenetics
equilibration
evolutionary developmental
   psychology (EDP)
gene
genetics
gene x environment (G x E)
   interactions
genome
heredity
information processing
   theory
meiosis
mitosis
modeling
monozygotic

natural selection
negative reinforcement
observable behaviors
operant conditioning
polygenetic
positive reinforcement
psychoanalytic theory
psychosocial theory
recessive traits
schema
sex-linked traits
social cognitive theory
sociocultural cognitive
   theory
vicarious learning
zone of proximal
   development

Introduction

Imagine yourself standing in the checkout line at a grocery store. The line is slow-moving, so as you wait your turn, it is hard to ignore a young child who is having a temper tantrum nearby. The child kicks and screams and lays on the floor and cries. Why? Did the child ask for a treat that was denied? Maybe it is not that simple. You speculate on why this behavior is occurring and what motivated it. Your own past experiences and knowledge influence your opinion. If you know the child, your opinion may be different than if the child is a stranger. Is the child tired or hungry? Is the child too young to understand? Does the child not get enough attention? Is this a behavior for which the child is typically rewarded? Is there a developmental challenge that is present?

We all have opinions about why people act the way they do. Your views about why situations occur and how people respond are often based on your current knowledge and past experiences. Child development researchers and scientists take these opinions a step further by exploring the many ways in which humans grow and develop. They observe people, perform experiments, and draw conclusions based on their own and others' studies. Using observation and experimentation, they formulate theories about why people act and behave in certain ways and how they change over time. Researchers study their subjects' genetic makeups and environments. Developmental researchers attempt to understand why behaviors occur and how growth and maturation happen. For example, what impacts do available economic resources have on a child's physical development? Does the onset of the gross motor ability to walk correlate to when a child learns to use small motor skills such as manipulating a crayon? Will a toddler who bites others have anger issues in middle childhood? If young children do not develop trust relationships with their caregivers, will they not have strong attachments later in life?

Why should you learn about developmental theories and the basics of genetics? Instead of relying only on your own limited personal experiences and observations, understanding developmental theories and the interplay of genetics and the environment will give you a broader picture of how people develop and change over time. That is the focus of this chapter.

2.1 Foundational Developmental Theories

Developmental researchers may have more knowledge and experience and use more scientific methods, but the process of conducting research is much like anyone's problem-solving when faced with a question. Researchers often start with an idea or a hypothesis—a specific prediction, forecast, or calculation—about what might happen. A hypothesis is not just a guess, but an informed premise founded on the work of previous research or observations from others. They then design a study to test their hypothesis. They observe people and perform experiments, all with the intent of collecting data. Once data are collected, they are then analyzed. Then, researchers draw conclusions and formulate explanations about why people act and behave the way they do and how their actions change over time. These ideas or models of thought are called **developmental theories.**

Although these are theories, not proven facts, they can be particularly useful to help you better understand what infants, children, and teens are capable of doing and why. Instead of relying on your own limited personal experiences and observations, understanding developmental theories will give you a broader picture. The developmental theories summarized in this chapter are just a brief overview of the many that exist. They will be revisited throughout the upcoming chapters. As you read about them, evaluate how the theorists' conclusions compare with your own life experiences.

Foundational developmental theories focus on how humans grow, mature, change, and develop over time. The four thought orientations or groupings discussed next include the psychoanalytic, cognitive, behavioral and social, and ecological foundational theories. Research is active in all these areas, as current researchers build upon or dispel the ideas of others.

Psychoanalytic Theories

Many theorists have held different ideas about how and why humans develop and change the way they do. Some theorists believe that extensive development happens at an unconscious level and is buried in emotions. These ideas are called psychoanalytic theories. Psychoanalytic theorists analyze the symbolic meanings behind behaviors. They often believe that early life experiences are important in shaping development.

Freud's Theory

Sigmund Freud (1856–1939) was the founder of and a pioneer in **psychoanalytic theory**. Intending to restore psychological health, he helped his patients talk through their dreams and associated issues. As he spoke with more patients, he began to create a developmental theory focused on early life experiences. He believed that what happens early in a person's life affects them for years, influencing later adult behavior. Freud published a plethora of work during his life. Because he did not author a definite or summary work, researchers focus on his works that highlighted pleasure-seeking themes such as oral or anal fixations. However, his work was much more comprehensive and significantly affected future studies on the impact of cultural determinants on development. In addition, his work on how early childhood experiences influence later adult development changed the way society thinks about how our environment and experiences shape how we develop (Sandler, 1997; Tauber, 2010). Freud is well known for his idea that the human personality, or the psyche, is multidimensional and includes three parts: the id, the ego, and the superego, each with distinct but overlapping functions

Part of the Human Personality or Psyche	Description and Role
Id	• Primitive and instinctual part of the mind that stores hidden memories and basic drives such as sexual arousal and aggression • Might be responsible for basic, primal urges • Present at birth • Includes unconscious behaviors and actions • Remains a force throughout life
Ego	• Mediates between the id and the superego • More realistic part of personality, but challenging • Includes judgments and ways of processing appropriate behavior • Develops last, toward the end of early childhood
Superego	• Integrates moral judgment • Operates a moral compass often based on punishments and rewards • Regulates the id so that impulsive, primal behaviors begin to be modified

Kato

Table 2.1 Freud's Theory: Three Parts of the Human Psyche

(see Table 2.1). As these three parts develop, children learn to control their basic, primal urges in socially appropriate ways.

Erikson's Psychosocial Theory

Erik Erikson (1902–1994) was one of the most influential developmental researchers of the twentieth century. Like all researchers, his work was inspired by the theorists who came before him. Freud's daughter, Anna, was a friend and mentor to Erikson, urging him to pursue scholarly work in human development (Mooney, 2013). His focus was on personality development and, more specifically, on how children develop the basis for emotional and social development supported by mental health. In his first book, *Childhood and Society* (1950), Erikson laid out his theory of how children progress through stages of social-emotional development. Each stage is based on a crisis that needs to be resolved psychologically as the child's needs are weighed against other people's needs. Later, Erikson expanded his stages to encompass the entire human lifespan (see Table 2.2).

According to Erikson's **psychosocial theory,** psychosocial development occurs during eight stages of life (Erikson, 1982; Salkind & Rasmussen, 2008). People face and must successfully resolve a psychological or social conflict at each stage. If they fail to do so, their unsuccessful resolution will affect future stages of their development, although they may still resolve stages later in life (Erikson, 1982; Sheehy & Forsythe, 2003).

In the first of Erickson's stages, an infant must resolve the conflict of trusting or not trusting others, mostly learned from physical comforts instead of apprehension and fear. Erikson termed this the trust-versus-mistrust stage that dominates during the first year of life. For example, a baby's sense of trust may be built on learning that crying consistently results in being fed and comforted. Developing this sense of trust as an infant allows the child to develop other trusting relationships in life and builds a sense of hope. When adult caregivers fail to respond to an infant, their behaviors contribute to an infant developing mistrust. Of course, a child also must gradually learn to meet their own needs.

According to Erikson's psychosocial theory, other stages follow sequentially. As toddlers, young children begin to assert their independence and will, termed the autonomy-versus-shame-and-doubt stage. During this stage, young children begin to discover that their actions and behaviors influence others. Erikson cautioned that if children are reprimanded or controlled too severely, they are more likely to experience shame and doubt.

In early childhood, preschoolers learn to develop initiative by conducting plans or taking advantage of others. Erikson termed this the initiative-versus-guilt stage. For example, at age 3, Claire wants her younger sister and neighbor to pretend and play school with her. She wants to be the teacher, and they are to be her students. They go along with her plan, but once Claire becomes bossy, they may lose interest. Claire needs to take the initiative to

Stage/Age	Task	Description	Strength Developed
Infancy (Birth to 1 year)	Trust versus mistrust	Infants learn about trust from caregivers who meet their needs, including food, attention, physical contact, interaction, and safety. When needs are unmet, they perceive the world as an unpredictable place and begin to mistrust the care of others.	Hope
Toddler (1 to 3 years)	Autonomy versus shame and doubt	Toddlers learn self-help skills, such as feeding, toileting, dressing, and undressing, which increases their confidence. Toddlers who lack control or independence may experience shame and doubt. Some caregivers punish toddlers for not doing things "right" while still learning new skills. This can undermine confidence and lead to feelings of shame.	Willpower
Early childhood (3 to 6 years)	Initiative versus guilt	Through make-believe play, discovery, and exploration, young children learn about the world and their place in it. They learn what is real and what is imaginary. They learn to take initiative to claim their place in the world. Too much criticism and punishment can result in feelings of guilt and shame and makes children less likely to experiment with adult tasks.	Purpose
Middle childhood (6 to 12 years)	Industry versus inferiority	Children develop competency both at school and at home. They develop a sense of self-confidence as they become competent in the outside world and learn to work and cooperate with others. Feelings of inferiority can surface if children consistently are compared or compare themselves negatively to others.	Competence
Adolescence (13 to 19 years or older)	Identity versus role confusion	Preteens and teens begin to understand and experiment with several different roles. A task during this stage is to integrate multiple roles such as sister, daughter, student, athlete, friend, and employee. If a central, or core, identity is not established, role confusion exists.	Fidelity
Young adulthood (19 to 40 years or older)	Intimacy versus isolation	During later adolescence and early adulthood, close relationships form that should involve sharing oneself emotionally. Success in this stage depends on success at earlier stages. Failure to establish intimacy results in emotional or psychological isolation.	Love
Middle adulthood (40 to 65 years)	Generativity versus self-absorption	Adults in middle adulthood begin to emphasize assisting others and improving the next generation. This can be done in many ways, including parenting, teaching or training others, or passing on cultural values. Failure to do so leads to self-absorption.	Care
Older adulthood (65 years and older)	Integrity versus despair	In the last stage of life, adults review their lives and reflect on its meaning. If people are satisfied with their life, there is a sense of integrity. Without it, feelings of despair may emerge as the end of life approaches.	Wisdom

Kato

Table 2.2 Erikson's Theory of Psychosocial Development

Figure 2.1 Young children often enjoy helping with household chores.
Do you remember wanting to help grown-ups when you were a young child?

accomplishing her original plan; but at the same time, she has to learn to make the game enjoyable for the other children. Likewise, according to Erikson's theory, young children also want to be involved in family chores (see Figure 2.1). A child may not have the skills to sweep the floor properly, but allowing them to demonstrate this initiative (without being made to feel guilty for any mistakes) is an essential part of development.

During their elementary school years, children must master social and academic skills, such as making friends and learning to read. These are examples of skills that are important throughout life. Erikson calls this the industry-versus-inferiority stage. Children who cannot keep up with their peers may feel inferior, or less important, hindering later development. During the teen years, individuals must resolve what Erikson called identity-versus-role-confusion. Teens figure out who they are as individuals. They are concerned about how others see them, and they begin to decide what they want to do in life. Failure to create a self-identity in adolescence and young adulthood results in role confusion or a lack of understanding of one's place in society.

Erikson eventually updated his theory to include stages of psychosocial development through adulthood. He believed that development occurs throughout a person's life, a relatively new concept during his time. He theorized that people are constantly changing and developing. He labeled early adulthood as the intimacy-versus-isolation stage, when people tend to find personal partners. In middle adulthood, the strength of caring is developed through what Erikson called the generativity-versus-stagnation stage. Even elderly adults must face conflicts as they try to assess their lives in what Erikson termed the integrity-versus-despair stage (Guthrie, 2003; Salkind & Rasmussen, 2008).

A Critique of Psychoanalytic Theories

Although Freud's theory is not considered scientifically sound and many criticize his work today, Freud opened the door to a new way of understanding human development. Subsequent researchers used his work to build their own psychoanalytic theories (Robinson, 1993). Some critics also agree that Erikson's theories are not supported by empirical research. Erikson himself touted his theory as a framework that defines the problem or question rather than a testable tool that is used to gather any information to answer the questions (Erikson, 1950, 1982).

Psychoanalytic theorists such as Freud and Erikson contributed to our understanding that human psychological development happens in stages, an important standard for understanding how humans develop. Most importantly, they contended that developmental stages happened within the context of family relationships, and they introduced the idea that there are unconscious aspects of the mind that influence development (Wright, 2002). Educators and other professionals in child development use Erikson's psychosocial theory framework to understand behaviors in children and teens. It is also used in psychoanalytic practice with people of all ages, especially in counseling individuals experiencing mental illness (Knight, 2017).

☑ CHECKPOINT

☐ What are the id, ego, and superego?

☐ What are the eight stages of Erikson's Theory of Psychosocial Development?

☐ Which of Erikson's stages are you currently in? Cite your evidence to support this.

Cognitive Theories

Some theorists believe that much development happens through complex thinking at a conscious level, as opposed to psychoanalytic theories that relate human development to the effects of early childhood experiences at the unconscious level. Cognitive theorists attempt to explain human behavior by understanding thought processes, especially related to learning. The scientific focus on how we process information, think, and learn is called **cognitive theory**. Cognitive researchers seek to explain the differences in how people think throughout the stages of life. They look for explanations of how cognition changes over the lifespan. Three main cognitive theories include cognitive development theory, sociocultural cognitive theory, and information processing theory.

Piaget's Cognitive Development Theory

One of the most well-known cognitive theory researchers is Jean Piaget (1896–1980), a Swiss researcher who sought to explain the differences in how people think throughout the stages of life. Piaget's **cognitive development theory** utilized

observations that led him to identify four stages of cognitive development (see Table 2.3). His studies showed that individuals' thinking skills are similar during any stage of life. At each new stage, individuals incorporate new experiences into what they know based on the skills they developed in previous stages. Piaget asserted that children are constantly building knowledge about the world around them. They are not "blank slates" but already have knowledge based on their surroundings. This knowledge is referred to as **schema**. For example, infants know how to suck on objects, and their schema includes things they can or cannot suck. As new cognitive learning takes place, children utilize **assimilation**, the process of taking in new information. For example, infants suck on an object such as a bottle, pacifier, finger, or toy rattle. In doing so, they learn about the differences in the experience of sucking on each object. They then use **accommodation**, the

Stage	Age	Description	Example
Sensorimotor	Birth to 2 years	Infants and toddlers begin to learn about the world through their senses. At first, learning relies on reflexes; but more purposeful movement later enhances learning. This stage is further divided into six substages that will be explored in Chapter 5.	
Preoperational	2 to 7 years	Toddlers and young children communicate through language. They recognize symbols and learn concepts. Both direct experiences and imaginative play are keys to learning. This stage will be explored further in Chapter 8.	
Concrete operational	7 to 11 years	Children learn to think logically. They can generalize, understand cause and effect, group and classify items, and suggest solutions to problems. This stage will be explored further in Chapter 11.	
Formal operational	11 years and older	Children and adolescents master both logical and abstract thinking. This includes making predictions and considering "what if" questions. This stage will be explored further in Chapter 14.	

Daxiao Productions/Shutterstock.com; Odua Images/Shutterstock.com; Collin Quinn Lomax/Shutterstock.com; Daisy Daisy/Shutterstock.com; Kato

Table 2.3 Piaget's Stages of Cognitive Development

process of incorporating the new information into their schema, as they develop preferences between objects based on their experiences with each object. An infant may prefer one bottle type over another with a different-shaped nipple.

Piaget used the term **equilibration** to describe the mechanism of balancing old and new cognitive understanding. For example, a young child may sleep in a crib; but when a new bed arrives, the child is introduced to a new idea or definition of sleeping space. It typically takes time for the child to meld the old and new information, finding equilibrium and matching the old and new definitions of a place to sleep. Piaget opened a world of wondering and learning about the cognitive development of infants and toddlers. His groundbreaking research recognized and respected the great potential in an infant's cognitive abilities. Researchers and developmental psychologists have refined and added to this knowledge over the decades (Barrouillet, 2015; Kenny, 2013; Morra, 2008).

By carefully documenting children's thinking skills at various ages, Piaget improved the understanding of how cognitive skills develop over time. Piaget called the first stage of cognitive development the sensorimotor stage. In this stage, infants move from simple motor reflexes to interacting with the world around them using their ever-growing motor skills such as reaching, rolling, creeping, and crawling—all significant signs of cognitive growth. Infants combine actions learned through using reflexes with motor skills to achieve more goals, which gradually become more complex as the brain matures and experiences increase over time (Mandler, 2004). An infant may begin to reach for an object such as a dangling toy and, after learning that jiggling the toy produces a song, may purposefully repeat the action. According to Piaget's theory, toddlers are still in the sensorimotor stage as they continue to put objects in their mouths and discover through their senses while developing their motor skills. Toddlers use discovery to solve problems. Although they may still figure things out using their senses, they also start developing more sophisticated thought processes as they model and imitate the behaviors of others (Lerner et al., 2013). For example, a toddler may solve the problem of fitting a square shape into a square hole after observing the action.

Piaget believed that the world expands for children in early childhood during the preoperational stage as they walk, talk, explore new places, and can reason and think about the world in ways that were not possible during infancy (Cohen, 2018). Piaget referred to this stage as *preoperational* because it represents a time when children's use of symbolic and logical thinking is growing, and they gradually begin to use reasoning and logic (Inhelder & Piaget, 1958). They learn to use symbols, or language, to understand the world around them as they gradually move from using intuition and primitive reasoning based on feelings to more rational and logical thinking (Barrouillet, 2015; Bjorklund, 2004). In this stage, Piaget believed that young children are challenged with the concept of the state of an object changing in size (volume, mass, number), which he termed **conservation**. They tend to be egocentric, or focused on their own perspective, and they are not able to understand that others have different thoughts and feelings. More recent research shows that children understand conservation at an earlier age than previously thought. They are capable of thinking about their own thinking, as well as recognizing that other people have their own thoughts and feelings at a much earlier age than Piaget proposed (Estes & Bartsch, 2017; Schaafsma et al., 2015; Wellman et al., 2011).

In Piaget's concrete operational stage, concrete thinking refers to the logical mental processing that emerges in middle childhood. Piaget's experiments showed that children between the ages of 6 and 11 learn to think in more complex ways than they did in early childhood. They begin to use more analytical thinking and respond to open-ended questions. At the same time, their ability to manipulate abstract concepts into three-dimensional models, conduct science experiments, hypothesize and assess, and understand and use time and spatial parameters increases (Cohen, 2018; Hopkins, 2011; McLeod, 2018a).

Piaget describes adolescent learning, the fourth and final stage in his cognitive theory, as the formal operations stage. He believed that this stage starts at the beginning of adolescence, when teens have reached their highest level of cognitive maturity, and continues throughout adulthood (Barrouillet, 2015). In this stage, teens can think in more abstract and less concrete ways than in earlier stages.

Vygotsky's Sociocultural Cognitive Theory

In his **sociocultural cognitive theory**, Lev Vygotsky (1896–1934) believed that children are social beings and develop their minds through interactions with primary caregivers, siblings, and others with whom they are in a close relationship. These social interactions and the surrounding culture are critical to an infant's cognitive development (Bullard, 2014; Legerstee et al., 2013). Through these social interactions, infants—and eventually children—learn not only by exploring their world through their senses but also by responding to and imitating others. When primary caregivers, educators, older peers or siblings, and other mentor figures help children at their current level of understanding, they learn more (Moore, 2010; Xu, 2019).

Vygotsky called this interface of learning the **zone of proximal development** (ZPD), or the level at which a child can learn with help (Barrouillet, 2015). Once a mentor can find the child's ZPD, the child is more likely to learn new skills without feeling overwhelmed. Once a child performs a task, scaffolding or mentor support can be decreased and eventually removed, resulting in a new ZPD (Vygotsky, 1978, 1993; Wertsch, 1984). For example, a young child cannot ride a bicycle. If a mentor helps, holding onto the bike as the child learns to balance, the mentor's support is gradually decreased and eventually eliminated as the child learns to ride the bike independently. You will learn more about scaffolding in Chapter 5. Vygotsky believed social interactions were crucial to learning a new skill or acquiring new knowledge or understanding (see Figure 2.2).

Vygotsky's work decades ago in Russia still informs early childhood educators today. Vygotsky saw children's imaginative play as a way to learn new skills (Bodrova & Leong, 1996; Wertsch & Sohmer, 1995). Learning is a social endeavor, and through relationships, young children learn about the world around them (Mahn & John-Steiner, 2012; Wink & Puteny, 2002). In middle childhood, during the school-age years, the pool of mentors continues to expand to include teachers, classmates, peers, coaches, and other mentors as they interact with children to guide or facilitate their learning (Barrouillet, 2015; Bates, 2019; Vygotsky, 1978, 1993). Later, adolescents learn new knowledge and skills through interactive exploration, cooperative learning with others, utilizing the scientific method, and general problem-solving (Bodrova & Leong, 1996; Wertsch & Sohmer, 1995).

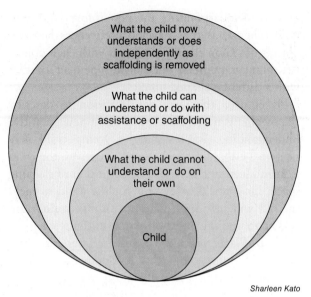

Sharleen Kato

Figure 2.2 Vygotsky's Zone of Proximal Development (ZPD) and Childhood Learning

Information Processing Theory

Information processing theory uses the analogy of the human brain functioning much like a computer. When given a problem to solve or a task to perform, the brain goes through a series of functions to reach a resolution. This includes the movement, storage, and transformation of information to reach an end goal or solution. Allen Newell, John Clifford Shaw, and Herbert Simon (1958) were among the first researchers to promote this theory. From the 1950s onward, a group of researchers from multiple backgrounds, including those in psychology and computer science, continued to progressively develop the theory (Klahr & Wallace, 1976; Vanlehn, 1991; Young, 1978). Information processing theory began as an attempt to understand the human brain as a problem-solving device that performed mental manipulations, including memory, perception, and language acquisition. Many researchers have used games and problem-solving puzzles as a way to understand how the human brain processes information at different stages of life (Anderson, 1995; Baylor & Gascon, 1973; Klahr & Siegler, 1978).

In comparing how a computer solves a problem to how the human brain solves a problem, information processing theory explains behavior as a function of memory and cognitive controls or rules (Ericsson & Simon, 1984). It is not age- or stage-based. Researchers learn about cognitive processes by observing human actions and the verbal reports of a person solving a problem or performing a task. Information processing theory has played a significant role in developing artificial intelligence (Drescher, 1991; Newell, 1970). Neuroscientists, those who study brain functions, are also expanding our understanding of how the brain processes information (David, 2019; Moustafa, 2018).

A Critique of Cognitive Theories

Although cognitive theories are continually being updated, modified, and expanded upon, the foundation of Piaget, Vygotsky, and similar theorists' work remains vital to our understanding of human development today. Although Piaget focused on an infant's maturation process, subsequent theorists have highlighted the importance of outside influences, including caregivers, on cognitive development. Cognitive theories continue to be significant because they are based on biological maturation and personal life stages. Thus, the focus is on the child's or youth's readiness to learn, not on what has already been taught. A child or teen should be biologically mature enough before being expected to solve a problem using internal thinking (Barrouillet, 2015; Hopkins, 2011; Wavering, 2011).

☑CHECKPOINT

- ☐ How did Piaget describe his four stages of learning?
- ☐ How does Vygotsky's sociocultural cognitive theory expand Piaget's cognitive theory?
- ☐ What is the zone of proximal development?
- ☐ How does information processing theory expand our view of cognitive processing?

Behavioral and Social Cognitive Theories

Behaviorism is the belief that forces in the environment determine a person's behavior. According to behaviorists, how a person behaves depends on what they have seen, modeled, been taught, or experienced. When an experience is encountered, an outcome will result. These results are called observable behaviors. **Observable behaviors** are the things people do and say or how they act. The behavior could be a verbal or facial response such as a smile or the act of following instructions. Social cognitive theory takes behaviorism further by offering a structure for understanding how people actively shape and are shaped by their environment, are motivated to learn, and self-regulate (Bandura, 1977, 1986, 1997, 2001; Schunk & Usher, 2019). According to behavioral and social cognitive theories, each interaction and stimuli from surroundings plays a part in a person's cognitive growth and development (Thornton, 2003; Moore, 2010).

Skinner's Operant Conditioning

When you have a favorable experience, such as getting a good grade on a class project or being complimented on a personal trait, you internalize the experience as positive. Psychologist B.F. Skinner (1904–1990) identified this basic principle as operant conditioning. **Operant conditioning** is simple: people tend to repeat behaviors that have a positive effect. It is a matter of reinforcement, a method of strengthening or encouraging behaviors. If you receive a good grade on a math project, you may use a similar strategy on a future project. Repeated high grades on tests and assignments may result in a belief that you are good at math (Skinner, 1953).

Skinner saw that operant conditioning takes more than just reinforcing the behavior. To make the behavior stick, the reinforcement must be gradually removed in an irregular pattern to make reinforcement unpredictable. He believed that support and unpredictability were crucial to learning. It is easy to see why behaviorism in the form of operant conditioning became so popular in American education. **Positive reinforcement** through rewards or incentives when children learn a new skill or behavior, followed by gradual removal of the support, is believed to result in a permanent behavioral change. **Negative reinforcement**, in the form of punishment or disincentives, is also thought to be especially important in guiding behaviors and learning. For example, children who have had a toy or privilege taken away after hitting another child may change their future behavior. However, if fear and intimidation are used in negative reinforcement, this may increase the negative behavior.

Bandura's Social Cognitive Theory

Albert Bandura (1925–2021) argued that people are much more complex than Skinner described. Bandura noted that children use both **enactive learning**, learning that comes from their own actions, and **vicarious learning**, learning that comes from observing others (Beswick, 2017; Summers, 2017). He asserted that people, whether children or adults, watch and imitate other people's behaviors, regardless of whether rewards or punishments are involved. While people are affected by rewards and punishments, their reactions to them are filtered by their perceptions, thoughts, and motivations. Bandura called this **social cognitive theory** (Bandura, 1977, 1986, 1997, 2001).

Social cognitive theorists believe that a child who observes a kind act may later imitate it toward another person. This is termed **modeling**, also known as imitation or observational learning. How people respond depends on their reactions and individualistic information processing. A child who observes kind behavior may become an empathic helper. On the other hand, the child may become a person who bullies others. It all depends on how the information is processed and the child's cognitive abilities (Bandura, 1977, 1986). Even very young children respond to experiences as opportunities, and the child's responses to them shape and mold the young child's brain. Thus, educational settings should offer stimulating opportunities and environments for exploration (Lerner et al., 2013; Wells, 2020; Xu, 2019).

A Critique of Behavioral and Social Cognitive Theories

Behaviorism and social cognitive theories acknowledge the importance of recognizing the three-fold influences on development: the person/cognition, behavior, and the environment. Ongoing research is exploring the specifics of these factors. For example, motivation for learning, self-regulation, and self-efficacy are three critical areas receiving interest (Schunk & Usher, 2019; Usher & Weidner, 2018). However, a continuing criticism of these theories is the need to emphasize diversity and the long-term effects of social and behavioral interventions (Schunk & DiBenedetto, 2020). In addition, they are not stage theories, making them more difficult to assign to ages or developmental stages.

Ecological Theory

In **ecological theory**, psychologist Urie Bronfenbrenner (1917–2005) proposes that a person's surrounding environment, interactions, and influences affect their growth and development (Bronfenbrenner, 1996; Moen et al., 1995; Shelton, 2019). Specifically, these influences occur in five different socio-historical cylinders surrounding an individual, including the microsystem, mesosystem, exosystem, macrosystem, and chronosystem (see Figure 2.3).

In the innermost circle or cylinder of Bronfenbrenner's model is the person with individual characteristics such as sex, chronological age, health, and other personal variables. The microsystem surrounds the individual; it is the person's most immediate or closest environment. For children and teens, this often includes the home and family and later the classroom and religious groups. Parents, siblings, other close family members, teachers, and peers are all a part of this sphere. Children learn and cognitively grow because of these social relationships and the environmental interactions and opportunities within their microsystem (Bronfenbrenner, 1996; Moen et al., 1995; Shelton, 2019).

The mesosystem provides linkages between the individual's microsystem and their exosystem. For example, interactions between primary caregivers and educators, or collaboration in learning between home and school, are connections between a child's mesosystem and exosystem. The exosystem includes an expanding environment where the individual lives, works, and interacts. For children, the exosystem consists of the parallel environments of the child's significant others, including primary caregivers, siblings, peers, neighbors, family, friends, the neighborhood or community, health and social welfare services, and mass media influences. For example, the child's parents' environment affects the child directly and indirectly. The influence is bidirectional, as each system affects the other.

The macrosystem is the surrounding environment that encircles an individual and includes cultural values and beliefs as well as social, political, and economic systems. It can also include religious beliefs in some cultures or events, such as wars.

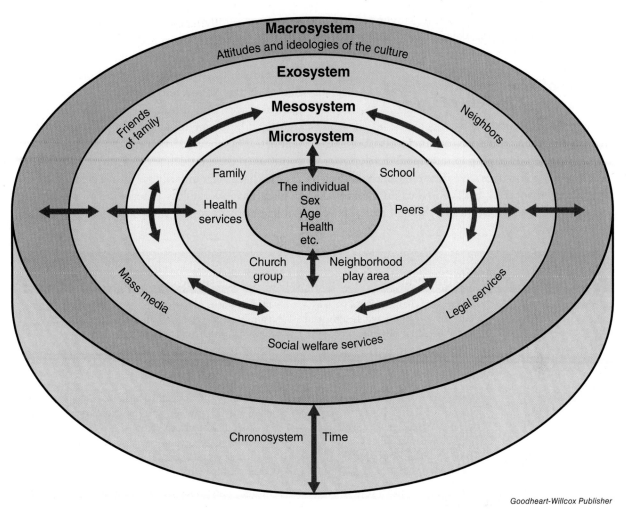

Figure 2.3 Bronfenbrenner's Ecological Theory with Examples of Factors That Influence Development Within Each Sphere

As globalization has become more dominant, interaction with the macrosystem is more common in children's and teens' everyday lives than it was in the past, primarily via social media.

The chronosystem is the overriding influence of time on the spheres. Historical differences, major life events, and shifts affect the child's environments and learning. These influences can be at the personal level, such as the death of a parent, or on a large scale, such as a global pandemic. Ecological theorists assert that social relationships and the surrounding environment greatly impact cognitive development and learning (Gray & MacBlain, 2015; Tach et al., 2020). Each of these spheres impacts a child's development (see Table 2.4).

A Critique of Ecological Theory

The ecological theory gives credence to the importance of a person's environment on human growth and development. It goes beyond the individual's closest or immediate environment to include growing circles of influence. Ecological theory can also be used throughout a person's life cycle. Critics cite the lack of inclusion of biological factors and the focus being primarily on sociocultural influences.

☑ CHECKPOINT

☐ Name and describe three behavioral and social cognitive theories.

☐ How did Bandura's theory build on Piaget's work? Why are they called *cognitive theories*?

□ What are the five socio-historical cylinders that may affect a child's development, according to Bronfenbrenner's ecological theory?

Voices of Women, Indigenous People, and People of Color

Foundational theories and ongoing research lend insight into the complexity of human development. However, when discussing foundational developmental theories, it sometimes seems that our understanding of human development has been based on traditional male perspectives. Historically, White males have been more readily accepted into higher education and professional guilds; more research funding has been awarded to them; and their publishing efforts have been more successful due to cultural bias. This does not mean that women and researchers representing all genders, races, and ethnicities have not contributed significantly to our understanding of human development. They have. However, sometimes they have contributed on the sidelines, assisting those researchers who have been unfairly given sole credit.

They have worked as practitioners in education, public or private health care, or human services such

Socio-historical cylinders	Description	Examples of Factors Within Sphere That May Impact the Developing Child
Microsystem	Individual characteristics such as sex, chronological age, health, and other personal variables	• Health status of the child • Family resources based on socioeconomic status • Opportunities offered based on child's sex • Developmental capabilities by age • Relationships between the child and family members, educators, or caregivers
Mesosystem	Immediate or closest environments, including primary caregivers, siblings, neighborhood, church or other religious community, and healthcare system	• Availability of community resources, such as parks, open spaces, beaches, and playgrounds • Accessibility of health care • Accessibility of quality educational opportunities, such as schools, libraries, and museums • Relationships with siblings and peers
Exosystem	Parallel environments of the child's significant others, such as their primary caregivers, educators, siblings, and peers	• Primary caregivers' workplace stress • Primary caregivers' work travel • Primary caregivers' income and benefits • Quality of extended family relationships such as between primary caregivers and grandparents • Health status of significant others • Primary caregivers' friends and coworkers
Macrosystem	Surrounding environment, which encircles an individual and includes cultural values and beliefs, social, political, and economic systems	• Child's socioeconomic status • Child's ethnicity • Resources of the child's geographic location • Ideologies of the larger culture within which the child resides, including political and economic systems • Laws and regulations
Chronosystem	Overriding influence of time on the spheres	• Primary caregivers' divorce • Death of an immediate family member • Changing the custodial status • Changing schools • Relocation • Climate changes • Global pandemics • Changes in political power and global relationships between counties

Kato

Table 2.4 Factors Within Bronfenbrenner's Ecological Theory Spheres That May Impact the Developing Child

as early childhood education. Although women, along with Black, Brown, and Indigenous people, are often not included in historical textbooks on developmental theories, their contributions were a significant part of history. Recent studies are looking at the invisibility or lack of representation of minority subjects in research and the lack of enough diverse voices asking the research questions, including several who are described next (Nishina & Witkow, 2019; Syed, 2016; Syed et al., 2018).

Inez Beverly Prosser

Inez Beverly Prosser (1895–1934) was the first female Black American to earn a PhD in psychology (Figure 2-4). She faced educational and cultural barriers that inspired her work, most notably on the impact of racially segregated schools on both Black and White children and adolescents (Benjamin et al., 2005). Her work eventually led to school desegregation; but during her lifetime, her work was often used to denounce the promotion of learning for Black children in the United States (Rose, 2007).

Wikimedia Common

Figure 2.5 Maria Montessori, 1914

Maria Montessori

Maria Montessori (1870–1952), Italy's first native-born female doctor, tried to find ways to help children who had difficulty learning (Figure 2-5). The students she worked with had medical conditions that may have kept them from learning. The teaching program she developed, now known as the Montessori method, has significantly affected young children. It remains well-recognized and accepted today. Montessori believed that young children are capable of great discovery and that sensory experiences should come before learning to read and write. The Montessori method provides opportunities for large- and fine-motor development and sensory exploration, along with language, science, art, geography, and math. Children direct their own learning with educators as their partners. Teachers encourage children to judge their progress and choose their interests (Giardiello, 2014; Mooney, 2013).

Anna Freud

Anna Freud (1895–1982) was the daughter of the well-known psychoanalyst, Sigmund Freud (Figure 2-6). Yet her work and contributions to the

Crisis Publishing Co., Public domain via Wikimedia Commons

Figure 2.4 Inez Beverly Prosser at Her 1933 Graduation

Figure 2.6 Anna Freud, 1957

Figure 2.7 Mary Ainsworth (center) playing with a child in 1973.

field of psychoanalysis have been significant. Her focus was on understanding children, especially within their home environment. She made a substantial impact on Erikson's thinking as well. Anna Freud practiced as a child psychoanalyst at the Vienna Psychoanalytic Institute. She and her family escaped from Vienna to London in 1938 during the Holocaust. During her over 40 years in London, she collaborated with an American friend, Dorothy Burlingham, to direct a war nursery that helped approximately 100 children made homeless by bombing raids and served as a psychoanalytic training program for child caregivers. Her prolific writing, most notably *The Writings of Anna Freud, Volumes I-VIII*, significantly influenced how children are studied, especially respecting family relationships when using psychoanalytic methods (Malberg & Raphael-Leff, 2012; Young-Bruehl, 2008).

Mary Ainsworth

Mary Ainsworth (1913–1999) was an American female psychologist specializing in infant-caretaker relationships (Figure 2-7). She collaborated extensively with fellow researcher John Bowlby on the effect of early-life experiences on later child development. She also focused on the significance of naturalistic observation as a means of collecting data about young children. Bowlby is often given sole credit for attachment theory—his idea on how young children form psychological attachments with their caregivers—however, Ainsworth also deserves credit because her evolving work added depth and meaning to this theory.

Using detailed observation as a means of study, she spent time living and learning in West Africa, most notably in Uganda, where she observed the interactional process of attachment between infants and mothers and the influences of the surrounding environment on these interactions. She detailed how a mother responds to a baby's distress signals as an antecedent to the attachment relationship. She then replicated and refined this methodology in the United States. Her now well-known method is termed the *strange situation procedure* (SSP). You will learn more about this in Chapter 6.

Using this methodology, researchers observed infants playing for 20 minutes while caregivers and strangers entered and left the room. The young children's reactions were observed and recorded. From these observations of their behaviors, young children were grouped into three different attachment categories: secure, insecure-resistant, and insecure-avoidant. Each category lent insight to the infant-caretaker relationship. This research has been foundational in understanding how young children attach to their caregivers and has spawned decades of follow-up research (Ainsworth et al., 2015; Van der Horst, 2011).

Mamie Phipps Clark

Mamie Phipps Clark (1917–1983) was a prominent Black American psychologist and educator who promoted strategies to enhance racial understanding and fight racial prejudice (Figure 2-8). Her research demonstrated that racial preference and bias showed up early in children's development, and these early racial prejudices and attitudes are not inherent but learned from others. She focused on recognizing strengths in others and promoting respectful relationships. She believed both traits could be learned successfully early in a child's life. She was also instrumental in shedding light on structural factors that oppress resource-disadvantaged children as well as societal attitudes of racial suppression. As a practitioner, Clark put her theories to use as the executive director of the Northside Center for Child Development in New York City, which she co-founded with her husband, Kenneth Bancroft Clark. Together, they combined their social welfare and psychology interests to understand child development better.

Mamie Phipps Clark played a significant role in the 1954 Supreme Court Decision of *Brown v. Board of Education of Topeka*, which ruled on the illegality of segregation by race in public schools. Through her research—particularly through her now-famous doll test, which asked children to choose a preferred doll among those of different skin colors—she demonstrated that racial prejudice and preference is learned from others at a young age. (Jackson, 2005; Jackson & Weidman, 2006; Pickren et al., 2012).

Martha Bernal

Martha Bernal (1931–2001) was the first female Latinx-American to earn a PhD in psychology in the US (Figure 2-9). Her parents emigrated from Mexico to Texas, where Dr. Bernal was born. She was a prolific writer and scholar. Her empirical research focused on ethnic socialization, the transmission of ethnic identification, and multicultural psychology (Bernal, 1985; Bernal & Knight, 1993). She was very vocal about injustices, especially equity, in using empirical research in child welfare. She made exceptional contributions that increased the understanding of ethnic minority psychology (Sanchez Korrol & Ruiz, 2006; Vásquez, 2002).

Wikimedia Common

Figure 2.8 Dr. Mamie Phipps Clark and Dr. Kenneth B. Clark

John Sunderland/Denver Post via Getty Images

Figure 2.9 Dr. Martha Bernal, left, and her colleague Gayla Margolin in 1975

Reiko Homma True

Reiko Homma True (1933–present) earned a doctorate in psychology and has spent her career focusing on the health and mental well-being of Asian Americans (Figure 2-10). Specifically, she focuses on issues related to Asian-American identity, helping to form the Asian-American Community Mental Health Program, located in Oakland, California. (Bayne-Smith, 1996; Drogin, 2019; Lee, 1997). She mentors Asian-American women pursuing educational and vocational goals. She also provides clinical services to those impacted by traumatic experiences, including natural disaster relief (American Psychological Association, 2006; Rayburn, 2010).

Nick Crettier/NickCrettier.com

Figure 2.10 Reiko Homma True

Global Perspectives

Spanking as a Form of Discipline

Over three decades ago, the United Nations (UN) Committee on the Rights of the Child called on all member states to ban corporal (physical) punishment of children, including spanking. As an alternative, they called on all states to institute educational programs on positive discipline (UNICEF, 2017). The rationale for the suggested ban included a plethora of studies that demonstrated the ineffectiveness of spanking and other corporal methods of changing behavior as well as the potential for increasing harm (Gershoff & Grogen-Kaylor, 2016). Spanking is associated with fewer long-term behavior changes compared to non-physical discipline strategies such as time-outs (Gershoff, 2017; Gershoff et al., 2018). Spanking has also been associated with childhood aggression and lower self-esteem at both the preschool and middle childhood stages of development (Gershoff et al., 2012; Hineline & Rosales-Ruiz, 2012; Lee et al., 2013).

In 2016, out of 197 countries surveyed, about two-thirds banned corporal punishment of children. However, nearly one-third allowed corporal punishment in schools in the form of spanking (Gershoff, 2017). Most countries in Europe, South America, and Asia have outlawed corporal punishment in schools, as have Greenland and New Zealand (Global Initiative to End All Corporal Punishment of Children, 2019). Only three industrial countries allow corporal punishment, including the United States, Australia, and the Republic of South Korea (Gershoff, 2017).

The American Academy of Pediatrics has published a policy statement that offers guidance for positive, effective, and age-appropriate discipline strategies. It advises against physical punishment and verbal abuse of children at any age (Sege & Siegel, 2019). Most pediatricians surveyed (94%) had negative attitudes toward spanking, and few expected positive outcomes from using this method of discipline (Taylor et al., 2018).

A vast amount of research has concluded that spanking is ineffective and may even be harmful to children. Most professional organizations and human rights organizations do not support any form of corporal punishment, including spanking. It is the least often used method of discipline, as reported by US parents of children under the age of 18. However, according to the Pew Research Center (2015), about 16% of parents say they spank their children at least some of the time. The number varies by race, income, and education.

To Think About:

• What are your views on spanking children? What influences your beliefs? Why do primary caregivers continue to use spanking to discipline children despite research that does not support it?

• How might cultural factors specifically contribute to the pervasiveness of this practice?

☑ CHECKPOINT

☐ Identify and describe the work of at least two theorists who have not often been included in history due to gender and/or racial bias.

☐ What are two reasons it is important to include the voices and experiences of diverse researchers?

☐ What are 10 things you think are essential to optimal growth and development? Where do your ideas come from? Are your statements empirically supported? Why or why not?

Apply Here!

A parent you are working with is engaging in a childcare practice that you question. The practice is not abusive, but you are concerned that it harms the child. You wonder if your concerns are culturally biased. How might you expand your knowledge of this parenting practice?

2.2 The Evolutionary Perspective

The evolutionary perspective draws on principles of evolution, or the gradual process in which living things change and develop over millions of years. Evolutionary perspective theorists believe that evolution influences every aspect of human development, including physical growth characteristics, cognitive abilities and functions, behaviors, and how people relate to each other, including the passing on of traits from generation to generation. They assert that through the process of evolution, humans became the dominant living organism on earth. Dominant theories within this perspective are natural selection and adaptive behavior and evolutionary developmental psychology.

Natural Selection and Adaptive Behavior

Natural selection and adaptive behavior are concepts used by biologists to organize their understanding of evolutionary processes and to facilitate their communication. Humans are not static; as a species, they evolve. Charles Darwin (1809–1882) traced all living organisms back to a simple, self-replicating molecule. Over time, some traits persisted through natural selection, and others did not.

Natural selection is the progression of sorting traits by reproductive success. As humans replicate through biologically producing offspring, a replication of units occurs, whether those units are molecules, cells, or individual characteristics or traits (Losos et al., 2013). These are inheritable units such as hair color, body proportions, and temperament, which is the foundation of personality. It should be noted that the word "selection" is misleading. Natural selection describes the reproductive success of traits or units passed on through generations. It does not eliminate undesirable traits. Natural selection works almost entirely within a species.

Adaptive behavior refers to the portion of evolutionary change in a trait driven by natural selection. In other words, those with the strongest traits adapt and change to the needs of the surrounding environment, while those with weaker traits may be more negatively impacted. Biological adaptations are made to protect and propagate the species (Muehlenbein, 2015; Stewart-Williams, 2018).

Evolutionary Developmental Psychology

Evolutionary developmental psychology (EDP) applies the basic principles of evolution by natural selection to our understanding of how humans develop. EDP emphasizes understanding cognition and human behaviors, combining the study of biology with environmental mechanisms (Buss, 2005; LaFreniere, 2010). As humans biologically develop their social and cognitive competencies, these competencies adapt to given environmental conditions. EDP, which began by studying adults, attempted to answer, "Why do humans behave and think the way they do?" (Machluf et al., 2014).

As the field of EDP grew, more theorists began to combine the concepts of biological development and psychological processes, including cognition. For example, EDP theorists may propose that young children have an innate instinct to speak a language. When combined with environmental influences, such as a parent or educator who engages the child in conversation, this instinct allows a young child to learn to communicate through language (Belsky et al., 1991; Chomsky, 1965; Ellis & Bjorklund, 2005). Likewise, in the United States and much of the world, young teen girls typically start menstruating (menarche) around age twelve. This is a biological development that is shared among groups of young girls. Historically, the average age for menarche in the United States has continued to decrease over time (Martinez, 2020). A girl's individual genetics also influences menarche. Factors such as a girl's quantity and quality of nutritional intake are environmental factors that also influence onset. The presence or absence of a father figure in the girl's life may also impact the age of menarche (Bjorklund & Pellegrini, 2000; Ellis & Bjorklund, 2005; Webster et al., 2014).

Evolutionary biology and developmental theory have not always been in agreement, however. For many years, the two fields were viewed as incompatible. In the past century, psychologists have understood that modern evolutionary theory that focuses on genetics could be applied to our understanding of human development, particularly in the realm of cognition and behaviors. Although development follows a biological pattern, and many traits are shared among people, every individual has a unique environment and social interactions that influence their cognition and behaviors (Bjorklund & Pellegrini, 2002; Ellis & Solms, 2018).

A firm evolutionary approach usually encounters the problem of genetic determinism, the idea that genes, not the environment, directly cause, regulate, or govern our cognition and behavior. Nothing can be done to alter the course of evolutionary development. However, evolutionary developmental theorists suggest that a developmental course can be changed when environmental interactions occur (Bjorklund & Pellegrini, 2002; Ellis & Solms, 2018).

A Critique of the Evolutionary Perspective

An evolutionary perspective is widely accepted today, but it is still just a theory. When Darwin was formulating his theory of evolution in the mid-1800s, he had no understanding of the biological role of DNA, the carrier of our individual genetic information. Today, our understanding of the science behind genetics is expanding rapidly as we learn more about the interaction between genetics, the environment, and development.

☑CHECKPOINT

- ☐ What are the origins of the evolutionary perspective in human development?

- ☐ What are natural selection and adaptive behavior? To which theorist are these ideas usually attributed?
- ☐ How does evolutionary developmental psychology expand on Darwin's theory?

Apply Here!

It is the first day of school! Imagine that you have just welcomed a new group of 3-year-olds into your early childhood classroom. Half of the children have never experienced a group care setting before, and they have been primarily in the care of a parent in the home before today. As an experienced teacher, you expect to observe varying excitement and anxiety levels in all the children. You know that they will all experience this transition differently. As an early childhood educator, how might you help the children transition between what is known and what is new? How much is controllable (environment), and how much is not controllable (inherited temperament)? Because each child is an individual, how would you help the whole class make this transition to a new class and teacher? List specific ideas.

lostinbids/E+ via Getty Images

2.3 Genetics and Development

For centuries, people assumed that physical traits were passed from biological parents to their children or offspring. A tall mother and a short father may have had a child of medium adult height. A mother with brown eyes and a father with blue eyes may have had a child with hazel-colored eyes. The idea that a child inherited half of the mother's traits and half of the father's traits in a sort of unified or mixed result remained the prominent way of thinking for much of modern history. But sometimes, the results did not seem so clear. A child of two brown-eyed parents might have blue or brown eyes with no trace of the other color. A child who had a biological parent with dark, curly hair may have straight, light-colored hair or straight, dark-colored hair. Children may inherit some characteristics but not others.

As far back as the mid-1800s, Gregor Mendel (1822-1884), often cited as the founding theorist of genetics, proposed his ideas about how physical traits are inherited through his studies of pea plants (Olby, 1985; Powar, 2007). **Heredity** is the transmission of characteristics from parents to their biological offspring. Research continued during the latter nineteenth century but then slowed until the mid-twentieth century. Then, post-World War II efforts to increase scientific exploration took the focus back to the study of genetics, especially in the health and medical fields. In the 1950s, scientists identified the double helix, the three-dimensional structure of **DNA** (deoxyribonucleic acid) that contains the genetic instructions in all living things. It completely changed the way scientists viewed heredity. **Genetics** is the field of study within biological sciences that examines how genes, the basic information for heredity, are passed from one generation to the next generation (Crick, 1962; Finlay, 2013; Moore, 1963; Muehlenbein, 2010).

Genes and Chromosomes

Conception occurs when a single cell or ovum is released from the female reproductive organs, the ovaries, and unites with a sperm cell from the male reproductive organs. The fertilized egg carries a human code that instructs the newly formed embryo to grow into a human being. Conception results in a newly formed **genome**, or a complete set of DNA, that establishes the hereditary makeup of the new individual and includes all the instructions that cause the embryo to grow. Life begins as a single cell, and within 24 hours of being fertilized, that cell starts dividing quickly into many cells, each cell carrying the instructions of its genetic code.

Cells are the basic building blocks of all living things, and the human body is composed of billions of cells. Inside each cell is the **cell nucleus**, like a command center, which instructs the cell to grow or change. Within the cell nucleus are the hereditary materials or DNA. As mentioned earlier, DNA is composed of two strands that wind around each other, often described as a twisting of two ladders, or a double helix (Chambers et al., 2019; Hood,

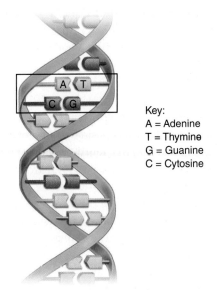

Key:
A = Adenine
T = Thymine
G = Guanine
C = Cytosine

©Body Scientific International

Figure 2.11 The Double Helix Structure of DNA and Complementary Bases

2010). DNA is made up of complementary bases referred to as A (adenine), T (thymine), G (guanine), and C (cytosine) that are attached to a sugar phosphate frame (see Figure 2.11). Although human DNA contains about three billion bases, 99% of them are shared, or are the same, between all individuals. The order or sequence of these bases is what impacts the outcome and makes each person unique (US National Library of Medicine, 2020).

A **gene** is the part of DNA that carries the blueprint information for life. Each human cell (except the ovum or sperm) contains 46 chromosomes, and structures within the cell nucleus consist of protein and DNA. Every human inherits one copy of each gene from each parent, resulting in 23 pairs; half of the chromosome pair comes from the mother and half from the father. Chromosomes contain a person's genes (Borry & Matthijs, 2016). Genes will impact how tall a person will be, their eye and hair color, and whether the person might have certain diseases.

Each pair of chromosomes is called an **autosome**. The 23rd pair, called the sex chromosome, determines whether a developing embryo will be biologically female or male. Using common designations, a female embryo is labeled XX, indicating the transmission of the same trait from both the mother and father that created the 23rd pair of chromosomes. A male embryo is labeled XY, indicating the transmission of an X chromosome from the mother and a Y chromosome from the father. As mentioned earlier, a person's complete set of DNA is called their genome. The genome includes all the necessary instructions that cause an embryo to be created from a single cell (Chamber et al., 2019; Running, 2015; Wallace, 2018).

The Human Genome Project (HGP), conducted between 1990–2003, is considered one of the most significant discoveries in scientific history. It involved the efforts of many international research scientists. The goal of the HGP was to sequence and map all 23 pairs of chromosomes in the human genetic plan. This project identified all the base pairs that constitute the chromosomes from pair 1 to 23. The strenuous efforts involved in this project were massive, like the earlier exploration in space. In addition, more than three million human genetic variations were identified (Berkowitz, 2020; Wallace, 2018).

In the past few decades, there has been an emphasis on the study of genetics to better understand heredity and its influence on human development. Before this, scientists focused on classical genetics, which concentrated on studying outward appearances such as stature or hair and eye color. Today, scientists study actual genes, a branch of science called *molecular genetics*. Researchers study different forms of genes, termed *alleles*, which produce variations in a genetically inherited trait, such as the amount of hair a person will have or eye color. They have also learned more about how genomes affect health and how to prevent disease (Lucchesi, 2019; Muehlenbein, 2010).

The Human Genome Project has, in many ways, transformed biology and medicine.

Today, additional characteristics such as temperament, intelligence, and mental health traits are being explored. For example, researchers consider the potential biological heredity of obesity, anxiety, aggression, introversion and extraversion, intellectual giftedness, and autism spectrum disorders.

☑ CHECKPOINT

- ☐ How does human life begin from a single cell?
- ☐ What is a *gene*, and where do genes reside in the body?
- ☐ What is the Human Genome Project? What impact has it had on understanding genetics?

Cell Division

Cells can replicate themselves and divide to keep an organism alive, growing, and thriving. Cells are constantly replenishing within the body. Sometimes, cells replenish to accommodate growth; other times, to replace damaged or aging cells. In the replenishing processes, the human body also creates cells for sexual reproduction. Cells divide using either the process of *mitosis* or the process of meiosis.

Mitosis is used to make new cells, identical replications, or *daughter* cells. One cell divides through a series of stages to make two replicated cells. Each cell has a complete set of 23 pairs of chromosomes (see Figure 2.12). Mitosis occurs in almost all cells, except specialized cells such as red blood cells, nerve cells, heart muscle cells, and gamete or sex cells. Cell division aids in keeping the human body alive, thriving, and healthy as bodies grow and adapt to changes in

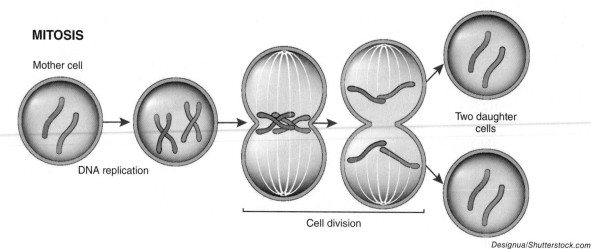

Designua/Shutterstock.com

Figure 2.12 Cell Division via Mitosis

the environment. Many body cells replenish in just a few days or weeks, such as skin cells that slough off and replenish frequently. Other cells may last years. Brain cells are an example of cells that have a long life. All human cells go through formation, growth, division, and eventual death (Muehlenbein, 2010; Running, 2015; Wallace, 2018).

Meiosis is needed for sexual reproduction to occur. Meiosis is a process of cell division that works differently than mitosis and only with gamete or sex cells. Gamete cells include the female ovum and the male sperm. When sex cells divide, they divide into four, each with 23 chromosomes. When one new cell from the parent ovum cell unites with one new cell from the parent sperm cell, the resulting new unified cell, or embryo, now has a full set of 46 chromosomes, found in 23 pairs (see Figure 2.13).

Guiding Genetic Principles in Human Development

Each person has their own genome, set at the moment of conception. This blueprint contains instructions for bodily features, growth patterns, and even temperament. How does the human body create a viable set of chromosomes or genes? Is it all by chance? As researchers study human genomes, more is learned about the principles that guide or determine an

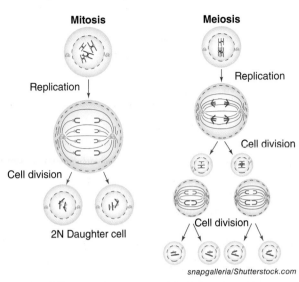

snapgalleria/Shutterstock.com

Figure 2.13 A Comparison of Cell Division via Mitosis and Meiosis

individual's characteristics. These include dominant and recessive genes, sex-linked genes, and polygenetic inheritance, discussed below.

Dominant traits are those that are expressed. For example, dark or brown eyes and hair genes are considered dominant because these traits are represented more often than light-colored hair and blue eyes, which are considered recessive traits (see Figure 2.14A). **Recessive traits** are those that are

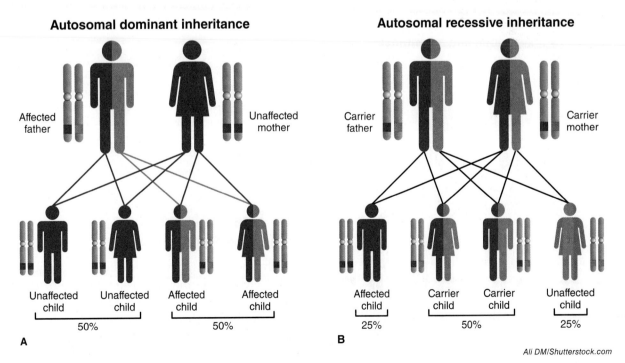

Ali DM/Shutterstock.com

Figure 2.14 Dominate Gene Inheritance (A) and Recessive Gene Inheritance (B)

overridden or influenced by dominant genes. When two recessive genes join, an unlikely recessive gene may prevail, such as two brown-eyed parents having a blue-eyed child (see Figure 2.14B).

Sex-linked traits are linked to X or Y chromosomes and can be dominant or recessive (see Figures 2.15 and 2.16). Hemophilia, fragile X syndrome, and muscular dystrophy are examples of X-linked genetic disorders. Because only males have a Y chromosome, Y-linked genetic disorders can only be passed from father to son. Genetic disorders are discussed more in Chapter 3. Genetic transmission of inherited genes is complex. The more scientists learn about genomes, the more there is an appreciation for the complex interactions when genes combine. This complex interaction is termed **polygenetic** (Korf, 2020). Height and eye and skin color are some examples of polygenic inheritance, as they are regulated by more than one gene.

The sequencing of the human genome revolutionized biology and is revolutionizing medicine practices. More work is needed to understand the complexities of relationships, especially concerning how mutation and abnormalities occur. Understanding how environmental factors play a role is critical, too. Lastly, the ethical, legal, and social implications and the subsequent development of policy options for public consideration are critical.

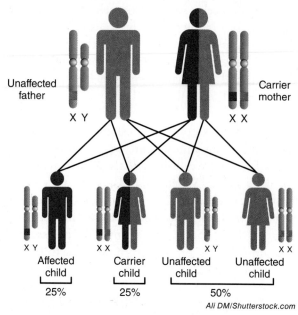

X-linked recessive inheritance

Unaffected father — X Y
Carrier mother — X X

Affected child — X Y — 25%
Carrier child — X X — 25%
Unaffected child — X Y — Unaffected child — X X — 50%

Ali DM/Shutterstock.com

Figure 2.16 Recessive X-Linked Gene Inheritance

☑ CHECKPOINT

☐ How is mitosis different than meiosis?

☐ What is the relationship between dominant and recessive genes?

☐ What are sex-linked traits?

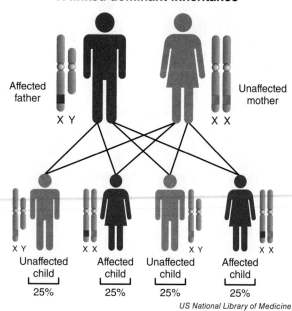

X-linked dominant inheritance

Affected father — X Y
Unaffected mother — X X

Unaffected child — X Y — 25%
Affected child — X X — 25%
Unaffected child — X Y — 25%
Affected child — X X — 25%

US National Library of Medicine

Figure 2.15 Dominant X-Linked Gene Inheritance

Apply Here!

Make a list of your personal traits, both internal traits such as your personality or temperament and physical traits such as your height or hair color. Are your identifiable characteristics influenced by your genes or the environment? If so, how much?

2.4 The Nature–Nurture Interaction

Which aspects of our bodies and behavior are genetically determined, and which are environmentally shaped? Is genetics or the environment more dominant? Can biology be shaped or altered by the environment? These are some of the critical issues in the nature versus nurture debate. Today, it is no longer considered a debate, a consideration of one versus

Practical Issues and Implications

DIY Genetics?

The popularity of citizen science or do-it-yourself (DIY) DNA testing shows that the average consumer is now involved in genetic testing. There are several direct-to-consumer test kits that can provide information on traits, health, and ancestry through a simple saliva sample. According to Pew Research, about 15% of US adults have used mail-in DNA testing. The vast majority, 87%, have used consumer genetic testing to learn more about their ancestry. Most report that they were not surprised by the results; although a significant number said they were surprised (40%), especially about their racial identification. Some have cited the desire to find lost or unknown relatives or learn more about their health. Nearly one-third of respondents reported learning about unknown relatives, even those who had hoped to remain unidentified. About one-quarter were surprised by the previously unknown health data revealed (Graf, 2020).

Genomic sequencing has also become a prominent tool used by scientists in multiple fields, including medicine and criminology. Data are often made public. Even criminal perpetrators have been identified, and long-unsolved cases have been solved (Guerrini et al., 2018; Kennett, 2019).

Globally, regions with the most interest in DNA testing are North America, Western Europe, and Australia. In Canada, the United States, and Australia, participants often cite showing proof of their Indigenous heritage as a motivation for taking the test. Participants also note a need to seek more information about their possible racial or ethnic heritage (Marcon et al., 2021). Sociologists and medical ethicists argue that the idea of "race as fixed" is a Westernized concept rather than race being viewed as malleable from a biomedical and sociopolitical perspective. On the other hand, some researchers are concerned that DNA tests may be used divisively, that the ideology of fixed race is being promoted even though DNA tests are often marketed as building bridges globally (Marcon et al., 2021; Roberts & Middleton, 2017; Roth et al., 2020; Suzuki & Vacano, 2018).

Genetic testing in the United States is regulated by the Food and Drug Administration (FDA), the Centers for Medicare and Medicaid Services (CMS), and the Federal Trade Commission (FTC). Tests are evaluated for their analytical validity (ability to predict the presence or absence of a gene), clinical validity (ability to connect a specific gene variant to disease risk), and clinical utility (likelihood of information leading to improved health outcomes). Although regulated, there is an acknowledgment that clinical validation of health-related genetic testing may raise significant ethical issues. For example, it might cause some people to overreact to the potential of a disease even if the actual disease is not present (White, 2019). Other concerns include biosafety and security matters, that is, the security of highly personal data being accidentally or unintentionally shared (Callaghan, 2019; Finney et al., 2012; Wiggins & Wilbanks, 2019).

As genetic testing becomes more accessible, scientists and consumer advocates call for more consumer education, especially in health-related genomics. Without diagnosis, treatment, and support from health professionals, information may be misconstrued because medical terminology and methodologies may be unfamiliar or unknown to the consumer. Interpretation and communication of research findings may also be misleading if they are not provided under a health care professional's guidance (Stoeklé et al., 2020; White, 2019; Whitley et al., 2020; Wiggins & Wilbanks, 2019).

However, sharing data through public engagement in research and data collection offers a rich opportunity for scientists to engage larger study cohorts. The large amount of data collected may help scientists solve the riddles of chronic illnesses and diseases faster than ever before. The possibilities are truly endless.

To Think About:

- Have you done genetic testing? If so, what motivated you to do so? If not, why not?
- Do you think that DNA tests could be helpful or harmful to an individual's mental health and well-being?
- What should be done with the collected data, and who should have access to the information? Does shared data invade privacy?
- How might future genome sequencing aid your understanding of how children and teens grow and mature?

the other, but an understanding that the interaction is complex and that humans are very diverse.

Scientists and researchers are finding ways in which the environment affects growth and development. Even though genes determine individual traits, the environment can affect certain traits. The environment affects social and emotional traits, and physical traits as well. For example, the human brain continues to grow and develop long after birth. When children experience positively stimulating and interactive environments, their brains physically respond differently than children who have been neglected or under-stimulated. As the brain develops critical pathways that are needed for strong connections, it affects children's cognitive skills. For example, learning is enhanced when information processing speed is supported by developing efficient brain pathways.

Behavioral Genetics

Behavioral genetics is a field of study exploring genetic and environmental contributions to human behavior. It is a field concerned with variation, questioning why one individual differs from another. Behavioral genetics often involves defining behavior outcomes, or phenotypes, and measuring the corresponding genetic influences, or genotypes. Classic behavioral geneticists often study twins or twins in adoption situations (Little et al., 2020; Than, 2016; Yashon & Cummings, 2020).

Twin studies are a classic way of comparing behaviors between two people who share the same or a similar genetic code. **Monozygotic** (MZ), or identical twins, are the only humans who share the same genetic code and genetic makeup, as each twin develops from the same fertilized ovum that later divided, subsequently sharing their mother's womb during prenatal development. Behavioral outcomes are also compared between **dizygotic** (DZ), or fraternal, twins. Fraternal twins share common parental genetic input; they are no more similar genetically than any other siblings. Their commonality is a shared environment in the uterus. Behavioral geneticists may compare identical twins to fraternal twins to understand the impact of genotypes on phenotypes. Some studies investigate the effect on twins raised in different environments, often referred to as an adoption study. Or they may look at differences between adoptive and biological siblings within a family (Jansen et al., 2015; Segal, 2012, 2017; Than, 2016).

Epigenetics

Epigenetics is the study of changes in DNA outcomes or phenotypes caused by something in the environment. It is a term used to describe genetics with a modified or enhanced expression due to these environmental factors. For example, a developing fetus carries a unique DNA sequence, but the specific prenatal environment may cause the expression of the gene to modify or change (Barua & Junaid, 2015; Kanherkar et al., 2014; Tabery, 2007, 2015). Maternal stress, lack of quality of nutritional intake, disease, injury, or lifestyle choices may alter the developing fetus's DNA. DNA is typically modified through chemical tags, chemical compounds, and proteins that can attach to DNA, which change its functional identity or expression. The response can be dynamic and flexible, causing temporary or permanent change (see Figure 2.17). The changes can be long-lasting, such as the expression of metabolic disease in adulthood (Roseboom, 2019; Tobi et al., 2018; US Centers for Disease Control and Prevention, 2020).

If a fetus is prenatally exposed to nicotine, there are potential long-term effects of lower birth weight, an increased risk of being overweight or obese by adolescence, an increased risk of insulin resistance, type 2 diabetes, and hypertension (Rogers, 2019). DNA alteration can cause permanent change that is passed down through generations. For example, grandchildren of women exposed to famine or other severe dietary restrictions are more likely to experience health complications later in life (Aiken et al., 2016; Tiffon, 2018). Other areas explored are epigenetic factors on lifelong obesity as a health issue (Ordavas, 2008). Although many environmental factors potentially cause epigenetic modulation (Figure 2.17), the impact is more significant on fetuses, as the child is still developing (Banik et al., 2017; National Scientific Council on the Developing Child, 2010).

Gene x Environment (G x E) Interaction

Mapping the human genome was a major scientific breakthrough that shed light on the vast complexity

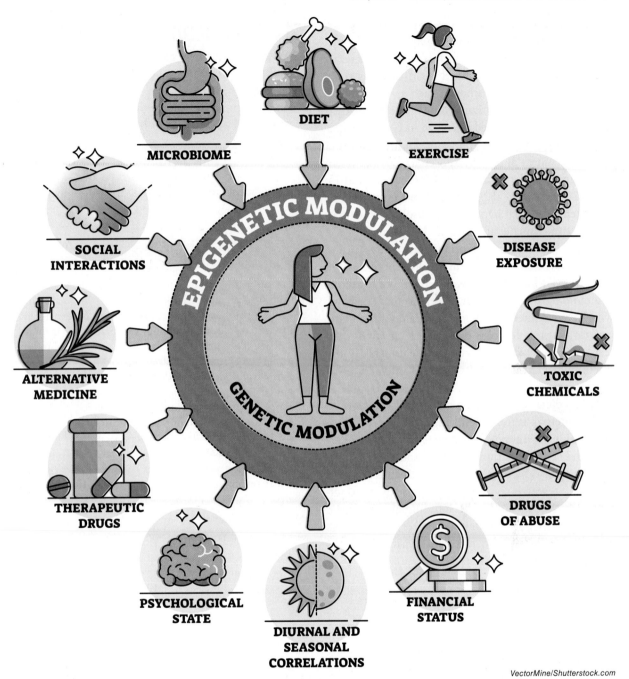

MICROBIOME

DIET

EXERCISE

SOCIAL INTERACTIONS

DISEASE EXPOSURE

ALTERNATIVE MEDICINE

EPIGENETIC MODULATION

GENETIC MODULATION

TOXIC CHEMICALS

THERAPEUTIC DRUGS

DRUGS OF ABUSE

PSYCHOLOGICAL STATE

DIURNAL AND SEASONAL CORRELATIONS

FINANCIAL STATUS

VectorMine/Shutterstock.com

Figure 2.17 Examples of Factors That Influence Epigenetic Modulation

of individual human genes and different responses to environmental variations. Epigenetics is an example of gene-environment effects. Genes often do not possess a one-to-one relationship with the characteristics they contribute, nor are environmental influences always predictable. Instead, the connections may be additive, multiplicative, or interactive. Studying epigenetics within a nuanced context of gene-by-environment interactions is known as **the gene x environment (G x E) interaction**. Simply put, instead of genes plus environmental factors, G x E presents genes multiplied by environmental factors in a dynamic way and over time (Barua & Junaid, 2015; Esposito et al., 2018; Fowler-Finn & Boutwell, 2019; Winham & Biernacka, 2013).

Environmental variations in gene response can result in physical, chemical, or biological modifications or changes. They can also result in different behavior patterns during various stages of life, which then influence genes and subsequent behaviors. Examples of environmental factors that may interact with genetics include chemical toxins such as those found in pesticides, a pathogen such as COVID-19, or extreme poverty or abuse. Some of the many areas that are receiving focused attention in G x E integrations include childhood and adult obesity (Qasim et al., 2018; Sulc et al., 2020; Sun et al., 2017), autism spectrum disorder (Chauhan & Chauhan, 2015; Haruvi-Lamdan et al., 2018; Pearson et al., 2016), and attention deficit hyperactivity disorder (Hartman et al., 2016; Posner et al., 2020; Sciberras et al., 2017).

G x E researchers see opportunities expanding at great speed in the medical field (Esposito et al., 2018; Fowler-Finn & Boutwell, 2019). For example, epidemiologists who study diseases may discover which environmental factors combined with specific genetic markers increase disease risk or strengthen resistance. G x E may also further the understanding of complex gene and environmental interactions in mental health. Pharmacologists may soon be able to tailor medications based on a person's genetic and environmental factors, resulting in more effective medications with fewer adverse reactions. Understanding the interactions of genes and the environment may also help prevent or cure future diseases. Although research regarding G x E has advanced scientific knowledge and understanding about genetic disorders, genetics and lifestyle choices, and genetics and disease, it has also revealed a vast expanse of unexplored terrain.

☑ CHECKPOINT

- What is behavioral genetics? How does this field of study relate to twin studies?
- Define epigenetics and give an example related to child development. How does this form of inquiry add to and enhance behavioral genetics?
- Summarize gene x environment (G x E) interaction and how it relates to and expands on behavioral genetics and epigenetics.

Apply Here!

As an early childhood educator, you have the opportunity to instruct not only the children in your care but also their primary caregivers. You often have parents who want to talk to you about their children, including various concerns such as language acquisition, toilet learning, and helping children deal with farewell and greeting transitions. Considering what you have learned about developmental cognitive and social learning theories, environmental influences, genetics, and G x E interaction, how might you give primary caregivers a broad overview of why behaviors occur, how genetic alterations or modifications happen, and how growth and maturation happen? Either compose a short summary statement or create an infographic that can be shared.

Summary

Developmental researchers and genetic scientists attempt to understand why behaviors occur, how genetic alterations or modifications happen, and how growth and maturation happen. Some examples include how a pregnant woman's lifestyle choices influence a developing fetus, how genetics affects the developing baby, or whether the environment in the uterus affects development in the later stages of childhood and adolescence. The upcoming chapters will apply these foundational developmental theories and explore the interactions between genetics and the environment. Chapter 3 starts at the beginning of the life cycle, with conception, pregnancy, and birth.

Learning Outcomes and Key Concepts

2.1 Describe the four foundational theories in human development.

- Psychoanalytic theorists analyze the symbolic meaning behind behaviors.
- Erikson's psychosocial theory includes eight life-stage social-emotional crises or tasks to solve.
- Cognitive theorists explain human behavior by understanding thought processes and learning.
- Piaget's cognitive developmental theory identifies four stages: sensorimotor, preoperational, operational, and formal.
- Vygotsky's sociocultural cognitive theory asserts that interactions with others in close relationships are critical to a child's cognitive development.
- Information processing theory uses the analogy of the human brain functioning much like a computer.
- Behaviorism and social cognitive theories acknowledge the importance of recognizing the three-fold influences of the person/cognition, behavior, and the environment.
- Bronfenbrenner's ecological theory asserts that surrounding environmental interactions influence human growth and development.

2.2 Identify some major theories related to the evolutionary perspective on human development.

- The evolutionary perspective is the gradual process in which living things change and develop over millions of years.
- Natural selection is a progression of sorting traits in which some traits persist and others do not.
- Adaptive behavior refers to the evolutionary change in a trait driven by natural selection and environmental adaptation.
- Evolutionary developmental psychology combines the study of biology and environmental mechanisms.
- DNA (deoxyribonucleic acid) contains the genetic instructions (or blueprint) for living things; and it has changed scientific views about heredity.

2.3 Explain how genetics influences human growth and development.

- Heredity is the transmission of characteristics from parents to their biological offspring.
- Genetics examines how genes pass from one generation to the next generation.
- A gene is a part of DNA that carries the blueprint information.
- Human cells (except the ovum or sperm) contain 46 chromosomes, one copy of each gene from each parent, resulting in the 23 pairs.
- The Human Genome Project, one of the most significant discoveries in scientific history, sequenced and mapped all 23 pairs of chromosomes in the human blueprint.
- Cells divide through mitosis or meiosis to keep organisms alive, growing, and thriving.
- Genes are classified as dominant, recessive, sex-linked, and polygenic.

2.4 Analyze the interaction between nature and nurture in human growth and development.

- Behavioral genetics attempts to explain the genetic and environmental contributions to human behavior.
- Twin studies compare behaviors of people who share the same or a similar genetic code.
- Epigenetics is the study of changes or modifications in DNA outcomes or phenotypes caused by something in the environment.

- Epigenetics has the most significant impact on embryos, fetuses, and young children.
- Gene x environment (G x E) interaction presents the concept of genes multiplied by environmental factors dynamically and over time.
- Environmental variations in gene response can result in physical, chemical, or biological changes.
- Environmental variations in gene response can also result in different behavior patterns during various stages of life, which then influence genes and subsequent behaviors.
- Opportunities for future research on the precise etiological pathways of G x E are expanding at breathtaking speed.

Chapter Review

1. If you were writing a blog about your emotional and social interactions with family and friends, what factors (such as sleep, stress, excitement, nutrition) have affected your interactions with others today? State your beliefs as a theory of why your day turned out the way it did.

2. Choose a news story about an event in your community, such as a large humanitarian donation, robbery, murder, new community playground, or child neglect case. Write a short opinion piece discussing your theory about what life events may have prompted the behavior.

3. Create a chart that describes and differentiates psychosocial and cognitive theories.

4. Design an infographic that describes the eight stages of Erikson's psychosocial theory.

5. Create a simple activity that could assess whether a young child was in Piaget's preoperational or operational stage of cognitive development.

6. Produce a case study that illustrates a young child learning a new skill using Vygotsky's sociocultural cognitive theory.

7. Explain how a primary caregiver could use behaviorism to get their child to stop whining.

8. Explain how a primary caregiver could use social learning theory to help their child become a good cook.

9. Illustrate or diagram Bronfenbrenner's ecological theory and fill in the concentric circles with examples from your life influences.

10. Define *evolutionary perspective* in human development. How does natural selection relate?

11. What significance did the Human Genome Project lend to understanding how genetics is related to human development?

12. Write a blog post about how the impact of expanding knowledge of epigenetics and gene x environment (G x E) interaction may influence understanding human development in the future.

Matching

Match the following terms with the correct definitions.

A. **Bronfenbrenner's ecological theory**

B. **Erikson's psychosocial theory**

C. **evolutionary developmental psychology**

D. **information processing theory**

E. **operant conditioning**

F. **psychoanalytic theory**

G. **social cognitive theory**

H. **Vygotsky's sociocultural cognitive theory**

1. Theory that the human brain goes through a series of movements or functions to solve a problem or task.

2. Theory that a baby will learn to repeat or stop his response to a stimulus.

3. Theory about the symbolic meaning behind behaviors and early life experiences as related to development.

4. Theory that interactions with the surrounding environments influence human growth and development.

5. Theory that learning is a social endeavor and young children learn about the world around them through relationships.

6. Theory that applies the basic principles of evolution by natural selection to our understanding of how humans develop.

7. Theory that development occurs during eight stages of life; at each stage, a psychological or social conflict must be successfully resolved.

8. Theory that people actively shape and are shaped by their environment, are motivated to learn, and self-regulate.

3

Pregnancy and Birth

Learning Outcomes

After studying this chapter, you will be able to:

3.1 Describe the three stages of pregnancy and the developmental milestones that occur in each stage.

3.2 Explain how health practices and lifestyle choices during conception and pregnancy influence the pregnant woman, developing fetus, and newborn.

3.3 Discuss how prenatal complications can affect the developing fetus and newborn.

3.4 Contrast the three stages of childbirth.

Key Terms

afterbirth stage
blastocyst
Braxton-Hicks contractions
breech birth
certified nurse-midwives
cesarean section
conception
congenital disorders
contractions
cystic fibrosis
dilation stage
doula
Down syndrome
effacement
embryo
embryonic period

episiotomy
expulsion stage
fetal alcohol spectrum
    disorders (FASDs)
fetal monitoring
fetal period
fetus
first trimester
forceps-assisted extraction
fragile X syndrome
germinal period
gestational diabetes
induced labor
low birthweight
maternal morbidity
maternal mortality

mutations
natural childbirth
obstetrician
oxygen deprivation
phenylketonuria (PKU)
placenta
preterm birth
Rh factor
sickle cell anemia
single-gene disorder
stillbirth
teratogens
third trimester
umbilical cord
vacuum extraction

Introduction

Imagine finding out you or someone close to you is pregnant. What thoughts and feelings would you have? What kinds of plans would you need to make? What would excite you or make you apprehensive? Some of us have personally experienced pregnancy and giving birth. Many have been in close relationships with someone who experienced pregnancy and childbirth. For others, these experiences are observed from afar or through reading and media.

Before you start reading, consider what you already know about pregnancy and childbirth. What are the best health and lifestyle practices before conception? What new knowledge has been discovered over the past generation? How does pregnancy proceed, and what are the steps or stages of childbirth? What determines healthy outcomes for baby and mother? As you proceed through the chapter, take note of content that is new and increases your knowledge base.

The story of human development begins even before conception, long before a fetus develops in the uterus. This chapter discusses various lifestyle choices made before pregnancy, the stages of prenatal development and care, and the birth process. Finally, you will explore prenatal and postpartum challenges.

3.1 Stages of Prenatal Development

There are many stages that a woman goes through during the nine months of pregnancy. Learning about her pregnancy is the first change that occurs, and this news may cause stress. Even planned pregnancies can cause stress as the woman wonders about how her life will change, whether she is ready to handle the additional responsibility, whether she has adequate available resources to care for the baby, and how her body will change.

First Trimester

The **first trimester** begins on the first day of a woman's last menstrual period and lasts until the end of the thirteenth week of pregnancy. Sometimes, a woman does not even realize she is pregnant during much of the first trimester, especially if her menstrual periods are irregular (a missed period is often the first indicator of pregnancy). Other signs of pregnancy may include fatigue, appetite, tender breasts, nausea, frequent urination, and mood changes. Although it may not be externally evident, a tremendous amount of change is going on inside of the mother's body (Mayo Clinic, 2020).

The first trimester includes both the germinal and the embryonic periods of prenatal development. The **germinal period** extends from conception until about two weeks later when implantation in the uterus occurs. **Conception** occurs when a sperm penetrates the egg or ovum. Within hours, this fertilized egg, now called a zygote, begins dividing—first into two cells, then into four cells, and after five days, into 64 to 128 cells referred to as a **blastocyst**. Within two weeks, the blastocyst will attach to the lining wall of the woman's uterus, a process called implantation (American College of Obstetricians and Gynecologists, 2016; Office on Women's Health, 2020; Mayo Clinic, 2020).

The next stage of the first trimester, or **embryonic period**, extends from the second to the ninth week of pregnancy, during which time the blastocyst is called an **embryo**. The embryo has three parts: the outermost layer or ectoderm, the middle layer or mesoderm, and the innermost layer or endoderm (see Table 3.1). These three layers are responsible for forming distinct parts of the developing body (American College of Obstetricians and Gynecologists, 2016; Mayo Clinic, 2020).

Early in this stage, an umbilical cord develops between the embryo and the uterine lining. The umbilical cord is attached to the **placenta**, an organ shaped like a sac attached to the uterus that provides nutrients from the mother. The **umbilical cord** is a tube of veins and arteries that connects the placenta with the embryo (at the site we later call the umbilicus, navel, or belly button). This lifeline will provide oxygen, nutrients, and water through the maternal blood supply to the developing embryo. As it develops, the embryo floats freely inside the placenta, surrounded by the amniotic fluid that protects it from shocks and movements and keeps the temperature constant as the mother carries on with life.

The development during the embryonic period is astonishing (see Table 3.2). The nervous system develops; the heart develops and begins to beat; and most body parts become identifiable, with the head being most dominant. During this earliest stage of life, regulation of gene expression and development may profoundly impact health and disease in later life. These epigenetic variations are primarily established in utero (Bogdarina et al., 2004; Gluckman et al., 2008).

One of the most critical milestones for a pregnant woman is when she emotionally shifts from viewing pregnancy as a change in her body to viewing her unborn child as a separate person. This perspective shift usually occurs after the first few months, during the germinal period, after "morning sickness" or the

Part of the Embryo	Body Parts/Systems That Develop
Ectoderm	Nervous system, ears, nose, eyes
Mesoderm	Bones, muscles, circulatory system, reproductive system
Endoderm	Digestive and respiratory systems

American College of Obstetricians and Gynecologists, 2016; Mayo Clinic, 2020

Table 3.1 Parts of the Embryo and Body Parts/Systems That Develop from Each

Weeks of Pregnancy	Developmental Milestones
1–4	• Conception: sperm and egg (ovum) unite; cells start dividing, creating the blastocyst • Implantation into the uterine lining occurs • Nervous system (brain and spinal cord) begins to develop, continues throughout pregnancy • Digestive system, heart, and circulatory system begin to form • Limb buds appear and later become arms and legs • Eyes and ears start forming • Heart begins to beat
5–8	• Major systems develop and function, including circulatory, digestive, nervous, and urinary systems • Tooth buds form • Eyes, nose, and ears are identifiable • Head continues rapid growth, appearing larger than rest of body • Arms and legs are distinguishable • Most body parts can be identified, including leg buds and hands
9–12	• Toes visible, elbows identifiable • Facial features well-formed • Eyelids, fingernails, and toenails form • Voice box forms • May be possible to determine sex from genitals • Head growth slows

Kato

Table 3.2 Overview of the First Trimester: Highlights in Prenatal Development

feeling of nausea passes (Han, 2013). By the time the mother reaches the end of this period, her body shows the effects of pregnancy with an enlarged abdomen, larger breasts, and expanding hips.

By the end of the first trimester, the embryo is fully formed with identifiable body parts; it is about three to four inches in length, weighing between half to one full pound (see Figure 3.1). Although the embryo has the appearance of a baby, it cannot yet survive outside the uterus (American College of Obstetricians and Gynecologists, 2016; Mayo Clinic, 2020).

Second Trimester

The second trimester begins the **fetal period**, which lasts through the second and third trimesters until birth. During this stage, the developing baby is now called a **fetus**. Body parts become more distinct, including arms and legs, fingers and toes, and

Fetal growth from 4 to 40 weeks

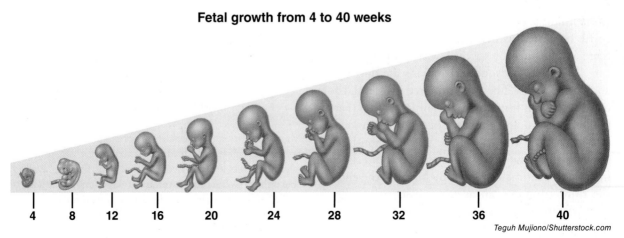

4	8	12	16	20	24	28	32	36	40

Teguh Mujiono/Shutterstock.com

Figure 3.1 Fetal Growth from 4 to 40 Weeks.

Weeks of Pregnancy	Developmental Milestones
12–16	• Eye movements • Limb movement becomes more coordinated • More muscles and bones form and develop • Transparent skin forms and gradually thickens • Scalp hair forms • Sucking reflex begins
16–20	• Ears begin hearing • Swallowing reflex begins • Taste buds form • Eyes face forward • Vernix caseosa covers body
20–24	• The mother can feel fetus's active movements • Sucking reflex becomes more developed • Lanugo, a fine, soft hair, covers the body • Fingerprints become distinct • Rapid eye movements develop

Kato

Table 3.3 Overview of the Second Trimester: Highlights in Prenatal Development

eyes and ears. Facial features become clear. When using ultrasound imaging, the bones of the developing fetus can be seen (see Table 3.3). Movements of the arms and legs become more coordinated, and the mother and sometimes other people can feel the fetus's movements. Even the sex of the baby can often be visually seen during the second trimester.

Many women report that the second trimester is the best part of their pregnancies, as morning sickness is often over and the body has not yet expanded to an uncomfortable state. When the second trimester ends, the developing fetus weighs one pound and may be 12 to 14 inches (approximately 30 to 35 centimeters) long. As the fetus increases in size, so does the mother.

Third Trimester

If the infant is born as early as the beginning of the **third trimester**, which includes weeks 24 to 40, there is a chance of survival with proper medical care. In other words, all fetal organs are developed and functioning. The last trimester is essential for increased organ function, especially the lungs. Fatty tissue develops, and the fetus becomes both longer and heavier. By the end of the seventh month, the fetus weighs about three pounds and is about sixteen inches (40 centimeters) long. By birth, at the end of the third trimester, an average newborn weighs 7 to 8 pounds and is about 20 inches (50 centimeters) long (Office on Women's Health, 2020; Mayo Clinic, 2020).

As the fetus grows and increases in weight over nine months, the mother's body prepares for labor and delivery, the birth process. Typically, this begins as the fetus positions itself in a head-down (cephalic) position. As the head moves into the pelvis, the mother often feels less pressure on her breathing and stomach. Sometimes women experience psychological changes, such as the desire to ready things for the upcoming new baby, sometimes called *nesting*.

☑ CHECKPOINT

☐ Describe how an embryo changes during the first trimester of pregnancy.

☐ In general terms, describe the order of prenatal growth and development of a baby.

☐ In comparison to the first trimester, how might a pregnant woman experience the middle stage of pregnancy?

☐ How does a fetus change during the third trimester of pregnancy?

Apply Here!

Many educational videos show prenatal development. Some are full-length features available for streaming, whereas others are short educational clips that are available online. Do an online search for videos and make a list of 5 to 10 videos that you might recommend for an audience of women who are experiencing their first pregnancy. Include a review summary for each video you select.

Practical Issues and Implications

Are Gender Reveal Parties Harmless?

Knowing the sex of a baby before birth has long been a preoccupation of expected parents and their extended family members. Before modern-day medical technology was available to identify a baby's sex prenatally, traditional customs, stories, and beliefs attempted to provide revelation. Did the expected mother carry the fetus low? Wide? Was she experiencing nausea or other discomforts? Customs and beliefs often are based on shared folk stories and unsubstantiated tales passed down between generations. Today, a baby's sex is often revealed through medical imaging long before birth.

In the age of social media, a US cultural phenomenon has exploded that creates an opportunity for parents to divulge the sex of their babies by planning elaborate "gender reveal" parties shared widely through social media. Sex is often assigned a social gender and a color. Pink frosting, smoke, or balloons let the party attendees know that the parents expect a baby of the female sex, whereas blue signifies they anticipate a baby of the male sex (see Figure 3.2) (Applequist, 2014; Pasche Guignard, 2015).

What started as a simple gesture became larger than life, involving pyrotechnics and potentially risky actions performed at celebratory gatherings. People are drawn to performance as a means of gaining approval and as a way of processing life's transitions. Having a child is a significant life transition. As a new social ritual, a gender reveal party offers a way to celebrate this upcoming life transition and a subjective way to demonstrate that the parents have the means to support the child (Applequist, 2014; Nahata, 2017; Pasche Guignard, 2015).

Critics of gender reveal parties note several issues. First, the reveal is about the physical attributes of sex features. It is not about gender, a socially constructed identity. Critics are also concerned that such a binary definition, even before birth, may harm the parents, the child, family

Mccalllk69/Shutterstock.com

Figure 3.2 At gender reveal parties, the sex of an expecting mother's baby is publicly announced in front of family and friends. *Do you think that gender reveal parties are helpful or harmful? If so, how and to whom?*

members, and the community at large by celebrating and ritualizing gendered identity, setting premature expectations and creating distress (Gieseler, 2018; Nahata, 2017).

To Think About:

- Have you ever attended a gender reveal party? If so, what were your impressions of it?
- Are parties and gatherings centered on revealing an unborn baby's sex to others harmful? Why or why not? If so, to whom, why, and how?
- How might this phenomenon impact someone of a lower socioeconomic standing who doesn't have the means to support a child?

3.2 Care and Lifestyle Before and During Pregnancy

Health and lifestyle behaviors can play a large part in the ability to conceive and the success of a pregnancy. Most importantly, these factors can play a large part in the health of a developing fetus and newborn. They may even have lifelong effects on both the mother and child's health and well-being. The pre-conception stage encompasses the months preceding pregnancy, anywhere from three months to one year prior. The length of a typical pregnancy is forty weeks because it includes the first day of the pregnant woman's last menstrual period, which is about two weeks before actual conception occurs.

Health Care and Lifestyle Before Conception

An important first consideration for a woman who is planning to become pregnant or suspects that she might be pregnant is to find quality medical care. Recent studies have confirmed that preconception care is critical in positive health outcomes for mothers and babies (Pentecost & Maurizio, 2020). If possible, a woman should have a thorough physical checkup before becoming pregnant to assess her health, which might also include genetic testing for the potential risk of congenital disabilities or disorders. During this time, any existing health problems will be observed and managed, including family health issues such as high blood pressure gestational diabetes, or sexually transmitted diseases (Lancet, 2018; Lane et al., 2014). When pregnancy is suspected, health care professionals can confirm the pregnancy and begin to offer care right away. Medical care in the form of counseling and education prior to conception leads to improved maternal and child outcomes and reduces risky behaviors (Jack et al., 2015).

Eating a well-balanced diet of healthy foods is essential during every stage of life. In addition, a woman's healthy body weight and physical fitness before conception can provide the right setting for optimal development of a fetus. Emphasis should be placed on the quality, not the quantity, of food consumed (King, 2016; Lancet, 2018). For example, health care providers recommend that a woman take an extra folic acid (folate) supplement before conception and throughout pregnancy because it promotes healthy brain and spinal cord development. The brain and nervous system are some of the earliest organs to develop during pregnancy, and folic acid is linked to a 70% reduction in congenital disabilities. (Lancet, 2018; Mastroiacovo & Leoncini, 2011). Taking prenatal vitamins and minerals also creates a more favorable environment for any future pregnancy, even impacting the likelihood of conception (Farquharson & Stephenson, 2010; Stephenson et al., 2018).

Recent studies have focused on the effects of maternal obesity on pregnancy outcomes. Obesity is an increasing global concern for women of childbearing age (Black et al., 2013). Being either underweight or overweight during the pre-pregnancy months negatively impacts the future mother and child (Stephenson et al., 2018). Maternal obesity before pregnancy is associated with greater risks of pregnancy-induced hypertension, greater birthweight of infants, and greater likelihood of cesarean delivery. It also increases the likelihood of **preterm** delivery; delivery before 38 weeks of gestation–the period from the time of conception until birth– or **stillbirth**, death of a fetus after 20 weeks gestation and prior to delivery (Blomberg, 2013; Schummers et al., 2015; Stothard et al., 2009). For mothers who have a normal pre-pregnancy weight, an increase of 25-35 pounds during pregnancy is recommended (Cantor et al., 2021).

It is critical that pregnant women avoid consuming alcohol, taking drugs (including over-the-counter and prescription drugs), and smoking. Even second-hand smoke should be avoided. These substances can cause significant harm to the developing fetus and possibly cause cognitive impairment throughout the child's life.

Chemical exposure can have lasting adverse effects. Exposure to heavy metals in utero can lead to stillbirth and problems in memory formation (US Centers for Disease Control and Prevention, 2019a, c). Avoiding these things *prior* to pregnancy can positively affect the future pregnancy as well (Lancet, 2018). The impact of these environmental risk factors may also influence epigenetic mechanisms, or the inherited genetic changes that impact future generations, as described in Chapter 2.

The concept of the relationship between preconception health and lifestyle behaviors and fetal and neonatal health has traditionally focused on women. However, increasing knowledge of biology and genetics emphasizes that health and lifestyle affect both the mother and the father due to their 50% to 50% genetic contribution (Stephenson et al., 2018). Although most research continues to focus on women as potential child bearers, men are increasingly becoming a focus of research involving the impact of paternal substance use, exposure to chemicals, and smoking on the developing fetus (Kotelchuck & Lu, 2017; Meng & Groth, 2018; Rutkowska et al., 2020).

Pregnancies are most successful when women begin at a healthy body weight, are active, and have social and emotional support from family members and friends. Mental health issues such as depression before conception have been linked to negative pregnancy outcomes (Thombre et al., 2015).

☑ CHECKPOINT

☐ In general terms, describe some lifestyle concerns that women who may become pregnant should consider. How might a woman's lifestyle choices impact a future pregnancy? Why should the lifestyles of men who may become fathers be considered, too?

☐ Why is medical care critical during pregnancy?

☐ How might a healthy maternal body weight during pregnancy impact pregnancy outcomes?

Nutrition During Pregnancy

During pregnancy, proper maternal nutrition is fundamental to the health of a growing embryo and fetus. As previously noted, the placenta forms early in pregnancy, just after implantation, and serves as a lifeline, delivering nutrition via the maternal blood supply. Because the fetus receives nutrients from foods, there are critical windows during organ development when nutrition is especially impactful. When there is inadequate nutrition consumption, the placenta works to garner nutrition from maternal stores, which places the mother at risk for adverse health (Mousa et al., 2019; Wyness et al., 2013). Although newborns can be at a normal birthweight even when the mother has had inadequate nutritional intake during pregnancy, negative health impacts often appear later in life, such as night blindness from insufficient vitamin A (Brown et al., 2010; McCauley et al., 2015). However, maternal undernutrition, inadequate food intake, and the poor nutritional quality of food are linked to poor fetal growth throughout the developing world (Mousa et al., 2019; Rao & Yajnik, 2010).

Researchers offer detailed recommendations about what comprises a healthy, well-balanced diet during pregnancy. The Academy of Nutrition and Dietetics (2020) recommends that pregnant women eat a well-rounded diet that includes whole grains, fruits and vegetables, lean protein, low fat or fat-free dairy products, and healthy monounsaturated and polyunsaturated fats. Healthy fats include those from nuts and seeds, canola and olive oils, or foods such as avocados. Avoiding added sugars and solid fats decreases the likelihood of unhealthy weight gain.

Three essential nutrients—folate (folic acid), iron, and calcium—are critical to healthy fetal growth and development. Although many pregnant women strive to eat healthy foods, most doctors recommend additional vitamin and mineral supplements (Lancet, 2018; Mastroiacovo & Leoncini, 2011). Prenatal vitamins, made just for pregnancy, contain extra folic acid, calcium, and iron. The additional supplements have several benefits (see Table 3.4). Folic acid (a vitamin) helps reduce brain and spinal cord congenital disabilities. Extra calcium helps build strong bones, teeth, and heart and nervous systems. Additional iron helps to increase the mother's blood supply and to reduce the chance of babies being born at low birthweight.

Pregnant women should avoid certain foods during pregnancy, including some fish and shellfish that contain high levels of mercury, undercooked meats, poultry (such as chicken), eggs, and unpasteurized milk products such as cheese (Academy of Nutrition and Dietetics 2020). These foods can

Nutrient	Description
Folic Acid (Folate)	• Reduces the risk of spinal cord congenital disabilities • Found in natural foods, such as green leafy vegetables, citrus fruits, and legumes • Found also in fortified foods, such as bread, pasta, and cereals • 400+ micrograms daily recommended; often through supplements
Iron	• Increases blood supply, moves oxygen • Found in natural foods, such as chicken, red meat, fish, spinach, some other green leafy vegetables, and beans • Found also in fortified foods, such as bread, pasta, corn products, and white rice • 27+ milligrams daily recommended, often through supplements
Calcium	• Builds healthy bones, teeth, heart, nerves, and muscles • Found in natural foods, such as low-fat or fat-free milk, yogurt, and cheese • Found also in fortified foods, such as cereals, juices, and other beverages • 1300+ micrograms daily for teen mothers, 1000+ micrograms daily for adult mothers recommended, often through supplements

Academy of Nutrition and Dietetics, 2020; Brown et al., 2010; Wyness et al., 2013

Table 3.4 Key Nutrients Needed During Pregnancy

cause food-related illnesses, such as salmonella or norovirus, which may affect the developing fetus (US Food and Drug Administration, 2020). Mercury has been linked to impaired brain development or cognitive delays, but only at excessive consumption levels (Hibbeln et al., 2018). The US Food and Drug Administration (2020) and the American Academy of Pediatrics (2012) recommend that pregnant women consume moderate amounts of mercury-free fish or shellfish. These foods have rich nutritional value as sources of omega-3 fatty acid, a substance that is widely understood to positively impact fetal neurodevelopment (Zhang et al., 2019; Devarshi et al., 2019).

When Food Is Scarce, Unsafe, or Nutritionally Inadequate

Food insecurity is the limited or uncertain availability of nutritionally adequate safe food. As is true throughout the world, many Americans face food insecurity, including pregnant women. In some neighborhoods, food markets or grocery stores simply do not exist. Dense urban or rural areas that have faced economic hardship may lack stores that stock fresh produce, healthy protein choices, or fresh dairy products. Sometimes, the only source of food products is a fast-food or convenience store that sells mostly snack food and beverages that are not nutritionally sound. Neighborhoods lacking adequate nutritious food sources are termed food deserts (see Figure 3.3). Food deserts are often associated with neighborhood racial segregation, health care disparity, and poverty (Howell et al., 2020; Moaddab et al., 2018; Rhone et al., 2017).

At any stage of life, food insecurity leads to adverse health outcomes for the mother and child, including stunted growth prenatally and in childhood, obesity throughout childhood to adulthood, and mental health concerns for the mother, including anxiety and depression (Cheu et al., 2020; Iqbal & Ali, 2021; Kelli et al., 2019). Women who live in food deserts while pregnant are at a higher risk for pregnancy morbidity, preeclampsia, gestational hypertension, gestational diabetes, preterm labor, and low birthweight babies (Karbin et al., 2021; Laraia et al., 2010; Tipton et al., 2020).

Health Services During Pregnancy

Besides proper nutrition, initiating early prenatal health care is critical for pregnant women. There are many options. The most common is being under the care of a medical doctor. **Obstetricians** are doctors who specialize in pregnancy and childbirth. Some women choose to use their family doctor (primary care provider) who also provides general prenatal care. Others prefer the services of a nurse practitioner (NP), a nurse with a graduate degree in advanced practice nursing, or a **certified nurse-midwife**

A

B

David J Garcia/Shutterstock.com; duckeesue/Shutterstock.com

Figure 3.3 Pregnant women and their families may experience food insecurity for many reasons. Some may live in rural areas and lack a car or easy access to public transportation, making a trip to a grocery store difficult (A). Others may live in urban neighborhoods where the closest stores offer limited options for obtaining nutritious foods like fresh fruits and vegetables (B).

(CNM). Midwives are nurses who specialize in pregnancy and birth. For healthy women, any of these medical professionals can provide good care. If, however, a woman is considered at risk for complications, she may be referred to a doctor who specializes in the condition (Thornton et al., 2009; US Department of Health and Human Services, 2020d; Zolotor & Carlough, 2014).

Expectant mothers are screened for potential health problems during the first medical exam, usually at around the eighth week of pregnancy. Providers will confirm the pregnancy and calculate a due date. The woman receives a complete physical exam, and blood and urine samples are taken. A physical examination can detect any reproductive tract abnormalities and screen for sexually transmitted infections. Health care professionals record the woman's height and weight and calculate her body mass index (BMI) to provide any necessary counseling related to obesity or diabetes concerns. Early consultation offers the opportunity for the medical provider to diagnose any health problems and provide an early cure or treatment if possible.

In the United States, a woman's age and race influence prenatal medical care or the lack thereof (see Figure 3.4). On average, teenagers and Native Americans are less likely to receive prenatal care than their counterparts. Mothers who do not receive early prenatal care are three times more likely to have low-weight babies and five times more likely to die than those who receive early prenatal care (US Department of Health and Human Services, 2020d).

After the first prenatal visit, health care exams are typically scheduled every month through week 28. In the last trimester, weeks 28 through 36, visit frequency increases to every two weeks. During the last month, at weeks 36 and beyond, weekly visits are the norm. During these visits, the health care provider records the woman's weight, measures her blood pressure, and detects the fetal heartbeat through Doppler ultrasound or an electronic monitor. The health care provider will also take measurements of the pregnant woman's abdomen, or the distance from the pubic bone to the top of the uterus, to determine the size of the growing fetus. Prenatal counseling and education are often included as best practices. For pregnant women who are over the age of 35 or those who are considered at high risk, more frequent medical exams may be needed (Thornton et al., 2009; US Department of Health and Human Services, 2020; Zolotor & Carlough, 2014).

Throughout pregnancy, several medical tests or screenings may be offered, depending on the individual patient's needs (Zolotor & Carlough, 2014). A few of these include screenings to detect birth disorders or to assess the overall health of the mother or fetus (see Table 3.5). Through routine blood tests, mismatches are detected. Sometimes, the **Rh factor** (the type of protein in red blood cells) does not match the baby's. A mismatch between the mother and fetus is of concern as incompatibility can cause miscarriage (infant death). In some cases, the newborn may become anemic or have an iron deficiency that may lead to serious complications without treatment. In other cases, the newborn experiences no harm. It all depends on the type and severity of the incompatibility. If the results are positive for the Rh factor incompatibility, mothers can be treated with Rh immune globulin during pregnancy and after delivery (American College of Obstetricians and Gynecologists, 2021).

Maternal and Prenatal Health care Inequities Related to Race

One of the most significant public health inequities in the United States is the disproportion of **maternal mortality**, or pregnancy-related death, for Black and Native American women (see Figure 3.5).

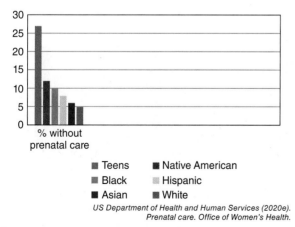

US Department of Health and Human Services (2020e). Prenatal care. Office of Women's Health.

Figure 3.4 Lack of Prenatal Care Averages by Age and Race

Timing	Screening	Method	Function/Detection
11–14 weeks	**First trimester screen**	Blood test and ultrasound imaging	• Chromosomal disorders • HIV • Rubella • Rh factor • Sexually transmitted infections (STI) • Human immunodeficiency virus (HIV) • Other problems, such as heart defects • Multiple births (twins, triplets, etc.)
14–20 weeks	**Amniocentesis***	Needle extraction of amniotic fluid	• Down syndrome • Cystic fibrosis • Spina bifida
15–20 weeks	**Maternal serum screen**	Blood test	• Chromosomal disorders • Neural tube defects
18–20 weeks	**Ultrasound**	Ultrasound imaging	• Problems with organs and systems • Confirm proper growth • Sex of baby
26–28 weeks	**Glucose challenge screening**	Blood test	• Risk of gestational diabetes
Third trimester	**Biophysical profile**	Blood test and stress test	• Overall health of the baby • Early delivery may be warranted

US Department of Health and Human Services, 2020

*Not considered a standard test.

Table 3.5 Examples of Prenatal Screenings

Black women in the United States are three to four times more likely to die from pregnancy or childbirth complications than their White counterparts (Jackson et al., 2020; Small et al., 2017). Preterm labor is twice as likely for Black women and 20% higher for Native American women when compared to White women. Black infants are also twice as likely to die in their first year of life than

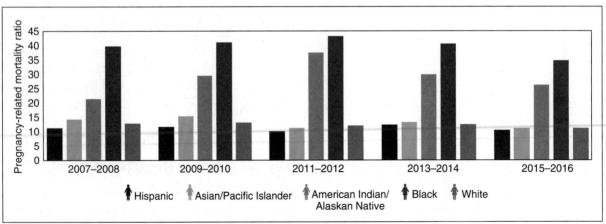

US Centers for Disease Control and Prevention

Figure 3.5 Pregnancy-Related Mortality Ratio by Race

White, non-Hispanic babies, with the highest mortality numbers occurring in the southern states (Kandasamy et al., 2020).

Large-scale economic system disparities, health care, and other policies have contributed to disproportionately higher rates of **maternal morbidity**, severe or life-threatening complications from pregnancy or childbirth. There is no evidence that complications in pregnancy or childbirth are from genetic differences, although chronic health differences may play a part (Lemke & Brown, 2020). Recent investigations suggest that while interventions are available to inhibit preterm birth and prevent adverse maternal outcomes, Black women and other women of color either have not had (or have not sought) equal access to these treatments (Rowley & Hogan, 2012). Although this is a complex issue, scientific evidence ties these chronic health differences to societal structural differences in health care (Jackson et al., 2020). When some women are persistently denied equal access to quality health care over time, they may develop a mistrust and skepticism about the value of health care. These feelings become ingrained. Even when they receive better health care, some of these individuals may perceive the care as substandard because it is hard to change systems that have been in place for generations (Rowley & Hogan, 2012).

Equal access to high-quality health care is essential, but some research indicates that it does not account for most of the higher maternal morbidity and mortality rates in communities of color (Davis, 2019). Longstanding racial issues that span generations have made it difficult to secure adequate employment with livable wages, career advancement, and equitable pay, making housing less secure. Those who experience living daily in a racially biased culture may suffer the consequences of poor health outcomes (Davis, 2019; Dominguez et al., 2008). Systemic racism may also lead to distrust of community resources and the health care system (Rowley & Hogan, 2012). Today, the United States ranks last among all developed countries in terms of access to community services (childcare, housing, and other resources). This lack of access exists despite evidence that links increases in public health spending to declines in inequitable, preventable adverse outcomes and death (Mays, 2011; Freedman & Kruk, 2014).

Lifestyle During Pregnancy

A healthy lifestyle is vital to positive health outcomes for the pregnant woman and the developing fetus. Good outcomes include an uncomplicated pregnancy and delivery and a healthy baby at birth. Choices associated with healthy outcomes include consuming nutritionally dense food, maintaining a healthy pregnancy weight and adequate weight gain, avoiding drugs and alcohol, healthy blood pressure, and having paid family employment (Chappell et al., 2013).

Although there is a lack of research on the issue, health care providers often encourage physical activity during pregnancy because it can offer a host of physical and mental health benefits. Positive outcomes include a reduced risk of gestational diabetes, gestational hypertension, and preeclampsia; lower likelihood of excessive weight gain during pregnancy; lower incidence of cesarean and preterm birth; lower incidence of low birthweight; and fewer symptoms of postpartum depression (ACOG, 2020; Dipietro, et al., 2019; Ferraro et al., 2012). Lack of physical activity during pregnancy is associated with greater weight gain and maternal obesity, gestational diabetes, and depression (Hui et al., 2014; Symons-Downs et al., 2012). However, starting and maintaining physical activity should be under the guidance of the pregnant woman's health care provider.

Anxiety, depressive behaviors, and stress are commonly seen in pregnant women and may be pre-existing conditions (Dunkel, 2010; Leight et al., 2010; Ross & Woods et al., 2010). Because women are undergoing significant physical and emotional changes during pregnancy, mental health issues are a major factor in their overall health and well-being. Stress is known to have negative effects at all stages of life, causing various emotional and physical disorders, including anxiety and depressive behaviors. The fact of pregnancy itself may cause stress, anxiety, or depression, especially in situations where the pregnancy is unwanted, unplanned, or the woman is experiencing an unstable domestic or financial environment. Stress has been associated with pregnancy complications such as preterm births and **low birthweights**, birthweights of less than 5.5 pounds (2500 grams) (Ding et al., 2014; World Health Organization, 2004). Pregnant women, especially near the end of pregnancy, also have a higher risk of being

LightField Studios/Shutterstock.com

Figure 3.6 Healthy pregnant women under a doctor's care are encouraged to spend 150 minutes each week performing moderate-intensity aerobic exercise. This should continue after pregnancy as well.
How many minutes per week do you spend exercising?

victims of domestic violence. Such abuse results in physical and mental harm to the mother and even higher levels of stress (Priya et al., 2019; Zheng et al., 2020).

One of the best ways to reduce stress during pregnancy is for the pregnant woman to be surrounded by a support group. Friends, medical professionals, and family can all help relieve stress by providing social and emotional support. Having an employer willing to accommodate any necessary job changes is also important. Finally, getting exercise, both aerobic and stretching exercises, can aid in wellness (see Figure 3.6). Together, these factors can reduce the chance of problems during pregnancy (Asselmann et al., 2020; Ding et al., 2014).

☑ CHECKPOINT

- ☐ Why is prenatal nutrition important for optimal results?
- ☐ How does receiving prenatal health care increase optimal results for pregnant women and their developing babies?

- ☐ What are three maternal prenatal lifestyle choices that have the potential to yield positive outcomes for the mother and baby?
- ☐ What are the effects of stress on pregnancy?

Apply Here!

You are helping at a food bank, distributing to families needing some extra assistance. A young immigrant woman approaches you. She tells you that she is pregnant. She is new to your community and unfamiliar with the neighborhood. She begins asking your advice on lifestyle choices, options, and resources. What advice do you give?

3.3 Potential Problems in Prenatal Development

Women have been giving birth since the beginning of time; and in most cases, pregnancy and birth go well. Sometimes, though, complications can make the pregnancy difficult. These problems range from family genetic disorders to environmental concerns, such as drug use or radiation exposure. Today, there are more treatments for potential problems than ever before.

Genetic Disorders

Disorders associated with faulty genes or chromosomes are termed **congenital disorders** and are inherited by the infant from the biological parents. Prenatal testing can determine the possibility of some genetic disorders before pregnancy occurs. Other disorders can be diagnosed during pregnancy, and some of these disorders can be treated. Other genetic disorders cannot be diagnosed prior to birth, nor can they be treated until after birth (US National Library of Medicine, 2020).

Genetic disorders happen for various reasons, many of which remain unknown (see Table 3.6). What is known, however, is that gene mutations, a change in the DNA sequence, cause some conditions. **Mutations** are permanent gene modifications involving some sort of substitution, deletion, or insertion (Pritchard & Korf, 2013). For example, **phenylketonuria (PKU)** is caused by two mutated genes that prevent the body from processing phenylalanine, an amino acid (US Department of Health and Human Services, 2020c).

Disorder	Description	Effects/Treatment
Cystic fibrosis	Caused by two faulty genes that interfere with the respiratory, digestive, and reproductive systems. The body cannot easily process mucus, which creates blockages within the body.	Causes digestive, reproductive, and respiratory issues. Effects range from mild to severe. No cure exists, but treatments are available and vary depending on symptoms. Treatments may include medications, exercise, and dietary supplements.
Down syndrome	Usually caused by an extra copy of the 22nd chromosome.	Causes severe cognitive disability and delayed language development. Effects are not uniform. Treatments may include surgery, education specialists, and specialized learning programs.
Fragile X syndrome	Caused by a faulty gene. The X chromosome is unstable (fragile) and usually breaks.	Effects range from a short attention span to a learning disability to severe cognitive disability. Treatments vary but may include specialized education and therapy.
Huntington's disease	Caused by an abnormal gene that provides instructions for producing a protein called *huntingtin*, which is suspected to play an important role in nerve cells in the brain.	Causes loss of physical control, memory, and ability to rationalize. Often leads to depression and death from complications. There is no cure, but medication is available to treat symptoms. Physical activity is also recommended.
Phenylketonuria (PKU)	Caused by two mutated genes that prevent the body from processing phenylalanine, an amino acid.	Effects include cognitive and developmental disabilities, seizures, and behavioral problems. When detected early, a modified (low phenylalanine) diet can prevent physical and cognitive damage.
Sickle-cell anemia	Caused by a recessive gene that alters the shape of red blood cell. Affected cells are bowed instead of circular and do not properly carry oxygen throughout the body.	Effects range from no effect—unless in high-altitude areas—to chronic illness to early death. Treatments include blood transfusions, penicillin, and proper medication.
Spina bifida	Caused by incomplete development and formation of the spine in utero.	Causes partial to complete paralysis and fluid buildup in the skull. Treatments include corrective surgery, physical therapy, and a modified diet.
Tay-Sachs disease	Caused by a recessive gene. The body is unable to break down certain types of fats, which build up in the system and can block neural transmissions.	Causes cognitive and physical deterioration that usually leads to early death. No cure exists, but a modified diet and medication can ease symptoms.

Goodheart-Willcox Publisher

Table 3.6 Examples of Genetic Disorders

Autosome conditions run in families and occur in one of the first 22 sets of chromosomes, either as a dominant or a recessive disorder. For dominant genetic disorders, if one parent carries the gene, the child has at least a 50% chance of inheriting the disease. Marfan syndrome, a condition affecting the body's connective tissue, is an example of an autosomal dominant disorder. For recessive genetic disorders, both parents must carry a recessive gene mutation. The child has a 25% chance of inheriting the disorder, even if the condition is not apparent in the parent. A child who has inherited a recessive gene mutation can pass the gene to their offspring. An example of an autosomal recessive disorder that is diagnosed after birth is **cystic fibrosis**. This is a condition that affects organs in the body due to thick mucus buildup making it difficult for internal organs to operate effectively (US Centers for Disease Control and Prevention, 2019a).

Sometimes, genetic disorders are not passed down. Instead, they may be seen for the first time in the family line as a mutation of one person's genes. These are called **single-gene disorders**. They may be present at birth, manifest later in life, or may be triggered by environmental triggers or exposure (US Centers for Disease Control, 2018). In this case, the child may have the gene mutation, even though the parents do not. **Sickle cell anemia** is an autosomal single-gene disorder that causes a shortage and change of red blood cells and affects the body in numerous negative ways, including pain and infections. Sickle cell anemia can be diagnosed before birth (US Centers for Disease Control and Prevention, 2019c).

Sometimes infants have cognitive disabilities because of an abnormal number of genes or chromosomes. **Down syndrome** is a genetic condition caused by an extra chromosome that results in distinct physical qualities and intellectual disabilities that cause cognitive delays. The risk of having a baby born with Down syndrome increases with the mother's age (US Department of Health and Human Services, 2020a). **Fragile X syndrome** is also caused by an inherited faulty gene. The X chromosome is unstable (fragile) and usually breaks, resulting in a range of developmental issues, including learning disabilities and cognitive impairment (US Department of Health and Human Services, 2020b). If untreated, PKU may also cause intellectual disability (US Department of Health and Human Services, 2020c).

There are many congenital defects that can be treated before or after birth. For example, some fetal heart problems may be detected before birth, and their treatment can be implemented immediately following birth, such as with a heart repair surgery or heart transplant. Some treatments can even occur before birth (US National Library of Medicine, 2020). Although congenital disabilities vary, stem cell transplantation is showing progress both before and after birth to treat or mitigate the impact of some congenital diseases (University of California, San Francisco, 2020).

Mother's Age

Even a woman's age during pregnancy can impact the most critical outcome of the pregnancy, the health of the developing fetus. Age can also affect the mother's pregnancy experience and her health. Age at both ends of the spectrum, younger mothers (under age 20) and older mothers (over age 35), can complicate pregnancies and births.

Teenage Mothers

Do teenagers intend to get pregnant? Some do not, but some do. Some societies take great lengths to prevent teen pregnancy, whereas pregnancy is considered a choice, or at least tolerated, in others (Checkland & Wong, 2016). In the United States, teenage pregnancy rates have declined over the last half-century since their peak in the 1950s, when teen mothers accounted for 96 out of every 1,000 live births to just over 18 of every 1,000 live births (Livingston, 2019). This drop may be due to more sex education, greater accessibility to birth control, economic and societal changes, or simply less sexual activity among teens. The data does not consider pregnancy termination such as miscarriages, stillbirth, or abortion. Most US teen pregnancies are unintended, although about 25% of these women experience a repeated pregnancy within two years (Black et al., 2012). Despite the planning or lack of planning, teen pregnancy creates consequences for both the mother and baby. Some social taboos and restrictions, such as social unacceptability or the lack of access to health care, keep pregnant teens from getting early prenatal care. The consumption of vitamins and a healthy diet are often started later in the pregnancy than desired. If the teen consumes alcohol or uses drugs, the negative impact is most significant during the early weeks of fetal development when the brain and spinal cord are developing (Lindberg et al., 2016; Martin et al., 2018; Sedgh et al., 2015).

Teen mothers are more likely to experience preterm labor and delivery, resulting in low birthweight babies. However, this is associated with age, not necessarily health (Ferré et al., 2016). Low birthweight babies face several challenges, including developmental delays that can last for many years. Teen pregnancy has also been associated with pregnancy-induced hypertension and sexually transmitted infections (Klein et al., 2005).

Early pregnancy may be hard on a teen mother and may cause lifelong negative health consequences, such as decreased physical and mental health. Physical health is not always impacted immediately but later in life. This is due to the social and economic life situations that are often associated with teen pregnancy. Some teen mothers experience decreased mental health during the prenatal and postnatal periods compared to older mothers (Black et al., 2012; Patel & Sen, 2012). Mothers just past puberty are especially at risk because their bodies and brains are still undergoing tremendous growth and change. When a teen mother is also supporting the growth and development of a baby, fewer nutrients are available for her own growth and development (Fisher & Lara-Torre, 2012; Satin et al., 1994).

The biggest concern for teen mothers is finding adequate emotional and social support (see Figure 3.7). In most developed countries, women give birth at a later age. For example, in Canada, Greece, Australia, South Korea, Japan, and Italy, the average age to give birth for the first time is over age 30. In the United States, the average age to give birth for the first time is 26.4 years of age (Livingston, 2018).

In the last two decades, the rates of adolescent pregnancies have fallen significantly worldwide (World Bank, 2020). In the United States, mothers who have babies in their teens are more likely to be socially and economically disadvantaged throughout their lives. It may increase stress, especially if social support systems are not in place. For this reason, many high schools now offer alternative school programs that allow teens to finish their schooling while learning parenting and life skills (Fisher & Lara-Torre, 2012; Leishman & Moir, 2007).

Mothers of Advanced Age

Medically, mothers of advanced age are pregnant women aged 35 or older. Many women choose to become pregnant after turning 35, and most have healthy babies. The odds of having a healthy baby decrease, however, when compared to younger mothers. It often takes longer to conceive, and the risk of having multiple fetuses (twins, triplets) increases (Sauer, 2015).

When a mother is older, the pregnancy can be harder on her. **Gestational diabetes**, a type of diabetes that occurs only during pregnancy, is more common. Older mothers are at a higher risk for miscarriage, the early loss of a pregnancy. They are also more likely to have problems with labor and to deliver their babies via **cesarean section** (surgical removal of the newborn) rather than through normal vaginal delivery (Carolan & Frankowska, 2011; Kenny et al., 2013; Magnus et al., 2019).

In some more recent studies, mothers considered to be of advanced age are defined as pregnant women who are 40 or older (see Figure 3.8). By this definition, pregnant women of advanced age are more likely to give birth to babies with congenital disabilities and abnormalities. There are two main reasons. One is exposure to environmental toxins such as second-hand smoke, cleaning chemicals, food pollutants, and medications that can affect a developing fetus. The second reason is the age of the fertilized egg, which may be more likely to have

Andy Dean Photography/Shutterstock.com

Figure 3.7 Adolescents who become pregnant in the United States face many challenges. How common is teen pregnancy in your community? What local resources exist to support pregnant teens in your community?

Rido/Shutterstock.com

Figure 3.8 Women who become pregnant over age 40 are considered to be of advanced age. What challenges do pregnant women in this category face? Do these challenges merit routine and invasive tests such as amniocentesis? Why or why not?

structural chromosomal abnormalities (Cimadomo et al., 2018; Grondahl et al., 2017). Women over 45 are also more likely to experience maternal mortality, often due to preexisting conditions or cesarean delivery (Troiano et al., 2019). There is some evidence that older fathers may also present health risks, such as increased risk of premature birth, low birthweight, and genetic abnormalities, due to aging sperm and a history of lifelong exposure to environmental toxins (Croen et al., 2007; Khandwala et al., 2018; Sigman, 2017). Because of these risks, additional prenatal testing is often done to prepare the mother and medical team and to provide proper care for the newborn.

If a woman's family history of preterm labor or stillbirth is known, special medical care during pregnancy may reduce the chances of occurrence. In addition, risk factors can alert medical care professionals to signs such as a mother's advanced age, infection, or stress so they can provide preventative guidance (Fretts, 2005; Spong, 2011).

Environmental Factors

Fetal exposure to harmful environments causes specific pregnancy problems and congenital disabilities. These environments include chemicals, viruses and infections, and medications. Alcohol, drugs, and cigarettes also create an adverse environment for both mother and fetus. It is hard to know exactly which agents in the environment cause problems as there may be a combination of several reasons (Vesterinen et al., 2017).

Because environmental toxins, called **teratogens**, can cause pregnancy problems and congenital disabilities, it is essential to limit contact with these hazards (see Figure 3.9). Cleaning supplies, garden fertilizers and other chemicals, poor sanitation, and even cat litter boxes can all contribute to adverse fetal health outcomes. Exposure to fertilizers and pesticides is of particular concern during early pregnancy as they can cause congenital disabilities (Addissie et al., 2020; Krauss & Hong, 2016). Pregnant women should avoid as many risky situations as possible, including being around people fighting infections or other illnesses. Although research supports the toxicity of many environmental elements, additional research still needs to be done to understand the complexity of interacting factors (Vesterinen et al., 2017).

Lead, Radiation, and Toxic Chemical Exposure

How can pregnant women be exposed to radiation, toxic chemicals, or lead? Sometimes exposure is in the workplace. Other times, it is in the home. For example, lead-based paint still exists in some older apartments and homes, although the United States banned its use in household paint in 1978 (US Centers for Disease Control and Prevention, 2021). Lead can also be found in older home renovations or repairs, auto refinishing, and plumbing. Sometimes foods, cosmetics, or other consumer products contain lead. Public water supplies are another potential source of lead exposure. In 2014, in Flint, Michigan, an economically distressed city, approximately 140,000 people were exposed to lead and other contaminants via their drinking water after the city changed drinking water suppliers (Ruckart et al.,

A

B

Mabeline72/Shutterstock.com; New Africa/Shutterstock.com

Figure 3.9 Exposure to teratogens in the environment like pesticides (A) or contact with soiled cat litter (B) may cause congenital disabilities or other abnormal conditions in a developing fetus. What are some ways a pregnant woman can avoid these environmental toxins? Why is this important?

Figure 3.10 In 2014, residents of Flint, Michigan, began complaining that their drinking water tasted and smelled bad. Tests of water samples eventually revealed that the water contained high levels of lead. Adults, including pregnant women, and nearly 9,000 children were exposed to lead-contaminated water for 18 months until a federal emergency was declared.
What are the long-term consequences of prenatal lead exposure? What are its effects on a developing infant or child?

2019). The government declared this a federal emergency in 2015, and the city changed its water source supplier. However, this time lag and the cumulative health effects of lead exposure on the population, particularly infants and children, remains a significant concern (see Figure 3.10) (Santucci & Scully, 2020). Lead exposure can cause miscarriage, preterm birth, low birthweight, childhood cognitive deficiencies, and behavior problems; lead may even damage the developing nervous system or other fetal organs (US Centers for Disease Control, 2019a).

Although some medical tests like X-rays use radiation, most do not expose a person to high enough levels of radiation to cause a health concern. Radiation used in cancer treatment does pose a health risk, however. Women exposed to too much radiation in medical settings have also shown higher chances of miscarriage. For all medical treatments performed, the radiographic technician should be aware that a woman is pregnant. High exposure is linked to growth deficiencies, physical malformations, diminished brain function, and cancer (Schull et al., 1990; US Centers for Disease Control, 2019; Wilcox et al., 1988).

Chemicals are pervasive in the environment; they can affect reproductive health and have a lasting developmental impact on a fetus (Sutton et al.,

2012). A good general rule for pregnant women is to avoid handling chemicals because much remains to be known about the impact of chemicals, especially in combination with other environmental and personal factors (Woodruff et al., 2010). Stress may even intensify the health effects of toxic chemical exposure (Vesterinen et al., 2017; Wilcox, 2010;).

Drug and Alcohol Use

Drugs are a significant environmental risk for both a pregnant woman and a developing fetus. Drug exposure can cause severe and long-term congenital disabilities, which can affect children for their entire lifetime. Drugs include illegal drugs, prescription and over-the-counter drugs, alcohol, and nicotine. Drugs do not only include those that are swallowed, injected, or inhaled by a pregnant woman. They can also have negative effects when they exist in the environment. For example, first and secondhand smoke (smoke exhaled by someone else) are established risk factors for spontaneous abortion, premature birth, low birthweight, orofacial clefts or deformities, and respiratory diseases during infancy (Honein et al., 2007; Merritt et al., 2012).

Drug use by cohabitating fathers can also have an adverse environmental effect on a developing fetus (DiFranza et al., 2004). A father's exposure to chemicals may even alter his sperm and subsequently the epigenetics of his offspring (Murphy et al., 2016; Rutkowska et al., 2020). The major drugs known to cause congenital disabilities are tobacco, marijuana, alcohol, heroin, methadone, cocaine, and a myriad of other drugs found and sold on the streets or online. Prescription and over-the-counter drugs, especially pain killers such as opioids, are also of concern, although many of their possible effects are still unknown (Hemingway et al., 2020; US Department of Health and Human Services, 2020a,d).

Nicotine is a drug found in cigarettes and other tobacco products. It is a stimulant that is easily absorbed in a pregnant woman's bloodstream and can have dire effects on a developing fetus. Once absorbed, it goes through the placenta and umbilical cord to the developing fetus. Because it is a stimulant, nicotine causes an increase in fetal activity. Mothers who smoke are more likely to have placenta problems and premature, low birthweight babies who are at a higher risk of death. Their babies are also more likely to have congenital abnormalities compared to babies born to mothers who do not smoke (Ion & Bernal, 2015; Pineles et al., 2014; Rua et al., 2014).

Marijuana or cannabis is the most common (frequently used) addictive drug in the United States. Because it is legal in many places, it is sometimes considered a harmless substance for pregnant women (National Institute on Drug Abuse, 2021). Pregnant women who use marijuana or cannabis are more likely to deliver premature infants of low birthweight who require time in neonatal intensive care (Hayatbakhsh et al., 2012). Infants exposed to cannabis in utero may also have neurological disorders, respiratory problems, and be slower to gain weight than their counterparts who have not been exposed to cannabis. There is evidence that prenatal cannabis use may also impact fetal cognitive development as demonstrated in a child's later attention and behavioral problems and poorer academic achievement and executive functioning skills (Jaques et al., 2014; Warner et al., 2014).

Alcohol is the drug that infants are most often exposed to before birth. It, too, has dire effects,

even when consumed in small amounts. Neither good prenatal nutrition nor good health care after birth can change the impact of prenatal exposure to alcohol on the fetus. Excessive maternal prenatal alcohol consumption is the leading cause of mental disability. Head and facial abnormalities and heart, brain, and skeletal damage are common symptoms of **Fetal Alcohol Spectrum Disorders (FASDs)**, prenatal exposure to alcohol. Heavy alcohol consumption is also associated with an increased risk of miscarriage, low birthweight, and preterm deliveries (DeVido et al., 2015; O'Leary et al., 2012; Srikartika & O'Leary, 2015). Because alcohol consumption is often combined with other risky behaviors such as smoking or drug use, the total impact of alcohol may be more significant than when considered alone (Hemingway et al., 2020).

Illicit drugs and misused prescription drugs and supplements can have the same devastating effects on the developing fetus as alcohol, namely preterm births and low birthweights (see Table 3.7). Because they, too, are exposed to the drug while in utero, newborns often must go through drug withdrawals

Factor	Possible Effects
Alcohol	Facial deformities Defective limbs Defective heart Below-average intelligence Disorders of intellectual development
Chemical solvents (such as paint thinners, degreasers, stain and varnish removers)	Preterm birth Miscarriage
Cocaine	Low birthweight Shorter birth length Smaller head circumference Slower motor development through infancy Slower growth through age 10 Excitability/irritability Neurological deficits Cognitive deficits Medical deficits Behavioral and attention issues
Heroin	Behavioral and attention issues Withdrawal issues Excitability/irritability Excessive crying Disturbed sleep Slower motor development

(Continued)
Kato

Table 3.7 The Impact of Environmental Factors on Fetal Development

Factor	Possible Effects
Marijuana	Preterm births Low birthweight Neurological disorders Respiratory problems Slow weight gain SIDS
Methamphetamine	Low birthweight Higher infant mortality Neurological deficits Cognitive deficits Behavioral and attention issues
Nicotine	Preterm births Low birthweight Congenital disorders Cardiovascular disorders
Pollution (harmful substances from sources such as smoke, asbestos, carbon monoxide, ozone and radon, chemical and smoke output from factories, dust, mold, and pollen)	Preterm births Low birthweight Stillbirth
Prescription opioids (painkillers including codeine, morphine, and oxycodone)	Congenital heart defects Fetal growth restrictions Gastroschisis (intestines stick outside the body) Glaucoma (optic nerve damage in eyes) Low birthweight Neural tube defects (spina bifida is the most common) Neonatal abstinence syndrome (withdrawal from the drug after birth) Miscarriage Placental abruption (placenta separates from the wall of the uterus before birth) Preterm labor and birth Stillbirth
Radiation, lead, or mercury	Miscarriage Congenital disorders

Kato

Table 3.7 Continued

after birth when the exposure is stopped. This painful process involves excessive sweating, sneezing, yawning, tremors, and shaking. Infants exposed to drugs in utero may have breathing and sucking or eating difficulties. They often cry incessantly, have trouble keeping food in their stomachs, have rigid bodies, and are hyperactive. In other words, their withdrawal experience is no different than that of adults. Those who survive the painful withdrawal process are more likely to die from sudden infant death syndrome (SIDS), and those who continue to survive will suffer lifelong consequences.

The timing and impact of exposure vary as teratogens affect parts of the fetus's body as it is forming (see Figure 3.11). For example, the central nervous system, heart, and limbs are most affected by teratogens after the first 4 to 5 weeks of prenatal development. This is past the germinal period but still within the period when women may not realize that they are pregnant. Early pregnancy confirmation gives a pregnant woman more opportunity to be aware of environmental hazards to her developing embryo and fetus. The brain is most affected during weeks 20 to 36 (Alwan et al., 2010).

CRITICAL PERIODS OF HUMAN DEVELOPMENT

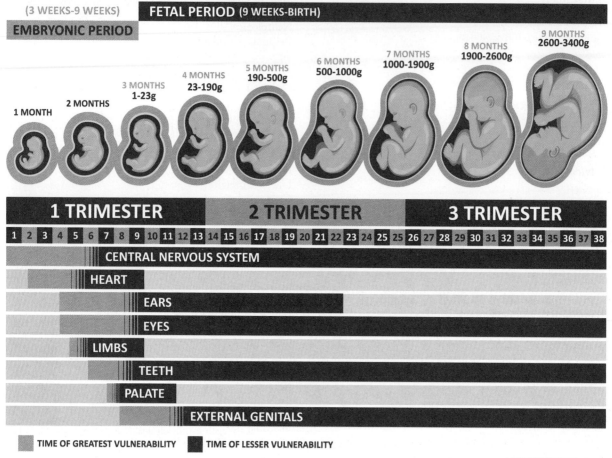

(3 WEEKS-9 WEEKS)
EMBRYONIC PERIOD
FETAL PERIOD (9 WEEKS-BIRTH)

1 MONTH
2 MONTHS
3 MONTHS 1-23g
4 MONTHS 23-190g
5 MONTHS 190-500g
6 MONTHS 500-1000g
7 MONTHS 1000-1900g
8 MONTHS 1900-2600g
9 MONTHS 2600-3400g

1 TRIMESTER | **2 TRIMESTER** | **3 TRIMESTER**

1 2 3 4 5 6 7 8 9 10 11 12 13 14 15 16 17 18 19 20 21 22 23 24 25 25 26 27 28 29 30 31 32 33 34 35 36 37 38

CENTRAL NERVOUS SYSTEM
HEART
EARS
EYES
LIMBS
TEETH
PALATE
EXTERNAL GENITALS

TIME OF GREATEST VULNERABILITY   TIME OF LESSER VULNERABILITY

logika600/Shutterstock.com

Figure 3.11 Critical Periods in Fetal Development
According to this chart, in which weeks of pregnancy is the fetus most impacted by the exposure to teratogens? How could awareness of these critical periods impact the lifestyle decisions of an expected mother?

The timing of teratogen exposure is important as there is a critical impact period. The level and length of exposure, known as the *threshold effect*, can also make a difference. In addition, the reciprocal influence of multiple teratogens such as smoking, malnutrition, and alcohol or drug use can magnify the impact. Individual genetics also plays a role in the effects of teratogens on a mother and the fetus (National Institute on Drug Abuse, 2020; US Department of Health and Human Services, 2020). Although a baby exposed to teratogens in utero may be born without apparent negative consequences, effects of prenatal teratogen exposure may show up years later. For example, prenatal drug exposure may result in childhood learning disabilities or mental health issues later in life (Goldfarb et al., 2020; Ross et al., 2015).

☑ CHECKPOINT

☐ Define *congenital disorders*. Name and describe two.

☐ What impact does a mother's age have on the health and well-being of her fetus? How do young teen mothers differ from mothers of advanced age?

☐ In what specific ways does heavy exposure to lead and radiation pose problems for a developing fetus?

☐ Alcohol and drugs can significantly influence the health of a fetus. Name three specific drugs and describe their potential impact on a developing fetus.

Apply Here!

Consider the following: A pregnant friend asks if you think it is okay for her to have "just a little" wine and "just a little" marijuana. How do you respond? What would inform your response?

3.4 Birth

After weeks and months of waiting, it is finally time for the birth process to begin! When a fetus is full-term (any time after 37 weeks), the mother

is usually more than ready to meet her new son or daughter. By now, the fetus should be in position, and the mother begins to feel slight changes in her health. Mild cramps, known as **Braxton-Hicks contractions**, start. She may feel slightly nauseous. She may feel that something is about to change (US National Library of Medicine, 2018a).

Labor

The first signs of real labor starting are felt and seen. Most women experience one or all the following: discharge of blood or mucus when the mucous plug

Global Perspectives

Global Maternal Mortality and Morbidity

Conception, prenatal development and growth, and childbirth have been part of the human experience since the beginning of time; they ensure the continuation of our species. Human beings have survived through abundance, hardship, ease, pandemics, and even times of war and violence. However, despite the normality of pregnancy and childbirth, it is historically the leading cause of death in childbearing-age women (World Health Organization, 2020).

Maternal mortality data are a key indicator of public health (Alkema et al., 2016; Say et al., 2014). Most cases of maternal mortality occur after the infant is delivered and are often due to postpartum hemorrhage, especially in the developing world (Kamali & Amin, 2016). Maternal mortality due to pregnancy or childbirth complications has been the focus of the United Nations Millennium Goals for several decades. As a result of these efforts to ensure universal access to reproductive health, the global maternal mortality ratio has declined by 38%, slightly less than 3% per year. Although this progress is significant, much more work is needed to create safe and equitable health care for women globally (Alkema et al., 2016; UNICEF, 2019).

Some regions of the world have made substantial progress toward reducing maternal mortality. Countries in South Asia reduced maternal mortality by almost 60%, and those in Sub-Saharan Africa reduced deaths by nearly 40% (UNICEF, 2019). Strategies focused on access to quality health care through partnerships formed between governments and development partners (UNICEF, 2015). As mentioned earlier, the United States has the highest maternal mortality rate among developed countries. Australia, New Zealand, Germany, France, Sweden, and Switzerland have lower maternal mortality rates (Admon et al., 2020). However, when compared to all countries

globally, the mortality rate is considered low, with about 17 per 100,000 live births (Joseph et al., 2021). Most of these deaths are considered preventable (Creanga et al., 2014; Joseph et al., 2021; Petersen et al., 2019).

Although maternal mortality rates have been declining and attempts are being made to reduce them further, there is still work to be done. Often unaccounted for is the issue of life-threatening complications that may seriously impact the future health of women and their babies. The number of severe maternal morbidity cases, especially in low- to middle-income countries, is rising (Benova et al., 2019; Geller et al., 2018). Even in the US, maternal morbidity has been steadily increasing in recent years (American College of Obstetricians and Gynecologists et al., 2016; Chen et al., 2021).

The United Nations Sustainable Goal for maternal mortality, established in 2016, was to reduce the mortality ratio to less than 70 per 100,000 live births by 2030 (Alkema et al., 2016). This goal is aggressive, but it is a critical public health priority. Although progress is being made to further reduce maternal mortality, the current pace may fall short of reaching the 2030 goal without more intentional partnerships and funding (Benova et al., 2019).

To Think About:

- If maternal morbidity is preventable in well-resourced countries, why might its incidence be growing in the US?
- Is maternal morbidity associated with social-economic class or race/ethnicity? If so, how?
- Locate the maternal morbidity data for your state or region by searching online. A good source of information is the Centers for Disease Control and Prevention website. Do the rates surprise you? What factors play into the incidence levels in your area?

falls out of the cervix, "water breaking" (passing of amniotic fluid), and the beginning of uncomfortable uterine **contractions** that last 30 to 60 seconds. Typically, contractions occur every 5 to 20 minutes during this stage. As labor progresses, these contractions become more intense and closer together (US National Library of Medicine, 2018a).

During the birth process, three stages prepare the mother for the delivery of her infant (see Figure 3.12). During the first stage of labor, the **dilation stage**, the cervix (opening to the uterus) thins, called **effacement**. At this stage, the cervix increases in diameter to allow for the baby to eventually pass through. The goal is for the cervix to dilate 10 centimeters, or about 4 inches in diameter. This stage can last hours. For women giving birth to their first infant, the average time for this labor stage typically ranges from 8 to 20 hours. It ranges 12 to 14 hours for women delivering their second or subsequent babies (Nirmal & Fraser, 2016). At this stage, local

**The Stages of Labor
Stage 1**

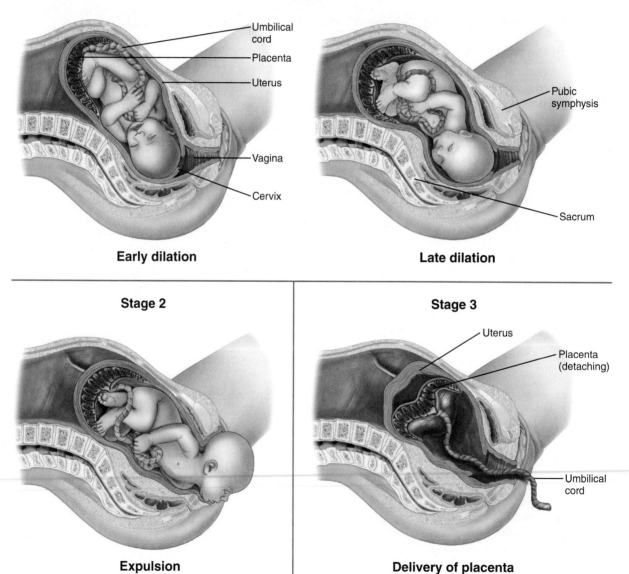

Early dilation

Late dilation

Stage 2

Stage 3

Expulsion

Delivery of placenta

©*Body Scientific International*

Figure 3.12 Stages of Childbirth Though the Birth Canal

anesthetics, medications that numb the pain in a specific region of the body, may be administered to control pain for the laboring woman.

Fetal monitoring is often used during labor to track the fetal heart rate and the mother's contractions and to alert the medical staff to any signs of the baby's distress. Typically, one monitor is strapped around the top of the mother's abdomen; the second monitor is inserted internally through the cervix and rests on top of the baby's head. However, recent concerns over best practices may change how fetal monitoring is done in the future (Rosenbaum et al., 2020).

Delivery

The second stage of the birth process is called the **expulsion stage**, or delivery. Once the mother's cervix is fully dilated, the fetus is ready to move through the birth canal (vagina). Usually, the baby's head appears first, quickly followed by the rest of the body. Delivery is much shorter than the labor stage and only lasts about 1.5 hours for first-time mothers and much less time for those who have given birth before (US Department of Health and Human Services, 2017; US National Library of Medicine, 2018b).

Sometimes the birth canal does not appear to stretch adequately to allow passage of the newborn without harm. When this is the case, an **episiotomy**, or surgical cut through the perineum, may be performed to allow the newborn to pass through more easily. The surgical cut is then quickly repaired with a few stitches. Episiotomies are performed far less routinely now as there is concern about infection and healing afterward; it is no longer considered a recommended practice by the American College of Obstetricians-Gynecologists (2006, 2019).

Although the American College of Obstetricians and Gynecologists (2019) recommends limited intervention strategies during the birth process, sometimes an intervention may be necessary, recognizing that each carries a risk to mother and/or the baby (see Table 3.8). **Cesarean birth**, commonly referred to as a *C-section*, involves removing the fetus from the uterus using a surgical procedure. **Forceps-assisted extraction** utilizes a scissor-shaped or tong-type of instrument to guide the newborn's head through the birth canal while the mother pushes. With **vacuum extraction**, the health care provider attaches a soft plastic cup with a handle to the baby's head

Intervention Method/Technique	Reported Reason for Use	Risks
Cesarean birth or C-section	• Difficult or long labor • High-risk pregnancy • Distressed fetus • Mother's request	• Involves invasive surgical risks (infection, pain, deep vein thrombosis, damage to urinary bladder/kidneys) • Longer recovery for the mother • Newborn breathing difficulties if born before 39 weeks • Low APGAR score for newborn
Forceps-assisted extraction	• Mother's cervix is fully dilated, but labor is not progressing • To help guide the baby's head through the birth canal • Baby is in danger • Exhausted mother	• Lack of expertise and training of medical personnel • Lacerations (tearing around the vagina, rectum, or urethra) • Short-term urinary incontinence • Increased blood loss • Skull or face injuries to the infant
Vacuum extraction	• Mother's cervix is fully dilated but labor is not progressing • To help guide the baby's head through the birth canal • Baby is in danger • Exhausted mother	• Lack of expertise and training of medical personnel • Lacerations (tearing around the vagina, rectum, or urethra) • Short-term urinary incontinence • Increased blood loss • Hematoma or bruising of baby's skull or face

Chapman & Charles, 2013; Dudenhausen et al., 2014; Foglia et al., 2021; Jansen et al., 2013

Table 3.8 Birth Intervention Strategies and Possible Risks

using suction and then gently pulls on the handle as the mother pushes through a contraction. Both forceps-assisted and vacuum extraction accelerate delivery when progress through the birth canal is slow or the baby shows signs of distress, addressing concerns for the baby's safety. In the United States, forceps-assisted and vacuum-assisted extraction are not often used, but cesarean deliveries have grown significantly in the past decade, often as an elective surgical procedure (Longe, 2018; Martin et al., 2015).

Global Perspectives

Global Rise of Cesarean Birth Deliveries

Sometimes babies are born using a surgical procedure called cesarean section. In 1990, cesarean births accounted for about 7% of all births (Betran et al., 2021). Historically used as a childbirth intervention to reduce maternal and infant mortality, cesarean birth has become commonplace, sometimes considered routine (Jansen et al., 2013). Globally, about 21% of mothers today, a little over one in every five, give birth through cesarean birth rather than the usual method of labor and vaginal delivery. The World Health Organization (2021) predicts that by 2030, nearly 30% of all births will take place by cesarean section.

Cesarean interventions may not be readily accessible in the least developed countries, even in dire situations when a woman's life is at risk. In sub-Saharan Africa, cesarean section births account for only about 5% of total births, despite high maternal mortality rates and the potential lifesaving results. In Latin America and the Caribbean, cesarean section births were as high as 43% of all births. In 2020, cesarean section births were more common than vaginal deliveries in Brazil, Cyprus, Egypt, Turkey, and the Dominican Republic (Betran et al., 2021; World Health Organization, 2021).

Cesarean section birth rates vary by country and within global regions (see Figure 3.13). In the Americas, Latin American countries reported higher rates of cesarean section births when compared to North American countries. Southern European countries such as Spain and Italy reported the highest rates when compared to the rest of Europe. Asian reports are varied, with most countries reporting 12% to 19% cesarean births, except for countries such as China, Japan, and South Korea that reported the highest. African countries reported the widest range, with Northern African countries such as Algeria, Egypt, Libya, and Morocco having the highest rates and sub-Saharan countries having the lowest (Betran et al., 2021; World Health Organization, 2021).

Although cesarean births are considered safe for mothers and infants when performed in optimal conditions by trained medical professionals (Keag et al., 2018; Sobhy et al., 2019), the World Health Organization (2021) estimates that only about 10% of births should involve cesarean interventions. The WHO's position is that most births should be vaginal deliveries. The American College of Obstetricians and Gynecologists (2019) recommends limited intervention strategies during the birth process. Despite these recommendations, however, rates of cesarean births have continued to grow due to a multitude of reasons.

There are many complex reasons for this increase, such as the attending physician or midwife's views and beliefs or expectations of the surrounding medical community. For example, interventions may lower risks of adverse outcomes or be less expensive than a long assisted labor, birth, and recovery. Sometimes, prevailing ideologies promote interventions over natural methods. Sometimes the reasons are not complex—a C-section is preferred by the pregnant woman or family. Convenience of planning and scheduling are often cited as reasons for the upward trend.

In the United States, a growing trend that has accompanied higher cesarean births is the concept of a family-centered birth. This practice may include allowing family members to view the procedure, using low lighting and minimal extraneous noise in the operating room, allowing access to their neonate after delivery, and encouraging early skin-to-skin contact between the baby and mother (Foglia et al., 2021; Schorn et al.,

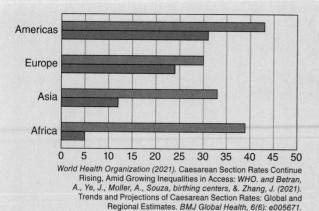

World Health Organization (2021). Caesarean Section Rates Continue Rising, Amid Growing Inequalities in Access: WHO. and Betran, A., Ye, J., Moller, A., Souza, birthing centers, &. Zhang, J. (2021). Trends and Projections of Caesarean Section Rates: Global and Regional Estimates. BMJ Global Health, 6(6): e005671.

Figure 3.13 Cesarean Birth Rate Ranges by Global Regions

2015). Despite these changes, the American College of Obstetricians and Gynecologists (2019) continues to partner with health care providers to reduce the trend (Kingdon et al., 2018).

To Think About:
Vaginal birth is a natural process, but in certain circumstances, a cesarean section may be required to protect the mother and baby's health.

- What is your reaction to learning about the growing prevalence of cesarean birth rates? Were you surprised? Why or why not? Why might you have had this reaction?
- What might be the impact of underusing C-sections as a birth intervention?
- What might be the impact of overusing C-sections as a birth intervention?

Afterbirth

The final stage of birth is called the **afterbirth stage**. The stage does not last very long, only a few minutes to an hour. During this final stage, the woman's uterus rapidly decreases in size, and the placenta detaches from the uterine wall and descends into the birth canal. The umbilical cord and the placenta are then expelled or delivered. The umbilical cord is cut, and the new baby is now a separate, independent human being (Figure 3.14) (Kamali & Amin, 2016).

Most births are "good" births. They go according to plan and result in a positive experience for both mother and baby (Arulkumaran, 2016). However, unexpected complications can sometimes occur, including preterm births, breech births, and emergencies requiring labor induction or an emergency C-section. Some neonates experience oxygen deprivation during the birth process. Others are determined to have Rh factor challenges that were not identified and monitored during pregnancy (Kilpatrick & Garrison, 2017; Lanni et al., 2017).

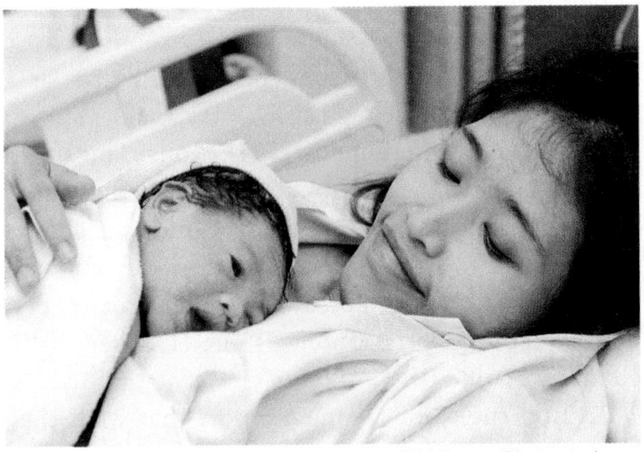

Preterm Birth

As previously discussed, newborns come earlier than expected (before 38 weeks gestation) for many reasons, including the mother's age, health, and exposure to environmental toxins. Preterm births also occur despite a woman's best efforts to provide the safest prenatal environment possible. Sometimes, they are a result of too much crowding, when twins or other multiple siblings struggle to share space inside the uterus.

Preterm infants are usually small in size and have a low birthweight of less than 5.8 pounds. A very low birthweight baby weighs less than 3.5 pounds and is at greater risk for many problems. The risk varies, however, depending on how early the baby comes. Newborns who are born prematurely require special attention and medical care.

Infants born after 28 weeks have the best chance of survival among premature babies. By then, all organs are developed and functioning. Each day after week 28 adds to the newborn's chances of good health and lessens the chance of developmental delays associated with early birth. For example, although the lungs are developed and functioning, each week after the 28th week prepares the lungs for better functioning outside of the uterus.

Premature infants often face developmental challenges, such as growing more slowly or crawling later than full-term infants; they may also be delayed in reaching other early milestones. Today, health care improvements have greatly improved the chances of preterm infants living normal lives (see Figure 3.15). So, by the time most premature babies

Arief Juwono/Shutterstock.com

Figure 3.14 Following delivery, the newborn is a separate, independent being.

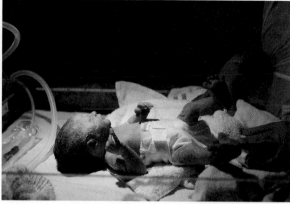

RMC42/Shutterstock.com

Figure 3.15 This premature newborn weighs only four pounds. Medical interventions, such as special care, monitoring, and treatment in a newborn intensive care unit (NICU), enable many infants born preterm to continue their physical development before they are released home.

reach toddlerhood, they have often caught up with their full-term counterparts.

Induced Labor

Sometimes it is necessary to start labor before the mother's body begins the birth process itself. To induce (begin) labor, a doctor may use medication or break the amniotic sac, signaling to the woman's body that labor should begin. Induction is considered when prolonged pregnancy poses a risk to the mother or baby. For example, when a pregnancy continues well past the expected due date, the fetus continues to grow and gain weight, and the extra weight and size may be detrimental to both the mother and baby. **Induced labor** has its drawbacks, however. One is more intense and includes painful labor contractions that create more stress for the fetus. Intense labor and fetal stress lead to the higher possibility of an emergency C-section, such as when a baby's oxygen supply is compromised during labor.

Breech Birth

Typically, fetuses turn head-down (called *cephalic presentation*) in the mother's uterus during the last few weeks of pregnancy in preparation for birth. When a baby does not turn, it is called a **breech birth**. Breech babies do not come through the birth canal in the typical headfirst fashion, so the birth attendant must carefully guide the delivery. Sometimes the infant comes feet first, sometimes crosswise, and sometimes buttocks first. Because delivering a newborn in any of these alternate positions can be difficult or dangerous, attempts like massage and outside prodding are often made before labor and delivery to get the fetus to turn head-down. Sometimes these interventions work; but more often, the breech baby is delivered by C-section.

Oxygen Deprivation

Sometimes fetal monitoring determines that a fetus is experiencing **oxygen deprivation**, or an interrupted flow of oxygen, which can cause brain damage or death. Causes of oxygen deprivation may include too much pressure on the newborn's blood vessels during the birth process, inadequate blood supply between the mother and fetus, or problems with the placenta or umbilical cord. Whatever the reason, medical professionals must move quickly to deliver the baby safely.

Childbirth Choices

Today women in the United States typically give birth at home, in a hospital, or in a birth center. Historically, childbirth occurred in the home, with newborns delivered by midwives, nurses, or doctors. During the twentieth century, as hospitals became more accessible to many pregnant women and pregnancy and childbirth were viewed in more medical terms, the number of hospital births increased dramatically. It became more likely for a newborn to be delivered by a physician than by a midwife, and the entire birth process became more controlled by technology, especially following the post-World War II emphasis on science. Then in the 1970s, increasingly, women wanted more choice, more holistic care, and support for experiencing childbirth as a natural process (McCool et al., 2002; Oakley, 2016; Panazzolo & Mohammed, 2011). Today, most US women give birth in hospitals with a medical doctor attending. However, a growing number choose to give birth in home-like family birth centers with a midwife attending. For low-risk pregnancies, evidence supports both options as safe (Dekker, 2013; Renfrew et al., 2014).

Around the world, women report that what they want most in childbirth is a positive experience that meets their preconceived ideas of giving birth to a healthy baby and feeling safe in the process. Better yet, they desire that their experiences exceed their expectations. Although many acknowledge that childbirth can feel scary or risky, most expectant mothers want to be involved in decision-making throughout the childbirth process. Local and familial attitudes combined with affordability, accessibility, and perception of quality influence these choices (Downe et al., 2018; Tuncalp et al., 2015).

In the US, many expectant mothers have choices about where and how they give birth. Some estimates indicate that at least 50% of women already have strong expectations for their desired childbirth experience before becoming pregnant (see Figure 3.16) (Regan et al., 2013). Some mothers choose **natural childbirth**. In natural childbirth, breathing and relaxation exercises are used to help the mother deal with pain instead of using medications. Often a partner or coach, such as a spouse, relative, or **doula**, helps the laboring woman focus.

In a common natural childbirth method, the Lamaze method, the partner helps the laboring woman keep track of the intensity and timing of her contractions while providing emotional support. Natural childbirth methods can be used in hospitals, birthing centers, or in-home births (McCool et al., 2002; Oakley, 2016; Panazzolo & Mohammed, 2011). Because there are many options, some expectant parents create a birth plan that describes what they expect during the labor process. They can decide about taking pain medications, delivering naturally, and inviting whom they want to be present at the birth.

Another choice is whether to use an obstetrician, a medical doctor who specializes in general family medicine, or a certified midwife (CM) or certified nurse-midwife (CNM) who specializes in holistic care with less reliance on technology. Medical doctors usually deliver babies in hospitals, while midwives typically deliver them in birthing centers or at the woman's home. CMs and CNMs usually work in close cooperation with medical professionals in case a complication arises. Many birthing centers are also associated with nearby hospitals. CNMs have an advanced level of education and training. The scope of practice for midwives varies according to US state law (Dekker, 2013; Renfrew et al., 2014).

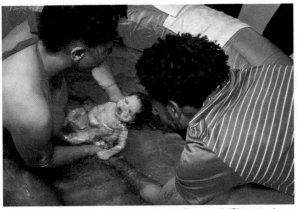

In The Light Photography/Shutterstock.com

Figure 3.16 Many pregnant women in the United States now have choices about how they would like to give birth. This couple chose a water birth in their home with the assistance of a midwife.

☑ CHECKPOINT

☐ Name and describe the three stages of labor.

☐ How long does each stage typically last?

☐ Identify and describe three potential complicating factors during childbirth that may impact outcomes for the mother and baby.

Apply Here!

Considering the social culture today, how might you predict the impact of societal events that will shape childbirth experience choices? Are you noticing any trends?

Summary

Pregnancy and birth are amazing life stages, but many factors can complicate them. These include the mother's age and health status, the baby's reaction to the birth, exposure to alcohol and drugs, and blood incompatibility, among other factors. Even so, most pregnancies are uncomplicated, resulting in the birth of a healthy baby. Unit 2 explores infants' growth and development, giving insight into physical, cognitive, and socioemotional development domains.

Learning Outcomes and Key Concepts

3.1 Describe the three stages of pregnancy and the developmental milestones that occur in each stage.

- The first trimester includes the germinal and the embryonic periods of development.
- The germinal period extends from conception until implantation, about two weeks later.
- The nervous system, heart, and most body parts develop in the embryonic period.
- The fetal period spans the second and third trimesters and lasts until birth.
- In the fetal period, arms and legs, fingers and toes, and eyes and ears become more distinct.
- The third trimester is important for increased organ function, especially the lungs. Fatty tissue develops as the fetus becomes both longer and heavier.
- As the mother's body prepares for labor and delivery, the fetus positions itself in a head-down position into the pelvis.

3.2 Explain how health practices and lifestyle choices during conception and pregnancy influence the pregnant woman, developing fetus, and newborn.

- Health and lifestyle behaviors can play a large part in conception and in the later health of a baby.
- Lifestyle choices may influence epigenetic mechanisms or the inherited genetic changes.
- Conception involves genetic contributions of both the biological mother and father.

- A growing embryo and fetus are entirely dependent on the mother for nutritional needs.
- Inadequate nutrition makes the placenta steal nutrition for the fetus from maternal stores.
- Key prenatal nutrients include folate, iron, and calcium, which are critical to healthy development.
- Early prenatal care can diagnose any health problems and possible treatment.
- Nutrition and healthy weight, healthy blood pressure, and paid family employment are associated with healthy pregnancy outcomes.
- A way to reduce stress during pregnancy is to surround the mother with a support group.

3.3 Discuss how prenatal complications can affect the developing fetus and newborn.

- Disorders associated with faulty genes or chromosomes are termed congenital disorders.
- A woman's age can affect her pregnancy and her own health as well as complicate childbirth.
- Teen mothers are more likely to experience preterm labor and low birthweight babies.
- Prenatal environmental concerns include teratogens such as chemicals, illness and infections, medications, alcohol, drugs, and cigarettes.
- Environmental toxins can cause pregnancy complications and birth defects.

3.4 Contrast the three stages of childbirth.

- The birth process begins with labor contractions.
- As labor continues, contractions become more intense and closer together.
- During labor, the cervix thins and dilates to ten centimeters.
- The head appears first, and intense pushing begins during the second, or delivery stage.
- The placenta and umbilical cord follow during the third or afterbirth stage.

Chapter Review

1. If a female friend or family member shared with you that she hopes to become pregnant in the next year and asked for advice, what would you tell her? Would your advice include recommendations for the potential father?

2. Design an infographic that communicates the importance of healthy lifestyle choices before pregnancy.

3. Describe the timing and changes that happen during the embryonic and fetal stages of prenatal development. How does the baby grow and change?

4. Name and describe three changes to the developing baby during the third trimester.

5. Write a newsletter article for expectant teen parents that defends the need for good nutrition choices during pregnancy.

6. In blog format, write a post that elaborates on how care during pregnancy, including medical care and a healthy lifestyle, can lead to positive outcomes for the mother and developing baby.

7. Name and define four genetic disorders that can affect a developing fetus.

8. Describe the potential impact of a mother's age on pregnancy and childbirth.

9. The use of drugs and other environmental toxins can gravely influence birth outcomes. Choose three environmental factors, and create a poster, handout, or potential social media post that offers a warning to expectant mothers.

10. In a visual format (chart, graphic, animation, or slides), depict and contrast the three stages of childbirth labor and delivery. Label each stage with descriptors.

11. Describe what happens during the third stage of childbirth. Why might this term be confusing to some?

Matching

Match the following terms with the correct definitions.

A. afterbirth stage

B. dilation stage

C. effacement

D. expulsion stage

E. first trimester

F. induced labor

G. Lamaze method

H. maternal morbidity

1. When a mother's cervix thins during labor

2. Labor that is hastened by medical intervention rather than occurring naturally

3. Natural childbirth method that focuses on relaxation techniques, using a focal point and an emotional coach

4. The last stage of birth, after delivery, when the placenta and umbilical cord are expelled

5. A women's experience with severe or life-threatening complications from pregnancy or childbirth

6. Begins at conception until about the twelfth week of pregnancy

7. Labor stage that causes the cervical opening to widen

8. The delivery stage of childbirth

Children change dramatically from infancy to the preschool stage.

Unit

2

Infants and the First Two Years (Ages 0–2)

Chapter 4: Infant Physical Development

Chapter 5: Infant Cognitive Development

Chapter 6: Infant Socioemotional Development

Chapter

4

Infant Physical Development

Learning Outcomes

After studying this chapter, you will be able to:

4.1 Describe the physical qualities of neonates and methods for assessing health and wellness following birth.

4.2 Explain the physical development of infants, including sensory abilities, bodily changes, and motor skills.

4.3 Summarize brain and nervous system development during infancy.

4.4 Recognize the determinants of health and wellness in infancy.

4.5 Identify disorders that may influence infant physical development.

Key Terms

abusive head trauma
Apgar score
Babinski reflex
brain stem
Brazelton Neonatal Behavioral Assessment Scale
cephalocaudal development
cerebellum
cerebral cortex
colostrum
crawling
creeping
extremely preterm (EPT)
failure to thrive
fine motor skills
frontal lobes
grasp reflex
gross (large) motor skills
infancy
kangaroo care
lanugo
lateralization
lobes
moderately preterm (MPT)
Moro reflex
myelin
Neonatal Intensive Care Unit Network Neurobehavioral Scale (NNNS)
neonates
neurons
occipital lobes
palmar grasp
parietal lobes
pincer grasp
prefrontal cortex
preterm
primitive reflexes
protective reflexes
proximodistal development
reflexes
rooting reflex
shaken baby syndrome
sound localization
stepping reflex
suck reflex
Sudden infant death syndrome (SIDS)
Sudden unexpected infant death (SUID)
synapses
temporal lobes
toddler
tonic reflex
vernix caseosa
well-baby exams

Introduction

Imagine that you unexpectedly became the caregiver of a newborn. How would your life change? What would the infant need from you? If you remained the child's primary caregiver, how much would you expect the child to grow and change in the first few months of life? Six months? A year? Two years?

Throughout infancy, infants undergo tremendous physical, cognitive, and socioemotional changes. They are utterly dependent on their caregivers to meet their basic needs and to provide social interaction. They are learning about how to survive in the world. They master an abundance of abilities and skills such as sitting, crawling, walking, and talking while learning to take nourishment from others and then to feed themselves. These small, dependent newborns grow, change, and become walking, talking, independent toddlers who know what they want. The first two years of life are called **infancy,** and infants are often called babies in the first year of life. The term **toddler** is a social construct, created and accepted by society, is used to describe infants once they begin walking, typically anywhere between 8 to 18 months. In this text, infancy will refer to the first two years of life.

The physical, cognitive, and socioemotional developmental changes during the two years of infancy and toddlerhood are astounding. This chapter discusses the typical markers of physical development for infants, ages 0 through 2 years, exploring how infants grow and change physically. Before you begin, recall all the information you already know about the physical development of infants. As you read this chapter, think of how the new information presented in the text matches or challenges your prior understanding of the topic. Think of direct connections between what you thought to be true and what is presented here.

4.1 The Neonate

It is the miracle of life. Since the beginning of humankind, infants have survived through all sorts of conditions. We are often amazed by the ability of humans to procreate, given the fragility and vulnerability of their young. And yet, newborns, or **neonates**, who are 4 weeks old or younger, are quite adaptable and resilient. They do more than cry, eat, and need diaper changes. In fact, evidence suggests that infants begin learning before birth and start adapting to their environment right after birth (Mennella, et al., 2001). At the same time, their physical growth and development are phenomenal.

Neonate Assessment

During a normal, uncomplicated birth, a mother can usually hold her newborn soon after birth. What will she see? Many neonates are covered in blood, a thin white coating called **vernix caseosa**, and fine, soft hair called **lanugo** (see Figure 4.1). Their heads are temporarily misshapen as they go through the birth canal, often producing a cone-shaped head. They often look bluish, purple, or red for the first few seconds or minutes as their bodies adjust to breathing. In some hospital settings, the newborn is often cleaned up quickly before being handed to the mother. In birthing centers, some hospitals, or in-home deliveries, the newborn may be immediately placed on the mother (Baston & Durward, 2010; Lomax, 2015; Tappero & Honeyfield, 2018). To many new mothers or biological parents, the

child is exquisitely beautiful, while for others, the introductory experience may feel strange, awkward, or unwanted.

In the United States, full-term neonates are typically about 18 to 22 inches long at birth and vary in weight, though they average at about 7 to 7.5 pounds in weight. In other cultures, median birthweights and lengths may differ from these averages. Variations in length and weight can be attributed to genetics, the mother's health status, and culture. Being a lower- or higher-than-average-size infant at birth often becomes a part of family folklore. But length and weight at birth do not necessarily relate to size later in life. When newborns have low birthweights, weighing less than 5.5 pounds (2,500 grams), most still show normal growth and development, although others have exceptionalities that will require specialized care (Bremner & Wachs, 2010; Brink, 2013 Gross, 2019).

Neonates born at less than 29 weeks' gestation are described as **extremely preterm (EPT)**; those born between 29- and 33-weeks' gestation are **moderately preterm (MPT)**. Finally, neonates who are born between 33- and 37-weeks' gestation are considered **preterm**. Preterm newborn infants require immediate interventions, such as thermal care to prevent heat loss, including immediately drying and wrapping them or providing skin-to-skin contact. Some preterm infants may need treatments to help them breathe or feed more easily. For both EPT and MPT neonates, the main cause of mortality is congenital malformation, accounting for 43% of infant deaths (Walsh et al., 2017). Early neonatal death, defined as infants who die in the first seven days of life, is a global problem. This is especially true in low- and middle-income countries where newborns may not receive the interventions they need to survive (Lee et al., 2017; Lehtonen et al., 2017).

Tests for the Health Status of Neonates

After birth, infants are tested to make sure that they are healthy. If not, interventions can be determined, planned, and started immediately. Ways of testing neonates' health status in the United States include the APGAR Scale, the Brazelton Neonatal Behavioral Assessment Scale, the Neonatal Intensive Care Unit Network Neurobehavioral Scale, and a neurological assessment of the neonate's reflexes.

FatCamera/E+ via Getty Images

Figure 4.1 Many newborns are covered in a thin white coating called vernix caseosa.

APGAR Scoring

One of the oldest tests still used today is an assessment of the newborn's overall health status. It is named after an obstetrical anesthesiologist, Dr. Virginia Apgar, who developed it in the early 1950s. The **Apgar score** is administered one minute after birth to assess the newborn's overall condition and determine if emergency medical intervention is needed. The Apgar is repeated five minutes later and then again every two to five minutes if the neonate fails to reach a score of seven. Each indicator receives a score between 0 and 2 (see Table 4.1). The neonate receives a total score somewhere between 0 and 10, with a score of 7 or higher indicating the newborn's health status is good and that additional medical care is not needed (Clayton & Crosby, 2006). The Apgar score assesses heart rate, respiratory effort, muscle tone, body color, and reflex response. Dr. Apgar used her name as an easy acronym to remember areas for scoring—A for general appearance, P for pulse, G for grimace or reflex response, A for activity level and muscle tone, and R for respiratory rate of breathing (Baston & Durward, 2010; Lomax, 2015; Tappero & Honeyfield, 2018).

The **Brazelton Neonatal Behavioral Assessment Scale**, developed by pediatrician Dr. T. Berry Brazelton, is another newborn assessment given a few days following birth to measure a newborn's reflexes and responses to light, sounds, and touch. Healthcare professionals observe the ability of each stimulus to catch the infant's attention and the infant's ability to be soothed. Results of this assessment of a newborn's reflexes and behavioral responses help determine if further evaluation into possible neurological concerns, including brain damage, is required (Lester et al., 2004).

The **Neonatal Intensive Care Unit Network Neurobehavioral Scale (NNNS)**, created by Brazelton in collaboration with others, assesses newborns at risk for neurological challenges due to premature birth or other known risk factors, such as prenatal drug exposure (Lester & others, 2004). The NNNS evaluates the infant's response to stress, their ability to respond to soothing care and to self-soothe, their observed reflexes and motor development, and their responses to stimulation from sights and sounds. Such assessments are essential so that medical professionals and primary caregivers can begin early intervention practices if concerns are identified (Brazelton & Nugent, 2011; Tappero & Honeyfield, 2018).

Neurological Assessment of Reflexes

Infants are born with **reflexes**, involuntary, spontaneous movements or actions that respond to a stimulus (see Table 4.2). For example, newborns typically have the reflex to suck when something is placed on the roof of their mouth, which is called the **suck reflex**. They move toward a bottle or their mother's breast when the side of their mouth is stroked, which is called the **rooting reflex**. The sucking and rooting reflexes are basic to survival (Adolph et al., 2010; Brink, 2013). Healthcare providers check an infant's reflexes in the hours and days following birth to determine if the brain and nervous system are working well.

Indicator	0 Points	1 Point	2 Points
A **Activity: Muscle tone**	Absent/lacking	Arms and legs flex, react	Active response
P **Pulse/Heartbeat**	Absent/lacking	Below 100 beats per minute	Over 100 beats per minute
G **Grimace: Reactions to stimulations (sneezing, coughing)**	Limp/floppy	Little or minimal response	Quick and ready response
A **Appearance: Skin color**	Pale or blue	Healthy body, although extremities may be blue	Healthy body color and pink at hands and feet
R **Respiration: Effort**	Absent/lacking	Irregular or slow	Vigorous/hearty cry

Table 4.1 The APGAR Neonatal Behavioral Assessment Scale

Reflex Name	Reflex Description	Examples
Moro or Startle Reflex	This reflex occurs when an infant is startled, such as by loud noises or quick movements. A typical newborn response might include lowering/dipping their head, throwing back their head, flailing arms and legs, pulling the limbs in toward the body, and crying. Named after a twentieth-century physician who first identified it, the Moro reflex typically subsides after the first few months of life (Brink, 2013).	 *Zhuravlev Andrey/Shutterstock.com*
Grasp Reflex	This occurs when the infant closes four fingers as if clasping an object when their palm is stroked. This reflex can be observed in utero and lasts until age 5–6 months; voluntary grasping usually follows. When the grasping reflect diminishes, an infant can more easily pick up small items such as food placed before them (US National Library of Medicine, 2020).	 *Whiskyy/Shutterstock.com*
Babinski Reflex	This is the response to stroking the bottom of infant's foot. During the first year, the typical response is reflexively spreading toes and lifting the big toe upward. After age 1, the typical infant response is to curl the toes downward following stroking. When the Babinski reflex continues past infancy or about age 2, it is termed a "positive Babinski response," which is often a sign of a possible neurological disorder requiring further testing for a diagnosis (Mercuri et al., 2005; Walker, 2018; Schor, 2020).	 *OMfotovideocontent/Shutterstock.com*
Tonic Reflex	Infants often lay on their backs with their heads turned to one side and with the arm and leg on the same side stretching outward. At the same time, the opposite arm and leg will be flexed. This common reflexive body posture lasts until 6 to 7 months (US National Library of Medicine, 2020).	 *Jordi Mora/Shutterstock.com*
Stepping Reflex *Also called **Walking Reflex or Dance Reflex**	When held upright with feet touching a solid surface, the infant appears to walk, step, or dance. This reflex usually occurs during the first couple months of life (Brink, 2015; Gross, 2019).	 *Hananeko_Studio/Shutterstock.com*

Table 4.2 Reflexes: Involuntary Movements or Actions

The reflexes present at birth are called **primitive reflexes**, and they are considered necessary for infant development or even survival (Modrell & Tadi, 2021). Primitive reflexes diminish over the first year of life, as voluntary motor skills replace involuntary movements. Because primitive reflexes are considered normal for newborns, testing an infant's primitive reflexes is often used as part of a neurological examination and assessment.

Protective reflexes are those that instinctively protect the body from harm. These reflexes include blinking when an object comes close to the eyes, gagging to prevent choking, pulling a body part away from something hot, resisting blockage of air passages, and extending arms to break a fall (Calciolari & Montirosso, 2013; Feldman & Chaves-Gnecco, 2018; Lean et al., 2017).

The Importance of Touch

It is well known that infants need to be touched and held. Research shows that infants deprived of touch show impaired growth and development (Ardiel & Rankin, 2010; Bigelow & Williams, 2020; Frank et al., 1996). In his classic study, psychologist Harry

Global Perspectives

Global Infant Mortality

Infants and toddlers are resilient, but they are also vulnerable. During the first month of life, an infant is most vulnerable and more at risk of dying than at any other point throughout infancy. According to the United Nations Children's Fund (UNICEF, 2019), the average global rate of infant deaths was 18 per 1,000 live births (newborns) in 2018 and 13 per 1,000 births from age 1 month to 1 year. UNICEF reported that, globally, 2.5 million children died in the first month of life in 2017. This amounted to approximately 7,000 neonatal deaths every day. Most of these deaths occurred during the first week of life. According to the World Health Organization (WHO, 2019), an infant's risk of dying during the first year of life was highest in the WHO African Region (51 per 1,000 live births). Most infant deaths were attributed to preterm birth complications, birthing difficulties, congenital anomalies, chronic diarrhea, and acute respiratory infections (WHO, 2018).

Although any infant mortality is tragic, the past three decades have shown a profound decrease in deaths. The global newborn mortality rate fell from 65 deaths per 1,000 live births in 1990 to 29 deaths per 1,000 live births in 2018 (WHO, 2019). Once an infant passes the first month of life, their chances for survival continue to increase. The reasons for the decline in the infant mortality rate are many, but most have to do with increasing community resources. These include skilled and accessible medical care, opportunities for immediate and exclusive breastfeeding, access to clean water, and community education on postnatal care, nutrition, and danger signs that an infant is in distress (WHO, 2018).

The death rate within the first year of life is often an indicator of population health. How does the United States compare to other countries? Infant mortality has decreased in the United States over the past two decades, but not within all demographic groups (Thakrar et al., 2018). Infants born in socioeconomically disadvantaged areas, rural areas, or some racial demographic groups were less likely to survive their first year of life compared to their advantaged, urban, and Asian or White, non-Hispanic counterparts (Probst et al., 2019).

As discussed in Chapter 3, Black infants are twice as likely to die in their first year of life than White, non-Hispanic babies (Kandasamy et al., 2020). US regional differences also play a part in infant mortality. For example, infants born in the southeast central region (Alabama, Kentucky, Mississippi, Tennessee) are twice as likely to die within the first year of life than those born in the northeast region (Maine, New York, New Jersey, Vermont, Massachusetts, Rhode Island, Connecticut, New Hampshire, Pennsylvania) (Chen et al., 2016; Thakrar et al., 2018). Although this is a complex issue, scientific evidence ties higher infant mortality to societal differences in health care socioeconomic and racial inequalities (Freedman & Kruk, 2014; Fuentes-Afflick et al., 2021; Mays et al., 2011).

To Think About:
- What resources does a newborn need to survive?
- What is the infant mortality rate in your state, county, or town? How would you go about finding this out?
- What factors/resources in your community might help or hinder the infant mortality rate?

Harlow (1958) demonstrated that even monkeys preferred warm, physical contact to food when given a choice. Early studies on institutionalized infants showed that receiving as little as twenty minutes of a caregiver's touch could make a significant positive impact on their development, such as improved educational and social interactions (Casler, 1965; MacLean, 2003; Rutter et al., 1998).

Cultures are primarily held together by relationships between people. Cultures, subcultures, or communities include shared experiences transferred from generation to generation. Sometimes, shared experiences are due to ethnically homogenous groups and less interaction with outside groups. Ethnically homogenous and isolated groups are less common in today's global society, but traditions may remain strong. We can learn a lot from cultures that are less familiar to us, especially concerning the

care of newborn infants related to caregiver physical responsiveness, proximity, closeness, and touch.

Many cultures tend to hand down parenting information, beliefs, and customs through conversations, instruction, or by example. Other cultures transfer parenting information less intimately through books, podcasts, social media, and apps. In some cultures, caregivers tend to respond immediately to crying infants rather than letting the infant cry it out. Instead, they use physical touch to soothe an upset infant. Hewlett & Lamb (2002) found that many cultures have physical contact with their infants up to about 80% of the time, while some western, industrialized cultures tend only to have direct bodily contact about 20% of the time (see Figure 4.2). This trend is changing as more primary caregivers are using traditional methods of "baby wearing" to maintain physical contact. A growing

A

B

C

AJ_Watt/E+ via Getty Images; ranplett/E+ via Getty Images; grinvalds/iStock via Getty Images plus

Figure 4.2 Caregivers may have direct bodily contact with their infants by utilizing wearable devices (A) or they may use equipment that offers independence (B, C).
What are the potential benefits to the caregiver and infant in each of the examples shown? Are there potential disadvantages?

amount of research shows the benefit to both infant and caregiver (Barry, 2019; Little et al., 2019).

Parents and educators can promote physical touch by picking up and holding, rocking, and gently massaging the baby. These practices positively affect the infant and build sensitivity in the caregiver (Moore et al., 2017). This is particularly valuable for caregivers helping infants who have difficult temperaments. In traditional cultures, infants are typically kept close by the mother during both nighttime and daytime hours, and this close-proximity care is consistent among the infant's parents, siblings, and other relatives or caretakers. Research shows that traditional cultures are doing it right; this proximity, often within sight and hearing range, can be comforting to very young infants (Bremner & Wachs, 2010; Brink, 2013; Gross, 2019).

In some family settings, breastfeeding tends to be on-demand whenever the infant responds or seeks it. Caregivers use skin-to-skin contact, or **kangaroo care**, to soothe and nurture infants, placing the infant's ear next to the primary caregiver's heart (see Figure 4.3). By listening to the caretaker's heartbeat, the baby regulates their own heart rate and breathing in response, which has a calming effect (Davies & Troy, 2020; Oster, 2019). Kangaroo care practices are now used in intensive care units worldwide.

Subsequent studies have shown that when kangaroo care is practiced early in life, later positive interactions occur, including biological bonding and attachment between infants and their primary caretakers (Feldman et al., 2002). For example, one study of premature infants showed that kangaroo care resulted in higher cognitive and motor skill development at 6 months of age (Feldman et al., 2002). Preterm infants who experience kangaroo care may sleep better, gain weight faster, and experience lower pain and stress levels (Als & McAnulty, 2011; Johnston et al., 2014; Jönsson et al., 2018; Scafidi et al., 1986). Sensitive and responsive caregiving supports infants' ability to better self-regulate when they reach the toddler years and beyond. In contrast, infants with lower levels of physical contact showed more distress, resulting in an underdeveloped genetic profile for their age (Kostandy & Ludington-Hoe, 2019; Moore et al., 2017).

Physical contact between newborn infants and their primary caregivers appears to lower stress in both. For example, studies show skin-to-skin contact causes the release of oxytocin, a hormone that promotes positive caregiver feelings as it soothes and calms the infant and caregiver (Chen et al., 2017; Uvnäs-Moberg et al., 2020; Xiaoli et al., 2019). Lowered caregiver stress results in higher sensitivity to their infants' needs, while caregivers experiencing stress are less sensitive to their infants' signals.

☑ CHECKPOINT

☐ Describe a neonate's physical characteristics.

☐ How is the health and wellness of a newborn determined?

☐ Name three factors that influence an infant's weight and length.

☐ Describe five newborn reflexes.

☐ Why is touch critical to newborn development?

4.2 Physical Qualities and Changes

Throughout the first two years of life, infants grow rapidly as they gain weight and length. Their proportions and facial features change, and their gross and fine motor skills improve. These changes are easy to observe as infants learn to hold their heads up, roll over, crawl, walk, and run. They learn how to grasp for and manipulate toys and eventually how to feed themselves. They eagerly explore their environment and learn other new skills in the process.

Tyler Olson/Shutterstock.com

Figure 4.3 Kangaroo care positions the infant's ear next to the primary caregiver's heart, which has a calming effect on the baby.

Apply Here!

Physical touch is an essential aspect of infant caregiving. Imagine that you are addressing a group of expectant parents in a workshop on infant care. How would you communicate the importance of touch in promoting optimal development in infants? What practical ideas might you share for incorporating more physical touch between caregivers and infants? Compare how the caregivers in Figure 4.4 differ in how they hold their infants. What are the commonalities? Should physical touch change throughout infancy? If so, how?

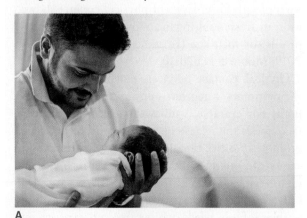

A

B

paulaphoto/Shutterstock.com; fizkes/Shutterstock.com

Figure 4.4 (A) Caregiver Holding a Newborn Infant; (B) Caregiver Holding a Toddler.

Infants also discover new ways to solve problems. They learn about themselves and others.

Sensory Skills

Infants use their senses—taste and oral exploration, sight, smell, touch, and hearing—to explore their environment and learn about the world. How do we know what infants can sense? Researchers conduct tests to see how neonates respond to changes in light, sounds, volume, texture, movement, and other stimuli. Some senses, like touch, are fully developed at birth, while others, like sight, take longer to develop. At birth, neonates can feel the touch of heat, cold, pressure, and pain (Johnston et al., 2014; Jönsson et al., 2018).

Infants are also born with a fully functioning sense of smell (olfaction). Researchers have found that they can even smell before birth, and there is nothing inferior about a newborn's sense of smell (Adam-Darque et al., 2018). When exposed to unpleasant odors such as ammonia or vinegar, infants typically react by turning their heads away. They prefer familiar smells from their own self and from their primary caregivers to new or unfamiliar odors (Loos et al., 2017; Schaal, 2005). Newborns orient themselves toward the smell of their mothers or primary caregivers, and they are drawn to breast milk over the smell of formula in their first few days (even breast milk that is not from their mother). Studies have shown that the smell of their mother's breast milk or other familiar scents can significantly calm a distressed baby (Loos et al., 2017; Nishitani et al., 2009).

If you have spent any time with infants, you know that most things in their hands end up in their mouths. It doesn't matter what it is—fingers, toes, toys, and other less palatable objects all end up in the mouth (see Figure 4.5). Their tactile sensors, in and around their mouths, are particularly useful for exploration. But can infants detect different tastes? That depends on taste buds responding to chemicals in the mouth, giving the sensation of sweet, sour,

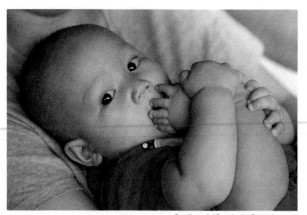

Saslistock/iStock via Getty Images

Figure 4.5 Infants explore their world through their senses. Putting objects and even toes in the mouth is a way to explore.

salty, bitter, and umami (a savory taste found in meats and milk products).

Infants can distinguish between tastes, showing a distinct preference for sweet flavors and distaste for bitter flavors (Cowart et al., 2004; Mennella et al., 2001; Mennella et al., 2009). For example, research has shown that neonates respond with a grimace when a sour or bitter taste is put on their tongues, whereas their lips relax when given a sweet taste. Interestingly, exposure to certain tastes in infancy is thought to affect taste preferences later in life. Infants may be exposed to various foods prenatally, depending on what the mother consumes.

Researchers acknowledge that the flavor world of infants is complex, particularly for those who are breastfed, as flavors found in both amniotic fluid and breast milk modify later food preferences (Beauchamp & Mennella, 2011). In addition, genetics also plays a role in these preferences. Likewise, a breastfed baby may be exposed to a wider variety of food due to their mother's food consumption, which may vary throughout the days and weeks. An exclusively formula-fed infant is not as exposed to taste differences because formula offers the baby a single flavor for every meal. As infants develop from newborns to toddlers, various flavor exposures can create familiarity, stimulate taste buds, and broaden taste preferences (Beauchamp & Mennella, 2009; Nguyen, 2019).

Hearing is critical in caregiver-infant communication. Before birth, infants learn the sound of their biological mother's voice. They continue to prefer the familiar voices of their caretakers, both for pitch and actual language, even though their hearing does not mature fully until about age 6 months (Erickson & Newman, 2017; Werker, 2018; Tsuji et al., 2019). Newborns and infants generally prefer higher-pitch over lower-pitch voices. They are drawn to music, develop preferences for musical styles, and react to changes in musical keys or tones. Speaking, humming, or singing softly in a low-volume voice can provide effective soothing for a distraught infant (Conrad et al., 2011). The sense of hearing continues to develop and refine over a child's first two years of life. For example, their ability to hear low-volume and mid- and low-range sounds increases. They also become more adept at **sound localization** abilities, or identifying where a sound originates (Middlebrooks, 2015).

Although neonates can see, sight or vision is their least developed sense. The reason is physiological as an infant's eye is structurally immature at birth. The muscles that control the lens, which help to focus, and the retina, the membrane that sends visual information to the brain through the optic nerve, are still undeveloped (Boyd, 2020). So, what does a newborn see? As a result of the underdeveloped eye, it is estimated that a neonate sees an object placed 20 feet away just as clearly as an adult with normal vision would see that object placed 600 feet away. Newborns tend to see objects that are in close proximity the clearest, about 7 to 9 inches away (Braddick & Atkinson, 2011). Neonates can focus on their caregiver's face, especially its perimeter, when at a close range. They cannot see distant objects as clearly as those close by during the first few months of life. After a couple of months, an infant can centralize on the face of another person (see Figure 4.6) (Baston & Durward, 2010; Braddick & Atkinson, 2011; Bushall, 2003).

A   B   C

Figure 4.6 Newborns tend to see objects that are close-up most clearly, and they can focus on their caregiver's face, especially its perimeter (A, B). After a couple of months, an infant can centralize on the face of another person. By their first birthday, most infants have close to normal adult vision (C).

During the first month or two, infants do not see colors clearly because the cone cells in the retina responsible for color vision are not yet fully formed. However, infants do see high contrasts such as black and white. By 8 weeks of age, infants begin to discriminate between some colors, such as distinguishing between red, white, and some blue-greens. Color distinction continues to develop through infancy as yellow, yellow-green, and purple become more distinctive over time (Kimura et al., 2010). Infants prefer patterns over random designs, and they like curved lines over straight lines. Once they can distinguish colors at about 5 months of age, they prefer colors over grays (see Figure 4.7).

An additional component of vision that develops in infancy is depth perception, the ability to discern the relative distance of an object. The classic experiment to determine infant depth perception was published in the *Scientific American* (Walk & Gibson, 1960). This experiment created a perceptual visual cliff by placing a piece of transparent plastic over a box, extending beyond the box edge so that it appeared that there was a ledge or drop-off. Infants who could creep and crawl were placed on the surface and encouraged to move forward. This classic experiment established that infants could perceive depth and would stop at or before the ledge by the time they learned to crawl. This experiment led to decades of further research on infant depth perception (Gibson, 2002; Gibson & Pick, 2000).

Depth perception requires binocular vision that occurs when each eye combines the image seen in both eyes into one image. Typically, infants develop binocular vision, and subsequently depth perception, at around age 2 to 3 months. This development happens just in time, because infants often start scooching, creeping, and eventually crawling soon thereafter. Depth perception can prevent a mobile infant from falling off the edge of a surface or from running into objects (Dahl et al., 2013).

Hayden Volkmar

Figure 4.7 What do infants see? Vision clarity matures during the first year of life, including clarity and color perception.

Age of Infant	Vision/Sight Growth and Development
Newborn	• Pupils constrict to avoid brightness. • Eyes see peripherally. • Pupils dilate after first couple of weeks. • Focused, central vision develops. • Infant begins to see light and dark variations. • Infant begins to see patterns. • Eyes focus on objects at a close distance. • Eyes focus attention on large objects and high-contrast colors.
2 to 4 Months	• Infant develops more coordination between eyes over time. • Eyes begin to follow a moving object. • Infant begins hand-eye coordination (around 3 months).
5 to 8 Months	• Infant has good color perception, although it is still developing. • Infant can see in three dimensions. • Depth perception has developed. • Infant recognizes caregivers and responds when seeing them. • Familiar people and objects from a distance can be recognized. • Sight recognition does not require seeing an entire object or person to identify.
9 to 12 Months	• Distance perception or near-sightedness develops. • Far-sightedness and ability to pick up small items develops. • Eye color is near completion, although timing varies and may continue for several years.

Boyd, K. (2020). Vision Development: Newborn to 12 Months. *American Academy of Ophthalmology.*

Table 4.3 Maturation of Vison in Infancy

Sight maturity happens quickly; sometime between 6 months and the first birthday, most infants can have close to normal 20/20 vision. By age one, the infant sees a distant object with the same clarity as a teen or an adult (see Table 4.3).

An infant's senses eventually become integrated; as one sense matures and develops, so do others. Together, input from the senses shapes the infant's brain (Dionne-Dostie et al., 2015; Lickliter, 2011; Monroy et al., 2019). As this happens, infants learn to predict the sensory consequences of their interactions with their environment. Imagine a 12-month-old sitting in a highchair with a plastic plate on the highchair tray. The infant pushes the plate to the floor, creating a loud noise, to the infant's delight. When a caregiver picks the plate up and places it back on the tray, the infant will likely repeat the motion, fascinated by the cause and effect of the action. These sensory interactions with the environment, especially those that are new or novel, aid in cognitive and motor skill development (Kayhan et al., 2019; Koster et al., 2020; Nagai, 2019; Stahl & Feigenson, 2015). The interdependency of infants' senses and their continued development through interaction with the environment is complex and adaptive. When one sense is thwarted, other sensory abilities may be enhanced or heightened (Bauer et al., 2017; Monroy et al., 2019). For example, an infant who is severely sight-impaired will likely develop a heightened sense of hearing, smell, and touch to better navigate their surroundings.

The development of the senses is critical to cognitive learning, social interaction, and safety. As one sense matures, it influences others and vice versa. For example, the sense of touch informs vision, and the sense of smell informs taste. As the senses work together and play off each other, the senses' multimodality, or coworking, increases (Lickliter, 2011; Murray et al., 2016; Walker-Andrews et al., 2013). Caregivers play an essential role in providing stimulating experiences that support optimal sensory development through environmental interactions (Day, 1982; Kayhan et al., 2019). When caregivers engage infants in developmentally appropriate sensory play, it builds brain pathways; supports language development, memory, and motor skills; and may calm and soothe. Table 4.4 offers suggestions on engaging infants and toddlers in developmentally appropriate sensory play; what other sensory activities might you add?

Age of Infant or Toddler	Suggested Activities
0–3 Months	• Use skin-to-skin contact. • Smile and respond to the infant. • Hang a mobile above the infant so they can observe color contrast and movement. • Touch and massage the infant's extremities. • Tickle or lightly touch the abdomen. • Use different voice sounds, pitches, and rhythms, including singing. • Play music. • Place a mirror so that the infant can see themselves. • Encourage the infant to hold and shake a rattle. • Share photos of familiar people or pets. • Talk to the infant during diaper changes, and verbally comment while lifting legs up and down, massaging the limbs, and playfully touching the infant's body trunk.
4–6 Months	• Place infant in different body positions, use up-and-down movements. • Support the infant in a standing position. • Expose the infant to different textures by touching and commenting on textures. • Roll a ball toward the baby and encourage them to return it. • Incorporate toys with rattles and bells.
7–9 Months	• Read and offer chunky board books for exploration. • Offer toys of different weights such as a solid, heavy ball and a light ball. • Offer, explore, and examine objects from varying distances. • Assist the infant so they can observe the environment from different positions or perspectives, such as in your arms, laying on their back, sitting on the floor, or crawling. • Investigate a variety of object shapes and colors.
10–12 Months	• Sing and assist the infant in using motions or clapping to songs such as "Head, Shoulders, Knees, and Toes." • Play peek-a-boo. • Offer stacking toys. • Create accessible obstacle courses for crawling over, under, and around objects. • Introduce new textures through food, toys, or clothing.
13–24 Months	• Create sensory tables with objects that can be safely explored. • Blow bubbles and encourage the infant to capture and pop them. • Offer appropriate finger foods in a variety of different colors and textures. • Offer toys the infant can safely sit on and move. • Explore and verbally describe colors and textures in nature.

Table 4.4 Suggestions for Sensory Play

Growth in Weight and Length

Over the first year of life, the infant will grow and change physically while coping and adjusting to the outside world. Right after birth, newborns tend to lose approximately 5% to 10% of their weight. However, they usually recover their weight by the end of the first week. Premature infants may lose up to 15% percent of their weight, but they should regain their weight in the first 10 to 15 days. Not recovering birthweight within these time frames may be a concerning sign and should be closely monitored by medical professionals.

As infants learn to suck, swallow, and digest their food, they grow quickly. In the first 4 months, most infants double their birthweight. They grow about 1 inch per month in length (height). By the end of the first year, the same baby might weigh 22 pounds and measure 40 inches long. That is, the child might triple in weight and double in length in just a year. This all happens in an orderly and predictable manner (Brink, 2013 Gross, 2019; US National Library of Medicine, 2020). However, an infant's growth often occurs in fits and starts. An infant may go for days without any measurable growth and then go through a rapid spurt.

In the first few months of life, growth in length and weight is used as a sign of health. Medical professionals can determine an infant's ideal weight by comparing their weight and length, age, and sex to national averages using the World Health Organization (WHO) reference charts (see Figures 4.8 and 4.9). Ideal body length and weight averages vary by country. The US Centers for Disease Control

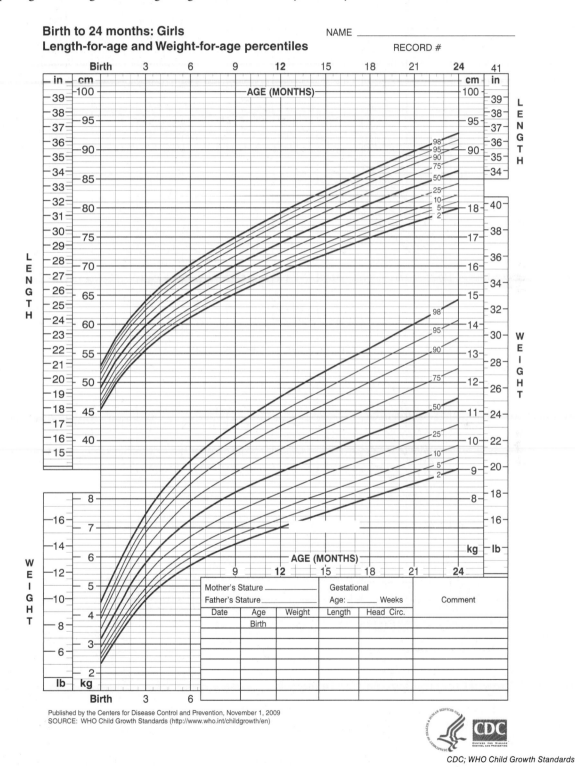

Birth to 24 months: Girls
Length-for-age and Weight-for-age percentiles

NAME _____

RECORD # _____

Published by the Centers for Disease Control and Prevention, November 1, 2009
SOURCE: WHO Child Growth Standards (http://www.who.int/childgrowth/en)

CDC; WHO Child Growth Standards

Figure 4.8 Growth Chart for Girls, Birth to 24 Months.

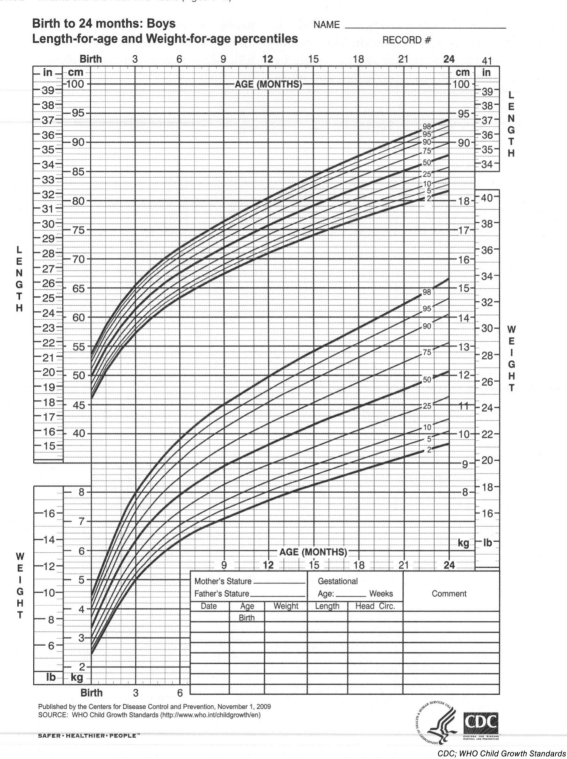

Birth to 24 months: Boys
Length-for-age and Weight-for-age percentiles

NAME _____

RECORD # _____

Published by the Centers for Disease Control and Prevention, November 1, 2009
SOURCE: WHO Child Growth Standards (http://www.who.int/childgrowth/en)

SAFER · HEALTHIER · PEOPLE™

CDC

CDC; WHO Child Growth Standards

Figure 4.9 Growth Chart for Boys, Birth to 24 Months

and Prevention also offers growth charts based on the actual growth of children nationally; but it is intended for children aged 2 and above.

When an infant does not meet recognized growth standards, they are said to have **failure to thrive**. If a doctor diagnoses failure to thrive, the infant's weight falls well below the ideal weight for an infant of that age. Possible causes of failure to thrive include conditions that prevent the absorption of nutrients, physical abnormalities that make it difficult to feed, organ malfunctions, and other specific medical conditions. Sometimes environmental factors such as neglect, abuse, trauma, or insufficient nutrition play a part in an infant's failure to thrive. Receiving consistent medical checkups to monitor growth during the first months and year of life is important to infant health (Brink, 2013; Gross, 2019; US National Library of Medicine, 2020).

As an infant's length and weight increase, bone and muscle growth must keep up. Newborn bones and muscles are soft and pliable. They are not strong enough to support weight or position changes such as sitting or crawling. Over time, cartilage solidifies into stronger and interconnected bones. This process occurs simultaneously with muscle growth, providing increased strength. Growth rates and achivements are influenced by both genetics and the infant's environment, both prenatally and neonatally, including nutrition, health, and exposure to stress (Kitsiou-Tzeli & Tzetis, 2017). Race and ethnicity also play a part; so, attention is being focused on more inclusive standards for assessing healthy growth and development (Buck et al., 2015). Racial or ethnic differences in US newborn birthweights are related more to maternal pregnancy weight gain, preterm birth rate, and maternal physical height, weight, and body composition than maternal age, socioeconomic conditions, or behavioral characteristics (Morisaki et al., 2017).

Although infants develop at their own pace, some common principles of development will be discussed throughout this chapter. One principle of physical growth and change is the proximodistal pattern of development. *Proximal* means near the center or midline while distal means farthest from the midline. In **proximodistal development**, infants first use the muscles at the core of their bodies before they can use muscles further out from their abdominal center (see Figure 4.10). This development occurs

Figure 4.10 In proximodistal development, infants first use the core muscles, followed by the muscles further out from their abdominal center. This infant has crept up to the desired object using abdominal core muscles, arms outstretched. The ability to grasp the object with the hand is still not possible.

from the core to the extremities (arms and legs) as gross motor skills develop before fine motor skills. For example, infants use their abdominal muscles, allowing them to sit up, before they can developmentally use their legs to walk. They can use their whole hands before controlling their fingers to pick up Cheerios® or other small items.

Bodily Proportions

An infant's bodily proportions also change during their first year. At birth, their head is large compared to the rest of their body. It is about one-fourth of their total body length throughout their first year. A newborn's skull has soft spots called *fontanelles*. One on the back of the head closes within the first couple of months, while a larger one on the top middle of the head closes toward the end of the first year. Gradually, by the end of the second year, a child's head is much more proportional to the size of the body. This process continues throughout early and middle childhood until adolescence, when the head-body ratio is at an adult proportion, or at about 1/7 of total body weight (Figaji, 2017). Throughout infancy, an increase in body weight often makes infants appear chubby, soft, and cuddly, which makes them especially endearing.

It is not a coincidence that an infant's head is disproportionately large; it relates to the process or sequencing of development. Infants develop from the top of the head down to their extremities, called **cephalocaudal development**, or head-to-tail growth (see Figure 4.11). The brain grows faster than the lower parts of the body. Following this development pattern, infants can use their hands before they can crawl and crawl before they can walk. Although cephalocaudal is a principle of development, it is not always rigidly or strictly followed because infants vary in their individual development (Bremner & Wachs, 2010; Brink, 2013; Gross, 2019).

As infants become toddlers around age 1 1/2, their bodily proportions change as their relative head size decreases from 1/4 to 1/5 of the total body length by age 2. Infants may continue to seem chubby, but they gradually lose their "baby fat" as their bodies lengthen. Arms, legs, hands, and feet also lengthen. By their second birthday, most toddlers weigh about 27 pounds and are just under 3 feet tall (32 to 35 inches). At this point, they are about half of their final adult height (US Centers for Disease Control and Prevention, 2010; US National Library of Medicine, 2020).

Facial Features

When someone says, "She has such a baby face!" what does that mean? Generally, it refers to a roundish facial shape, soft features, large eyes, soft skin—exactly what is common for infants in their first year. Although their eyes are large in proportion to their other facial features, their noses are small. Infants are born with about 20 deciduous (baby) teeth, not yet erupted through their gums. Their teeth do not typically begin to erupt until at least 6 months of age. But once teeth eruption begins, it continues at a rapid pace throughout the first 2 years (see Figure 4.12) (American Dental Association, 2020). The first two bottom teeth usually erupt first, quickly followed by the top two teeth (Lockman & Tamis-LeMonda, 2020). Many infants become fussy as they deal with the pain and soreness of teeth breaking through their gums.

During the toddler years, more teeth develop. Gaining teeth can contribute to a changing facial profile and a growing ability to bite and chew. By

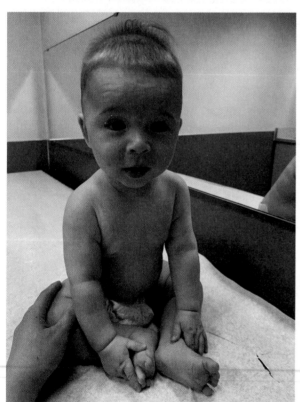

Sharleen Kato

Figure 4.11 In cephalocaudal development, infants develop from the top of the head down to their extremities. Control of the neck muscles comes before control of the shoulders, which helps an infant roll over. Abdominal control comes next, enabling the infant to sit up.

fizkes/iStock via Getty Images Plus

Figure 4.12 Throughout infancy, teeth erupt through the gums. By the end of infancy, most infants have all their primary teeth except for their second molars.

Teeth	Erupt	Lost/replaced
Central lower incisors	6–10 months	6–7 years
Central upper incisors	8–12 months	6–7 years
Lateral upper incisors (adjacent to central incisors)	9–13 months	7–8 years
Lateral lower incisors (adjacent to central incisors)	10–16 months	7–8 years
First upper molar	13–19 months	9–11 years
First lower molar	14-18 months	9–11 years
Upper canine (cuspid)	16–22 months	10–12 years
Lower canine (cuspid)	17–23 months	9–12 years
Second lower molar	23–31 months	10–12 years

American Dental Association, 2020

Table 4.5 Typical Tooth Eruption Timing in Infancy

the time toddlers reach their second birthdays, most have all their primary teeth, except their second molars (see Table 4.5). This changes the look of their smile and facial features (Bremner & Wachs, 2010; Brink, 2013; Gross, 2019). The emergence of teeth during infancy requires the need for dental care, which involves gently cleaning teeth with a soft cloth and eliminating sugar intake. A visit to a dentist is recommended before the first birthday (American Academy of Pediatrics, 2014; American Academy of Pediatric Dentistry, 2016; US Department of Health and Human Services Oral Health Coordinating Committee, 2019).

☑CHECKPOINT

- ☐ What can a newborn feel, smell, hear, and taste? How about a 6-month-old?
- ☐ Why should caregivers engage infants in sensory play and exploration?
- ☐ Name and describe two common principles of physical growth and development.
- ☐ How do bodily proportions and facial features change during infancy?
- ☐ How might you describe the sequences of teething and tooth eruption during early infancy to a new caregiver?

Infant Motor Skills

Infants are fascinating to watch. The physical qualities and changes that occur over the first year are sequential and predictable, although infants develop at their own pace and on a schedule that is individually "normal." Three interacting elements underlie motor development: brain maturation, muscle strength, and practice. This points to the fact that everything in development is both nature and nurture. During the first year, infants develop both their fine and gross motor skills at a rapid pace.

Gross or large motor skills involve more significant muscle movements such as creeping forward, crawling, walking, and jumping. Later in life, they include skipping, hopping, kicking a ball, or hitting a baseball. **Fine motor skills** include small movements using fingers and toes (Dionne-Dostie et al., 2015; Gross, 2019). For example, holding a bottle, picking up toys and food items, and holding a spoon are fine motor skills. Later in life, fine motor skills include abilities such as buttoning a shirt, tying shoes, brushing teeth, holding a pencil, and using a video game controller (see Table 4.6). As described earlier, proximodistal and cephalocaudal development are related to gross and fine motor skill development.

Both gross and fine motor skill development are linked to infants' interactions with their environment. When an infant or toddler perceives something in their environment that motivates them to act, they then become a problem solver. This early problem-solving results in motor skill development (Adolph et al., 2010). For example, when a toy is set in front of an infant during "tummy time" (when infants are placed on their abdomens), they may attempt to grab the toy. With repeated attempts, coordination improves, and gross motor skills build. An important job of an infant caregiver, both at

Age	Skill
1 month  Jani Bryson/iStock.com	• Focuses on objects in close range, about 8 to 12 inches from eyes • Recognizes some sounds and voices • Has little control of arms • Lifts arms to mouth and eyes • Makes a tightly closed fist • Will turn to face sounds and noises • Dislikes strong smells
3 months  Aliwak/Shutterstock.com	• Supports the upper body with arms when on stomach • Kicks legs • Uses leg muscles to resist flat surface at feet • Grasps and holds ring • Hands predominately open and relaxed • Reaches for dangling ring • Fingers hand in play • Uses a palmar grasp
4 to 7 months  Anetta/Shutterstock.com	• Reaches for objects • Moves an object from one hand to the other • Strengthens ability to follow objects in motion • Closes hand on a dangling ring
8 to 12 months  Anton Gvozdikov/Shutterstock.com	• Creeps on stomach • Crawls on stomach • Moves from sitting to crawling position • Creeps up and down stairs • Uses a neat pincer grasp • Plays Pattycake • Attempts to self-feed using a spoon or a cup • Scribbles spontaneously (10–21 months, typically 14 months) • Pulls to stand with support
13 to 18 months Felix Mizioznikov/Shutterstock.com	• Stands with little support • Takes first steps (or earlier) • Walks without assistance • Pushes or pulls objects while sitting • Dances in standing position for short periods
24 months  Jordi Mora/Shutterstock.com	• Carries items while walking or pulls a toy behind • Runs short distances • Walks backward • Kicks a ball • Uses blocks to build • Stands on toes • Uses a pincer grasp and a cup with handles to self-feed • Undresses self

Kato

Table 4.6 Summary of Infant Physical Milestones

home and in a daycare setting, is to provide appropriate environmental stimulation and motivation to help them develop motor skills. Stimulating home environments and supportive primary caretakers enhance both fine and gross motor skills (Cacola et al., 2011; Flores et al., 2019).

Gross Motor Skill Development

Newborns cannot support their heads without help. By as early as one month, newborns can begin to lift their heads slightly. By four months, they can hold their heads steady, and by six months, they can balance their heads while in an upright position. During those same 6 months, infants learn to roll over. Creeping and crawling come next (see Figure 4.13).

Creeping is a commonly used term to describe a dragging movement that is accomplished by infants

A

B

Figure 4.13 (A) Infants creep by laying on their stomachs and pulling themselves forward to explore their environment. (B) Infants crawl by lifting their knees and arms to move themselves forward.

pulling forward using their arms and shoulders while lying on their stomachs. **Crawling** describes movement that uses the hands and knees to pull the body forward while the stomach is raised off the ground. No two infants creep or crawl in the same way. Their unique efforts to move forward can be quite entertaining as some use coordinated movements to alternate lifting the arms and knees while others seem to drag themselves along (Dionne-Dostie et al., 2015; Gross, 2019).

At the same time they are learning to creep and crawl, infants learn to sit without support. They are holding their heads steady, and their abdominal muscles become stronger. Soon they will be able to support themselves when leaning against an object such as a piece of furniture. Before long, they are pulling themselves up to a standing position, leaning against a support, and taking side steps around it. Next, a baby will begin standing without support and begin the process of walking, taking a few tentative steps, and after much trial and error, taking the first actual steps. Some infants skip the crawling stage altogether and go from creeping to standing and walking. This continues until the baby easily walks alone. In their newfound independence, toddlers explore the world with much enthusiasm.

Toddlers learn many new gross and fine motor skills. In addition to walking, toddlers also learn to pull a toy on a string, run for short distances, kick, throw, walk backward, and climb stairs more easily, mastering each skill on their own individual schedules (see Figure 4.14). Some learn to walk early, others learn later. Likely these developmental milestones are both programmed by genetics and learned through interactions with their caregivers and environment. As toddlers explore their world, they move constantly. They fall and get back up many times an hour. Caregivers should provide toddlers with a safe environment, but they should also encourage this active exploration as much as possible (Haibach-Beach et al., 2018; Payne & Isaacs, 2016).

Fine Motor Skill Development

Infants first reach for people and things. Then, they grasp things. Remember, at birth, a newborn's movements are reflexive. Reaching and grasping attempts are significant because they demonstrate that the baby has developed beyond reacting to stimuli and is now actively interacting with the world around

Sharleen Kato

Figure 4.14 Infants develop both gross and fine motor skills that enable them to sit up and begin to feed themselves.

them using motor skills (Haibach-Beach et al., 2018; Payne & Isaacs, 2016). Like gross motor skill development, fine motor skill development moves in a sequential order following proximodistal and cephalocaudal principles of development. Infants first move their shoulders and elbows toward things. Next, they move their hands by rotating their wrists. This is a common attempt for infants who are sitting and supporting themselves. They reach out their arms to their caregiver, rotate their wrists and hands, and verbalize their desire for contact.

Next, infants learn to coordinate their fingers and thumb (Lipkin, 2009). The thumb and forefinger coordinate first, followed by using all their fingers. Infants use the **palmar grasp** when they use all their fingers to grab an object into the palm of their hand (see Figure 4.15A). This reflex is present at birth, and it can be seen when an infant grasps and wraps their hand around a caregiver's finger. Imagine a baby eating small food items from their high chair tray. The baby scoops the items into a fist; however, caregivers must often uncurl their fingers to reach the food. Infants next move on to using the **pincer grasp**. When picking up small items such as bits of food on their high chair tray, they use their forefinger and

thumb, much like children and adults do (see Figure 4.15B). Once they master the pincer grasp, toddlers can feed themselves finger foods. They can hold a cup with handles. They can take off their diapers and other clothing items (Dionne-Dostie et al., 2015; Gross, 2019).

Caregivers may occasionally walk in on just-wakened toddlers only to find them in their cribs with clothes and diapers removed and anything else within reach in their hands. During toddlerhood, infants become multitaskers—using both large and fine motor skills, often in unrelated tasks (see Figure 4.16). Primary caregivers and educators must keep medications, small objects that may cause choking, and other toxic substances out of reach. Because their fine-motor skills develop so quickly, toddlers often surprise their caregivers with these new skills.

A

B

Yaoinlove/Shutterstock.com; DUSITARA STOCKER/Shutterstock.com

Figure 4.15 (A) Baby Demonstrating a Palmar Grasp; (B) Baby Demonstrating a Pincer Grasp.

Sharleen Kato

Figure 4.16 Toddlers begin coordinating large and fine motor skills. They often multitask, such as this young child driving a toy car and blowing bubbles at the same time.

☑CHECKPOINT

☐ What three elements are required for motor development?

☐ What gross motor skills develop in the first two years of life? Identify a typical milestone for a 1-month-old, 3-month-old, 6-month-old, 12-month-old, and 18-month-old.

☐ What fine motor skills develop in the first two years of life? Identify a typical milestone for a 1-month-old, 3-month-old, 6-month-old, 12-month-old, and 18-month-old.

Apply Here!

Fourteen-month-old Jordan has been in your care for two weeks and is warming up to you. But he is still hesitant around the other four children in your care. These peers range in age from 11 to 14 months. All of Jordan's peers have begun to walk during the last two months. Jordan is getting around by crawling and standing, but he is not yet walking. Jordan's mother has become concerned. She has noticed that Jordan is the only one in the classroom who is not yet walking. She is worried that "something might be wrong with Jordan." As an educator or caretaker, how might you address her concerns?

4.3 Brain and Nervous System Development

As you learned previously in Chapter 3, the brain and nervous system begin to develop within days of conception. This growth and development continue throughout prenatal development and following birth. The newborn's brain is perfect for what it needs to do—learn about the world. However, brain and nervous system development do not stop there, as only the brain stem is complete at birth. During infancy, both the brain and nervous system continue to develop rapidly (Dean et al., 2018; Diamond et al., 2011).

How fast are infants' brains growing? At birth, a neonate's brain is about 25% of the size or mass of an adult brain. By the end of infancy at age two, it is about 75% of adult size. But brain development is not limited to increases in size or changes in structure. It also includes the connections and pathways forming during this critical stage of development.

Structure of the Infant Brain

Knowing information about early brain development can help educators and primary caregivers understand infant development and how best to nurture their growth. It can be helpful to divide the human brain into three parts: the brain stem, the cerebellum, and the cerebral cortex (see Figure 4.17). Each part has a distinct function, yet the parts synchronize when we think, feel, perceive, read, process, interpret, and perform many other brain functions. Although scientists have identified specific brain centers, such as the area where emotions are processed or language is learned or used, the brain consists of complex interdependent parts. The **brain stem** serves to carry messages from the spinal cord to the upper brain. It resembles a tree trunk in shape and, as mentioned earlier, develops prenatally. The brain stem is critical to life as it controls reflexes and involuntary processes like heart rate and breathing (Breedlove & Watson, 2020; Dean et al., 2019; Fine, 2019).

The **cerebellum** is located behind the brain stem and below the upper brain and occupies the largest area of the human brain. It is involved in gross motor skills, including balance, posture, and coordination. It also plays a part in fine motor skills.

Human Brain

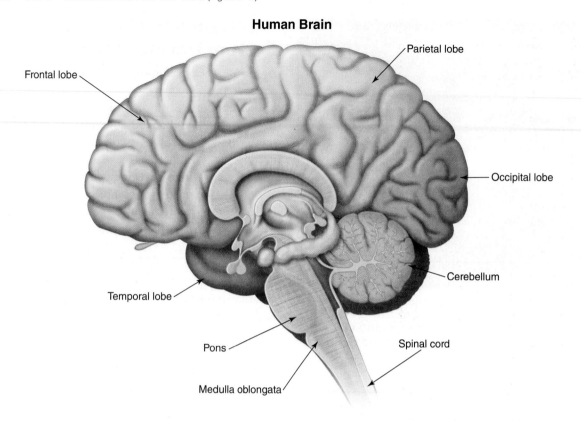

©*Body Scientific International*

Figure 4.17 The human brain has three parts: the brain stem, the cerebellum, and the cerebral cortex.

The **cerebral cortex** occupies the front part of the brain and regulates the perceptions of touch, pressure, temperature, and pain. The cerebral cortex grows dramatically during infancy, especially the visual and auditory areas. It can be divided into a right and a left hemisphere; each side of the brain or hemisphere has four smaller units called **lobes**. These lobes are in both hemispheres, although not identical in anatomy or function. The specialized functioning of the left and right brain hemispheres is termed **lateralization**. Brain lateralization refers to how cognitive processes are typically more dominant on one side of the brain than the other. However, the two sides are connected, and communication occurs between both sides.

The **occipital lobes** control vision. The **parietal lobes** interpret sensory information, such as sensations like cold, heat, touch, pressure, and pain. The **frontal lobes** are associated with executive functions such as planning, organizing, memory, abstract thinking, and impulse control. The **temporal lobes** are involved with language skills, hearing, and social

understanding. For example, the temporal lobes help us understand facial expressions.

An area of the brain that has had a lot of attention in recent years is the frontal lobe, often referred to as the **prefrontal cortex**, the front portion of the cerebral cortex located behind the eyes and forehead. The prefrontal cortex helps us keep attention, stay motivated, practice self-control, and focus on goals. Caregivers of infants and young children are not surprised to learn that this lobe is one of the last parts of the brain to develop. You will learn more about the prefrontal cortex in Chapter 13.

In addition to these three major parts of the brain, the inner brain behind the cerebral cortex includes a collection of small but critically important structures. The limbic system, which consists of structures that contribute to brain functioning, involves instinctive behaviors and reactions such as emotions and memory. The hypothalamus, sometimes referred to as the "control center" of the brain, regulates our responses to stress through the production of specific hormones. The hippocampus contributes to spatial learning, short- and long-term memory, and navigation. The amygdala, another part of the limbic system, appraises threats and initiates the body's stress response (Breedlove & Watson, 2020; Dean et al., 2019; Fine, 2019).

Infant Brain Wiring

As neuroscientists continue to study the brain's structure or architecture, they have made tremendous progress in locating specific areas that contribute to its functioning. Brain architecture includes parts, but it is also a network of interconnections. Those that are used become stronger, those that are less used are eventually eliminated. As you just learned, the individual regions that comprise the brain work together to perform specific functions; these independent parts must communicate with each other and with the rest of the body. To do so, the brain processes information through "wiring"—forming networks of specialized nerve cells called **neurons**. Neurons communicate with each other by using electrical and chemical signals, termed *neurotransmitters*, to connect parts of the brain. Neuron communication creates pathways or **synapses** within the brain (Barkovich & Raybaud, 2019; Numan, 2020; Perlman et al., 2019).

Neurons contain a nucleus and long tail-like fibers (axons and dendrites) that aid in communication (see Figure 4.18). The axon fiber carries information away from the neuron cell body and transmits it at the synapse to the dendrite of another neuron via an electrochemical impulse. The dendrites receive information from other neurons and then process the information in their neuron body. Some axon fibers are covered with a protective sheath of **myelin**, a substance made of fat and protein. The process of myelination, or encasing axons with myelin, starts prenatally and continues to occur rapidly during the first two years of life before slowing down. Myelin helps speed up the communication between neurons; as more neurons are myelinated, brain processing increases throughout infancy (Barkovich & Raybaud, 2019; Knickmeyer et al., 2008; Numan, 2020; Perlman et al., 2019).

The formation of synapses is fundamental to an infant's brain development. This peaks at about 4 months of age. This network of synapses formed prenatally and during infancy will eventually determine the development of behavior and cognitive functions. An infant's brain contains more brain cells, or neurons, than the adult brain. They are immersed in their environment and social interactions, taking in everything around them. Many of these unnecessary connections will eventually be eliminated later in development. This process of building pathways and refining or redirecting them later is often termed "blooming and pruning." Brain research indicates that this process varies by brain part. It also differs individually in timing due to genetics and varied life experiences (Barkovich & Raybaud, 2019; Brink, 2013; Numan, 2020; Perlman et al., 2019; Sakai, 2020).

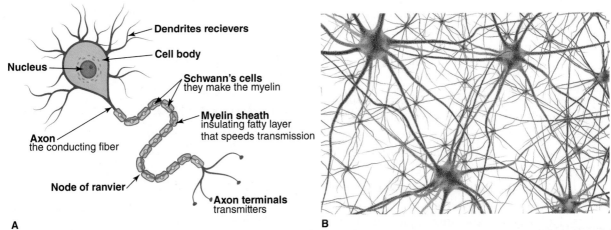

A   B

IconicBestiary/iStock via Getty Images Plus; Volodymyr Horbovyy/iStock via Getty Images Plus

Figure 4.18 (A) The parts of a neuron include the nucleus, cell body, dendrites, and axon. The Schwann's cells make myelin that helps speed up nerve impulses along the axon. (B) Neurons in the brain form a network of synapses.

Early Life Experiences and the Brain

Primary caregivers, educators, and medical professionals have long sensed that children are affected by their surroundings, even as young as infants (Calkins, 2015). Environmental factors such as stress and poverty can negatively impact a child in the long term. The impacts of neglect and abuse on a child are far-reaching. Recent research shows that negative experiences can affect the development of the brain during infancy. Infant caregivers can and should provide an environment that encourages optimal brain development during these first years (Gao et al., 2017; Legerstee et al., 2013; Lockman & Tamis-LeMonda, 2020). In an optimal environment, the caregiver would do the following:

- Offer positive sensory stimulation that uses all five senses. When used in brief intervals, sensory pathways in the brain become stronger.
- Use soothing and comforting skin-to-skin touch.
- Engage the infant in frequent conversation, speaking in a rhythmic, lyrical way while smiling and making eye contact.

Recently, researchers have been able to see changes in specific areas of the brains of adolescents and adults who suffered severe abuse as children. Challenges associated with severe childhood abuse include increased risks of psychiatric disorders such as aggressiveness, anxiety, and depression, as well as more frequent substance abuse and suicide (Bick & Nelson, 2016; Lutz et al., 2017). In addition, the lack of socioeconomic resources, such as inadequate housing, stimulating play areas, quality early childhood education, trauma-informed practices, and mental health support likely contribute to impeding optimal brain physical development (Hackman & Farah, 2009; Hanson et al., 2013; Noble et al., 2007;).

As you learned in Chapter 3, exposure to teratogens, or environmental toxins, prenatally or early in life, can have a devastating and lifelong effect on the architecture of the developing brain, potentially causing pregnancy problems and congenital disabilities. Infants' brains are far more susceptible to the negative impact of environmental toxins than adults' brains. This includes exposure to heavy metals, mercury, lead, manganese, and organophosphates that are commonly found in pesticides. Several sources may cause exposure, including contaminated water or food and synthetic materials such as paint. Exposure can negatively impact neurotransmitters in the brain, which carry signals from one cell to another (Gao et al., 2017; National Scientific Council on the Developing Child, 2006).

Caregivers should always handle infants carefully and avoid head injuries. A baby should never be shaken because the jostling can cause brain swelling, hemorrhaging (bleeding) inside the brain, and brain damage. Traditionally referred to as **shaken baby syndrome**, but now more aptly called **abusive head trauma**, the resulting brain injury from rough handling is one of the leading causes of death among young infants. These tragic injuries affect hundreds of infants in the United States each year and should be avoided at all costs (National Institute of Neurological Disorders and Stroke, 2020). Many states offer training for primary caregivers and early childhood educators that may include head trauma prevention and care, safe sleeping practices, and child abuse prevention, recognition, and treatment.

Although there is still much to be learned about the specific impact of environmental factors on brain development, it is important for primary caregivers and educators to keep up with current brain research. It is known that infants who engage in physical activity and are spoken to and encouraged to verbalize for themselves (cooing, babbling) are more apt to develop strong brain pathways. Likewise, neglected infants fail to thrive both physically and cognitively. Caregivers may be able to help infants and children who are at risk and to undo the effects of early environmental hardships, neglect, or maltreatment. On the other hand, disorders of the brain may be the origin of many neurological challenges and diseases rather than environmental factors (Batalle et al., 2017).

☑ CHECKPOINT

☐ What are three main structures of the brain?

☐ How does the formation of synapses relate to infant brain development?

☐ How can primary caregivers and early childhood educators encourage an infant's brain development during the first year?

☐ Create a checklist of activities or behaviors that caregivers can incorporate to help create brain-shaping experiences.

Apply Here!

Providing an environment that promotes brain development may include educational toys, as seen in the childcare settings in Figure 4.19 (A–B). The environment may also include simple items that are used in the home on a daily basis, such as safe plastic containers or wood utensils, exploring clean laundry, or interacting with siblings (see Figure 4.19 C–D). What are the benefits to the infant(s) as seen in each of the examples shown? What are the similarities seen in each of the examples shown? How might a caregiver encourage infants' interaction with their environments to support brain development in these examples?

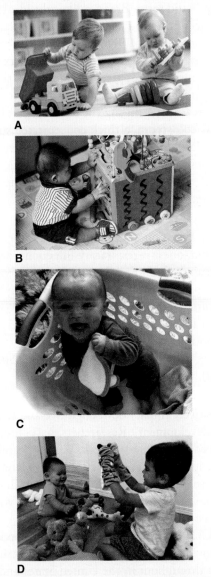

A

B

C

D

Oksana Kuzmina/Shutterstock.com;
jirawat phueksriphan/Shutterstock.com; Kato; Kato

Figure 4.19 What are the benefits in each example?

4.4 Infant Health and Wellness

Keeping infants safe while providing nutrition, sleep, play, and adequate medical and dental care are determinants of health and critical for optimal physical growth and development. Because infants' bodies continue to develop rapidly during infancy, carcinogens, toxic or unhealthy water and air, or chemical exposure may have detrimental effects on physical development. Infants require intervention to keep them healthy and safe in their environments, free of exposure to toxins or other dangers (Landrigan & Landrigan, 2018; National Scientific Council on the Developing Child, 2006). Best practice also includes providing optimal health care.

Medical and Dental Care

Regular medical care should be provided to babies throughout infancy, not just when the child is sick. Preventive and regular medical exams, or **well-baby exams**, focus on observing how an infant is growing and changing and whether or not the child is meeting recommended developmental milestones (American Academy of Pediatrics, 2018; US Centers for Disease Control and Prevention, 2020; World Health Organization, 2017). Medical oversight is crucial for infants born preterm to intercept or intervene in any health issues (Coathup et al., 2020). Well-baby exams also provide opportunities to identify problems and begin interventions (Lipkin & Macias, 2020). Primary caregivers may use checkups to seek advice about nutrition, sleep, or other concerns such as bowel movements and urination, spitting up food, excessive crying, diaper rash, or teething. Infants may also need medical care for common communicable diseases such as ear infections and respiratory tract illnesses. These types of illnesses peak at about age one and then slowly decline in frequency throughout the second year. Likewise, gastrointestinal issues such as colic and constipation are more common during the first year of life, occurring in up to half of all US infants (Vandenplas et al., 2019).

Some infants in the United States receive well-baby exams at recommended schedules readily agreed upon by medical professionals (see Table 4.7). However, many others do not. Infants born to and raised by mothers, either single or married, who are

Age	Ranges
The first week visit	3 to 5 days old
1 month old	7 days to <1 month
2 months old	1 month <3 months
4 months old	3 months to <5 months
6 months old	5 months to <8 months
9 months old	8 months to <11 months
12 months old	11 months to <17 months

American Academy of Pediatrics

Table 4.7 Recommended Schedule for Well-Baby Exams

economically disadvantaged are much more likely to receive little or no well-baby care in the United States (Iin, 2009; Odgers, 2015; Rauscher & Rangel, 2020). Because income disparity is often tied to race, Black, Brown, or Native American infants often receive less or inferior care (Manduca, 2018).

Toddlers, or children ages 1 to 2, also require regular medical care. The American Academy of Pediatrics recommends checkups at 12, 18, and 24 months, and then yearly after that to ensure toddlers are growing and thriving as they should. When visiting a healthcare professional, primary caregivers can ask questions about their toddler's growth, language, toilet training, and other developmental expectations (American Academy of Pediatrics, 2014).

Dental visits often begin by the first birthday and then repeat every six months afterward. Dentists clean teeth and repair them when necessary. Dentists can also show caregivers how to care for toddlers' teeth properly. Older toddlers may "help" primary caregivers as they begin learning how to brush their teeth.

Although this idea is controversial for some, most medical professionals encourage that children be vaccinated on a regular schedule throughout childhood (see Table 4.8). Whether given as shots or orally, vaccinations produce or boost immunity to a specific disease such as measles or mumps. According to the US Centers for Disease Control and Prevention (CDC, 2020), immunizing infants and children also helps protect the community's health, including schools and care centers. This is especially true for children who cannot be immunized, such as newborns who are too young to be vaccinated or those who cannot receive certain vaccines for medical reasons.

Nutrition and Feeding

Good, well-balanced nutrition is critical at any stage of development, but especially during infancy and the growing years of childhood. Infants' needs are quite different from the nutritional needs of children or adults (USDA, 2020). Because newborns are just learning to suck and swallow, their nutrition must come in liquid form. Breast milk is the ideal food for infants (Simkin et al., 2018). The American Academy of Pediatrics (2019) recommends that infants be exclusively breastfed for about the first six months and to continue breastfeeding alongside the introduction of complementary foods for at least one year. Initial breast milk during the first week of lactation contains **colostrum**, a thick concentrated substance that contains high concentrations of nutrients and antibodies (American Academy of Pediatrics, 2012). Some of the benefits of breastfeeding include the following:

- Protection against disease
- Lower likelihood of developing infant asthma, obesity, respiratory infections, and gastrointestinal infections
- Development of stronger bones, making it easier to learn to stand and walk
- Easier transition to solid foods
- Lower likelihood of obesity later in life (Thompson et al., 2020; Wambach & Spencer, 2021).

In addition to its nutritional benefits, breastfeeding can positively impact both cognitive and socioemotional development. Researchers have found that breastfeeding for even 4 weeks is significantly associated with higher cognitive test scores later in life, and these benefits increase over time (Borro and Iacovou, 2012; Thompson et al., 2020; Wambach & Spencer, 2021).

The CDC published a Breastfeeding Report Card that provided data on breastfeeding practices and support throughout in the United States and its territories in 2019. The data from this report showed that, although most infants receive some breastmilk

Immunization Name	Purpose	Month Inoculation Is Given
Hepatitis B	Prevents a type of contagious liver infection	Three to four doses: at birth, within first 2 months, and between 6 to 18 months
Rotavirus	Prevents a virus that causes diarrhea; doses are swallowed, not injected	Two to three doses: at months 2, 4, and 6 if necessary
Diphtheria, tetanus, and pertussis	Prevents bacteria that causes diphtheria, a sickness that creates thick mucus in the back of the throat; also prevents tetanus (lockjaw) and pertussis (whooping cough)	Five doses: at months 2, 4, and 6, and between months 15 through 18; the fourth dose may be administered at 12 months if 6 months have passed since the third dose; the fifth dose is administered between ages 4–6
Hemophilus influenzae type b	Prevents bacteria that causes meningitis, pneumonia, and interference with the respiration system, other infections, or death from these complications	Three to four doses: at months 2, 4, and 6, and between months 12 and 15; a dose at month 6 may not be needed, which a doctor will help determine
Pneumococcal (pneumonia)	Prevents bacteria that causes pneumonia, meningitis, and blood infections, which can all be fatal to infants and children	Four doses: at months 2, 4, and 6, and between months 12 and 15
Inactivated poliovirus	Prevents a virus that causes polio, which causes paralysis and stiff joints; also prevents meningitis	Four doses: at months 2, 4, and between months 6 through 18; a fourth dose is given between the ages of 4 to 6
Influenza inactivated	Prevents the virus that causes the flu	Dose at 6 months and yearly afterwards.
Measles, mumps, and rubella	Prevents the virus that causes • measles—fever, rash, eye irritation, cough • mumps—fever, swollen glands, muscle pain • rubella—fever and rash	Two doses: between months 12 to 15, and again between the ages of 4 to 6; the second dose may be given earlier if one month passes in between the first and second doses
Varicella (chicken pox)	Prevents the chicken pox disease, which causes itching, rashes, and a fever	Two doses: between months 12 and 15; again between the ages of 4 to 6
Hepatitis A	Prevents a type of spreadable liver disease	Two doses: at month 12, and 6 to 18 months after the first dose
Meningococcal	Given in special circumstances to infants living in countries with epidemics, who travel internationally, or those who have an improperly functioning spleen	Dates given vary depending on the reason for this inoculation

Note: Recommendations are reviewed and updated regularly. Check for updates at the American Academy of Pediatrics (www.aap.org).

American Academy of Pediatrics

Table 4.8 Recommended Immunizations from Birth through Age 2

early in life, most are not exclusively breastfed or breastfed as long as recommended. Younger women who become mothers in their early twenties are less likely to breastfeed than older mothers. Fewer non-Hispanic Black infants are breastfed compared with Hispanic and non-Hispanic White infants. Racial differences may be influenced by corporate sway through advertising or product giveaways, cultural norms and values, laws that vary by state, and the media (Freeman, 2020). Infants who qualify for and receive the Special Supplemental Nutrition Program for Women, Infants, and Children (WIC) are less likely to be breastfed than infants ineligible for this federal program because formula is provided for free. Because of this statistic, WIC participants have access to a number of resources, including nutrition and breastfeeding counseling (US Department of Agriculture, Food and Nutrition Service, 2020).

Time, privacy, encouragement, and educational resources can help women commence and continue breastfeeding. Employers, childcare providers, and other community members can create environments that accommodate breastfeeding mothers, such as providing private, clean spaces where they can nurse or pump breast milk. Because the personal and societal barriers to breastfeeding can be complex, the US Surgeon General has made a Call to Action (2011) to change how the culture considers and talks about breastfeeding. This includes hospital lactation support after the child's birth and ongoing support and education. It also includes family and community support from infant caregivers, providing incentives for employers to accommodate breastfeeding mothers and changing public opinion to promote breastfeeding for at least the first 6 months and ideally for the first year of life (see Figure 4.20) (Simkin et al., 2018; Thompson et al., 2020; Wambach & Spencer, 2021; World Health Organization, 2017).

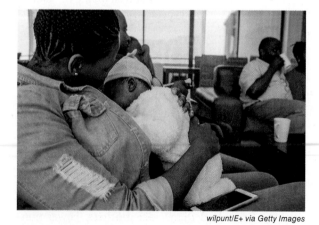

wilpunt/E+ via Getty Images

Figure 4.20 Time, privacy, encouragement, and social support from family members and friends can encourage the practice of breastfeeding.

For a variety of reasons, some primary caregivers feed their infants formula. Sometimes it is not possible for a mother to breastfeed. Adoption, surrogacy, low milk production, health issues, and medication use can make breastfeeding difficult or impossible. In these cases, careful selection of a nutritious formula can meet an infant's nutritional needs. Other life situations, such as working several jobs, lack of support from a partner, or even personal choice, influence the decision about whether to breastfeed. Extended family members, friends, and others surrounding a family need to respect and support the caregiver's decision about the best way to nurture their infant.

As infants develop over the first year, they can handle solid foods when combined with a liquid nutrient such as breast milk or formula (Siega-Riz et al., 2010; Taveras et al., 2009). Because infants grow and develop during infancy faster than at any other time in their lives, adequate intake of protein and iron is essential. When breast milk or fortified baby formula is concluded too early, it is difficult for infants to receive proper nutrition, which negatively impacts their growth and development (Biesalski & Black, 2016).

After babies reach the age of 6 months, it is important that their primary caregivers have access to affordable supplemental baby food, followed by nutritious food for toddlers. WIC, which is administered through a number of state agencies, including hospitals, schools, Indian Health Services facilities, and county health communities, is funded with grants from the US government. Specialized infant formula, baby food, fruits and vegetables, dairy products, protein products, and whole-grain products are some of the nutritious foods made available to eligible mothers and young children. WIC offers health and immunization screenings and substance abuse screenings, among other services.

Infants in the toddler stage have progressed beyond baby foods. They learn to feed themselves and use a cup (see Figure 4.21). Toddlers can also eat foods prepared for the family rather than requiring separate food. They can pick up bite-sized foods and chew and swallow various solid foods. Toddlers' stomachs are small, and they prefer to eat small portions many times during the day. Long periods between meals do not sustain them well as their energy needs are high. Their taste buds are more sensitive than those

Figure 4.21 Toddlers learn to feed themselves by using a cup (A) AND with utensils (B)

of adults, and caregivers often interpret this as picky behavior. An assortment of flavors and textures can help toddlers enjoy a wider variety of foods (Avena, & Ferreira, 2018).

To promote bone growth and strength, toddlers typically need to drink 2 cups of whole milk each day. They also need to eat a variety of nutritious foods, including plenty of fruits and vegetables. Eating an excessive number of foods that are high in calories and low in nutritional value, such as junk foods, can cause toddlers to gain too much weight. It is also when food allergies may appear (Sicherer, 2011). Physicians can help determine a toddler's nutritional needs based on their height, weight, and physical activity level (Wyness et al., 2013).

Toddlers are known for being fussy eaters. They may dislike, refuse, or play with their food. With patience, caregivers can address these issues. The following are tips to help prevent feeding issues:

- Offer food on a predictable schedule so the toddler is likely to be hungry.
- Respond to the child's feeding needs in prompt, emotionally supportive ways.
- Serve foods in smaller portions. Limit the amount of food on the plate; too much food can be overwhelming.
- Use finger foods and avoid mixing foods in dishes such as casseroles or salads. Toddlers prefer foods to be separated.
- Introduce a new food by placing the food alongside favorite foods.
- Make sure the toddler is comfortable during mealtimes.
- Ensure that the food is at a proper height, that the plate is within reach, and that the toddler's feet are on a high-chair footrest or on the floor.
- Provide toddler-friendly flatware, including larger, softer forks and spoons, and smaller, graspable cups.
- Limit distractions during mealtime. Toddlers are easily distracted by music or the television.
- Correct behavior when toddlers begin to play with food. Explain that the food is for eating and not for playing. When you see the toddler is finished eating, take the plate away before they begin to play with food.
- Allow the toddler to eat the foods on the plate in any order.

Primary caregivers and educators should maintain a positive attitude during mealtimes, model positive eating habits, and help the toddler when needed. If the toddler does not know how to self-feed, guide them to help with the feeding process. Toddlers also like colorful foods with fun shapes. Visit www.chooseMyPlate.gov to view the food requirements of toddlers.

Infants and Sleep

Newborn infants sleep most of the day and night. Typically, they sleep for about 3 hours and are awake for 1 hour, repeating the pattern around the clock, which results in 16–17 hours of sleep per day. Half of that sleep time is spent in rapid eye movement (REM) sleep, which is more active than deep sleep (Dereymaeker et al., 2017). This sleeping pattern

Practical Issues and Implications

Toddlers as "Foodies"

Infants have a long-held reputation of being averse to new, and especially spicy, foods. But market trends show that many young children are actually food connoisseurs. When infants are old enough to have developed the necessary skills, they easily transition to family table food. This often includes a variety of food items and types, including those that are unique to the family's cultural traditions. Some childcare centers offer a broad range of ethnic food varieties.

Like the adult food market, the organic movement has impacted baby food. Many consumers desire fruits and vegetables from growers that abstain from using chemicals in growing their produce. Many also seek additive-, dye-, and preservative-free foods.

Food packaging for children has evolved through the years. Squeeze pouches filled with vegetable, fruit, and grain "smoothies" are increasingly popular. Sweet potatoes, carrots, pear, apple, blueberry, banana, flax, and oats are a few popular ingredients. Many food manufacturers are jumping on the trend for naturally grown foods, so baby food has become a big business. For example, in 2018, worldwide baby food sales amounted to over $59 billion; between 2018 and 2023, baby food sales worldwide are projected to increase by 5.4% per year (Degenhard, 2019).

Think About It:

- What are the trends you are seeing in infant food products?
- Do they primarily focus on convenience, nutrition, or taste preferences?
- Is nutrition or marketing the primary focus?

can be very inconsistent as infants adjust to changes in their health and environment. Although this pattern works for the infant's needs, caregivers often find it difficult. During this time, it is essential for caregivers to be patient with their infants and responsive to their cries (McHale et al., 2017; Simkin et al., 2018).

Some infants appear over-alert and cannot achieve restful sleep. They may fuss or cry regularly. Caregivers can help struggling infants by assisting them to self-regulate. The swaddling technique is both a traditional and current practice among new primary caregivers (see Figure 4.22). By wrapping them tightly in a light blanket, forming a cocoon that only exposes their head, the infant feels a sense of security and calmness that simulates their recent pre-birth state in utero (Adolph et al., 2010; Simkin et al., 2018). Many caregivers find that a gentle rocking in a vertical position may enhance the calming effect of swaddling. As the infant develops, the swaddling time is reduced until it is no longer needed.

An infant's sleep needs change over the first few months of life. At age 3 or 4 months, infants sleep more at night than during the day, often 6–7 hours per night with a morning and afternoon nap. At 4 months to 12 months, infants should sleep 12 to 16 hours per 24 hours (including naps) on a regular basis (Paruthi et al., 2016). By 6 months, many infants begin sleeping through the night plus continuing daytime naps. Their rapid eye movement (REM) sleep decreases at the same time.

After 6 months of age, physical development, culture, and caregiving practices play a more significant role in infant sleep patterns. As infants grow, their stomachs can hold larger amounts for longer periods of time, especially if solid foods are introduced in the second 6 months. They also often adapt to the schedule of the household, following its sleeping and waking patterns more closely. In some cultures, infants are carried more, resulting in lighter sleeping throughout the day. Preparing infants for sleep time by singing and rocking them contributes to self-regulatory behavior and an ability to fall asleep as they mature (American Academy of Pediatrics, 2014).

Toddlers often need about 11 to 14 hours of sleep per 24 hours, including naps (Paruthi et al., 2016). They usually have more regular sleep schedules than during infancy, and they sleep for longer periods of time. However, it may be difficult to get them into bed or to transition from wake time to sleep time. Research shows that if the bedtime routine is more consistent, toddlers will wake during the night less often (Covington et al., 2019; Kitsaras et al., 2018). More consistent sleep in the early years is associated with later neurocognitive cognitive development, including language acquisition and socioemotional and physical health (Mindell & Williamson, 2018).

Primary caregivers often need to help toddlers calm down and relax before sleep time; evening

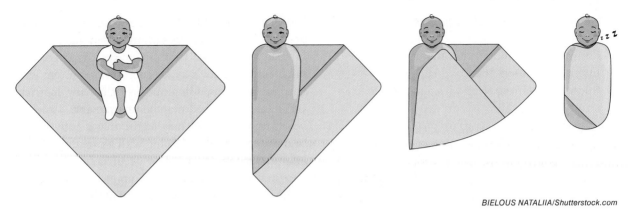

Figure 4.22 Wrapping or swaddling a young infant snugly can calm their nerves.

rituals such as bath time or story times can help. Toddlers may become fearful and have nightmares. When this occurs, toddlers need comforting to feel safe and secure. Placing a night-light in the room or sleeping with a stuffed animal can often help toddlers feel safe. At times, toddlers will get out of bed during the night simply to see what is happening. Primary caregivers may often need to firmly but calmly prompt toddlers to return to bed so they can get the sleep they need (Gradisar et al., 2016).

The practice of training a child to sleep alone is based on ideologies that claim more independence and infant safety. Co-sleeping does not necessarily mean sleeping in the same bed, but it may include sleeping in the same room or in close vicinity as recommended by the American Academy of Pediatrics (Moon et al., 2016). Although sleep routines, including scheduled naps or rest times, are practiced in most early childhood care facilities in the United States, a more naturalistic approach to sleep and body rhythms may be practiced at home (Gross-Loh, 2013). This is another example of the importance of family and non-custodial caregiver communication about expectations, ideals, and practices to support healthy sleep habits (Harvey, 2021). Chapter 6 explores infant and child sleep culture further.

Sudden Unexpected Infant Death and Sudden Infant Death Syndrome

Sudden unexpected infant death (SUID) and **sudden infant death syndrome (SIDS)** refer to an infant's unexplained death, usually during the first year. SUID occurs from various means, including suffocation, an infection or virus that impedes breathing, entrapment between objects, ingestion of an object that blocks breathing, or other diseases or trauma (US Department of Health and Human Services, 2021). SIDS is a type of SUID where the cause of death is unknown. Over 95% of SIDS occurs in infants aged 6 months or younger (Duncan & Byard, 2018; Kinney & Thach, 2009). The risk of SIDS is highest when an infant is between 2 and 4 months (Duncan & Byard, 2018; Fleming et al., 2015).

New research indicates SIDS may be related to an irregularity in the infant's sleeping pattern, resulting in the inability to awake from sleep (Duncan & Byard, 2018). Another possible cause is a buildup of carbon dioxide in the infant's bloodstream. No definitive cause of SIDS is yet known, and most believe the cause is multifactorial and usually determined by eliminating other causes of death (Duncan & Byard, 2018). Several other factors that may increase the potential of SIDS include the following:

- Exposure to alcohol, tobacco, or other drugs during pregnancy
- Exposure to secondhand smoke after birth
- Lack of prenatal care
- Teen pregnancy
- Premature or multiple births

On the other hand, the following precautions may help to prevent SIDS (Moon, 2016; Carlin & Moon, 2017; Sidebotham et al., 2018; Cohen, 2019):

- Place infants to sleep on their backs. Do not allow infants to sleep on their stomachs. "Back to sleep" is a good way to remember this important precaution.
- Ensure that bedding is not too soft and pillows or stuffed animals are not in the crib.

- Do not allow infants to sleep in the same bed as caregivers.
- Ensure that the room is not too warm and that infants do not feel hot.
- Allow the infant to sleep with a pacifier to keep airways open.

In the United States, SUIDS, including SIDS, are more prevalent in minority groups (Leu et al., 2020). This may be attributed to a lack of knowledge, financial struggles, or cultural beliefs that do not align with recommended care practices. Studies have shown that infant mortality rates decline when hospitals and birth centers communicate recommended sleep practices. However, even with increased public health campaigns and education, financial struggles or cultural expectations may discourage or prevent safe sleeping practices. Obtaining a firm baby mattress and a safe infant bed may be unattainable. Cultural beliefs and traditions may advise that a baby would be more comfortable sleeping with a caregiver or that infant mortality is a random occurrence rather than preventable (Leu et al., 2020; Kim & Pearson-Shaver, 2021; Stiffler et al., 2018). Figure 4.23 shows an example of a safe sleep environment.

What Does A **Safe Sleep Environment** Look Like?

The image below shows a safe infant sleep environment.

Baby's sleep area is in the same room, next to where parents sleep.

Use a firm and flat sleep surface, such as a mattress in a safety-approved crib*, covered by a fitted sheet.

Baby should not sleep in an adult bed, on a couch, or on a chair alone, with you, or with anyone else.

Do not smoke or let anyone else smoke around your baby.

Do not put pillows, blankets, sheepskins, or crib bumpers anywhere in your baby's sleep area.

Keep soft objects, toys, and loose bedding out of your baby's sleep area. Make sure nothing covers the baby's head.

Dress your baby in sleep clothing, such as a wearable blanket. Do not use a loose blanket, and do not overbundle.

Always place your baby on his or her back to sleep, for naps and at night.

NIH Eunice Kennedy Shriver National Institute of Child Health and Human Development

SAFE TO SLEEP

* A crib, bassinet, portable crib, or play yard that follows the safety standards of the Consumer Product Safety Commission (CPSC) is recommended. For information on crib safety, contact the CPSC at **1-800-638-2772** or http://www.cpsc.gov.

National Institute of Child Health and Human Development

Figure 4.23 This infographic developed by the National Institutes of Health provides tips to caregivers on best practices for creating a safe sleep environment for an infant.

Toilet Learning in Toddlerhood

One of the most controversial topics in early childhood is when to initiate and how to teach toileting skills to children. Many experts agree that toilet learning should not start until the young child is ready and able to exert bodily control so as not to cause anxiety or stress (Hallas, 2019).

How do primary caregivers know when children are ready to begin toilet learning? A toddler's maturity in other domains is necessary for successful toilet training. These include cognitive understanding, social awareness, physical sensing of the urge to go, and language development. For example, social awareness, desire for approval, and self-mastery are the skills and aptitudes needed for toilet training (Kaerts et al., 2012; Kiddoo, 2012). One common sign that a child might be ready for toilet learning is when they recognize their need to "go." A child might also feel more uncomfortable wearing diapers.

To be successful, children must be able to follow simple directions and demonstrate some bodily control. Usually, this does not happen until a child is at least 18 months of age, and the process typically takes months to complete. Even after training is complete, accidents may occur for months or years before a young child can stay dry overnight. Many children can stay dry after age 5, but some, especially boys, lag (Hallas, 2019; Halligan & Luyben, 2009; Kaerts et al., 2012). The process of toilet learning is another example of the importance of family and non-custodial caregiver communication about expectations, ideals, and common or shared practices to support healthy and effective toilet training.

☑CHECKPOINT

☐ Why are well-baby exams recommended? What is vaccination, and what is its purpose?

☐ What is the ideal food for infants? Why?

☐ About how many hours of sleep do infants need each day?

☐ What are SUID and SIDS? What are some ways they can be prevented?

☐ Describe factors that might indicate that an infant is ready for toilet training.

Apply Here!

As a care provider, how can you provide emotional support to the sleep-deprived parents of a newborn baby? How can you provide information and support for parents who are starting to toilet train their toddler?

4.5 Infants with Disorders Related to Physical Development

Although everyone develops at slightly different rates, primary caregivers and early childhood educators should note an infant's difficulties in reaching developmental milestones (see Figure 4.24). If a developmental delay is evident, the infant may be displaying signs of a disability, such as a loss of hearing. Hearing impairment can be present at birth or may develop from an illness, head injury, or other accident. Signs of hearing impairment include a lack of babbling, lack of attention to noise, and other language delays. In cases where hearing loss exists at birth, the infant may need to learn sign language. If an infant has reduced hearing ability, hearing aids, surgery, and other therapies are available to enhance hearing ability (American Academy of Pediatrics, 2012; US Centers for Disease Control and Prevention, 2019; US Department of Education, Office of Special Education Programs, 2019).

Another physical and cognitive disability that may become apparent during the infant years is cerebral

Olesia Bilkei/Shutterstock.com

Figures 4.24 Sensory development is important for all infants, regardless of their abilities or sensory impairments.

palsy. This condition develops due to brain damage, which may have occurred during fetal development, the birthing process, or shortly after birth. Because brain damage affects motor skills and language development, signs of cerebral palsy may include significant delays or difficulties in swallowing, sitting up, walking, and using speech. Cerebral palsy becomes noticeable as the child grows and misses developmental milestones. Cerebral palsy is not curable; but it can be treated with speech and physical therapies, medications, and specialized education (Goldstein & Reynolds, 2011; Levitt & Addison, 2019).

Other disabilities that impact physical development include muscular dystrophy, cystic fibrosis, and blindness, described in Table 4.9. Note that this list is not meant to be exhaustive; it is a representative sample of the conditions. Being aware of these potential special needs increases the likelihood of early treatment, which may improve the child's long-term well-being. Other conditions that may be classified as cognitive, such as Down syndrome, may also impact physical growth and development, and are discussed in Chapter 5.

☑ CHECKPOINT

☐ What is cerebral palsy? How can cerebral palsy be treated?

☐ List and describe three or more other diseases or conditions that may influence infant physical growth and development.

☐ What are some potential signs of physical disability?

Apply Here!

Consider all that you have learned about sensory development throughout the chapter. Remember, when caregivers engage infants in developmentally appropriate sensory play, it builds brain pathways and supports language development, memory, and motor skills. Now imagine that an infant diagnosed with a particular sensory impairment was recently placed in your care. How might you go about learning more about this specific sensory impairment? How would you modify the environment in ways that could still support sensory development? Review Table 4.4 and consider which suggestions you could use and which ones might need modification for a specific sensory impairment such as sight or hearing.

Disease, Disorder or Developmental Challenge	Description	Medical Intervention or Treatment
Cerebral palsy	A muscle and movement disorder caused by a prenatal abnormality or disruption in brain development; types vary depending on which part of the brain is affected and include stiff muscles (spasticity), uncontrollable movements (dyskinesia), and poor balance and coordination (ataxia); most common form is muscle spasticity	Occupational therapy, a caregiving environment that promotes physical development
Cystic fibrosis	A genetic disorder that affects the lungs, pancreas, and other body organs due to thick mucus buildup, making it difficult for internal organs to operate effectively	Minimizing contact with germs, since the mucus obstructs the airways and traps germs, including bacteria that may lead to infections, inflammation, or respiratory failure
Deafness and blindness	Simultaneous hearing and visual impairments	Caregiving environment that promotes communication strategies between child and others
Deafness	A hearing impairment that causes difficulties in processing linguistic information, with or without hearing amplification	Caregiving environment that promotes alternative language strategies between child and others

(Continued)

US Department of Education, Office of Special Education Programs, 2019

Table 4.9 Conditions and Disorders Related to Physical Growth and Development

Disease, Disorder or Developmental Challenge	Description	Medical Intervention or Treatment
Visual impairment including blindness	An impairment in vision that includes both partial sight and blindness even with eyeglasses or medical procedures/surgery	Medical care and occupational therapy; a caregiving environment that promotes sensory development, physical exploration, and communication
Hearing impairment	A hearing deficiency that is not deafness but impairs the processing of linguistic information whether permanently or periodically	Medical devices such as a hearing aid or cochlear implants; a caregiving environment that promotes alternative language strategies between the child and others
Fetal alcohol syndrome	A collection of conditions that result from prenatal exposure to alcohol through maternal consumption; symptoms vary by timing and quantity of exposure, but often include central nervous system (CNS) problems, minor facial feature defects, growth problems, birth defects, and cognitive issues such as learning, memory, attention span, vision, hearing, or communication challenges	Treatment depends on the specific condition and severity; medical care can include medication and occupational therapy focusing on learning
Miscellaneous medical conditions	Serious conditions such as cancer, cleft palate, or heart defects that may affect the physical development of a child due to illness, surgeries, and other medical procedures	Treatment depends on the specific condition, as well as caring and knowledgeable caregivers
Muscular dystrophy	A complex genetic disease that causes muscles to weaken over time; part of its complexity is that it can appear at different life stages, vary in severity, and impact different muscle groups	Early intervention is critical; occupational therapy and a caregiving environment that promotes physical development
Neonatal abstinence syndrome	Prenatal exposure to opioid and other drugs, such as such as heroin, codeine, oxycodone (Oxycontin), and methadone that cause a host of drug withdrawal symptoms; symptoms include excessive crying, irritability, seizures, and a variety of sleep, feeding, and breathing issues	Medical care that monitors the overall health of the infant and includes medication to treat withdrawal symptoms; a caregiving environment that promotes skin-to-skin contact, reduced light and noise stimulation, and gentle rocking
Orthopedic impairment	Impairments of the skeleton, including the bones, joints, muscles, ligaments, and nerves, including those caused by congenital anomalies or by amputation, burns, or fractures	Occupational therapy, a caregiving environment that promotes physical development
Sensory integration difficulties	Difficulty tolerating or processing sensory information such as sound, taste, sight, or touch; not diagnosed as a disorder typically associated with autism spectrum disorders, attention-deficit/hyperactivity disorder, developmental coordination disorders, and childhood anxiety disorder	Medical care and occupational therapy focusing on integrating the senses

US Department of Education, Office of Special Education Programs, 2019

Table 4.9 Continued

Summary

Infants experience significant growth and development from birth. Height, weight, limbs, and teeth continue to grow. They use their senses—taste and oral exploration, sight, smell, touch, and sounds—to learn about the world. During infancy, both the brain and nervous system continue to develop rapidly. Both gross and fine motor skills develop sequentially, keeping many infants in constant motion as they begin to creep, crawl, walk, run, use the pincer grasp, and scribble.

An infant's interaction with the environment is vital; cognitive and socioemotional development are strongly tied to physical development and exploration. In the upcoming chapters, you will learn how infants who engage in physical activity to explore their environment and those who have caregivers who interact with them and encourage them to explore are more apt to develop strong brain pathways. As you begin the next chapter, consider how cognitive changes intersect with physical changes and vice-versa.

Learning Outcomes and Key Concepts

4.1 Describe the physical qualities of neonates and methods for assessing health and wellness following birth.

- Newborns are adaptable and resilient and begin adapting to their environment right after birth.
- Average newborns are about 20" long and weigh about 7 to 7.5 pounds.
- Genetics, health status, and culture influence variations in length and weight.
- Infants deprived of physical touch have impaired growth and development.
- Newborns can feel heat, cold, pressure, and pain.
- Newborn hearing does not mature fully until about halfway through the first year of life.
- Newborns' sense of smell is well developed, and they prefer familiar smells.
- Newborns' vision takes up to a year to mature to the adult level.

4.2 Explain the physical development of infants, including sensory abilities, bodily changes, and motor skills.

- Infants can distinguish between tastes, showing a distinct preference for sweet flavors.
- Breastfed infants are exposed to a larger variety of foods than a baby who is formula-fed.
- Infants show voice preferences, but hearing does not fully mature for about 6 months.
- Vision is the least developed sense for infants, as eyes are structurally immature at birth.
- An infant can triple in weight and double in length in the first year of life.
- First teeth erupt around 6 months of age then continue at a rapid pace throughout infancy.
- Gross and fine motor skill development are linked to interaction with the environment.

4.3 Summarize brain and nervous system development during infancy.

- During infancy, both the brain and nervous system continue to develop rapidly.
- The brain has three distinct, synchronous parts: brain stem, cerebellum, and cerebral cortex.
- The limbic system involves instinctive behaviors and reactions.
- Brain synapses are formed quickly and peak at about 4 months of age.
- Negative experiences can affect the development of the brain during infancy.
- Abusive head trauma from rough handling is a leading cause of death among young infants.

4.4 Recognize the determinants of health and wellness in infancy.

- Infants require preventive and regular medical care throughout infancy.
- Recommended vaccinations produce immunity to specific diseases.
- If possible, infants should be exclusively breastfed for the first 6 months.
- Breastfeeding provides many nutritional benefits, but it may also positively affects cognitive and socioemotional development.

- Infants' sleep needs change dramatically over time, although sleep remains important.
- Toilet learning should not start until the young child is ready and able to exert bodily control.
- Sudden infant death syndrome (SIDS) is an unexplained cause of death of an infant.

4.5 Identify some disorders that may influence infant physical development.

- Caregivers should note a child's difficulties in reaching developmental milestones.
- Signs of hearing impairment include a lack of babbling, attention to noise, and language delays.
- Cerebral palsy may include significant delays in swallowing, sitting up, walking, or speech.
- Other disabilities include cystic fibrosis, muscular dystrophy, and physical impairments.

Chapter Review

1. Name and describe how a neonate's health and well-being are typically assessed soon after birth. Provide two specific examples of assessments.
2. How do infants use their senses to familiarize themselves with their environment and with their caregivers? Be as specific as possible.
3. How does motor activity develop during infancy?
4. Identify the physical developmental milestones achieved during the infant years.
5. Explain why regular and preventive medical care is essential during infancy. What are some of the risks for infants who do not receive such care?
6. Create a case study that demonstrates successful toddler toilet learning.
7. Write a newsletter article for expectant teen parents that defends a decision to breastfeed infants.

Matching

Match the following terms with the correct definitions.

A. brain stem
B. cerebellum
C. cerebral cortex
D. frontal lobe
E. hippocampus
F. hypothalamus
G. left hemisphere
H. limbic system
I. lobes
J. occipital lobe

1. the four smaller units within the right and left hemispheres of the cerebral cortex
2. the interrelated areas of the brain used in emotions, instinctive behaviors and reactions, and some other behaviors
3. the back of each cerebral hemisphere, containing the centers of vision and reading ability
4. occupies the front part of the brain and regulates the perception of touch, pressure, temperature, and pain
5. the part of the brain in the back lower area of the cerebrum that regulates muscle coordination, movement, posture, and balance
6. the front, top regions of each of the cerebral hemispheres that regulate emotions, problem-solving, executive functions, and voluntary movements
7. the base of the brain that connects the brain's cerebrum to the spinal cord and controls many instinctive and motor functions
8. a part of the brain's limbic system that contributes to spatial learning, short- and long-term memory, and navigation
9. sometimes referred to as the "control center" of the brain and regulates responses to stress through the production of specific hormones
10. the left part of the cerebral cortex

5

Infant Cognitive Development

Learning Outcomes

After studying this chapter, you will be able to:

5.1 Describe ways that infants learn about their world.

5.2 Summarize social and behavioral cognition in infancy.

5.3 Explain how language is learned, including the developmental language milestones often achieved during infancy.

5.4 Identify some disorders that may influence infant cognitive development.

Key Terms

child-directed speech
delayed imitation
expanding technique
holophrases
imitation
infantile amnesia
interactionist theory

intermodal perception
labeling
language acquisition device (LAD)
memory
mirror neurons
neuroplasticity

object permanence
recast
receptive language
scaffolding
serve-and-return interaction
telegraphic speech
vocabulary spurt

Introduction

Have you ever engaged in peek-a-boo with an infant? If so, you have witnessed the delight of repeated wonder when the person or object is revealed. Over time, this game between a caregiver and infant loses its impact as the element of surprise fades away. This is a sign of learning. But how do infants learn? What do infants know? Can they organize or remember?

Physical, cognitive, and socioemotional development go hand in hand. As infants explore their world, their learning increases as they organize their experiences. They learn to integrate what they sense (see, hear, feel, smell, and taste) with motor skills (actions). Infants are active learners, not passive recipients of information. Their perceptions are also profoundly influenced by their experiences. When studying infant cognitive development, some researchers focus on innate abilities while others focus on the impact of learning and experience. Both types of research contribute to our understanding of the cognitive development of infants

As you read this chapter, think of how the new information presented in the text matches or challenges your prior understanding of infant cognitive development. Think of the direct connections between what you already know about infant physical development and what you will learn about infant cognitive and, eventually, socioemotional development. Learning and building on what is already known is how an infant's senses and cognitive functioning mature and develop.

5.1 How Infants Learn

What do we know about how infants think and learn? As described in Chapter 4, infants' brains go through tremendous physical development and changes. During infancy, neurons in the brain proliferate and form a network of interconnected pathways. In fact, during infancy, the brain makes more connections than it will ever need. During the second year of infancy, the neuron pathways continue to develop. Some neurons are reinforced, while others are trimmed away. Just as is done when pruning a rose bush, trimming away unnecessary branches helps strengthen those that need it most. Experiences strengthen the most relevant connections and eliminate those that are no longer used. These adaptive changes make the brain more efficient (Kolb et al., 2017; Sakai, 2020). These physical changes within the brain result in observable and measurable cognitive changes during infancy and beyond.

When infants begin to crawl or scoot, they may be fearless about going over the edge of a bed, changing table, or other ledges. However, once infants begin crawling, caution replaces this fearlessness.

As described in Chapter 4, very young infants seem drawn to exploring a ledge rather than fearful of it. However, they become more cautious at about 9 months of age and avoid drop-off ledges. Researchers believe this avoidance has more to do with natural cognitive maturation than with negative experiences or newly acquired depth perception. However, individual temperament may also play a part (Adolph et al., 2014; Dahl et al., 2013; Ueno et al., 2012). What remains to be discovered is why this usually develops between ages 7 to 12 months rather than earlier. Some believe it may be tied to an innate need to explore.

Infants love to put objects into their mouths, exploring how they taste and feel. They touch, feel, and move things around. They respond to sensations and stimuli. For example, an infant may respond to a toy's loud rattle by turning and looking as a caregiver shakes it nearby. The toy's bright colors, the sound it emits, and the caregiver's voice may motivate the child to reach out. The infant then integrates what they touch and feel into other experiences they have had, such as the color and sound of an object, the caregiver's personality, and previous experiences of cause and effect.

New research shows that infant babbling changes how primary caregivers respond and speak to their infants. A caregiver may use shorter sentences or even one-word responses when responding to the infant's babbling. This suggests that infants are participants in shaping their learning environments (Elmlinger et al., 2019). With each new sensory exploration, infants integrate the information they obtain, and cognitive development occurs. The process of bringing together input from multiple senses is called **intermodal perception** (Baillargeon, 2004; Cohen, 2018). Throughout infancy and beyond, infants play a critical role in directing their own dynamic learning (Begus et al., 2014; Xu, 2019).

As described in Chapter 4, an infant's brain architecture includes a network of interconnections formed of specialized nerve cells called neurons. Neuron communication creates pathways or synapses within the brain (Barkovich & Raybaud, 2019; Numan, 2020; Perlman et al., 2019). **Mirror neurons** are a type of neuron that modify their activity when another person expresses emotion or performs a specific action. Neonates can recreate a caregiver's facial expression by replicating the caregiver's action

LaylaBird/iStock via Getty Images Plus

Figure 5.1 Mirror neurons modify their activity when the infant observes a specific motor action or another person expresses an emotion. This is shown here as the infant recreates their caregiver's facial expression.

of slowly and repeatedly sticking out their tongue (see Figure 5.1) (Arturo et al., 2016; Simpson et al., 2014). Later, after a caregiver raises and waves their hand and says, "bye-bye," an infant may lift an arm and eventually wave their hand. Likewise, infants may cry or feel sad when they observe sadness in others. They often laugh when they hear and see others laugh. Mirror neurons are not simply modeling or replicating the behaviors of others; powerful brain mechanisms allow imitation when mirror neurons are activated (Kilner & Lemon, 2013; Marshall & Meltzoff, 2014).

Infancy is considered a critical time for cognitive development. The young brain displays a heightened sensitivity to external stimuli that instructs and helps the infant adapt to their surroundings. This sensitivity is termed **neuroplasticity** or, more commonly, brain plasticity. Neuroplasticity refers to the brain's ability to undergo structural and neurochemical changes. It is not simply brain maturation, but a complex process that makes the developing brain especially sensitive to a wide range of experiences (Ismail et al., 2017; Kobl, 2018). During this sensitive period, the infant's brain is responsive and active; learning takes place faster and easier than at other times in life, especially in terms of sensation and language development. This makes infancy a prime time for exposure to sensory stimulation and language (Fandakova & Hartley, 2020). It also makes infancy a critical time in terms of the negative influences of poverty, neglect, caregiver stress, and inadequate infant care. These environmental triggers have been linked to psychological disorders later in life (Inguaggiato et al., 2017; Weyandt et al., 2020).

Piaget's Cognitive Developmental Theory

Jean Piaget placed a new focus on the cognitive development of infants. He was a groundbreaker in seeing great potential in an infant's cognitive abilities; and his work has been refined and added to since it was originally presented. Piaget theorized that the sequential nature of motor skill development and experiences directly relate to an infant's cognitive development. As described in Chapter 2, Piaget called this first stage of cognitive development the sensorimotor stage. In this stage, infants move from exhibiting reflexes to interacting with the world around them using their growing motor skills. Reaching, rolling, creeping, and crawling are significant signs of cognitive growth. Infants combine actions learned by using reflexes with motor skills to achieve additional goals. Their thinking is organized through concepts. These concepts are simple at first, but they gradually become more complex as their brains mature and their experiences increase over time (Barrouillet, 2015; Kenny, 2013; Mandler, 2004; Morra, 2008).

According to Piaget's theory, older infants who begin to walk, or toddlers, are still in the sensorimotor stage. Like younger infants, toddlers put objects in their mouths and discover through their senses, but they use their developing motor skills even more. Toddlers use discovery to solve problems such as building a tower out of blocks or running a toy car over a hurdle. Around 18 to 24 months, toddlers still figure things out using their senses, and they also start developing more sophisticated thought processes. For example, a toddler may stop to think about fitting a large object through a small opening rather than just physically testing to see if the object fits (Lerner et al., 2013).

Piaget's Six Stages of Sensorimotor Development

Piaget believed that an infant's sensorimotor development was orderly and consisted of six stages. The stages begin with reflexive reactions to environmental stimuli, and they gradually progress until the

final stage concludes with the beginnings of symbolic thought. Piaget often paired these steps into three overall stages: reflex and primary circular reactions, secondary circular reactions, and tertiary reactions (see Figure 5.2) (Lerner et al., 2013).

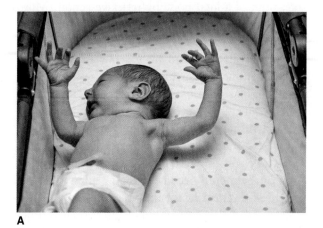

A

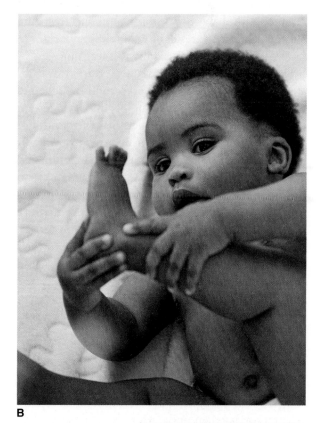

B

Andrey Zhuravlev/iStock via Getty Images Plus; PeopleImages/iStock via Getty Images Plus

Figure 5.2 Piaget believed that infant cognitive development was orderly, beginning with reflexive reactions to environmental stimuli (A) and gradually progressing until they start to focus on how their own bodies can impact their surroundings (B).

Infants, usually between birth to 4 months, are in the simple reflex stage (substage 1) and primary circular stage (substage 2). It is easiest to understand these stages when visualizing a baby's reactions to stimuli. At substage 1, the newborn will startle at the sound of a loud noise by reflexive action (Moro reflex). Usually, within 1 to 4 months, infants lying on their backs will react to a caregiver talking or singing directly to them by moving arms and legs in circular motions, which is substage 2, the primary circular reaction stage. These reactions seem simple, but they lay important foundations for present and future learning as infants respond to their immediate surroundings. An infant learns through trial and error—sometimes the waving of a hand in front of the mouth becomes rubbing a hand against the cheek. Eventually, the infant learns to place a fist in the mouth. Later, they might insert their thumb. This trial and error of infant learning becomes goal oriented as the baby moves from thumb sucking being a coincidence to the result of a plan. It is important to note that the infant is initiating this learning.

During the secondary circular reactions (substage 3) and coordination of secondary schemes (substage 4) stages, an infant begins to focus on how their own body can impact their surroundings. The infant may then start to focus on how their actions impact objects and other environmental events. Thus, primary circular reactions focus on the infant's body, whereas secondary circular reactions are repetitive reactions focused on the qualities of objects. The infant does the same action repeatedly, looking for a cause-and-effect reaction to their movements. These stages typically occur between 4 and 8 months of age. Toys that respond to the infant's actions, such as those that light up, rattle, or play music when the infant touches or shakes it, promote secondary circular reactions.

Object permanence, one of Piaget's core ideas, is the understanding that something still exists even when it is out of sight or can no longer be heard or touched. For example, a newborn does not respond when a toy is taken out of view, but a 6-month-old does. An 8-month-old will likely yank the blanket off a favorite toy when the toy has been covered, delighted and expecting to see it beneath. Piaget believed that understanding object permanence was an essential cognitive milestone during the first year of life, typically occurring around 8 months of age.

Piaget described the tertiary circular reaction stage (substage 5) as a time of purposeful exploration. Typically, this exploratory, almost scientific, behavior begins in earnest between ages 12 to 18 months. A baby or toddler may drop utensils or even a plate off a high chair tray just to see what happens. The infant may kick off shoes or pull off socks while riding in a car seat. An infant may shriek just to see the impact on others or to hear the sound. Through this trial-and-error experimentation, infants learn how things work and how others react to actions. Repetition helps learning, and experimentation may continue despite caregivers' negative reactions. However, finally, the infant will understand what is socially acceptable. The infant will begin responding to situations appropriately or using objects correctly.

Piaget described the invention of new means through mental combinations stage (substage 6) as the transitionary stage between the sensorimotor stage of infant cognitive development and the next pre-operational stage. During substage 6, toddlers begin to use symbolic thought. At about 18 months of age, toddlers begin mentally problem-solving rather than relying solely on the physical trial and error of earlier substages. For example, when something the toddler desires is out of their reach, they may devise a plan for getting around barriers to get the object. By this time, they are well on their way to using words as a form of symbolism (Goswami, 2010; Marti & Rodriguez, 2012; Miller, 2016; Singer & Revenson, 1996). Table 5.1 summarizes Piaget's six stages of sensorimotor development.

What Have We Learned Since Piaget?

Piaget introduced cognitive development as a process involving distinct and identifiable stages. Many researchers and developmental psychologists have added to this knowledge over the past decades. Some have even disregarded or disagreed with aspects of his theory. For others, further research has provided additional understanding.

Some researchers found that the concept of object permanence was understood at a younger age than Piaget proposed (Baillargeon et al., 1985; Baillargeon, 2004; Bogartz, 2000; Cohen, 2018). Infants as young as 4 months may show distress when an object is taken away, indicating their understanding that the object still exists. Current research is looking at how infants perceive objective permanence and

Piaget's Sensorimotor Sub-Stage	Age	Description
Simple reflex	Neonate	Reflexive movements
Primary circular	1–4 months	Movements of arms and legs in circular motion, related to the infant experiencing their own body
Secondary circular reactions	4–8 months	Movements in relation to objects that are intentional, such as placing a fist or pacifier in the mouth to suck on after unintentionally experiencing the pleasure before
Coordination of secondary schemes	8–12 months	Infant is more mobile, exploring environments and reactions with repeated actions such as shaking a rattle or other toy that makes noise
Tertiary circular reactions	12–18 months	Making purposeful actions while trying new ways to use their own body, such as yelling or dropping objects
Invention of new means through mental combinations	18–24 months	Transitioning toward Piaget's next stage, when symbolism is used to represent thoughts, such as using words or gestures

Kato

Table 5.1 Piaget's Six Stages of Sensorimotor Development

predict consequences of their own or others' actions, such as in a game where a person hides, then reappears and says, "peek-a-boo", or when a toy is a covered by a blanket (see Figure 5.3) (Koster et al., 2020).

One key research finding is that infants are born with an ability to coordinate the process of inter-modal perception, the bringing together of input from multiple senses. In other words, the ability to learn is inherent in newborns, and evidence suggests that fetuses learn in utero. Instead of happening in the first few months, as Piaget proposed, researchers now believe that infants have an innate ability to integrate

Odua Images/Shutterstock.com

Figure 5.3 Why does the game of peek-a-boo continue to bring pleasure to both infants and caregivers? How might infants learn to predict consequences through this game?

multiple senses. In addition, many researchers believe that infants are not as stage-bound as Piaget proposed; they claim that each individual infant cognitively develops in their unique way (Kenny, 2013).

Many critics proclaim that Piaget's theory of cognitive development is not specific enough. Piaget has been considered a pioneer in this field, but his initial sample was limited to his own six children. The combination of added knowledge, time, and continued experimentation lends itself to forthcoming details and understanding (Barrouillet, 2015; Marti & Rodriguez, 2012; Morra, 2008). Other critics focus on timing issues with some of his ideas. For example, Piaget thought that children began portraying **delayed imitation** at around 18 months. Delayed imitation is duplicating or copying another person's behavior after some time has passed instead of immediately. Research suggests that this occurs much earlier, even in infants as young as 9 or 10 months. Piaget also proposed that toddlers did not understand computational concepts, such as more or less, small or big, and tall or short, until after 2 years of age. More recent research shows that children may understand these concepts as early as 9 months of age (Christodoulou et al., 2017; Hespos & vanMarle, 2012). As caregivers count objects aloud, infants notice and remember. They understand numerical concepts far earlier than they can verbalize names (Wang & Feigenson, 2019).

Practical Issues and Implications

Is There an Easy Formula for Creating a "Smart Baby"?

When asked, many primary caregivers say that what they really want for their babies is for them to become happy adults. Although unstated, some caregivers may also hope that their child will be smart, bright, precocious, and academically gifted. Most researchers believe that an infant's intelligence is a product of both nature (genetics) and nurture (experiences). In the early 2000s, some entrepreneurs capitalized on the desire of some primary caregivers to have intelligent children by offering products that claimed to encourage intellectual development, even superiority, in young children, usually in the form of videos, games, and recordings.

What seems too good to be true is often just that. Instant formulas for creating a smart baby are similar to weight-loss plans that proclaim one can lose weight without diet or exercise. The early 2000s was a time when society was just learning about the impact of screen time on infant cognitive development. Many technologies were new, such as videos that could be displayed on smaller screens and placed in front of the infant. Product sales and promotions were tantalizing to parents wanting an easy way to create a smart baby. But these products' claims could not withstand scientific scrutiny; some companies folded because of lawsuits, while others were forced to rescind their false claims.

Around the same time, John Medina, a developmental molecular biologist, became fascinated with how the human brain works. In his book, *Brain Rules for Baby*, he describes how a child's brain develops—and how you can enhance it through experiences and interactions. Medina concluded that there is no one smart gene. Intelligence is not a simple concept, and in many ways, it is unmeasurable. He strongly advised caregivers not to expose infants to any screen time before 2 years of age. Instead, he proposed nurturing cognitive development through interactive talk and play. He encouraged breastfeeding to further help with cognitive development. As infants grow into toddlers and later enter preschool years, Medina encouraged primary caregivers to create a feeling of safety for them to promote the development of self-control—both of which are tied to cognitive development.

The American Academy of Pediatrics (AAP, 2016) recommends that caregivers refrain from exposing infants under 18 months to screen media. However, the AAP makes an exception to video chatting media for infants ages 0–18 months, but only with caregiver oversight. Viewing high-quality screen media is currently approved for infants between 18 and 24 months. The AAP also recommends that caregivers and toddlers interact with the media together (see Figure 5.4). The rationale is that toddlers

A

B

Julief514/iStock via Getty Images Plus; Jetta Productions Inc/DigitalVision via Getty Images Plus

Figure 5.4 Screen devices may be used as a learning and communication tool (A, B). What are the benefits of including caregiver interaction during infant screen use?

find screen media confusing without interaction with caregivers (American Psychological Association, 2020; Ashton et al., 2019; Strouse et al., 2018).

Current research does not support a quick fix to enhance cognitive development (Barrouillet, 2015; Cohen, 2018). Instead, face-to-face, interactive, and secure relationships over time best foster cognitive development. Stimulating environments that offer opportunities for exploration and abundant stimuli for the senses also reinforce it. Primary caregivers and educators can best nurture and enhance learning in infants using these methods. Most importantly, especially during infancy, learning is an active social activity. Effective caregivers praise an infant's attempts to learn new things. Enhancing cognitive development in infants goes back to the basics of social interaction and stimulation of the senses.

Think About It:

- Why do infant brain-enhancing products continue to lure new primary caregivers? How might they be appealing to toddlers in early childhood education programs? What are the pros and cons?

- Do you think that having a smart baby is a global or a Western ideal? Why?

Although Piaget's theory is continually updated, modified, and expanded, its foundation remains essential. In particular, although Piaget focused on an infant's maturation process as an individual, subsequent theorists have highlighted the importance of acknowledging outside influences, including caregivers and environmental factors, on an infant's cognitive development.

☑ CHECKPOINT

- ☐ What are Piaget's six stages of sensorimotor development?
- ☐ What is *object permanence*? Why is it used as a marker for tracking infant cognitive development?
- ☐ List and describe three specific post-Piaget findings on infant cognitive development.

Apply Here!

If you have access, take some time to sit and observe a neonate, baby, or toddler. If you do not have access, plenty of online videos are available showing infants interacting with caregivers. Do an online search and find examples of infants and toddlers engaging in conversation with others through facial expressions, crying, gestures, babbling, or spoken words. Summarize what you observe or experience. How do caregivers engage in conversations with infants? If an infant is presented with an item that is not familiar, in what ways do they respond? How do infants engage with, respond to, and reciprocate messages and gestures? In what ways do you observe infants learning about unfamiliar objects?

5.2 Social and Behavioral Cognition

Infants naturally learn from their primary caregivers, their closest and most important social relationships. They first learn about their primary caregiver and then about the world around them. Because infants have a keen sense of smell, they subsequently use this ability to identify their caregivers. This often happens within the first couple weeks of life (Adam-Darque et al., 2019). Touch and individual voice qualities also help the infant develop recognition. Sight is a critical part of recognizing other humans. When newborns view a human face, their eyes track around the perimeter or outer edges of the

Anna Kraynova/Shutterstock.com

Figure 5.5 Infants naturally learn about their primary caregivers as they interact together. What might the infant be learning about the caregiver in this setting?

face. Within the first 2 months, their eyes begin to focus on the center of the face, in the spot between the eyes and nose (see Figure 5.5). This visual focus on the center of a face continues throughout life and is an integral part of understanding communication (Braddick & Atkinson, 2011; Kimura et al., 2010).

When the senses of smell, touch, and sight are combined, the infant will often react with emotion as a sign of recognition (Bushall, 2003). If you have ever been greeted by a smiling baby who attempts to communicate with you through cooing sounds, smiles, or by outstretched arms, you know how wonderful it feels to have an infant communicate that they know you with facial expressions and body movements. By 2 years of age, that same infant might greet you verbally by calling your name.

Infants' genetic blueprint (what they are born with), social relationships, and environmental experiences shape their cognitive development. The most significant impact of brain-shaping relationships and experiences occurs during infancy. These first years form the foundation for a lifetime of learning (Center on the Developing Child at Harvard University, 2016; Wells, 2020; Xu, 2019). Because of this, infant maltreatment, exposure to toxic stress, or other forms of adversity in early life can negatively alter brain architecture in infants (Child Welfare Information Gateway, 2015; Garner, 2013; Hostinar et al., 2012; Orr & Kaufman, 2014). Brain architecture changes may include reduced brain activity, differences in overall brain volume, or lower volume white and gray matter in several brain areas (Bick, 2016; Nelson et al., 2020; Pierce et al., 2019).

Social relationships are essential in infant cognitive development because human interactions reinforce learning, especially when interactions are imitated or repeated. **Imitation** is an advanced behavior that occurs when one person observes and replicates another person's behavior; it often serves as a tool for infant learning. **Serve-and-return interaction**, the relationship between caregivers and infants, is like a game of volleyball or tennis. One person (infant or caregiver) sends a message, the other responds, and the interaction continues to volley. Often, this volleying includes imitation while adding to a message. Even neonates can imitate and participate in serve-and-return interactions through their eye-tracking and emotional expressions. If a caregiver smiles and interacts with an infant in a bright, happy manner, the infant will likely respond with a happy smile. If the emotion is combined with caregiver vocalizations, the infant will likely respond with vocalizations appropriate for their developmental age such as cooing, babbling, or laughing. For infants and their caregivers, serve-and-return becomes a natural interaction (see Figure 5.6). In the volleying back and forth, they learn to respond to and even predict each other's needs and responses (Cohen, 2018; Goswami, 2010; Legerstee et al., 2013; Wells, 2020; Xu, 2019).

As infants begin to integrate symbolic language through their expressions, bodily responses, imitation, and eventually spoken language, it enhances their social relationships and their understanding of the environment. It even subsequently changes the brain's neurotransmission. Infant social learning and the act of imitation are crucial parts of social survival that create brain changes and set infants up for the challenges ahead in life (Gopnik, 2016; Lally & Mangione, 2017; Meltzoff & Marshall, 2018).

The idea that learning is social is not new. As Lev Vygotsky theorized, caregivers are instrumental in an infant's learning (see Chapter 2). Vygotsky believed that children are social beings and develop their minds through interactions with primary caregivers, siblings, educators, and others in close relationships. This social interaction is critical to an infant's cognitive development (Bullard, 2014; Legerstee et al., 2013). Through these interactions, infants learn not only by exploring their world through their senses, but also by responding to and imitating others (Moore, 2010; Xu, 2019).

If social interaction is critical to infant cognitive development, what happens when intervening factors make the caregiving environment less optimal? Primary caregiver stress or mental illness, lack of adequate nutrition, unstable housing, and lack of quality childcare options may impact an infant's social learning environment. As a result, the infant's brain wiring may be affected, changing their cognitive trajectory for life, including the way they communicate (Betancourt et al., 2016; Blair & Raver, 2012, 2016; Hirsh-Pasek et al., 2015; Johnson et al., 2016). Many of these factors are present in situations

A   **B**

Alvarog1970/iStock via Getty Images Plus; Wavebreakmedia/iStock via Getty Images Plus

Figure 5.6 Infant and caregiver interactions reinforce learning through imitation and serve-and-return communications (A, B).
How are imitation and serve-and-return occurring in the interactions shown?

where poverty reduces resources and contributes to stress and anxiety in primary caregivers.

As introduced in Chapter 2, Vygotsky described the zone of proximal development (ZPD), or the level at which a child can learn with assistance (Barrouillet, 2015). **Scaffolding** helps bridge what an infant can cognitively understand or do and their developmental potential for understanding or doing. Much scaffolding may be necessary at first, but as the child performs a task more frequently, the scaffolding can be decreased and eventually removed, at which point a new ZPD forms (Vygotsky, 1978, 1993; Wertsch, 1984; Wertsch & Sohmer, 1995). When caregivers utilize the ZPD and assist infants at their current level of understanding, they break down the learning into smaller, attainable steps.

For example, caregivers may use scaffolding to help an infant learn to stand faster than if the infant was attempting it without help. Using scaffolding when the infant is developmentally ready, or in the ZPD, a caregiver helps by holding the infant upright or encouraging and providing props to lean against as they learn to balance. The mentor's support gradually decreases and eventually disappears as the child learns to stand independently and without support. Or a caregiver might assist an infant by holding a lidded cup with handles to the infant's mouth until the infant can manage the action independently. As a result of utilizing the ZPD, infants learn more quickly as they attain new skills without feeling overwhelmed (Moore, 2010; Xu, 2019).

How caregivers scaffold an infant is dependent on the cultural and social setting. Some parents use direct verbal instruction, or they physically guide motor skill development (see Figure 5.7). Others may use more facial expressions and gestures to guide learning (Gogate et al., 2015). As babies become toddlers, primary caregivers continue to influence their cognitive development significantly; and as toddlers become more social, peers may also provide an opportunity for further learning (Jung & Recchia, 2013; Mermelshtine, 2017; Williams et al., 2019).

Behaviorism

With new stimuli and with positive and negative responses, each interaction an infant has with another person plays a part in their learning. In a classic and well-known study, 2- to 3-week-old

Dragon Images/Shutterstock.com

Figure 5.7 How are the caregivers providing scaffolding and social support to this infant who is learning to walk independently?

infants were able to imitate the facial gestures of their adult caregivers (Meltzoff & Moore, 1977). The study demonstrated that even newborns could copy facial expressions; when the researcher held a newborn's face close to his own and slowly stuck out his tongue, each newborn imitated this behavior.

Human interaction is learned through experiences, especially when tied to human-to-human experiences (Lerner et al., 2013; Wells, 2020; Xu, 2019). One way that infants learn from experience is through operant conditioning, B.F. Skinner's theory (Skinner, 1953). For example, an infant responds to a stimulus. Depending on the result of their response, the infant will learn to repeat or stop this response. Imagine a primary caregiver singing a happy song to an infant who smiles and babbles in reply. The caregiver responds with a smile and words of praise, and the baby learns that these actions show a positive relationship with the caregiver. In essence, the caregiver is modeling behavior.

Modeling and imitation are essential parts of cognitive development for infants. Caregivers model responses to stimuli. Infants pay attention and imitate what they see and experience. Faces, voices, and physical touch are powerful communication tools used in creating effective learning environments for infants (Bandura, 1977; Moore, 2010; Thornton, 2003).

Infants are not pawns in the game of learning; they play an active role in deciding what will capture their attention and hold it and what the response might be. In other words, an infant may receive opportunities to interact with stimuli, but it is the infant's choice whether to respond or not, even at a very early age. They use their senses to perceive stimuli. How the infant responds is based on motivation, maturation, and experiences. Opportunities and the infant's response to them are what shape and mold the infant's brain (Center on the Developing Child at Harvard University, 2016; Wells, 2020; Xu, 2019).

Social Learning and Memory

Memory is central to cognition and cognitive development. Yet, the idea of **infantile amnesia**, the inability of adults to remember past episodic social events from infancy and early childhood, has been widely held for most of modern history. More current research shows that infantile amnesia is not necessarily true, but it is complicated (Legerstee et al., 2013). **Memory** is often defined as recalling experiences or thoughts from the past. Learning is considered forward moving through integrating new concepts. Differentiating between learning and memory really depends on definitions. An infant can learn how a toy operates, and it may require memory to repeat the action, but what differentiates it from learning? Likewise, remembering a face, reacting to a story that was heard as an infant or even in utero, or experiencing familiarity with a family pet is learning that requires memory (Reynolds & Romano, 2016).

Memory abilities develop over time, and even infants show indications that experiences become familiar or remembered (Bauer and Pathman, 2008). By age 6 months, infants begin to demonstrate even more familiarity with or memory of certain objects or people (Bauer & Pathman, 2008). Their memories are not always long-lasting, but as they develop, they are retained longer (Bauer, 2015; Madsen & Kim, 2016; Mullally & Maguire, 2014). This process is the same throughout life and explains why it is unusual for teens and adults to have memories of events much earlier than their third birthdays. As with adults, infants are more likely to make memories the closer the experience was in time. For example, depending on your age, your memories of your first day of high school may be sharp, or they may have faded with time. If that first day was emotional or traumatic, your likelihood of retaining a clear memory increases. Likewise, a 2-year-old will have clearer memories of an emotional experience at age one, but they are less likely to retain it with the same clarity once they are in grade school (see Figure 5.8).

DTeibe Photography/Shutterstock.com

Figure 5.8 How much of this experience would you expect this infant to remember? Will memories be short- or long-term? What might help memories of the family dog become long-term memories?

During the first months of infancy, the brain's prefrontal cortex (where memory storage of events occurs) is still immature, but that does not mean that infants cannot remember. Dramatic changes occur in the brain areas connected to memory in the first two years of life. Understanding infants' memories is complicated because they do not vocalize their thoughts using words. However, researchers gain insight into what infants remember by measuring and observing responses. Just as in older children, teens, and adults, using patterns and repetition increases the likelihood of remembering people and actions (Peterson et al., 2011; Rovee-Collier & Cuevas, 2009). As is true throughout life, what captures an infant's attention is most likely to be recalled, at least in the short term (Reynolds & Ramono, 2016; Ross-Sheehy et al., 2011; Simmering, 2012).

☑ CHECKPOINT

- ☐ Describe the interplay between genetics, social relationships, and environmental experiences in infant cognitive development.
- ☐ How do caregivers play a part in infant cognitive development?
- ☐ What is *operant conditioning*? Give an example from your observation of infants.
- ☐ What is the current thinking on childhood amnesia? Can infants remember? Why might the study of memory in infants be challenging to researchers?
- ☐ What is the impact of neglect on infant cognition?

Global Perspectives

Infant Maltreatment: Neglect

Infant mortality rates decreased dramatically between 1990 and 2018 (World Health Organization, 2019). This is good news. However, many infants are born into poverty conditions or lack adequate nutrition, which, as discussed previously, negatively affects brain development. Although infant mortality has decreased substantially, the ability of surviving newborns to thrive and meet their developmental potential is often impaired due to the same adverse environmental factors that negatively impact the optimal functioning of their primary caregivers (Spratt et al., 2012). Stress often affects the caregiver; subsequently, it may place the infant at risk for neglect. Infant neglect refers to inadequately providing the basic needs of food, housing, and safety. Neglect and abuse are associated with many disorders across the lifespan. These include poor health status, stunted cognitive and socioemotional development, and neurodevelopmental disorders such as attention-deficit/hyperactivity disorder (Zeanah & Humphreys, 2018).

Infant and child neglect are pervasive worldwide (Kobulsky et al., 2020). For example, El-Kogali & Krafft (2015) found that infants living in the conflict-ridden areas of the Middle East and North Africa are frequently prevented from engaging with parents in activities that promote learning. Specifically, two-thirds of children in the Republic of Yemen and about 60% of children in Djibouti were neglected or deprived of parental interaction, resulting in developmental delays in childhood cognitive development. Girma et al. (2019) looked at maternal depression in low- and middle-income countries where over 90% of children live. They found that it is relatively common in these countries, often negatively affecting a mother's ability to function in her caregiving role. Risk factors such as war or conflict, disasters, violence, migration, societal acceptance of spousal abuse, and a high prevalence of HIV/AIDS may contribute to maternal depression and, subsequently, infant neglect. Likewise, infants in institutional childcare settings, such as those in Romanian orphanages who were neglected and did not have caregiver engagement, demonstrated lower cognitive and language scores later in childhood. (Nelson et al., 2014; Spratt et al., 2012).

Infant neglect is an issue in the United States as well, where more than 75% of reported child maltreatment involves neglect (Burge et al., 2019; Logan-Greene, 2018). There is no federal definition of *neglect*, and states define it differently, so actual numbers are hard to establish. In the United States, infant neglect refers to inadequately providing basic needs and supervision and insufficiently providing for the infant's emotional and medical needs. The link between poverty and neglect of infant needs is well established (Lee et al., 2021). Neglect is also likely prevalent in more wealthy families, but because of resources to combat or thwart any investigations, rates of actual existence are not known (Logan-Greene, 2018). Regardless of socioeconomic standing, families that exhibit chronic or ongoing infant neglect are more likely to have younger parents, more children, higher rates of mental health issues, domestic violence, and parental cognitive development issues (Logan-Greene & Semanchin Jones, 2018). Mental health issues such as depression have been associated with infant neglect in the United States (Dubowitz, 2013; Lee, 2013). Postpartum depression can alter responses in mothers, making them less likely to accurately read their infant's social cues and respond to their needs (Brummelte & Galea, 2016; Nguyen et al., 2019).

The Committee on Global Strategy for Women's, Children's and Adolescents' Health—2016–2030 (World Health Organization, 2019a, 2019b) is working to provide a blueprint to ensure every newborn and mother survives and thrives. Even so, infant and child neglect continues to be widespread throughout the world. Because the scope, form, and definition of neglect vary, the task is challenging (Kobulsky et al., 2020).

To Think About:

- How would you define child neglect? Does it only mean failure to meet basic needs? Does it include socioemotional stimulation and care? Does it involve showing love, affection, or nurturing?

- Have you observed infant and child neglect in your community? What form does it take?

- Sometimes parents provide basic needs, but social interaction between the infant and caregiver is minimal due to caregiver distraction. What is the most common cause of caregiver distraction or inattention during infant care in your community? What is the societal cost of infant neglect or caregiver inattention?

Apply Here!

Have you observed people around you who are distracted by their smartphones? If so, what impact does their distraction have on their effective communication with or attention to those around them? How might smartphones and other screen technologies be distracting when caring for infants? Be specific. For example, these distractions may affect the caregiver's direct eye contact and interaction with infants. How can you ensure that the infants in your care receive more interaction or face time?

GrapeImages/E+ via Getty Images

5.3 Language Development

Fetuses start learning language in utero, even as early as 10 weeks before birth; and this ability develops rapidly during the first year (Moon et al., 2013, Werker & Hensch, 2015).

When they are just a few days old, newborns use language processing skills similar to those that adults use (Ferry et al., 2016). As infants interact with others, they begin to associate symbols with their thoughts. These symbols are found in words or language. Language is a basic form of communication. As language ability increases, deeper interactions occur between the infant and caregivers. Learning to communicate using language is universal. Throughout history, cultures, and geographic locations, infants learn to communicate in their caregivers' language(s). These early language perceptions shape infant cognitive development (Carey, 2009; Kidd & Hayden, 2015; Perszyk & Waxman, 2019).

Exposure to language and individual preferences contributes to language learning. Before birth, fetuses show a preference for their biological mother's voice over the voice of another female or the father (Begus et al., 2016; DeCasper and Fifer, 1980; Lee & Kisilevsky, 2014). Newborns prefer human speech to digitally synthesized speech, and they prefer their native language to others (Vouloumanos et al., 2010). For example, if the native language is English or Spanish, one study found that 2-day-old infants prefer their native language over an unfamiliar one (Moon et al., 1993). However, infants do not show preferences for languages that are more similar in prosody (stress, intonation, and rhythm). For example, Dutch and English are more similar in prosody than English and Spanish. At 2 months of age, infants do not readily distinguish between two similar languages, but they do by 5 months of age (Mehler et al., 1988). There is no meaning attached to the language the fetus hears, but a fetus acquires the typical prosodic pattern of the language heard. Infants continue to learn the overall prosody of their native language, and even infant cries subtly vary based on language patterns. By age 10 months, an infant's babbling resembles their native language, and listeners can distinguish it as similar to the native language spoken around them (Mampe et al., 2009; Vouloumanos et al., 2010).

How do infants learn language? Much is still unknown, but here are some things we do know. Infants must be biologically ready to learn language (Chomsky, 1965; Hoff, 2014; Tamis-LeMonda et al., 2018). Their brains must be at a certain developmental level to form words of a particular language, both in terms of meaning and the physical ability to form certain sounds (see Figure 5.9) (Hagoort, 2019; Traxler et al., 2012). Infants learn language from interactions with other humans, so no interactions would mean no language learning (August et al., 2005; Kroeger & Nelson, 2006). If an infant is not exposed to language during infancy when brain pathways are developing and neuroplasticity allows the infant to discern distinct word sounds (phonetics), it is much harder to learn later in life (Berken et al., 2017; Li et al., 2014). Lastly, infants understand language long before they, themselves, can form words. This is termed **receptive language**. Most infants recognize their name when they are as young as 5 months. Talking to infants is critical to their language development and overall learning (see Figure 5.11) (Clancy & Finlay, 2001; Tamis-LeMonda et al., 2018).

FatCamera/E+ via Getty Images

Figure 5.9 Infants are exposed to language in many ways. Besides verbal interactions, what other ways are they exposed to language?

Language Learning Theories

Infants and children worldwide learn language at around the same age and follow a very similar process. They do not just learn any language; they learn the language of their primary caregivers. So, is language learning mostly a component of nature or nurture? What makes learning language possible? Over time, theorists have formed their own opinions. Theorists can be grouped into three categories regarding what influences language learning: nativist or biological, environmental, and interactionist. This next section walks through each theory.

Nativist or Biological Theories

Even without sophisticated language mentoring, infants learn to communicate through language. They are born to talk. Nativists believe that this ability to understand complex language and talk is biologically based. The ability to learn language is inherent in infants (Grover et al., 2019).

An early theorist, linguist Noam Chomsky (1965), transformed the field of linguistics by considering the acquisition of language as a uniquely human, biologically-based cognitive capability. His views were transformative, as the commonly held belief was that an infant's mind was like a blank slate. Instead, Chomsky held that infants were innately able to learn language. He termed the hypothetical biological part of the human brain that enables infants to

detect the sounds of language as the **language acquisition device (LAD)**. The LAD was not one identifiable area of the brain but instead a predisposition. For example, toddlers are predisposed to ask questions, innately understand grammar, and know that language provides symbols for communication.

Research has shown that specific brain areas are prone to be used for language acquisition (Gleason & Ratner, 2017; Shafer & Garrido-Nag, 2007). There are also critical periods when infants listen and practice language. Infants start emulating sounds within the first few months of life, and they may be structuring words at around 20 months of age (Birdsong, 2018). Brain research supports the concept that language acquisition has critical periods. Specifically, phonological, or sound patterns and grammatical understanding, are best learned during the first year of life (Friedmann & Rusou, 2015; Werker & Hensch, 2015).

Nativist brain research focuses on parts of the brain impacted when an aphasia, or brain communication disorder, is present, and how language communication is difficult (Bear et al., 2016; Edwards, 2005). The Broca's and Wernicke's areas of the brain are related to aphasias. The Broca's area, located in the frontal lobe, helps humans produce speech. The Wernicke's area is located in the temporal lobe near the brain's center and helps humans process spoken language (see Figure 5.10) (Raymer & Gonzalez-Rothi, 2018; Small, 2018).

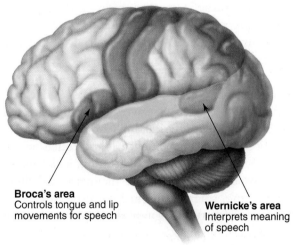

Broca's area Controls tongue and lip movements for speech

Wernicke's area Interprets meaning of speech

© Body Scientific International

Figure 5.10 These are two regions in the brain related to speech. How do these regions support speech acquisition?

Environmental Theories

Environmentalist researchers suggest that instead of having a language-specific mechanism for language processing, children simply utilize general cognitive and learning principles to acquire language. They learn languages from hearing and mimicking those in their environment (Barton and Brophy-Herb, 2004).

Environment plays a significant part in infant language acquisition. Surprisingly, recent studies show that infants with an older sibling develop language skills more slowly than firstborn infants, particularly those with older brothers (Havron et al., 2019). Mothers who are satisfied in their marital relationship spend more time talking to their infants than those who are dissatisfied or unhappy (Fink et al., 2019). Infant peers also play a role in language acquisition. For example, toddlers exposed to other toddlers were better at learning new words or names for objects and understanding language patterns (Bernier and White, 2019).

Primary caregivers and educators use many forms of speech to encourage language development. Many of these techniques are universal, including labeling, recasting, or expanding language conversations with infants (see Figure 5.11). Caregivers use **labeling** to name things, animals, and people (Grover et al., 2019). Examples are "There is your mommy!" "Where is the dog? Yes, right there." Caregivers **recast** by rephrasing a young child's verbal message while including more information such as "the dog is soft and fuzzy." Caregivers utilize the **expanding technique** when they add to what was verbalized when responding, "Did you say kitty?" "That is a kitty, and it is soft and furry."

Newborns prefer speech directed at them over communication directed toward other adults (Cooper and Aslin, 1990). When caregivers use **child-directed speech**—animated, lyrical, higher-pitched speech—it captures infants' attention. Child-directed speech not only captures an infant's attention, it also maintains a social interaction with the infant. Labeling, questioning, singing, and making expressive facial features all nurture language development through human relationships.

Approaching language acquisition from the perspective of environmental influences emphasizes the effects of all caregivers and surrounding influences. It lessens the perceived effect of biological influences.

Daniela Jovanovska-Hristovska/E+ via Getty Images; AJ_Watt/E+ via Getty Images

Figure 5.11 What do caregivers typically talk to infants about? How does it change as they mature?

Interactionist Theories

Most researchers today believe that language acquisition is a product of both biological and environmental influences. This is termed the **interactionist theory** of language learning (Balari & Lorenzo, 2015; Traxler et al., 2012). In the interactionist theory of language development, social communication between the infant and others supports the biological underpinnings of language-learning readiness.

Biological readiness and social interaction work together to aid and support infant language development (Kugiumutzakis, 2017; Lytle & Kuhl, 2017).

Infants are surrounded by language from the moment they are born, and they are receptive to language from the start. Even though language acquisition develops universally at the same life stages, each child learns language at a different pace, even within the same family (Cristia et al., 2014). This supports the understanding that language acquisition has a biological basis.

However, infants do not begin to acquire language on their own. Language acquisition requires and depends on human interaction. Otherwise, language abilities would not vary depending on the quality and amount of interaction between caregivers and infants (Conrad et al., 2021; Hagoort, 2019; Spencer et al., 2016). This supports the understanding that language acquisition has an environmental basis. Language development allows humans to express thoughts and influence others. When an infant cries or babbles, a caregiver responds. Infants can make links between their expressions and others' behaviors. For example, when an infant learns to point to an object of interest, a caregiver responds with a comment, description, or action. Thus, communication occurs and is directed by the infant (Begus et al., 2014; Goupil et al., 2016; Xu, 2019).

Finding a definitive answer to the question of language acquisition is far from conclusive, as our current understanding of the language development process is still immature. Table 5.2 summarizes the major theories of language development.

The Process of Language Learning

Infants produce sounds from birth. Crying is the first step in language development as infants learn to cry differently based on their particular need. As primary caregivers know, a hungry cry is different from a tired cry. Infants cry when distressed, or the cry may signal a different need (see Figure 5.12). But as language progresses, it becomes much more complex. Words become precise, grammar is complicated, and cognitive development and language are critically linked. The link between language and cognition starts in the first 3 to 4 months of life (Perszyk & Waxman, 2019).

Language development continues to be social. Between 2 and 4 months, most infants begin to coo,

FamVeld/Shutterstock.com

Figure 5.12 For young infants, crying is their primary means of communication.
Why might this baby be distressed?

Language Development Theories	Description
Nativist or biological theories	Infants are born with an innate ability to learn language. This has been shown throughout history and in all cultures and languages. The timing of language learning is part of the infant's genetic makeup, and certain parts of the brain contribute to language learning.
Environmental theories	Infants learn language by observing and imitating others and through reinforcement and nurturing. Language is learned gradually over time. As language skills develop, infants modify their language.
Interactionist theories	Infants are born with an innate ability to learn language that progresses over time as they physically grow and mature. A critical part of language learning is social interaction. Together, biology and environment promote infant language learning.

Kato

Table 5.2 Theories of Language Development

a sound made at the back of the throat, most often in response to something pleasurable, such as a sibling singing or talking to them (Oller et al., 1976; Topping et al., 2013). By age 6 months, infants babble, producing a string of consonants and vowels. Babbling, the vocalization of repeated syllables such as ba-ba or ma-ma, is the first step toward symbolic languages (Cohen & Billard, 2018; Orr, E., & Geva, 2015). The most common first babble is "ba, bab, ba…" a sound easily formed by the mouth. Imagine a caregiver responding to the babbling by talking back or responding to the baby. The infant will respond back to the caregiver with another string of babble, and so the interaction continues. The more a caregiver engages with the infant's babbling, the more likely the child's vocabulary will be more extensive when they later communicate with words (Lopez et al., 2020; Werwach et al., 2021). When babbling combines with gesturing such as finger-pointing, symbolic and goal-oriented communication occurs (see Figure 5.13) (Cohen & Billard, 2018; Elmlinger et al., 2019). Babbling is an essential step in language acquisition. It is considered the only universal language that is heard across cultures with only slight variations, mostly caregiver directed (Cychosz et al., 2021).

Many infants begin to communicate between ages 8 to 12 months through gestures such as pointing (Gullberg & De Bot, 2008). Waving bye-bye, blowing kisses, and shaking their heads are common forms of communication that infants learn (see Figure 5.14). This is a good time for infants to begin

A

B

MIA Studio/Shutterstock.com; Maica/iStock via Getty Images Plus

Figure 5.14 Between ages 8 and 12 months, many infants learn begin to communicate through gestures such as waving (A) or blowing kisses (B). What other gestures do caregivers typically teach infants?

yaoinlove/iStock via Getty Images Plus

Figure 5.13 Caregivers can play a major role in helping infants and young children identify and learn the names of objects and living things around them.

learning baby sign language as a form of communication, which will be discussed further in the next subsection.

In the second year, many toddlers use words to identify their caregivers—*dada* and *mama* are often the first combinations. Since primary caregivers usually respond enthusiastically the first few times these sounds are spoken, the infant quickly associates these sounds with their father and mother. Around their first birthday, infants begin to use single words to communicate different objects or people. They begin to name familiar items, including animals, foods, toys, and people. They even begin to speak their names and the names of others, although often in delightfully unique ways (Swingley, 2009; Tamis-LeMonda et al., 2018). A toddler may call a sibling named Alex *Ah Ah,* later becoming *Ayicks.* This adaptation works until the toddler can pronounce the difficult letter *L* sound.

Toddlers often use one word to describe a whole group of things, such as the word "dog" to describe every animal seen at the zoo. These are called **holophrases**, and they increase quickly. From about 18 months of age through much of early childhood, children learn dozens of new holophrases each month (Clancy & Finlay, 2001; Tamis-LeMonda et al., 2018).

Although infants begin to say their first words at about the one-year mark, they add words slowly. However, at about 17 or 18 months of age, a rapid and productive explosion of words becomes part of their vocabularies as words take on meaning or symbolism (Smith, 2013; Yu, 2014). This object-naming explosion is referred to as a **vocabulary spurt**, when infants learn productive vocabulary at a rate as high as 10 new words every 2 weeks (Roy et al., 2015; Samuelson & McMurray, 2017). Although this concept has been long established, more recent research has explored whether infants are merely learning object- and people-naming words or if they are comprehending the vast variations of words learned. Research indicates that the toddler stage of vocabulary spurts is more complex than initially thought. It includes sophisticated word comprehension that comes from integrating auditory and social inputs before and during this stage (Kucker et al., 2015; Ramírez-Esparza et al., 2017; Song et al., 2018).

In the last quarter of infancy, at about 18 to 24 months of age, toddlers begin to combine words into two-word combinations, called **telegraphic speech**. A toddler might say, "Daddy, up!" which means, "Daddy, I want you to pick me up!" Although telegraphic speech dramatically improves communication, some toddlers struggle to express the idea of past or present tense (see Table 5.3).

Baby Sign Language and Gesturing

Baby sign language uses manual signing; it allows infants to communicate emotions, desires, and even to identify objects before, or along with, learning spoken language (see Figure 5.15). Baby sign language may be an effective additional communication tool that can enhance vocal language learning for infants. For example, an infant may learn to sign "all done" by putting the ends of their fingertips together, letting a caregiver know when they are finished eating. The availability of empirical research on how best to enhance an infant's verbal language development is limited. Still, many primary caregivers and educators believe that teaching and practicing baby sign language can help infants express themselves before

Age	Form of Communication
Birth	Crying is a means of communication.
2–4 months	Cooing begins.
5–6 months	First receptive word is understood, and babbling begins.
8–12 months	Hand language is used to indicate needs and interests, with gestures such as pointing, waving, head shaking or nodding comprehension begins.
13 months	First word is spoken, and holophrases are used.
18–24 months	Word explosion begins, with rapid expansion of receptive language, including two-word speech combinations and telegraphic speech.

Kato

Table 5.3 Infant Language Development Milestones

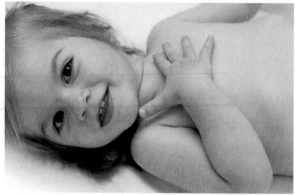

Anya Ponti/Shutterstock.com

Figure 5.15 Infants can learn simple baby sign language gestures to help them communicate their emotions and needs. This toddler is saying "I love you" through baby sign language.

they have spoken language ability (Thompson et al., 2007). Advocates of practicing baby sign language with infants suggest the following advantages to teaching infants simple sign language:

- adds another vehicle for the expression of emotions, needs, and demands
- reduces frustration in developing verbal skills
- adds additional opportunity for interaction between infant and caregiver
- develops fine motor skills

Baby sign language for hearing infants is not as complex as other sign languages, such as American Sign Language (ASL), typically used in the deaf or hearing-impaired community, which maintains its own grammar and sentence structure. ASL inspires baby sign language, yet it is simpler and usually includes a limited number of gestures. However, it is more complex than simple gestures such as pointing.

The Early Childhood Education arena often uses alternative communication systems, such as gesturing or baby sign language, because they may aid expressive language communication, especially when several infants are being cared for simultaneously. Baby sign language may also be beneficial as a communication aid between caregivers and infants who have disorders, such as Down syndrome, which makes verbal communication challenging (Neil & Jones, 2018; Smith et al., 2020).

Baby sign language is most effective when caregivers accompany it with spoken language. It should also be kept simple and interactive. As infants increase their spoken language abilities, caregivers will often decrease their use of baby sign language as it becomes less necessary.

Bilingual Language Learning

Some families raise their children bilingually, or with the ability to speak two languages fluidly. Some infant caretakers and early childhood education providers also offer bilingual language exposure. A family might raise their child bilingually to connect to family or community heritage, enhance cognitive ability, promote multiculturalism, and provide an advantage in a global economy. Learning multiple languages at an early age also helps develop phonemes in those languages, such as the rolling r sound in Spanish (Nicoladis & Montanari, 2016; Ortega & De Houwer, 2019).

As an infant is exposed to language during infancy, when brain pathways are developing neuroplasticity, it allows them to discern distinct word sounds, or phonetics (Berken et al., 2017; Li et al., 2014). This ability to perceive different phonetics persists until the end of early childhood and as a result, infants and young children can fluently learn other languages without an accent. This ability declines at about age seven or eight (Friedmann & Rusou, 2015; Purves et al., 2001; Werker & Hensch, 2015). Today, many toddlers and young children are exposed to two or more languages in their daily lives. Thus, research has switched from exclusively studying infants of a dominant native language to infants who are simultaneously exposed to two or more languages. Young children who are exposed to, practice, and learn multiple languages are equally able to learn vocabulary and grammar rules for each language (Hartshorne et al., 2018; Nicoladis & Montanari, 2016).

Because infants as young as six months can begin distinguishing between two languages (Burns et al., 2007; Kuhl et al., 2003), bilingual caregivers should use both languages from the start. When a toddler is learning two languages simultaneously, some primary caregivers become concerned that the toddler may confuse the languages. They may report a delay in the toddler's ability to speak. Experts agree that this delay is temporary, and not all children raised bilingually experience speech delays. In the long term, bilingual infants have a more extensive vocabulary than their monolingual counterparts. Spoken communication may be slightly delayed, but it is not an indicator that one language should be chosen over the other. Eventually, the child will be fluid in both languages (Grover et al., 2019; Hoff et al., 2012).

Understanding a language is the foundation for the ability to speak the language. If a primary caregiver verbally names an object in either language, and the toddler can identify the object, then bilingual education is successful. Early childhood education settings, such as daycare or preschool, may be a convenient way to expose infants to a second language.

The Impact of Language on Computational Understanding

Language helps infants learn computational skills when they understand the meaning of number words such as *one, two, three,* and beyond. When number names are verbally reinforced and connected to objects, infants begin to make an inductive jump to number computation. The ability to understand grouping objects follows, such as learning that 2 objects become a pair. Even infants as young as 3 months old begin to comprehend pairs (Anderson et al., 2018). When a caregiver demonstrates how objects are added or subtracted from a group of objects, the infant observes the resulting new sum. Surprisingly, computational skills begin in the early months of life, long before infants can talk; but it is through social language that these concepts are realized (Carey, 2009, 2014; Sarnecka & Carey, 2008). However, it is unknown if infants transfer number meaning from one kind of object to another (Spelke, 2017). For example, can an infant translate the numerical concept of 3 teddy bears to a different object, such as 3 carrots?

Another type of computational understanding is the concept of cause and effect. As infants watch a sequence of events, they process the event. A caretaker's description may further enhance their understanding of the event. Interactions with others help reinforce the concept. Language links to understanding spatial dimensions as caretakers name the concepts of big and small or short and tall (Henik et al., 2017). Geometric principles are used in shape naming, such as identifying squares, circles, and triangles. Manipulating shapes and noting the connections between shapes is tied to cognitive development (Cesana-Arlotti et al., 2018; Denison et al., 2013; Wellman et al., 2016).

Creating interest and curiosity in computational learning and language are critical because infants are natural information seekers. Toward the end of the first year, infants are drawn to experiences or objects that are somewhat, but not too, unpredictable (Goupil et al., 2016; Kidd et al., 2012; Stahl and Feigenson, 2015).

The Impact of Reading on Language Learning

Social interaction has a huge impact on learning. Reading is one way to build this interaction, and many suggest that it should begin as early as the first weeks of life (Council on Early Childhood, 2014). Infants love books for many reasons. They love the cuddling and interaction that occurs when someone reads them a book. As they grow and mature, they like seeing colors and pictures, and they like turning pages. They enjoy identifying objects and interacting with the reader. They do not have the patience or the mental ability to sit and listen to a story without visual and physical interaction. Books and reading are excellent ways to build bonds between the caregiver and active toddler while encouraging the use of language.

Reading to infants increases their understanding of pictures and print as symbols of ideas and thoughts. It enhances vocabulary and teaches how books work in their native languages (Durkin, 2011; Horowitz-Kraus & Hutton, 2015). For example, is a book read front to back or back to front? Are lines read left to right or right to left? Should books be read page by page? How do stories progress? Learning how a book is followed offers cultural competency as well as preliteracy skills. Reading with infants provides fine motor skill practice as they learn to touch and turn pages (High & Klass, 2014).

Daily reading to infants is vital because it has been shown to increase an infant's vocabulary, critical thinking, and preparation for school (see Figure 5.16) (Horowitz-Kraus & Hutton, 2015; Horowitz-Kraus et al., 2018; Hutton et al., 2020).

The social relationship between the infant and caregiver is strengthened as the caregiver points out and names objects and asks the child to identify what they see on the page (High & Klass, 2014; Torr, 2020).

AJ_Watt/E+ via Getty Images; SDI Productions/E+ via Getty Images

Figure 5.16 Reading to infants has many benefits, including supporting language acquisition. What are some benefits of daily reading with infants?

☑CHECKPOINT

- ☐ When do infants show signs of understanding receptive language?
- ☐ Describe the general timeline of infant language development, using specific terminology when possible.
- ☐ Compare the nativist, environmental, and interactionist theories of language development.
- ☐ What is meant by the terms babbling and vocabulary spurt? When do these actions typically appear and what role do they play in language acquisition?
- ☐ How might you counsel a parent who is concerned that their child will become confused if their partner uses two languages at home?
- ☐ Given the opportunity, would you support or oppose the use of baby signing in a childcare setting. Why?

Apply Here!

What languages are typically spoken in your community? Do you speak multiple languages? If so, when were these languages learned? What do you consider to be your primary or first language? If possible, interview the parent of a bilingual child. Ask them about the challenges and rewards of raising a child bilingually. Did the child experience a speech delay? Was the delay temporary? Then, interview a person who was raised bilingually. Compare the interviews with the parent and the individual raised bilingually. As an alternative to conducting an interview, write a newsletter for parents of infants in your care. How might you describe good practices for promoting language development in infants? Would you encourage or discourage bilingualism? Why or why not?

5.4 Infants with Disorders or Delays Related to Cognitive Development

Common milestones in cognitive development can be observed as infants reach certain ages within the first 2 years of life (see Table 5.4). By age 3 months, most infants coo to show their enjoyment, respond to sounds, and move their arms in circles in response to an interaction. Between ages four and seven months, most infants know their names and can distinguish between two similar languages. Other milestones, as discussed earlier, also become apparent. But what if those milestones are unmet? What if the infant does not babble or seem to understand simple requests? Measuring infant cognitive abilities may be done through simple observation. Although anyone can make observations, valid and credible assessments should be made by trained professionals (Mackin et al., 2017).

Assessing Cognitive Abilities

Primary caregivers and healthcare professionals often need and rely on accurate assessments to make good care decisions for infants. However, determining an infant's cognitive abilities when their language and motor skills are limited and developing can be challenging. Infants cannot answer surveys, offer opinions, express their reasoning, or share memories.

One of the primary assessment tools to measure infant cognitive development is the Bayley's scales of infant and toddler development, which focuses on identifying risk factors for cognitive delay (Bayley & Aylward, 2019). It is often considered the gold

Age	Skill
1 month 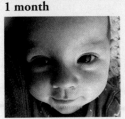 Sharleen Kato	• Identifies caregiver through sense of smell • Responds to caregiver's voice • Cries when wants a need addressed • Mimics facial expressions • Prefers human speech to digitally synthesized speech • Prefers their own native language to others
3 months  Jani Bryson/iStock.com	• Follows objects in motion • Responds to sounds • Unaware of a visual drop-off • Uses primary circular movements • Coos as a form of communication
4 to 7 months  Aliwak/Shutterstock.com	• Recognizes own name • Places objects in their mouth to learn about them • Shows interest in and responds to mirrors • Displays caution of a visual drop-off • Uses secondary circular reactions • Distinguishes between two similar languages • Begins using receptive language
12 months  Anetta/Shutterstock.com	• Follows simple instructions • Uses delayed imitation • Understands that words have meanings • Understands simple requests • Shows interest in learning about objects and their names • Enjoys music and attempts to sing • Uses coordination of secondary schemes • Uses hand language or gestures to indicate needs
18 months  Anton Gvozdikov/Shutterstock.com	• Understands the purpose of everyday items • Identifies objects and body parts • Refuses food or toys by shaking their head or using hands to push the food away • Points to images or objects • Understands object permanence • Asks questions by raising their voice at the end of sentence • Uses tertiary circular reactions • Begins invention of new means through mental combinations • Speaks first words followed by a rapid expansion of vocabulary
24 months  Felix Mizioznikov/Shutterstock.com	• Identifies objects when prompted by caregivers • Tries to pronounce and repeat words in surrounding conversations • Begins to organize objects by color or shape • Uses discovery to solve problems • Uses invention of new means through mental combinations • Increases receptive language quickly • Uses telegraphic speech

Table 5.4 Summary of Infant Cognitive Milestones

Areas of Measure	Ages	Strengths	Challenges
• Attention, memory, visual preferences, exploration, manipulation, and concept formation • Receptive and expressive language (subtest) • Large and fine motor skills (subtest)	16 days to 42 months	• Studies confirm reliability and validity across cultures • Quick to administer (15–20 minutes)	• Assessor training needed • Must combine with medical and neurological assessments • Assessment tailored to age with subtests for language and motor skills

Adapted from: Balasundaram & Avulakunta, 2021 and Del Rosario et al., 2021

Table 5.5 The Bayley's Scales of Infant and Toddler Development

standard for infant cognitive assessment (Mackin et al., 2017; Morgan et al., 2019; Spencer-Smith et al., 2015). Bayley's scales of infant and toddler development assesses cognitive measures including attention, memory, visual preferences, exploration, manipulation, and concept formation. It also measures receptive and expressive language and motor skills (see Table 5.5). When combined with social-environmental analysis and medical or neurological assessments, this assessment tool is considered both reliable and valid (Mackin et al., 2017). Other infant cognitive assessments include the Mayes motor-free compilation and the Fagan test of infant intelligence.

This scale appears to be an effective tool for assessing the cognitive abilities of extremely preterm infants and for use with infants who have motor development concerns as a result of cerebral palsy (Brito et al., 2019; dos Santos et al., 2013; Morgan et al., 2019). It is considered an effective assessment tool cross-culturally, specifically as used in Bangladesh, Brazil, India, Nepal, Pakistan, Peru, and South Africa (Pendergast et al., 2018; Ranjitkar et al., 2018). However, The Bayley's scales of infant and toddler development is not necessarily predictive of future cognitive functioning (Spencer-Smith et al., 2015).

Conditions and Disorders

When an infant's intellectual functioning level is significantly below the average for their chronological age, it may be a sign of an intellectual or cognitive disability or delay. Although there are many causes for challenges and delays, they can generally be traced to three general causes: genetic abnormalities, prenatal or birth problems, and health problems caused by the natural or social environment.

Intellectual disabilities may be a consequence of genetic inheritance, such as Down syndrome, fragile X syndrome, or phenylketonuria (PKU), to name some examples. Cognitive disabilities are usually diagnosed soon after birth using neonatal screening (Heward et al., 2017; Kauffman et al., 2017).

Sometimes intellectual disabilities are the result of abnormal prenatal development. This may be a functional problem because the cells divide irregularly as the fetus develops. Other conditions may be caused by the biological mother's health during pregnancy, particularly if exposed to certain diseases or viruses. Other times, it is due to the mother's exposure to teratogens or what she consumes during pregnancy. Alcohol and illicit substances or medications can cause profound cognitive impairments such as fetal alcohol syndrome (FAS). Cognitive impairments in infants can also be traced to problems during birth. The most common is when oxygen is cut off during the birthing process or when the newly expelled baby cannot breathe on their own for too long after birth (Chen, 2014; Heward et al., 2017; Kauffman et al., 2017).

An infant's environment can also impair cognitive development. For example, exposure to harmful chemicals such as lead, which is found in paint, pipes, and other materials in older homes, can impact an infant's brain development. Exposure to measles, whooping cough, or meningitis may cause delays or impairment. Some infants may be subjected to physical harm in their living environment (Grandjean & Landrigan, 2014). Infants who are victims of physical abuse or neglect may lack necessary medical care. They may be cognitively impaired due to an accident that caused brain injury. Many infants worldwide experience malnutrition or starvation, which may impair brain development during this critically important stage of life. The effects of these congenital conditions are irreversible. However, nurturing and stimulating caregiving can help infants with cognitive disabilities meet their full potential both in infancy and in the years beyond (Omnigraphics, 2016; U.S. Department of Health and Human Services, 2019 a,b,c).

☑ CHECKPOINT

- ☐ List and describe three diseases or conditions that may impact an infant's cognitive development.
- ☐ What are some of the major cognitive milestones for the first year of life? The second?
- ☐ Describe the usage and usefulness of the Bayley's scales of infant and toddler development.

Apply Here!

Infants learn by exploring and interacting with their environment. Imagine that you have been tasked with designing an infant care room at a community center, church, hospital, university, or workplace. How might you create a physical classroom that promotes a supportive environment for cognitive development for all the infants and toddlers in your care? How would you divide the space? What furnishings would you choose? What would make the environment intellectually stimulating? What would your top design priorities be? Justify your reasoning.

Summary

During the first year of infancy, neurons in the brain grow and sprout branches, and the brain makes more connections than it will ever need. The neuron pathways continue to develop during the second year of infancy. While some are reinforced, others are trimmed away. This physical change results in observable and measurable cognitive changes during infancy. Using sensory exploration, infants integrate the information obtained; and cognitive development occurs through intermodal perception, the process of bringing together input from multiple senses. As infants interact with others, they associate symbols with their thoughts. These symbols, found in words or language, facilitate learning as an active social activity.

An infant's interaction with the environment and with other people is vital. As you will discover in upcoming chapters, both the biological and social aspects of cognitive development are strongly tied to socioemotional development. As you begin the next chapter, consider how cognitive changes intersect with how an infant perceives the self in relation to others and forms social relationships. The intersections will prove fascinating.

Learning Outcomes and Key Concepts

5.1 Describe ways that infants learn about their world.

- Neurons in the brain grow pathways, more connections than needed.
- As the neuron pathways continue to develop, some are reinforced, while others are trimmed.
- Infants learn by putting objects in their mouths, exploring the way the objects taste and feel.
- Intermodal perception is the process of bringing together input from multiple senses.
- Infants play a critical role in directing their own dynamic learning.
- Medical and neurological screenings and tools assess cognitive abilities.
- Piaget theorized that motor skill development and experiences directly relate to cognition.
- In Piaget's sensorimotor stage, infants move from reflexes to interacting with the world.
- Post-Piagetian theorists highlight the importance of outside influences and timing.

5.2   Summarize social and behavioral cognition in infancy.

- Infants naturally learn from their primary caregivers first, using their senses.
- Social relationships reinforce learning, as infants imitate or repeat interactions.
- Serve-and-return interaction describes the relationship between caregivers and infants.
- Vygotsky believed that minds develop through interactions with caregivers and others.
- Caregiver resource limits, stress, and mental illness negatively affect cognitive development.
- Vygotsky's zone of proximal development is the level at which a child can learn with help.
- Using operant conditioning, an infant responds to a stimulus, repeating or stopping a response.
- Memory abilities develop over time, and even young infants show indications of memory.

5.3   Explain how language is learned, including the developmental language milestones often achieved during infancy.

- Infants start learning language while still in the womb.
- Newborns prefer human speech to digitally synthesized speech.
- Infant brains must be at a certain development level to form words and certain sounds.
- Infants who do not interact with other humans do not learn a language.
- Chomsky's language acquisition device is the part of the human brain that enables language.
- There are specific areas of the brain that are prone to enhance language acquisition.
- There may be critical biological stages in infancy when language is learned.
- Caregivers use many forms of speech to encourage language development.
- Universal language techniques include labeling and expanding infant language conversations.
- Infants who are invited to engage in conversation acquire greater language skills.
- Many caregivers believe that sign language can help infants express needs before they are able to speak.
- Young infants can begin to distinguish between two languages.
- Language helps computational skills, including the meaning of number words and cause-and-effect.
- Reading to infants increases their understanding of symbols and enhances vocabulary.

5.4   Identify some disorders that may influence infant cognitive development.

- Genetics, environment, and pregnancy or birth issues cause intellectual disabilities and delays.
- Abnormal genes cause Down syndrome, Fragile X syndrome and phenylketonuria (PKU).
- Alcohol and drugs can cause profound cognitive impairments such as fetal alcohol syndrome disorder.
- Environment can impair cognitive development. For example, children may be exposed to harmful chemicals.
- Exposure to lead, measles, whooping cough, or meningitis may cause delays or impairment.
- Physical harm through accidents may cause cognitive delays or impairments.
- Physical abuse such as head injuries or neglect may cognitively impair infants.
- Malnutrition or starvation impairs brain development during this critical stage of life.

Chapter Review

1. Describe how neonates, babies, and toddlers learn about their world.

2. Do an online search and find an image (chart, infographic, figure, or photo) that visually portrays an aspect of infant cognitive development that was described in this chapter.

3. How would you describe the ability to remember experiences during infancy and toddlerhood to the parent of a newborn?

4. How does the environment impact infant learning? How might you create an environment that promotes cognitive development for infants?

5. Create a checklist of activities or behaviors that caregivers of infants can incorporate to help create brain-shaping experiences.

6. Cell phones and other screen time are technologies that may distract from caregivers having direct eye contact and interaction with infants. Observe what you see around you. How can infants in your care receive more interaction or face time?

7. Describe the process, methods, and importance of language development in infancy.

8. Describe how genetics, the environment, and pregnancy or birth issues may cause intellectual disabilities and delays. Give two examples of disabilities from each cause.

Matching

Match the following terms with the correct definitions.

A. child-directed speech

B. delayed imitation

C. expanding techniques

D. holophrase

E. imitation

F. language acquisition device

G. recasting

H. receptive language

I. telegraphic speech

1. A technique used when infant caregivers add to what was verbalized by an infant when responding back

2. Chomsky's theory that a biological part of the human brain enables infants to detect the sounds of language

3. Understanding language before one has the ability to form words

4. Duplicating or copying the behavior of another person after some time has passed

5. Term used to describe speech pattern when toddlers begin to combine words into two-word combinations

6. When toddlers often use one word to describe a whole group of things

7. Animated, lyrical, higher-pitched speech used by caregivers to captures the attention of infants

8. An advanced behavior that occurs when one person observes and replicates another person's behavior

9. Rephrasing a young child's verbal message back while including more information

6

Infant Socioemotional Development

Learning Outcomes

After studying this chapter, you will be able to:

6.1 Describe how infants and their caregivers forge relationships in infancy.

6.2 Summarize critical components of infant socioemotional growth and development.

6.3 Explain how interactions with an expanding world impact an infant's socioemotional development.

6.4 Identify some disorders that may influence infant socioemotional development.

antibias early childhood
  programs
associate play
autism spectrum disorder
  (ASD)
bonding
colic
custodial grandparent
disinhibited social
  engagement disorder
exploratory play

highly reactive
  temperament
insecure-ambivalent
insecure-avoidant
insecure-resistant
onlooker play
personality
play
postpartum anxiety
postpartum depression
postpartum period

prosocial behaviors
reactive attachment disorder
securely attached
social referencing
solitary play
strange situation
synchrony
temperament
transracial adoption
trust versus mistrust
unoccupied play

Introduction

Have you held a newborn baby? Have you ever tried to figure out a newborn's needs by listening to the rhythms of their crying? How do you communicate with a newborn when you do not yet share a language? Infants are social people. Just as in any later stage of life, infants need to be talked to, listened to, and interacted with on many levels. They need care and nuturing. They need to have their basic needs met, not neglected. They need to feel safe. They need to feel love and affection. All these needs require social interaction.

An infant's socioemotional development is critical to physical and cognitive growth. Playing, talking, bonding with, and attaching to others and understanding themselves all affect these other areas of growth. As infants enter their second year of life, their relationships with others become more reciprocal, as more two-way interaction occurs. Primary caregivers begin to direct toddlers' behavior more than they did during their first year. They respond to toddlers' behaviors and attempt to shape future behaviors. "Don't touch," "Hot!" and "Wait for me" are common commands caregivers use when guiding toddlers. At the same time, toddlers are reaching toward independence. Sitting on a parent's lap for long periods becomes much more difficult as toddlers want to explore their world. Singing songs, playing games, and practicing large motor skills are essential to family relationships and to developing socioemotionally.

Although all infants develop socioemotionally at their own unique pace, certain developmental milestones occur throughout infancy. For example, 2-month-old infants smile at familiar people, and many 10-month-olds show distress when separated from their primary caregiver. Infants learn to control their emotions and look to their caregivers to model emotional reactions.

This chapter explores socioemotional development throughout the first two years of life. As you read this chapter, think of how the information that you have already learned about infants' physical and cognitive development connects with what you learn about socioemotional development. The three domains (physical, cognitive, and socioemotional) intertwine and are interdependent, as one domain does not develop without the others.

6.1 Forging a Relationship: Infant-Caregiver Bonding

Bonding is the reciprocal emotional connection a primary caregiver develops with a child. Researchers believe that bonding is dynamic and bidirectional and that the bonding process actually begins in utero. Attachment between an infant and their caregivers is critical for survival and for the initial encoding of infants' lifelong social, emotional, and cognitive capabilities. Primary caretakers of newborns, whether they are birth mothers, biological fathers, adoptive parents, grandparents, or other family members who assume a caretaking role, tend to naturally bond with their infants by holding, feeding, and responding to their infants' needs. Caretakers smile at, seek eye contact with, and talk or sing to their infants, and they look for signals that their infants are responding. Healthy, full-term infants are seemingly programmed to respond by reaching for breast or bottle, crying, making eye contact, and creating other cues for the caregiver to respond to (Brown et al., 2019; Gholampour et al., 2020; Shiller, 2017).

Bonding has two main functions—to ensure survival and to facilitate cognitive and emotional development (Sullivan et al., 2011). This critical bonding relationship plays out later in infancy. As children near their first birthdays, a more complex form of highly specific attachment develops that will be discussed later in this chapter (see Figure 6.1).

When a primary caregiver consistently responds to an infant's needs, a lifelong attachment and a trusting relationship develop (Johnson, 2013; Kinsey & Hupcey, 2013; Rossen et al., 2019; Scism & Cobb, 2017).

If the optimal period to bond begins right after birth, what happens when an infant is born prematurely, is sick, or when the mother or father are unable to bond due to physical or mental health needs? What happens if the infant is given into another's care, such as with adoption, surrogacy, or foster care? Bonding can still occur. Researchers have found that human infants have many opportunities to bond with their primary caregivers throughout their first year of life.

Responsive contact and care are critical, however, even during the first couple hours of life (Bienfait et al., 2011; Dodwell, 2010; Johnson, 2013). Therefore, newborn care providers in medical facilities will create opportunities for primary caregivers to bond with their infants through skin-to-skin contact (see Figure 6.2). Research also supports the theory that caregivers who adopt toddlers and older children can form normal attachment relationships through warm, responsive interactions (Baker & McGrath, 2011).

The process of caregiver bonding with an infant involves neurological changes. Studies show that a change occurs in a biological mother's brain later in pregnancy when neural circuits regulate maternal motivation to bond with their infant. (Numan,

A

B

Figure 6.1 The dynamic and bidirectional bonding process between infants and caregivers facilitates cognitive and emotional development in infants and socioemotional expression in caregivers (A, B).

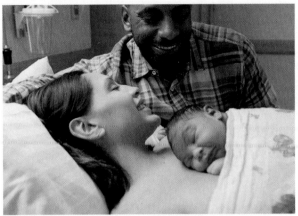

SelectStock/iStock via Getty Images Plus

Figure 6.2 The bonding process between caregivers and infants starts early, often right after birth.

2020; Rilling, 2013). Research further indicates that neurological changes can also occur in fathers' and other caretakers' brains that motivate bonding (Li et al., 2018; Mascaro et al., 2014). Considerable evidence links the hormone oxytocin to caregiver bonding (Li et al., 2017; Rilling, 2013; Rutherford et al., 2017). Typically, studies that determine primary caregiver bonding measure their responsiveness to an infant's crying.

Primary caregiver bonding is complex; caregivers may struggle to bond with their infants, and sometimes interventions are needed to facilitate the bond. When a new mother or other primary caregiver is stressed, their brain may not adapt as readily to an emotional attachment with their infant, and bonding may be delayed (Kim, 2020). Likewise, mental health issues, especially anxiety and depression, may negatively influence caregiver-infant bonding, especially if the caregiver is ambivalent or did not choose to become the caregiver (Kinsey & Hupcey, 2013; Kinsey et al., 2014; Rados et al., 2020). Caregivers who have difficulty accurately reading social visual cues, such as infant facial expressions, may also struggle with bonding. Fortunately, various early psychological interventions may help bonding occur (Dickinson et al., 2020; Rossen et al., 2019; Scism & Cobb, 2017; Tichelman et al., 2019).

Bonding forms a critical foundation in infants for future development and the ability to form healthy relationships as an adult. Bonding can occur throughout life but is especially important during this stage as it helps family members to adjust during the transition of introducing a new infant into the home. For some primary caregivers, bonding with the infant occurs immediately, while for others, it takes some time. Bonding has a greater chance of success when caregivers spend time with the infant and build confidence in forecasting and meeting their infant's needs (see Figure 6.3).

Bringing Baby Home

The trip home can be a significant event for infants born in hospitals or other birthing centers. Caregivers often choose special newborn clothes for this event, gather necessary items like blankets and diapers, and arrange for transportation. But these details are often easy to manage. Once caregivers arrive home with a new baby, a time of adjustment awaits.

Family Adjustments

Family structures that welcome newborns home vary widely. Two parents, single parents, foster parents, grandparents, and other extended family members may all be primary caregivers. It takes time for caregivers and others living in a home to adjust to a new baby's temperament, schedule, and needs. Mothers who have just given birth need to make physical and psychological adjustments.

The **postpartum period** usually lasts at least six weeks. After delivery, a huge hormonal shift occurs within the mother. She may be overwhelmed with fatigue, stress from this new demanding role, and sometimes sadness from the "let down" after all

Bartosz Hadyniak/E+ via Getty Images

Figure 6.3 Bonding occurs when caregivers spend time interacting with their infants, learning their rhythms and needs.

the excitement of waiting. Stress may come from changing work and family care logistics, such as working to fit a newborn into existing work schedules, caretaking of other family members, concerns about childcare, or the lack of sufficient maternity, paternity, or general employment leave (Burtle & Bezruchka, 2016; Petts, 2018). For caregivers of newborns with physical or developmental disabilities, the adjustment period will be even more challenging (Balakrishnan et al., 2011; Grunberg, 2019; Treyvaud et al., 2013).

Feelings of melancholy, exhaustion, and stress are a normal part of caring for a newborn. Caring for a newborn can cause **postpartum anxiety**, as caregivers worry over all that is involved. Common worries include whether the infant is getting enough to eat, sleeping enough or too much, or crying too much or not enough. The caregiver may also have concerns about being personally able to provide adequate care. Although postpartum anxiety is often invisible to others, it is very real to the parent experiencing it. It can be especially difficult for those who have experienced prior loss due to miscarriage or stillbirth, or for those who had difficulty getting pregnant or experienced extreme anxiety before pregnancy (Ali, 2018; Giannandrea et al., 2013). About one in five US mothers experience postpartum anxiety, with levels periodically spiking due to hormone level changes (Liu et al., 2021).

When feelings of sadness, fatigue, and stress last more than a few weeks, a new mother may need to seek medical help. **Postpartum depression** is an intense mental health issue that affects about 5% of US postpartum women (U.S. Department of Health & Human Services, 2020b). Postpartum depression may manifest as feelings of hopelessness, thoughts of death or suicide, sleep disorders, mood swings, difficulty concentrating, sadness and crying, and heightened fears. These feelings can last months or even years after the birth of a baby (Putnick et al., 2020). Many factors influence the presence of postpartum depression, and it is crucial for mothers to find medical treatment for themselves and for the sake of their infants (Norhayati et al., 2015).

New fathers also experience a period of adjustment, and many report feelings of being overwhelmed with a new sense of responsibility. Like mothers, they are challenged by work and family balance issues. Role expectations often change, and responsibilities within the family often shift (Leavitt et al., 2017; McCubbin & Figley, 2014). In a collection of studies focusing on new parents, Shapiro et al. (2015) found that 67% of couples had become very unhappy during the first 3 years of their baby's life, while only 33% remained content. Some researchers assert that several factors account for this relationship dissatisfaction, including the following:

- Even though both parents may be working harder, they both feel unacknowledged.
- The conflict between parents often increases in intensity and frequency during the first year after a child's birth.
- For many mothers, sexual desire drops during the first year, especially if she is nursing.
- Many mothers become highly involved with their new infant and, as a result, are extremely fatigued and emotionally distant from their partners.
- Parenthood often changes personal identities, values, and goals for both caregivers (Gottman & Gottman, 2008).

These researchers also found that couples who could navigate the everyday stressors of new parenthood were happier than those who could not. For new mothers, not succumbing to unrealistic expectations of motherhood helped in the transition (Meeussen & Van Laar, 2018; Newman & Henderson, 2014). New caregivers who could not navigate stressors were unhappy and overwhelmed in their new roles. Friends, partners, extended family, and community resources can help in the daunting transition to parenthood. Social support is critical for relieving stress, and it can be as simple as offering encouragement, sharing the excitement of new infant milestones achieved, or lending a listening ear. Sometimes challenges may increase or collide, such as when new parenthood occurred during the COVID-19 pandemic (Joy et al., 2020).

Single-Parent Families

Approximately 40% of newborns in the United States are born to single mothers (Martin et al., 2019). According to the Pew Research Foundation (Kramer, 2019), the United States has the highest rate of single-parent families globally, headed by both single mothers or single fathers. Family adjustments with a new baby are hard in two-parent families, and those challenges are only likely to increase for single parents. For example, financial and social support may be inadequate if only one parent can provide for the family. According to the Annie E. Casey Foundation, in 2016 about 32% of single-parent families lived in poverty versus just 7% of two-parent families (2018). Being overwhelmed with responsibilities combined with feelings of insecurity can make bonding difficult.

Even when fathers do not live in the household, their involvement with the new family member is critical to the health and emotional wellbeing of the infant throughout life (Adamsons & Johnson, 2013). The quality of a father's relationship with their infant is associated with infant cognitive development. The more quality indicators reported—such as time spent together and interactions through basic care, such as feeding, diapering, comforting, and playing—the higher infant cognitive achievement as well as parental mental health (Rolle et al., 2019; Sethna et al., 2017; Shorey & Ang, 2019).

Global Perspectives

Global Infant Caregiver Diversity and Antibias Early Childhood Programs

It is essential for infant caregivers to have an awareness and respect for diverse global infant caretaking practices. The National Association for the Education of Young Children (2020) recommends that all early childhood caregivers develop trusting, respectful, culturally responsive, and affirming partnerships with the children and families that they serve. These practices that actively respect and honor children and their families are an integral part of **antibias early childhood programs** (Derman-Sparks & Leekeenan, 2015; Nimmo, 2015). Antibias early childhood programs help caregivers better understand the specific needs of infants in their care (Kaiser & Rasminsky, 2019). They also strengthen the relationship with an infant's family while building trust and support between the infant and caregiver (Ray, 2015; US Department of Health and Human Services, 2020.

There are many similarities between infant caregiving practices worldwide, primarily related to keeping infants alive and thriving. However, many differences exist in daily cultural practices (see Figure 6.4). Some differences center on beliefs about verbal interactions, approaches to sleeping arrangements, and practices and general ideas about what infants need (LeVine & LeVine, 2016; Passe, 2020; Trawick-Smith, 2018). For example, many agrarian (farming) societies, such as in rural Senegal, focus less on intense interactions between an infant and a caregiver and more on exposing an infant to language that is naturally occurring all around them (Weber et al., 2017). Other cultural differences may include whether to give indirect or direct instruction to toddlers and varying expectations related to an infant or child's response and compliance. In China, giving instructions to a toddler may be direct and nonnegotiable. Most of the world practices infant-parent co-sleeping, so those who do are puzzled by the those who choose to sleep separately. A naturalistic approach to sleep and body rhythms is practiced and preferred over scheduled naps or bedtimes in many parts of the world. One of the most significant differences in infant caregiving practices is the ideology behind and preference for stimulating versus soothing infant interactions. For example, in many African cultures and in Mexico, infant caregivers express the importance of soothing care. Interaction occurs casually as a matter of daily activities with many family members who wear or hold infants close to the body. Infants tend to be integrated into the daily happenings of family life rather than family life focusing on the infant (Gross-Loh, 2013; LeVine & LeVine, 2016).

In the United States, caregivers tend to provide stimulating environments for infants because they believe this will best aid their development. Caregivers stress the importance of verbal interaction with an infant. This interaction is ideally face-to-face, direct, engaging, and often simulates a conversation, even before the infant can respond verbally. Facial expressions become a part of the dialogue as caregivers react to all an infant's cues. This interaction is often considered crucially important to an infant's language acquisition. Toys and other stimulating experiences, along with conversational interactions between caregivers and their infants, are often prized and encouraged. Parents often place infants in strollers rather than carry them or use floor play sets, sit-up chairs, and swings to entertain them.

In the United States, training a child to sleep alone is based on the idea that it is safer and promotes infant independence (Gross-Loh, 2013). The American Academy of Pediatrics recommends co-sleeping in the same room or nearby (Moon et al., 2016). Caregivers often schedule an infant's sleep, including specified nap- and bedtimes. Bedtime routines that involve taking a warm bath, wearing pajamas, bedtimes stories, and other sometimes elaborate behaviors are often a part of infant sleep routines. Training an infant to self-soothe or cry it

(Continued)

Mrs_ya/Shutterstock.com; dikkenss/Shutterstock.com; Ekaterina Pokrovsky/Shutterstock.com; hadynyah/E+ via Getty Images

Figure 6.4 There are many similarities between infant caregiving practices around the world, and there are also many differences in daily cultural practices caregiving.
What similarities and differences do you observe in these caregiver-infant practices?

out is a US practice that involves allowing a monitored infant to cry themselves to sleep. Infant sleep patterns are an anxiety-ridden focus of many US parents (Bilgin & Wolke, 2020; Shimizu & Teti, 2018).

During infancy, a plethora of diverse caregiving practices may surface. Toilet learning, dealing with temper tantrums, and co-parenting among community members are just a few examples of situations that demonstrate cultural variation in values and practice. Providing an environment that includes respect for the infant's unique cultural background and family influences is what is best for the infant's social development and feelings of security (Derman-Sparks et al., 2020; Passe, 2020; Trawick-Smith, 2018). In the end, it is about relationship-based caregiving (Sosinsky et al., 2016).

To Think About:

• How did your parent/guardian soothe you as a child? Were the methods used more stimulating or more

calming? Can you identify other caretaking practices or biases that you learned through your own cultural upbringing?

• If possible, interview a person in your social circle who represents a different culture. If possible, choose a person who has immigrated to the United States as an adult. Ask about parenting practices in their home culture, and ask if there are any differences they identify between their native culture and your current community culture. Are they aware of differences in how parents care for their infant children, especially regarding communication between parents and young children, expectations for sleeping, or ideologies about how to best support optimal infant and toddler development?

• How can you become more informed about diverse caregiving practices? Identify an action that you can take today that would increase your knowledge.

Other Family Members

Primary caregivers are not the only ones adjusting to a new family member. Other children in the household, including siblings and stepsiblings, must adjust (see Figure 6.5). It takes time to care for and nurture infants, especially neonates. Since this time is usually given by primary caregivers, other children can feel left out or cheated during what should be their time. Younger children often struggle to understand that their new sibling is here to stay. For older children, increased responsibilities may be unwelcome.

Extended family members, including grandparents, aunts, uncles, and cousins, may also need to adjust to the new family member. In some family configurations, extended family members share the same dwelling or live nearby, while others may be geographically spread out. Grandparents may play a vital role in caring for a new infant depending on the amount of contact, behaviors, and support offered (Sadruddin et al., 2019). Some grandparents are **custodial grandparents**, or the primary legal caregivers. Custodial grandparents are very effective in their caretaking roles despite added stress or competing aging or health issues. Possible contributing factors to positive outcomes include more life experience, resiliency, social networks, and financial resources (Ge & Adesman, 2017; Hayslip et al., 2014; Hayslip et al., 2015).

Across cultures, early relationships with parents and extended family caregivers, including grandparents, lay a foundation for social, cognitive, and emotional development (McHale, 2007; McHale et al., 2014) As each member of the family adjusts to new roles and relationships, the new member eventually becomes a welcomed part of the family (see Figure 6.6).

☑ CHECKPOINT

☐ How do caregivers and infants bond? What are the benefits of these bonds?

☐ How might the arrival of a new baby impact home life for mothers? Fathers? Extended family members?

☐ What challenges do caregivers face that might impede bonding with a newborn infant?

☐ How might culture and traditions impact family dynamics between generations?

☐ Imagine that a friend or family member who recently gave birth shows signs of postpartum depression. What might be some signs? What advice might you share with the new mother or her support partners?

Rosie Parsons/Shutterstock.com

Figure 6.5 Do you have memories of a younger sibling entering your world? Have you observed the introduction of a sibling to a family? What kind of adjustments were made for older siblings and other family members?

Apply Here!

Survey friends and acquaintances to find out how many of them come from homes that included the influence of extended family, two-parent households, single-parent households, parents of the same gender or transgender, or other family structures. How did their family structure affect parenting styles or expectations? How might you to handle a situation where a grandparent (or other caregiver) contradicts the primary caretaker in an Early Childhood Education setting?

MBI/Shutterstock.com

Figure 6.6 Multigenerational families include children, parents, guardians, grandparents, or other older adults in the extended family. They may live together or just be in frequent contact. What are some benefits of these relationships to the young child? To the caregivers?

6.2 Socioemotional Development in Infancy

In the twentieth century, psychologist Erik Erikson became known for describing the eight stages of socioemotional development, which covered the entire lifespan from infancy to old age. In his classic work, *Childhood and Society* (1950), Erikson went beyond Sigmund Freud's notion of psychosexual development (1923, 1961) and instead focused on socioemotional development that encompasses social relationships. In terms of how people develop socially and emotionally, this includes an individual's relationships with others and their own personal identity and sense of place in the world (Bee, 1992; Lally & Mangione, 2017; Miller, 2016;).

Erikson's first stage, **trust versus mistrust**, encompasses the first 18 to 24 months of life (see Table 6.1). During this stage, the infant is dependent on primary caregivers to provide them with stability through consistent care. Infants develop trust as this constant care becomes predictable and reliable. When trust develops between infants and caregivers, infants feel secure, safe, and not threatened. If an infant feels secure, they can transfer this trust to other relationships. Trust can translate to the virtue of hope, a sense that if a new crisis arises, someone will be there to meet needs (Bee, 1992; Gross & Humphreys, 1992).

When caregivers are inconsistent, unpredictable, and unreliable, infants develop mistrust, resulting in increased anxiety or insecurity. An infant's distrust of their primary caregivers can carry into other relationships, just like trust can. Mistrust also lessens hope, which can lead to fear and insecurities later in life (Bee, 1992; Gross & Humphreys, 1992). When an infant experiences extreme deprivation of social interactions that build trust, this experience alters their brain structure at the cellular and molecular levels, leading to behavioral and psychological issues later in life (Nelson et al., 2019).

Erikson's second stage, **autonomy versus shame and doubt**, encompasses the middle of the first year of life through about age 3 (Lewis & Able, 2020). During this stage, the toddler begins to understand the consequences of their actions. Caregivers can offer choices and encourage a toddler's efforts to gain age-appropriate autonomy and personal control (Gloeckler et al., 2014; La Paro & Gloeckler, 2016; Lippard & LaParo, 2018). If independence is encouraged by a caregiver, a growing sense of autonomy results. If, instead, a caregiver discourages independence, this may result in an infant feeling shame

Erikson's Stage/Age	Caregiver Actions	Potential Result(s)
Trust versus mistrust (0–18 months)	Responsive Predictable Reliable Visual contact Touch	Trust Feeling safe, secure, not threatened Hope Stability
Autonomy versus shame and doubt (18–months–3 years)	Offer choices Encourage efforts Celebrate accomplishments Avoid shaming	Autonomy Independence Understanding consequences Personal control

Kato

Table 6.1 Erikson's Socioemotional Development Theory Applied to Infancy

or doubting their own ability to act independently. This stage is essential in early childhood and will be further explored in Chapter 9.

Infant Attachment to Caregivers

Bonding is a term commonly used to describe the growing affection and desire of a caregiver to nurture an infant. Attachment refers to an infant's growing perception of connection, security, and trust in the caregiver-infant reciprocal relationship (Ettenberger et al., 2021; Mihelic et al., 2017). Like bonding, attachment refers to the strong emotional bond one individual feels for another. Psychologist John Bowlby (1969, 1973) proposed that all primates are born with an innate bias toward becoming attached to their mothers or another primary attachment figure. This is especially evident in dangerous or stressful situations. However, the need to attach to a caregiver is universal for human infants. Psychologist Mary Ainsworth (1967), in her Ugandan studies, suggested that parental sensitivity may be considered the crux of the attachment process. Ainsworth and her colleagues (1978) used a now well-known procedure to measure an infant's attachment to their caregiver called the **strange situation**. The researchers exposed the infants to three "strange" components of stressful situations, including a strange environment, interaction with a stranger, and two short separations from the primary caregiver. Researchers then observed how the infant responded when reunited with the caregiver.

Researchers identified three patterns of attachment based on this study. **Securely attached** infants actively engaged with their primary caregiver upon reunion while communicating their distress over the situation and then returning to play. **Insecure-avoidant** infants seemed to ignore or avoid the caregiver following reunion. Other times, the insecure-avoidant infant may not even be bothered by the parent/caregiver leaving or returning. **Insecure-resistant,** sometimes called **insecure-ambivalent**, infants sought proximity closeness after reuniting with their caregiver, but they were still resistant and difficult to be soothed and calmed (Rosmalen et al., 2015).

Ainsworth (1967) also found that three precursors appeared to be especially important to an infant's ability to attach: (1) infants whose mothers breastfed more often tended to be more securely attached; (2) infants whose mothers spent a lot of time with them and included them in everyday activities also tended to develop secure attachments; (3) and infants whose mothers had realistic and optimistic views of them also tended to have strong attachments. In these scenarios, the mothers seemed less anxious and better able to respond to their infants' specific expressions of emotions and foster a secure bond. The crucial factor was the sensitivity of the mother when perceiving and responding to her infant's attachment behavior signals. The appropriateness and promptness of her responses were key (Rosmalen et al., 2015).

The importance of the reciprocal attachment relationship between the caregiver and infant continues to be reinforced as a critical component of socioemotional development, as insecure attachment has been associated with many adverse outcomes later in life, including problems with social relationships and anxiety (Bakermans-Kranenburg, 2008; Cassidy & Shaver, 2016; Kerns & Brumariu, 2014; Zeanah & Gleason, 2015). Secure attachment in infancy may moderate negative behaviors throughout childhood and early adolescence (Boldt et al., 2017). Primary caregiver sensitivity and attention to infant needs appear to be vital in providing an optimal environment for infants to form caregiver attachments (see Figure 6.7). Although early research focused on the infant-mother relationship, later research confirmed that infants can form multiple attachments to other caregivers. The attachment relationships share the commonality of being frequent, if not daily or

FotoDuets/Shutterstock.com

Figure 6.7 Securely attached infants seek comfort from caregivers. The appropriateness and promptness of the caregiver's responses build and reinforce connection, security, and trust.

intimate, and involving caring for the infant's basic needs (Cassidy & Shaver, 2016; Perry et al., 2017; Steinfeld, 2020; Zeegers et al., 2017).

Researchers have continued to examine the impact of an infant not forming an attachment to their primary caregivers and the possibility of using interventions to help young children create secure attachments. For example, they developed assessments to evaluate the strength of caregiver-child attachment. Young children with specific symptoms related to attachment difficulty, such as rarely seeking or responding to emotional comfort or lacking strong emotional responses to others, infrequently expressing positive emotions, or being socially withdrawn, might be given the diagnosis, **reactive attachment disorder** (RAD) (Hanson & Spratt, 2000). For infants, RAD became associated with child abuse and neglect as a possible psychological consequence of the trauma (Horner, 2008). Children with another attachment disorder, **disinhibited social engagement disorder** (DSED), in contrast, demonstrate a pattern of behavior in which they show no inhibition in approaching and interacting with unfamiliar adults, including hugging or sitting in the laps of strangers. DSED is not a matter of having an extroverted personality or being uninhibited, but a willingness to be separated from their primary caregiver without any hesitancy or concern (Lehmann et al., 2020; Zeanah & Gleason, 2015). Although symptoms of attachment disorders may be similar to some genetic disorders, the etiologies or causes are different, and a child may be diagnosed with both (Mayes et al., 2017). Likewise, methods of successful intervention are also receiving continued attention. Most of these methods involve care that emphasizes intense caregiver sensitivity, eliminating any form of trauma such as abuse or neglect, narrowing outside influences for a given period, and restoring stability to the young child (Ellis et al., 2021; Gonzalez et al., 2012; Lehmann et al., 2020).

Practical Issues and Implications

Transracial Adoptions

Transracial adoption is when adoptive parents and adoptive children do not share the same racial identities. Historically, there have been critics who argue that parents and children should racially match, otherwise the adopted children will face difficult identity formation. They will always feel separate from their adoptive families. Although many biological or non-adoptive parents and children do not share the same racial identities, transracial adoption families often receive the most criticism (Godon-Decoteau & Ramsey, 2017).

Critics of transracial adoption often focus on either children adopted from Asian countries into an all-White family or domestic adoptions that include a Black child adopted into an all-White family (Fong & McRoy, 2016; McKee, 2019; Montgomery & Powell, 2018). Their main criticism is that Black children should only be adopted by Black families, White children should only be adopted by White families, and Asian and Latinx children should only be adopted by same-race families (Mariner, 2019; Raleigh, 2018).

However, these are just the opinions of certain critics. Transracial adoption, like any adoption, can be very successful. And like any adoption, there can be challenges, whether due to race or other circumstances. Research supports this. It highlights the need for communication about race issues, stating that such conversations are critically important within transracial families (Hamilton, et al., 2015; Hasberry, 2019; Montgomery & Jordan, 2017). Further research found that how effectively adoptive mothers understand and experience diversity is a significant influence on their approach to the racial or ethnic socialization of their children (Barn, 2013). The study concluded that effective transracial parents should rely on extended family and community support and societal discourse about race issues (see Figure 6.8) (Montgomery, J.E., Jordan, 2018; Reynolds & Wing, 2020).

Early childhood educators and caregivers can play a critical role in reducing microaggressions against transracial adoptive families and promoting antibias care for infants and their families. Microaggressions include perpetuating and reinforcing biases, myths, images, and stories about adoption and adoptees. A microaggression can be as simple as asking if the infant knows their biological parents. Microaggressions include implicitly biased ideologies, such as subconsciously thinking that White parents are "saving" an adopted non-White infant from harm, or that a Black parent has questionable motives when seen with their adopted White infant in public. Microaggressions support and perpetuate structural racism about adoption and ultimately harm children (Baden, 2016; Branco, 2021).

Figure 6.8 Effective transracial parents and caregivers should rely on extended family and community support, along with societal discourse about race issues.
What resources might early childhood educators offer to parents?

To Think About:

- How might systematic racism play a part in the lived experience of transracial families?
- Do you think you carry any implicit bias towards transracial families, by either criticizing or assigning undue "fairytale" images to their narrative? If so, how can you change these preconceptions and offer antibias care?
- List some specific, practical ways caregivers can support transracial adoptees and parents. For ideas, visit the US Department of Health and Human Services, Child Welfare Information Gateway online.

☑CHECKPOINT

☐ Describe the two stages of Erikson's socioemotional development theory during infancy.

☐ What is the difference between bonding and infant attachment?

☐ Describe the three patterns of attachment. How does attachment relate to optimal infant socioemotional development?

Temperament and Personality

Temperament, the unique individual differences in how we interact with the world, is persistent throughout life. Temperament includes emotional reactions or moods, and infants are born with their temperaments intact. It is a biological predisposition. **Personality** is related to what and why infants do the things they do. Personality includes temperament, but it can be swayed and shaped by experiences (Buss et al., 2019; Shiner et al., 2012). Personality development takes time, and although temperament can be observed early, personality typically becomes more evident after infancy and does not fully form until late childhood, or ages 10–11, and into adulthood (Bornstein et al., 2015). Although temperament and personality are related, personality does not affect temperament; but temperament and lived experiences affect personality (Tang et al., 2020). Psychologist Carol Dweck (2017) proposed that personality does begin to develop during infancy, motivated by the infant's imperative to fulfill three basic needs: the need to predict events, the need to act on events, and the need to accept and engage people in their environment. Temperament, or predispositions, influence how an infant seeks to meet these three needs through emotions and actions. How these are displayed become the visible parts of personality (Planalp & Goldsmith, 2020; Schmidt et al., 2019).

For many decades, the work of psychologists Alexander Thomas and Stella Chess (1977) has been cited for their description of nine traits in children that may shed light on understanding an infant's temperament. These include the following behaviors:

- activity level
- rhythmicity (biological regularity)
- approach or withdrawal
- adaptability to changes
- threshold of responsiveness to stimuli
- intensity of emotional reactions to situations
- quality of mood (positive or negative)
- distractibility
- attention span and persistence

From these behaviors, Thomas and Chess identified that about 60% to 65% of infants have one of three basic temperaments. These include what they termed *easy babies, difficult babies,* and *slow-to-warm-up babies.* These descriptors were used to describe an infant's basic temperament in relation to the primary caregivers. When infant and caregiver are coordinated, it is referred to as "goodness of fit," and it is often assumed that bonding is easier between the caregiver and infant (Chess & Thomas, 1996, 1999; Goldsmith et al., 1987). These descriptors became pervasive in Westernized culture and are still often used today to describe infants, especially newborns, informally. However, because these terms carry value-laden meaning, professionals today tend to use words like *easy, active,* and *slow-to-warm-up* when describing basic temperament types (see Table 6.2).

Recently, more emphasis has been placed on how to measure and classify temperament in infants and toddlers objectively. Typically, these measuring devices include questionnaires or interviews with primary caregivers or others in close contact with the child, focusing on descriptions of infant behaviors and reactions (Enlow et al., 2016; Freund, 2018; Putnam & Gartstein, 2017). A baby or toddler may be naturally shy or hesitant to experience unfamiliar things, or they may be highly interactive. A child's temperament behaviors include emotional intensity, activity level, reaction to new people, reaction to change, and frustration tolerance (see Figure 6.9). Although one temperament variable is no better or worse than

Basic Temperament Type	Possible Outward Signs
Easy	Flexible Happy Calm Easy-going Adaptable Regular sleep habits Regular eating habits
Active	Fussy Fearful Feisty Easily disturbed or upset Easily stimulated Intense reactions Irregular sleep habits Irregular eating habits
Slow-to-warm-up	Cautious of new experiences Cautious of new people Hesitant Observant May withdraw or react negatively to new people or experiences May warm up over time Fussy Less active Difficulty with transitions

Table 6.2 Temperament Behaviors and Examples

Figure 6.9 How might you help a baby or toddler who may be naturally shy and hesitant to experience unfamiliar things or interact with others? How can you encourage them to adjust to new situations and interactions? Specifically, how might you adjust the environment or introduce new situations and people?

another, some behaviors may be more difficult for primary caretakers or childcare providers to manage. For example, an infant who is intense or reactive may require more calming attention and care. A toddler who exhibits a high activity level may be a good match for a caregiver who shares the trait, but it could be challenging for one who does not. For optimal infant development, caregivers can support and help infants build on their strengths (see Table 6.3) (Dalimonte-Merckling & Brophy-Herb, 2018; Shigeto & Voltaire, 2020; Wittmer & Peterson, 2017). Caretakers must diligently self-question to prevent positive or negative unspoken or implicit bias toward an infant based on characteristics such as temperament, gender, race, ethnicity, or socioeconomic class. This self-awareness is critical to providing antibiased care (Derman-Sparks & LeeKeenan, 2015; Derman-Sparks et al., 2020).

An infant's innate temperament affects how caregivers respond, especially if the baby's temperament is different from their own (Clark et al., 2000). Infants with **highly reactive temperaments** tend to react with intense fear, anger, or other emotions to environmental changes such as a loud noise, new people, or climate changes. One researcher found that infants classified as highly reactive became less so when their caregivers were responsive (Ursache et al., 2012). However, when caregivers were less responsive, they became overwhelmed with fear, anxiety, and other emotions. The relationship between the caregiver's psychological factors, such as satisfaction or frustration, is bidirectional when related to the infant's temperament. In other words, they impact each other.

Mothers' preconceptions of their infant's temperament during pregnancy may impact the child's personality because the mother influences the infant, and the infant reacts (Schwaba, 2019; Van Aken et al., 2007). For example, a mother who perceives that her developing baby is extra active in the womb may continue to assume that after the baby is born. Likewise, the same study demonstrated that a father's caregiving style may be a bidirectional influence on an infant's temperament and related personality development (Wittig & Rodriguez, 2019). If a caretaker expects an infant to respond to a situation with hesitancy, and the infant fulfills this expectation, this behavior may be reinforced; the infant may display more fear when strangers enter their environment. However, caretakers may help to play a moderating role. Infants may play a moderating role in their caregivers' behaviors, too, as some caregivers may tailor their reactions based on the infant's behaviors (Aunola et al., 2013; 2015; Brenning, 2019; Casalin et al., 2014a, 2014b).

Environment and culture also play a part in how caretakers receive an infant's temperament. Some of the "temperamental" differences identified in children may be culturally biased (Kirchhoff et al., 2019). For example, in some cultures, quietness and low reactivity may be valued. Other cultures may value high responsiveness and activity levels. Culture, both in larger surrounding society and individual families, can influence what behaviors a caregiver deems acceptable or unacceptable in children (Ashdown & Faherty, 2020; Josselson, 2019; Senzaki et al., 2021). A caregiver's values, including acceptable and unacceptable behaviors associated with temperament, are communicated to the infant repeatedly and over time (Albert & Trommsdorff, 2014; Super et al., 2020).

As the infant gives clues to personal preferences and a primary caregiver responds in either an affirming or negative way, the infant's brain learns how to regulate emotions, and the caretaker learns how to best meet the infant's needs. Environment will also shape and mold the baby's temperament and eventual personality over time, but the tendency to approach the world in the same manner remains constant.

Temperament Behaviors	Descriptors of Associated Behaviors	Examples of Enriching Caregiving Environments
Emotional intensity	High intensity: • strong reactions, negative or positive Low intensity: • subdued reactions, • muted reactions	• Create calming environment • Moderate noise and activity levels • Offer one-on-one time • Respond to infant's emotions • Offer comfort when distressed
Activity level	High activity: • lots of movement, • squirmy Low activity: • prefers less noise • prefers less movement	• Offer space for movement and exploration • Offer varying levels of activity engagement • Create spaces for quiet play • Offer indoor and outdoor activities • Offer encouragement to explore
Reaction to new people	High reactivity: • eagerly approaches • engaged Low reactivity: • hesitant • withdrawn	• Talk through transitions • Allow new introductions to occur at preferred pace • Model positivity in caregiver responses and bodily reactions and gestures • Offer comfort when fearful • Offer encouragement when engaged
Reaction to change	Strong reaction: • resists • cries Mild reaction: • able to adjust • adaptability	• Create a predictable schedule for eating, elimination, and sleeping • Make transitions smooth • Give toddlers choices in transitions • Be flexible based on infant's needs • Offer comfort when distressed
Frustration tolerance	High tolerance: • persistent • focused Low tolerance: • frustration • leaves task	• Provide stimulating but developmentally appropriate activities • Offer encouragement • Provide scaffolding • Avoid comparisons between infants • Offer comfort and verbal reinforcement of feelings

Kato

Table 6.3 Temperament Behaviors, Descriptors, and Examples of Caregiving Environments

Emotions

Infant emotions have biological and neuroscientific origins, and they are shaped by temperament, experiences, and social interactions (Barrett et al., 2016). As early as birth, some emotions such as pleasure or disgust are displayed. Around 2 months of age, most infants display some type of smile. Within a few months, infants show anger, wariness, and delight; in the latter half of the first year, infants may display shyness, fear, and anxiety (Brody et al., 2016; Lewis, 2016; Mesquita et al., 2016).

Some early interactions between infants and primary caregivers are described as **synchrony**, which includes the swift, harmonized, and smooth exchange of responses between an infant and caregiver.

Synchrony requires the attentiveness of each participant as they respond to each other moment-by-moment (see Figure 6.10). Over time, this synchrony increases, as can be seen in their responsive facial expressions, body movements and positions, and vocalizations (Carmas et al., 2016; Legerstee et al., 2013; Lerner et al., 2013; Soussignan et al., 2018). However, if primary caregivers attempt to control their infant's emotions daily, the reaction is often negative, and they cannot achieve synchrony (Aunola et al., 2013).

Even at an early age, infants can show some control over their emotions as they learn to respond to the world around them (Buss et al., 2019; Fischer & Manstead, 2016). Infants develop the ability to

Ivan Lonan/Shutterstock.com

Figure 6.10 How might this interaction between infant and caregiver be used to describe synchrony?

connect emotions with facial cues from caregivers (Palama et al., 2018). These emotional interactions and experiences can be mutually connected, as the infant's brain is molded to reinforce responses, while the caregivers react based on reinforced experiences (Schore, 2015; Soussignan et al., 2018). Children gradually learn to control their emotions, but the foundation laid during the first year continues throughout the upcoming years. Toddlers learn how to exert some control over their emotions, and their self-regulation abilities expand. Learning emotional self-regulation, starting in infancy, offers psychological protective factors, especially important for young children who are at risk (Norona & Tung, 2021).

Crying as a Means of Expression

Infants express their emotions in many ways, including showing signs of distress and pleasure through facial expressions, vocalizations, and body posture. One of infants' most common vocalization tools is crying, an emotional expression used as soon as they enter the world. Infants need to have their basic needs met and will cry to make their needs known (Bremner & Wachs, 2010; Saarni et al., 2006; Witherington & Crichton, 2007). When an infant's period or length of crying is relatively short and can be resolved or answered by meeting the infant's needs, caregivers become proficient at "reading" their infant's cries. Longer periods of crying can be stressful to both the infant and caregiver.

Even so, the caregiver's responsiveness is critical and may have long-term consequences on the quality of infant-caregiver attachment (Rousseau et al., 2020).

Extensive infant crying is not unusual during the first few months of life. **Colic** is a term used to describe the prolonged and unexplained bouts of crying and distress in young infants. It occurs in approximately 20% of newborns globally and 10% to 20% of infants in the United States, as reported by pediatricians (Akhnikh et al., 2014; St. James-Roberts et al., 2013; Wolke et al., 2017). The incidence of reported colic is highest during the first 4 months, peaking around 6 weeks of age and dropping significantly after 8 to 9 weeks. A newborn with colic may cry for about two hours straight (see Figure 6.11). After 6 weeks, the duration typically decreases to about one hour (Wolke et al., 2017).

The cause of colic is still unknown despite the amount of research done on this common condition. Possible causes under investigation are neurogenic, dietary, gastrointestinal, microbial, and social issues. Management of colic is also being explored, including environmental factors and pharmacological possibilities (Partty et al., 2017; St. James-Roberts et al., 2013; Zeevenhooven et al., 2018). What is known is that the consequences of caring for an infant with colic are stressful and may negatively impact family relationships during this crucial time. Caregivers

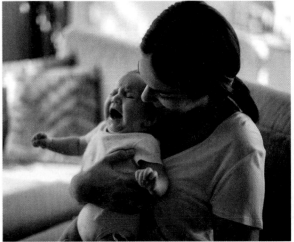

damircudic/E+ via Getty Images

Figure 6.11 Some newborns experience colic, a term used to describe the prolonged and unexplained bouts of crying and distress in young infants.

may need to seek medical care to consider any associated feeding problems or other issues (Wolke et al., 2017).

Support, education, and reassurance for caregivers are vital (Botha et al., 2019; Rousseau et al., 2020). Early childhood educators and caregivers should quickly acknowledge how stressful an infant with colic can be on family members. They can remind parents that colic affects many infants and is short-lived. They can also encourage parents to make crying infants comfortable, to swaddle if that helps, and to provide other comforting tactics such as a pacifier, massage, background white noise, warm baths, gentle rocking, and humming or softly singing (Lam et al., 2019; Wolke et al., 2017). Infant caregivers should experiment with different tips and techniques for soothing a crying infant (see Table 6.4 and Figure 6.12).

Social Referencing

Many of our relationships focus on sharing emotions. Infants imitate emotions as they learn to express their feelings by observing others' reactions to events. Infants can be fascinating to observe, especially when they are watching and responding to their caregivers. Infants take cues from their caregivers' responses to inform their own responses to ambiguous events or new interactions in their environment. They then adjust their own emotional responses and behavior. This active process is **social referencing** (Hertenstein, 2011). Even 6-month-olds use social referencing when faced with ambiguous emotional situations, and they become more proficient the more they do it over time (Mireault et al., 2014; Soussignan et al., 2018). Babies may wonder if the new person who entered the room is safe, if reaching for that new toy is okay, if the caregiver's crying and sadness is a cause for distress, or if smiling and laughing is the appropriate response. This simple act of taking cues from other people's voices, facial expressions, and body language comprises social referencing. (Baker & McGrath, 2012; Barrett et al., 2016; Carmas et al., 2016; Soussignan et al., 2018).

As one might expect, the act of social referencing changes and develops throughout infancy. Walden & Ogan (1988) found in their study that infants, 6 to 9 months of age, referenced or looked at their caregiver for clues most often when the caregiver expressed positive reactions. Older infants, 14 to 22 months of age, looked at their caregiver for clues most often when the caregiver displayed fearful reactions toward a stimulus. In a different study, Walden & Baxter (1989) also found that the child's age and the context of the social referencing mattered. Infants more readily accept and use positive clues in the latter half of their first year of life, whereas toddlers more often reference negative responses.

Assess if the infant is hungry, and if so, feed the infant	Introduce white noise	Place the infant in a baby carrier against the body
Change the infant's diaper if wet or dirty	Try different movements such as gentle rocking or gentle, quick bouncing	Experiment with different safe positions of holding the infant
Gently pat the infant's back to relive potential trapped gas	Consider whether the infant is too warm or cold and adjust clothing as necessary	Change the infant's view by looking out a window or walking around the home or outside
Reduce sensory inputs, including lights, noises, textures	Swaddle the infant	Offer a pacifier or other safe object to suck
Provide a comfort item such as a soft, lightweight blanket	Hum or sing a lullaby	Use an infant swing to provide gentle and consistent movement
Calmly talk to the baby and use facial expressions	Offer infant isolation and a chance to self-soothe, especially if tired	Give the infant a warm bath

Kato

Table 6.4 Tips for Soothing a Crying Baby

Figure 6.12 Tips for comforting a crying newborn include swaddling (A), experimenting with different positions (B), and offering something to suck on, such as a pacifier (C).

Infants are infamously curious and active participants in their learning. They realize that pointing to an object or person is an effective way to get a response from a caregiver. Caregivers naturally respond with commentary about the object or person, which provides the infant with data on how to behave or respond (Kovacs et al., 2014; Lucca & Wilbourn, 2018). Or infants may activate feedback by handing a toy, book, or other object to the caregiver (see Figure 6.13) (Bazhydai et al., 2020; Boundy et al., 2016). Infants learn appropriate emotions by following the cues of their caregivers. Is this funny? Should I smile or laugh? Throughout infancy and into toddlerhood, they learn to identify their most reliable resources of good informational cues and favor those caregivers they perceive can best provide this information (Brosseau-Liard & Poulin-Dubois, 2014; Crivello et al., 2018). As language develops, toddlers begin to seek verbal confirmation of cues, the precursor to the coming questions of why? in early childhood (Bazhydai et al., 2020; Harris et al., 2017; Harris et al., 2018).

BananaStock/BananaStock via Getty Images Plus

Figure 6.13 An infant uses a pointing gesture to indicate an object of interest to others.

☑ CHECKPOINT

- How does Erikson's theory of trust versus mistrust play out in infancy?
- Describe attachment theory. How does attachment differ from bonding?
- How does synchrony shape emotional responses for both infants and caregivers?
- Can an infant's temperament change over time? If so, how?
- What are the first emotions to appear in infants?
- What is social referencing?

Apply Here!

Review the tips found in Table 6.4. Have you had any personal experience using these tips for comforting a crying infant? How effective were they? Did you make any modifications? If so, were the modifications based on the infant's circumstances or temperament? What advice would you give to parents who are dealing with a fussy baby? Besides stopping the crying, what might other goals be? If you have observed others who have a knack for soothing a crying baby, what techniques, behaviors, or persona do they have in common?

6.3 An Expanding World

An infant's world begins to expand at birth. Medical professionals, primary caregivers, and extended family members and friends enter their lives, and thus, the journey of expanding social circles begins. Many infants receive care from extended family or childcare professionals soon after birth. As discussed earlier, wariness of others, in particular strangers, is an indicator of infant-caregiver attachment. Caregivers, whether parents, family members, or childcare providers, play an important role in helping an infant interact with others in their expanding world through emotional expression and social referencing (Wittmer & Honig, 2020). In the end, it is a matter of helping infants feel comfortable exploring their world, including navigating ever-expanding social relationships.

Infant Peer Relationships

It may seem premature to discuss peer relationships at this earliest stage of life, but infants have been observed reacting to their peers as young as 6 months of age (Hay et al., 1983; Hay et al., 2018). Infants demonstrate preferences for those who are similar to themselves, such as those who use the same language, over those who are different from them (Hamlin et al., 2013; Mahajan & Wynn, 2012). They can also react to a peer's distress (Hay et al., 1981; Hay et al., 2018). Around age 1, infants even show preference toward others who exhibit **prosocial behaviors**, behaviors that help or benefit another person, over those who do not. Especially during the second year of life, infants make dramatic developments in their ability to understand emotions beyond just those of their immediate caregivers (Hammond & Brownell, 2018; Hay et al., 2018; Paulus, 2018).

Exhibiting prosocial behaviors, or a concern for others, is one way of demonstrating peer relationships. During the second year of life, toddlers may show helping behaviors, and their prosocial behaviors begin to develop further as they start to understand the emotions of others (see Figure 6.14) (Hammond & Brownell, 2018; Hay et al., 2018; Paulus, 2018). Toddlers' prosocial behaviors tend to focus on instrumental actions, such as giving a comfort toy to a distressed peer. With these actions, toddlers are forming the foundation for later empathic or emotion-based reactions as they learn what works and what does not (Hepach & Warneken, 2018;

Waugh & Brownell, 2017). Sometimes prosocial behaviors may come in the form of disengagement or non-participation in interactions that are perceived as socially negative (Lin & Janice, 2020). They may turn their attention away, or older infants may crawl or move away. Toddlers tend to favor actions in others (third parties) that defend or stand up against negative social behaviors (Geraci, 2020; Hamlin & Wynn, 2011). Altruistic prosocial behaviors, which cost the giver something personally, tend to be understood later (Hammond & Brownell, 2018; Hay et al., 2018; Paulus, 2018). For example, when a toddler reacts with anger and physical force at an object taken away from them, a caregiver may model prosocial behavior in the offender by helping the child return the object. A caregiver can model empathic behavior when responding to an infant's distress. Caregivers can play a significant role in promoting social interaction and prosocial behaviors (see Figure 6.15).

The Importance of Play

Play is an integral part of infant and child development in all three domains: physical, cognitive, and socioemotional. Play enhances both gross- and fine-motor-skill development in various ways when infants crawl after toys or pick up blocks. Play enhances cognitive development when infants integrate sensual experiences, utilize memory, and problem-solve. Because play often involves interaction with others and helps create strong infant-caregiver bonds, it enhances an infant's socioemotional development as well

gradyreese/E+ via Getty Images; lostinbids/E+ via Getty Images

Figure 6.14 Infants use prosocial behavior when they share food as a way to help or benefit another person.

Sharleen Kato

Figure 6.15 Caregiver Behaviors That Promote Social Interaction and Prosocial Behaviors

(Ginsburg, 2007). Infants learn about their expanding world through different types of play: exploratory, play with caregivers, and play alongside peers (Bruner et al., 1976; Hassinger-Das, 2017; Yogman et al., 2018).

Exploratory play is a physical type of play that infants use when discovering their environment. Typically, they engage their whole bodies and all senses in exploratory play. They grasp and explore objects with their mouths and pull on objects to see what happens. As infants mature, they become more confident; they gradually gain the physical skills to interact with their environment and the cognitive ability to perceive their world through their senses. In this process, both fine and gross motor skills become more refined. Infants are more mobile, and many objects are suddenly within their reach. In the socioemotional realm, infants engage more frequently with their primary caretakers and then with others around them. This social exposure is critical for encouraging and modeling how to interact with the environment and people in it. Social referencing is a crucial component of both exploratory play and caregiver-infant communication. Caregivers should provide opportunities for safe exploration and encourage it through words, gestures, and, if needed, some assistance (Toub et al., 2016; Weisberg et al., 2016; Yogman et al., 2018).

The acknowledgment that play is critical to optimal growth and development was first noted in the early twentieth century when Mildred Parten proposed six stages of young children's play practices, two of which are common in infancy (see Table 6.5) (Bernard, 1970; Parten, 1933). Her work continues to be cited today (Biddle et al., 2014). Although the two infant stages are considered linear, with infants progressing through them one after the other, the stages build on each other. Play development will continue throughout early childhood as more physical, cognitive, and socioemotional abilities and skills enhance play. Chapter 9 describes stages four through six in greater detail.

Infants take their cues from caregivers as to whether they should pursue exploration. In their first year, infants learn how to engage in unoccupied

Type of Play	Typical Age Range of Initiation	Examples of Play Activities
Unoccupied	Birth to 3 months	Focusing on an object, person, or animal; staring at a mobile overhead; holding and mouthing a toy; responding to caregiver interactions
Solitary play	3 months through end of infancy, age 2.5 years	Engaging with an object or animal; reaching for a nearby animal to pet, rolling a ball; shaking or drumming to create noise; exploring the environment
Onlooker play	Age 2.5 to 3.5 years	Observing other's play with interest; typically, decision-making is disconnected from peers, as goals may or may not be similar
Parallel play	Age 3.5 to 4 years	Observing other's play; playing side by side but often with different goals or purposes; may be distanced
Associate play	Age 4 to 4.5 years	When resources are shared, decisions are made together, and play may be similar in context
Cooperative play	Age 4.5 and up	Sharing a common goal such as solving a problem or producing an artistic outcome, such as a play or musical

Kato and Biddle et al., 2014

Table 6.5 Types of Play

play and eventually solitary play. **Unoccupied play** happens when a baby observes and focuses on an object or activity. For example, a 3-month-old may lie in a crib watching the toy mobile hung above (see Figure 6.16). Although unoccupied play may seem inactive, it is still significant because it engages an infant's senses and cognition (Scott & Cogburn, 2021; Weisberg et al., 2016; Yogman et al., 2018).

Solitary play happens when an infant plays alone. For example, a baby may sit and play with toy blocks without interacting with others. Solitary play teaches independence and autonomy as infants discover play that is personally interesting or pleasing (Scott & Cogburn, 2021; Yogman et al., 2018). Reaching the solitary play milestone in socioemotional development is the precursor for parallel play, which includes side-by-side play activities. In **associate play**, toddlers may not be playing with or sharing a toy, but they are playing side-by-side. In this stage, the concept of "mine" becomes real (see Figure 6.17) (Biddle et al., 2014; Ginsburg, 2007).

Infants use **onlooker play** starting at about age 2 1/2 when they observe other children but are not yet participating (see Figure 6.18). Instead, they are learning how to play with objects and toys or by watching others play with them. Another example of onlooker play is observing others engaged in activities such as playing the violin, dancing, or singing (Ginsburg, 2007).

When encouraging play with infants and toddlers, caregivers should select developmentally appropriate games and activities that promote physical, cognitive, and socioemotional development. Play activities should incorporate the infant's developmental

Figure 6.16 Toy mobiles are a common tool for promoting unoccupied play as an infant observes and focuses on the object's shapes, colors, and movement.

A

B

Figure 6.17 Solitary play happens when an infant plays alone (A), whereas associate play includes engaging in play side by side (B).

Lisa5201/E+ via Getty Images

Figure 6.18 Infants participate in onlooker play when they observe but do not engage in another's play.

SeventyFour/Shutterstock.com

Figure 6.19 Infants enjoy exploring the world through sensory play with different textures, smells, and colors found in a variety of materials.

level (Hassinger-Das et al., 2017; Yogman et al., 2018). For example, infants are very active and still developing fine motor skills. Therefore, large, soft items are often easier for them to grasp. Picture books with sounds stimulate cognitive development, especially when the sound links to a picture. Infants love to see themselves, and safe plastic mirrors can entertain them and intrigue their senses. Mirrors can also reflect an infant's growing sense of self as being separate from others. In the classic study, Lewis & Brooks-Gunn (1978) placed a red dot on infants' noses, ranging in ages from 9 to 24 months, and then encouraged them to look at themselves in a mirror. The older infants knew that they were looking at their own reflections. But how did the researchers know? The older infants looked and touched their noses when viewing their reflection, while those younger than 9 months viewed their own reflections but did not touch their nose.

Exploration is at the heart of play, and play is crucial to an infant's growth and development in all realms. Because infants are in the sensorimotor stage of cognitive development, they enjoy exploring with their senses. Under caregiver supervision, toddlers enjoy the sensual experience of texture tables where they can dig in dry rice or sand. Water tables stimulate toddlers' senses while they pour and dump water. As infants learn about their bodies, they use all their senses, and the understanding of cause and effect increases (see Figure 6.19). Even throwing food off the high chair tray onto the floor teaches physical, cognitive, and socioemotional skills (Hassinger-Das et al., 2017; Yogman et al., 2018).

Music as an Instrument of Play

Music can enhance infant play as early childhood songs are familiar, funny, sometimes silly, and catchy. Preschoolers love to sing songs, perform hand motions, and use their bodies to execute dance moves. It is all a familiar part of early childhood, and many performers have established musical careers based on the appeal of music to both infants and their caregivers. Music can be used as an intervention tool for encouraging growth and development in preterm infants, pain management, and supporting infants with socioemotional special needs (Brandt, 2013; Edwards, 2016; Noocker-Ribaupierre, 2004). Much research has been conducted over the years focusing on the importance of exposing young children to music. It is a form of communication, a precursor to language, a tool for creative expression, and when it is combined with rhythmic movements it can foster gross-motor development (Trehub, 2010). Researchers have also found that music's positive and therapeutic effects on children may begin much earlier, even before birth (Edwards, 2011).

Infants are soothed by the sound of lullabies, especially if sung by the familiar voices of their caregivers. Hospital intensive care units have effectively used music therapy to calm and lower stress in premature babies (Meltzoff & Moore, 1977). Infants react to hearing the same songs after birth that they became familiar with while in utero. Early music exposure can have a long-term positive impact on cognitive and social development. It can enrich language skills, attention span, reasoning, and even mathematical understanding (Tafuri et al., 2008). As infants are rocked or swayed, the caregiver-child relationship is also enhanced.

Music nurtures creativity, self-expression, and self-esteem in the toddler and preschool years and beyond; it even promotes mental health. Infants develop complex listening skills by listening to music sung by caregivers. It can also help develop problem-solving skills, even shaping brain pathways (Wong et al., 2007; Zhao & Kuhl, 2016). For example, when infants create music through age-appropriate instruments (or instruments of their own making), they learn how to manipulate the instrument and how to beat or bang a rhythm (see Figure 6.20) (Hannon & Trehub, 2005; McPherson, 2016).

☑ CHECKPOINT

- ☐ When do infants begin to show prosocial behaviors?
- ☐ How might play with peers look for infants and toddlers?
- ☐ How might a caregiver encourage infant exploration and play?
- ☐ How does exposure to music benefit infants and toddlers?

Apply Here!

Imagine that a new parent of an infant in your daycare witnesses you singing silly songs and shaking a rattle in rhythm with their baby. The parent then makes the comment "I never feel comfortable doing that, as I am not musical and do not know the words to many appealing songs. Besides, I have a bad singing voice." How would you help this parent?

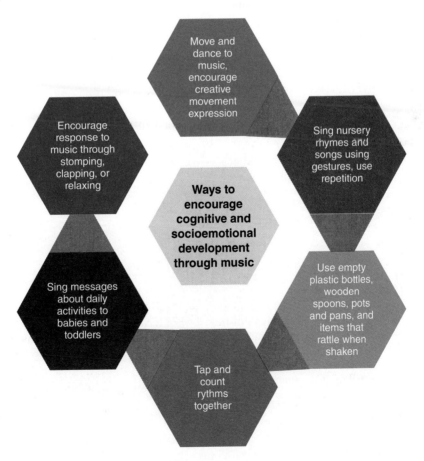

Sharleen Kato

Figure 6.20 Ways to Encourage Infant Cognitive and Socioemotional Development through Music

6.4 Infants with Disorders or Delays Related to Socioemotional Development

As infants reach certain ages within the first 2 years of life, they demonstrate common, observable milestones in socioemotional development (see Table 6.6). Most infants begin to show enjoyment when interacting with caregivers by age 3 months. They may smile, coo, and interact with their caregiver's focused attention. Other milestones, as discussed earlier in the chapter, also become apparent. But what if those milestones are not reached? What if the infant does not crave eye contact or is distressed by social interaction?

According to Stanford Children's Health (2020), about 17% of children experience developmental delays. Many of these are diagnosed before the school years. Because they spend so much time with the infants in their care, primary caregivers and early childcare providers are the best frontline experts for noticing whether an infant seems to be falling short of meeting socioemotional milestones. When delays are suspected, pediatricians and other medical professionals can assist with assessment and diagnosis and offer interventions (Lipkin & Macias, 2020).

In the first three months of life, most infants start to interact with their caregivers through eye contact, smiles, and gestures. They may imitate their

Age	Socioemotional Milestones
1 month  Goodheart-Willcox Publisher	• Prefers the attention and faces of people over toys and other objects • Tries to look at caregiver • Briefly calms self by sucking hand • Can be calmed or comforted by caregiver
3 months  ©iStock.com/Jani Bryson	• Focuses on faces and watches closely • Smiles at people • Smiles spontaneously • Expresses more emotions • Copies facial expressions
4 to 7 months  Aliwak/Shutterstock.com	• Recognizes differences in emotions through changes in voice • Likes play and may be distressed when it ends • Enjoys playful interactions with caretakers and others who are familiar • Enjoys viewing themself in a mirror • Knows familiar faces • Recognizes strangers • Demonstrates social referencing

(Continued)

Age	Socioemotional Milestones
8 to 12 months  *Bruno D'Andrea/ Shutterstock.com*	• Becomes shy or fearful around new people • Demonstrates separation anxiety and shows a preference for the regular caregiver by becoming clingy • Shows disinterest in some objects and pushes them away • Enjoys peek-a-boo and similar games • Has favorite toys, books, and songs
12 months  *Anetta/Shutterstock.com*	• Shows favoritism and attachment to toys, objects, and people • Cries or shows distress when separated from a caregiver • Is hesitant or fearful around strangers • Enjoys interactive games and songs • Repeats sounds • Begins responding with *no* • Exhibits fear • Works to get the attention of caregivers through sounds or gestures • Watches caregivers for responses to actions • Begins to assist in self-dressing by lifting legs or raising arms • *As infants move into the second year of life, emotions such as fear, anger, and joy may begin to intensify with increased energy or activity level, vocalizations, and resistant behaviors or unwillingness to comply with requests.*
18 months  *Anton Gvozdikov/ Shutterstock.com*	• Demonstrates desire to share objects of interest with caregivers • Shares observations of interest by pointing • Exhibits temper tantrums • Demonstrates comfort and affection toward familiar people • May be afraid of unfamiliar people or places, becoming clingy • Enjoys exploring, especially in proximity to the caregiver • Begins simple pretend play such as moving a toy train or feeding a doll
24 months  *Felix Mizioznikov/ Shutterstock.com*	• Develops self-awareness • Mimics or copies the behavior of others • Shows interest in other children • Gets excited and active around other children • Engages in parallel play with others • Shows defiant or disobedient behavior • Becomes more independent

Kato; US Centers for Disease Control and Prevention, 2020

Table 6.6 Socioemotional Developmental Milestones in Infancy

caregiver's expressions and become distressed when the caregiver's attention ends. By 7 months, most infants can respond to their names and to the different emotions of others communicated through voice. By age 1, most infants become shy around strangers; by age 2, they can imitate the moods and emotions of the people around them. By the age of 2, most infants have reached these milestones, despite differences in temperament (National Institute of Mental Health, 2020).

Delays may be related to physical or cognitive issues, or they may be considered socioemotional developmental delays, some of which may fall under the umbrella diagnosis of **autism spectrum disorder (ASD).** ASD was previously referred to as autism, Asperger's syndrome, pervasive developmental disorder (PDD), and other names. It includes disorders that can cause a child to have difficulty communicating with others and may include repetitive behaviors and eventual language problems (American Psychiatric Association, 2013; Chen, 2019; Donahue & Crassons, 2020). When infants are not meeting socioemotional developmental milestones, it is important to communicate caregiver concerns to medical professionals.

According to the American Association of Pediatrics (Hyman et al., 2020), the frequency of ASD in the United States is about 1 in 59 children (approximately 1.7%). The causes of ASD are unknown, but some researchers believe it is related to genes and the environment. Other risk factors for ASD include a sibling diagnosed with ASD, older parents, low birthweight, and other genetic conditions such as Down syndrome or fragile X syndrome (National Institute of Mental Health, 2020).

By the time an infant nears age 2, doctors can diagnose ASD by looking at the infant's socioemotional behavior and development. The American Academy of Pediatrics recommends screening all infants for developmental delays at their 9-, 18-, and 24- or 30-month well-child visits. They also recommend specifically screening for ASD at a child's 18- and 24-month well-child visits. It is essential that assessment be done as soon as possible so that a diagnosis can be made. Intervention or treatment such as occupational therapy or medical treatment can then begin. Early intervention may give a child the best chance at learning new skills, and it can offer caregiver support and education (Zwaigenbaum et al., 2015).

☑ CHECKPOINT

☐ What are some of the major socioemotional milestones for the first year of life? The second?

☐ How is an autism spectrum disorder (ASD) diagnosed?

☐ What is the advantage of having an early diagnosis of ASD?

Apply Here!

Review what you have learned about socioemotional development through infancy, ages 0–2. Create an infographic that includes photos or images showing examples of socioemotional developmental stages seen in play behaviors through infancy. Your infographic should include depictions of social interactions with others.

Summary

Socioemotional development in infancy is a stage of developing either trust or mistrust with others, specifically caregivers. The relationship between an infant and primary caregiver is critical for an infant's survival; it also influences the initial encoding of their lifelong social, emotional, and cognitive capabilities. As is true for all stages of human life, infants need to be talked to, listened to, and interacted with on many levels. Being dependent on their caregivers for survival, they need to be cared for and nurtured and to have their basic needs met, not neglected. They need to feel safe and to feel love and affection. All these needs require social interaction. Infants'

socioemotional development is critical and related to their physical and cognitive growth.

As infants mature, they become proficient at social referencing or taking cues from the caregiver's emotive displays and using them to form reactions to the environment. As infants enter their second year of life, relationships with others become much more reciprocal and more two-way interaction occurs. Caregivers begin to direct toddlers' behavior more than when they were babies, and toddlers become much less passive, reaching toward independence.

Exploration is at the heart of play, and as infants move into early childhood, it is crucial to their growth and development in all realms. As you will learn in the next unit, as infants move to early child-hood, they learn about their bodies, use all of their senses, and increase their understanding of cause and effect in terms of themselves, objects, and relationships to others. The adventure awaits!

Learning Outcomes with Key Concepts

6.1 Describe how infants and their caregivers forge relationships in infancy.

- Bonding is the reciprocal emotional connection that a parent or caregiver develops with a child.
- Responsive care is critical, especially during the first couple of hours of life.
- Bonding and attachment continue to develop throughout the first year of life.
- Postpartum depression is a mental health issue that manifests itself in many ways.
- New fathers report feelings of being overwhelmed with a sense of responsibility.
- Grandparents may play a vital care role depending on the contact and support offered.

6.2 Summarize critical components of infant socioemotional growth and development.

- Synchrony is the harmonized, smooth exchange of responses between infants and caregivers.
- Temperament is the unique way infants interact with the world that is persistent throughout life.
- Temperaments are biological, but experiences may shape personality.
- Highly reactive infants tend to react with intense emotions to environmental changes.
- Emotions are neuroscientific in origin and shaped by temperament and social experiences.
- Erickson's socioemotional development during infancy is the trust versus mistrust stage.
- Infants innately attach to primary caregivers, especially under perceived danger.
- Infants learn how to express emotions through observing and using social referencing.

6.3 Explain how interactions with an expanding world impact an infant's socioemotional development.

- Infants react to their peers when they are as young as 6 months of age, including their peers' distress.
- Infants show preference towards others who exhibit prosocial behaviors over those who do not.
- Toddlers may demonstrate prosocial or helping behaviors.
- Play enhances physical development through eye and hand coordination and fine- and gross- motor skill development.
- Play enhances cognitive development as infants integrate sensual experiences, utilize memory, and problem-solve.
- Socioemotional development is enhanced as play often involves interaction with others, and play helps to create strong infant-caregiver bonds.
- Infants engage in unoccupied, solitary, and then onlooker play.

6.4 Identify some disorders that may influence infant socioemotional development.

- Common or typical milestones in socioemotional development can be observed throughout infancy.
- By 3 months of age, most infants begin to show enjoyment in interacting with caregivers.
- Caregivers may notice if infants in their care meet or fall short of socioemotional milestones.
- Parents should report socioemotional milestones delays to medical professionals.
- Autism spectrum disorders include disorders that cause difficulty communicating with others.
- Screenings for developmental delays are done at 9-, 18-, and 24- or 30 month well-child visits.
- Early diagnosis and intervention, along with caregiver support and education, is optimal.

Chapter Review

1. Describe the ways that neonates, babies, and toddlers connect socially and emotionally with their caregivers and others.

2. Grandparents may play a vital role in both supporting new parents and in acting as caregivers for infants. How might grandparents be most helpful?

3. How does culture impact caregiving practices? What practices might you be inclined to explore further?

4. How would you describe the timing and the significance of infant-caregiver attachment?

5. Describe Erikson's theory of trust versus mistrust and how it could impact caregiver behaviors.

6. How does infant temperament potentially impact caregivers? How might caregivers impact an infant's temperament?

7. Provide a compelling argument for the importance of play.

Matching

Match the following terms with the correct definitions.

A. autism spectrum disorder

B. disinhibited social engagement disorder

C. highly reactive temperament

D. insecure-ambivalent

E. insecure-avoidant

F. reactive attachment disorder

G. securely attached

1. Infants who tend to react with intense fear, anger, or other emotions to environmental changes such as a loud noise, new people, or changes in climate

2. Infants who seem to ignore or avoid the caregiver following reunion after a short separation

3. When an infant does not form attachment to their primary caregivers

4. Infants who actively engage with their caregiver upon reunion after a short separation while communicating their distress over the situation and then returning to play

5. A number of disorders that can cause a child to have difficulty communicating with others, to perform repetitive behaviors, and have language problems as they get older

6. Infants who seek proximity or closeness after reuniting with their caregiver after a short separation but are still resistant and difficult to be soothed and calmed

7. A pattern of behavior in which young children show no inhibition in approaching and interacting with unfamiliar adult

Unit

3

Early Childhood (Ages 2–6)

Chapter 7: Early Childhood: Physical Development

Chapter 8: Early Childhood: Cognitive Development

Chapter 9: Early Childhood: Socioemotional Development

Chapter

7

Early Childhood: Physical Development

Learning Outcomes

After studying this chapter, you will be able to:

7.1 Describe how young children grow and change physically.

7.2 Explain how the gross- and fine-motor skills developed during early childhood are continuous, sequential, and interrelated.

7.3 Explain the relationship between the brain's physical changes and cognitive development in early childhood.

7.4 Discuss the importance of health and wellness in the early childhood years and the effects of interaction between individuals and their environment.

7.5 Summarize indicators of child abuse and neglect and the role of caregivers in advocating for children who have experienced trauma.

Introduction

What activities might you plan if you were to spend a day with a 3-year-old and the weather outside looked inviting? Where would you go? How would your plans change if a 2-, 4-, 5-, or 6-year-old were to join you? Do you have the physical energy to keep up? If you have spent the day with a preschool-age child, you know they are full of energy, seeking exploration and nonstop movement. At age 2, children typically enter early childhood; they have the skills to walk and run, and they eventually learn to run, hop, and skip, developing new physical skills as they gain independence and physical competence.

The development process during early childhood is gradual and not as dramatic as seen during infancy. Even so, the physical growth and maturation that occur during early childhood, often called the **preschool years**, is astounding. As in infancy, the developmental domains are interrelated as young children go through physical, cognitive, and socioemotional changes that depend on each domain. Development does not happen in the same way, at the same time, for all children. Children will develop certain skills or abilities faster or slower than other children. Some children will walk or climb earlier, while others experience delays in their physical accomplishments. Does it matter?

As you read this chapter, consider how each change during early childhood builds on what you have learned about infant physical growth and development. Also, consider how this growth and development might form a foundation for physical development later in life.

7.1 Physical Characteristics and Growth

At age 2, toddlers still have the rounded features that make them cuddly throughout infancy. Infants' heads are relatively large and their limbs are short compared to their bodies. Between ages 2 and 3, children dramatically change in body proportions as they transform from baby to child (American Academy of Pediatrics, 2014). By age 3, children may gain a more athletic, leaner body. Both boys and girls appear slimmer as the trunks of their bodies lengthen (Drummond, 2020; Voigt et al., 2018).

Their stomachs become more defined due to newly acquired muscle mass and core strength development. This is particularly true among boys who have more muscle mass on average than girls, even at this young age. The legs and arms of both sexes lengthen relative to their body heights. Although their heads are still large in proportion to their bodies, children in this stage are not as top-heavy. For most by age 6, their body proportions are becoming more similar to those of an adult (Feldman, 2017; Hay, 2020; Voigt et al., 2018) (see Figure 7.1).

Children tend to grow at a gradual, steady pace during early childhood. According to the American

SolStock/E+ via Getty Images

Figure 7.1 Two-year-old children have the rounded features of infancy, whereas 5-year-old children are growing taller and leaner.

Academy of Pediatrics (2014), they add an average of 2.5 in. (6 cm) in height and about 4 lb. (2 kg) in body weight each year (see Table 7.1). Children grow at their own individual pace, and differences are apparent, especially during the second and third years of life. Girls grow slightly slower than boys during this stage (National Institute of Health, 2020).

Individual differences in both height and weight become more apparent during early childhood. Sometimes these differences are due to heredity. A father who is short in stature may have a son who is also shorter. Short height is usually physiological and linked to genetics. Other times, these differences are due to the environment. A child who does not have access to health care or nutritious food may fail to thrive and show below-average growth (Laraque-Arena & Stanton, 2019; Miall & Smith, 2016). Usually, differences in growth rates are a combination of heredity and environment. It becomes a concern when growth falls off or stops.

If parents or guardians notice a pronounced lapse in growth over time, they should discuss their concerns with a physician to rule out physical causes. Problems could be kidney or liver disease, recurrent infections, or, in rare cases, hormonal gland disorders or gastrointestinal complications due to certain chronic illnesses (American Academy of Pediatrics, 2014). Of course, if underlying causes are determined, physicians may then prescribe interventions (Hay, 2020; Kliegman et al., 2020; Maaks et al., 2020).

Facial features are also slimmer in early childhood compared to infants' chubby faces. With a complete set of baby teeth, toothy smiles are common. By the age of 3, most children have their complete first set of teeth. As they reach the end of their early childhood by age 6, their baby teeth begin to fall out, producing gaps in their smiles. Each missing tooth is perceived as an achievement toward becoming a big girl or boy. Over time, as adult teeth replace baby teeth, facial features change again. However, most of these changes in facial appearance happen during middle childhood (Koch, 2017; Nowak et al., 2019).

Height and Weight Averages in Early Childhood				
Age (Years)	Height (in inches)*		Weight (in pounds)*	
	Girls	Boys	Girls	Boys
3	37	37½	31¾	31¾
3½	38½	39¼	34	34
4	39¾	40½	34	36½
4½	41¼	41¾	37¾	38½
5	42½	43	40	41¾
5½	43¾	44¼	42	43

*Height and weight measurements are averages. Each child develops at a slightly different rate.

G-W Teaching.

Table 7.1 Height and Weight Averages in Early Childhood

☑ CHECKPOINT

☐ What are the years that encompass early childhood?

☐ What physical changes occur in early childhood?

☐ How would you describe the sequences of physical growth and development during early childhood to a new parent or primary caregiver?

7.2 Motor Skill Development

Young children are known for their energy and increasing their physical skills. Their energy keeps them moving—running, skipping, hopping, climbing, and even performing summersaults, handstands, and other feats that challenge adults. Motor skills are the physical abilities or capacities to perform physical tasks such as walking, running, jumping, kicking a ball, operating utensils, brushing teeth, turning a lever, and other hand operations. Motor skills considered fundamental, the basis for all other movement patterns, are categorized into functional types (see Table 7.2). These include locomotor (ability to move the body), balance, and manipulative skills. Manipulative skills refer to the ability to handle an object and include object control and fine-motor skills (Kokstein et al., 2017).

In early childhood, over a period of a few years, the toddlers' slow, robot-like walking transforms into running, twirling, and dancing. Motor functions develop over time, as young children are both physically and cognitively able to perform new tasks. For example, 2-year-olds may have trouble understanding how LEGO® pieces work together. Their lack of manual dexterity and hand-eye coordination makes building with these toy blocks difficult as well. But by the end of early childhood, at about age 6, young children can both conceptualize how puzzle pieces work together while also picking up and properly placing age-appropriate building block pieces together.

While motor functions develop as young children are physically and cognitively able, acquired motor skills also affect physical and cognitive development (Figure 7.2). For example, as a child learns to climb a ladder to access a playground slide, acquiring gross-motor skills leads to better physical coordination and cognitive problem solving (Lubans et al., 2010). Developing fine-motor skills such as holding a pencil affects the physical development of the brain for future academic success and learning (Carlson et al., 2013; Grissmer et al., 2010; James, 2010).

Motor skills are also associated with socioemotional development. Young children who demonstrated higher social engagement skills showed more advancement in both motor and cognitive skills by the end of the preschool stage (Rojas et al., 2020). As children improve their ability to manage feelings and emotions to assist with goal-directed actions, their motor skills may be positively affected. For example, learning to ride a bike may require managing fears and frustrations. In addition, young children who are around older peers and demonstrate early self-regulation or self-control skills can show more advanced motor skills as well as language development (Blair & Raver, 2015; DeLay et al., 2016).

Type of Fundamental Motor Skill	Examples
Locomotor	Running, skipping, hopping
Balance	Standing on one leg, climbing on an object, twisting
Manipulative: object control	Kicking, throwing, catching
Manipulative: fine-motor skills	Holding a fork, spoon, or chopstick; holding a cup, holding a toothbrush; holding a crayon or marker, using scissors, or performing a sewing or lacing task

Kato; Kokstein et al., 2017; Lubans et al., 2010

Table 7.2 Fundamental Motor Skills

Figure 7.2 Young children use gross-motor skills as they explore their world.

The theory of Albert Bandura gives insight into how children learn motor skills. Children hone their motor skills through observation, trial and error, and guided practice (Bandura, 1986; Carroll & Bandura, 1990). Bandura's theory of observational learning includes:

1. Being biologically able to perform a motor skill.
2. Observing a motor behavior demonstrated by others.
3. Forming a mental image of the motor skill being performed.
4. Imitating or replicating the motor skill.
5. Repeating and practicing the motor skill.

Gross-Motor Skills

Gross-motor skills rely on the development of larger muscle movements that typically involve the whole body. Gross-motor skills develop rapidly during the early childhood years. For example, at age 2, most children are walking, albeit with more of a toddling, wide-legged approach to navigating their way. Between 2 and 3 years of age, their gait becomes faster, their balance is better, and their ability to navigate around obstacles improves significantly. By age 3, children are also more confident in their abilities. They add simple movements such as jumping, hopping, and twirling. Their bodies are more muscular and less rounded and chubby. Their bones are stronger as they gain more mass or density. Bone sturdiness and muscular development enhance their abilities to throw or catch a ball, run, jump, climb a playground jungle gym, and participate in other activities that require large motor skills (Draper & Stratton, 2019; Haywood & Getchell, 2020; Kramer et al., 2020).

Throughout early childhood, gross-motor skills become more refined. This refinement of skills takes practice and balance and shows postural control. **Postural control** involves achieving and maintaining a state of balance while performing an activity.

Young children can demonstrate postural control by stabilizing themselves as they jump up and down or stand on one foot. By the time children reach the end of this stage, they are capable of learning many activities that require coordination (Faigenbaum et al., 2020; Kramer et al., 2020). For example, they can learn to ride a bike, throw and catch a ball, shoot a basketball, or skate.

Age-appropriate gross-motor skill competency milestones assess a young child's overall developmental health (see Table 7.3).

Developing gross-motor skill competency combined with physical activity promotes better health practices throughout an individual's lifetime (Utesch et al., 2019). Preschool-age children who test high in motor skill competence tend to continue to show motor skill competence and to be more physically active throughout life. In contrast, those demonstrating poor competency tend to be less physically active and continue to be challenged in motor skill competency later in life (Barnett et al., 2008, 2009; Haga, 2009; Haugen & Johansen, 2018).

Parent- or teacher-led physical activity plays a part in gross-motor skill development. When young children are encouraged to develop motor skill competence, they tend to choose active play over sedentary play when given a choice during free and unstructured playtime (Tsuda et al., 2020). Families that engage in active lifestyles, such as outdoor exploration, indoor dancing, or other forms of active movement, model an active versus sedentary lifestyle. In the early childhood classroom, educators can incorporate physical activity and movement throughout the day by encouraging children to use playground equipment, creating obstacle courses that require climbing, jumping, or hopping, or providing opportunities for moving the body to music.

Fine-Motor Skills

Fine-motor skills involve performing skills with hands and fingers. These movements use smaller muscles and often require **hand-eye coordination** or the ability to use visual input to guide a hand activity. **Manual dexterity** is the ability to coordinate fine-motor skills more quickly and efficiently. Two-year-olds often enjoy squeezing, squishing, pulling, and rolling playdough. They can hold a crayon and scribble on clothing. Two-year-olds can stack blocks and push play cars. They often enjoy opening and closing containers and can easily open storage cupboards. By age 3, children can often draw a circle or an X; some children can form letters. They can color with crayons, hold a fork or spoon, and pull on simple clothing. Putting easy puzzles together is a good activity for building hand-eye coordination.

Children can even start learning to play a musical instrument. Although they are not yet ready to read music, children can often replicate music they have heard. Some researchers believe that the sensory connection between fine-motor skills and hearing

Age in Years	Gross-Motor Skill Milestone
2	Runs Jumps Kicks Throws a ball overhand, three feet forward Walks up stairs without holding the railing
3	Pedals a tricycle Walks down stairs without holding the railing Walks up stairs, alternating feet, without holding the railing
4	Hops Walks down stairs, alternating feet, no railing Walks backwards in a line
5	Catches a ball Balances on one foot Performs sit-ups Skips

Kato

Table 7.3 Gross Motor Skill Development Milestones

creates a perfect environment for learning a musical instrument at this young age (Miendlarzewska & Tros, 2014; Musco, 2010).

By age 4, children can often copy alphabet letters, dress and undress independently, fold a piece of paper into triangles, and build a tower of blocks. By age 5, children can often write their names, string beads, use scissors, and hold a pencil or chopsticks correctly (see Figure 7.3). Young children who have access to technology may also have an advantage in developing fine-motor skills, especially when used with caregiver oversight and under restrictive time guidelines (Souto et al., 2020). Age-appropriate fine-motor skill milestones are used to assess a young child's overall developmental health (see Table 7.4). If a child cannot scribble with a large crayon by

A

B

C

D

Raul Teran Aquino/iStock via Getty Images Plus; zGel/iStock via Getty Images Plus; Alina Demidenko/iStock via Getty Images Plus; kali9/E+ via Getty Images

Figure 7.3 Fine-motor skills develop over time. With repetition and practice, young children develop the muscles and coordination to perform exceedingly difficult tasks.

Age in Years	Fine-Motor Skill Milestone
2	Copies a vertical line Stacks six cubes Uses a spoon Helps with getting dressed
3	Copies a horizontal line or circle Stacks 10 cubes Uses a spoon and fork well Drinks from an open cup Removes their socks and shoes Undresses Indicates when urinary or bowel movement occurs
4	Copies an X Draws a two-to-four-part person Cuts paper in half Dresses themselves if there are no buttons Indicates the need for urinary void
5	Copies square Draws a 10-part person Colors between lines Grasps a pencil with three fingers Washes and dries hands thoroughly

Kato

Table 7.4 Fine-Motor Skill Development Milestones

the end of the fourth year, and there are no known reasons, the child may be lagging in motor skill development (Dosman et al., 2012; US Centers for Disease Control and Prevention, 2020d).

As young children develop their fine-motor skills, the preference for handedness (being left- or right-handed) becomes more apparent. Most young children show a strong preference, with most children being right-handed. About 10% show left-handed preference; and left-handedness is more common in boys than in girls (de Kovel & Francks, 2019). Studies have shown that right- or left-handedness can even be observed early in utero; about 90% of fetuses favor reaching with a dominant right hand, mirroring the same occurrence in infants (Faurie & Raymond, 2004). Recently, researchers established that left- or right-handedness differences are visible in the brain (Wiberg et al., 2019). Infants may favor one hand or the other, but they are still prone to switching back and forth. Typically, children tend to show a dominance of handedness between ages 3 and 4 through more sophisticated fine-motor skill development (Fagard & Lockman, 2005). This dominance preference correlates with young

children beginning preschool activities that involve fine-motor skill development.

Some early studies claimed that left-handed children performed significantly worse in many areas of development, including motor skill development (Johnston et al., 2009). More recent research indicates that left-handedness is a complex trait, influenced by multiple factors, including genetics, environment, and even by chance (Armour et al., 2014 de Kovel & Francks, 2019; Sha et al., 2021). The environment may play a large part in the impact of left-handedness in a dominantly right-handed environment. For example, if left-handed children are only offered right-handed tools, such as scissors, or placed in dining table positions that favor right-handedness, they may face more obstacles in motor skill development.

Some researchers and theorists have claimed that motor skill competency is based on biological sex. However, no definitive studies demonstrate that motor skill competency, such as boys being better at gross-motor skills or girls being better at fine-motor skills, correlates to biological sex (Kokstejn et al., 2017). However, when age was a variable in comparing young preschool boys and girls, girls tended to outperform boys in overall motor skill competency, manual dexterity, aiming and catching objects, and balance. In older preschool children, these differences tended to disappear, except for aiming and catching, in which boys tended to outperform girls (Kokstein et al., 2017; Vlacho & Bonoti, 2014).

It is recommended that parents or guardians should act early by consulting a doctor if they have concerns about lagging motor skills. For example, by the end of the fourth year, if a child cannot jump in place and there are no known reasons, the primary caregiver might seek a medical opinion (Dosman et al., 2012; Houwen et al., 2021; US Centers for Disease Control and Prevention, 2020d). Early childhood educators can assist primary caregivers by monitoring and documenting the motor skill development of children in their care.

When young children struggle to coordinate their gross- or fine-motor abilities, this difficulty may indicate other delays or disorders, such as autism spectrum disorder and attention-deficit/hyperactivity disorder (Athanasiadou et al., 2020; Kaiser et al., 2015; Visser et al., 2016). These connections are likely biological and associated with genes for muscle and brain functioning. Thus, early intervention can make a difference in motor skill development and achievement (Fliers et al., 2012; Heinrichs-Graham & Wilson, 2015; McLeod et al., 2014). When caregivers focus on helping young children learn gross-motor skills, it pays off in fine-motor skill development and increases both cognitive and communication skills. For example, assisting children to form the letter *T* with their bodies by standing tall and stretching out arms to each side combines gross-motor skills with the perception of a concept the child can reference when learning to write a *T* while using their fine-motor skills (Cheyne et al., 2014; Cook et al., 2019; Johnson et al., 2020; Valla et al., 2020).

Practical Issues and Implications

Encouraging Motor Skill Development: Play Spaces for All

Guidance, support, and encouragement are essential factors in young children acquiring new motor skills. Ideally, primary caregivers and educators share the role of providing preschool children with opportunities and tools for growth followed by guidance and praise (Kramer et al., 2020; Palmer et al., 2020). Classroom play areas, play equipment, and outdoor playgrounds may offer preschoolers places to explore, engage, and build motor skills. Giving young children opportunities to run and climb, especially on child-friendly playgrounds, can help them develop these skills as they learn how to navigate spaces with their bodies (Palmer et al., 2020). Just as all children have different physical and cognitive abilities, so do very young children. Sometimes these differences can make access and interaction with play spaces challenging. But it doesn't have to be that way. Using universal design principles can make classroom play equipment, playground equipment, and outdoor spaces accessible to all (Brillante & Nemeth, 2018; Darragh, 2007; Yantzi et al., 2010).

Universal design is the concept that play spaces and equipment should be flexible, versatile, and useable for everyone. Universal design allows all children to participate rather than being defined by their differing physical abilities (Darragh, 2007; Kang et al., 2017). Children can use the play equipment in varied and creative ways, allowing the imagination to flow without concern for using it in one right way (Dinnebeil et al., 2013; Kaderavek, 2009). In the past, designing for special needs involved creating play spaces and modifying them for a particular need. For example, a playground slide might have a ramp built beside the traditional ladder. In universal design, instead of modifying play spaces and equipment to meet a special need, everything is designed to be used by all (see Figure 7.4). For example, a structure might incorporate a ramp as an approach for all children, not as an add-on. In doing so, a young child is not identified primarily by their physical ability but by their desire to play. Universal design for all includes making play spaces and equipment with adequate size and space for approach, flexibility in use, simplicity, intuitiveness, and allowance for tolerance and error in use (Flores, 2008; Kang et al., 2017).

US federal mandates require that all children have access to learning in the least restrictive environment possible. Many parents of young children with a disability still report a lack of readily available inclusive play facilities for their children (Stanton-Chapman & Schmidt 2017, 2019). This disparity occurs despite

A   B

Figure 7.4 Universally designed play spaces welcome children of all abilities to participate in activities and not be defined by their differing physical abilities.
What makes these play equipment examples inclusive?

the Americans with Disabilities Act that aims to ensure all children have access to outdoor play equipment (US Department of Education, 2015). When teachers and care providers are committed to creating play spaces accessible by all, they advance more creative ways for young children to socialize and learn together. In the end, it serves to create an antibiased, equitable social learning environment where all young children can belong (Darragh, 2007).

To Think About:

• Why is it essential to create play spaces for young children of all abilities?

• What perceived factors might discourage universal design of school, neighborhood, or community play areas?

• Are the local play facilities in your neighborhood or community accessible to young children of all abilities?

☑CHECKPOINT

☐ What are motor skills? Name some developmental milestones in gross- and fine-motor skill development during early childhood.

☐ Describe gross- and fine-motor skills milestones that might be expected of a child starting kindergarten at age 5.

☐ Why is it a concern when young children struggle to coordinate their gross- or fine-motor skills?

☐ What are hand-eye coordination and manual dexterity? How do they relate to motor skill development?

☐ How does postural control relate to motor functions? Give an example of this relationship.

Copyright Goodheart-Willcox Co., Inc.

Apply Here!

Choose a physical activity that a preschooler might engage in, such as learning to ride a bike, building a blanket fort, or mounting a climbing wall. Identify the physical developmental gross- and fine-motor skills needed to achieve the chosen task. How do these gradually and sequentially acquired skills affect the three domains of development?

7.3 Growth and Development of the Brain

As described in detail in Chapter 4, the major parts of the brain include the brain stem, cerebellum, and cerebral cortex, each with a distinct yet synchronized function. The brain stem serves to carry messages from the spinal cord to the upper brain, and it is critical to life as it controls reflexes and involuntary processes like heart rate and breathing. The cerebellum has a role in gross-motor skills, including balance, posture, and coordination, and it plays a part in fine-motor skills. The cerebral cortex regulates the perceptions of touch, pressure, temperature, and pain, and is divided into the right and left hemispheres. The prefrontal part of the cerebral cortex helps people stay attentive, motivated, practice self-control, and focus on goals.

The specialized functioning of the left and right brain hemispheres of the cerebral cortex is termed *lateralization*, referring to how cognitive processes are typically more dominant on one side of the brain than the other. The limbic system includes various brain structures that contribute to brain functioning and instinctive behaviors and reactions, such as emotions and memory. The hypothalamus, sometimes referred to as the *control center* of the brain, regulates our responses to stress through the production of specific hormones.

Children's brains continue to grow and change physically in both size and function during the preschool years. By the time children reach 5 years of age, their brains have increased to about 90% of their eventual adult size (Dekaban, 1978; Leigh, 2004). As it does in infancy, the early childhood brain processes information through wiring—forming networks of specialized neurons that communicate with each other via electrical and chemical pathways that connect parts of the brain (Barkovich & Raybaud, 2019; Perlman et al., 2019). According

to Harvard University's Center on the Developing Child (2007), more than 1 million new neural connections are formed every second during the first few years of life. These pathways are reduced during the preschool years as the brain becomes more sophisticated (Sakai, 2020). The process of building pathways and refining or redirecting them later is often termed "blooming and pruning." Brain research indicates that this process varies by brain part. The timing of this process also varies by individual due to genetics and varied life experiences (Brink, 2013).

As discussed in Chapter 3, brain development is affected and shaped by both biological genes and lived experiences during early childhood. Genes provide a blueprint for brain development, but experiences shape and reinforce development. Responsive caregivers who encourage dynamic back and forth interactions help to create brain-shaping experiences. For example, when a young child interacts with a toy, a caregiver might respond with a smile or frown, look of surprise, or verbal exclamation. The child will then perceive that response and react. When high levels of stress are present in the surrounding environment, it can change the young child's perception, reactions, or responses and, ultimately, their brain architecture. Sometimes, lower socioeconomic resources may contribute to environmental factors that impede optimal brain physical development (Bick & Nelson, 2016; Hackman & Farah, 2009). For example, a child may not have access to a stimulating environment or quality childcare.

Exposure to environmental toxins can have a devastating lifelong effect on the developing brain's architecture. Toxins include heavy metals like mercury, lead, and manganese; organophosphates commonly found in pesticides; or contaminated water or food (Harvard University Center on the Developing Child (2007). Studies have shown that young children in unsafe, unstable, and resource-limited environments may develop fewer neurological pathways than those living in safe, stable, and nurturing environments. Such children may also be less healthy and less successful in school and life (Center on the Developing Child at Harvard University, 2016).

Young children are in constant motion and actively involved in learning about their world. They enjoy meeting new people, learning new concepts, and having new experiences. Evidence indicates that a loving, caring environment is a positive factor for stimulating brain development (National Academies of Sciences, 2016) (see Figure 7.5). Similarly, perceived stress due to the child's environment or relationships is proven to interfere with the wiring of neuron pathways. The people within a child's environment are instrumental in helping the child learn and develop when a child's brain is most receptive to learning. You will learn more about these windows of opportunity in Chapter 8. Repetition in activities is also vital to solidifying a developmental task (Conkbayir, 2017; Sortino, 2017). To continue stimulating all types of development, caregivers, family members, and teachers should offer a variety of learning sources.

In early childhood, the brain undergoes rapid growth compelled by a child's acquisition and integration of skills across the physical, cognitive, and psychomotor domains. Development in all domains is integrated across brain neural circuitry. This allows for young children to learn increasingly complex skills and tasks over time (Conkbayir, 2017; Sortino, 2017). Skill acquisition depends on children being ready to learn, and it can be envisioned as a developmental trajectory. It also depends on their health and wellness.

☑CHECKPOINT

☐ What biological factors influence physical brain architecture in early childhood?

☐ How does stress influence brain architecture?

☐ In early childhood, what factors affect skill development most directly?

MIA Studio/Shutterstock.com

Figure 7.5 Responsive caregivers who encourage dynamic back and forth interactions with young children help to create brain-shaping experiences through volleying reactions, including facial expressions, gestures, behaviors, and verbal responses.

Apply Here!

Create an infographic that visually and effectively communicates the growth and development of the brain during the preschool years. Consider how this infographic might aid communication between early childhood educators and parents or guardians. Could it be posted on the walls of the classroom? Could it be included in a newsletter?

7.4 Health and Wellness

Because young children are so physically active, good nutrition and adequate sleep are essential. Young children learn what to eat, how to eat, and when to eat as they learn to associate food with emotions. Food becomes a part of social interaction, and they eat from the choices provided by their primary caregivers or other family or community members. They learn how to care for themselves as their large and fine-motor skills develop. This is a time when primary caregivers, educators, and other adults help young children begin the lifelong task of self-care for optimal health and wellness.

Physical Activity and Play

Dancing, hopping, skipping, running, jumping, and climbing—young children love to actively play. Toddlers and young children tend to engage naturally in more physically active play than older children when given a chance (Birch et al., 2011). Engaging in physical play activities reaps many benefits, such as developing stronger muscles and bones and overall healthier body composition. Activity also encourages children's attempts to try new moves, developing self-confidence.

Active children also have fewer chronic diseases such as obesity, cardiovascular disease, and type 2 diabetes mellitus later in life (Fernandes & Zanesco, 2010; Keech et al., 2018; Milteer & Ginsburg, 2012). When it is a part of a preschooler's daily activities, being physically active becomes a lifestyle (see Figure 7.6). For optimal health, preschoolers should engage in about 3 hours of light, moderate, or vigorous activity per day (Birch et al., 2011; US Department of Health and Human Services, 2018).

Physical activity and play are essential to a child's physical, cognitive, and socioemotional development.

A

B

Figure 7.6 When young children have the chance and space to play, they tend to be more physically active and less sedentary.

Some researchers say that active play is really a young child's main job. In studies assessing the effects of physical activity and play on motor skills, 80% reported significant improvements in gross-motor skill development and cognitive development when young children engaged in active play throughout each day (Zeng et al., 2017). Improvements included positive changes in attention, memory, and language learning. Physical activity also gives young children the chance to actively play with other children, offering them opportunities to build social skills.

Despite the known benefits of physical activity, studies show that children today often do not get enough opportunities for physical play. Many young children in the United States and worldwide fail to meet physical activity guidelines (Chang & Kim, 2017; US Department of Health and Human Services, 2018). Young children often sit in strollers instead of walking. Sedentary lifestyles for young children can also be caused by television watching, too much screen time, structured and scheduled activities, and primary caregivers' fears of outdoor exploration. A lack of physical activity can negatively affect young children with weight gain, excess body fat, high blood pressure, bad cholesterol, cardiovascular diseases, and bone health problems in childhood and continuing through life (Campbell & Hesketh, 2007; Pandita et al., 2016).

Young children who live in poverty are the most susceptible to not having opportunities to play actively. They may be deprived of safe places to play in dense urban neighborhoods. In rural areas, they may lack contact with other children or lack adequate supervision to keep them safe. This deficiency, combined with being deprived of education, health care, and socioeconomic resources, has a lifelong detrimental impact (Milteer & Ginsburg, 2012). Caregivers in childcare settings can play an essential role in giving young children a chance to engage in physical activity and play. This might include giving children unstructured free time where they can interact directly with each other. When children play together without direct adult supervision, more physical activity often occurs (Ginsburg, 2007). Young children also demonstrate more physically active play when they are allowed outside rather than staying inside. Unfortunately, though, sometimes outdoor play is prohibited due to unsafe neighborhoods or a lack of play equipment or open spaces (Chang & Kim, 2017; Lindsay et al., 2017).

Primary caregivers and other family members who model active behaviors can positively affect children (Chen et al., 2020). In addition to the benefits of physical activity, caregivers who play with their young children have the opportunity to see through their eyes and build stronger bonds with them. Spending time outdoors in an unstructured environment can be helpful, too. Young children need supervision, but they should also be able to play within social and safety limits that allow for exploration and challenge (Wiseman et al., 2019).

Practical Issues and Implications

Outdoor Preschools or Nature Schools

Most people agree that outdoor play is good for young children. They run freely, hop, skip, climb, and explore when they are outdoors. There is room to kick a ball, ride a scooter, or climb on playground equipment. There are also opportunities to look under a rock, collect leaves, follow an insect, or watch a duck make a pattern in the water as it swims away. Most early childcare providers and preschools make it a point to get children outside when the weather permits. But what if they instead encouraged outdoor play in any weather? Can preschool centers operate entirely in the great outdoors?

Outdoor education is a given in many parts of the world, while more developed countries embrace the preconceived notion of preschool education being set within walls. However, developed countries such as Sweden, Denmark, and Germany have been leading the way in promoting outdoor education for many years. Across the United States, a movement by proponents of outdoor preschool education has been going on for decades (Nabhan & Trimble, 1994; Wilson, 2000). Most of these are nature-based programs where 25% to 50% of the class day occurs outside, though they are not full-time outdoor classrooms (Larimore, 2016). Sometimes, these schools are called **nature schools**, **forest schools,** or schools without walls (see Figure 7.7). Outdoor preschools go beyond the occasional nature walks or playground time. Children incorporate outdoor learning for the entire day. They learn to take risks and how to dress for the weather. They then engage with the weather. They see life and death in nature while observing growth and restoration.

Overall, outdoor education keeps young children more physically active at a time when physical activity is tied to learning (Ansari et al., 2015; Wenner, 2009; Wilson, 2000). Proponents cite advantages of outdoor preschools, including the health benefits of more vigorous and sustained physical play that fully engages fine- and gross-motor skills and improves balance and core strength. Being outdoors may also strengthen a child's immune system. Comparisons between students in conventional indoor preschools and outdoor preschools showed no difference between the two in the number of illnesses or serious injuries. Girls had slightly more minor injuries in nature schools when compared to conventional preschools, but boys did not (Frenkel et al., 2019; Hashikawa et al., 2015). However, according to a national survey conducted by the North American Association for Environmental Education (2017), outdoor preschools are primarily private, expensive, and lack diversity. Most children enrolled are White, middle-class, and from urban or suburban neighborhoods.

A

B

C

lp-studio/Shutterstock.com; Imgorthand/E+ via Getty Images; Herlanzer/Shutterstock.com

Figure 7.7 Outdoor preschools give young children the opportunity to explore and learn from the natural world.

(Continued)

Conducting preschool education outdoors offers learning opportunities, especially for problem-solving. As children explore the outdoors, they become more focused and observant and are better able to self-regulate. They engage in decision-making, become aware of the natural environment around them, and experince a sense of wonder in how the world functions (Wilson, 1993). Some proponents point to the socioemotional benefits, including reducing stress and anxiety, from learning through outdoor play. Others propose that outdoor education builds special social bonds among the participants (Ginsburg, 2007; MacQuarrie et al., 2015).

To Think About:

- What factors might discourage outdoor classrooms? How many of these factors are based on research, and how many on tradition?
- Would an outdoor classroom work in an urban setting? Why or why not?
- Imagine that you could plan a half-day block for preschool students in an outdoor setting. How would you organize this time?

☑CHECKPOINT

- ☐ How much physical activity should young children get each day?
- ☐ How does physical activity promote healthy body composition and boost general health and wellness in young children?
- ☐ How does physical activity promote other areas of development, including cognitive and socioemotional development in young children? Give two examples.
- ☐ Why do some young children not get enough physical activity during their day? How can early childhood educators help to alleviate this problem?

Nutritional Needs

Young children need adequate calories from dense nutritional foods to grow and develop physically, cognitively, and socioemotionally. Their dietary needs for essential vitamins and minerals are like those of teens and adults. They need well-rounded diets; and as physically active, growing children, they require adequate calories. According to the US Department of Agriculture's (2020a) Choose My Plate recommendation, young children's caloric needs vary by gender, age, and activity level as shown in Table 7.5.

Sometimes referred to as the "just right phenomenon," young children may be very particular about

Age and Gender	<30 min activity	30–60 min activity	60 min activity
Girl age 2	1000	1000	1000
Boy age 2	1000	1000	1000
Girl age 3	1000	1200	1200
Boy age 3	1000	1400	1400
Girl age 4	1200	1400	1400
Boy age 4	1200	1400	1600
Girl age 5	1200	1400	1600
Boy age 5	1200	1400	1600

US Department of Agriculture (2020a). Choose My Plate.

Table 7.5 Activity and Calories Needed

sensory intake with strong preferences for textures, colors, and tastes. Food intake is no exception. These preferences affect eating patterns because young children's food preferences indicate that they most prefer energy-dense foods, particularly sweet and salty foods, and least prefer vegetables (Grimm et al., 2014; Johnson, 2016; Samuel et al., 2018). As young children become more independent, their food preferences often become more pronounced. Part of their perceived pickiness comes from their acute ability to taste. The taste buds on their tongues rejuvenate or are replaced at a much faster pace than they do in adolescents or adults. Besides taste, they may have preferences for textures, enjoying those that are most familiar. A well-balanced diet in early childhood should include a large variety of fruits and vegetables, whole grains, protein, and dairy (see Figure 7.8). These food choices promote a healthy eating style and provide the nutrients their bodies need. Added sugars, sodium, and saturated fats should be limited in the diet of young children (US Department of Agriculture, 2020b).

Because early childhood is such an essential time for exploration, introducing a variety of nutritional food choices can have lasting positive effects for children and caregivers and play an important role in promoting and establishing healthy eating behaviors during preschool and beyond (see Table 7.6). This is true in family situations as well as preschool or care settings (Cooper & Contento, 2019;

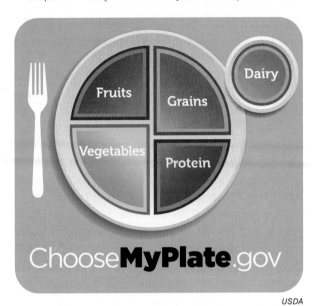

USDA

Figure 7.8 My Plate Dietary Recommendations for Children.

Kim et al., 2019; Metcalfe & Fiese, 2018). Providing well-balanced meals is vital during this critical time of growth because young children eat smaller amounts than older children and adults due to their smaller stomach sizes. They also have lower caloric intake needs when compared to infants because of their slower growth rate (Eilender, 2016; More, 2013; Wood et al., 2020). In some cultures, such as

Encourage Healthy Eating	Tips for Picky Eaters
Model and encourage healthy eating behaviors.	Offer a variety of food choices.
Offer water, milk, and low-fat or fat-free beverages.	Offer small portions for both meals and snacks.
Sit at the table when eating and choose foods wisely to prevent choking hazards.	Serve a new food alongside a familiar food.
Try new foods together.	Realize that it may take a dozen or more tries for a picky eater to accept a new food.
Involve preschoolers in shopping choices and food preparation.	Think "big picture" by trying to balance suggested amounts over serval days.
Offer opportunities to make choices between healthy food options.	Include preschoolers in food prep so that they can use their other senses to explore unfamiliar foods.

Kato; US Department of Agriculture (2020a). Choose My Plate. https://www.choosemyplate.gov/browse-by-audience/ view-all-audiences/children/health-and-nutrition-information/preschoolers-food-groups

Table 7.6 Ways to Encourage Healthy and Less Picky Eating

the United States, primary caregivers may consider healthy snacks between meals to be necessary. In other cultures, eating family meals together regularly is practiced at an early age, and caregivers do not cook young children special meals or allow them to skip eating things that are served.

Many children in the United States are not eating nutritious diets, and their consumption of sugars, fat, and sodium far exceed the recommended guidelines (Wang et al., 2018). Many diets consist of foods filled with too much sugar and fat and without an adequate intake of fruits, vegetables, whole grains, and low-fat or nonfat milk and other dairy products (Fox, et al., 2010; Siega-Riz, et al., 2010). Sweetened beverages, such as sodas and juices, are also an issue as sugar-sweetened beverages and 100% fruit juice consumption negatively affect s the healthy weight status of young children (Bleich & Vercammen, 2018; Crowe-White et al., 2016). As a result of unhealthy eating, many preschool-age children may have excessive weight gain, with the prevalence of preschool-age child obesity at about 14% in the United States and other economically rich countries (Bradlee et al., 2010; Frank, 2008; Volger et al., 2018). This has long-term effects because overweight and obese children are more likely to become obese adolescents and adults (Birken & Hamilton, 2014; Taveras et al., 2009).

In early childhood, the eating habits of primary caregivers strongly influence the eating preferences of their children (see Figure 7.9). Eating meals on a regular schedule, decreasing distractions such as television, reducing stress from conflicts during meals, and offering healthy choices can have positive long-term effects on a person's eating habits. On the other hand, when meals become forced or restrictive, the consequences can be harmful. Obesity is a negative effect linked to both permissiveness, with the young child having complete control over how much to eat, and food restrictiveness, with the caregiver having tight control over what and how much is consumed (Hassink, 2014; Isong et al., 2018). Another risk factor for obesity in the United States is race and/or ethnicity. Black children were at the highest risk for obesity, whereas Asian American children were at the lowest risk (Hales et al., 2018). Socioeconomic gaps were identified as an important contributor to these disparities, as children in lower socioeconomic groups

martinedoucet/E+ via Getty Images

Figure 7.9 Young children can be included in food acquisition, including inspecting and choosing healthy food options.

had less access to healthy food. (Hales et al., 2018). However, medical, family, and community interventions have proven effective in early childhood obesity prevention (Volger et al., 2018).

Although expanding a preschooler's food preferences is a goal during early childhood, the reality of the growing number of children with food allergies is also a concern. By some estimates, 6% to 8% of children in the United States have food allergies (Ierodiakonou et al., 2016; Sicherer, 2011). For unclear reasons, more children are experiencing food intolerance or allergies than in the past. Examples of common foods most likely to cause allergies include tree nuts, milk, eggs, peanuts, wheat, soy, sesame, fish, and shellfish. Restricted eating habits to mitigate food allergies, such as avoiding lactose-containing foods or following a gluten-free diet to manage celiac disease, can make it challenging for a child to get essential nutrients in their diet. If this is not carefully monitored, it will affect growth and development (Meyer et al., 2012). Food intolerances can also affect a child in other ways, including digestive or behavioral problems and skin reactions. Food allergies can cause serious reactions, including severe breathing problems, anaphylaxis, or death. There are internal immune mechanisms underlying food allergy (Brough et al., 2020). Even being in the proximity of certain foods can cause reactions for some children.

Pediatricians and dietitians can offer support and education for caregivers of preschoolers with food intolerances or allergies. While several food groups may cause allergies, peanut and other tree nut allergies tend to receive much media attention, as foods with nuts or nut oils are common in children's diets (Custovic, 2015). Through awareness of their students' food allergies, educators can help keep children safe and avoid adverse reactions.

Global Perspectives

Early Childhood Hunger and Malnutrition

According to the United Nations Children's Fund's (UNICEF) state of the world's children report (2021), around 200 million children under the age of 5 are either undernourished or overweight because they are not fed food that nurtures proper development. In this report, UNICEF reports a triple threat that includes undernutrition, overweight young children, and malnutrition from foods that lack essential nutrients. The World Health Organization (2021) reported that 149 million children under 5 years of age (22%) were chronically undernourished as of 2020. One of the United Nations Sustainable Goals established in 2016 focuses on ending poverty. Specifically, the target is to end all forms of malnutrition for children under age 5 and for pregnant or lactating women by 2030. Reaching this goal would be life-altering for millions of young children. A lack of food results in underweight children. However, in children who are obese or appear to have normal body weight, malnutrition may be masked.

Early childhood hunger and malnutrition have compounding physical, emotional, cognitive, behavioral, and educational consequences (American Academy of Pediatrics, 2015). It is well documented that the early years of a child's life, from birth to age 5, are a critical window of opportunity for optimal brain development that lasts a lifetime (Hassink, 2014). For a young child's brain to develop properly, fuel in the form of nutritious food is needed. The lack of adequate nutrition, or malnutrition, leads to long-ranging and often chronic conditions. These include asthma, iron-deficiency anemia, dental/oral health challenges, and other detriments to a child's overall health status (Kirkpatrick et al., 2010). Hungry young children are also more likely to suffer from stomachaches, headaches, and the common cold than their well-fed counterparts. Hungry preschoolers are also more than twice as likely to have behavioral problems (Coleman-Jensen, 2018; UNICEF, 2020).

Living in poverty can greatly affect food availability. Without adequate economic resources, caregivers simply cannot feed their young children well. In addition to not having enough fuel for the brain to develop and function well, a lack of nutrition also involves the socioemotional influence of stress on early development. The stress from being hungry in early childhood may increase behavioral problems and affect relationships throughout life (Hines et al., 2021; Kirkpatrick et al., 2010). For young children who are born into poverty, they face even tougher odds, as they are more likely to be disadvantaged from being born prematurely and at lower birthweights (UNICEF, 2019).

The United States has a longstanding federal government program designed to help parents provide their children with adequate nutritional resources during these critical developmental years. The Special Supplemental Nutrition Program for Women, Infants, and Children (WIC), which began in 1974, is a program of the Food and Nutrition Service of the US Department of Agriculture (2020b). It is intended to support the healthcare and nutrition of low-income pregnant women, breastfeeding women, and children under 5. Young children who have participated in WIC programs have been shown more likely to:

- be in excellent health compared to their counterparts who have not participated
- be food secure
- have healthy body weight and height for their age
- have fewer developmental delays than their counterparts who have not participated
- be at less risk for language and motor skill delays.

There are similar results for both working and non-working parents (Carlson & Neuberger, 2015; Soneji & Beltrán-Sánchez, 2019). Even so, young children continue to go hungry and be malnourished in the United States when WIC resources are not accessed or available for whatever reason.

All the progress made by efforts of the United Nations and in the United States through WIC may be set back several years due to the COVID-19 global pandemic.

(Continued)

The economic ramifications, including loss of income and lockdown measures that interrupted food supply chains, negatively affected the diets of young children as well as pregnant and nursing mothers (United Nations, 2021).

To Think About:

- How prevalent is food insecurity, hunger, and poverty in your community? Did childhood hunger increase during the COVID-19 global pandemic? If so, why?
- What programs are in place in your community to assist families with young children?
- What role might an early childhood educator play in addressing or helping young children who are hungry?

☑ CHECKPOINT

- ☐ How do the nutritional needs of preschoolers differ from those of adults?
- ☐ Describe what is meant by the *just right phenomenon*. How does it relate to food intake?
- ☐ Why are preschoolers sometimes picky eaters? How might caregivers help expand a preschooler's food choices? Give two examples.
- ☐ Why are restrictive or controlling caregiver tactics, such as making a child finish everything on their plate, not recommended?

Sleep

Establishing a healthy, regular sleep routine helps ensure a preschooler is getting enough sleep. On average, young children need between 10 and 13 hours of sleep over a 24-hour period, including naps (American Academy of Pediatrics, 2016). Because preschoolers are very active, they may also need one nap per day, especially during their younger years. Lack of sleep affects young children just like it affects teens and adults (McHale et al., 2017). On a short-term basis, it can cause moodiness, irritability, overactivity, inattention, and increased risk of injury. On a long-term basis, too little sleep is linked with storing extra body weight and developing type 2 diabetes mellitus (Weisenberger, 2020). Sometimes, physical conditions or disorders may interfere with a preschool child's ability to sleep, such as epilepsy, restless leg syndrome, autism spectrum disorder, attention-deficit hyperactivity disorder, or the effects of stress or abuse (Carrioon, 2019; Gregory, 2018; Sturmey & Didden, 2014).

Parents and guardians may demonstrate cultural variations in their values and practices related to their child's sleeping habits. As discussed in Chapters 4 and 6, the practice of training a child to sleep alone is based on ideologies related to developing a child's independence and promoting safer sleep conditions. Co-sleeping includes sleeping in the same room or in close proximity to a child as recommended by the American Academy of Pediatrics (Moon et al., 2016). Some families may share a family bed with infants and older children. In addition to physical sleeping arrangements, families may have a variety of bedtime expectations and routines, ranging from structured to unstructured. Most US early childhood education centers tend to establish sleep routines for the young children in their care, including scheduled naps or rest times, even though a more naturalistic approach to sleep and body rhythms may be practiced in homes (Gross-Loh, 2013). Thus, it is essential for families and early childhood caregivers to communicate about expectations, ideals, and practices to support healthy sleep habits (Harvey, 2021). Providing an environment that includes respect for a young child's unique cultural background and family influences promotes social development and feelings of security (Derman-Sparks et al., 2020; Passe, 2020).

Young children have vivid imaginations and may experience memorable dreams and nightmares. During this time, preschoolers may have trouble sleeping. To feel comfortable and secure, children may wish to take a favorite stuffed animal, special blanket or pillow, or another personal item to sleep. However, establishing consistent pre-nap or bedtime routines are shown to result in better sleep outcomes (Johnson & Campbell, 2016). This includes quicker sleep onset, longer sleep duration, earlier bedtimes, and fewer nighttime awakenings (Mindell, 2015; Spock & Needlman, 2018).

Some young children experience sleep disorders, including sleepwalking and night terrors. Sleepwalking is common, as children may partially wake and wander without being fully aware of their whereabouts and may be slow in speech and responses. About one-third of young children experience sleepwalking at least once (Boyden et al., 2018; Moreno, 2015). Night terrors involve periods of intense fear when a young child may cry or scream while partially awake. They may show physiological signs of extreme fear such as a racing heartbeat or sweating and may thrash their bodies around. Night terrors differ from bad dreams, as the child is more difficult to console when experiencing night terrors. Night terrors affect just over half of children at some point (Petit et al., 2015). It is recommended that caretakers gently guide a young sleepwalker back to bed without waking the child. In the case of night terrors, they should try not to wake a child but remain calm while making sure that the child is safe and cannot hurt themself (Petit et al., 2015). Most children eventually outgrow these sleep disorders, but they should be treated if there are underlying conditions. Identified triggering factors should be avoided, such as irregular sleep schedules, fatigue, illness, fever, and stress or anxiety (Leung et al., 2020).

Early childhood educators can help reinforce the child's home sleeping practices or even help the child's primary caregivers determine the best sleep and nap patterns for their child. Having both the home and preschool or care environment reinforce sleep and awake habits can keep the child more in sync, making transitions between school and home smoother. Early childhood educators can help with sleep transitions by being aware of and supportive of familiar routines when possible.

Toilet Learning

Methods of teaching young children toilet learning have varied over the last 120 years, ranging from passive and unstructured, to structured and even coercive, to child-centered (Spock & Needlman, 2018; Hutchings, 2019). Pediatrician, Dr. Brazelton (1962) developed a child readiness approach that began with observing when a child was physiologically

ready and the primary caregivers were emotionally ready to help the child transition to more independence. Brazelton argued that readiness of both the child and the caregiver, along with a supportive social environment, was key to successful toilet learning. He found that when children started toilet learning at around 18 months of age, they typically achieved continence, or the ability to control urination, by age 28.5 months, although the progress of toilet learning varies among individual children.

By age 3, most preschoolers significantly improve their ability to control bathroom habits. They understand the need to use the bathroom and can communicate this to caregivers. According to the Canadian Pediatric Society (2000), most young children in the Western world are toilet trained between ages 2 and 4, with girls often trained earlier than boys. Urinary training comes before bowel training, which may lag by months. Likewise, daytime toilet learning may be accomplished long before nighttime control.

Although preschoolers usually make significant progress in toilet learning, they still have accidents. Difficulty in controlling bathroom habits overnight is called **enuresis** or bed-wetting. Enuresis is a common condition for preschoolers and improves with time. Evidence suggests that more disorders of elimination, such as enuresis or urinary tract infections, may develop in children who toilet train late, after age 4. Overnight accidents may be the result of by drinking too much liquid before bedtime, heavy sleep, fear of the dark, or a combination of factors (Hutchings, 2019; Kiddoo, 2012; Shelov et al., 2014).

Some children face toileting challenges due to physical or medical conditions such as Down syndrome, cerebral palsy, or autism. Others face extra challenges due to cognitive or socioemotional conditions such as autism spectrum disorders. These special needs may present delays or limitations in toilet learning. Behavioral therapy and alternatives to punishment are recommended (Graziano, 2017; Pearsall et al., 2012; Sturmey & Didden, 2014; Wilde, 2015).

Early childhood educators can help reinforce the child's home toilet learning practices or even help the child's parents or guardians determine when starting the process is developmentally appropriate. Coordinating the home and school or care environments reinforces learning for the child. Caregivers can help ease difficulties in the preschooler's toileting habits to help avoid accidents. Preschoolers often need to be reminded or asked if they need a trip to the bathroom before activities, car rides, going to a new place, or bedtime. They also need periodic reminders throughout the day. To help ease overnight accidents, caregivers should limit liquids at night and create a dimly lit pathway to the bathroom. A nightlight in a preschooler's room, dim hallways lights, and a light in the bathroom can make for a friendly, safe trip at night. As preschoolers continue to grow and develop, they will be able to master toilet learning skills (Hutchings, 2019; Shelov et al., 2014; Spock & Needlman, 2018).

Medical and Dental Care

The American Academy of Pediatrics recommends annual well-child checkups to ensure that preschoolers grow and thrive as expected (US Centers for Disease Control and Prevention, 2020e). During a wellness visit, primary caregivers can ask questions about their preschooler's development. Healthcare professionals have an opportunity to interact with the child to assess any developmental or health concerns and to offer preventive care including vaccines against preventable illness (American Academy of Pediatrics, 2018).

Vaccines were developed to protect infants, young children, and people in general from diseases such as measles, mumps, diphtheria, rubella, polio, tetanus, whooping cough (pertussis), and others (see Table 7.7). Vaccinations produce or boost a person's immunity to specific diseases and help to protect the health of the community, including schools and care centers (US Centers for Disease Control and Prevention, 2020e). According to the US Centers for Disease Control and Prevention (2017), four important reasons for young children to be immunized follow:

- **Immunizations can save the lives of children and others they encounter.** For example, polio has not been seen in the United States since 1979. When parents choose not to immunize, they put other children at risk for diseases that could be eradicated, particularly infants who are too young to receive vaccinations.
- **Immunizations are safe and effective.** Side effects, if any, are mild. Science has demonstrated that the myths surrounding vaccinations are unfounded. Choosing not to vaccinate children can leave them and others in danger of contracting devastating diseases (Abramson et al., 2018; Klass, 2020; Shally-Jensen, 2020).

Infants: Ages 0–1	Toddlers: Ages 1–3	Early Childhood: Ages 2–6
Diphtheria, tetanus, and pertussis (DTaP), 3 doses	Diphtheria, tetanus, and pertussis (DtaP)	Diphtheria, tetanus, and pertussis (DtaP)
Measles, mumps, rubella (MMR)	Measles, mumps, rubella (MMR)	Measles, mumps, rubella (MMR)
Polio (IPV), 3 doses	Polio (IPV)	Polio (IPV)
Flu vaccine, every year starting at age 6 months	Flu vaccine, every year	Flu vaccine, every year
Hepatitis A (Hep A)	Hepatitis A (Hep A)	-
Hepatitis B (Hep B), 3 doses	Hepatitis B (Hep B)	-
Pneumococcal (PCV13), 3 doses	Pneumococcal (PCV13)	-
Haemophilus influenzae type b (Hib), 3 doses	-	-
Rotavirus (RV), 3 doses	-	-
-	Chickenpox (varicella)	Chickenpox (varicella)

Kato; US Centers for Disease Control (2017). *Growing Up with Vaccines: What Should Parents Know?* https://www.cdc.gov/vaccines/growing/toddler-vaccines.html

Table 7.7 Common Early Childhood Immunizations

- **Immunizations can prevent loss of time and income for families.** They help avoid prolonged disabilities from illness, lost time at work, medical bills, or long-term disability care for family members. Without proper vaccinations, young children can be denied attendance at schools or daycare facilities.
- **Immunization protects future generations.** Through immunization, diseases that kill or disable can be reduced or eliminated. Smallpox no longer exists in the world. Rubella (German measles) has also been greatly reduced.

In the preschool years, children are more frequently outside the home, and they have opportunities to interact more with peers than they may have during infancy. In the United States, most 3- and 4-year-olds are in full-time childcare settings, typically more than 10 hours per day (Augustine et al., 2013). The effect is that young children in childcare settings get sick more often than those cared for in their homes. These illnesses include gastrointestinal tract illnesses, upper respiratory infections, and ear infections. According to the American Academy of Pediatrics (2017), some of the most common early childhood illnesses include the following:

- bacterial sinusitis
- bronchiolitis (wheezing)
- bronchitis
- common cold
- cough
- ear pain
- skin infection
- sore throat
- urinary tract infection

On the positive side, children in childcare settings are more likely to receive medical care when necessary. Primary caregivers are more likely to be educated on preventive measures (American Academy of Pediatrics, 2017). However, income inequality affects the availability of health care for young children and perpetuates the persistence of racial economic disparities (Manduca, 2018; Odgers, 2015).

As discussed in Chapter 4, many young children do not receive adequate medical care and wellness oversight. In the United States, children living in poverty are much less likely to receive routine care or annual wellness check-ups. Because income disparity is often tied to race, children who are Black, Brown, or Indigenous often receive less or inferior health care than their White counterparts (Manduca, 2018; Odgers, 2015; Rauscher & Rangel, 2020).

Children begin learning how to brush their own teeth and even floss during the preschool years. Dental caries (tooth decay, cavities) is one of the most common chronic health concerns of early childhood. Because of this, young children should visit their dentist every six months (Chi, 2017; Koch, 2017; Nowak et al., 2019). Children who live in poverty in the United States are the most likely to have dental caries because they may have less access to dental care (Dooley et al., 2016). A child's age also significantly affects the occurrence of dental caries when dental visits start later than recommended (Gupta et al., 2018). When tooth decay begins early, preschoolers experience the pain and ill effects of poor dental care that can last a lifetime.

In the United States, fluorinated water is mandated in public water supplies, resulting in reduced dental caries and stronger teeth (US Centers for Disease Control, 2020b). In some areas of the world, including the United States, where many people use well water, water may not be treated with fluoride and dental care may not be readily accessible (Mouradian et al., 2000). Disparities exist in the United States regarding access to dental care. However, especially for young children who are taught good dental hygiene at home or in childcare centers, techniques combined with regular use of fluoride toothpaste significantly reduce caries. Having a dentist apply topical fluorides and sealants is also effective (Chi, 2017; Koch, 2017; Nowak et al., 2019).

☑ CHECKPOINT

- ☐ How much sleep should young children get each day?
- ☐ What are two sleep disorders that may affect a preschooler's sleep?
- ☐ How might a caregiver determine toilet learning readiness in a young child? Give two examples.
- ☐ When and how often should preschoolers receive medical care? Why are vaccinations considered an essential part of healthcare during early childhood?
- ☐ Ideally, how often should a preschooler have a dental checkup? What dental hygiene habits should young children be taught?

Environmental Hazards

As you learned in Chapter 4, young children may be more affected by environmental hazards than older children and adults. The World Health Organization (2017) reported that, in 2015, more than a quarter of the 5.9 million deaths of children under age 5 years were preventable. Because young children's bodies are developing rapidly, their exposure to carcinogens, toxic or unhealthy water and air, or chemicals have detrimental effects (Landrigan & Landrigan, 2018). Therefore, primary caregivers, educators, and others must ensure children's environments are healthy and safe. The US Environmental Protection Agency (EPA, 2020) offers important tips on how caregivers can protect young children from many environmental risks (see Table 7.8).

The EPA also offers tips and recommendations for creating healthy environments and providing protection from too much sun and heat, mosquitos, ticks, and storms and floods. Creating healthy environments for young children is critical, as their nervous and immune systems are still developing. They have less control over their environments than adults, spend more time on the ground; and because of their rapid growth, they breathe more air and consume more water and food in proportion to their body weight (Landrigan & Landrigan, 2018; Levy et al., 2018).

Hazards, Injuries, and Accidents

Young children are dependent on their caregivers to keep them safe. They are physically active and inquisitive. When everything around them seems new and interesting, children are motivated to explore. But, without life experience and knowledge, they need

Environmental Hazard	Recommendations
Carbon monoxide poisoning	• Install CO alarms in living, working space. • Only use fuel-burning appliances such as barbeques and grills outdoors. • Never sleep in rooms with an unvented gas or kerosene space heater. • Check and clean chimneys once per year. • Do not leave children in running cars in enclosed spaces such as garages.
Chemical poisoning	• Store all chemicals out of reach of children. • If a child has consumed or inhaled toxic chemicals, call 911. • Check labels to provide information to responders. • Properly dispose of toxic household chemicals. • Call the Poison Control Center at 1-800-222-1222.
Contaminated fish	• Stay informed and be aware of any fish advisories, beach closings, or drinking water advisories and refrain from visits or use if advised. • Properly dispose of toxic household chemicals that could pollute the lakes, rivers, and stream habitats of fish.
Lead poisoning	• Test living or working spaces for lead if built before 1978. • Wash children's hands and toys, pacifiers, and bottles frequently. • Wash floors and windowsills frequently. • Use cold water whenever possible for drinking and cooking. • Have children tested for lead by healthcare professionals.
Mercury	• Avoid serving children fish with high mercury levels, such as king mackerel, marlin, orange roughy, shark, swordfish, tilefish, ahi tuna, and bigeye tuna. • Use digital thermometers rather than mercury thermometers.
Pesticides	• Store all pesticides out of reach of children. • Store all food items safely to discourage pests. • Avoid outdoor play in areas where pesticides were applied. • Wash all fruits and vegetables before consuming.

Kato; US Environmental Protection Agency, 2020.

Table 7.8 Environmental Risks in Early Childhood

protection to avoid hazards, injuries, and accidents, some of which can be life-threatening, life-altering, or even life-ending. In the United States, many laws and regulations exist to protect children from harm as described below. Even so, the greatest areas of danger for young children include toys with small parts, improperly manufactured or installed car seats or booster seats, swimming pools or areas with water, bicycles and other riding equipment, firearms, fire safety, medications, and other poisons. Adult supervision is critical during the early childhood years.

Toys

Buying toys that are developmentally appropriate and safe for young children is also critical. In the United States, toys must be labeled as age-appropriate. For example, toys with small pieces that might be swallowed are not recommended for children under age 3. Toy manufacturers, distributors, and sellers must comply with the Child Safety Protection Act as enforced by the US Product Safety Commission (2020). Even so, caregivers must be diligent in ensuring that available toys are safe and appropriate, especially when young children interact with others or less familiar settings. Because many toys are acquired from others, purchased at yard sales, or bought at thrift or discount stores, extra care must be taken to make sure that these toys are safe. Sometimes, these toys have been recalled by government agencies due to safety concerns, are defective, or they are missing pieces through wear and tear.

Car Seats and Booster Seats

According to the US Department of Transportation (2020), nearly 116,000 US children under 12 were injured in 2017. Over 600 children died in car accidents. As a result, the department makes strong recommendations concerning child safety in cars. Infants, 12 months and younger, should always ride in a rear-facing car seat. Young children, ages 1–3, should continue to ride in rear-facing car seats until they have outgrown the seat by recommended height and weight. Only then should young children be placed in front-facing car seats. Young children older than 3 should continue riding in car seats until their height and weight exceed recommendations. Only then should they begin using a booster seat (see Figure 7.10). Although federal recommendations are given and car and booster seats are consumer

Figure 7.10 Car seats are essential beyond infancy.

products that are regulated by the Consumer Product Safety Commission, there are no federal regulations on car seat use. Instead, each state legislates car and booster seat use.

Swimming Pools and Water Safety

According to the US Centers for Disease Control and Prevention (2020c) and reported by the American Academy of Pediatrics (Pickering, 2014), young children between the ages of 1 and 4 have the highest rate of drowning than any other group in the United States. Most drownings happen in home swimming pools. Recommendations for minimizing these deaths include:

- placing fences and locked gates as barriers to pool access
- ensuring careful adult supervision for all water activities
- using appropriate personal flotation devices
- teaching water skills early
- ensuring adult supervisors know cardiopulmonary resuscitation (CPR)

The CDC (2020c) offers healthy and safe swimming tips for using pools, hot tubs/spas, and water playgrounds.

Bicycles, Tricycles, and Scooters

Young children need right-sized and age-appropriate bikes, trikes, and scooters. Providing safe places for their use that are away from traffic is essential. Helmets are also critical for preventing head injuries (see Figure 7.11). To date, no federal law requirements

romrodinka/iStock via Getty Images Plus

Figure 7.11 Helmets can protect the head from injury.

related to helmets for young children exist. However, many states, but far from all, do require helmets for children. In an early study, it was predicted that bike helmet legislation for children could reduce child bicycle fatalities by about 15% (Grant & Rutner, 2004). A study by Kraemer (2016) found that after bike legislation was introduced in several states, there were significant decreases in head or traumatic brain injury. Unfortunately, the number of people heeding these legislative mandates was negatively affect ed by racial, ethnic, and economic factors.

Fire Safety

According to the CDC (2019), about 300 US children are treated for burn-related injuries each day. Younger children tend to be scalded from hot liquids or steam more frequently, whereas older children tend to suffer from burns from flames. Caregivers should be careful when cooking or filling bathtubs for young children and supervise them around fireplaces, stoves, campfires, candles, or other flame sources. Consumer laws, such as the Flammable Fabrics Act, require that all children's sleepwear, size 0 to 14, be flame resistant.

Firearms

Nearly 1,300 children die from firearms, and 6,000 are treated for gunshot wounds each year in the United States (Fowler et al., 2017). Older children and boys are most affected. The American Academy of Child and Adolescent Psychiatry (2014) recommends that all firearms be stored in locked gun lockers with ammunition stored separately. Caregivers should never leave guns attended, even when cleaning.

Medications and Other Toxic Substances

Sometimes, just as environmental hazards may appeal to young children, prescription and over-the-counter medication may also attract them. Consumer products, such as laundry detergent capsules, may also be enticing. Why? Young children may mistake medicines or other consumer goods as food products. Bright and colorful items are particularly enticing. According to the CDC (2020a), approximately 60,000 US children under 5 years of age visit hospital emergency rooms each year after ingesting or overdosing on medications. The CDC (2020a) recommends storing medications out of reach of young children, never referring to medicine as candy, and ensuring that all medicines are in child-proof packaging. If children consume medications or other non-food consumer products, caregivers should call to get medical help right away.

☑ CHECKPOINT

☐ What are some of the top environmental hazards that threaten young children? Why are preschoolers particularly susceptible to environmental hazards?

☐ What are some of the top accident or potential injury hazards that affect young children? How can they be avoided?

☐ Name three US regulations or legislative acts that directly relate to keeping young children safe.

Apply Here!

Your friends are parenting a 3-year-old child, Simon. The preschool that Simon attends requires that children receive the influenza inoculation. One friend says that she never received the flu shot as a child, and she turned out to be a healthy child and adult. On the other hand, your other friend, her partner, is determined to get every immunization available for Simon to be precautious, believing that vaccinations are absolutely necessary. Their state recommends but does not require all children to receive the influenza inoculation. Now the COVID-19 vaccination is also recommended. They have turned to you for advice.

- What other factors should they take into consideration before deciding?
- What are the benefits of receiving the flu shot? Are there possible disadvantages?
- How would you advise your friends?

7.5 Child Abuse, Neglect, and Trauma

Young children need care. They need adequate food, clothing, and a place to feel safe and call home. They require education and nurturing, and they need to feel love. They also need protection from danger. Sadly, many children experience abuse and neglect by adults. According to the US Department of Health and Human Services (2019a), about 3.5 million children were the subjects of abuse or neglect investigations in 2017. Within this group, almost 80% were reported as neglected, about one-fifth as physically abused, and a little over 8% as sexually abused. Infants and young children are the most susceptible to maltreatment in the forms of abuse and neglect. Child abuse and neglect are global issues that cross national borders and socioeconomic lines (van Duin et al., 2018). Both direct and indirect costs affect the victim and society as a whole (Peterson et al., 2018).

Child abuse occurs when someone in power, such as a parent, extended family member, teacher, or another adult, inflicts violence on a child (minor). Child abuse involves inflicting harm, and it includes physical, emotional, and sexual abuse as well as neglect. **Physical abuse** involves injury through slapping, kicking, hitting, beating, shaking, biting, punching, or other means. The US Department of Health and Human Services (2019a) advises educators, professional caregivers, and service providers to suspect physical abuse when a child displays multiple or repeated injuries. If the child has many unexplained bruises or hides bruises under clothing, professional service providers should suspect abuse. Likewise, if a child has repeated injuries such as broken bones, cuts, or scrapes, abuse may be a cause (Hamilton-Giachritsis & Pellai, 2017; Shipman et al., 2017).

Harm that causes serious cognitive, behavioral, or emotional problems is **emotional abuse**. Emotional abuse can be as harmful to a child as physical abuse and have lifelong effects (Cicchetti et al., 2016; Doyle & Cicchetti, 2017). Many times, physical and emotional abuse exist together. When children display signs of emotional abuse, this often also confirms question signs of physical injuries as child abuse. Signs of emotional abuse are often easier to identify in older children and teens as they

can articulate concerns. For this reason, emotional abuse will be discussed more fully in later chapters. Both physical and emotional abuse used in a sexual manner is **sexual abuse** and includes all kinds of inappropriate behavior toward or with a child, including touching and sexual acts. It can also include exposure to pornography. Many times, children who experience sexual abuse act out their abuse by being overtly sexual. They may inappropriately touch or confront another child or even an adult. For children who are sexually abused, these behaviors are learned and modeled to them. These behaviors go beyond the normal curiosity of children and teens.

Neglect is a type of endangerment or harm to a child resulting from a caregiver's failure to provide basic needs, including physical, medical, educational, or emotional support. There are often news reports of children left unattended or without proper care (Shipman et al., 2017). Evidence suggests that psychological outcomes from abuse and neglect can vary according to the relationship between the child and the perpetrator, the duration and severity of the abuse or neglect, and the type of abuse (Bryce et al., 2019; US Department of Health and Human Services, 2019a).

Why Are Children Abused?

People often wonder why children, the most vulnerable members of society, experience abuse. The answer is that they are easy targets. They are the targets of anger and wrath from frustrated and stressed adults. Because children are less powerful and often lack the ability to defend themselves, the abuse goes unreported. The vulnerable never deserve abuse, nor do they ever ask for it. Abuse and neglect are behaviors that victimize. Although most children who experience abuse do not grow up to become abusers, the cycle of child abuse may repeat itself in future generations because of learned behaviors. For instance, when children experience abuse, they may begin to think this behavior is normal. Caregivers can help turn this tide by modeling nurturing caregiving (McCrory et al., 2017; Wekerle et al., 2019).

According to the US Department of Health and Human Services (2015), risk factors linked to child abuse and neglect include:

- parental lack of understanding of child development, parenting skills, and children's needs
- substance abuse or mental health issues in the family
- temporary caregivers in the home
- intimate partner violence
- parenting stress

Community violence is also a risk factor for child abuse and neglect. Children who live in neighborhoods that experience more violence may also be more likely to face abuse. Some family situations may increase susceptibility to child abuse and spousal abuse (or intimate partner abuse). Most of these factors relate to stress. Economic distress brought on by unemployment, inadequate pay, or family illness is often associated with abuse. Primary caregiver personality issues are often factors, such as a need for control, low self-esteem, anger issues, social isolation, or difficulty coping with stress (Goddard et al., 2017; Painter & Scannapieco, 2021).

Child abuse does not have to repeat itself; it is possible to both stop and prevent it (Munro, 2020; O'Hare, 2021). According to the US Department of Health and Human Services (2019b), in contrast to risk factors that increase the danger for abuse, **protective factors** help lessen the risk of child abuse and neglect and help promote family resilience and optimal child development (see Table 7.9). Parent education is the key to stopping abuse because it increases the parents' understanding of children. Learning about developmental stages can help parents have more reasonable expectations for their children's behavior. It also includes showing parents how to guide and discipline their children appropriately and effectively (McCrory et al., 2017; Wekerle et al., 2019).

Because abusive behaviors are often linked to stress, community resources are valuable. Local government sources, schools, hospitals, health centers, religious organizations, and law enforcement agencies can make referrals to counselors who specialize in intimate partner violence (and other forms of domestic violence) and child abuse. They can also make referrals to others community resources that can lower family stress, including financial resources, childcare, housing, and food assistance (Westman, 2019).

Although anyone can report child neglect or abuse, **mandated reporters** must legally report suspected instances of child neglect and abuse. Mandated reporters include people in occupations that involve working with children, such as teachers, counselors, nurses, administrators, special education professionals, and social workers. Whether or not someone is a mandated reporter, if they are in a situation where they suspect neglect or abuse of a child, they have an ethical responsibility to report the concern (Shipman et al., 2017; Waite & Ryan, 2020). If someone suspects a child is being abused or neglected, they must contact their supervisor, local child protective services, or a law enforcement agency so professionals can evaluate the situation. Most states provide emergency hotlines to report child abuse, and the national 911 emergency service

Individual Protective Factors	Family Protective Factors	Community Protective Factors
• Caregivers who create relationships with children that are safe, positive, and nurturing • Provision of basic needs such as food and shelter • Education availability and support • Access to health services • Caregivers who have stable financial income or steady employment • Caregivers who have earned a college degree	• Established support networks • Stable and positive community relationships • House rules that are established and enforced • Present caregivers that are interested in and monitor children • Role models in extended family members or other outside adults	• High-quality preschools • Safe childcare options • Family-friendly work opportunities • Stable and affordable housing • Accessible medical and mental health care • Financial and emergency support services

US Centers for Disease Control and Prevention.
https://www.cdc.gov/violenceprevention/childabuseandneglect/riskprotectivefactors.html#Protective%20Factors

Table 7.9 Factors That Help Lessen the Risk of Child Abuse and Neglect

may also be used for reporting. In addition, the US Department of Health and Human Services (2019b) provides an abundance of information for teachers, caregivers, family, and other community members who desire more resources or avenues for reporting including the Childhelp® National Child Abuse Hotline. The hotline is open 24 hours a day, 7 days a week. All calls to Childhelp are anonymous. Crisis counselors are available to take calls, answer questions, make referrals, and connect the caller with emergency social and support services. Childhelp is an important resource to remember for teachers and care providers of children and teens.

Trauma-Informed Caregiving

Young children experience trauma from all forms of abuse and neglect. They also experience trauma through domestic partner violence, poverty that includes hunger or housing instability, displacement from natural disaster, observing violence and war, separation from or death of caregivers, or other forms of adverse childhood experiences (ACEs). Household substance abuse, mental illness, and parental separation or divorce may also cause trauma (McCrory et al., 2017; Painter & Scannapieco, 2021). Young children who experience intense distress may manifest many forms of maladaptive behavior, including mental health issues, risky behaviors, and developmental challenges (see Table 7.10).

Interdisciplinary research focused on the effect of ACEs on young children has demonstrated that the effect is both immediate and long-term (Godoy et al., 2020, Holman et al., 2016; Merrick et al., 2018). Young children who experience trauma may have lifelong altered brain architecture. These negative changes may be seen in the structure, function, and connectivity of different brain areas (Cross et al., 2017; Danese & Lewis, 2017; McCrory et al., 2017).

Trauma-informed care (TIC) involves understanding, identifying, and responding to the effects of trauma on children and teens. The American Academy of Pediatrics (2020) and the US Department of Health and Human Services (2020) offer many important guidelines for primary caregivers, foster parents, medical care providers, and caregivers to properly care for children who experience trauma (see Figure 7.12). The goals of TIC include engaging caregivers in trauma education, avoiding triggers that might cause continuing trauma, developing trust, and most importantly, taking care not to add more trauma when addressing needs. Young children are susceptible to long-term consequences as their brains are still developing. However, they are also resilient. With patient, stable, and repetitious TIC practices, traumatized children may recover and thrive (Erdman et al., 2020; O'Hare, 2021; Osofsky et al., 2018). Tips for providing supportive trauma-informed care in early childhood settings include (Statman-Weil, 2015):

- providing stability through daily routines
- inviting and modeling respectful communication

Mental Health Issues	Risky Behaviors	Development
Anxiety and depression	Addictive behaviors	Poor physical health
Stress tolerance	Increase in craving reactivity or strong, conscious desires	Early puberty
Schizophrenia, mood disorders, and posttraumatic stress disorder (PTSD)	Propensity to engage in sexual behaviors	Cardiovascular disease symptoms
Sleep disorders	Inclination to behaviors that produce or lead to crime later in life	Insecure/avoidant attachment styles
Atypical physiological regulations of stress	Susceptibility to engage in atypical sexual behaviors or sexual deviance later in life	Cognitive delays and challenges in memory, processing, self-regulation

Kato. McCrory et al., 2017; Painter & Scannapieco, 2021.

Table 7.10 Potential Manifestations of Trauma Maladaptation

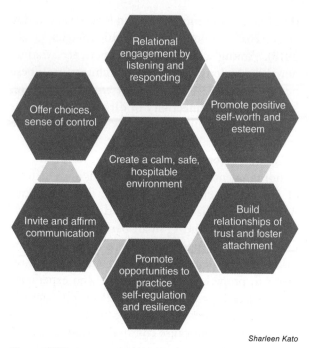

Sharleen Kato

Figure 7.12 Creating a Trauma-Informed Care Environment.

- giving warnings if unusual occurrences or schedule changes will occur
- being warm, affectionate, nurturing, and flexible toward traumatized children
- being creative and resourceful in helping children deal with transitions
- empowering children to make developmentally appropriate decisions or choices, giving them control over their circumstances when possible
- being sensitive to a child's tendency to reenact experiences
- providing positive encouragement and guidance

Professional care providers should also work with the child's family and outside specialists (such as a trauma specialist or a child therapist) to learn how to best support the child.

☑ CHECKPOINT

☐ What are the different forms of child abuse?

☐ Who are mandated reporters of suspected child abuse or neglect? How should it be reported?

☐ Child abuse and neglect have immediate effects. What are some potential lifelong impacts on a child's physical health?

☐ What types of adverse childhood experiences are considered trauma?

☐ Why are young children especially susceptible to trauma?

☐ List and describe some of the characteristics of trauma-informed care.

Apply Here!

Imagine that you have just taken two siblings, a 5-year-old and a 3-year-old, into your care facility. The siblings were removed from their parental home due to neglect and abuse and have been placed in foster care. Both children are reluctant to express their needs, whether expressing an interest in a toy or choosing a snack option. The older sibling will sometimes scream and throw tantrums, and the younger sibling is very fearful and hesitant. Thinking about the principles of trauma-informed care, how might you physically rearrange your caregiving space to create a safer environment, both perceived and actual? What practices might you implement into daily activities, both one-on-one with the children and in groups? What types of toys and play might you encourage?

Summary

During the early childhood years, physical development transforms toddlers into school-age children as they undergo tremendous developmental changes. Although children develop in similar ways, each child is an individual. Preschool children continue to gain more control over small muscles and fine-motor skills. They learn to hold a pencil and crayon, use scissors, brush their teeth, and dress. At the same time, their gross-motor skills continue to improve as they learn to hop, skip, jump, and throw a ball. Each child will follow a different timeline of physical developmental milestones, and physical development does not happen without supporting cognitive and socioemotional development. As you move into the following chapters, notice how physical development lays the foundation for learning and social relationships as young children learn their colors and the alphabet, expand their vocabularies, care for themselves, and relate to others.

Learning Outcomes and Key Concepts

7.1 Describe how young children grow and change physically.

- Compared to infancy, the development process during early childhood is gradual; and it does not happen in the same way, at the same time, for all children.
- During early childhood, children tend to grow at a steady pace.
- Both boys and girls appear slimmer as the trunks of their bodies lengthen and body fat diminishes, their stomachs are less rounded with newly acquired muscle mass.
- For both boys and girls, their legs and arms lengthen compared to their body height.
- By the end of this stage, their body proportions begin to become more like those of an adult than they were during infancy.

7.2 Explain how gross- and fine-motor skills developed during early childhood are continuous, sequential, and interrelated.

- Gross- and fine-motor skills are acquired sequentially.

- Through observation, trial and error, and guided practice, young children hone their motor skills, the physical abilities or capacities to perform physical tasks.
- Gross-motor skills, which involve the development of larger muscle movements, include walking and climbing.
- Gross-motor skills typically develop rapidly during the early childhood years.
- Fine-motor skills, involving the hand and fingers, develop as hand-eye coordination grows.
- Acquiring motor skills affects the physical development of the brain and subsequently both cognitive and physical development.

7.3 Explain the relationship between the brain's physical changes and cognitive development in early childhood.

- Brain development is affected and shaped by both genetics and lived experiences in early childhood.
- Stress can negatively affect physical brain development.
- Responsive caregivers who encourage dynamic back-and-forth interactions with young children help create brain-shaping experiences.

7.4 Discuss the importance of health and wellness in the early childhood years and the effects of interaction between individuals and their environment.

- Playful activities are essential to physical development in early childhood, as they build muscles and bones and result in healthier body compositions and overall wellness.
- Because young children are so physically active, good nutrition and adequate sleep are essential.
- Young children learn what to eat, how to eat, and when to eat as they learn to associate food with emotions.
- Food becomes a part of social interactions, and they eat from the choices provided by their parent or other caregivers.
- Adequate sleep and learning to control body functions are essential in early childhood.
- Children in early childhood need regular dental and medical care.

- Without life experience and knowledge, young children need help and protection to avoid hazards, injuries, and accidents.
- Young children may be more affected by environmental dangers than older children and adults.

7.5 Summarize indicators of child abuse and neglect and the role of caregivers in advocating for children who have experienced trauma.

- Young children are the most affect ed by potentially traumatic events in their lives.
- Child abuse is violence inflicted by someone in power, such as a parent, family member, or caregiver.
- Neglect results from failure to provide basic needs, including physical, medical, or emotional support.
- Infants and young children are the most susceptible to maltreatment in the forms of abuse and neglect.
- Trauma may manifest in many ways, including mental health issues, risky behaviors, and developmental challenges.
- Intense trauma may result in lifelong altered brain architecture.
- Traumatized children may recover and thrive if they are treated with patience and offered stable and repetitious TIC practices.

Chapter Review

1. List five ways that children grow and change physically in early childhood.
2. Describe the physical attributes of young children and their caregiver needs for promoting optimal growth and development.

3. Which is most impactful on brain development in early childhood—genetics or lived experiences? Be prepared to defend your answer.
4. If you were writing a newsletter for parents of young children in your care, how might you describe young children's nutritional and physical activity/play needs?
5. Why do young children in childcare settings get sick more often than those cared for in their homes? Should this be considered positive or negative? Why?
6. How might environmental factors affect the health and well-being of young children? How can these risks be avoided?

Matching

Match the following terms with the correct definitions.

A. manual dexterity
B. motor skills
C. postural control
D. fine-motor skills
E. hand-eye coordination

1. The ability to achieve and maintain a state of balance while performing an activity
2. Using visual input to guide a hand activity
3. Physical abilities or capacities to perform physical tasks
4. The ability to coordinate fine-motor skills more quickly and efficiently
5. Abilities that involve performing skills with the hand and fingers

A child in a wooden obstacle course at an adventure playground challenges his large motor skills leading to better physical coordination and cognitive problem solving.

8

Early Childhood: Cognitive Development

Learning Outcomes

After studying this chapter, you will be able to:

8.1 Demonstrate knowledge of current research findings on how early childhood brain development and growth impacts cognitive functions and learning.

8.2 Explain major cognitive theories of early childhood development.

8.3 Describe the impact of young children's social relationships and their environment on cognitive growth and learning.

8.4 Discuss how children learn language and identify cognitive developmental language milestones often achieved during early childhood.

8.5 Recognize indicators of school readiness.

Introduction

Young children are known for asking, "Why?" There are so many questions: Why is the sky blue? Why are snowflakes white? Why do leaves fall off trees? Why is there a baby in her stomach? Why is he sick? Why do cats catch mice? How do you respond to these constant questions?

Throughout early childhood, ages 2 to 6, children seek rational answers through observation and experience to explain what they believe. Brain development occurs quickly and dramatically as children learn about themselves and their world. Colors and shapes, letters and numbers, words, and gestures, all become a part of learning concepts to communicate through language development.

Overall, early childhood is a time of profound cognitive development, closely tied to the physical and socioemotional realms. Physical development, especially in the refinement of gross- and fine-motor skills, allows children to explore their world. Learning continues to be interactive and reliant on social relationships. Together, these three developmental realms mature together as a young child's cognitive abilities expand. How can you foster cognitive growth and development in young children? As you journey through this chapter, you will make connections between what you know and what is new to you.

8.1 Brain Growth and Development

During the early years, especially ages 0–5, the human brain goes through tremendous physical development and change (Conkbayir, 2017; Harvard University Center on the Developing Child, 2007; Nelson et al., 2006). As you learned in Unit 2, brain neurons grow and form synapses (pathways) throughout infancy, making more connections than the brain will ever need. By the age of 5, a typical child's brain has created more than 100 billion synapses (Cohen, 2018; Miller & Cummings, 2007).

The process of creating these pathways is called **synaptogenesis** and is programmed by genes.

After infancy, these neuron pathways continue to develop (see Figure 8.1). Some are reinforced, while others that are less used or unneeded are trimmed away. The young child's brain continues to expand at an incredible rate despite all this pruning and trimming of neurons, resulting in observable and measurable cognitive changes during early childhood (Harvard University Center on the Developing Child, 2007; Nelson et al., 2006). When young children are given opportunities to have stimulating experiences that reinforce new pathways, such as chances to

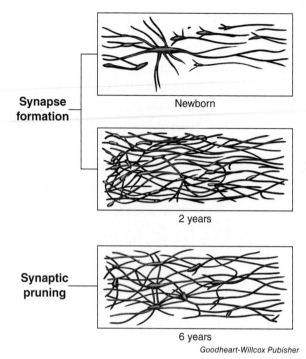

Synapse formation

Newborn

2 years

Synaptic pruning

6 years

Goodheart-Willcox Pubisher

Figure 8.1 Brain Neuron Pathways.
How do neuron pathways change between newborns, 2-year-olds, and 6-year-olds?

problem-solve when playing age-appropriate games or physically climbing on play equipment, it makes the pathways stronger and faster (Bauer & Pathman, 2008; Conkbayir, 2017; Gallagher, 2005).

Neuron pathways peak in early childhood but not all at the same time. For example, the visual cortex peak is reached in the first few months of life, but neuron pathways in the prefrontal cortex do not peak until a toddler's second year of life, although development continues (Huttenlocher & Dabholkar, 1997; Conkbayir, 2017). The more time lapses before a brain region peaks in neural pathways, the more plastic or moldable that area remains. Experiences do shape neural pathways in early childhood (Cohen, 2018; Tierney & Nelson, 2009).

Once the synapses reach a peak in each brain region, the overabundance of synapses begins the process of pruning the pathways that are unused or not needed after new ones have formed (Nelson et al., 2006). Whereas genes drive the synaptogenesis stage, the pruning backstage relies on a child's experiences interacting with their environment and the people around them (Gallagher, 2005; Tierney & Nelson, 2009). Experience helps fine-tune brain

functioning, and although this process does not stop throughout life, the pruning that happens in early childhood affects the brain's efficiency. In early childhood, genes and experiences together form brain architecture for life (Bessieres et al., 2020; Conkbayir, 2017; Sortino, 2017).

Physical brain development combined with environmental experiences creates inherently dynamic times of learning in early childhood. As you learned in Chapter 5, neuroplasticity, or **brain plasticity**, refers to the malleability or adaptability of the young brain as it undergoes structural changes while responding to environmental experiences. It is a complex process between experiences and biology, including genetics, molecular and cellular mechanisms, and the synaptic pathways that are formed and pruned. This neuroplasticity offers tremendous learning opportunities, but it also means that the preschooler's brain is hypersensitive to environmental experiences, both positive and negative (Banich & Compton, 2018; Bessieres, et al., 2020; Sale, 2016).

Windows of Opportunity

As a child's brain continues to develop during early childhood, **windows of opportunity**, or sensitive periods for optimizing the development of critical skills, exist. Windows of opportunity are ideal times when the child's brain is most receptive to learning because specific neurological pathways are not yet complete. The lengths of time for physical, cognitive, and socioemotional developmental windows vary. The length of the optimal impact on sensitive periods varies, too. As you learned in Chapter 6, the optimal time for developing the brain wiring for building trust between primary caregivers and their children occurs within the first 12 months of the child's life. In contrast, the optimal time for building the brain wiring for learning motor and language skills is during the first 24 months of life.

Some windows of opportunity are open from birth and continue throughout the childhood years into adulthood. Other windows of opportunity may only be open for a few months or years. If these windows are missed, it is sometimes difficult, but not impossible, for children to develop these abilities later (Giedd, & Rapoport, 2010; Herschensohn, 2007; Kuhl, 2004; Kuhn, 2005;). Research about the timing of these sensitive time periods is ongoing; however, newer research shows another window of opportunity for learning happens during adolescence and adulthood (Knoll et al., 2016).

Windows of opportunity during the early childhood years provide a favorable time frame for primary caregivers and educators to expose children to stimulating experiences and teach many life skills. Some of these will be explored further in this chapter, and others more relevant to socioemotional development are covered in Chapter 9. These life skills include:

- *Conversational skills.* Speaking to young children using grammatically correct language sets the stage for having good language skills later in life. Young learners can also learn a second language more easily at this age than they can in later years.
- *Self-control.* The preschool years are a critical time for learning self-control. Primary caregivers and teachers can take advantage of this opportunity by creating experiences in which self-control has a positive outcome, and caregivers or teachers provide both encouragement and praise.
- *Initiative and self-esteem.* Young children want to please their caregivers and teachers and are eager to be industrious. Letting young children help with simple tasks—such as setting the table for snack time or putting away toys—is one way to build self-esteem.
- *Pre-literacy and a love for learning.* Early childhood is a prime time to promote language acquisition and understanding. Primary caregivers and teachers can talk and promote conversation, ask questions, sing songs, or read to young children and encourage them to read books back to build their self-esteem.
- *Friendship and sharing.* Interactions with other children during the preschool years help children to learn the value of friendships and sharing. Primary caregivers and teachers can take advantage of this window by providing guided opportunities for young children to interact and play together.
- *Conflict management and regulation of emotions.* When young children learn to identify emotions in themselves and others, they can better self-regulate in later years. Primary caregivers and teachers can help young children with this process by helping them name and identify emotions, recognize when emotions are present, and think about how emotions affect themselves and others.
- *Problem-solving and decision-making.* Learning decision-making and problem-solving skills early in life sets the foundation for dealing with more complicated challenges as children mature. Young children enjoy having choices because this gives them a sense of control. Caregivers and teachers can provide young children with simple decisions, such as picking which book to read, what to wear, when to play, and what to eat for a snack. Likewise, caregivers and teachers can offer young children problems to solve that require thinking through the potential consequences of choices and weighing which one is best. As developmentally appropriate, options should be limited.

Recognizing that early childhood lends itself to foundational learning opportunities is not new. However, the realization that all young children may not have access to experiences that promote optimal cognitive development is gaining new attention (Mackes et al., 2020; Nelson et al., 2019). During the 1960s in the United States, the federal government developed an early childhood education program called **Head Start** to support children who lacked available quality learning opportunities due to social and economic challenges. Head Start is a government preschool program that serves the needs of young children, especially those who are economically disadvantaged, as defined by the US Department of Health and Human Services (2020). This program continues to positively affect young children and their families today (Puma et al., 2010).

From a global perspective, the World Health Organization dared to declare that attention to early childhood learning could serve as a powerful equalizer in societies. Many countries followed with interventions for young children (Irwin et al., 2007). In 2009, the Race to the Top–Early Learning Challenge was introduced in the United States. This legislation gave money to states that could show progress in providing access to quality education and interventions to young children at risk or challenged by financial or social barriers (Puma et al., 2010). UNICEF (2017) followed with their First 1,000 Days campaign; and many countries expanded this focus to the first 2,000 days, an effort that focuses on development from conception through early childhood.

Providing children with basic needs, including nutrition, housing, safety, and security, followed by rich experiences and activities throughout early childhood, will stimulate brain growth and development. Caregivers are encouraged to take advantage of these windows of opportunity when the brain is undergoing remarkable growth. Public interest in these findings on brain development has been widely reported and used globally to build support for high-quality early childhood intervention and education (Abadzi, 2006; Heckman, 2006; UNICEF, 2016).

☑CHECKPOINT

☐ What is brain plasticity?

☐ Identify specific ways the brain continues to grow and mature during early childhood.

☐ How is a young child's brain affected when exposed to stimulating experiences?

☐ When does the formation of neural pathways peak in brain development? Does it happen all at once? If not, how does it occur, and what is the effect on learning?

☐ Define *windows of opportunity* or sensitive periods for learning in early childhood. How might understanding these windows inform interactions between caregivers and young children? How might missing these windows or sensitive periods impact a young child's future?

Apply Here!

Write a public service announcement (PSA) to raise awareness about the windows of opportunity for learning in early childhood. Consider a message that is instructional, informative, and inspiring to those with young children in their care.

8.2 Early Childhood Cognitive Theories

Many researchers have been fascinated with the cognitive development of young children long before brain scans and neuroimaging. Developing theories about how young children learn still provides a way to organize findings and to help give meaning to many observations and study results. The theories of Piaget and Vygotsky were explored in Chapters 2 and 5; this chapter will cover how these theories relate to the preschool years. In recent years, *theory of mind* is an example of the work done by researchers who are moving our understanding of cognitive development in early childhood forward. **Theory of mind** involves a child's ability to understand that another person's knowledge, emotions, intentions, beliefs, or motivations are part of that person and may not correlate with their own knowledge, emotions, intentions, beliefs, or motivations.

Piaget's Cognitive Theory

During early childhood, the world expands for children as they walk, talk, explore new places, and can reason and think about the world in ways that were not possible at earlier stages (Cohen, 2018). In his cognitive theory, Jean Piaget called this the **preoperational stage** of thinking. *Operations* refer to formal or logical mental processes. Piaget referred to this stage as *preoperational* because it represents a time when children's use of symbolic and logical thinking is growing, but they are only beginning to use reasoning and logic (Inhelder & Piaget, 1958).

As children move from the sensorimotor stage of infancy into the preoperational stage of early childhood, they continue to explore their world. Learning increases rapidly as they organize their experiences. They learn to use symbols, or language, as a way of understanding the world around them. Language may be spoken or serve as an object or symbol for something else. For example, when playing with a toy farm set, a child understands that a miniature toy cow represents a life-sized living cow. As young children enter the preoperational stage of thinking, they gradually move from using intuition and primitive reasoning, based on their feelings, to more rational and logical thinking (Barrouillet, 2015; Bjorklund, 2004).

Three characteristics mark the preoperational stage: centration, lack of conservation, and egocentrism. **Centration** is the tendency to focus on just one aspect of something seen. This concentration on one part of an object hinders a young child from understanding conservation, or how an object may be transformed. **Conservation** refers to an ability to follow the transformations of viewed objects—that objects can remain the same even if the way they look changes (Wadsworth, 2003). For example, consider two apples of the same size offered to a young child and an older sibling. One apple is cut into four pieces and the other into five pieces. The younger child might focus on the overall number of pieces, thinking that more pieces means more apple rather than the fact that both apples are the same size. According to Piaget, a child in the preoperational thought stage does not yet recognize that the apple's volume is the same, or reversible, whether it is cut or remains whole, the concept of reversibility in transformation. Piaget believed that young children were illogical, and that logical thinking did not surface until much later in childhood. However, many researchers today think that Piaget underestimated the precocious logical knowledge already present in young children that is enhanced through their experiences (Catilla et al., 2021; Houde & Borst, 2015).

Piaget acknowledged that although a child may develop new cognitive abilities simultaneously, they often learn them in different ways or orders. For example, he used the term **horizontal decalage** to describe how young children learn conservation. Horizontal decalage refers to a child's understanding of conservation of volume, then conservation of mass, and finally, conservation of number. In other words, cognitive understanding of conservation does not automatically turn on understanding in all areas. Instead, a child learns conservation in a non-simultaneous manner throughout the learning stage.

In the preoperational stage, young children find it difficult to see transformations as they are challenged to apply conservation. Piaget demonstrated this difficulty, or inability to follow transformations, by pouring the contents of a short glass of water into a taller, thinner glass. To young children, the second glass may appear to have more liquid, even when they observe the transformation or see the water from the short glass being poured into the taller glass (see Figure 8.2). Piaget also showed that

Conservation Task	Original Presentation	Transformation
Number	Are there the same number in each row? 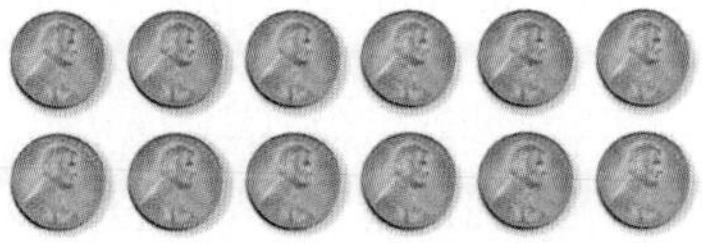	Are there still the same number in each row or does one row have more? 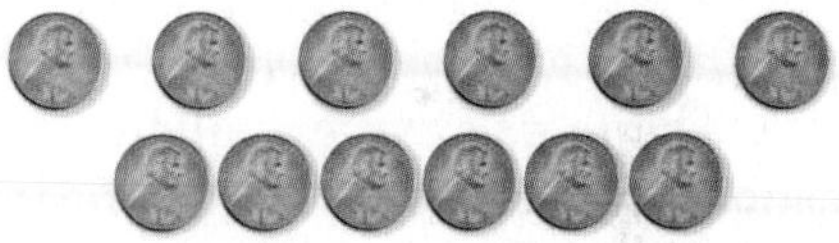
Mass	Is there the same amount in each ball? 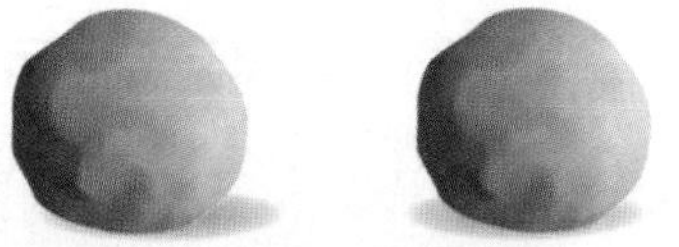	Does each piece still have the same amount or does one have more? 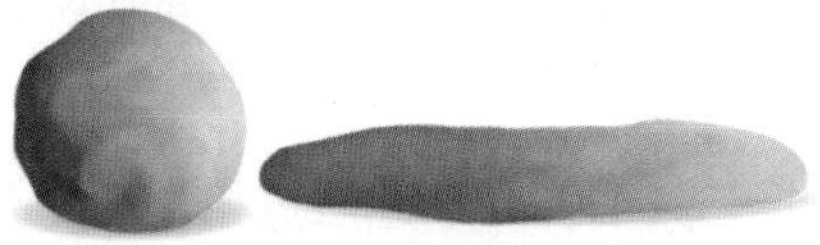
Liquid	Is there the same amount in each glass? 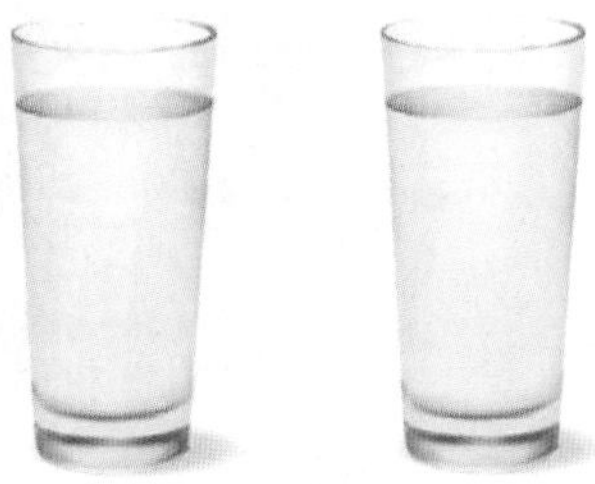	Does each glass still have the same amount of liquid or does one have more? 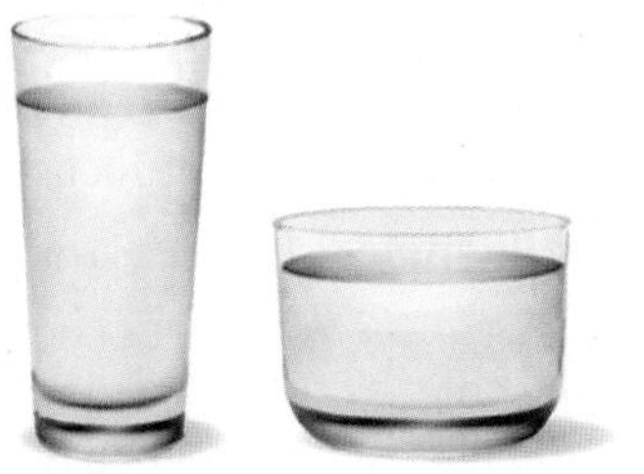

Goodheart-Willcox Publisher

Figure 8.2 Piaget Conservation and Transformations.

children have difficulty understanding conservation or transformation with mass, numbers, length, weight, and area. For example, a young child might observe the same ten blocks taking up more space when separated over a larger area than when placed close together.

Part of preoperational thought involves **egocentrism**, an inability to take another person's perspective. Egocentrism may come from a child's difficulty in perceiving transformations and understanding the thoughts and feelings of others. Instead, young children often focus on their own subjective experiences. This is especially true if the other person's thoughts are different from the preschooler's thoughts or if the person's thoughts do not match their facial expressions or behaviors. For example, a preschooler may not understand that an older sibling is annoyed with their behavior if the sibling is smiling and speaking in a gentle voice when telling them to stop. It is most effective to use clear communication with young children.

Although Piaget's work provides the foundation for much understanding about young children, more recent research shows that children understand conservation at an earlier age than previously thought. They are capable of thinking about their own thinking much earlier than Piaget proposed (Estes & Bartsch, 2017; Schaafsma et al., 2015; Wellman et al., 2011). The more exposure children have to transformations of objects, such as the formation of the same amount of clay into different shapes, the more quickly they understand that things remain the same (Bullard, 2014; Thornton, 2003). As you will discover in Chapter 9, children at this age are also more capable of understanding others' thoughts and feelings than previously recognized.

Critics of Piaget's cognitive development theory often focus on his small sample size and the use of his own children when conducting research. However, many researchers still laud his work today, and it continues to influence how young children are educated (Wavering, 2011). For example, based on Piaget's theories, early childhood best practices focus on:

- stressing thinking processes rather than end products
- recognizing the child's critical role in learning
- appreciating the child's developmental stage while using developmentally appropriate responses

- appreciating individual differences in children's cognitive abilities (Bjorklund, 2004; Slavin, 2009)

Vygotsky's Sociocultural Theory

As discussed in Chapters 2 and 5, Lev Vygotsky's sociocultural theory of cognitive development stressed the importance of social interaction in learning with the concepts of the zone of proximal development and scaffolding. When caregivers and others help children at their level, they learn more through a process of scaffolding. Scaffolding helps bridge what a young child can cognitively understand and their developmental potential for understanding. Vygotsky called this interface of learning *the zone of proximal development* (ZPD), or the level at which a child can learn with help (Barrouillet, 2015). Once a caregiver can find the child's ZPD, the child is more likely to learn new skills without feeling overwhelmed (see Figure 8.3). Once a child performs a task, scaffolding can be decreased and eventually removed resulting in a new ZPD (Vygotsky, 1978, 1993; Wertsch, 1984).

In his sociocultural theory, Vygotsky believed that children learn what they know through social interaction. As brain pathways are pruned and refined, gross-motor skills develop. These increasing skills allow young children to interact more freely with their world. Vygotsky theorized that as children play, the objects they use encourage imaginative thinking. Their understanding of concepts moves from realistic to more abstract. Vygotsky saw children's **imaginative play** as a way to learn new skills

Jacob Lund/Shutterstock.com

Figure 8.3 The zone of proximal development. How is the relationship between this child and caregiver demonstrating the ZPD in action?

(Bodrova & Leong, 1996; Wertsch & Sohmer, 1995). When young children use symbolic play, they use their highest levels of abstract thinking. For example, a child may make an inanimate object, like a stuffed bear, animate by creating a story about the stuffed bear talking to a stuffed lion. Or they may use an object in a symbolic way, such as using a banana as a sword or gun. Vygotsky noted that self-guiding speech, sometimes referred to as private speech or "self-talk," occurs when young children employ this type of symbolic play. In doing so, they often express and even control emotions in ways not seen in social-guided speech led by caregivers and others (Colliver & Veraksa, 2021; Smolucha & Smolucha, 2021).

Vygotsky's work still informs early childhood education today. Learning is a social endeavor. Through relationships, young children learn about the world around them (Mahn & John-Steiner, 2012; Wink & Puteny, 2002). Primary caregivers and teachers should provide as many opportunities for creative and imaginative play as possible. Providing children with props, such as dress-up clothes or empty boxes, might spur their imaginations. Sometimes, children need nothing but free, uninhibited time and space. Primary caregivers should let young children direct the play, allowing time to interact with others as well as time to play alone.

Theory of Mind

By ages 4 or 5, children begin to understand that others may have different needs. They begin to realize that sometimes things do not appear as they seem. These incongruities can lead to "false beliefs," and that people may hide their true feelings and emotions. Theory of mind (ToM) is children's awareness that others may think differently and that another person's knowledge, emotions, intentions, beliefs, or motivations may not correlate with their own (Peterson et al., 2012; Westby & Robinson, 2014). ToM involves the ability to understand that another person's knowledge, emotions, intentions, beliefs, or motivations may not correlate with their own. ToM also includes the child's ability to think about their own mental state. It is strongly tied to both cognitive development and socioemotional development because it relates to social relationships and emotional regulation and understanding (Figure 8.4). Language ability also facilitates the development of theory of mind (Dunn, 1996).

Robert Kneschke/Shutterstock.com

Figure 8.4 A preschooler watches as another child takes a turn in a building game. How does this example illustrate ToM? How is the observing child demonstrating their own emotional regulation and understanding while anticipating the motivation of the child observed?

The first glimpses of theory of mind occur in infancy when toddlers begin to use toys in a way that gives inanimate objects emotional displays, such as making a toy elephant cry because it is sad. ToM becomes most apparent and measurable as children become more proficient at understanding why a person acts in a certain way (Bartsch & Wellman, 1995; Meltzoff et al., 1999). For example, a young child may see a peer crying while playing alone. The observing child might ask, "Why are you crying? Are you sad?" As theory of mind abilities become more sophisticated though the preschool years, young children learn how to assess others' thoughts and actions.

Around the age of 4, children begin to understand that an event or object may not match what the child knows to be true (Kloo et al., 2010). Imagine an early childhood educator sitting with a child who is filling an empty cookie tin with beads, buttons, and assorted craft items. The teacher asks the child what classmates might think is in the cookie tin. "Cookies!" the child exclaims in response, understanding that others might think an object has a different use than what they are using it for.

Accuracy may or may not correlate with a young child's ToM and understanding that although others have their own perceived reality, the child's interpretation of an action may be rightly or wrongly assessed (Wellman & Liu, 2004). For example, young children may think that their primary caregiver is angry with another person if they hear very formal language and observe gestures that do not include smiles. Or a child who has just received serious instructions to stop an unwanted behavior may think their mother is happy when she suddenly smiles and greets a neighbor. As a result, the child may continue the unwanted behavior while their mother is interacting with the stranger. Over time, the young child will learn that outside displays of emotion when interacting with one person may not always match the non-displayed emotions.

Theory of mind is a complex phenomenon that illuminates many aspects of early childhood development. For example, language abilities at age 3 may predict a child's theory of mind in early adolescence (Ebert, 2017). In young children with developmental delays or disabilities such as autism spectrum disorders, theory of mind may be delayed or not fully reached (Astington, 2003; Hoogenhout & Malcolm-Smith, 2016; Mazz et al., 2017). Theory of mind may be linked to executive functioning abilities such as brainstorming, planning, and executing ideas. Preschoolers often use these functions as they engage in play such as deciding what to build with blocks, doing the construction, and then evaluating whether their plan was effective. Preschoolers with more advanced executive functioning skills may be better able to understand and move between the multiple perspectives of others (Best & Miller, 2010).

Primary caregivers and early childhood educators can play an important role in helping young children develop ToM (Lecce & Devine, 2021; Mueller & File, 2020; Wellman, 2014). ToM improves both cognitive and social development. For example, caregivers can demonstrate and model social competence by:

- verbally commenting on their own feeling and emotions
- verbally commenting and responding to others' perceived feelings and emotions
- asking clarifying or investigative questions about others' feelings, emotions, behaviors, or opinions
- encouraging and complimenting prosocial behaviors, such a showing concern, empathy, or understanding for others
- validating positive choices and behaviors
- initiating and encouraging children to wonder and ponder over others' perspectives

- using books and pretend play to stimulate conversations that support ToM
- encouraging civil behavior and manners for the sake of others

☑ CHECKPOINT

☐ Describe Piaget's preoperational stage of cognitive development.

☐ How do caregivers play a part in early childhood cognitive development?

☐ Explain Vygotsky's sociocultural theory of cognitive development as applied to early childhood.

☐ Describe a specific way that a caregiver might use the zone of proximal development (ZPD) to help a young child learn a new skill.

☐ Express how a young child might exhibit theory of mind.

Apply Here!

Create a training slide show to demonstrate Piaget's preoperational thought, Vygotsky's ZPD, and theory of mind in practice. As much as possible, include visuals such as illustrations, photographs, or video clips you find.

Practical Issues and Implications

Is Sharing Just Caring or Is It More?

Many prosocial behaviors, which will be further discussed in Chapter 9, are taught in early childhood. An often-used instructional phrase of caregivers is that "sharing is caring!" Sharing is a prosocial behavior valued in many cultures including the United States. But do parental expectations match what a young child is cognitively capable to do? In a large-scale survey of US parents of preschoolers (ZERO TO THREE, 2016), 43% of parents believed that young children could share and take turns with others by the age of 2, and 71% believed that young children could do this by age 3. In reality, the ability to share and take turns with others does not develop until between ages 3.5 to 4 years (Moore et al., 2001; ZERO TO THREE, 2016). This is not a matter of caring but of cognition.

Many recent researchers have linked sharing with language development, math concepts, and theory of mind. Young children need to understand math concepts to think about fairness and distribution. They need language to communicate intentions and feelings. They need a theory of mind that is developed to the point of understanding others' mental states (Conte et al., 2018; Cowell et al., 2015; Wu & Su, 2014). Even so, some recent research begins to question the impact of cognitive readiness to share because theory of mind may have the opposite effect. A young child may decide not to share but, instead, to be competitive or to show favoritism (Lenz & Paulus, 2021; Moore et al., 2001; Nilsen & Valcke, 2018). It is shown that modeling and instruction from peers and caregivers, even in the form of reading books about sharing or role-playing during pretend play, can assist a young child's understanding of the concept (Worle et al., 2020; Okanda & Taniguchi, 2020).

To Think About:

- What is your earliest memory about learning how to share?
- How might you approach teaching preschoolers about sharing resources, such as snacks or toys?
- When would you start emphasizing sharing to young children? What are your expectations?

8.3 The Social Nature of Cognitive Development

Young children learn by imitating what others do, and by experimenting, exploring, and engaging in fantasy and play. In early childhood, learning is a social endeavor. They watch and observe. They copy what they see, they question, and they want to know why. Young children are active participants in their own learning, but they also depend on others—primary caregivers, siblings, peers, extended family members, and others.

The Role of Imaginative Pretend Play

Fantasy stories, make-believe fairies, incredible superheroes, bogeymen and monsters—the world of creative make-believe abounds in early childhood. Do you remember any favorite movies, television shows, or books that took you to another time and place as a young child? Did you play dress-up, act

out stories, or insist on being called by another name to fit the character you played? Imagination is so much a part of early childhood that movies have been made about the fantasies and fears of this stage. Some young children even create fantasy playmates or "invisible friends." These pretend peers can seem very real to young children as they carry on conversations and care for the imaginary friend's needs. These imaginary friendships contribute to a young child's cognitive development, especially in relation to a developing theory of mind (Aguiar et al., 2017; Dore & Lillard, 2015; Thompson & Goldstein, 2019).

Imaginative or **pretend play** that involves make-believe has an important role in early childhood. It goes much beyond keeping a young child physically active; it facilitates cognitive, emotional, and social growth both in relationships and self-identity (Barnett, 1990; Tsao, 2002; Milteer & Ginsburg, 2012). Play enhances cognitive development as young children use executive functions in planning, creating, building, and problem-solving while they use symbols to create figurative meaning (Coolahan et al., 2000; Erickson, 1985; Tamis-LeMonda et al., 2004). Imaginative play often involves movement that facilitates motor development, offering the physical health benefits of exercise and activity (Figure 8.5). It is also child-directed and changes in content as children develop from 2-year-olds to 6-year-olds in later preschool years (see Table 8.1).

Alexander_Safonov/Shutterstock.com

Figure 8.5 Preschool children love pretend or imaginary play.
How might cognitive development be enhanced in this child's play? How is the child incorporating self-identity, problem-solving, and known experiences into play?

Age Cohorts	Typical Themes of Pretend Play
Younger preschoolers	• Imitating and expanding on familiar stories from families: mothers, fathers, children, siblings, and other family roles • Using familiar objects in unique ways • Imitating cats, dogs, and other animals • Storytelling about getting lost, safety concerns, or about scary experiences • Storytelling about getting hurt and caretaking • Storytelling about favorite characters from a variety of media and books • Exploring new or budding interests, such as camping or trains
Older preschoolers, kindergarteners	• Imitating and expanding on familiar and more complex stories from families: mothers, fathers, children, siblings, and other family roles in situations such as marriage, parenthood, work, celebrations • Imitating and expanding on familiar and more complex stories from daily life: medical checkups, school, restaurants • Using familiar objects in unique ways, especially to feel powerful and capable • Storytelling to work through highly emotional or scary experiences such as monsters, bad guys, or even death • Storytelling about favorite characters from a variety of media and books, expanding on stories and playing roles such as princesses or fantasy space characters • Storytelling about adventure, such as space travel or travel by sea • Creating more complex narratives around growing or burgeoning interests, such as dinosaurs or specific animals or pets

Table 8.1 Typical Themes of Pretend Play by Preschool Age Cohorts

As will be discussed further in Chapter 9, play facilitates socioemotional development both in enhancing relationships and role exploration (Band & Weisz, 1988; Henry, 1990; Hurwitz, 2002). Sadly, all young children do not get the opportunity to play. Over-scheduling, too much emphasis on unimaginative academic learning, overworked single parents, a lack of outdoor play spaces or unsafe environments for outside play, and other stressful environments may make play a limited or nonexistent reality for some young children (Shonkoff & Phillips, 2000). Pretend play is important for all children and has even been shown to provide a positive protective factor for young children at risk (Thibodeau-Nielsen et al., 2020).

The Role of Imitation

Like infants, young children learn from experiences or through operant conditioning, as discussed in Chapter 2 (Skinner, 1953). Modeling and imitation are important parts of cognitive development as young children pay attention and imitate what they

see and experience. Young children naturally learn from others. A young child might copy a father's way of walking with his hands behind his back, a family's custom of offering a prayer of thanksgiving before eating a meal, flipping hair off the face, speaking to a younger sibling or pet in a softer tone, or swaying and dancing to a lively beat. They also may imitate what they see by biting a peer, kicking a sibling, or cursing. Although imitation has been demonstrated in newborns as discussed in Chapter 5, imitation takes on a whole new level of intensity and frequency that intersects motor, cognitive, and social-emotional developmental skills in early childhood (Jones, 2009).

Caregivers can provide scaffolding for preschoolers to learn appropriate imitation behaviors (Figure 8.6). The more engaged and encouraging caregivers are, providing positive opportunities for young children to imitate, the more effective and flexible the learning becomes (Clegg & Legare, 2016). Young children are judicious regarding whom and what they imitate. That does not mean that their imitations

A

B

Figure 8.6 Young Children Learn About Culture through Observation and Imitation.
What might these young children be learning about their own culture? How have you personally learned about your own culture through observation and imitation?

are logical, however. Often, they will imitate a caregiver's actions even if the actions are not necessary, inefficient, or incorrect (Clay & Tennie, 2017). This is termed **over-imitation.** Although there are often actions or behaviors that caregivers prefer not to be copied, young children will imitate them anyway because it is a fundamental cognitive process of learning (Lyons et al., 2007).

Learning through imitation offers children at this stage opportunities to learn the traditions and customs of everyday life. It also offers them the opportunity to engage in socioemotional learning, an important part of cognitive ability and the foundation for later academic success (Vann, 2015).

The Role of Memory

Hearing whimsical stories or recounting actual events often creates an entertaining partnership in early childhood. As language abilities increase, so do the shared stories, observations, and accounts of events past. Preschoolers begin to think about what they are thinking, termed **metacognition.** They also begin to think about what they remember, or **metamemory.** Verbal young children may begin a story with, "I was 'membering….'"

Memory can be divided into several categories. First is **working memory,** defined as information that is useable in the present (Gade et al., 2017; Imuta et al., 2013; Wang & Gulgoz, 2019). Working memory allows humans to remember things for a few seconds. It is usually a small amount of information,

and it is remembered for a short amount of time. For example, a preschooler may be asked to return a toy to a storage bin at the end of playtime. The child may remember this instruction for a few seconds and no longer. Working memory improves throughout early childhood as preschoolers are able to retain larger amounts of data for a longer amount of time. Working memory aids in increasing executive skills during early childhood including planning, comprehension, and problem-solving (Bauer, 2014; Bauer & Larkina, 2014; Cowan, 2014).

Memories that can be accessed over a longer time frame or even over a lifetime are called **long-term memory.** Long-term memory includes both declarative memory and non-declarative memory. **Declarative memory,** sometimes referred to as explicit memory, are memory skills that are with us from birth such as a memory for familiar faces (Mullally & Maguire, 2014). **Non-declarative memories** relate to skills that have been so integrated into subconscious thought that children perform them without thinking (Bauer & Pathman, 2008; Wessel et al., 2019). For example, once a child learns how to drink from a cup, the child recalls this skill even if they do not execute it perfectly each time. Of course, memories are built from all the senses, not just vision. Throughout early childhood, long-term memory abilities grow and include things like the names of people, objects, and learned skills. With these new abilities come cognitive growth and development.

The Role of Self-Regulation

During the preschool years, temper tantrums tend to decrease as preschoolers gain more self-regulation over their overwhelming emotions. **Self-regulation**, sometimes referred to as self-control, is the ability to manage thoughts, feelings, and emotions to assist with goal-directed actions. It includes not becoming so overwhelmed with emotions or strong feelings that goals are impeded. Self-regulation is tied to all dimensions of development, including physical and socioemotional development. But it is strongly associated with cognitive development because it requires more sophisticated cognitive processes and metacognition. Mostly, it requires an ability to focus and sustain one's attention on a task (Blair & Raver, 2015; Guillory et al., 2018).

In classic research studies conducted at Stanford University in the 1960s, young children were put in a situation where they were given a treat. They were then told that if they delayed eating the treat for a given amount of time, another treat would follow. Some children were able to wait for the extra treat, while others ate the first treat immediately. It was an experiment in delayed gratification and a measurement of self-control. During the decades since then, this study has been replicated many times with different children, different treats, and different time-delay expectations. These studies have not only given insight into the ability of some young children to practice self-regulation, but they have also explored individual differences and the possible effects on future academic success. Young children who exhibit self-regulation in the preschool years tend to perform better later in school, have better future relationships, and are less likely to struggle with impulse control and addiction (Eigsti, et al., 2006; Gomes & Livesey, 2008; Lemmon & Moore, 2007). More recent studies confirm that self-regulation has a foundational role in promoting well-being across the lifespan, including higher academic achievement, positive interpersonal behaviors, increased mental health, and overall healthy living as seen in lower levels of obesity, aggressive and criminal behaviors, and substance abuse later in life (Allan et al., 2014; Lonigan et al., 2017; Robson et al., 2020).

Caregivers can play an important role in helping young children recognize, practice, and gain control of their emotions and feelings. While doing so, it is important to remember the cognitive and social developmental abilities of the child at a given age. For example, between ages 2 to 3 1/2 years, children begin desiring to do things independently and to figure things out on their own. "Let me do it!" is a common phrase. During this age, children begin to understand and identify emotions in others or in characters they encounter in books or media. They can remember rules for a short period of time, refocus attention when needed (but only for a minute or so), and can sometimes refocus to another activity or toy when their attention has been disrupted. Around ages 5 to 6, children may not only recognize their own emotions and feelings, but they may apply strategies to regulate their emotions and feelings. They can follow more than one instruction at a time, and their attention span increases. During increased socialization with peers, they begin to realize that self-regulation can aid them in meeting personal goals (McLaughlin et al., 2017; Spira & Fischel, 2007; Williford et al., 2013). In addition, play, physical activity, and support and encouragement from caregivers positively affect increased self-regulation skills (see Figure 8.7) (Cadima et al., 2018; Savina, 2020; Silkenbeumer et al., 2018). Chapter 9 discusses tips for encouraging and helping young children gain self-regulation skills.

The Role of Executive Function

Children ages 2 to 6 are beginning to engage in abstract or inferential thinking, an important ability needed to solve complex problems that require executive functioning, such as planning, problem-solving, reasoning, social judgment, and moral decision-making. **Executive function** relies on imitation or instruction, memory, and self-regulation, and it enhances young children's growing abilities to tackle increasingly complex problems or tasks (Ackerman & Friedman-Krauss, 2017; Davies & Troy, 2020; Doebel, 2020) (see Figure 8.8). They move from following very simple instructions to instructions involving several steps. For example, the instruction to "put the toy in the basket" may evolve to a more complex instruction such as "put the cars in this basket and the bears in that basket."

Although young children can engage in executive functioning, it is in middle childhood, ages 6 to 11,

AaronAmat/iStock via Getty Images Plus

Figure 8.7 Caregivers can help young children recognize and gain control of their emotions.

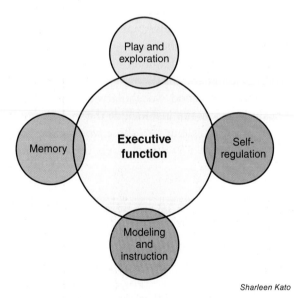

Sharleen Kato

Figure 8.8 Critical Components of Executive Function. Executive function is made up of many parts, including self-regulation, learning from the modeling and instruction of others, using both short-term and long-term memory. It is practiced and reinforced through play and exploration in the preschool years.
How might a preschooler use executive function when engaging in dramatic play such as performing a skit or musical?

that this ability grows and matures significantly (Semrus-Clikeman, 2010; Doebel, 2020). However, the foundation is laid in early childhood. Executive thinking relies on imitation, metacognition, working memory, and self-regulation, all of which are enhanced by pretend play and imagination. In pretend play, young children can experiment with solutions, role play, set goals, experiment, solve problems, and evaluate whether their solution worked (Doebel, 2020; Kalkusch et al., 2020; Rand & Morrow, 2021).

☑ CHECKPOINT

☐ Name three ways in which social relationships might affect cognitive growth and learning during early childhood.

☐ Describe how modeling and imitation affect cognitive development during early childhood.

☐ Explain how metacognition and metamemory affect cognitive development as applied to early childhood.

☐ How does self-regulation relate to early childhood learning?

☐ Describe how imaginative play can aid cognitive development in early childhood.

Apply Here!

School readiness has more to do with socioemotional skills and less to do with cognitive milestones. When schools face long-term closures due to natural disasters, civil unrest, or health concerns such as pandemics, young children may be deprived of opportunities to develop these skills through play. What are some creative and practical ways to help families and caregivers continue to offer young children opportunities to develop cooperative skills, such as learning to take turns and share, negotiate, and develop self-control? How might you make up for lost time in situations where preschoolers have missed out on chances to play with other children?

8.4 Language Development

Intelligible, or understandable, speech is a milestone of early childhood cognitive development. Speech allows children to communicate their needs and emotions to caregivers and others. Language is not only essential to communication, but it is an important part of cognitive development in early childhood.

Children first learn to communicate their needs to others. They learn to name people, animals, and colors. They learn simple counting. They learn to identify and sound out the alphabet, and they eventually learn to read. As this happens, children can focus on their inward thoughts. They think about what they are thinking (metacognition). But language learning begins far earlier than during the preschool years. It begins early in infancy when an infant hears language being spoken, long before the child begins communicating through spoken words (Cheour et al., 2004; Kuhl, 2011). Language acquisition gives symbolic meaning to thoughts. Learning language is particularly enhanced by developing cognitive abilities in early childhood (Adlof & Hogan, 2019; Hjetland et al., 2019; US Department of Health & Human Services, 2020).

In early childhood, and even as far back as infancy, children begin to learn that words are symbols. A *boat* represents an object that floats in the water. They also learn that words carry meaning through tone, intonation, and the emotions associated with types of speech. Tone is the attitude or message of a spoken word. For example, children learn early how a word sounds when a caregiver speaks in anger or with joy. This is tone. They also learn that intonation or the rise and fall of speaking can communicate meaning. They begin to associate emotional meaning to words such as *kitty* or *monster* (Kuhl, 2007, 2011).

By the time children grow out of toddlerhood, closer to 3 years of age, they can produce many of the sounds in language, although some of the consonant sounds may be delayed (see Table 8.2). **Phonology** refers to the sounds that make up words. After children have mastered the combination of sounds that make up words in a language, they move to morphology (Hulit et al., 2019; Ladefoged, 2001; Lyster et al., 2021).

Morphology includes word structures and formations. For example, the verb *go* becomes *goes* when used in third-person form. It becomes tricky when the word form changes into a completely different sound, such as when *go* becomes *went* when used in the past tense. Learning morphology takes time, instruction, trial, and error. Young children should be encouraged in their attempts to use their newly developing language skills. **Syntax** refers to sentence structure, or when words are combined to form grammatical sentences. Preschoolers learn to lengthen their sentences by adding conjunctions, prepositions, and clauses. *Semantics* refers to the meaning of words, whereas *pragmatics* refers to using language properly (Hulit et al., 2019; Ladefoged, 2001; Lyster et al., 2021).

In early childhood, vocabulary expands quickly. Vocabulary does not just include the spoken words a child uses or says, but also those words they understand (see Figure 8.9). Preschoolers use many nouns

Age	Sound and Examples
3 years	h—home, hug, doghouse m—man, hammer, hum n—now, penny, run p—play, hippo, pop w—with, water, wow
4 years	b—ball, baby, tub k—cat, chicken, kick f—fun, telephone, stuff g—girl, wagon, tag
5 years	d—dog, middle, hand ng—finger, sing y—yellow, onion, story

G-W Publishers

Table 8.2 Sounds Preschoolers Master

Figure 8.9 Young children increase word recognition or vocabulary when caregivers read books to them.

as they name objects and people. The use of verbs, adjectives, pronouns, and locations come later. As young children begin to question, they ask why, who, and where. By age 3, they use possessive concepts with words such as *me* or *mine*. Two-word sentences become three-or-more-word sentences. The use of tense, past or present, and plural forms of words increases as the child matures. They also give voice to inanimate objects such as dolls or stuffed animals (Hayes, 2016; Hoff, 2014; US Department of Health and Human Services, 2020).

As they learn language, many young children have a delightfully unique way of speaking as they gain language skills. Instead of saying "a couple of minutes ago," a child might say "a couple of whiles ago." Or I "goed" to the store rather than "I went to the store." A 3-year-old might respond to the question, "What did you do this morning?" quite literally with, "Nothing, my life is empty." The receiver of this message can appreciate the double meaning of this child's response, even when the child does not. Children acquire the subtle social meaning of language, phrases, and sayings over time. It is like the process for adults learning a foreign language. Although individual expressions of language can be charming and fascinating to consider, language usually occurs in a consistent order. Typically, young children learn phonology, followed by morphology, syntax, semantics, and, finally, the pragmatic use of language (Hayes, 2016; Hulit et al., 2019; US Department of Health and Human Services, 2020).

Between ages 3 to 4, children continue increasing their vocabularies as they listen and mimic what they hear from others, words that are read to them from books, or words that they hear on television shows or films. They begin to use more connecting words such as *because, and, if,* or even *actually.* They begin to organize and group things with labels such as *toys, vegetables,* or things belonging to another person, such as *mommy's things.* Likewise, several siblings may be labeled as *sisters* rather than by their individual names (Hayes, 2016; Hulit et al., 2019; US Department of Health and Human Services, 2020).

An important part of socioemotional development is when preschoolers learn to label emotions. Naming basic emotions such as *happy* or *sad* can help young children self-regulate. It can also aid them in increasing emotional labeling as they become aware of more sophisticated emotions such as *disappointed* or *excited*, linking them to behaviors or reactions. Young children soak up language learning as they listen and observe those around them. They play with language as they sing songs they have learned or composed on their own, make rhymes, or purposefully and jokingly say words incorrectly. As they begin to play more with peers, they may begin to form their own play language, descriptive words, or rules for play (Hayes, 2016; Brodin & Renblad, 2020; Hulit et al., 2019).

Between ages 4 and 5, preschoolers are often very talkative as their language abilities progress quickly. They follow simple instructions, moving from one-step instructions such as "put your markers in the bin" to two-step instructions such as "put your book back on the bookshelf and then come and wash your hands before lunch." They can use comparison speech such as *longer* or *taller* or *shorter*. They learn to negotiate through words. Pronunciation of speech sounds become clearer. And delightfully, they expand their conversational skills through modeling and direct instruction (Brodin & Renblad, 2020; Hulit et al., 2019; US Department of Health and Human Services, 2020). Table 8.3 summarizes some speech and language development milestones for preschoolers.

Many young children can learn multiple languages, making them bi- or even trilingual. As discussed in Chapter 5, the ability to perceive different language phonetics persists until the end of early

Age	Language Skills
2–3 years	• Communicates with words that close caregivers or other family members can understand • Has their own word for most objects and people • Can name and ask for objects or responses • Uses phrases that contain two or three words
3–4 years	• Listens to videos, television, or music at the same level as other family or class members • Hears when their name is called, even from another room • Can answer simple investigative questions, such as who, what where, how, and why • Shares or talks about things that have happened during the day at school, on play dates, excursions, or at home • Speaks easily with longer, four-word sentences
4–5 years	• Can listen to short stories and recall simple details when asked • Hears and understands what caregivers and family members say around them • Includes details when forming sentences • Tells their own stories • Uses rhyming words, some letters, and numbers • Pronounces most sounds correctly although they may have lingering problems with a few sounds such as *l, s, r, v, z, ch, sh*, and *th* • Uses more adultlike grammar in speech

US Department of Health & Human Services (2020)

Table 8.3 Speech and Language Developmental Milestones

childhood. As a result, young children can fluently learn other languages, even without an accent. After the preschool years, at about age 7 or 8, this ability declines (Friedmann & Rusou, 2015; Purves et al., 2001; Werker & Hensch, 2015).

Learning language is complex; but through experimentation, social interaction, and modeling, young children can learn quickly. Experts estimate that a child learns a new word during every waking hour, resulting in a vocabulary of over 14,000 words at the end of early childhood. Language involves speech, but it is also connected to literacy, or the ability to read and write. It also includes interpreting and decoding what others say and interpreting their meaning (Hulit et al., 2019). Not only are they learning words and their meanings, they are learning to understand the basic rules of language use just in time to enter school (Brodin & Renblad, 2020; Hayes, 2016; Hoff, 2014).

Preschool Humor

It has been said that there is no funnier being on earth than a 3-year-old child. Imaginative conversations, fresh new observations about the world around them, and uninhibited reactions can be a source of humor. Young children enjoy the humor

in daily life events. In the earlier years of this stage, children enjoy the funny sounds and faces made by others. Silly facial expressions, physical antics of known characters, such as Big Bird from the television show Sesame Street, or surprise movements such as hiding and being found can all cause peals of laughter. Although humor may create pleasure or happiness, it is serious business because humor aids cognitive development in early childhood (Miller, 2017).

Humor is a cognitive process in that it involves the perception, interpretation, and identification of a stimulus that has incongruities (Martin & Ford, 2018). It may involve theory of mind as it causes a child to see from another person's perspective or identify the irony of something being incongruent with expectations (Angeleri & Airenti, 2014). For example, a tree might be blue, a cow might say *meow*, a bird may wear sunglasses, or a tiger might fly. Identifying perceptions of incongruity as a cognitive mechanism are minimally necessary for all forms of humor.

The beauty of humor is that it not only aids cognitive development, but it begins early in life as part of social relationships (Filippova, E., & Astington, 2010; Hoicka & Akhtar, 2012). An infant responds to caregivers playing peek-a-boo with a cloth over their face or blowing a noisy sound on the infant's stomach. Socially laughing at incongruous events usually emerges at about 4 years of age (Martin & Ford, 2018). As children enter the preschool years and beyond, humor becomes more developed as cognitive capacities develop, specifically in the prefrontal cortex of the brain, which is associated with reward seeking. Funny images become part of language as preschoolers learn the mechanics of telling a joke (Goel & Dolan, 2001; Paine et al., 2020; Wise, 2004).

As language grows, so does the ability to manipulate it to achieve humorous results. In early childhood, language that focuses on words used or spoken inappropriately becomes humorous. For example, an adult cartoon animal that speaks in "baby talk" might be seen as funny. Humor can be used positively as a form of self-expression and language development. Expanding language abilities aid the process, and humor can add to or diffuse emotions (Goswami, 2010; Martin & Ford, 2018).

Around ages 4 to 5, as children near the end of early childhood, they may become more interested in humor that centers on bodily functions and characteristics. They have usually mastered their own toileting and bodily functions and, as a result, jokes about "farting" and other bodily mishaps become humorous to them. As they become aware of the differences between boys and girls, a fascination and curiosity often take the form of humor about these differences (see Figure 8.10). The fascination with bodily humor gives primary caregivers, families, teachers, peer groups, and significant others a practical opportunity to influence social development and socialization processes that help children become successful members of their society (Gavin, 2015; Saracho & Spodek, 2007; Stenius et al., 2021).

☑ CHECKPOINT

☐ Explain how language acquisition relates to cognitive development in early childhood.

☐ Identify the cognitive developmental language milestones often achieved by age 3, between the ages 3 and 4, and between the ages 4 and 5.

☐ What do preschoolers find to be humorous? How does humor support cognitive development in young children?

New Africa/Shutterstock.com

Figure 8.10 Preschool children find humor in the unexpected, including incongruent social roles, word usage, body humor, and jokes. Why might these two preschoolers find this situation humorous? How might the depicted interactions influence their social development and socialization processes?

Apply Here!

Take time to listen to a conversation between two young children that are about the same age. This might include children you know personally, or a video recording found online. Observe how their conversation proceeds, noting:

- their ages
- the topic or subject matter of their conversation
- common types of words (nouns, verbs, adjectives) used
- whether their interactions are mostly observations, commands, or dialogue
- whether they indicate enjoyment and humor or are task-oriented
- whether each partner is mostly talking, mostly listening, or if there is an exchange
- whether there a noticeable power differential between the two conversation partners; if yes, how so
- whether the conversation changes the behaviors or emotions of the participants

For comparison, observe another pair of young children representing a different age or stage in early childhood. For example, compare 3-year-old and 6-year-old conversation partners. What differences do you notice?

8.5 School Readiness

As noted previously, the early childhood years are described as the preschool years, the years that children prepare to enter school. How is a child best prepared for school? It takes more than learning the names of colors, identifying the alphabet, or knowing how to spell their own name to ready a child to enter school. In some of the most recent research on school readiness, a child's cognitive knowledge is not the sole focus. Instead, health and wellness along with social and emotional competence, especially self-regulation skills, are considered foundational to a young child's preparation for school (Blair, 2002; Blair & Raver, 2015; Coolahan, 2000).

Preparing to be ready for school begins at birth. Preparation comes through a nurturing and resourced home environment, availability of high-quality preschool programs, and available and accessible intervention support efforts for children at risk (US Department of Health and Human Services, 2021). Children must be treated as individuals. Also, appropriate expectations for school readiness should be broadly defined for parents and caregivers to help all children be ready to succeed at the set legal chronological age. School readiness should not be based on the mastery of skills (Williams & Lerner, 2019). The focus of preparing a child to begin school should go beyond the individual child's readiness to that of the family, school, and community to support each child (see Figure 8.11).

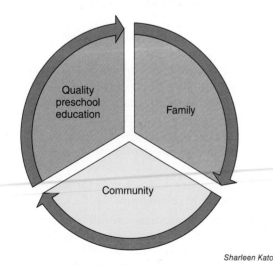

Sharleen Kato

Figure 8.11 School Readiness, A Community Endeavor. How might all three factors work together to prepare a young child to start elementary school?

Quality preschool programs and stimulating home and community environments can provide opportunities that prepare young children for learning. School readiness experiences include sensory development, socioemotional development, and early language, literacy, and math skills. "Use your words" is a common phrase spoken to preschoolers, and it is not without merit. Language skills have been found to increase a young child's ability to self-regulate. Primary caregivers and other family members can play a critical role in providing encouragement, comfort, and verbal descriptions of observed self-regulatory behaviors to the young children in their care (Brodin & Renblad, 2020; Vallotton & Ayoub, 2011).

One way that young children learn language and increase their self-regulation and vocabulary is to have adults and older children read books to them. Books provide a wonderful world of language. Recent researchers estimate that when a child is read five books a day, the child will enter kindergarten having been exposed to about one million additional words compared to peers who have not been read to (Logan et al., 2019). Words used in children's books are often different than the everyday language used at home, as imaginative creatures and talking animals are described. If the reader engages with the child while reading, such as by pausing to ask the child questions, using different voices to narrate different characters, or pointing out illustrations, this creates a positive social exchange that provides a positive orientation for learning while developing both pre-literacy and executive skills (Ferrer & McArdle, 2004; O'Keefe, 2014).

Most children begin to recognize and identify letters of the alphabet by age 2 (Rabiner & Huang, 1993; Skibbe et al., 2019). By age 5, most can identify many if not all letters of the alphabet and can write their own names (see Figure 8.12). Some can also write their phone number or address, depending on the length. There is a rapid progression in a short amount of time from marking an X to writing one's name or simple words. All of this occurs during the few short years of early childhood (see Table 8.4). (Whitehead, 2010).

Learning math skills are tied to increasing executive function skills and school readiness (Welsh et al., 2010). Counting and learning to identify shapes in early childhood are math competencies. Math competency is critically important in early childhood to prepare young children for the school

yaoinlove/iStock via Getty Images Plus

Figure 8.12 Learning the alphabet can include tactile activities or games.

years—so much so that some researchers have asserted that competence with math concepts such as counting, less, and more may be one of the most predictable indicators of future academic success (Nguyen et al., 2016).

Some primary caregivers and teachers put a lot of effort into teaching young children academic skills at a young age. For some parents, a child's proficiency in concepts like letter recognition or counting is like a contest to show how smart their child is. Although it is not harmful to teach a receptive child to read at an early age, most experts agree that early childhood education should focus on the whole child, emphasizing a child's physical, emotional, and social needs

Age	Developmental Milestone
2 years  *Nadezhda1906/iStock via Getty Images Plus*	• Identifies objects when prompted by caregivers • Tries to pronounce and repeat words in surrounding conversations • Begins to organize objects by colors or shape • Uses discovery to solve problems • Refuses food or toys by shaking their head, using hands to push away, or saying "No"
3 years *Perfect Angle Images/ Shutterstock.com*	• Speaks in sentences between five and six words in length • Begins to put puzzles with large pieces together • Organizes items by color or shape • Begins to count • Follows more complex instructions
4 years *kapley/iStock via Getty Images Plus*	• Remembers portions of stories • Can predict a story's ending • Differentiates between real and make-believe • Identifies colors by name • Uses intuition to solve problems • Understands the concept of opposites • Counts to 10 or higher • Uses different tenses in language other than present tense • Understands and interacts with programs or websites on a computer
5 years  *ziggy_mars/Shutterstock.com*	• Remembers their own name and address • Writes their own name • Has a higher attention span • Recognizes some written words • Wants to be like classmates/peers • Can draw a stick-person figure consisting of six parts (2 arms, 2 legs, head, body)

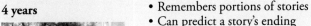

G-W Publishers; Kato

Table 8.4 Early Childhood Cognitive/Intellectual Developmental Milestones

as well as intellectual needs. With this in mind, early childhood education should focus on the process of learning rather than on the results alone (Pianta et al., 2007).

In addition to cognitive skills, social, emotional, and physical development prepare a child for school. Learning to share, follow simple instructions, verbalize thoughts and needs, and interact with other children are all important social skills that help a young child in later school years. Likewise, appropriate physical development as seen in fine- and gross-motor skills is important (Diamond, 2000; Bart et al., 2007). Abilities such as holding eating utensils to feed oneself, holding a pencil and crayon, using scissors, and turning the pages in a book are important fine-motor skills. Gross-motor skills such as jumping, hopping, and balancing are related to social and cognitive abilities. Socially, motor skills help children to fit in with their peers. Cognitively, motor development is related to learning. If a child is behind in gross-motor skills, providing them with extra help in this area enhances their cognitive skills (Grissmer et al., 2010; Wolfgang et al., 2003).

Because all areas of development are important to a child's school readiness, preschool programs are available to kids who are at risk for not being ready for school. Head Start is one example. By providing young children opportunities to learn school readiness skills, these programs prepare them for success in the next developmental stage, middle childhood. Participating in classroom-based early childhood education has a substantial positive effect on young children (Camilli et al., 2010; Gorey, 2001; National Association for the Education of Young Children, 2009). Children who attend preschool are better prepared to start kindergarten and require less remedial catch-up when compared to their peers who do not attend preschool. In a more recent study (McCoy et al., 2017), researchers found that participation in preschool can significantly reduce the number of children who need special education support once they enter school.

Preschool participation also increases high school graduation rates. This is good news, because individuals who fail to complete high school earn significantly less than their peers who successfully graduate. In addition to earning significantly less over a lifetime, a lower educational achievement level ends up costing governments more in services. When studies compared the costs of mandatory preschool versus the positive effect on the student's long-term earnings and potential contributions to society, they concluded that the long-term benefits of preschool far outweighed the costs. This was especially true for young children who came from under-resourced families (Cates et al., 2016; Chapman et al., 2011; McCoy et al., 2017). The good news is that more children in the United States are enrolled in early childhood education programs as many states are investing to make preschool feasible for more families. Unfortunately, though, more than half of the young children who come from low-income families are still not enrolled in preschool programs because of the lack of their universal availability or prohibitive costs (Hahn et al., 2016; O'Connor & Fernandez, 2006).

Global Perspectives

Preschool for All?

Early childhood education and care services are important for cognitive learning, physical development, and socio-emotional development and wellness. How does early childhood education and care compare around the world? Specific examples may be hard to come by as early childhood education can occur in preschools, childcare facilities, and care relationships within the home.

A report to the United Nations (UN) on the global history of early childhood education and care confirmed the importance of these opportunities, not only for a young child's cognitive development and socialization but also for providing an essential service to their employed parents (see Figure 8.13) (Kamerman, 2006). This study featured historical touch points, including the social protection policies in Europe and Africa during the 1960s to 1980s and the global policy effects of the 1990s between World Bank, UNESCO, UNICEF, and other global organizations within the United Nations. Offering free or subsidized early childhood education and care to families with young children has attributed to more women entering the workforce, fewer concerns about inequities among children and families, a decline in birthrates, and an appreciation for the impact that

MBI/Shutterstock.com

Figure 8.13 Early childhood education can enhance cognitive learning, physical development, and socioemotional development.

high-quality early childhood education and care can have over a lifetime.

Since 2016, the United Nations Sustainable Development Goals have included a challenge to countries across the globe to provide quality early childhood education and care by 2030 (UNICEF, 2020). This is a very bold goal, as it is estimated that about half of young children around the world lack access to quality preschool education or care (UNICEF, 2020). The motivation for

change is the understanding that children who fall behind in early childhood are affected for the rest of their lives, particularly in academic endeavors (Garcia et al., 2016). They often struggle in primary school, drop out of secondary school, and fall behind socially (UNICEF, 2019).

Although there is agreement that quality early childhood education and care are critically important, progress has been slow and disparities between high- and low-income countries are great. In fact, among the countries surveyed, over 80% of young children in high-income countries were enrolled in preschool, whereas only 22% were enrolled in low-income countries. Even if the UN goal is met by 2030, the disparities and gaps will likely remain as half of the world's children will still not have access (UNICEF, 2019). Even within the high-income countries, there is a disparity in how much is spent on early childhood education. Some countries spend significantly more than others and some significantly less. For example, Norway and Sweden spend nearly 2 percent of their gross domestic product on preschool education and care, whereas the United States spends only 0.4 percent (Samuels, 2017).

In the United States, public spending on early childhood education and care programs varies widely. Families utilize both private and public preschool education for 3- and 4-year old children, but at varying rates (see Figure 8.14). While a few states offer universal,

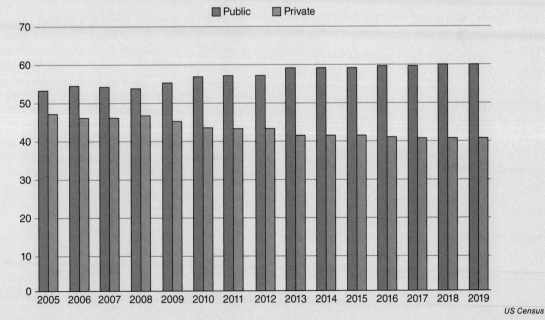

US Census

Figure 8.14 Public and private preschool enrollment in the United States between 2005 and 2019.

(Continued)

fully funded pre-kindergarten programs, mostly intended for 4-year-old children, most states do not. In other words, pre-kindergarten classroom learning opportunities are not available to all children due to cost or other accessibility restrictions, such as transportation and location (Parker, 2018). Because of the disparities, many children enter kindergarten developmentally behind by about a year as compared to those who have had access to quality pre-kindergarten education and care. This often traps children in a cycle of always being behind and never catching up academically (US Department of Education, 2015). Although the percentage of young children in the United States partaking in preschool education increased to 54% in 2019, the rate suddenly dropped to 40% participating in preschool education in 2020 during the COVID-19 pandemic. For infant and toddler care, it dropped by 25% (McElrath, 2021).

Creating an environment that supports early childhood education and care requires several things. First, it is important to see preschool as a right for every child. Second, it is essential to create strong public financial support to both train teachers and to pay for the operating expenses of running programs. Third, it is critical to make connections early with families and communities while making quality early childhood education accessible to all (Bos et al., 2017).

To Think About:

- Is preschool state-funded in your state? If so, is it limited to a particular group? If not, what do you perceive to be the barriers?
- If early childhood education became a norm, how might that impact society? How might it affect your own community?
- What specific benefits might you expect in global or international relationships?
- How might global early childhood education affect global migration?

☑ CHECKPOINT

- ☐ Explain why social and emotional competence are of primary importance when determining a young child's school readiness.
- ☐ Describe how language skills are tied to the ability to self-regulate.
- ☐ Identify the specific school readiness skills that are tied to basic math competencies such as counting.
- ☐ Name at least three social skills that contribute toward school readiness. Based on what you know about early childhood cognitive development, how might these skills be taught to young children?

Apply Here!

What types of preschool opportunities exist in your immediate community? If you had the responsibility of finding a preschool for a 3-year-old in your neighborhood, which program would you choose? Why? If early childhood is such an important time of learning, should preschool be mandatory? If so, how should it be financially supported? Is the inequity in early childhood education a matter of financial resources only, or are there other factors at play? If so, what might those factors include? What choices should be made available to parents? Write a statement that supports your viewpoint, citing information learned from your careful reading of this chapter.

Summary

Young children are eager to learn, and they are often talkative, humorous, imaginative, and playful. Their vocabulary grows rapidly as they communicate with family, caregivers, and peers. They learn their colors, the alphabet, and how to care for themselves and others. Young children are creative in their play, dreaming up imaginary friends and fantasy make-believe stories.

Children learn to hop, skip, jump, and throw a ball. They continue to gain more control over their small muscles and develop fine-motor skills. They can hold a pencil and crayon, use scissors, brush their teeth, and dress themselves as their physical and cognitive development domains work together.

In Chapter 9, you will explore young children's socioemotional development, including how they strive toward autonomy and industriousness, becoming less dependent and beginning to exert their will. Children simultaneously grow and change in all three developmental domains—physical, cognitive, and socioemotional.

Learning Outcomes and Key Concepts

8.1 Demonstrate knowledge of current research findings on how early childhood brain development and growth impacts cognitive functions and learning.

- Young children learn about their world through their senses, cognitive functions, social interactions, observations, and experiences.
- As their brains physically change, their cognitive functions grow and mature, too.
- By the age of 5, more than 100 billion neuron connections or synapses have been made in the young child's brain.
- The brain continues to expand at an incredible rate despite the pruning and trimming of neurons, resulting in observable and measurable cognitive changes.
- When children are given the opportunity to have stimulating experiences that reinforce new brain pathways, it makes the pathways stronger and faster.

- Neuron pathways peak in early childhood but not all at the same time.
- In early childhood, genes and experiences together form brain architecture for life.
- Windows of opportunity during the early childhood years provide a favorable time frame to teach many life skills.

8.2 Explain major cognitive theories of early childhood development.

- Piaget called early childhood the preoperational stage of cognitive development.
- Piaget believed this stage represents a time when children's use of symbolic and logical thinking grows.
- Recent research shows that conservation is understood at an earlier age than previously thought.
- Piaget's work influenced today's early childhood best practices focusing on thinking rather than accomplishments.
- Vygotsky's sociocultural theory of cognitive development posed the importance of social interaction in learning.
- The zone of proximal development (ZPD) emphasized the importance of caregiver-provided scaffolding.
- Theory of mind is used to understand another person's knowledge, emotions, or motivations that may differ from one's own.

8.3 Describe the impact of young children's social relationships and their environment on cognitive growth and learning.

- Modeling and imitation are important tools in cognitive development for young children.
- Young children are judicious but not always logical about who and what they imitate.
- Learning through imitation offers young children opportunities to learn the traditions and customs of everyday life.
- Preschoolers begin to think about thinking and memory, often referred to as metacognition and metamemory.
- Self-regulation is tied to all dimensions of development, including cognitive development.
- Cognitive development is enhanced through imaginative play.

- Young children begin to give meaning to symbols through using language and imaginative play.

8.4 Discuss how children learn language and identify cognitive developmental language milestones often achieved during early childhood.

- Language is not only essential to communication, but also an important part of cognitive development in early childhood.
- Young children begin to learn the symbolic nature of words and that words carry meaning through tone, intonation, and emotions.
- By age 3, most children can produce many of the sounds in language, although some of the consonant sounds may be delayed.
- By age 3, many children use possessives, three-word sentences, tense, and plural forms of words.
- Between 3 and 4 years of age, children continue to increase their vocabularies as they listen to and mimic what they hear from others.
- Between 4 and 5 years of age, children are conversational, can follow instructions, use comparison speech, and negotiate through words.

8.5 Recognize indicators of school readiness.

- Social and emotional competence are seen as foundational to school readiness.
- Language skills in early childhood have been found to increase a young child's ability to self-regulate.
- Learning math skills, such as counting and identifying simple shapes, is tied to increasing executive function skills.
- Learning to share, follow instructions, verbalize thoughts and needs, and peer relations are all important social skills.

Chapter Review

1. By the age of 5, more than 100 billion neuron connections or synapses have been made in the young child's brain. How do these expansive connections affect brain functions in early childhood?

2. Name two factors that contribute to learning in early childhood.

3. What are two tenets of Piaget's preoperational cognitive theory? Give examples of these tenets demonstrated in the real life of a preschooler.

4. Define the *zone of proximal development* (ZPD). Describe how ZPD relates to caregivers of young children.

5. Create a case study of a young child and caregiver relationship that illustrates theory of mind.

6. How do experiences interact with brain development and growth to promote learning in early childhood?

7. If you were writing a newsletter for parents of young children in your care, how might you describe the process, methods, and importance of language development in young children?

8. Explain why social and emotional competence are seen as foundational to school readiness.

Matching

Match the following terms with the correct definitions.

A. centration

B. conservation

C. declarative memory

D. egocentrism

E. long-term memory

F. metacognition

G. metamemory

H. non-declarative memories

1. Thinking about one's own thinking

2. The inability to take another person's perspective

3. The self-awareness of one's own memory

4. The ability to follow transformations of viewed objects and the ability to understand that the properties of objects can remain the same even if the way they look changes

5. Memory skills that are with us from birth

6. Memories that relate to skills that have been so integrated into subconscious thought that children perform them without thinking

7. These memories can be accessed over a longer time frame or even over a lifetime and include both declarative memory and non-declarative memory

8. The tendency to focus on just one aspect of something seen

9

Early Childhood: Socioemotional Development

Learning Outcomes

After studying this chapter, you will be able to:

9.1 Analyze the theories related to socioemotional development in early childhood and how these theories are demonstrated in a young child's life.

9.2 Describe the relationships between a young child's cognitive and socioemotional development and how the interplay between domains affects overall development.

9.3 Explain how a young child's relationship with their primary caregivers affects their socioemotional development.

9.4 Identify ways in which a young child's relationship with siblings affects their socioemotional development.

9.5 Identify ways in which a young child's peer relationships affect their socioemotional development.

9.6 Describe moral development and spirituality during early childhood.

Key Terms

authoritarian style
authoritative style
autonomy versus shame
  and doubt
empathy
ethnicity
gender
gender identity
gender roles
ideal self

initiative versus guilt
morality
parenting style
peer relationships
permissive style
personal identity
preconventional morality
prosocial behaviors
racial identity

rough-and-tumble play
school–family partnerships
self-esteem
self-image
sense of identity
social emotional learning
  (SEL)
social identity
spirituality

Introduction

What is your earliest memory? Who was with you? What were you doing? Is it a positive memory or one that saddens or frustrates you? During early childhood, children discover themselves and the people around them. They rely on their caregivers for affection and warmth, basic care, and guidance on how to relate to the people in the world around them. They learn who they are in the context of child–caregiver, family, peer, and other relationships. As they explore their social world, they learn to express their personal identity. They learn to express emotions as they dance, run, tell stories, share secrets, and explore their world. They have an abundance of energy.

How do those who knew you as a young child describe your temperament? Were you thrill-seeking? Shy? Friendly to strangers? Slow-to-warm up? Did you have budding friendships? Many young children are bold risk-takers, they forget previous failures and readily repeat their attempts at new activities. Others are very cautious and need encouragement to interact with others. Although present from birth, a young child's temperament and developing personality become more apparent to others during early childhood. Children see themselves as their own person, separate from their parents and siblings.

The preschool years are a social stage of life. Regardless of individual temperament, young children learn about the people, relationships, and cultural life around them and where they fit in (Bilmes, 2012). This chapter explores how children at this stage form close relationships with others, express and regulate emotions in socially and culturally appropriate ways, and develop a sense of identity in the context of family, community, and culture.

9.1 Socioemotional Theories

Developing social and emotional skills, both a part of psychosocial development, is critical to leading a healthy life. Socioemotional development affects a young child's overall well-being today and for life because it sets the stage for all relationships and social interactions. It affects later school readiness and success, relationships with others, positive or deviant social behaviors, and mental health throughout life (Bandura, 1977; Blair & Raver, 2016; Darling-Churchill & Lippman, 2016; Williams & Lerner, 2019).

Awareness of oneself and others is often divided into three main categories: self-image, self-esteem, and the concept of the ideal self (Cowie, 2012). **Self-image** is how the child perceives their social identity, or the roles that they play as a son or daughter, brother or sister, grandchild, student, or friend. **Self-esteem** is how children conceptualize their own value to others and themself. The **ideal self** is a child's concept of how they want to be seen in a social context, including the power they can exert. None of these concepts exist independently; they exist within the context of social and emotional development. How the self-concept develops in early childhood and throughout life has long been the subject of research inquiry (Dowling, 2014; Lerner et al., 2013; Schore, 2015).

As discussed in Chapter 5, theorist Erik Erikson asserted that the main socioemotional task accomplished in the first two years of life is the development of trust between the infant and primary caregiver. Primary caregivers help their babies or toddlers develop trust by responding to their needs. By volleying back and forth in response to each other, caregivers and infants simultaneously communicate needs and expectations. Erikson believed that the patterns that develop early in life remain with the individual, and personal weaknesses and strengths come from the struggles presented at each stage of development (Erikson, 1950). The strengths that can potentially come from these socioemotional struggles in early childhood include hope, willpower, and purpose (see Table 9.1).

Primary caregivers help their young children become independent and have a strong sense of self. Erikson described the second stage of socioemotional development as **autonomy versus shame and doubt**. This stage typically lasts from about 18 months to about 3 years of age. During this stage, young children begin to strive for independence. Sometimes, to the despair of primary caregivers, they are known to say "no" frequently and with enthusiasm. They learn to separate themselves from others, demonstrating their own will and personal preferences (Mooney, 2013). This is an essential process as young children learn what is acceptable behavior and what is not. The goal at this stage is to develop a sense of autonomy, but some children learn to feel a sense of shame.

In the third stage of Erikson's theory of socioemotional development, preschoolers begin to see themselves as their own person, separate from their parents and siblings and initiating their own actions. Erikson described this stage as **initiative versus guilt**. Preschoolers can be exuberant and enthusiastic about trying new things that they see others do, such as sweeping the floor, setting the table, or entertaining a younger sibling. In their eagerness to do things independently, they often make mistakes. For example, a child may knock over a cup of milk as they try to set the table. This type of mistake can cause feelings of guilt and lower a child's self-esteem, especially if a caregiver reacts negatively by scolding the child. On the other hand, through caregiver encouragement, the experience can create a sense of purpose in the child as they learn new skills (Cowie, 2012; Dowling, 2014; Lerner et al., 2013; Lindon, 2012; Robinson, 2008; Schore, 2015). The caregiver helps the child wipe up the milk and gives them the opportunity to try setting the table again. Table 9.2 provides additional examples of stages two and three.

Age	Stage	Strength Developed
0–12 months	Trust versus mistrust	Hope
1–3 years	Autonomy versus shame and doubt	Willpower
3–6 years	Initiative versus guilt	Purpose

Table 9.1 Erikson's Early Childhood Socioemotional Tasks and Strengths

Stage	Examples
Autonomy versus shame and doubt (1–3 years)	Toddlers learn how to control their physical bodies by feeding, toileting, dressing and undressing, and making strides in physical development. As toddlers learn new skills, they become self-confident. A lack of control or independence can make them feel shame and doubt. Often this is caused by caregivers punishing them for not doing things correctly.
Initiative versus guilt (ages 3–6)	Through discovery and exploration, young children learn about the world and their place in it. They learn what is real and what is imaginary. They learn to take initiative for their place in the world. Criticism and punishment can promote a sense of guilt.

Kato

Table 9.2 Erikson's Theory of Socioemotional Development in Early Childhood

Although Erikson's work continues to be a foundation for understanding young children's social and emotional development, more recent researchers have continued to expand and refine his work. For example, researchers have explored strong correlations between language and cognitive development, particularly language abilities, as being foundational to autonomy seeking (Maree, 2021; Tamis-LeMonda et al., 2004; Weiner et al., 2012). While a 2-year-old may be known for saying "No!" the 3- and 4-year-old may communicate their independence using phrases and sentences.

Language as a part of cognitive development also plays a role in helping children learn how to identify emotions such as pride, shame, or guilt. Attributing words to emotions may help young children recognize and understand their emotional state. This plays a large part in Erikson's autonomy versus shame and doubt stage (Mascolo & Fischer, 2007; Weiner et al., 2012). In addition, language can help children create a self-identity, particularly in the areas of gender and race. Language can also reflect how the child positively or negatively perceives that identity (Perry et al., 2019; Stanford Children's Health, 2020; Zosuls et al., 2016).

Applied Socioemotional Theory

Preschool mental health has been the subject of research for the past several decades, especially regarding childhood attachment and socialization disorders. Socioemotional theories focusing on well-being emerged, and educators often applied this growing knowledge to prevention-based early childhood programs (Bufferd et al., 2012; McLuckie et al., 2019). Research has identified that adverse childhood experiences (ACEs), as discussed in Chapters 1 and 4, may be associated with mental disorders that present as precursors to life-long challenges.

Prevention techniques that include environmental changes, caregiver education, medical and wellness care, and mental health counseling for children and their families show promise. More study is needed to understand factors that put young children at risk for mental health issues. Some researchers focus on behavioral issues (Dettmer et al., 2020; Posthumus et al., 2012). Others focus on family members' mental health, such as caregivers who struggle with depression or substance abuse. Other research focuses on environmental factors, such as poverty, violence, or abuse (Painter & Scannapieco, 2021).

Another applied area of socioemotional theory is the work of researchers and educators to understand how preschool-aged children learn social and emotional skills (Gershon & Pellitteri, 2018). **Social emotional learning (SEL)** is the process of developing the self-awareness, self-regulation, interpersonal, and decision-making skills to be effective in personal relationships (Botvin & Griffen, 2004; Dettmer et al., 2020; Jennings & Greenberg, 2009). Upcoming chapters that focus on childhood and adolescence will discuss SEL at great length, as it has been a focus in education for many years. In recent years, however, more emphasis has been placed on the positive effects of incorporating SEL theory in early childhood education, especially for at-risk children (Rivers et al., 2013). The intervention techniques for early childhood may vary from those used in elementary and secondary schools (Murano et al., 2020; Sklad et al., 2012). SEL includes helping young children deal with conflict, anger, and self-regulation of emotions, and encouraging them to demonstrate pro-social behaviors (Ferrier et al., 2014; Koplow, 2021; Webster-Stratton et al., 2008).

☑CHECKPOINT

☐ How would you describe socioemotional development in your own words? Why is it critical for primary caregivers and early childhood educators to pay attention to this developmental domain?

☐ Describe the two stages included in Erikson's early childhood socioemotional development. What two strengths are associated with these stages?

Apply Here!

Create an infographic that communicates classroom rules or expectations for children in a pre-kindergarten or kindergarten setting. Use words or images as appropriate. Then, consider the following questions:

• Do these rules primarily benefit the children or the teacher?

• Are these expectations based on personal or cultural values? If so, how?

• Will these rules be difficult to learn or enforce? Why or why not?

• Do your expectations build community?

Global Perspectives

Becoming Social

Primary caregivers, family members, and community members all play a part in young children's socialization. But when compared globally, are their goals the same? The answer may be yes or may be no. The United Nations General Assembly mandates UNICEF to advocate for the protection of children's rights and to help children reach their full potential in all domains of development as citizens of families and communities (Tobin, 2019). UNICEF works in over 190 countries worldwide, and the vast majority agree that children's ability to thrive is most important (UNICEF, 2020). In another study of 14 countries, most parents agreed that their goal for their children was for them to be successful and contributing members of their community (Gartstein & Putnam, 2019). How do these goals play out in how young children are socialized?

One common way to examine differences among cultural values is the view on individualism and collectivism. Individualistic cultures value independence; they socialize children to care for themselves, grow confident in their abilities, and become independent adults. Individualistic cultures consider freedom and autonomy essential both for parents and children. For example, in the United States, children have traditionally been taught to sleep separately from their parents. In times of distress, they learn to self-soothe (Ashdown & Faherty, 2020; Byrd, 2012; Guerda, 2016). However, this is not every child's experience in the United States, and customs within families and communities continue to change.

When cultures emphasize collectivism, they may also focus on teaching manners, demonstrating responsibility toward others, and balancing assertiveness and kindness.

Collectivist cultures value living in a community with others. Members of the community recognize the importance of considering the impact of their actions on others within the community. For example, young children in Japan learn about empathy from an early age with a focus on how their actions affect another person and their community as a whole (LeVine & LeVine, 2016). Taiwan is often considered a collectivist society, although it is important to avoid overgeneralizing any country.

Researchers have found that, because of globalization, individualism appears to be increasing worldwide, whereas collectivism may be slightly decreasing (Henri et al., 2017). However, there are still ample differences in cultures regarding individualism versus collectivism. Countries such as South Korea and Chile also place great value on the well-being of family, schools, and other community groups over individual concerns (Foo, 2019; Gross-Loh, 2013; Low & Tsang, 2019).

The concept of self-esteem also varies among cultures. While immediate caregivers influence self-esteem development in young children, as children mature, the outside influences affecting their self-esteem become more critical (Hosogi et al., 2012). In the United States, helping a child build high self-esteem, or the feeling of self-appreciation, is viewed as necessary in the child's social adjustment and health. In contrast, low self-esteem is associated with aggression and other antisocial behaviors (Donnellan et al., 2005). Adults often lavishly and frequently praise children, believing that this will result in high self-esteem. Many primary caregivers think that having a strong

sutlafk/Shutterstock.com

Figure 9.1 Young children often initiate or look for ways to help with household chores as they explore their social world.

sense of self will give their children an advantage in social relationships (Figure 9.1). In some cases, parents may consider their child's self-esteem to be a measure of their own self-worth (Assor & Tal, 2012).

In contrast, children in Sweden are encouraged to see themselves as valuable community members but not necessarily as special. Taiwanese parents do not necessarily value building self-esteem or self-affirmation through compliments and abundant praise as highly as in the United States. In Germany, parents are sometimes perplexed by American parents' desire to give young children so many choices (Gross-Loh, 2013). In a study of children and teens in the Netherlands, researchers (Brummelman et al., 2017) found that inflated positive praise lowers a child's

self-esteem and may result in higher narcissism (self-centeredness) in the teen years. These same researchers later found that narcissism could be mitigated if the praise children received was positive and realistic, but not inflated (Brummelman & Sedikides, 2020).

Teaching self-reliance is another way children worldwide are socialized; but this varies by culture, mostly in relation to developmental timing. Parents' cultural values are strongly connected to the specific ways they socialize their children (Gartstein & Putnam, 2019). For example, in many societies based on farming or agriculture, children become caregivers of younger family members, or they may begin performing chores such as fetching water or caring for livestock. Having these responsibilities at a young age may lead to more self-reliance. However, the effects of more available schooling, irrigation, and other technological advances on agrarian societies have made these socialization avenues more challenging when teaching the social value of responsibility. Communities continue to adapt their methods of enforcing shared social values (LeVine & LeVine, 2016).

Children in the United States often learn self-reliance through the cultural emphasis on individualism versus collectivism, as discussed above. However, US parents or caregivers may also practice dominant decision-making control rather than child-led decision-making. This is counterproductive, leading to less self-reliance and lower self-esteem in young children (Obradovic et al., 2021). It is impossible to separate cultural beliefs and values from a young child's socialization. But they should not be overly generalized, especially in this increasingly globalized world. Even though countries and communities may share the same cultural values, how parents and caregivers translate, rank, and communicate these values varies (Gartstein & Putnam, 2019; Gielen & Roopnarine, 2004).

To Think About:

- How did you learn about empathy, self-esteem, and self-reliance as a preschooler?

- In your encounters with young children and families, what parenting practices have you observed that are different from practices in your own culture? Do these differences make sense to you? Why or why not?

- As a future childcare provider, why is it essential for you to understand different parenting practices? How can expanding your cultural understanding provide more optimal care for young children?

9.2 Emotions, Identity, and Empathy

It is difficult, if not impossible, to separate socioemotional development from cognitive development. For example, children need to be cognitively able to understand that another person is a separate being, capable of their own thoughts and feelings, to be able to develop empathy. They require language skills to improve the articulation of their emotions to others (Schoon et al., 2010). Children learn how to express love through culture (Albert & Trommsdorff, 2014). Cognitive development is intertwined, and all developmental domains depend on each other (Bandura, 1977; Darling-Churchill & Lippman, 2016; Williams & Lerner, 2019).

Although a discussion of socioemotional development may include many skills and abilities, a few areas have particularly fascinated researchers. These include how young children learn to express and control their emotions in socially and culturally appropriate ways, how they learn to feel and express empathy, and how they form a self-identity in relation to others within their social circles (Darling-Churchill & Lippman, 2016; Lally & Mangione, 2017).

Emotions

Like all humans at every stage of life, preschoolers experience various emotions. As they mature cognitively, they become more aware of their feelings.

Often, those feelings may seem overwhelming. Young children may even be a bit surprised by their strong feelings. When they were infants, they were not able or expected to control their emotions. However, as young children, they are now expected to do so. Preschoolers often verbally and physically act out their emotions. They may react strongly to changes or transitions in their environment or daily activities by shouting, kicking, or thrashing (see Figure 9.2) (Blair & Raver, 2016; Darling-Churchill & Lippman, 2016; Williams & Lerner, 2019). Young children's maturing cognitive abilities combined with caregiver modeling, encouragement, and support create opportunities for them to learn to self-regulate emotions (Chaplin & Aldao, 2013).

Although learning emotional self-regulation is an essential part of early childhood and beyond, emotional expression is also important. Suppressing or not allowing children to express emotions, as opposed to regulating emotions, can thwart optimal socioemotional development throughout life (Gross & Cassidy, 2019). Culture must be considered when making value assessments of emotional expressions, as standards for acceptable expression of emotions may vary among families represented in an early childhood education class (Vaishali & Walker, 2019).

Preschool boys are more prone than girls to physically act out strong and more negative emotions (Brody & Hall, 2008; Chaplin & Aldao, 2013). Transitioning from one play activity to another,

A

B

Arlee.P/Shutterstock.com; Laura Crazy/Shutterstock.com

Figure 9.2 Young children often display strong emotions, verbally and physically acting out their emotions.

separating from others at naptime or bedtimes, or not receiving the choice they desired can cause strong negative reactions from both boys and girls. Likewise, positive emotions from pleasant experiences can be intense, and yet change quickly to fear. In early childhood, healthy emotional development includes learning to recognize and name emotions and self-regulate emotions as socially appropriate (Ho & Funk, 2018). Learning self-regulation is a process, not a one-time event. The following list provides some recommendations for encouraging self-regulation in preschoolers. What methods have you found to be most successful?

- Provide a warm, respectful, and emotionally and physically safe environment.
- Ask questions and then listen and be responsive, paraphrasing responses.
- Identify and name emotions by using specific descriptive words.
- Validate the child's feelings.
- Help the child consider what is triggering their emotions.
- Encourage and praise self-efficacy, their belief in their own capacity to self-regulate.
- Provide opportunities to explore and practice new skills without fear of punishment if mistakes are made.
- Provide occasions to practice problem-solving and executive skills.

Preschoolers are easily pleased and like to please others. They seek emotional approval and attention from others, especially primary caregivers, siblings, and teachers (Bai et al., 2015). They often enjoy demonstrating what they know, although they may be shy around strangers. They show attachment to primary caregivers and teachers and can experience stress when they are separated. Although attachment may look different than it did in toddlerhood, preschoolers still prefer the care and company of familiar adults to that of others (Brazelton & Cramer, 1991; Cassidy, 2008).

Fears, both real and imaginary, increase during the preschool years. Young children continue to fear the dark and unknown things or places. Like toddlerhood, preschoolers will imagine scary things and people. They also develop new fears of getting hurt. Examples are visits to the doctor and dentist, being bitten by an insect or animal, and loud noises

such as thunderstorms. They may also fear fire, large bodies of water, and other situations that may seem hurtful. Primary caregivers can help young children learn self-regulation skills to combat these real or imagined fears (Berti & Cigla, 2022; Joseph & Strain, 2010).

When preschoolers experience fear, anger, jealousy, or sadness, they may express their emotions physically or verbally. Temper tantrums peak during ages 2 to 3, but they can still occur in the later preschool years (Potegal et al., 2003; Solter, 1992). Preschoolers may yell and cry, but they are less likely to bite, kick, or lay on the floor, as a toddler might do. Preschoolers have increased vocabularies, so they will use words more often than temper tantrums to express their feelings.

Many caregivers are familiar with the renowned temper tantrums of 2- to 3-year-olds. Although tantrums may be common in early childhood, only about 10% of preschoolers have daily tantrums (Wakschlag et al., 2012). They tend to decrease through the preschool years, as young children mature in regulating emotions and communicating their needs verbally (Manning et al., 2019; Sisterhen & Wy, 2021). Even so, tantrums can be disruptive in families and early childhood classrooms. Tantrums come from frustration and often turn to anger and acting out, sometimes by physical aggression (Louis et al., 2021). A preschool child throwing a tantrum is often hungry, tired, wanting attention, desiring something they cannot have, or avoiding something they do not want to do. Parents and early childhood educators should remain calm and not be reactive during a tantrum.

To manage tantrums, giving choices is often a recommended way of helping young children develop autonomy and the strength of willpower in a socially conventional way. Table 9.3 provides other tips and recommendations for dealing with tantrums in the immediate and long term. No one method may work every time and with every child. Sometimes, verbal interaction with the child during a tantrum only exacerbates their anger. Other times, it may be the most effective manner to deal with the tantrum, especially if the young child is feeling unheard. Tantrums may require immediate responses from caregivers, especially if a child or others are in danger of being physically hurt. However, it is most effective to think about long-term goals as young children

Caregiver Responses and Behaviors During the Tantrum	Caregiver Responses and Behaviors in the Long Term
• Stay calm. • Keep the child safe. • Determine the cause of the distress by observation. • Determine the cause of the distress by asking the child. • Distance or redirect the child's focus. • If appropriate, eliminate or alter the source of distress. • Verbally paraphrase the child's response to their source of distress. • Be prompt and brief with any disciplinary measures. • If necessary, remove the child from the source of distress, such as implementing a time out; but keep the child in your eyesight, especially in public. • Do not respond back aggressively with hitting, slapping, or biting back.	• Establish clear expectations of appropriate social behavior. • Compliment children when they behave appropriately, especially during times of disappointment or frustration. • Identify the emotions of anger and frustration, both personally and as observed in the child. • Maintain open communication with the child about most matters. • Model healthy ways to deal with personal anger and frustration. • Help young children to prepare for schedule transitions.

Adapted from Cowie, 2012; Dowling, 2014; Lerner et al., 2013; Schore, 2015

Table 9.3 Short- and Long-Term Methods of Diffusing or Preventing Temper Tantrums

learn self-regulation and socially appropriate ways to communicate feelings.

Preschoolers' actions are often caused by issues provoking emotional responses. Family conflicts, relocating to a new area, and social problems are examples of stressful events that could trigger responses. Understanding the preschooler's concerns can help adults address the preschooler's emotions. Talking about preschoolers' concerns and feelings can help soothe preschoolers while preparing them for interacting with other children (Ashiabi, 2000; Dacey & Fiore, 2000; Dennis, 2006). Eventually, a young child's growing ability to express and regulate emotions appropriately leads to more satisfying social relationships and success in school (Herdon et al., 2013; Ross, 2017).

Identity

Young children's **sense of identity**, or who they believe themselves to be, advances as they cognitively understand their relationships with others. It is thought that when a young child has a positive self-identity, or **self-esteem**, it builds the foundation for relationships with caregivers, siblings, peers, and others both during early childhood and throughout life. Temperament, the environment, and other people's values shape young children's self-identity and their subsequent feelings about their perceived identity (Rambura, 2015).

Personal identity refers to self-identity shaped by individual temperament and subjective feelings about how one compares to others (Warin & Adriany, 2017). Young children build personal identity through their relationships with others (Milica, 2014). As they interact with others and make observations about these experiences, young children begin to perceive who they are (see Figure 9.3). This includes their role in the family structure, their way of reacting in situations, their perceived power and control, and the characters they play in social

EpicStockMedia/Shutterstock.com

Figure 9.3 Through play, young children form a perception of who they are, leading to personal identity.
How might playing dress-up contribute to a preschooler's sense of identity?

encounters. For example, a child might think of themselves as shy, or smart, or kind.

Identity that is built from referencing others around the child, such as identifying with gender, age, ethnic background, race, and religious background, is called **social identity** (Milica, 2014). Social identity includes the sense of belonging (Rogoff, 2003). Having a sense of personal identity and feeling positive about one's identity can give a young child insight into the feelings of others toward their own identity and emotions (Bennett, 2011). Like adults, young children's identities may be multiple and complex, changing over time and dependent on relationships and circumstances (Solomon, 2016).

Gender Identity

As young children develop their identities, they begin to identify with gender; this process is called **gender identity**. Although gender is often associated with biological differences, it is much more fluid than identifying sex chromosomes or genital characteristics (Ehrensaft, 2011; Piper, 2018). **Gender** is the expressed identity related to how the surrounding society defines men or women. For example, a young child can identify as a boy or a girl. How that identity plays out socially is considered gender. While biology dictates sex, gender identity comes from biology and interaction with the social environment (Hines, 2011; Klubeck et al., 2017; Lynch, 2018).

During early childhood, children also learn the expectations of being a girl or a boy. They learn what is expected of them in how they should act, feel, look, or appear, and what should be of interest to them. These are called **gender roles**. How does this happen? This topic goes back to the nature versus nurture debate. Biology is the basis for some gender roles. Much is based on what children are taught or how they are socialized by primary caregivers, siblings, peers, teachers, and others in their larger community (see Figure 9.4) (Eschenfelder, 2019; Foss, 2019; Lynch, 2018).

Rawpixel/iStock via Getty Images Plus

Figure 9.4 Young children enjoy dressing up in costumes. Do gender roles influence these costumes? If so, how?

As children interact more with peers, this gives them a new source of information about gender. Peers tend to use forms of punishment and rewards for behaviors that are deemed gender appropriate according to the rules formed by different friendship groups. Often, these expectations are unspoken, but the reactions are easy to read. If a young boy chooses a princess costume for a party, the response of his peers may communicate to him that this choice is socially unacceptable because he is a boy (Solomon, 2016). Because young children are in a dynamic stage of exploration in identity development, gender can be fluid and changing (Brown & Jones, 2001). Even so, male/female gender binary remains a default perspective in most cultures and is reinforced by societal norms even if it is becoming less rigid (Bennett, 2011; Brill & Pepper, 2008; Thomas, 2019).

In most countries, children are given a legal designation of male or female gender—their gender assignment—at birth. This designation is usually based on a visual inspection of a newborn's primary sex characteristics (anatomy) or on chromosome analysis before birth. The combination of a child's anatomy, chromosomes, hormones, and genes will all influence how their body develops (physiology). However, children may not become conscious of their own gender identity until they reach between ages 18–30 months (Halim et al., 2016). Children do not tend to assign stereotyped gender roles to others until they are in early childhood, ages 3–5 years old (Carroll, 2019; Ruble et al., 2006).

As children grow older, some develop a gender identity that matches their initial designation (*cisgender*), and some develop a gender identity that differs from their initial designation (*gender expansive* or *gender creative*). Gender identity may remain fixed or change over time (Carroll, 2019; Ruble et al., 2006). Children's internal sense of their gender identity can affect their gender expression, which refers to how they communicate their gender identity through behavior, clothing, hairstyle, and voice. It may also affect their gender attribution, which is the assumption that observers make about a child's gender, based on their gender expression.

For children who develop a gender identity that matches their initial gender designation, their gender expression often aligns with that gender identity. A child who is designated as a girl at birth, for example, might continue to feel, dress, and act like what is culturally considered appropriate for a girl as she grows older. Or she may choose not to comply with cultural expectations. Children whose gender identity or gender expression does not align with their initial designation may feel confused or upset when others make assumptions about their gender, misclassify them by using inaccurate pronouns, or expect them to exhibit certain gender-stereotyped behaviors. Primary caregivers and teachers can support healthy gender development by becoming aware of the full spectrum of gender experience so that they are well prepared to care for gender expansive children (Keo-Meier & Ehrensaft, 2018). Gender expansive children develop better mental health when adults support them in expressing their authentic gender identities (Carroll, 2019).

Ethnic and Racial Identity

In addition to parents and peers, the larger culture also affects how children view their identity. Children are motivated to fit in with others in society. They want to be included. Television, movies, music, advertisements, and toys are just some of the cultural influences that affect young children's views of themselves (Eschenfelder, 2019; Foss, 2019; Milica, 2014). Children develop a socially based racial or ethnic identity during the preschool years based on group membership. Creating a **racial identity** is an ongoing process of determining the racial or ethnic groups to which one belongs or does not belong. Social race identity may or may not be biologically based. When it is not, it is based on a shared culture such as language and traditions (Swanson et al., 2009). **Ethnicity**, sometimes considered distinct from race, is related to cultural groups that share social and cultural traditions, language, and communication styles (Quintana, 2007; Byrd, 2012).

Race Differentiation

Do young children naturally place value on others based on race or ethnicity? If so, then must this value judgment be unlearned as a child is socialized? Or, is placing value when differentiating between outward racial characteristics and ethnic practices something that is taught as young children are socialized? Does racism harm young children? These questions have been the focus of research over recent years. Children as early as infancy can distinguish between racial phenotypes or observable characteristics of a given race or ethnic group (Sangrigoli & De Schonen, 2004; Vogel et al., 2012; Xiao et al., 2018).

Distinguishing characteristics among people may demonstrate a child's cognitive skills in differentiation or their desire to create order and meaning to things observed. It might not be linked to learned racism, the social valuing of physical characteristics, or assigning meaning (Swanson et al., 2009). Racism, the system of socially giving rank value to different races, places unfair and unwarranted advantages on some groups of people and disadvantages on others (Macintosh et al., 2013). For example, by ages 4 to 5, a young child may already be socialized to show a preference for White children over Black children (Perszyk et al., 2019).

Although young infants may demonstrate preferences, does that assume bias? Not necessarily. The environment dramatically influences children's developing thinking and behavior (Rogoff, 2003; Rollin, 2019). Young children watch and learn from those around them. When they view and experience racism around them in their home, they make assumptions about how things and people are valued. This includes inputs from peers, family members, and authority figures, including what they see, hear, experience in their schools, and the distribution of economic resources (Trent et al., 2019).

Racism towards children can show up in three ways: institutional, personally meditated, and personally internalized into a child's social identity. As a result, effective management and education are needed so that primary caregivers and teachers are aware of displaying subtle attitudes, preferences, and behaviors that create negative social identity awareness at a young age. For example, research has shown that Black children are more likely to receive poor evaluations of their behavior than their peers when a White teacher assesses them rather than a Black teacher (Bates & Glick, 2013; Healey & Stepnick, 2020). The American Academy of Pediatrics (AAP, Trent et al., 2019) asserts that when children are affected by racism, whether as a victim or as a perpetrator, the impact is negative on the child's social development and society. The AAP also affirms that racism is not always overt but can manifest in subtle and even unintended ways. For example, an educator might repeatedly not pick a Hispanic child to read aloud or always call on an Asian child for the correct answer.

Empathy and Prosocial Behaviors

Empathy, the ability to comprehend another person's emotional state and, in response, have a similar emotion, is critical in shaping children's socioemotional development and their relationships with others (Decety et al., 2018; Stern & Cassidy, 2018). Young children develop helping or empathic behaviors very early in life (Paulus, 2014; Moore et al., 2015; Vaish, 2018). For example, toddlers may help their caregiver with putting on clothing or show care by patting their caregiver's back. By the time children enter the preschool years, they are cognitively, socially, and emotionally developing **prosocial behaviors**. Prosocial behaviors are those voluntary behaviors intended to benefit others (see Figure 9.5) (Haley, 2014).

Pavel Kobysh/Shutterstock.com

Figure 9.5 Young children demonstrate prosocial behavior through perspective-taking, such as when they recognize a need of another.

An essential part of prosocial behavior is the ability to take another person's perspective, or theory of mind, as discussed previously. As a young child becomes more capable of perspective-taking, they become more apt to develop empathy (Dettmer et al., 2020; Stern & Cassidy, 2018). However, identifying with and feeling a similar emotion does not necessarily guarantee prosocial behavior (Eisenberg & Strayer, 1987; Eisenberg & Fabes, 1998). Empathy goes beyond simply identifying someone else's feelings, it means reacting to another person in a compassionate or helping manner.

Although empathy may be an inherent human trait, prosocial behavior is learned over time and includes helping, sharing, and comforting others. Children learn prosocial behaviors through modeling. When encouraged and modeled in the home and classroom by primary caregivers, teachers, and peers, prosocial behaviors increase (Dunfield, 2014; Paulus et al., 2020; Spinrad & Gal, 2018). As a child matures, these behaviors become a part of their socioemotional development and even part of their neurological wiring (Abraham et al., 2018; Vaish, 2018). For example, a young child might see a peer take a toy out of a friend's hands. In response, the child might share a different toy with the friend. If the friend starts crying, the child may comfort the friend or participate in their distress by crying

too, or vocally sharing similar feelings. Figure 9.6 includes suggestions for promoting empathy and prosocial behaviors in the early childhood education classroom.

Young children can exhibit a sense of fairness, even as young as toddlers (Williams & Moore, 2014). By the preschool age, they notice when resources such as toys or food are dispersed unequally. They may take the initiative to share resources when given the opportunity, which marks the beginning of moral decision-making (Sommerville et al., 2012; Vaish, 2018). Primary caregivers and educators, including preschool teachers, play a significant role in helping young children develop empathy and prosocial behaviors (see Figure 9.7). Empathy toward others begins from the start of life with nurturing and

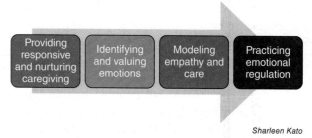

Sharleen Kato

Figure 9.7 Encouraging empathic behaviors in preschool children is not a one-time event but a continuing process.

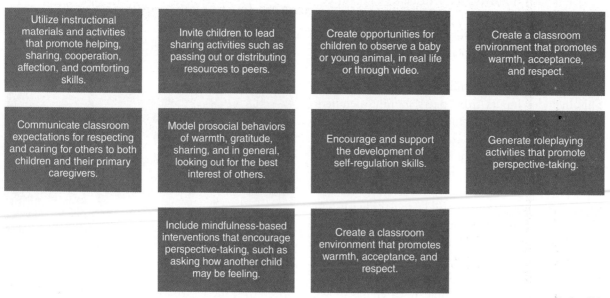

Sharleen Kato

Figure 9.6 Ways to Promote Young Children's Empathy and Prosocial Behaviors
Have you used any of these methods to promote prosocial behaviors? Which ones? Can you provide specific details?

empathic care from primary caregivers, which then combines with modeling, emotional learning, and practicing self-regulation (Decety et al., 2018; Spinrad & Gal, 2018; Stern & Cassidy, 2018).

☑CHECKPOINT

- ☐ What are typical ways preschoolers experience fear, anger, jealousy, or sadness?
- ☐ What are the component parts of identity development, and how do young children develop an identity?
- ☐ Define the terms gender, gender identity, and gender roles. How does socialization affect gender identity?
- ☐ Brainstorm specific ways that primary caregivers and teachers can support healthy gender development for young children in their care.
- ☐ Is social race identity biologically based? What is socially based racial or ethnic identity dependent on?
- ☐ What is empathy? How does it relate to prosocial behaviors?

Apply Here!

Books abound for young children that focus on socioemotional development. Gender, racial and ethnic identity and expression, identifying and regulating emotions, and prosocial behaviors are topics of children's books. They often feature beautiful photographs, artwork, animation, and drawings that capture the richness of these topics. Choose one socioemotional development topic and create a booklist for caregivers that highlights engaging books for young children. Consider age levels, and define your audience (board books, picture books, or beginning reader books).

9.3 Relationships with Caregivers

Children spend most of their time at home or in care settings during the preschool years. The role of parenting and caregiving changes, sometimes becoming more complex, as children become more social and independent. Young children need support, encouragement, and instruction to become socially and emotionally competent. They need to try new tasks on their own even though they may fail. Family members can provide this support and encouragement. As young children become more independent, their sense of self and their confidence grows (Harter, 2012; Stipek, 1995). Caregivers and teachers influence a young child's development in all domains (Kirby & Hodges, 2018; Sanders & Morawska, 2018).

Because young children learn in the context of relationships, primary caregivers and teachers are critical players in their emotional and social development as young children spend a large amount of their lives in their care. The trust relationship between securely attached primary caregivers and infants is essential in early childhood when young children navigate social relationships and learn new skills (see Figure 9.8) (Doyle & Cicchetti, 2017; Raikes & Edwards 2009). When young children are learning in a trusting, attached relationship, they tend to explore

A

B

digitalskillet/Shutterstock.com; DisobeyArt/Shutterstock.com

Figure 9.8 Caregivers encourage positive emotional and social development through shared experiences.

more, ask more questions, engage in problem-solving, and be more apt to identify and express their feelings with others (Gordon & Browne, 2014). Some practitioners in early childhood learning recommend consistently offering warmth, respect, and care to young children (Ho & Funk, 2018). When young children are maltreated and fail to develop trust in their caregivers, or when that trust erodes, this negatively affects their socioemotional development. Insecure attachment in early childhood manifests in feelings of unworthiness, lack of trust in relationships, and antisocial or aggressive behaviors (Cicchetti, D., & Toth, 2015; Doyle & Cicchetti, 2017; Sherman et al., 2015).

Caregiving/Parenting Styles

Primary caregivers' approach when guiding and socializing their children is known as their **parenting style**. Parenting styles are directly observable behaviors used to socialize children (Kuppens & Ceulemans, 2019). Three common parenting styles include the **authoritarian style**, the **permissive style**, and the **authoritative style** (see Table 9.4). Researchers have been studying parenting styles for years, largely under Dr. Diana Baumrind, a clinical psychologist, who noticed that preschool children's distinct behaviors were often related to their caregivers' socialization and guidance practices (Baumrind, 1967, 1971, 1989).

Over time, Dr. Baumrind began observing the effects of two influencing factors, parental or caregiver warmth and control (Maccoby & Martin, 1983). Caregiver warmth included a range of behaviors such as showing emotional availability, responsiveness, and involvement in the child's activities. Higher or more frequent demonstrations of warmth reap positive developmental outcomes, such as long-term mental health and well-being (Gerhardt et al., 2021; Moran et al., 2018). Low, absent, or infrequent demonstrations of warmth have been repeatedly connected to negative developmental outcomes, including depression, anxiety, lower self-esteem, aggression, and later delinquency and substance abuse (Asmussen, 2011; Kuppens & Ceulemans, 2019; Scheier et al., 2014). Caregivers demonstrate control when they use behaviors that attempt to manage, regulate, or govern the child, either psychologically or behaviorally. Excessive control over a child has been linked to negative developmental outcomes such as deviant behavior, aggression, anxiety, or passiveness (Asmussen, 2011; Scheier et al., 2014). Insufficient control has been connected to caregiver permissiveness, which may result in more behavior problems or lower self-esteem in preschoolers. However, the results of this correlation have not been conclusive and are complex (Pinquart & Gerke, 2019). Most research has supported that some amount of control when socializing a child results in positive developmental outcomes (Asmussen, 2011; Sclafani, 2012).

Considering warmth and control as influencing factors lends more depth to the complexity of understanding complex human behaviors. For example,

Parenting/Caregiving Style	Description
Authoritarian style	An *authoritarian style* tends to be controlling and corrective. Caregivers who use this parenting style tend to be strict and expect obedience without discussion. Children with authoritarian caregivers may not understand why they are asked to behave a certain way.
Permissive style	A *permissive style* lets children control situations, making decisions with few limits or controls. Caregivers who use this style tend to be more like friends than parents. Children with few limitations may have trouble getting along with others because they are only used to following their own rules.
Authoritative style	Giving choices and encouraging children to practice decision-making are common practices for caregivers using the *authoritative style* (also called the *democratic style*). Caregivers who use this style offer support while setting clear limits. These limits may be strict, but they are set in a warm and responsive manner. Caregivers communicate their rationale for expectations in age-appropriate ways.

Kato

Table 9.4 Three Main Parenting Styles

although the authoritarian parenting style may be seen as less than ideal, this style may be effective in some cultures, such as in South Korea and China, if parental warmth is high (Liu & Wang, 2015; Xing et al., 2019). Most experts agree that if combined with a sense of warmth, caring, and the child's best interests, any type of involved parenting can be effective. A surrounding community that supports the parenting style is also essential. Parenting and caregiving are culturally biased. Geographic location, local practices and customs, religious background, economics, personal experiences, and education influence parenting style (Doepke & Zilibotti, 2019; Foo, 2019; Sorkhabi & Mandara, 2013). For most parents, methods may vary based on the situation, their own emotions, the child's emotional state, perceived threat to the child, or the amount of energy they are willing to exert.

In a daycare or preschool setting, the professional caregivers and the children they serve may come from different cultural settings. Effective caregiving requires teachers to be sensitive to and appreciative of these cultural differences (Ashdown & Faherty, 2020; Moore et al., 2018). How teachers demonstrate sensitivity may vary day to day or hour to hour. Caregiving that is consistent over time and situations is most effective and provides the most stable, secure environment for a child. Young children need support, encouragement, and instruction to become independent. They need to try new tasks on their own, even though they may fail. Caregivers can provide this guidance and encouragement through

positive guidance techniques (see Figure 9.9) (Doyle & Cicchetti, 2017; Kirby & Hodges, 2018; Raikes & Edwards 2009; Sanders & Morawska, 2018).

Socioemotional Learning in Guiding Behavior

Transitioning from caring for children's needs to guiding their behaviors requires an understanding of how young children see their world. To allow for more autonomy, primary caregivers and educators can help children learn to make decisions and how to interact with others appropriately. As described earlier, social emotional learning (SEL) is the process of developing basic social and emotional competencies (Albright et al., 2011).

There are many practical ways that primary caregivers and educators can model or directly teach socioemotional learning. For example, they can coach children on-the-spot as they encounter new or challenging social experiences, such as navigating a relationship with a peer. Or it might be seen by carefully selecting educational materials such as books, activities, and media that support SEL (Ho & Funk, 2018; Jones & Doolittle, 2017; McClelland et al., 2017).

Because many young children spend much of their time away from home in childcare settings, primary caregivers and educators should work together to ensure congruence in expectations and values. Caregivers and educators may share reports about daily activities, interactions they have observed, developmental milestones, or any concerns they might have

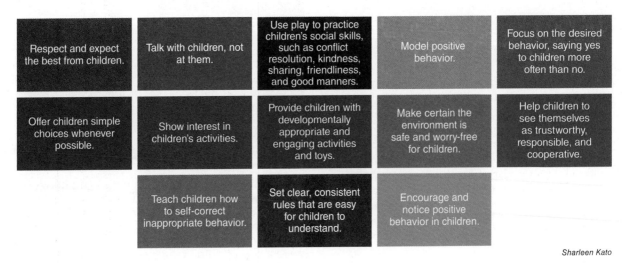

Sharleen Kato

Figure 9.9 Early Childhood Guidance Techniques

about the child's well-being in their care. Primary caregivers may likewise report any changes in home life, health, wellness, developmental milestones concerns, or worries or questions about their child's well-being. These interactions are referred to as **school–family partnerships** (SFP) (Albright et al., 2011). For example, SFPs can focus on instructing, encouraging, and reinforcing SEL skills within the home and in childcare settings, as well as within the broader social arena, including:

- self-awareness
- social awareness
- self-management
- relationship skills

The effort to collaborate with caregivers is worth it. When parents and professional caregivers mutually agree upon appropriate social behavior and provide direct instruction, cues, encouragement, and modeling, young children improve their social skills over time compared to their peers (Ashdown & Faherty, 2020; Moore et al., 2018).

☑CHECKPOINT

- ☐ Why are secure parent and caregiver-child attachments necessary in the preschool years?
- ☐ Describe the three main caregiving/parenting socialization styles.
- ☐ What is social emotional learning (SEL)? Give an example of how a teacher might model it.
- ☐ Define school-family partnerships (SFP). List and describe several socialization skills SFP can enhance.

Apply Here!

Think of a situation that you have observed in which a caregiver intentionally focused on the identity development of a young child. This might include something you have observed in life, a memory from your own life, or an example from a television program, movie, or online source. Then, create a case study of a young child and caregiver relationship that illustrates how relationships between a young child's cognitive, social, and emotional development play a part in identity formation. Include specific ideas such as activities, conversations, books, games, or other media. Include gender and racial identity considerations.

9.4 Relationships with Siblings

Siblings are often a social fixture in the lives of preschoolers. Many gain new siblings during this time. Others are born into a family and live with siblings from the moment they enter the world. Sibling relationships are often one of the most influential social connections in early childhood. Studies have shown that sibling relationships may even influence a child's social development more than parental or later peer relationships (Brook et al., 1990; Campione-Barr, 2017; Hindle et al., 2014).

Siblings can be playmates, confidants, competitors, opponents, and the focus of social comparisons. In all, siblings can profoundly affect a young child's socioemotional development (Dunn, 1983; McHale et al., 2012). Sibling relationships can play an essential role in influencing the power positions within a family (McHale et al., 2006). For example, when a new baby joins the family, the preschooler may experience changes in their personal position as parents suddenly direct their attention and resources to the infant's needs. This can result in both adjustment problems as well as positive development. Older siblings can create norms and expectations for younger siblings to follow (Campione-Barr, 2017; Hindle et al., 2014).

Frequent conflicts occur between siblings, especially in the preschool years. Often, these conflicts center on sharing toys, food, playmates, or even parents (see Figure 9.10). New baby siblings can be a

Figure 9.10 Frequent conflicts between siblings and between peers often occur over ownership and use of toys, including sharing and taking turns during the preschool years.
Did you have sibling or peer conflicts when you were a young child? What was the source of the conflicts?

concern for many young children. Primary caregivers often work hard to prepare their young children for the new baby's arrival. A preschooler's reaction to a new sibling can best be described as unpredictable, despite caregivers' best efforts. But these conflicts can help young children develop skills in perspective-taking, emotional self-regulation, problem-solving, and even persuasion that they can use throughout life (Brown et al., 1996; Dunn, 1983; Howe et al., 2002; Updegraff et al., 2002; Youngblade & Dunn, 1995).

Some children welcome their baby siblings with open arms and a sense of nurturing. They see themselves as the older sibling and caretaker, separate from the needy infant. Other young children act out and regress in their behavior, vying for their parent's attention. If siblings have similar temperaments, there may be less conflict in the home. When personalities contrast, sibling conflicts often exist. This is not just true in early childhood, but throughout life (Campione-Barr, 2017; Updegraff et al., 2010).

When sibling conflict is high over an extended period, it can negatively affect family dynamics, such as increased aggressive behavior between siblings and peers (Bank et al., 2004; Criss & Shaw, 2005; Wojciak & Gamboni, 2020). Negative sibling relationships have even been attributed to substance abuse during adolescence (Fagan & Najman, 2005). Within the family, daily sibling conflicts are common. Young children are capable of settling these disagreements, but they often do not. Young children do not naturally apologize for their wrongdoing, but they can learn to do so over time. They are more likely to resolve conflicts if a parent or other caregiver is present. Modeling problem-solving and conflict resolution for young children is effective. So are warm, responsive parental relationships (Campione-Barr, 2017; Dunn, 1983).

One area of sibling conflict that is difficult for a child to overcome is a perceived differential treatment, when a primary caregiver seems to favor one child over another, even if they do not share the same home (Brody & Stoneman, 1994; Shanahan et al., 2008). However, if the young child perceives a logical reason for this difference, such as the sibling is a baby and needs more care, the child is less likely to be negatively affected (McHale et al., 2005). In a study looking at young children who had siblings with disabilities, in this case Down syndrome, the children were well-adjusted to living with their siblings and possible differing parental expectations or treatment (O'Brien et al., 2009). In the same study, the impact of siblings with cancer or autism spectrum disorders was less clear. Still, researchers found that interventions from healthcare professionals to help young children understand the needs of their siblings were a positive moderating factor. Young children need to know the reasons for differential treatment from parents, whether due to age, special needs, or even ordinal position in a cultural context (Kowal & Kramer, 1997; Wojciak & Gamboni, 2020).

Each sibling relationship is unique and complex, with many dynamic forces shaping it. These relationships can be simultaneously positive and negative. However, it is known that the loss of a sibling can have a profound effect on surviving siblings (Berman, 2009). Sibling relationships in early childhood are shaped by many factors, including the direct relationship between siblings, the family, and the larger environment. These relationships are dynamic and change over time (Hindle et al., 2014; Updegraff et al., 2010).

☑ CHECKPOINT

- ☐ What role do siblings play in a preschooler's socioemotional development?
- ☐ How do sibling relationships rank compared to parent, peer, and extended family relationships during early childhood?
- ☐ Describe typical sibling conflicts involving preschoolers and siblings.
- ☐ How can family dynamics be planned to decrease sibling conflict?

Apply Here!

Today, you have two siblings in your care. Four-year-old Jack is playing next to 2-year-old sibling Ollie. Ollie picks up a toy zebra and puts it on Jack's head. Jack begins to sing a song, creating the lyrics, "No zebras in my hair, no zebras in my hair, no, no, no, no, NO ZEBRAS IN MY HAIR!" Ollie laughs, takes it off Jack's head, and puts it on his own head. You notice this event, especially because these siblings often get into disputes over toys; but this is a pleasant interaction. You tell Jack that you like the song. Jack then says, "Oh, it is a very old song that is sung before holidays. I knew it since before I was born."

(Continued)

- On another day, Jack reacts differently. He yells at Oliver, "Take that Zebra OFF my head!" and pushes Ollie away. Why might the reaction be different on another day?
- Sibling relationships between young children ebb and flow just like they do in any stage of life. What have been your most effective ways of helping young siblings communicate and care for each other? Are these universal values?
- How might sibling relationships be enhanced in early childhood?

9.5 Relationships with Peers

Fort building, playing dress-up, acting out roles, playing tag, and hide-and-go-seek are all a part of preschool years. Play continues to be critical to optimal growth and development during the preschool years, but peers become a part of the mix. As introduced in Chapter 6, sociologist Mildred Parten's proposed six stages of play (Bernard, 1970; Biddle et al., 2014; Parten, 1933), with four of the six types most common during the preschool years (see Table 9.5). Although progression through the stages is considered linear, each new stage offers more to a child's repertoire as the child's physical, cognitive, and socioemotional abilities and skills develop and enhance play in a social context. All children develop at their own pace, and play behaviors are no different. Young children who have frequent opportunities to play with siblings or peers may move more quickly into associate or cooperative types of play. Likewise, children who do not have many

Type of Play	Typical Age Range of Initiation	Examples of Play Activities
Onlooker play	Age 2.5–3.5 years	Observing others' play with interest; typically, decision-making is disconnected from peers, goals may or may not be similar. Examples might include: • playing in the same vicinity with a shared pool of toys such as stacking blocks; • separately playing on playground equipment; or • jointly using a sensory table or sandbox, but playing independently.
Parallel play	Age 3.5–4 years	Observing others' play; playing side by side or near each other, but often with different goals or purposes; may be distanced. Examples might include: • playing in the same vicinity with a shared pool of toys, • creating artwork in the same vicinity, each with their own supplies; or • watching another pull or in some way interact with a toy.
Associate play	Age 4–4.5 years	When resources are shared, decisions are made together, and play may be similar in context. Examples might include: • playing together with a shared pool of toys such as train cars using the same track, making informal rules about the direction but not sharing goals for creating new track formations; • separately but concurrently making pretend meals in a play kitchen; • riding bikes or scooters together on the same area or surface; • sharing art materials in the same physical space; or • chasing bubbles in the same vicinity.
Cooperative play	Age 4.5 and up	Sharing a common goal, such as solving a problem, with more interaction about common goals than in associate play. Examples might include: • creating a musical or theater production with a storyline, costumes, and props; • jointly planning, creating, and completing a group art project together; • building a fort out of cushions and blankets together; or • taking turns on playground equipment.

Kato; Biddle et al., 2014

Table 9.5 Types of Play

opportunities to play socially may be delayed (Lindsey & Berks, 2019; Ramani, 2012; Yogman et al., 2018). Associate and cooperative play demand more communication skills and teach children about cooperation, sharing, decision-making, group work, problem-solving, negotiation, and self-advocacy (Yogman et al., 2018).

Ask 4-year-olds who their best friends are, and they can give you a ready answer. But peer relationships can begin much earlier, even during infancy, when babies exhibit preferences toward some peers over others (Hay et al., 1999). **Peer relationships** are social connections between like-age individuals (see Figure 9.11). They can occur in pairs or in groups. Aggression toward peers can also be displayed as early as infancy, indicating that peer preferences are formed early in life (Hay & Castle, 2000; Rubin et al., 2003).

Peer relationships in the form of friendships can positively affect a young child's development. Friendships help children learn how to interact socially and express emotions. Friendships in early childhood provide joy as children play together, share secrets, defend each other, and explore their world. These interactions help children learn how to share and get along with others. Friendships provide support when a child is feeling happy or sad. Friendships also help young children learn about people who are different from them. In recent years, researchers have appreciated the complexity of friendships in early childhood. In many ways, they are very similar to adult friendships (Coelho et al., 2017; Fabes et al., 2009; Ginsburg, 2007).

Young children play differently with friends than with primary caregivers or other adults. They can distinguish the difference between these relationships from a young age (Kernan & Singer, 2010; Yogman et al., 2018). They may begin by playing independently alongside their peers in more constructive play, such as building with construction blocks, putting together puzzles, or creating a piece of art out of clay (parallel play). But as young children develop cognitively, socially, and emotionally, they begin engaging their peers in their play.

By ages 5 to 6, children move from associative play (interacting while involved in parallel play) to cooperative play. They might build something together or make up elaborate rules to play (Ginsburg, 2007; Yogman et al., 2018). Peer relationships, especially friendships, can enhance imaginary play as children take on roles in their complex creative stories. Playing school, doctor, or acting out family roles are part of early childhood (Ginsburg, 2007; Mottweiler & Taylor, 2014). **Rough-and-tumble play**, an active and vigorous form of physical play, can aid in children's social abilities to negotiate, communicate, create rules, and regulate emotions (see Figure 9.12). Rough-and-tumble play, often seen in later preschool years, can encourage children to take risks and experience cause and effect when practiced in a safe environment (Hart & Tannock, 2019; Pellis et al., 2010; Yogman et al., 2018).

As a young child's understanding and skills develop, peer relationship skills are learned over time. Some young children are drawn to peer interactions and readily engage, whereas others are shy or hesitant. However, forming peer relationships is not dependent on having an outgoing personality; it requires a sense of identity as peer relationships often center on meeting the young child's goals. Subconsciously, identifying and working toward these goals builds competence in effective peer group entry, conflict resolution, and maintaining play over time (Guralnick, 2010; Sette et al., 2019; Thibodeau et al., 2016).

Some young children have difficulty forming relationships with peers. Although peer relationships are affected by many factors, both within the child and the larger environment, peer acceptance

FatCamera/iStock via Getty Images Plus

Figure 9.11 Early Childhood Friendships.
Do you remember who your playmates were in early childhood? What games or activities did you engage in together? Where did your ideas for play come from?

Figure 9.12 How can rough-and-tumble play aid in a young child's optimal development?

is most directly related to the young child's behavior toward others (Conte et al., 2018). For example, highly aggressive children are less often accepted by their peers (Coelho et al., 2017; Crick et al., 1997). Preschool girls show more relational aggression than boys, such as not including a peer in play activities, although boys show more physical and verbal aggression (Ostrov & Keating, 2004). An overall lack of prosocial behaviors also negatively affects a child's peer relationships (Fabes et al., 1997; Guralnick, 2010; Hay et al., 1999).

Primary caregivers and teachers can help young children learn friendship and effective peer interaction skills. Still, it is most effective to lay the foundations early, starting in the toddler years. These include regulating emotions, practicing self-regulation, understanding cause and effect, imitating others, and building language or communication skills (Conte et al., 2018; Guralnick, 2010; Ladd, 2005). Secure attachment formed from responsive, caregiver–child relationships results in more empathic child–peer relationships (Stern & Cassidy, 2018). During the preschool years, primary caregivers and teachers can help children practice and expand their abilities to effectively and positively interact with peers by modeling relationships, listening, encouraging, and offering support (Qu et al., 2015; Yogman et al., 2018).

"She took my toy!" "That is mine!" "I was first!" are phrases commonly heard along with grabbing, pushing, and other aggressive behaviors as children negotiate conflicts. Young children are concerned with their own rights over important things, including toys, food, space, and attention from others, especially caregivers. An essential aspect of learning social interaction skills is learning to negotiate conflict. Conflict negotiation skills are necessary throughout life, but early childhood sets the foundation for learning these skills. Primary caregivers and early childhood educators may help children by:

- approaching conflict calmly, acknowledging that it is a natural part of social interaction
- helping children articulate what their concerns are, such as a possession being taken or something else that is interpreted as an afront on their space or rights
- listening, and paraphrasing their responses
- assisting young children in articulating how this affront makes them feel by using words that express emotions, such as mad, sad, angry, or frustrated
- helping children to problem-solve or come up with solutions to care for each child's needs and desires
- encouraging children to agree upon a solution, implement it, and, if not successful, to continue in negotiations
- acknowledging and encouraging children when conflict negotiation skills are observed

Of course, 2-year-olds are developmentally different from 6-year-olds in their cognitive ability to recognize and name emotions. They also vary widely in their ability to problem-solve. The ability to articulate and comprehend conflict resolution matures over time, typically over a lifetime. Through developmental maturity, caregiver guidance, reinforcement, and practice, the foundation for conflict resolution is laid.

Learning peer relationship skills helps young children better understand themselves. It is key to forming their self-concept. Early positive peer relationships even affect long-term mental health (Ladd & Troop-Gordon, 2003). The friendship skills learned in early childhood often carry forward through middle childhood and beyond.

☑ CHECKPOINT

- ☐ List and describe typical forms of play during the preschool years. How do the different types of play relate to each other? Give specific examples.
- ☐ What role do peers play in a preschooler's socioemotional development?
- ☐ How are friendships formed in early childhood?
- ☐ Why are positive relationships important to a young child's socioemotional development?

Apply Here!

Imagine that three 4-year-olds are in your care. They join an already established group of three other children who have been in your care for several months. You observe the children during play. Most of the children are happily playing in the same area, imagining and reenacting a story that you read to them from a book a few days ago. Two of the new children join in, lending their ideas to the evolving story being played out. One of the new children is holding back, refusing invitations to join in even though showing great interest by following the other children's actions. How would you respond? Would you experiment with ways to involve the child in the group play? If so, how?

Practical Issues and Implications

Expelled from Preschool?

Preschool children are full of wonder, curiosity, and energy. At the same time, they can be challenging to adults as they learn social and emotional skills within their own cultural contexts. When frustration mounts, tantrums, defiance, and even aggression are not uncommon. Although challenging behaviors can be difficult within families, they are particularly difficult within preschools when there are many children to manage.

Occasional or even frequent challenging behavior is a normal part of social and emotional development during the preschool years. It is also seen more often in young children living in poverty or with other adverse childhood experiences. As a result, children who observe domestic violence in their homes, are poor, live with family members who abuse substances, or face physical or mental health issues may need more care in helping them learn social skills (Zeng et al., 2019). But it may not just be the children who need extra attention; teachers, too may need more time, attention, and learning to increase sensitivity against biased reactions.

A large multistate study from the Yale University Child Study Center found that preschool children are more than three times more likely to be expelled from school than their K–12 counterparts (US Department of Health and Human Services, 2014). The study also found that 4-year-olds were twice as likely to be expelled from preschool than their 3-year-old classmates, and that boys were four-and-a-half times more likely to be expelled from preschool than girls. Overall, the study found that about 250 children are expelled from preschool each day in America. This study and others also found that Black preschoolers were twice as likely to be expelled as were their White or Latino peers, and they were five times more likely to be expelled than their Asian classmates (Miller et al., 2017; Novoa & Malik, 2018).

In preschool settings, challenging behavior can be disruptive for all. This is especially true when temper tantrums or aggressive behaviors make others feel unsafe or concerned for a child's safety. Challenging behaviors in preschool settings may have less to do with the setting itself than with the child's family environment or their primary caregiver's style or behaviors (Umami & Sari, 2020). For the child who is misbehaving, it can lead to more preschool expulsions and less academic success later in childhood and adolescence (Conte et al., 2018; Vitiello & Williford, 2020). When children are disruptive, they tend to be less engaged in the tasks or play activities going on around them (Bulotsky-Shearer et al., 2011). When aggression and lack of attention are

(Continued)

combined, children fall behind academically. This takes the focus off of positive learning for all children (Coolahan et al., 2000; Gross et al., 2019; Ingoldsby et al., 1999). Teacher intervention in the form of guiding children in learning and practicing self-regulation and other social skills can help young children succeed not only in preschool, but in life (Ho & Funk, 2018; Lippard et al., 2018). In the Yale study, factors that contributed to higher rates of challenging behavior included higher student-to-teacher ratios, teacher job stressors, and longer school days related to offering extended care (Gilliam, 2005).

What can early childhood teachers do to alleviate the problem of disruptive behavior? Five practical ways to create an environment that helps young children and lowers the bias against some children include the following:

- learning about students' and families' cultural values and practices by spending time and asking questions
- developing, clearly communicating, and setting behavior expectations in a consistent and equitable manner
- attempting to take the child's perspective whenever possible to gain greater insight
- teaching and modeling empathy
- using circle times, group activities, and curricula such as books to discuss conflict (Price & Steed, 2016; Umami & Sari, 2020)

To Think About:

- How might teachers and primary caregivers teach prosocial behaviors in a more culturally sensitive way?
- How might a teacher know if bias affects their evaluation of a young child's behavior?

9.6 Moral and Spiritual Development

"Did you eat the cookies I laid out on the counter?" The preschooler with facial cookie crumbs answers, "Not me!" Most primary caregivers of preschoolers are aware of their ability to state untruths even in the presence of strong evidence against their statements. Are young children who lie or tell distorted truths headed for a life of crime? Likely not, based on these behaviors. During the preschool years, young children develop both morally and spiritually.

Moral development is not the same as having good manners or adhering to social conventions when interacting with others, although these attributes may play a part. **Morality** is more complex, dealing with concepts of justice, welfare, and the rights of others (Smetana, 2013). Young children are beginning to navigate the complexities and diversity of living socially. Primary caregivers and educators play essential roles in helping them navigate the conceptual, affective, and relational foundations (Thompson, 2012).

Moral Development

Can young children make morally right or wrong decisions? Learning what is considered culturally right or wrong is a process that has intrigued researchers for years. Jean Piaget (1932) included moral development in his stages of cognitive development, and Lawrence Kohlberg (1981) further developed Piaget's foundational work. Early childhood is when moral reasoning goes through significant development (Brown et al., 2019). According to Kolberg's theory of moral development, younger children respond to rewards and punishments instead of making ethical decisions. They are in Kohlberg's first level of moral development called **preconventional morality**. For example, a child may share toys with a playmate to avoid punishment, not because the child is motivated by a sense of caring for the playmate. Over time, young children want to make a good impression on adults. Because of their increased cognitive skills, they are also capable of making up tall tales to avoid punishment. They are often concerned about what their parents think of them and whether they are labeled as good or bad.

Kohlberg theorized that children could tell the difference between right and wrong. Although their judgment is often based on potential rewards and punishments rather than universal moral truths or family values, they start to care more about doing what is right. For example, a 5-year-old may decide to do a task out of concern for helping a caregiver rather than because they fear punishment. Kohlberg's theory focuses on the cognitive aspects of justice and reasoning when a young child faces a moral decision. A young child may look at a moral decision as a choice between "right" or "wrong," "good" or "bad," or whether or not rules were followed.

In contrast to Kohlberg, more recent theorists focus on the affective or emotional aspects of moral decision-making, such as social relationships, rather than on justice and reasoning (Gibbs, 2014; Hoffman, 2000). Social relationships include considering the child's psychological needs, altruism towards others, and maintaining or enhancing human relationships (Ma, 2013). Critiques of Kolberg's theory often note the importance of taking a cultural-developmental approach because standards for moral decision-making vary by culture (Jensen, 2015). For example, in some cultures, maintaining and respecting individual needs is valued more highly than collectivism, or giving priority to the needs of the group. Young children develop a sense of moral identity, giving them their place in the world. The development of moral identity in early childhood assists in the child's ability to form positive relationships and benefits the community at large (Lapsley & Narváez, 2004).

Spiritual Development

Spirituality can be described as an authentic expression of humanity, addressing and pondering life's existential questions. These are the questions about life, death, and human existence that individuals ask throughout their lives, including during early childhood. Upon losing a family member, young children might ask, "Where did she go?" or "Where is he now?" Asking these questions is a part of being human, not necessarily related to religion. Engaging in spiritual questions with preschoolers addresses the child's whole development—physically, cognitively, and emotionally and socially within the socioemotional domain (Daly, 2004; King & Boyatzis, 2015). Around the world and throughout history, spirituality has played a significant role in human growth and maturation alongside physical, cognitive, social, and emotional development (Benson et al., 2005; Fowler, 1981; Russo-Netzer, 2018).

Spirituality is not the same as following religious beliefs and practices, although for many, this is an integral part of spiritual awareness (Giesenberg, 2000; Yust et al., 2006). Instead, spirituality can be broadly defined as the emotional, social, and cognitive connections between people and the natural world. It includes views on hope, forgiveness, life, and death that give meaning to human existence (Russo-Netzer, 2018). It also provides self-awareness, world awareness, meaningful social relationships and traditions (Eaude, 2003). Spirituality is a subject that many primary caregivers approach with trepidation, as it is often politically and culturally tied to religion (Best, 2000). This has been especially true in the United States and other Western countries over the past 75 years (Giesenberg, 2000). However, this has not necessarily been the same around the world.

In a study, the Pew Research Center posed a series of questions to 30,133 people in 27 countries, including "Does religion play a more or less important role than in the past?" along with similar questions about gender, the importance of family ties, and diversity (Poushter & Fetterolf, 2019). The study found that globally, most cultures favor gender equity but are less in favor of more diversity, and most do not oppose a stronger or more prominent role of religion in their society. The study also found that most surveyed believe that societal ties to family and religion have diminished. Of those respondents saying religion is becoming culturally more important than in prior years, increases ranged from 7% in Spain to 65% in Nigeria. Of those who responded that religion was becoming more important, a significant number also reported that religion was important to them personally.

Early childhood may offer a natural time to address spiritual development. Preschoolers have an extraordinary sense of awe and wonder about the world around them that may lead to more positive social and emotional outcomes (Eaude, 2005; Russo-Netzer, 2018). A cross-cultural study of spirituality in children found that a focus on spirituality, as defined by children themselves, was linked to higher reports of happiness. However, happiness was not correlated with religious practices or higher wealth (Holder et al., 2010). When spirituality is linked to religion, it can offer a social connection between others and help to form a young child's social identity (Benson et al., 2005).

Not addressing spiritual development may ignore a crucial part of healthy development, leaving children at a disadvantage later. Spiritual growth differs from other developmental processes in that it offers the element of an act of choice (Russo-Netzer, 2018; Shek, 2012). Spiritual development is not only nurtured through religious education but through all cultural modes of real-life socialization, including families, media, and schools (Ng, 2012; Ubani, 2013; Watson et al., 2014). Expressions of spirituality are diverse but essential to the whole child's development (Mata-McMahon et al., 2020; Ubani & Murtonen, 2018; Watson et al., 2014). Commonalities often exist despite differences in expressions (see Table 9.6).

☑ CHECKPOINT

☐ According to Kohlberg, preschool children are in what stage of moral development? Describe this stage.

☐ According to Kohlberg, when do young children typically know the difference between right and wrong?

☐ How might you define spirituality in young children? What might it include?

Apply Here!

Charlotte, a 4-year-old in your care, told you this morning that her great-grandfather died. She announces to the class that her grandfather is now in heaven. Another child says, "No, he went to sleep." Another pipes up to tell the class that his body would probably be burned up in a fire. You hear the conversation going towards where the great-grandfather's body really is now. When might you step in? Would you join the conversation, or would you let the children finish their conversation and ponder? Consider the following:

- Why do early childhood educators sometimes avoid the topic of spirituality? How are morality, spirituality, religion, and culture tied together?

- How might spirituality offer an important pathway in antibias education as it intersects with race, ethnicity, or immigrant status?

Spiritual Expression	Examples
Love	• Care • Nurturing • Compassion • Wisdom
Association	• Relationships with family, peers, teachers, or other caregivers • Connection to nature, earth • Being part of a larger community • Feeling connection to something greater
Positive feelings	• Wonder, joy, happiness • Mystery and wonder • Acknowledging invisibility • Pondering big questions
Moral development	• Valuing diversity • Resiliency • Core values

Adams et al., 2016; Mata-McMahon et al., 2018; Schein, 2017

Table 9.6 Children's Expressions of Spirituality

Summary

Children ages 2 to 6 undergo tremendous socio-emotional developmental changes. Young children are eager to connect socially and are often talkative, humorous, imaginative, and love to play. Their vocabulary proliferates as they communicate with family, caregivers, and peers. They see themselves as their own person, separate from others. As they work toward autonomy, they become less dependent and begin to exert their will. They take initiative and like to be helpers with tasks. They also have an increased awareness of their own and others' perceived self-image or social identity, self-esteem or perceived self-value, and the concept of the ideal self. Spiritual development emerges during early childhood when young children become more aware of the interconnectedness between people and their world.

Authoritative parents and caregivers are most effective in guiding and supporting their preschool children in decision-making by providing firm expectations. The socioemotional development skills learned in early childhood lay the foundation for later success in academic learning and social relationships. Of utmost importance is learning self-regulation skills, as it helps young children focus on physical needs, cognitive learning, and social relationships throughout life. This period of life is described as the preschool years, as these years directly affect the physical, cognitive, and socioemotional development as they enter the school years of middle childhood.

Learning Outcomes and Key Concepts

9.1 Analyze the theories related to socioemotional development in early childhood and how these theories are demonstrated in a young child's life.

- Awareness of oneself and the awareness of others includes self-image or social identity, self-esteem or perceived self-value, and the concept of the ideal self.
- Autonomy versus shame/doubt is Erikson's second socio-emotional stage when young children begin to see themselves as separate from their caregivers, typically from ages 1.5 to about 3 years.

- Initiative versus guilt is Erikson's third stage of socio-emotional development, when preschoolers begin to see themselves as their own person, separate from their parents and siblings.
- More recent researchers have focused on the strong correlations between cognitive and socioemotional development, particularly language abilities.

9.2 Describe the relationships between a young child's cognitive and socioemotional development and how the interplay between domains affects overall development.

- Young children, like all humans, are complex beings and as such, it is difficult, if not impossible, to separate social and emotional development from cognitive development.
- A young child's growing ability to express and regulate emotions appropriately leads to more satisfying social relationships and their success later in school.
- A young child's self-identity and their subsequent feelings about identity are shaped by their temperament as well as the social relationships around them.
- Gender identity in early childhood can be fluid and changing, but a default perspective in most cultures is based on sexual characteristics and social roles.
- Like gender, race is dictated by biology, but racial identity comes from both biology and interaction with the social environment.
- Although empathy may be a human trait, prosocial behavior is learned over time and includes helping, sharing, and comforting others.

9.3 Explain how a young child's relationship with their primary caregivers affects their socioemotional development.

- Because young children learn in the context of relationships, parents and caregivers are critical players in their emotional and social development.
- Transitioning from caring for children's needs to guiding their behavior requires an understanding of how young children see their world.
- Parents can help children learn to make decisions themselves and how to appropriately interact with others.

9.4 Identify ways in which a young child's relationship with siblings affects overall development.

- Sibling relationships are often one of the most influential social connections in early childhood; they may even be more influential on a child's social development than parental or later peer relationships.
- In the preschool years, frequent conflicts between siblings occur centering on sharing toys, food, playmates, or even their parents.
- Sibling conflicts can be mitigated by helping young children develop skills in perspective taking, emotional self-regulation, and problem-solving.

9.5 Identify ways in which a young child's peer relationships affect their socioemotional development.

- Peer relationships are social connections between like-age individuals; they begin early in life, showing preferences as early as infancy.
- Peer relationships can positively affect a young child's development as friendships help children learn how to interact socially.
- Although peer relationships are affected by many factors, both within the child and the larger environment, peer acceptance is most directly related to the young child's behavior toward others.

9.6 Describe moral development and spirituality during early childhood.

- Early childhood is a time when moral reasoning goes through important development.
- Morality is complex, dealing with concepts of justice, welfare, and the rights of others.
- According to Kohlberg, young children first respond to rewards and punishments before they can make moral decisions.
- Besides justice and reasoning, affective aspects should be considered in early childhood moral decision-making.
- Preschoolers' awe and wonder about the world around them may lead to more positive social and emotional outcomes.

Chapter Review

1. How do young children's cognitive, social, and emotional development interact in their identity formation? How does one area inform the other? Give a life example.

2. Name and describe Erikson's two stages of socioemotional development in early childhood. Provide two examples of how each stage might play out in a young child's everyday activities.

3. Describe three ways that cognitive development correlates with socioemotional development in young children. Give specific examples.

4. List and describe how a young child's family relationships influence the child's socioemotional development. What role should parents and caregivers play in enhancing positive relationships between siblings?

5. If two siblings, both in early childhood, are in conflict, what are the likely sources of conflict? How might a caregiver best diffuse sibling conflicts? Provide a specific example of a conflict and a proposed way of diffusing it.

6. List and describe the ways in which a young child's peer relationships can positively affect the child's socioemotional development.

7. If you were writing a newsletter for parents of preschoolers, how might you describe a young child's ability to make moral decisions? How might a parent help a child make moral decisions?

Matching

Match the following terms with the correct definitions.

A. self-esteem   **D. personal identity**

B. self-image   **E. ideal self**

C. sense of identity

1. Who a person believes themselves to be
2. The roles that a person plays, such as child, parent, brother or sister, grandchild, student, or friend
3. How a person conceptualizes their own personal value to others and to themselves
4. How a person wants to be seen in a social context, including the power they can exert
5. Self-identity shaped by individual temperament and subjective feelings about how they compare to others

Unit

4

Middle Childhood (Ages 6–11)

Chapter 10: Middle Childhood: Physical Development

Chapter 11: Middle Childhood: Cognitive Development

Chapter 12: Middle Childhood: Socioemotional Development

10

Middle Childhood: Physical Development

Learning Outcomes

After studying this chapter, you will be able to:

10.1 Describe the ways children in middle childhood grow and change physically.

10.2 Discuss how the gross- and fine-motor skills developed during middle childhood are continuous, sequential, and interrelated.

10.3 Explain the relationship between the brain's physical changes and cognitive development in middle childhood.

10.4 Discuss the importance of health and wellness in the middle childhood years and the effects of interaction between individuals and their environment.

Key Terms

body mass index (BMI)
cybersex trafficking
food desert
growing pains
healthy weight

obese
overweight
prepubescence
precocious puberty
proprioception

puberty
sex trafficking
sexual assault
sexuality education
unintended injuries

Introduction

It may be hard to imagine middle childhood without imagining school and the expansion of social relationships, learning, and play. Children ages 6 to 11 experience many firsts—starting school, spending more time with friends and away from the family, learning to ride a bike, and even beginning sports, theater, or music participation. So much happens during these years that relates to physical growth and development.

During middle childhood, children are growing and active. Physically, growth continues to be a measure of health. What games or activities do you remember playing during recess in elementary school? Do you know what children are commonly playing today? Games of chase, playground ball games, and playground equipment often draw school-age children. What does this tell you about gross- and fine-motor skill development in middle childhood? How do the growth trajectories change between early and middle childhood? How is physical growth and change preparing a child for adolescence? How might physical activity be another important indicator of physical, cognitive, and socioemotional development?

As children enter middle childhood, sometimes called the school years, they are just becoming independent beings who gradually progress toward the greater independence of adolescence and young adulthood. Fine- and gross-motor skills develop rapidly. Although their physical growth appears to slow down compared to the explosive growth that occurred during infancy and early childhood, children in this stage are experiencing a lot of internal growth, and the brain changes are dramatic.

This chapter discusses the developmental milestones that occur in middle childhood. As discussed in other chapters, this process does not happen in the same way, at the same time, for all children. Some children grow or develop certain skills or abilities faster or slower than other children. These differences are normal and expected.

10.1 Physical Characteristics and Growth

Compared to the fast pace of growth from birth through age 5, increases in height and weight are more gradual but steadily increase during the middle childhood stage. This slower and steadier growth prepares for rapid growth later in adolescence. Although differences exist, most children in the United States grow 2 to 3 in. and gain 4 to 5 lbs. per year throughout middle childhood. Six-year-old boys and girls are, on average, about 48 to 49 lbs. and about 42 in. tall. By age 11, both boys and girls are still similar sizes, weighing between 52 to 74 lbs. and measuring about 50 to 55 in. in height (Davies & Troy, 2020; Humphrey, 2003). These measurements can vary widely, especially in the later years of middle childhood, when **puberty**, the transition to sexual maturity, often begins. Heredity or genetics, nutrition, physical activity, environmental factors, health issues, parenting, and hormones all play a part in a child's height, weight, and growth patterns during middle childhood (Alderman et al., 2017; Balantekin et al., 2020; Ben-Joseph, 2020).

Table 10.1 shows the 25th, 50th, and 97th percentiles in stature (height) for both boys and girls in middle childhood. If a child's weight is at the 50th percentile in height, that means that out of 100 average children of the same age, 50 will be taller, and 50 will be shorter. If a child's weight is at the 75th percentile in height, only 25 children will be taller out of 100 average children of the same age, and 75 will be shorter. Similarly, if a child's weight is at the 97th percentile in height, which means that out of 100 average children of the same age, only three will be taller and 97 shorter (see Table 10.2).

Globally, height and weight averages vary by ethnicity and nationality. Massive data collected from over 2,000 population-based studies (in over 200 countries and territories comparing height and weight measurements in 65 million children and

teen participants) showed that growth in middle childhood is primarily affected by social, nutritional, and environmental factors in the home, at school, and in the larger community (NCD Risk Factor Collaboration, 2020). Genetics accounts for these variations in height and weight (Paciorek et al., 2013; Sawyer, 2020). For example, a child with a biological parent who is tall is genetically inclined to be tall, too. Genetics may play an increasing role in individual growth patterns as children move toward adolescence (Dubois et al., 2012; Jelenkovic et al., 2016). The age of onset of puberty during middle childhood also is a factor in weight and height gain (Limony et al., 2015).

Children's growth is sequential despite the individual variations, following similar patterns. Around ages 6 to 7, children's bodies begin to look longer and leaner than they appeared during early childhood. Boys and girls are of similar size during the first few years of middle childhood, although boys are slightly larger than girls as their legs and arms lengthen, and muscles grow (Davies & Troy, 2020). This growth can be painful, and as many as

Stature in Centimeters (Approximate Feet/Inches)						
Age in Years (Months)	**Boys**	**Girls**	**Boys**	**Girls**	**Boys**	**Girls**
6–11 years	25th percentile	25th percentile	50th percentile	50th percentile	97th percentile	97th percentile
6 (72)	112 (3'8")	111 (3'8")	115 (3'9")	115 (3'9")	125 (4'1")	125 (4'1")
7 (84)	118 (3'10")	118 (3'10")	122 (4')	121 (3'11")	132 (4'4")	132 (4'4")
8 (96)	124 (4'1")	123 (4')	128 (4'2")	127 (4'2")	139 (4'7")	139 (4'7")
9 (108)	129 (4'3")	128 (4'2")	133 (4'5")	133 (4'4")	145 (4'9")	145 (4'9")
10 (120)	134 (4'5")	133 (4'4")	138 (4'6")	138 (4'6")	151 (4'11")	151 (4'11")
11 (132)	139 (4'7")	139 (4'7")	143 (4'8")	144 (4'8")	157 (5'2")	158 (5'2")

US Centers for Disease Control and Prevention (2020a)

Table 10.1 Stature for Age Chart: US Boys and Girls
How might knowing the wide variation among children in middle childhood be helpful to educators or other caregivers?

Weight in Kilograms (Approximate Pounds)						
Age in Years (Months)	Boys	Girls	Boys	Girls	Boys	Girls
6–11 years	25th percentile	25th percentile	50th percentile	50th percentile	97th percentile	97th percentile
6 (72)	19 (41lbs.)	18 (40 lbs.)	20 (44 lbs.)	20 (44 lbs.)	28 (62 lbs.)	28 (62 lbs.)
7 (84)	21 (46 lbs.)	20 (44 lbs.)	23 (50 lbs.)	22 (48 lbs.)	32 (73 lbs.)	33 (73 lbs.)
8 (96)	23 (51 lbs.)	23 (50 lbs.)	25 (55 lbs.)	25 (55 lbs.)	37 (82 lbs.)	38 (84 lbs.)
9 (108)	25 (55 lbs.)	25 (55 lbs.)	28 (62 lbs.)	29 (63 lbs.)	43 (95 lbs.)	44 (97 lbs.)
10 (120)	28 (62 lbs.)	29 (63 lbs.)	32 (70 lbs.)	33 (73 lbs.)	49 (108 lbs.)	51 (112 lbs.)
11 (132)	31 (68 lbs.)	32 (70 lbs.)	36 (80 lbs.)	37 (82 lbs.)	56 (123 lbs.)	58 (128 lbs.)

US Centers for Disease Control and Prevention, 2020a

Table 10.2 Weight for Age Chart: US Boys and Girls
How might you explain the variation in height between boys and girls in middle childhood?

37% of children entering middle childhood experience **growing pains**. Despite its name, this pain felt in the legs and sometimes arms, predominantly at night, is not related to the growth of muscles or bones. Growing pains have no known cause, and the pain is usually short-lived, lasting just minutes or hours. There is no single diagnostic test or treatment for complaints of growing pains, although it is one of the most frequently reported health concerns (Evans, 2008). Massage may offer pain relief for some children (Evans, 2008; Evans & Scutter, 2004).

Most 8- and 9-year-olds continue to experience steady growth, with girls tending to have slightly more significant gains than boys. Proper nutrition is a crucial factor. Physical growth shows more individual variation during this stage than at younger ages (see Figure 10.1). By the end of middle childhood, significant variation in height can exist between the same age children—just look at any fifth-grade classroom photo. When the children are arranged in rows from shortest to tallest, the differences between the tallest and shortest children can be remarkable.

Alex Tihonovs/Shutterstock.com

Figure 10.1 Children vary individually in growth patterns.
How did genetic factors impact your physical growth during middle childhood?

As children near the end of middle childhood at ages 10 to 11, individual differences in size and physical maturity become even more apparent. Some children experience a characteristic growth spurt leading up to puberty, while others maintain the look and size of children.

Besides growth in height and weight, other physical changes occur during middle childhood. The toothless smile of a first or second grader is one of the happiest smiles you will find (see Figure 10.2). Over several years, each baby tooth falls out, and a larger permanent one replaces it. As the child's jaw grows to its adult size, it changes the facial contours, and additional permanent teeth, including molars, may erupt. In addition, children may experience a mid-stage growth spurt with an accompanying increase in muscle mass and body fat, with their overall appearance becoming less baby-like.

Prepubescence and Precocious Puberty

The primary reason for the variations in height and weight during middle childhood is the wide range of ages at which puberty begins. Although visible signs of puberty, such as breast development or facial hair, do not typically appear until ages 10 to 14 for girls and ages 12 to 16 in boys, internal hormonal changes begin occurring during middle childhood. The internal process of puberty typically starts at around age 8 for girls and ages 9 to 10 for boys, a period called **prepubescence**, during which the body begins preparing for the changes that will occur during puberty.

Most children in middle childhood will show early puberty signs, such as increased sweat production and noticeable body odor. Other early signs of puberty include the development of axillary (underarm) body hair, facial hair, and breast budding (girls). Boys' voices may also begin to change toward the end of middle childhood, which is related to male sex hormones. Again, variation exists among children, as some show distinct outward signs of puberty as early as ages 8 or 9 while others may not show signs until well into their teen years. During this time, growth can be very uneven. A child's hands or feet may grow to about adult size before the rest of their body catches up. Girls tend to develop ahead of boys, and some tower over their male classmates. Depending on the timing of these physical changes, this can be a time of uncertainty or growing self-confidence (Ben-Joseph, 2020; Davies & Troy, 2020; Lassi et al., 2017). See Chapter 13 for a more detailed discussion of puberty.

Although adolescence is often associated with the onset of puberty, the age when puberty begins has declined significantly over the past 150 years. It usually begins in middle childhood for both girls and boys, although this may be more difficult to visually determine in boys (Kim & Smith, 1999; Pierce & Hardy, 2012). Many factors influence this earlier age, including genetics, race, nutrition, body fat, and environmental stress. Although the age when puberty begins has been getting younger, some evolutionary biologists believe that later onset occurred in previous times due to poorer nutrition and increased infections. They propose that the early onset of puberty may be biologically appropriate, although this idea is still under debate (Gluckman & Hanson, 2006; Labe & Fuhrmann, 2020).

Even though puberty onset is happening earlier than in previous generations, there is still significant individual variation. This difference in timing between individuals ranges between 4 and 5 years (Pierce & Hardy, 2012). For many primary caregivers, the early onset of puberty raises social and emotional concerns about their children, but it may also present health concerns. Researchers are concerned that early puberty may be associated with an increase in chronic disease later in life (Pierce & Hardy, 2012). For example, potential increased risks for breast and ovarian cancers, obesity, and diabetes are associated with early puberty (Gong et al., 2013; Pierce et al., 2011).

The term **precocious puberty** describes puberty that occurs before 8 years in girls and 9 years in boys, outside the range of early puberty (Berberoglu, 2009). It includes the combination of accelerated

Figure 10.2 The grins of children in middle childhood change as baby teeth fall out and adult teeth replace them.

growth in stature and early development of secondary sexual characteristics. Precocious puberty has primarily been associated with increased risk for poor psychosocial, behavioral, and physical health during adolescence and later in early adulthood for girls and boys (Hoyt et al., 2020; Kota & Ejaz, 2021). For example, precocious puberty is associated with short stature or height in adulthood, as early growth is sometimes not supported by sufficient bone growth to match early and rapid growth in height (Mayo Clinic, 2021).

According to the Mayo Clinic (2021), the cause of precocious puberty is unknown. Sometimes, it is associated with hormone disorders, brain abnormalities or injuries, tumors, or infections in specific circumstances. Less commonly, problems with the ovaries, testicles, adrenal glands, or pituitary gland may cause precocious puberty. Precocious puberty is more common in girls than boys, especially in obese girls. It is also more common among Black children, children exposed to sex hormones used in medical treatments, or children who received radiation therapy of the central nervous system (Mayo Clinic, 2021).

While many of the risk factors for precocious puberty are unavoidable, prevention methods include helping children maintain a healthy body weight and avoiding any supplements that contain sex hormones such as estrogen or testosterone. Diagnosis is essential, and treatment for precocious puberty may include prescribed medication to delay further development (Cheuiche et al., 2021; Fuqua, 2013; Kaplowitz et al., 2016).

Changing Bodies: Sex Education in Middle Childhood

Individual states have authority over if, what, and how public schools teach sex education in the United States. In recent years, a handful of states have adopted **sexuality education** that begins in kindergarten and continues throughout high school. Sexuality education differs from the sex education that comes in later school years; it does not directly teach about sex or birth control. Instead, it focuses on using correct body terminology, exploring topics related to body respect and consent, and in some states, gender expression (Igras et al., 2014).

Middle childhood is often when elementary schools incorporate a sex education curriculum to present content on how bodies change throughout puberty. Typically, these programs segregate boys and girls and offer specialized course content that focuses on what to expect when their bodies begin to mature sexually, including changes in body secretions and sweat, development of acne, and pubic and underarm hair. The curriculum includes menarche, the beginning of a menstrual cycle, and breast development for girls. It covers genital growth and functioning for boys. Schools often offer this instruction just before adolescence, when a child is around 10 to 11 years old (Lindberg et al., 2006).

Sex education curricula at the middle and high school level typically expand to include a discussion of overall body composition changes and subsequent feelings and emotions of romantic relationships. Most programs incorporate information about birth control choices and/or abstinence, sexual abuse, pornography, online safety, HIV-AIDS, and other sexually transmitted infections (Lindberg et al., 2006).

Sex Ed for Social Change (2020), or SIECUS, offers national sex education standards for kindergarten through grade 12 students. These national standards include content about physical changes, including anatomy and physiology, puberty, adolescent sexual development, and sexual health. Social and emotional standards include healthy relationships, gender identity and expression, sexual orientation and identity, and interpersonal violence and prevention. Topics are introduced at developmentally appropriate levels. Individual states still have authority over implementing any educational standards, including sex education. According to the Guttmacher Institute (2020), 27 states mandate sex and HIV education in schools, 2 states require only sex education, and 10 states mandate only HIV education. There is political disagreement across state lines and even within states and communities. Family expectations and societal values factor into state requirements (Flores & Barroso, 2017).

According to a Planned Parenthood (2020) poll, most US parents surveyed support sex education in middle schools (93%) and high schools (96%). But what about in elementary school? In the same poll, over half of parents reported that they began talking to their children about the topics listed above before they were 10 years of age, and 80% reported doing so before their child turned 13.

Global Perspectives

The Rise of Childhood Sexual Assault and Sex Trafficking

Human trafficking has grown exponentially and exists in every country and across all races and ethnicities, genders, and socioeconomic levels. Children may be subjected to sexual violence. Children are dependents, and others in power, such as family members or other caregivers, may abuse them and control their physical bodies. According to the United Nations on Drugs and Crime (2021), one in five people who are human trafficked are children. In poorer nations, children are those who are most trafficked. Worldwide, humans are bought and sold, as their bodies are used as a commodity or currency. In these cases, children are not given agency over their physical bodies, and they are often forced into sexual exploitation or forced labor (see Figure 10.3).

Sex trafficking involves coercion, force, deception, and deceit to engage people in commercial sex (see Figure 10.4). They are trapped and controlled. Children can be coerced or deceived into relationships, or they are given or sold by others for use in sex trafficking. When primary caregivers are trafficked, their children become innocent bystanders; and they are sometimes groomed to follow the same path (US Department of Justice, 2017). Children are vulnerable to trafficking initiated by strangers, too, especially when their activities are unmonitored.

Sexual assault is defined as sexual activity without consent or not freely given. Nearly 20% of US women report having experienced attempted or completed rape in their lifetimes, and about 25% of US men have

Atjanan Charoensiri/Shutterstock.com

Figure 10.4 Human bodies should not be used as currency.
How does society suffer from this type of harmful exploitation of children?

experienced sexual violence. Although sexual violence can occur at all life stages, nearly 13% of females who experience sexual violence (an estimated 3.2 million) are age 10 or younger. Likewise, almost 25% of males who experience sexual violence report the first occurrences against them before the age of 10 (Smith et al., 2018; US Centers for Disease Control and Prevention, 2017).

In the United States, bus stops, shopping malls, and social media are common sources for luring children into harmful, abusive, and controlling situations and relationships. The effects of sexual violence against children are devastating and costly; and they impact millions of people in the United States alone. Caregivers, family members, or trusted individuals often commit sexual assault against children, making it particularly abhorrent. Children are often ashamed, scared, or embarrassed. They usually do not fully comprehend what is happening, and they are not developmentally prepared to give consent. They often do not have the knowledge or skills to report or contact authorities, especially when caregivers have normalized sexual assault against them. Sexual assault is not normal. It is a type of child abuse (David-Ferdon et al., 2016; Smith et al., 2018; US Centers for Disease Control., 2017).

The key to sex trafficking is taking away people's control. They feel trapped or controlled with threats, promises of protection, or economic opportunities to pay off debts, assurance of care, or shaming and isolation (US Department of Justice, 2017). Although

Tinnakorn jorruang/Shutterstock.com

Figure 10.3 Children involved in human trafficking can be subjected to forced labor in unsafe conditions.

child sex trafficking exists on every continent, children living in poverty are especially vulnerable. **Cybersex trafficking**, or exploitation through photos, webcams, videos, or other online platforms, is growing exponentially worldwide (International Justice Mission, 2020).

Experiencing sexual trauma is a type of adverse childhood experience (ACE). It can impact how a child thinks, acts, and feels. It can affect physical health because children are exposed to sexually transmitted infections and diseases. It will also affect mental health during childhood and throughout life (Palines et al., 2020). Many researchers and policymakers believe it is possible to prevent sexual assault and sex trafficking through coordination between local, federal, and international authorities (Walts, 20217). Most efforts focus first on raising awareness and increasing education to make it clear that perpetrators' actions are wrong, harmful, and punishable by law (National Center for Missing and Exploited Children, 2020; US Department of Justice, 2017).

Educators and other caregivers can play an essential role in protecting vulnerable children from human trafficking and sexual assault. First, they can be aware of potential risk factors and warning signs (see Table 10.3) (Development Services Group, 2016; Fedina et al., 2019). Second, they can help create a classroom culture of trust and safety. In doing so, socioemotional skills and social media safety are incorporated and reinforced in the curriculum. This includes focusing on healthy relationships, anti-bullying, and interpersonal violence prevention. Research continues on policies and best practices for reducing and eliminating all sexual assault and trafficking—particularly crimes against vulnerable children.

There are many ways that communities can implement practices that encourage healthy and non-abusive or non-exploitive relationships with children (David-Ferdon et al., 2016; US Centers for Disease Control., 2017; Smith et al., 2018). These include working to

- increase education in schools and community groups;
- foster safe home and school environments;
- improve monitoring in schools and other child services;
- designate safe places and people for reporting in schools;
- train teachers and other caregivers to be aware of signs of sexual assault and trafficking;
- increase health screenings during medical exams; and
- act to shut down businesses that profit from children being abused and exploited.

To Think About:

- Are you familiar with any child trafficking or sexual assault cases that have taken place within your community or city? Were there factors that made this child or these children particularly vulnerable to exploitation and abuse?
- How might awareness of sexual assault and trafficking be increased in your community? How would you follow up on concerns or hunches about a child's vulnerability?
- What resources and services are available in your community to people who have experienced sexual assault and trafficking?

Risk Factors	Warning Signs
Poverty	Controlling parents or caregivers
Family instability	Reporting excessive chores/responsibilities
Housing instability	Changes in friends
Family history of abuse	Social isolation or withdrawal
Family substance abuse	Absence of out-of-school peer interaction
Child welfare involvement	School absenteeism
Family or child gang involvement	Reported trauma or abuse
Trauma	Unauthorized immigrant status

Table 10.3 Childhood Trafficking: Potential Risk Factors and Warning Signs

☑ CHECKPOINT

☐ What are the years that encompass middle childhood?

☐ What bodily changes occur in middle childhood? How do they differ between girls and boys?

☐ When do individual variations in size and maturity become most apparent in middle childhood?

Apply Here!

Bodies change in many ways during middle childhood. Children grow taller and increase in weight, and experience the changes brought on by puberty. These changes can be perplexing and even confusing for children. Friends and family may comment on growth patterns. Peers and others may tease children about bodily changes. Children who mature early may experience increased or inappropriate expectations, exhibit delinquent behavior, or face learning challenges. Girls who show signs of early sexual maturation may more often have deviant peer relationships and may experience harsher parenting (Klopack et al., 2020; Labe & Fuhrmann, 2020). Helping children understand normal bodily changes is the objective of sex education in schools. How and what is taught, however, is controversial. Based on your knowledge of children, consider your personal and professional stance on the following:

- Which one (or both) should be taught in schools—sex education or sexuality education? Why?

- Should sex education or sexuality education begin in middle childhood? At the start or end of middle childhood? Why?

- Who should decide? How does this decision play into the best interests of the child?

10.2 Motor Skill Development

Throughout middle childhood, children quickly gain gross-motor skills. Children at this age have an abundance of energy they can devote to physical exercise and play rather than growth. They run, jump, climb, dodge people and objects, and build structures. They become involved in more sophisticated activities, including playing kickball or tetherball at school or in their free time. Children may participate in organized team sports like soccer, baseball, hockey, cheerleading, and football, or in individual sports such as gymnastics, ice-skating, dance, or martial arts. School-age children become stronger, and their hand-eye coordination improves (Faigenbaum et al., 2020; Haugen & Johansen, 2018).

As children reach the later years of middle childhood, they enter a stage of rapid fine-motor skill development as their ability to manipulate small objects increases. Their ability to hold a pen or pencil and write more legibly and fluidly improves. They become more adept at using video game controls, and they can handily manipulate arts and crafts materials to create art pieces and models. However, although hand-eye coordination develops further during this stage, it is still not at a teen or adult level. For example, a child at this stage can see an object, like a tennis ball, coming directly toward them; but they will still have difficulty determining its speed and direction when it is thrown near but not at them (Faigenbaum et al., 2020; Haugen & Johansen, 2018; Stricker, 2009).

As in early childhood, motor functions develop as older children are physically and cognitively more able to perform gross- and fine-motor physical tasks (Haywood & Getchell, 2020). For example, a 2-year-old's cognitive inability to understand how puzzle pieces work together combined with a lack of manual dexterity and hand-eye coordination makes solving a jigsaw puzzle difficult. By contrast, a 10-year-old can both conceptualize and problem-solve how the complex puzzle pieces work together. The 10-year-old also has the fine motor skills to fit the small puzzle pieces together. Table 10.4 includes examples of gross- and fine-motor skill milestones that occur throughout middle childhood.

While many children progressively develop gross- and fine-motor skills as they age, others do not. A failure to meet a milestone may indicate delayed development in other domains (Ghassabian et al., 2016). In middle childhood, motor skills increase as children become faster, more adept, and stronger. This improvement continues through adolescence into young adulthood, when motor skills increase in speed and agility (Draper & Stratton, 2019; Leverson et al., 2012). As in early childhood development, home environments, especially socioeconomic standing, influence a child's motor skills acquisition, especially if they lack ready access to toys and other manipulatives such as art supplies or

Age in Years	Gross-Motor Skill Milestones	Fine-Motor Skill Milestones
Ages 6–7 *EvgeniiAnd/iStock via Getty Images Plus* *Muralinath/iStock via Getty Images Plus*	• Jumps forward 10 to 12 times without falling • Hangs on a bar for at least five seconds • Walks heel-to-toe in a straight line • Walks up stairs while holding an object • Catches a small ball using hands only • Somersaults • Hops for a ten-foot distance • Balances on a beam • Quickly walks or runs lightly on toes • Skips using a skipping rope • Rides a two-wheeled bike or scooter • Throws or kicks a ball toward a target or goal	• Copies basic shapes like squares, circles, and triangles • Uses scissors to cut simple shapes • Draws recognizable pictures of common items like houses, people, animals • Colors within lines rather than scribbling across lines • Uses a glue stick to adhere objects • Uses three fingers to hold a pencil, using the thumb to direct motion • Gets dressed by themsleves • Independently opens packages • Brushes teeth with assistance • Performs simple household chores, such as setting a table, making a bed, or sweeping a floor • Forms most letters correctly, and later, words • Writes on a line • Prints their name clearly • Uses more controlled pencil movements • Forms most numbers • Uses one hand consistently to perform fine-motor tasks • Uses eating utensils correctly • Demonstrates good stamina for writing • Builds with small construction toys and other blocks independently • Ties shoelaces
Ages 7–9 *Image Source/Photodisc via Getty Images* *Motortion/iStock via Getty Images Plus*	• Displays more developed ball skills; can manipulate smaller-sized balls • Demonstrates more mature throwing and catching patterns • Participates in advanced game play, such as jump rope, four square, and hopscotch • Coordinates movements in team games • Runs up and down the stairs	• Maintains the legibility of handwriting for the entirety of a story • Constructs more complex structures with building toys • Manipulates small objects with increasing sophistication • Performs hand-eye coordination in-person and virtually using controllers or keyboards • Manipulates musical instruments more easily • Performs all self-grooming activities such as combing hair, brushing teeth, bathing • Uses cooking tools to prepare simple food recipes

(Continued)

Table 10.4 Gross- and Fine-Motor Skill Milestones in Middle Childhood

Age in Years	Gross-Motor Skill Milestones	Fine-Motor Skill Milestones
Ages 9–11 *FatCamera/iStock via Getty Images Plus* *miodrag igniatovic/ E+ via Getty Images*	• Performs rhythmic and graceful movements • Produces movements that are adultlike in general	• Performs all self-grooming activities, such as showering and washing hair or putting on deodorant • Uses cooking tools to prepare more complex food recipes

Table 10.4 Continued

sports and play equipment. Teachers and primary caregivers can play essential roles in helping children develop gross- and fine-motor skills (Maiano et al., 2019; Yang et al., 2021).

Gross-Motor Skills

Gross-motor skills develop rapidly during the middle childhood years, as muscular control with large objects becomes more effective. Arms and legs lengthen and muscles become stronger, making large muscle movements more operative. Endurance, physical stamina, and reaction time, the time between a stimulus and a response, improves (Haywood & Getchell, 2020).

Gross-motor skills are an essential part of middle childhood, as peer relationships become more significant than during earlier life stages. Playing physical games like tag or capture the flag, participating on sports teams or in school physical education classes, and using play equipment during recess time gives children opportunities to show off their gross-motor skills. Many children value athletic ability and associate it with competence and popularity.

When children lack gross-motor skill abilities, they may be socially rejected or teased by their peers (Davies & Troy, 2020; Tsuda et al., 2020). Many adults can remember a sense of anxiety and dread as they waited and were ultimately not chosen for a playground team because they lacked coordination or athleticism. Children who struggle

with gross-motor skill proficiency are often termed clumsy. These children may perform gross-motor skill tasks awkwardly or without skill or elegance. Research demonstrates that children who exhibit difficulty with gross-motor skills may have more fundamental developmental deficits in integrating their senses, visual processing, and perception or awareness of the position and movement of the body. Smoothly integrating these senses is termed **proprioception** (Hamilton, 2002; Yang et al., 2021).

Proprioception results from sensory receptors in the nervous system sending detailed messages to the brain about what the body is doing and where it is positioned. The brain processes these messages and coordinates vision and the nervous and vestibular (inner ear) systems to create a perception of where the body is, how it is moving, and how to maintain balance. For example, imagine a child climbing up a ladder to a playground slide. The child's nervous system tells their brain they are climbing and how their legs are bending with each step up. The child's sensory, nervous, and vestibular systems work together to inform the child when to adjust their body left or right to maintain balance. Once reaching the top, the child reorganizes to stand and maintain balance, sit, and position themselves to slide down. Using proprioception, the child smoothly anticipates and experiences a landing at the end of the slide.

The ability to stabilize the body through proprioception develops progressively and significantly during middle childhood (Pierret et al., 2020). Children who are challenged with proprioception may demonstrate uncoordinated movements and gross-motor skills, or they may have balance issues (Chu 2017; Kaviraja, 2021). Sometimes such children are wrongly treated as if they are exhibiting a behavior problem when they are simply struggling. Problems with proprioception are also associated with medical conditions such as cerebral palsy, autism, Down syndrome, and developmental disorders (Blanche et al., 2012; Fortin et al., 2021).

While activities led by primary caregivers contribute to the development of gross-motor skills during this stage, the role of educators in this process becomes particularly important because children spend much of their lives inside classrooms and on playgrounds. When school-age children are encouraged to develop motor skill competence by actively using their large muscles, they tend to choose vigorous play over sedentary play when given a choice during free and unstructured time (Tsuda et al., 2020). Active group games and activities that involve running, jumping, skipping, throwing, or dancing can facilitate gross-motor development and add interest to the learning environment (see Figure 10.5).

Fine-Motor Skills

Fine-motor skills involve performing skills with hands and fingers, such as grasping, holding, and manipulating (see Figure 10.6). Such skills often require hand-eye coordination or using visual input to guide a hand activity. Manual dexterity is the ability to coordinate fine-motor skills more quickly and efficiently. Much of the fine-motor skills development that begins in early childhood proves to be a valuable foundation for increasing fine-motor skills in middle childhood (Berk, 2013; Cameron et al., 2016).

Hand-eye coordination and manual dexterity skills grow, often exponentially, in middle childhood. Children improve their self-care skills, such

A

B

Figure 10. 6 In middle childhood, fine-motor skills advance.
What are some common activities that might help children learn a variety of fine-motor skill movements, especially using their hands in different ways?

Figure 10.5 Children use gross-motor skills while playing simple games such as tug-of-war. These activities build both muscle strength and motor skills.
What are some popular activities children you know are playing that improve gross-motor skills?

as effectively brushing their teeth, combing their hair, using eating utensils, and putting on their shoes with ease. They also become more skilled at manipulating art materials and picking up small objects like beads, sequins, and jewelry. They use their fine-motor skills to build and construct projects such as complex creations with Legos® or other building systems. Or they might follow recipes as they measure and pour ingredients into a bowl, mix by hand or with kitchen equipment, and shape the food item as directed. They become more proficient at playing games with small pieces, such as checkers or chess. They become more adept at using controls and keyboards on video or computer games.

Handwriting involves motor and perceptual skills that involve many brain systems, which makes it a complex cognitive activity (Arnold et al., 2017; James & Berninger, 2019). One of the most critical areas of fine-motor skill development, especially related to cognitive development and school success, is the ability to use a writing instrument such as a pencil or pen (Dinehart, 2015; Konnikova, 2014). Handwriting can include block lettering or cursive writing that connects letters in a flowing manner. Cursive writing is often used as an effective tool for learning. It has been associated with later academic success, likely due to its rhythmic and flowing nature that helps children coordinate their motor and perceptual skills (Askvik et al., 2020; MacKenzie, 2019; Semeraro et al., 2019).

Fine-motor skills are not independent of gross-motor skills. Children need to use their larger arm muscles to develop their hand and finger skills. A blending of gross- and fine-motor skill development occurs as both work in unison (Berk, 2013). The fine-motor skill development related to learning how to write also depends on cognitive, language, and literacy skills (Cadoret et al., 2018; Oberer et al., 2017).

As with delays in gross-motor skill development, poor fine-motor skills can lead to difficulties in academic achievement, which can then be associated with increased anxiety and poor self-esteem (Gaul & Issartel, 2016; Katagiri et al., 2021). For example, a child may be embarrassed by their inexpert abilities using an eating utensil or video game controller. Possible causes of delays or deficits in fine-motor skill development may include vision problems or conditions such as dyspraxia, Down syndrome, or

muscular dystrophy. Interventions such as physical or occupational therapy can increase fine-motor skill abilities (Maiano et al., 2019). School-age children with poor motor skills often need help dressing, feeding, or attending to other personal care activities, which may result in teasing from peers. Giving children the practical and repeated practice of using tweezers, tongs, and spoons may improve their fine-motor skills over time (Rule & Stewart, 2002).

☑ CHECKPOINT

- ☐ Describe some milestones in the development of gross- and fine-motor skills during middle childhood.
- ☐ How do gross-motor skills continue to develop during middle childhood?
- ☐ When gross-motor skills develop in an atypical or slower manner, why might this be a concern?
- ☐ How do fine-motor skills relate to life skills and school success?

Apply Here!

Imagine that you have a new student in your third-grade classroom. This child appears to have strong gross-motor skill development, as seen in the child's ease in learning choreography for a class musical, ability to complete fitness requirements, and an apparent athleticism in sports activities on the playground and in extracurricular sports activities. The child is interested in professional sports teams, including baseball, football, and basketball, and is involved in modern dance, demonstrating balance, strength, and hand-eye coordination. Although you have noticed these well-developed abilities, you have also noticed that the child seems to lag behind peers in fine-motor skill development. Holding a pen or pencil, using eating utensils, or manipulating art materials seem to challenge the child, and the skills the child has are more typical of a preschool child. Consider the following:

- Why is fine-motor skill development important?
- After eliminating any medical causes, how might you as a teacher or caregiver provide opportunities for the child to practice fine-motor skills?
- How might you help the child increase fine-motor hand-eye coordination? Consider interventions or activities that might appeal to this child's interests and gross-motor skill successes. Make a list of at least three to five captivating activities that could be incorporated into the child's daily activities.

10.3 Growth and Development of the Brain

After the spectacular growth of the brain during early childhood, sometimes middle childhood brain development is perceived as slow and steady, a quiet time before the remarkable changes that occur during adolescence. But middle childhood is far from a stagnant time in brain development. During this stage, the brain rapidly increases in volume. It approaches a peak of gray matter volume and white matter volume and integrity (Barkovich & Raybaud, 2019; Del Giudice, 2014; Giedd & Rapoport, 2010). Gray matter, mostly located on the outer parts of the brain, peaks in volume in middle childhood and then decreases throughout life. Gray matter is responsible for much of brain processing, allowing humans to perform normal daily functions. White matter contains bundles of axons, which are the long, lean projections of nerve cells covered in myelin, a white waxy substance (see Figure 10.7). White matter relays messages between the gray matter parts of the brain. It keeps developing well into adulthood (Berman, 2021; Dufford & Kim, 2017; Mercadante & Tadi, 2021).

As the brain increases in volume, children can engage in more difficult cognitive tasks. Much of the brain volume growth during middle childhood occurs in the frontal cortex of the cerebrum. In this area, executive functions such as planning, problem-solving, reasoning, social judgment, and moral decision-making occur. The prefrontal cortex also increases language acquisition (Hayiou-Thomas et al., 2012; Sowell et al., 2004; Stiles & Jernigan, 2010). Executive functioning ability results in children learning to plan their play activities and manage their responsibilities such as homework or chores. It is a work in progress, however.

Hormones affect brain development in middle childhood (Laube et al., 2020). Around ages 6 to 7, the adrenal glands begin secreting higher amounts of androgens, sex hormones in both girls and boys. This stage in middle childhood is termed *adrenarche*. Although the effects of these hormones are easiest to see in physical body changes toward the end of middle childhood, they also impact the brain throughout middle childhood. Most dramatically, these increases in androgens activate sexually differentiated brain pathways that did not exist in early childhood (Del Giudice, 2014; Hochberg, 2010).

Boys' brains are on average 10% to 15% larger and heavier than girls' brains. Whereas boys' brains contain on average 6 times the amount of gray matter, girls have nearly 10 times the amount of white matter compared to boys' brains (Bonomo, 2010). Both gray and white matter are related to intelligence. But structural differences in the brain, as seen in electronic imaging, show that boys' and girls' brains develop differently (Lenroot et al., 2007). Research indicates that the significant differences between girls and boys are the brain's structure and the sequence of development in the different brain regions (Sowell et al., 2004). The sex differences in physical brain development may also affect motor skills and special senses. For example, on average, boys develop spatial memory about 4 years earlier than girls. Girls, on average, develop fine-motor and language skills about 6 years earlier than boys (Hamilton et al., 1999).

Although brain development in middle childhood does not often get the same attention as the changes that occur during early childhood and adolescence, the physical changes are significant (Del Giudice, 2014; Laube et al., 2020). Educators and primary caregivers should use caution when making assumptions about differences in brain development and

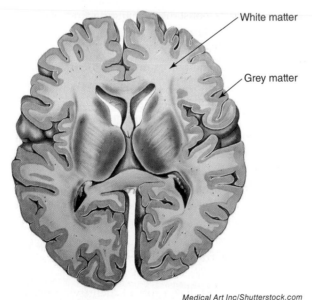

White matter

Grey matter

Medical Art Inc/Shutterstock.com

Figure 10.7 The Brain. Brain gray matter is mostly on the outer edges of the human brain while white matter forms the deep recesses.

their impact. The human brain is malleable (adaptable), and nurture plays an essential role from the moment a child enters the world. Environmental factors, such as social or educational deprivation, lack of quality nutrition, and stress, can alter anatomical brain development (Farah, 2017; Grayson & Fair, 2017; Hair et al., 2015). Childhood socioeconomic status (SES) also impacts brain development and mental health, especially brain functions associated with emotional processing, memory, and language (Dufford et al., 2020; Mackey et al., 2015; McDermott et al., 2019). Chapter 11 further explores these brain differences and their effect on learning.

☑ CHECKPOINT

- ☐ How does the brain continue to develop in middle childhood?
- ☐ How do sex differences affect brain development in middle childhood?
- ☐ How might sex differences affect motor skills and sensory perceptions in middle childhood?

Apply Here!

Design one physical obstacle course for a 6-year-old and one for an 11-year-old. It might include hopping, jumping, climbing, or even using equipment such as a trike, bike, scooter, skateboard, or other playground equipment such as balls and nets. The obstacles should be challenging but doable.

- How do the obstacle courses fundamentally differ between age groups?
- What do they have in common?
- How did you decide the appropriateness of activities or component parts of the courses?
- Given time and opportunity, build the obstacle course and test the appropriateness for motor skill levels at different stages/ages of middle childhood.

10.4 Health and Wellness

Health and wellness continue to be important in middle childhood as children spend their days in school and other activities outside the home. They are exposed to germs and illnesses that they might not have been previously. They need physical activity to maintain good health. They also need plenty of sleep and good nutrition to maintain activity, growth, physical and dental health, and cognitive functioning. Middle childhood is an essential time to teach health and wellness self-care as these are skills that can last a lifetime.

Keeping children safe and healthy is a complex endeavor. Healthy development across the lifespan has four major components. These include supportive public policy, caregiver and community resources, safe living and learning settings, and individual biological health. Public policies must support children and families. Caregiver and community resources must provide the time for quality child–caregiver interactions, commitment to shared oversight and protection of children, and the financial support for children and families to thrive. Primary caregivers must have the skills and knowledge to offer good care to their children that meets their health and wellness needs. Responsive, healthy, and supportive relationships and access to quality nutrition are essential for children to be safe and healthy. In addition, healthy home environments are critical. Healthy home environments provide safe environments with access to physical, cognitive, and socioemotional resources (Center on the Developing Child, Harvard University, 2021; Jones et al., 2017; Schmeer & Yoon, 2016).

These four components seem straightforward, but as the world is constantly changing and evolving, new issues arise that display the complexity of ensuring healthy development across the lifespan, especially for children. For example, dramatic changes related to the COVID-19 pandemic were disruptive for children. The pandemic caused school interruptions, modifications, or even prolonged closures and cancellations that affected learning and social relationships (Hoffman & Miller, 2020). The pandemic stretched caretaker and community resources. Family lifestyles and socioeconomic status changed when caretakers became sick and lost or changed jobs. These COVID-19-related disruptions also affected children's physical growth and development. This was especially true in cases where schools served as a child's primary source of nutrition and health care. Schools also play a role in identifying neglect or abuse (Abramson, 2020; Anderson & Caseman, 2020). Educators had less direct contact with their students, making it difficult to assess learning and comprehension or if their basic needs were being met. Most rose to the challenge, adapting to a constantly evolving situation and problem-solving ways to provide essential care and promote healthy development among their students.

Physical Activity and Play

Children need about 60 minutes of moderate to vigorous daily aerobic physical activity to grow strong bones and muscles (see Figure 10.8) (US Department of Agriculture, 2020). Only one in three children are physically active every day (The Child & Adolescent Health Measurement Initiative, 2016). Key factors contributing to low levels of physical activity may be that 44 of the 50 states in the United States do not require physical education in every school grade, kindergarten through grade 12. Also, many children do not have a park, playground, or fitness center near their homes (National Association for Sport and Physical Education/American Heart Association, 2012; SHAPE America, 2016; US Department of Health and Human Services, 2020b). This inactivity during school hours, combined with an excessive amount of screen time—sometimes over 7 hours per day—leads to sedentary lifestyles during a phase of life that should be filled with running, jumping, climbing, and overall movement.

As discussed in Chapter 7, children who live in poverty are most susceptible to not having opportunities for active play due to a lack of safe places. This

MBI/Shutterstock.com

Figure 10.8 Children need time and access to physical activity.
Does your community provide adequate resources and encouragement for children to engage in physical activity and play?

shortage, combined with disadvantages in health care and socioeconomic resources, has a lifelong detrimental impact (Barnett et al., 2018; Milteer & Ginsburg, 2012; Tremblay et al., 2011). However, with adequate resources, encouragement, and modeling from family, educators, and other caregivers, children in middle childhood can lead active lifestyles sustained throughout life.

Benefits of Physical Activity

There are several known benefits for children who engage in physical activity and active play. Physical activity positively affects bone mineral content, improving bone strength and density (Gunter et al., 2013; Proia et al., 2021). The positive impact occurs in the hips, spine, and whole-body bone mineral content for boys. In girls, it results in significant increases in the density of hip bone and whole-body bone mineral content (Janz et al., 2008). Engaging in regular physical activity during middle childhood may also positively affect later adult behavior, as adults who were active as children are more likely to be active adults. This correlation is stronger when activity is in leisure or play activities or transport such as biking or running (Cleland et al., 2012).

Scheduled versus Unscheduled Play

In the United States, some children may spend their free time away from school scheduled with numerous activities such as playing on soccer, baseball, or football teams; performing in cheerleading or dance; competing in swim meets; or perfecting martial arts moves. While these activities keep a child active, overscheduling can have adverse effects, such as anxiety, especially when the activities are adult-initiated rather than child-led (Melman et al., 2007). In other words, when children can choose their extracurricular activities, they demonstrate less stress than when they share that decision-making with their parents (Carbonaro & Maloney, 2019; Watchman & Spencer-Cavaliere, 2017). However, the reported number of hours of homework is the single most significant predictor of activity-related stress (Brown et al., 2011).

Just as in early childhood, children ages 6 to 11 need time for free and creative play because it is an integral part of their physical, cognitive, and socioemotional development. Free play gives children time to build forts, play on playground equipment, ride bikes, hike, and play make-believe games. Free play is important to developing physical, cognitive, and psychomotor skills, as imagination comes into play (see Figure 10.9). Free play activities are associated with experimentation, recovery from mistakes or miscalculations, and exploration. They may lower stress as children learn to test their physical and social boundaries (Al-Yateem & Rossiter, 2017; Lee et al., 2020a; Lee et al., 2020b). When structured activities such as participation in team sports combine with free play, they are much more effective in helping children achieve healthy bodies than the passive play of video or computer games (Ginsburg, 2007; Knell et al., 2019).

Even with the known benefits of activity, elementary school recess may become a relic of the past. For years, scheduled recess time during the regular school day has decreased in elementary schools. Schools are allotting more time to core subjects and standardized testing. Since the late 1980s, the National Association for Sport and Physical Education (NASPE) has periodically compiled the Shape of the Nation® report that surveys, reviews, and measures physical education policies in the American education system. In its 2016 report, only 16% of US state and local educational boards required recess in elementary school. Like free play time outside of school, the benefits of recess offer children

JackF/iStock via Getty Images Plus

Figure 10.9 When children engage in unstructured play, they often find new and creative ways to use play equipment, engage in new social interactions, and form new games or rules of play.

a break from their schoolwork and opportunities to play, explore, imagine, physically move, and socialize (American Academy of Pediatrics, 2013; US Centers for Disease Control and Prevention, 2019). Educators and primary caregivers can help support children to develop healthy fitness behaviors early in life. They may also provide significant interventions that will lower the risk of children becoming lower-fit youth (Babic et al., 2014; de Souza et al., 2014; True et al., 2021).

Practical Issues and Implications

Screen Time and Physical Health and Wellness

Most children today live in a world that offers many opportunities for accessing media via computer screen time. Many spend hours each day in front of screens (see Figure 10.10). For example, one study found that daily screen time for children and youth under age 18 continues to increase, with half of the children and youth surveyed surpassing two hours a day spent focused on smartphones, computers, video games, and other devices (Saunders, T. J., & Vallance, 2017). Children's recreational screen time increased significantly during the COVID-19 global pandemic. Recreational use doubled from pre-pandemic estimates for families facing economic stress or when

parents were essential workers. In addition, many children's schools were operating remotely, although these estimates did not include educational screen time (Eales et al., 2021; Korhonen, 2021; McArthur et al., 2021).

Smartphones, social media, video games, and even educational gamification strategies offer many benefits, exposing children to new ideas and information. They may gain increased social contact with peers and family members, which often results in social support or exposure to health and wellness information. Active video games, which require whole body motion to participate, may also positively impact children's fundamental motor skills and physical fitness (Liu et al., 2020; Sween et al., 2014).

Dejan Dundjerski/Shutterstock.com

Figure 10.10 Children often playing video games together.
What are some benefits of children playing together, either in person or remotely? What are some of the drawbacks? Can you identify any video games that integrate physical activity?

On the other hand, media usage and screen time also have negative consequences. They may expose children to unsafe situations, such as developmentally inappropriate online relationships with older teens or adults. They may limit rather than expand healthy social relationships and impede educational achievement. This is especially true when a child spends excessive time on social media rather than physically interacting with peers, reading books, or pursuing other academic interests (Jahic et al., 2021). Mental health concerns associated with an abundance of screen time include anxiety, depression, and behavioral issues like increased aggressive behavior (Carson et al., 2016; Dahlgren et al., 2021). As a result, many experts advocate creating policies that emphasize digital safety and etiquette beyond mere knowledge about and access to technology (American Academy of Pediatrics, 2016; Hurwitz & Schmitt, 2020; Van Deursen et al., 2014). Such policies would apply to school and home use.

How are media usage and screen time associated with physical development in middle childhood? One concern is that it makes children more sedentary. Screen time is associated with several health concerns, including obesity, reduced physical activity and physical fitness levels, and less and lower-quality sleep.

To Think About:

- What comes to mind when you hear the term *video games*? How often do you play video games?
- Do you think video games cause children to exhibit more or less aggressive behavior? Can video games be good for relieving stress?
- How might social media and screen time diminish or improve health and physical wellness for children? As a caregiver, how might you counteract these effects?

Nutritional Needs

In middle childhood, as throughout life, good nutrition is vital to physical growth and development, cognitive functioning, and general health and wellness. Recommendations for a well-balanced diet include a variety of fruits and vegetables, whole grains, low and non-fat dairy products, a variety of proteins, and healthy oils (see Figure 10.11). Each food group provides a range of nutrients and should be consumed in nutrition-dense forms. Food and beverages should maintain caloric balance to support normal growth and development without promoting excess weight gain (US Department of Agriculture, 2020a; US Department of Health and Human Services, 2015).

In the United States, children and teens consume on average 40% of their daily calories as empty calories through foods and beverages with added sugars and unhealthy fats (Reedy & Krebs-Smith, 2010). Growth in middle childhood is highly dependent on nutrition, especially the intake of micronutrients, including essential vitamins and minerals (Lassi et al., 2017). Children who experience delayed growth are more at risk for chronic illnesses during adolescence and adulthood. Unmet nutritional needs during early and middle childhood may stunt a child's growth and delay puberty (Solimon et al., 2014). Girls are particularly affected by their childhood **body mass index (BMI)** and percentage of body fat. When these numbers are

U.S. Department of Health and Human Services and U.S. Department of Agriculture, 2015; U.S. Department of Agriculture, 2020a

Figure 10.11 The USDA created this child-friendly graphic to promote the five food groups. How might educators use this graphic in a nutritional activity for children?

high, the onset of puberty is likely to be earlier (Lassi et al., 2017).

Inadequate nutrition may impact cognitive functioning. This is especially true in relation to learning, as academic performance improves when children meet their nutritional needs and decreases when they cannot meet them (Hoyland et al., 2009; Rampersaud et al., 2005; Taras, 2005). Likewise, inadequate hydration may impact cognitive functioning in children, particularly memory and attention (Edmonds & Jeffes, 2009).

Caloric requirements increase during middle childhood to accommodate larger bodies and more muscle mass, ranging from 1,200 to 2,200 calories per day. Boys typically need slightly more calories than girls to maintain energy and health. A child's required calories depend on age, weight, height, sex, and activity level. Tables 10.5 and 10.6 include recommended daily caloric intake for school-age children

from the US Department of Agriculture's Choose My Plate Dietary Guidelines (2020).

Environmental Influences on Healthy Eating

Primary caregivers and other family members significantly influence what children eat. This influence begins with the choices that primary caregivers typically make when purchasing or obtaining food and beverage items for the home (see Figure 10.12). Having healthy options is critical. What is served, when, and in what quantity also plays a part in whether a diet is healthy or not. Food choice is related to many factors, such as culture and ethnicity, socioeconomic status, and access to affordable healthy food choices. In some cultures, particularly in the United States, the mentality that "bigger is better" prevails with large portion sizes. Energy-dense foods have a large number of calories per serving, typically

Boys' Age in Years	Daily Calories Needed When Sedentary	Daily Calories Needed When Moderately Active	Daily Calories Needed When Highly Active
6	1,400	1,600	1,800
7	1,400	1,600	1,800
8	1,400	1,600	2,000
9	1,600	1,800	2,000
10	1,600	1,800	2,200
11	1,800	2,000	2,200

US Department of Agriculture, 2020a

Table 10.5 Daily Caloric Needs for Boys

Girls' Age in Years	Daily Calories Needed When Sedentary	Daily Calories Needed When Moderately Active	Daily Calories Needed When Highly Active
6	1200	1400	1600
7	1200	1400	1800
8	1400	1600	1800
9	1400	1600	2000
10	1400	1800	2000
11	1600	1800	2000

US Department of Agriculture, 2020a

Table 10.6 Daily Caloric Needs for Girls

MBI/Shutterstock.com

Figure 10.12 Providing choices and modeling can help children make healthy food choices.

packed with sugars and fats. Examples of such food choices include ice cream, donuts, potato chips, or other sugary or high-fat foods.

On the other hand, nutrient-dense foods provide a high nutrient value with low added sugar and fat. For example, two cups of broccoli, a nutrient-dense food, provides the same calories as a pat of butter but it is much more filling. Foods are not good or bad, but they should be evaluated based on their contribution to a healthy diet that provides sufficient nutrients for children to grow (Drewnowski et al., 2019; US Department of Agriculture, 2020). The availability of food choices can positively or negatively affect a child's eating behaviors, causing them to eat more or less nutritious food. Lack of healthy food choices also negatively affects children's health and weight status (Banfield et al., 2016; Movassagh et al., 2017).

Modeling from family members and peers can also positively impact eating choices. When children see adults eating fruits, vegetables, and dairy products, their intake of similar food choices also goes up (Balantekin et al., 2020; Larsen et al., 2018). Likewise, when children observe their peers eating vegetables, their consumption of vegetables goes up, too (Birch et al., 2007; Helsel et al., 2019). Although rewards and punishments for making healthy eating choices can impact children, the impact is often not positive.

For example, children whose food choices are highly controlled and who are punished when they fail to follow expectations often do not learn self-regulatory behaviors related to eating. The result may be disordered or unhealthy eating over time (Boswell et al., 2019; Haddad et al., 2018). Likewise, when children are rewarded for eating only healthy foods, they may eventually dislike those same foods (Balantekin et al., 2020; Birch et al., 2007). When primary caregivers are controlling and restrictive regarding their own food intake, such as deeming foods good or bad, this behavior may have negative impacts on their children's food intake and weight status (Rollins et al., 2014; Scaglioni et al., 2018). Although researchers know peers and siblings may negatively influence children's and adolescents' healthy eating behavior, they have more to discover through ongoing research (Anderson-Steeves et al., 2016; Watts et al., 2018).

Schools can play a major role in influencing healthy food consumption behaviors and providing quality nutrition. Children in this age group spend much of the day away from home in school settings. Schools may also be the primary source of regular meals for many children. For example, the US Department of Agriculture sponsors a federal school breakfast and lunch program that is free or price-reduced for school children who qualify based on their household income (US Department of Agriculture, 2020b). Another national resource, the BackPack food program, sends free healthy food home with school children inside backpacks, providing their families with the resources to make meals (https://www.feedingamerica.org/our-work/hunger-relief-programs/backpack-program).

Food availability is an essential part of keeping children healthy. Some children live in a **food desert**, or neighborhoods that do not have grocery stores or food markets that offer fresh produce or other healthy and affordable food choices for children in their home environment. Food deserts may include urban areas that lack grocery stores or suburban or rural areas that require transportation to reach markets. See Chapter 3 for more information on food deserts.

The Rise of Childhood Obesity

Approximately 34% of US children are **overweight** or **obese**, which means they have an abnormal or excessive accumulation of body fat (Ogden et al., 2014). According to the US Centers for Disease Control and Prevention (CDC, 2018), over 12 million children and adolescents are obese in the United States. These numbers have not always been this high. In the five decades between 1950 and 2010, childhood obesity quadrupled (Field, 2017; Hales et al., 2018; Skinner & Skelton, 2014).

In middle childhood, school-age children naturally gain weight through muscle and fat and increase stature as part of natural growth and development. Children grow at different rates, and the addition of muscle or body fat body composition varies by child. Because of this, determining when a child is overweight or obese is not as defined as it might be in adulthood. While the CDC publishes growth charts (2018, 2020a) to determine weight percentiles by gender and age, a child's body mass index (BMI) is the best indicator of weight status. The BMI is related to the child's age and body weight relative to height. According to the US Department of Health and Human Services (2020c), being at a **healthy weight**, overweight, or obese can be determined using the BMI Percentile Calculator for Children. However, calculating BMI can be tricky. Using the following general guidelines as a starting place can give initial insight into BMI percentages:

- Healthy weight: 5th to 84th percentile
- Overweight: 85th to 94th percentile
- Obese: 95th percentile or higher

Because puberty often begins in middle childhood, related changes in body composition should be considered. In puberty, girls tend to increase in weight and body fat, whereas boys tend to increase in weight and muscle mass. Because muscle weighs more than fat, boys can be falsely classified as overweight or obese more often than warranted (Field, 2017).

Race and ethnicity also affect childhood obesity rates. Asian girls have the lowest incidence of being overweight or obese, whereas Latino boys have the highest rates (Ogden et al., 2014). Socioeconomic class also impacts obesity prevalence in children, as nearly half of children living in poverty are classified as overweight or obese (Levi et al., 2010; Schmeer & Piperata 2017; Wang & Zhang, 2006). Often this is due to the unavailability of healthy food choices, poor income, and a lack of education. Food marketing campaigns that promote unhealthy food products, such as sugary drinks, more often to lower-resourced groups may also contribute to childhood obesity (Cassaday et al., 2015). Sometimes childhood obesity is associated with a lack of available community or neighborhood spaces for physical activity. Lower-level socioeconomic communities may offer fewer safe playgrounds, open spaces, community pools, beaches, and other ways of accessing outdoor activities (An et al., 2017; Kim et al., 2019; Sanders et al., 2015). For children with disabilities, the incidence rate for obesity is much higher, more than 38% more than for children without disabilities (US Department of Health and Human Services, 2020a).

Childhood obesity has become a public health crisis worldwide, especially in Western and industrialized countries (Wang & Lim, 2012). According to the World Health Organization (2020), obesity is considered one of the most significant public health issues of the twenty-first century (Wang & Lobstein, 2006).

The factors that impact a child being overweight or obese are complex and go beyond activity level, food intake, and food availability. Race, ethnicity, genetics, gender, socioeconomic class, health, and other factors may all play a role (Field, 2017). What makes it more complicated is understanding how these factors interplay. Continued research and understanding are needed to help children maintain healthy weights. Failure to do so will create tremendous health costs associated with increased chronic illnesses such as cardiovascular disease, type 2 diabetes mellitus, asthma, sleep apnea, and fatty liver disease (Barlow, 2007; Levi et al., 2010; US Centers for Disease Control and Prevention, 2021).

Sleep

Children need time to be creative, reflect, and decompress. They also need good sleep. On average, school-age children need between 9 and 12 hours of sleep over 24 hours (American Academy of Pediatrics, 2016). Because most school-age children spend many hours learning in school, adequate sleep is critical to physical and cognitive development. Establishing a healthy, regular sleep routine is important to ensure that the child gets enough sleep. Lack of sleep affects children just as it affects teens and adults. On a short-term basis, it can cause moodiness and irritability, overactivity, inattention, and an increased risk of injury. On a long-term basis, too little sleep is linked to children storing extra body weight and developing type 2 diabetes mellitus (Lee et al., 2019; Weisenberger, 2020). Recent studies have also linked a lack of sleep with mental issues such as anxiety and depression, either as a cause or as a result (Agathão et al., 2020).

In general, middle childhood is a time of good sleep. This is especially true when primary caregivers help children to maintain a daily routine that includes predictable times for school, play, meals, and relaxation. Bedtime routines that are calming and relaxing and increase the probability of uninterrupted sleep, such as reducing liquid intake before bedtime, remain important. Bed wetting, or nocturnal enuresis, may awaken children and disturb their sleep patterns.

Physical activity, especially if it is done outside in the fresh air, can improve sleep patterns. Organizing homework and extracurricular activities at predictable times ending before bedtime can also help with relaxation leading up to bedtime. In addition, eliminating all screen time for at least one hour before sleep can prepare the child's brain for good sleep (American Academy of Pediatrics, 2016). For children living in unstable homes, the opportunity for obtaining good sleep may not be possible due to changing relationship dynamics, hunger, lack of a regular sleeping space, or worry (Bagley et al., 2015; Doane et al., 2019).

Medical and Dental Care

Most children ages 6 to 11 are generally healthy because immunizations given during early childhood and before the start of the school years prevent many of the diseases that affected children in the past, like smallpox, measles, and mumps. In the United States, pneumonia, influenza, and ear infections are the most common ailments that require children to miss school (Biehl, 2002; Flais, 2019). Access to regular medical care continues to be important, and annual wellness checkups can set a child up for lifelong good health and wellness habits. Checkups include physical assessment and developmental assessments of mental health and cognitive concerns, as needed.

Health care providers also conduct hearing and vision tests and blood pressure and anemia screening. Approximately 20% of school-age children require medical care for chronic conditions. Allergies are the leading condition of school-age children, impacting approximately 21%, followed by asthma at approximately 9% (Parasuraman et al., 2020). Socioeconomic disadvantage is a predictor of delayed physical development and associated with poorer health for children (McCoy et al., 2016; Minh et al., 2017; Sun et al., 2017). For example, low socioeconomic status (SES) has strong associations with adverse health outcomes, including a higher incidence and severity of asthma in school-age children (see Figure 10.13) (Chen et al., 2017; Schreier & Chen, 2013).

Primary caregivers typically accompany children to their health care visits, providing additional information to their health care providers. Over time, however, children should be encouraged to

participate in discussions with medical professionals about their health which makes rapport important (Flais, 2019). In the United States, the National Education Association (NEA) encourages school districts and state oversite agencies to focus on the health of the whole child by setting up school wellness policies that promote physical and emotional health for students (Howley & Rosales, 2017). This includes employing registered professional school nurses as a resource.

Good dental care is critical during middle childhood, as caries (cavities or tooth decay) are among the most common diseases in middle childhood, affecting about 20% of children in this age group. The impact of tooth decay is significant. The subsequent pain that it causes can negatively affect a child's daily life, from school attendance to speaking and eating, possibly leading to malnutrition. Tooth decay affects low-income children in greater percentages than those from high-income families (US Centers for Disease Control, 2020).

Proper dental care helps prevent cavities. Drinking fluoridated tap water and brushing two or more times a day with fluoride toothpaste can lower a child's risk of developing caries. Oral hygiene is especially important as adult teeth erupt. Applying dental sealants to the back teeth has also been shown to prevent cavities by 80% (National Institute of Dental and Craniofacial Research, 2018).

The American Academy of Pediatrics (2019) recommends that children begin regularly visiting a dentist as toddlers. They should continue with yearly checkups and cleanings after that. In addition, children should avoid sugary foods and drinks. Besides good oral hygiene, other recommendations include keeping children away from secondhand smoke, which can cause dental caries, especially in primary teeth (Dhanuka & Vasthare, 2019).

Wearing braces, orthodontics, or oral appliances to straighten teeth is common in middle childhood. Upon a dentist's recommendation, children usually see an orthodontist by the age of 7, as most treatment begins between 9 and 14 (The American Association of Orthodontists, 2013). The most common reasons for using orthodontics during middle childhood are crooked or crowded teeth or teeth that protrude. Early treatment may also eliminate habits that are causing the problems (Dowshen, 2014 Prabhakar et al., 2014).

JPC-PROD/Shutterstock.com

Figure 10.13 This child with asthma is using an inhaler to open air passages. Approximately 8% of US children live with asthma (Pate et al., 2021). How common is asthma in your school or workplace?

Age-Related Hazards, Injuries, and Accidents

Children become more independent and developmentally able to engage in physical activities with less caregiver participation and oversite during middle childhood. As a result, they sometimes experience **unintended injuries**, or injuries that were not inflicted purposefully through such means as assault or abuse. Participation in team sports may create more opportunities for accidental injuries. Broken bones, head injuries including concussions, and injuries from burns or falls are most common. In the United States, the leading causes of injuries in middle childhood are related to transportation—riding a bicycle or other self-transport, being hit as a pedestrian, or riding as a passenger in a vehicle involved in an accident.

The five leading causes of death for children ages 6 to 11 are unintended injuries, followed by cancer, congenital disabilities, homicide, and heart disease. Boys have more injuries than girls, and most involve falls, cuts, or being pierced by an object (Biehl et al., 2002; Tupetz et al., 2020). In the United States, being a vehicle occupant is the most common source of serious injuries for school-age children, and it is the leading cause of death (US Centers for Disease Control, 2008; Tupetz et al., 2020). Around the world, millions of children are maimed or killed from unintended injuries each year (Alonge & Hyder, 2014). These injuries tend to fall into seven categories:

- road traffic: inflicted as a vehicle passenger, pedestrian, bicyclist, or from other moving transportation
- falls
- drownings
- fire burns
- poisoning
- exposure to firearms or sharp mechanical objects such as knives, swords, machinery
- adverse medical treatment

More than half of childhood fatalities from unintended injuries happen in lower-income countries such as those in Western sub-Saharan Africa and South Asia. Most of these come from road traffic injuries but burns and falls also significantly contribute. Boys are unintentionally injured more than girls, although girls are more often injured due to burns. The risk of burns is especially true in low-income countries, where girls are more likely to participate in cooking chores using fire or poor-quality stoves (Alonge & Hyder, 2014; Tupetz et al., 2020). However, even in high-income countries, 40% of child deaths occur because of unintended injuries (Harvey et al., 2009).

The United Nations Sustainable Development Goals emphasize middle childhood health and well-being. Although the goals do not include childhood injuries, two indirect sub-goals may decrease unintended injuries. These include increasing the proportion of populations with access to electricity, thus reducing the incidence of burns, and increasing coverage of essential health services (UNICEF, 2020). More responsiveness is still needed as increased urbanization creates more slums and unsafe living conditions for children (World Health Organization, 2016).

According to the World Health Organization (2016), some things can help decrease the frequency of unintentional childhood injuries and death in middle childhood (see Table 10.7).

☑ CHECKPOINT

- ☐ Why are physical activity and play critical to development in middle childhood? How much physical activity is recommended?
- ☐ Describe how nutritional needs in middle childhood compare with adulthood.
- ☐ Why is good sleep essential in middle childhood? What are some common reasons for sleep deprivation in children?
- ☐ How often should children receive preventive medical and dental care? What are the most common illnesses that impact school-age children?
- ☐ Why are unintentional injuries common in middle childhood? Name five ways to reduce unintended injuries in middle childhood.

Apply Here!

Write a health and wellness newsletter for parents of school-age children enrolled in an after-school care program. How will you describe children's physical activity, sleep, and nutrition needs? Include specific advice for encouraging health and wellness in a bulleted list form and include at least one infographic, illustration, or photograph to emphasize your points.

Making roadways safer for children	• Adding crosswalks, bike lanes, crossing signals • Enforcing bicycle helmet laws • Reducing traffic density when possible
Passenger transportation	• Reducing driving incidents through enforced driving under the influence of alcohol or other substances (DUI) or while intoxicated (DWI) laws • Expanding child safety seat laws to cover middle childhood • Enforcing child safety seat protection laws, including seat belts
Home environment protection	• Installing fire, smoke, and carbon monoxide alarms • Placing fencing around swimming pools • Legislating and enforcing child-protective containers and packaging • Ensuring safe storage of guns and other weapons
Community or neighborhood environment	• Maintaining playground equipment that meets safety standards • Increasing communication about new environmental dangers at parks and other public sites • Increasing education of risk management through media campaigns • Supporting policies and legislation

World Health Organization, 2016

Table 10.7 Ways to Lower Childhood Unintended Injuries

Summary

In middle childhood, a slow and steady increase in height and weight prepares children for rapid growth later in adolescence. Genetics, nutrition, physical activity, environmental factors, health issues, and hormones all play a part in height, weight, and growth patterns. These individual differences often become even more apparent toward the end of middle childhood as puberty nears. School-age children quickly gain motor skills as they are physically and cognitively more able, and their hand-eye coordination improves. Brain changes are dramatic, making it possible for children to engage in increasingly complex cognitive tasks. As children spend much of their day in school and other activities outside the home, health and wellness continue to be necessary. They are exposed to germs and illnesses that they might not have been exposed to previously and need physical activity and play opportunities, adequate sleep and nutrition, and regular physical and dental health care. As they become more independent, childhood is an essential time to teach health and wellness self-care skills that can last a lifetime. As you move through the next chapters, consider how physical development lays a foundation for learning and social relationships as children progress through the school years, forming relationships with peers and others outside the home.

Learning Outcomes and Key Concepts

10.1   Describe the ways children in middle childhood grow and change physically.

- Increases in height and weight slow down but remain steady.
- Slower and steadier growth serves as preparation for rapid growth later in adolescence.
- Children grow 2 to 3 in. and gain 4 to 5 lbs. per year.
- Heredity or genetics, nutrition, physical activity, environmental factors, health issues, and hormones all play a part in height, weight, and growth patterns.
- Individual variation in size and maturity becomes even more apparent as puberty comes closer.
- The onset of early puberty may be due to genetics, race, nutrition, body fat, and environmental stress.

10.2 Discuss how the gross- and fine-motor skills developed during middle childhood are continuous, sequential, and interrelated.

- Children quickly gain several motor skills as they are physically and cognitively more able.
- They become stronger, and their hand-eye coordination improves.
- Rapid fine-motor skill development occurs as the ability to manipulate small objects increases.
- Both gross- and fine-motor skills continue to be an indicator of milestones reached or delayed development in other domains.
- Poor motor skills can lead to difficulties in academic achievement, increased anxiety, and poor self-esteem.

10.3 Explain the relationship between the brain's physical changes and cognitive development in middle childhood.

- The brain undergoes rapid growth in volume as it approaches a peak of gray and white matter.
- Children can engage in more difficult cognitive tasks as the brain increases in volume.
- Much of the brain volume growth occurs in the frontal cortex area, where executive functions occur.
- Adrenal glands secrete higher amounts of androgens, which activate sexually differentiated brain pathways.
- Brain structure and the sequence of development differ between girls and boys.

10.4 Discuss the importance of health and wellness in the middle childhood years and the effects of interaction between individuals and their environment.

- About 60 minutes of physical activity is needed each day for children to grow strong bones and muscles.
- Physical growth and development, cognitive functioning, and general health and wellness require a well-balanced diet.
- Forty percent of daily calories are empty calories with little nutritional density, added sugars, and unhealthy fats.
- Approximately 34% of US children are considered overweight or obese.

- Pneumonia, influenza, and ear infections are the most common ailments that require school absences.
- The leading causes of death are unintended injuries or accidents.

Chapter Review

1. Name three physical attributes of middle childhood.
2. List five factors that might impact a child's height, weight, and growth patterns.
3. Make an argument against the commonly held belief that brain development is not as spectacular during middle childhood as compared to early childhood or adolescence.
4. How does the development of fine-motor skills impact success in school? Give specific examples.
5. Defend the need for physical activity, free play, or recess time for school-age children.
6. Why might childhood obesity be considered an equity issue?
7. What types and sources of injuries are common during middle childhood? What precautions might you communicate to a newly hired coach?

Matching

Match the following terms with the correct definitions.

A. adrenarche   D. healthy weight

B. androgens   E. overweight

C. body mass index

1. A male sex hormone, secreted by the adrenal glands
2. The awakening stage of the endocrine system and the beginning of puberty
3. BMI is in the 85th to 94th percentile for gender, age, and height
4. A calculation that includes a person's age and body weight relative to height
5. BMI is in the 5th to 84th percentile for gender, age, and height

Chapter

11

Middle Childhood:
Cognitive Development

Learning Outcomes

After studying this chapter, you will be able to:

11.1 Explain how the major cognitive theories progress from early childhood to middle childhood.

11.2 Demonstrate knowledge of current research findings on how development and growth affects cognition functions and learning in middle childhood.

11.3 Discuss how children learn language and identify the cognitive developmental language milestones often achieved during middle childhood.

11.4 Describe factors that impede learning, including learning challenges and disabilities.

Key Terms

attention-deficit/
  hyperactivity disorder
  (ADHD)
classification
cognitive flexibility
communities of practice
concentration
concrete operational stage
concrete thinking
conservation

expressive language
gifted
highly talented
inferential thinking
internalization
language modalities
literacy
neurodevelopmental
  disorders

operational thinking
phonics
pragmatics
processing speed
receptive language
rote learning
semantics
seriation
transitivity

Introduction

By the time children enter elementary school, their brains are almost at full adult size. Brain pathways become stronger. The brain's frontal lobe grows significantly, making it easier for children to complete increasingly complex cognitive tasks. Think back to your elementary school days. What were your favorite subjects? Who were your favorite teachers? How were you growing, learning, and relating to others? Think of children you have known since birth and who are now in middle childhood. What can they now understand that they could not before? Is learning a social process? If so, how? How do relationships with primary caregivers, siblings, and peers influence learning in school-age children?

Children at the beginning of this stage are generally eager to learn. They are excited about starting school, and they want to do well. Curiosity and a desire for independence drive them. They simply want to understand the world and learn new skills. Succeeding at learning increases their feelings of competence. They believe that they can accomplish what they try to do.

As children enter 3rd and 4th grades, they face new challenges in school as learning becomes more complex. Although most children are still eager learners, many educators note that some students begin to lose interest and enthusiasm. If they fall behind in their studies, catching up becomes more difficult because the pace of learning continues to increase. By the end of middle childhood, around age 11, many children enter middle school, where learning expectations become even more difficult and demanding.

As you read this chapter, think about what you might expect in learning patterns compared to earlier stages of childhood. How are school-age children developmentally ready to learn?

11.1 Middle Childhood Cognitive Theories

Developing theories about how children learn is a way to organize findings and to help give meaning to many observations and study results. As you learned in Chapter 2, Jean Piaget (1896–1980) was one of the earliest researchers to focus on cognitive developmental theory and how children change from early to middle childhood. Lev Vygotsky (1896–1934) focused on the social nature of cognitive development, continuing his work on how learning is a social endeavor. Theory of mind involves the ability to understand that another person's knowledge, emotions, intentions, beliefs, or motivations may not correlate with one's own.

Piaget's Concrete Operational Stage Development

Piaget viewed cognitive changes as a progressive reorganization of mental processes happening in stages and shaped by biology and experiences (McLeod, 2018). As you will recall from Chapter 2, in Piaget's theory, **conservation** refers to the fact that something can remain the same (its properties are conserved), even if the way it looks changes (transformation). Young children can only focus on how things appear or on only one aspect at a time. For example, a 5-year-old believes that a tall, narrow milk bottle contains more milk than a short, wide bottle, even after observing the teacher pour the same amount of milk into each bottle. The greater height of the milk in the taller bottle makes it appear as if it holds more milk. At about age 7, most children begin to consider multiple aspects of the bottle when solving the same problem. They may take both height and width into account. This is one of the signals of improved thinking skills that indicates a shift in Piaget's **concrete operational stage**.

Understanding a sequence of steps is the basis of the ability to plan. At the beginning of this stage, at around age 6 or 7, most children can follow simple two-step directions. This ability builds to the understanding of multistep instructions by the end of second grade. A first-grade teacher may instruct students to "put your pencil down and place your paper on my desk." At the end of second grade, a teacher might add "and line up at the door" to that instruction. Children also begin to base their own plans on simple sequences. For example, a child may decide in advance how long to play a game with a friend before taking a break for a snack.

In Piaget's concrete operational stage, **concrete thinking** refers to logical mental processing based on the physical characteristics that the senses perceive. Concrete thinking is limited to the logical perceptions of the concrete or real world. **Operational thinking** refers to problem-solving without having to encounter or experience the problem, either in the physical world or personally. In other words, problems can be solved in the mind. The problem may be hypothetical in operational thinking, not part of the child's real or concrete world. Unlike in early childhood, children now understand that the properties of objects can remain the same even if the way they look changes (Barrouillet, 2015). Compared to the preoperational stage of early childhood, the concrete operational period is marked by the predominance of logic rather than perception (Hopkins, 2011; McLeod, 2018; Miller, 2010).

Piaget's experiments showed that children between the ages of 6 and 11 also learn to think in more complex ways. They begin to use more analytical thinking. They can respond to open-ended questions that require more than a one-word or one-phrase answer, a "yes" or "no." For example, children can now answer "how can we solve this problem?" or "what would happen if…?" At the same time, they are able to manipulate abstract concepts into three-dimensional models, conduct science experiments, hypothesize and test, and understand and use time and spatial parameters (Cohan, 2018; Hopkins, 2011; McLeod, 2018).

Piaget noted the development of the following essential skills during this period (see Figures 11.1 and 11.2):

- **seriation**: the ability to place objects in order by a characteristic, such as smallest to largest
- **classification**: the ability to sort items by one or more common characteristics (Children at this stage can identify objects with two or more features, such as separating all the small green balls from a group of balls of mixed colors and sizes.)
- **conservation**: the ability to understand that a simple change in the shape of an object does not change its volume (Water poured into a container of a different shape is still the same amount; a flattened ball of clay retains the same amount of clay.)

Figure 11.1 In middle childhood, children begin to understand Piaget's idea of conservation. If all the colors of modeling clay pictured above are of the same volume, how might this photo depict conservation?

Figure 11.2 This child is arranging chairs in an order that makes sense to her. Which of Piaget's skills might this photo depict?

- **transitivity:** the ability to understand that relationships between two objects can extend to a third object. (For instance, if Ashley is taller than Jorge, and Jorge is taller than Tomi, then Ashley is taller than Tomi.) (Miller, 2010)

As discussed in Chapter 5, Piaget opened a world of wondering and learning about cognitive development in children. He was a groundbreaker in introducing cognitive development as a process involving distinct and identifiable stages. Many researchers and developmental psychologists have added to this knowledge over the past decades, and some have disagreed with his timing of the stages. They have discovered that children are capable of complex thinking much sooner than Piaget originally proposed (Barrouillet, 2015; Cohen, 2018; Marti & Rodriguez, 2012). However, Piaget's work continues to be significant because it is based upon biological maturation and stages, not on the learning itself. Thus, the focus is on the child's readiness to learn, not on what the child has learned. A child needs to be biologically mature enough before being expected to solve a problem using internal thinking. According to Piaget, this typically does not happen until middle childhood (Hopkins, 2011; Houde, 2019).

Vygotsky and Middle Childhood Learning

Vygotsky's sociocultural theory of cognitive development posed the importance of social interaction with others in facilitating learning. As you learned in Chapter 2, the theory focused on concepts of the zone of proximal development and learning scaffolding. In middle childhood, the world of other people expands to teachers, classmates, peers, coaches, and other mentors. Vygotsky's concept of the zone of proximal development (ZPD), or the level at which a child can learn with help, continues to be important in learning during the school-age years.

Vygotsky believed that children's understanding of concepts moves from realistic to more abstract during early childhood, and this process continues in middle childhood. He believed that the thought patterns of people nearby, conveyed through language, influence a child's ways of thinking. Vygotsky asserted that children acquire knowledge and learn how to think through culture. Language is a critical component of learning. Children first learn from the language of others; then, they gradually use their own inner language, or private speech, to guide and control their actions. He called this process of moving from social language to self-talk **internalization** (Morin, 2012; Vygotsky, 1978). For example, a child may learn about friendships from others, but they then begin to internalize and act on their own evolving definition of friendship.

As described in Chapter 8, Vygotsky saw children's imaginative play as a way to learn new skills. When children in imaginative play, they use their highest levels of symbolic or abstract thinking; examples include creating a stage play dramatization or pretending to be fictional characters such as superheroes (see Figure 11.3) (Colliver & Veraksa, 2021; Smolucha & Smolucha, 2021; Wertsch & Sohmer, 1995). Imaginative play becomes less common for children in later elementary school grades. However, there are still opportunities for children to learn within a social context through cooperative learning with others, utilizing the scientific method, and general problem-solving. When working with others on a task, each learner has different knowledge and skills, and together they can accomplish the task (Pritchard, 2008; Schunk, 2012).

Because formal schooling generally begins during the middle childhood years, it offers opportunities for children to meld social relationships and their environment with cognitive development. Primary caregivers and educators can interact with children to guide or facilitate their learning (Bates, 2019; Leonard, 2002).

Silvia Moraleja/Shutterstock.com

Figure 11.3 These children are obviously involved in imaginative play.
What were some of your favorite imaginative ways to play when you were a school-age child?

☑ CHECKPOINT

☐ Describe Piaget's concrete operational stage of cognitive development.

☐ Explain Vygotsky's sociocultural theory of cognitive development as applied to elementary school classroom settings.

☐ Describe an example of a caregiver using the zone of proximal development (ZPD) to help a school-age child learn a new life skill.

☐ Social learning takes on new meaning in middle childhood. How do Piaget and Vygotsky's cognitive theories explain changes in middle childhood compared to early childhood?

Global Perspectives

Global Primary Education: Lack of School Attendance and Chronic Absenteeism

Around the world, primary education for children ages 6 to 11 focuses on the basics of reading, writing, and math. Primary education inherently and often intentionally includes socioemotional learning as children as well. This is because the importance of interacting with peers, and it is essential for reducing extreme poverty and promoting positive social changes (UNICEF, 2020).

Globally, not all children have access to primary education due to financial, health, or safety issues. Sometimes the lack of financial resources to pay for transportation, school fees, or required uniforms prevents regular and consistent school attendance (United Nations, 2015; UNESCO, 2015, 2021). Sometimes lack of a safe environment may result in poor attendance or even prevent children from attending primary school. UNICEF's "The State of the World's Children" (2019) reports that one in five young children are malnourished, and two out of three are at risk of malnutrition. Hunger and lack of

financial resources often cause poor attendance in primary school.

Violence also takes place against children in many settings, and it may be a barrier to children attending primary school. According to UNICEF (2020), the top causes of global violence against children include armed violence, child labor, and child recruitment by armed forces or armed groups. The United Nations reports that children are becoming more affected by violence as conflicts and wars are lasting longer and claiming the lives of more children and young teens than in the past. Particularly vulnerable groups are children who lack parental care, live with disabilities, or live separately from family members in emergencies (UNESCO, 2021; United Nations, 2015).

Increasing access to primary education, especially for girls, was part of the United Nations Sustainable Goals of 1990–2015. In 2018, the United Nations reported that about 91% of children in developing countries were enrolled in primary school. Most of the children who were not enrolled were concentrated in developing countries. Children from wealthier countries are more likely to attend primary school (Programme for International Student Assessment, 2018). The impact of the global COVID-19 pandemic on long-term school attendance is not yet fully known (Khan & Ahmed, 2021).

A lack of primary school attendance is a concern even in wealthy nations. In the United States, where primary school is free, and transportation is often provided, 16% or more of US students are chronically absent (Kearney et al., 2019). When transportation is not provided or easily available, it may create a barrier to attendance for some children. This truancy means that children miss school fifteen or more days per year. The number increases as children age and enter middle school, especially students who are diverse learners, live in poverty, and have a physical or cognitive disability (US Department of Education, 2019). Most states define chronic absenteeism as missing 10% or more of school days (Che et al., 2015).

Chronic absenteeism is prevalent in US schools. Even among the youngest students in kindergarten and first grade, chronic absenteeism correlates with lower academic success in later grades. It also correlates with poor socioemotional outcomes whether the absences are excused or unexcused (Garcia & Weiss, 2018; Gottfried, 2019; Ready, 2010). Chronic truancy, even when supported or sanctioned by primary caregivers, can impede regularly paced instruction and learning (Allen et al., 2018).

Educators can play a significant role in encouraging children to stay in school. It begins by noticing absences and communicating that any child's absence results in a loss of community for everyone as well as the child. In primary school, educators can work with the child's family or guardians to facilitate school attendance. Communications can reveal impediments or reasons for school absences, such as parental stress or health issues (Claessens, et al., 2015). Educators may also discover a child's concerns related to school attendance, such as a fear of bullies or anxiety. It can also give educators the opportunity to solve identified issues with the child's primary caregivers, sometimes through connecting with needed resources (Garcia & Weiss, 2018).

To Think About:

- Why is primary education considered essential by the United Nations? How does it affect the labor force and society in general?
- What keeps children from regularly attending primary school in countries like the United States, where school attendance is mandatory and free?
- Can you identify barriers or issues directly affecting school attendance or chronic absenteeism for children in your primary schools, neighborhoods, and communities?
- How might educators respond to absenteeism in proactive and hospitable ways?

The Social Nature of Cognitive Development

Like Vygotsky, other later theorists, including Jerome Bruner (1973) and Urie Bronfenbrenner (1996), held beliefs that social relationships and the surrounding environment have a tremendous impact on cognitive development and learning (Gray & MacBlain, 2015; Margolis, 2020). Bruner (1915–2016) furthered Vygotsky's idea of social scaffolding by laying out specific ways for educators to provide temporary support to help children learn. These include modeling tasks for learners to observe, breaking tasks down into manageable steps, utilizing visual aids, and using prompting questions to encourage thinking and discovery (Bruner, 1973). Bronfenbrenner (1917–2005) asserted that overall development, specifically learning, is influenced by five socio-historical spheres: the micro-, meso-, exo-, macro-, and chronosystems (see Table 11.1) (Moen et al., 1995).

Jean Lave and Etienne Wenger (1998) stress the importance of active participation in the practices of social communities, or **communities of practice**. In these communities, children (and subsequently adolescents and adults) create a common identity as they share ideas and knowledge over time or with practice (Fisher et al., 2021; Lave, 1991; Lave & Wenger, 1998). In later work, Wenger (2018) includes four aspects of learning that integrate social participation into the process of learning and of knowing. Children and adults derive knowledge in a social context that provides meaning, practice, community, and identity (see Table 11.2). Educators often play an essential role in establishing communities of practice by creating an inviting and respectful classroom learning culture. Examples include morning circle

Sociohistorical Sphere	Description
Microsystem	This is the child's most immediate environment, including family and classroom. Primary caregivers, siblings, other close family members, educators, and classmates are part of this sphere. Children learn and cognitively grow because of these social relationships.
Mesosystem	This environment includes the linkages between the microsystems and macrosystems. For example, interactions between primary caregivers and educators, or collaboration in learning between home and school, are examples of links or connections.
Exosystem	This involves the parallel environments of the child's significant others, such as their primary caregivers, educators, siblings, and peers.
Macrosystem	The largest environment comprises cultural values and beliefs and social, political, and economic systems. It can also include religious beliefs in some cultures or events such as wars.
Chronosystem	This is the overriding influence of time on the spheres. Historical differences, developments, and shifts affect the environments and learning.

Kato

Table 11.1 Bronfenbrenner's Theory of Sociohistorical Spheres and Middle Childhood Learning

Social Aspect	Description
Meaning	This is how children and others communicate about life experiences, their meaningfulness, and how these experiences relate to the world.
Practice	This involves how children and others communicate about shared resources that give meaning, such as perspectives, frameworks, social resources, and history, to what is being learned.
Community	Children and others communicate about social configurations, worth, and competence to create community.
Identity	This is how children and others communicate about their own personal identity in relation to the larger community.

Wenger, 2018

Table 11.2 Aspects of Wenger's Social Learning Theory Applied to Children

times and show-and-tell or sharing times in younger grades; peer "shout outs" or acknowledgments of good effort in academic learning in older grades; greeting each student as they enter the classroom; and developing school or class mascots or slogans for everyone's use.

Communities of practice in elementary school environments promote theory of mind (ToM) (Lecce et al., 2014; Imuta et al., 2016; Smogorzewska et al., 2020). As described in Chapter 8, ToM involves understanding that another person's knowledge, emotions, intentions, beliefs, or motivations may not correlate with one's own. ToM continues to be strongly tied to cognitive and psychosocial development in middle childhood (Estes & Bartsch, 2017). ToM relates to social relationships, along with emotional regulation and executive functioning (Devine & Hughes, 2016; Devine et al., 2016). The development of ToM continues to facilitate a child's language aptitude because it relates to their increasing abilities to understand metaphors, or figures of speech, and the ability to infer meaning from messages. It is also related to a child's social competence and motivation to engage socially (Devine & Apperly, 2021). In other words, the more a child is capable of understanding another person's perspective, the more they are motivated to engage in social learning. Children who are assessed and rated with higher levels of ToM may have a lower interpretive bias or less of an inclination to incorrectly interpret ambiguous cues in social scenarios (Moldovan & Visu-Petra, 2021).

As described in Chapter 2, social cognitive theory offers a structure for understanding how people actively shape and are shaped by their environment, are motivated to learn, and able to self-regulate (Bandura, 2001; Schunk & Usher, 2019). Each interaction with another person, along with stimuli from the environment, plays a part in a child's cognitive growth and development (Lecce et al., 2017; Osterhaus & Koerber, 2021).

Children ages 6 to 11 gradually become more aware of their own feelings and others'. Developing this socioemotional learning (SEL) requires cognitive sophistication and intelligence. It also coincides with the ability to have insight, empathize, and communicate or articulate personal feelings. SEL includes (Gueldner et al., 2020):

- understanding the self
- understanding and getting along with others
- understanding social situations and relationships
- making altruistic, ethical, or moral decisions

Empirical evidence-based studies have shown that including SEL in a classroom environment positively affects cognitive development and learning (Madden-Dent & Oliver, 2021; Tomson et al., 2018). Chapter 12 further explores methods for teaching socioemotional skills and assessing socioemotional growth.

As the twentieth century turned and medical advances offered new insight into actual brain functioning, much research on middle childhood cognitive development focused on the brain and was made possible by sophisticated medical imaging. This new understanding continues to give insight and explanation of middle childhood cognitive development and learning (Wilmshurst, 2012).

☑CHECKPOINT

- ☐ What are three ways social relationships might affect cognitive growth and learning during middle childhood?
- ☐ Describe specific ways educators can provide social scaffolding to facilitate learning.

- ☐ How does theory of mind facilitate language ability during middle childhood?
- ☐ What are the four components of social emotional learning (SEL)? How does it relate to middle childhood cognitive development?

Apply Here!

Most kids begin kindergarten between the ages of 5 and 6 years of age. By then, a child's language is developed to the point where words can convey thoughts and events. Kids are talkative, humorous, imaginative, and great at exploration in middle childhood. They are learning in relationship with their teachers and peers. Consider one of the following activities:

- Using descriptive language, write about a distinct memory from your early formal school years, preferably one of your first school-age memories. Include parallels between your memory and what you have learned in the text. You may want to begin by describing your favorite elementary teacher and a favorite assignment or activity in which you participated. Who were your school friends? Do you remember specific knowledge learned from these friendships? Record your memories in written form.

- Using open-ended prompts, interview a young student in middle childhood about their favorite current classroom teachers, peers, or activities. If possible, help the child write or draw responses.

- How does descriptive language change? How might the emphasis or focus on experiences change over time? How do expanding language abilities enrich communication? How do language and social relationships affect learning?

11.2 Brain Development and Cognitive Functioning

Chapter 10 described the physical changes in the brain during middle childhood, such as the brain's rapid growth in the volume of both gray and white matter. Gray matter is responsible for much of brain processing, allowing humans to perform normal daily functions. White matter relays messages between the gray matter parts of the brain. As the brain grows in size, neural connections between its different parts flourish, while it prunes away any unused connections that proliferated during early childhood. This fine-tuning enables children at this stage to engage in more complex cognitive tasks (Barkovich & Raybaud, 2019; Del Giudice, 2014; Goswami, 2010).

The maturation of white matter, which takes up nearly half of the brain, makes up for many of the complex brain transformations that occur during this stage and into adolescence (Buyanova & Arsalidou, 2021). These are biological changes that affect learning. Some researchers find that biological or genetic factors, combined with experience, play a more significant role in middle childhood academic performance than in earlier life stages (Malanchini et al., 2020; Sowell et al., 2004). Language skills and other abstract representations increase, as do emotions (Hayiou-Thomas et al., 2014). As discussed in Chapter 10, motor skills are related to brain development, and differences are seen between boys and girls in brain volume and types of brain matter (Bonomo, 2010; Lenroot et al., 2007).

The physical changes in the brain during middle childhood are significant because they impact learning and cognition (Andre et al., 2020; Del Giudice, 2014; Houston et al., 2014). Links between the hypothalamus and amygdala help coordinate emotions. The brain becomes more efficient, and improvements are seen in cognitive flexibility, working memory, and **processing speed** (Buyanova & Arsalidou, 2021). White matter creates connectivity between parts of the brain, and communication between these parts becomes faster (Wendelken et al., 2017). Changes in the brain also affect the motivation to learn and the ability to concentrate; as a result, executive functioning increases (Andre et al., 2020; Ostroff, 2012).

In middle childhood, children are learning to concentrate and focus. Selective attention is the ability to choose and give preference to processing specific information while at the same time suppressing irrelevant or distracting information. For example, an 8-year-old can finish a math problem and temporarily ignore their rumbling stomach. Selective attention is associated with brain development during this stage, including improved working memory, increased coordination between parts of the brain, and the continuing maturation of the prefrontal cortex (Isbell et al., 2017; Reuter et al., 2019).

Cognitive Flexibility

Children at this age demonstrate improved **cognitive flexibility**, also called *plasticity*, which is the ability to switch back and forth between mental tasks. Cognitive flexibility develops over time, starting in early childhood but increasing significantly during middle childhood (Buttelmann & Karbach, 2017; Fandakova & Hartley, 2020). As children become more cognitively flexible, they can better shift their attention and focus between tasks and adapt to new situations. For example, if they are working on a class project and the time comes to shift focus to another subject, older children are often better at making these shifts than younger children. Likewise, they can also discard new information that does not apply to the task at hand (Monsell, 2003; Zatorre et al., 2012). For example, if children are highly engaged in an art project, they may ignore the opportunity to integrate newly offered tips or available tools if they are not part of their envisioned plan.

Cognitive flexibility is vital in school settings because children are often required to move from one task to another. When children struggle with cognitive flexibility, they sometimes struggle academically, especially in reading and math (Magalhaes et al., 2020; Titz & Karbach, 2014). For example, studies have shown that cognitive flexibility correlates with patterning performance, a component of both reading and math (Bock et al., 2018; Burgoyne et al., 2017).

Because cognitive flexibility is an important part of executive functioning, particularly in problem-solving tasks, providing opportunities for children to build their task-switching skills is essential in middle childhood. The good news is that school-age children can improve cognitive flexibility with intervention (Buttelmann & Karbach, 2017). Some ways that educators might encourage cognitive flexibility include:

- asking open-ended questions
- brainstorming different methods for solving problems
- switching up or altering daily routines
- offering a variety of perspectives on an issue or topic
- linking old knowledge with new learning
- encouraging risk-taking
- integrating songs and music in learning

- playing games, especially those that promote recognizing patterns or that encourage guessing or riddles

Working Memory

In Chapter 8, you learned how memory can be divided into several categories, including working memory and long-term memory. Working memory is a small amount of information that is useable in the present or retained for a short time (Bauer & Pathman, 2020). In early childhood, children may struggle with working memory as they often forget an event or instruction soon after it occurs. However, during middle childhood, their working memory improves dramatically and becomes stronger. For example, imagine that a child is reading a story out loud. When the child comes across an unknown word, the child receives instruction on its correct pronunciation and learns how to pronounce the given word. This memory is stored and utilized as the child continues reading the story. Eventually, the child may retain the word's pronunciation as the knowledge moves into long-term memory. Likewise, a child may remember a math computation and subsequently use it to solve a more complicated math problem. Over time, this allows children to retain larger amounts of data for a longer amount of time. Working memory aids in increasing executive skills during middle childhood, including problem-solving, especially in math (Cowan, 2014; Visu-Petraa et al., 2011).

Improvements in working memory capacity do not mean that children do not become distracted. They do. During the first half of middle childhood, distraction and lack of focus can be challenging, especially for 6- or 7-year-old children. Working memory improves as the brain's prefrontal region develops (Semrud-Clikeman, 2010). Rehearsing and practicing can help children retain memories longer. Ensuring that the child is focused and listening can also help build working memory (Diamond & Lee, 2011). For example, learning lines, playing a part, and performing in a classroom play about national historical events can help reinforce the retainment of historical dates and events, especially as rehearsals and interactions with other peer actors support learning.

Excessive stress from living in poverty can affect working memory in children, typically associated with brain inflammation (Kokosi et al., 2020, 2021). Inflammation refers to over-activation of the immune system leading to brain degradation, which may result in less effective executive functioning in middle childhood. These consequences are blamed on the toxic nature of stress that many children living in poverty experience (Blair & Raver, 2016). Imaging studies have detected a decrease in total gray matter in the brains of children under stress. More significantly, lagging maturation in the frontal and temporal lobes is associated explicitly with the effects of poverty stress on children (Hair et al., 2015). Stress is also associated with affective disorders such as depression and behavioral problems in children (Flouri et al., 2019, 2020).

Improving working memory can be beneficial for children with learning challenges because it helps them maintain and rearrange information, assess the value of new information, and decide whether to keep the information or discard it. Working memory also assists a learner in remembering information while completing a different task. Many children with **attention-deficit/hyperactivity disorder (ADHD)**, for example, struggle with reordering information and performing dual tasks (Fosco et al., 2020; Ramos et al., 2020). Children with developmental dyslexia, a hereditary visual disability that affects reading, may have deficits in verbal working memory. Children with developmental coordination disorder, a condition affecting physical coordination, may have deficits in visuospatial working memory (Biotteau et al., 2017; Maziero et al., 2020). Interventions, especially those focusing on visual perception exercises, such as memory games, have been found helpful in increasing working memory (Maziero et al., 2020; Narimani et al., 2020).

Long-term memory is memory data that can be accessed over a longer time frame, or even over a lifetime. It includes both declarative memory and non-declarative memory. As described in Chapter 8, declarative memories are with us from birth, such as a memory of familiar faces. Non-declarative memories relate to skills that have been so integrated into subconscious thought that, over time, we perform them without thinking, such as recognizing the letters of the alphabet (Bauer & Pathman, 2020; Wessel et al., 2019). Throughout middle childhood, long-term memory abilities grow and include the names of people, objects, vocabulary, multiplication tables, other math computations, facts, trivia, and learned skills (Allen et al., 2020; Bauer & Pathman, 2020;

Clearman et al., 2017). With these new abilities comes cognitive growth and development. Children can remember and use facts to write a report on a given topic, utilize complex strategies and rules to play board or video games, write and perform an original play or theater presentation, create a new recipe using culinary knowledge, or engage in a plethora of other activities that combine both working and long-term memories (see Figure 11.4). As what children learn merges and consolidates, knowledge is stored in long-term memory (Gazzaniga & Magnun, 2014).

Processing Speed

Processing speed is the ability to complete a task with relative speed and accuracy. Working memory affects processing speeds (Jacobson et al., 2011). During middle childhood, the ability to mentally manipulate information or data becomes faster as children mature (Buttelmann & Karbach, 2017). These improvements also happen as a result of the maturing brain. The middle childhood brain is in constant change, as *myelination*, the process of forming a myelin sheath around nerves, allows nerve impulses to move more quickly (see Figure 11.5). These sheaths are composed of protein and lipids that increase conduction speed and transmission between the left and right hemispheres of the brain (Knudsen, 2004).

Concentration

Concentration, or focus, is the ability to pay attention to something while ignoring other competing stimuli. Compared to early childhood, concentration

Oksana Shufrych/Shutterstock.com

Figure 11.4 Games like chess offer moments of intensive thinking and anticipation.
How does memory play a part in playing games like chess?

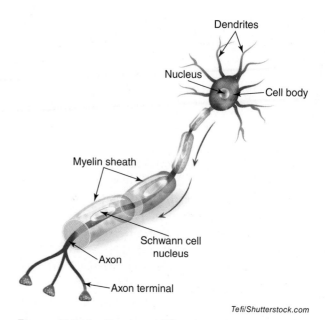
Tefil/Shutterstock.com

Figure 11.5 Myelination of Nerves

increases and improves as children mature throughout middle childhood. This improvement is easy to see when comparing a 6-year-old to an 11-year-old. As a child's brain develops, thoughts and actions become more regulated, even when there are competing stimuli (Hetherington et al., 2006). For example, a 6-year-old asked to clean up toys might become distracted from the task with each toy they see or handle. An 8-year-old is more likely to stay on task, especially with help; and an 11-year-old can get the job done with little assistance (Davies & Troy, 2020).

The ability to focus or concentrate attention may be related to parts of the brain creating complex networks that affect attention-related activities (Posner & Rothbart, 2007). These complex connections help the brain be alert to new stimuli, orient to the new stimuli, and manage appropriate actions or reactions. Should the new stimuli cause the brain to refocus? Should the brain ignore it and keep attention on the problem at hand? Various parts of the brain work together to manage these decisions (Corbetta & Shulman, 2002; Meltzer, 2011).

Executive Functions

At ages 6 or 7, learning is often by rote or automatic. **Rote learning** is a method of learning by memorizing information, which often uses repetition as a means. Examples include memorizing addition or subtraction tables or phonetic sounds of letters. Songs, rhymes, and math "hand tricks" may help children remember information. As children approach adolescence, they move away from rote learning and become better able to use **inferential thinking**—the ability to combine different ideas, discuss their merits or characteristics, and draw conclusions (Ostroff, 2012; Semrud-Clikeman, 2010). For example, if a 6-year-old is shown a photo of a setting and asked to infer the details and motivations of what is depicted, they would likely offer details about what they see in the photo. In contrast, a 10-year-old may infer motivation for depicted actions (see Figure 11.6).

Inferential thinking is the crucial ability to solve complex problems that require executive functioning such as planning, problem-solving, reasoning, social judgment, and moral decision-making. Although young children can engage in executive functioning, this ability grows and matures significantly during middle childhood. Evidence suggests that this advance is likely due to the maturation of the brain's frontal lobes and the neuron connections made over time (Davies & Troy, 2020; Doebel, 2020; Semrus-Clikeman, 2010).

Growing abilities in executive functioning allow children to tackle increasingly complex problems or tasks that require coordination between knowledge, people, and other resources (Davies & Troy, 2020). For example, they can follow increasingly more detailed instructions and listen and respond to the expertise of primary caregivers, educators, or coaches. Children slowly master the ability to solve complex tasks as their executive functioning skills mature and confidence grows (Davies & Troy, 2020; Doebel, 2020; Semrud-Clikeman, 2010). Working memory and the ability to focus play a part in expanding executive skills.

☑ CHECKPOINT

☐ Identify specific ways the brain continues to grow and mature during middle childhood.

☐ What differences have been seen in the physical brain development of boys and girls during middle childhood?

☐ What three brain changes affect how a child's brain functions during middle childhood?

☐ What brain changes influence the ability to solve more complex problems by using executive functioning during middle childhood?

Apply Here!

Choose a game that you might recommend for someone to play with children in middle childhood. It could be a board game, card game, or video game. Games that require cognitive reasoning, inference, or predictive skills may provide the most interesting observations. Make sure that participants can understand the game objective when you choose a game. Which game did you choose? Why?

If you have the opportunity, play the game with children who are just entering middle childhood, ages 6 to 7, and again with children who are at the end of middle childhood, ages 10 and 11. If possible, do not mix the groups; it will be difficult to separate modeling or intimidation between various age participants. Play several rounds of the game with the children. Report on the following:

- Name and describe the game chosen. List and describe the ages of the children who participate.
- How well do the children understand the game objective? Does this vary by age?
- Does this game require language or math skills? If so, describe.
- How strategic are the children in playing the game? Does this vary by age?
- Do the children utilize working memory, concentration or focus, or executive organizational skills? If so, how?
- For which age group is this game most appropriate? What did you base your assessment on?

tamara_kulikova/iStock via Getty Images Plus

Figure 11.6 As a child observes this photo, inferential thinking may lead to drawing conclusions about what is seen, how it came to be, or how things might change under different circumstances. A 6-year-old looking at this photo might describe a boy lying on a dock staring at the water. In contrast, a 10-year-old might speculate that the boy lost something in the water or is looking for fish.

Practical Issues and Implications

Gifted and Highly Talented Children

According to the National Association for Gifted Children (2020), **gifted** children are those with the capacity to perform at levels higher than their peers in one or more common academic domains, such as math, science, or language arts (reading or writing). Peers include those in the same age group, with the same experience level, and the same environmental constructs. **Highly talented** children demonstrate exceptional capacity in creative expression, such as in music, art and design; dramatic arts; or other creative endeavors (Kim et al., 2013; Pfeiffer, 2015). Although general intelligence is associated with genetics and brain development that is cultivated by environment (Simonton, 2005), giftedness is much more complex and likely associated most closely with genetics, as seen in particular brain differences that emerge over time (Rinaldi & Karmiloff-Smith, 2017; Schmitt et al., 2019).

Giftedness and exceptional talent are different from being academically bright or hardworking. The definitions of giftedness and talent used by educational systems vary significantly across countries and even within countries. Generally, giftedness equates to high academic ability, whereas exceptional talent can include artistic achievement and performance (Vidergor & Harris, 2015). Approximately 6% of US children enrolled in public schools are identified as gifted or talented (US Department of Education, 2016). Because many gifted and talented children are enrolled in private schools or are home-schooled, the exact number of children in this category is difficult to establish. Gifted and talented children come from all racial, ethnic, and socioeconomic populations (US Department of Education, 2016).

Giftedness or exceptional talent are not considered disabilities, but these children in the middle childhood years may receive an individualized education program (IEP), a written plan for providing a student with the most appropriate learning opportunity. Gifted or exceptional students need support and guidance as they sometimes feel different from their peers (Wood & Peterson, 2018). They can also have learning and processing disorders that create a "double exceptionality" (Kaufman, 2018). For example, a child diagnosed with autism spectrum disorder may also be gifted. As with all children, gifted and highly talented children need support and guidance in their cognitive, physical, and psychosocial development (Eckert & Robbins, 2016; Information Resources Management Association, 2016; Vidergor & Harris, 2015). (More details about IEPs are provided at the end of the chapter.)

To Think About:

- Should public schools be required to offer support services for gifted and highly talented children?
- Should all children be mainstreamed, or included in regular classrooms with their peers, or should special programming be provided for children to succeed?

11.3 Language Learning

Language is composed of symbols that communicate meaning. It includes comprehension or **receptive language** and production or **expressive language** (Klee & Stokes, 2011; Owens, 2020). Although children in early childhood make tremendous strides in verbal communication, school-age children also begin to use language to read and write. When children enter school at around age 6, they often know over 2,000 words. They will learn about 3,000 to 5,000 new words per year (Berman, 2007). By ages 10 or 11, vocabulary accelerates at great speed. By the 5th or 6th grade, children learn about 20 new words a day and know a total of about 40,000 words

(Berman, 2007). Although they can pronounce nearly all sounds in their native languages, children at this stage sometimes still have challenges with longer words, especially during the younger years of middle childhood. Wang (2014) summarizes the language changes demonstrated in middle childhood to include:

- *lexical diversity:* the use of different types of words such as nouns, verbs, adverbs, and adjectives that have similar meanings (For example, a child might use synonyms for *yell*, such as *shout, cry, scream*, or *holler.*)
- *lexical complexity:* the use of more multisyllabic words, such as *cooperation, difference*, or *instrument*

- *lexical density:* the use of linguistic complexity, which is calculated by dividing the number of content words by the total number of words

In middle childhood, children learn to understand that words can have more than one meaning and become more proficient at using verb tenses (Singleton & Shulman, 2020; Wang, 2014). They can understand syntax (sentence structure), grammar, and rules of speaking and writing. The sentences children speak and write start to become more complex in structure (see Table 11.3). For example, they begin **pragmatics**, using oral parts of speech more efficiently and correctly, such as nouns, verbs, adjectives, pronouns, adjectives, and conjunctions. They also begin to identify their use and function as they enter later elementary school grades. They understand **semantics**, the multiple meanings of words; they appreciate jokes and riddles; and they both tell and enjoy more complex jokes and stories (Davies & Troy, 2020).

Sometimes children lag in meeting language acquisition milestones. Language skill delays in middle childhood are a concern because they are often correlated with academic and social functioning problems (Conti-Ramsden et al., 2009; Whitehouse et al., 2009). When children enter school with lower language skills, this deficit often predicts later reading skill challenges, reading comprehension difficulties, and even math learning disabilities (Cain, 2006; Catts et al., 2006). Lagging language skills in middle childhood are not always associated with being a later-than-expected talker in early childhood. Instead, delays in language skills may be more complex and environmentally shaped as the child enters the school years (Poll & Miller, 2013; Singleton & Shulman, 2020).

Language modalities are the means of, or processes for, expressing language. Writing, reading, and verbal speech are all types of communication or language modalities. Speaking and writing are both forms of language; but writing often becomes more complex than spoken language as writing skills increase. At the same time, reading informs speaking, and speaking informs writing. Typically, by age 9 or 10, a child's spoken language does not resemble their written language. Written language tends to be much more complex, requiring the coordination of multiple abilities, including recognizing symbols, speaking, writing, reading, expressing, conjecturing, discerning, understanding, and evaluating (Singleton & Shulman, 2020; Wang, 2014). The relationship between spoken and written language

Language Concept	Development During Middle Childhood
Morphology: **word structures and formations such as plural or singular form**	Children hone language skills as they use word structures, singularities, or pluralities correctly (Davies & Troy, 2020).
Pragmatics: **using language properly**	Increased usage of correct language, including lexical density and proper sentence structure, is progressively demonstrated as children gain language skills throughout middle childhood (Wang, 2014).
Syntax: **the proper order of words in a phrase or sentence**	Children learn to lengthen their sentences by adding conjunctions, prepositions, and clauses. But learning syntax requires a level of cognitive sophistication not usually reached until ages 6 or 7 when they acquire the ability to reverse their thoughts. This helps them to understand transformations in syntax (Elkind & Weiner, 1978; Ladefoged, 2001; Lenneberg, 1967).
Semantics: **the meaning of words**	By the age of 10, children can use skills to break down unfamiliar words and phrases to deduce their meanings. They do this by analyzing the smaller parts (morphemes) and relating them back together (Ravid, 2004).
Vocabulary: **known meaning of words**	From age 7 forward, vocabulary increases greatly as it becomes vivid, descriptive, and more differentiated (Berman, 2007).

Kato

Table 11.3 Language Development Milestones in Middle Childhood

is reciprocal in that learning done in one affects the other. For example, the more a child writes, the more spoken vocabulary expands. Likewise, the more vocabulary expands, the more fluent the child becomes in expressing ideas in written form. To not further compound delays, early intervention may be necessary for some children with speech and language disorders or delays. (see Table 11.4).

Reading and Writing

As children learn to read, they decode the symbols of written language and their phonology. *Phonology* is the science of the fundamental sounds and combinations of sounds in a language. **Phonics** is a teaching method using phonology (see Figure 11.7). Phonological coding of sounds and combinations of sounds is crucial to word recognition (Melby-Lervag et al., 2012; Snowling & Hulme, 2005). For this reason, during early childhood, many educators and primary caregivers focus on phonology or language sound decoding as they teach children to read.

Learning how to write goes hand-in-hand with learning to read. As children learn to read words, they also learn to write. Writing requires some skills that are different from reading skills, however. For example, as discussed in Chapter 10, children need fine-motor skills to hold a marker, crayon, or pencil and to form letters. Children in early school grades may write some letters backward or incorrectly, such as confusing the letters d and b. Typically, most children have mastered writing the alphabet letters correctly

Nilobon Sweeney/Shutterstock.com

Figure 11.7 Phonics help new readers learn sounds and sound combinations to decode or recognize words.
Did you learn phonics when you were learning to read?

when they reach the end of 2nd grade. Throughout middle childhood, children become increasingly proficient at putting thoughts together into words and sentences (see Figure 11.8). They begin to understand language structure, such as nouns and verbs; and they often learn capitalization, punctuation, and sentence structure as well (Bowyer-Crane et al., 2008; Byrne & Fielding-Barnsley, 1989; Muter et al., 2004).

As children expand their abilities to use oral language learning in both listening and speaking, they become more literate as they explore and make sense of written forms (see Figure 11.9). Reading and writing

Type of Disorder or Delay	Description	Examples
Speech disorders	Challenges forming sounds or words correctly and/or difficulties in smoothly making words or sentences such as in stammering or stuttering	Stuttering, apraxia, lisping
Language disorders	Difficulties understanding the meaning of spoken language (receptive language) or communicating their own thoughts (expressive language)	Aphasia, auditory processing disorder
Language delays	Difficulties or delays in oral speech when compared to average milestones	Missed milestones, such as not babbling by 15 months, not talking by age 2, poor articulation

Kato

Table 11.4 Speech and Language Disorders and Delays

Rido/Shutterstock.com

Figure 11.8 In middle childhood, writing proficiency increases.
What are some writing activities that may help children put their thoughts together into words and sentences?

wavebreakmedia/Shutterstock.com

Figure 11.9 Listening to stories increases receptive language and vocabulary.
Do you remember favorite stories that your teachers read aloud? What appealed to you more—the book content or the storyteller's skill?

skills within a cultural and language construct are termed **literacy**. Learning literacy skills begins much earlier than middle childhood, as even very young children are in the process of becoming literate when they learn to decode symbols and their meanings (Whitehead, 2010). Reading involves books and signage, all other print mediums, and digital media such as toys, games, and tablets (Hall, 2013).

Although some children learn to read before entering school, most begin the process during kindergarten through third grade. First and second graders may make great strides in their reading abilities. By the time they reach the end of 2nd grade, many children are competent readers enjoying chapter books. Some children may be just beginning to read chapter books, while others are struggling and still reading picture books. Although some children may require extra assistance, most can read by the time they reach about age 9, or third grade (Hulme & Snowling, 2015).

The time between kindergarten and third grade appears to be a critical period for learning to read (Wang, 2014). When researchers looked at potential contributing factors influencing reading literacy to predict reading difficulties, they noted that brain imaging scans found fewer white matter clusters in the brains of children who struggled with learning to read than those who did not struggle (Dahhan et al., 2016). The amount of white matter that a child begins with in kindergarten does not appear

to make a difference. Instead, it is what happens to brain white matter between kindergarten and 3rd grade that affects learning to read. Researchers have also looked at other potential factors related to reading proficiency or lack thereof, including genetics, environmental factors, early childhood language ability, and overall cognitive capacity (Myers et al., 2014; Pennington & Olson, 2005; Plomin & Kovas, 2005). Thus, children who struggle to learn to read may have extenuating factors that need attention. For some children, causal risk factors, such as dyslexia, may also contribute to severe reading problems (Hulme & Snowling, 2015; Miller et al., 2018).

Some children in elementary school are independent readers. They may read chapter books and enjoy complex stories (see Figure 11.10) (Hall, 2013; Ng & Bartlett, 2017; Snowling & Hulme, 2005). Book series are often popular with this age group. Many may enjoy reading stories about children their age or slightly older who play a part in adventures or fantasies. They also often enjoy reading stories about animals. For many children, reading can be a creative experience that stimulates dreams about becoming a crime solver, a scientist, or a mountain climber. Reading can take them into another world, another time, or another culture.

By ages 10 to 11, children are often proficient readers. They may spend hours of free time pleasure reading. Reading competence is essential in 5th and 6th grade as it forms the foundation for

wavebreakmedia/Shutterstock.com

Figure 11.10 Children may enjoy reading chapter books and more complex stories in older elementary grades.
Do you remember book series from your elementary school days? Which genres were most popular?

upper grades (Hall, 2013; Snowling & Hulme, 2005). Reading has a positive effect in all academic areas. Instructions are better understood when reading ability and comprehension are high. Vocabulary increases when children read. However, some children struggle with reading throughout middle childhood, and their challenges may result from a specific condition or disorder, as you will learn in the next section.

Some children face not just the challenge of learning to speak, read, and write in one language, but through either necessity or enrichment choice, may learn two or more languages. Due to brain plasticity, a child's ability to learn a second language is at its peak from about age 10 until 18 (Oliver & Azkarai, 2017; Smith, 2018). Children who are dual language learners may simultaneously activate two or more languages, switching back and forth between them. The experience of switching between languages may have positive cognitive benefits as the brain responds by building networks to accommodate the challenge (Mohades et al., 2015).

In the United States, students with limited English proficiency (LEP) may have difficulty communicating effectively in English because it is not their native or primary language. A term often synonymous with LEP is English language learners (ELL). The National Education Association (2020) predicted that by 2025, 25% of US children in classrooms will

be an ELL. These students must learn English while also mastering the content of their regular classes. This process involves developing reading and writing skills and verbal communication. In addition to general vocabulary, every subject area has its specialized terms. Understanding also depends on learning about popular culture, such as holidays and traditions, television and movies, music, magazines, and fashion. Learning English is not an easy process, and anxiety may negatively affect learning (Teimouri et al., 2019). Teachers monitor students on their progress to help determine what additional support they may need (Alanis et al., 2021; Reyes et al., 2010).

☑ CHECKPOINT

☐ What are two components of language learning?

☐ What are three examples of a language modality?

☐ What are the component parts of child literacy?

☐ What cognitive developmental language milestones do children often achieve by age 9? Age 11?

☐ What challenges do students with LEP experience in the classroom?

Apply Here!

Create a list of recommended books by elementary school grade levels. First, choose a genre (category) and reading level. The genre might support a reading interest such as fiction, mysteries, or interactive stories. Or it might focus on a particular animal or creature, such as a cat, horse, or dinosaur. If it is nonfiction, it might expand knowledge about science, cooking, or technology. It might consist of books that focus on socioemotional learning, such as kindness, friendship, or other prosocial behaviors. Then, to collect information to create your list, consider:

- interviewing children
- interviewing a school or children's librarian
- researching literacy websites
- scanning online book retailer rankings
- reading publisher recommendations

Practical Issues and Implications

School for All? Inequity in America

A large study conducted by the Annie E. Casey Foundation (2013) found that if children are reading on grade level by the end of 3rd grade, they will be more likely to succeed academically and graduate from high school. Yet, in a US national study conducted by the National Assessment of Educational Progress (2019), sometimes referred to as The Nation's Report Card, only 18% of Black 4th-graders scored proficient or above in reading, whereas 45% of White and 55% of Asian/Pacific Islander 4th-graders scored proficient or higher. As a comparison, the study showed that 23% of Hispanic 4th-grade students scored proficient or above in reading (see Figure 11.11). More sobering, the scores for all students decreased compared to data collected two years prior. These gaps put children at a disadvantage to succeed academically, and they lower children's chances of graduating from high school.

Several factors contribute to lower achievement levels among all children. These include lower socioeconomic levels, including poverty, lower school quality, stressful family dynamics, and unsafe or less-resourced neighborhoods. Black children and others who are socially and economically disadvantaged are more likely to experience these factors, especially poverty (Morsy & Rothstein, 2019). However, when these factors are leveled, Black teens are still significantly more likely to drop out of high school than are their White counterparts (Calzada et al., 2015; Ford & Moore, 2013; Hernandez, 2011).

The US has one of the widest gaps worldwide among rich nations between high-achieving and low-achieving students (UNICEF, 2020). Although this report showed even wider gaps for children who were non-native to their given country of residence, this is not true for Black children in America. Non-native Black children fare better academically than Black children born in the United States (Crosby & Dunbar, 2012).

According to the Economic Policy Institute, socioeconomic levels are the single biggest factor that impacts school achievement in the United States (Annie E. Casey Foundation, 2008, 2020; Garcia & Weiss, 2017). However, looking beyond income, two factors surfaced that may significantly affect all children. These included improved school readiness and better classroom quality that focuses on academic preparation and culturally aware socioemotional learning (Calzada et al., 2015; Wexler, 2019). Studies show that improving early childhood education, including preschool and kindergarten, will better prepare children in the United States to succeed in school (Hahn et al., 2014, 2015). Other school reformists call for educators to adopt a social justice approach that is culturally responsive and inclusive (Ford & Moore, 2013).

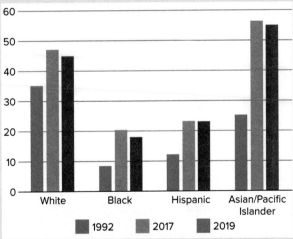

National Assessment of Educational Progess (NAEP), 2019

Figure 11.11 Trend in Percentage of US 4th-Graders at or above NAEP-Proficient Reading Levels, by Race/Ethnicity

*1992 dates are significantly different (p<.05) from the selected focal year

To Think About:

- Are the effects of poverty so powerful that it is unrealistic to expect educators to overcome them?
- Have you seen strategies to combat poverty used in your community? How did they work?
- What roles could caregivers, teachers, and other service providers play in fighting this inequity of resources or opportunities?

11.4 Learning Challenges and Disabilities

According to the US Centers for Disease Control and Prevention (2020), about 1 in 6 children between the ages of 3 and 17 have a cognitive challenge that affects their learning. Between 2009 and 2017, the prevalence of developmental disabilities increased with overrepresentation in some lower SES demographic groups (Zablotsky et al., 2019). These changes in demographic groups may be due to access to health care and reporting (Cortiella & Horowitz, 2015; Gargiulo & Kilgo, 2020). Learning disabilities include a broad range of physical, intellectual, social, and behavioral challenges that affect learning. The effects of these conditions can range from minimal to severe. They include the following:

- *Developmental disabilities*: These are severe long-term (often lifelong) disabilities that can affect intellectual, abilities, socioemotional abilities, or physical functioning, or all three domains. Some of these disabilities are physical, such as hearing or vision loss, and are present from birth.
- *Intellectual disabilities*: This group of disorders is characterized by limited cognitive ability that occurs before age 18. Intellectual disabilities may have a physical cause, such as cerebral palsy, or a nonphysical cause, such as a lack of stimulation and responsiveness from adults.

- *Learning disorders*: These are processing problems that involve the central nervous system. Children with learning disorders generally have average to above-average intelligence; however, challenges in processing information may interfere with learning, such as math (dyscalculia), reading (dyslexia), and writing (dysgraphia).

Some developmental disabilities result from environment or injury, but many have neurological or genetic origins, such as autism spectrum disorder (ASD) and attention-deficit/hyperactivity disorder (ADHD). These are termed **neurodevelopmental disorders** and share these common factors (Bishop & Rutter, 2008; McGill et al., 2020):

- tend to lessen with age but continue at least in a milder form through adulthood
- impact more boys than girls
- traced through family historical accounts

Learning disorders, specifically, affect at least 1 in 10 US schoolchildren, according to the American Academy of Child and Adolescent Psychiatry (2019). Identifying learning disorders takes a team approach. The caregiver team generally includes parents/guardians, teachers, educational specialists, and medical and mental health professionals. For the best outcomes, team members work together to identify the specific types of learning disabilities, their severity, and interventions or treatment options (see Table 11.5) (Wang & Singer, 2016).

Global Perspectives

Meeting the Needs of All Children in the Classroom

In the United States, Section 504 of the Rehabilitation Act of 1973 lists federal civil rights legislation that guarantees certain protections and rights to people with disabilities and prohibits discrimination based on disability. Section 504 protects people with disabilities across their lifespan, including their rights to education, employment, public access to buildings, and transportation. This law set precedents for subsequent legislation for people with disabilities. The US Department of Education's Office for Civil Rights enforces Section 504 in public elementary and secondary schools.

In 1975, the US Congress passed the Education for All Handicapped Children Act (EAHCA). This law required public schools to provide students with a free appropriate public education (FAPE) in the least restrictive environment possible. The statute was renamed the Individuals with Disabilities Education Act (IDEA) in the 1990s. It is administered by the US Department of Education Office of Special Education, which provides funding for special education programs. To qualify for services under the IDEA, children must have disabilities that adversely affect their educational performance.

Part of the IDEA requires that public schools create an individualized education program (IEP) for each student who meets one or more of the 13 specific criteria listed in the legislation. A team that includes the child's primary caregivers, one or more regular classroom teachers, a special education teacher, and a school counselor, psychologist, or administrator develops an IEP (Twachtman-Cullen, D., & J. Twachtman-Bassett, 2011). An IEP is a written plan for providing a student with the most appropriate opportunities for learning between ages 3 and 21. It describes the student's level of performance and how their disability affects academic performance. It sets educational goals and objectives. The plan describes specific accommodations or modifications to the environment, learning strategies, or materials to help the student succeed in the classroom. For example, a student who is blind might need braille copies of textbooks or have written texts converted to spoken voice. The IEP specifies services the student needs to succeed in the classroom, such as a teacher aide, occupational therapy, or speech therapy.

The goal of an IEP is to provide the least restrictive, most effective learning environment for the student to succeed. However, in some classrooms, school districts, and states, this has been interpreted as providing a minimal level of support. To address this inequity, the US Supreme Court ruled in 2018 that children with IEPs should receive education in a regular classroom with the intent of grade-level advancement.

Sometimes educators and primary caregivers think of IEPs as a vehicle only for children who are moderately to severely learning impaired due to diagnosed learning challenges or disabilities. However, some psychologists and educators assert that IEPs could also be valuable for supporting children who are mildly to moderately impaired, especially regarding improving behavior such as children with ADHD (Bakken et al., 2012; Davis, 2018).

In addition to the laws just described, the United States has enacted other legislation related to education over the last twenty years. For example, the No Child Left Behind (NCLB) Act of 2002 measured and tracked the success of public-school children by requiring regular testing of reading and math comprehension each year from 3rd grade through 8th grade. The 2015 Every Student Succeeds Act (ESSA) revised the NCLB Act by expanding educational opportunities and improving student outcomes for disadvantaged and high-needs students. Together, these acts extended the 50-year-old Elementary and Secondary Education Act (ESEA), the national education law that commits to equal opportunity for all students.

☑ CHECKPOINT

- ☐ How prevalent are learning disabilities in middle childhood?
- ☐ What are the three broad categories of special needs that affect learning in middle childhood?
- ☐ What role should educators play in identifying learning disabilities in school-age children?
- ☐ Name and describe three intellectual disabilities or disorders of middle childhood learners and how schools might meet their needs.

Apply Here!

Choose a learning challenge or condition about which you would like to know more, especially regarding the most current research for caregivers and teachers. Produce a presentation in a slide format that care practitioners could use for training. Consider a message that is instructional, informative, and inspiring to those with children in their care.

Disability or Disorder	Characteristic Indicators	Diagnostic Tests	Instructional Strategies or Accommodation
Intellectual disability	• Difficulty or lack of understanding new concepts • Slowness or struggle when processing data • Organizational challenges • Below average intellectual functioning • Difficulty keeping up	Prenatal screening; or a team approach including: • Home and classroom observation • Medical exam • Mental health exam • Genetic and neurological testing • Intelligence or cognitive testing • Adaptive behavior assessment • Family history	• Physical, speech, and occupational therapy • Special education classes • Psychological counseling • Inclusive classroom environment that includes differential teaching methods • Mentoring
Learning disorders	• Problems with reading, writing, or math (*dyslexia, dysgraphia,* and *dyscalculia*) • Poor memory • Attention problems • Time-management problems	• School testing/ evaluation • Healthcare behavioral assessment • Parent/guardian observations and feedback • Evaluation of response to academic interventions	• Early intervention from an education specialist • Extra classroom help • Individualized instruction • Special education classes • Healthcare provider support for behavioral issues • Psychological counseling • Inclusive classroom that includes differential methods • Mentoring
Emotional/behavioral disability	• Inappropriate expressions for age • Overwhelming anxiety, fear, nervousness • Inappropriate expression of anger • Learning challenges not caused by other disabilities • Overwhelming sadness and depression • Bullying or victimization • Irrational obsessions	A team approach including • Home and classroom observation • Medical exam • Mental health exam	• Special or alternative education classes • Psychological counseling
Attention deficient hyperactivity (ADHD)	• Moves quickly from one activity to the next • Forgetful • Difficulty following directions • Impulsive • Overreacts to situations and feelings • Difficulty sitting still	A team approach including: • Home and classroom observation • Medical exam • Mental health exam • Behavioral rating scale • Conners' Continuous Performance Test • MOXO-CPT	• Adhere to strict schedules • Utilize and offer organizational tools • Praise appropriate behavior • Vary instruction modes • Build in physical "breaks" • Utilize kinesthetic methods of teaching

Kato

Table 11.5 Learning Disabilities and Interventions

Disability or Disorder	Characteristic Indicators	Diagnostic Tests	Instructional Strategies or Accommodation
Autism spectrum disorder (ASD)	• Difficulty expressing emotion • Difficulty making friends • Compulsive interest in one subject area • Lack of eye contact • Honesty to a fault or without regard to or understanding of social norms • Appears distant or remote • High intellectual functioning	A team approach including: • Home and classroom observation • Medical exam • Mental health exam	• Special education classes • Psychological counseling • Inclusive classroom environment that includes differential teaching methods • Mentoring • Adhere to strict schedules • Utilize and offer interpersonal communication tools
Communication disorder	• Difficulty expressing ideas, thoughts • Inappropriate or incorrect use of words • Frustration over others' lack of understanding their message • Misunderstanding or inappropriate use of facial gestures or nonverbal cues	A team approach including: • Home and classroom observation • Medical exam • Mental health exam	• Physical, speech, and occupational therapy • Special education classes • Psychological counseling • Inclusive classroom environment that includes differential teaching methods • Offer printed instruction to reinforce verbal instructions
Hearing loss or deafness	• Diminished or loss of hearing • Unresponsive to loud noises or voices • Lack of startle reflex • Inappropriate or incorrect use of words • Incorrect pronunciation of words	• Observation • Hearing test • Medical exam	• Use visual images to relay messages • Integrate sign language • Use subtitles on audiovisual presentations • Use signage in classroom • Offer printed instruction to complement verbal instructions
Low vision	• Diminished or loss of vision • Unresponsive to visual cues • Squinting • Inability to read or low-level reading • Illiteracy	• Observation • Vision test • Medical exam	• Seat in well-lit areas of classroom • Offer additional or more focused light source • Offer nonvisual means of communication such as tactile or auditory methods • Arrange classroom for easier physical movement

Kato

Table 11.5 Continued

Summary

When children enter elementary school, their brains are almost full adult size, and neural pathways become stronger. They have an easier time completing increasingly complex cognitive tasks, and they are generally eager to learn and start school. Children at this stage make tremendous strides in oral communication and begin using language to read and write. They tend to be curious, and their desire for independence drives them to understand the world and learn new skills. Succeeding at learning increases their feelings of competence, and they believe they can accomplish anything they try to do. Their ability to concentrate and focus grows. Their thinking shifts to using logical ways of mental processing rather than relying on their perceptions. They can solve problems without personally experiencing them. They can also learn cooperatively within a social setting.

Students' interest and enthusiasm for learning may dip as academic expectations become more complex and demanding by ages 10 or 11. At the same time, they are more aware of their feelings and have increased capacities for insight, empathy, and communicating personal feelings. As in each stage of life, cognitive development in middle childhood ties to other domains. As you move into Chapter 12, note how physical and cognitive development influence socioemotional development.

Learning Outcomes and Key Concepts

11.1 Explain how the major cognitive theories progress from early childhood to middle childhood.

- Piaget's experiments showed that children between the ages of 6 to 11 are learning to think in more complex ways.
- Piaget theorized that children are in the concrete operational stage during middle childhood.
- The concrete operational period is marked by the predominance of logic rather than relying predominantly on perceptions.
- In Piaget's concrete operational stage, concrete thinking refers to logical ways of mental processing.
- Operational thinking refers to the ability to solve problems without having to experience the problem.
- Vygotsky's social learning theory can be seen in school classrooms when cooperative learning and general problem-solving offer opportunities for children to learn within a social setting.
- Bruner laid out specific ways to provide scaffolding, including modeling tasks, breaking tasks into manageable steps, utilizing visual aids, and using prompt questions to encourage thinking.
- Bronfenbrenner's sociohistorical spheres that affect learning include the micro-, meso-, exo-, macro-, and chronosystems.
- Communities of practice create a common identity as they share ideas and knowledge over time or with practice.
- Language ability continues to be facilitated by the development of theory of mind (ToM).
- Using social emotional learning (SEL), children become more aware of their own feelings; they have an increased ability to have insight, empathize, and communicate personal feelings.
- Empirical evidence-based studies have shown that including SEL in a classroom environment positively impacts cognitive development and learning.

11.2 Demonstrate knowledge of current research findings on how development and growth affects cognitive functions and learning in middle childhood.

- In middle childhood, both gray and white matter brain volume grows while connections between parts flourish, enabling children to engage in more complex cognitive tasks.
- Sex differences are seen between boys and girls in brain volume, types of brain matter, and the sequence of development in the different regions of the brain.
- As seen in cognitive flexibility, working memory, and processing speed, the brain becomes more efficient as white matter creates connectivity between brain parts.
- Improved cognitive flexibility is seen as children are better able to switch back and forth between cognitive tasks.

- In middle childhood, working memory improves dramatically, aiding learning.
- Mentally manipulating information or data becomes faster as myelination allows nerve impulses to move more quickly in middle childhood.
- The ability to focus or expand attention may be related to the back (posterior) and front (anterior) parts of the brain creating complex networks that affect attention-related activities.
- Increased ability in solving complex problems or executive functioning is likely due to maturation of the brain's frontal lobes and neuron connections.

11.3 Discuss how children learn language and identify cognitive developmental language milestones often achieved during middle childhood.

- Children learn about 3,000 to 5,000 new words per year; by the latter years of middle childhood, vocabulary accelerates at great speed as they know about 40,000 words.
- Middle childhood language increases lexical diversity (use of different types of words), lexical complexity (use of more multisyllabic words), and lexical density.
- Language skill delays correlate with academic and social functioning problems and may predict later reading skill and comprehension difficulties and even math learning.
- By age 9 or 10, spoken language does not resemble written language because written language tends to be much more complex, requiring coordination of multiple abilities.
- As children learn to read, they decode the symbols of written language and their phonology, which is crucial to word recognition and stringing together words into sentences.
- Writing requires some skills that are different from reading, such as fine-motor skills.
- Most children have mastered writing their letters correctly by the time they reach the end of 2nd grade, and they then become increasingly proficient at putting thoughts into words and sentences.

- Some children learn to read before school, but most begin the process between kindergarten and 3rd grade; most can read by the time they reach about age 9.
- Children who struggle with reading comprehension may have less white matter in one specific area of their brain combined with adverse environmental factors.

11.4 Describe factors that impede learning, including learning challenges and disabilities.

- About 1 out of 6 US children live with developmental disabilities, intellectual disabilities, or learning disorders.
- Some developmental disabilities result from the environment or an injury, but many have neurological or genetic origins.
- Identifying learning disorders should include input from parents/guardians, teachers, educational specialists, and medical and mental health professionals.

Chapter Review

1. Name three ways that learning happens in middle childhood that differs from learning in early childhood.
2. How would you describe the brain changes and subsequent cognitive abilities during middle childhood to a new after-school caregiver?
3. Design an infographic that describes/illustrates the cognitive attributes of school-age children and how their caregivers or teachers can promote optimal cognitive growth and development.
4. If you were holding a workshop for parents of children in your care, how might you describe the process, methods, and importance of literacy/language development in young children? Why is there such a significant variation in reading ability?
5. Knowing what you know now, how might you go about helping a child learn to read and write?

Matching

Match the following terms with the correct definitions related to cognitive theories.

A. classification

B. concrete thinking

C. conservation

D. inferential thinking

E. internalization

F. operational thinking

G. concrete operational stage

H. seriation

I. transitivity

J. social learning theory

1. Ways of thinking influenced by the thought patterns of those around them
2. A cognitive stage marked by the predominance of logic, rather than relying on perceptions
3. The ability to combine different ideas, discuss the merits or characteristics of different ideas, or draw conclusions
4. Zone of proximal development
5. The ability to understand that relationships between two objects can extend to a third object
6. The ability to solve problems without having to encounter or experience the problem either in the physical world or personally
7. The ability to understand that a simple change in the shape of an object does not change its volume
8. The ability to place objects in order by a characteristic
9. The ability to sort items by one or more characteristics they have in common
10. Logical ways of mental processing

Match the following terms with the correct definitions related to literacy/language development.

A. expressive language

B. language modalities

C. lexical complexity

D. lexical density

E. lexical diversity

F. literacy

G. morphology

H. phonology

I. pragmatics

J. receptive language

K. semantics

L. syntax

M. vocabulary

1. Language comprehension
2. The use of more multisyllabic words
3. Language that is produced
4. The proper order of words in a phrase or sentence
5. The meaning of words
6. Using language properly
7. Known meaning of words
8. The use of different types of words that have similar meanings
9. The use of linguistic complexity
10. Reading and writing skills, within a cultural and language construct
11. Word structures and formations such as plural or singular form
12. The science of the fundamental sounds and combinations of sounds in a language
13. The means or processes for expressing language

Children with exceptional talent may express themselves through performing.

12

Middle Childhood:
Socioemotional Development

Learning Outcomes

After studying this chapter, you will be able to:

12.1 Analyze the socioemotional theories related to learning in middle childhood.

12.2 Explain how socioemotional learning influences physical and cognitive development and academic success.

12.3 Discuss how a school-age child's relationships with their primary caregivers and teachers influences their socioemotional development.

12.4 Identify ways in which a school-age child's relationship with siblings affects their socioemotional development.

12.5 Identify ways in which a school-age child's peer relationships affect their socioemotional development.

12.6 Describe moral developmental theory and milestones often achieved during middle childhood.

Key Terms

bullying	full siblings	protective factors
care perspective	half siblings	reciprocity
civic duty	industry versus inferiority	self-awareness
conventional reasoning	stage	self-efficacy
cyberbullying	moral agency	self-management
dyads	preadolescents	social awareness
dyad friendships	preteens	stigma bullying

Introduction

Think about why socioemotional development in middle childhood affected you. Did you have family chores or responsibilities during middle childhood? How did your relationships with parents, teachers, siblings, and peers change as you matured? Who were your best friends in middle childhood? Are you still friends with them now? Did you have a favorite teacher? How did gaining emotional and social skills help you in your social relationships and moral decision-making?

In middle childhood, developmental changes and maturation contribute significantly to who children will become as adolescents or adults. While school-age children still rely heavily on their primary caregivers, their social lives expand as they strive to figure out who they are, what roles they play, and how their lives matter. They may spend more time away from family as they begin elementary school. As a result, many new relationships with peers, teachers, coaches, and others outside the home influence how they view themselves.

As their thought processes become more rational, school-age children try to figure out how people and things work. In doing so, they become more self-aware and more aware of the feelings and emotions of those around them. Although traditionally considered a trouble-free stage of life, middle childhood brings many new and complex experiences and learning—school, peers, rules, and academic expectations. Children can be very industrious, but they can feel overwhelmed by the tasks and expectations set before them.

Socioemotional development includes acquiring social skills and attitudes, learning how to care about others, and developing both self-confidence and self-esteem. This chapter explores how the physical and cognitive changes that occur throughout middle childhood affect the development of these skills.

12.1 Socioemotional Theories

Interactions with others expand the social environment and the child's place within it. As in earlier life stages, developing social and emotional skills are critical to leading a healthy life. It is well-acknowledged that socioemotional development affects a child's overall well-being both in the moment and for life. It sets the stage for most relationships, social interactions and behaviors, and mental health (Blair & Raver, 2015; Darling-Churchill & Lippman, 2016; Williams & Lerner, 2019). It also lays the foundation for cognitive and physical development.

An awareness of self and of others is often divided into three main tenets: self-image, self-esteem, and the concept of the ideal self (Cowie, 2012). Self-image includes a person's social identity, or the roles they play, such as being the child of a parent, a sibling, a grandchild, student, or friend. Self-esteem refers to a person's subjective perception of their value. The concept of the ideal self includes how children want to be seen in a social context, including the power they can exert over others (see Figure 12.1). None of these exist independently, but all exist within the context of social and emotional development as school-age children continue to experiment and define, evaluate, and adjust their thoughts and actions. They seek a self-identity to place themselves within a social context. Studies show that these concepts begin early in infancy and grow and develop throughout life (Dowling, 2014; Lerner et al., 2013; Schore, 2015).

During middle childhood, children learn how to do more things for themselves. They garner new self-care skills, such as personal grooming or preparing a snack. Their organizational skills expand as they learn to focus and complete classroom assignments. They become more competent in meeting cultural expectations and in interactions with others, such as using appropriate greetings, asking for assistance, or using communication technologies. In school, they face expectations of learning how to read and write with growing competence. Successfully learning new skills can lead to a sense of confidence, or **self-efficacy**, a feeling that they can master a situation that will yield favorable results. On the other hand, if a child fails to learn a new skill or does not perform it as well as their peers, cultural expectations can lead to feelings of inferiority (McCormick & Scherer, 2018).

As discussed in Chapter 9, theorist Erik Erikson asserted that the main socioemotional tasks faced in early childhood are developing autonomy (versus shame and doubt) and establishing initiative (versus guilt). Children begin to see themselves as autonomous or separate from their primary caregivers, and they assert themselves through words and actions. When they are successful, the strengths that can potentially come from these socioemotional struggles include a sense of hope, willpower, and purpose. Failure, on the other hand, may lead to feelings of shame, doubt about their abilities, and guilt about trying.

In middle childhood, the focus shifts to facing the tension of the **industry versus inferiority stage** (see Table 12.1), as children seek competence or the ability to accomplish something successfully (Erikson, 1950). As children develop a sense of industry, competence and feelings of worth are strongly tied together. Competence may be measured in aptitude, proficiency, ability, or fitness in demonstrating a skill. School-age children pursue recognition measured by being acknowledged when they learn new skills or accomplish new goals, both in school and at home. Demonstrating competence may also include completing family chores, such as drying dishes, or assuming other increasing responsibilities, like feeding the family pet (see Figure 12.2).

Gaining competency in tasks may include physical, intellectual, or social tasks. A child may learn to self-pack a lunch or prepare a simple meal. They may be able to stay at home alone for a brief time; this accomplishment can extend into longer periods as children exhibit competence during the later years of middle childhood. As children increase

Self-image	Self-esteem	Ideal self
• Social identity • Roles	• Subjective feelings about self • Perception of own value	• Other's perception • Power or agency

Goodheart-Willcox Publisher

Figure 12.1 The Concept of Self in the Context of Others: Three Main Parts
How might these parts work both together and independently?

Age	Stage	Strength Developed
0–12 months	Trust versus mistrust	Hope
1–3 years	Autonomy versus shame and doubt	Willpower
3–6 years	Initiative versus guilt	Purpose
6–11 years	Industry versus inferiority	Competency

Kato

Table 12.1 Erikson's Early and Middle Childhood Socioemotional Tasks and Strengths

A   **B**

fizkes/Shutterstock.com; Waraporn Chokchaiworarat/Shutterstock.com

Figure 12.2 In middle childhood, children can help with household tasks, especially (A) with supervision at younger ages and (B) with less supervision as they get older.
With supervision, which household chores might be reasonable for a 6- or 7-year-old? Which household chores might be appropriate for a 10- or 11-year-old to complete without close supervision?

their competency, they are motivated by praise and recognition of their growing independence and abilities (Glowiak & Mayfield, 2016; McCormick & Scherer, 2018). When children feel incompetent, such as when they struggle with academic endeavors, it may negatively affect their mental health (Deighton et al., 2018; Panayiotou & Humphrey, 2017).

One aspect of developing competency is the motivation to try something one or more times (Wigfield & Eccles, 2002). Broussard and Garrison (2004) observe that when faced with the opportunity to learn a new skill, a child's motivation tends to be organized around three questions:

- Can I do this task?
- Do I want to do this task, and why?
- What do I have to do to succeed in this task?

Learning new tasks generally requires motivation, emotional self-regulation, and a sense of self. It also requires a child's ability to focus and utilize executive functioning skills, such as goal setting, time management, and evaluation (Devine & Apperly, 2021).

Children tend to thrive when they work on home, school, and extracurricular activities that offer them room to gain competency and industry. They enjoy acknowledgment and encouragement to explore (Broussard & Garrison, 2004). This does not mean that a child should receive constant attention and praise. When caregivers provide reassurance and give children a sense that they trust them, children develop a sense of competence and confidence in their ability to work toward achieving a new skill (Gonzalez-DeHass & Willems, 2012; Medina, 2014). When encouragement and recognition are rare, children develop a sense of inferiority and low self-esteem. Ideally, through recognition and encouragement, a healthy work ethic and positive self-esteem results (Gonzalez-DeHass & Williams, 2012).

☑ CHECKPOINT

☐ Describe the middle childhood stage included in Erikson's early childhood socioemotional development. What strength is associated with this stage?

☐ Besides motivation, what other socioemotional factors affect a child's ability to learn a new skill?

☐ What three questions do children ask when faced with the potential of learning a new skill?

☐ What are some practical ways that educators might encourage or motivate students in middle childhood to develop new skills?

Apply Here!

Theorists often agree that school-age children need to feel competent and industrious, instead of inferior, for optimal socioemotional growth and development. Rather than just praise alone, children measure their competency by being acknowledged when new skills are learned or accomplished. Imagine that you are helping a school-age child learn a new skill. The skill might be athletic, such as hitting a ball with a bat, or require problem-solving, such as planning and making breakfast for another person. Consider three things you may say to the child that would be purely praise. Next, consider three statements that could encourage their competency. How do these two types of responses fundamentally differ?

Global Perspectives

Does Child Labor Still Exist?

Around the world, children are thrust into adult roles; this includes participating in the labor force to contribute to family income. Despite global family policies that make the exploitation of children through child labor illegal, it continues (Greenbaum & Brodrick, 2017). Child labor is most common in developing regions, including countries in Asia, Africa, and Latin America, where, combined, over 90% of children become child laborers (Radfar et al., 2018).

For many years, the continuation of childhood labor was attributed to poor economies and diverse cultural expectations. To explain the persistence of child labor despite lowering global poverty levels, Sakar & Sakar (2016) performed an economic modeling of child labor across many countries, including the United States. They found that income inequality within a society was the key factor to its continuing practice. They asserted that efforts to decrease income inequality, along with strong anti-child labor legislation, were more effective than attempting to change views on child labor. Tied to income inequality were fewer opportunities for free secondary education that could improve the health of child workers and combat child labor in the long term.

Child labor is difficult to identify, particularly in agricultural markets where migrant workers are regularly employed. Globally, it is estimated that there are over one billion adult migrant farm workers, many of whom have children in tow (Jan et al., 2017). Farm workers are often invisible to the public, and they may work long hours under diverse circumstances. Around the world, many migrant farm workers are underpaid and sometimes perform dangerous tasks. Because many migrant families have children who lack proper identification, their ages may be misreported, so children often begin working before it is legal. Children of migrants may also be ineligible for education or health services, depending on the country in which they are living (Ramos, 2018).

The United Nations considers child labor illegal, although cultural definitions of what constitutes *labor* or *work* may vary by country (Radfar et al., 2018). Around the world, children may labor in hazardous settings, including mines, brick kilns, and fisheries (see Figure 12.3). In some countries, children even serve as soldiers (Ramos, 2018). In the United States, child labor is illegal and considered a type of child trafficking. However, it still exists, especially in household servitude and janitorial or cleaning services, as informal settings can make it easy to go largely unnoticed (Greenbaum & Bodrick, 2017).

Child labor is attractive to employers because children can be paid low wages or not paid at all. They lack the power, experience, and knowledge to advocate for fair pay. This also makes children vulnerable to added corrupt practices, including other forms of human trafficking. To mitigate the adverse effects on children and families, many governments are adopting more holistic approaches to combating child labor. Efforts include providing free education, better health care, community resources, and better laws, regulations, and policies that support the well-being of children (Basu et al., 2010; Jan et al., 2017). Child labor is not new and has existed throughout history. With these efforts, there is hope for long-term well-being and the betterment of children's

Figure 12.3 Here are some examples of child labor: (A) a young girl working in a brick factory in Nepal and (B) a young boy working in a garment factory in India.

lives and subsequent societal benefits (Beegle et al., 2004; Miller, 2010; Radfar et al., 2018).

Does child labor ever have a positive impact? Sometimes. When children participate in voluntary labor that is not excessive or forced, they may develop a sense of industry. Their competence and feelings of worth may be measured in their aptitude, proficiency, ability, or fitness in demonstrating skills. When children help in farming communities, involvement during harvest times may build a sense of community or family identity. In some areas, including the United States, schools may adjust schedules so that children can be involved in the harvest.

For example, in Caribou, Maine, schools close for three or four weeks each fall for the potato harvest. Many children participate in the community harvest, and the break is titled "Potato Recess" (Johnson-Smith, 2021).

To Think About:

- Child labor is illegal in the United States. Are you aware of any child labor that is not recognized as such in your community? Are there expectations of unpaid work?

- How might family expectations of paid or unpaid labor affect children in your community?

12.2 Socioemotional: Cognitive, Social, and Emotional Development

Socioemotionally, school-age children mature rapidly. They are often eager, friendly, and responsible. They can also be irritable, hurtful, and careless. Their improving cognitive skills allow them to complete more complex tasks, such as organizing their living spaces, games, homework, or other school responsibilities. They also have more involvement in social friendship groups. Having duties at home and school gives them a sense of accomplishment (Bosacki, 2016).

Although praise and encouragement continue to be necessary, children in this stage begin to be sensitive and discerning about instruction from others. Children do not want others to be condescending or talk down to them. They are beginning to appreciate

reasonable explanations, since they are becoming more rational thinkers. They care more about how others perceive them than they did in previous life stages (Blair & Raver, 2015; Darling-Churchill & Lippman, 2016; Williams & Lerner, 2019). When children move into the later stage of middle childhood, ages 10 to 11, they are often tagged as **preadolescents** or **preteens**. As these terms suggest, they have an interesting and challenging blend of childlike and teen characteristics.

As in earlier stages of development, socioemotional development is closely tied to cognitive and physical development. Socioemotional development includes gaining the social and emotional skills that allow integrating with others within families, schools, and other social relationships (Domitrovich et al., 2017; Gueldner et al., 2020). Cultural traditions, norms, and values inform children about how they should act, care for and treat others, care for themselves, and make moral decisions. During middle childhood, a critical part of socioemotional development is learning the social-emotional learning (SEL) skills required for effective personal relationships. These skills include self-awareness, social awareness, self-management, relationship skills, and responsible decision-making (see Figure 12.4). These skills positively affect their overall success and make it easier for them to navigate life's challenges (Albright et al., 2011; Hoerr, 2020; Kostelnik et al., 2015). As discussed in previous chapters, SEL has become an essential and valued practice in children's education (Dwecket al., 2014; Jones et al., 2017a).

The benefits of integrating SEL in middle childhood are many. For example, children learn to articulate their own needs more effectively and have a better sense of self as their awareness grows. They are better able to self-discipline and regulate their emotions and impulses. They can better resolve conflict (Duckworth & Yeager, 2015; Smith & Low, 2013). However, SEL does not happen overnight. It is a process that occurs with classroom, school, caregiver, family, and community support and reinforcement (see Figure 12.5).

Developing Self-Awareness

Self-awareness is a child's assessment or view of self. Childhood is a critical time for developing self-awareness. Prosocial behaviors associated with self-awareness include diligence or persistence, assertiveness or confidence, and a sense of citizenship or social responsibility (Thompson et al., 2018). Children who positively perceive themselves often feel capable and worthwhile and are more likely to act in ways that enhance their abilities. Those who develop a negative self-concept often adopt self-defeating behaviors (Orth & Robins, 2019; Scherrer & Preckel, 2019).

Erikson's description of the conflict at the stage of industry versus inferiority links to self-concept (Erikson, 1950). Children have the drive to learn new skills and become more independent. They want to be seen as competent, skilled, and valuable. When adults help them succeed, their sense of competence gives them the self-confidence to keep meeting new challenges and mastering additional skills.

In middle childhood, a sense of identity advances as children are cognitively better able to understand their relationships with others. Self-identity and subsequent feelings about their perceived identity are shaped by individual temperament and the environment and values of the social relationships around them (Milica, 2014; Rambura, 2015; Warin & Adriany, 2017). As school-age children's social sphere grows beyond their immediate families, they have access to more input from others about how they might be perceived in their role in the classroom structure, their way of reacting in situations, their perceived power and control, and the characters they play in social encounters (Madden-Dent & Oliver, 2021). Based on this input, a child might begin to label themselves as *popular, funny, shy, smart, athletic, clumsy, musical,* or *kind.* In addition, social identity concerning gender, age, ethnic background or race, and religious background continues to grow and expand (Rogoff, 2003; Solomon, 2016).

During middle childhood, children can identify that race and ethnicity are a multidimensional construct involving labels and presumptions. For example, they can understand that ethnicity includes how people live, the foods they eat, and how family members celebrate events. On the other hand, race is a social construct that includes ways society categorizes people, such as by their skin color or geographical ancestry. They begin to self-identify with racial and ethnic groups, but they also understand that these categories are flexible and changing

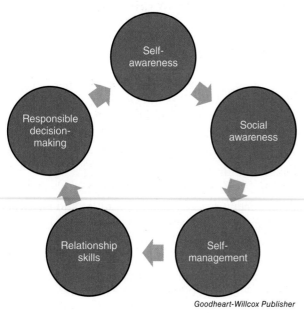

Goodheart-Willcox Publisher

Figure 12.4 Social Emotional Learning Domains

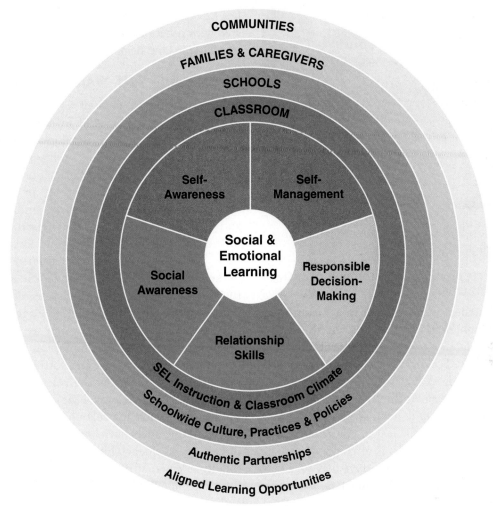

©2021 CASEL. Social and Emotional Learning Framework. All rights reserved. casel.org

Figure 12.5 Socioemotional learning is supported by classrooms, schools, families and caregivers, and communities.

(Derlan et al., 2016). Input from family, peers, teachers, and others can shape a child's self-identity and personal awareness (McCormick & Scherer, 2018).

Because self-awareness includes the ability to accurately assess one's strengths and limitations, roles, and influence over self and others, it can help facilitate goal setting and achievement. Possessing self-awareness can lend a sense of optimism and an internal sense of control. It goes together with social awareness, as you will see next.

Developing Social Awareness

Social awareness is the ability to take another person's perspective or to sense what a group of people may think. As discussed in earlier childhood development stages, a significant milestone

is understanding that another person's knowledge, emotions, intentions, beliefs, or motivations belong to that person. They may not correlate with one's feelings or opinions. Social awareness also includes the understanding that groups may act together and act with shared rather than individual beliefs. Social awareness is strongly tied to cognitive development, emotional regulation, and language ability (Housman, 2017). It may also be linked to executive functioning abilities such as brainstorming, planning, and executing ideas. Children with more advanced executive functioning skills may be better able to understand the perspectives of others, even multiple perspectives (see Figure 12.6) (Best & Miller, 2010; Madden-Dent & Oliver, 2021).

Prostock-studio/Shutterstock.com

Figure 12.6 Children enjoy working together on a school project.
How might having multiple perspectives in school group projects promote brainstorming, planning, and executing ideas?

Social awareness is not created in a vacuum but evolves through social interactions. At this stage, children desperately want to feel a sense of belonging and competence. Feelings of competence primarily depend on gaining skills, especially at school, and on acceptance by peers. At the same time, school-age children may be full of doubts, avoiding new tasks to prevent or cope with the fear of failure. Dressing, acting, or talking like others is often an attempt to ensure acceptance. Criticizing others may be a way to look better in comparison with them. Competition is exciting, but it brings the possibility of not measuring up. No wonder emotions can be close to the surface during this stage (Milica, 2014; Rambura, 2015; Warin & Adriany, 2017).

Social awareness naturally leads to social comparison. Children ask themselves questions such as, "Who is the better reader—my friend or me?" Or they may ask questions such as, "Are my toys as good as their toys?" "Who is invited to Kelly's birthday party? Why was I not invited?" "Who can run the fastest?" These self-evaluations and social comparisons may be related to both environment and genetics. There may be a heritability factor in how much a child compares themself to others (Becht et al., 2021; Denny et al., 2012; van Drunen et al., 2021).

Social awareness is associated with exercising self-regulation of emotions and demonstrating empathy (Thompson et al., 2018). Empathy is the ability to understand the thoughts and feelings of another person. Empathy seeks connection and increases relational understanding. Sympathy focuses on pitying or feeling sorry for another person. Empathy is associated with other prosocial behaviors such as cooperating, sharing, and helping others (Telzer et al., 2018).

Developing Self-Management

Self-management, or self-regulation, continues to be an essential SEL skill in middle childhood. Self-management includes developing self-awareness and social awareness while managing oneself in accordance with the social expectations and ethical norms of behavior. It consists of an understanding that social resources exist in families, schools, and communities and that those resources may be utilized to help self-manage behaviors and emotions. In other words, self-management is accomplished with the help of and under the influence of social community. Children may see effective self-management, or the lack of self-management, modeled by watching media. They may see the story of a child who manages to accomplish an incredible feat through self-management and fortitude. They may see someone who breaks the rules and suffers the consequences or gets away with it. Media can play a significant influencing role on children's social values, beliefs, and behaviors, including expectations of self-management (Huesmann & Taylor, 2011; Stiglic & Viner, 2019).

One component of self-management is handling and expressing emotions. Just as in early childhood, school-age children may express their feelings physically or verbally (see Figure 12.7). They may use subtle or overt ways to provoke emotional responses, such as ignoring instructions or questions. Family conflicts, relocating to a new area, and school social problems, such as bullying, are examples of stressful events that could trigger emotional responses (Madden-Dent & Oliver, 2021). Fear is a powerful emotion that evolves as children age. While younger children tend to fear the dark, animals, and unfamiliar places, the fears school-age children experience begin to change. They may fear the potential loss or death of primary caregivers, fire, large bodies of water, and other situations that seem hurtful. New experiences and cognitive maturation often cause fears to center around tragedy and loss, stress related to unstable homes, or underlying medical conditions.

Learning self-management skills during middle childhood is one indicator of a child's well-being and positive mental health (Pollard & Lee, 2003; Scales

Collin Quinn Lomax/Shutterstock.com

Figure 12.7 Children may express their emotions physically or verbally.
What do you think the conflict might be about? How might an adult caregiver help this frustrated child express emotions in a socially appropriate and effective way?

et al., 2004; Thompson et al., 2018). Self-management helps children to control their emotions and regulate appropriate interactions with others. It also enables them to accomplish tasks and goals. But learning to self-manage does not happen on its own. Educators can help children develop self-management skills by providing small achievable goals, integrating effective classroom routines, providing positive feedback and reinforcement, monitoring behaviors, and providing opportunities for children to assess and celebrate their progress toward goals (Balaghi et al., 2021; Briesch et al., 2019; Busacca et al., 2015). Children continue to learn in a social context throughout the school-age years; thus, modeling and reinforcement remain significant contributors to social learning (Kostelnik et al., 2015; McClelland et al., 2017; Taylor et al., 2017).

Developing Relationship Skills

Establishing and maintaining healthy and rewarding relationships with diverse individuals is a crucial SEL skill that children can develop during middle childhood. SEL includes communicating clearly, listening actively, cooperating, resisting inappropriate social pressure, negotiating conflict constructively, and seeking and offering help when needed. Friendships and social groups form. Social cliques or clubs, "best friends," and social status and popularity are a part of middle childhood as children negotiate relationships and establish self-worth (Holder & Coleman, 2015; Maunder & Monks, 2019).

Relationship and friendship skills are learned from others and through personal experience. Primary caregivers, teachers, and other mentors can play a significant role in helping children learn relationship skills (Hay et al., 2004; Kostelnik et al., 2015). Educators can help children build relationships by being intentional about forming social groups. For example, they can form students into pairs and small working groups to work on projects together. They can create opportunities for students to share information about themselves and to learn about their peers. Having healthy and rewarding relationships during middle childhood can provide a sense of security, intimacy, and trust. It can also aid in building other prosocial behaviors (Rubin et al., 2006). As children age and mature, relationships become increasingly important to mental well-being (Furman & Buhrmester, 1985; Telzer et al., 2018; Thomson et al., 2018).

Moral Decision-Making

Making productive and respectful choices is another essential SEL skill that children learn. Decisions may include choices about personal behavior, social interactions, and their subsequent consequences. Considerations may include the effects of decisions on self and others, safety, and expectations of others or societal norms.

Including SEL in the elementary school classroom environment is vital as evidence-based studies have shown that its inclusion positively impacts cognitive development and learning (Hansen, 2018; Sanchez, 2021). SEL can enhance self-awareness, self-management, social awareness, relationship skills, and decision-making in middle childhood and beyond (Espelage et al., 2015; Keelan, 2020; Stalker et al., 2018). Practical ways educators can promote SEL activities include integrating welcoming activities, facilitating engagement with children and between classmates, and focusing on optimistic closures that encourage children to appreciate what they have accomplished individually and collectively (Rowell, 2021).

Teaching SEL, particularly in schools and care settings, can have a tremendous effect on children. When SEL is part of the classroom, it can boost resilience and counteract some adverse childhood experiences, especially poverty (Sanchez, 2021). The impacts of racism and social marginalization can be mitigated or improved as children learn to respect each other as individuals (Verschelden & Lomotey, 2021).

Practical Issues and Implications

Children and Mental Health

According to the National Alliance on Mental Illness (2020), the prevalence of mental health issues continues to increase worldwide, especially in the United States. Whether this is due to an actual increase in numbers, better diagnosis abilities, or less stigma related to a diagnosis is unknown. Are children likewise facing growing numbers of mental health issues? According to the US Centers for Disease Control and Prevention (2020), mental health issues are widespread and growing in numbers. Approximately one in every six children aged 2 to 8 years have a diagnosed mental, behavioral, or developmental disorder (Cree et al., 2018; Ghandour et al., 2018; Holbrook et al., 2017). Mental health issues are most common among children who live in poverty and receive less treatment due to a lack of accessible health care (Cree et al., 2018).

Children's mental health issues are defined as serious changes in typical behavior that negatively affect how they behave, manage their emotions, and learn (Bitsko et al., 2018). The most prevalent mental disorders include anxiety, depression, and attention-deficit hyperactivity disorder (ADHD), which is associated with impulsiveness, hyperactivity, and inattention (Bhandari, 2018). Diagnosed anxiety and depression have increased significantly among school-age children ages 6 to 11; and they have become even more common as children enter adolescence (see Figure 12.8) (Cree et al., 2018).

Depression and generalized anxiety are two of the most common mental health concerns in middle childhood, and this stage is often considered the starting point of lifetime struggles with these mental health disorders (Bitsko et al., 2018; Holbrook et al., 2017). Depression symptoms may include sadness, changes in appetite or sleep patterns, and loss of interest and pleasure in activities or relationships. Generalized anxiety symptoms often include excessive worry. Depression and generalized anxiety often co-exist and can negatively affect children's lives, including their family relationships, academic achievement, and peer relationships. Medical diagnosis and comprehensive treatment are important; and careful monitoring may have a lifelong impact.

Before the COVID-19 global pandemic, the incidence rate of anxiety and depression among children was about 11% to 12%. After COVID-19 was declared a pandemic and school children experienced school closures, quarantine, and family isolation and stress, a large global study indicated that incidence rates of depression

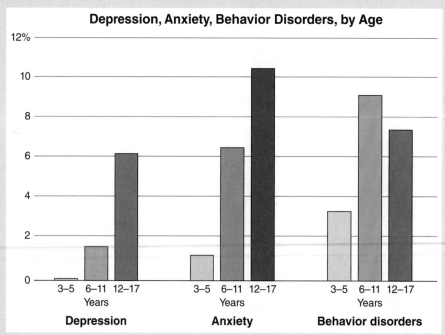

National Center on Birth Defects and Developmental Disabilities, Centers for Disease Control and Prevention

Figure 12.8 Depression, Anxiety, and Behavior Disorders in Children

and generalized anxiety among children may have more than doubled (Lee, 2020; Racine et al., 2021; Singh et al., 2020).

As seen in Figure 12.8, behavior disorders, such as oppositional defiant disorder or conduct disorder, are the most common type of mental health concern during middle childhood (US Centers for Disease Control, 2020). Conduct disorders go beyond children misbehaving. It is common for all children to struggle with behavior as they learn self-awareness and social-awareness skills. Conduct disorders go beyond bouts of misconduct to prolonged and sustained antisocial behaviors (Cree et al., 2018; Ghandour et al., 2018; Perou et al., 2013).

Middle childhood is a time for learning how to live in a social setting. Conduct disorders make this challenging because they may include aggressive or violent behaviors, such as hitting or kicking, abusing, bullying, intimidating people or animals, or harming with weapons. Conduct disorders may also include behaviors such as inflicting damage on property, breaking the rules or laws, or running away from school or home (Bhandari, 2018). Children with conduct disorders often lack empathy for others. They may demonstrate an absence of guilt, blame others for their actions, or lack caring about their school performance (Bhandari, 2018). Conduct disorders typically present before age 10 and affect more boys than girls (Meier et al., 2011). When children who have conduct disorders act out, it can result in school problems and expulsions, legal or criminal consequences, and harm to others.

The cause of conduct disorders in children is unknown. Still, likely culprits include genetics, cognitive deficits, and learning disabilities, functional brain abnormalities that affect the regulation of emotions, and a myriad of environmental issues, including stress from adverse childhood experiences (Holbrook et al., 2017; Meier et al., 2011; Perou et al., 2013). In addition, it is unknown how much other mental health disorders, such as oppositional defiant disorder, explosive disorder, antisocial personality disorder, pyromania, and kleptomania, are disorders that may be related to conduct (Bhandari, 2018).

Although the number of children who are challenged with conduct disorders has increased, it is difficult to gain a firm grip on the number of children affected. Research on causes, the correlation between other types of mental illness, and best treatment outcomes is ongoing; but it remains a staggering task. The US Centers for Disease Control and Prevention (2020) completed a comprehensive report on estimates of children with specific mental disorders between 2005–2011 that laid the groundwork for future data collection (American Psychiatric Association, 2013; Perou et al., 2013). This report aimed to join forces among the agencies serving children to understand the prevalence, treatment, and impact on children's growth and development over time.

To Think About:

- Why do you think mental health issues are increasing in middle childhood?

- Can integrating social emotional learning into schools and communities help alleviate the burden of helping children with mental health issues? If so, how? If not, why not?

☑ CHECKPOINT

- ☐ Name the five skill categories of social emotional learning.
- ☐ What are the component parts of identity development, and when do children begin to develop an identity?
- ☐ How does cognitive development affect self-awareness?
- ☐ Why is social awareness essential in middle childhood socioemotional development?
- ☐ Define self-management SEL skills. Why are these skills important? Give several examples.
- ☐ What are the primary social relationships experienced in middle childhood? How do children best learn social relationship skills?

Apply Here!

Collectible toys such as baseball cards, stuffed animals, and dolls or action figures are often trendy and faddish during middle childhood, especially during the middle years of elementary school. Examples from the past include Beanie Babies®, Fidget Spinners®, Zhu Pets®, and Pokeman® cards. Gather a group of adults and lead a class discussion on what they remember as big trends and how they felt about this trend. Ask those with younger siblings or who interact with kids to comment on current trends. Or pick a fad from a specific era, then search online to find commentaries from people who remember this trend. Why do you think fads hold such great appeal to school-age children? What role do these trends play in socioemotional development? How do trends change as children mature?

12.3 Relationships with Primary Caregivers and Teachers

Despite the widening social circles and the lessening of direct supervision, the influence of primary caregivers on their children remains strong in middle childhood (Bosmans et al., 2007, 2009; Lansford et al., 2021b). During middle childhood, relationships with primary caregivers remain essential in a child's socioemotional development (Allen, 2008; McHale et al., 2003). However, as SEL skills expand and mature, intimate relationships within the family change. Children begin to spend less time in direct contact with caregivers and more time with teachers, peers, coaches, and other external relationships. They gradually become more autonomous as this stage forms the transition from early childhood to adolescence.

Although children are becoming more independent and spending more time with peers, they still rely on their families for physical and mental health, cognitive stimulation, and socioemotional development (Collins & Madsen, 2019; Lam et al., 2014). Families provide food, clothing, shelter, and access to health care. They monitor and oversee the physical health, safety, and well-being of children. Families also provide opportunities for children to develop cognitively. For example, families foster cognitive and linguistic development by engaging children in conversation or encouraging verbal expression. Some families encourage reading and academic pursuits. They help children learn problem-solving independently in age-appropriate ways (Mermelshtine, 2017; Pinquart, 2016).

Families also shape social relationships, including what it means to be in a relationship with others, to communicate needs, and how to treat others (Yuill & Carr, 2018). For example, families model how to deal with conflict, negotiate needs and wants, and care for each other. They can help children nurture friendships with peers by guiding and providing opportunities for peer interactions. Families affect the development of self-identity and self-esteem. They foster children's self-regulatory skills, serving as a rich learning and practice environment while they transition between early childhood and adolescence (Barreto-Zarza et al., 2021; Morawska et al., 2019).

The quality of the family context impacts the household influence on the child. Financial stress, abuse, neglect, parent education level, income level, and restrictive or controlling parent behavior can greatly reduce the quality of the family environment for children (Julien et al., 2017; Ursache & Noble, 2016). However, even in adverse situations, families teach children how to react to or manage stress directly and indirectly. Overall, families have the potential to provide stability in the lives of children.

Relationships with Primary Caregivers

Primary caregivers remain the primary source of attachment during middle childhood. Even as children approach adolescence, they prefer their parents over their peers for emotional support (Bosmans & Kerns, 2015; Schul et al., 2003; Seibert & Kerns, 2009).

For school-age children, strong parent-child relationships have been shown to increase children's abilities to concentrate, form positive social relationships with others, and exhibit more trust (Bosmans & Kerns, 2015; Seibert & Kerns, 2009). When children perceive hostility from their primary caregivers, it is often associated with feelings of rejection (Khaleque & Rhoner, 2011; Rohner, 2004). Primary caregivers can provide warmth and encouragement using positive parenting or guidance techniques (Kirby & Hodges, 2018; Sanders & Morawska, 2018).

Families come in many forms. According to Pew Research (2015), living with two heterosexual parents has become less common in the previous few decades for US children, while living with two same-sex parents has become more common. Children in the United States also have fewer siblings than in years past. The birthrate has decreased, including fewer **full siblings** (share the same biological parents) but more **half siblings** (share only one biological parent) than in previous decades. Parents are less likely to be married and more likely to cohabitate than in previous generations (see Figure 12.9).

Because nearly 50% of marriages end in divorce, many children are raised by single parents, or blended families may form. Blended families include stepparents, stepchildren, and stepsiblings. Stepchildren are minors whose biological or adoptive parent marries someone who is not their birth parent. A child's stepparent is someone who married the

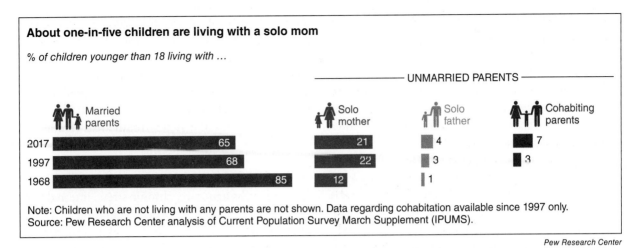

Figure 12.9 The number of children in the United States who live with married parents continues to decrease, while the percentage of children living with unmarried, cohabiting parents increases.

child's legal parent. Blended families may include stepsiblings, children who are not biologically related but are related through their parent and stepparent's marriage.

The likelihood of living in poverty is significantly lower for children living in married two-parent living arrangements (Pew Research, 2018) (see Figure 12.10). As changes in the family structure occur, such as through death, divorce, or remarriage, changes in parent-child relationships will occur (Cherlin, 2009; Parker et al., 2015). According to the Pew Research Center (2018, children with less-educated parents are less likely to live in two-parent households. These changes have trended over the past 60 years, and the United States now has the highest rate of children living in single-parent households than any other country (Kramer, 2021; Pew Research, 2015).

With family structural changes occurring over the past several decades, it became far less common for children to have one primary caregiver who stayed home caring for the family. However, this trend has recently been changing in both single- and two-parent families; there are now more stay-at-home parents (US Department of Labor, 2021). Having a stay-at-home parent is associated with higher academic achievement in middle childhood and potentially lower family stress levels (Bettinger et al., 2014).

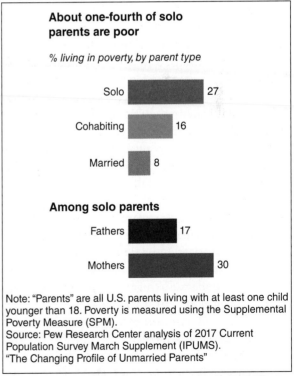

Figure 12.10 Poverty is more common for children living with a solo parent or cohabiting parents than for children living with married parents.

Nevertheless, the primary caregivers of most school-age children are now engaged in the outside labor force, either working remotely or on-site. Among more highly educated two-parent families, this has often resulted in more equal sharing of parenting duties and increased opportunities for extracurricular activities after-school. On the other hand, in lower socioeconomic situations, children whose parents work outside the home may experience added stress, especially when parents' working conditions are stressful. If parents hold multiple jobs or work night hours, quality time together may be minimized, and time spent with other adults such as teachers and out-of-school caregivers may increase (Parker et al., 2015).

Sometimes situations arise when children must live with and be cared for by people who are not the child's primary caregivers or extended family. In the United States, foster care is a temporary service provided by individual states for children who cannot live with their families. Between 2009 and 2019, the number of US children in foster care remained stable. The lack of increase was likely due to more children being reunited with primary caregivers or placed with extended family members such as grandparents, adult siblings, or aunts and uncles than placed in state foster care. During this same period, the percentage of White, Hispanic, and multiracial children entering foster care increased while the rates of Black children decreased (Child Welfare Information Gateway, 2021). The most common age of a child entering foster care is between ages 6 and 7, and children remain in foster care for about 20 months on average (US Department of Health and Human Services, 2020).

Children living in foster care often face several challenges. Placements may require them to change neighborhoods and schools. They may leave primary caregivers and friends, and they sometimes are separated from siblings. These challenges place children at risk for academic struggles and mental health issues (Gypen et al., 2017). As children age, they are more at risk for criminal justice involvement and substance abuse (Fawley-King et al., 2017). However, if children are in contact with their biological parents while in foster care, the distress lessens (Boyle, 2017).

Besides the upheaval of changing home environments, many children in foster care have experienced abuse or neglect and carry the effects of the trauma. As discussed in Chapter 7, the effect of adverse trauma is both immediate and long-term in the health and well-being of children. Children who experience trauma may have life-long altered brain architecture that changes the structure, function, and connectivity of different brain areas (Danese & Lewis, 2017; McCrory et al., 2017).

Resilience

In any family structure, chronic stress, internal conflict, or lack of support when separation or family changes occur will negatively affect how a child adjusts (Brown et al., 2015; Cicchetti, 2016; Southwick, et al., 2011). Many early studies proposed that children who experienced parental divorce, remarriage, changing cohabitation relationships, or single parenthood were at a greater risk for mental health and behavioral issues. More recent studies support the resiliency of children to withstand changes (Ager, 2013; Greene et al., 2012; Walsh, 2016). According to Harvard University's Center on the Developing Child (2020), the single most significant factor impacting a child's resilience, the ability to overcome adversity, is having at least one stable and committed relationship with a supportive parent, guardian, caregiver, or other adult who offers them security and stability. In contrast, children who lack a stable relationship with a primary caregiver may experience instability or a sense of household chaos or disorganization (Garrett-Peters et al., 2016; Hong et al., 2021; Marsh et al., 2020).

Failure to form a secure emotional bond with a primary caregiver may be the result of numerous factors. These include authoritative parenting styles, parental mental health issues such as depression or anxiety, and verbal or physical conflict, all of which have the most negative developmental effect on children (Brown et al., 2015; Helton & Smith, 2013). They also represent risk factors that increase the chances that a child may experience adverse childhood experiences (ACEs).

Children vary in the way they react to trauma and adverse experiences. Sometimes children demonstrate resiliency to adverse conditions due to protective factors. **Protective factors** include characteristics that make positive outcomes more likely for children and reduce the likelihood of adverse childhood experiences (ACEs), such as abuse or neglect.

Examples of protective factors might include living with a parent who meets the child's basic needs of food, shelter, and health; living in a family where adults show an interest in the child; and living in a safe community (see Figure 12.11). It is important to note that these factors do not place blame on the child but instead give insight into why children may differ in how adverse experiences affect them. Protective factors are related to a child's temperament and skills but, most importantly, to the family and community supports or resources that accentuate their strengths while also recognizing areas where they need support (see Table 12.2) (Child Welfare Gateway, 2020; Dixon et al., 2017; Statman-Weil, 2020).

Children who lack strong connections with primary caregivers may lead them to seek out peers for emotional support. However, if children prematurely rely on peers for attachment and security, they may experience poorer social outcomes, such as lack of focus, lower levels of self-regulation, or anxiety and other mental health issues as they progress through middle childhood and adolescence (Allen, 2008; Khaleque & Rhoner, 2011).

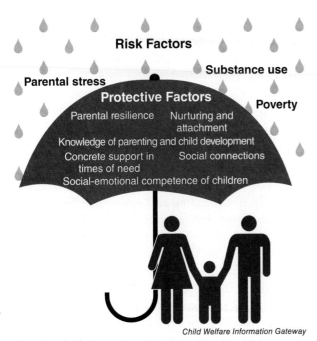

Child Welfare Information Gateway

Figure 12.11 Protective factors may serve as a covering or deterrent to environmental risk factors for adverse childhood experiences such as parental stress, substance abuse, or poverty. *What other risk factors might you add?*

Parenting Styles

As described in Chapter 9, primary caregivers offer warmth and encouragement in secure parent-child relationships. Caregivers demonstrate warmth through many behaviors, such as being emotionally available, responding to a child's needs, and taking an interest in a child's activities. Mutual trust is a crucial factor in secure parent-child relationships (Bosmans, 2015). Warmth and friendliness (low hostility) also play essential roles; children, especially girls, who experience warmth in these relationships may exhibit less depression in middle childhood or preadolescence (Hipwell et al., 2008; Pinquart, 2017; Rothernberg et al. 2020). At the same time, when children perceive hostility in these relationships, they may be more likely to be rule breakers later in childhood and adolescence (Trang & Tuppett, 2020). In a large global study on the impact of perceived parental warmth between parents and children, researchers found significant correlations between warmth, psychological adjustment, and overall mental health (Khaleque, 2013), including:

- positive self-esteem
- higher confidence
- higher emotional responsiveness
- appropriately increasing independence
- more emotional stability
- less hostility and aggression

Children who maintain close relationships with primary caregivers, especially when parents work together to make joint decisions, have many advantages. They also show more interest in exploring new and challenging situations even if the risk of failure is moderate to high (Burke et al., 2008; McHale et al., 2003). Strong parent-child relationships also positively affect peer relationships regarding ego resiliency and ego control, which are critical for forming peer relationships (Van den Berg et al., 2017). They are also associated with working memory and executive control functions (Devine et al., 2016; de Wilde et al., 2016; Lecce et al., 2020).

Relationships with Teachers

As in parent-child relationships, attachment may play an essential role in the relationships between children as students and their teachers (Verschueren, 2015).

Domain	Potential Risks for Trauma and ACEs	Potential Strengths or Protective Factors Reducing the Likelihood of Trauma and ACEs
Individual child protective factors	• Mental health issues such as anxiety, depression, low self-esteem • Attachment issues • Low social skills • Difficult temperament • Shyness • Behavioral issues/challenges • Self-regulation challenges • High need for approval from others	• High self-esteem • High academic achievement • High intelligence • Engagement with others through social relationships • Self-regulation skills • Coping skills • Problem-solving skills
Family protective factors	• Mental health issues in the household • Suicide or suicide attempts within the household • Inadequate or neglectful parenting; low supervision of children • Abuse or neglect within family • Housing and/or food instability • Substance abuse • Divorce • Financial crisis, unemployment	• Supportive relationships • Predictable routines and roles • Established rules and boundaries • Established and known values • Crisis coping skills and problem-solving
Community protective factors	• Community violence • High community crime • Peer rejection or bullying • Rejection from adults • Failing or unfunded schools	• Supportive and encouraging communities • Sense of community culture and belonging • Healthy school culture • Physical safety • Psychological safety • Community behavioral expectations • Shared religious identity

Kato

Table 12.2. Protective Factors, Risks, and Strengths by Domain

Attachment necessitates a responsiveness that builds trust. When children recognize and perceive responsiveness from their teachers, their social and academic performance improves (Brock et al., 2008; Pianta et al., 2003; Rimm-Kaufman et al., 2007). This attachment to a teacher may involve feeling encouraged, heard, and respected. As children spend more time in school classrooms, the impact of teacher-child relationships increases (Solomon et al., 2012).

The relationships between teachers and school-age children have long been a subject of fascination. They have been associated with early school adjustment and strong peer relationships (Urhahne, 2019; Wilder, 2014). In a large-scale study by the Gates Foundation (Cantrell & Kane, 2013), effective teachers, as partially measured in strong teacher-child relationships, were seen to have more effect on children's academic success than any other relationship in the children's lives. For example, good teacher-child relationships positively affect reading and prosocial skills. Positive child-teacher-parent relationships strongly impact academic success. These relationships may even affect future economic success (Chetty et al., 2014; Rimm-Kaufman et al., 2007).

Although the responsibility for creating positive teacher-child relationships is firmly on the teacher, characteristics of school-age children may also play a part. For example, more problematic behaviors at home and extenuating internal issues, such as emotional or learning challenges, may negatively affect teacher-child relationships (Henricsson & Rydell, 2004; O'Connor et al., 2012). Gender may also play a part, as girls are more likely than boys to have closer relationships with their teachers (Baker, 2006; Hughes et al., 2001; Williford et al., 2013). In addition, girls are often more affected by negative relationships or conflicts with their teacher than boys, especially negatively impacting academics (Curby et al., 2009). Overall, a teacher's effect on children's growth and development is significant (Rimm-Kaufman & Chiu, 2007). Teachers can do many things to create positive teacher-child relationships in the school setting, including (Rimm-Kaufman, 2010):

- demonstrating enjoyment and positivity in interacting with the child
- exhibiting responsive and respectful interactions
- establishing familiarity with the child's background, interests, strengths, and challenges
- offering encouragement, help, and support to a child
- avoiding showing irritability or frustration with the child
- encouraging the development and use of SEL skills in all relationships
- giving meaningful feedback

There are many practical ways that both primary caregivers and teachers can model or directly teach SEL skills during middle childhood. For example, they can coach children on-the-spot as they encounter new or challenging experiences. Or they might carefully select and provide access to educational materials such as books, activities, and media that support SEL (Jones et al., 2017b; McClelland et al., 2017). When parents, teachers, or other caregivers mutually agree on appropriate social behaviors and also provide direct instruction, cues, encouragement, and modeling, children improve their social skills over time (see Figure 12.12). The positive effect of these efforts on the child, family, classroom, school, neighborhood, and society are significant (Duckworth & Yeager, 2015; Dweck, 2016; Jones et al., 2017a).

☑ CHECKPOINT

- ☐ How does the perception of parental warmth or hostility affect a child?
- ☐ In what areas of development do teachers affect children most?
- ☐ Describe specific ways that teachers might influence positive teacher-student relationships.

MBI/Shutterstock.com

Figure 12.12 Educators can model appropriate social behaviors and provide encouragement. Do you remember a favorite teacher from your elementary school days who went beyond imparting knowledge and who modeled social behaviors or attitudes?

Apply Here!

Parents and teachers play vital roles in a child's socioemotional development. Consider the following socioemotional attributes. How might parents and teachers encourage these traits? Give five bulleted ideas/activities/practices that parents could use in developing these traits in their children. Note that most will be repeated and practiced over time.

1. Positive self-esteem
2. Higher confidence
3. Higher emotional responsiveness
4. Appropriately increasing independence
5. More emotional stability
6. Less hostility and aggression

12.4 Relationships with Siblings

For many children, siblings are a significant part of their lives. Sibling relationships are a common experience during middle childhood, but these relationships are also some of the longest continuous relationships children will experience in their lifetimes (Knop, 2020).

New siblings may enter the life of a school-age child when siblings are born, adopted, or fostered into the family. As families change over time, new stepsiblings might enter the family structure. Sometimes siblings are lost through family changes, transitions, or death. With each change, new dynamics form. The youngest sibling may become an older sibling. An only child may become a sibling. Roles, expectations, power, and even physical well-being may change when siblings are gained or lost but also as siblings mature and develop. For example, in an extensive study on the impact of sibling death on the remaining child, an increased risk of all-cause death (death from any cause) was found, especially among siblings who were close in age or the same sex (Yu et al., 2017).

Parents play a significant role in helping children learn how to have positive sibling relationships (Buist et al., 2013; Gamble & Yu, 2014; Modry-Mandell et al., 2007). Parents also influence sibling relationships when they indirectly serve as models in family relationships, positively and negatively affecting sibling relationships (Whiteman et al., 2011).

Sibling relationships are powerful factors in children's socioemotional development (see Figure 12.13). Good quality relationships can provide children with a way of learning social skills (Downey & Condron 2004; Howe & Recchia, 2014; Waid et al., 2020). For example, engaging in pretend play helps siblings build social competence in the early years of middle childhood as they try out different fictional roles (Howe & Bruno, 2010). Siblings may also provide emotional support to each other. Children learn to understand and control their own emotions and learn to better understand the emotions of others through sibling relationships (Kramer, 2014). When there is high warmth demonstrated between siblings, there is a greater likelihood that both siblings will follow similar life outcomes, such as attending college (Sun et al., 2019). Although a long-held assumption considered older siblings and primary caregivers as the primary socializing influences on younger children, recent research shows the influence is two-way. Younger siblings are an important socializing factor for older siblings, too, especially regarding learning empathy skills (Jambon et al., 2018). For example, an older sibling might remember what it felt like to be excluded because they were "too young" and be empathic to their younger sibling having the same experience.

Siblings can also negatively affect each other in power relationships, teasing, or even bullying (Wolke et al., 2015). **Bullying** is repeated aggressive behavior inflicted by someone who holds perceived power over the other. It is known to cause psychological and social damage, although it appears to be a common part of family practices within US culture (Eriksen & Jensen, 2009; Skinner & Kowalski, 2013; Wolke et al., 2015). Approximately half of children report bullying from siblings, and most say that it occurs in front of primary caregivers (Wolke et al., 2015).

Children who are excessively bullied, or bullied more than three times per week, by siblings were twice as likely to struggle with mental health issues such as depression or anxiety. They were also more likely to engage in self-harm practices in their teens than their non-bullied peers (Bowes et al., 2014). This is especially true for children with developmental disabilities who are bullied by siblings (Toseeb et al., 2018; Tucker et al., 2017). The negative behavior of one sibling may also serve as a model for other siblings. For example, when a child demonstrates antisocial, deviant, or risky behaviors, their sibling is more likely to follow suit and behave similarly. Sibling influence on negative behaviors may be even more influential than genetics, parents, or peers (Laursen et al., 2016; Waid et al., 2020).

The characteristics of each sibling may play a part in the relationship dynamics as well. For example, in an extensive review of literature, O'Brien et al. (2009) found that children who have siblings with chronic health or developmental issues may be significantly impacted. Children with a sibling who has

Alena Ozerova/Shutterstock.com

Figure 12.13 Sibling relationships can be positive or negative factors in socioemotional development.

Down syndrome tended to adjust well to living with their sibling; they even demonstrated more empathy toward others. However, their conclusions offered conflicting information on the adjustment of siblings of children with cancer and autism. In another large international study, about 8% of children who had siblings with disabilities suffered from mental health disorders possibly caused by greater psychological stress to the family (Caliendo et al., 2020).

Sibling relationships share a unique intimacy during childhood as their lives often follow similar paths, including the availability of social-economic resources, life experiences, and family expectations (Brody & Stoneman, 1987; Campione-Barr & Killoren, 2015). Children learn how to communicate emotions through sibling relationships, although sometimes it is through highly charged interactions that yield conflict (Abuhatoum & Howe, 2013; Carpendale & Lewis, 2004). Jealousy between siblings is far from uncommon as they often vie for similar resources and have a need for control (Howe et al., 2003; Meunier et al., 2012; Richmond et al., 2005). Sometimes the control is directed at relationships with primary caregivers. Other times perceived parental favoritism between siblings is a source of conflict (Brody & Stoneman, 1987; Meunier et al., 2012; Ross & Lazinki, 2014).

☑ CHECKPOINT

☐ What role do siblings play in a child's socioemotional development? Do you think there are potential benefits or drawbacks to being an only child?

☐ What are the known benefits of having strong sibling relationships during middle childhood? What might be some negative effects of negative sibling relationships?

☐ How may sibling relationships change based on each sibling's development, individual needs, and characteristics?

Apply Here!

List and describe how a child's relationship with siblings may both positively and negatively affect socioemotional development. How should parents having this knowledge respond? What role should parents play in enhancing positive relationships between siblings?

12.5 Relationships with Peers

Around ages 6 to 7, friends are often defined as playmates, and children form ties with peers who share interests or play styles. For example, two children may share an interest in collecting the same trading cards. As children mature, they increasingly view their peers as important sources of closeness or intimacy and companionship. Girls in middle childhood report intimacy and sharing confidences as an essential part of peer friendships (Erdley & Day, 2017; Erwin, 2013). As this happens, friendships sometimes develop between pairs or groups. Although family influence on peer interactions and friendship formation continues, the effect lessens as children increasingly learn to participate in the give and take of power and status within peer relationships (Hruschka, 2010; Marcone et al., 2015; Rawlins, 1992).

As in other life stages, children consider others to be friends when they perceive positive feelings for one another. Positive emotions may evolve from parallels in background, such as ethnicity, neighborhoods, or similarities in interests or skills (Erdley & Day, 2017; Erwin, 2013). Children interested in sports may be attracted to other children interested in sports. Children are also most often attracted to others who look or act like them or whom they aspire to be like. As children mature, the concept of friendship changes from "someone I play with" to "someone I can share my thoughts with or count on." Although definitions of friendships may change as children mature, they continue to want friendships that provide positive experiences (Bagwell & Schmidt, 2011). Children learn social norms and practice SEL skills, such as appropriate self-regulation and social awareness, within peer relationships.

The perks that come from having peer relationships or friendships are significant. Peer relationships help children feel connected to others who share their age and many life experiences. It creates a sense of group belonging, sometimes referred to as peer culture (see Figure 12.14) (Baumeister & Leary, 1995). Studies show that children who have at least one other peer accepting them show more positive internal mental health, including higher self-confidence, less anxiety and depression, and less loneliness (Devine & Apperly, 2021; Jiang

MBI/Shutterstock.com

Figure 12.14 Peer relationships are important to socioemotional development in middle childhood.
What are some specific things that children learn from each other?

et al., 2015). When children feel better about themselves, they exhibit more prosocial behavior and connectedness. Children who feel connected are less likely to be bullied and are happier in general. In essence, peer relationships can provide a protective social factor. These benefits extend into adolescence (Kendrick et al., 2012; Van Lier & Koot, 2010).

Peer relationships can exist within larger social environments, such as in a school, classroom, or on a team. Peer relationships also include small groups and **dyads**, or two-person relationships. Peer acceptance, status, and ranking are essential factors in peer relationships. Some children are better liked than others. They are picked to be partners in class projects or on teams. However, even less socially popular children benefit from two-person, or **dyad friendships** that demonstrate **reciprocity**, meaning the friends are mutually dependent and reliant on each other. Dyad friendships result in higher perceived self-worth and higher friendship quality, including mutual respect, warmth, and trust (Bagwell & Schmidt, 2011; Maunder & Monks, 2019). Dyad friendships can predict how positively a child feels toward the larger social group (Rudolph et al., 1995; Zimmer-Gembeck et al., 2010). Peer acceptance also predicts more positive attitudes toward and engagement in school (Betts et al., 2012; Boulton et al., 2011).

On the other hand, peer relationships can affect children negatively when rejection or unhealthy relationships occur. Failure to connect with peers also has adverse effects on a child's socioemotional development, including lower self-esteem and higher degrees of reported loneliness (Lafko et al., 2015; Laursen et al., 2007; Wang et al., 2018). When low peer interaction is related to a lack of SEL skills, interventions can be effective in helping children develop reciprocal peer relationships. When low peer interaction comes from peer rejection, the impact can be significant. Bullying may also be a result (Jiang et al., 2015; Sakyi et al., 2015).

Choosing inappropriate friends can be detrimental to a child's well-being. Numerous studies show that negative peer relationships correlate with delinquent, oppositional, and rule- or law-breaking behaviors that extend into adolescence and beyond (Coie & Miller-Johnson, 2001; Decker & Van Winkle, 1996). The positive effects of peer relationships and group participation may be offset or nullified by deviant peer influences (Guilford-Smith, et al., 2005). In addition, conflict in friendships, sometimes because of power differentials and peer pressure to engage in harmful behaviors, is associated with self-reported school stress during middle childhood (Wang & Fletcher, 2017). Peer pressure is especially strong when it includes temptations to deviate from conventional norms (Killen et al., 2013).

As children get closer to adolescence, social issues such as friendship conflicts and academic challenges may promote an increasing reliance on peers for support and less on parents (Vandevivere et al., 2015). Although children may rely less on parents for help in peer struggles, they may continue to seek out parent relationships for comfort and security in stressful situations. Overall, middle childhood is a crucial stage for learning how to build relationships with peers. Not developing peer relationship skills may result in rejection, victimization, friendlessness, and social isolation (Betts et al., 2012; Schwartz et al., 2015). Learning to have high-quality peer relationships during middle childhood may be an indicator of broader SEL skills that affect the quality of life through adulthood (Fink et al., 2015; Lecce et al., 2020).

Global Perspectives

The Power of Bullying

Bullying is not a new phenomenon; it has been around for generations as a part of the childhood and adolescence experience. Traditionally, bullying includes aggressive dominance as shown in physical, mental, or verbal intimidation or threats that result in fear and insecurity for the receiver. In more recent times, bullying also includes aggressive behaviors or defamation using social media or other digital means, referred to as **cyberbullying**. This includes posting unwanted statements about a person or posting unwelcome or false images with the intent to harm. According to the US Department of Health and Human Services (2017), the effects of bullying include increased depression and anxiety, substance abuse, suicidal thoughts or actions, and subsequently, lower academic achievement and earning potential (Copeland et al., 2013; Wolke et al., 2013).

Childhood bullying is a global concern (United Nations, 2016). However, according to the National Institutes of Health (2020), reported bullying among US children and teens has decreased slightly over the past two decades. This decline may be due to increased emphasis on socioemotional learning in schools, including learning how to show empathy and respect for others. Even so, more than one in five US children and teens report being actively bullied by siblings, peers, and others.

Who are the bully-victims? Research identifies them as children who have lower social capital or power, lack self-confidence or social skills, and stand apart from their peers in any way or form. This is termed **stigma bullying**.

For example, in a large US study of bullying, over one-third of teens who identify as lesbian, gay, or bisexual reported being bullied (The National Institute of Health, 2020). In middle childhood, bullying may include homophobic language and name-calling (Darwich et al., 2012; Kann et al., 2016). Another predominant form of stigma bullying centers on race and ethnicity and socioeconomic status (Pascoe & Smart-Richman, 2009; Williams & Mohammed, 2009). Adults often counsel children to ignore the bullying, fight back, or work to fit in better with their peers. However, newer research shows that these actions may be ineffective. Instead, strategies now emphasize stopping the bully's behavior (Cook et al., 2010). Programs that prove to be the most effective in stopping bullying involve the whole school and community focusing on cultural change (Swartz, 2016).

Why do children bully, and what is its impact? Children who bully are seeking dominance (Dodge et al., 2006). They are often well-connected within the peer community and may hold legitimate power (Guerra et al., 2011). Some have been exposed themselves to domestic violence and bullying by primary caregivers or family members against others (Baldry, 2003). But the negative impact is clear. Bullying impedes the socioemotional development of the receiver and the bully alike (Rodkin & Espelage, 2015). It also negatively affects any observers' physical and mental health over time and affects their sense of safety and security (Gini & Pozzoli, 2009; Rivers et al., 2009; Rosenthal et al., 2015).

☑CHECKPOINT

- ☐ What role do peers play in a child's socioemotional development?
- ☐ Why are positive relationships important to a young child's development? How do poor peer relationships affect school-age children?
- ☐ What role does peer pressure play in negative peer relationships? What are the long-term effects?
- ☐ What are the different forms of bullying? Discuss some strategies to counteract bullying.

Apply Here!

Create a series of infographics, memes, or other illustrative forms to communicate friendship skills to school-age children. These can be communicated in print or digital formats. Consider the following:

- the specific age group or grade targeted and why
- the appropriate and typical peer-related issues to address
- positive ways to communicate friendship skill building
- problem-solving or conflict resolution skills
- icebreaker ideas
- ways to nurture friendships

12.6 Moral Development

By the time children enter the school-age years, they can recognize how their actions affect others. Termed **moral agency**, children begin to understand how their intentions may be justified or mitigated by extenuating circumstances. In middle childhood, moral reasoning goes through significant development, especially concerning others. As their social relationships expand, they encounter more situations that require them to make morally right or wrong decisions, show compassion, and demonstrate empathy. As children become more independent, they face questions such as, "Should I break the rules even though no one else can see me? Who am I responsible for in my actions and behaviors—just myself or also the needs of others? How should I respond when I see injustice?" The process of children learning what is considered culturally right or wrong is a subject that has intrigued researchers for years (Bosacki, 2016; Jensen, 2015).

As you learned in Chapter 9, Jean Piaget (1932) included moral development in his stages of cognitive development. Lawrence Kohlberg (1981) further developed his foundational work. According to Kohlberg's theory of moral development, younger school-age children (ages 6 to 7) respond to rewards and punishments instead of making moral decisions. In Kohlberg's first level of moral development, preconventional morality, children may demonstrate prosocial behaviors to avoid punishment, not because they are motivated by a sense of caring or morals. Kohlberg theorized that children could tell the difference between right and wrong by age 8 or 9, and they start to care more about doing what is morally right. However, their judgment is still often based on potential rewards and punishments rather than universal moral truths or family values.

By ages 10 to 11, children enter the **conventional reasoning** stage, when social relationships, rules, and conformity become more critical. They often seek others' approval when making moral decisions that have a social impact. Having a reputation of being a "good person" becomes increasingly important and a driver in publicly demonstrating prosocial behaviors. Rules and laws become important as children strive to maintain group social order. They begin to make decisions based on how they would like others to treat them (Gibbs, 2014).

In early childhood, young children learn that it is possible to deceive another person by telling a lie or being dishonest. Toward the end of early childhood, children begin to understand the social conventions around honesty, especially if primary caregivers and other family members model them (Gingo, 2017; Lee, 2013). Punitive measures to discourage lying tend to have the opposite effect. They can enhance or encourage deceptive behaviors as children attempt to avoid punishment (Talwar & Lee, 2011).

By middle childhood, the concept of honesty may become more complex (Jambon & Smetana, 2014). On the one hand, older children understand the difference between telling the truth and lying. The vast majority publicly denounce the behavior, saying it is wrong to lie (Talwar & Lee, 2011). However, school-age children also begin to understand and practice the art of intentional acts of deception. For example, they begin to leave out information if it serves them, especially when doing so is meant to protect the feelings of their primary caregivers, teachers, or even siblings and peers (Carl & Bussey, 2019; Ding et al., 2014; Gingo, 2017). In the school environment, studies show that making an honesty pact with students that outlines behavioral expectations reduces cheating and other forms of dishonesty (Heyman et al., 2015).

Practicing moral behavior necessitates the presence of SEL skills, including personal awareness, social awareness, and a desire to be in social relationships. Carol Gilligan's **care perspective** theory of moral decision-making focuses on the attention to and nurturing of others (Gilligan, 1982; Gilligan, 1988; Skuse et al., 2017). Concerns for social conventions such as justice and care for others and the child's perceived role or responsibility in social relationships also play a part in developing a sense of **civic duty**. This is a sense of one's obligation and responsibility toward others, even if the actions are not reciprocated (see Figure 12.15) (Crocetti et al., 2012; Gibbs, 2014; Nucci, 2013). In middle childhood, children become better able to show care and compassion, altruism, and justice (Gibbs, 2014).

Theorists tend to use a whole child view of moral decision-making that involves children's cognition, emotions, goals, and environmental contexts (Lansford et al., 2021a; Vozzola, 2014). Many researchers have conducted studies to further understand the complexity of contributing factors such as

Rawpixel.com/Shutterstock.com

Figure 12.15 Children may show concern for their community and care for others by participating in community service.

environmental and individual attributes. For example, research notes a modest association between religious involvement and moral development. Religious practices and traditions model and teach children ethical behaviors. However, an individual child's actions may have more to do with their personal attributes, such as perfectionism, than their moral development (De Souza, 2014; Flett & Hewitt, 2014). Sex may also play a part in moral behavior, as girls tend to demonstrate compassion or nurturing behaviors earlier than boys. However, determining whether this difference is due to socialization or brain biology is complex (Hyde, 2014).

Recent research has also focused on brain structure and maturation as precursors to moral behavior (Decety & Cowell, 2018; Wildeboer et al., 2018). An interesting focus has been on mirror neurons, those brain connections that respond to or "mirror" another person's emotional experience (Rizzolatti & Fabbri-Destro, 2008; Waters & Tucker, 2013). When a child observes someone doing something kind, generous, or empathic, mirror neurons may respond by mimicking the same emotions and subsequent behaviors (Amodio & Ratner, 2013). The exact areas of the brain that empower this activity are still being debated (Wellman, 2014).

☑ CHECKPOINT

☐ According to Kohlberg, in which stages of moral development are school-age children? Describe these stages.

☐ What insights have more recent moral development theorists contributed?

☐ How has more recent brain structure knowledge contributed toward understanding moral development in middle childhood?

Apply Here!

Charlie, a 7-year-old in your care, reported that several personal things were missing, including a coat, colored pencils, and new glue stick. Consider the following:

- Are you dealing with a classroom theft issue?
- What other potential reasons might there be for the items to be missing?
- How might your suspicions be supported by what you know about middle childhood cognitive and socioemotional development? Be specific.
- How might you go about unraveling the mystery?
- Should this be a problem to solve with Charlie or with the whole group/class of children? Why?

Practical Issues and Implications

Why So Sexy So Soon?

Do young girls grow up too quickly? Is the display of sexualized behaviors, idealized body image, and appearance concerns growing? Is it the result of an onslaught of sexualized media images and messaging? Some think so. Both the American Psychological Association's *Report of the APA Task Force on the Sexualization of Girls* (2007) and the UK Government Report, *Letting Children be Children* (Bailey, 2011), emphasize media as a significant contributing environmental factor that encourages body objectification of young girls. Although the reports found that objectification also affects boys, the number of boys involved is far fewer (Lamb & Koven, 2019). These influences start early in Western culture through models that promote stereotypical standards of beauty and body ideals (Slater & Tiggemann, 2016; Slater et al., 2017).

The media, in its various forms, exposes children to sexualized messaging. In the United States, media use is high. According to the Pew Research Center (2015), 9 out of 10 parents with children ages 6 to 17 say their kids watch online videos, stream movies, or play videos every day and often for extended periods (see Figure 12.16). Consumer products directed at younger audiences may also be contributors. These include toys, classic fairy tale books, video games, and all forms of messaging that encourage the sexualization and objectification of girls (Rice et al., 2016; Smolak & Murnen, 2011).

In addition to media, other negative influences may exist in the home and among close relationships. Parents, siblings, teachers, peers, coaches, and others may also play a part in young girls learning to objectify themselves. For example, a peer group may focus on dieting or comparing their physical traits with others. Or adults may pay more subtle attention to a child's appearance-related characteristics and show disapproval if the child falls outside of the ideal (Collins et al., 2017; Hart et al., 2014).

Mothers may also affect a child's self-image. Research shows that when mothers strive to achieve cultural ideals of beauty or display sexualized behaviors, their daughters notice and may model this behavior. As a result, daughters are likewise more concerned about achieving their own idealized and sexualized appearance cues. Focusing on material goods and services related to beauty also increases girls' interest in sexualized self-images (Slater & Tiggemann, 2016a).

Why does it matter? Developmentally, the early objectification of girls has negative consequences. These include disordered eating, early sexual behaviors, depression, negative comparisons to peers, and increased interest in cosmetic surgery (Anschutz et al., 2012; Collins et al., 2017). School-age girls (and boys) are not cognitively prepared to evaluate messages from the media or their social relationships critically. Children are particularly vulnerable to these messages as they actively form their self-identity, including gender identity and social roles. For example, social media can positively influence children's self-perception by creating a constructive self-image. It can also influence children negatively through self-objectification, body dissatisfaction, and body shame (Pacilli et al., 2019; Slater & Tiggeman, 2016b). When girls internalize sexualization and objectification, they may self-limit their aspirations and goals (Slater et al., 2017; Tzampazi et al., 2013). Yet, media literacy interventions and lessons often begin in middle school

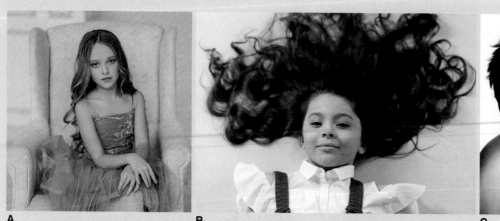

A   B   C

jozzeppe/iStock via Getty Images Plus; Just dance/Shutterstock.com; Ixepop/Shutterstock.com

Figure 12.16 Do these images appear sexualized to you? If so, how? If not, why not?

or high school rather than in early and middle childhood (Watson & Vaughn, 2006; Lamb & Koven, 2019).

To Think About:

- Do you believe social media has influenced the objectification of girls? If so, how?

- Should media literacy intervention strategies occur sooner in early to middle childhood? Are children able to comprehend and exercise judgment or discernment?

Summary

Children's social lives expand as they strive to figure out who they are, what roles they play, and how their lives matter during middle childhood. They may spend more time away from family, and new relationships with others outside the home influence how they view themselves. As their social lives expand, their thought processes become more rational. They try to figure out how people and things work as they become more self-aware and conscious of others' feelings.

The school-age years can bring abundant new and complex experiences. As a result, children may feel overwhelmed by the tasks and expectations. Improving cognitive and socioemotional skills allow them to complete more complex tasks and organize responsibilities. They have a greater ability to accurately assess their strengths, limitations, roles, and influence over others. This may result in better self-regulation, confidence, and self-efficacy. Throughout this stage, children learn to recognize how their actions affect family members, peers, teachers, and others. They discover how extenuating circumstances might justify or mitigate their intentions. The school years of middle childhood prepare children physically, cognitively, and socioemotionally to move into the next stage of life—adolescence.

Learning Outcomes and Key Concepts

12.1   Analyze the socioemotional theories related to learning in middle childhood.

- Socioemotional development affects a child's overall well-being as it sets the stage for all social interactions, positive or deviant social behaviors, and mental health throughout life.
- During middle childhood, children begin to learn how to do things for themselves, leading to a sense of confidence, or self-efficacy.
- Industry versus inferiority is Erikson's fourth stage of socioemotional development, when children face the task of feeling competent or incompetent.
- Learning new tasks requires motivation, emotional self-regulation, a sense of self, focus, and executive functioning skills.

12.2   Explain how socioemotional learning influences physical and cognitive development and academic success.

- Improving cognitive skills allows children to complete more complex tasks, organize responsibilities, and participate in social groups.
- Socioemotional development includes gaining the social and emotional skills required to integrate with others within families, schools, and other social relationships.
- Social-emotional learning (SEL) is a critical part of socioemotional development and includes developing self-awareness, self-regulation, and interpersonal skills.
- Self-awareness includes accurately assessing one's strengths and limitations, roles, and influence over self and others.
- Social awareness is associated with self-regulation, empathy, cooperation, sharing, and exercising self-regulation of emotions.
- Self-management helps children regulate their emotions, exhibit appropriate interactions with others, and accomplish tasks and goals.

12.3 Discuss how a school-age child's relationships with their primary caregivers and teachers influence their socioemotional development.

- Parents and caregivers remain the primary source of attachment during middle childhood. Even as children approach adolescence, they prefer parents over peers for support.
- Children who prematurely rely on peers for attachment and security may experience poorer social outcomes such as lack of focus, lower levels of self-regulation, or anxiety.
- Secure parent-child relationships include trust, warmth, and encouragement without hostility.
- Attachment plays a role in child-teacher relationships. Children with responsive teachers show improved social and academic performance.
- Strong teacher-child relationships may affect children's academic and future economic success more than any other relationship.
- A child's environment, such as problematic behaviors at home or extenuating issues, contributes to their relationships.

12.4 Identify ways in which a school-age child's relationship with siblings affects their socioemotional development.

- Sibling relationships are a common experience during middle childhood and are some of the longest continuous relationships children will experience in their lifetimes.
- Good quality sibling relationships are powerful factors in children's socioemotional development; they can be a source of learning social skills and of emotional support.
- Siblings can affect each other negatively, even more than genetics, parents, or peers, when a sibling demonstrates antisocial, deviant, or risky behaviors.
- Children learn to communicate emotions through sibling relationships as interactions may yield conflict, jealousy, power and control, or perceived parental favoritism.

12.5 Identify ways in which a school-age child's peer relationships affect their socioemotional development.

- Children learn social norms and practice appropriate self-regulation and social awareness within peer relationships.

- Parent-child relationships affect the formation of peer relationships, especially regarding a child's ego resiliency and ego control within a social context.
- Peer relationships help children feel connected, create a sense of group belonging, and influence more positive internal mental health.
- Being disconnected from peers may negatively affect children, causing increased anxiety, depression, lower self-esteem, and higher degrees of reported loneliness.

12.6 Describe moral developmental theory and milestones often achieved during middle childhood.

- Children can recognize how their actions affect others and how their intentions might be justified or mitigated by extenuating circumstances.
- According to Kohlberg, children's conformity to social relationships, rules, and expectations becomes essential when making moral decisions.
- Concerns for social conventions, such as justice and care, play a part in moral decision-making, including perceived duty, obligation, and responsibility toward others.
- When a child observes someone doing something kind, generous, or empathic, mirror neurons may respond by mimicking the same emotions and subsequent behaviors.

Chapter Review

1. If you were writing a blog about how socioemotional development affects a child's overall well-being in middle childhood and beyond, what would your main points be?

2. Name and describe Erikson's stages of socioemotional development in middle childhood. Provide two examples of how these stages might play out in a child's everyday activities.

3. How do school-age children's cognitive, social, and emotional development interact with their identity formation? How does one area inform the other? Give a life example.

4. During middle childhood, children begin to learn how to do things for themselves. How do they best learn? Why is it important for a child's overall well-being to learn to do things for themselves? Be specific.

5. Identify and describe the component parts of social-emotional learning (SEL). How might you model SEL when playing a game with a school-age child?

6. How do peer relationships rank in comparison to parent, sibling, and extended family relationships during early childhood? How is this information useful in understanding the behavioral motivations of school-age children?

7. If you were writing a newsletter for parents of school-age children, how might you describe a child's ability to make moral decisions? How might a parent help a child make moral decisions?

Matching

Match the following terms with the correct definitions.

A. moral agency

B. self-awareness

C. self-efficacy

D. self-management

E. social awareness

F. social-emotional learning

1. Confidence in oneself that proficiency in a situation is achievable and can yield favorable results

2. Also known as self-regulation

3. A sense of how moral actions and decision affect others

4. The process of developing self-awareness, self-regulation, and interpersonal skills needed to be effective in social relationships

5. A child's own assessment or view of self that includes personal identity and the perceived roles in a social situation

6. The ability to take the perspective of another person or group of people

MBI/Shutterstock.com

As children develop self-awareness, they also develop a sense of responsibility and begin to feel capable.

13

Adolescence: Physical Development

Learning Outcomes

After studying this chapter, you will be able to:

13.1 Outline how the onset of puberty begins the process toward adulthood and how these changes are continuous, sequential, and interrelated.

13.2 Describe the ways that teens grow and change physically.

13.3 Explain the relationship between the brain's physical changes and cognitive development in adolescence.

13.4 Summarize the importance of health and wellness in the teen years.

adolescence

adrenarche

androgens

asynchrony

circadian rhythms

estrogen

gonads

hormones

menarche

menstruation

opioids

pituitary gland

postpubescence

prepubescence

pubescence

sedentary

spermarche

testosterone

Introduction

Recall all the information you already know about the physical development of adolescents, either from your own lived experience or from observing others. Think back to when you were going through puberty. Did your peers experience it in the same way that you did? Were the physical and maturity growth differences stark or more subtle? Are there memories that make you cringe?

Adolescence is the stage in life when humans go through the transforming process of changing from children to adults. It is a time when teens are just starting to move toward the independence of young adulthood. The early teen years, ages 12 to 13, are followed by the middle teens, ages 14 to 16, and the later teens, ages 17 to 19. A 13-year-old in the 7th grade is profoundly different from a 17-year-old high school senior.

Except for infancy, the rate of physical growth and change in adolescence is unlike any other period in life. Changes occur in height, weight, muscle development, and secondary sexual characteristics. The brain also changes in form and function. Although all teens go through similar physical changes, no two teens have the same experiences or develop in the same way. Physical changes are the most apparent in early adolescence; but cognitive, social, and emotional changes are significant throughout adolescence. This chapter discusses the typical markers of the physical development process in adolescence, a process—as you will see—that is far from uneventful.

13.1 The Onset of Puberty

Puberty starts the physical transformation from a child to an adult capable of reproduction. Puberty is not synonymous with adolescence, however. Adolescence is a chronological stage of life, whereas puberty is the bodily transformation toward sexual maturity. Although the onset of adolescence at age 12 and puberty often coincide, the start of puberty does not define adolescence. Instead, timing varies among individuals. As you learned in Chapter 10, a child may start puberty in middle childhood (ages 10 or 11) or well into adolescence (Galvan, 2018; Kipke, 1999).

Puberty is a long, sequential process controlled by hormones and associated with changes in body shape and size, mood and behaviors, and cognitive processing. It is typically divided into three stages that include:

- **prepubescence**, when the body is preparing for the initial onset of puberty
- **pubescence**, when sex hormones increase, physical changes (primary and secondary sex characteristics) appear, and puberty is in process
- **postpubescence**, when puberty gradually subsides (McCormick & Scherer, 2018; Sisk & Romeo, 2020).

As discussed in Chapter 10, prepubescence often begins around age 8 for girls and ages 9 or 10 for boys, as the body prepares for its upcoming physical changes. The length of time between puberty's onset and sexual maturation varies based on many factors, including genetics and age at onset (Sisk & Romeo, 2020).

Puberty begins in both sexes when the hypothalamus in the brain starts to release gonadotropin-releasing hormone (GnRH) to the **pituitary gland**, located at the base of the brain. **Hormones** are chemical messengers released into the bloodstream that stimulate specific cells into action. GnRH stimulates the pituitary gland to secrete two puberty-inducing hormones, luteinizing hormone (LH) and follicle-stimulating hormone (FSH) (Best & Ban, 2021; Bordini & Rosenfield, 2011). LH and FSH circulate in the blood and cause the **gonads** (reproductive glands) to release a group of sex hormones called **androgens**. Androgens cause the reproductive organs to mature; they also cause the other physical changes of puberty. In addition to the gonads, the adrenal glands (located on the kidneys) also produce androgens. Adrenal androgen production begins at around age 8 in a stage called **adrenarche**. During adrenarche, children begin to grow pubic and underarm hair, and they sweat more, resulting in increased body odor (Best & Ban, 2021; Montemayor, 2019).

The hypothalamus, pituitary gland, and gonads are called the hypothalamic–pituitary–gonadal (HPG) axis when discussed as one entity. The HPG axis is responsible for a cascading release of sex hormones from the ovaries (female gonads) or the testes (male gonads) (Sisk & Romeo, 2020). Fluctuations or changes in one axis component affect the whole HPG axis.

While biological males and females produce androgens, males typically have higher levels than females. The testes produce the androgen **testosterone** and sperm (male reproductive cells). The ovaries produce androgens which are converted into a form of the hormone **estrogen**. The ovaries also produce the hormone progesterone and eggs (ovum, female reproductive cells). Males and females make both testosterone and estrogen, and the ratio varies by individual. When adolescents begin releasing testosterone and estrogen by way of the testes and ovaries, noticeable body changes occur. This stage of puberty

is gonadarche. During gonadarche, girls experience their first menstrual cycle, called **menarche**, and a boy experiences his first involuntary ejaculation of semen, or **spermarche**, typically nocturnally.

In girls, one of the first outward signs of puberty is breast development. Hair begins to grow in the pubic region and armpits. Menstruation eventually begins. **Menstruation** is the normal vaginal bleeding that occurs as part of a woman's monthly cycle when the uterus sheds its lining in the absence of a fertilized egg. When menstruation begins, the end of puberty for girls is near; bodies will continue to mature, however (Galván, 2018; Sisk & Romeo, 2020). For boys, the first outward signs of puberty include the penis and testicles growing larger, followed by hair growth in the pubic region and armpits. Muscle development, facial hair, and a deepening voice are also signs in boys. These outward puberty signs are often seen in girls between ages 10 and 14 and in boys between 12 and 16 (National Institutes of Health, 2019). Table 13.1 presents some additional physical changes that occur during puberty.

The age and timing of puberty varies by individual (see Figure 13.1). In most cultures, puberty now occurs at a younger age in the twentieth and twenty-first centuries than it did during the nineteenth century, occurring around age 10 instead of age 16 or 17 (Demerath et al., 2004; Klopack et al., 2020; Morris et al., 2011).

Biology influences physical maturation and growth patterns; children must be biologically

Prostock-studio/Shutterstock.com

Figure 13.1 The age of onset for puberty varies among adolescents.
Do you remember noticing the differences in physical development among peers when you were a young teen? How did that make you feel?

Physical Change	Girls	Boys
Typical onset	Most experience puberty between the ages of 9 and 13, usually before boys begin puberty.	Most experience puberty between the ages of 10 and 16.
Body shape	• Hips get wider. • Waist gets smaller. • Fat builds up in the stomach, buttocks, and legs. • The body develops a more curved shape. • Breasts grow in size and shape; this is often the first area of growth during puberty. • It may be necessary to begin wearing a bra.	• Shoulders grow broader. • Muscles get bigger. • The body gains more weight.
Body size	• Both boys and girls grow taller. • Arms, legs, hands, and feet may grow faster than rest of body. • Both boys and girls may feel clumsier because of these changes.	• Both boys and girls grow taller. • Arms, legs, hands, and feet may grow faster than rest of body. • Both boys and girls may feel clumsier because of these changes.
Hair	• Hair grows under the arms, on the legs, and in the pubic area. • Hair growth begins shortly after breast development. • Some may begin shaving legs and armpits.	• Hair grows under the arms, on the legs, and in the pubic area. • Chest hair may appear in some during puberty (or years later). • Some may begin shaving facial hair.
Skin	• Both boys' and girls' skin becomes oilier. • Their bodies will sweat more. • Acne or pimples may develop.	• Both boys' and girls' skin becomes oilier. • Their bodies will sweat more. • Acne or pimples may develop.
Other changes	Menstruation (period)	Penis
	• Menarche begins for most girls between the ages of 9 and 16. • Menstruation occurs monthly. It may start out on an irregular schedule, having a period one month and not the next; but it develops into a more regular schedule. • Most periods last from 3 to 7 days. • Many may feel discomfort before, during, or after a period.	• Penis and testicles get larger. • Boys may experience more erections (hardening of the penis). • The body will begin to produce sperm during puberty. **Voice** • Boys' voices become deeper. • Their voices may start cracking for a period of time.

American Academy of Pediatrics, 2014; Kowal-Connelly, 2019

Table 13.1 Puberty Physical Changes in Adolescence

ready for puberty to begin. Biological factors such as genetics, ethnicity, nutrition, and body fat percentage may play a part in its onset, timing, and duration. Genetic and ethnicity factors may be significant (Morris et al., 2011). In the United States, Black and Latinx girls start to menstruate earlier than White or Asian girls (Biro et al., 2018; Deardorff et al., 2014). Nutrition may also play a part in puberty's onset; children who eat high-fat diets or are obese may experience an earlier onset of puberty, especially girls (Cheng et al., 2010;

De Leonibus et al., 2014; Nokoff et al., 2019). Some studies have indicated that high activity levels as seen in high-level athletes may delay the onset (Kipke, 1999; Labe & Fuhrman, 2020; Middeldorp, 2020). Likewise, girls who are malnourished or lack proper nutrition experience delayed onset (Biro et al., 2018; Deardorff et al., 2014). Stress in early life also plays a role in the timing of puberty. Studies have associated stress with both precocious (early) puberty and delayed puberty (Maharaja, 2018; Sisk & Romeo, 2020).

☑ CHECKPOINT

☐ Define puberty. What initiates it?

☐ What are the three stages of puberty? What bodily changes occur at each stage?

☐ How does puberty differ between males and females regarding onset, timing, and body changes?

Sexual Maturity

As teens go through puberty in early to middle adolescence, their bodies continue to change and eventually reach sexual maturity. These physical changes are interwoven with cognitive and socioemotional changes that will be discussed in subsequent chapters. As adolescents are reaching physical sexual maturity earlier than in generations past, primary caregivers, educators, and society have become concerned about early sexual activity, or sexual activity initiated before the age of 16. Physical changes may place teens under undue pressure to participate in sexual activity, either from themselves or others. When sexual activity starts early, there is more time for unplanned pregnancies to occur, for exposure to sexually transmitted viruses and infections, and for increased vulnerability to sexual abuse (Sisk & Romeo, 2020; Tulloch & Kaufman, 2013).

Increased interest in sexual activity is a normal part of adolescence. Teens benefit from open conversations, education, and supportive scaffolding from adults when sexually maturity begins (Korem, 2019). Physiologically, hormonal levels and brain development contribute to an increased interest and desire to participate in sexual activities. Intimacy in relationships also increases when teens age (Pringle et al., 2017; Suleiman et al., 2015). Studies indicate that about half of teens, ages 15 to 19, report they have engaged in some form of sexual activity. In addition to vaginal-penile intercourse, this may include having oral and anal sex, viewing pornography, and participating in *sexting*, which means sending sexually explicit content through a smartphone or other technological device (Abma & Martinez, 2017; Sedgh et al., 2015). Because sexual maturity occurs before a teen's brain is fully developed, there may be a lag in judgment and increased risk-taking. Sexual activity can leave teens who are not socially or emotionally ready vulnerable to peer pressure and abuse (Pringle et al., 2017; Suleiman et al., 2017).

Pregnancy

Sexual intercourse is associated with consequences such as unplanned pregnancy, potential sexual abuse, and sexually transmitted diseases. In the

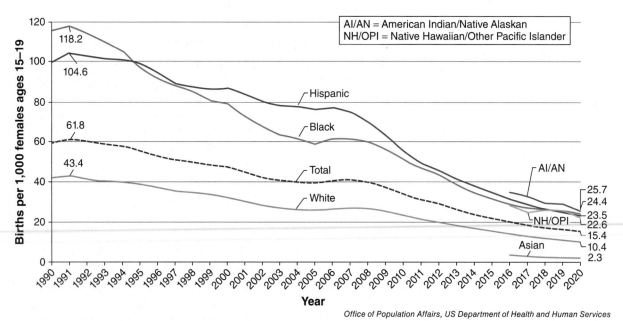

Office of Population Affairs, US Department of Health and Human Services

Figure 13.2 The chart shows the birth rates from 1990–2020 per 1,0000 females ages 15–19 in the United States and categorized by race or heritage.
What overarching societal trends may be influencing these decreases across population groups?

United States, across racial categories, teen pregnancies have decreased dramatically in the past two decades (see Figure 13.2). As described in Chapter 3, teen pregnancy may have adverse effects on both the teen mother and the baby. Teen mothers are more likely to give birth to low birthweight or preterm babies; they are also at a higher risk for eclampsia and other infections during pregnancy (Ferré et al., 2016; World Health Organization, 2016). Teen pregnancy may negatively impact the mother's health because she is still growing and developing herself; and the pregnancy results in fewer available nutrients for her own growth and development. Socially, teen pregnancies can negatively impact both teen mothers and fathers, if they remain involved. Teenage parents are less likely to graduate from high school. They may also have significantly lower earnings than their counterparts who begin having children in their twenties. For example, a teen parent may be under considerable stress from juggling school responsibilities, experiencing interrupted sleep from caring for the baby, financial concerns, and missing out on typical teen social activities because of parenting responsibilities. For teen mothers, these disparities extend into middle adulthood, which may lead to long-term health issues (US Department of Health and Human Services, 2021; Zajacova & Lawrence, 2018).

Contraception

Although reported teen sexual activity has decreased slightly in the last decade, the use of contraception may be the primary reason for the significant decline in teen pregnancy (Lindberg et al., 2018). Teen contraceptive use is high in the United States, with about 90% of teen girls and 94% of teen boys reporting its use during their most recent sexual intercourse (Witwer et al., 2018). The American College of Obstetricians and Gynecologists (2017) recommends that teens use any FDA-approved contraceptives. Besides condoms and prescription birth control pills, contraception methods include long-acting reversible contraception (LARC), such as intrauterine devices (IUDs) and implants. Teens use condoms most often, likely due to ease of use, access, cost, and confidentiality (Frost & Lindberg, 2019; Szucs et al., 2020). Teens who can discuss contraceptive measures with primary caregivers, health care providers, or other trusted adults are more likely to use contraception consistently. They are also less

likely to become pregnant or impregnate another (Amialchuk & Gerhardinger, 2015; Hasstedt, 2018). Contraception decreases the likelihood of pregnancy, and condoms can reduce the risk of sexually transmitted diseases.

Sexually Transmitted Diseases

Sexually transmitted diseases include both sexually transmitted infections (STIs), such as chlamydia infections, and sexually transmitted viruses (STVs), such as genital herpes simplex and human papillomavirus (HPV). Globally, STIs and STVs are particularly prevalent in the teen population (World Health Organization, 2021). In the United States, the incidence of diagnosed sexually transmitted infections and viruses has risen since 2014, with about half of the reported STIs diagnosed in teens (Shannon & Klausner, 2018; US Centers for Disease Control and Prevention, 2021b). Although teens make up approximately 50% of diagnosed STIs, teens represent only a quarter of the total population.

Rates and types of diseases vary greatly based on geographical areas of the United States. These differences are often attributed to differences in health care, the availability of health education, or the prevalence of risky sexual behaviors, such as unprotected sex or sex with multiple partners. Because of the potential long-term effects of STIs and STVs, medical care for infected teens is particularly important (see Table 13.2). Screening and medical management after diagnosis are essential to the health and welfare of teens. But concerns for confidentiality, a lack of knowledge, or lack of access to available screenings keep many teens from getting proper care (Jefferson et al., 2021; Matkins, 2013).

Sexual Abuse and Assault

According to the Rape, Abuse & Incest National Network (RAINN, 2021), teen girls ages 16 to 19 are four times more likely to be victims of rape, attempted rape, or sexual assault than females in other age groups. Teen males are victims, too, but at a much lower incidence rate. Teens with vulnerabilities, such as special needs or learning difficulties, may be particularly at risk for sexual exploitation (Child Welfare Information Gateway, 2018; Forsyth & Rogstad, 2015). Sexual abuse and assault may be

Sexually Transmitted Disease (STIs and STVs)	Possible Symptoms	Possible Treatment	Potential Long-Term Effects if Untreated
Chlamydia infection	Vaginal or penile discharge and burning with urination	Usually curable with regimens of antibiotics	May lead to pelvic inflammatory disease (PID), possible deadly ectopic pregnancies, and long-term infertility in both men and women; increases an individual's chance of getting or giving HIV
Genital herpes simplex virus (HSV)	Painful sores or ulcerations on the external genitalia and mouth	No known cure: antiviral medications can treat or prevent symptomatic recurrences	Lifelong condition that includes recurring episodes of symptoms
Gonorrhea infection	Vaginal or penile discharge and burning with urination	Usually curable with regimens of antibiotics; potential to become antibiotic resistant, however	May lead to pelvic inflammatory disease (PID), possible deadly ectopic pregnancies, and long-term infertility in both men and women; can spread to the blood or joints and become life-threatening; increases an individual's chance of getting or giving HIV
Human papillomavirus (HPV)	Often asymptomatic	Preventive vaccination; no known cure	Possible genital warts and cervical, vaginal, penile, or anal cancers
Syphilis infection	Lesions or rash on skin	Usually curable with regimens of antibiotics	Long-term concerns such as eye or brain damage; more stillbirths, preterm, and low birthweight babies in pregnancies
Human immunodeficiency virus (HIV) and acquired immunodeficiency syndrome (AIDS)	Spread by contact with an HIV-infected person through certain bodily fluids, unprotected sex, or sharing injection drug paraphernalia; no reliable HIV symptoms, diagnosis confirmed through testing	Antiretroviral therapy (ART) medication to prevent transmission and ensure longer and healthier life	Untreated, may lead to AIDS, which has no cure; lifespan after diagnosis typically short

Kato

Table 13.2 Why Medical Diagnosis and Treatment of STDs Matters

perpetrated by adults or peers, often in the context of personal, romantic relationships or what is called date rape. The behavior often includes bullying and harassment, either overtly or subtly, through repetitive requests or pleading invitations intended to "wear the victim down." Those who abuse are most often people within a teen's social framework, such as family members, family friends, and other familiar people (Edwards et al., 2017; Rape, Abuse & Incest National Network, 2021). Social media may render teens more vulnerable to sexual violence, breaking down social inhibitions and victim resistance (Maas et al., 2019; Sanderson & Weathers, 2020). There is often less adult supervision at a time when teens may have limited self-regulation and immature judgment skills.

The impact of sexual abuse on teens is long-lasting. Those who have been sexually abused are more likely to abuse drugs and experience post-traumatic stress disorder (PTSD) or depression as adults (Rape, Abuse & Incest National Network, 2021). Educators, parents, and other caregivers can play a critical role in teaching teens about sexual abuse and supporting those who are victims (Edwards et al., 2019). Educators, in particular, must be responsible bystanders. They must notice situations that may be problematic, assume responsibility to act, create a plan of action, and choose to intervene or act. Supportive bystander actions are associated with higher levels of trust between teens and caregivers, increased reporting, and more equity in reporting (Banyard, 2011, 2016; Edwards et al., 2017). In many US states, educators and other care professionals are considered mandatory reporters; they are required by law to report suspected abuse of minors.

☑ CHECKPOINT

☐ Name three sexually transmitted infections or diseases (STIs and STVs) and their potential long-term impact if left untreated.

☐ What are three risky outcomes associated with teen sexual activity?

☐ What may make teens particularly susceptible or vulnerable to risky sexual behaviors?

Apply Here!

Create an infographic for school-age children that describes the process of puberty, including expected bodily changes and timing.

Global Perspectives

The Physical Health and Well-Being of Teen Girls

According to the World Health Organization (2020), approximately 1 in 6 of the world's population are adolescents who, for the most part, are healthy. However, 90% of teens live in low- and middle-income countries where many health-related concerns are prevalent (UNICEF, 2020). For example, teens in these countries are more susceptible to infectious diseases like malaria, diarrheal diseases, and HIV/AIDS when compared to their counterparts in high-income countries. They are also often the least likely members of their communities to have access to treatment. Unprotected sex, sex with multiple partners, or sex with a partner who has other partners all increase HIV/AIDS infection susceptibility rates. Globally, adolescents are the only age group where HIV/AIDS is still rising (UNICEF, 2020).

HIV/AIDS and other sexually transmitted infections disproportionately affect teen girls (Kalamar et al., 2016). There are several possible explanations for this disparity. One is biological; the skin of the female vulva may be prone to tears and lacerations, creating access points for infections (Shannon & Klausner, 2018). Contributing social factors may include a greater likelihood of transactional sexual relationships between teenage girls and their sexual partners, sexual violence when lack of consent, or a sexual partner's nondisclosure of sexual history or health status (Dellar et al., 2015; Nankinga et al., 2016).

Teen pregnancy and childbirth continue to raise health concerns for many female teens worldwide, especially in low and middle-income countries. Each year, millions of teen girls give birth or have unsafe abortions, and both rates are expected to rise. Most of these pregnancies are unintended (Hindin et al., 2016; Sedgh et al., 2015). Besides negative social and economic consequences, mortality rates are higher for teen mothers than for older mothers. Their babies are more often born with adverse health conditions (Blanc, 2014; Pradhan et al., 2015). A lack of easily accessible sexual health education and birth control options, practices of early marriage, and cultural views preventing girls and women from managing their sexual activity all play a part in this continuing health concern. These factors also help cause the spread of HIV/AIDs among teen girls (Dellar et al., 2015; Nankinga et al., 2016; Raj & Boehmer, 2013).

Many health-related problems that impact teen girls are preventable. Sexual and reproductive education can help empower teens with knowledge. Effective birth control can slow the teen pregnancy rate, and condoms can lower HIV/AIDS infection rates (Darroch et al., 2016). Vaccines can also slow the spread of some sexually transmitted diseases. It is also especially important to eliminate violence against girls and women, which requires systematic changes on personal, social, political, and economic levels. Advocating for teen girls' physical health and well-being is essential at the global, national, and local level to ensure optimal development for this generation and subsequent generations.

To Think About:

- Why are teen girls particularly susceptible to sexually transmitted diseases and infections?
- How are these health concerns also reflected in teen girls in developed countries?
- How do global concerns impact the lives of teen girls locally?

13.2 Physical Characteristics and Growth

Because the onset of puberty is individualized and varied, growth happens in height (stature) and weight on different schedules (see Figures 13.3 and 13.4). Growth does not always occur in an orderly way. It usually begins with the feet and hands, followed by legs and arms, which often grow at different rates. A young teen, for example, may have long legs and short arms, or the reverse. This is called **asynchrony**—the lack of simultaneous occurrence. In early adolescence, teens often look and feel uncoordinated because of rapid changes in their body proportions. Getting used to rapid changes, such as longer legs or larger feet, can cause a growing teen to feel clumsy.

Growth spurts, or rapid increases in height and weight, happen during adolescence. During puberty, teens often experience rapid growth lasting two to three years, which gets them closer to their adult height, especially girls. Both boys and girls are close to their adult height by high school. However, full adult height is usually achieved after puberty, especially for boys (Best & Ban, 2021; National Institutes of Health, 2019; Steinberg, 2014). Adolescents can grow as much as 3 to 4 in. a year, resulting in a potential height increase of 10 in. (25 cm) during adolescence (Gavin, 2018). Because girls typically commence puberty earlier than boys, they often experience a rapid growth spurt during later childhood and early adolescence. After menarche, they typically grow another 1 to 2 in., reaching their full adult height by ages 14 or 15 (Marcin, 2019).

Boys usually experience the onset of puberty slightly later than girls. With their later growth pattern, males have larger gains in height. They often do not stop growing until about age 16, and they may continue to grow an inch or two up to early adulthood at about age 21 (Brusie, 2019). In addition, males' shoulders broaden, they build more muscle mass, and their voices change and deepen.

Significant weight gains during adolescence increase both muscle mass and fat tissue. Weight gain can happen quickly during puberty. The ratio between height and weight, or body mass index (BMI), can vary significantly for the same teen progressing through puberty (Ben-Joseph, 2020; Johns Hopkins Medicine, 2020). Likewise, growth in stature and weight can happen at a slow and steady rate. A teen may experience a sudden growth spurt followed by a period of little change. BMI ratios are calculated the same way for children as they are for adults, but there are slight differences in calculations for female and male teens (Brusie, 2019; Johns Hopkins Medicine, 2020; Marcin, 2019).

Along with growth in stature, weight, and muscle mass, fine- and gross-motor development continues during the teen years (see Figure 13.5). The heart doubles in size and lung capacity increases, giving both females and males greater strength and endurance (Ben-Joseph, 2020; Marcin, 2019). Although the athletic abilities of male and female teens overlap, and both sexes are capable of athletic feats, boys generally become faster and stronger than girls due to their changing body composition. The observation that boys can also jump higher and throw farther than girls may not only be affected by their body size and composition, but by the amount of physical activity that boys have versus girls (McCormick & Scherer, 2018; US Department of Health and Human Services,

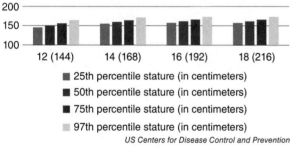

Stature by Age in Years (months)

- 25th percentile stature (in centimeters)
- 50th percentile stature (in centimeters)
- 75th percentile stature (in centimeters)
- 97th percentile stature (in centimeters)

US Centers for Disease Control and Prevention

Figure. 13.3 Stature for Females Age Chart

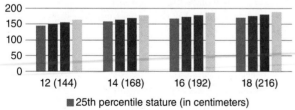

Stature by Age in Years (months)

- 25th percentile stature (in centimeters)
- 50th percentile stature (in centimeters)
- 75th percentile stature (in centimeters)
- 97th percentile stature (in centimeters)

US Centers for Disease Control and Prevention

Figure. 13.4 Stature for Males Age Chart

MBI/Shutterstock.com

Figure 13.5
Do you think it is a good idea beginning in adolescence to separate boys and girls in their physical education classes and sports teams? Why or why not?

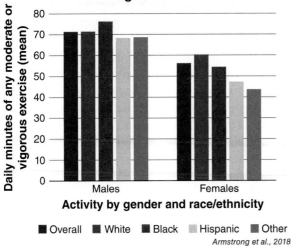

Daily Physical Activity of Adolescents Aged 12–17

Daily minutes of any moderate or vigorous exercise (mean)

Activity by gender and race/ethnicity

■ Overall   ■ White   ■ Black   ■ Hispanic   ■ Other

Armstrong et al., 2018

Figure 13.6
Why might physical activity level vary by race and gender?

2017). Because of these differences, physical education classes and sports teams often separate boys and girls beginning in adolescence.

Activity levels vary by race and gender (see Figure 13.6). For example, many girls become less physically active during adolescence (Corder et al., 2015; Edwardson et al., 2013). Gender differences in teen activity levels may start early, with cultural gender norms playing a large part in girls. Eventually, women may be less inclined to participate in sports or other physical activities (Cla, 2018). It is not necessarily that physical activity is of less interest or a less chosen activity for teen girls; it may relate to cultural expectations that girls spend more time contributing to household chores and caring for family members (Bann et al., 2019).

Inadequate physical activity levels among all teens are a concern in the United States and throughout the world. For example, the World Health Organization found that over 80% of teens do not get sufficient physical activity. The results did not vary significantly by household income levels in each country, including in the United States (Guthold et al., 2020). However, activity levels within different regions within the United States may vary, with teens in some areas getting less or more physical exercise and activity than other regions. Likewise, race and ethnicity may play a part in differences in activity levels. This may be due to social factors such as family modeling, family expectations about caring for family members or household chores, weight, psychological well-being, the need to financially contribute to family income, or expected focus on academic pursuits outside of school (Belcher et al., 2010; Harding et al., 2015; Straatmann et al., 2016). Evidence shows that some of the best ways to combat these decreasing levels include:

- integrating physical activity into the school day
- including health education in school curricula
- offering safe community spaces, such as bike trails or skate parks (see Figure 13.7) (Heath et al., 2012; Lucas et al., 2021).

Duttagupta M K/Shutterstock.com

Figure 13.7 Dedicated urban areas, like this skatepark in Denver, CO, may inspire teens and others to be physically active. They also provide safe spaces for teens to socialize.
What are the benefits of providing outdoor space for teens to be physically active? What are the risks?

☑ CHECKPOINT

- ☐ How do growth patterns in adolescence compare to growth during early and middle childhood?
- ☐ Describe how typical growth patterns may differ between boys and girls in adolescence. When is full adult stature typically achieved?
- ☐ Define *asynchrony*. Describe how it may look in a young teen.

Apply Here!

Imagine that you have two young teens in your care. One is short in stature and has not yet begun to show any outward signs of puberty. The other teen is on the other end of height and weight averages for age and gender. They have not only gone through puberty, but their body resembles that of a mature teen. These young teens are struggling both emotionally and socially in similar and different ways. What kinds of issues do you think they are dealing with? What might you offer as a way of encouragement and opportunity for these two teens? They share similar hobbies, interests, and levels of cognitive maturity.

13.3 How the Teen Brain Develops

With the onset of puberty, sex hormones create more changes in a teen's brain anatomy and circuitry.

During adolescence, anatomical brain changes are dramatic, resembling the changes during early childhood. Some gray matter decreases while white matter significantly increases (Perrin et al., 2008). This includes further myelination of synapses that lend flexibility and plasticity to brain functioning (Asato et al., 2010; Herting et al., 2012; National Institutes of Health, 2020). As you discovered in Chapter 8, plasticity means that the brain can change, modify, adapt, and respond to its environment. The most significant changes occur in the frontal lobe and parietal cortex, and both play a large part in executive functioning (Sturman & Moghaddam, 2011; National Institutes of Health, 2020). The brain also reaches its largest volume during adolescence. This happens at about age 11 for girls and age 14 for boys.

Although the process of brain transformation accelerates at puberty, it does not stop at the end of adolescence but continues into young adulthood (Jensen & Nutt, 2015). The brain is not considered fully developed until a person is in their mid-twenties, with the prefrontal cortex one of the last regions to fully develop (see Figure 13.8) (National Institutes of Health, 2020). During adolescence, dramatic brain growth and refinement play significant roles in language, executive functioning, emotions, and overall cognitive functioning. However, because the adolescent brain is still developing, it may be particularly vulnerable

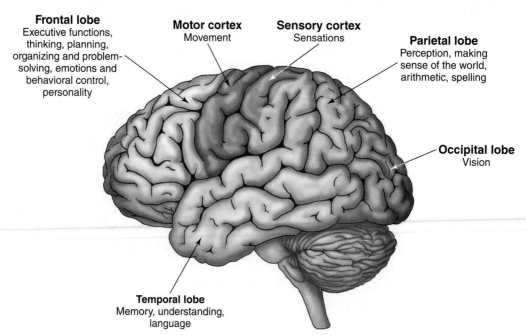

Frontal lobe
Executive functions, thinking, planning, organizing and problem-solving, emotions and behavioral control, personality

Motor cortex
Movement

Sensory cortex
Sensations

Parietal lobe
Perception, making sense of the world, arithmetic, spelling

Occipital lobe
Vision

Temporal lobe
Memory, understanding, language

miha de/Shutterstock.com

Figure 13.8 The Human Brain: Impact of the Later-Developing Prefrontal Cortex

to chronic or prolonged stress. Chronic or prolonged stress may cause fluctuating neural or endocrine responses, often referred to as *allostatic load*. Over time, a heightened allostatic load negatively affects physical and mental health (Ersig et al., 2021; Whelan et al., 2021). This may illuminate why some mental disorders such as anxiety, depression, schizophrenia, and possibly even eating disorders develop during adolescence (National Institutes of Health, 2020).

Because the developing teen brain is highly malleable, teens may be particularly vulnerable to the effect of drugs on their cognitive functioning (Fuhrmann et al., 2015). (This will be discussed further in Chapter 14.) A teen's prefrontal cortex, the part of the brain that exerts behavioral control, is slower in developing than other parts of the brain. This can result in more impulsive behaviors and makes teens more prone to developing addictions (Potenza, 2013; Rutherford et al., 2010). From the subtle cognitive and emotional impairments that occur over time as the teen's plastic brain molds to repeated experiences, these changes then support the initiation, increase, and maintenance of the addiction cycle

(Argyriou et al., 2018). Other neurological changes that contribute to addiction may include socioemotional processing difficulties, working memory disruptions, increased anxiety, and a heightened risk for addiction in adulthood (Salmanzadeh et al., 2020).

Teens may be addicted to many things, such as video games, pornography, alcohol, food, or smartphone use. Addiction treatment is complex because the problem likely consists of multiple overlapping factors. Potential causes might include adverse childhood experiences (ACEs), quality of early caregiver attachment, social environmental factors, sleep patterns, genetics, and individual brain functioning and development (Logan et al., 2018; Singh & Gupta, 2017; Strathearn et al., 2019). Therapies that treat the underlying behaviors that may be causing the addiction may be effective for some adolescents. Examples include family therapy (multidimensional, multisystemic, brief strategic), cognitive behavioral therapy, or twelve-step programs. In many teen addictions, such as opioid addiction, medication combined with behavioral treatments may be most effective (Hadland et al., 2018; Saloner et al., 2017).

Practical Issues and Implications

The Impact of Opioid Drugs on the Teen Brain

Opioids are a class of addictive drugs (see Table 13.3). Legal and effective prescription pain medications, given for sports injuries or after medical procedures, are common oral forms of opioids. When misused, opioids may negatively affect teens' physical and cognitive development. Teens may access prescribed opioids like oxycodone or codeine through the family medicine cabinet or obtain them illegally on the street. Heroin, an illicit and illegal drug injected into veins, is typically purchased on the street or shared among friends and family members.

Synthetic forms of opioids, such as methadone and fentanyl, have also appeared more recently. They are often prescribed for severe pain, making access to this class of drugs even easier. Synthetic forms of opioids are stronger, thus more dangerous than other opioids when used recreationally. In 2019, over 10 million people in the United States over the age of 12 had an opioid use disorder (US Centers for Disease Control and Prevention, 2021d). Fentanyl lacing of other street drugs is the cause of many overdoses. Of every three drug overdoses in the United States, two were opioid-related (US Centers for Disease Control

Type of Opioids	Examples of Drug Names
Natural opioids	Morphine Codeine
Semi-synthetic opioids	Oxycodone Heroin Hydrocodone Hydromorphone Oxymorphone
Methadone	Methadone
Synthetic opioids	Tramadol Fentanyl

Hedegard et al., 2020

Table 13.3 Types of Opioids

and Prevention, 2021). Illicit drug use, including opioids, among US students rose dramatically in the past decades. However, the numbers of students reporting drug use dropped significantly during the global pandemic in 2021 (see Figure 13.9). (US Centers for Disease Control and Prevention, 2020). Whether this decrease in teen drug use will continue remains unknown.

(Continued)

Although the impact of opioid drugs on the normal development of the maturing adolescent brain is not yet fully known, growing evidence suggests that these substances may negatively impact its plasticity (Winters & Arria, 2011). The National Institute on Drug Abuse (2020) describes that opioids may impact the teen brain by

- interfering with how neurons send, receive, and process signals via neurotransmitters
- increasing large surges of dopamine, training the brain to seek drugs at the expense of other needs
- impacting the basal ganglia, or pleasure-seeking center, by diminishing sensitivity to desire, thus making it harder to feel pleasure from anything besides the drug
- influencing the developing and maturing prefrontal cortex, reducing impulse control over time

- sensitizing the extended amygdala so the teen increasingly seeks opioids to buffer feelings of unease, irritability, and anxiety

To Think About:

- Why does the opioid drug epidemic present a serious concern for impending adolescent growth and development?
- Which drugs or other forms of teen addiction are prevalent in your community?
- How might teachers, primary caregivers, and the larger community help educate children and teens on the negative side effects of opioid drug use? Have you experienced educational prevention measures that have been successful?

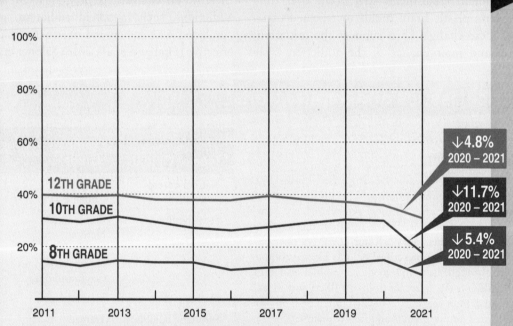

U.S. Students Reporting Any Past-Year Illicit Drug Use*

↓4.8%
2020 – 2021

↓11.7%
2020 – 2021

↓5.4%
2020 – 2021

12TH GRADE
10TH GRADE
8TH GRADE

*Illicit drug use in this survey was defined as use of marijuana, LSD, other hallucinogens, crack, other cocaine, or heroin; or any use of narcotics other than heroin, amphetamines, sedatives (barbiturates), or tranquilizers not under a doctor's orders.

Source: 2021 Monitoring the Future Survey

National Institute on Drug Abuse

nida.nih.gov

National Institute on Drug Abuse

Figure 13.9 High School Students' Reported Drug Use

☑CHECKPOINT

☐ How is brain development during adolescence similar to brain development in early childhood?

☐ Describe how gray and white matter change and how they impact brain functioning.

☐ When is the human brain typically considered fully developed? What is the last area to develop? How does this impact teen development? For instance, what type of things can you do with students this age to capture this new ability?

Apply Here!

Imagine that you are writing a letter to a group of older children or young tweens. You hope to give them more insight into how their bodies will grow and change in the upcoming years of adolescence. What would your main points be? How would you encourage them? How might you give insight into embracing rapid or slow bodily changes?

13.4 Teen Health and Wellness

With so many bodily changes happening during the adolescent years, health and wellness are critically important. Because teens are becoming increasingly independent and cognitively sophisticated, health and wellness become more of a personal responsibility and a matter of personal agency, or a sense of self-control or power over life choices. However, learning to care for one's health and wellness is a gradual process. Because of their increasing cognitive skills and rapidly growing repertoire of social and emotional skills, younger teens need to develop appropriate health and wellness self-care because these are skills that can last a lifetime (Hamilton et al., 2017; Patel et al., 2016).

Physical Activity

Similar to middle childhood, teens continue to need about 60 minutes of moderate to vigorous aerobic physical activity each day to grow strong bones and muscles and to maintain a healthy BMI (US Department of Health and Human Services, 2018; US Office of Disease Prevention and Health Promotion, 2019). Physical activity positively affects bone

mineral accrual by increasing bone mass content. This development has a beneficial effect on the hips and spine. This is critical during these growing years and may help prevent the future development of osteoporosis (Alghadir et al., 2015; Fonseca et al., 2008; Zulfarina et al., 2016). As compared to **sedentary** or inactive teens, teens who are physically active may demonstrate:

- improved cardiovascular health (Ekelund et al., 2012; US Department of Health and Human Services, 2018),
- better mental health, including increased self-confidence and reduced stress (Biddle & Asare, 2011; Duncan et al., 2012)
- higher academic performance (Singh et al., 2012)

Despite the significant benefits of physical activity, only one in three children are physically active every day. The situation becomes more dire during adolescence, when teens spend more sedentary time in school with fewer breaks for recess or active play than in earlier years. Teens may also spend more unsupervised time engaging in other passive activities such as playing video games or engaging with social media and other technologies (see Figure 13.10) (Broderson et al., 2007; Corder et al., 2015). For many teens, other possible deterrents to regular physical activity may include opposing or nonsupportive cultural values, living in unsafe neighborhoods, and a lack of resources or encouragement (Armstrong et al., 2018; Trent et al., 2019). In the United States, physical activity drops significantly in the teen years. Current rates may even be at a historically low level, with the highest level of sedentary

Motortion Films/Shutterstock.com

Figure 13.10 Many teens spend their free time engaged in sedentary activities. Gaming is one type of sedentary activity.
What are other common sedentary activities for teens?

Aerobic Activity	Strength Training	Bone Strenthening
• 3 X or more per week; 20-minute intervals • Includes brisk walking, swimming, running, dancing, or other activities that elevate heart level	• 3 X or more per week • Includes weight lifting, yoga, Pilates, resistance bands among other activities that strengthen muscles	• 3 X or more per week • Includes running, playing basketball, jumping rope, playing tennis, or other activities that strengthen bones

US Department of Health and Human Services, 2018.

Figure 13.11 Recommended Physical Activity for Teens

lifestyles ever observed in a teen cohort (Hamilton et al., 2017; Weston et al., 1997).

Although many teens are physically active through organized or team sports, achieving an adequate activity level is possible through everyday activities (see Figure 13.11). Walking or riding a bike to school, rather than driving or riding a bus, participating in school physical education programs, and participating in household chores can effectively combat a sedentary lifestyle. The 60 minutes of moderate to vigorous activity can be achieved by getting 20 minutes of aerobic activity three times per week combined with strength training and bone-strengthening activities. Teens can also combine daily non-sedentary activities, aerobic activities, strength training, and bone strengthening throughout the day to achieve the 60-minute goal (US Department of Health and Human Services, 2017).

While physical activity is essential, teens should heed medical advice when starting an exercise plan. Strength training, in particular, should be well-supervised to ensure teens use the proper form and technique and engage in developmentally appropriate activities (Dahab & MacCambridge, 2009; Miller et al., 2011). An adolescent's ability to gain muscular strength does not dramatically change during puberty when height and weight increase. Instead, it is a progressive process dependent on age and physical development (Behringer et al., 2010; Morton et al., 2016; Verloigne et al., 2014).

Because teens spend so much time in school, physical education and after-school activities can provide effective ways to stay active during school days. Learning through adult modeling is an effective way to increase a teen's physical activity level. Even peer pressure may encourage teens to maintain adequate physical activity levels (Vorhees et al., 2005). The results are worth it; studies show that physical activity and sports participation in childhood and adolescence positively affect active lifestyles in adulthood (Hamilton et al., 2012). This correlation is even stronger when teens demonstrate self-efficacy and enjoyment from physical activity (US Department of Health and Human Services, 2018; US Office of Disease Prevention and Health Promotion, 2019).

Practical Issues and Implications

Protecting the Head and Brain from Injuries

As teens become more physically active, often engaging in high-impact sports such as soccer, football, hockey, or lacrosse, it is essential to protect the head, brain, and mouth from injury. Although head and mouth injuries can cause pain, scars, and broken or lost teeth, brain injuries are particularly concerning. A concussion or traumatic brain injury may occur when the brain undergoes trauma through the impact of a tackle, jolt, hit, or knock to the head. A concussion is caused by the brain bouncing or twisting inside the skull, creating chemical changes and damaging brain cells (US Centers for Disease Control and Prevention, 2019). Signs of possible concussion or head injury include:

- confusion
- clumsy movements
- losing consciousness
- mood, behavior, or personality changes
- loss of memory
- headaches
- balance issues
- blurry vision
- sleepiness or sluggishness

Getting immediate medical care following an impact to the head is critical. Severe brain injuries may have long-term effects, including cognitive changes in thinking and memory and speech, hearing, or vision changes. Coordination and balance issues may be long-lasting. In addition, severe brain injuries can affect a teen's emotions long-term (Kerr et al., 2014).

Protective equipment is essential in preventing concussions during sports. Mouthguards, headgear, helmets, and face shields may protect against, but not prevent all, head injuries (Navarro, 2011). Primary caregivers, athletes, and coaches must learn how to prevent head injuries and handle head injuries properly (Rivara et al., 2014; US Centers for Disease Control and Prevention, 2021a). Properly caring for teens with head injuries requires a team approach, involving the teen, their primary caregivers, educators, school nurses, and medical professionals. Educators can play an essential role by monitoring changes in the injured teen and reporting any changes to primary caregivers (US Centers for Disease Control and Prevention, 2021a).

To Think About:

- Have you ever had or known someone with a concussion? How did it affect your or that person's ability to learn?
- How can primary caregivers, coaches, and other care providers play a part in increasing community awareness about teen head injuries? List specific strategies.

Nutritional Needs

Proper nutrition is as vital during adolescence as it is in earlier life stages. It promotes physical growth and development, cognitive functioning, and general health and wellness. Inadequate nutrition may lead to impaired development and stunted growth.

A well-balanced diet includes a variety of fruits and vegetables, whole grains, low and non-fat dairy products, a variety of proteins, and healthy oils. As discussed in previous chapters, each of the five food groups provides a range of nutrients and should be consumed in nutrition-dense forms.

As dependents, teens sometimes lack control over what they eat and may be subject to family food choices, although independence may be growing (Ziegler et al., 2021). How teens interact, value, or symbolize food is based on complex interactions in social relationships and the media (see Figure 13.12). Besides food familiarity and availability, other factors such as self and group identity, gender, cultural prohibitions, and religion influence dietary choices (Monterrosa et al., 2020; Ziegler et al., 2021).

Caloric requirements during adolescence increase from those in middle childhood. They range from 2,000 to 3,000 calories per day depending on age,

Dragon Images/Shutterstock.com

Figure 13.12 Family mealtimes and how families interact around food have a large influence on a teen's nutritional choices.
How did your family traditions for eating or not eating together affect you? Were your practices based on choice or logistics?

activity level, and sex. Teen boys typically need slightly more calories than girls to maintain energy and healthy growth, especially in their later teen years, ages 16 to 19 (see Table 13.4). For teen girls, recommended daily caloric intake requirements are lower, unless a teen is pregnant or highly active,

Boys Age in Years	When Sedentary	When Moderately Active	When Highly Active
13–15	2,000–2,200	2,200–2,400	2,600–3,000
16–18	2,200–2,400	2,600–2,800	3,000–3,200
19	2,400–2,600	2,600–2,800	2,800–3,000

Guidelines for estimating energy requirements during adolescence are based on sex, age, height, weight, and level of physical activity.

Adapted from *Dietary Reference Intakes: The Essential Guide to Nutrient Requirements*

Table 13.4 Daily Caloric Needs for Teen Boys

Girls Age in Years	When Sedentary	When Moderately Active	When Highly Active
13–15	1,600–1,800	2,000–2,200	2,200–2,400
16–18	1,800–2,000	2,000–2,200	2,400–2,600
19	2,000–2,200	2,200–2,400	2,400–2,600

Guidelines for estimating energy requirements during adolescence are based on sex, age, height, weight, and level of physical activity.

Adapted from *Dietary Reference Intakes: The Essential Guide to Nutrient Requirements*

Table 13.5 Daily Caloric Needs for Teen Girls

which means that calorie needs increase significantly (see Table 13.5).

As their self-efficacy grows, teens become more responsible for their own selection and consumption of food compared to earlier stages of life. Many teens learn food preparation skills; they are often in charge of personal and family food shopping. Unfortunately, as teens assume more responsibility for their nutrition, diet quality tends to decline, particularly in teen girls. This lack of proper nutrition is a concern both for a teen's health and society in general, as teenage girls and young women bear children who then experience the adverse effects of a poor diet (Dietary Guidelines Advisory Committee, 2020). With less dependence on parental authority, more sedentary lifestyles, and peer pressure to conform, many teens make food and beverage choices that are less nutritionally dense. Teens are often bombarded at school and in other social arenas with unhealthy foods in vending machines or fast-food restaurants and with beverages such as soft drinks and specialty coffees. In addition, pubertal growth stimulates appetite (Gidding et al., 2006). Many teens in prosperous cultures consume diets consisting of excess fat and added sugars with fewer micronutrients, such as vitamins A, D, C, folic acid, calcium, iron, zinc, and potassium. The most common micronutrient deficiency among adolescents is iron (Chelsey et al., 2019; Gidding et al., 2006; Salam et al., 2016a, 2016b).

While the nutritional value of foods consumed tends to decline in adolescence, the prevalence of obesity increases. According to the Dietary Guidelines Advisory Committee (2020), over 20% of US teens, ages 12 to 19 years, can be classified as obese or having excess body fat as measured by BMI (ratio of body weight to height). This is compared to 13% of young children and 18% of grade-school children. If a teen is overweight or obese, it can affect both their immediate and future health (Barlow et al., 2007;

Kesten et al., 2011). Obesity impacts teens both physically and emotionally, as will be discussed in Chapter 15. Obese teens show increased incidences of hypertension, diabetes, sleep apnea, cardiovascular and digestive diseases, and cancers compared to their healthy weight counterparts (Reinehr, 2018; Sharma et al., 2019). Obesity impacts a teen's overall physical health, increasing the likelihood that obesity will continue into adulthood and increase personal and public health care costs (Sanyaolu et al., 2019).

In contrast, disordered eating patterns, such as anorexia nervosa and bulimia nervosa, may also become health issues when teens excessively restrict their diets or purge. Anorexia nervosa involves restricted caloric intake relative to energy requirements. Individuals with this condition severely limit their food intake or only consume certain foods because they consider themselves overweight. Bulimia nervosa refers to food intake over and above what is normal in a short time period with a sense of lack of control over food intake. This *binging* is followed by repeated use of inappropriate compensatory behaviors, such as self-induced vomiting (*purging*), misusing laxatives, diuretics or other medications, or excessively exercising. Anorexia nervosa and bulimia nervosa are two eating disorders on the rise in the United States, impacting approximately one in ten teens and young women (American Academy of Child and Adolescent Psychiatry, 2021).

Eating disorders also occur in males, but less often. Other eating disorders include binge eating disorders, characterized by quick, large food intake with a sense of lack of control, predictive of becoming overweight or obese. Individuals with avoidant restricted food intake disorders limit or curb their consumption of select foods based on fears, sensory aversion, or beliefs (Herpertz-Dahlmann, 2015; Marzilli et al., 2018). These eating disorders share a preoccupation with food and body image distortion. Disordered eating can have adverse effects on teens' physical and psychological health and well-being and even cause death (see Table 13.6). As will be discussed in Chapter 15, disordered eating always has ramifications for socioemotional development.

Effective treatment for teens with disordered eating requires a comprehensive team approach. This includes medical care from a primary care physician, nutritional counseling, individual and family therapy, and the oversight of a psychiatrist trained to diagnose and treat eating disorders (American Academy of Child and Adolescent Psychiatry, 2021; Hornberger & Lane, 2020).

Inadequate nutrition during adolescence is a critical global issue. Globally, one-third of teens

Eating Disorder	Description	Impact on Physical Growth and Development

Anorexia nervosa (AN)	Restricted caloric intake relative to energy requirements	• Low body weight for age, sex, growth, and overall physical health
		• Sample of potential health issues:
		  • amenorrhea (no menstrual period)
		  • anemia (low red blood cell count)
		  • anxiety
		  • congestive heart failure
		  • constipation
		  • decreased cardiac muscle mass
		  • dehydration
		  • depression
		  • electrolyte abnormalities
		  • growth retardation
		  • hypoglycemia (low blood sugar)
		  • obsessive–compulsive symptoms
		  • pancreatitis
		  • seizures
		  • testicular atrophy (shrinking of testicles)

Binge eating disorder (BED)	Excessive food intake	• Anxiety • Depression • Excessive or unexplained weight gain • Hypothyroidism

Bulimia nervosa (BN)	Excessive food intake followed by purging	• Anxiety
		• Depression
		• Excessive or unexplained weight gain or loss
		• Hypothyroidism
		• Related to vomiting or laxative use:
		  • dental erosions
		  • edema (swelling, especially hands, feet, ankles)
		  • esophageal or gastric rupture
		  • esophagitis
		  • fluid and electrolytes disturbance
		  • gastroesophageal reflux
		  • laxative dependence
		  • night sweats
		  • obesity
		  • seizures

Avoidant restricted food intake disorders (ARFIP)	Interrupted eating patterns such as avoidance or noninterest in eating or food; sometimes based on sensory avoidance	• Anxiety • Depression • Failure to achieve growth or weight standards • Failure to meet appropriate nutritional and/or energy needs • Weight loss

Haltom, 2018; Hornberger & Lane, 2020; Yearwood et al., 2021

Table 13.6 How Eating Disorders Impact Teen Physical and Mental Health

experience food insecurity resulting in poor health (Nguyen et al., 2017). On the continent of Africa in 2015, 45% of the world's 1.2 million overall adolescent deaths occurred (Askeer et al., 2019). While mental health, accidents, and infectious diseases contributed to this high number, the lack of adequate nutrition also played a significant role in adolescent mortality (Chelsey et al., 2019). A main concern is a general lack of accessible food. Lack of access to nutritious food is another factor, such as in food deserts, situations of domestic food insecurity, or poverty-stricken neighborhoods. As a result, overweight and obese teens account for one-third of teens globally; and this situation is considered a major global health concern (Askeer et al., 2017).

Proper nutrition and fitness are linked to many health benefits for adolescents. These include maintaining a healthy weight during growth spurts, reducing risks of developing high blood pressure and diabetes, and decreasing chances of early death (Reilly & Kelly, 2011). Other positive benefits include healthier brain functioning and reduced chances of depression and drug use. Eating well and exercising regularly also enhances sleep, reduces stress, and improves overall health. Adequately nourished teens also show improved school attendance (Burrows et al., 2017; Patton et al., 2016). Girls who have a healthy weight before pregnancy experience better labor and delivery outcomes, including decreased maternal mortality (World Health Organization, 2020).

Peers and social media may often provide inaccurate and harmful information related to nutrition or health, which influences teens. As noted previously, parental instruction and modeling related to food choices can positively or negatively affect a teen's nutritional intake. School health programs that focus on the role of personal behavior in making healthy choices can have a positive impact on a teen's nutritional intake and overall outlook on health (Salam et al., 2016a, 2016b).

Aligning schools, public health resources, and families to increase health promotion may have the most positive impact on teens' holistic health, including their physical, cognitive, and socioemotional health. For example, the Whole School, Whole Community, Whole Child (WSCC) model creates collaboration and synergy among schools, families, and public health providers (see Figure 13.13) (US Centers for Disease Control and Prevention, 2021d).

Sleep

During adolescence, when much physical growth and maturation occur, teens need 8 to 10 hours of sleep every 24 hours (Paruthi et al., 2016). However, according to the US Centers for Disease Control and Prevention (2020), 6 out of 10 middle school students (12- to 14-year-olds) and 7 out of 10 high school students (15- to 19-year-olds) do not get enough sleep or get less than 8 hours per night (Wheaton et al., 2018).

Why do teens not get enough sleep? Both environment and biology play a part. Distractions from school, family, peers, and employment expectations often bombard teens and compete for their time. This is often in the form of social media that keeps teens from falling asleep or wakes them up as new posts or messages arrive. Teens living in unstable environments due to homelessness, violence, transient household members, and financial or food instability may experience poor sleep quality, as will those with conditions like asthma or epilepsy (Doane et al., 2019; Fowler et al., 2015; Sivertsen et al., 2009).

Biology also plays a large part in sleep quality. Humans have internal clocks that influence sleep cycles, appetite, hormonal changes, and body temperature. These 24-hour cycles are termed **circadian rhythms**. For teens, circadian rhythms change with puberty and impact a teen's sleep signals, sleep quality, and sleep timing (Cirelli & Tononi, 2008; Owens, 2014). The pubescent change in teens' circadian rhythms causes them to feel sleepy a few hours later than they did in middle childhood. This means that someone who felt sleepy around 8:00 p.m. as a 10-year-old might not feel sleepy until 10:00 p.m. as a teenager. The teen subsequently stays up later.

Sleep is critical to the health and well-being of people of all ages, but it is vital during physical growth and development. Adolescents require the restorative properties of adequate sleep to undergo hormonal changes, bone and muscle growth, and brain architecture re-wiring (Brand & Kirov, 2011). When teens do not get enough sleep, the impact can be significant. The most noticeable effect may be daytime drowsiness, low energy, and lower academic performance. Inadequate sleep also contributes to poorer health outcomes, including a greater likelihood of

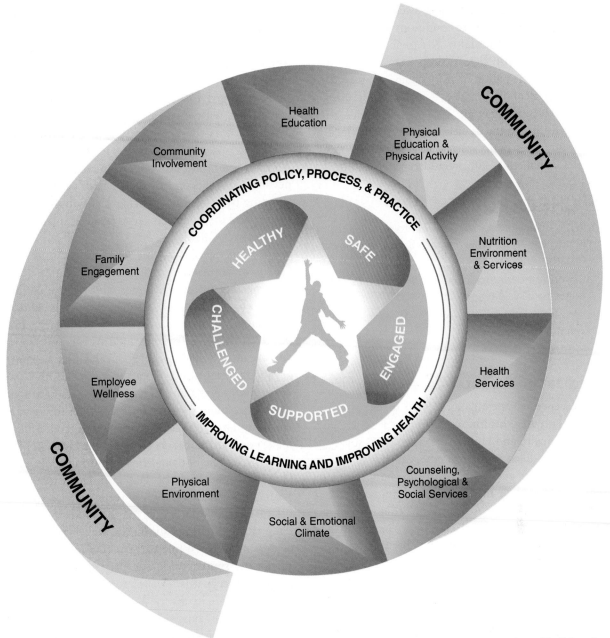

Figure 13.13 The WSCC model includes 10 components of evidence-based school policies and practices. Where might your community improve?

obesity (Brand & Kirov, 2011; Chaput & Dutil, 2016; Lowry et al., 2012).

As with anyone, a lack of adequate sleep affects mood, the ability to concentrate and focus, and energy levels, which ultimately impact academic performance and social relationships. Over time, the negative effects of inadequate sleep grow, affecting cognitive growth and development as seen in

everyday functioning and problem-solving. For example, sleep-deprived teens may have a lower capacity to concentrate and focus (Brand & Kirov, 2011; Lowry et al., 2012).

Lack of sleep also affects a teen's social and emotional well-being. It has been linked with increased suicides and suicide attempts (Fitzgerald et al., 2009; Liu et al., 2019). It has been associated with increased mental health issues, including stress, anxiety, and depression, although these conditions may also cause inadequate sleep (McMakin & Alfano, 2015; Patton et al., 2016). Insufficient sleep may also lead to increased participation in risky behaviors, including drugs and alcohol (Brand & Kirov, 2011; Jamieson et al., 2020; Zhang et al., 2017). These issues often continue into young adulthood because the lack of sleep may alter brain functioning (Bonanno et al., 2019; Chehal et al., 2021; Gaudreault et al., 2019).

☑ CHECKPOINT

☐ Why is physical activity critical to development in adolescence? How much physical activity is recommended?

☐ Describe how nutritional needs in adolescence relate to physical and cognitive development.

☐ Why is good sleep essential in adolescence? What are some common reasons for sleep deprivation in teens?

Medical and Dental Care

Adolescence is generally considered to be a time of optimal physical health. According to a US Department of Health and Human Services (2018) survey of parents of adolescents, 88% reported that their teen was overall in good health. Teens change rapidly, however, and their medical needs change, too. As a result, the American Academy of Pediatrics recommends continued annual check-ups, including any needed immunizations, typically between ages 11 to 14, 15 to 17, and 18 to 21 (Hagan et al., 2017). In the teen years, discussions about participation in risky behaviors, nutritional intake and habits, physical activity, sexual health, and mental health issues are important to overall health. Although teens tend to be healthy, good health oversight can have lasting positive impacts on their future health and well-being. When health needs are unmet during adolescence due to economic disparity, negligent caregivers, unfamiliarity with health care resources, or other challenges, it can change the trajectory of health status throughout adulthood, including the prevalence of chronic illnesses (Hargreaves et al., 2015).

The teen years are a period of transition from medical care that focuses on children to care that focuses on adults. This includes the types of services needed and the transition to the self-management of health care. Primary caregivers typically accompany young teens to their visits with medical professionals. They provide additional information about the teen's health history or status to the health care provider as needed. Over time, however, teens should be encouraged to participate more and engage in discussions with medical professionals about their own health as they practice and hone self-efficacy skills (Banspach et al., 2016; Hagan et al., 2017). Another important component in facilitating teens' personal management of their health care is understanding their personal confidentiality rights related to care and insurance coverage (American Academy of Pediatrics, 2016).

The American Academy of Pediatric Dentistry (2020) recommends continued twice yearly dental care check-ups, teeth cleanings, and the use of fluoride toothpaste for teens. It also recommends continuing dental education as a part of the secondary school health curriculum. Topics include instruction on good dental care and information about the negative effects of tobacco, drugs, and alcohol on dental health.

The unique characteristics of teenagers can make dental care more complex for them than for younger children. This complexity comes from tendencies to make poor nutritional choices combined with a potentially higher rate of dental cavities during adolescence (American Academy of Pediatric Dentistry, 2015; Freeman & Sheiham, 1997). Teens are also more at risk for facial injuries related to sports and other potentially risky activities resulting in broken facial bones or missing teeth. While participating in sports, teens should use sport-specific and properly-fitted mouthguards or faceguards. Lack of access to regular dental care can result in dental problems, including tooth or mouth pain, missed school, heart disease, overall health, and even death (Sil & Kwok, 2017).

Certain societal or cultural practices may complicate dental care for teens. Teens are often concerned about beauty standards, and some cultures promote the ideal of straight, white teeth (Khalid & Quiñonez, 2015). Wearing braces or other oral appliances can make regular brushing and flossing more difficult, resulting in noncompliance and subsequent tooth decay. Self-expressive practices such as mouth and tongue piercing or tongue splitting can also harm oral health. These practices may cause excessive bleeding, swelling, infection, and tooth damage (Hennequin-Hoenderdos et al., 2016; Studen-Pavlovich et al., 2012).

Tobacco use in the form of cigarettes, chewing tobacco, or e-cigarettes (vaping) is prevalent among teens. Vaping is prevalent among teens, with over 11% of US high school students (1.72 million) and nearly 3% of middle school students (320,000) reporting frequent use (Park-Lee et al., 2021). E-cigarettes utilize electronic devices, sometimes called *mods* or *e-hooka*, that heat nicotine-containing liquid, flavorings, and other chemicals, then release it as an aerosol. The added flavorings, such as cotton candy, banana split, or Hawaiian punch, help increase vaping's appeal to adolescents.

Tobacco products cause dental problems like tooth decay, receding gums, bone and jaw damage, tooth loss, and periodontal disease. They may also cause oral and lung cancers (American Dental Association, 2021). Nicotine may damage a teen's developing brain, including learning, memory, and impulse control (National Academies of Sciences, Engineering, and Medicine, 2018; US Department of Health and Human Services, 2016). Almost all lifetime tobacco product use begins during adolescence or the early adulthood years, and these habits often continue through life (Gentzke et al., 2019; Sun et al., 2021).

Wearing braces, orthodontics, or oral appliances to straighten teeth is common in adolescence, especially in the United States. Most orthodontic treatment begins before age 14, according to the American Association of Orthodontists (2013). Typically, orthodontic work is commenced due to crooked or crowded teeth or teeth that protrude. Although orthodontic work may start in later adolescence, earlier treatment may be successful in eliminating habits that are causing the problems (Dowshen, 2014; Prabhakar et al., 2014).

Age-Related Injuries and Deaths

US teens are generally healthy. Despite accounting for 12.8% of the population, they account for just 1% of annual deaths (US Census Bureau, 2019). The leading causes of death for US teens are unintentional injuries (accidents), homicide, and suicide. According to the CDC (2018) the ten leading causes of teen deaths are:

- Motor vehicle crash
- Firearm-related injury by suicide or homicide, by unintentional or undetermined intent
- Cancer
- Suffocation by unintentional suicide
- Drowning
- Drug overdose or poisoning by suicide or unintentional suicide
- Congenital anomalies
- Heart disease
- Fire or burns
- Chronic lower respiratory disease

For all other age groups, the leading causes of death are heart disease, cancer, and unintentional injuries (Xu et al., 2018). Violence is the underlying theme affecting teen deaths, and it disproportionally includes the use of alcohol, drugs, or firearms. At age 12, boys are almost 50% more likely to die than girls, and by age 19, they are three times as likely to die as females of the same age. Rural teens are more likely to die from car accidents, burns, or suffocation, while their urban counterparts are more likely to die from firearms or other forms of violence (Cunningham et al., 2018; Curtin et al., 2018; Xu et al., 2018).

Participating in risky behaviors, not uncommon during the teen years, combined with inexperience, can play a lethal role in unintentional injuries. The number of deaths that occur from accidents accounts for about 80% of teen deaths, with car accidents being the most common cause, followed by poisoning and drowning (Xu et al., 2018). Unintentional poisonings include drug overdoses, which account for approximately 90% of teen poisoning deaths (Curtin et al., 2018).

Suicide is the second leading cause of death for teens in the United States (Curtin et al., 2018). Since 2005, death rates via suicide have grown for teen and all adult age groups in the United States (Steele et al., 2018). The death rates by suicide doubled between late 2007 and 2016 for teens ages 11 to 15 but decreased between 2018 and 2019 (Ramchand et al., 2021). This was the first national decline in mortality among teens reported since 1999. Although suicide rates are low compared to the general population during early adolescence, ages 10 to 14, the rates climb during older adolescence and early adulthood. Among older teens, approximately 17% of high school students reported seriously considering suicide, and almost 15% of those made plans to carry it out during the year surveyed (Kann et al., 2018). Males are four times more likely to commit suicide than females (National Institute of Mental

Health, 2022). In 2020, during the global pandemic and the move to remote learning, suicide rates for young teen males increased by 13% (Curtin et al., 2021). The reasons behind teen suicide are complex and likely due to an interplay of many factors. These may include biology, family history, parental divorce, peer victimization and bullying, and media idealization and ideation (Holland et al., 2017; Holt et al., 2015).

Homicide is just slightly less common than suicide as a means of teen death, although differences vary when broken down by racial/ethnic groups. Homicide is most often through firearms, followed by cutting or stabbings. In fact, almost 90% of homicides occur from firearms, and Black males are especially susceptible to dying in this manner (Cunningham et al., 2018; Curtin et al., 2018). Over 90% of teen girls who die by homicide do so at the hands of an intimate partner (Adhia et al., 2019).

Globally, unintentional injuries, especially road-related accidents, account for most adolescent deaths, including driver, passenger, and pedestrian accidents. HIV/AIDS, suicide, lower respiratory infections, and interpersonal violence follow as top reasons for teen deaths globally. Most of these deaths are preventable (World Health Organization, 2018).

Global Perspectives

Teen Mortality and Race

Violence related to homicide and other firearm-related incidents accounts for most deaths of teen Black males (Cunningham et al., 2018; Curtin et al., 2018). Teen death rates in the United States vary by race. White teens are more likely to die from car crashes or suicide than Black teens. Black teen boys, ages 15 to 19, have the highest death rates of any teen group when compared by sex and race.

Recent studies have shown that police violence is the leading cause of death in the United States for Black teens and especially for Black young men (Buehler, 2017; Edwards et al., 2019). The number of deaths far exceeds numbers from all other racial and ethnic groups, although Black adolescent and young adult females are also more likely to die from police violence than their White, Latino, or Asian counterparts. For all Brown and Black teens, the odds of dying from police violence are higher than their White counterparts (Buehler, 2017; Edwards et al., 2019). Black teens are also more likely to be incarcerated than White teens. Black male teens account for 30% of juvenile arrests and 37% of imprisoned minors; but they make up 58% of incarcerated teens sent to adult prisons (Nittle, 2020).

Black and Hispanic teens are much more likely to be exposed to violence in their communities than White teens, including fatal violence inflicted by community members (Slopen et al., 2016). The impact of a racially imbalanced justice system has a profound negative effect on the wellness and health of all teens, their families, and the police officers who work in the communities (Galovski et al., 2016; Wildeman & Wang, 2017). Living in fear also negatively affects the mental health of teens and their family members. The overall mental health of community members is affected by increased violent deaths and racism. This impact may begin very early in life, as studies show that pregnant women exhibit more depression when racism is present in their community. This depression later negatively impacts the infant or child (Gentile, 2017; Jackson et al., 2017; O'Leary et al., 2019). Studies have linked a significant increase in childhood suicides among Black children to increased community violence and societal racism (Cunningham et al., 2018; Curtin et al., 2018). Overall, teens, their families, and communities suffer when violence and racism persist. Loss of life in adolescence robs communities of a future (Galovski et al., 2016; Wildman & Wang, 2017).

☑CHECKPOINT

☐ How often should teens receive preventive medical and dental care? How do medical needs change in adolescence compared to the needs of school-age children?

☐ What are the leading causes of teen deaths in the United States? How do they vary by race? Globally?

☐ What is the role of educators within a community to prevent violence or advocate for change?

Apply Here!

If you were writing a newsletter for teens, how might you describe the physical activity, sleep, and nutritional needs of adolescence? How might you convince teens that sleep is important? How could you help them assess their own sleep deterrents, such as social media, video games, over-scheduling, or worry? Include specific advice for encouraging health and wellness and suggest problem-solving activities for teens to make personal change.

Summary

Teens experience significant growth and development, but because puberty onset is individualized and varied, timing of when growth occurs in height and weight varies. Puberty also begins sexual maturation, and hormones initiate brain changes. Permanent changes to a teen's brain anatomy and circuitry occur as the production of brain synapses vigorously increases, followed by pruning in the prefrontal cortex and other areas. Along with myelination, these changes lend flexibility and plasticity to the functioning of the teen brain. Because the teen brain is still developing, it may be especially vulnerable to stress and mental disorders such as anxiety, depression, schizophrenia, and eating disorders. At the same time, teens are becoming increasingly independent and cognitively sophisticated. Thus, health and wellness become a matter of personal agency as teens make their own personal care decisions.

With your newly gained knowledge, how might you summarize the dominant health and wellness concerns of adolescence? In upcoming chapters, the knowledge you have gained about adolescent physical growth and development will be fundamental to your learning about adolescent cognitive and socioemotional development.

Learning Outcomes and Key Concepts

13.1 Outline how the onset of puberty begins the process toward adulthood and how these changes are continuous, sequential, and interrelated.

- Puberty is the physical transformation from being a child to an adult capable of reproduction.

- Timing varies in terms of when puberty starts; it could be in middle childhood or well into adolescence.
- Puberty is typically divided into three stages: prepubescence, pubescence, and postpubescence.
- Hormones control puberty and cause changes in body shape and size, mood and behaviors, and cognition.
- Puberty onset often begins in middle childhood, just after age 8 for girls and around ages 9 or 10 for boys, and long before any changes are detected externally.
- Factors such as genetics, ethnicity, nutrition, and body fat may play a part in the onset, timing, and duration of puberty.

13.2 Describe the ways that teens grow and change physically.

- Because puberty onset is individualized and varied, when growth occurs in height (stature) and weight varies among teens.
- Adolescents can grow as much as 3 to 4 in. in a year resulting in a potential height increase of 10 in. or 25 cm.
- After menarche, girls typically grow another 1 to 2 in., reaching their full adult height by ages 14 or 15.
- Boys typically do not stop growing until about age 16, although many continue to grow an inch or two up to early adulthood.
- Significant weight gains increase both muscle mass and fat tissue.
- Weight gain can occur quickly during puberty, or it may progress at a slow and steady rate with growth spurts along the way.
- Growth does not always occur in an orderly way.

13.3 Explain the relationship between the brain's physical changes and cognitive development in adolescence.

- Once puberty begins, hormones initiate brain changes that create permanent changes to a teen's brain anatomy and circuitry.
- The production of brain synapses vigorously increases, followed by pruning in the prefrontal cortex and other areas.
- Some brain gray matter decreases while white matter significantly increases.
- Further myelination of brain synapses lends flexibility and plasticity to the functioning of the teen brain.
- Brain transformation begins at puberty and continues into young adulthood.
- The adolescent brain is still developing and may be particularly vulnerable to stress and mental disorders such as anxiety, depression, schizophrenia, and eating disorders.

13.4 Summarize the importance of health and wellness in the teen years.

- Because teens are becoming increasingly independent and cognitively sophisticated, health and wellness become a personal endeavor and a matter of personal agency.
- Teens need about 60 minutes of moderate to vigorous aerobic physical activity each day to grow strong bones and muscles and maintain a healthy BMI.
- Good nutrition promotes physical growth and development, cognitive functioning, and general health and wellness.
- Teen caloric requirements range from 2,000 to 3,000 calories per day depending on age, activity level, and sex.
- For teens, circadian rhythms change with puberty and may impact a teen's sleep signals, quality of sleep, and timing of sleep.
- In the United States, adolescence is considered to be a stage of optimal physical health, but regular medical and dental care is still recommended.

- The leading causes of death for teens in the United States are unintentional injuries, suicide, and homicide, often from car crashes or firearms.
- Globally, unintentional injuries, especially road-related accidents, account for most adolescent deaths.
- In the United States, Black teen boys have the highest rates of death.
- The impact of a racially imbalanced justice system has a profound negative impact on the wellness and health of all teens, their families, and communities.

Chapter Review

1. Define and contrast *adolescence* and *puberty*.
2. Name and describe the three stages of puberty.
3. List five factors that might impact the onset of puberty.
4. Answer an email correspondence from a fictional teen who is concerned about not developing as quickly as peers are developing. How would you respond?
5. What might a typical growth pattern look like for teen girls and teen boys?
6. Provide an activity level recommendation for a teen. What might this look like throughout a day?
7. Defend the need for physical activity and physical education in middle schools and high schools.
8. How do medical and dental needs change from middle childhood to adolescence?
9. Explain why teens often have sleep issues and appear tired or sluggish during the day.
10. What are the leading causes of death for US teens? Globally? What do these causes have in common?

Matching

Match the following terms with the correct definitions.

A. adrenarche

B. circadian rhythms

C. estrogen

D. hormones

E. pituitary gland

F. testosterone

1. The primary type of female sex hormones

2. Chemical messengers that are secreted by the endocrine system into the bloodstream

3. Change with puberty and impact sleep signals

4. A gland located at the base of the brain that signals the endocrine system to release hormones

5. The primary type of male sex hormones

6. Pubescence, or when adrenal androgen production begins

14

Adolescence:
Cognitive Development

Learning Outcomes

After studying this chapter, you will be able to:

14.1 Summarize some major cognitive theories related to learning during adolescence.

14.2 Describe how knowledge of current research findings applies to adolescent brain development and growth.

14.3 Connect how brain maturation and growth impact cognitive characteristics and functioning, emotions, and risk-taking.

14.4 Analyze the impact of adolescents' interactions, social relationships, and school environment on cognitive growth and learning.

Chapter opener image credit: MStudioImages/E+ via Getty Images

Key Terms

abstract thinking
amygdala
convergent thinking
critical thinking
divergent thinking
dyscalculia
dysgraphia
dyslexia
fixed mindset

formal operations stage
growth mindset
hypocrisy
hypothetical-deductive
  reason
interdisciplinary learning
limbic system
mental schemata
metacognition

multitasking
parallel instructional design
prefrontal cortex
problem-based learning
processing issues
project-based learning
pseudostupidity
reciprocal determinism
triadic reciprocity

Introduction

By the time a child reaches early adolescence, elementary school may seem like ancient history. Most early teens are in middle school or junior high school and are ages 12 to 14. With the change in school settings, school expectations increase scholastically and socially. Do you remember your first day of middle school or junior high? What about your first day of high school? You changed considerably since those first days of school—and not just physically—but in how you think and learn.

The teen years include a significant age span. Adolescence is the stage in life when humans go through the transforming process of changing from children to adults. By the end of this time period, teens are in their last couple of years of high school and likely facing significant family, occupational, and educational changes. With the anticipated changes accompanying high school graduation, expectations increase academically, vocationally, and socially.

Chapter 13 summarized the physical changes in adolescence, including brain development. Consider how physical and cognitive development are related in adolescence. Does puberty affect cognitive development? How do cognitive abilities from early adolescence compare to those of later adolescence? School is a large part of adolescent life. What do you remember about middle school and high school classrooms? What were you learning in your classes?

How has the way you process information and learn changed since then? Recall all the information you already know about the cognitive development of adolescents. As you read this chapter, think of how the new information presented in the text matches or challenges your prior understanding of the topic.

14.1 Cognitive Theories

Theories about how adolescents learn is a way to organize findings and give meaning to many observations and study results. As you learned in Chapter 2, Jean Piaget was one of the earliest researchers to focus on cognitive developmental theory, while Lev Vygotsky and other social learning theorists focused on the social nature of cognitive development. Information processing theory explores the complex and internal process of learning and problem-solving.

Piaget's Concrete Operational Stage Development

Although Piaget's theory is one of the earliest theories about cognitive development, his view of intellectual changes that evolve in stages, shaped by biology and personal experiences, is still relevant to understanding adolescent cognitive development today (Hopkins, 2011; McLeod, 2018). In the concrete operational stage of middle childhood, *concrete* thinking refers to logical mental processing. *Operational* thinking refers to solving a problem without the need to encounter or experience the situation beforehand. In other words, problems are solved logically and do not require having lived through an experience. Rational thought, rather than perception, dominates the concrete operational period (Hopkins, 2011; McLeod, 2018; Miller, 2010).

Piaget describes adolescent learning as the **formal operations stage**, the fourth and final stage in his theory of cognitive development. He believed that this stage starts at the beginning of adolescence, when teens have reached their highest level of cognitive maturity, and continues throughout adulthood (Barrouillet, 2015; Piaget, 1950). Young teens at the beginning of this stage change considerably as they move from middle childhood into adolescence. They can gradually think in more abstract and less concrete ways.

Abstract thinking involves complex thought (see Figure 14.1). As teens' abstract thinking abilities increase, they can understand ideas that have no physical references, such as ideas about freedom or morality. They can talk about love or beauty as an abstract concept, not just connected to certain behaviors or physical characteristics. Abstract thinking is a powerful tool because it includes a variety of skills, including the ability to

- grasp universal abstract concepts such as honor or respect;
- think about the future;
- consider multiple solutions to problems and the potential consequences of each;
- figure out why things are the way they are;
- understand complex math problems; and
- think critically about their own thinking processes—**metacognition**.

In adolescence, teens can hypothesize, theorize, test, and make conclusions, even when ideas may seem in conflict (Barrouillet, 2015).

While younger children often learn through trial and error, teens can use **hypothetical-deductive reason**. They can form a hypothesis based on what logically may occur rather than relying on what has

Zimiri/Shutterstock.com

Figure 14.1 The ability to think abstractly enables this teen to work through complex math problems.

occurred. Hypothetical-deductive reasoning allows teens to engage in scientific reasoning and logic, a method of reasoning or using argumentation. Teens speculate or imagine what *could be* at a more complex level. They can suppose, forecast, or form a rational hypothesis about future events and the impact of current behaviors or actions. They often question or ask for a rationale or reason for others' behaviors.

As teens move from the concrete operational stage to the formal operational stage, their mental ideas may not coincide with what they physically observe. Because of this, teens may be quick to call out **hypocrisy**, a situation in which someone pretends to believe something but does the opposite (Crone, 2016; Thapar, 2015). That is why teens are so quick to call out their parents or teachers when they perceive an inconsistency between instructions or advice given and personal behaviors. For example, a parent may encourage their teen to not worry about the unknown while demonstrating stress and worry themselves.

If teens can use hypothetical-deductive reasoning, why do they not plan to do their homework in a reasonable and logical way? Why are they risk-takers—driving over the speed limit or not wearing a helmet when biking? Why do they make inappropriate choices? Why do caretakers often ask, "What were you thinking?" Psychologist David Elkind (1978) coined the term **pseudostupidity** to describe a teen's tendency to overlook obvious answers due to inexperience rather than cognitive ability.

Although teens demonstrate the executive functioning ability to plan, their inexperience in planning may play a large part in their unrealistic expectations or their sense of invulnerability. This may play out in their tendency to overlook the obvious, such as calculating the time necessary to finish a homework assignment; so, they may put off completing their homework until it becomes a crisis. Or they may be unable to make appropriate choices. These tendencies are a normal part of teen cognitive development (Amsel & Smetana, 2011; Elkind, 1967).

Social Learning Theory

Cognitive theories are directed toward an increased understanding of the role of social relationships in cognitive development. Social learning theory acknowledges the importance of mental processes and the interaction and impact of the environment in determining a person's behavioral responses (Bandura, 1977).

Vygotsky's sociocultural theory of cognitive development stressed the importance of social interaction with others in facilitating learning. Vygotsky also believed that children's understanding of concepts moves from the realistic to the more abstract as they approach adolescence (Barrouillet, 2015; Vygotsky, 1993). Adolescents acquire new knowledge and skills through exploration, cooperative learning, utilization of the scientific method, and general problem-solving (Bodrova & Leong, 1996; Wertsch & Sohmer, 1995).

Other theorists, including Jerome Bruner (1973) and Urie Bronfenbrenner (1996), also believed that social relationships and the surrounding environment have a tremendous impact on cognitive

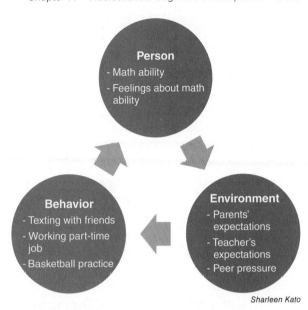

Sharleen Kato

Figure 14.2 This figure shows the triadic reciprocity of learning applied to completing a math homework assignment.

development and learning (Blakemore & Mills, 2014; Gray & MacBlain, 2015). **Reciprocal determinism** examines the relationship between three different variables—person, environment, and behavior. This interaction among the variables is termed **triadic reciprocity** (see Figure 14.2) (Bates, 2019; Kihlstrom & Harackiewicz, 1990; Murty et al., 2016). As self-efficacy skills are built during adolescence, how the variables interact depends on the individual. In other words, teens have more agency in how much or how little these variables interact when compared to childhood.

For example, educators know that teens may not meet the expectations imposed upon them, such as the expectation that they will understand an algebraic formula. Instead, their efficacy or ability to learn (propensity to understand mathematical concepts) is in relationship with their interactions with others (peers, teachers, parents, media) and their behaviors (focused attention, time spent studying). These three interrelated parts will work together (triadic reciprocity) to impact their learning more than imposed standards or expectations.

Information Processing Theory

As described in Chapter 2, information processing theory uses the analogy of the human brain functioning much like a computer, performing movements or functions to come to problem resolution. In the process, the brain stores and transforms information to reach an end goal or solution. Information processing theorists acknowledge that learning is a complex and internal process. Unlike Piaget's theory, information processing theory does not rely on the idea of learning as a set of stages but as a process of problem-solving. The brain accepts information, uses memory storage, and then retrieves information when needed. Thus, the brain stores reactions to stimuli over time and uses them in learning. For example, teens who have secure attachments to parents early in life are less likely to be involved in bullying behavior during later childhood and adolescence (Murphy et al., 2017).

When faced with a stimulus or problem, teens are often bombarded with information. This includes their perceptions of things and associated emotions or visual and auditory stimuli. The input can be brief, typically within seconds; and the teen will process or encode the stimuli and place their understanding in short-term memory. If the stimuli are deemed important, the learning will be moved to long-term memory. The learning will connect with other long-term memories and become part of the teen's **mental schemata,** the cognitive structure representing generic knowledge (Westwood, 2014). If the stimuli and process stay in short-term memory, the learning will be forgotten and deemed useless. The mental schemata contains a lifetime of responses to stimuli that have been categorized. Executive functioning plays a role because the teen controls and directs their attention, perception, coding, and retrieving of information.

Cognitively, teens can better focus their attention and more quickly process information, retrieve memories, and execute decisions than they could in childhood (Capuzzi & Stauffer, 2016; Johnson & Proctor, 2004). They can see relationships between events, actions, and thoughts. When combined with abstract thinking and hypothetical-deductive reasoning, teens process input from the environment and their own personal experiences when responding to stimuli (see Figure 14.3). For example, a teen living in a war zone will process differently than a teen living in safe conditions (UNICEF, 2017). A teen exposed to reading at a higher level will process and encode new words, and the familiarity with those words will become automated with practice. The teen reader may then devise a strategy for responding to foreign words in a challenging text and respond contextually.

Brain researchers try to understand how the human brain mentally processes at different stages of life (Moustafa, 2018). Neuroscientists, those who study brain functions, are expanding our understanding of how the adolescent brain processes information (David, 2019; Moustafa, 2018; Rolls, 2016). Their work intends to broaden our understanding of what is involved in performing an act or solving a problem by using magnetic resonance imaging (MRI) to look at the brain in action and see what factors lead to a response (Johnson & Proctor, 2004). Although teens are often viewed as irrational risk-takers, some studies indicate that they may make more conservative and risk-averse choices than adults, when viewed from an information processing perspective (Kwak et al., 2015).

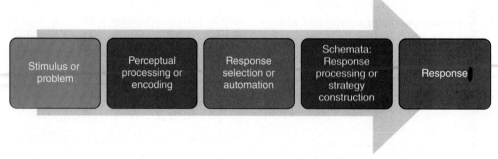

Sharleen Kato

Figure 14.3 Information Processing. Consider how a teen might go through information processing when confronted with a situation that causes stress, such as an impending school exam.
How might anxiety become their response? How might confidence and calm become their response?

✅ CHECKPOINT

- [ ] How did Piaget describe formal operations?
- [ ] How did social learning theory expand Piaget's cognitive theory?
- [ ] How does triadic reciprocity function in adolescent learning?
- [ ] How do perceptions and memory play roles in information processing theory?

Apply Here!

Social learning takes on new meaning in adolescence. Think of a significant learning experience from your adolescence. It could involve proficiency in a skill, completing a project or task, or learning new interpersonal competencies. Think about how you as a person, your behaviors, your social relationships, and the surrounding environment impacted your learning. Draw and complete the triadic reciprocity of learning model (Figure 14.2) to illustrate your learning.

Practical Issues and Implications

Can Smartphones Make Teens Smarter?

Smartphones are more than a communication tool as they enable users to access information easily and quickly. In the United States, teen smartphone usage is just about universal. According to Pew Research (2018), over 95% of teens own or have access to a smartphone. Unlike computer and tablet device use, which are tied to family income and parental education level, smartphone ownership crosses socioeconomic backgrounds and different genders, races, and ethnicities. In this report, 45% of teens say that they use their smartphone "almost constantly," a statistic that doubled since a similar poll five years earlier. Girls and Latinx teens were the most likely to report using their phones at this high rate.

How are teens using their smartphones? Smartphones are ubiquitous, always on the body, and they play a part in almost all aspects of life. They are the one thing that connects everything—entertainment, information access, communication, and even bodily functions with apps that monitor exercise, food intake, sleep, and waking. According to Schaeffer (2019), 9 out of 10 teens use their smartphones to pass the time. Approximately 84% of the teens surveyed use them to connect with other people, and 83% of teens said they use their phones to "learn new things."

But do smartphones make teens smarter? Some experts say no. Some assert that for teens, even being in the presence of their phones reduces their cognitive capacity (Ward et al., 2017). Smartphones potentially create a "brain drain" in two ways: first, by reducing available working memory capacity due to overreliance on the device, and second, by lowering functional fluid intelligence, the ability to think and reason quickly and abstractly to solve problems. Repeated reliance on the smartphone causes intelligence to crystalize or stagnate. Fluid intelligence relies on multiple novel input sources without heavily relying on past experiences. These researchers

also propose that the anxiety caused by the need to be constantly engaged with or monitor a smartphone can take attention away from a focus on school and reduce higher-level cognitive functioning (Ward et al., 2017). Smartphones may also be associated with more significant relationship anxiety and peer aggression (Cyr et al., 2015; Grøntved et al., 2015).

Smartphones are one of the first pieces of technology that profoundly shifted the relationship between the user and the product, transcending the limits of defined space and time. Personal computers were used in specific places, especially before laptop computers became lighter and more affordable. On the other hand, smartphones can be used anytime, anywhere, and are typically never far from their users (see Figure 14.4). That may be the biggest distraction. So, should smartphones be banned in classroom settings? The answer to this question is hotly debated.

In 2018, the French government banned personal phones in schools from preschool through 9th grade—even at afterschool activities, including sports (Langley, 2019). In England, a ban on phones in schools led to higher test scores (Beland & Murphy, 2015). In the United States, there is evidence that students take better notes, retain more detailed information, and score higher on tests when smartphones are banned in the classroom (Kuznekoff & Titsworth, 2013).

Smartphones may be distracting. They may even change the neuropathways in a teen's developing brain because the adolescent brain is still under construction. Even so, smartphones are likely not going away. Many people advocate allowing students smartphone access. They say smartphones can enhance learning by making information more readily accessible. They may also promote independent learning. Parents also like being able to reach their children at any time of the day.

(Continued)

insta_photos/Shutterstock.com

Figure 14.4
Are smartphones an essential communication tool for teens or a distraction in school settings?

Ultimately, people say that enforcing smartphone bans is not possible because they are ubiquitous.

To Think About

- Are smartphones an essential tool for effective daily living in today's world? How might usage aid or impede cognitive development?
- How much do you depend on your smartphone? In what ways does it aid your learning and focus? In what ways does it detract from your learning and focus?
- In your opinion, should smartphone use be encouraged or limited in adolescence? If so, when and how?
- How might a caregiver best guide a young teen in the appropriate use of a smartphone?

14.2 Using Medical Technology to Understand the Teen Brain

For nearly a century, the predominant thinking was that the human brain had reached its full growth by the time a child reached puberty and adolescence. However, advanced brain imaging has revealed that the teenage brain has much more maturing to do. Medical technologies offer insight into the neuro-development of the adolescent brain, especially the finding that the **prefrontal cortex** is still busy developing and continues to develop until it reaches maturity around age 26, clearly into young adulthood

(Choudhury, 2010; Foulkes & Blakemore, 2018; Murty et al., 2016). Located at the front of the brain behind the forehead, the prefrontal cortex is responsible for executive functioning, the ability to organize, plan, demonstrate self-control, problem-solve, judge, and be self-aware (see Figure 14.5).

Brain imaging has also shown that the adolescent brain demonstrates increased plasticity compared to the brain during adulthood. This means that it can change or modify, adapt, and respond to its environment. Although the brain does not grow substantially larger during the teen years, increased connectivity between different brain regions does occur (Casey et al., 2008; Luna et al., 2004). This involves the

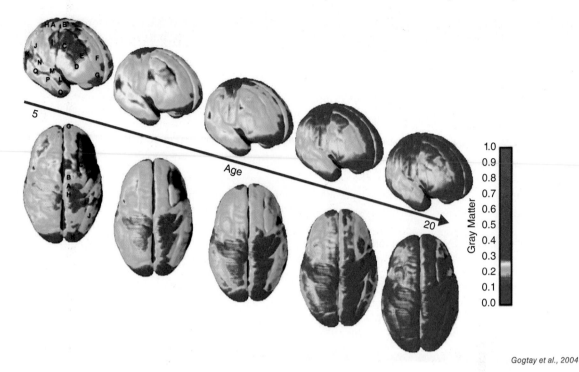

Gogtay et al., 2004

Figure 14.5 The human brain changes over time.
How does this illustration of the changing brain through childhood and adolescence illustrate what is known about teen cognition and behavior?

increase in myelin, a fatty substance that covers nerve cells and aids in communication between brain regions by speeding up the transmission of signals between them (Choudhury, 2010). This further myelination of synapses lends flexibility and plasticity to the functioning of the adolescent brain (Asato et al., 2010; Lebel & Beaulieu, 2011; Lebel et al., 2008). Teens are often quick in computing, problem-solving, evaluating, critiquing, and memorizing information. Because brain plasticity involves responding to environmental factors, the adolescent plasticity window offers educators an opportunity to provide experienced-based learning (Fuchs & Flugge, 2014).

Although the adolescent brain does not fully mature until after adolescence and into young adulthood, the **limbic system** has already reached maturity during adolescence. The limbic system refers to structures within the cerebrum that control motivation and feelings of reward (Arain et al., 2013; Choudhury, 2010; Steinberg, 2008). The **amygdala**, a part of the limbic system responsible for emotional reactions such as anger, develops early. The prefrontal cortex, which affects judgment, is still

developing. This mismatch may cause some teens to take uncalculated risks or make unwise decisions, causing their parents or teachers to ask, "What were you thinking?" (Casey & Caudle, 2013; Mata et al., 2016; Romer et al., 2017).

While the limbic system is much more mature in teen brains than the prefrontal cortex part of the brain, there is a danger in oversimplifying this relationship. The limbic system includes many parts (see Table 14.1 and Figure 14.6). Although each part of the limbic system shares the overarching commonality of regulating emotions, each plays a distinctive role.

Sometimes teens, with their underdeveloped prefrontal cortex, are not able to control their emotions; they can be irrational and moody. Certainly, adults have long observed young teens' unpredictable emotions and behaviors. Some days they act like kids, while other days they act more like adults. In the past, these swings in behavior were blamed on hormonal changes. Today, scientists believe that brain development also plays a significant role in emotional variability. As a teen matures through adolescence, emotions become more controlled by the prefrontal cortex (Mills et al., 2014; Spear & Silveri, 2016).

Brain Structure	Regulates
Amygdala	Emotional responses, memory, fear, and hormonal secretions
Cingulate gyrus	Emotional responses and the regulation of aggressive behaviors
Fornix	White matter that connects the hippocampus and hypothalamus
Hippocampus	Sends memories out for long-term storage
Hypothalamus	Regulates adrenaline for energy and emotional responses such as anger, happiness, or exhilaration
Olfactory cortex	Identifies odors
Thalamus	Relays sensory perception and motor function information and impacts alertness and sleep

Botteron, 2020; Spear & Silveri, 2016

Table 14.1 The Limbic System Structures

Limbic System

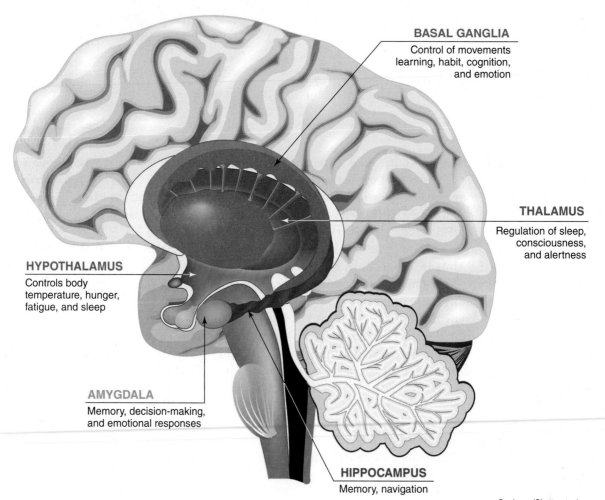

BASAL GANGLIA
Control of movements
learning, habit, cognition,
and emotion

THALAMUS
Regulation of sleep,
consciousness,
and alertness

HYPOTHALAMUS
Controls body
temperature, hunger,
fatigue, and sleep

AMYGDALA
Memory, decision-making,
and emotional responses

HIPPOCAMPUS
Memory, navigation

Designua/Shutterstock.com

Figure 14.6 The components of the limbic system control different cognitive and physical body functions.
Why does understanding the development and role of the limbic system help educators meet the needs of teens in their care?

☑CHECKPOINT

☐ How has medical brain imaging added to the knowledge and understanding of teen brains?

☐ What specific changes to a teen's brain contribute to cognitive functioning?

☐ Describe the function and roles of white matter connections, the prefrontal cortex, and the limbic system to adolescent brain cognitive development.

Apply Here!

Knowing about how the physical brain changes during adolescence can help teens understand themselves better. Attributes include emotional regulation, risky behaviors, and decision-making. There are a plethora of online materials, including streaming educational videos, that offer insight into the mechanics of the teen brain. Make a list of the sources you've reviewed that could be useful for sharing with teens, along with their corresponding descriptions and links.

14.3 Cognitive Characteristics and Growth

Do teens think differently than children? They do. They think faster, and they solve problems differently. Teens can come up with multiple solutions to problems. Teens think creatively and abstractly about questions such as, "What would happen if…." (Feiler & Stabio, 2018; Luna et al., 2004). They can connect how they feel to what they are thinking. They think about the causes of injustice, and they change their behavior to adjust (American Academy of Child and Adolescent Psychiatry, 2016). For example, many teens become vegetarians out of their concern for animals.

During adolescence, anatomical brain changes are dramatic. They resemble the changes during early childhood, when the production of nerve synapses or pathways vigorously increases. As the brain develops, the most significant changes occur in the frontal lobe and parietal cortex, which play a large part in executive functioning abilities (Kuhn, 2009; National Institutes of Health, 2020; Sturman & Moghaddam, 2011). As in early childhood, pruning follows an increase in synapses. This includes further myelination of the synapses, which lend flexibility and plasticity to the functioning of the adolescent brain (Asato et al., 2020; Herting et al., 2012; National Institutes of Health, 2020).

The physical changes in the brain during adolescence are significant because they influence learning and cognition (Del Giudice, 2014; Houston et al., 2014; Mah & Ford-Jones, 2012). The brain becomes more efficient, and teens demonstrate improvements in cognitive flexibility, working memory, and processing speed (Bialystok & Craik, 2006). Increasing white matter creates connectivity between parts of the brain, and communication between these parts becomes faster (Kuhn, 2009; Wendelken et al., 2012). Changes in the brain also affect the motivation to learn and the ability to concentrate. As a result, executive functioning increases, particularly with regard to critical thinking and problem-solving skills (Jensen & Nutt, 2015; Ostroff, 2012).

Creativity, including idea generation, original insights and solutions, and divergent thinking, develops gradually and linearly between childhood and adulthood. As they progress toward increased creative problem-solving, adolescents exhibit an increased ability to address open-ended challenges (Kuhn, 2009; Giedd, 2014). Open-ended challenges are questions that encourage expanded responses and allow teens to reason, consider, and reflect. Some examples of open-ended questions include, "What would you do if…?" or "What do you think of…?" and "How did you decide on…?" Some researchers have found that **divergent thinking**, the ability to brainstorm and come up with creative possibilities, peaks in middle adolescence at around ages 15 to 16 (see Figure 14.7) (Kleibeuker et al., 2013a, 2013b). Teens may be effectively trained to use more divergent thinking skills as their brains develop (Stevenson et al., 2014).

As their brains mature, adolescents become better at **critical thinking**—making a judgment when presented with complex problems or circumstances. They brainstorm solution possibilities using divergent thinking and hone those possibilities using convergent thinking. **Convergent thinking** focuses on finding a single best answer to a problem or question. For example, when taking a multiple-choice exam, convergent thinking skills are critical in discerning the best answer among multiple possibilities. Using convergent thinking, adolescents reason and form new ideas or questions from what they already know (Kuhn, 2009). They are better able to compare and debate ideas, often to the despair of their primary

Rawpixel.com/Shutterstock.com

Figure 14.7 Learning in teams can positively affect motivation to learn. Executive functioning increases, particularly for critical thinking and problem-solving. Working in teams can promote increased creativity, idea generation, original insights, novel solutions, and divergent thinking. *What are some disadvantages of working in teams?*

caregivers or teachers. As they mature, teens can consider the views of others. They become more aware of the process of thinking, or thinking about thinking, or metacognition (Giedd, 20004; Siegel, 2015).

The ability to remember continues to develop throughout adolescence, and teens can remember more things for longer than children can. Repetition and exposure to opportunities to remember and recall information increase this ability. Around middle adolescence, ages 14 to 15, most teens have reached an adult level of memory (Crone, 2016).

As described previously, the maturing adolescent brain is plastic or pliable; as a result, it is primed for learning. Teens can adapt to new learning opportunities, such as those offered by complex problems or new technologies. As new learning is presented, the adolescent brain is shaped by these new learning experiences (Choudhury & Wannyn, 2022; National Institutes of Health, 2020). Because the teenage brain is in transition, it may be more resilient in its ability to change, adapt, and respond to new environmental stimuli than in later life (National Institutes of Health, 2020).

Cognitive changes occur gradually throughout adolescence. The foundation is laid for these changes in early adolescence as the brain forms new connections. Older teens can better consider complex and abstract problems found in math, political issues, and other areas (Arsenio & Willems, 2017).

On the other hand, brain scans show that teen brains work differently than adult brains when making

decisions or solving problems (Kuhn, 2009). They are more likely to rely on the limbic system, using their emotions to make decisions impulsively, rather than by using the prefrontal cortex, which would make them more thoughtful. Teens are more apt to misread or misinterpret facial cues or the social emotions of others than their adult counterparts (American Academy of Child and Adolescent Psychiatry, 2016). As a result, teens are often described as risk-takers. Chapter 15 will discuss adolescent risk-taking in the context of emotions.

Cognition, Emotions, and Risk-Taking

As a result of the brain scan research that was done in the early twenty-first century, it became common to generalize about teens' emotional states. Because the amygdala develops more quickly than the prefrontal cortex, adolescents' brains function differently than adult brains (Casey et al., 2008; Choudhury, 2010). As stated previously, their actions are guided more by emotions when making decisions or solving problems. They are more likely to act on impulse without thinking about the possible consequences of their actions. They can easily become overly emotional. They are also more likely to engage in risky, dangerous behaviors, such as experimenting with drugs and alcohol, not using protective equipment, participating in sexually risky behavior, or driving too fast (American Academy of Child and Adolescent Psychiatry, 2016).

Teens are known to be sensation-seeking because of their attraction to novel and exciting experiences regardless of their evident dangers (see Figure 14.8)

Ipatov/Shutterstock.com

Figure 14.8 Risky or thrill-inducing activities often attract teens. *Based on what you have learned about adolescent development, why might these activities appeal to teens?*

(Vijayakumar et al., 2018; Zuckerman, 2007). As a result, teens are often described as risk-takers, and frequently not in positive terms. Some view risk-taking as a characteristic that declines from childhood to adulthood when more executive reasoning and experience come into play. Instead of adolescence being a peak in risk-taking, it is instead viewed as a point in the continuum when more independence and less supervision makes it appear to be at a peak (Romer et al., 2017). Exaggerated risk-taking does not have to be a given, and many teens go through adolescence without exhibiting high-risk behaviors.

Global Perspectives

Is Teen Risky Behavior a Global Issue?

Taking selfie photos from precarious perches, driving too fast, engaging in unprotected sex, and experimenting with drugs, such as cocaine, inhalants, heroin, methamphetamines, steroids, or prescription medicines—these are all the risky behaviors of teens and young adults that are observed in the United States. In fact, US teenagers and young adults typically take more risks than any other age group studied (Freund et al., 2021; Steinberg, 2008). Are such behaviors universal around the globe or does culture socialize them? The answer is yes and no (Mata et al., 2016; Skeen et al., 2019).

In a survey study of world values, data from 77 countries reveals that the propensity for risk-taking tends to peak in the teen and young adult years but declines across the lifespan in the majority of countries (Mata et al., 2016). However, the data also showed that in countries where teens experience high levels of hardship, higher levels of risk-taking are present. The risk-taking in these situations may stay consistently high as teens mature through life. For example, teens may engage in dangerous or risky employment if laws or governmental regulations are not in place to protect them. Hardships include civil unrest, poverty, and the presence of violence. This flatter age-risk curve suggests that hardship may be an environmental influence and guide in lifelong risk-taking strategies.

Why do teens from relatively low hardship environments still take risks, even when the risks pose high stakes and the potential for overwhelmingly negative outcomes (see Figure 14.9)? Early developmental theorists believed that teens and young adults engage in risky behaviors because their brains are not mature enough to evaluate risk to make good decisions (Baumrind, 1987; Berns et al., 2009; Heinrich et al., 2016). Others attributed risky behaviors to inexperience, such as jumping in a cold river on a sunny day not knowing that water can remain cold far into the summer season. Thus, schools and teachers, parents, religious groups, coaches, and other community leaders began focusing on efforts to provide more education to teens and young adults about the consequences of indulging in risky behaviors. A lot of focus was put into these efforts in the 1990s and early 2000s, but teens still tended to continue these behaviors (Kann et al., 2014).

In more recent years, brain scans have shown several changes in the brain during puberty that may contribute to these behaviors. Teens are more sensitive to the rewards of peer relationships than adults (Chein et al., 2011). In a teen's brain, peer relationships may trump the odds of adverse outcomes from taking risks (Romer, 2010; Romer et al., 2017). Teens may fear being left out socially if they do not participate in risky behaviors. Teen brains are still developing in the prefrontal cortex, and most specifically the right ventrolateral prefrontal cortex, which may be important in helping reduce distress when one is excluded by peers (Blakemore & Mills, 2014).

A less-mature ability to self-regulate may also be an important factor in teen risk-taking behavior (Casey & Caudle, 2013; Jewett et al., 2021). For example, when driving alone or with an adult, teens drove carefully. However, when paired with peers, teens were much more likely to demonstrate risky driving behaviors. This

MBI/Shutterstock.com

Figure 14.9 Sometimes engaging in risky or illegal behaviors can create a social bond between teens.
Can you identify risky teen behaviors in your community that create a sense of group identity by those who participate?

(Continued)

was especially true for younger teens and less true for older teens (Gardner & Steinberg, 2006).

To Think About

- What kind of risks did you take as a teen? What motivated you to take these risks? Would you make these same decisions today? Why or why not?

- Why do teens take more risks than adults do? Does teen risk-taking create any positive outcomes? If so, how?

- Does global social media influence risk-taking? If so, how?

Global Perspectives

Do Cognitive Gender Differences Exist in Math and Science?

In a report commissioned by the United Nations Educational, Scientific and Cultural Organization (UNESCO, 2017), several startling findings revealed the following:

- Since 1903, only 17 women versus 572 men have won the Nobel Prize for physics, chemistry, or medicine.

- Only 28% of the world's researchers are women.

- Girls appear to lose interest in science, technology, engineering, and mathematics (STEM) topics as they age, particularly between early and late adolescence, but especially apparent in upper secondary education.

In creating their report entitled Cracking the Code: Girls' and Women's Education in Science, Technology, Engineering and Mathematics (STEM), UNESCO researchers were motivated to address this lower participation and learning achievement.

Despite ongoing popular beliefs, research on neuroscience, including hormones, brain structure, brain development, and genetics, does not support gender differences in innate abilities to understand and engage in STEM subjects. Findings instead support the impact of environmental factors that shape the brain. Too many girls and underrepresented minorities are held back by discrimination, biases, and social norms that influence the quality of education they are offered and the subjects they choose to study (Chemers et al., 2011; Cheryan et al., 2009; Else-Quest et al., 2013).

In an extensive survey, over half of Americans believed that STEM jobs offered higher pay and more prestige than other jobs. Still, approximately the same number believed that STEM jobs offered less flexibility and work/life balance (see Figure 14.10) (Funk & Parker, 2018). For many teen girls, choosing not to pursue STEM opportunities in middle school, high school, or at the university level may

Most Americans believe STEM employment offers better pay than other industries

% of U.S. adults who say that, compared with jobs in other industries, jobs in science, technology, engineering, and math …

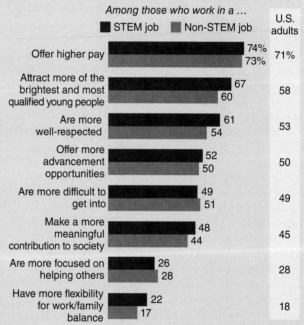

Note: Respondents who gave other responses or who did not give an answer are not shown.
Source: Survey of U.S. adults conducted July 11-Aug. 10, 2017. "Women and Men in STEM Often at Odds Over Workplace Equity"

PEW RESEARCH CENTER

Funk & Parker, 2018

Figure 14.10 How Americans View STEM Careers

have more to do with cultural stereotypes that fail to promote careers in STEM-related fields than to personal efficacy and ability (Cheryan et al., 2015; Hughes et al., 2013; Kessels, 2015). Although media roles have recently begun to promote girls and women in STEM subjects, such as movies about female scientists and mathematicians, changing cultural role modeling takes time (Steinke, 2017).

Social support plays an essential role in encouraging teen girls to pursue STEM fields, such as educational opportunities for pursuing interest in STEM subjects (Rice et al., 2013). For example, peer mentoring and friendships can positively influence whether girls pursue STEM coursework or careers by helping them feel a sense of belonging (see Figure 14.11) (Riegle-Crumb et al., 2006; Riegle-Crumb & Morton, 2017; Robnett & Leaper, 2013). Primary caregiver and teacher encouragement can also be a positive influence in counteracting gender social expectations (Heddy & Sinatra, 2017; Rozek et al., 2015). Lastly, promoting a sense of self-efficacy in girls that their contributions in STEM careers are valuable and needed in society is crucial (Brown et al., 2016; Flowers & Banda, 2016).

MBI/Shutterstock.com

Figure 14.11 Peer mentoring and friendships can positively influence whether girls pursue STEM coursework careers by helping them feel a sense of belonging through teamwork and group problem-solving.

☑CHECKPOINT

- ☐ What are three cognitive improvements that occur in the adolescent brain?
- ☐ How do critical thinking, divergent thinking, and convergent thinking impact creative problem-solving?
- ☐ How do younger and older teens differ in their cognitive functioning?
- ☐ Do cognitive gender differences exist in math and science? Give three points to support your answer.
- ☐ How does cognition, including brain and socioemotional development, influence risky behaviors in teens?

Apply Here!

How would you describe the brain changes and subsequent cognitive abilities during middle adolescence to a new high school teaching assistant or mentor? Write a descriptive summary or create a descriptive slide presentation.

Global Perspectives

Secondary Education for All

According to 2019 UNICEF data, only four out of five older children and teens are enrolled in lower secondary school, the equivalent of US middle school, worldwide. Globally, most countries have achieved increased access to primary school education, especially after concerted efforts by the United Nations Millennium Development Goals project that spanned 1990 to 2015. These goals were agreed upon by all the world's countries and leading development institutions. They have spurred unparalleled efforts to meet the needs of the world's poorest people. One of the eight goals was to make sure that, by 2015, children everywhere, regardless of gender, would be able to complete primary schooling. The results of these efforts were outstanding (see Figure 14.12). Enrollment in primary education in developing regions went from 83% in 2000 to 91% in 2015 (United Nations, 2016).

Primary education sets a foundation for reading, writing, and mathematical literacy, and the United Nations' results have been outstanding. However, although great strides have been made in offering primary education to girls and boys, some world areas still lag, especially regarding offering equal access to girls. These are primarily located in sub-Saharan Africa, the Middle East, and South Asia, typically in the poorest communities (UNICEF, 2019).

Secondary education is dependent on first completing primary education. Most teens in the United States and worldwide are enrolled in secondary education in the form of middle school or high school. However, globally, distinct gaps exist. Poor children are the least likely to attend secondary school, and this is especially true for poor rural children and teens, which reduces opportunities to improve their quality of life.

Over the past decade, the number of children and teens attending schools has increased significantly. However, the gender gap still exists. Globally, more boys receive both primary and secondary education than girls (UNICEF, 2019). The data show that progress toward universal secondary education has slowed since 2011, with the most significant challenges being in sub-Saharan Africa and South Asia. In particular, more than 60% of teens in Chad, Niger, and Tanzania are not enrolled in secondary school (UNICEF, 2019). In Afghanistan, multiple decades of sustained conflict have devastated the education system, especially in rural areas and especially for girls (Fore, 2021).

Although receiving a secondary education is seen as critical to improving quality of life (Glewwe & Muralidharan, 2016; Lee & Lee, 2016), research has found that the number of years of schooling is less important than educational achievement, measured by mean test scores (Delgado et al. 2014). Quality of education is critical. How can quality be measured globally and across cultures? One way is by using data gathered from the Program for International Student Assessment (PISA, 2019). This international assessment measured 32 million 15-year-old students' reading, mathematics, and science literacy in 79 participating countries (see Figure 14.13). In most low-income countries that UNICEF supports, more than half of the students measured failed to reach the minimum level of performance in mathematics. Although overall PISA measured test scores are improving, improvement is slow. One of the eight United Nations' sustainable development goals in 2016 is to "ensure free, equitable and quality primary and secondary education to all and equal access to affordable and quality technical and vocational education such as university."

To Think About

- Do you agree that access to primary education for all children should be a global priority? Why or why not?
- We live in a global world where many ideologies, consumer products, and opportunities intertwine. How does access to secondary education or the lack thereof impact your community?
- What are the perceived barriers to obtaining a secondary education in your community?

Mamunur Rashid/Shutterstock.com

Figure 14.12 Students wearing face masks attend their class at the Azimpur Government Girls School and College in Dhaka, Bangladesh, on September 12, 2021. Some dress or appearance codes are traditional, while others may be short-term or in response to current events.

Education system	Average score		Education system	Average score	
B-S-J-Z (China)[1]	555	⬆	Turkey[2]	466	⬇
Singapore	549	⬆	Slovak Republic	458	⬇
Macao (China)	525	⬆	Greece	457	⬇
Hong Kong (China)	524	⬆	Chile	452	⬇
Estonia	523	⬆	Malta	448	⬇
Canada	520	⬆	Serbia	439	⬇
Finland	520	⬆	United Arab Emirates	432	⬇
Ireland	518	⬆	Romania[2]	428	⬇
Korea, Republic of	514		Uruguay	427	⬇
Poland	512		Costa Rica[2]	426	⬇
Sweden	506		Cyprus	424	⬇
New Zealand	506		Moldova, Republic of	424	⬇
United States	**505**		Montenegro, Republic of	421	⬇
United Kingdom	504		Mexico[2]	420	⬇
Japan	504		Bulgaria[2]	420	⬇
Australia	503		Jordan[2]	419	⬇
Chinese Taipei	503		Malaysia[2]	415	⬇
Denmark	501		Brazil[2]	413	⬇
Norway	499		Colombia[2]	412	⬇
Germany	498		Brunei Darussalam	408	⬇
Slovenia	495	⬇	Qatar	407	⬇
Belgium	493	⬇	Albania	405	⬇
France	493	⬇	Bosnia and Herzegovina	403	⬇
Portugal	492	⬇	Argentina	402	⬇
Czech Republic	490	⬇	Peru[2]	401	⬇
Netherlands	485	⬇	Saudi Arabia	399	⬇
Austria	484	⬇	Thailand[2]	393	⬇
Switzerland	484	⬇	North Macedonia	393	⬇
Croatia	479	⬇	Baku (Azerbaijan)[3]	389	⬇
Latvia	479	⬇	Kazakhstan	387	⬇
Russian Federation	479	⬇	Georgia	380	⬇
Italy	476	⬇	Panama[2]	377	⬇
Hungary	476	⬇	Indonesia	371	⬇
Lithuania	476	⬇	Morocco[2]	359	⬇
Iceland	474	⬇	Lebanon	353	⬇
Belarus	474	⬇	Kosovo	353	⬇
Israel	470	⬇	Dominican Republic[2]	342	⬇
Luxembourg	470	⬇	Philippines[2]	340	⬇
Ukraine	466	⬇			

National Center for Education Statistics

Figure 14.13 Average Scores of 15-Year-Old Students on the Program for International Student Assessment (PISA) Reading Literacy Scale, 2018. The up arrows indicate scores significantly higher than the United States; the down arrows signify scores significantly lower.

14.4 Cognitive Development in the School Context

How does cognitive development affect student learning in middle school and high school settings? Younger teens experience many changes as they leave elementary school and move into the middle school grades. As a middle school educator describes, young teens may be self-conscious, social, and sensitive (Chandler, 2018). Teens may be challenged by difficult contradictions—they are hoping that "nobody looks at me" and "they notice

MBI/Shutterstock.com

Figure 14.14
How might these students be employing systematic, rational problem-solving while also maintaining flexible thinking as they move between classes, academic demands of different subjects, and varying teaching styles?

me" (Chandler, 2018). Teens in early adolescence can study a subject with intense interest and focus. They begin to question the status quo, especially rules enforced by adults. They begin to test values and think about the meaning behind others' expectations (Armstrong, 2016; Spear & Silveri, 2016). In many ways, teens are cognitively vulnerable because they are more apt to develop psychiatric disorders during this stage (Colizzi et al., 2020; Paus et al., 2008). On the other hand, there are tremendous windows of opportunity for cognitive growth as the brain is in transition (Anderson, 2003; Knoll et al., 2016).

By middle adolescence, most teens in this age group are in the beginning years of high school. They have become abstract thinkers and can use complex thinking skills (see Figure 14.14). They are systematic, rational problem-solvers and more flexible thinkers (Crone & Dahl, 2012; McLeod, 2010). Higher-level math, class discussions and debates, and independent class projects are appropriate for middle teens. They initiate and carry out tasks and projects often with little or no supervision (Demetriou et al., 2002). They can research topics and report to others on what they have learned. Educators can encourage problem-solving skills by offering opportunities for them to use their executive function skills and by emphasizing convergent, divergent, and critical thinking in the classroom (see Table 14.2).

Middle School: Younger to Mid-Teens

Middle school years are a crucial time to help mold a plastic, fluid, and maturing teen brain. Educators can use various practical and applied activities to help teens learn and practice abstract thinking. Such activities also involve memory, which aids cognitive development (Fandakova & Bunge, 2016). They also may include:

- using arts and creative imagination activities;
- using emotional regulation skill-building exercises;
- setting appropriate developmental expectations;
- helping younger teens focus on growth mindset goals;
- integrating humor and laughter in learning activities;
- mixing in opportunities for fitness and physical activity; and
- creating an environment that promotes inclusion and belonging.

Effective learning occurs when activities and teaching methods allow teens to express themselves artistically, whether through drama, music, art, dance, or other creative ways. Especially when movement in involved, middle school teens are better able to concentrate, learn, apply new content, and their memory improves (Fandakova & Gruber, 2020). Using the creative and expressive arts can maximize the limbic system's potential subsequent emotional expression in young teens (Armstrong, 2016; Brown & Knowles, 2007; Caissy, 2002).

As teens struggle with intense emotions they do not understand, helping them recognize and identify their feelings facilitates their understanding of their reactions to events and experiences. A thorough description of how the teen brain is changing and maturing is often helpful in giving young teens appreciation for what they are experiencing. Social emotional learning (SEL) is vital during this stage.

Empirical evidence-based studies have shown that including SEL in a classroom environment positively impacts cognitive development and learning (Hansen, 2018; Sanchez, 2021; Tomson et al., 2018). For example, classroom bullying, which peaks during the middle school years, is related to poor academic performance (Bellmore et al., 2017; Copeland et al., 2013). In an

Problem-Solving Type	Examples of Methods
Divergent thinking	• Suggesting brainstorming and explorative activities • Creating opportunities to invent games or products • Encouraging students to pursue their own ideas • Offering opportunities for free or creative writing responses • Integrating music and other expressive arts • Reframing case studies to imagine another viewpoint
Convergent thinking	• Using logic-based problems or case studies • Including games that require rational or logical decision-making • Using projects that involve completing necessary step-by step instructions • Integrating story problems that require materials from a variety of diverse resources to be made into a coherent and unified product • Offering case studies that require students to resolve, explain, identify, or define the problem • Including multiple-choice questions
Critical thinking	• Exploring "why" questions • Comparing and contrasting ideas • Considering alternatives to problems • Assigning group projects • Making connections to a real-life situation • Identifying patterns
Executive functioning	• Minimizing classroom distractions by eliminating clutter • Posting a daily schedule • Providing visual supports and reminders, such as calendars and bulleted to-do lists • Clearly articulating expectations • Offering clear instructions • Providing encouragement and support

Kato

Table 14.2 Ways Educators Might Promote Problem-Solving Skills

SEL classroom environment, teens can talk about what is happening when emotions become overwhelming. It gives them a renewed sense of control (Gestsdottir & Lerner, 2008; Siegel, 2015). An emphasis on SEL also enhances self-awareness, self-management, social awareness, relationship skills, and decision-making—key components of anti-bullying behavior (see Table 14.3) (Espelage et al., 2015; Keelan, 2020; Stalker et al., 2018).

Setting expectations and guidelines early in the school year aids in reducing conflict between young teens, who are seeking independence, and their teachers and primary caregivers. By clearly setting standards and expectations, there is less room for misunderstanding. If emotions rise, there is less reason for the teens to feel that consequences are reasonable or that they are being judged unfairly.

Understanding that success in life comes from hard work, motivation, and passion is termed a **growth mindset**. Believing that success mainly comes from innate talent or genetic traits and abilities is termed a **fixed mindset**. Teens taught to focus on a growth mindset often feel in control and achieve more success academically, socially, and emotionally throughout adolescence (Dweck, 2006; Meruelo et al., 2019). Teens who focus on a fixed mindset rely on their natural talents, believing that they are either good at something or not. Educators can help students use a growth mindset that focuses on effort and creative thinking to improve academic performance. They can do this by encouraging and praising effort and hard work, even if the starting point is a fixed mindset (Alvarado et al., 2019; Dweck, 2006; Smith et al., 2018). Evidence supports that interventions can increase a growth mindset, resulting in improved learning and academic achievement, which then becomes a motivation for learning. Interventions

Social-Emotional Skill Category	Components
Self-awareness	• Perceiving themselves accurately • Recognizing emotions • Identifying specific emotions • Recognizing personal strengths • Identifying personal needs • Realizing personal values • Developing agency or self-efficacy
Self-management	• Self-regulation • Self-discipline • Stress management • Goal-setting skills • Organizational skills
Social awareness	• Respect for others • Perspective-taking • Empathy
Relationship skills	• Communication • Engagement with others • Cooperation • Responsibility • Conflict management • Negotiation skills • Refusal skills
Decision-making	• Problem-solving skills • Personal responsibility • Social responsibility • Ethical responsibility • Evaluation skills • Reflection

Kato

Table 14.3 Social-Emotional Skill Categories and Component Parts.
What skills might you add?

SpeedKingz/Shutterstock.com

Figure 14.15 Educators can help create a positive environment for learning that is inclusive and gives everyone a sense of belonging.
How might the educator in the photo be creating a positive environment? What parameters and expectations might an educator establish to make group projects meaningful and effective for teens?

may even change the brain's physiological functioning in terms of how it solves problems (Ng, 2018; Sun et al., 2021). Grit, a sense of courage and resolve, and a growth mindset can help students persist, even under adverse circumstances (Hochanadel & Finamore, 2015).

Physical activity can also play a significant role in a young teen's cognitive development. It can reduce stress and anxiety, thus providing a more conducive learning environment (Dubuc et al., 2020; García-Hermoso & Marina, 2017). Some effective educators consider adding humor into interactions with middle school teens. Humor and laughter can

relieve stress, as long as it is sensitive and does not exclude or negatively focus on another person or group. Young teens often feel awkward with their changing physical bodies and strong emotions. Sharing funny video clips, cartoons, or stories that are culturally sensitive and appropriate can relieve stress and model appropriate social behaviors (Armstrong, 2016; Brown & Knowles, 2007; Caissy, 2002).

Young teens can be self-conscious, sensitive, and social—all at the same time. They are beginning to make new friendships with peers. They are often unsure of themselves. To create a positive environment for learning, consider ways that can make a classroom environment inclusive and give everyone a sense of belonging (Brown & Knowles, 2007; Caissy, 2002; Chandler, 2018). For example, educators can create a classroom culture that is hospitable, inviting, and respectful by establishing clear expectations and modeling positive social interactions (see Figure 14.15).

Applying learning to oneself is an effective way to help young teens learn and connect with new content. For example, asking students to respond with their personal opinions on a controversial topic, choose a favorite character in a story, or write a reflective response to an experience are ways that can make learning more personal for teens.

☑ CHECKPOINT

☐ What effective education practices can aid adolescent learning in middle school?

☐ What is the difference between a fixed and a growth mindset?

☐ Identify at least three SEL skill categories and give examples of skills that would reflect each.

Apply Here!

Based on what you have learned about cognitive development thus far, how might you approach this debate question with adolescent students: "Should teens be tried and sentenced as adults in courts of law after committing a violent crime?" If this question was proposed in the secondary school classroom, how might you facilitate discussion? Would you bring in differing points of view? Create debates? Have students gather information? If so, from whom or from where?

High School: Middle to Older Teens

Teens can think about their future rather than just the present. Older teens are often better able to understand the long-term effects of their decisions. They may begin to think seriously about career goals, or at least the short-term future, as they remember the past and envision their potential future (Blakemore & Robbins, 2012; Schacter et al., 2007). Older teens can plan, organize, and schedule their own time. Because so many life opportunities and challenges present themselves to older teens, sometimes decision-making can seem overwhelming. In short, older teens think very much like young adults; the major difference is that the parts of the brain that regulate emotions are still developing. Thus, although they are competent, they may be inconsistent in performing tasks as the demands of growing independence and social expectations increase (Crone & Dahl, 2012). They can exhibit great flexibility and compromise and juggle many things at once, including school, work, outside activities, and friends. Sometimes these multiple roles can become overwhelming. Teens may reject goals set by others, such as their primary caregivers, teachers, coaches, or even peers (Dahl, 2004; Dweck, 2006; Ernst, 2014).

In high school, most teens become more skilled at complex thinking skills, and they have an increased ability to take on other perspectives (Choudhury, 2010). They are becoming more systematic, rational problem-solvers, and with extended working memory, they can identify and analyze multiple options (Raghubar et al., 2010). They enjoy trying new ideas and possibilities (Keating, 1990). As a result, the pace of learning is rapid. Students are expected to be more independent than in their earlier years. Some teens may begin to lose interest in academic pursuits unless assignments are complex, challenging, and related to real-life problems (Dawes & Larson, 2011; Halpern, 2009; Vedder-Weis & Fortuc, 2011). Positive relationships with teachers can be an especially helpful because they can encourage and guide their students (De Wit et al., 2010).

Sometimes academic performance declines during adolescence and added stress may be a culprit. As teens mature, their goals are more often based on personal values than on the expectations of others (Davidow et al., 2018). For example, they may struggle with goals that compete for their time (see Figure 14.16). Family responsibilities, such as caring for younger siblings or contributing to their family's financial well-being, may conflict with their academic goals. Goals related to their social life may conflict with goals related to their extracurricular activities, such as participating in sports or music. They may often experience the impact of **multitasking**, or trying to do many things simultaneously. Many teens might say they can effectively listen to music, text, check their online profiles, and write an essay for tomorrow's class at the same time. However, the evidence

sturti/E+ via Getty Images

Figure 14.16 Teens may hold a variety of responsible and potentially conflicting roles such as student, employee, or family caregiver to younger siblings.

shows that a lack of focus is bound to make writing that essay take longer and lower its quality.

School provides a forum for teens to become more independent from their primary caregivers, learn in a social context, and increase their cognitive abilities and skills. But sometimes, high school students choose to drop out or leave school prior to completion. Many factors play into this decision. Adverse childhood experiences (ACEs) are associated with an increased risk for dropping out of school. This is true even if the ACE occurred in early childhood, as they are with mental health issues such as depression (Dupere et al., 2018; Morrow & Villodas, 2018). Poverty and rural location are key risk factors for high school dropout rates. A lack of resources, including a lack of local peers, creates hardships and barriers to community. Rural areas may leave teens isolated from one another (Wils et al., 2019). Students may drop out of school due to social or academic challenges, especially those related to linguistic or cultural diversity (Choe, 2021; Kim et al., 2020). Even health plays a part, as the COVID-19 global pandemic increased school dropout rates (Chatterji & Li, 2021).

According to the US Department of Education (2021), the dropout rate remains consistent at about 5%, a reduction from a 10% rate in the previous decade. The rate is level among geographic regions of the United States. However, it does vary by race/ethnicity (see Figure 14.17). In 2019, the dropout status in the United States was lowest among White teens, at less than 4%, and highest among Latinx teens, at 6.5%. Males are more likely than females to drop out of high school, as are students with disability status (US Department of Education, 2021).

In the United States, there is an acknowledged racial and gender disparity in school punitive actions. Black and Brown male teens are disproportionately suspended as compared to White teens (Bottiani et al., 2018; Gwathney, 2021; Payne & Welch, 2015). During suspensions, teens' routines are disrupted; they lose out on academic instruction; and many miss out on school-sponsored nutrition programs. Zero-tolerance suspensions, which do not offer second chances, are often precursors to teens dropping out.

The economic impacts of dropping out of high school are high. Students without a secondary education set themselves up for a lifetime of lower earnings. The social consequences can be high, too, as social stigma is often associated with lower levels of education. There is hope, however. Interventions for combatting the dropout problem are becoming more available and common. Most importantly, interventions are making a positive difference. For example, providing mental health assessment and care, offering language support, focusing on SEL, increasing school safety, and reducing commute times between rural teens and community schools have all shown promise in reducing dropout rates (Rumberger, 2020; Wils et al., 2019).

Disorders or Challenges Related to Cognitive Development

According to The National Center for Learning Disabilities (2020), one in five people nationwide is challenged with learning and attention issues. Although many such issues become apparent when children enter school, some become more obvious when they enter adolescence. Other times, they are not even diagnosed until much later in life. Teens with learning challenges may also struggle with organization and decision-making, lowered self-esteem, and bullying. Primary caregivers, educators, and other adult advocates can play a critical supporting role. Adults can empower teens by helping them establish routines and identify and focus on their strengths, while also encouraging them to do things they love to do. Teens with learning challenges also require expert guidance from medical and educational specialists (Patrick, 2020).

In addition to the learning disabilities discussed in previous chapters, four additional learning challenges exist that may have been diagnosed in childhood and can become more apparent in adolescence when teens enter middle and high school. These include **dyscalculia**, **dysgraphia**, **dyslexia**, and cognitive **processing issues** (see Table 14.4).

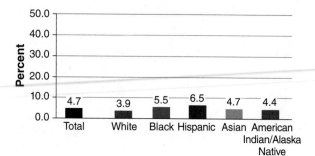

Figure 14.17
How do US dropout rates differ by race/ethnicity? Why might these differences occur?

Learning Disability	Description
Dyscalculia	Dyscalculia is difficulty learning math, including understanding time span and other abstract measurements, such as days, weeks, or months of the year. Challenges typically appear in early childhood when children are attempting to learn basic number ordering and math computation;but dyscalculia may be more challenging in adolescence when math learning becomes more abstract with the study of algebra and calculus. Students may have trouble learning time and performing addition, subtraction, multiplication, and fractions. The challenges may be more pronounced when teens must estimate, make exact calculations, use decimals, or decipher graphs and charts (US Department of Health and Human Services, 2019).
Dysgraphia	Dysgraphia is difficulty with organizing ideas. Challenges typically show up early, when children learning writing and composition; but they often become more pronounced in middle school and high school due to higher expectations for both organizing and communicating thoughts through writing (US Department of Health and Human Services, 2020).
Dyslexia	Dyslexia is a learning disorder that makes it difficult to decode speech sounds and how they relate to spoken or written (phonology) words, despite possessing intellectual and visual skills in the normal range. Because a part of the brain is involved, there is no current cure; but intervention can help (Hulme & Snowling, 2015; Mayo Clinic, 2020).
Processing issues	Children who struggle with processing issues often need more time to translate auditory and visual information. Sometimes they are challenged with words, comprehension, or replication of what they see or hear. As teens, the expectation of audio or visual data processing speed may increase, causing more stress for the teen who needs more time to process information (The National Center for Learning Disabilities, 2020).

Kato

Table 14.4 Select Learning Disorders or Challenges in Adolescence Educational Settings

Practical Issues and Implications

Interdisciplinary Learning

Human rights, global warming, food scarcity, lack of clean water, pesticide use, racial profiling, migration, or homelessness are huge, complex issues that face our world. These are examples of real-world problems that demand creative solutions. Problem solutions require multiple perspectives and the application of various disciplines. Breaking big world problems down into real-life community issues presents a rich learning opportunity for teens to hone their critical thinking skills and further promote executive functioning (Geier et al., 2008; Sawyer, 2014).

Interdisciplinary learning is an educational process that integrates two or more subject areas to nurture heightened learning in each of the subject areas involved. It often includes core disciplines such as reading, writing, mathematics, science, technology, and social studies. In short, an interdisciplinary approach is an educational method that incorporates knowledge and skills from multiple areas or disciplines (Szostak, 2007; Youngblood, 2007). Learning may focus on a problem to solve, such as in **problem-based learning**, or a project to complete, such as in **project-based learning**. In both instances, learning starts with stating a question or posing a problem that needs solving (Krajcik & Shin, 2014; Lu et al., 2014).

Interdisciplinary learning often occurs in teams when each team member can independently research solutions and then dialogue and decide as a team (see Figure 14.18). As a result, teens often feel more connected and in control of their learning (Boyer & Bishop, 2004; Szostak, 2007). Another way to integrate interdisciplinary learning is to introduce thematic units. For example, global warming may be the broad topic from which all subjects contribute. This is referred to as **parallel instructional design** (Youngblood, 2007).

Interdisciplinary teaching methods often work best when they are student-led. If students voice concern about an issue in their community, educators may find ways to use their interest as a catalyst for integrative learning. For example, if historical bigotry or bullying is an issue addressed in a social studies class, English class students might look at bullied characters in a story and reflect upon their own responses when experiencing or witnessing bullying. Students may then strategize to find solutions to bullying in their own community.

(Continued)

Figure 14.18 Teens are capable of working together in teams to problem-solve and complete a learning project.

Implementing these large themes works well to unite the school (Sawyer, 2014; Szostak, 2007; Youngblood, 2007).

Why is interdisciplinary learning valued today? Because the world is complex. Most of the problems people face do not fall under just one academic discipline, such as English or mathematics. Educators and students can use real-world situations to promote learning in meaningful ways. They can dig deeper into topics. By using multiple sources of information, perspective widens. Interdisciplinary learning, especially when problem-based or project-based, allows teens to utilize and expand problem-solving skills that mirror complex social situations. At the same time, they can experience learning under the guidance of adults who can provide scaffolding to help teens start learning at the appropriate levels (Krajcik & Shin, 2014).

To Think About

- What are some current local, state, or national issues that can provide opportunities for middle school and high school students to partake in interdisciplinary learning?

- Should the identified issues be approached as problem-based or project-based learning opportunities? Why?

- What are the tangible benefits of interdisciplinary learning for teens related to their cognitive development?

☑ CHECKPOINT

- ☐ How do the educational needs of high school students differ from those of middle school students?

- ☐ Are high school drop-out rates increasing or decreasing in the United States? Why?

- ☐ What are three potential learning challenges that might impact teens?

Apply Here!

Kimi, a 15-year-old with whom you have a supportive care relationship, told you about some academic challenges, including a failed quiz and a lower than desired grade on a classroom project. Imagine how Kimi might respond to this issue using a fixed and growth mindset. Provide three examples of what Kimi might say in response to the situation.

Summary

As their brains undergo tremendous development, teens show increased cognitive plasticity so that they can change or modify, adapt, and respond to their environment more effectively than before. Although the prefrontal cortex does not reach maturity until around age 26, its continual development during adolescence improves teens' abilities to organize, plan, demonstrate self-control, problem-solve, and discern. Increased myelination in the brain promotes better connectivity and cognitive processing, flexibility, working memory, and processing speed. As the limbic system reaches maturity, adolescents are better able to focus on abstract thinking. They can hypothesize, theorize, test, and make conclusions, even when ideas may seem in conflict. Social relationships and the surrounding environment greatly impact cognitive development and learning in adolescence. By ages 18 to 19, teens become more skilled at complex thought and the ability to take another person's perspective.

You have learned a lot about cognitive development in childhood and adolescence. Reflect on what you have learned. How do the ways teens learn differ from childhood learning? What cognitive skills are gained through the adolescent years that offer an enhanced ability to solve complex problems? As you move to Chapter 15, consider how physical and cognitive development are interrelated and how this relationship may impact socioemotional development.

Learning Outcomes and Key Concepts

14.1 Summarize some major cognitive theories related to learning in adolescence.

- Piaget describes the formal operations stage, the fourth and final stage in his cognitive theory, when teens reach their highest level of cognitive maturity.
- Piaget's theory focuses on abstract thinking, which allows teens to hypothesize, theorize, test, and make conclusions, even when ideas may seem in conflict.
- Social learning theorists assert that social relationships and the surrounding environment greatly affect cognitive development and learning in adolescence.
- Reciprocal determinism examines the relationship between person, environment, and behavior on adolescent cognitive development.
- Due to growing self-efficacy skills in adolescence, the individual teen is most responsible for how the variables of self, the environment, and behavior interact.

14.2 Describe how knowledge of current research findings applies to adolescent brain development and growth.

- Medical technologies offer insight into the neurodevelopment of the adolescent brain.
- The prefrontal cortex area of the brain continues to develop until it reaches maturity around age 26, clearly into young adulthood.
- The prefrontal cortex aids the abilities to organize, plan, demonstrate self-control, problem-solve, and discern.
- The adolescent brain demonstrates increased plasticity so that it can change or modify, adapt, and respond to its environment.
- The brain does not grow substantially larger during the teen years, but better connectivity occurs through an increase in myelination.
- The limbic system regions of the brain that control motivation and reward reach maturity during adolescence.

14.3 Connect how brain maturation and growth impact cognitive characteristics and functioning, emotions, and risk-taking.

- The teen brain becomes more efficient with improvements in cognitive flexibility, working memory, and processing speed.
- Changes in the brain affect the motivation to learn, working and long-term memory, and the ability to concentrate.
- Executive functioning increases, particularly in critical thinking and problem-solving abilities.
- Adolescents exhibit an increased ability to address open-ended challenges, using both divergent and convergent thinking.
- Teens often rely on the limbic system, utilizing emotions to make decisions that are made quickly, sometimes on impulse.

14.4 Analyze the impact of adolescents' interactions, social relationships, and school environment on cognitive growth and learning.

- Higher-level math, class discussions and debates, and independent class projects are appropriate for middle teens.
- The middle school years provide a crucial time for molding a plastic, fluid, and maturing teen brain.
- In middle school, various types of practical and applied activities help teens learn and practice abstract thinking.
- Including social emotional learning is important in a classroom environment because it positively impacts cognitive development and learning for teens.
- Teens with a growth mindset often feel in control and achieve more success academically, socially, and emotionally.
- Older teens become more skilled at complex thought, the ability to take another perspective, and identifying and analyzing multiple options.
- School provides a forum for teens to become more independent, learn in a social context, and increase their cognitive abilities and skills.

Chapter Review

1. Give examples of three ways learning happens in early adolescence that differ from late adolescence.
2. Name and describe three brain maturation changes that influence learning in the teen years.
3. Create a case study about classroom peer relationships that illustrates how social emotional learning (SEL) aids cognitive development in adolescence.
4. Design an infographic that describes/illustrates the cognitive attributes of high school-age teens and how their caregivers or teachers can promote optimal cognitive growth and development.
5. If you were writing a newsletter for incoming middle school students, how might you encourage them to succeed in their academic pursuits? Include a checklist of tips.
6. Describe how engaging teens in challenging activities, including interdisciplinary learning, can strengthen the brain's ability to function swiftly and effectively.

Matching

Match the following terms with the correct definitions related to cognitive theories.

A. limbic system   D. plasticity
B. metacognition   E. prefrontal cortex
C. myelination

1. The region at the front of the brain responsible for the abilities to organize, plan, demonstrate self-control, problem-solve, judge, and to be self-aware
2. A fatty substance that covers nerve cells and aids in communication between brain regions
3. The brain's ability to change or modify, adapt, and respond to its environment
4. Regions of the brain that control motivation and reward
5. The ability to think about one's own thinking

Match the following terms with the correct definitions related to literacy/language development:

A. convergent thinking   D. dysgraphia
B. critical thinking   E. dyscalculia
C. divergent thinking

1. A learning challenge characterized by difficulty with organizing ideas
2. A learning challenge characterized by difficulty learning math, including understanding the concepts of time spans and other abstract measurements, such as days, weeks, or months of the year
3. Making a judgment when presented with a complex problem or circumstances
4. Thought processes that bring together information focused on solving a problem
5. The ability to brainstorm and come up with different creative possibilities

Motortion Films/Shutterstock.com

Many relationship changes happen in the teen years, both with family members and peers.

15

Adolescence:
Socioemotional Development

Learning Outcomes

After studying this chapter, you will be able to:

15.1 Describe common theories related to an adolescent's socioemotional development.

15.2 Discuss how the interplay among the cognitive, social, and emotional domains affects a teen's overall development.

15.3 Explain how a teen's relationship with family members influences their socioemotional development.

15.4 Describe the influence of a teen's peer relationships on their socioemotional development.

15.5 Explain the moral development milestones often achieved during adolescence.

15.6 Discuss the socioemotional determinants of successfully transitioning to adulthood during older adolescence and early adulthood.

Chapter opener image credit: track5/E+ via Getty Images

Key Terms:

at-risk
body image
care perspective
conventional reasoning
dysmorphic disorder
egocentrism
emerging adulthood
fidelity
gender dysphoria
gender identity
idealized self

identity achievement
identity diffusion
identity foreclosure
identity moratorium
imaginary audience
individuation
marginalization
moral atmosphere
moral identity
occupational identity
personal fable

political identity
post-conventional morality
role confusion
self-identity
sexual identity
sexual orientation
social clock
storm and stress
transgender

Introduction

A lot happens during the adolescent years. What do you remember about experiencing puberty, turning thirteen, or learning that you were now a teenager? Did you meet these new experiences with excitement, fear, or indifference? Did your family expect more of you? Did you have increased independence? Reflect on the adolescent experiences that brought you the most joy, the most sorrow, the most anxiety, and the most courage. Were special relationships involved in each of these scenarios?

Adolescence encompasses the long journey from the early teen years to the transition into young adulthood as many physical and cognitive changes affect socioemotional development. Young teens traverse the unparalleled changes of puberty with emotions that ride up and down, sometimes dramatically. But as they mature, they can better cope with life's challenges. Hormones contribute to the emotional rollercoaster, but the developing brain also plays a part. Relationships within the family begin to change as teens become more independent and autonomous and focus on establishing a self-identity. Peers become extremely important to teens who want to fit in and be accepted. Teens grow more capable of understanding how others feel, and they tend to be less self-absorbed than younger children. They are more comfortable interacting with others, including those of the other sex. Older teens are more emotionally stable in their social interactions and less moody, yet they can still be withdrawn or emotional as they face life decisions and stresses.

As you read this chapter, think about which scenarios are likely to be normative for most teens. How might their relationships with primary caregivers, teachers, siblings, and peers change throughout adolescence? How do teens make moral and ethical decisions? What impact do these decisions have on occupational and other life choices? What are the main socioemotional issues that older adolescents face as they transition to adulthood?

15.1 Socioemotional Theories

Theorist Erik Erikson asserted that the main socio-emotional crisis children in middle childhood face is the tension between industry and inferiority. They work to master new skills and struggle with feelings of inferiority if their efforts fail. As children become more competent, they transition to identifying their place in the world and how it relates to others—they develop a **self-identity**. Erikson described this fifth stage of his eight life stages in his psychosocial development as *identity versus role confusion*; it is the last stage before adulthood (Erikson, 1950). During this stage, teens answer the big question, "Who am I?" They need to explore who they are as individuals and where they fit into society. Part of Erikson's theory described how a teen's identity is instrumental in relating to others despite their differences. In doing so, this process is critical in developing a final identity. **Fidelity** is ultimately the personal strength that comes from creating one's self-identity and relating to the self-identities of others (see Table 15.1).

Erikson proposed that forming a self-identity occurs through an adolescent's experimentation with different behaviors, activities, personas, and roles. He termed this phase of exploration as an **identity moratorium** when teens put self-identity on hold as they try on different identities. For example, teens may experiment with their physical appearance by changing their hairstyles and trying out different types of clothing and body adornments such as piercings or tattoos (see Figure 15.1). Through this experimentation process, teens can eventually develop a strong sense of who they are, termed **identity achievement**, that sets them up for healthy adulthood. Failure to create a self-identity results in **role confusion**, a lack of understanding of one's place in society. Erikson emphasized that

Motortion Films/Shutterstock.com

Figure 15.1 As teens try on different identities, they may experiment with changes to their physical appearance. *Did you experiment with your appearance as a teen? If so, how?*

pushing a teen into claiming a self-identity without giving them room for exploration, such as by enforcing strict guidelines on behavior expectations, could lead to rebellion and confusion (Erikson, 1950).

Psychologist James Marcia (1980, 2010) expanded on Erikson's work to propose four identity statuses based on a teen's exploratory behaviors and a teen's commitment to an identity (see Table 15.2). Depending on the absence or presence of these two variables—exploration and commitment—the result could be *identity moratorium, identity achievement, identity diffusion*, or *identity foreclosure*.

As described previously, identity moratorium occurs when an adolescent explores different roles and personas without committing to a final identity. For example, a teen may take on the persona of a studious introvert one day and outgoing extrovert the next day, depending on with whom, and in what situations, the interactions take place. They may dress up as the persona, even changing the way they speak and their overall attitude to explore

Age	Stage	Strength Developed
0–12 months	1: Trust versus mistrust	Hope
1–3 years	2: Autonomy versus shame and doubt	Willpower
3–6 years	3: Initiative versus guilt	Purpose
6–11 years	4: Industry versus inferiority	Competency
12–19	5: Identity versus role confusion	Fidelity

Erikson, 1993

Table 15.1 Erikson's Childhood and Adolescence Socioemotional Tasks and Strengths

Commitment to identity and roles		Present	Absent
	Present	Identity achievement status (crisis is over)	Foreclosure status
	Absent	Identity moratorium status (crisis is occurring)	Identity diffusion status
		Exploration of identity and roles	

Marcia, 2010

Table 15.2 Marcia's Four Identity Statuses

new identities. Adolescence is a time for exploration with the end goal of refining self-identity in preparation for adulthood. Identity achievement occurs when exploration and commitment to an identity are both present.

James Marcia proposed that identity moratorium and identity achievement happen in a repeating cycle throughout adolescence, as a teen finds more clarity about who they are through trial and error. When exploration is absent, but a commitment to an identity is present, teens may experience **identity foreclosure**—committing to an identity before they have fully explored it. This often happens as a result of the perceived or real expectations of others. Committing to an identity without fully exploring "the fit" results in making premature identity decisions without adequate evaluation. For example, a teen might believe that they are not good at math and thus think that some technical jobs are not open to them. They could thereby miss opportunities to explore creative and applied math subjects, such as computer science, data analytics, or business. Or teens may not explore options and foreclose on a premature identity when culture dictates what they can and cannot do based on their gender and or race and ethnicity.

Lastly, James Marcia proposed that **identity diffusion**, or identity confusion, occurs when both exploration and commitment to an identity are absent. A teen who doesn't have or doesn't take opportunities to explore their identity may feel perplexed, bewildered, or confused about their role within their families, school, and in society in general (Montgomery, 2021). Depression is also associated with identity diffusion (Bogaerts et al. 2021; Meca et al., 2019).

Recent research in socioemotional developmental theory has supported Erikson's work on identity

development as a crucial factor during adolescence. At the same time, some have proposed extending the timing of the identity moratorium well into young adulthood, arguing that few teens leave adolescence with a strong sense of self-identity (Berzonsky, 2011; McLean & Pasupathi, 2012; Whitbourne, 2002).

In the years since the work of Erikson, many researchers have sought a deeper understanding of how identity develops during adolescence (Becht et al., 2021; Carlsson et al., 2016; McClean & Syed, 2015). Teens and adults play formal roles, such as student, musician, athlete, employee, and informal roles, such as daughter, son, sister, brother, grandchild. All these roles are integrated and interdependent upon each other, even when a teen's outward display of roles varies widely. Theorists continue to view identity formation in adolescence as a complex process that involves numerous factors. This is especially true considering the reciprocal relationships between identity formation and the environment and within social relationships. Kaplan and Garner (2017) integrated the theories of many when they proposed the *complex dynamic systems model* of identity development. In this model, the teen's action related to role identity is at the center, surrounded by emotions. The complex dynamic system forms from four interdependent spheres. These include the teen's ontological beliefs (reason for being) and their epistemological beliefs (ways of knowing); their purposes and goals; their self-perceptions; and their perceived action possibilities. Surrounding these interactions within the complex dynamic system are the teen's disposition or temperament, the teen's domain or sphere of control, and the greater society and culture. The model captures the complexity and dynamic nature of adolescent identity development.

☑CHECKPOINT

☐ Describe the adolescent stage included in Erikson's psychosocial development theory. What strength is associated with this stage?

☐ What question do adolescents ask themselves during Erikson's fifth psychosocial stage? What is a consequence of role confusion?

☐ What is an identity moratorium? How might it play out in a teen's development?

☐ Name the four interdependent spheres in Kaplan and Garner's complex dynamic systems model that represent variables in a teen's identity formation. To learn more about this model, you can search online to find the article *A Complex Dynamic Systems Perspective on Identity and its Development: The Dynamic Systems Model of Role Identity.*

Apply Here!

As a faculty representative, Chris will soon be giving a welcoming speech to first-year high school students. Watching the students stream into the building, Chris feels a mixture of interest, amusement, and empathy. Chris is thinking, *"They are all sizes and shapes. Some are arriving in groups, chatting animatedly, but sticking close together. Others are coming alone, seeming to know no one, and trying to be invisible. Their conversations range from bragging to answering questions with only a nod. Most of the first-years are very self-conscious. I wish that instead of making a formal speech today, I could whisper in the ear of every undersize first-year student: Don't give up. Your time will come!"*
Consider:

• How do Erikson's stages of socioemotional development in adolescence relate to what Chris is observing?

• Provide two examples of how a teen might feel perplexed, bewildered, or confused about the identity roles as they begin high school.

Practical Issues and Implications

Disordered Body Image

A simple definition of **body image** is one's awareness, beliefs, judgments, and feelings about one's body. Body image is a part of self-identity. It is related to how a person presents themself to others. As teens develop a sense of identity, especially as the physical body grows and matures, creating a healthy body image is important but sometimes challenging (see Figure 15.2). The topic of body image, especially related to teens, has been one of fascination for decades. It has included input from psychologists, sociologists, medical professionals, and media researchers (Grogan, 2017; Markey, 2010). Body image can be realistic, distorted, or somewhere in between. However, body image distortion is so widespread and pervasive in teen girls that it is sometimes viewed as normative, especially in the early and middle teen years (Markey, 2010; McIntosh-Dalmedo et al., 2018). The early years of adolescence are when physical bodies are changing rapidly, and the pace of body changes varies significantly between individuals. The start and length of sexual physical maturation vary greatly. Some teens enter puberty in middle childhood (ages 10 or 11), while others do not start until well into adolescence (Galvan, 2018; Kipke, 1999). Genetics, ethnicity, nutrition, body fat percentage, and even stress play a part in the timing of physical and sexual maturation. This can make it challenging for teens to overlay the realities of a maturing body with the expectations of others as well as cultural ideals (Andrew et al., 2016; Markey, 2010). Although teen boys' bodies are also changing, studies show boys are more likely to have a positive body image because of these body changes, especially with gaining weight and muscle (Archibald et al., 2003; Hoffmann & Warschburger, 2017).

Having a healthy body image is linked to many positive outcomes, including intuitive eating, perception of others as judging them positively, higher self-esteem, better mental health, and lower incidents of body objectification (Andrew et al., 2016). Likewise, harmful outcomes may result from a negative body image, including an increased likelihood of low self-esteem, depression, and obesity (Paxton et al., 2006). Many studies have involved females, specifically teen girls and young women. They focus on the connection between negative body image and eating disorders and practices, such as excessive dieting or anorexia nervosa and bulimia, both considered psychiatric disorders that require treatment (Stice & Shaw, 2002). Negative body image links to an increased likelihood of drug, alcohol, and tobacco use (Andrew et al., 2016). Excessive body image distortion is termed body **dysmorphic disorder**, a distinct mental disorder that causes an overwhelming preoccupation with physical appearance (Cash, 2011).

In the past, much research on teen girls' negative body image and disordered eating focused on media's unrealistic ideals of beauty, exemplified by thin, White, and blonde female models and celebrities (Anderson & Jiang, 2018; Jones, 2001; Strahan et al., 2006). Later research

A   B

Figure 15.2 Perceptions of body image may vary based on many factors. (A) How a teen girl views her changing body is often influenced by implicit and explicit messages within close relationships. (B) Teen boys may make comparisons between their own weight and muscle gains to that of their peers. What influenced your perception of your own changing body during early adolescence?

has shown that the influence of others within a teen's social circle is even more powerful than these media images (Cooley et al., 2008; Crespo et al., 2010). Images of idealized bodies became more prolific as social media allowed teens to share pictures of themselves that were edited to be the most flattering possible. These studies showed that manipulated online photos led to lower reported body satisfaction in teen girls (Fardouly & Vartanian, 2015; Kleemans et al., 2018; Tiggemann & Slater, 2013).

Other studies have focused on how closer relationships within families, friendships, and romantic relationships affect body image. Both implicit and explicit messages within close relationships influence how a teen girl views her changing body (Tiggeman, 2011). Relationship messaging focused on the teen's appearance or modeled through a parent or peers' body image perception is influential. For example, studies have shown that when mothers communicate dissatisfaction with their bodies, or focus on dieting rather than healthy eating, it contributes to a teen's negative body image (Cooley et al., 2008). Likewise, negative communication or teasing about body changes from siblings, peers, or romantic partners helps create a negative body image in teens (Rohde et al., 2015). Teen girls who are involved in romantic relationships and judgmental peer friendships are more likely to engage in dieting behaviors and to have a negative body image (Voelker et al., 2015; Webb & Zimmer-Gembeck, 2014).

Recent research has shown that there may be a connection between peer acceptance and hormones related to low body image in teen girls. Progesterone, a hormone released by the female ovaries, may regulate the relationship between peer approval and body image. The higher the progesterone levels, the more vulnerable the teen girl may be to body image distortion (Forney et al., 2019). Therapy that uses a cognitive-behavioral perspective and medical intervention shows promise in treating teens and adults who experience body dysmorphic disorder (Cash, 2011; Dalhoff et al., 2019; Tylka & Wood-Barcalow, 2015).

To Think About

- Do you think that cultural perceptions of the ideal body have changed over the last ten years? If so, how?

- In your opinion, do you think that teens' propensity toward having a negative body image will change in future generations? Why or why not?

- Teen boys have a greater likelihood of having a positive body image than teen girls. Can you identify factors that might influence this difference? Do you think that this is changing? Why or why not?

- Will more access to social media or other technologies help or hinder a teen's perception of their body?

15.2 Psychosocial: Cognitive, Social, and Emotional Development

As teens transition to adulthood, the most significant point in their socioemotional development is becoming more independent and autonomous (McCormick & Scherer, 2018; Milevsky, 2015). Opportunities for employment and new friendships open up when teens provide their own transportation by driving a car or negotiating a public transit system. During this time, teens focus on establishing a self-identity. In later years, teens have an increased ability to behave appropriately or responsibly in the eyes of their peers, the adults in their lives, and, most importantly, themselves. They become more secure in their identity and more independent and self-reliant. They can better analyze their social interactions and those of others.

At the same time, however, teens may often feel compared to others. They often feel judged; frequently, this is combined with reactionary feelings of embarrassment. Piaget introduced the concept of adolescent egocentricity in his work on cognitive theory, but David Elkind (1967) expanded on the concept. Elkind theorized that teens are primarily concerned with themselves. Within this intense self-focus, some teens may believe that others are enamored and fascinated with their actions, appearance, and behavior. He termed this self-focus **egocentrism**. That is, teens tend to think intensely about themselves, their well-being, and how they compare to others. They often view themselves as special and unique, and they believe they possess feelings that no one else can understand. Teens also care tremendously about what others think of them (Crone, 2016; Harter, 2012).

In fact, during this period, teens tend to see themselves as the main character on the stage of life. Young teens are dealing with changing bodies and unfamiliar feelings that cause acute self-consciousness (Guzman & Nishina, 2014). This leads them to assume that everyone, or an **imaginary audience**, is paying attention to them. Since they think that everyone is watching them, young teens often excessively focus on how they appear to others. Are they dressed right? Are they saying the right things? Their strong desire to fit in makes them painfully self-focused (Chandler, 2018; Elkind, 1967). They want to fit in and stand out from

Zivica Kerkez/Shutterstock.com

Figure 15.3 Sharing a common interest or goal can help teens fit in with a group.

the crowd (see Figure 15.3). As Erikson theorized, they may frequently "try on" new appearances, hobbies, and interests.

Middle teens frequently resort to **personal fable**, a thinking pattern related to cognitive function. In a personal fable, a teen will distort and inflate their opinion of themselves and their importance. For example, they may believe they are on their way to becoming a social media pop star, a major league baseball player, or a real estate tycoon. The danger of a personal fable is that this thinking may lead to a teen's belief that they are invincible. Many middle and older teens believe that bad things will never happen to them because they are unique and special. This may cause them to take dangerous risks such as experimenting with illicit drugs or engaging in hazardous outdoor activities such as cliff diving (Berns et al., 2009; Brand et al., 2006).

Since the part of the brain that regulates emotions and impulse control is not fully developed in adolescence, teens are often considered immature. Adults may often ask, "Why don't you act your age?" In fact, teens are behaving exactly their age (Mills et al., 2014; Spear, 2010, 2013; Spear & Silveri, 2016).

Personality Development

As discussed in Chapter 6, children are born with a certain temperament. Temperament, the unique individual differences in the ways people respond to and interact with the world, is persistent throughout life (Thomas & Chess, 1977). This is why each child shows differences in affect or emotion, activity level, focus, and self-regulation (Rothbart & Bates,

Openness to Experiences	Conscientiousness	Extraversion	Agreeability	Neuroticism
• Curious • Creative • Imaginative • Adventurous	• Responsible • Accountable • Perseverance • Orderly	• Positive emotions • Dominance • Social • Outward focus	• Cooperative • Helpful • Accommodating • Kind	• Negative emotions • Stressed • Tendency toward anxiety or depression • Internal focus

Caspi et al., 2005; McAdams & Pals, 2006; McCrae & John, 1992

Table 15.3 The Big Five Personality Traits. Each person is a blend of the five traits. Which traits do you possess?

2006). Personality is broader than temperament; it is affected by temperament, life experiences, and learning (McAdams & Pals, 2006). Personality includes personal narratives or history, ways of adapting to challenges or change, and stable patterns or traits (Klimstra, 2013). Theorists often describe personality using the big five traits: openness to experiences, conscientiousness, extraversion, agreeability, and neuroticism (Caspi et al., 2005; McAdams & Pals, 2006; McCrae & John, 1992). Although every individual is different, each personality trait shares some commonalities or tendencies (see Table 15.3). Most people are a mix of personality traits.

By the time a child enters adolescence, maturing cognitive abilities combined with lived experience begin to meld as teens refine self-identity, which is a component of personality. Identity formation during adolescence is key to personality development and change (Klimstra, 2013).

Self-identity Development Domains

Even when it is in transition, self-identify is essential to a teen's mental health and social relationships (Berzonsky, 2011; Erikson, 1950; McLean & Pasupathi, 2012). It is normal for teens to swing back and forth between feeling like they have achieved an identity to exploring different roles and personas. Fluctuating easily between states of identity achievement and identity moratorium or exploration, typical during adolescence, can lower anxiety, the risk of depression and suicide, and decrease neurotic symptoms (Arnett et al., 2014; Claveirole & Gaughan, 2011; Crocetti et al., 2009).

Part of developing self-identity during adolescence involves separating from primary caregivers. This process of **individuation** involves complex mechanisms that require the redefinition of relationships, rather than their dissolution (Butterfield et al., 2021;

Koepke et al., 2012). For example, a teen may shift the intensity of a close relationship with a parent to a peer by choosing to share private information with a friend instead of their mother. As relationships with others, especially peers, become more prominent, these friendships feed into teen identity development (Jones et al., 2014; Ragelienė, 2016). Whether in person or virtually through social media, peer relationships greatly influence individual identity formation through interaction and communication (Reid & Boyer, 2013; Van Doeselaar et al., 2018).

The larger culture also affects how teens view their identity as they are motivated to be included or fit in with others in society. Identity formation, started in childhood, expands in adolescence as teens determine the racial or ethnic groups to which they do or do not belong (see Figure 15.4). Social race is based on shared cultures, such as language and traditions, and ethnicity is related to cultural groups that share social and cultural traditions, language,

Marko Subotin/Shutterstock.com

Figure 15.4 Ethnic identity often means personal habits, adornments, or behaviors.
As a teen, how did you begin to blend your family's ethnic heritage or culture with your own lived experiences?

and communication styles. Growing autonomy in adolescence may make teens more interested in their racial or ethnic identity. Or, they may be less interested as they explore different identities and seek independence (Cama & Sehgal, 2021). Recent studies show that teens with a strong ethnic-racial identity through cultural socialization have better socioemotional and academic outcomes than those with low or moderate levels of ethnic-racial identity and socialization. Those who have experienced being perceived as part of a model minority group, such as stereotypes of Asians being smart, may fare better than those who are not. Those with low racial or ethnic identity and socialization tend to experience more prejudice or bias from others (Atkin et al., 2019; Xie et al., 2021).

Many factors influence the complex process of creating a self-identity (Crocetti et al., 2017; Kaplan & Garner, 2017). Overall shifting self-identity includes a combination of sub-identities. These include gender, race and ethnicity, occupational aims, political views, religious or spiritual leanings, and sexual identity. Self-identity affects how teens view their own emotions, body image, and perceived intellectual abilities (McClean & Syed, 2015). It also includes social roles and responsibilities, perceived competencies, and challenges. Ultimately, self-identity shapes self-esteem, the assessment of oneself. Although self-identity begins early in life, three areas that become especially important during adolescence include sexual identity, occupational identity, and political identity. Forming an identity in these areas comes subtly from day-to-day interactions, learning, and experiences (Becht et al., 2021; Galliher et al., 2017).

Sexual Identity

As teens mature physically and sexually, gender identity and sexual orientation become an integral part of overall **sexual identity** (Erikson, 1950). **Gender identity** refers to a person's mental concept about their gender, whether woman, man, or something else (Roselli, 2018). Gender identity development reflects a complex interchange between a person's biology, culture, and environmental factors (Olson-Kennedy et al., 2016). For most teens, gender identity correlates with body features such as males having a penis or females having a vagina. The onset of puberty may create incongruence between physical body development and the teen's gender identity

if a teen does not feel like they identify with their biological gender. However, sometimes it does not. This is termed **gender dysphoria**. If the teen accepts this incongruence, they may identify as **transgender**. If, instead, the incongruence causes them distress, they may consider hormone treatments or cosmetic surgery to create more harmony between their physical sex characteristics and their identity (de Graaf & Carmichael, 2019; Olson-Kennedy et al., 2016).

Sexual orientation refers to a persistent pattern of social, emotional, romantic, or sexual attraction to women, men, or both sexes. Although culture and environment play a part in establishing sexual orientation, it may also have a biological component (Bailey et al., 2016; Bao & Swaab, 2011; Fisher et al., 2017). Both gender identity and sexual orientation create sexual identity. For teens, sexual identity involves the question, "How do I relate to others sexually?"

Sexual identity often plays out in relationships as teens present themselves to the world or engage in sexually intimate relationships. LGBTQ+ is an acronym that stands for lesbian, gay, bisexual, transgender, questioning (or queer), and other (see Table 15.4). An individual's sexual behavior is often moderated by their perceived acceptance by others. For some,

Term	Definition
Lesbian	Woman who feels romantic love or sexual attraction to other women
Gay	Usually refers to men who feel romantic love or sexual attraction to other men but sometimes used in reference to a lesbian
Bisexual	Suggests an attraction to all genders including transgender
Transgender	Transgender describes gender identity that differs from what is typically associated with the sex assigned at birth
Queer	An umbrella term for anyone who is non-cisgender (not aligned with their assigned birth sex) or is other than heterosexual
+ (plus)	Includes intersex, asexual, and other identity combinations

Kato

Table 15.4 Definitions of LGBTQ+ Terms

using personal pronouns such as she, her, he, him, they, or their is an important way of acknowledging acceptance.

Teen girls still experience the traditional double standard as their peer acceptance ratings decrease when they are involved in sexual relationships compared to teen boys (Allison & Risman, 2013; Kreager et al., 2016). Teens who sexually identify as lesbian, gay, bisexual, transgender, or other may find themselves in the minority. As a result, they may encounter stigma or rejection by peers, family members, or others. Despite these experiences, most teens navigate these obstacles and develop a mentally healthy sexual identity in adulthood (Saewyc, 2011; Stynes et al., 2021).

Occupational Identity

Occupational identity refers to a teen finding their purpose or place in the world. Questions are asked such as, "What can I contribute to the world?" and "What are my talents and skills?" Establishing an occupational identity may be one of the most challenging aspects of creating a self-identity during adolescence (Chavez, 2016; Lin et al., 2018). It includes making decisions about how to live as an adult in society through paid or unpaid work or through service to others. By creating an occupational identity, teens make decisions about their education, family relationships, and the type of occupation or work they will pursue.

Work contributes to identity, and status is associated with different kinds of work, such as office work or manual labor and career fields such as childcare or medicine. At the same time, teens identify others and make assumptions about others' characteristics based on stereotypes about their line of work, gender, both positive and negative, although not always accurately (Daniels & Sherman, 2016). For teens facing **marginalization**, or relegation to an unimportant or powerless position, there may be more real or perceived boundaries for establishing an occupational identity as there may be fewer opportunities for exploration (Sumner et al., 2018).

Political Identity

As teen brains mature, they are better able to utilize abstract thinking and to solve complex problems. Establishing a **political identity** is an essential part of adolescence that continues through adulthood.

Political identity includes the development of social responsibility and agency. In establishing a political identity, teens will ask, "What do I stand for?" and "What do I believe to be true?" For example, teens may establish a political stance about racial issues, global warming, or animal rights. With every major life transition, teens must re-establish who they are and how to be true to themselves and the world in which they live. Political identity plays a large part in developing positive relationships with others. It is also related to moral development (Porter, 2013; Wolak & Stapleton, 2020).

Political identity is socially constructed as it is influenced by primary caregivers, mentors, peers, culture, school experiences, and community or civic engagement (Cech, 2017; Kelly, 2018; Schulz, 2006). This strong influence may be particularly true for political party affiliation and voting as teens reach voting age (Hufer et al., 2020). Helping, serving, or civic experiences also contribute to forming a teen's political identity (Yates & Youniss, 1998). Because most teens live at home with family and attend school, their political ideals and worldviews are often similar to these influencers. However, as teens become more independent and autonomous toward the end of adolescence, their views may become more divergent (Hufer et al., 2020).

By young adulthood, most people can accurately describe their own political and spiritual or religious beliefs with some degree of accuracy. They know their own likes and dislikes, tastes and preferences. They may know what they are good at, what they struggle with, and how they relate to others. This does not happen overnight; it is a gradual process, as young adults experience education, the political expressions of others, the workforce, and family transitions.

☑ CHECKPOINT

☐ How do egocentrism, personal fable, and invincibility relate to adolescent socioemotional development?

☐ How are temperament and personality related? Which is more stable?

☐ Why is self-identity important to healthy socioemotional development during adolescence? Name some factors that influence it.

15.3 Family Relationships

Some have viewed adolescence as a stage of life when conflict within the family and other close relationships is inevitable. Early in the twentieth century, psychologist Stanley Hall called this time **storm and stress**. The term highlights the intensity of conflicts between teens who are struggling for independence and who are highly sensitive at the same time (Arnett, 2006). This negative description of adolescence was pervasive for decades and served as a warning to primary caregivers and siblings alike. Although conflict is inevitable in any close relationship, recent research has demonstrated that conflict is not necessarily problematic for teens.

Most relationships between teens and family members are reported to be harmonious and satisfying (Adams et al., 1989; Whiteman et al., 2011). Typical disagreements tend to focus on short-lived things such as household chores, time spent with peers, emotional moodiness, or personal habits or choices (Allison, 2000). Conflict between teens and primary caregivers tends to peak during the early years of adolescence. The frequency and intensity of disputes tend to flatten as teens mature and parents or guardians become more comfortable with their growing independence as relationships ebb and flow over time (Allison, 2000; Boele et al., 2019a; Pinquart, 2017a, 2017b).

When the members of a family believe their relationships with each other are strong, this offers the potential for many positive outcomes (see Figure 15.5). For example, teens who perceive positive relationships with their primary caregivers are less likely to experience depression during adolescence and later during midlife (Chen & Harris, 2019). This was measured using teens' perceptions of high family cohesion and low levels of family conflict

A

B

C

PamelaJoeMcFarlane/E+ via Getty Images; Jaren Jai Wicklund/Shutterstock.com; MBI/Shutterstock.com

Figure 15.5 Family units can offer a sense of belonging to members.
As a teen, how did you spend time with your family? How did it change from childhood?

within their own families. When teens experience acceptance or warmth from their primary caregivers, they often demonstrate less negative externalizing behavior, such as sarcasm or belligerence.

Positive parent-teen relationships and the inverse relationship with negative externalizing behaviors extend past adolescence into young adulthood (Roelofs et al., 2006; Sequeira et al., 2019; White & Renk, 2012). In addition, teen-parent harmony may vary by culture, as measured by the level or quantity of praise, encouragement, or communicated responsibilities and expectations (Chen & Harris, 2019; Lansford et al., 2021; Whiteman et al., 2011). However, when teens perceive and report the existence of hostility with primary caregivers, more behavioral problems such as defiance or negative interactions both within the family and externally are likely (Richman & Stocker, 2006; Van Holland De Graaf et al., 2018).

Sibling relationships are complex, and as each sibling presents individual needs, temperament, capabilities, motivations, and desires, the conflicts between teens and their siblings rise and fall (McHale et al., 2006; Waid et al., 2020). These relationships can be the source of conflict within family systems. Sibling relationships tend to be less close and intense as teens approach the end of adolescence and become more autonomous and independent (McHale et al., 2006; Odudu et al., 2020).

Families face transitions as their members grow, mature, and experience life. Transitions in roles and responsibilities have a particularly significant effect on the quality of these relationships (Boele et al., 2019a; Schulenberg et al., 2003; Whiteman et al., 2011). Transitions such as experiencing puberty, changing schools, obtaining a driver's license, getting a job, and developing intimate peer relationships are all examples of transitional changes that may occur within a teen's life. Likewise, transitions in the lives of other family members may also occur.

Normative transitions, especially during early and middle adolescence, are significant within families as each family member adjusts to changing roles. For example, as children become teens, they may have more decision-making and care responsibilities within their family (Allison, 2000; Butterfield et al., 2019; Schulenberg et al., 2003). Family transitions during later adolescence also affect family relationships. This occurs as teens begin to take on more adult-like roles, such as in employment, school responsibilities, and family social relationships.

As teens transition toward young adulthood, they often report improving relationships with parents, guardians, and other family members compared to earlier adolescent years (Crone, 2016; Whiteman et al., 2011). Most research has either focused on the teen preparing to leave home and establish independence or on the primary caregiver who no longer has dependent children living in the family home. Some recent research explores the positive and negative effect of this transition on younger siblings (Whiteman et al., 2011). Birth order and gender influence these relationships as some sisters and younger siblings report more closeness or intimacy in their relationships during adolescence (Becht et al., 2021; Kim et al., 2006).

Global Perspectives

The Impact of Family Poverty and Homelessness on Teens

The impact of poverty on teens is significant. Teens who experience low socioeconomic status (SES), whose families experience stress related to resource instability, are often considered at risk of pronounced emotional and social harm (Giano et al., 2020; Hyde, 2005). Because adolescents become more independent and autonomous as they mature, they may be subject to family socioeconomic decisions that affect them more than their younger siblings. For example, families may expect working-age teens to contribute financially or participate in family decision-making.

Some teens experience housing insecurity due to high housing costs relative to their family's income, overcrowding, poor housing quality, and/or unstable neighborhoods. Housing insecurity takes many forms, including frequent moves or relocations, sometimes without warning such as with eviction. It can include homelessness, temporarily living with friends and relatives, shelter living, or transitional housing, all of which provide temporary housing for certain sectors of the homeless population (Embleton et al., 2016; Heinze et al., 2012). These resources are often not as welcoming or even available to families with adolescent children. As a result, families may

(Continued)

separate in their attempts to find housing. According to the National Conference of State Legislatures (2019), 1 in every 30 teens in the United States is homeless and unaccompanied by a primary caregiver in any given year.

For most teens facing homelessness, the causes of family separation include relationship incompatibility, conflict, abuse, or the inability of primary caregivers to provide care (Buccieri, 2019; Heinze et al., 2012; Hyde, 2005). The Pew Trust Research Foundation (Wiltz, 2017) reports that nearly 40% of teens who face homelessness sexually identify as lesbian, gay, bisexual, or transgender; they often leave home due to being dismissed, disowned, or shunned by their families. A third of these teens report having to exchange sex for their basic needs, whereas homeless heterosexual teens report less than 10% of sex as currency. Other causes of teen homelessness include aging out of foster care, mental health issues, pregnancy, trouble with the law, or substance abuse by the teen or primary caregiver (Ferguson, 2009; Heinze et al., 2012; National Conference of State Legislatures, 2019).

Homelessness can profoundly affect a teen's physical, cognitive, and socioemotional development. Besides the increased possibility of malnutrition, poor hygiene, substance abuse, and unattended medical and dental needs, teens who are homeless often face threats to their physical well-being. Violence, in the form of assault, abuse, rape, and homicide, is not uncommon among homeless youth, and many teens protect themselves by formulating their own "street families" (Smith, 2008). These impacts are often physically visible.

Behavioral symptoms that show cognitive and socioemotional delays include low self-esteem, being withdrawn or listless, hostility or aggression, and fatigue. In addition, teens facing homelessness often have difficulty trusting others, are emotionally needy, drop out of school, and are forced to make decisions that are typically beyond their maturity level (Buckner & Bassuk, 2001; Schmitz & Tyler, 2016). Teens facing homelessness may also lose control, resulting in bossy, promiscuous, or risky behaviors. These negative effects often set a teen up for disadvantage throughout life, not the least being a lack of hope for the future (Hughes et al., 2010).

☑ CHECKPOINT

- ☐ How and why do warm, supportive relationships between teens and parents continue to be important in adolescence?
- ☐ How do most teens perceive their relationships with parents or guardians? How do life transitions influence these relationships?
- ☐ During which part of adolescence do most teen-parent conflicts occur? What are the typical topics of conflict?
- ☐ How do sibling relationships change during the teen years?
- ☐ How might family poverty and homelessness affect teens?

Apply Here!

Describe how you have seen positive teen-parent relationships play out in the lives of people you know as the teen matured from early to late adolescence. Choose three to five relationships that you are personally familiar with or have observed. Write a descriptive story about each one. How do your stories relate to the content learned so far about adolescent physical, cognitive, and social development? How might teens' positive or negative relationships with parents or guardians influence these relationships and others throughout their whole lives?

Global Perspectives

What Is the Connection Between Teens and Violence?

According to the World Health Organization (2020), youth violence is a key health issue for teens worldwide. Homicide is the fourth-leading cause of death among teens, representing over 42% of all homicides, with the vast majority involving teen males. Most perpetrators are male, too. Firearms, gangs, and bullying often play a part in the violence, resulting in homicide or physical, psychological, or social trauma and injury.

School shootings have increased in recent years in the United States, Brazil, Finland, Germany, Greece, and other countries where teens may find access to firearms (Kellner, 2018). The epidemic proportions of violence have been associated with mental health issues, violence in the media, and gun legislation (Flannery et al., 2013; Rowhani-Rahbar & Moe, 2019). Males are the most frequent offenders. They often cite emotional rage due to their feelings of victimization, often from bullying.

Gangs are groups who share a common identity and who are involved in delinquent or unlawful behavior. Fights and aggression or harm caused by weapons such as knives or guns are often associated with gangs and territorial rule. Gangs are not just a US phenomenon; they are common worldwide and include all demographics, urban and rural. Teens are often motivated to join gangs to connect with others. But the consequences can be dire, ranging from exposure to violence, drugs and other substances, and other criminal activities (American Academy of Child and Adolescent Psychiatry, 2016). Results can include incarceration, harm to self or family, and even death.

As teens collectively experience the critical period of self-identity development, peer aggression may surface as they seek to find their place, especially in peer power relationships. Bullying may be defined as dominance-oriented aggressive behaviors focused on and repeated toward the victim. Although conflict among peers is normal as social relationships change, aggressive power relationships in the form of bullying can result in emotional or physical harm (Menesini & Salmivalli, 2017; Reijntjes et al., 2016; Rodkin et al., 2015).

Bullying, too, is seen worldwide, especially among teens (Espelage et al., 2021; Smith et al., 2016). In the United States, nearly 25% of teens in public school reported weekly bullying among students (Wang et al., 2020). Although teen bullying traditionally involved physical proximity, social media has introduced a new generation of cyberbullying. Cyberbullying uses electronic means to demean, embarrass, threaten, or harass victims.

Gender inequality increases vulnerability to violence (Blondeel et al., 2018; Namy et al., 2017). Violence directed toward women and girls is of particular concern around the world, especially in low- and middle-income settings. In a study that examined global patterns of violence, as well as attitudes and social norms in 190 countries (UNICEF, 2014), findings included the following:

- More than 1 in 3 teen girls report experiencing bullying regularly.
- Approximately 25% of teen girls say that they have been the victims of physical violence.
- At least 1 in 10 teen girls report having been subjected to forced intercourse or sexual acts.
- Approximately 1 in 3 teens have been victims of physical, emotional, or sexual violence inflicted by their intimate partner.
- About 3 in 10 adults worldwide believe that physical punishment is necessary to raise or educate children properly.
- Almost half of teen girls report that the practice of a husband beating his wife is justified.

A variety of risk factors have been attributed to teen violence. Factors related to the individual teen include behavioral and learning disorders, low educational achievement, crime involvement, and family violence exposure. Some risk factors from close relationships include low parental involvement and attachment, delinquent peers, or gang membership. Other risk factors that exacerbate teen violence are impoverished communities, or those having a high degree of income inequity, and those that give easy access to firearms, drugs, and alcohol (Skrzypiec et al., 2020; Wiseman, 2021). It is known that teens are particularly vulnerable to violence due to their lack of social, economic, and political power (Chiang et al., 2021; Lopez et al., 2008).

To Think About

- Based on what you know about adolescent physical, cognitive, and socioemotional development, why are teens particularly vulnerable to both inflicting and being victims of violence?
- Are there demographic profiles of teens who are particularly vulnerable to victimization?
- Have you personally known someone who has been affected by bullying? Have you encountered antiviolence programs that have been effective in your school or community? How can teachers help students who are subjected to bullying?

15.4 Peer Relationships

Family relationships influence how teens interact with their peers. Primary caregivers in particular are the first role models for children in maintaining and nurturing relationships (Boele et al., 2019b; Van der Graaff et al., 2014). Children and teens learn how to trust and care for others and deal with interpersonal conflict through these first relationships. Peer friendships differ from family relationships, however, as they offer more opportunity to engage with high levels of equality, intimacy, and trust (Boele et al., 2019b; Smith, 2015; Smith & Rose, 2011).

Positive relationships with peers are critical to mental health during adolescence and are specifically shown to decrease the potential for depression in teens, especially among girls (Cicchetti & Toth, 2016; Hankin, 2005; Rice & Mulkeen, 1995). Quality relationships with mothers are critical to peer acceptance and lower depression rates for daughters (Alto et al., 2018; Romund et al., 2016). Peer relationships may offer a protective factor for teens who are at-risk. **At-risk** is a term used to describe children or teens who are considered to have a higher probability of struggling, failing, or dropping out of school, or facing other circumstances that may jeopardize life choices and opportunities. This may include serious health issues, homelessness, teen pregnancy, incarceration, or limited job prospects.

Close and supportive relationships that have low conflict can offer protective safeguards or buffers against risky decision-making. They can increase resiliency and provide a high degree of satisfaction (Grych et al., 2015; Lerner et al., 2009). As a result, positive peer relationships increase self-esteem, social competence, social emotional learning (SEL) skills, and independence or autonomy (Lafko et al., 2015; Moses & Villodas, 2017; Oberle et al., 2010). In addition, positive peer relationships increase academic achievement and involvement (Vaquera & Kao, 2008).

Although teen peer relationships offer many protective factors, they pose possible risk factors when quality is low by leading to more risky behaviors. (Moses & Villodas, 2017; Rudolph et al., 2016). For example, teens with friends who drink alcohol, smoke tobacco, misuse other substances, or are involved in traumatic sexual relationships are more likely to engage in these behaviors themselves (Patterson et al., 2000; Rose, 2008; Spencer et al., 2021).

As relationships within the family begin to change and peers become increasingly important, teens want to fit in with the crowd, be accepted, and also hold high-ranking status within peer groups (Cillessen & Mayeux 2004; Devine & Apperly, 2021; Rubin et al., 2006). Peer popularity refers to a person's prominence or visibility within their peer group (Cillessen et al., 2011). When a teen lacks prominence or visibility, they may consider themselves unpopular. Likeability, or peer acceptance, is sometimes a part of popularity, but popularity may also be established and maintained through dominance or negative behaviors. Likeability is also related to peer acceptance and rejection, especially for younger teens (LaFontana & Cillessen, 2010; van den Berg et al., 2015).

For younger teens, such as those ages 13 to 15, peer popularity is very important and is often perceived by the number of friends a teen has accumulated, whether in person or virtually. Friends often have similar tastes in music, fashion, hobbies, sports, or other activities. In younger adolescence, peers are more influential than ever before. Being popular often overrides the need to follow the rules, meet parental or teacher expectations, or live up to their own personal values (Waldrip et al., 2008; Wentzel et al., 2004). The mechanisms of peer popularity, peer acceptance or rejection, or aggressive peer behaviors are complex. They likely include added contextual factors, such as the racial or ethnic composition of the neighborhood and school environment (Graham & Echols, 2018; Meuwese et al., 2017; Rosenthal & Kobak, 2010).

Peer romantic relationships can result in positive self-worth and improved skills in creating intimate relationships, especially in middle to late adolescence (see Figure 15.6) (Laursen & Mooney, 2007; Xia et al., 2018). On the other hand, these relationships can have a great negative impact when they include an abundance of conflict, power differentials, or abuse (Collins, 2003; Zimmer-Gembeck et al., 2001).

Other factors that influence whether a teen romantic relationship has primarily positive or negative outcomes are whether the relationship is experienced independently—the couple on their own—or within a larger social group. Romantic relationships

SpeedKingz/Shutterstock.com

Figure 15.6 Peer relationships can result in positive self-worth and improved skills in creating social relationships, especially in middle to late adolescence.

that separate teens from the larger social group tend to have more negative outcomes, including anxiety and depression (Collibee & Furman, 2015; Kansky & Allen, 2018). These positive and negative outcomes tend to influence peer and family relationship quality, self-esteem, and overall mental health, behavior issues, and academic achievement (Laursen & Mooney, 2007).

Primary caregivers and educators may play essential roles in helping teens develop quality peer relationships that are low in conflict. This includes modeling compassion for others, communicating emotions and needs, and demonstrating conflict management skills. Primary caregivers indirectly shape how teens think about their peers, both in the selection of their own friendships and the emphasis they place on these relationships (Lee et al., 2016). For example, a parent might make an extra effort to spend time with a friend, which demonstrates the value of prioritizing personal relationships. Or a parent might share a story about a recent conflict they are having with a friend and describe to their teen how they are handling it.

Primary caregivers can also help in orchestrating teen social relationships. For example, primary caregivers who participate in their teenagers' education may help their children select coursework that creates communities where friendships are formed between like-minded teens (Frank et al., 2013). Parents may also encourage teens to try new activities where they will have opportunities to interact with peers who have similar interests.

Educators, coaches, and other supportive adults can aid teens in mediating conflict and promoting SEL skills (Gregory et al., 2014; Wang & Eccles, 2012). Learning empathy, the capacity to understand or feel what another person is experiencing, is an important factor in teens' peer relationships, lending closeness and relationship quality and lowering levels of aggression (Alleman et al., 2015; Eisenberg et al. 2010). Parents and teachers can also help teens navigate appropriate displays of empathy by modeling acceptance and respectful relationships within family and academic environments (Batanova & Loukas, 2016; Bornstein & Lamb, 2011; Mikami et al., 2011). However, recent studies show that empathy is not the only strong variable in adolescent peer relationships. It is a complex and multi-layered variable to measure, but it may be one piece of SEL skills related to quality peer relationships (Portt et al., 2020). Relationship skills also include other SEL skills such as responsible decision-making, social awareness, and self-management (Yang et al., 2020).

☑ CHECKPOINT

- ☐ How do teen peer relationships differ from relationships with family members?
- ☐ What mental health benefits do quality peer relationships offer teens?
- ☐ What role does conflict play in teen romantic relationships?
- ☐ How can parents, guardians, and other mentors help teens foster positive peer relationships?

Apply Here!

What a difference a few months can make! As a healthcare provider, Tay was noticing a trend with the group of notoriously rowdy 7th graders she worked with. They were starting to act more civil, encouraging, supportive, and kind to each other. Verbal taunts and acts of excluding others had diminished. They were doing their best academically. Tay was proud of each of her students individually and proud of them collectively.

From the outside, many would guess that this class of 7th graders would struggle socially and academically as most were living in poverty. Some were challenged with unstable housing, and food was sometimes scarce. Tay suspected that in the upcoming colder months, some may not have adequate or warm enough clothing

(Continued)

to wear. Tay also knew that several of them came from violent homes, and the larger community in general was known for high levels of violence. Tay took this as a challenge to provide services to these 7th graders. This school and community were where Tay wanted to serve and support the group to thrive academically and socially.

Tay privately vowed to do everything possible to create an environment where the 7th graders would feel safe—even a reprieve from the challenges in their own lives. Tay knew that it had to include more than how she treated them, but also how they learned to treat each other. Tay decided to begin with helping them identify and express their feelings, and then use that understanding to take on the perspectives of others. Respect, empathy, and self-regulation became the underlying theme of all group meetings. Tay used news stories, books, social media, journal writing, film, and discussions to create an environment that promoted positive social behaviors. Tay created group expectations and rules of civil behavior with their input.

Tay looked out over the group of 7th graders and felt so proud of them. A few weeks ago, they had been talking about the problems of bullying and intimidation. This led to a discussion about feeling left out. Tay had shared a story with them about a school group who had created their own social media site where teens could sit out when feeling excluded and others could join to keep them company.

The group quickly latched on to this idea, creating their own version of the "friendship site." Their site was designed so that teens could connect when feeling lonely. At first Tay wondered if it would really work once the novelty wore off. But much to Tay's delight, almost every day there were new "encouragement buddies" being formed. It was a simple solution—but one that the kids owned. Consider:

- What are some of the peer challenges that affect the lives of younger teens?
- In what ways do school or other group settings help or hinder social relationships?

Practical Issues and Implications

Alone Together: Is Teen Loneliness Typical or Linked to Social Media?

Today's teens are socially connected. In a 2018 Pew Research study, 95% of US teens reported having access to a smartphone, and 45% say they are online "almost constantly" using YouTube, Instagram, Snapchat, or the most current social media platform (Anderson & Jiang, 2018). This reflects nearly a 21% increase in social media usage in the 7 years between 2011 and 2017 (Twenge et al., 2019). Teens check on friends and acquaintances, follow influencers and celebrities, view the latest video clips and memes, and post about their lives. Teen social interaction and support are linked to many positive outcomes, including increased mental and physical health (Breiner et al., 2018; Cicchetti & Toth, 2016; Hankin, 2005; Rice & Mulkeen, 1995).

If they are so connected, why are teens reportedly so lonely? Loneliness, an emotional state of feeling disconnected socially, is common during adolescence (Blakemore, 2012; Mund et al., 2020; Qualter et al., 2013). Reported feelings of loneliness climb from childhood and through adolescence and early adulthood before finally decreasing after age 50. Despite social media connections, it does not appear that these trends are changing (Mund et al., 2020). In fact, loneliness among Americans is higher than ever reported previously, with more than 1 in 10 Americans reporting being lonely (Bialik, 2018).

Sometimes loneliness is linked to situational or external experiences, such as abuse, neglect, bullying, boredom, or societal events, such as a global pandemic that socially distances people (Knopf, 2020; Loades et al., 2020). At other times, loneliness is linked to internal mental health factors, such as personality or genetics. These external and internal factors are often linked (Mahon et al., 2006). The COVID-19 global pandemic combined internal and external factors for many teens in a devastating way as they faced school closures, family financial crises, and the absence of social activities (Cohen et al., 2021; de Figueiredo et al., 2021; Rogers et al., 2021).

When loneliness becomes overwhelming, there are many impacts, including decreased mental and physical health, academic failure, and lower life satisfaction. It can also lead to serious issues such as disordered eating or addictive behaviors resulting in substance abuse, self-harming, anxiety, depression, and even suicide (Kong & You, 2013; Mund et al., 2020; Qualter et al., 2013). Across gender and socio-economic lines, 7 out of 10 US teens report concern for their own or their peers' mental health, especially related to anxiety and depression (Horowitz & Graf, 2019).

Some studies find that social media usage may be linked to teens' feelings of loneliness and depression because teens spend less time physically together, especially without a planned agenda of activities (McCrae et al., 2017; Nowland et al., 2018; Twenge et al., 2019). In addition, if most of their interactions happen online, teens may not be learning to hone socioemotional skills, such as eye contact or active listening, to enhance in-person interactions when they do occur (Twenge et al., 2019). Other studies argue that social media provides an enhanced opportunity for teens who may be shy or emotionally reserved, offsetting their feelings of loneliness and increasing the probability of in-person interaction afterwards while building self-esteem and their sense of self (Beyens et al., 2020; Lima et al., 2017; Lui et al., 2017).

What do teens think? In a large national study, about one-third of US teens surveyed found social media had a mostly positive effect on their lives, allowing them to stay connected and lowering stress levels (see Figure 15.7). About 25% said that it has a negative influence. Social media use has become a pervasive and ubiquitous aspect of teen life. During the COVID-19 pandemic, teens worldwide found themselves separated, often participating in remote or online classroom learning. Teen loneliness, feelings of isolation, and mental health concerns increased dramatically, despite being connected through social media (Ellis et al., 2020; Stephenson, 2021).

To Think About

- Did you experience loneliness as a teen? Did social media make you feel more connected or less connected with others? Why?

- Social media is an important tool for connecting socially and for learning. It can also promote isolation. Can social media be enhanced or combined with in-person interactions to better enhance adolescent socioemotional development? If so, how?

- Did you experience unexpected remote learning during the COVID-19 pandemic? If so, how did this affect your learning? Did social media help you feel connected during the pandemic or removed from others? How?

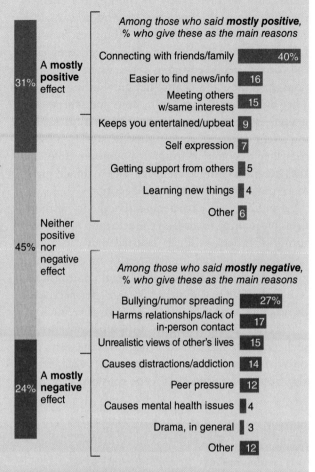

Survey conducted March 7-April 10, 2018
Note: Responses have been coded into categories. Figures may add up to more than 100% because multiple responses were allowed.

Pew Research Center

Figure 15.7 This is what teens say about the positive and negatives of social media on their relationships.
What do you think?

15.5 Moral Development

Moral development undergoes significant changes during the teen years. As cognitive and socioemotional development occur, teens' beliefs about right and wrong and what is fair and right continue to evolve. As younger teens move from concrete to more abstract thinking, they begin to think in all-or-nothing terms. This type of thinking may affect moral reasoning. For example, when taking a political view, moral thinking tends to take on a strong stance with no room for variances or nuances. The concepts of justice and equity become intriguing as teens interact with others (da Silva Pinho et al., 2021).

Jean Piaget (1932) included moral development in his stages of cognitive development. Lawrence Kohlberg (1981) further developed Piaget's foundational work. According to Kohlberg's theory of moral development, adolescents are more likely to consider the effect of their decisions and actions on others instead of making ethical decisions with only their self-interest in mind. In late childhood and early adolescence, teens enter the **conventional reasoning** stage, when social relationships, rules, and conformity grow in importance. They often seek approval from peers and others when making moral decisions that have social impact. Having a reputation of being a "good person" or a "troublemaker" becomes increasingly important. Rules and laws become central as teens strive to maintain group social order or create a separate identity.

Carol Gilligan's **care perspective** theory of moral decision-making focuses on the attention to and nurturing of others. Gilligan asserted that psychology had repeatedly and systematically misunderstood girls and women's motives and moral commitments (Gilligan, 1982, 1988). This care perspective is increasingly common in adolescence (Davis, 2018; Skuse et al., 2017). Concerns for social conventions, such as justice and care for others, and the teen's perceived role or responsibility in social relationships also become important as teens consider their civic duty, or obligation and responsibility toward others (Crocetti et al., 2012; Gibbs, 2014; Nucci, 2013). In early adolescence, as in later childhood, teens continue to show care and compassion, altruism, and justice (Fett et al., 2014; Gibbs, 2014).

Young teens are just beginning to make moral decisions based on universal principles. Universal principles include collective ideas such as the ethics of right and wrong, justice, equality, freedom, and human rights. Kohlberg termed this the **post-conventional morality** stage. Teens may begin to believe that it is wrong to cheat or steal, because the act can negatively affect others. Previously, in middle childhood, they may have based that decision on whether they were likely to be caught, perceived differently, or breaking the rules. This transformation, however, is far from complete. Most young adolescents still struggle with whether to report a friend for breaking a rule or law, such as cheating on a test or shoplifting. As teens move into post-conventional morality, mutual social expectations or obligations and the effect of decisions or actions on society come into play (see Table 15.5) (Chopik et al., 2017; Moshman, 2011).

Stage/Focus	Description	Perspective	Typical age
1: Heteronomous morality	Following rules, obedience, punishment, and reward; the child is more likely to ask, "How will this decision affect (benefit or hurt) me?"	Autonomous	0–6
2: Individualism and exchange	Enlightened self-interest, acknowledging others' interests to get needs met; the child is more likely to ask, "How will this decision affect (benefit or hurt) me or give others what they want?" (Will I get approval from my mother and make her happy, too?)	Relationship between self and others	6–10
3: Mutual expectations	Moral social obligation, fulfilling expectations of others, perceived role responsibilities; the child is more likely to ask, "Will this decision affect (benefit or hurt) others around me or give them what they want?"	Relationships between others, groups	10+
4: Social system	Considering the moral decision impact on society as a whole; the child is likely to ask, "Will this decision affect (benefit or hurt) society as a whole such as in breaking a law?"	Beyond personal relationships to abstract understanding of social institutions	12+
5: Social contract	Found in complex societies, transcending culture, and permitting cross-cultural analyses; the individual is most likely to ask, "Will this decision affect (benefit or hurt) society on a large scale? Is it universally right or wrong?"	Universal truth through complex analysis	Adulthood, may not be reached

Chopik et al., 2017; Moshman, 2011

Table 15.5 Kohlberg's Moral Development Stages

A   B

Figure 15.8 Teens are often idealistic and concerned about their impact on the world. (A) Greta Thunberg and (B) Malala Yousafzai are examples of teen moral influencers.
Can you identify teen moral influencers within your school or community?

As noted previously, teens tend to see moral decisions in all-or-nothing terms. For example, it is typical for middle teens to label inconsistencies they see in adults as hypocrisy or acting in contradiction to a person's stated beliefs or values. In contrast, older teens can recognize nuances and may no longer see situations as an all-or-nothing choice. They are often idealistic and concerned about their impact on the world. They can embrace moral issues with conviction (Moshman, 2011; Mestre et al., 2018). Cross-cultural studies support the theory that teens throughout the world typically enter the post-conventional morality stage as they move from a self-focus to societally and other-focused moral decision-making (Snarey & Keljo, 1991; Thoma et al., 2019; Turiel, 2002). Malala Yousafzai and Greta Thunberg are both examples of teen moral influencers because they stood for the universal truths of justice, truth, and equality (see Figure 15.8). Malala Yousafzai stood as a Pakistani education advocate, demanding justice and equality in girls' education. Greta Thunberg, a Swedish teen, challenged world leaders to take immediate action for climate change.

Establishing Personal Values and Moral Identity

One of the most important tasks during adolescence is the development of personal values and a related code of conduct. This becomes a part of **moral identity** (Hardy et al., 2014). Primary caregivers must help their children learn positive values and appropriate behavior during childhood. Children

respond, but they do so mainly to get approval and praise from their parents and other adults. During adolescence, teens must decide what type of people they will be. This involves evaluating, choosing, and committing to specific values and ideals. This is not a quick or easy process, and it requires time for reflection. It also takes place at a time when so much else is going on in teens' lives (Miller et al., 2012; Recchia et al., 2014).

Establishing values is strongly influenced by culture and religious traditions. In adolescence, asking questions is common. To teens, establishing personal values often seems contradictory. Media may portray a "think of yourself first" lifestyle as personally rewarding. At the same time, many teens are developing more empathy and finding real satisfaction in helping others, such as through service projects. They may adhere to religious beliefs that run counter-culture.

Teens' increasing ability to analyze and reason causes them to reexamine the beliefs and rules of their families and those of the larger culture and society. This can be difficult for primary caregivers because teens sometimes seem to ignore all they have learned about right and wrong. They want and need to understand the reasons behind the beliefs of the adults in their lives. However, teens may tend to push them away in an attempt to become independent or autonomous (Pasupathi et al., 2007; Reinders & Youniss, 2006).

Recent research has shown that moral development during adolescence is complex and multidimensional (Hardy et al., 2014; Hart & Carlo,

2005). Many variables contribute to moral development, including social norms, belief systems, and overarching cultural values. For example, teens who hold strong religious beliefs within a larger cultural context are shown to be less likely to engage in viewing or consuming pornography (Hardy et al., 2013b). This environmental influence is termed the **moral atmosphere** (Hart & Carlo, 2005). There appears to be some similarity among global cultures in defining what morality entails, including such factors as courage, justice, humanity, temperance, and wisdom. However, how these are applied in teen moral decision-making is not yet understood (Thoma et al., 2019).

Moral development is also personal. When a teen begins to form a moral identity, making decisions becomes a part of how the teen perceives their moral self (Lapsley, 2008; Walker, 2004). It becomes a part of doing the "right" or consistent thing as a part of self-identity (Hardy et al., 2014). Ultimately, teens must consider what kind of adult they want to be. What are their personal goals? Many look to role models, people who have the characteristics they would like to exhibit. Even role models change with more maturity. For a 13-year-old, it may be the latest star. For a 17-year-old, a role model is more likely to be someone with values or an outlook they want to emulate. Integrating personal ideology and self-imposed expectations of behaviors or actions is the **idealized self**. In early adolescence, the ideal self may be based on celebrities or acquaintances. As teens mature, their ideal self is often formulated around close relationships or role models within the family, school, and community (Dunkel & Anthis, 2001; Oyserman & James, 2011). Establishing an idealized self may provide purpose in life and validate social role expectations (Boele et al., 2019b; Hardy et al., 2013a; Schwartz et al., 2011).

☑ CHECKPOINT

☐ How does Kohlberg's post-conventional morality stage differ from his conventional stage?

☐ Describe the care perspective of moral decision-making.

☐ What are teens likely to consider when making moral decisions and actions?

Apply Here!

Imagine that you have been asked to visit a high school leadership class to discuss personal decision-making. How might you describe the process of making tough or controversial decisions? What examples might you use? What or who should be considered when making tough decisions? What or who is most important to consider when making a tough decision? Make a list of at least three challenging or difficult decisions that students will likely face as they go through their high school years.

15.6 Older Adolescence and Emerging Adulthood

In many countries, including the United States, the law often treats teens as adults when they become 18 years of age. They reach important milestones, such as being eligible to vote. They can also be tried as adults in a court of law. However, upon reaching their 18th birthday, teens do not suddenly become independent adults. The transition from teen to independent adult varies for everyone. This transitional stage of **emerging adulthood** typically occurs between ages 19 and 26.

For many people, the self-definition of adulthood does not happen until they meet certain social roles and expectations. Social relationships are the main supports that help youth circumnavigate adolescence and the transition to adulthood (Zarrett & Eccles, 2006). Social expectations of late adolescence and adulthood vary by culture and are often tied to **social clock** expectations, or cultural expectations of when major life milestones should occur. These expectations may include completing an education, living alone, establishing a career, marrying, or having children. Family members often reinforce these social clock expectations (Arnett, 2007; Laible et al., 2004).

Despite familial and cultural expectations, there comes a time when young adults must claim responsibility for their well-being. Many young adults leave their parental homes and establish their independent lifestyles. Some less-advantaged teens may need to assume financial responsibility to support the family or become caretakers of others. Making good decisions and taking care of one's needs and the needs of others become more evident (Arnett, 2001; Crocetti et al., 2017). Older teens often become more responsible for making decisions that can affect their lifestyle for years to come (Laible, 2007). Some teens may decide to continue with education and attend a college or university. Others may pursue a career option immediately after high school. Joining the military or traveling abroad are still other options.

Late adolescence and emerging adulthood are often a time of experimentation (Kloep, 2015). Since older teens are dealing with many new transitions, they may experience new emotions, and these changes can be challenging. Leaving a well-known environment for an entirely new location with new people can be intimidating and stressful. Young adults may feel fear, anxiety, and depression. Adjusting may be difficult. On the other hand, life transitions can be perceived as exciting, as older teens establish their adult identities and manage their own lives. They gain new friends, experiences, and knowledge. Feeling a range of emotions is common and normal during this time, especially when environments and living situations change.

Gaining independence is just beginning in the late teen years. At this time, teens are building the many skills necessary to become self-sufficient adults. Older teens typically feel like they have reached the stage of full maturity. As a result, they expect others to treat them as adults, especially as they make day-to-day decisions (Laible, 2007). In addition to brain development and maturity, the hormones that drive the body's push toward physical maturity also set in motion the drive for autonomy, independence that includes personal responsibility and decision-making. Teens must become individuals and less dependent on their families. They must develop a personal identity with their own beliefs and goals. Their increasing cognitive abilities help them with this process (Laible et al., 2004).

For older teens, the question of what they will do after high school is a more immediate decision. Is college a goal? Is occupational training a good idea? Will they seek employment? Teachers, school counselors, employers, primary caregivers, and other adults play an important role in helping teens navigate the decisions they are making during this stage, but ultimately the goals must be the teens' own (Arnett, 2007; Becht et al., 2021; Hair et al., 2008).

☑ CHECKPOINT

- ☐ Identify and describe the characteristics of the emerging adulthood stage.
- ☐ How does the concept of social clock affect development?
- ☐ What does gaining independence in late adolescence involve?

Apply Here!

Interview several older teens or reflect on your own life as an older teen. Ask older teens to predict what their life might look like at age 30. For example, have them calculate time to finish a college degree or vocational training, to save for housing, to establish a long-term relationship, to be established in a career, to have children. This will help students to be more realistic about their ideas, especially concerning lifestyle and income.

Summary

As a teen's cognitive abilities and increased lived experiences merge, one of the main tasks in adolescent socioemotional development is developing and refining a self-identity. This may be a key to personality development and change later in life. Through the process of experimenting with different behaviors, activities, personas, and roles, teens identify who they are and how they relate to others. Relationships with others are important, as teens learn to integrate their own personal disposition, social context, worldview or beliefs, purposes and goals, self-perceptions, and possible actions.

Relationships between teens and their family members are generally harmonious and satisfying. But positive peer friendships often offer higher levels of equality, intimacy, and trust. As teens mature, they become less egocentric and are more likely than before to consider the impact of their decisions and actions on others instead of only on themselves. They are more likely to enter into relationships outside the immediate family. However, the social expectations of late adolescence and adulthood vary by culture and are often tied to social clock expectations.

As in other stages of life, physical growth and development, cognitive development, and socioemotional development are interrelated, each domain depending on the others. As you reflect on what you have learned, how do you view your own experiences as a teen? Does your newly gained knowledge offer insight? If so, how? Think back through the stages of childhood and teen development covered in this chapter and all previous chapters. How can your increased knowledge positively impact your professional relationships with infants, children, and teens? How might it affect your collegial and personal relationships?

Learning Outcomes and Key Concepts

15.1 Describe common theories related to an adolescent's socioemotional development.

- Erik Erikson asserted that the main socioemotional task faced during adolescence is developing a self-identity versus role confusion.
- Erikson's work proposed four identity statuses: identity moratorium, identity achievement, identity diffusion, and identity foreclosure.
- Self-identity is determined through the process of experimenting with different behaviors, activities, personas, and roles.
- Recent research proposes extending the timing of identity moratorium well into young adulthood; it cites that few teens leave adolescence with a strong sense of self-identity.
- The complex dynamic systems approach integrates disposition, social context, along with worldview or beliefs, purposes and goals, self-perceptions, and perceived possible actions.

15.2 Discuss how the interplay among the cognitive, social, and emotional domains affect a teen's overall development.

- Maturing cognitive abilities combined with lived experience begin to meld as teens refine self-identity.
- Identity formation during adolescence is a key to personality development and change.

- Identity includes gender, racial and ethnic, occupational, political, and sexual components.
- In adolescence, emotions gradually become more controlled by the brain's prefrontal cortex, not just the limbic system.
- Risk-taking behaviors are due to the imbalance in maturity states between the limbic system and the prefrontal cortex.

15.3 Explain how a teen's relationship with family members influences their socioemotional development.

- Relationships between teens and their family members are generally harmonious and satisfying.
- Teens who perceive positive relationships with their parents are less likely to experience depression during adolescence or later.
- Sibling relationships are complex, and the conflicts between teens and their siblings ebb and flow.
- The impact of normative transitions is significant within families, as each family member adjusts to change.
- Older teens have more positive relationships with parents and family compared to younger teens.

15.4 Describe the influence of a teen's peer relationships on their socioemotional development.

- Peer friendships differ from family relationships in that there are higher levels of equality, intimacy, and trust.
- Positive relationships with peers are critical to teen mental health, decreasing the potential for depression, especially among girls.
- For teens who have experienced adverse childhood experiences, peer relationships may offer a protection from further trauma.
- Close, supportive, and low-conflict peer relationships offer buffers against risky decision-making; they also increase resiliency.
- Romantic relationships can result in positive self-worth, or they may have a negative effect if there is conflict, power differentials, or abuse.
- Parents and teachers help teens develop quality relationships by modeling warmth, conflict management, and sharing emotions and needs.

15.5 Explain the moral development milestones often achieved during adolescence.

- As cognitive and socioemotional development occur, teens' beliefs about what is right and wrong or fair and unjust continue to evolve.
- Teens are more likely to consider the impact of their decisions and actions on others instead of only on themselves.
- Kohlberg theorized that in the post-conventional morality stage, universal principles are used to make moral decisions.
- The care perspective theory of moral decision-making focuses on the care and nurturing of others.
- Teens evaluate, choose, and commit to specific values and ideals when creating a moral identity.

15.6 Discuss the socioemotional determinants of successfully transitioning to adulthood during older adolescence and early adulthood.

- Emerging adulthood is the transition from teen to independent adulthood, which typically occurs between ages 19 through 26.
- Social expectations of late adolescence and adulthood vary by culture and are often tied to social clock expectations.

Chapter Review

1. If you were writing a blog about how socioemotional development affects a teen's overall well-being in adolescence and beyond, what would be your main points?
2. If you were assigned to lead a middle school study skills group, what socioemotional considerations should be addressed?
3. Multiple domains of development such as gender and race are a part of identity development. What other domains should be included? Why is identity development during adolescence a primary focus of optimal socioemotional development for teens?
4. How do teens' cognitive, physical, social, and emotional development interact with their identity formation? How does one area inform the other? Give a life example.
5. What two components comprise sexual identity? How do the concepts of sexual identity and body image relate to each other? Be specific.
6. Explain why teens are physiologically more prone to risky behaviors than are children or adults.
7. Justify the importance of peer friendships in adolescence. If you were to write an advice blog for young teens about friendships, what would it say?
8. Create two case studies of a teen and parent relationship that illustrates how relationships change during a teen's cognitive, social, and emotional development from early to late adolescence.
9. List and describe the ways in which teens' relationships with siblings may positively or negatively affect their socioemotional development. What role should parents play in enhancing positive relationships between siblings?
10. How do peer relationships rank in comparison to parent, sibling, and extended family relationships during adolescence? How is this information useful in understanding the behavioral motivations of teens?
11. If two peers in a romantic relationship are in conflict, how might it influence a teen's identity development? Provide a specific example of a conflict and a proposed way of diffusing it.
12. How do the three domains—physical, cognitive, and socioemotional—prepare a teen for independent, emerging adulthood?

Matching

Match the following terms with the correct definitions.

A. gender identity

B. idealized self

C. identity achievement

D. identity diffusion

E. identity foreclosure

F. identity moratorium

G. individuation

H. role confusion

1. A complex process of self-identity during adolescence that involves separating from parents or guardians and requires redefinition of relationships, not dissolution of relationships

2. When exploration is absent but commitment to an identity is present, resulting in a person making premature identity decisions without adequate exploration and evaluation

3. When both exploration and commitment to an identity are absent and identity confusion occurs

4. When, through experimentation, teens develop a strong sense of identity

5. Failure to create a self-identity, resulting in a lack of understanding of one's place in society

6. A person's mental conception about their gender be it woman, man, or something else

7. When self-identity exploration is present but commitment to an identity is absent

8. The integration of both personal ideology and self-imposed expectations of behaviors or actions

Glossary

A

abstract thinking. High-level thought processes that utilize executive functions. (14)

abusive head trauma. A more descriptive term for shaken baby syndrome. (4)

accommodation. Described by Piaget as the process whereby children incorporate new information into their schema. (2)

adaptive behavior. Evolutionary change in a trait driven by natural selection so that those with the strongest traits adapt and change to the needs of the surrounding environment. (2)

adolescence. The stage in life when humans go through the transforming process of changing from children to adults, typically between ages 12 to 19. (13)

adrenarche. Another name for prepubescence. (13)

adverse childhood experience (ACE). When young children and teens experience potentially traumatic events in their lives. (1)

afterbirth stage. The last stage of birth, after delivery, when the placenta and umbilical cord are expelled. (3)

amygdala. A part of the brain's limbic system responsible for emotional reactions such as anger or joy. (14)

androgens. The primary type of male sex hormones. (13)

antibias early childhood programs. Programs that develop trusting, respectful, culturally responsive, and affirming partnerships with the children and families that they serve. (6)

Apgar scale. An assessment of a newborn's overall health. (4)

assimilation. The process of children taking in new information. (2)

associate play. When an infant plays side-by-side with another child, whether or not they are engaging or sharing toys. (6)

asynchrony. At different times; in the case of body growth, not in simultaneous occurrence. (13)

at-risk. Having a greater probability of being harmed in some way due to adverse circumstances such as exposure to poverty, abuse, or racism. (15)

attention-deficit/hyperactivity disorder (ADHD). A wide range of neurological differences causing challenges in concentration, hyperactivity, and impulsivity. (11)

authoritarian style. A parenting style that tends to be controlling and corrective. (9)

authoritative style. A parenting style that tends to give choices and encourages children to practice decision-making; also called the *democratic style*. (9)

autism spectrum disorders (ASD). A number of disorders that cause a child to have difficulty communicating with others, use repetitive behaviors and, difficulty with language. (6)

autonomy versus shame and doubt. Erikson's socio-emotional stage when young children begin to see themselves as separate from their caregivers, typically lasting from about 18 months to about 3 years of age. (9)

autosome. A pair of chromosomes. (2)

B

Babinski reflex. In the first year, a reflex of infants to respond by spreading their toes and lifting their big toe upward when the bottom of the foot is stroked; after the first year, to curl the toes downward. (4)

behavioral genetics. Field of study that attempts to explain the genetic and environmental contributions to human behavior. (2)

behaviorism. Theory that people's behavior depends on what they have seen, modeled, experienced, or been taught. (2)

big data. Large-scale collection of quantitative data used in developmental research lends itself to better understanding the complexities of social factors such as socioeconomic demographics. (1)

blastocyst. A fertilized egg divided into cells. (3)

body image. The awareness, beliefs, judgments, and feelings about one's own body. (15)

body mass index (BMI). A calculation that includes a person's age and body weight relative to height. (10)

bonding. The reciprocal emotional connection that a parent or caregiver develops with a child. (6)

brain plasticity. The malleability or adaptability of the young brain as it undergoes structural changes and maturation while responding to environmental experiences. (8)

brain stem. The base of the brain that connects the brain's cerebrum to the spinal cord and controls many instinctive and motor functions. (4)

Braxton-Hicks contractions. The first mild contractions that begin labor, sometimes weeks before actual labor begins. (3)

Brazelton Neonatal Behavioral Assessment Scale. A test that measures a baby's reflexes and responses to light, sounds, and touch to evaluate possible neurological concerns including brain damage. (4)

breech birth. The baby is in an upright rather than a head-down position through birth. (3)

bullying. Repeated aggressive behavior inflicted by someone who holds power over another. (12)

C

caesarean section. Surgical procedure to remove the baby from the womb. (3)

care perspective. Gilligan's theory of moral decision-making that focuses on the attention to and nurturing of others. (12)

care perspective. A theory of moral decision-making focused on the attention to and nurturing of others. (15)

case studies. Collection methods that look at a single individual's life experience and evaluates that individual's response within the scenario. (1)

cell. The biological building block of all living things. (2)

cell nucleus. A cell's command center, which instructs the cell to grow or change. (2)

centration. The tendency to focus on just one aspect of something seen. (8)

cephalocaudal development. Infants' physical growth and changes occurring at the top of the body first and working their way down. (4)

cerebellum. The part of the brain in the back lower part of the cerebrum that regulates muscle coordination, movement, posture, and balance. (4)

cerebral cortex. Occupies the front part of the brain and regulates the perception of touch, pressure, temperature, and pain. (4)

certified nurse midwives. Nurses who specialize in pregnancy and birth (3)

child abuse. Inflicting harm on a child or teen that may include physical, emotional, and sexual mistreatment. (7)

child-directed speech. Animated, lyrical, higher-pitched speech used by caregivers to capture the attention of infants. (5)

chronological age. Age determined by days, months, and years lived. (1)

circadian rhythms. Humans' internal clocks that influence sleep cycles, appetite, hormonal changes, and body temperature. (13)

civic duty. One's duty, obligation, and responsibility toward others even if the actions are not reciprocated. (12)

classification. The ability to sort items by one or more characteristics they have in common. (11)

cognition. Thinking, sensing, memorizing, and organizing ideas, thoughts, and actions and other mental processes involving thought and knowledge. (1)

cognitive development. The study of neurological and psychological development that includes information processing, perception, memory, language, and adaptive learning or the ability to build on previous experiences and knowledge. (1)

cognitive development theory. Piaget's theory that there are four stages of cognitive development. (2)

cognitive flexibility. The ability to switch back and forth between cognitive tasks. (11)

cognitive theory. The scientific focus on how human beings process information, think, and learn. (2)

cohort group. People born to a certain generation that share common historical experiences and ideologies. (1)

colic. A term used to describe prolonged and unexplained bouts of crying and distress in young infants. (6)

colostrum. An ingredient in breast milk that contains high concentrations of nutrients and antibodies. (4)

communities of practice. Groups or communities that create a common identity as they share ideas and knowledge over time or with practice. (11)

concentration. The ability to pay attention to something while ignoring other competing stimuli. (11)

conception. When the female egg is fertilized by sperm. (3)

concrete operational stage. A cognitive stage marked by the predominance of logic rather than relying on perceptions. (11)

concrete thinking. Logical ways of mental processing. (11)

congenital disorders. Genetic disorders that are inherited or passed down from biological parents to a baby. (3)

conservation. Term for understanding that quantity does not change even when a substance's form is altered. (2)

conservation. The ability to follow transformations of viewed objects and the ability to understand that the properties of objects can remain the same even if the way they look changes. (8)

contractions. Tightening of the uterus during the labor process of birth. (3)

conventional reasoning. Kohlberg's moral development stage when social relationships, rules, and conformity become more important. (12)

conventional reasoning. Kohlberg's theory of moral development in which social relationships, rules, and conformity become more important when making moral decisions that have social impact. (15)

convergent thinking. A form of thinking that focuses on finding a single best answer to a problem or question. (14)

correlational studies. Research studies that determine relationships between variables. (1)

crawling. Term used to describe using the hands and knees to pull the body forward while the stomach is raised off the ground. (4)

creeping. Dragging movement accomplished by pulling the arms and shoulders forward while lying on the stomach. (4)

critical thinking. Making a judgment when presented with a complex problem or circumstances. (14)

cross-sectional studies. Research studies that compare groups of various ages at the same time. (1)

custodial grandparent. Grandparents who are primary caregivers. (6)

cyberbullying. Aggressive behaviors or defamation using social media or other digital means. (12)

cybersex trafficking. Sex trafficking that includes exploitation through photos, webcams, videos, or other online platforms. (10)

cystic fibrosis. Genetic disorder that causes a thick mucus buildup on internal organs, making it difficult for them to operate effectively. (3)

D

declarative memory. Sometimes referred to as explicit memory; memory skills that are with us from birth such as a memory for familiar faces. (8)

delayed imitation. Duplicating or copying the behavior of another person after some time has passed, rather than immediately. (5)

dependent variable. Factors that are *dependent* on the independent variable in a research study. (1)

descriptive data. Information that describes people and situations, such as their age, attitudes, or behaviors. (1)

descriptive studies. Research studies that do not rely on the manipulation of variables, but describe human growth and development through observations, case studies, or surveys. (1)

development. The gradual increase in skills and abilities that occur over a lifetime. (1)

developmental theories. Conclusions based on observations or data about why people act and behave the way they do and how they change over time. (2)

developmentally appropriate practices (DAP). A framework or approach to working with young children that is based on knowledge of how children learn and develop at different ages and stages. (1)

dilation stage. Labor stage that causes the cervical opening to widen. (3)

disinhibited social engagement disorder. A pattern of behavior in which young children show no inhibition in approaching and interacting with unfamiliar adults. (6)

divergent thinking. The ability to brainstorm and produce creative possibilities. (14)

dizygotic. Two separate and distinct embryos. (2)

DNA. Deoxyribonucleic acid that contains the genetic instructions in all living things. (2)

dominant traits. Traits that come from genes exerting an overriding influence on other recessive genes. (2)

doula. An emotional coach used by some mothers during childbirth. (3)

Down syndrome. Genetic disorder caused by a chromosomal defect, resulting in impaired intellectual development. (3)

dyad friendships. Two-person friendly relationships. (12)

dyads. Two-person relationships. (12)

dyscalculia. A learning challenge characterized by difficulty learning math including understanding the concepts of time spans and other abstract measurements, such as days, weeks, or months of the year. (14)

dysgraphia. A learning challenge characterized by difficulty with organizing and expressing ideas that makes writing difficult. (14)

dyslexia. A learning disorder that makes it difficult to decode speech sounds and how they relate to spoken or written (phonology) words, despite possessing intellectual and visual skills in the normal range. (14)

dysmorphic disorder. Excessive body image distortion; a distinct mental disorder that causes overwhelming preoccupation with physical appearance. (15)

E

ecological theory. Bronfenbrenner's theory that interactions with the surrounding environments influence human growth and development. (2)

effacement. When a mother's cervix thins during labor. (3)

egocentrism. The inability to take another person's perspective. (8)

egocentrism. Self-focus that causes a person to think intensely about their own self, well-being, and comparisons to others. (15)

embryo. The developing baby during the embryonic period. (3)

embryonic period. Pregnancy stage extending from conception to the ninth week of pregnancy. (3)

emerging adulthood. The transition from teen to independent adult, which typically occurs between ages 19 and 26. (15)

emotional abuse. Harm that causes serious cognitive, behavioral, or emotional problems. (7)

empathy. The ability to comprehend another person's emotional state and have a similar emotion in response. (9)

enactive learning. Bandura's term for children's learning that comes because of their own actions. (2)

enuresis. Nighttime bedwetting or difficulty in controlling bathroom habits; a common condition for preschoolers that improves with time. (7)

epigenetics. The study of changes in phenotypes by something other than changes in DNA sequencing. (2)

episiotomy. Surgical cut that allows the baby to pass through the birth canal more easily during delivery. (3)

equilibration. Piaget's term for the balancing of old and new cognitive understanding. (2)

estrogen. The primary type of female sex hormone. (13)

ethics. Moral principles that govern a person when conducting research experiments. (1)

ethnicity. Shared social and cultural traditions, language, and communication styles. (9)

evolutionary developmental psychology. Theory that applies the principles of evolution by natural selection to our understanding of how humans develop. (2)

executive function. Complex thinking that involves planning, problem-solving, reasoning, social judgment, and moral decision-making. (8)

expanding technique. When infant caregivers add to what was verbalized by an infant when responding back. (5)

experimental research. Research studies that explore cause-and-effect relationships. (1)

exploratory play. Physical exploration of the environment. (6)

expressive language. Language that is produced. (11)

expulsion stage. Delivery stage of childbirth. (3)

extremely preterm. Neonates born at less than 29 weeks' gestation. (4)

F

failure to thrive. A lack of normal physical growth and development. (4)

fetal alcohol spectrum disorder (FASD). Disorder of intellectual development caused by prenatal exposure to alcohol. (3)

fetal monitoring. Tracking a baby's heart rate and the mother's contractions; alerts the medical staff to any signs of distress. (3)

fetal period. Pregnancy stage that extends from the ninth week of pregnancy until birth at the end of the third trimester. (3)

fetus. The developing baby during the fetal period. (3)

fidelity. Strength that comes from creating a self-identity and relating to others with their own identities. (15)

fine-motor skills. Small muscle movements using fingers and toes. (4)

first trimester. Begins at conception until about the ninth week of pregnancy. (3)

fixed mindset. Believing that success only comes from innate talent or genetic traits and abilities outside of one's control. (14)

food desert. Neighborhoods without grocery stores or food markets that offer fresh produce or other healthy and affordable food choices. (10)

forceps-assisted extraction. A form of delivery that utilizes a tong-type instrument to guide the newborn's head through the birth canal while the mother pushes. (3)

forest schools. Classroom learning that occurs completely outdoors; sometimes called *nature schools.* (7)

formal operations stage. The fourth and final stage in Piaget's cognitive theory, when teens reach their highest level of cognitive maturity. (14)

fragile X syndrome. Genetic condition resulting in a range of developmental issues including learning disabilities and cognitive impairment. (3)

frontal lobes. The front, top regions of each of the cerebral hemispheres that regulate emotions, problem-solving, executive functions, and voluntary movements. (4)

full siblings. Siblings who share same parents. (12)

G

gender. Usually associated with biological differences of the female or male sex; much more fluid than the identification of sex chromosomes or genital characteristics. (9)

gender dysphoria. When gender identity does not correlate with physical body birth features and causes emotional distress. (15)

gender identity. The expressed identity in how one views one's own gender. (9)

gender identity. A person's mental conception about their gender, be it woman, man, or something else. (15)

gender roles. The expectations that are associated with being a girl or a boy expressed in ways of acting, feelings, and interests. (9)

gene. Part of DNA that carries the blueprint information within chromosomes. (2)

gene × environment (G × E) interactions. The field of study that explores genes multiplied by environmental factors in a dynamic way and over time. (2)

genetics. Field of biological science that examines how genes are passed from one generation to the next generation. (2)

genome. A person's complete set of DNA. (2)

germinal period. Pregnancy stage that extends from conception until about two weeks later when implantation in the uterus occurs. (3)

gestational diabetes. Type of diabetes that occurs only during pregnancy. (3)

gifted. Those with the capacity to perform at levels higher than their peers in one or more common academic domain. (11)

gonads. The reproductive glands such the ovaries or testes. (13)

grasp reflex. A reflex of newborns to close their hand in a grasp when the palm is stroked. (4)

gross-(or large) motor skills. Larger muscle movements such as crawling, walking, and jumping. (4)

growing pains. Anecdotal reports of limbs hurting during the growth periods of middle childhood (non-diagnostic). (10)

growth. Physical changes in size, such as gains in height and weight. (1)

growth mindset. Understanding that successes in life come from hard work, motivation, and passion. (14)

H

half siblings. Siblings who share one same parent. (12)

hand-eye coordination. Using visual input to guide a hand activity. (7)

Head Start. A US federal government preschool program that serves the needs of young children, especially those who are disadvantaged. (8)

healthy weight. BMI is in the 5th to 84th percentile for gender, age, and height. (10)

heredity. The transmission of characteristics from parents to their biological offspring. (2)

highly reactive temperament. Tendency to react with intense fear, anger, or other emotions to environmental changes such as a loud noise, new people, or changes in climate. (6)

highly talented. Children who demonstrate exceptional capacity in creative expression. (11)

holophrases. When toddlers often use one word to describe a whole group of things. (5)

horizontal decalage. The non-simultaneous manner of learning throughout a learning stage. (8)

hormones. Chemical messengers that are secreted by the endocrine system into the bloodstream to stimulate specific cells into action. (13)

human development. A gradual process in which people grow and change from birth to death. (1)

hypocrisy. A situation in which someone pretends to believe something but does the opposite. (14)

hypothetical-deductive reason. A learning method that uses argumentation, hypothetical-deductive or scientific reasoning, and logic. (14)

I

ideal self. How a person wants to be seen in a social context, including the power they can exert. (9)

idealized self. The integration of both personal ideology and self-imposed expectations of behaviors or actions. (15)

identity achievement. When teens develop a strong sense of identity through experimentation. (15)

identity diffusion. When both exploration and commitment to an identity are absent and identity confusion occurs. (15)

identity foreclosure. When exploration is absent, but commitment to an identity is present; making premature identity decisions without adequate exploration and evaluation. (15)

identity moratorium. When teens put self-identity efforts on hold as they "try on" different identities. (15)

imaginary audience. Seeing oneself as the main character on the stage of life and that others are always watching, comparing, and judging. (15)

imaginative play. A type of play that involves make-believe or pretend activities. (8)

imitation. An advanced behavior that occurs when one person observes and replicates another person's behavior. (5)

independent variable. Represents the cause or reason for an outcome in a research study. (1)

individuation. A complex process of self-identity during adolescence that involves separating from parents or guardians and a redefinition (not dissolution) of relationships. (15)

induced labor. Labor hastened by medical intervention. (3)

industry versus inferiority stage. Erickson's stage of emotional-social development that focuses on the tension between the feeling of being industrious versus inferior as children seek to become competent. (12)

infancy. The first 2 years of life. (4)

infantile amnesia. The theory that infants have an inability to remember past events; although a widely held concept, more current research shows this is not necessarily true. (5)

inferential thinking. The ability to combine different ideas, discuss the merits or characteristics of different ideas, or draw conclusions. (11)

information processing theory. Theory that the human brain goes through a series of movements or functions to solve a problem. (2)

initiative versus guilt. Erikson's socioemotional stage when preschoolers begin to assert their power and control over the world and see themselves as a productive person. (9)

insecure-ambivalent. Infants who seek closeness after reuniting with their caregiver after a short separation but who are difficult to soothe and calm. Also called *insecure resistant*. (6)

insecure-avoidant. Infants who seem to ignore or avoid the caregiver following reunion after a short separation. (6)

interactionist theory. Belief that language acquisition is a product of both biological readiness and environmental influence. (5)

interdisciplinary learning. Learning that occurs in thematic units when two or more subject areas are combined to nurture heightened learning in each of the subject areas involved. (14)

intermodal perception. The ability to coordinate or bring together input from multiple senses. (5)

internalization. Ways of thinking that are influenced by the thought patterns of people in the environment. (11)

K

kangaroo care. Skin-to-skin contact used to soothe and nurture infants by placing the infant's ear next to the parent or caregiver's heart. (4)

L

labeling. Naming things, animals, and people. (5)

language acquisition device. Chomsky's theory that there is a specific part of the human brain that enables infants to detect the sounds of language. (5)

language modalities. Means or processes for expressing language. (11)

lanugo. Fine, soft hair that may cover a newborn's limbs and body. (4)

lateralization. Term used to describe the specialized functioning of the left and right brain hemispheres. (4)

left hemisphere. The left half of the cerebrum that controls language and speech. (4)

lifespan development. Human development that extends from birth to old age or death. (1)

limbic system. Regions of the brain that control motivation and reward. (14)

literacy. Reading and writing skills, within a cultural and language construct. (11)

lobes. Four smaller units in each hemisphere of the brain. (4)

longitudinal studies. Research studies that focus on the same individuals who are observed over time. (1)

long-term memory. Memories that can be accessed over a longer time frame or even over a lifetime; includes both declarative memory and non-declarative memory. (8)

low birthweight. Weight at birth less than 5.5 pounds or 2,500 grams. (3)

M

mandated reporters. People who legally must report suspected instances of child neglect and abuse. (7)

manual dexterity. The ability to coordinate fine-motor skills more quickly and efficiently. (7)

marginalization. Perceived or real relegation to an unimportant or powerless position in social groups. (15)

maternal morbidity. A woman's experience with severe or life-threatening complications from pregnancy or childbirth. (3)

maternal mortality. A woman's death due to complications from pregnancy or childbirth. (3)

meiosis. When sex cells divide into four, each with 23 chromosomes without pairs. (2)

memory. Recalling experiences or thoughts from the past. (5)

menarche. The initial onset of menstruation. (13)

menstruation. The normal vaginal bleeding that occurs as part of a woman's monthly cycle when she releases an unfertilized egg. (13)

mental schemata. Cognitive structure representing generic knowledge including lifetime of responses to stimuli that have been categorized. (14)

metacognition. Thinking about one's own thinking. (8)

metacognition. To think critically about one's own thinking processes. (14)

metamemory. The self-awareness of one's own memory. (8)

mirror neurons. A type of neuron that modifies its activity when a specific motor action is observed or an emotion is expressed by another person. (5)

mitosis. When one cell divides to make another duplicate cell. (2)

mixed data collection methods. Collection methods that combine both quantitative and qualitative methods to provide a deeper and more complex picture. (1)

modeling. Imitation of a behavior or response. (2)

moderately preterm. Infants born between 29 and 33 weeks' gestation. (4)

monozygotic. One complete embryo that divides. (2)

moral agency. A sense of how moral actions and decisions affect others. (12)

moral atmosphere. Morals communicated through the social environment or cultural influences. (15)

moral identity. The development of personal values and a related code of conduct that becomes a part of self-identity. (15)

morality. The distinction between right and wrong behaviors; the complexity of dealing with concepts of justice, welfare, and the rights of others. (9)

Moro reflex. A reflex of newborns to startle. (4)

morphology. Word structures and formations. (8)

motor skills. Body movements that depend on increasing strength and coordination. (1)

multitasking. Attempting to do many tasks at the same time. (14)

mutations. Permanent gene modifications involving some sort of substitution, deletion, or insertion. (3)

myelin. A protective sheath made of fat and protein substance that covers axon fibers and helps speed up the communication between neurons. (4)

N

natural childbirth. Birth procedures that focus on relaxation techniques instead of medication to deal with pain. (3)

natural selection. A progression of sorting traits according to reproductive success. (2)

nature schools. Classroom learning that occurs completely outdoors; sometimes called *forest schools*. (7)

nature versus nurture debate. The question that asks whether a person's personality traits, abilities, skills, and tastes are a result of genetics (what they were born with) or a result of their environment (a person's surroundings and the people in it). (1)

negative reinforcement. Repeated punishment or disincentives used to guide behavior. (2)

neglect. Endangerment of or harm to a child resulting from a caregiver's failure to provide basic needs, including physical, medical, educational, or emotional support. (7)

Neonatal Intensive Care Unit Network Neurobehavioral Scale (NNNS). Assesses newborns at risk for neurological challenges due to premature birth or other known risk factors, such as prenatal drug exposure. (4)

neonates. Babies who are 4 weeks old or younger. (4)

neurodevelopmental disorders. Developmental disabilities that are the result of environment or injury or have neurological or genetic origins. (11)

neurons. Nerve cells. (4)

neuroplasticity. Refers to the ability of the brain to undergo structural and neurochemical changes. (5)

non-declarative memories. Memories that relate to skills that have been so integrated into subconscious thought that children perform without thinking. (8)

O

obese. BMI is in the 95th percentile or higher for gender, age, and height. (10)

object permanence. Understanding that something still exists even when it is out of sight or can no longer be heard or touched. (5)

observable behaviors. Things people do and say or how they act. (2)

obstetrician. Medical doctor who specializes in pregnancy and birth. (3)

occipital lobe. The back of each cerebral hemisphere containing centers of vision and reading ability. (4)

occupational identity. A part of self-identity development that includes making decisions about how to live as an adult in society through paid or unpaid work or service to others. (15)

onlooker play. When an infant observes the play of others, while not actually playing themselves. (6)

operant conditioning. Theory that depending on the result, a baby will learn to repeat or stop their response to a stimulus. (2)

operational thinking. The ability to solve problems without having to encounter or experience the problem either in the physical world or personally. (11)

opioids. A class of drugs that includes prescription pain killers and illicit drugs that are addictive. (13)

over-imitation. Copying a caregiver's actions even if it is known that the actions are not necessary, inefficient, or incorrect. (8)

overweight. BMI is in the 85th to 94th percentile for gender, age, and height. (10)

oxygen deprivation. When the baby's flow of oxygen is interrupted during the birth process. (3)

P

palmar grasp. Term used to describe when a baby picks up an object using all the fingers to bring it into the palm of their hand. (4)

parallel instructional design. Interdisciplinary learning that is integrated to introduce thematic units. (14)

parenting style. Behaviors that are directly observable and used to socialize children. (9)

parietal lobe. The middle lobe of each cerebral hemisphere containing sensory centers. (4)

peer relationships. Social connections between like-aged individuals. (9)

permissive style. A parenting style that tends to let children control situations, making decisions with few limits or controls. (9)

personal fable. A thinking pattern related to cognitive function when the opinion of oneself and importance are distorted or inflated. (15)

personal identity. Self-identity shaped by individual temperament and subjective feelings about how they compare to others. (9)

personality. Distinctive behaviors that define what and why infants do the things they do. (6)

phenylketonuria (PKU). Genetic condition that prevents the body from processing phenylalanine, an amino acid; left untreated, may cause intellectual disability. (3)

phonics. Teaching method using phonology. (11)

phonology. The sounds that make up words. (8)

physical abuse. Mistreatment that involves inflicting injury through slapping, kicking, hitting, beating, shaking, biting, punching or other means. (7)

physical development. Includes all growth and bodily changes that occur as a child or adolescent grows and matures. (1)

physiological measures. Data collection tools that evaluate bodily functions or changes such as blood tests, magnetic resonance imaging (MRI), hearing tests, and other medical testing. (1)

pincer grasp. Term used to describe when an infant picks up small items using the forefinger and thumb. (4)

pituitary gland. A gland located at the base of the brain that signals the endocrine system to release hormones. (13)

placenta. A mass attached to the uterus and the umbilical that provides nutrients from the mother to the baby. (3)

play. Enjoyable activities that are sustained by the child. (6)

political identity. A part of self-identity development that includes the development of social responsibility and agency. (15)

polygenetic. Complex gene interactions. (2)

positive reinforcement. Repeated rewards or incentives used to guide behavior. (2)

post-conventional morality. Kohlberg's theory of moral development in which moral decisions are based on universal principles. (15)

postpartum anxiety. Overwhelming worry over providing adequate care for a newborn. (6)

postpartum depression. Mental health depression that manifests itself after giving birth. (6)

postpartum period. Period following birth that usually lasts six weeks. (6)

postpubescence. When puberty gradually subsides. (13)

postural control. The ability to achieve and maintain a state of balance while performing an activity. (7)

pragmatics. Using language properly. (11)

preadolescents. Stage when children move into the later end of middle childhood and exhibit an interesting and challenging blend of child- and teen-like characteristics. (12)

precocious puberty. The onset of puberty prior to typical early timing and includes the combination of both accelerated growth in stature and early development of secondary sexual characteristics. (10)

preconventional morality. Kohlberg's stage of moral development when young children respond to rewards and punishments instead of making moral decisions. (9)

prefrontal cortex. The front section of the brain's cortex that aids in attention, motivation, self-control, and focus. (4)

prefrontal cortex. The region at the front of the brain responsible for the abilities to organize, plan, demonstrate self-control, problem-solve, judge, and to be self-aware. (14)

preoperational. Piaget's stage representing a time prior to the operational stage when children use reason and logic. (8)

prepubescence. A period in which the internal process of puberty typically starts at around age 8 for girls and ages 9 to 10 for boys. (10)

preschool years. Early childhood years, generally between 2 to 6 years of age. (7)

preteens. Another term for preadolescents. (12)

pretend play. A type of play that involves make-believe or imaginative activities. (8)

preterm birth. Babies born prior to 28 weeks gestation. (3)

preterm. Neonates who are born between 33 and 37 weeks' gestation. (4)

primitive reflexes. Involuntary, spontaneous movements or actions that are present at birth but diminish during the first year of life. (4)

problem-based learning. Learning that focuses on a problem to solve. (14)

processing issues. Needing more time to translate auditory and visual information. (14)

processing speed. The ability to complete a task with relative speed and accuracy. (11)

project-based learning. Learning that focuses on a project to complete. (14)

proprioception. Integration of senses, visual processing, and perception or awareness of the position and movement of the body. (10)

prosocial behaviors. Helping behaviors toward others. (6)

prosocial behaviors. Voluntary behaviors that are intended to benefit others. (9)

protective factors. Dynamics that reduce the risk of child abuse and neglect and help promote family resilience and the optimal development of children. (7)

protective factors. Individual, family, or community characteristics that have been shown to make positive outcomes more likely for children and to reduce the likelihood of adverse experiences such as abuse or neglect. (12)

protective reflexes. Involuntary, spontaneous movements or actions that instinctively protect the body from harm. (4)

proximodistal development. Development of the muscles at the core of infants' bodies before they can use muscles further out from their abdominal center. (4)

pseudostupidity. A teen's tendency to overlook obvious answers due to inexperience rather than cognitive ability, resulting in inappropriate choices. (14)

psychoanalytic theory. Theory that early life experiences relate to development and there is a symbolic meaning behind behaviors. (2)

psychosocial theory. Erikson's theory that development occurs during eight stages of life, each stage resolving a psychological or social conflict. (2)

puberty. The transition to sexual maturity making one capable of reproduction that occurs over time. (10)

pubescence. When hormones increase, the appearance of physical changes are seen, and puberty is in process. (13)

Q

qualitative data. Data that focus on understanding the complexities of social relationships, customs, and social norms. (1)

quantitative data. Data that emphasize objective mathematical or numerical measurements. (1)

R

racial identity. An ongoing process of determining the racial or ethnic groups within which one belongs. (9)

reactive attachment disorder. When an infant does not form an attachment to their primary caregivers. (6)

recast. To rephrase a young child's verbal message back while including more information. (5)

receptive language. Understanding language before one has the ability to form words. (5)

receptive language. Language comprehension. (11)

recessive traits. Traits being overridden or influenced by dominant genes. (2)

reciprocal determinism. The relationship between person, environment, and behaviors that impacts cognitive development. (14)

reciprocity. Relationships characterized by mutual dependence, reliance, and benefits. (12)

reflexes. Involuntary, spontaneous movements or actions that occur in response to a stimulus. (4)

rh factor. When the type of protein in red blood cells between the mother and baby do not match. (3)

role confusion. Failure to create a self-identity resulting in a lack of understanding of one's place in society. (15)

rooting reflex. A reflex of newborns to move toward a bottle or their mother's breast when the side of their mouth is stroked. (4)

rote learning. A method of learning by memorizing information; often uses repetition as a means. (11)

rough and tumble play. An active and vigorous form of physical play, often seen in later preschool years. (9)

S

scaffolding. When caregivers and older peers or siblings help children by beginning at their level, they learn more. (5)

schema. Basic units of knowledge that relate to how something is perceived or known. (2)

school–family partnerships. When parents and caregivers work together to ensure congruence of expectations and values. (9)

securely attached. Infants who actively engage with their caregiver upon reunion after a short separation while communicating their distress over the situation and then returning to play. (6)

sedentary. Inactive, mostly sitting or lying down. (13)

self-awareness. A child's own assessment or view of self that includes personal identity and the perceived roles in a social situation. (12)

self-efficacy. Confidence in oneself that proficiency in a situation is achievable and can yield favorable results. (12)

self-esteem. How a person conceptualizes their own personal value. (9)

self-identity. Identifying one's place in the world and how it relates to others. (15)

self-image. The roles that a person plays, such as child, parent, brother or sister, grandchild, student, or friend. (9)

self-management. Also known as self-regulation. (12)

self-regulation. The ability to manage thoughts, feelings, or emotions to assist goal-directed actions; sometimes referred to as self-control. (8)

semantics. The meaning of words. (11)

sense of identity. Who a person believes themself to be. (9)

sensorimotor stage. Stage when infants move from exhibiting reflexes to interacting with the world around them. (5)

seriation. The ability to place objects in order by a characteristic, such as smallest to largest. (11)

serve-and-return interaction. The communication relationship between caregivers and infants is like a game of volleyball or tennis. (5)

sex trafficking. When coercion, force, deception, and deceit are used to engage people in commercial sex acts. (10)

sex-linked traits. Traits associated with X or Y chromosomes. (2)

sexual abuse. Mistreatment that includes all kinds of inappropriate behavior toward or with a child including touching and sexual acts or exposure to pornography. (7)

sexual assault. Sexual activity that occurs without consent or not freely given. (10)

sexual identity. A person's mental conception about gender identity and sexual orientation. (15)

sexual orientation. A person's persistent pattern of social, emotional, romantic, or sexual attractions to women, men, or both sexes. (15)

sexuality education. Curriculum that focuses on using correct body terminology, body respect and consent, and in some states, gender expression. (10)

shaken baby syndrome. When an infant brain experiences swelling and brain injury from rough handling. (4)

sickle cell anemia. An autosomal single-gene disorder that causes a shortage and change of red blood cells. (3)

single-gene disorder. A mutation of one person's genes that has not yet been seen in a family line. (3)

social age. Expectations about how and when a child should be able to perform tasks. (1)

social awareness. The ability to take the perspective of another person or group of people. (12)

social clock. Refers to cultural expectations of when major life milestones should occur. (15)

social cognitive theory. Theory that people actively shape and are shaped by their environment. (2)

social emotional learning (SEL). The process of developing basic social and emotional competencies that assist children, teens, and adults in all areas of life. (9)

social emotional learning. The process of developing self-awareness, self-regulation, and interpersonal skills needed to be effective in social relationships. (12)

social identity. Identity built from referencing those around the child; involves identification with gender, age, ethnic background or race, and religious background. (9)

social referencing. Taking cues from a caregiver's emotive displays and using them to form their own reactions. (6)

sociocultural cognitive development theory. Vygotsky's theory that learning is a social endeavor; children learn about the world through relationships. (2)

socioemotional development. The growth and maturation of identity, social relationships, emotions, and feelings. (1)

socioemotional development. Development that includes a young child's ability to form close relationships with adults and peers, to express and regulate emotions in socially and culturally appropriate ways, and to develop a sense of identity in the context of family, community, and culture. (9)

solitary play. Play without interaction with others. (6)

sound localization. Ability to identify where a sound is originating. (4)

spermarche. When a boy experiences his first involuntary ejaculation of semen, typically nocturnally. (13)

spirituality. An authentic expression of humanity, addressing and pondering life's existential questions about life, death, and human existence. (9)

standardized tests. Data collection assessment tools that are used to measure differences, abilities, attitudes, or other factors across large swaths of people. (1)

stepping reflex. Young infants' reflex to appear to walk, step, or dance when held upright with feet touching a solid surface. (4)

stigma bullying. Bullied children who have lower social capital or power, are lacking in self-confidence or social skills, or who stand apart from their peers in any way or form. (12)

stillbirth. Delivery of a deceased baby after 20 weeks' gestation. (3)

storm and stress. A termed used by American psychologist G. Stanley Hall highlighting the intensity of conflicts for teens who are struggling for independence. (15)

strange situation. Procedure used to assess an infant's attachment to the caregiver by exposing the infant to a strange experience. (6)

suck reflex. Reflex of newborns to suck when something is placed on the roof of their mouth. (4)

sudden infant death syndrome. Unexplained death of an infant usually during the first year of life. Also called *sudden unexpected infant death*. (4)

synapses. Site where electric nerve impulses are transmitted and received between two nerve cells (neurons). (4)

synaptogenesis. When the neurons in the brain grow and sprout branches or pathways throughout infancy, making more connections than the brain will ever need. (8)

synchrony. The swift, synchronized, and smooth exchange of responses between an infant and caregiver. (6)

syntax. Sentence structure, or when words are combined to form grammatical sentences. (8)

T

telegraphic speech. Speech pattern used when toddlers begin to combine words into two-word combinations. (5)

temperament. The ways that people interact with the world; biologically based and persistent throughout life. (6)

temporal lobes. The lower sides of each cerebral hemisphere used for hearing and memory. (4)

teratogens. Any agent, such as an environmental toxin, that can negatively impact the development of an embryo or fetus. (3)

testosterone. An androgen. (13)

theory of mind. The ability to understand that knowledge, emotions, intentions, beliefs, or motivations come from another person and may not correlate with their own. (8)

third trimester. Weeks 24 to 40 of a pregnancy. (3)

toddler. A socially constructed term used to describe infants once they begin walking, typically anywhere between 8 to 18 months. (4)

tonic reflex. Reflex of newborns to lay with their head turned to one side with the arm on the same side stretching outward. (4)

transgender. When gender identity does not correlate with physical body birth features. (15)

transitivity. The ability to understand that relationships between two objects can extend to a third object. (11)

transracial adoption. Adoptive parents and adoptive children do not share the same racial identities. (6)

trauma-informed care (TIC). Understanding, identification, and responsiveness to the effects of trauma on children and teens in one's care. (7)

triadic reciprocity. The impact of a person on the interactions between self, environment, and behavior. (14)

trust versus mistrust. Erickson's psychosocial development stage that encompasses the first 18 to 24 months of life. (6)

U

umbilical cord. Tube of veins and arteries that connect the placenta to the baby. (3)

unintended injuries. Injuries that occur accidently through falls, burns, drowning, traffic, calamities, or other inadvertent means. (10)

universal design. A concept that creates spaces and equipment that are flexible and versatile and can be used by anyone. (7)

unoccupied play. A baby observes and focuses on an object or activity. (6)

V

vacuum extraction. A form of delivery in which a health care provider attaches a soft plastic cup with a handle to the baby's head using suction and then gently pulls on the handle as the mother pushes through a contraction. (3)

vernix caseosa. A thin white coating that covers infants at birth. (4)

vicarious learning. Term for learning that results from observing or modeling after others. (2)

vocabulary spurt. Stage when infants are learning productive vocabulary at a rapid rate, up to 10 words every 2 weeks. (5)

W

well-baby exams. Preventive, regular medical exams focused on infant growth and attainment of developmental milestones. (4)

windows of opportunity. The time frames for optimizing the development of critical skills as the brain continues to develop. (8)

working memory. Memories of information that is useable in the present; things remembered for a short amount of time. (8)

working memory. Storage of a small amount of information that is useable in the present or retained for a short time. (11)

Z

zone of proximal development. The level at which a child can learn with help; when scaffolding can be decreased and eventually removed. (2)

References

Chapter 1

Addis, C. (2003). *Jefferson's vision for education, 1760–1845*. Peter Lang.

Alfano, C., & Beidel, D. (2014). *Comprehensive evidence-based interventions for children and adolescents*. Wiley.

Alford, B., Rollins, K., Padrón, Y., & Waxman, H. (2016). Using systematic classroom observation to explore student engagement as a function of teachers' developmentally appropriate instructional practices (DAIP) in ethnically diverse pre-kindergarten through second-grade classrooms. *Early Childhood Education Journal, 44*, 623–635.

Allen, A. (2017). *The transatlantic kindergarten: Education and women's movements in Germany and the United States*. Oxford.

Alonge, O., & Hyder, A. (2014). Reducing the global burden of childhood unintentional injuries. *Archives of Disease in Childhood, 99*(1), 62.

American Academy of Pediatrics (2014). *Caring for your baby and young child: Birth to age 5*. Bantam.

American Academy of Pediatrics (2020). *Trauma guide*. https://www.aap.org/en-us/advocacy-and-policy/aap-health-initiatives/healthy-foster-care-america/Pages/Trauma-Guide.aspx#foster

American Psychological Association (2017). *Ethical principles of psychologists and code of conduct*. http://www.apa.org/ethics/code/index.html

Baker, A., & Charvat, B. (2008). *Research methods in child welfare*. Columbia University Press.

Banati, P., & Lansford, J. (2018). *Handbook of adolescent development research and its impact on global policy*. Oxford University Press.

Barkovich, A., & Raybaud, C. (2019). *Pediatric neuroimaging*. Wolters Kluwer.

Barros, R., Silver, E., & Stein, R. (2009). School recess and group classroom behavior. *Pediatrics, 123*(2), 431–436.

Barrouillet, P. (2015). Theories of cognitive development: From Piaget to today. *Developmental Review, 38*(C), 1–12.

Bergen, D., Davis, D. R., & Abbitt, J. T. (2016). *Technology play and brain development: Infancy to adolescence and future implications*. Routledge, Taylor & Francis Group.

Berkowitz, R., Moore, H., Astor, R., & Benbenishty, R. (2017). A research synthesis of the associations between socioeconomic background, inequality, school climate, and academic achievement. *Review of Educational Research, 87*(2), 425–469.

Bilmes, J. (2012). *Beyond behavior management: The six life skills children need*. Redleaf.

Black, M., Walker, S., & Fernald, L. & the Lancet Early Childhood Development Series Steering Committee (2017). Early childhood development coming of age: Science through the life course. *Lancet, 389*(10064): 77–90.

Blair, C., & Raver, C. (2015). School readiness and self-regulation: A developmental psychobiological approach. *Annual Review of Psychology, 66*, 711–731.

Boomsma, D., Busjahn, A., & Peltonen, L. (2002). Classical twin studies and beyond. *Nature Reviews Genetics, 3*(11), 872–882.

Borrero, N., & Yeh, C. (2011). The multidimensionality of ethnic identity among urban high school youth. *Identity: An International Journal of Theory and Research, 11*, 114–135.

Bosmans, G., & Kerns, K. (2015). Attachment in middle childhood: Progress and prospects. *New Directions for Child and Adolescent Development, 148*: 1–14.

Bradley, R. (2019). Socioeconomic status effects. In S. Hupp & J. Jewell (Eds.) *The encyclopedia of child and adolescent development*. Wiley.

Bredekamp, S. (1987). *Developmentally appropriate practice in early childhood programs serving children from birth through age 8*. NAEYC.

Bredekamp, S. (2005). Play and school readiness. *Educational Perspectives, 38*, 18–26.

Bremner, J., & Wachs, T. (2010). *The Wiley-Blackwell handbook of infant development*. Wiley-Blackwell.

Brink, S. (2013). *The fourth trimester: Understanding, protecting and nurturing an infant through the first three months*. University of California Press.

Brownson, R., Colditz, G., & Proctor, E. (2018). *Dissemination and implementation research in health: Translating science to practice*. Oxford University Press.

Budiman, A. (2020). *Americans are more positive about the long-term rise in US racial and ethnic diversity than in 2016*. Pew Research Center. https://www.pewresearch.org/fact-tank/2020/10/01/americans-are-more-positive-about-the-long-term-rise-in-u-s-racial-and-ethnic-diversity-than-in-2016/

Burniat, W. (2002). *Child and adolescent obesity: Causes and consequences, prevention and management*. Cambridge University Press.

Calkins, S. (2015). *Handbook of infant biopsychosocial development*. The Guilford.

Casey, B., Getz, S., & Galvan, A. (2008). The adolescent brain. *Developmental Review, 28*(1), 62–77.

Causadias, J., Joseph, A., Vitriol, A., & Atkin, L. (2018). The cultural (mis)attribution bias in developmental psychology in the United States. *Journal of Applied Developmental Psychology, 59*, 65–74.

Center on the Developing Child at Harvard University (2017a). *InBrief: The science of resilience*. https://developingchild.harvard.edu/resources/inbrief-the-science-of-resilience.

Center on the Developing Child at Harvard University (2017b). *Three principles to improve outcomes for children and families*. http://www.developingchild.harvard.edu

Centers for Disease Control and Prevention (2021). *Adverse childhood experiences prevention strategy*. National Center for Injury Prevention and Control.

Choudhury, S. (2010). Culturing the adolescent brain: What can neuroscience learn from anthropology? *Social Cognitive Affective Neuroscience, 5*, 159–167.

Cozby, P., & Bates, S. (2020). *Methods in behavioral research*. McGraw-Hill Education.

Criss, M., & Shaw, D. (2005). Sibling relationships as contexts for delinquency training in low-income families. *Journal of Family Psychology, 19,* 592–600.

Darling-Churchill, K., & Lippman, L. (2016). Early childhood social and emotional development: Advancing the field of measurement. *Journal of Applied Developmental Psychology, 45*, 1–7.

Davies, D., & Troy, M. (2020). *Child development: A practitioner's guide.* Guilford.

Davis-Kean, P., & Jager, J., III (2017). From small to big: Methods for incorporating large scale data into developmental science. *Monographs Society Research in Child Development, 82*, 31–45.

Debs, M. (2019). *Diverse families, desirable schools. Public Montessori in the era of school choice.* Harvard Education.

Demuth, C. (2015). New directions in qualitative research in psychology. *Integrative Psychological and Behavioral Science, 49*, 125–133.

Diamond, A., Casey, B., & Munakata, Y. (2011). *Developmental cognitive neuroscience.* Oxford Press.

Dickson-Swift, V., James, E., & Liamputtong, P. (2008). *Undertaking sensitive research in the health and social sciences: Managing boundaries, emotions and risks.* Cambridge University Press.

Dua, T., Tomlinson, M., Tablante, E., Britto, P., Yousfzai, A., Daelmans, B., & Darmstadt, G. (2016). Global research priorities to accelerate early child development in the sustainable development era. *The Lancet: Global Health, 4*(12), E887–E889.

Dube, S., Felitti, V., Dong, M., Chapman, D., Giles, W., & Anda, R. (2003). Childhood abuse, neglect, and household dysfunction and the risk of illicit drug use: The adverse childhood experiences study. *Pediatrics, 111*(3), 564–572.

Dunn, J. (1983). Sibling relationships in early childhood. *Child Development, 54*(4), 787–811.

Dunn, L., Kontos, S., & ERIC Clearinghouse on Elementary Early Childhood Education (1997). *Developmentally appropriate practice: What does research tell us?* ERIC Clearinghouse on Elementary and Early Childhood Education, University of Illinois.

Ellis, G., & M. Solms (2018). *Beyond evolutionary psychology: How and why neuropsychological modules arise.* Cambridge University Press.

Erikson E. (1982). *The life cycle completed.* Norton.

Fagan, A., & Najman, J. (2005). The relative contributions of parental and sibling substance use to adolescent tobacco, alcohol, and other drug use. *Journal of Drug Issues, 35*, 869–884.

Farah, M. (2018). Socioeconomic status and the brain: Prospects for neuroscience-informed policy. *National Review of Neuroscience, 19*, 428–438.

Fegert, J., Vitiello, B., Plener, P., & Clemens, V. (2020). Challenges and burden of the Coronavirus 2019 (COVID-19) pandemic for child and adolescent mental health: A narrative review to highlight clinical and research needs in the acute phase and the long return to normality. *Child and Adolescent Psychiatry and Mental Health, 14*, 20.

Felitti V. J. (2002). The relation between adverse childhood experiences and adult health: Turning gold into lead. *The Permanente Journal, 6*(1), 44–47.

Feinman, S., Roberts, D., Hsieh, K., Sawyer, D., & Swanson, D. (1992). A critical review of social referencing in infancy. In S. Feinman (Ed). *Social referencing and the social construction of reality in infancy.* Springer.

Fife, B. (2013). *Old school still matters: Lessons from history to reform public education in America.* Praeger.

Finn, C., & T. Rebarber (1992). *Education reform in the '90s.* Macmillan.

Follari, L. (2019). *Foundations and best practices in early childhood education: History, theories, and approaches to learning.* Pearson.

Franciosi, R. (2014). *The rise and fall of American public schools: The political economy of public education in the twentieth century.* Praeger.

Fraser, J. (2014). *The school in the United States: A documentary history.* Routledge.

Freedman, L., & M. Kruk (2014). Disrespect and abuse of women in childbirth: Challenging the global quality and accountability agendas. *Lancet, 384*, e42–44.

Galovski, T., Peterson, Z., Beagley, M., Strasshofer, D., Held, P., & Fletcher, T. (2016). Exposure to violence during Ferguson protests: Mental health effects for law enforcement and community members. *Journal of Traumatic Stress, 29*, 283–292.

Gartstein, M., & Putnam, S. (2019). *Toddlers, parents, and culture: Findings from the joint effort toddler temperament consortium.* Routledge.

Gerde, H., Schachter, R., & Wasik B., (2013). Using the scientific method to guide learning: An integrated approach to early childhood curriculum. *Early Childhood Education Journal, 41*(5), 315–323.

Ginsburg, K. (2007). The importance of play in promoting healthy child development and maintaining strong parent-child bonds. *Pediatrics, 119*(1), 181–192.

Godoy, L., Frankfurter, C., Cooper, M., Lay, C., Maunder, R., & Farkouh, M. (2020). Association of adverse childhood experiences with cardiovascular disease later in life: A review. *JAMA Cardiology,* https://jamanetwork.com/journals/jamacardiology/article-abstract/2773390

Gonzalez-DeHass, A. (2020). *Parent involvement for motivated learners: Encouraging self-directed and resilient students.* Routledge.

Gonzalez-DeHass, A., & Willems, P. (2013). *Theories in educational psychology concise guide to meaning and practice.* Rowman & Littlefield Education.

Good, T. (2008). *21st century education: A reference handbook.* Sage.

Good, T., & The National Society for the Study of Education (2000). *American education: Yesterday, today, and tomorrow.* National Society for the Study of Education.

Gough, B., & Lyons, A. (2016). The future of qualitative research in psychology: Accentuating the positive. *Integrative Psychological and Behavioral Science, 50*, 234–243.

Gray, C., & MacBlain, S. (2015). *Learning theories in childhood.* Sage.

Gross, D. (2019). *Infancy: Development from birth to age 3.* Rowman & Littlefield.

Guhn, M., Janus, M., Enns, J., Brownell, M., Forer1, B., Duku, E., Muhajarine, N., & Raos, R. (2016). Examining the social determinants of children's developmental health: Protocol for building a pan-Canadian population-based monitoring system for early childhood development. *BMJ Open, 6*, e012020.

Gunasekare, U. (2015). Mixed research method as the third research paradigm: A literature review. *International Journal of Science and Research, 4*, 361–368.

Guthrie, J. (2003). *Encyclopedia of education.* Macmillan Reference USA.

Hagan, J., Shaw, J., & Duncan, P. (2017). *Bright futures: Guidelines for health supervision of infants, children and adolescents.* American Academy of Pediatrics.

Haibach-Beach, P., Reid, G., & Collier, D. (2018). *Motor learning and development.* Human Kinetics.

Haight, W., Bidwell, L., Marshall, J., & Khatiwoda, P. (2014). Implementing the crossover youth practice model in diverse contexts: Child welfare and juvenile justice professionals' experiences of multisystem collaborations. *Children and Youth Services Review, 39,* 91–100.

Hanson, J., Hair, N., Shen, D., Shi, F., Gilmore, J., Wolfe, B., & Pollak, S. (2013). Family poverty affects the rate of human infant brain growth. *PLOS ONE, 8*(12), e80954.

Hargreaves, D., Elliott, M., Viner, R., Richmond, T., & Schuster, M. (2015). Unmet health care need in US adolescents and adult health outcomes. *Pediatrics, 136*(3), 513–520.

Harter, S. (2006). The self. In W. Damon, R. Lerner, & N. Eisenberg (Eds.), *Handbook of child psychology.* John Wiley & Sons.

Harvard University Center on the Developing Child (2007). *The science of early childhood development (InBrief).* www.developingchild.harvard.edu

Heath, D., & Oxford Analytica (1986). *America in perspective: Major trends in the United States through the 1990s.* Houghton Mifflin.

Hertzman, C., & Boyce, T. (2010). How experience gets under the skin to create gradients in developmental health. *Annual Review of Public Health, 31*(1), 329–347.

Hilton, T., Fawson, P., Sullivan, T., & DeJong, C. (2020). *Applied social research: A tool for the human services.* Springer.

Hinitz, B., & Miller, S. (2013). *The hidden history of early childhood education.* Routledge.

Holder, M., & Coleman, B. (2015). Children's friendships and positive well-being. In M. Demir (Ed.), *Friendship and happiness: Across the lifespan and cultures.* Springer.

Holman, D., Ports, K., Buchanan, N., Hawkins, N., Merrick, M., & Trivers, K. (2016). The association between adverse childhood experiences and risk for cancer in adulthood: A systematic review of the literature. *Pediatrics,* S81–S91.

Hosken, D. (2019). *Genes and behaviour: Beyond nature-nurture.* John Wiley & Sons.

Hosogi, M., Okada, A., Fujii, C., Noguchi, K., & Watanabe, K. (2012). Importance and usefulness of evaluating self-esteem in children. *BioPsychoSocial Medicine, 6,* 9.

International Organization for Migration (2017). *Migration and migrants: A global overview. World Migration Report 2018.* IOM.

Ivankova, N., Creswell, J., & Clark, V. (2016). Foundations and approaches to mixed methods research. In K. Maree (Ed.), *First steps in research.* Van Schaick Publishers.

Jaffa, T., & McDermott, B. (2007). *Eating disorders in children and adolescents* (Cambridge child and adolescent psychiatry series). Cambridge University Press.

Jones, N., Platt, M., Mize, K., & Hardin, J. (2020). *Conducting research in developmental psychology: A topical guide for research methods utilized across the lifespan.* Routledge.

Karr-Morse, R., & Wiley, M. (2012). *Scared sick: The role of childhood trauma in adult disease.* Basic Books.

Kenny, D. (2013). *Bringing up baby: The psychoanalytic infant comes of age.* Karnac.

Kostelnik, M., Soderman, A., Whiren, A., Rupiper, M., & Gregory, K. (2015). *Guiding children's social development and learning: Theory and skills.* Cengage.

Lake, A., & Chan, M. (2014). Putting science into practice for early child development. *Lancet, 385,* 1816–1817.

Lamb, M. (2015). Toward developmentally aware practices in the legal system: Progress, challenge, and promise. *American Psychologist, 70,* 686–693.

Lascarides, V., & Hinitz, B. (2011). *History of early childhood education.* Routledge.

Lee, A., & Brann, L. (2015). Influence of cultural beliefs on infant feeding, postpartum and childcare practices among Chinese-American mothers in New York City. *Journal of Community Health, 40*(3).

Lee, D., & Jackson, M. (2017). The simultaneous effects of socioeconomic disadvantage and child health on children's cognitive development. *Demography, 54,* 1845–1871.

Legerstee, M., Haley, D., & Bornstein, M. (2013). *The infant mind: Origins of the social brain.* Guilford.

Lemke, M., & Brown, K. (2020). Syndemic perspectives to guide black maternal health research and prevention during the COVID-19 pandemic. *Maternal and Child Health Journal, 24*(9), 1093–1098.

Lerner, R., Easterbrooks, M.. Mistry, J., & Weiner, I. (2013). Developmental psychology. *Handbook of psychology.* John Wiley & Sons.

Leversen, J., Haga, M., & Sigmundsson, H. (2012). From children to adults: Motor Performance across the life-span. *PLOS ONE, 7*(6), e38830.

LeVine, R., & LeVine, S. (2016). *Do parents matter?* Public Affairs.

Levitt, H., Motulsky, S., Wertz, F., Morrow, S., & Ponterotto, J. (2017). Recommendations for designing and reviewing qualitative research in psychology: Promoting methodological integrity. *Qualitative Psychology, 4,* 2–22.

Lovasi, G., Diez Roux, A., & Kolker, J. (2021). *Urban public health: A research toolkit for practice and impact.* Oxford University Press.

Lubans, D., Morgan, P., Cliff, D., Barnett, L., & Okely, A. (2010). Fundamental movement skills in children and adolescents: Review of associated health benefits. *Sports Medicine, 40*(12), 1019–1035.

Mandler, J. (2004). *The foundations of mind: Origins of conceptual thought.* Oxford University Press.

Maunder, R., & Monks, C. (2019). Friendships in middle childhood: Links to peer and school identification, and general self-worth. *British Journal of Developmental Psychology, 37,* 211–229.

Mays, S. (2011). Evidence links increases in public health spending to declines in preventable deaths. *Health Affairs, 30*(8), 1585–1593.

McClure, K. (2020). *Selecting and describing your research instruments.* American Psychological Association.

McCormick, C., & Scherer, D. (2018). *Child and adolescent development for educators.* Guilford.

McCoy, D., Peet, E., Ezzati, M., Danaei, G., Black, M., Sudfeld, C., Fawzi, W., & Fink, G. (2016). Early childhood developmental status in low- and middle-income countries: National, regional, and global prevalence estimates using predictive modeling. *PLoS Medicine, 13*(6), e1002034.

McGuinn, P. (2006). *No child left behind and the transformation of federal education policy, 1965–2005.* University of Kansas.

McHale, J. P. (2007). *Charting the bumpy road of coparenthood: Understanding the challenges of family life.* Zero to Three Press.

McHale, J., Dinh, K., & Rao N., (2014). Understanding co-parenting and family systems among East and Southeast Asian heritage families. In H. Selin (Ed.), *Parenting across cultures: Childrearing, motherhood and fatherhood in non-Western cultures.* Springer.

McHale, S., Updegraff, K., & Whiteman, S. (2012). Sibling relationships and influences in childhood and adolescence. *Journal of Marriage and the Family, 74*(5), 913–930.

Mennella, J., Jagnow, C., & Beauchamp, G. (2001). Prenatal and postnatal flavor learning by human infants. *Pediatrics, 107*, E88.

Merrick, M., Ford, D., Ports, K., & Guinn, A. (2018). Prevalence of adverse childhood experiences from the 2011-2014 behavioral risk factor surveillance system in 23 states. *JAMA Pediatrics, 172*(11), 1038–1044.

Meschke, L., Peter, C., & Bartholomae, S. (2012). Developmentally appropriate practice to promote healthy adolescent development integrating research and practice. *Child Youth Care Forum, 41*, 89–108.

Miller-Cotto, D., & Byrnes, J. (2016). Ethnic/racial identity and academic achievement: A meta-analytic review. *Developmental Review, 41*, 51–70.

Minh, A., Muhajarine, N., Janus, M., Brownell, M., & Guhn, M. (2017). A review of neighborhood effects and early child development: How, where, and for whom, do neighborhoods matter? *Health & Place, 46*, 155–174.

Moen, P., Elder, G., Lüscher, K., & Bronfenbrenner, U. (1995). *Examining lives in context: Perspectives on the ecology of human development.* American Psychological Association.

Mondale, S., Patton, S., Streep, M., Tyack, D., Anderson, J., Cuban, L., Kaestle, C., Ravitch, D., & Bernard, S. (2001). *School: The story of American public education.* Beacon.

Moore, C., Paulus, M., & Williams, A. (2015). *Sugar and spice, and everything nice: Exploring prosocial development through infancy and early childhood.* Frontiers Media.

Moore, S., McEwen, L., Quirt, J., Morin, A., Mah, S., Barr, R., Boyce, W., & Kobor, M. (2017). Epigenetic correlates of neonatal contact in humans. *Development and Psychopathology, 29*(5), 1517.

Morra, S. (2008). *Cognitive development: Neo-Piagetian perspectives.* New York: Lawrence Erlbaum Associates.

Morsa, M., Gagnayre, R., Pomey, M., Deccache, C., & Lombrail, P. (2020). Developmentally appropriate patient education during transition: A study of healthcare providers' and parents' perspective. *Health Education Journal, 79*(4), 377–389.

Nasaw, D. (1979). *Schooled to order: A social history of public schooling in the United States.* Oxford.

National Academies of Sciences, Engineering, and Medicine (2018). *How people learn II: Learners, contexts, and cultures.* The National Academies Press.

National Association for the Education of Young Children (2020). *Professional standards and competencies for early childhood educators.* NAEYC. https://naeyc.org/resources/positionstatements/professional-standards-competencies

National Association for the Education of Young Children (2021). 10 effective DAP teaching strategies https://www.naeyc.org/resources/topics/dap/10-effective-dap-teaching-strategies

National Commission on Social, Emotional, and Academic Development (2019). *From a nation at risk to a nation at hope.* The Aspen Institute.

National Institutes of Health (2019). *Puberty.* US National Library of Medicine. https://medlineplus.gov/puberty.html

Nordhagen, S. (2020). Food supply chains and child and adolescent diets: A review. *Global Food Security, 27,* 100443.

Oster, E. (2019). *Crib sheet: A data-driven guide to better, more relaxed parenting, from birth to preschool.* Penguin Press.

Paradies, Y., Ben, J., Denson, N., Elias, A., Priest, N., Pieterse, A., Gupta, A., Kelaher, M., & Gee, G. (2015). Racism as a determinant of health: A systematic review and meta-analysis. *PLOS ONE, 10*, e0138511.

Parker, K. & Igielink, R. (2020). *On the cusp of adulthood and facing an uncertain future: what we know about gen z so far.* Pew Research Center. https://www.pewresearch.org/social-trends/2020/05/14/on-the-cusp-of-adulthood-and-facing-an-uncertain-future-what-we-know-about-gen-z-so-far-2

Pastorello, K. (2014). *The progressives: Activism and reform in American society, 1893–1917.* John Wiley.

Pauker, K., Apfelbaum, E., & Spitzer, B. (2015). When societal norms and social identity collide: The race talk dilemma for racial minority children. *Social Psychological and Personality Science, 6*, 887–895.

Payne, V., & Isaacs, L. (2016). *Human motor development: A lifespan approach.* Holcomb Hathaway.

Perszyk, D., Lei, R., Bodenhausen, G., Richeson, J., & Waxman, S. (2019). Bias at the intersection of race and gender: Evidence from preschool-aged children. *Developmental Science, 22*, e12788.

Pew Research Center (2015). *The whys and how of generations research.* https://www.pewresearch.org/politics/2015/09/03/the-whys-and-hows-of-generations-research/#:~:text=%20The%20Whys%20and%20Hows%20of%20Generations%20Research,and%20Marijuana%20Legalization.%20Views%20on%20the...%20More%20

Pinsker, J. (2020). Oh no, they've come up with another generation label: How much do members of "Generation Alpha," or any generation, really have in common? *The Atlantic.* https://www.theatlantic.com/family/archive/2020/02/generation-after-gen-z-named-alpha/606862/

Pritchard, A. (2008). *Ways of learning: Learning theories and learning styles in the classroom.* Routledge.

Raikes, H. & Edwards, C. (2009). *Extending the dance in infant and toddler caregiving: Enhancing attachment and relationships.* Brookes.

Ramey, J. (2012). *Child care in black and white: Working parents and the history of orphanages.* University of Illinois.

Reid, J., Kagan, S., & Scott-Little, C. (2017). New understandings of cultural diversity and the implications for early childhood policy, pedagogy, and practice. *Early Child Development and Care, 189*(6), 976–989.

Rielly, E. (2003). *The 1960s.* Greenwood.

Robinson, M. (2008). *Child development 0-8: A journey through the early years.* Open University Press, McGraw Hill.

Rosen, M., Sheridan, M., Sambrook, K., Meltzoff, A., & McLaughlin, K. (2018). Socioeconomic disparities in academic achievement: A multi-modal investigation of neural mechanisms in children and adolescents. *NeuroImage, 173*, 298–310.

Rury, J. (2005). *Urban education in the United States: A historical reader.* Palgrave MacMillan.

Rymsza-Pawlowska, M. (2017). *History comes alive: Public history and popular culture in the 1970s.* University of North Carolina.

Sagert, K. (2007). *The 1970s*. Greenwood.

Salam, R., Das, J., Lassi, Z. & Z. Bhutta (2016a). Adolescent health and well-being: Background and methodology for review of potential interventions. *Journal of Adolescent Health, 59*(Suppl. 4):S4–S10.

Salam, R., Das, J., Lassi, Z., & Bhutta, Z. (2016b). Adolescent health interventions: Conclusions, evidence gaps, and research priorities. *Journal of Adolescent Health, 59*(Suppl. 4), S88–S92.

Salkind, N., & Rasmussen, K. (2008). *Encyclopedia of educational psychology*. Sage.

Samuel, L. (2012). *The American dream: A cultural history*. Syracuse University Press.

Sanders, K., & Farago, F. (2018) Developmentally appropriate practice in the twenty-first century. In M. Fleer & B. van Oers (Eds.), *International handbook of early childhood education*. Springer.

Scholtz, S. E., de Klerk, W., & de Beer, L. (2020). The use of research methods in psychological research: A systematized review. *Frontiers in Research Metrics and Analytics, 5*.

Schunk, D. (2012). *Learning theories: An educational perspective*. Pearson.

Segal, N. (2012). *Born together—reared apart: The landmark Minnesota twin study*. Harvard University Press.

Segal, N. (2017). *Twin mythconceptions*. Academic Press.

Seibert, A., & Kerns, K. (2009). Attachment figures in middle childhood. *International Journal of Behavioral Development, 33*, 347–355.

Sharma, R., Gaffey, M., Alderman, H., Bassani, D., Bogard, K., Darmstadt, G., Das, J., de Graft-Johnson, J., Hamadani, J., Horton, S., Huicho, L., Hussein, J., Lye, S., Pérez-Escamilla, R., Proulx, K., Marfo, K., Mathews-Hanna, V., Mclean, M., Rahman, A., Silver, K., Singla, D., Sherry, K., & Powell, G. (2021). *Determined: The 400-year struggle for black equality*. Virginia Museum of History & Culture in Association with D Giles Limited.

Shin, K., Cho, S., Shin, Y., & Park, K. (2016). Effects of early childhood peer relationships on adolescent mental health: A 6- to 8-year follow-up study in South Korea. *Psychiatry Investigation, 13*(4), 383–388.

Shonkoff, J. (2016). Capitalizing on advances in science to reduce the health consequences of early childhood adversity. *JAMA Pediatrics, 170*(10), 1003–1007.

Shonkoff, J., Boyce, W., & McEwen, B. (2009). Neuroscience, molecular biology, and the childhood roots of health disparities: Building a new framework for health promotion and disease prevention. *JAMA, 301*(21), 2252–2259.

Sibley, B., & Etnier, J. (2003). The relationship between physical activity and cognition in children: A meta-analysis. *Pediatric Exercise Science, 15*, 243–256.

Skinner, E., Kindermann, T., & Mashburn, A. (2019). *Lifespan developmental systems: Meta-theory, methodology and the study of applied problems*. Routledge.

Slopen, N., Shonkoff, J., & Albert, M. (2016). Racial disparities in child adversity in the US: Interactions with family immigration history and income. *American Journal of Preventive Medicine, 50*(1), 47–56.

Soliman, A., Sanctis, V., & Elalaily, R. (2014). Nutrition and pubertal development. *Indian Journal of Endocrinology and Metabolism, 18*, S39–47.

Spring, J. (2018). *The American school: From the Puritans to the Trump era*. Routledge.

Steinberg, L. (2014). *Age of opportunity: Lessons from the new science of adolescence*. Houghton, Mifflin, Harcourt.

Sullivan, R., Perry, R., Sloan, A., Kleinhaus, K., & Burtchen, N. (2011). Infant bonding and attachment to the caregiver: Insights from basic and clinical science. *Clinics in Perinatology, 38*(4), 643–655.

Sun, Y., Mensah, F., Azzopardi, P., Patton, G., & Wake, M. (2017). Childhood social disadvantage and pubertal timing: A national birth cohort from Australia. *Pediatrics, 139*(6).

Svetlova, M., Nichols, S., & Brownell, C. (2010). Toddlers' prosocial behavior: From instrumental to empathic to altruistic helping. *Child Development, 81*(6), 1814–1827.

Tabery, J. (2014). *Beyond versus: The struggle to understand the interaction of nature and nurture*. MIT Press.

Thigpen, C., & Funk, C. (2020). *Younger, more educated US adults are more likely to take part in citizen science research*. Pew Research. https://www.pewresearch.org/fact-tank/2020/06/25/younger-more-educated-u-s-adults-are-more-likely-to-take-part-in-citizen-science-research/

Tomlinson, M., Darmstadt, G., Yousafzai, A., Daelmans, B., Britto, P., Gordon, S., Tablante, E., & Dua, T. (2019). Global research priorities to accelerate programming to improve early childhood development in the sustainable development era: A CHNRI exercise. *Journal of Global Health, 9*(3), 020703.

Truesdale, K., Matheson, D., JaKa, M., McAleer, S., Sommer, E., & Pratt, C. (2019). Baseline diet quality of predominantly minority children and adolescents from households characterized by low socioeconomic status in the childhood obesity prevention and treatment research (COPTR) consortium. *BMC Nutrition, 5*, 38.

Ungar, M. (2015). Practitioner review: Diagnosing childhood resilience—A systemic approach to the diagnosis of adaptation in adverse social and physical ecologies. *Journal of Child Psychology and Psychiatry, 56*, 4–17.

UNICEF (2014). *Hidden in plain sight: A statistical analysis of violence against children*. https://www.unicef.org/publications/index_74865.html

UNICEF (2020). *Huge inequality in educational achievement in every rich nation*. https://www.unicef.org/media/media_19241.html

United Nations (2018). *United Nations millennium goals 4: Reduce child mortality*. http://www.un.org/millenniumgoals/childhealth.shtml

United Nations (2019). *Migration policy institute tabulation of data from the United Nations, department of economic and social affairs, trends in international migrant stock*. www.un.org/en/development/desa/population/migration/data/estimates2/estimates19.asp

Urban, W., & Wagoner, J. (2014). *American education: A history*. Routledge.

US Department of Health and Human Services (2020). *Healthy people 2020*. http://www.healthypeople.gov/2020/default.aspx

US Department of Justice (2017). *Sex trafficking*. https://www.justice.gov/criminal-ceos/child-sex-trafficking

Vaish, A. (2018). Sophisticated concern in early childhood. In N. Roughley & T. Schramme (Eds.), *Forms of fellow feeling: Empathy, sympathy, concern and moral agency*. Cambridge University Press.

van IJzendoorn, M., & Bakermans-Kranenburg, M. (2008). Maternal sensitivity and infant temperament in the formation of attachment. *Theories of Infant Development*. Blackwell.

Vogel, M., Monesson, A., & Scott, L. (2012). Building biases in infancy: The influence of race on face and voice emotion matching. *Developmental Science, 5*(3), 359–372, 375.

Vries, S. L., Hoeve, M., Assink, M., Stams, G. J. J., & Asscher, J. J. (2015). Practitioner review: Effective ingredients of prevention programs for youth at risk of persistent juvenile delinquency– Recommendations for clinical practice. *Journal of Child Psychology and Psychiatry, 56*, 108–121.

Wang, X. (2014). *Understanding language and literacy development: Diverse learners in the classroom*. John Wiley.

Wells, K. (2020). Cognitive development. *Gale Encyclopedia of Children's Health: Infancy through Adolescence*. Gale Research, Inc.

White, R., Nair, R., & Bradley, R. (2018). Theorizing the benefits and costs of adaptive cultures for development. *American Psychologist, 73*(6), 727–739.

Whitfield, C., Anda, R., Dube, S., & Felitti, V. (2003). Violent childhood experiences and the risk of intimate partner violence in adults: Assessment in a large health maintenance organization. *Journal of Interpersonal Violence, 18*(2), 166–185.

Wildeman, C., & Wang, E. (2017). Mass incarceration, public health, and widening inequality in the U.S.A. *Lancet, 389*, 1464–1474.

Williams, P., & Lerner, M. (2019). School readiness. *Pediatrics, 144*(2).

Williamson, D., Thompson, T., Anda, R., Dietz, W., & Felitti, V. (2002). Body weight, obesity, and self-reported abuse in childhood. *International Journal of Obesity, 26*, 1075–1082.

Willingham, D. (2009). Ask the cognitive psychologist: What is developmentally appropriate practice? *American Educator*, 34–39.

Woo, S., Tay, L., & Proctor, R. W. (2020). *Big data in psychological research*. American Psychological Association.

Xiao, N., Quinn, P., Liu, S., Ge, L., Pascalis, O., & Lee, K. (2018). Older but not younger infants associate own-race faces with happy music and other-race faces with sad music. *Developmental Science, 21*(2).

Xu, F. (2019). Towards a rational constructivist theory of cognitive development. *Psychological Review, 126*(6), 841–864.

Yates, T., Ostrosky, M., Cheatham, G., Fettig, A., Shaffer, L., & Santos, R. (2008). *Research synthesis on screening and assessing social-emotional competence*. Center on the Social Emotional Foundations for Early Learning. http://csefel.vanderbilt.edu/documents/rs_screening_assessment.pdf

Zeiders, K., Causadias, J., & White, R. (2018). The health correlates of culture: Examining the association between ethnic-racial identity and diurnal cortisol slopes. *The Journal of Adolescent Health: Official Publication of the Society for Adolescent Medicine, 62*(3), 349–351.

Chapter 2

Aiken, C., Tarry-Adkins, J., & Ozanne, S. (2016). Transgenerational effects of maternal diet on metabolic and reproductive ageing. *Mammalian Genome, 27*(7-8), 430–439.

Ainsworth, M., Blehar, M., Waters, E., & Wall, S. (2015). *Patterns of attachment: A psychological study of the strange situation*. Psychology Press/Taylor & Francis Group.

American Psychological Association. (2006). Reiko Homma True. *Monitor on Psychology, 37*(2). http://www.apa.org/monitor/feb06/true

Anderson, J.R. (1995). *Learning and memory: An integrated approach*. Wiley & Sons, Inc.

Bandura, A. (1977). *Social learning theory*. Prentice Hall.

Bandura, A. (1986). *Social foundations of thought and action: A social cognitive theory*. Prentice-Hall.

Bandura, A. (1997). *Self-efficacy: The exercise of control*. Freeman.

Bandura, A. (2001). Social cognitive theory: An agentic perspective. *Annual Review of Psychology, 52*, 1–26.

Banik, A., Kandilya, D., Ramya, S., Stünkel, W., Chong, Y., & Dheen, S. T. (2017). Maternal factors that induce epigenetic changes contribute to neurological disorders in offspring. *Genes, 8*(6), 150.

Barrouillet, P. (2015). Theories of cognitive development: From Piaget to today. *Developmental Review, 38*(C), 1–12.

Barua, S., & Junaid, M. (2015). Lifestyle, pregnancy and epigenetic effects. *Epigenomics, 7*, 85–102.

Bates, B. (2019). *Learning theories simplified*. Sage.

Baylor, G., & Gascon, J. (1973). An information processing theory of aspects of the development of weight seriation in children. *Cognitive Psychology, 6*, 1–40.

Bayne-Smith, M. (1996). *Race, gender, and health*. Sage.

Belsky, J., Steinberg, L., & Draper, P. (1991). Childhood experience, interpersonal development, and reproductive strategy: An evolutionary theory of socialization. *Child Development, 62*, 647–670.

Benjamin, L., Henry, K., & McMahon, L. (2005). Inez Beverly Prosser and the education of African Americans. *Journal of the History of the Behavioral Sciences, 41*(1), 43–62.

Berkowitz, A. (2020). Playing the genome card. *Journal of Neurogenetics, 34*(1), 189–197.

Bernal, M., & Educational Resources Information Center (1985). *Issues in the training of minority psychologists*. Indiana University Press.

Bernal, M., & Knight, G. (1993). *Ethnic identity: Formation and transmission among Hispanics and other minorities*. State University of New York Press.

Beswick, D. (2017). *Cognitive motivation: From curiosity to identity, purpose and meaning*. Cambridge University Press.

Bjorklund, D. (2004). *Children's thinking: Cognitive development and individual differences*. Wadsworth Publishing.

Bjorklund, D., & Pellegrini, A. (2000). Child development and evolutionary psychology. *Child Development, 71*, 1687–1708.

Bjorklund, D., & Pellegrini, A. (2002). *The origins of human nature: Evolutionary developmental psychology*. American Psychological Association.

Bodrova, E., & Leong, D. (1996). *Tools of the mind: The Vygotskian approach to early childhood education*. Merrill.

Borry, P., & Matthijs, G. (2016). *The human recipe: Understanding your genes in today's society*. Leuven University Press.

Bronfenbrenner, U. (1996). *The ecology of human development experiments by nature and design*. Harvard University Press.

Bullard, J. (2014). *Creating environments for learning: Birth to age eight*. Pearson.

Buss, D. (2005). *The handbook of evolutionary psychology*. John Wiley & Sons.

Callaghan, T. (2019). Responsible genetic genealogy. *Science, 366,* 155.

Chambers, D., Huang, C., & Matthews, G. (2019). *Basic physiology for anaesthetists.* Cambridge University Press.

Chauhan, A., & Chauhan, V. (2015). Increased vulnerability to oxidative stress and mitochondrial dysfunction in autism. In S. Fatemi (Ed.), *The molecular basis of autism: Contemporary clinical neuroscience.* New York: Springer.

Chomsky., N. (1965). *Aspects of the theory of syntax.* MIT Press.

Cohen, D. (2018). *How the child's mind develops.* Routledge.

Crick, F. (1962). The genetic code. *Scientific American, 207,* 66–74.

Darwin, C., 1859. *On the origin of species by means of natural selection.* John Murray.

David, A. (2019). *The secret life of the brain: Unlocking the mysteries of the mind.* Firefly.

Drescher, G.L. (1991). *Made-up mind. A constructivist approach to artificial intelligence.* MIT Press.

Drogin, E. (2019). *Ethical conflicts in psychology.* American Psychological Association.

Elliott, S., & Davis, J. (2020). Challenging taken-for-granted ideas in early childhood education: A critique of Bronfenbrenner's ecological systems theory in the age of post-humanism. In A. Cutter-Mackenzie-Knowles, K. Malone, & E. Barratt Hacking (Eds.), *Research handbook on childhood nature.* Springer.

Ellis, B., & Bjorklund, D. (2005). *Origins of the social mind: Evolutionary psychology and child development.* Guilford.

Ericsson, K., & Simon, H. (1984). *Protocol analysis.* MIT Press.

Erikson, E. (1950). *Childhood and society.* Norton.

Erikson, E. (1982). *The life cycle completed.* Norton.

Esposito, G., Azhari, A., & Borelli, J. (2018). Gene × environment interaction in developmental disorders: Where do we stand and what's next? *Frontiers in Psychology, 9,* 2036.

Estes, D., & Bartsch, K. (2017). Theory of mind: A foundational component of human general intelligence. *Behavioral Brain Science, 40,* e201.

Finlay, G. (2013). *Human evolution: Genes, genealogies and phylogenies.* Cambridge University Press.

Finney Rutten, L., Gollust, S., Naveed, S., & Moser, P. (2012). Increasing public awareness of direct-to-consumer genetic tests: Health care access, internet use, and population density correlates. *Journal of Cancer Epidemiology,* 309109.

Fowler-Finn, K., & Boutwell, B. (2019). Using variation in heritability estimates as a test of G × E in behavioral research: A brief research note. *Behavior Genetics, 49.*

Gershoff, E. (2010). More harm than good: A summary of scientific research on the intended and unintended effects of corporal punishment on children. *Law and Contemporary Problems, 73,* 33–58.

Gershoff, E. (2017). School corporal punishment in global perspective: Prevalence, outcomes, and efforts at intervention. *Psychology, Health & Medicine, 22*(1), 224–239.

Gershoff, E., Goodman, G., Miller-Perrin, C., Holden, G., Jackson, Y., & Kazdin, A. (2018). The strength of the causal evidence against physical punishment of children and its implications for parents, psychologists, and policymakers. *American Psychologist, 73*(5), 626–638.

Gershoff, E., & Grogan-Kaylor, A. (2016). Spanking and child outcomes: Old controversies and new meta-analyses. *Journal of Family Psychology, 30*(4), 453–469.

Gershoff, E., Lansford, J., Sexton, H., Davis-Kean, P., & Sameroff, E. (2012). Longitudinal links between spanking and children's externalizing behaviors in a national sample of White, Black, Hispanic, and Asian American families. *Child Development, 83,* 838–843.

Giardiello, P. (2014). *Pioneers in early childhood education: The roots and legacies of Rachel and Margaret McMillan, Maria Montessori and Susan Isaacs.* Routledge.

Global Initiative to End All Corporal Punishment of Children (2019). *States which have prohibited all corporal punishment.* Retrieved at: http://www.endcorporalpunishment.org/progress/prohibiting-states/

Graf, N. (2020). *Mail-in DNA test results bring surprises about family history for many users.* Pew Research Center. https://www.pewresearch.org/

Gray, C., & MacBlain, S. (2015). *Learning theories in childhood.* Sage.

Guerrini, C., Robinson, J., Petersen, D., & McGuire, A. (2018). Should police have access to genetic genealogy databases? Capturing the golden state killer and other criminals using a controversial new forensic technique. *PLoS Biol, 16*(10), e2006906.

Guthrie, J. (2003). *Encyclopedia of education.* Macmillan.

Hineline, P., & Rosales-Ruiz, J. (2012). Behavior in relation to aversive events: Punishment and negative reinforcement. In G. Madden, W. Dube, T. Hackenberg, G. Hanley, & K. Lattal (Eds.), *APA handbook of behavior analysis.* American Psychological Association.

Hood, K. (2010). *Handbook of developmental science, behavior, and genetics.* Wiley-Blackwell.

Hopkins, J. (2011). The enduring influence of Jean Piaget. *Psychological Science.* psychologicalscience.org/observer/jean-piaget

Inhelder, B., & Piaget, J. (1958). The growth of logical thinking from childhood to adolescence: An essay on the construction of formal operational structures. *Psychology Press, 22.*

Jackson, J. (2005). *Social scientists for social justice: Making the case against segregation.* New York University Press.

Jackson, J., & Weidman, N. (2006). *Race, racism, and science: Social impact and interaction.* Rutgers University Press.

Jansen, A., Mous, S., White, T., Posthuma, D., & Polderman, T. (2015). What twin studies tell us about the heritability of brain development, morphology, and function: A review. *Neuropsychology Review, 25*(1), 27–46.

Kanherkar, R. R., Bhatia-Dey, N., & Csoka, A. B. (2014). Epigenetics across the human lifespan. *Frontiers in cell and developmental biology, 2,* 49. https://doi.org/10.3389/fcell.2014.00049

Kennett, D. (2019). Using genetic genealogy databases in missing persons cases and to develop suspect leads in violent crimes. *Forensic Science International, 301,* 107–117.

Kenny, D. (2013). *Bringing up baby: The psychoanalytic infant comes of age.* Karnac.

Klahr, D., & Siegler, R. (1978). The representation of children's knowledge. In H. W. Reese & L. P. Lipsitt (Eds.), *Advances in Children Development,* 12. Academic Press.

Klahr, D., & Wallace, J. (1976). *Cognitive development: An information processing view.* Lawrence Erlbaum Associates.

Knight, Z. (2017). A proposed model of psychodynamic psychotherapy linked to Erik Erikson's eight stages of psychosocial development. *Clinical Psychology & Psychotherapy, 24*(5), 1047–1058.

Korf, B. (2020). Principles of genetics. In L. Goldman & A. Schafer (Eds.), *Goldman-Cecil medicine.* Elsevier.

LaFreniere, P. (2010). *Adaptive origins: Evolution and human development.* Psychology Press.

Lal, S. (2002). Giving children security: Mamie Phipps Clark and the racialization of child psychology. *The American Psychologist, 57*(1), 20–28.

Lee, E. (1997). *Working with Asian Americans: A guide for clinicians.* Guilford.

Lee, S., Altschul, I., & Gershoff, E. (2013). Does warmth moderate longitudinal associations between maternal spanking and child aggression in early childhood? *Developmental Psychology, 49*(11), 2017–2028.

Legerstee, M., Haley, D., and Bornstein, M. (2013). *The infant mind: Origins of the social brain.* Guilford.

Lerner, R., Easterbrooks, M., Mistry, J., & Weiner, I. (2013). Developmental psychology. In *Handbook of psychology.* John Wiley & Sons.

Little, C. W., Larsen, S., Byrne, B., Logan, J. A. R., Olson, R. K., & Coventry, W. L. (2020). Exploring the influence of early childhood education and care on the etiology of achievement. *Behavior Genetics, 50*(6), 387–400.

Losos, J., Baum, D., Hoekstra, H., Lenski, R., Moore, A., Peichel, C., Schluter, D., & Whitlock, M. (2013). *The Princeton guide to evolution.* Princeton University Press.

Lucchesi, J. (2019). *Epigenetics, nuclear organization and gene function: With implications of epigenetic regulation and genetic architecture for human development and health.* Oxford University Press.

Machluf, K., Liddle. J., & Bjorklund, D. (2014, April). An introduction to evolutionary developmental psychology. *Evolutionary Psychology.*

Mahn, H., & John-Steiner, V. (2012). Vygotsky and sociocultural approaches to teaching and learning. In *Handbook of psychology.* John Wiley.

Malberg, N., & Raphael-Leff, J. (2012). *The Anna Freud tradition: Lines of development—Evolution and theory and practice over the decades.* Karnac Books.

Mandler, J. (2004). *The foundations of mind: Origins of conceptual thought.* Oxford University Press.

Marcon, A., Rachul, C., & Caulfield, T. (2021). The consumer representation of DNA ancestry testing on YouTube. *New Genetics and Society, 40*(2), 133–154.

Martinez, G. (2020). Trends and patterns in menarche in the United States: 1995 through 2013–2017. *National Health Statistics Reports, 146,* 1–12.

McLeod, S. (2018a). Jean Piaget's theory and stages of cognitive development. *Simply Psychology.* simplypsychology.org/piaget.html

McLeod, S. (2018b). *Pavlov's dogs. Simply Psychology.* Retrieved at: ttps://www.simplypsychology.org/pavlov.html

Moen, P., Elder, G., Lüscher, K. & U. Bronfenbrenner (1995). *Examining lives in context: Perspectives on the ecology of human development.* American Psychological Association.

Mooney, C. (2013). *Theories of childhood: An introduction to Dewey, Montessori, Erikson, Piaget, and Vygotsky.* Redleaf.

Moore, C. (2010). Social cognition in infancy. *Encyclopedia on early childhood development.* http://www.child-encyclopedia.com/social-cognition/according-experts/social-cognition-infancy

Moore, J. (1963). *Heredity and development.* Oxford University Press.

Morra, S. (2008). *Cognitive development: Neo-Piagetian perspectives.* Lawrence Erlbaum Associates.

Moustafa, A. (2018). *Computational models of brain and behavior.* John Wiley & Sons.

Muehlenbein, M. (2010). *Human evolutionary biology.* Cambridge University Press.

Muehlenbein, M. (2015). *Basics in human evolution.* Academic Press.

National Scientific Council on the Developing Child (2010). *Early experiences can alter gene expression and affect long-term development: Working paper no. 10.* www.developingchild.harvard.edu.

Newell, A. (1970). Remarks on the relationship between artificial intelligence and cognitive psychology. In R. Barneji & M. Mesarovic (Eds.), *Theoretical approaches to non-numerical problem solving.* Springer-Verlag.

Newell, A., Shaw, J., & Simon, H. (1958). Elements of a theory of human problem solving. *Psychological Review, 65*(3), 151–166.

Newell, A., & Simon, H. (1972). *Human problem solving.* Prentice Hall.

Nishina, A.. & Witkow, M. (2019). Why developmental researchers should care about biracial, multiracial, and multiethnic youth. *Child Development Perspectives, 14.*

Olby, R. (1985). *Origins of Mendelism.* Chicago University Press.

Ordovas, J. (2008). Genotype-phenotype associations: Modulation by diet and obesity. *Obesity, 16* (Suppl 3), S40–S46.

Pearson, B., Simon, J., McCoy, E., Salazar, G., Fragola, G., & Zylka, M. (2016). Identification of chemicals that mimic transcriptional changes associated with autism, brain aging and neurodegeneration. *Nature Communications, 7,* 11173.

Pew Research Center (2015). *Parenting in America.* https://www.pewsocialtrends.org/2015/12/17/parenting-in-america/

Pickren, W., Dewsbury, D., & Wertheimer, M. (2012*). Portraits of pioneers in developmental psychology.* Taylor & Francis.

Posner, J., Polanczyk, G., & Sonuga-Barke, E. (2020). Attention-deficit hyperactivity disorder. *Lancet, 395*(10222), 450–462.

Powar, C. (2007). *Genetics (Volume I).* Himalaya Publishing.

Pritchard, D., & Korf, B. (2013). *Medical genetics at a glance.* Wiley-Blackwell.

Qasim, A., Turcotte, M., de Souza, R., Samaan, M., Champredon, D., Dushoff, J., Speakman, J., & Meyre, D. (2018). On the origin of obesity: Identifying the biological, environmental and cultural drivers of genetic risk among human populations. *Obesity Reviews, 19*(2), 121–149.

Rayburn, C. (2010). *A handbook for women mentors: Transcending barriers of stereotype, race, and ethnicity.* Praeger.

Roberts, J., & Middleton, A. (2017). Genetics in the 21st century: Implications for patients, consumers and citizens. *F1000Research, 6,* 2020.

Robinson, M. R. et al. (2017). LifeLines Cohort Study. Genotype-covariate interaction effects and the heritability of adult body mass index. *Nat. Genet. 49,* 1174–1181.

Robinson, P. (1993). *Freud and his critics.* University of California.

Rogers, J. (2019). Smoking and pregnancy: Epigenetics and developmental origins of the metabolic syndrome. *Birth Defects Research, 111,* 1259–1269.

Rose, A. (2007). The discovery of southern childhoods: Psychology and the transformation of schooling in the Jim Crow South. *Historical Psychology, 10*(3), 249–278.

Roseboom, T. (2019). Epidemiological evidence for the developmental origins of health and disease: Effects of prenatal undernutrition in humans. *The Journal of Endocrinology, 242*(1), T135–T144.

Roth, W., Yaylaci, S., Jaffe, K., & Richardson, L. (2020). Do genetic ancestry tests increase racial essentialism? Findings from a randomized controlled trial. *PLOS ONE, 15*(1), 1–17.

Running, M. (2015). *A primer on cell and molecular biology.* Momentum Press.

Salkind, N., & Rasmussen, K. (2008). *Encyclopedia of educational psychology.* Sage.

Sánchez Korrol, V., & Ruíz, V. (2006). *Latinas in the United States: A historical encyclopedia.* Indiana University Press.

Sandler, J. (1997). *Freud's models of the mind: An introduction.* Karnac Books.

Schaafsma, S., Pfaff, D., Spunt, R., & Adolphs, R. (2015). Deconstructing and reconstructing theory of mind. *Trends in Cognitive Science, 19*(2), 65–72.

Schunk, D., & DiBenedetto, M. (2020). Motivation and social cognitive theory. *Contemporary Educational Psychology, 60.*

Schunk, D., & Usher, E. (2019). Social cognitive theory and motivation. In R. Ryan (Ed.), *The Oxford handbook of human motivation.* Oxford University Press.

Sciberras, E., Mulraney, M., Silva, D., & Coghill, D. (2017). Prenatal risk factors and the etiology of ADHD: Review of existing evidence. *Current Psychiatry Reports, 19,* 1.

Segal, N. (2012). *Born together—reared apart: The landmark Minnesota twin study.* Harvard University Press.

Segal, N. (2017). *Twin mythconceptions.* Academic Press.

Sege, R., & Siegel, B. (2019). Council on child abuse and neglect; Committee on psychosocial aspects of child and family health. Effective discipline to raise healthy children. *Pediatrics, 142*(6), e20183112.

Sheehy, N., & Forsythe, A. (2003). *Fifty key thinkers in psychology.* Routledge.

Shelton, L. (2019). *The Bronfenbrenner primer: A guide to develecology.* Routledge.

Skinner, B. F. (1953). *Science and human behaviour.* The Macmillan Company.

Stewart-Williams, S. (2018). *The ape that understood the universe: How the mind and culture evolve.* Cambridge University Press.

Stoeklé, H. C., Charlier, P., Mamzer-Bruneel, M. F., Hervé, C., & Vogt, G. (2020). Systemic modelling in bioethics. *New Bioethics, 26*(3), 197–209.

Sulc, J., Mounier, N., Günther, F., Winkler, T., Wood, A., Frayling, T., Heid, I., Robinson, M., & Kutalik, Z. (2020). Quantification of the overall contribution of gene-environment interaction for obesity-related traits. *Nature Communication, 11,* 1385.

Summers, R. (2017). *Social psychology: How other people influence our thoughts and actions.* Greenwood.

Sun, X., Li, P., Yang, X, Li, W., Qiu, X., & Zhu, S. (2017). From genetics and epigenetics to the future of precision treatment for obesity. *Gastroenterology Report, 5*(4), 266–270.

Suzuki, K., & Von Vacano, D. (2018). *Reconsidering race: Social science perspectives on racial categories in the age of genomics.* Oxford.

Syed, M. (2016). Power and agency in conceptualizing life stages as master narratives. *Human Development, 59,* 317–323.

Syed, M., Santos, C., Yoo, H. C., & Juang, L. (2018). Invisibility of racial/ethnic minorities in developmental science: Implications for research and institutional practices. *American Psychologist, 73*(6), 812–826.

Tabery, J. (2007). Biometric and developmental gene-environment interactions: Looking back, moving forward. *Development and Psychopathology, 19*(4), 961–976.

Tabery, J. (2015). Debating interaction: The history, and an explanation. *International Journal of Epidemiology, 44*(4), 1117–1123.

Tabery, J., & Griffiths, P. E. (2010). In K. E. Hood, C. T. Halpern, G. Greenberg, & R. M. Lerner (Eds.), *Handbook of developmental science, behavior, and genetics.* Wiley-Blackwell.

Tach, L., Dunifon, R., & Miller, D. (2020). *Confronting inequality: How policies and practices shape children's opportunities.* American Psychological Association.

Tauber, A. (2010). *Freud, the reluctant philosopher.* Princeton University Press.

Taylor, C., Fleckman, J., Scholer, S., & Branco, N. (2018). US pediatricians' attitudes, beliefs, and perceived injunctive norms about spanking. *Journal of Developmental and Behavioral Pediatrics, 39*(7), 564–572.

Than, K. (2016). *A brief history of twin studies.* Smithsonian Magazine. https://www.smithsonianmag.com/science-nature/brief-history-twin-studies-180958281/

Thornton, S. (2003). *Growing minds: An introduction to children's cognitive development.* Palgrave Macmillan.

Tiffon, C. (2018). The impact of nutrition and environmental epigenetics on human health and disease. *International Journal of Molecular Sciences, 19*(11), 3425.

Tobi, E., Slieker, R., Luijk R., Dekkers, K., Stein, A., Xu, K., & Slagboom, P. (2018). DNA methylation as a mediator of the association between prenatal adversity and risk factors for metabolic disease in adulthood. *Science Advances, 4,* eaao4364.

UNICEF (2017). *A familiar face: Violence in the lives of children and adolescents.*

US Centers for Disease Control and Prevention (2020). *Genomics and Human Health.* www.cdc.gov/genomics/disease/epigenetics.htm

US National Institute of Health (2020). *About genomics. National human genome research institute.* https://www.genome.gov

US National Institute of Health (2020). *US National Medical Library.* https://medlineplus.gov/genetics/understanding/basics/dna/

Usher, E., & Weidner, B. (2018). Sociocultural influences on self-efficacy development. In D. Liem & D. McInerney (Eds.), *Big theories revisited.* Information Age Publishing.

Van der Horst, F. (2011). *John Bowlby: From psychoanalysis to ethology: Unravelling the roots of attachment theory.* Wiley-Blackwell.

Vanlehn, K. (1991). Rule acquisition events in the discovery of problem-solving strategies. *Cognitive Science, 15,* 1–47.

Vásquez, M. (2002). Martha E. Bernal (1931–2001). *American Psychologist, 57,* 880–888.

Vygotsky, L. (1978). *Mind and society: The development of higher mental processes.* Harvard University Press.

Vygotsky, L. (1993). *The collected works of L. S. Vygotsky, Vols. 1 and 2.* Plenum Press.

Wallace, B. (2018). *The search for the gene.* Cornell University Press.

Wavering, M.J. (2011). Piaget's logic of meanings: Still relevant today. *School Science and Mathematics, 111,* 249–252.

Webster, G., Graber, J., Gesselman, A., Crosier, B., & Schember, T. (2014). A life history theory of father absence and menarche: A meta-analysis. *Evolutionary Psychology, 12,* 273–294.

Wellman, H., Fuxi, F., & Peterson, C. (2011). Sequential progressions in a theory of mind scale: Longitudinal perspectives. *Child Development, 82*(3), 780–792.

Wellman, H., & Liu, D. (2004). Scaling of theory-of-mind tasks. *Child Development, 75*(2), 523–541.

Wells, K. (2020). Cognitive development. In *Gale encyclopedia of children's health: Infancy through adolescence.* https://www.encyclopedia.com

Wertsch, J., & Sohmer, R. (1995). Vygotsky on learning and development. *Human Development, 38,* 332–337.

White, L. (2019). A neglected ethical issue in citizen science and DIY biology. *American Journal of Bioethics, 19*(8), 46–48.

Whitley, K., Tueller, J., & Weber, K. (2020). Genomics education in the era of personal genomics: Academic, professional, and public considerations. *International Journal of Molecular Sciences, 21*(3), 768.

Wiggins, A., & Wilbanks, J. (2019). The rise of citizen science in health and biomedical research. *The American Journal of Bioethics, 19,* 8, 3–14.

Winham, S., & Biernacka, J. (*2013*). Gene-environment interactions in genome-wide association studies: Current approaches and new directions. *Journal of Child Psychology and Psychiatry, and Allied Disciplines, 54(10),* 1120–1134.

Wink, J., & Puteny A. (2002). *A vision to Vygotsky.* Allyn & Bacon.

World Health Organization (2015). *Global initiative to end all corporal punishment of children. Prohibiting and eliminating corporal punishment: A key health issue in addressing violence against children.* www.who.int/topics/violence/Global-Initiative-End-All-Corporal-Punishment-children.pdf

Wright, E. (2002). *Psychoanalytic criticism theory in practice.* Routledge.

Xu, F. (2019). Towards a rational constructivist theory of cognitive development. *Psychological Review, 126*(6), 841–864.

Yashon, R., & Cummings, M. (2020). *Genetics and human behavior.* Momentum Press Health.

Young, R.M. (1978). Strategies and the structure of cognitive skill. In G. Underwood (Ed.), *Strategies of information processing.* Academic Press.

Young-Bruehl, E. (2008). *Anna Freud: A biography.* Yale University Press.

Chapter 3

Academy of Nutrition and Dietetics (2020). *Eating right during pregnancy.* https://www.eatright.org/health/pregnancy/what-to-eat-when-expecting/eating-right-during-pregnancy

Addissie, Y., Kruszka, P., Troia, A., Wong, Z., Everson, J., Kozel, B., Lipinski, R., Malecki, K., & Muenke, M. (2020). Prenatal exposure to pesticides and risk for holoprosencephaly: A case-control study. *Environmental Health, 19*(1), 65.

Admon, L., Dalton, V., Kolenic, G., Ettner, S., Tilea, A., Haffajee, R., Brownlee, R., Zochowski, M., Tabb, K., Muzik, M., & Zivin, K. (2021). Trends in suicidality 1 year before and after birth among commercially insured childbearing individuals in the United States, 2006–2017. *JAMA Psychiatry, 78*(2), 171–176

Alkema, L., Chou, D., Hogan, D., Zhang, S., Moller, A. B., Gemmill, A., Fat, D., Boerma, T., Temmerman, M., Mathers, C., Say, L., & United Nations Maternal Mortality Estimation Inter-Agency Group (2016). Global, regional, and national levels and trends in maternal mortality between 1990 and 2015, with scenario-based projections to 2030: A systematic analysis by the U.N. maternal mortality estimation inter-agency group. *Lancet, 387*(10017), 462–474.

Almeling, R., & Waggoner, M. (2013). More and less than equal: How men factor in the reproductive equation. *Gender and Society, 27,* 821–842.

Alwan, S., Bleyl, S., Brent, R., Chambers, C., Daston, G., Faustman, E., Finnell, R., Fraser, F., Freidman, J., Fugh-Berman, A., Graham, J., John & Hales, B., Hansen, D., Holmes, L., Hood, R., Kavlock, R., Knudsen, T., Lary, J., & Weringer, E. (2010). *Teratology primer.* Department of Pediatrics Faculty Papers. Thomas Jefferson University. https://www.scribd.com/document/439539611/teratology-primer-pdf

American Academy of Pediatrics, American College of Obstetricians and Gynecologists (2012). *Guidelines for perinatal care.*

American College of Obstetricians and Gynecologists. (2006). ACOG Practice Bulletin: Episiotomy: Clinical Management Guidelines for Obstetrician-Gynecologists. *Obstetrics & Gynecology, 107*(4), 957–962.

American College of Obstetricians and Gynecologists (2016). *Your pregnancy and childbirth month to month.*

American College of Obstetricians and Gynecologists (2019). *Approaches to limit intervention during labor and birth.* Committee Opinion, Number 766. https://www.acog.org/-/media/project/acog/acogorg/clinical/files/committee-opinion/articles/2019/02/approaches-to-limit-intervention-during-labor-and-birth.pdf

American College of Obstetricians and Gynecologists (2021). *The rh factor: How it can affect your pregnancy.* https://www.acog.org/womens-health/faqs/the-rh-factor-how-it-can-affect-your-pregnancy

American College of Obstetricians and Gynecologists and the Society for Maternal–Fetal Medicine, Kilpatrick, S., & Ecker, J. (2016). Severe maternal morbidity: Screening and review. *American Journal of Obstetrics and Gynecology, 215*(3), B17–B22.

Applequist, J. (2014). Pinterest, gender reveal parties, and the binary: Reducing an impending arrival to 'pink' or 'blue'. *Pennsylvania Communication Annual, 70,* 51–65.

Arulkumaran, S. (2016). *Best practice in labour and delivery*. New York: Cambridge University Press.

Asselmann, E., Kunas, S., Wittchen, H., & Martini, J. (2020). Maternal personality, social support, and changes in depressive, anxiety, and stress symptoms during pregnancy and after delivery: A prospective-longitudinal study. *PLOS ONE, 15*(8), 1–18.

Aviram, A., Hod, M., & Yogev, Y. (2011). Maternal obesity: Implications for pregnancy outcome and long-term risks. *International Journal of Gynecology & Obstetrics, 115*(1), S6–S10.

Benova, L., Moller, A., & Moran, A. (2019). What gets measured better gets done better: The landscape of validation of global maternal and newborn health indicators through key informant interviews. *PLOS ONE, 14*(11), e0224746.

Betran, A., Ye, J., Moller, A., Souza, J., & Zhang, J. (2021). Trends and projections of caesarean section rates: Global and regional estimates. *BMJ Global Health, 6*(6), e005671.

Black, A., Fleming, N., & Rome, E. (2012). *Pregnancy in adolescents*. American Academy of Pediatrics.

Black, R., Victora, C., Walker, S., Bhutta, Z., Christian, P., Onis, M., Ezzati, M., Grantham-McGregor, S., Katz, J., Martorell, R., Uauy, R., & Maternal and Child Nutrition Study Group (2013). Maternal and child undernutrition and overweight in low-income and middle-income countries. *Lancet, 382*(9890), 427–451.

Blomberg, M. (2013). Maternal obesity, mode of delivery, and neonatal outcome. *Obstetrics and Gynecology, 122*(1), 50–55.

Bogdarina, I., Murphy, H., Burns, S., & Clark, A. (2004). Investigation of the role of epigenetic modification of the rat glucokinase gene in fetal programming. *Life Sciences, 74*(11), 1407–1415.

Brown, L., Regnault, T., Rozance, P., Barry, J., & Hay, W. (2010). Pregnancy and feto-placental growth: Macronutrients. In M. Symonds & M. Ramsay (Eds.), *Maternal-fetal nutrition during pregnancy and lactation*. Cambridge University Press.

Cantor, A., Jungbauer, R., McDonagh, M., Blazina, I., Marshall, N., Weeks, C., Fu, R., LeBlanc, E., & Chou, R. (2021). Counseling and behavioral interventions for healthy weight and weight gain in pregnancy: Evidence report and systematic review for the US preventive services task force. *JAMA, 325*(20), 2094–2109.

Carolan, M., & Frankowska, D. (2011). Advanced maternal age and adverse perinatal outcome: A review of the evidence. *Midwifery, 27*, 793–801.

Chapman, V., & Charles, C. (2013). *The midwife's labour and birth handbook*. Wiley–Blackwell.

Chappell, L., Seed, P., Myers, J., Taylor, R., Kenny, L., Dekker, G., Walker, J., McCowan, L., North, R., & Poston, L. (2013). Exploration and confirmation of factors associated with uncomplicated pregnancy in nulliparous women: Prospective cohort study. *British Medical Journal, 49*(2) 47.

Checkland, D., & Wong, J. (2016). *Teen pregnancy and parenting: Social and ethical issues*. University of Toronto Press.

Chen, J., Cox, S., Kuklina, E., Ferre, C., Barfield, W., & Li, R. (2021). Assessment of incidence and factors associated with severe maternal morbidity after delivery discharge among women in the US. *JAMA Network Open, 4*(2), e2036148.

Cheu, L., Yee, L., & Kominiarek, M. (2020). Food insecurity during pregnancy and gestational weight gain. *American Journal of Obstetrics & Gynecology, 2*(1), 100068.

Cimadomo, D., Fabozzi, G., Vaiarelli, A., Ubaldi, N., Ubaldi, F., & Rienzi, L. (2018). Impact of maternal age on oocyte and embryo competence. *Frontiers in Endocrinology, 9*, 327.

Creanga, A., Berg, C., Ko, J., Farr, S. L., Tong, V., Bruce, F., & Callaghan, W. (2014). Maternal mortality and morbidity in the United States: Where are we now? *Journal of Women's Health, 23*(1), 3–9.

Croen, L., Najjar, D., Fireman, B., & Grether, J. (2007). Maternal and paternal age and risk of autism spectrum disorders. *Archives of Pediatrics & Adolescent Medicine, 161*(4), 334–340.

Davis, D. (2019). Obstetric racism: The racial politics of pregnancy, labor, and birthing. *Medical Anthropology, 38*(7), 560–573.

Dekker, R. (2013). *Evidence confirms birth centers provide top-notch care*. American Association of Birth Centers. https://www.birthcenters.org/page/NBCSII

Devarshi, P., Grant, R., Ikonte, C., & Hazels Mitmesser, S. (2019). Maternal omega-3 nutrition, placental transfer and fetal brain development in gestational diabetes and preeclampsia. *Nutrients, 11*(5), 1107.

DeVido, J., Bogunovic, O., & Weiss, R. (2015). Alcohol use disorders in pregnancy. *Harvard Review of Psychiatry, 23*(2), 112–121.

DiFranza, J., Aligne, C., & Weitzman, M. (2004). Prenatal and postnatal environmental tobacco smoke exposure and children's health. *Pediatrics, 113*(4), 1007–1015.

Ding, X., Wu, Y., Xu, S., Zhu, R., Jia X., Zhang, S., Huang, K., Zhu, P., Hao, J., & Tao, F. (2014). Maternal anxiety during pregnancy and adverse birth outcomes: A systematic review and meta-analysis of prospective cohort studies. *Journal of Affective Disorders, 159*, 103–110.

Dipietro, L., Evenson, K., Bloodgood, B., Sprow, K., Troiano, R., Piercy, K., Vaux-Bjerke, A., Powell, K., & 2018 Physical Activity Guidelines Advisory Committee (2019). Benefits of physical activity during pregnancy and postpartum: An umbrella review. *Medicine and Science in Sports and Exercise, 51*(6), 1292–1302.

Dominguez, T., Dunkel-Schetter, C., Glynn, L., Hobel, C., & Sandman, C. (2008). Racial differences in birth outcomes: The role of general, pregnancy, and racism stress. *Health Psychology, 27*(2), 194–203.

Dorr, P., Khouw, V. M., Chervenak, F., Grunebaum, A., Jacquemyn, Y., & Nijhuis, J. (2017). *Obstetric interventions*. Cambridge University Press.

Downe, S., Finlayson, K., Oladapo, O., Bonet, M., & Gülmezoglu, A. (2018). What matters to women during childbirth: A systematic qualitative review. *PLOS ONE, 13*(5), e0197791.

Dudenhausen, J., Travis, S., Obladen, M., & Pschyrembel, W. (2014). *Practical obstetrics*. De Gruyter.

Dunkel, S. (2010). Psychological science on pregnancy: Stress processes, biopsychosocial models, and emerging research issues. *Annual Review of Psychology, 62*, 531–558.

Farquharson, R., & Stephenson, M. (2010). *Early pregnancy*. Cambridge University Press.

Ferraro, Z., Gaudet, L., & Adamo, K. (2012). The potential impact of physical activity during pregnancy on maternal and neonatal outcomes. *Obstetrical & Gynecological Survey, 67*(2), 99–110.

Fisher, M., & Lara-Torre, E. (2012). *Adolescent gynecology*. American Academy of Pediatrics.

Foglia, L., Nielsen, P., Deering, S., & Galan, H. (2021). Operative vaginal delivery. In M. Landon, H. Galan, & E. Jauniaux (Eds.), *Gabbe's obstetrics: Normal and problem pregnancies*. Elsevier.

Freedman, L., & Kruk, M. (2014). Disrespect and abuse of women in childbirth: Challenging the global quality and accountability agendas. *Lancet, 384,* e42–e44.

Fretts, R. (2005). Etiology and prevention of stillbirth. *Obstetrics & Gynecology, 193*(6), 1923–1935.

Geller, S., Koch, A., Garland, C., MacDonald, E., Storey, F., & Lawton, B. (2018). A global view of severe maternal morbidity: Moving beyond maternal mortality. *Reproductive Health, 15*(Suppl 1), 98.

Gieseler, C. (2018). Gender-reveal parties: Performing community identity in pink and blue. *Journal of Gender Studies, 27*(6), 661–671.

Gluckman, P., Hanson, M., Cooper, C., & Thornburg, K. (2008). Effect of in utero and early-life conditions on adult health and disease. *The New England Journal of Medicine, 359*(1), 61–73.

Godfrey, K., Gluckman, P., & Hanson, M. (2010). Developmental origins of metabolic disease: Life course and intergenerational perspectives. *Trends in Endocrinology and Metabolism, 21,* 199–205.

Goldfarb, S., Stanwood, G., Flynn, H., & Graham, D. (2020). Developmental opioid exposures: Neurobiological underpinnings, behavioral impacts, and policy implications. *Experimental Biology and Medicine, 245*(2), 131–137.

Grondahl, M., Christiansen, S., Kesmodel, U., Agerholm, I., Lemmen, J., Lundstrøm, P., Bogstad, J., Raaschou-Jensen, M., & Ladelund, S. (2017). Effect of women's age on embryo morphology, cleavage rate and competence: A multicenter cohort study. *PLOS ONE, 12*(4), e0172456.

Han, S. (2013). *Pregnancy in practice: Expectation and experience in the contemporary US.* Berghahn Books.

Hayatbakhsh, M., Flenady, V., Gibbons. K., Kingsbury, A., Hurrion, E., Mamun, A., & Najman, J. (2012). Birth outcomes associated with cannabis use before and during pregnancy. *Pediatric Research, 71*(2), 215–219.

Hemingway, A., Davies, S., Jirikowic ,T., & Olson, E. M. (2020). What proportion of the brain structural and functional abnormalities observed among children with fetal alcohol spectrum disorder is explained by their prenatal alcohol exposure and their other prenatal and postnatal risks? *Advances in Pediatric Research, 7,* 41.

Hibbeln, J., Gregory, S., Iles-Caven, Y., Taylor, C., Emond, A., & Golding, J. (2018). Total mercury exposure in early pregnancy has no adverse association with scholastic ability of the offspring particularly if the mother eats fish. *Environment International, 116,* 108–115.

Honein, M., Rasmussen, S., Reefhuis, J., Romitti, P., Lammer, E., Sun, L., & Correa, A. (2007). Maternal smoking, environmental tobacco smoke, and the risk of oral clefts. *Epidemiology, 18,* 226–233.

Howell, E., Egorova, N., Janevic, T., Brodman, M., Balbierz, A, Zeitlin J., & Hebert, P. (2020). Race and ethnicity, medical insurance, and within-hospital severe maternal morbidity disparities. *Obstetrics and Gynecology, 135*(2), 285–293.

Hui, A., Back, L., Ludwig, S., Gardiner, P., Sevenhuysen, G., Dean, H., Sellers, E., & Shen, G. (2014). Effects of lifestyle intervention on dietary intake, physical activity level, and gestational weight gain in pregnant women with different pre-pregnancy body mass index in a randomized control trial. *BMC Pregnancy and Childbirth, 14,* 331.

Ion, R., & Bernal, A. (2015). Smoking and preterm birth. *Reproductive Sciences, 22*(8), 918–926.

Iqbal, S., & Ali, I. (2021). Maternal food insecurity in low-income countries: Revisiting its causes and consequences for maternal and neonatal health. *Journal of Agriculture and Food Research, 3,* 100091.

Jack, B., Bickmore, T., Hempstead, M., Yinusa-Nyahkoon,L., Sadikova, E., Mitchell, S., Gardiner, P., Adigun, F., Penti, B., Schulman, D,. & Damus, K. (2015). Reducing preconception risks among African American women with conversational agent technology. *The Journal of the American Board of Family Medicine, 28*(4), 441–451.

Jackson, F., Rashied-Henry, K., Braveman, P., Dominguez, T., Ramos, D., Maseru, N., Darity, W., Waddell, L., Warne, D., Legaz, G., Gupta, R., & James, A. (2020). A prematurity collaborative birth equity consensus statement for mothers and babies. *Maternal and Child Health Journal, 24*(10), 1231–1237.

Jaques, S., Kingsbury, A., Henshcke, P., Chomchai, C., Clews, S., Falconer, J., Abdel-Latif, M., Feller, J., & Oei, J. (2014). Cannabis, the pregnant woman and her child: Weeding out the myths. *Journal of Perinatology, 34*(6), 417–424.

Jansen, L., Gibson, M., Bowles, B., & Leach, (2013). First do no harm: Interventions during childbirth. *The Journal of Perinatal Education, 22*(2), 83–92.

Joseph, K., Boutin, A., Lisonkova, S., Muraca, G., Razaz, N., John, S., Mehrabadi, A., Sabr, Y., Ananth, C., & Schisterman, E. (2021). Maternal mortality in the United States: Recent trends, current status, and future considerations. *Obstetrics and Gynecology, 137*(5), 763–771.

Kamali, H., & Amin, P. (2016). Management of the third stage of labour. In S. Arulkumaran (Ed.), *Best practice in labour and delivery.* Cambridge University Press.

Kandasamy, V., Hirai, A., Kaufman, J., James, A., & Kotelchuck, M. (2020). Regional variation in Black infant mortality: The contribution of contextual factors. *PLOS ONE, 15*(8), e0237314.

Karbin, K., Khorramrouz, F., Farkhani, E., Sobhani, S., Mosalmanzadeh, N., Shahriari, Z., & Ranjbar, G. (2021). Household food insecurity during pregnancy as a predictor of anthropometric indices failures in infants aged less than six months: A retrospective longitudinal study. *Public Health Nutrition,* 1–24.

Keag, O., Norman, J., & Stock, S. (2018). Long-term risks and benefits associated with cesarean delivery for mother, baby, and subsequent pregnancies: Systematic review and meta-analysis. *PLoS Medicine, 15*(1), e1002494.

Kelli, H., Kim, J., Samman Tahhan, A., Liu, C., Ko, Y., Hammadah, M., Sullivan, S, Sandesara, P., Alkhoder, A., Choudhary, F., & Gafeer, M. (2019). Living in food deserts and adverse cardiovascular outcomes in patients with cardiovascular disease. *Journal of the American Heart Association, 8*(4), e010694.

Kenny, L., Lavender, T., McNamee, R., O'Neill, S., Mills, T., & Khashan, A. (2013). Advanced maternal age and adverse pregnancy outcome: Evidence from a large contemporary cohort. *PLOS ONE, 8*(2), e56583.

Khandwala, Y., Baker, V., Shaw, G., Stevenson, D., Lu, Y., & Eisenberg, M. (2018). Association of paternal age with perinatal outcomes between 2007 and 2016 in the United States: Population based cohort study. *BMJ, 363,* k4372.

Kilpatrick, S., & Garrison, E. (2017). Normal labor and delivery. In S. Gabbe (Ed.), *Obstetrics: Normal and problem pregnancies.* Elsevier.

King, J. (2016). A summary of pathways or mechanisms linking preconception maternal nutrition with birth outcomes. *Journal of Nutrition, 146*, 1437S–1444S.

Kingdon, C., Downe, S., & Betran, A.P. (2018). Women's and communities' views of targeted educational interventions to reduce unnecessary caesarean section: A qualitative evidence synthesis. *Reproductive Health, 15*(1), 1–14.

Klein, J., & Committee on Adolescent Pediatrics (2005). Adolescent pregnancy: Current trends and issues. *American Academy of Pediatrics, 116*(1), 281–286.

Kotelchuck, M., & Lu, M. (2017). Father's role in preconception health. *Maternal and Child Health Journal, 21*, 2025–2039.

Krauss, R., & Hong, M. (2016). Gene–environment interactions and the etiology of birth defects. In P. Wassarman (Ed.), *Current Topics in Developmental Biology, 116*, 569–580.

Lancet (2018). Campaigning for preconception health. *Lancet, 391*, 1749.

Lane, M., Robker, R., & Robertson, S. (2014). Parenting from before conception. *Science, 345*, 756–760.

Lanni, S., Gherman, R., & Gonik, B. (2017). Malpresentations. In S. Gabbe (Ed.), *Obstetrics: Normal and problem pregnancies.* Elsevier.

Laraia, B., Siega-Riz, A., & Gundersen, C. (2010). Household food insecurity is associated with self-reported pre-gravid weight status, gestational weight gain, and pregnancy complications. *Journal of the American Dietetic Association, 110*(5), 692–701.

Leight, K., Fitelson, E., Weston, C., & Wisner, K. (2010). Childbirth and mental disorders. *International Review of Psychiatry, 22*, 453–471.

Leishman, J., & James, J. Moir (2007). *Pre-teen and teenage pregnancy a twenty-first century reality.* M&K Update.

Lemke, M., & Brown, K. (2020). Syndemic perspectives to guide black maternal health research and prevention during the COVID-19 pandemic. *Maternal and Child Health Journal, 24*(9), 1093–1098.

Li, N., Liu, E., Guo, J., Pan, L., Li, B., Wang, P., Liu, J., Wang, Y., Liu, G., Baccarelli, A., Hou, L., & Hu, G. (2013). Maternal pre-pregnancy body mass index and gestational weight gain on pregnancy outcomes. *PLOS ONE, 8*(12), e82310.

Lindberg, L., Santelli, J., & Desai, S. (2016). Understanding the decline in adolescent fertility in the United States, 2007–2012. *Journal of Adolescent Health, 59*(5), 1–7.

Livingston, G. (2019). *US women are postponing motherhood, but not as much as those in most other developed nations.* Pew Research. https://www.pewresearch.org/fact-tank/2018/06/28/u-s-women-are-postponing-motherhood-but-not-as-much-as-those-in-most-other-developed-nations/

Longe, J. (2018). *The Gale encyclopedia of nursing and allied health.* Gale Virtual Reference Library.

Magnus, M., Wilcox, A., Morken, N., Weinberg, C., & Håberg, S. (2019). Role of maternal age and pregnancy history in risk of miscarriage: Prospective register based study. *British Journal of Medicine, 364*, l869.

Martin, J., Hamilton, B., Osterman, M., Curtin, S., & Matthews, T. (2015). Births: Final data for 2013. *National Vital Statistics Reports, 64,* (1).

Martin, J., Hamilton, B., & Osterman, M. (2018). Births in the United States, 2017. *NCHS Data Brief,* (318), 1–8.

Mastroiacovo, P., & Leoncini, E. (2011). More folic acid, the five questions: Why, who, when, how much, and how. *Biofactors, 37*(4), 272–279.

Mayo Clinic (2020). *Pregnancy: First trimester.* https://www.mayoclinic.org/healthy-lifestyle/pregnancy-week-by-week/in-depth/pregnancy/art-20047208

Mays, S. (2011). Evidence links increases in public health spending to declines in preventable deaths. *Health Affairs, 30*(8), 1585–1593.

McCauley, M., van den Broek, N., Dou, L., & Othman, M. (2015). Vitamin A supplementation during pregnancy for maternal and newborn outcomes. *The Cochrane Database of Systematic Reviews,* (10), CD008666.

McCool, W., & Simeone, S. (2002). Birth in the United States: An overview of trends past and present. *Nursing Clinics of North America, 37*(4), 735–746.

Meng, Y., & Groth, S. (2018). Fathers count: The impact of paternal risk factors on birth outcomes. *Maternal and Child Health Journal, 22*(3), 401–408.

Merritt, T., Mazela, J., Adamczak, A., & Merritt, T. (2012). The impact of second-hand tobacco smoke exposure on pregnancy outcomes, infant health, and the threat of third-hand smoke exposure to our environment and to our children. *Przeglad Lekarski, 69*(10), 717–720.

Moaddab, A, Dildy, G., Brown, H., Bateni, Z., Belfort, M., Sangi-Haghpeykar, H., & Clark, S. (2018). Health care disparity and pregnancy-related mortality in the United States, 2005–2014. *Obstetrics and Gynecology, 131*(4), 707–712.

Mousa, A., Naqash, A., & Lim, S. (2019). Macronutrient and micronutrient intake during pregnancy: An overview of recent evidence. *Nutrients, 11*(2), 443.

Murphy, K., Jenkins, T., & Carrell, D. (2016). How the father might epigenetically program the risk for developmental origins of health and disease effects in his offspring. In C. Rosenfeld, (Ed.), *The epigenome and developmental origins of health and disease.* Elsevier.

Nahata, L. (2017). The gender reveal: Implications of a cultural tradition for pediatric health. *Pediatrics, 140*(6), e20171834.

National Institute on Drug Abuse (2020). *Substance use while pregnant and breastfeeding.* https://www.drugabuse.gov/publications/research-reports/substance-use-in-women/substance-use-while-pregnant-breastfeeding

National Institute on Drug Abuse (2021). *What is the scope of marijuana use in the United States?* https://www.drugabuse.gov/publications/research-reports/marijuana/what-scope-marijuana-use-in-united-states

Nirmal, D., & Fraser, D. (2016). The first stage of labour. In S. Arulkumaran (Ed.), *Best practice in labour and delivery.* Cambridge University Press.

Oakley, A. (2016). The sociology of childbirth: An autobiographical journey through four decades of research. *Sociology of Health and Illness, 38*, 689–705.

Office on Women's Health. (2012). *Prenatal care fact sheet.* http://www.womenshealth.gov/publications/our-publications/fact-sheet/prenatal-care.html

Office on Women's Health (2020). *Stages of pregnancy.* US Department of Health and Human Services. https://www.womenshealth.gov/pregnancy/youre-pregnant-now-what/stages-pregnancy

O'Leary, C., Jacoby, P., D'Antoine, H., Bartu, A., & Bower, C. (2012). Heavy prenatal alcohol exposure and increased risk of stillbirth. *BJOG, 119*(8), 945–952.

Panazzolo, M., & Mohammed, R. (2011). Birthing trends in American society and women's choices. *Race, Gender & Class, 18*(3/4), 268–283.

Pasche Guignard, F. (2015). A gendered bun in the oven. The gender-reveal party as a new ritualization during pregnancy. *Studies in Religion/Sciences Religieuses, 44*(4), 479–500.

Patel, P., & Sen, B. (2012). Teen motherhood and long-term health consequences. *Maternal Child Health Journal, 16*, 1063–1071.

Pentecost, M., & Maurizio, M. (2020). It's never too early: Preconception care and postgenomic models of life. *Frontiers in Sociology, 5*. https://www.frontiersin.org/article/10.3389/fsoc.2020.00021

Petersen, E., Davis, N., Goodman, D., Cox, S., Mayes, N., Johnston, E., Syverson, C., Seed, K., Shapiro-Mendoza, C., Callaghan, W., & Barfield, W. (2019). Vital signs: Pregnancy-related deaths, United States, 2011–2015, and strategies for prevention, 13 states, 2013–2017. *Morbidity and Mortality Weekly Report, 68*(18), 423–429.

Pineles, B., Park, E., & Samet, J. (2014). Systematic review and meta-analysis of miscarriage and maternal exposure to tobacco smoke during pregnancy. *American Journal of Epidemiology, 179*(7), 807–823.

Pritchard, D., & Korf, B. R. (2013). Medical genetics at a glance (3rd ed., *At a Glance*). Chichester, England: Wiley-Blackwell.

Priya, A., Chaturvedi, S., Bhasin, S., Bhatia, M., & Radhakrishnan, G. (2019). Are pregnant women also vulnerable to domestic violence? A community-based enquiry for prevalence and predictors of domestic violence among pregnant women. *Journal of Family Medicine and Primary Care, 8*(5), 1575.

Quesada, O., Gotman, N., Howell, H., Funai, E., Rounsaville, B., & Yonkers, K. (2012). Prenatal hazardous substance use and adverse birth outcomes. *The Journal of Maternal-Fetal & Neonatal Medicine, 25*(8), 1222–1227.

Rao, S., & Yajnik, C. (2010). Maternal diets in the developing world. In M. Symonds & M. Ramsay (Eds.), *Maternal-fetal nutrition during pregnancy and lactation*. Cambridge University Press.

Regan, M., McElroy, K., & Moore, K. (2013). Choice? Factors that influence women's decision making for childbirth. *The Journal of Perinatal Education, 22*(3), 171–180.

Renfrew, M., McFadden, A., Bastos, M., Campbell, J., Channon, A., Cheung, N., Silva, D., Downe, S., Kennedy, H., Malata, A., McCormick, F., Wick, L., & Declercq, E. (2014). Midwifery and quality care: Findings from a new evidence-informed framework for maternal and newborn care. *Lancet, 384*, 1129–1145.

Rhone, A., Ver Ploeg, M., Dicken, C., Williams, R., & Breneman, V. (2017). Low-income and low-supermarket-access census tracts, 2010–2015. *Economic Information Bulletin, 165*, 1–5.

Rosenbaum, A., Smith, R., Hade, E., Gupta, A., Yilmaz, A., & Cackovic, M. (2020). Use and experiences with external fetal monitoring devices among obstetrical providers. *Journal of Maternal-Fetal & Neonatal Medicine, 33*(14), 2348–2353.

Ross, E., Graham, D., Money, K., & Stanwood, G. (2015). Developmental consequences of fetal exposure to drugs: What we know and what we still must learn. *Neuropsychopharmacology, 40*(1), 61–87.

Rowley, D., & Hogan, V. (2012). Disparities in infant mortality and effective, equitable care: Are infants suffering from benign neglect? *Annual Review of Public Health, 33*, 75–87.

Rua, E., Porto, M., Ramos, J., Nogueira, B., Meyrelles, S., Vasquez, E., & Pereira, T. (2014). Effects of tobacco smoking during pregnancy on oxidative stress in the umbilical cord and mononuclear blood cells of neonates. *Journal of Biomedical Science, 21*, 105.

Ruckart, P., Ettinger, A., Hanna-Attisha, M., Jones, N., Davis, S., & Breysse, P. (2019). The Flint water crisis: A coordinated public health emergency response and recovery initiative. *Journal of Public Health Management and Practice, 25*(Suppl 1), S84–S90.

Rutkowska, J., Lagisz, M., Bonduriansky, R., & Nakagawa, S. (2020). Mapping the past, present and future research landscape of paternal effects. *BMC Biology, 18*, 183.

Santucci, R. J., Jr., & Scully, J. R. (2020). The pervasive threat of lead (Pb) in drinking water: Unmasking and pursuing scientific factors that govern lead release. *Proceedings of the National Academy of Sciences of the United States of America, 117*(38), 23211–23218.

Satin, A., Leveno, K., Sherman, M., Reedy, N., Lowe, T., & McIntire, D. (1994). Maternal youth and pregnancy outcomes: Middle school versus high school age groups compared with women beyond the teen years. *American Journal of Obstetrics and Gynecology, 171*, 184–187.

Sauer, M. (2015). Reproduction at an advanced maternal age and maternal health. *Fertility and Sterility, 103*, 1136.

Say, L., Chou, D., Gemmill, A., Tunçalp, O., Moller, A., Daniels, J, Gulmezoglu, A., Temmerman, M., & Alkema, L. (2014). Global causes of maternal death: A WHO systematic analysis. *The Lancet. Global health, 2*(6), e323–e333.

Schummers, L., Hutcheon, J., Bodnar, L., Lieberman, E., & Himes, K. (2015). Risk of adverse pregnancy outcomes by pre-pregnancy body mass index: A population-based study to inform pre-pregnancy weight loss counseling. *Obstetrics and Gynecology, 125*(1), 133–143.

Schull, W., Norton, S., & Jensh, R. (1990). Ionizing radiation and the developing brain. *Neurotoxicology and Teratology, 12*(3), 249–260.

Schorn, M., Moore, E., Spetalnick, B., & Morad, A. (2015). Implementing family-centered cesarean birth. *Journal of Midwifery and Women's Health, 60*, 682–690

Sedgh, G., Finer, L., Bankole, A., Eilers, M., & Singh, S. (2015). Adolescent pregnancy, birth, and abortion rates across countries: Levels and recent trends. *Journal of Adolescent Health, 56*(2), 223–230.

Sigman, M. (2017). What to do with older prospective fathers: The risks of advanced paternal age. *Fertility and Sterility, 107*, 299.

Small, M., Allen, T., & Brown, H. (2017). Global disparities in maternal morbidity and mortality. *Seminars in Perinatology, 41*(5), 318–322.

Sobhy, S., Arroyo-Manzano, D., Murugesu, N., Karthikeyan, G., Kumar, V., Kaur, I., Fernandez, E., Gundabattula, S., Betran, A., Khan, K., Zamora, J., & Thangaratinam, S. (2019). Maternal and perinatal mortality and complications associated with caesarean section in low-income and middle-income countries: A systematic review and meta-analysis. *The Lancet, 393*(10184), 1973–1982.

Soltani, H., Smith, D., & Olander, E. (2017). Weight, lifestyle, and health during pregnancy and beyond. *Journal of Pregnancy*, 4981283.

Spong, C. (2011). *Stillbirth prediction, prevention and management.* Wiley.

Srikartika, V., & O'Leary, C. (2015). Pregnancy outcomes of mothers with an alcohol-related diagnosis: A population-based cohort study for the period 1983–2007. *BJOG, 122*(6), 795–804.

Stephenson, J., Heslehurst, N., Hall, J., Schoenaker, D., Hutchinson, J., Cade, J., Poston, L., Barrett, G., Crozier, S., Barker, M., Kumaran, K., Yajnik, C., Baird, J., & Mishra, G. (2018). Before the beginning: Nutrition and lifestyle in the preconception period and its importance for future health. *Lancet, 391*(10132), 1830–1841.

Stothard, K., Tennant, P., Bell, R., & Rankin, J. (2009). Maternal overweight and obesity and the risk of congenital anomalies: A systematic review and meta-analysis. *JAMA, 301*(6), 636–650.

Sutton, P., Woodruff, T., Perron, J., Stotland, N., Conry, J., Miller, M., & Giudice, L. (2012). Toxic environmental chemicals: The role of reproductive health professionals in preventing harmful exposures. *American Journal of Obstetrics and Gynecology, 207,* 164–73.

Symons-Downs, D., Chasan-Taber, L., Evenson, K., Leiferman, J., & Yeo, S. (2012). Physical activity and pregnancy: Past and present evidence and future recommendations. *Research Quarterly for Exercise and Sport, 83*(4), 485–502.

Thombre, M., Talge, N. & C. Holzman (2015). Association between pre-pregnancy depression/anxiety symptoms and hypertensive disorders of pregnancy. *Journal of Women's Health, 24*(3), 228–236.

Thornton, Y., Smarkola, C., Kopacz, S., & Ishoof, S. (2009). Perinatal outcomes in nutritionally monitored obese pregnant women. *Journal of the National Medical Association, 101*(6), 569–577.

Thorp, J., & Grantz, K. (2019). Clinical aspects of normal and abnormal labor. In R. Resnik, J. Iams, C. Lockwood, T. Moore, M. Greene, J. Copel, and Silver, R. (Eds). *Creasy and Resnik's Maternal-Fetal Medicine: Principles and Practice.* Philadelphia, PA: Elsevier.

Tipton, M., Wagner, S., Dixon, A., Westbay, L., Darji, H., & Graziano, S. (2020). Association of living in a food desert with pregnancy morbidity. *Obstetrics and Gynecology, 136*(1), 140–145.

Troiano, N., Witcher, P., Baird, S., & Association of Women's Health, Obstetric, Neonatal Nurses (2019). *High-risk & critical care: Obstetrics.* New York: Lippincott Williams & Wilkins.

Tunçalp, O., Were, W., MacLennan, C., Oladapo, O., Gulmezoglu, A., Bahl, R., Daelmans, B., Mathai, M., Say, L., Kristensen, F., Temmerman, M., & Bustreo, F. (2015). Quality of care for pregnant women and newborns—the WHO vision. *British Journal of Obstetrics and Gynecology, 122*(8), 1045–1049.

UNICEF (2015). *Strategies toward ending preventable maternal mortality.* https://data.unicef.org/resources/strategies-toward-ending-preventable-maternal-mortality/

UNICEF (2019). *Maternal mortality.* https://data.unicef.org/topic/maternal-health/maternal-mortality/

University of California, San Francisco (2020). *Inherited genetic diseases: Stem cell treatments.* Benioff Children's Hospital. https://fetus.ucsf.edu/stem-cells

US Centers for Disease Control and Prevention (2010). *Guidelines for the identification and management of lead exposure in pregnant and lactating women.* https://www.cdc.gov/nceh/lead/publications/leadandpregnancy2010.pdf

US Centers for Disease Control and Prevention (2018). *Genetic disorders.* https://www.genome.gov/For-Patients-and-Families/Genetic-Disorders

US Centers for Disease Control and Prevention (2019a). *Childhood lead poisoning prevention.* https://www.cdc.gov/nceh/lead/prevention/pregnant.htm

US Centers for Disease Control and Prevention (2019b). *Cystic fibrosis.* https://www.cdc.gov/genomics/disease/cystic_fibrosis.htm

US Centers for Disease Control and Prevention (2019c). *Radiation and pregnancy: Information for clinicians.* National Center for Environmental Health Agency for Toxic Substances and Disease Registry. https://www.cdc.gov/nceh/radiation/emergencies/pdf/303779–A_2019_Radiation-and-Pregnancy_508.pdf

US Centers for Disease Control and Prevention (20219d). *Sickle cell disease.* https://www.cdc.gov/ncbddd/sicklecell/facts.html

US Centers for Disease Control and Prevention (2021). *Lead in paint.* https://www.cdc.gov/nceh/lead/prevention/sources/paint.htm#:~:text=Lead%2Dbased%20paints%20were%20banned,have%20some%20lead%2Dbased%20paint

US Department of Health and Human Services (2017). *What are the stages of labor?* Eunice Kennedy Shriver National Institute of Child Health and Human Development. https://www.nichd.nih.gov/health/topics/labor-delivery/topicinfo/stages

US Department of Health and Human Services (2020a). *Commonly used drug charts.* National Institute on Drug Abuse. https://www.drugabuse.gov/drug-topics/commonly-used-drugs-charts

US Department of Health and Human Services (2020b). *Down syndrome.* https://ghr.nlm.nih.gov/condition/down-syndrome

US Department of Health and Human Services (2020c). *Fragile X.* https://ghr.nlm.nih.gov/condition/fragile-x-syndrome#resources

US Department of Health and Human Services (2020d). *Phenylketonuria.* https://ghr.nlm.nih.gov/condition/phenylketonuria

US Department of Health and Human Services (2020e). *Prenatal care.* Office of Women's Health. https://www.womenshealth.gov/a-z-topics/prenatal-care

US Food and Drug Administration (2020). *2015–2020 Dietary guidelines for Americans.* https://health.gov/dietaryguidelines/2015/guidelines/

US National Library of Medicine (2018a). *Am I in labor?* Medline Plus. https://medlineplus.gov/ency/patientinstructions/000508.htm

US National Library of Medicine (2018b). *Your baby in the birth canal.* Medline Plus. https://medlineplus.gov/ency/article/002060.htm

US National Library of Medicine (2018c). *Childbirth problems.* Medline Plus. https://medlineplus.gov/childbirthproblems.html

US National Library of Medicine (2020). *How are genetic conditions treated or managed?* https://ghr.nlm.nih.gov/primer/consult/treatment

Vesterinen, H., Morello-Frosch, R., Sen, S., Zeise, L., & Woodruff, T. (2017). Cumulative effects of prenatal-exposure to exogenous chemicals and psychosocial stress on fetal growth: Systematic-review of the human and animal evidence. *PLOS ONE, 12*(7), e0176331.

Warner, T., Roussos-Ross, D., & Behnke, M. (2014). It's not your mother's marijuana: Effects on maternal fetal health and the developing child. *Clinical Perinatology, 41*(4), 877–894.

Wilcox, A. (2010). *Fertility and pregnancy: An epidemiologic perspective.* Oxford University Press.

Wilcox, A., Weinberg, C., O'Connor, J., Baird, D., Schlatterer, J., Canfield, R., Armstrong, E., & Nisula, B. (1988). Incidence of early loss of pregnancy. *New England Journal of Medicine, 319*(4), 189–194.

Woodruff, T., Schwartz, J., & Giudice, L. (2010). Research agenda for environmental reproductive health in the 21st century. *Journal of Epidemiology and Community Health, 64,* 307–310.

Woods, S. M., Melville, J. L., Guo, Y., Fan, M. Y., & Gavin, A. (2010). Psychosocial stress during pregnancy. *American Journal of Obstetrics and Gynecology, 202*(1), 61.e1-61.e7

World Bank Data (2020). *Adolescent fertility rate (Births per 1,000 women ages 15–19).* https://data.worldbank.org/indicator/SP.ADO.TFRT

World Health Organization (2004). *International statistical classification of diseases and related health problems.* https://www.who.int/classifications/icd/ICD10Volume2_en_2010.pdf

World Health Organization (2020). *Maternal mortality ratio.* https://www.who.int/healthinfo/statistics/indmaternalmortality/en/

World Health Organization (2021). Caesarean section rates continue to rise, amid growing inequalities in access. https://www.who.int/news/item/16-06-2021-caesarean-section-rates-continue-to-rise-amid-growing-inequalities-in-access-who#:~:text=Worldwide%20caesarean%20section%20rates%20have,increasing%20over%20this%20current%20decade.

Wyness, L., Stanner, S., Buttriss, J., & British Nutrition Foundation (2013). *Nutrition and development: Short and long term consequences for health.* Wiley-Blackwell for the British Nutrition Foundation.

Zhang, C., & Ning, Y. (2011). Effect of dietary and lifestyle factors on the risk of gestational diabetes: Review of epidemiologic evidence. *American Journal of Clinical Nutrition, 94* (supplement 6), 1975S–1979S.

Zhang, Z., Fulgoni, V., Kris-Etherton, P., & Mitmesser, S. (2019). Dietary intakes of EPA and DHA omega-3 fatty acids among US childbearing-age and pregnant women: An analysis of NHANES, 2001–2014. *Nutrients, 10*(4), 416.

Zheng, B., Zhu, X., Hu, Z., Zhou, W., Yu., Y., Yin, S., & Xu, H. (2020). The prevalence of domestic violence and its association with family factors: A cross-sectional study among pregnant women in urban communities of Hengyang City, China. *BMC Public Health,* 20, 620.

Zolotor, A., & Carlough, M. (2014). Update on prenatal care. *American Family Physician, 89*(3), 199–208.

Chapter 4

Adam-Darque, A., Grouiller, F., Vasung, L., Leuchter R., Pollien, P., Lazeyras, F., & Huppi, P. (2018). MRI-based neuronal response to new odorants in the newborn brain. *Cerebral Cortex, 28*(8), 2901–2907.

Adolf, K., Berger, S., Baston, H., & Durward, H. (2010). *Examination of the newborn: A practical guide.* Routledge.

Adolph, K., & Berger, S. (2005). Physical and motor development. In M. Bornstein & M. Lamb (Eds.), *Developmental science: An advanced textbook.* Psychology Press/Taylor & Francis.

Adolph, K., Karasik, L., & Tamis-LeMonda, C. (2010). Moving between cultures: Cross-cultural research on motor development. In M. Borstein & L. Cote (Ed.), *Handbook of cross-cultural developmental science, domains of development across cultures.* Psychology Press.

Als, H., & McAnulty, G. B. (2011). The newborn individualized developmental care and assessment program (NIDCAP) with kangaroo mother care (KMC): Comprehensive care for preterm infants. *Current Women's Health Reviews, 7*(3), 288–301.

American Academy of Pediatrics (2014). American Academy of Pediatrics section on oral health. Maintaining and improving the oral health of young children. *Pediatrics, 34*(6), 1224–1229.

American Academy of Pediatrics (2014). *Caring for your baby and young child: Birth to age 5.* Bantam.

American Academy of Pediatrics (2018). *AAP schedule of well-child care visits.* https://www.healthychildren.org/English/family-life/health-management/Pages/Well-Child-Care-A-Check-Up-for-Success.aspx

American Academy of Pediatrics (2019). Where we stand: Breastfeeding. *Caring for your baby and young child: Birth to age 5.* https://publications.aap.org/aapbooks/book/568/Caring-for-Your-Baby-and-Young-Child-Birth-to-Age

Ardiel, E., & Rankin, C. (2010). The importance of touch in development. *Paediatrics & Child Health, 15*(3), 153–156.

Avena, N., & Ferreira, C. (2018). *What to feed your baby & toddler: A month-by-month guide to support your child's health & development.* Ten Speed Press.

Barkovich, A., & Raybaud, C. (2019). *Pediatric neuroimaging.* Wolters Kluwer.

Baston, H., & Durward, H. (2010). *Examination of the newborn: A practical guide.* Routledge.

Batalle, A., Edwards, D., & O'Muircheartaigh, J. (2017). Annual research review: Not just a small adult brain: Understanding later neurodevelopment through imaging the neonatal brain. *Journal of Child Psychology and Psychiatry, 59*(4), 350–371.

Bauer, C., Hirsch, G., Zajac, L., Koo, B., Collignon, O., & Merabet, L. (2017). Multimodal MR-imaging reveals large-scale structural and functional connectivity changes in profound early blindness. *PLOS ONE, 12*(3), e0173064.

Beauchamp, G., & Mennella, J. (2009). Early flavor learning and its impact on later feeding behavior. *Journal of Pediatric Gastroenterology and Nutrition,* 48, S25-S30.

Beauchamp, G., & Mennella, J. (2011). Flavor perception in human infants: Development and functional significance. *Digestion, 83,* 1–6.

Bergman, T. (1996). *Precious time: Children living with muscular dystrophy.* Gareth Stevens.

Bick, J., & Nelson, C. (2016). Early adverse experiences and the developing brain. *Neuropsychopharmacology,* 41, 177–196. https://www.nature.com/articles/ npp2015252.

Biesalski, H., & Black, R. (2016). *Hidden hunger: Malnutrition and the first 1,000 days of life: Causes, consequences, and solutions.* Karger.

Bigelow, A., & Williams, L. (2020). To have and to hold: Effects of physical contact on infants and their caregivers. *Infant Behavior & Development, 61,* 101494.

Borro, M., & Iacovou, A. (2012). The effect of breastfeeding on children's cognitive and noncognitive development. *Labour Economics, 19*(4), 496–515.

Boyd, K. (2020). *Vision development: Newborn to 12 months.* American Academy of Ophthalmology. https://www.aao.org/eye-health/tips-prevention/baby-vision-development-first-year

Braddick, O., & Atkinson, J. (2011). Development of human visual function. *Vision Research, 5*(13), 1588–1609.

Brazelton T., & Nugent, J. (2011). Neonatal behavioural assessment scale. *Clinics in Developmental Medicine, 137*(4).

Breedlove, S., & Watson, N. (2020). *Behavioral Neuroscience.* Sinauer Associates.

Bremner, J., & Wachs, T. (2010). *The Wiley-Blackwell handbook of infant development.* Wiley-Blackwell.

Brink, S. (2013). *The fourth trimester: Understanding, protecting and nurturing an infant through the first three months.* University of California Press.

Buck, L., Grewal, J., Albert, P., Sciscione, A., Wing, D., Grobman, W., Newman, R., Wapner, R., D'Alton, M., Skupski, D., Nageotte, M., Ranzini, A., Owen, J., Chien, E., Craigo, S., Hediger, M., Kim, S., Zhang, C., & Grantz, K. (2015). Racial/ethnic standards for fetal growth: The NICHD fetal growth studies. *American Journal of Obstetrics and Gynecology, 213*(4), 449.e1-41. https://doi.org/10.1016/j.ajog.2015.08.032

Bushall, I. (2003). Newborn face recognition. In O. Pascalis & A. Slater (Eds.), *The development of face processing in infancy and early childhood*, 41-53. Nova Science Publishers.

Calciolari, G., & Montirosso, R. (2013). Neonatal neurobehavioral assessment in healthy and at-risk infants. *Early Human Development, 89,* S58–S59.

Calkins, S. (2015). *Handbook of infant biopsychosocial development.* Guilford.

Carlin, R., & Moon, R. (2017). Risk factors, protective factors, and current recommendations to reduce sudden infant death syndrome: A review. *JAMA Pediatrics, 171*(2), 175–180.

Casler, L. (1965). The effects of extra tactile stimulation on a group of institutionalized infants. *Genetic Psychological Monographs, 71,* 137–175.

Chen, A., Oster, E., & Williams, H. (2016). Why is infant mortality higher in the United States than in Europe? *American Economic Journal, 8*(2), 89–124.

Chen, E., Gau, M., Liu, C., & Lee, T. (2017). Effects of father-neonate skin-to-skin contact on attachment: A randomized controlled trial. *Nursing Research and Practice,* 1–8.

Clayton, R., & Crosby, R. (2006). Measurement in health promotion. In R. Crosby, R. diClemente, & L. Salazar (Eds.), *Research methods in health promotion.* Wiley.

Coathup, V., Boyle, E., Carson, C., Johnson, S., Kurinzcuk, J., Macfarlane, A., Petrou, S., Rivero-Arias, O., & Quigley, M. (2020). Gestational age and hospital admissions during childhood: Population based, record linkage study in England (TIGAR study). BMJ, m4075.

Cohen, M. (2019*). Investigation of sudden infant death syndrome.* Cambridge University Press.

Conrad, N., Walsh, J., Allen, J., & Tsang, C. (2011). Examining infants' preferences for tempo in lullabies and play songs. *Canadian Journal of Experimental Psychology, 65*(3), 168–172.

Covington, L., Rogers, V., Armstrong, B., Storr, C., & Black, M. (2019). Toddler bedtime routines and associations with nighttime sleep duration, and maternal and household factors. *Journal of Clinical Sleep Medicine,15*(6), 865–871.

Cowart, B., Beauchamp, G., & Mennella, J. (2003). Development of taste and smell in the neonate. *Fetal and Neonatal Physiology, 3*(2), 1819–1827.

Dahl, A., Campos, J., Anderson, D., Uchiyama, I., Witherington, D., Ueno, M., Poutrain-Lejeune, L., & Barbu-Roth, M. (2013). The epigenesist of wariness of heights. *Psychological Science, 24*(7), 1361–1367.

Davies, D., & Troy, M. (2020*). Child development: A practitioner's guide.* Guilford.

Day, S. (1982). Mother-infant activities as providers of sensory stimulation. *The American Journal of Occupational Therapy, 36*(9), 579–585.

Dean, D., Planalp, E., Wooten, W., Schmidt, C., Kecskemeti, S., Frye, C., Schmidt, N., Goldsmith, H., Alexander, A., & Davidson, R. (2018). Investigation of brain structure in the 1-month infant. *Brain Structure & Function, 223*(4), 1953–1970.

Degenhard, J. (2019). Food report 2019: Baby food. *Statista Consumer Market Outlook—Segment Report.* https://www.statista.com/study/48837/food-report-baby-food

Dereymaeker, A., Pillay, K., Vervisch, J., De Vos, M., Van Huffel, S., Jansen, K., & Naulaers, G. (2017). Review of sleep-EEG in preterm and term neonates. *Early Human Development, 113,* 87–103.

Diamond, A., Casey, B., & Munakata, Y. (2011). *Developmental cognitive neuroscience.* Oxford Press.

Dionne-Dostie, E., Paquette, N., Lassonde, M., & Gallagher, A. (2015). Multisensory integration and child neurodevelopment. *Brain Sciences, 5*(1), 32–57.

Duncan, J., & Byard, R. (2018). Sudden infant death syndrome: An overview. In J. Duncan & R. Byard (Eds.), *SIDS sudden infant and early childhood death: The past, the present and the future.* The University of Adelaide Press.

Erickson, L., & Newman, R. (2017). Influences of background noise on infants and children *Current Directions in Psychological Science, 26*(5), 451–457.

Feldman, H., & Chaves-Gnecco, D. (2018). Developmental/behavioral pediatrics. In B. Zitelli, S. McIntire, & A. Nowalk (Eds*.), Zitelli and Davis' atlas of pediatric physical diagnosis.* Elsevier.

Feldman, R., Eidelman, A., Sirota, L., & Weller, A. (2002). Comparison of skin-to-skin (kangaroo) and traditional care: Parenting outcomes and preterm infant development. *Pediatrics, 110,* 16–26.

Figaji A. (2017). Anatomical and physiological differences between children and adults relevant to traumatic brain injury and the implications for clinical assessment and care. *Frontiers in Neurology, 8,* 685.

Fine, R. (2019). *Receptors in the evolution and development of the brain: Matter into mind.* Academic Press.

Fleming, P., Blair, P., & Pease, A. (2015). Sudden unexpected death in infancy: Etiology, pathophysiology, epidemiology and prevention in 2015. *Archives of Disease in Childhood, 100*(10), 984–988.

Frank, D., Klass, P., Earls, F., & Eisenberg, L. (1996). Infants and young children in orphanages: One view from pediatrics and child psychiatry. *Pediatrics, 97,* 569–578.

Freeman, A. (2020). *Skimmed: Breastfeeding, race, and injustice.* Stanford University Press.

Fuentes-Afflick, E., Perrin, J., Moley, K., Díaz, A., McCormick, M., & Lu, M. (2021). Optimizing health and well-being for women and children. *Health Affairs, 40*(2), 212–218.

Gao, W., Lin, W., Grewen, K., & Gilmore, J. (2017). Functional connectivity of the infant human brain: Plastic and modifiable. *The Neuroscientist, 23*(2), 169–184.

Gibson, E., & Pick, A. (2000). *Perceptual learning and development: An ecological approach to perceptual learning and development.* Oxford.

Goldstein, S., & Reynolds, C. (2011). *Handbook of neurodevelopmental and genetic disorders in children.* Guilford.

Gradisar, M., Jackson, K., Spurrier, N., Gibson, J., Whitham, J., Williams, A., Dolby, R., & Kennaway, D. (2016). Behavioral interventions for infant sleep problems: A randomized controlled trial. *Pediatrics, 137*(6), e20151486.

Gross, D. (2019). *Infancy: Development from birth to age 3.* Lanham: Rowman & Littlefield.

Hackman, D., & Farah, M. (2009). Socioeconomic status and the developing brain. *Trends in Cognitive Sciences, 13,* 65–73.

Haibach-Beach, P., Reid, G., & Collier, D. (2018). *Motor learning and development.* Human Kinetics.

Hallas, D. (2019). *Behavioral pediatric healthcare for nurse practitioners: A growth and developmental approach to intercepting abnormal behaviors.* Springer.

Halligan, S., & Luyben, P. (2009). Prompts, feedback, positive reinforcement, and potty training. *Journal of Prevention & Intervention in the Community, 37*(3), 177–186.

Hanson, J., Hair, N., Shen, D., Shi, F., Gilmore, J., Wolfe, B., & Pollak, S. (2013). Family poverty affects the rate of human infant brain growth. *PLOS ONE, 8*(12), e80954.

Harlow, H. (1958). The nature of love. *The American Psychologist, 13*(2), 673–685.

Harvey, H. (2021). Encouraging healthy sleep habits. National Association for the Education of Young Children (NAEYC). https://www.naeyc.org/our-work/families/encouraging-healthy-sleep-habits

Hewlett B., & Lamb, M. (2002). Integrating evolution, culture and developmental psychology: Explaining caregiver-infant proximity and responsiveness in Central Africa and the USA. In H. Keller, Y. Poortinga, & A. Scholmerich (Eds.), *Between culture and biology: Perspectives on ontogenetic development.* Cambridge University Press.

Horsley, A., Cunningham, S., & Innes, J. (2015). *Cystic fibrosis.* Oxford University Press.

Johnston, C., Campbell-Yeo, M., Fernandes, A., Inglis, D., Streiner, D., & Zee, R. (2014). Skin-to-skin care for procedural pain in neonates. *The Cochrane Database of Systematic Reviews*, (1), CD008435.

Jönsson, E., Kotilahti, K., Heiskala, J., Wasling, H., Olausson, H., Croy, I., Mustaniemi, H., Hiltunen, P., Tuulari, J., Scheinin, N., Karlsson, L., Karlsson, H., & Nissilä, I. (2018). Affective and non-affective touch evoke differential brain responses in 2-month-old infants. *Neuroimage, 169,* 162–171.

Kaerts, N., Van Hal, G., Vermandel, A., & Wyndaele, J. (2012). Readiness signs used to define the proper moment to start toilet training: A review of the literature. *Neurourology and Urodynamics, 27*(3), 162–166.

Kayhan, E., Hunnius, S., O'Reilly, J., & Bekkering, H. (2019). Infants differentially update their internal models of a dynamic environment. *Cognition, 186,* 139–146.

Kiddoo, D. (2012). Toilet training children: When to start and how to train. *Canadian Medical Association Journal, 184*(5), 511–512.

Kim, H., & Pearson-Shaver, A. (2021). Sudden infant death syndrome. StatPearls Publishing. https://www.ncbi.nlm.nih.gov/books/NBK560807/

Kimura, A., Wada, Y., Yang, J., Otsuka, Y., Dan, I., Masuda, T., Kanazawa, S., & Yamaguchi, M. (2010). Infants' recognition of objects using canonical color. *Journal of Experimental Child Psychology, 105*(3), 256–263.

Kinney, H., & Thach, B. (2009). The sudden infant death syndrome. *New England Journal of Medicine, 361*(8), 795–805.

Kinzler, K., Dupoux, E., & Spelke, E. (2007). The native language of social cognition. *Proceedings of the National Academy of Sciences of the United States of America, 104,* 12577–12580.

Kitsaras, G., Goodwin, M., Allan, J., Kelly, M., & Pretty, I. (2018). Bedtime routines, child wellbeing, & development. *BMC Public Health, 18*(1), 386.

Kitsiou-Tzeli, S., & Tzetis, M. (2017). Maternal epigenetics and fetal and neonatal growth, *Current Opinion in Endocrinology & Diabetes and Obesity, 24*(1), 43–46.

Knickmeyer, R., Gouttard, S., Kang, C., Evans, D., Wilber K., Smith, J., Hamer, R., Lin, W., Gerig, G., & Gilmore, J. (2008). A structural MRI study of human brain development from birth to 2 years. *Journal of Neuroscience, 28,* 12176–12182.

Kostandy, R., & Ludington-Hoe, S. (2019). The evolution of the science of kangaroo (mother) care (skin-to-skin contact). *Birth Defects Research, 111*(15), 1032–1043.

Koster, M., Kayhan, E., Langeloh, M., & Hoehl, S. (2020). Making sense of the world: Infant learning from a predictive processing perspective. *Perspectives on Psychological Science, 15*(3), 562–571.

Landrigan, P., & Landrigan, M. (2018). *Children and environmental toxins: What everyone needs to know.* Oxford University Press.

Lean, R., Smyser, C., & Rogers, C. (2017). Assessment: The newborn. *Child and Adolescent Psychiatric Clinics of North America, 26*(3), 427–440.

Lee, A., Panchal, P., Folger, L., Whelan, H., Whelan, R., Rosner, B., Blencowe, H., & Lawn, J. (2017). Diagnostic accuracy of neonatal assessment for gestational age determination: A systematic review. *Pediatrics, 140*(6), e20171423.

Legerstee, M., Haley, D., & Bornstein, M. (2013*). The infant mind: Origins of the social brain.* Guilford.

Lehtonen, L., Gimeno, A., Parra-Llorca, A., & Vento, M. (2017). Early neonatal death: A challenge worldwide. *Seminars in Fetal and Neonatal Medicine, 22*(3), 153–160.

Lester, B., Tronick, E., & Brazelton, T. (2004). The neonatal intensive care unit network neurobehavioral scale (NNNS*). Pediatrics, 113,* 641–667.

Leu, R., Raol, N., & Harford, K. (2020). Racial and ethnic disparities in sudden unexpected infant death and sudden infant death syndrome rates in the USA: A complex problem mired in a deeply entangled web. *Current Sleep Medicine Report, 6,* 232–238.

Levitt, S., & Addison, A. (2019). *Treatment of cerebral palsy and motor delay*. Wiley-Blackwell.

Lickliter, R. (2011). The integrated development of sensory organization. *Clinics in Perinatology, 38*(4), 591–603.

Lipkin, P. (2009). Motor development and dysfunction. In *Developmental-Behavioral Pediatrics*, 643–652. Elsevier Inc.. https://doi.org/10.1016/B978-1-4160-3370-7.00066-3

Lipkin, P., & Macias, M. (2020). Council on children with disabilities, section on developmental and behavioral pediatrics promoting optimal development: Identifying infants and young children with developmental disorders through developmental surveillance and screening. *Pediatrics, 145*(1), e20193449.

Little, E., Legare, C., & Carver, L. (2019). Culture, carrying, and communication: Beliefs and behavior associated with babywearing. *Infant Behavior & Development, 57*.

Lockman, J., & Tamis-LeMonda, C. (2020). *The Cambridge handbook of infant development: Brain, behavior, and cultural context*. Cambridge University Press.

Lomax, A. (2015). *Examination of the newborn: An evidence-based guide*. Wiley.

Loos, H., Doucet, S., Védrines, F., Sharapa, C., Soussignan, R., Durand, K., Sagot, P., Buettner, A., & Schaal, B. (2017). Responses of human neonates to highly diluted odorants from sweat. *Journal of Chemical Ecology, 43*(1), 106–117.

Lutz, P., Tanti, A., Gasecka, A., Barnett-Burns, S., Kim, J., Zhou, Y., Gang, G., Wakid, M., Shaw, M., Almeida, D., Chay, M., Yang, J., Larivière, V., M'Boutchou, M., van Kempen, L., Yerko, V., Prud'homme, J., Davoli, M., Vaillancourt, K., Théroux, J., Bramoullé, A., Zhang, T., Meaney, M., Ernst, C., Côté, D., Mechawar, N., & Turecki, G. (2017). Association of a history of child abuse with impaired myelination in the anterior cingulate cortex: Convergent epigenetic, transcriptional, and morphological evidence. *American Journal of Psychiatry, 174*(12), 1185–1194.

MacLean, K. (2003). The impact of institutionalization on child development. *Development and Psychopathology, 15*, 853–884.

Manduca, R. (2018). Income inequality and the persistence of racial economic disparities. *Sociological Science, 5*, 8.

McHale, S., King, V., & Buxton, O. (2017). *Family contexts of sleep and health across the life course* (National Symposium on Family Issues, v. 8). Springer.

Mennella, J., Forestell, C., Morgan, L., & Beauchamp, G. (2009). Early milk feeding influences taste acceptance and liking during infancy. *American Journal of Clinical Nutrition, 90*, 780S–788S.

Mennella, J., Jagnow, C., & Beauchamp, G. (2001). Prenatal and postnatal flavor learning by human infants. *Pediatrics, 107*, E88.

Mercuri, E., Ricci, D., Pane, M., & Baranello, G. (2005). The neurological examination of the newborn baby. *Early Human Development, 81*(12), 947–956.

Middlebrooks, J. (2015). Sound localization. *Handbook of Clinical Neurology, 129*, 99–116.

Mindell, J., & Williamson, A. (2018). Benefits of a bedtime routine in young children: Sleep, development, and beyond. *Sleep Medicine Reviews, 40*, 93–108.

Modrell, A., & Tadi, P. (2021). *Primitive reflexes*. StatPearls Publishing. https://www.ncbi.nlm.nih.gov/books/NBK554606/

Monroy, C., Shafto, C., Castellanos, I., Bergeson, T., & Houston, D. (2019). Visual habituation in deaf and hearing infants. *PLOS ONE, 14*(2), e0209265.

Moon, R., & Task Force on Sudden Infant Death Syndrome (2016). SIDS and other sleep-related infant deaths: Evidence base for 2016 updated recommendations for a safe infant sleeping environment. *Pediatrics, 138*(5), e20153275.

Moore, S., McEwen, L., Quirt, J., Morin, A., Mah, S., Barr, R., Boyce, W., & Kobor, M. (2017). Epigenetic correlates of neonatal contact in humans. *Development and Psychopathology, 29*(5), 1517.

Morisaki, N., Kawachi, I., Oken, E., & Fujiwara, T. (2017). Social and anthropometric factors explaining racial/ethnical differences in birth weight in the United States. *Scientific Reports, 7*(1), 1–8.

Murray, M., Lewkowicz, D., Amedi, A., & Wallace, M. (2016). Multisensory processes: A balancing act across the lifespan. *Trends in Neuroscience, 39*(8), 567–579.

Nagai, Y. (2019). Predictive learning: Its key role in early cognitive development. *Philosophical Transactions of the Royal Society B: Biological Sciences, 374*(1771).

National Institute of Neurological Disorders and Stroke (2020). *Shaken baby syndrome information page*. https://www.ninds.nih.gov/Disorders/All-Disorders/Shaken-Baby-Syndrome-Information-Page

National Scientific Council on the Developing Child (2006). *Early exposure to toxic substances damages brain architecture: Working paper no. 4*. www.developingchild.harvard.edu.

Nguyen, A. (2019). Making taste public: Ethnographies of food and the senses. *Food, Culture & Society, 22*(3), 380–381.

Nishitani, S., Miyamura, T., Tagawa, M., Sumi, M., Takase, R., Doi, H., Moriuchi, H., & Shinohara, K. (2009). The calming effect of a maternal breast milk odor on the human newborn infant. *Neuroscience Research, 63*(1), 66–71.

Noble, K., McCandliss, B., & Farah, M. (2007). Socioeconomic gradients predict individual differences in neurocognitive abilities. *Developmental Science, 10*, 464–480.

Numan, M. (2020). *The parental brain: Mechanisms, development, and evolution*. Oxford University Press.

Odgers, C. (2015). Income inequality and the developing child: Is it all relative? *American Psychologist, 70*, 722–731.

Oster, E. (2019). *Crib sheet: A data-driven guide to better, more relaxed parenting, from birth to preschool*. Penguin Press.

Payne, V., & Isaacs, L. (2016). *Human motor development: A lifespan approach*. Holcomb Hathaway.

Paruthi, S., Brooks, L., D'Ambrosio, C., Hall, W., Kotagal, S., Lloyd, R., Malow, B., Maski, K., Nichols, C., Quan, S., Rosen, C., Troester, M., & Wise, M. (2016). Recommended amount of sleep for pediatric populations: A consensus statement of the American Academy of Sleep Medicine. *Journal of Clinical Sleep Medicine, 12*(6),785–786.

Perlman, J., Cilio, M., & Polin, R. (2019). *Neurology: Neonatology questions and controversies*. Elsevier.

Probst, J., Zahnd, W., & Breneman, C. (2019). Declines in pediatric mortality fall short for rural US children. *Health Affairs, 38*(12), 2069–2076.

Rauscher, E., & Rangel, D. (2020). Rising organization for economic co-operation and development, (2017). Health status indicators: Kaiser Family Foundation analysis of data from OECD. *OECD Health Statistics Database*. http://www.healthsystemtracker.org/chart-collection/infant-mortality-u-s-compare-countries/#item-start.

Rutter, M.,, & the English and Romanian Adoptees (ERA) Study Team (1998). Developmental catch-up, and deficit, following adoption after severe global early privation. *Journal of Child Psychology and Psychiatry, 39,* 465–476.

Sakai, J. (2020). Core concept: How synaptic pruning shapes neural wiring during development and, possibly, in disease. *Proceedings of the National Academy of Sciences, 117*(28), 16096–16099.

Scafidi, F., Field, T., Schanberg, S., Bauer, C., Vega-Lahr, N., Garcie, R., Poirier, J., Nystrom, G., & Kuhn, C. (1986). Effects of tactile/kinesthetic stimulation and sleep/wake behavior of preterm neonates. *Infant Behavior and Development, 9,* 91–105.

Schaal, B. (2005). From amnion to colostrum to milk: Odor bridging in early developmental transitions. In B. Hopkins & S. Johnson (Eds.), *Prenatal development of postnatal functions.* Praeger.

Schor, N. (2020). Neurological evaluation. In R. Kliegman,, J. St. Geme, N. Blum, S. Shah, R. Tasker, & K. Wilson (Eds.), *Nelson textbook of pediatrics.* Elsevier.

Shulman, S. (2004). The history of pediatric infectious diseases. *Pediatric Research, 55,* 163–176.

Sicherer, S. (2011). Epidemiology of food allergy. *The Journal of Allergy and Clinical Immunology, 127*(3), 594–602.

Sidebotham, P., Bates, F., Ellis, C., & Lyus, L. (2018). Preventive strategies for sudden infant death syndrome. In J. Duncan & R. Byard (Eds.), *SIDS sudden infant and early childhood death: The past, the present and the future.* University of Adelaide Press.

Siega-Riz, A., Deming, D., Reidy, C., Fox, M., Condon, E., & Briefel, R. (2010). Food consumption patterns of infants and toddlers: Where are we now? *Journal of the American Dietetic Association, 110*(12), S38–S51.

Simkin, P., Whalley, J., Keppler, A., Durham, J., & Bolding, A. (2018). *Pregnancy, childbirth, and the newborn: The complete guide.* Da Capo Lifelong.

Stahl, A., & Feigenson, L. (2015). Observing the unexpected enhances infants' learning and exploration. *Science, 348*(6230), 91–94.

Stiffler, D., Ayres, B., Fauvergue, C., & Cullen, D. (2018). Sudden infant death and sleep practices in the Black community. *Journal for Specialists in Pediatric Nursing, 23*(2), e12213.

Tappero, E., & Honeyfield, M. (2018). *Physical assessment of the newborn.* Springer.

Taveras, E., Rifas-Shiman, S., Belfort, M., Kleinman, K., Oken, E., & Gillman, M. (2009). Weight status in the first 6 months of life and obesity at 3 years of age. *Pediatrics, 123*(4), 1177–1183.

Thakrar, A., Forrest, A., Maltenfort, M., & Forrest, C. (2018). Child mortality in the US and 19 OECD comparator nations: A 50-year time-trend analysis. *Health Affairs, 37*(1), 140–149.

Thompson, J., Manore, M., & Vaughan, L. (2020). *The science of nutrition.* Pearson.

UNICEF (2019). *Levels and trends in child mortality,* United Nations Inter-Agency Group for Child Mortality Estimation. https://childmortality.org/wp-content/uploads/2019/10/UN-IGME-Child-Mortality-Report-2019.pdf

US Centers for Disease Control and Prevention (2019). *Breastfeeding.* Division of Nutrition, Physical Activity, and Obesity, National Center for Chronic Disease Prevention and Health Promotion. https://www.cdc.gov/breastfeeding/index.htm

US Centers for Disease Control and Prevention (2010). *WHO growth standards are recommended for use in the US for infants and children 0 to 2 years of age.* https://www.cdc.gov/growthcharts/who_charts.htm

US Centers for Disease Control and Prevention (2020). *Well-child visits are essential.* https://www.cdc.gov/vaccines/parents/why-vaccinate/well-child-visits.html

US Department of Agriculture, Food and Nutrition Service (2020). *The special supplemental nutrition assistance program for women, infants and children (WIC).* https://www.fns.usda.gov/wic

US Department of Education, Office of Special Education Programs (2019). *Disabilities that qualify infants, toddlers, children, and youth for services under IDEA.* WETA-TV. http://www.ldonline.org/article/12399

US Department of Health and Human Services Oral Health Coordinating Committee (2019). US Department of Health and Human Services Oral Health Strategic Framework, 2014-2017. *Public Health Reports, 131*(2), 242–257. https://www.ncbi.nlm.nih.gov/pmc/articles/PMC4765973/

US Department of Health and Human Services (2021). *Common SIDS and SUID terms and definitions.* https://safetosleep.nichd.nih.gov/safesleepbasics/SIDS/Common

US National Library of Medicine (2019). *Babinski reflex.* US Department of Health and Human Services National Institutes of Health. https://medlineplus.gov/ency/article/003294.htm

US National Library of Medicine (2020). *Normal growth and development.* National Institute of Health. https://medlineplus.gov/ency/article/002456.htm

US Surgeon General, Centers for Disease Control and Prevention, Office on Women's Health (2011). *The surgeon general's call to action to support breastfeeding.* https://www.ncbi.nlm.nih.gov/books/NBK52679/

US Surgeon General, Centers for Disease Control and Prevention (2019). *What is cerebral palsy?* https://www.cdc.gov/ncbddd/cp/facts.html

US Surgeon General, Centers for Disease Control and Prevention (2019). *What is muscular dystrophy?* (2019). https://www.cdc.gov/ncbddd/cp/facts.html

Uvnäs-Moberg, K. (2003). *The oxytocin factor: Tapping the hormone of calm, love, and healing.* Da Capo Press.

Uvnäs-Moberg, K., Handlin, L., & Petersson, M. (2015). Self-soothing behaviors with particular reference to oxytocin release induced by non-noxious sensory stimulation. *Frontiers in Psychology, 5.*

Uvnäs-Moberg, K., Handlin, L., & Petersson, M. (2020). Neuroendocrine mechanisms involved in the physiological effects caused by skin-to-skin contact: With a particular focus on the oxytocinergic system. *Infant Behavior and Development, 61.*

Vandenplas, Y., Hauser, B., & Salvatore, S. (2019). Functional gastrointestinal disorders in infancy: Impact on the health of the infant and family. *Pediatric Gastroenterology, Hepatology & Nutrition, 22*(3), 207–216.

Walk, R., & Gibson, E. (1960). *The "visual cliff."* https://www.scientificamerican.com/article/the-visual-cliff/

Walker, R. (2018). Nervous system. In M. Glynn & W. Drake (Eds.), *Hutchison's clinical methods.* Elsevier.

Walker-Andrews, A., Lewkowicz D., & Lickliter, R. (2013). *The development of intersensory perception: Comparative perspectives.* Psychology Press.

Walsh, M., Bell, E., Kandefer, S., Saha, S., Carlo, W., Laptook, A., Sánchez, P., Stoll, B., Shankaran, S., Van Meurs, K., Cook, N., Higgins, R., Das, A., Newman, N., Schibler, K., Schmidt, B., Cotton, C., Poindexter, B., Watterberg, K., & Truog, W. (2017). Neonatal outcomes of moderately preterm infants compared to extremely preterm infants. *Pediatric Research, 82*, 297–304.

Wambach, K., & Spencer, B. (2021). *Breastfeeding and human lactation.* Jones & Bartlett Learning.

Werker, J. (2018). Perceptual beginnings to language acquisition. *Applied Psycholinguistics, 39*(4), 703–728.

World Health Organization (2017). *Guidelines on infant health.* https://www.who.int/publications/i/item/978924150437

World Health Organization (2018). *Infant mortality.* http://www.who.int/gho/child_health/mortality/neonatal_infant_text/en/

Wyness, L., Stanner, S., Buttriss, J., & British Nutrition Foundation (2013). *Nutrition and development: Short and long term consequences for health.* Wiley-Blackwell.

Xiaoli, H., Liling, C., & Li, Z. (2019). Effects of paternal skin-to-skin contact in newborns and fathers after cesarean delivery. *The Journal of Perinatal & Neonatal Nursing, 33*(1), 68–73.

Chapter 5

Adam-Darque, A., Grouiller, F., Vasung, L., Leuchter R., Pollien, P., Lazeyras, F., & Huppi, P. (2018). MRI-based neuronal response to new odorants in the newborn brain. *Cerebral Cortex, 28*(8), 2901–2907.

American Academy of Pediatrics (2016). *Where we stand: Screen time.* https://www.healthychildren.org/English/family-life/Media/Pages/Where-We-Stand-TV-Viewing-Time.aspx

American Psychological Association (2020). What do we really know about kids and screens? *Monitor on Psychology, 51*(3). http://www.apa.org/monitor/2020/04/cover-kids-screens

Anderson, E., Chang, Y., Hespos, S., & Gentner, D. (2018). Comparison within pairs promotes analogical abstraction in three-month-olds. *Cognition, 176*, 74–86.

Arturo, D., Morban, H., & Cruz, N. (2016). Copying the development: Mirror neurons in child development. *Medwave, 16*(5), e6466.

Ashton, J., & Beattie, R. (2019). Screen time in children and adolescents: Is there evidence to guide parents and policy? *The Lancet Child & Adolescent Health, 3*(5), 292–294.

August, D., Carlo, M., Dressler, C., & Snow, C. (2005). The critical role of vocabulary development for English language learners. *Learning Disabilities Research & Practice, 20*, 50–57.

Baillargeon, R. (2004). Infants' physical world. *Current Directions in Psychological Science, 13*, 89–94.

Baillargeon R. (2008). Innate ideas revisited: For a principle of persistence in infants' physical reasoning. *Perspectives on Psychological Science, 3*(1), 2–13.

Baillargeon, R., Spelke, E., & Wasserman, S. (1985). Object permanence in five-month-old infants. *Cognition, 20*(3), 191–208.

Baillargeon, R. (1987). Object permanence in 3 ½-and 4 ½-month-old infants. *Developmental Psychology, 23*(5), 655–664.

Balari, S., & Lorenzo, G. (2015). Should it stay or should it go? A critical reflection on the critical period for language. *Biolinguistics, 9*, 8–42.

Balasundaram, P., & Avulakunta, I. D. (2021) Bayley scales of infant and toddler development. In *StatPearls.* StatPearls Publishing.

Bandura, A. (1977). *Social learning theory.* Prentice Hall.

Barkovich, A., & Raybaud, C. (2019). *Pediatric neuroimaging.* Wolters Kluwer.

Barrouillet, P. (2015). Theories of cognitive development: From Piaget to today. *Developmental Review, 38*(C), 1–12.

Barton, L., & Brophy-Herb, H. (2004). *Learning to read the world: Language and literacy in the first three years.* Zero to Three.

Bauer, P. (2015). A complementary processes account of the development of childhood amnesia and a personal past. *Psychological Review, 122*, 204–231.

Bauer, P., & Pathman, T. (2008). Memory and early brain development. In R. Tremblay, M. Boivin, & R. Peters, *Encyclopedia on early childhood development.* http://www.child-encyclopedia.com/brain/according-experts/memory-and-early-brain-development

Bayley, N., & Aylward, G. (2019). *Bayley scales of infant and toddler development screening test.* Pearson.

Bear, M., Connors, B., & Paradiso, M. (2016). *Neuroscience: Exploring the brain.* Wolters Kluwer.

Begus, K., Gliga, T., & Southgate, V. (2014). Infants learn what they want to learn: Responding to infant pointing leads to superior learning. *PLOS ONE, 9*, e108817.

Begus, K., Gliga, T., & Southgate, V. (2016). Infants' preferences for native speakers are associated with an expectation of information. *Proceedings of the National Academy of Sciences, 113*, 12397–12402.

Berken, J., Gracco, V., & Klein, D. (2017). Early bilingualism, language attainment, and brain development. *Neuropsychologia, 98*, 220–227.

Bernier, D., & White, K. (2019). Toddlers' sensitivity to phonetic detail in child speech. *Journal of Experimental Child Psychology, 185*, 128.

Betancourt, L., Avants, B., Farah, M., Brodsky, N., Wu, J., Ashtari, M., & Hurt, H. (2016). Effect of socioeconomic status(es) disparity on neural development in female African-American infants at age 1 month. *Developmental Science, 19*, 947–956.

Bick, J., & Nelson, C. (2016). Early adverse experiences and the developing brain. *Neuropsychopharmacology, 41*, 177–196.

Birdsong, D. (2018). Plasticity, variability and age in second language acquisition and bilingualism. *Frontiers in Psychology.* https://www.frontiersin.org/articles/10.3389/fpsyg.2018.00081/ful

Blair, C., & Raver, C. (2012). Child development in the context of adversity: Experiential canalization of brain and behavior. *American Psychologist, 67*, 309–318.

Blair, C., & Raver, C. (2016). Poverty, stress, and brain development: New directions for prevention and intervention. *Academic Pediatrics, 1*, S30–S36.

Bogartz, R. (2000). Object permanence in infants. *Infancy, 1*(4), 387–388.

Braddick, O., & Atkinson, J. (2011). Development of human visual function. *Vision Research, 5*(13), 1588–1609.

Brito, H., & Noble, K. (2014). Socioeconomic status and structural brain development. *Frontiers in Neuroscience, 8*, 276.

Brito, N., Fifer, W., Amso, D., Barr, R., Bell, M., Calkins, S., Flynn, A., Montgomery-Downs, H., Oakes, L., Richards, J., Samuelson, L., & Colombo, J. (2019). Beyond the Bayley: Neurocognitive assessments of development during infancy and toddlerhood. *Developmental Neuropsychology, 44*(2), 220–247.

Brummelte, S., & Galea, L. (2016). Postpartum depression: etiology, treatment and consequences for maternal care. *Hormones and Behavior, 77*, 153–166.

Bullard, J. (2014). *Creating environments for learning: Birth to age eight.* Pearson.

Burns, T., Yoshida, K., Hill, K., & Werker, J. (2007). The development of phonetic representation in bilingual and monolingual infants. *Applied Psycholinguistics, 28*(3), 455–474.

Burge, L., Louis, P., & Giardino, A. (2019). Neglect and failure to thrive. In A. Giardino, M. Lyn, & E. Giardino (Eds.), *A practical guide to the evaluation of child physical abuse and neglect.* Springer.

Bushall, I. (2003). Newborn face recognition. In O. Pascalis & A. Slater (Eds.), *The development of face processing in infancy and early childhood.* Nova Science Publishers.

Carey, S. (2009). *The origins of concepts.* Oxford University Press.

Carey, S. (2014). On learning new primitives in the language of thought: Reply to Rey. *Mind & Language, 29*, 133–166.

Cesana-Arlotti, N., Martín, A., Téglás, E., Vorobyova, L., Cetnarski, R., & Bonatti, L. (2018). Precursors of logical reasoning in preverbal human infants. *Science, 359*, 1263–1266.

Chen, D. (2014). *Essential elements in early intervention: Visual impairment and multiple disabilities.* AFB Press.

Child Welfare Information Gateway (2015). *Understanding the effects of maltreatment on brain development.* US Department of Health and Human Services, Children's Bureau.

Chomsky, N. (1965). *Aspects of the theory of syntax.* MIT Press.

Christodoulou, J., Lac, A., & Moore, D. (2017). Babies and math: A meta-analysis of infants' simple arithmetic competence. *Developmental Psychology, 53*(8), 1405.

Clancy, B., & Finlay, B. (2001). *Neural correlates of early language learning.* https://www.researchgate.net/publication/254400675_Neural_correlates_of_early_language_learning

Cohen, D. (2018). *How the child's mind develops.* Routledge.

Cohen, L., & Billard, A. (2018). Social babbling: The emergence of symbolic gestures and words. *Neural Networks, 106*, 194–204.

Conrad, S., Hartig, A., & Santelmann, L. (2021). *The Cambridge introduction to applied linguistics.* Cambridge University Press.

Cooper, R., & Aslin, R. (1990). Preference for infant directed speech in the first month after birth. *Child Development 61*(5), 1584–1595.

Cychosz, M., Cristia, A., Bergelson, E., Casillas, M., Baudet, G., Warlaumont, A., Scaff, C., Yankowitz, L., & Seidl, A. (2021). Vocal development in a large-scale crosslinguistic corpus. *Developmental Science, 24*(5), e13090.

Dahl, A., Campos, J., Anderson, D., Uchiyama, I., Witherington, D., Ueno, M., Poutrain-Lejeune, L., & Barbu-Roth, M. (2013). The epigenesis of wariness of heights. *Psychological Science, 24* (7), 1361.

DeCasper, A., & Fifer, W. (1980). Of human bonding: Newborns prefer their mothers' voices. *Science, 208*(4448), 1174–1176.

Del Rosario, C., Slevin, M., Molloy, E. J., Quigley, J., & Nixon, E. (2021). How to use the Bayley Scales of Infant and Toddler Development. *Archives of disease in childhood. Education and practice edition, 106*(2), 108–112. https://doi.org/10.1136/archdischild-2020-319063

dos Santos, L., de Kieviet, E., Konigs, J., van Elburg, M., & Oosterlaan, J. (2013). Predictive value of the Bayley scales of infant development on development of very preterm/very low birth weight children: A meta-analysis. *Early Human Development, 89*(7), 487–496.

Dubowitz, H. (2013). Neglect in children. *Pediatric Annals, 42*(4), 73–77.

Durkin, M. (2011). *From infancy to the elderly: Communication throughout the ages.* Nova Science.

Edwards, S. (2005). *Fluent aphasia.* Cambridge University Press.

El-Kogali, S., & Krafft, C. (2015). *Expanding opportunities for the next generation: Early childhood development in the Middle East and North Africa.* World Bank Group. https://elibrary.worldbank.org/doi/book/10.1596/978–1–4648–0323–9#

Elmlinger, S., Schwade, J., & Goldstein, M. (2019). The ecology of prelinguistic vocal learning: Parents simplify the structure of their speech in response to babbling. *Journal of Child Language, 46*(05), 998.

Fandakova, Y., & Hartley, C. (2020). Mechanisms of learning and plasticity in childhood and adolescence. *Developmental Cognitive Neuroscience, 42*, 100764.

Ferry, A., Flo, A., Brusini, P., Cattarossi, L., Macagno, F., Nespor, M., & Mehler, J. (2016). On the edge of language acquisition: Inherent constraints on encoding multisyllabic sequences in the neonate brain. *Developmental Science, 19*(3).

Fink, E., Browne, W., Kirk, I., & Hughes, C. (2019). Couple relationship quality and the infant home language environment: Gender-specific findings. *Journal of Family Psychology.* https://psycnet.apa.org/fulltext/2019–49285–001.html

Friedmann, N., & Rusou, D. (2015). Critical period for first language: The crucial role of language input during the first year of life. *Current Opinion in Neurobiology, 35,* 27–34.

Garner, A. (2013). Home visiting and the biology of toxic stress: Opportunities to address early childhood adversity. *Pediatrics, 132,* S65–S73.

Girma, S., Fikadu, T., & Abdisa, E. (2019). Maternal common mental disorder as predictors of stunting among children aged 6–59 months in Western Ethiopia: A case-control study. *International Journal of Pediatrics, 10,* 1–8.

Gleason, J., & Ratner, N. (2017). *The development of language.* Pearson.

Gopnik, A. (2016). *The gardener and the carpenter: What the new science of child development tells us about the relationship between parents and children.* Farrar, Straus, and Giroux.

Goswami, U. (2010). *The Wiley-Blackwell handbook of childhood cognitive development.* Wiley-Blackwell.

Goupil, L., Romand-Monnier, M., & Kouider, S. (2016). Infants ask for help when they know they don't know. *Proceedings of the National Academy of Sciences of the United States of America, 113,* 3492–3496.

Grandjean, P., & Landrigan, P. (2014). Neurobehavioural effects of developmental toxicity. *Lancet Neurology, 13,* 330–338.

Grover, V., Uccelli, P., Rowe, M., & Lieven, E. (2019). *Learning through language: Towards an educationally informed theory of language learning.* Cambridge University Press.

Gullberg, M., & De Bot, K. (2008). Gestures in language development. *Gesture, 8*(2).

Hagoort, P. (2019). *Human language: From genes and brains to behavior.* The MIT Press.

Hartshorne, J., Tenenbaum, J., & Pinker, S. (2018). A critical period for second language acquisition: Evidence from 2/3 million English speakers. *Cognition, 177,* 263–277.

Havron, N., Ramus, F., Heude, B., Forhan, A., Cristia, A., & Hugo, P. (2019). The effect of siblings on language development as a function of age difference and sex. *Psychological Science, 30*(9), 1333–1343.

Henik, A., Gliksman, Y., Kallai, A., & Leibovich, T. (2017). Size perception and the foundation of numerical processing. *Current Directions in Psychological Science, 26*, 45–51.

Hespos, S., & vanMarle, K. (2012). Physics for infants: Characterizing the origins of knowledge about objects, substances, and number. *Cognitive Science, 3*(1), 19–27.

Heward, W., Alber, S., & Konrad, M. (2017). *Exceptional children: An introduction to special education.* Pearson.

High, P., & Klass, P. (2014). Literacy promotion: An essential component of primary care pediatric practice. *Pediatrics, 134*(2), 404–409.

Hoff, E. (2014). *Language development.* Wadsworth Cengage Learning.

Hoff, E., Core, C., Place, S., Rumiche, R., Senor, M., & Parra, M. (2012). Dual language exposure and early bilingual development. *Journal of Child Language, 39*(1), 1–27.

Horowitz-Kraus, T., & Hutton, J. S. (2015). From emergent literacy to reading: How learning to read changes a child's brain. *Acta Paediatrica, 104*(7), 648–656.

Horowitz-Kraus, T., Hutton, J., Phelan, K., & Holland, S. (2018). Maternal reading fluency is positively associated with greater functional connectivity between the child's future reading network and regions related to executive functions and language processing in preschool-age children. *Brain and Cognition, 121*, 17–23.

Hostinar, C., Stellern, S., Schaefer, C., Carlson, S., & Gunnar, M. (2012). Associations between early life adversity and executive function in children adopted internationally from orphanages. *Proceedings of the National Academy of Sciences of the United States of America, 109*, 17208–17212.

Hutton, J., Dudley, J., Horowitz-Kraus, T., DeWitt, T., & Holland, S. (2020). Associations between home literacy environment, brain white matter integrity and cognitive abilities in preschool-age children. *Acta Paediatrica, 109*, 1376–1386.

Inguaggiato, E., Sgandurra, G., & Cioni, G. (2017). Brain plasticity early development: Implications for early intervention in neurodevelopmental disorders. *Neuropsychiatrie de l'Enfance et de l'Adolescence, 65*(5), 299–306.

Ismail, F., Fatemi, A., & Johnston, M. (2017). Cerebral plasticity: Windows of opportunity in the developing brain. *European Journal of Paediatric Neurology, 21*(1), 23–48.

Johnson, S., Riis, J., & Noble, K. (2016). State of the art review: Poverty and the developing brain. *Pediatrics, 137*, e20153075.

Jung, J., & Recchia, S. (2013). Scaffolding infants' play through empowering and individualizing teaching practices. *Early Education and Development, 24*(6), 829–850.

Kauffman, J., Hallahan, D., & Pullen, P. (2017). *Handbook of special education.* Routledge.

Kenny, D. (2013). *Bringing up baby: The psychoanalytic infant comes of age.* Karnac.

Kidd, C., & Hayden, B. (2015). The psychology and neuroscience of curiosity. *Neuron, 88*, 449–460.

Kidd, C., Piantadosi, S., & Aslin, R. (2012). The Goldilocks effect: Human infants allocate attention to visual sequences that are neither too simple nor too complex. *PLOS ONE, 7*, e36399.

Kilner, J., & Lemon, R. (2013). What we know currently about mirror neurons. *Current Biology, 23*(23), R1057–R1062.

Kimura, A., Wada, Y., Yang, J., Otsuka, Y., Dan, I., Masuda, T., Kanazawa, S., & Yamaguchi, M. (2010). Infants' recognition of objects using canonical color, *Journal of Experimental Child Psychology, 105*(3), 256–263.

Kobulsky, J., Dubowitz, H., & Xu, Y. (2020). The global challenge of the neglect of children. *Child Abuse & Neglect, 110*(1), 104296.

Kolb, B. (2018). Brain plasticity and experience. In R. Gibb & B. Kolb (Eds.), *The neurobiology of brain and behavioral development.* Academic Press.

Kolb, B., Harker, A., & Gibb, R. (2017). Principles of plasticity in the developing brain. *Developmental Medicine and Child Neurology, 59*(12), 1218–1223.

Koster, M., Kayhan, E., Langeloh, M., & Hoehl, S. (2020). Making sense of the world: Infant learning from a predictive processing perspective. *Perspectives on Psychological Science, 15*(3), 562–571.

Kroeger, K., & Nelson, W. (2006). A Language programme to increase the verbal production of a child dually diagnosed with Down syndrome and autism. *Journal of Intellectual Disability Research, 50*, 101–108.

Kugiumutzakis, G. (2017). Intersubjective vocal imitation in early mother-infant interaction. *New Perspectives in Early Communicative Development.* Routledge.

Kucker, S., McMurray, B., & Samuelson, L. (2015). Slowing down fast mapping: Redefining the dynamics of word learning. *Child Development Perspectives, 9*(2), 74–78.

Kuhl, P., Tsao F., & Liu, H. (2003). Foreign language experience in infancy: Effects of short term exposure and social interaction on phonetic learning. *Proceedings of the National Academy of Sciences of the United States of America, 100*(15), 9096–9101.

Lally, J., & Mangione, P. (2017). Caring relationships: The heart of early brain development. *Young Children, 72*(2).

Lee, G., & Kisilevsky, B. (2014). Fetuses respond to father's voice but prefer mother's voice after birth. *Developmental Psychobiology, 56*(1), 1–11.

Lee, S. (2013). Paternal and household characteristics associated with child neglect and child protective services involvement. *Journal of Social Service Research, 39*(2), 171–187.

Lee, S., Ward, K.P., Lee, J., & Rodriguez, C. (2021). Parental social isolation and child maltreatment risk during the COVID-19 pandemic. *Journal of Family Violence*, 1–12.

Legerstee, M., Haley, D., & Bornstein, M. (2013). *The infant mind: Origins of the social brain.* Guilford.

Lerner, R., Easterbrooks, M., Mistry, J., & Weiner, I. (2013). Developmental psychology. *Handbook of psychology.* John Wiley & Sons.

Li, P., Legault, J., & Litcofsky, K. (2014). Neuroplasticity as a function of second language learning: Anatomical changes in the human brain. *Cortex, 58*, 301–324.

Logan-Greene, P., & Semanchin Jones, A. (2018). Predicting chronic neglect: Understanding risk and protective factors for CPS-involved families. *Child & Family Social Work, 23*(2), 264–272.

Lopez, L., Walle, E., Pretzer, G., & Warlaumont, A. (2020). Adult responses to infant prelinguistic vocalizations are associated with infant vocabulary: A home observation study. *PLOS ONE, 15*(11), e0242232.

Lytle, S., & Kuhl, P. (2017). Social interaction and language acquisition: Toward a neurobiological view. *The handbook of psycholinguistics*. Wiley.

Mackin, R., Ben Fadel, N., Feberova, J., Murray, L., Nair, A., Kuehn, S., Barrowman, N., & Daboval, T. (2017). ASQ3 and/or the Bayley-III to support clinicians' decision making. *PLOS ONE, 12*(2), e0170171.

Madsen, H., & Kim, J. (2016). Ontogeny of memory: An update on 40 years of work on infantile amnesia. *Behavioral Brain Research, 298*, 4–14.

Mampe, B., Friederici, A., Christophe, A., & Wermke, K. (2009). Newborns' cry melody is shaped by their native language. *Current Biology, 19*, 1994–1997.

Mandler, J. (2004). *The foundations of mind: Origins of conceptual thought*. Oxford University Press.

Marshall, P., & Meltzoff, A. (2014). Neural mirroring mechanisms and imitation in human infants. *Philosophical Transactions of the Royal Society of London. Series B, Biological Sciences, 369*(1644), 20130620.

Marti, E., & Rodríguez, C. (2012). *After Piaget*. Transaction.

Medina, John (2014). *Brain rules for babies*. Pear Press.

Mehler, J., Jusczyk, P., Lambertz, G., Halsted, N., Bertoncini, J., & Tison, A. (1988). A precursor of language acquisition in young infants. *Cognition, 29*(2), 143–178.

Meltzoff, A., & Moore, M. (1977). Imitation of facial and manual gestures by human neonates. *Science, 198*, 75–78.

Meltzoff, P., & Marshall, J. (2018). Human infant imitation as a social survival circuit. *Current Opinion in Behavioral Sciences, 24*, 130–136.

Miller, P. (2016). *Theories of developmental psychology*. Worth, Macmillan Learning.

Moon, C., Cooper, R., & Fifer, W. (1993). Two-day-olds prefer their native language. *Infant Behavior and Development, 16*(4), 495–500.

Moon, C., Lagercrantz, H., & Kuhl, P. (2013). Language experienced in utero affects vowel perception after birth: A two-country study. *Acta Paediatrica, 102*(3), 156–160.

Moore, C. (2010). Social cognition in infancy. *Encyclopedia on Early Childhood Development*. http://www.child-encyclopedia.com/social-cognition/according-experts/social-cognition-infancy.

Morgan, C., Honan, I., Allsop, A., Novak, I., & Badawi, N. (2019). Psychometric properties of assessments of cognition in infants with cerebral palsy or motor impairment: A systematic review. *Journal of Pediatric Psychology, 44*(2), 238–252.

Morra, S. (2008). *Cognitive development: Neo-Piagetian perspectives*. Lawrence Erlbaum Associates.

Mullally, S., & Maguire, E. (2014). Learning to remember: The early ontogeny of episodic memory. *Developmental Cognitive Neuroscience, 9*, 12–29.

Neil, N., & Jones, E. (2018). Communication intervention for individuals with Down syndrome: Systematic review and meta-analysis. *Developmental Neurorehabilitation, 21*(1), 1–12.

Nelson, C., Fox, N., & Zeanah, C. (2014). *Romania's abandoned children: Deprivation, brain development, and the struggle for recovery*. Harvard University Press.

Nelson, C., Scott, R., Bhutta, Z., Harris, N. B., Danese, A., & Samara, M. (2020). Adversity in childhood is linked to mental and physical health throughout life. *BMJ, 371*, m3048.

Nguyen, A., Hoyer, E., Rajhans, P., Strathearn, L., & Kim, S. (2019). A tumultuous transition to motherhood: Altered brain and hormonal responses in mothers with postpartum depression. *Journal of Neuroendocrinology, 31*(9), e12794.

Nicoladis, E., & Montanari, S. (2016). *Bilingualism across the lifespan: Factors moderating language proficiency*. American Psychological Association.

Numan, M. (2020). *The parental brain: Mechanisms, development, and evolution*. Oxford University Press.

Oller, D., Wieman, L., Doyle, W., & Ross, C. (1976). Infant babbling and speech. *Journal of Child Language, 3*(1), 1–11.

Omnigraphics, Inc. (2016). *Disabilities sourcebook*.

Orr, C., & Kaufman, J. (2014). Neuroscience and child maltreatment: The role of epigenetics in risk and resilience in maltreated children. *Social Policy Report, 28*(1), 22–24.

Orr, E., & Geva, R. (2015). Symbolic play and language development. *Infant Behavior and Development, 38*, 147–161.

Ortega, L., & De Houwer, A. (2019). *The Cambridge handbook of bilingualism*. Cambridge University Press.

Pendergast, L., Schaefer, B., Murray-Kolb, L., Svensen, E., Shrestha, R., Rasheed, M., Scharf, R., Kosek, M., Vasquez, A., Maphula, A., Costa, H., Rasmussen, Z., Yousafzai, A., Tofail, F., Seidman, J., & The MAL-ED Network Investigators (2018). Assessing development across cultures: Invariance of the Bayley-III scales across seven international MAL-ED sites. *School Psychology Quarterly, 33*(4), 604–614.

Perlman, J., Cilio, M., & Polin, R. (2019). *Neurology: Neonatology questions and controversies*. Elsevier.

Perszyk, D., & Waxman, S. (2019). Infants' advances in speech perception shape their earliest links between language and cognition. *Scientific Reports, 9*, 3293.

Peterson, C., Warren, K., & Short, M. (2011). Infantile amnesia across the years: A 2-year follow-up of children's earliest memories. *Child Development, 82*, 1092–1105.

Pierce, L., Thompson, B., Gharib, A., Schlueter, L., Reilly, E., Valdes, V., Roberts, S., Conroy, K., Levitt, P., & Nelson, C. (2019). Association of perceived maternal stress during the perinatal period with electroencephalography patterns in 2-month-old infants. *JAMA Pediatrics, 173*(6), 561–570.

Purves, D., Augustine, G., Fitzpatrick D, Katz, L., LaMantia, A., McNamara, J., & Williams, S. (2001). The development of language: A critical period in humans. *Neuroscience*. https://www.ncbi.nlm.nih.gov/books/NBK11007/

Ramírez-Esparza, N., García-Sierra, A., & Kuhl, P. (2017). Look who's talking now! Parentese speech, social context, and language development across time. *Frontiers in Psychology, 8*, 1008.

Ranjitkar, S., Kvestad, I., Strand, T., Ulak, M., Shrestha, M., Chandyo, R., Shrestha Laxman, S., & Hysing, M. (2018). Acceptability and reliability of the Bayley Scales of Infant and Toddler Development-III among children in Bhaktapur, Nepal. *Frontiers in Psychology, 9*, 1265.

Raymer, A., & Gonzalez-Rothi, L. (2018). *The Oxford handbook of aphasia and language disorders*. Oxford University Press.

Reynolds, G., & Romano, A. (2016). The development of attention systems and working memory in infancy. *Frontiers in Systems Neuroscience, 10*. https://www.frontiersin.org/articles/10.3389/fnsys.2016.00015/full

Ross-Sheehy, S., Oakes, L., & Luck, S. (2011). Exogenous attention influences visual short-term memory in infants. *Developmental Science, 14,* 490–501.

Rovee-Collier, C., & Cuevas, K. (2009). Multiple memory systems are unnecessary to account for infant memory development: An ecological model. *Developmental Psychology, 45,* 160–174.

Roy, B., Frank, M., Decamp, P., Miller, M., & Roy, D. (2015). Predicting the birth of a spoken word. *Proceedings of the National Academy of Sciences of the United States of America, 112*(41), 12663–12668.

Sakai, J. (2020). Core concept: How synaptic pruning shapes neural wiring during development and, possibly, in disease. *Proceedings of the National Academy of Sciences, 117*(28), 16096–16099.

Samuelson, L., & McMurray, B. (2017). What does it take to learn a word? *Wiley Interdisciplinary Reviews. Cognitive Science, 8*(1–2),e1421.

Sarnecka, B., & Carey, S. (2008). How counting represents number: What children must learn and when they learn it. *Cognition, 108,* 662–674.

Sarnecka, B., Kamenskaya, V., Yamana, Y., Ogura, T., & Yudovina, Y. (2007). From grammatical number to exact numbers: Early meanings of 'one,' 'two,' and 'three' in English, Russian, and Japanese. *Cognitive Psychology, 55,* 136–168.

Shafer, V., & Garrido-Nag, K. (2007). The neurodevelopmental basis of speech and language. In M. Shatz & E. Hoff (Eds.), *The handbook of language development.* Blackwell.

Simmering, V. (2012). The development of visual working memory capacity during early childhood. *Journal of Experimental Child Psychology, 111,* 695–707.

Simpson, E., Fox, N., Tramacere A, & Ferrari, P. (2014a). Neonatal imitation and an epigenetic account of mirror neuron development. *Behavioral and Brain Sciences, 37*(2), 220.

Singer, D., & Revenson, T. (1996). *A Piaget primer: How a child thinks.* Plume.

Skinner, B. F. (1953). *Science and human behaviour.* The Macmillan Company.

Small, J. (2018). *Neuroradiology: Spectrum and evolution of disease.* Elsevier.

Smith, E., Hokstad, S., & Næss, K. (2020). Children with Down syndrome can benefit from language interventions: Results from a systematic review and meta-analysis. *Journal of Communication Disorders, 85,* 105992.

Smith, L. (2013). It's all connected: Pathways in visual object recognition and early noun learning. *The American Psychologist, 68*(8), 618–629.

Song, J., Demuth, K., & Morgan, J. (2018). Input and processing factors affecting infants' vocabulary size at 19 and 25 months. *Frontiers in Psychology, 9,* 2398.

Spelke, E. (2017). Core knowledge, language, and number. *Language Learning and Development, 13,* 147–170.

Spencer-Smith, M., Spittle, A., Lee, K., Doyle, L., & Anderson, P. (2015). *Pediatrics, 135*(5), e1258–e1265.

Spratt, E., Friedenberg, S., Swenson, C., Larosa, A., De Bellis, M., Macias, M., Summer, A., Hulsey, T., Runyan, D., & Brady, K. (2012). The effects of early neglect on cognitive, language, and behavioral functioning in childhood. *Psychology, 3*(2), 175–182.

Stahl, A., & Feigenson, L. (2015). Observing the unexpected enhances infants' learning and exploration. *Science, 348*(6230), 91–94.

Strouse, G., Georgene, L., Troseth, K., O'Doherty, M., & Saylor, M. (2018). Co-viewing supports toddlers' word learning from contingent and noncontingent video. *Journal of Experimental Child Psychology, 166,* 310–326.

Swingley, D. (2009). Contributions of infant word learning to language development. *Philosophical Transactions of the Royal Society of London. Series B, Biological Sciences, 364*(1536), 3617–3632.

Tamis-LeMonda, C., Kuchirko, Y., & Suh, D. (2018). Taking center stage: Infants' active role in language leaning. active learning from infancy to childhood. In L. Levine & J. Munsch (Eds.), *Child development from infancy to adolescence: An active learning approach.* Sage Publishers.

Thompson, R., Cotnoir-Bichelman, N., McKerchar, P., Tate, T., & Dancho, K. (2007). Enhancing early communication through infant sign training. *Journal of Applied Behavior Analysis, 40*(1), 15–23.

Thornton, S. (2003). *Growing minds: An introduction to children's cognitive development.* Palgrave Macmillan.

Topping, K., Dekhinet, R., & Zeedyk, S. (2013). Parent–infant interaction and children's language development. *Educational Psychology, 33.*

Torr, J. (2020). How 'shared' is shared reading: Book-focused infant–educator interactions in long day-care centres. *Journal of Early Childhood Literacy, 20*(4), 815–838.

Traxler, M., Boudewyn, M., & Loudermilk, J. (2012). What's special about human language? The contents of the "narrow language faculty" revisited. *Language and Linguistics Compass, 6*(10), 611–621.

Ueno, M., Uchiyama, I., Campos, J., Dahl, A., & Anderson, D. (2012). The organization of wariness of heights in experienced crawlers. *Infancy, 17*(4), 376–392.

US Centers for Disease Control and Prevention (2019). *Fetal alcohol spectrum disorders.* National Center on Birth Defects and Developmental Disabilities. https://www.cdc.gov/ncbddd/fasd/data.html

US Department of Health & Human Services (2019a). *Down syndrome.* https://ghr.nlm.nih.gov/condition/down-syndrome

US Department of Health & Human Services (2019b). *Fragile X.* https://ghr.nlm.nih.gov/condition/fragile-x-syndrome#resources

US Department of Health & Human Services (2019c). *Phenylketonuria.* https://ghr.nlm.nih.gov/condition/phenylketonuria

Vouloumanos, A., Hauser, M., Werker, J., & Martin, A. (2010). The tuning of human neonates' preference for speech. *Child Development, 81,* 517–527.

Vygotsky, L. (1978). *Mind and society: The development of higher mental processes.* Harvard University Press.

Vygotsky, L. (1993). *The collected works of L. S. Vygotsky* (Vols. 1 and 2). Plenum Press.

Wang, J., & Feigenson, L. (2019). Infants recognize counting as numerically relevant. *Developmental Science, 22,* 6.

Wellman, H., Kushnir, T., Xu, F., & Brink, K. (2016). Infants use statistical sampling to understand the psychological world. *Infancy, 21,* 668–676.

Wells, K. (2020). Cognitive development. *Gale encyclopedia of children's health: Infancy through adolescence.* https://www.encyclopedia.com

Werker, J., & Hensch, T. (2015). Critical periods in speech perception: New directions. *Annual Review of Psychology, 66,* 173–196.

Wertsch, J. (1984). *Culture, communication and cognition: Vygotskian perspectives.* Cambridge University Press.

Wertsch, J., & Sohmer, R. (1995). Vygotsky on learning and development. *Human Development, 38,* 332–337.

Werwach, A., Mürbe, D., Schaadt, G., & Männel, C. (2021). Infants' vocalizations at 6 months predict their productive vocabulary at one year. *Infant Behavior & Development, 64,* 101588.

Weyandt, L., Clarkin, C., Holding, E., May, S., Marraccini, M., Gudmundsdottir, B., Shepard, E., & Thompson, L. (2020). Neuroplasticity in children and adolescents in response to treatment intervention: A systematic review of the literature. *Clinical and Translational Neuroscience,* July-December, 1–20.

Xu, F. (2019). Towards a rational constructivist theory of cognitive development. *Psychological Review, 126*(6), 841–864.

Yu, C. (2014). Linking words to world: An embodiment perspective. *The Routledge handbook of embodied cognition.* Routledge.

Zeanah, C., & Humphreys, K. (2018). Child abuse and neglect. *Journal of the American Academy of Child & Adolescent Psychiatry, 57*(9), 637–644.

Chapter 6

Adamsons, K., & Johnson, S. (2013). An updated and expanded meta-analysis of nonresident fathering and child well-being. *Journal of Family Psychology, 27*(4), 589–599.

Ainsworth, M. D. (1967). *Infancy in Uganda: Infant care and the growth of love.* Johns Hopkins University Press.

Ainsworth, M., Blehar, M., Waters, E., & Wall, S. (1978). *Patterns of attachment: A psychological study of the strange situation.* Erlbaum.

Akhnikh, S., Engelberts, A., Sleuwen, B., Lhoir, M., & Benninga, M. (2014). The excessively crying infant: Etiology and treatment. *Pediatric Annals, 43,* e69–e75.

Albert, I., & Trommsdorff, G. (2014). The role of culture in social development over the lifespan: An interpersonal relations approach. *Online Readings in Psychology and Culture, 6*(2).

Ali, E. (2018). Women's experiences with postpartum anxiety disorders: A narrative literature review. *International Journal of Women's Health, 10,* 237–249.

Ashdown, B., & Faherty, A. (2020). *Parents and caregivers across cultures: Positive development from infancy through adulthood.* Springer.

Aunola, K., Tolvanen, A., Viljaranta, J., & Nurmi, J. (2013). Psychological control in daily parent–child interactions increases children's negative emotions. *Journal of Family Psychology, 27,* 453–462.

Baden, A. (2016). "Do you know your real parents?" and other adoption microaggressions, *Adoption Quarterly, 19*(1), 1–25.

Baker, B., & McGrath, J. (2011). Maternal-infant synchrony: An integrated review of the literature. *Neonatal, Pediatric & Child Health Nursing, 14*(3), 2–13.

Balakrishnan, A., Stephens, B., Burke, R., Yatchmink, Y., Alksninis, B., Tucker, R., Cavanaugha, E., Marc A., Collins, B., & Vohr, R. (2011). Impact of very low birth weight infants on the family at 3 months corrected age. *Early Human Development, 87,* 31–35.

Barn, R. (2013). 'Doing the right thing': Transracial adoption in the USA. *Ethnic and Racial Studies, 36*(8), 1273–1291.

Barrett, L., Lewis, M., & Haviland-Jones, J. (Eds.). (2016). *Handbook of emotions.* Guilford.

Bazhydai, M., Westermann, G., & Parise, E. (2020). "I don't know but I know who to ask:" 12-month-olds actively seek information from knowledgeable adults. *Developmental Science, 23*(5), 1–10.

Bee, H. L. (1992). *The developing child.* HarperCollins.

Bernard, J. (1970). Mildred Parten Newhall 1902–1970. *American Sociologist, 5*(4), 383.

Biddle, G., Garcia Nevares, A., Roundtree Henderson, W., & Valero-Kerrick, A. (2014). *Early childhood education: Becoming a professional.* Sage.

Bienfait, M., Maury, M., Haquet, A., Faillie, J., Franc, N., Combes, C., Daude, H., Picaud, J., Rideau, A., & Cambonie, G. (2011). Pertinence of the self-report mother-to-infant bonding scale in the neonatal unit of a maternity ward. *Early Human Development, 87*(4), 281–287.

Bilgin, A., & Wolke, D. (2020). Parental use of 'cry it out' in infants: No adverse effects on attachment and behavioural development at 18 months. *Journal of Child Psychology and Psychiatry, 61,* 1184–1193.

Boccia, M., & Campos, J. (1989). Maternal emotional signals, social referencing, and infants' reactions to strangers. *New Directions for Child Development, 44,* 25–49.

Boldt, L., Kochanska, G., & Jonas, K. (2017). Infant attachment moderates paths from early negativity to preadolescent outcomes for children and parents. *Child Development, 88,* 584–596.

Bornstein, M., Putnick, D., Gartstein, M., Hahn, C., Auestad, N., & O'Connor, D. (2015). Infant temperament: Stability by age, gender, birth order, term status, and socioeconomic status. *Child Development, 86,* 844–863.

Botha, E., Joronen, K., & Kaunonen, M. (2019). The consequences of having an excessively crying infant in the family: An integrative literature review. *Scandinavian Journal of Caring Science, 33*(4), 779–790.

Boundy, L., Cameron-Faulkner, T., & Theakston, A. (2016). Exploring early communicative behaviours: A fine-grained analysis of infant shows and gives. *Infant Behavior and Development, 44,* 86–97.

Bowlby, J. (1969). Attachment. *Attachment and loss* (Vol. 1). Penguin.

Bowlby, J. (1973). Separation: Anxiety and anger. *Attachment and loss.* (Vol. 2). Penguin.

Bradt, J. (2013). *Guidelines for music therapy practice in pediatric care.* Barcelona.

Branco, S. (2021). Relational–cultural theory: A supportive framework for transracial adoptive families. *The Family Journal.* https://doi.org/10.1177/10664807211028986

Bremner, J., & Wachs, T. (2010). *The Wiley-Blackwell handbook of infant development* (Vol. 1). Wiley-Blackwell.

Brenning, K., Soenens, B., Mabbe, E., & Vansteenkiste, M. (2019). Ups and downs in the joy of motherhood: Maternal well-being as a function of psychological needs, personality, and infant temperament. *Journal of Happiness Studies, 20,* 229–250.

Brenning, K., Soenens, B., & Vansteenkiste, M. (2015). What's your motivation to be pregnant? Examining relations between pregnant women's motives for having a child and their prenatal functioning. *Journal of Family Psychology, 29,* 755–765.

Brody, L., Hall, J., & Stokes, L. (2016). Gender and emotion: Theory, findings, and context. In L. Barret, M. Lewis, & J. Haviland-Jones (Eds.), *Handbook of emotions*. Guilford.

Brosseau-Liard, P., & Poulin-Dubois, D. (2014). Sensitivity to confidence cues increases during the second year of life. *Infancy, 19*, 461–475.

Brown, C., McMullen, M., & File, N. (2019). *The Wiley handbook of early childhood care and education*. Wiley-Blackwell.

Bruner, J., Jolly, A., & Sylva, K. (1976). *Play: Its role in development and evolution*. Basic Books.

Burtle, A., & Bezruchka, S. (2016). Population health and paid parental leave: What the United States can learn from two decades of research. *Healthcare, 4*(2), 30.

Buss, K., Pérez-Edgar, K., Vallorani, A., & Anaya, B. (2019). Emotion reactivity and regulation: A developmental model of links between temperament and personality. In D. McAdams, R. Shiner, & J. Tackett (Eds.), *Handbook of personality development*. Guilford.

Carmas, L., Fatani, S., Fraumeni, B,. & Shuster, M. (2016). The development of facial expressions: Current perspectives on infant emotions. In L. Barret, M. Lewis, & J. Haviland-Jones (Eds.), *Handbook of emotions*. Guilford.

Casalin, S., Luyten, P., Besser, A. Wouters, S., & Vliegen, N. (2014a). A longitudinal cross-lagged study of the role of parental self-criticism, dependency, depression, and parenting stress in the development of child negative affectivity. *Self and Identity, 13*, 491–511.

Casalin, S., Tang, E., Vliegen, N., & Luyten, P. (2014b). Parental personality, stress generation, and infant temperament in emergent parent-child relationships: Evidence for a moderated mediation model. *Journal of Social and Clinical Psychology, 33*, 270–291.

Cassidy, J., & Shaver, P. (2016). *Handbook of attachment: Theory, research, and clinical applications*. The Guilford.

Chen, J. (2019). Autism spectrum disorder. In C. Zeanah (Ed.), *Handbook of infant mental health*. The Guilford.

Chess, S., & Thomas, A. (1996). *Temperament theory and practice*. Brunner/Mazel.

Chess, S., & Thomas, A. (1999). *Goodness of fit*. Brunner-Routledge.

Clark, A., Kochanska, G., & Ready, R. (2000). Mothers' personality and its interaction with child temperament as predictors of parenting behavior. *Journal of Personality and Social Psychology, 79*(2), 274–285.

Crivello, C., Phillips, S., & Poulin-Dubois, D. (2018). Selective social learning in infancy: Looking for mechanisms. *Developmental Science, 21*, e12592.

Dalimonte-Merckling, D., & Brophy-Herb, H. (2018). A person-centered approach to child temperament and parenting, *Child Development, 90*(5), 1702–1717.

Davies, D., & M. Troy (2020). *Child development: A practitioner's guide*. Guilford.

Derman-Sparks, L., & LeeKeenan, D. (2015). *Leading anti-bias early childhood programs*. Teachers College Press.

Derman-Sparks, L., Edwards, J., Goins, C., & the National Association for the Education of Young Children (2020). *Anti-bias education for young children & ourselves*. National Association for the Education of Young Children.

Dickinson, C., Whittingham, K., Sheffield, J., Wotherspoon, J., & Boyd, R. (2020). Efficacy of interventions to improve psychological adjustment for parents of infants with or at risk of neurodevelopmental disability: A systematic review. *Infant Mental Health Journal, 41*(5), 697–722.

Dodwell, M. (2010). *The effects of postnatal separation on mother-infant interaction*. http://www.nct.org.uk/sites/ default/files/ related_documents/dodwell-effects-of-postnatal-separation-on-mother-infant-interaction-21-.pdf

Donahue, K., & Crassons, K. (2020). *Right from the start: A practical guide for helping young children with autism*. Rowman & Littlefield.

Dweck, C. (2017). From needs to goals and representations: Foundations for a unified theory of motivation, personality, and development. *Psychological Review, 124*(6), 689–719.

Edwards, J. (2011). *Music therapy and parent-infant bonding*. Oxford University Press.

Edwards, J. (2016). *The Oxford handbook of music therapy*. Oxford University Press.

Ellis, E., Yilanli, M., & Saadabadi, A. (2021). Reactive attachment disorder. StatPearls Publishing. https://www.ncbi.nlm.nih.gov/ books/NBK537155/

Enlow, M., Matthew, T., White, K., Cabrera, I., & Wright, R. (2016). The infant behavior questionnaire-revised: Factor structure in a culturally and socio-demographically diverse sample in the United States. *Infant Behavior and Development, 43*, 24–35.

Erikson, E. (1950). *Childhood and society*. Norton & Company.

Ettenberger, M., Bieleninik, L., Epstein, S., & Elefant, C. (2021). Defining attachment and bonding: Overlaps, differences and implications for music therapy clinical practice and research in the neonatal intensive care unit (NICU). *International Journal of Environmental Research and Public Health, 18*(4), 1733.

Fischer, A., & Manstead, A. (2016). Social functions of emotion and emotion regulation. In L. Barret, M. Lewis, & J. Haviland-Jones (Eds.), *Handbook of emotions*. Guilford.

Fong, R., & McRoy, R. (2016). *Transracial and intercountry adoptions: Cultural guidance for professionals*. Columbia University Press.

Freud, S. (1961). The ego and the id. In J. Strachey (Ed. & Trans.), *The standard edition of the complete psychological works of Sigmund Freud* (Vol. 19, pp. 3–66). Hogarth Press. (Original work published 1923)

Freund, J. (2018). Early temperament in parental report and scientific observation, *Early Child Development and Care, 189*(14), 2318–2333.

Ge, W., & Adesman, A. (2017). Grandparents raising grandchildren: A primer for pediatricians. *Current Opinion in Pediatrics, 29*(3), 379–384.

Geraci, A. (2020). How do toddlers evaluate defensive actions toward third parties? *Infancy, 25*(6), 910–926.

Gholampour, F., Madelon, M., Riem, M., & van den Heuvel, M. I. (2020). Maternal brain in the process of maternal-infant bonding: Review of the literature. *Social Neuroscience, 15*(4), 380–384.

Giannandrea, S., Cerulli, C., Anson, E., & Chaudron, L. (2013). Increased risk for postpartum psychiatric disorders among women with past pregnancy loss. *Journal of Women's Health, 22*(9), 760–768.

Ginsburg, K. (2007). The importance of play in promoting healthy child development and maintaining strong parent-child bonds. *Pediatrics, 119*(1), 181–192.

Gloeckler, L., Cassell, J., & Malkus, A. (2014). An analysis of teacher practices with toddlers during social conflicts. *Early Child Development and Care, 184*(5), 749–765.

Godon-Decoteau, D., & Ramsey, P. (2017). Positive and negative aspects of transracial adoption: An exploratory study from Korean transracial adoptees' perspectives. *Adoption Quarterly 21*(1), 17–40.

Goldsmith, H., Buss, A., Plomin, R., Rothbart, M., Thomas, A., Chess, S., Hinde, R., & McCall, R. (1987). What is temperament? Four approaches. *Child Development, 58*(2), 505–529.

Gonzalez, A., Jenkins, J., Steiner, M., & Fleming, A. (2012). Maternal early life experiences and parenting: The mediating role of cortisol and executive function. *Journal of the American Academy of Child & Adolescent Psychiatry, 51*(7), 673–682.

Gottman, J., & Gottman, J. (2008). *And baby makes three*. Crown/ Three Rivers Press.

Gross-Loh, C. (2013). *Parenting without borders: Surprising lessons parents around the world can teach us*. Avery.

Gross, R., & Humphreys, P. (1992). *Psychology: The science of mind and behaviour*. Hodder & Stoughton.

Grunberg, V., Geller, P., Bonacquisti, A., & Patterson, C. (2019). NICU infant health severity and family outcomes: A systematic review of assessments and findings in psychosocial research. *Journal of Perinatology, 39*, 156–172.

Hamilton, E., Samek, D., Keyes, M., McGue, M., & Iacono, W. (2015). Identity development in a transracial environment: Racial/ethnic minority adoptees in Minnesota, *Adoption Quarterly, 18*(3), 217–233.

Hamlin, J., & Wynn, K. (2011). Young infants prefer prosocial to antisocial others. *Cognitive Development, 26*(1), 30–39.

Hamlin, J., Mahajan, N., Liberman, Z., & Wynn, K. (2013). Not like me = bad: Infants prefer those who harm dissimilar others. *Psychological Science, 24*, 589–594.

Hammond, S., & Brownell, C. (2018). Happily unhelpful: Infants' everyday helping and its connections to early prosocial development. *Frontiers in Psychology, 9*, 1770.

Hannon, E., & Trehub, S. (2005). Tuning in to musical rhythms: Infants learn more readily than adults. *Proceedings of the National Academy of Sciences, 102*(35), 12639–12643.

Hanson, R., & Spratt, E. (2000). Reactive attachment disorder: What we know about the disorder and implications for treatment. *Child Maltreatment, 5*(2), 137–145.

Harris, P., Bartz, D., & Rowe, M. (2017). Young children communicate their ignorance and ask questions. *Proceedings of the National Academy of Sciences of the United States of America, 114*, 7884–7891.

Harris, P., Koenig, M., Corriveau, K., & Jaswal, V. (2018). Cognitive foundations of learning from testimony. *Annual Review of Psychology, 69*, 251–273.

Hasberry, A. (2019). Self-acceptance in Black and White. *Education Sciences 9*(2), 143.

Hassinger-Das, B., Toub, T., Zosh, J., Michnick, J., Golinkoff, R., & Hirsh-Pasek, K. (2017). More than just fun: A place for games in joyful learning. *Journal of the Study of Educational Development, 40*(2), 191–218.

Hay, D., Caplan, M., & Nash, A. (2018). *The beginnings of peer relations*. In W. Bukowski, B. Laursen, & K. Rubin (Eds.), *Handbook of peer interactions, relationships, and groups*. Guilford.

Hay, D., Nash, A., & J. Pedersen (1981). Responses of six-month-olds to the distress of their peers. *Child Development, 52*(3), 1071–1075.

Hay, D., Nash, A., & Pedersen, J. (1983). Interaction between six-month-old peers. *Child Development, 54*(3), 557–562.

Hayslip, B., Blumenthal, H., & Garner, A. (2014). Health and grandparent-grandchild well-being: One-year longitudinal findings for custodial grandfamilies. *Journal of Aging and Health, 26*, 559–582.

Hayslip, B., Blumenthal, H., & Garner, A. (2015). Social support and grandparent caregiver health: One-year longitudinal findings for grandparents raising their grandchildren. *The Journals of Gerontology, 70*, 804–812.

Hepach, R., & Warneken, F. (2018). Early development can reveal the foundation of human prosociality. *Current Opinion in Psychology, 20*, iv–viii.

Hertenstein, M. (2011). Social referencing. In S. Goldstein & J. Naglieri (Eds.), *Encyclopedia of child behavior and development*. Springer.

Hyman, S., Levy, S., & Myers, S. (2020). Identification, evaluation, and management of children with autism spectrum disorder. *Pediatrics, 145*(1), 2019–3447.

Johnson, K. (2013). Maternal–infant bonding: A review of literature. *International Journal of Childbirth Education, 28*, 17–22.

Josselson, R. (2019). The dialogic development of personality: Narrative, culture, and the study of lives. In D. McAdams, R. Shiner, & J. Tackett (Eds.), *Handbook of personality development*. Guilford.

Joy, P., Aston, M., Price, S., Sim, M., Ollivier, R., Benoit, B., Akbari-Nassaji, N., & Iduye, D. (2020). Blessings and curses: Exploring the experiences of new mothers during the COVID-19 pandemic. *Nursing Reports, 10*, 207–219.

Kaiser, B., & Rasminsky, J. (2019). Valuing diversity: Developing a deeper understanding of all young children's behavior. *Teaching Young Children, 13*(2). https://www.naeyc.org/resources/pubs/ tyc/dec2019/valuing-diversity-developing-understanding-behavior

Keating, D. (2011). *Nature and nurture in early child development*. Cambridge University Press.

Kerns, K., & Brumariu, L. (2014). Is insecure parent-child attachment a risk factor for the development of anxiety in childhood or adolescence? *Child Development Perspectives, 8*(1), 12–17.

Kim, P. (2020). How stress can influence brain adaptations to motherhood, *Frontiers in Neuroendocrinology, 60*, 10087510.

Kinsey, C., Baptiste-Roberts, K., Zhu, J., & Kjerulff, K. (2014). Birth-related, psychosocial, and emotional correlates of positive maternal–infant bonding in a cohort of first-time mothers. *Midwifery, 30*, e188–e194.

Kinsey, C., & Hupcey, J. (2013). State of the science of maternal–infant bonding: A principle-based concept analysis. *Midwifery, 29*, 1314–1320.

Kirchhoff, C., Desmarais, E., Putnam, S., & Gartstein, M. (2019). Similarities and differences between Western cultures: Toddler temperament and parent-child interactions in the United States (US) and Germany. *Infant Behavior & Development, 57*, 101366.

Kovacs, A., Tauzin, T., Teglas, E., Gergely, G., & Csibra, G. (2014). Pointing as epistemic request: 12-month-olds point to receive new information. *Infancy, 19*, 543–557.

Kramer, S. (2019). *US has world's highest rate of children living in single-parent households.* PEW Research Foundation. https://www.pewresearch.org/fact-tank/2019/12/12/u-s-children-more-likely-than-children-in-other-countries-to-live-with-just-one-parent/

Lally, J., & Mangione, P. (2017). Caring relationships: The heart of early brain development. *Young Children, 72*(2).

Lam, T., Chan, P., & Goh, L. (2019). Approach to infantile colic in primary care. *Singapore Medical Journal, 60*(1), 12–16.

La Paro, K., & Gloeckler, L. (2016). The context of child care for toddlers: The "experience expectable environment." *Early Childhood Education Journal, 44*(2), 147–153.

Leavitt, C., McDaniel, B., Maas, M., & Feinberg, M. (2017). Parenting stress and sexual satisfaction among first-time parents: A dyadic approach. *Sex Roles, 76*(5–6), 346–355.

Legerstee, M., Haley, D., & Bornstein, M. (2013). *The infant mind: Origins of the social brain.* Guilford.

Lehmann, S., Monette, S., Egger, H., Breivik, K., Young, D., Davidson, C., & Minnis, H. (2020). Development and examination of the reactive attachment disorder and disinhibited social engagement disorder assessment interview. *Assessment, 27*(4), 749–765.

Lengua, L., Gartstein, M., & Prinzie, P. (2019). Culture, context, and the development of traits. In D. McAdams, R. Shiner, & J. Tackett (Eds.), *Handbook of personality development.* Guilford.

Lerner, R., Easterbrooks, M., Mistry, J., & Weiner, I. (2013). Developmental psychology. *Handbook of psychology.* John Wiley & Sons.

LeVine, R., & LeVine, S. (2016). *Do parents matter?* Public Affairs.

Lewis, M. (2016). The emergence of human emotions. In L. Barret, M. Lewis, & J. Haviland-Jones (Eds.), *Handbook of emotions.* Guilford.

Lewis, S., & Abell, S. (2020). Autonomy versus shame and doubt. In V. Zeigler-Hill & T. Shackelford (Eds.), *Encyclopedia of personality and individual differences.* Springer.

Li, T., Chen, X., Mascaro, J., Haroon, E., & Rilling, J. (2017). Intranasal oxytocin, but not vasopressin, augments neural responses to toddlers in human fathers. *Hormones and Behavior, 93*, 193–202.

Li, T., Horta, M., Mascaro, J., Bijanki, K., Arnal, L., Adams, M., Barr, R., & Rilling, J. (2018). Explaining individual variation in paternal brain responses to infant cries. *Physiology & Behavior, 193*(Pt A), 43–54.

Lin, H., & Janice, J. (2020). Disengagement is as revealing as prosocial action for young children's responding to strangers in distress: How personal distress and empathic concern come into play. *International Journal of Behavioral Development, 44*(6), 515–524.

Lipkin, P., & Macias, M. (2020). Promoting optimal development: Identifying infants and young children with developmental disorders through developmental surveillance and screening. *Pediatrics, 145*(1), e20193449.

Lippard, C., & La Paro, K. (2018) Middle toddlerhood: Autonomy and peer awareness in the context of families and child care. In A. Morris & A. Williamson (Eds.), *Building early social and emotional relationships with infants and toddlers.* Springer.

Liu, C., Erdei, C., & Mittal, L. (2021). Risk factors for depression, anxiety, and PTSD symptoms in perinatal women during the COVID-19 pandemic. *Psychiatry Research, 295*, 113552.

Lucca, K., & Wilbourn, M. (2018). Communicating to learn: Infants' pointing gestures result in optimal learning. *Child Development, 89*, 941–960.

Mahajan, N., & Wynn, K. (2012). Origins of "us" versus "them:" Prelinguistic infants prefer similar others. *Cognition, 124*, 227–233.

Mariner, K. (2019). *Contingent kinship: The flows and futures of adoption in the United States.* University of California Press.

Martin, J., Hamilton, B., Osterman, M., & Driscoll, A. (2019). Births: Final data for 2018. *National Vital Statistics Reports, 68*(13). https://www.cdc.gov/nchs/data/nvsr/nvsr68_13-508.pdf

Mascaro, J., Hackett, P., Gouzoules, H., Lori, A., & Rilling, J. (2014). Behavioral and genetic correlates of the neural response to infant crying among human fathers. *Social Cognitive and Affective Neuroscience, 9*(11), 1704–1712.

Mayes, S., Calhoun, S., Waschbusch, D., & Baweja, R. (2017). Autism and reactive attachment/disinhibited social engagement disorders: Co-occurrence and differentiation. *Clinical Child Psychology and Psychiatry, 22*(4), 620–631.

McCubbin, H., & Figley, C. (2014). *Stress and the family: Coping with normative transitions.* Routledge.

McHale, J. (2007). *Charting the bumpy road of coparenthood: Understanding the challenges of family life.* Zero to Three Press.

McHale, J., Dinh, K., & Rao, N. (2014). Understanding co-parenting and family systems among East and Southeast Asian heritage families. In H. Selin (Ed.), *Parenting across cultures: Childrearing, motherhood and fatherhood in non-Western cultures.* Springer.

McKee, K. (2019*). Disrupting kinship: Transnational politics of Korean adoption in the United States.* University of Illinois Press.

McPherson, G. (2016). *The child as musician: A handbook of musical development.* Oxford University Press.

Meeussen, L., & Van Laar, C. (2018). Feeling pressure to be a perfect mother relates to parental burnout and career ambitions. *Frontiers in Psychology, 9*, 2113.

Mesquita, B., De Leersnyder, J., & Boiger, M. (2016). The cultural psychology of emotions. In L.Barret, M. Lewis, & J. Haviland-Jones (Eds.), *Handbook of emotions.* Guilford.

Mihelic, M., Morawska, A., & Filus, A. (2017). Effects of early parenting interventions on parents and infants: A meta-analytic review. *Journal of Child and Family Studies, 26*(6), 1507–1526.

Miller, P. (2016). *Theories of developmental psychology.* Worth, Macmillian Learning.

Mireault, G., Crockenberg, S., Sparrow, J., Pettinato, C., Woodard, K., & Malzac, K. (2014). Social looking, social referencing and humor perception in 6- and 12-month-old infants. *Infant Behavior & Development, 37*(4), 536–545.

Montgomery, J., & Jordan, N. (2018). Racial–ethnic socialization and transracial adoptee outcomes: A systematic research synthesis. *Child and Adolescent Social Work Journal, 35*(5), 439–458.

Montgomery, M., & Powell, I. (2018). *Saving international adoption: An argument from economics and personal experience.* Vanderbilt University Press.

Moon, R., & Task Force on Sudden Infant Death Syndrome (2016). SIDS and other sleep-related infant deaths: Evidence base for 2016 updated recommendations for a safe infant sleeping environment. *Pediatrics, 138*(5), e20153275.

National Association for the Education of Young Children (2020). *Professional standards and competencies for early childhood educators.* https://www.naeyc.org/resources/position-statements/professional-standards-competencies

Newman, H., & Henderson, A. (2014). The modern mystique: Institutional mediation of hegemonic motherhood. *Sociological Inquiry, 84,* 472–491.

Nimmo, J. (2015). Building anti-bias early childhood programs: The leader's role. *Young Children, 70,* 42–45.

Noocker-Ribaupierre, M. (2004). *Music therapy for premature and newborn infants.* Barcelona.

Norhayati, M., Hazlina, N., Asrenee, A., & Emilin, W. (2015). Magnitude and risk factors for postpartum symptoms: A literature review. *Journal of Affective Disorders, 175,* 34–52.

Norona, Z., & Tung, I. (2021). Developmental patterns of emotion regulation in toddlerhood: Examining predictors of change and long-term resilience. *Infant Mental Health Journal, 42*(1), 5–20.

Numan, M. (2020). *The parental brain: Mechanisms, development, and evolution.* Oxford University Press.

Palama, A., Malsert, J., & Gentaz, E. (2018). Are 6-month-old human infants able to transfer emotional information (happy or angry) from voices to faces? An eye-tracking study. *PLOS ONE, 13*(4), e0194579.

Parten, M. (1933). Leadership among preschool children. *Journal of Abnormal and Social Psychology, 27*(4), 430–440.

Partty, A., Kalliomaki, M., Salminen, S., & Isolauri, E. (2017). Infantile colic is associated with low-grade systemic inflammation. *Journal of Pediatric Gastroenterology and Nutrition, 64,* 691–695.

Passe, A. (2020). *Creating diversity-rich environments for young children.* Redleaf Press.

Paulus, M. (2018). The multidimensional nature of early prosocial behavior: A motivational perspective. *Current Opinion in Psychology, 20,* 111–116.

Perry, R., Blair, C., & Sullivan, R. (2017). Neurobiology of infant attachment: Attachment despite adversity and parental programming of emotionality. *Current Opinion in Psychology, 17,* 1–6.

Petts, R. (2018). Time off after childbirth and mothers' risk of depression, parenting stress, and parenting practices. *Journal of Family Issues, 39*(7), 1827–1854.

Planalp, E., & Goldsmith, H. (2020). Observed profiles of infant temperament stability, heritability, and associations with parenting. *Child Development, 91,* e563–e580.

Putnam, S., & Gartstein, M. (2017). Aggregate temperament scores from multiple countries: Associations with aggregate personality traits, cultural dimensions, and allelic frequency. *Journal of Research in Personality, 67,* 157–170.

Putnick, D., Sundaram, R., Bell, E., Ghassabian, A., Goldstein, R., Robinson, S., Vafai, Y., Gilman, S., & Yeung, E. (2020). Trajectories of maternal postpartum depressive symptoms. *Pediatrics, 146*(5), e20200857.

Rados, S., Marijana, M., Anđelinovic, M., Cartolovni, A., & Ayers, S. (2020). The role of posttraumatic stress and depression symptoms in mother-infant bonding. *Journal of Affective Disorders, 268,* 134–140.

Raleigh, E. (2018). *Selling transracial adoption families, markets, and the color line.* Temple University Press.

Ray, A. (2015). *Culture as the lens through which children learn best: Implications for policies to improve teaching.* BUILD Initiative & Center on Enhancing Early Learning Outcomes Conference Learning Table on State Policy to Improve Teaching and Children's Learning.

Reynolds, J., & Wing, H. (2020). Transracial adoption and transracial socialization: Clinical implications and recommendations. In E. Congress & M. Gonzalez (Eds.), *Multicultural perspectives in working with families: A handbook for the helping professions.* Springer.

Rilling, J. (2013). The neural and hormonal bases of human parental care. *Neuropsychologia, 51*(4), 731–747.

Rossen, L., Mattick, R., Wilson, J., Mattick, R., Clare, P., Burns, L., Allsop, S., Elliott, E., Jacobs, S., Olsson, C., & Hutchinson, D. (2019). Mother–infant bonding and emotional availability at 12-months of age: The role of early postnatal bonding, maternal substance use and mental health. *Maternal and Child Health Journal, 23,* 1686–1698.

Rousseau, S., Feldman, T., Harroy, L., Avisar, N., Wolf, M., Bador, K., & Frenkel, T. (2020). High emotionality to infant cry: Associations with adult attachment, gender, and age. *Early Child Development & Care, 190*(15), 2449–2458.

Rutherford, H., Maupin, A., Landi, N., Potenza, M., & Mayes, L. (2017). Parental reflective functioning and the neural correlates of processing infant affective cues. *Social Neuroscience, 12*(5), 519–529.

Saarni, C., Campos, J., Camras, L., & Witherington, D. (2006). Emotional development: Action, communication, and understanding. In W. Damon, R. Lerner, & N. Eisenberg (Eds.) *Handbook of child psychology. Social, emotional and personality development* (Vol. 3). Wiley.

Sadruddin, A., Ponguta, L., Zonderman, A., Wiley, K., Grimshaw, A.. & Panter-Brick, C. (2019). How do grandparents influence child health and development? A systematic review. *Social Science & Medicine, 239,* 112476.

Schore, Allan. (2015). *Affect regulation and the origin of the self.* Routledge.

Schmidt, N., Brooker, R., Carroll, I., Gagne, J., Luo, Z., Planalp, E., Sarkisian, K., Schmidt, C., Van Hulle, C., Lemery-Chalfant, K., & Goldsmith, H. (2019). Longitudinal research at the interface of affective neuroscience, developmental psychopathology, health and behavioral genetics: Findings from the Wisconsin twin project. *Twin Research and Human Genetics, 22*(4), 233–239.

Schwaba, T. (2019). Temperament and personality trait development in the family: Interactions and transactions with parenting from infancy through adolescence. In D. McAdams, R. Shiner, & J. Tackett (Eds.), *Handbook of personality development.* Guilford.

Scism, A., & Cobb, R. (2017). Integrative review of factors and interventions that influence early father–infant bonding. *Journal of Obstetric, Gynecologic & Neonatal Nursing, 46*(2), 163–170.

Senzaki, S., Shimizu, Y., & Calma-Birling, D. (2021). The development of temperament and maternal perception of child: A cross-cultural examination in the United States and Japan. *Personality and Individual Differences, 170*, 110407.

Sethna, V., Perry, E., Domoney, J., Iles, J., Psychogiou, L., Rowbotham, N., Stein, A., Murray, L., & Ramchandani, P. (2017). Father-child interactions at 3 months and 24 months contributions to children's cognitive development at 24 months. *Infant Mental Health Journal, 38*(3): 378–390.

Shapiro, A., Gottman, J., & Fink, B. (2015). Short-term change in couples' conflict following a transition to parenthood intervention. *Couple and Family Psychology: Research and Practice, 4*(4), 239–251.

Shigeto, A., & Voltaire, M. (2020). Role of the family in personality development. In V. Zeigler-Hill & T. Shackelford (Eds.), *Encyclopedia of personality and individual differences*. Springer.

Shiller, V. (2017). *The attachment bond: Affectional ties across the lifespan*. Lexington Books.

Shimizu, M., & Teti, D. M. (2018). Infant sleeping arrangements, Social criticism, and maternal distress in the first year. *Infant and Child Development, 27*(3), e2080.

Shiner, R., Buss, K., McClowry, S., Putnam, S., Saudino, K., & Zentner, M. (2012). What is temperament now? Assessing progress in temperament research on the twenty-fifth anniversary of Goldsmith. *Child Developmental Perspectives, 6*, 436–444.

Shorey, S., & Ang, L. (2019). Experiences, needs, and perceptions of paternal involvement during the first year after their infants' birth: A meta-synthesis. *PLOS One, 14*(1), e0210388.

Sosinsky, L., Ruprecht, K., Horm, D., Kriener-Althen, K., Vogel, C., & Halle, T. (2016). *Including relationship-based care practices in infant-toddler care: Implications for practice and policy*. Brief prepared for the Office of Planning, Research & Evaluation, Administration for Children and Families, U.S. Department of Health and Human Services. http://www.acf.hhs.gov/sites/default/files/opre/nitr_inquire_may_2016_070616_b508compliant.pdf

Soussignan, R., Dollion, N., Schaal, B., Durand, K., Reissland N., & Baudouin, J. (2018). Mimicking emotions: How 3–12-month-old infants use the facial expressions and eyes of a model. *Cognition and Emotion, 32*(4), 827–842.

St. James-Roberts, I., Alvarez, M., & Hovish, K. (2013). Emergence of a developmental explanation for prolonged crying in 1- to 4-month-old infants: Review of the evidence. *Journal of Pediatric Gastroenterology and Nutrition, 57*, S30–S36.

Stanford Children's Health (2020). *Your child's social and emotional development*. https://www.stanfordchildrens.org/en/topic/default?id=your-childs-social-and-emotional-development-1–4521

Steinfeld, M. (2020). *Bonding is essential for normal infant development*. UC Davis Health Medical Center. https://health.ucdavis.edu/medicalcenter/healthtips/20100114_infant-bonding.html

Sullivan, R., Perry, R., Sloan, A., Kleinhaus, K., & Burtchen, N. (2011). Infant bonding and attachment to the caregiver: Insights from basic and clinical science. *Clinics in Perinatology, 38*(4), 643–655.

Super, C., Harkness, S., Bonichini, S., Welles, B., Zylicz, P., Bermúdez, M., & Palacios, J. (2020). Developmental continuity and change in the cultural construction of the "difficult child": A study in six western cultures. *New Directions for Child and Adolescent Development, 170*, 43–68.

Tafuri, J., Welch, G., & Hawkins, E. (2008). *Infant musicality: New research for educators and parents*. Ashgate.

Tang, A., Crawford, H., Morales, S., Degnan, K., Pine, D., & Fox, N. (2020). Infant behavioral inhibition predicts personality and social outcomes three decades later. *Proceedings of the National Academy of Sciences, 117*(18), 9800–9807.

Thomas, A., & Chess, S. (1977). *Temperament and development*. Brunner/Mazel.

Tichelman, E., Westerneng, M., Witteveen, A., van Baar, A., van der Horst, H., de Jonge, A., Berger, M., Schellevis, F., Burger, H., & Peters, L. (2019). Correlates of prenatal and postnatal mother-to-infant bonding quality: A systematic review. *PLOS ONE, 14*(9), e0222998.

Toub, T., Rajan, V., Golinkoff, R., & Hirsh-Pasek, K. (2016). Playful learning: A solution to the play versus learning dichotomy. In D. Berch & D. Geary (Eds.), *Evolutionary perspectives on education and child development*. Springer.

Trawick-Smith, J. (2018). *Early childhood development: A multicultural perspective*. Pearson Education.

Trehub, S. (2010). In the beginning: A brief history of infant music perception. *Music Science. Musicae Scientiae, 14*(2), 71–87.

Treyvaud, K., Doyle, L., Lee, K., Roberts, G., Cheong, J., Inder, T., & Anderson, P. (2013). Family functioning, burden and parenting stress 2 years after very preterm birth. *Early Human Development, 87*, 427–431.

Ursache, A., Blair, C., Stifter, C., & Voegtline, K. (2012). Emotional reactivity and regulation in infancy interact to predict executive functioning in early childhood. *Developmental Psychology, 49*(1), 127–137.

US Centers for Disease Control (2020). *CDC's Developmental Milestones*. US Department of Health and Human Services. https://www.cdc.gov/ncbddd/actearly/milestones/index.html

US Department of Health and Human Services (2020). *Supporting transracial and transcultural adoptive families*. https://www.childwelfare.gov/topics/adoption/adoptive/family-type/diversefamilies/

Van Aken, C., Junger, M., Verhoeven, M., van Aken, M., & Dekovic, M. (2007). The interactive effects of temperament and maternal parenting on toddlers' externalizing behaviors. *Infant & Child Development, 16*(5), 553–572.

Walden, T., & Baxter, A. (1989). The effect of context and age on social referencing. *Child Development, 60*(6), 1511–1518.

Walden, T., & Ogan, T. (1988). The development of social referencing. *Child Development, 59*(5), 1230–1240.

Waugh, W., & Brownell, C. (2017). "Help yourself!" What can toddlers' helping failures tell us about the development of prosocial behavior? *Infancy, 22*(5), 665–680.

Weber, A., Fernald, A., & Diop, Y. (2017). When cultural norms discourage talking to babies: Effectiveness of a parenting program in rural Senegal. *Child Development, 88*(5), 1513–1526.

Weisberg, D., Hirsh-Pasek, K., Golinkoff, R., Kittredge, A., & Klahr, D. (2016). Guided play: Principles and practices. *Current Directions in Psychological Science, 25*(3), 177–182.

Witherington, D., & Crichton, J. (2007). Frameworks for understanding emotions and their development: Functionalist and dynamic systems approaches. *Emotion, 7*, 628–637.

Wittig, S., & Rodriguez, C. (2019). Emerging behavior problems: Bidirectional relations between maternal and paternal parenting styles with infant temperament. *Developmental Psychology, 55*(6), 1199–1210.

Wittmer, D., & Honig, A. (2020). *Day to day the relationship way: Creating responsive programs for infants and toddlers.* National Association for the Education of Young Children.

Wittmer, D., & Petersen, S. (2017). *Infant and toddler development and responsive program planning: A relationship-based approach.* Pearson.

Wolke, D., Bilgin, A., & Samara, M. (2017). Systematic review and meta-analysis: Fussing and crying durations and prevalence of colic in infants. *Journal of Pediatrics, 185*, 55–61.

Wong, P., Skoe, E., Russo, N., Dees, T., & Kraus, N. (2007). Musical experience shapes human brainstem encoding of linguistic pitch patterns. *Nature Neuroscience, 10*(4), 420–422.

Yogman, M., Garner, A., Hutchinson, J., Hirsh-Pasek, K., & Golinkoff, R. (2018). The power of play: A pediatric role in enhancing development in young children. Committee on the Psychological Aspects of Child and Family Health, Council on Communications and Media. *Pediatrics, 142*(3), e20182058.

Zeanah, C., & Gleason, M. (2015). Annual research review: Attachment disorders in early childhood: Clinical presentation, causes, correlates, and treatment. *Journal of Child Psychology and Psychiatry, and Allied Disciplines, 56*(3), 207–222.

Zeegers, M., Colonnesi, C., Stams, G., & Meins, E. (2017). Mind matters: A meta-analysis on parental mentalization and sensitivity as predictors of infant–parent attachment. *Psychological Bulletin, 143*(12), 1245–1272.

Zeevenhooven, J., Browne, P., L'Hoir, M., de Weerth, C., & Benninga, M. (2018). Infant colic: Mechanisms and management. *Nature Reviews Gastroenterology & Hepatology, 15*, 479–496.

Zhao, T., & Kuhl, P. (2016). Musical intervention enhances infants' neural processing of temporal structure in music and speech. *Proceedings of the National Academy of Sciences, 113*, 5212–5217.

Zwaigenbaum, L., Bauman, M., Fein, D., Pierce, K., Buie, T., Davis, P., Newschaffer, C., Robins, D., Wetherby, A., Choueiri, R., Kasari, C., Stone, W., Yirmiya, N., Estes, A., Hansen, R., McPartland, J., Natowicz, M., Carter, A., Granpeesheh, D., Mailloux, Z., Smith, S., & Wagner, R. (2015). Early screening of autism spectrum disorder: Recommendations for practice and research. *Pediatrics, 136*(Supplement 1), S41–S59.

Chapter 7

Abramson, B., Thomas, J., Safir, P., & American Health Lawyers Association (2018). *Vaccine, vaccination, and immunization law.* American Health Lawyers Association.

American Academy of Child and Adolescent Psychiatry (2014). *Firearms and children*, 37. https://www.aacap.org/AACAP/Families_and_Youth/Facts_for_Families/FFF-Guide/Children-And-Firearms-037.aspx

American Academy of Pediatrics (2014). *Caring for your baby and young child: Birth to age 5.* Bantam.

American Academy of Pediatrics (2017). *10 common childhood illnesses and their treatments.* https://www.healthychildren.org/English/health-issues/conditions/treatments/Pages/10-Common-Childhood-Illnesses-and-Their-Treatments.aspx

American Academy of Pediatrics (2018). *AAP schedule of well-child care visits.* https://www.healthychildren.org/English/family-life/health-management/Pages/Well-Child-Care-A-Check-Up-for-Success.aspx

American Academy of Pediatrics (2020). *Safety for your child: 5 years.* https://www.healthychildren.org/English/ages-stages/preschool/Pages/Safety-for-Your-Child-5-Years.aspx

Armour, J., Davison, A., & McManus, I. (2014). Genome-wide association study of handedness excludes simple genetic models. *Heredity, 112*(3), 221–225.

Athanasiadou, A., Buitelaar, J., Brovedani, P., Chorna, O., Fulceri, F., Guzzetta, A., & Scattoni, M. (2020). Early motor signs of attention-deficit hyperactivity disorder: A systematic review. *European Child & Adolescent Psychiatry, 29*(7), 903–916.

Augustine, J., Crosnoe, R., & Gordon, R. (2013). Early child care and illness among preschoolers. *Journal of Health and Social Behavior, 54*(3), 315–334.

Bandura A. (1986). Observational learning. In A. Bandura (Ed.), *Social foundations of thought and action: A social cognitive theory.* Prentice-Hall.

Barkovich, A., & Raybaud, C. (2019). *Pediatric neuroimaging.* Wolters Kluwer.

Barnett, L., Morgan, P., van Beurden, E., & Beard, J. (2008). Perceived sports competence mediates the relationship between childhood motor skill proficiency and adolescent physical activity and fitness: A longitudinal assessment. *The International Journal of Behavioral Nutrition and Physical Activity, 5*(1), 40.

Barnett, L., van Beurden, E., Morgan, P., Brooks, L., & Beard, J. (2009). Childhood motor skill proficiency as a predictor of adolescent physical activity. *Journal of Adolescent Health, 44*(3), 252–259.

Bick, J., & Nelson, C. (2016). Early adverse experiences and the developing brain. *Neuropsychopharmacology, 41*, 177–196.

Birch, L., Burns, A., Parker, L., & Institute of Medicine Committee on Obesity Prevention Policies for Young Children (2011). *Early childhood obesity prevention policies.* National Academies Press.

Birken, C., & Hamilton, J. (2014). Obesity in a young child. *CMAJ: Canadian Medical Association Journal, 186*(6), 443–444.

Blair, C., & Raver, C. (2015). School readiness and self-regulation: A developmental psychobiological approach. *Annual Review of Psychology, 66*, 711–731.

Bleich, S., & Vercammen, K. (2018). The negative impact of sugar-sweetened beverages on children's health: An update of the literature. *BMC Obesity, 5*(1).

Boyden, S., Pott, M., & Starks, P. (2018). An evolutionary perspective on night terrors. *Evolution, Medicine, and Public Health*, 2018(1), 100–105.

Bradlee, M., Singer, M., Qureshi, M., & Moore, L. (2010). Food group intake and central obesity among children and adolescents in the third national health and nutrition examination survey (NHANES III). *Public Health Nutrition, 13*(6), 797–805.

Brazelton, T. (1962). A child-oriented approach to toilet training. *Pediatrics, 29*, 121–128.

Brillante, P., & Nemeth, K. (2018). *Universal design for learning in the early childhood classroom: Teaching children of all languages, cultures and abilities, Birth–8 years.* Routledge.

Brough, H., Nadeau, K., Sindher, S., Alkotob, S., Chan, S., Bahnson, H., Leung, D., & Lack, G. (2020). Epicutaneous sensitization in the development of food allergy: What is the evidence and how can this be prevented? *Allergy, 75*(9), 2185–2205.

Bryce, I., Robinson, Y., & Petherick, W. (2019). *Child abuse and neglect: Forensic issues in evidence, impact and management.* Academic Press.

Campbell, K., & Hesketh, K. (2007). Strategies which aim to positively impact on weight, physical activity, diet and sedentary behaviors in children from zero to five years: A systematic review of the literature. *Obesity Review, 8*(4), 327–338.

Canadian Pediatric Society (2000). Toilet learning: Anticipatory guidance with a child-oriented approach. *Pediatrics & Child Health, 5*(6), 333–335.

Carlson, A., Rowe, E., & Curby, T. (2013). Disentangling fine motor skills'relation to academic achievement: The differential impact of visual-spatial integration and visual motor coordination. *Journal of Genetic Psychology, 175,* 514–533.

Carlson, S., & Neuberger, Z. (2015). *WIC works: Addressing the nutrition and health needs of low-income families for 40 years.* Center on Budget and Policy Priorities. https://www.cbpp.org/research/food-assistance/wic-works-addressing-the-nutrition-and-health-needs-of-low-income-families

Carrioon, V. (2019). *Assessing and treating youth exposed to traumatic stress.* American Psychiatric Association Publishing.

Carroll, W., & Bandura, A. (1990). Representational guidance of action production in observational learning: A causal analysis. *Journal of Motor Behavior, 22,* 85–97.

Chang, S., & Kim, K. (2017). A review of factors limiting physical activity among young children from low-income families. *Journal of Exercise Rehabilitation, 13*(4), 375–377.

Chen, C., Ahlqvist, V., Henriksson, P., Magnusson, C., & Berglind, D. (2020). Preschool environment and preschool teacher's physical activity and their association with children's activity levels at preschool. *PLOS ONE, 15*(10), 1–16.

Cheyne, D., Jobst, C., Tesan, G., Crain, S., & Johnson, B. (2014). Movement-related neuromagnetic fields in preschool age children. *Human Brain Mapping, 35*(9), 4858–4875.

Chi, D. (2017). *Evidence-based pediatric dentistry.* Elsevier.

Choi, E., Lee, J., & Hwang, J. (2018). Fruit and vegetable intakes in relation to behavioral outcomes associated with a nutrition education intervention in preschoolers. *Nutrition Research and Practice, 12,* 521–526.

Cicchetti, D., Hetzel, S., Rogosch, F., Handley, E., & Toth, S. (2016). An investigation of child maltreatment and epigenetic mechanisms of mental and physical health risk. *Development and Psychopathology, 28,* 1305–1317.

Coleman-Jensen, A. (2018). *Household food security in the United States in 2017.* US Department of Agriculture. Economic Research Report Number 256. https://www.ers.usda.gov/webdocs/publications/90023/err-256.pdf?v=0

Conkbayir, M. (2017). *Early childhood and neuroscience: Theory, research and implications for practice.* Bloomsbury Academic.

Cook, C., Howard, S., Scerif, G., Twine, R., Kahn, K., Norris, S., & Draper, C. (2019). Associations of physical activity and gross motor skills with executive function in preschool children from low-income South African settings. *Developmental Science, 22,* e12820.

Cooper, C., & Contento, I. (2019). Urban preschool teachers' nutrition beliefs, mealtime practices, and associations with training. *Journal of Nutrition Education and Behavior, 51*(9), 1047–1057.

Cross, D., Fani, N., Powers, A., & Bradley, B. (2017). Neurobiological development in the context of childhood trauma. *Clinical Psychology, 24*(2), 111–124.

Crowe-White, K., O'Neil, C., Parrott, J., Benson-Davies, S., Droke, E., Gutschall, M., Stote, K., Wolfram, T., & Ziegler, P. (2016). Impact of 100% fruit juice consumption on diet and weight status of children: An evidence-based review. *Critical Reviews in Food Science and Nutrition, 56*(5), 871–884.

Custovic, A. (2015). To what extent is allergen exposure a risk factor for the development of allergic disease? *Clinical & Experimental Allergy, 45,* 54–62.

Danese, A., & Lewis, S. (2017). Psychoneuroimmunology of early-life stress: The hidden wounds of childhood trauma? *Neuropsychopharmacology, 42*(1), 99–114.

Darragh, J. (2007). Universal design for early childhood education: Ensuring access and equity for all. *Early Childhood Education Journal, 35,* 167–171.

Dekaban, A. S. (1978). Changes in brain weights during the span of human life: Relation of brain weights to body heights and body weights. *Annals of Neurology, 4*(4), 345–356.

de Kovel, C., & Francks, C. (2019). The molecular genetics of hand preference revisited. *Scientific Reports, 9*(1), 5986.

DeLay, D., Hanish, L., Martin, C., & R. Fabes, R. (2016). Peer effects on head start children's preschool competency. *Developmental Psychology, 52*(1), 58.

Derman-Sparks, L., Edwards, J., Goins, C., & the National Association for the Education of Young Children (2020). *Anti-bias education for young children & ourselves.* National Association for the Education of Young Children.

Dinnebeil, L., Boat, M., & Bae, Y. (2013). Integrating principles of universal design into the early childhood curriculum. *Dimensions Early Child, 41,* 3–14.

Dooley, D., Moultrie, N., Heckman, B., Gansky, S., Potter, M., & Walsh, M. (2016). Oral health prevention and toddler well-child care: Routine integration in a safety net system. *Pediatrics, 137*(1).

Dosman, C. F., Andrews, D., & Goulden, K. J. (2012). Evidence-based milestone ages as a framework for developmental surveillance. *Pediatrics & Child Health, 17*(10), 561–568.

Doyle, C., & Cicchetti, D. (2017). From the cradle to the grave: The effect of adverse caregiving environments on attachment and relationships throughout the lifespan. *Clinical Psychology: Science and Practice, 24*(2), 203–217.

Draper, N., & Stratton, G. (2019). *Physical activity: A multi-disciplinary introduction.* Routledge.

Drummond, M. (2020). *Boys' bodies: Sport, health and physical activity.* Palgrave Macmillan.

Eilender, E. (2016). *Nutrition throughout the lifecycle.* Momentum Press.

Erdman, S., Colker, Laura J., & Winter, E. (2020). *Trauma & young children: Teaching strategies to support & empower.* The National Association for the Education of Young Children.

Fagard, J., & Lockman, J. (2005). The effect of task constraints on infants' (bi)manual strategy for grasping and exploring objects. *Infant Behavior and Development, 28*(3), 305–315.

Faigenbaum, A., Lloyd, R., Oliver, J., & American College of Sports Medicine (2020). *Essentials of youth fitness*. Human Kinetics.

Faurie, C., & Raymond, M. (2004). Handedness frequency over more than ten thousand years. *Proceedings of the Royal Society B: Biological Sciences, 271*, S43– S45.

Feldman, R. (2017). *Development across the life span*. Pearson.

Fernandes, R., & Zanesco, A. (2010). Early physical activity promotes lower prevalence of chronic diseases in adulthood. *Hypertension Research, 33*, 926–931.

Fliers, E., Vasquez, A., Poelmans, G., Rommelse, N., Altink, M., & Buschgens, C. (2012). Genome-wide association study of motor coordination problems in ADHD identifies genes for brain and muscle function. *The World Journal of Biological Psychiatry, 3*, 211–222.

Flores, M. (2008). Universal design in elementary and middle school: Designing classrooms and instructional practices to ensure access to learning for all students. *Childhood Education, 84*(4).

Fowler, K., Dahlberg, L., Haileyesus, T., Gutierrez, C., & Bacon, S. (2017). Childhood firearm injuries in the United States. *Pediatrics, 140*(1).

Fox, M., Condon, R., Briefel, K., & Deming, D. (2010). Food consumption patterns of young preschoolers: Are they starting off on the right path? *Journal of the American Dietetic Association, 110*(12), S52–S59.

Frank, G. (2008). Changes in women, infants, and children (WIC) food packages: An opportunity to address obesity. *Obesity Management, 4*(6), 333–337.

Frenkel, H., Tandon, P., Frumkin, H., & Vander Stoep, A. (2019). Illnesses and injuries at nature preschools. *Environment & Behavior, 51*(8), 936–965.

Ginsburg, K. (2007). The importance of play in promoting healthy child development and maintaining strong parent-child bonds. *Pediatrics, 119*(1), 182–191.

Goddard, C., Broadley, K., & Hunt, S. (2017). Children's services. In L. Dixon, D. Perkins, C. Hamilton-Giachritsis, & L. Craig (Eds.). *The Wiley handbook of what works in child maltreatment: An evidence-based approach to assessment and intervention in child protection*. Wiley-Blackwell.

Godoy, L., Frankfurter, C., Cooper, M., Lay, C., Maunder, R., & Farkouh, M. (2020). Association of adverse childhood experiences with cardiovascular disease later in life: A review. *JAMA Cardiology, 6*(2), 228–235.

Grant, D., & Rutner, S. (2004). The effect of bicycle helmet legislation on bicycling fatalities. *Journal of Policy Analysis and Management, 23*(3), 595–611.

Graziano, A. (2017). *Behavior therapy with children*. Routledge.

Gregory, A. (2018). *Nodding off: The science of sleep from cradle to grave*. Bloomsbury Sigma.

Grimm, K., Kim, S., Yaroch, A., & Scanlon, K. (2014). Fruit and vegetable intake during infancy and early childhood. *Pediatrics, 134*(Supplement 1), S63–S69.

Grissmer, D., Grimm, K., Aiyer, S., Murrah, W., & Steele, J. (2010). Fine motor skills and early comprehension of the world: Two new school readiness indicators. *Developmental Psychology, 46*, 1008–1017.

Gross-Loh, C. (2013). *Parenting without borders: Surprising lessons parents around the world can teach us*. Avery.

Gupta, N., Vujicic, M., Yarbrough, C., & Harrison, B. (2018). Disparities in untreated caries among children and adults in the US, 2011–2014. *BMC Oral Health, 18*, 30.

Hackman, D., & Farah, M. (2009). Socioeconomic status and the developing brain. *Trends in Cognitive Sciences, 13*, 65–73.

Haga, M. (2009). Physical fitness in children with high motor competence is different from that in children with low motor competence. *Physical Therapy, 89*(10), 1089–1097.

Hales, C., Fryar, C., Carroll, M., Freedman, D., & Ogden, C. (2018). Trends in obesity and severe obesity prevalence in US youth and adults by sex and age, 2007–2008 to 2015–2016. *JAMA, 319*(16), 1723–1725.

Hamilton-Giachritsis, C., & Pellai, A. (2017). Child abuse and neglect. In L. Dixon, D. Perkins, C. Hamilton-Giachritsis, & L. Craig (Eds.), *The Wiley handbook of what works in child maltreatment: An evidence-based approach to assessment and intervention in child protection*. Wiley-Blackwell.

Harvard University Center on the Developing Child (2007). *The Science of Early Childhood Development (InBrief)*. www.developingchild.harvard.edu

Hashikawa, A., Newton, M., Cunningham, R., & Stevens, M. (2015). Unintentional injuries in child care centers in the United States: A systematic review. *Journal of Child Health Care, 19*, 93–105.

Hassink, S. (2014). *Pediatric obesity: Prevention, intervention, and treatment strategies for primary care*. American Academy of Pediatrics.

Haugen, T., & Johansen, B. (2018). Difference in physical fitness in children with initially high and low gross motor competence: A ten-year follow-up study. *Human Movement Science, 62*, 143–149.

Hay, W. (2020). *Current diagnosis & treatment: Pediatrics*. McGraw-Hill Medical.

Haywood, K., & Getchell, N. (2020). *Life span motor development*. Human Kinetics.

Heinrichs-Graham, E., & Wilson, T. (2015). Coding complexity in the human motor circuit. *Human Brain Mapping, 36*(12), 5155–5167.

Hines, C., Markowitz, A., & Johnson, A. (2021). Food insecurity: What are its effects, why, and what can policy do about it? *Policy Insights from the Behavioral and Brain Sciences, 8*(2), 127–135.

Holman, D., Ports, K., Buchanan, N., Hawkins, N., Merrick, M., & Trivers, K. (2016). The association between adverse childhood experiences and risk for cancer in adulthood: A systematic review of the literature. *Pediatrics*, S81–S91.

Houwen, S., Kamphorst, E., van der Veer, G., & Cantell, M. (2021). The degree of stability in motor performance in preschool children and its association with child-related variables. *Human Movement Science, 75*.

Hutchings, J. (2019). *The positive parenting handbook: Developing happy and confident children*. Routledge.

Ierodiakonou, D., Garcia-Larsen, V., Logan, A., Groome, A., Cunha, S., Chivinge, J., Robinson, Z., Geoghegan, N., Jarrold, K., Reeves, T., Tagiyeva-Milne, N., Nurmatov, U., Trivella, M., Leonardi-Bee, & Boyle, R. (2016). Timing of allergenic food introduction to the infant diet and risk of allergic or autoimmune disease: A systematic review and meta-analysis. *JAMA, 316*, 1181–1192.

Isong, A., Rao, S., Bind, M., Avenda, M., Kawachi, I., & Richmond, T. (2018). *Obesity: Stigma, trends, and interventions.* American Academy of Pediatrics.

James, K. (2010). Sensori-motor experience leads to changes in visual processing in the developing brain. *Developmental Science, 13,* 279–288.

Johnson, B., Jobst, C., Al-Loos, R., He, W., & Cheyne, D. (2020). Individual differences in motor development during early childhood: An MEG study. *Developmental Science, 23,* e12935.

Johnson, C., & Campbell, J. (2016). *Sleep monsters and superheroes: Empowering children through creative dreamplay.* Praeger.

Johnson, S. (2016). Developmental and environmental influences on young children's vegetable preferences and consumption. *Advances in Nutrition, 7*(1), 220S–231S.

Johnston, D., Nicholls, M. E., Shah, M., & Shields, M. A. (2009). Nature's experiment? Handedness and early childhood development. *Demography, 46*(2), 281–301.

Justice, L., Petscher, Y., Schatschneider, C., & Mashburn, A. (2011). Peer effects in preschool classrooms: Is children's language growth associated with their classmates' skills? *Child Development, 82*(6), 1768–1777.

Kaderavek, J. (2009). Perspectives from the field of early childhood special education. *Language, Speech & Hearing Services in Schools, 40*(4), 403–405.

Kaiser, M., Schoemaker, M., Albaret, J., & Geuze, R. (2015). What is the evidence of impaired motor skills and motor control among children with attention deficit hyperactivity disorder (ADHD)? Systematic review of the literature. *Research in Developmental Disabilities, 36*(C), 338–357.

Kang, L., Hsieh, M., Liao, L., & Hwang, A. (2017). Environmental barriers to participation of preschool children with and without physical disabilities. *International Journal of Environmental Research and Public Health, 14*(5), 518.

Keech, J., Hatzis, D., Kavanagh, D., White, K., & Hamilton, K. (2018). Parents' role constructions for facilitating physical activity-related behaviours in their young children. *Australian Journal of Psychology, 70*(3), 246–257.

Kiddoo, D. (2012). Toilet training children: When to start and how to train. *CMAJ: Canadian Medical Association Journal, 184*(5), 511–512.

Kim, J., Kim, G., Park, J., Wang, Y., & Lim, H. (2019). Effectiveness of teacher-led nutritional lessons in altering dietary habits and nutritional status in preschool children: Adoption of a NASA mission X-based program. *Nutrients, 11,* 1590.

Kirkpatrick, S., McIntyre, L., & Potestio, M. (2010). Child hunger and long-term adverse consequences for health. *Archives of Pediatrics & Adolescent Medicine, 164*(8), 754–762.

Klass, P. (2020). *A good time to be born: How science and public health gave children a future.* Norton.

Kliegman, R., Stanton, B., St. Geme, J., Schor, N., Behrman, R., & Nelson, W. (2020). *Nelson textbook of pediatrics.* Elsevier.

Koch, G. (2017). *Pediatric dentistry: A clinical approach.* Wiley-Blackwell.

Kokstein, J., Musalek, M., & Tufano, J. (2017). Are sex differences in fundamental motor skills uniform throughout the entire preschool period? *PLOS ONE, 12*(4), e0176556.

Kraemer, J. (2016). Bicycle helmet laws and persistent racial and ethnic helmet use disparities among urban high school students: A repeated cross-sectional analysis. *Injury Epidemiology, 3*(1), 21.

Kramer, P., Hinojosa, J., & Howe, T. (2020). *Frames of reference for pediatric occupational therapy.* Wolters Kluwer.

Landrigan, P., & Landrigan, M. (2018). *Children and environmental toxins: What everyone needs to know.* Oxford University Press.

Laraque-Arena, D., & Stanton, B. (2019). *Principles of global child health: Education and research.* American Academy of Pediatrics.

Larimore, R. (2016). Defining nature-based preschools. *The International Journal of Early Childhood Environmental Education, 4*(1), 32. https://dimensionsfoundation.org/wp-content/uploads/2016/10/IJECEE-41-Complete-Issue.pdf

Leigh, S. (2004). Brain growth, life history, and cognition in primate and human evolution. *American Journal of Primatology, 62*(3), 139–164.

Leung, A., Leung, A., Wong, A., & Hon, K. (2020). Sleep terrors: An updated review. *Current Pediatric Reviews, 16*(3), 176–182.

Levy, B., Wegman, D., Baron, S., Sokas, Rosemary. K., & McStowe, H. (2018). *Occupational and environmental health: Recognizing and preventing disease and injury.* Oxford University Press.

Lindsay, A., Greaney, M., Wallington, S., Mesa, T., & Salas, C. (2017). A review of early influences on physical activity and sedentary behaviors of preschool-age children in high-income countries. *Journal for Specialists in Pediatric Nursing, 22*(3), 101–111.

Lubans, D., Morgan, P., Cliff, D., Barnett, L., & Okely, A. (2010). Fundamental movement skills in children and adolescents: Review of associated health benefits. *Sports Medicine, 40*(12), 1019–1035.

Maaks, D., Starr, N., Brady, M., Gaylord, N., Driessnack, M., & Duderstadt, K. (2020). *Burns' pediatric primary care.* Elsevier.

MacQuarrie, S., Nugent, C., & Warden, C. (2015). Learning with nature and learning from others: Nature as setting and resource for early childhood education. *Journal of Adventure Education and Outdoor Learning, 15*(1), 1–23.

Manduca, R. (2018). Income inequality and the persistence of racial economic disparities. *Sociological Science, 5,* 8.

Matwiejczyk, L., Mehta, K., Scott, J., Tonkin, E., & Coveney, J. (2018). Characteristics of effective interventions promoting healthy eating for pre-schoolers in childcare settings: An umbrella review. *Nutrients, 10,* 293.

McCrory, E., Palmer, A., & Puetz, V. (2017). The neurobiology and genetics of childhood maltreatment. In L. Dixon, D. Perkins, C. Hamilton-Giachritsis, & L. Craig (Eds.). *The Wiley handbook of what works in child maltreatment: An evidence-based approach to assessment and intervention in child protection.* Wiley-Blackwell.

McHale, S., King, V., & Buxton, O. (2017). *Family contexts of sleep and health across the life course.* Springer.

McLeod, K., Langevin, L., Goodyear, B., & Dewey, D. (2014). Functional connectivity of neural motor networks is disrupted in children with developmental coordination disorder and attention-deficit/hyperactivity disorder. *NeuroImage: Clinical, 4,* 566–575.

Merrick, M., Ford, D., Ports, K., & Guinn, A. (2018). Prevalence of adverse childhood experiences from the 2011–2014 behavioral risk factor surveillance system in 23 states. *JAMA Pediatrics, 172*(11), 1038–1044.

Metcalfe, J., & Fiese, B. (2018). Family food involvement is related to healthier dietary intake in preschool-aged children. *Appetite, 126*, 195–200.

Meyer, R., Venter, C., Fox, A., & Shah, N. (2012). Practical dietary management of protein energy malnutrition in young children with cow's milk protein allergy. *Pediatric Allergy and Immunology, 23*(4), 307–314.

Miall, L., & Smith, D. (2016). *Paediatrics at a glance.* Wiley Blackwell.

Miendlarzewska, E., & Trost, W. (2014). How musical training affects cognitive development: Rhythm, reward and other modulating variables. *Frontiers in Neuroscience, 7*, 279.

Milteer, R., & Ginsburg, K. (2012). The importance of play in promoting healthy child development and maintaining strong parent-child bond: Focus on children in poverty. *Pediatrics, 129*(1), e204–e213.

Mindell, J., Li, A., Sadeh, A., Kwon, R., & Goh, D. (2015). Bedtime routines for young children: A dose-dependent association with sleep outcomes. *Sleep, 38*(5), 717–722.

Moon, R., & Task Force on Sudden Infant Death Syndrome (2016). SIDS and other sleep-related infant deaths: Evidence base for 2016 updated recommendations for a safe infant sleeping environment. *Pediatrics, 138*(5), e20153275.

More, J. (2013). *Infant, child and adolescent nutrition: A practical handbook.* CRC Press.

Moreno, M. (2015). Sleep terrors and sleepwalking: Common parasomnias of childhood. *JAMA Pediatrics, 169*(7), 704.

Mouradian, W., Wehr, E., & Crall, J. (2000). Disparities in children's oral health and access to dental care. *JAMA, 284*(20), 2625–2631.

Munro, E. (2020). *Effective child protection.* Sage.

Musco, A. (2010). Playing by ear: Is expert opinion supported by research? *Bulletin of the Council for Research in Music Education, 184*, 49–64.

Nabhan, G., & Trimble, S. (1994). *The geography of childhood: Why children need wild places.* Beacon Press.

North American Association for Environmental Education (2017). *Nature preschools and forest kindergartens: 2017 national survey.*

Nowak, A., Christensen, J., Mabry, T., Townsend, J., & Wells, M. (2019). *Pediatric dentistry: Infancy through adolescence.* Elsevier.

Odgers, C. (2015). Income inequality and the developing child: Is it all relative? *American Psychologist, 70*, 722–731.

Oh, S., Yu, Y., Choi, H., & Kim, K. (2012). Implementation and evaluation of nutrition education programs focusing on increasing vegetables, fruits and dairy foods consumption for preschool children. *Korean Journal of Community Nutrition, 17*, 517.

O'Hare, T. (2021). *Evidence-based practices for social workers: An interdisciplinary approach.* Oxford University Press.

Osofsky, J., & Groves, B. (2018). *Violence and trauma in the lives of children.* Praeger.

Painter, K., & Scannapieco, M. (2021). *Understanding the mental health problems of children and adolescents: A guide for social workers.* Oxford University Press.

Palmer, K., Miller, A., Meehan, S., & Robinson, L. (2020). The motor skills at playtime intervention improves children's locomotor skills: A feasibility study. *Child: Care, Health & Development, 46*(5), 599–606.

Pandita, A., Sharma, D., Pandita, D., Pawar, S., Tariq, M., & Kaul, A. (2016). Childhood obesity: Prevention is better than cure. *Diabetes, Metabolic Syndrome and Obesity: Targets and Therapy, 9*, 83–89.

Passe, A. (2020). *Creating diversity-rich environments for young children.* Redleaf Press.

Pearsall, C., & Central Washington University. Office of Graduate Studies Research. (2012). *A punishment-free, toilet-training protocol for children with developmental disabilities.* Central Washington University.

Perlman, J., Cilio, M., & Polin, R. (2019). *Neurology: Neonatology questions and controversies.* Elsevier.

Peterson, C., Florence, C., & Klevens, J. (2018). The economic burden of child maltreatment in the United States, 2015. *Child Abuse & Neglect, 86*, 178–183.

Petit, D., Pennestri, M., Paquet, J., Desautels, A., Zadra, A., Vitaro, F., Tremblay, R., Boivin, M., & Montplaisir, J. (2015). Childhood sleepwalking and sleep terrors: A longitudinal study of prevalence and familial aggregation. *JAMA Pediatrics, 169*(7), 653–658.

Pickering, L. (2014). CDC offers tips to prevent illness, injury while swimming. *AAP News, 35*(7), 10.

Rauscher, E., & Rangel, D. (2020). Rising Organization for Economic Co-operation and Development, 2017. Health status indicators: Kaiser Family Foundation analysis of data from OECD. *OECD Health Statistics Database.* http://www.healthsystemtracker.org/chart-collection/infant-mortality-u-s-compare-countries/#item-start.

Rojas, N., Yoshikawa, H., Morris, P., Kamboukos, D., Dawson-Mcclure, S., & Brotman, L. (2020). The association of peer behavioral regulation with motor-cognitive readiness skills in preschool. *Early Childhood Research Quarterly, 51*, 153–163.

Samuel, T., Musa-Veloso, K., Ho, M., Venditti, C., & Shahkhalili-Dulloo, Y. (2018). A narrative review of childhood picky eating and its relationship to food intakes, nutritional status, and growth. *Nutrients, 10*(12), 1992.

Sha, Z., Pepe, A., Schijven, D., Carrión-Castillo, A., Roe, J., Westerhausen, R., Joliot, M., Fisher, S., Crivello, F., & Francks, C. (2021). Handedness and its genetic influences are associated with structural asymmetries of the cerebral cortex in 31,864 individuals. *Proceedings of the National Academy of Sciences, 118*(47), e2113095118.

Shally-Jensen, M. (2020). *Pandemics, plagues & public health.* Salem Press.

Shelov, S., Trubo, R., Altmann, T., & Hannemann, R. (2014). *Caring for your baby and young child: Birth to age 5.* Bantam Books.

Shipman, S., Hankins, J., Sanchez, R., & Speck, P. (2017). Introduction to child maltreatment. In R. Alexander, D. Faugno, & P. Speck (Eds.), *Child abuse: Quick reference for health care, social service, and law enforcement professionals.* STM Learning.

Sicherer, S. (2011). Epidemiology of food allergy. *The Journal of Allergy and Clinical Immunology, 127*(3), 594–602.

Siega-Riz, A., Deming, D., Reidy, C., Fox, M., Condon, E., & Briefel, R. (2010). Food consumption patterns of infants and toddlers: Where are we now? *Journal of the American Dietetic Association, 110*(12), S38–S51.

Soneji, S., & Beltrán-Sánchez, H. (2019). Association of special supplemental nutrition program for women, infants, and children with preterm birth and infant mortality. *JAMA Network Open, 2*(12), e1916722.

Sortino, D. (2017). *A guide to how your child learns: Understanding the brain from infancy to young adulthood.* Rowman & Littlefield.

Souto, P., Santos, J., Leite, H., Hadders-Algra, M., Guedes, S., Nobre, J., Santos, L., & Morais, R. (2020). Tablet use in young children is associated with advanced fine motor skills. *Journal of Motor Behavior, 52*(2), 196–203.

Spock, B., & Needlman, R. (2018). *Dr. Spock's baby and child care.* Gallery Books.

Stanton-Chapman, T., & Schmidt, E. (2017). Caregiver perceptions of inclusive playgrounds targeting toddlers and preschoolers with disabilities: Has recent international and national policy improved overall satisfaction? *Journal of Research in Special Educational Needs, 17*(4), 237–246.

Stanton-Chapman, T., & Schmidt, E. (2019). Building playgrounds for children of all abilities: Legal requirements and professional recommendations. *Early Childhood Education, 47,* 509–517.

Statman-Weil, K. (2015). Creating trauma sensitive classrooms. *Young Children, 70*(2).

Sturmey, P., & Didden, R. (2014). *Evidence-based practice and intellectual disabilities.* Wiley-Blackwell.

Taveras, E., Rifas-Shiman, S., Belfort, M., Kleinman, K., Oken, E., & Gillman, M. (2009). Weight status in the first 6 months of life and obesity at 3 years of age. *Pediatrics, 123*(4), 1177–1183.

Tsuda, E., Goodway, J., Famelia, R., & Brian, A. (2020). Relationship between fundamental motor skill competence, perceived physical competence and free-play physical activity in children. *Research Quarterly for Exercise & Sport, 91*(1), 55–63.

UNICEF. (2020). *Children, food and nutrition: Growing well in a changing world.*

UNICEF (2021). *The state of the world's children.* https://www.unicef.org/eu/reports/state-worlds-children-2021

United Nations (2021). *Policy brief: The impact of COVID-19 on children.* https://www.un.org/sites/un2.un.org/files/policy_brief_on_covid_impact_on_children_16_april_2020.pdf

US Centers for Disease Control and Prevention (2017). *Five important reasons to vaccinate your child.* https://www.cdc.gov/vaccines/partners/childhood/matte-articles-5-reasons.html

US Centers for Disease Control and Prevention (2019). *Burn prevention.* https://www.cdc.gov/safechild/burns/index.html

US Centers for Disease Control and Prevention (2020a). *Adverse drug events in children.* https://www.cdc.gov/medicationsafety/parents_childrenadversedrugevents.html

US Centers for Disease Control and Prevention (2020b). *Community water fluoridation.* https://www.cdc.gov/fluoridation/index.html

US Centers for Disease Control and Prevention (2020c). *Healthy and safe swimming.* https://www.cdc.gov/features/healthyswimming/index.html

US Centers for Disease Control and Prevention (2020d). *Important milestones: Your child by four years.* https://www.cdc.gov/ncbddd/actearly/milestones/milestones-4yr.html

US Centers for Disease Control and Prevention (2020e). *Well-child visits are essential.* https://www.cdc.gov/vaccines/parents/why-vaccinate/well-child-visits.html

US Centers for Disease Control and Prevention (2022). *Risk and protective factors.* https://www.cdc.gov/violenceprevention/childabuseandneglect/riskprotectivefactors.html#Protective%20Factors

US Department of Agriculture (2020a). *Choose my plate.* https://www.choosemyplate.gov/browse-by-audience/view-all-audiences/children/health-and-nutrition-information/preschoolers-food-group

US Department of Agriculture (2020b). Food and Nutrition Service. *The special supplemental nutrition assistance program for women, infants and children (WIC).* https://www.fns.usda.gov/wic

US Department of Education (2015). *About IDEA.* https://sites.ed.gov/idea/about-idea/#ADA

US Department of Health and Human Services (2015). *Promoting protective factors for victims of child abuse and neglect: A guide for practitioners.* https://www.childwelfare.gov/pubs/factsheets/victimscan/

US Department of Health and Human Services (2019a). *Child abuse, neglect.* https://www.acf.hhs.gov/media/press/2019/child-abuse-neglect-data-released

US Department of Health and Human Services (2019b). *Risk and protective factors.* https://training.cfsrportal.acf.hhs.gov/section-2-understanding-child-welfare-system/2984

US Department of Health and Human Services (2020). *Resources on trauma for caregivers and families.* https://www.childwelfare.gov/topics/responding/trauma/caregivers/

US Department of Transportation (2020). National Highway and Traffic Safety Administration. *Car seats and booster seats.* https://www.nhtsa.gov/equipment/car-seats-and-booster-seats

US Environmental Protection Agency (2020). *Children's health: What you can do to protect children from environmental risks.* https://www.epa.gov/children/what-you-can-do-protect-children-environmental-risks

US Product Safety Commission (2020). *Regulations and laws.* https://www.cpsc.gov/Regulations-Laws--Standards/Statutes/

Utesch, T., Bardid, F., Büsch, D., & Strauss, B. (2019). The relationship between motor competence and physical fitness from early childhood to early adulthood: A meta-analysis. *Sports Medicine, 49*(4), 541–551.

Valla, L., Slinning, K., Kalleson, R., Wentzel-Larsen, T., & Riiser, K. (2020). Motor skills and later communication development in early childhood: Results from a population-based study. *Child: Care, Health, and Development, 46,* 407–413.

Van Duin, E., Verlinden, E., Vrolijk-Bosschaart, T., Diehle, J., Verhoeff, A., Brilleslijper-Kater, S., & Lindauer, R. (2018). Sexual abuse in very young children: A psychological assessment in the Amsterdam sexual abuse case study. *European Journal of Psychotraumatology, 9*(1), 1503524.

Visser, J., Rommelse, N., Greven, C., & Buitelaar, J. (2016). Autism spectrum disorder and attention-deficit/hyperactivity disorder in early childhood: A review of unique and shared characteristics and developmental antecedents. *Neuroscience & Biobehavioral Reviews, 65,* 229–263.

Vlacho, F., Papadimitriou, A., & Bonoti, F. (2014). An investigation of age and gender differences in preschool children's specific motor skills. *European Psychomotricity Journal, 6*(1), 16–18.

Voigt, R., Macias, M., Myers, S., & Tapia, C. (2018). *Developmental and behavioral pediatrics.* American Academy of Pediatrics.

Volger, S., Rigassio Radler, D., & Rothpletz-Puglia, P. (2018). Early childhood obesity prevention efforts through a life course health development perspective: A scoping review. *PLOS ONE, 13*(12), e0209787.

Waite, R., & Ryan, R. (2020). *Adverse childhood experiences: What students and health professionals need to know.* Routledge.

Wang, Y., Guglielmo, D., & Welsh, J. (2018). Consumption of sugars, saturated fat, and sodium among US children from infancy through preschool age,. National Health and Nutrition Examination Survey 2009–2014, *The American Journal of Clinical Nutrition, 108*(4), 868–877.

Weisenberger, J. (2020). How sleep habits affect healthy weight. *Academy of Nutrition and Dietetics.* https://www.eatright.org/health/weight-loss/overweight-and-obesity/how-sleep-habits-affect-healthy-weight

Wenner, M. (2009). The serious need for play. *Scientific American Mind, 20*(1), 22–29.

Wekerle, C., Wolfe, D., Cohen, J., Bromberg, D., & Murray, L. (2019). *Childhood maltreatment.* Hogrefe.

Westman, J. (2019). *Dealing with child abuse and neglect as public health problems: Prevention and the role of juvenile ageism.* Springer.

Wiberg, A., Ng, M., Omran, Y., Alfaro-Almagro, F., McCarthy, P., Marchini, J., Bennett, D., Smith, S., Douaud, G., & Furniss, D. (2019). Handedness, language areas and neuropsychiatric diseases: Insights from brain imaging and genetics. *Brain, 142*(10), 2938–2947.

Wilde, K. (2015). *Autistic logistics: A parent's guide to tackling bedtime, toilet training, tantrums, hitting, and other everyday challenges.* Jessica Kingsley.

Wilson, R. (1993). *Fostering a sense of wonder during the early childhood years.* Greyden Press.

Wilson, R. (2000). The wonders of nature: Honoring children's ways of knowing. *Early Childhood News, 6*(9), 16–19.

Wood, A., Blissett, J., Brunstrom, J., Carnell, S., Faith, M., Fisher, J., Hayman, L., Khalsa, A., Hughes, S., Miller, A. & Momin, S. (2020). Caregiver influences on eating behaviors in young children: A scientific statement from the American Heart Association. *Journal of the American Heart Association, 9*(10), p.e014520.

World Health Organization (2017). *Guidelines on infant health.* https://www.who.int/publications/i/item/978924150437

World Health Organization (2021). *Malnutrition.* https://www.who.int/news-room/fact-sheets/detail/malnutrition

Yantzi, N., Young, N., & McKeever, P. (2010). The suitability of school playgrounds for physically disabled children. *Children's Geographies, 8*, 65–78.

Zeng, N., Ayyub, M., Sun, H., Wen, X., Xiang, P., & Gao, Z. (2017). Effects of physical activity on motor skills and cognitive development in early childhood: A systematic review. *BioMed Research International.* https://www.ncbi.nlm.nih.gov/pmc/articles/PMC5745693/

Chapter 8

Abadzi, H. (2006). *Efficient learning for the poor: Insights from the frontier of cognitive neuroscience.* Washington, DC: World Bank.

Ackerman, D. J., & Friedman-Krauss, A. H. (2017). Preschoolers' executive function: Importance, contributors, research needs and assessment options. *ETS Research Report Series*, 1–24.

Adlof, S., & Hogan, T. (2019). If we don't look, we won't see: Measuring language development to inform literacy instruction. *Policy Insights from the Behavioral and Brain Sciences, 6*(2), 210–217.

Aguiar, N., Mottweiler, C., Taylor, M., & Fisher, P. (2017). The imaginary companions created by children who have lived in foster care. *Imagination, Cognition, and Personality, 36*(4), 340–355.

Allan, N., Hume, L., Allan, D., Farrington, A., & Lonigan, C. (2014). Relations between inhibitory control and the development of academic skills in preschool and kindergarten: A meta-analysis. *Developmental Psychology, 50*, 2368–2379.

Angeleri, R., & Airenti, G. (2014). The development of joke and irony understanding: A study with 3- to 6-year-old children. *Canadian Journal of Experimental Psychology, 68*(2), 133–146.

Astington, J. (2003). Sometimes necessary, never sufficient: False-belief understanding and social competence. In B. Repacholi & V. Slaughter (Eds.), *Individual differences in theory of mind: implications for typical and atypical development.* Psychology Press.

Band, E., & Weisz, J. (1988). How to feel better when it feels bad: Children's perspectives on coping with everyday stress. *Developmental Psychology, 24*, 247–253.

Banich, M., & Compton, R. (2018). *Cognitive neuroscience.* Cambridge University Press.

Barnett, L. (1990). Developmental benefits of play for children. *Journal of Leisure Research, 22*, 138–153.

Barrouillet, P. (2015). Theories of cognitive development: From Piaget to today. *Developmental Review, 38*(C), 1–12.

Bart, O., Hajami, D., & Bar-Haim, Y. (2007). Predicting school adjustment from motor abilities in kindergarten. *Infant & Child Development, 16*, 597–615.

Bartsch, K., & Wellman, H. (1995). *Children talk about the mind.* Oxford University Press.

Bauer, P. (2014). The development of forgetting: Childhood amnesia. In P. Bauer & R. Fivush (Eds.), *The Wiley handbook on the development of children's memory.* Wiley-Blackwell.

Bauer, P., & Larkina, M. (2014). The onset of childhood amnesia in childhood: A prospective investigation of the course and determinants of forgetting of early-life events. *Memory, 22*(8), 907–24.

Bauer, P., & Pathman, T. (2008). Memory and early brain development. *Encyclopedia on Early Childhood Development.* www.child-encyclopedia.com/brain/according-experts/memory-and-early-brain-development

Bessieres, B., Travaglia, A., Mowery, T., Zhang, X., & Alberini, C. (2020). Early life experiences selectively mature learning and memory abilities. *Nature Communications, 11*(1), 628.

Best, J., & Miller, P. (2010). A developmental perspective on executive function. *Child Development, 81*(6), 1641–1660.

Bjorklund, D. (2004). *Children's thinking: Cognitive development and individual differences.* Wadsworth Publishing.

Blair, C. (2002). School readiness: Integrating cognition and emotion in a neurobiological conceptualization of children's functioning at school entry. *American Psychologist, 57*(2), 111–127.

Blair, C., & Raver, C. (2015). School readiness and self-regulation: A developmental psychobiological approach. *Annual Review of Psychology, 66*, 711–731.

Bodrova, E., & Leong, D. (1996). *Tools of the mind: The Vygotskian approach to early childhood education.* Merrill.

Bos, H., Fain, G., & Rein, E. (2017). Five things we can learn from pre-k in other countries. *American Institute for Research.* https://www.air.org/resource/five-things-we-can-learn-pre-k-other-countries

Brodin, J., & Renblad, K. (2020). Improvement of preschool children's speech and language skills. *Early Child Development and Care, 190*(14), 2205–2213.

Bruer, J. (2015). Brookings Institute. Windows of opportunity: Their seductive appeal. *Evidence Speaks Reports, 1*(5).

Bullard, J. (2014). *Creating environments for learning: Birth to age eight.* Pearson.

Cadima, J., Barros, S., Ferreira, T., Serra-Lemos, M., Leal, T., & Verschueren, K. (2018). Bidirectional associations between vocabulary and self-regulation in preschool and their interplay with teacher-child closeness and autonomy support. *Early Childhood Research Quarterly, 46*(1), 75–86.

Camilli, G., Vargas, S., Ryan, S., & Barnett, W. (2010). Meta-analysis of the effects of early education interventions on cognitive and social development. *Teachers College Record, 112*(3), 579–620.

Cates, C., Weisleder, A., & Mendelsohn, A. (2016). Mitigating the effects of family poverty on early child development through parenting interventions in primary care. *Academic Pediatrics, 16(3),* S112–S120.

Chapman, C., Laird, J., Ifill, N., & Kewal-Ramani, A. (2011). *Trends in high school dropout and completion rates in the United States: 1972–2009* (Compendium report NCES 2012–006). National Center for Education Statistics.

Cheour, M., Imada, T., Taulu, S., Ahonen, A., Salonen, J., & Kuhl, P. (2004). Magnetoencephalography is feasible for infant assessment of auditory discrimination. *Experimental Neurology, 190,* S44–S51.

Clay, Z., & Tennie, C. (2017). Is over-imitation a uniquely human phenomenon? Insights from human children as compared to bonobos. *Child Development, 89.*

Clegg, J., & Legare C. (2016). Parents scaffold flexible imitation in early childhood. *Journal of Experimental Child Psychology, 153.*

Cohen, D. (2018). *How the child's mind develops.* Routledge.

Colliver, Y., & Veraksa, N. (2021). Vygotsky's contributions to understandings of emotional development through early childhood play. *Early Child Development and Care,* 1–15.

Conkbayir, M. (2017). *Early childhood and neuroscience: Theory, research and implications for practice.* Bloomsbury Academic.

Conte, E., Grazzani, I., & Pepe, A. (2018). Social cognition, language, and prosocial behaviors: A multitrait mixed-methods study in early childhood. *Early Education and Development, 29,* 1–17.

Coolahan, K., Fantuzzo, J., Mendez, J., & McDermott, P. (2000). Preschool peer interactions and readiness to learn: Relationships between classroom peer play and learning behaviors and conduct. *Journal of Education Psychology, 92,* 458–465.

Cowan, N. (2014). Working memory underpins cognitive development, learning, and education. *Educational Psychology Review, 26*(2), 197–223.

Cowell, J., Samek, A., List, J., & Decety, J. (2015). The curious relation between theory of mind and sharing in preschool age children. *PLOS ONE, 10*(2), e0117947.

Davies, D., & Troy, M. (2020). *Child development: A practitioner's guide.* Guilford.

de Villiers, J. G., & de Villiers, P. A. (2014). The role of language in theory of mind development. *Topics in Language Disorders, 34*(4), 313–328.

Diamond, A. (2000). Close interrelation of motor development and cognitive development and of the cerebellum and prefrontal cortex. *Child Development, 1,* 44–56.

Doebel, S. (2020). Rethinking executive function and its development. *Perspectives on Psychological Science, 15*(4), 942–956.

Dore, R., & Lillard, A. (2015). Theory of mind and children's engagement in fantasy worlds. *Imagination, Cognition and Personality, 34*(3), 230–242.

Dunn, J. (1996). Children's relationships: Bridging the divide between cognitive and social development. *Journal of Child Psychology and Psychiatry, 37*(5), 507–518.

Ebert, S. (2017). Theory of mind, language, and reading: Developmental relations from early childhood to early adolescence. *Journal of Experimental Child Psychology, 164,* 225–238.

Eigsti, I., Zayas, V., Mischel, W., Shoda, Y., Ayduk, O., Dadlani, M., Davidson, M., Aber, L. & Casey, B. (2006). Predicting cognitive control from preschool to late adolescence and young adulthood. *Psychological Science, 17*(6), 483.

Erickson, R. (1985). Play contributes to the full emotional development of the child. *Education, 105,* 261–263.

Estes, D., & Bartsch, K. (2017). Theory of mind: A foundational component of human general intelligence. *Behavioral Brain Science, 40,* e201.

Fernyhough, C. (2008). Getting Vygotskian about theory of mind: Mediation, dialogue, and the development of social understanding. *Developmental Review, 28*(2), 225–262.

Ferrer, E., & McArdle, J. (2004). An experimental analysis of dynamic hypotheses about cognitive abilities and achievement from childhood to early adulthood. *Developmental Psychology, 40*(6), 935–952.

Filippova, E., & Astington, J. (2010). Children's understanding of social-cognitive and social-communicative aspects of discourse irony. *Child Development, 8,* 913–928.

Gade, M., Zoelch, C., & Seitz-Stein, K. (2017). Training of visual-spatial working memory in preschool children. *Advances in Cognitive Psychology, 13*(2), 177–187.

Gallagher, K. (2005). Brain research and early childhood development: A primer for developmentally appropriate practice. *Young Children, 60*(4), 12–20.

Gavin, M. (2015). Encouraging your child's sense of humor. *Kid's Health from Nemours.* https://kidshealth.org/

Giedd, J., & Rapoport, J. (2010). Structural MRI of pediatric brain development: What have we learned and where are we going? *Neuron, 67,* 728–734.

Gmitrova, V. (2013). Teaching to play performing a main role—Effective method of pretend play facilitation in preschool-age children. *Early Child Development and Care, 183*(11), 1705–1719.

Goel, V., & Dolan, R. (2001). The functional anatomy of humor: Segregating cognitive and affective components. *Nature Neuroscience, 4,* 237–238.

Gomes, L., & Livesey, D. (2008). Exploring the link between impulsivity and peer relations in 5- and 6-year-old children. *Child: Care, Health and Development,* 763–764.

Gorey, K. (2001). Early childhood education: A meta-analytic affirmation of the short-and long-term benefits of educational opportunity. *School Psychology Quarterly, 16*(1), 9–30.

Goswami, U. (2010). *The Wiley-Blackwell handbook of childhood cognitive development.* Wiley-Blackwell.

Grissmer, D., Grimm, K., Aiyer, S., Murrah, W., & Steele, J. (2010). Fine motor skills and early comprehension of the world: Two new school readiness indicators. *Developmental Psychology, 46*(5), 1008–1017.

Guillory, S., Gliga, T., & Kaldy, Z. (2018). Quantifying attentional effects on the fidelity and biases of visual working memory in young children. *Journal of Experimental Child Psychology, 167,* 146–161.

Hahn, R., Barnett, W., Knopf, J., Truman, B., Johnson, R., Fielding, J., Muntaner, C., Jones, C., Fullilove, M., & Hunt, P. (2016). Community Preventive Services Task Force. Early childhood education to promote health equity: A community guide systematic review. *Journal of Public Health Management and Practice, 22*(5), E1–E8.

Hayes, C. (2016). *Language, literacy and communication in the early years: A critical foundation.* Critical Publishing.

Heckman, J. (2006). Skill formation and the economics of investing in disadvantaged children. *Science, 312,* 1900–1902.

Henry, M. (1990). More than just play: The significance of mutually directed adult, child activity. *Early Child Development and Care, 60,* 35–51.

Herschensohn, J. (2007). *Language development and age.* Cambridge University Press.

Hjetland, H., Lervag, A., Lyster, S., Hagtvet, B., Hulme, C., & Melby-Lervag, M. (2019). Pathways to reading comprehension: A longitudinal study from 4 to 9 years of age. *Journal of Educational Psychology, 111*(5), 751–763.

Hoff, E. (2014). *Language development.* Wadsworth Cengage Learning.

Hoicka, E., & Akhtar, N. (2012). Early humour production. *British Journal of Developmental Psychology, 30,* 586–603.

Hoogenhout, M., & Malcolm-Smith, S. (2016). Theory of mind predicts severity level in autism. *Autism, 21*(2), 242–252.

Houde, O., & Borst, G. (2015). Evidence for an inhibitory-control theory of the reasoning brain. *Frontiers in Human Neuroscience, 9,* 148.

Hulit, L., Fahey, K., & Howard, M. (2019). *Born to talk: An introduction to speech and language development.* Pearson.

Hurwitz, S. (2002). To be successful: Let them play! *Child Education, 79,* 101–102.

Huttenlocher, P., & Dabholkar, A. (1997). Regional differences in synaptogenesis in human cerebral cortex. *The Journal of Comparative Neurology, 387,* 167–178.

Imuta, K., Scarf, D., & Hayne, H. (2013). The effect of verbal reminders on memory reactivation in 2-, 3-, and 4-year-old children. *Developmental Psychology, 49*(6), 1058–1065.

Inhelder, B., & Piaget, J. (1958). The growth of logical thinking from childhood to adolescence: An essay on the construction of formal operational structures. *Psychology Press, 22.*

Irwin, L, Siddiqi, A., & Hertzman, C. (2007). *Early child development: A powerful equalizer.* World Health Organization. https://apps.who.int/iris/bitstream/handle/10665/69729/a91213.pdf.jsessionid=5BDE4565A76EA90FFB1A420EE4B83777?sequence=1

Jones, S. (2009). The development of imitation in infancy. *Philosophical Transactions of the Royal Society of London. Series B, Biological Sciences, 364*(1528), 2325–2335.

Kalkusch, I., Jaggy, A., Burkhardt, C., Bossi, B., Sticca, F., & Perren, S. (2020). Promoting social pretend play in preschool age: Is providing roleplay material enough? *Early Education and Development, 31.*

Kamerman, S. (2006). *A global history of early childhood education and care.* United Nations Educational, Scientific and Cultural Organization. http://unesdoc.unesco.org/images/0014/001474/147470e.pdf.

Kloo, D., Perner, J., & Gritzer, T. (2010). Object-based set-shifting in preschoolers: Relations to theory of mind. In B. Sokol et al. (eds.), *Self and social regulation: Social interaction and the development of social understanding and executive functions.* Oxford University Press.

Knoll, L., Fuhrmann, D., Sakhardande, A., Stamp, F., Speekenbrink, M., & Blakemore, S. (2016). A window of opportunity for cognitive training in adolescence. *Psychological Science, 27*(12).

Kuhl, P. (2004). Early language acquisition: Cracking the speech code. *Nature Reviews Neuroscience, 5,* 831–843.

Kuhl, P. (2007). Is speech learning "gated" by the social brain? *Developmental Science, 10,* 110–120.

Kuhl, P. (2011). Early language learning and literacy: Neuroscience implications for education. mind, brain and education. *The Official Journal of the International Mind, Brain, and Education Society, 5*(3), 128–142.

Kuhn, D. (2005). *Education for thinking.* Harvard University Press.

Ladefoged, P. (2001). *Vowels and consonants: An introduction to the sounds of language.* Blackwell Publishers.

Lemmon, K., & Moore, C. (2007). The development of prudence in the face of varying future rewards. *Developmental Science, 10*(4), 502–511.

Lenz, S., & Paulus, M. (2021). Friendship is more than strategic reciprocity: Preschoolers' selective sharing with friends cannot be reduced to strategic concerns. *Journal of Experimental Child Psychology, 206*(2), 105101.

Logan, J., Justice, L., Melike-Yumus, L., & Chaparro-Moreno, J. (2019). When children are not read to at home: The million word gap. *Journal of Developmental & Behavioral Pediatrics, 40*(5), 383–386.

Lonigan, C., Spiegel, J., Goodrich, J., Morris, B., Osborne, C., Lerner, M., & Phillips, B. (2017). Does preschool self-regulation predict later behavior problems in general or specific problem behaviors? *Journal of Abnormal Child Psychology, 45,* 1491–1502.

Lyons, D., Young, A., & Keil, F. (2007). The hidden structure of overimitation. *Proceedings of the National Academy of Sciences, 104*(50), 19751–19756.

Lyster, S., Snowling, M., Hulme, C., & Lervag, A. (2021). Preschool phonological, morphological and semantic skills explain it all: Following reading development through a 9-year period. *Journal of Research in Reading, 44,* 175–188.

Mackes, N., Golm, D., Sarkar, S., Kumsta, R., Rutter, M., Fairchild, G., Mehta, M., Sonuga-Barke, E., & ERA Young Adult Follow-up team (2020). Early childhood deprivation is associated with alterations in adult brain structure despite subsequent environmental enrichment. *Proceedings of the National Academy of Sciences of the United States of America, 117*(1), 641–649.

Mahn, H., & John-Steiner, V. (2012). Vygotsky and sociocultural approaches to teaching and learning. *Handbook of Psychology.* John Wiley.

Martin, R., & Ford, T. (2018). *The psychology of humor.* Academic Press.

Mazz, M., Mariano, M., Peretti, S., Masedu, F., Pino, M., & Valenti, M. (2017). The role of theory of mind on social information processing in children with autism spectrum disorders: A mediation analysis. *Journal of Autism and Developmental Disorders, 47*, 1369–1379.

McCoy, D., Yoshikawa, H., Ziol-Guest, K., Duncan, G., Schindler, H., Magnuson, K., Yang, R., Koepp, K., & Shonkoff, J. (2017). Impacts of early childhood education on medium- and long-term educational outcomes. *Educational Researcher, 46*(8), 474–487.

McElrath, K. (2021). *Heightened focus on early childhood education programs as preschool enrollment increased before COVID-19*. US Census Bureau. https://www.census.gov/library/stories/2021/11/pre-pandemic-early-childhood-enrollment-expanded-as-more-enrolled-public-preschool.html

McLaughlin, T., Aspden, K., & Clarke, L. (2017). How do teachers support children's social-emotional competence? Strategies for teachers. *Early Childhood Folio, 21*, 21–27.

Meltzoff, A., Gopnik, A., & Repacholi, B. (1999). Toddlers' understanding of intentions, desires, and emotions: Explorations of the dark ages. In P. Zelazo et al. (Eds.), *Developing theories of intention: Social understanding and self-control*. Erlbaum.

Miller, B., & Cummings, J. (2007). *The human frontal lobes*. Guilford.

Milteer, R., & Ginsburg, K. (2012). The importance of play in promoting healthy child development and maintaining strong parent-child bond: Focus on children in poverty. *Pediatrics, 129*(1), e204–e213.

Moore, C., Barresi, J., & Thompson, C. (2001). The cognitive basis of future-oriented prosocial behavior. *Social Development, 7*, 198–218.

Mueller, J., & File, N. (2020). *Curriculum in early childhood education: Re-examined, reclaimed, renewed*. Routledge.

Mullally, S., & Maguire, E. (2014). Learning to remember: The early ontogeny of episodic memory. *Developmental Cognitive Neuroscience, 9*, 12–29.

National Association for the Education of Young Children (2009). *School readiness*. naeyc.org/positionstatements/school_readiness

Nelson, C., de Haan, M., & Thomas, K. (2006). Neural bases of cognitive development. *Handbook of Child Psychology*. John Wiley.

Nelson, C., Zeanah, C., & Fox, N. (2019). How early experience shapes human development: The case of psychosocial deprivation. *Neural Plasticity*, 1676285.

Nguyen, T., Watts, T., Duncan, G., Clements, D., Smara, J., Wolfe, C., & Spitler, M. (2016). Which preschool mathematics competencies are most predictive of fifth grade achievement? *Early Childhood Research Quarterly, 36*, 550–560.

Nilsen, E., & Valcke, A. (2018). Children's sharing with collaborators versus competitors: The impact of theory of mind and executive functioning. *Journal of Applied Developmental Psychology, 58*, 38–48.

O'Connor, C., & Fernandez, S. (2006). Race, class, and disproportionality: Reevaluating the relationship between poverty and special education placement. *Educational Researcher, 35*(6), 6–11.

Okanda, M., & Taniguchi, K. (2020). Children's response biases to results of object sharing. *Applied Cognitive Psychology, 34*(5), 1013–1019.

O'Keefe, L. (2014). Parents who read to their children nurture more than literary skills *American Academy of Pediatrics News*. https://www.aappublications.org/content/early/2014/06/24/aapnews.20140624–2

Paine, A., Karajian, G., Hashmi, S., Persram, R., & Howe, N. (2020). "Where's your bum brain?" Humor, social understanding, and sibling relationship quality in early childhood. *Social Development, 1*.

Parker, E. (2018). *How states fund pre-k: A primer for policymakers*. Education Commission of the States. https://www.ecs.org/wp-content/uploads/How-States-Fund-Pre-K_A-Primer-for-Policymakers.pdf

Peterson, C., Wellman, H., & Slaughter, V. (2012). The mind behind the message: Advancing theory-of-mind scales for typically developing children, and those with deafness, autism, or Asperger syndrome. *Child Development, 83*(2), 469–485.

Pianta, R., Cox, M., & Snow, K. (2007). *School readiness and the transition to kindergarten in the era of accountability*. Brookes.

Puma, M., Bell, S., Cook, R., & Heid, C. (2010). *Head start impact study final report executive summary*. US Department of Health and Human Services. https://www.acf.hhs.gov/sites/default/files/opre/executive_summary_final_508.pdf

Rabiner, L., & Huang, B. (1993). *Fundamentals of speech recognition*. Prentice Hall.

Rand, M., & Morrow, L. (2021). The contribution of play experiences in early literacy: Expanding the science of reading. *Reading Research Quarterly*, https://doi.org/10.1002/rrq.383

Robson, D., Allen, M., & Howard, S. (2020). Self-regulation in childhood as a predictor of future outcomes: A meta-analytic review. *Psychological Bulletin, 146*(4), 324–354.

Sale, A. (2016). *Environmental experience and plasticity of the developing brain*. Wiley/Blackwell.

Samuels, C. (2017). Which countries spend the most on early-childhood education? *Education Week*. http://blogs.edweek.org/edweek/early_years/2017/06/what_countries_spend_the_most_on_early_childhood_education.html

Saracho, O., & Spodek, B. (2007). *Contemporary perspectives on socialization and social development in early childhood education*. Information Age Publishing.

Savina, E. (2020). Self-regulation in preschool and early elementary classrooms: Why it is important and how to promote it. *Early Childhood Education Journal, 31*, 1–9.

Schaafsma, S., Pfaff, D., Spunt, R., & Adolphs, R. (2015). Deconstructing and reconstructing theory of mind. *Trends in Cognitive Science, 19*(2), 65–72.

Shonkoff, J., & Phillips, D. (2000). *From neurons to neighborhoods: The science of early childhood development*. National Academy Press.

Siegel, D., & Bryson, T. (2011). *The whole brain child: 12 revolutionary strategies to nurture your child's developing mind*. Delacorte Press.

Silkenbeumer, J., Eva-Maria Schiller, E., & Kartner, J. (2018). Co- and self-regulation of emotions in the preschool setting. *Early Childhood Research Quarterly, 44*, 72–81.

Skibbe, L., Montroy, J., Ryan, P., Bowles, F., & Morrison, J. (2019). Self-regulation and the development of literacy and language achievement from preschool through second grade. *Early Childhood Research Quarterly, 46*, 240–251.

Skinner, B. F. (1953). *Science and human behaviour*. The Macmillan Company.

Slavin, R. (2009). *Educational psychology: Theory and practice.* Pearson.

Smolucha, L., & Smolucha, F. (2021). Vygotsky's theory in-play: Early childhood education. *Early Child Development and Care, 32.*

Sortino, D. (2017). *A guide to how your child learns: Understanding the brain from infancy to young adulthood.* Rowman & Littlefield.

Spira, E., & Fischel, J. (2007). The impact of preschool inattention, hyperactivity, and impulsivity on social and academic development: A review. *Journal of Child Psychology and Psychiatry, 46*(7), 755.

Stenius, T., Karlsson, L., & Sivenius, A. (2021). Young children's humour in play and moments of everyday life in ECEC centres. *Scandinavian Journal of Educational Research*, 1–15.

Tamis-LeMonda, C., Shannon, J., Cabrera, N., & Lamb, M. (2004). Fathers and mothers at play with their 2- and 3-year-olds: Contributions to language and cognitive development. *Child Development, 75*, 1806–1820.

Thibodeau-Nielsen, R. B., Gilpin, A. T., Palermo, F., Nancarrow, A. F., Farrell, C. B., Turley, D., DeCaro, J. A., Lochman, J. E., & Boxmeyer, C. L. (2020). Pretend play as a protective factor for developing executive functions among children living in poverty. *Cognitive Development, 56*, 100964.

Thompson, B., & Goldstein, T. (2019). Disentangling pretend play measurement: Defining the essential elements and developmental progression of pretense. *Developmental Review, 52*, 24–41.

Thornton, S. (2003). *Growing minds: An introduction to children's cognitive development.* Palgrave Macmillan.

Tierney, A., & Nelson, C. (2009). Brain development and the role of experience in the early years. *ZERO TO THREE, 30*(2), 9–13.

Tsao, L. (2002). How much do we know about the importance of play in child development? *Child Education, 78*, 230–233.

UNICEF (2016). *The state of the world's children 2016: A fair chance for every child.*

UNICEF (2017). *First 1000 days the critical window to ensure that children survive and thrive.* https://www.unicef.org/southafrica/SAF_brief_1000days.pdf

UNICEF (2019). *A world ready to learn: Prioritizing quality early childhood education.* https://www.unicef.org/education/early-childhood-education

UNICEF (2020). *Early childhood education: Every child deserves access to quality early childhood education.* https://www.unicef.org/education/early-childhood-education

US Department of Health and Human Services (2020). *Office of Head Start.* https://www.acf.hhs.gov/ohs

US Department of Health and Human Services (2021). *Head Start: School readiness.* https://eclkc.ohs.acf.hhs.gov/school-readiness

Vann, K. (2015). Early childhood education: Teachers' perspectives, effective programs and impacts on cognitive development. *Nova Science Publishers.*

Vallotton, C., & Ayoub, C. (2011). Use your words: The role of language in the development of toddlers' self-regulation. *Early Childhood Research Quarterly, 26*(2), 169–181.

Vygotsky, L. (1978). *Mind and society: The development of higher mental processes.* Harvard University Press.

Vygotsky, L. (1993). *The collected works of L. S. Vygotsky* (Vols. 1 and 2). Plenum Press.

Wadsworth, B. (2003). *Piaget's theory of cognitive and affective development: Foundations of constructivism.* Allyn & Bacon.

Wang, Q., & Gulgoz, S. (2019). New perspectives on childhood memory: Introduction to the special issue. *Memory, 27*(1), 1–5.

Wavering, M.J. (2011). Piaget's logic of meanings: Still relevant today. *School Science and Mathematics, 111*, 249–252.

Wellman, H. (2014). *Making minds: How theory of mind develops.* Oxford Series in Cognitive Development. Oxford University.

Wellman, H., Fuxi, F., & Peterson, C. (2011). Sequential progressions in a theory of mind scale: Longitudinal perspectives. *Child Development, 82*(3), 780–792.

Wellman, H., & Liu, D. (2004). Scaling of theory-of-mind tasks. *Child Development, 75*(2), 523–541.

Welsh, J., Nix, R., Bierman, K., Blair, C., & Nelson, K. (2010). The development of executive function and gains in academic school readiness for children in low-income families. *Journal of Educational Psychology, 102*, 43–53.

Wertsch, J. (1984). *Culture, communication and cognition: Vygotskian perspectives.* Cambridge University Press.

Wertsch, J., & Sohmer, R. (1995). Vygotsky on learning and development. *Human Development, 38*, 332–337.

Wessel, I., Schweig, T., & Huntjens, R. (2019). Manipulating the reported age in earliest memories. *Memory, 27*(1), 6–18.

Westby, C. (2014). Social-emotional bases of pragmatic and communication development. In N. Singleton & B. Shulman (eds.), *Language development: Foundations, processes and clinical applications* (2nd ed., pp. 119–142). Jones & Bartlett Learning.

Westby, C., & Robinson, L. (2014). A developmental perspective for promoting theory of mind. *Topics in Language Disorders, 34*(4), 362–383.

Whitehead, M. (2010). *Language and literacy in the early years 0–7.* Sage Publications.

Williams, G., & Lerner, M. (2019). School readiness. *Pediatrics, 144*(2), e20191766.

Williford, A., Whittaker, J., Vitiello, V., & Downer, J. (2013). Children's engagement within the preschool classroom and their development of self-regulation. *Early Education and Development, 24*(2), 162–187.

Wink, J., & Puteny, A. (2002). *A vision to Vygotsky.* Allyn & Bacon.

Wise, R. (2004). Dopamine, learning and motivation. *Nature Reviews Neuroscience, 5*, 483–494.

Wolfgang, C., Stannard, L., & Jones, I. (2003). Advanced constructional play with Legos among preschoolers as a predictor of later school achievement in mathematics. *Early Child Development and Care, 173*, 467–475.

Worle, M., Essler, S., & Paulus, M. (2020). Paying it back and forward: The impact of experiencing and observing others' sharing and stinginess on preschoolers' own sharing behavior and expectations. *Journal of Experimental Child Psychology, 198*, 104886.

Wu, Z., & Su, Y. (2014). How do preschoolers' sharing behaviors relate to their theory of mind understanding? *Journal of Experimental Child Psychology, 120*, 73–86.

ZERO TO THREE (2016). Tuning In. *ZERO TO THREE's National parent survey.* https://www.zerotothree.org/parenting/national-parent-survey

Chapter 9

Abraham, E., Gal, R., Zagoory-Sharon, O., & Feldman, R. (2018). Empathy networks in the parental brain and their long-term effects on children's stress reactivity and behavior adaptation. *Neuropsychologia, 116*(A), 75–85.

Adams, K., Bull, R., & Maynes, M. (2016). Early childhood spirituality in education: Towards an understanding of the distinctive features of young children's spirituality. *European Early Childhood Education Research Journal, 24*(5), 1–15.

Albert, I., & Trommsdorff, G. (2014). The role of culture in social development over the lifespan: An interpersonal relations approach. *Online Readings in Psychology and Culture, 6*(2).

Albright, M., Weissberg, R., & Dusenbury, L. (2011). *School-family partnership strategies to enhance children's social, emotional, and academic growth*. National Center for Mental Health Promotion and Youth Violence Prevention, Education Development Center.

Ashdown, B., & Faherty, A. (2020). *Parents and caregivers across cultures: Positive development from infancy through adulthood*. Springer.

Ashiabi, G. (2000). Promoting the emotional development of preschoolers. *Early Childhood Education Journal, 28*(2), 79–84.

Asmussen, K. (2011). *The evidence-based parenting practitioner's handbook*. Routledge.

Assor, A., & Tal, K. (2012). When parents' affection depends on child's achievement: Parental conditional positive regard, self-aggrandizement, shame and coping in adolescents. *Journal of Adolescence, 35*, 249–260.

Bai, S., Repetti, R., & Sperling, J. (2015). Children's expressions of positive emotions are sustained by smiling, touching and playing with parents and siblings: A naturalistic observational study of family life. *Developmental Psychology, 52*, 88–101.

Bandura, A. (1977). *Social learning theory*. Prentice-Hall.

Bank, L., Burraston, B., & Snyder, J. (2004). Sibling conflict and ineffective parenting as predictors of adolescent boys' antisocial behavior and peer difficulties: Additive and interactional effects. *Journal of Research on Adolescence, 14*, 99–125.

Bates, L., & Glick, J. (2013). Does it matter if teachers and schools match the student? Racial and ethnic disparities in problem behaviors. *Social Science Research, 42*(5), 1180–1190.

Baumrind, D. (1967). Child care practices anteceding three patterns of preschool behaviour. *Genetic Psychology Monographs, 75*, 43–88.

Baumrind, D. (1971). Current patterns of parental authority. *Developmental Psychology, 4*, 1–103.

Baumrind, D. (1989). Rearing competent children. In W. Damon (Ed.), *Child development today and tomorrow*. Jossey-Bass.

Bennett, M. (2011). Children's social identities. *Infant and Child Development, 20*, 353–363.

Benson, P., Roehlkepartain, E., King, P., & Wagener, L. (2005). *The handbook of spiritual development in childhood and adolescence*. Sage.

Berman, C. (2009). *When a brother or sister dies: Looking back, moving forward*. Praeger.

Bernard, J. (1970). Mildred Parten Newhall 1902–1970. *American Sociologist, 5*(4), 383.

Best, R. (2000). *Education for spiritual, moral, social, and cultural development*. Continuum.

Biddle, G., Garcia Nevares, A., Roundtree Henderson, W., & Valero-Kerrick, A. (2014). *Early childhood education: Becoming a professional*. Sage.

Bilmes, J. (2012). *Beyond behavior management: The six life skills children need*. Redleaf.

Blair, C., & Raver, C. (2016). Poverty, stress, and brain development: New directions for prevention and intervention. *Academy of Pediatrics, 16*(3).

Brazelton, T., & Cramer, B. (1991). *The earliest relationship: Parents, infants and the drama of early attachment*. Routledge.

Brill, S., & Pepper, R. (2008). *The transgender child: A handbook for families and professionals*. Cleis Press.

Brody, G., & Stoneman, Z. (1994). Sibling relationships and their association with parental differential treatment. In E. Hetherington, D. Reiss, & R. Plomin (Eds.), *Separate social world of siblings: The impact of the nonshared environment on development*. Erlbaum.

Brody, L., & Hall, J. (2008). Gender and emotions in context. In M. Lewis, J. Haviland-Jones, & L. Barrett (Eds.), *Handbook of emotions*. Guilford.

Brook, J., Whiteman, M., Gordon, A., & Brook, D. (1990). The role of older brothers in younger brothers' drug use viewed in the context of parent and peer influences. *Journal of Genetic Psychology, 151*, 59–75.

Brown, C., McMullen, M., & File, N. (2019). *The Wiley handbook of early childhood care and education*. Wiley-Blackwell/John Wiley & Sons.

Brown, J., Donelan-McCall, N., & Dunn, J. (1996). Why talk about mental states? The significance of children's conversations with friends, siblings, and mothers. *Child Development, 67*, 836–849.

Brown, T., & Jones, L. (2001). *Action research and postmodernism: Congruence and critique*. Conducting Educational Research Series. Open University Press.

Brummelman, E., & Sedikides, C. (2020). Raising children with high self-esteem (but not narcissism). *Child Developmental Perspectives, 14*, 83–89.

Brummelman, E., Nelemans, S., Thomaes, S., & de Castro, B.O. (2017). When parents' praise inflates, Children's self-esteem deflates. *Child Development, 88*, 1799–1809.

Bufferd, S., Dougherty, L., Carlson, G., Rose S., & Klein, D. (2012). Psychiatric disorders in preschoolers: Continuity from ages 3 to 6. *American Journal of Psychiatry, 169*(11), 1157–1164.

Bulotsky-Shearer, R., Fernandez, V., Dominguez, X., & Rouse, H. (2011). Behavior problems in learning activities and social interactions in Head Start classrooms and early reading, mathematics, and approaches to learning. *School Psychology Review, 40*.

Campione-Barr, N. (2017). *Power, control, and influence in sibling relationships across development*. Jossey-Bass.

Carroll, J. (2019). *Sexuality now: Embracing diversity*. Cenage.

Cassidy, J. (2008). The nature of the child's ties. In J. Cassidy & P. Shaver (Eds.). *Handbook of attachment: Theory, research, and clinical applications*. Guilford.

Chaplin, T., & Aldao, A. (2013). Gender differences in emotion expression in children: A meta-analytic review. *Psychological Bulletin, 139*, 735–765.

Cicchetti, D., & Toth, S. (2015). Child maltreatment. In M. Lamb (Ed.), *Handbook of child psychology and developmental science*. Wiley.

Coelho, L., Torres, N., Fernandes, C., & Santos, A. (2017). Quality of play, social acceptance and reciprocal friendship in preschool children, *European Early Childhood Education Research Journal, 25*(6), 812–823.

Conte, E., Grazzani, I., & Pepe, A. (2018). Social cognition, language, and prosocial behaviors: A multitrait mixed-methods study in early childhood. *Early Education and Development,* 1–17.

Coolahan, K., Fantuzzo, J., Mendez, J., & McDermott, P. (2000). Preschool peer interactions and readiness to learn: Relationships between classroom peer play and learning behaviors and conduct. *Journal of Education Psychology, 92,* 458–465.

Cowie, H. (2012). *From birth to sixteen: Children's health, social, emotional and linguistic development.* Routledge.

Crick, N., Casas, J., & Mosher, M. (1997). Relational and overt aggression in preschool. *Developmental Psychology, 33*(4), 579–588.

Criss, M., Pettit, G., Bates, J., Dodge, K., & Lapp, A. (2002). Family adversity, positive peer relationships, and children's externalizing behavior: A longitudinal perspective on risk and resilience. *Child Development, 73*(4), 1220–1237.

Criss, M., & Shaw, D. (2005). Sibling relationships as contexts for delinquency training in low-income families. *Journal of Family Psychology, 19,* 592–600.

Dacey, J., & Fiore, L. (2000). *Your anxious child.* Jossey-Bass/Wiley.

Daly, M. (2004). *Developing the whole child: The importance of the emotional, social, moral, and spiritual in early years education and care.* The Edwin Mellen Press.

Darling-Churchill, K., & Lippman, L. (2016). Early childhood social and emotional development: Advancing the field of measurement. *Journal of Applied Developmental Psychology, 45,* 1–7.

Decety, J., Meidenbauer, K., & Cowell, J. (2018). The development of cognitive empathy and concern in preschool children: A behavioral neuroscience investigation. *Developmental Science, 21*(3), e12570.

Dennis, T. (2006). Emotional self-regulation in preschoolers: The interplay of child approach reactivity, parenting, and control capacities. *Developmental Psychology, 42*(1), 84–97.

Doepke, M., & Zilibotti, F. (2019). *Love, money & parenting: How economics explains the way we raise our kids.* Princeton University Press.

Donnellan, M., Trzesniewski, K., Robins, R., Moffitt, T., & Caspi, A. (2005). Low self-esteem is related to aggression, antisocial behavior, and delinquency. *Psychological Science, 16,* 328–335.

Dowling, M. (2014). *Young children's personal, social and emotional development.* Sage.

Doyle, C., & Cicchetti, D. (2017). From the cradle to the grave: The effect of adverse caregiving environments on attachment and relationships throughout the lifespan. *Clinical Psychology: Science and Practice, 24*(2), 203–217.

Dunfield, K. (2014). A construct divided: Prosocial behavior as helping, sharing, and comforting subtypes. *Frontiers in Psychology, 5.*

Dunn, J. (1983). Sibling relationships in early childhood. *Child Development, 54*(4), 787–811.

Eaude, T. (2003). Shining lights in unexpected corners: New angles on young children's spiritual development. *International Journal of Children's Spirituality, 8*(2), 151–162.

Eaude, T. (2005). Strangely familiar? Teachers making sense of young children's spiritual development. *Early Years, 25*(3), 237–248.

Ehrensaft, D. (2011). *Gender born, gender made: Raising healthy gender-nonconforming children.* The Experiment.

Eisenberg, N., & Fabes, R. (1998). Prosocial development. In W. Damon, & N. Eisenberg (Eds.), *Handbook of child psychology: Social, emotional, and personality development,* 3, 701–778, Wiley.

Eisenberg, N., & Strayer, J. (1987). *Empathy and its development.* Cambridge University Press.

Erikson, E. (1950). *Childhood and society.* Norton & Company.

Eschenfelder, C. (2019). Updating classic toys—guys and dolls: Gender-inclusive toy marketing in Baby Alive, the Easy-Bake Oven, and G.I. Joe. In K. Foss (Ed.) *Beyond princess culture: Gender and children's marketing.* Peter Lang.

Fabes, R., Martin, C., & Hanish, L. (2009). Children's behaviors and interactions with peers. In K. Rubin, W. Bukowski, & B. Laursen (Eds.) *Handbook of peer interactions, relationships, and groups.* Guilford.

Fagan, A., & Najman, J. (2005). The relative contributions of parental and sibling substance use to adolescent tobacco, alcohol, and other drug use. *Journal of Drug Issues, 35,* 869–884.

Ferrier, D., Bassett H., & Denham, S. (2014). Relations between executive function and emotionality in preschoolers: Exploring a transitive cognition-emotion linkage. *Frontiers in Psychology, 5,* 1–12.

Foo, K. (2019). *Intercultural parenting: How Eastern and Western parenting styles affect child development.* Routledge.

Foss, K. (2019). Constructing gender in childhood—Pink or blue? The gendering of children's marketing. In K. Foss (Ed.), *Beyond princess culture: Gender and children's marketing.* Peter Lang.

Fowler, J. (1981). *Stages of faith: The psychology of human development.* Harper & Row.

Gartstein, M., & Putnam, S. (2019). *Toddlers, parents, and culture: Findings from the joint effort toddler temperament consortium.* Routledge.

Gerhardt, M., Feng, X., & Chan, M. (2021). Long-term association of parental warmth with depression and obesity: Mediation by conscientiousness. *Health Psychology, 40*(3), 188–195.

Gershon, P., & Pellitteri, J. (2018). Promoting emotional intelligence in preschool education: A review of programs. *International Journal of Emotional Education, 10*(2), 264.

Gibbs, J. (2014). *Moral development and reality: Beyond the theories of Kohlberg, Hoffman, and Haidt.* Oxford University Press.

Gielen, U., & Roopnarine, J. (2004). *Childhood and adolescence: Cross-cultural perspectives and applications.* Praeger.

Giesenberg, A. (2000). Spiritual development and young children, *European Early Childhood Education Research Journal, 8*(2), 23–37.

Gilliam, W. (2005). *Prekindergarteners left behind: Expulsion rates in state prekindergarten systems.* Yale University Child Study Center. FCD Policy Brief Series No. 3. https://www.fcd-us.org/assets/2016/04/ExpulsionPolicyBrief.pdf

Ginsburg, K. (2007). The importance of play in promoting healthy child development and maintaining strong parent-child bonds. *Pediatrics, 119(1),* 181–192.

Gordon, A., & Browne, K. (2014). *Beginnings and beyond: Foundations in early childhood education.* Cengage.

Gross, J., & Cassidy, J. (2019). Expressive suppression of negative emotions in children and adolescents: Theory, data, and a guide for future research. *Developmental Psychology, 55*(9), 1938–1950.

Gross-Loh, C. (2013). *Parenting without borders: Surprising lessons parents around the world can teach us.* Avery Publishing.

Guerda, N. (2016). *Contemporary parenting: A global perspective.* Routledge.

Guralnick, M. (2010). Early intervention approaches to enhance the peer-related social competence of young children with developmental delays: A historical perspective. *Infants and Young Children, 23*(2), 73–83.

Haley, P. (2014). Evolution, prosocial behavior, and altruism: A roadmap for understanding where the proximate meets the ultimate. In L. Padilla-Walker & G. Carlo (Eds.), *Prosocial development: A multidimensional approach.* Oxford University Press.

Hart, J., & Tannock, M. (2019). *Rough play: Past, present and potential.* In P. Smith & J. Roopnarine (Eds.), *The Cambridge handbook of play: Developmental and disciplinary perspectives.* Cambridge University Press.

Harter, S. (2012). *The construction of the self: Developmental and sociocultural foundations.* Guilford.

Hay, D., & Castle, J. (2000). Toddlers' use of force against familiar peers: A precursor to serious aggression? *Child Development, 71*(2), 457–467.

Hay, D., Castle, J., Davies, L, Demetriou, H., & Stimson, C. (1999). Prosocial action in very early childhood. *Journal of Child Psychology and Psychiatry, 40*(6), 906–916.

Healey, J., & Stepnick, A. (2020). *Diversity and society: Race, ethnicity, and gender.* Sage.

Henri, C., Santos, M., & Varnum, I. (2017). Global increases in individualism. *Psychological Science, 28*, 9.

Hindle, D., Sherwin-White, S., & Rustin, M. (2014). *Sibling matters: A psychoanalytic, developmental, and systemic approach.* Karnac Books.

Hines, M. (2011). Gender development and the human brain. *Annual Review of Neuroscience, 34*, 69–88.

Ho, J., & Funk, S. (2018). Promoting young children's social and emotional health. *Young Children, 73*(1).

Hoffman, M. (2000). *Empathy and moral development: Implications for caring and justice.* Cambridge University.

Holder, M., Coleman, B., & Wallace, J. (2010). Spirituality, religiousness, and happiness in children aged 8–12 years. *Journal of Happiness Studies, 11*, 131–150.

Hosogi, M., Okada, A., Fujii, C., Noguchi, K., & Watanabe, K. (2012). Importance and usefulness of evaluating self-esteem in children. *BioPsychoSocial Medicine, 6*, 9.

Howe, N., Rinaldi, C., Jennings, M., & Petrakos, H. (2002). No! The Lambs can stay out because they got cozies! Constructive and destructive sibling conflict, pretend play, and social understanding. *Child Development, 73*, 1460–1473.

Ingoldsby, E., Shaw, D., Owens, E., & Winslow, E. (1999). *Journal of Abnormal Child Psychology, 27*(5), 343–356.

Jensen, L. (2015). *Moral development in a global world research from a cultural-developmental perspective.* Cambridge University Press.

Jones, S., & Doolittle, E. (2017). *Social and emotional learning: Introducing the issue. The future of children: Social and emotional learning.* The Wallace Foundation, *27*(1). https://www.wallacefoundation.org/knowledge-center/Documents/FOC-Spring-Vol27-No1-Compiled-Future-of-Children-spring-2017.pdf

Joseph, G., & Strain, P. (2010). Teaching young children interpersonal problem solving skills. *Young Exceptional Children, 13*(3).

Keo-Meier, C., & Ehrensaft, D. (2018). *The gender affirmative model: An interdisciplinary approach to supporting transgender and gender expansive children.* American Psychological Association.

Kernan, M., & Singer, E. (2010). *Peer relationships in early childhood education and care.* Routledge.

King, P., & Boyatzis, C. (2015). Religious and spiritual development. In R. Lerner (Ed)., *Handbook of child psychology and developmental science.* John Wiley and Sons.

Kirby G., & Hodges, J. (2018). Parenting of preschool and school-aged children. In M. Sanders & A. Morawska (Eds.), *Handbook of parenting and child development across the lifespan.* Springer.

Klubeck, M., Fuentes, K., & Kim-Prieto, C. (2017). Gender development, theories of. In K. Nadal (Ed.), *The SAGE encyclopedia of psychology and gender.* Sage.

Kohlberg, L. (1981). *Essays on moral development* (Vol. 1). *The philosophy of moral development.* Harper & Row.

Koplow, L. (2021). *Emotionally responsive practice: A path for schools that heal, infancy-grade 6.* Teachers College.

Kowal, A., & Kramer, L. (1997). Children's understanding of parental differential treatment. *Child Development, 68*, 113–126.

Kuppens, S., & Ceulemans, E. (2019). Parenting styles: A closer look at a well-known concept. *Journal of Child and Family Studies, 28*, 168–181.

Ladd, G. (2005). *Children's peer relations and social competence: A century of progress.* Yale University Press.

Ladd, G., & Troop-Gordon, W. (2003). The role of chronic peer difficulties in the development of children's psychological adjustment problems. *Child Development, 74*(5), 1344–1367.

Lally, J., & Mangione, P. (2017). Caring relationships: The heart of early brain development. *Young Children, 72*(2).

Lapsley, D., & Narváez, D. (2004). *Moral development, self, and identity.* Lawrence Erlbaum Associates.

Lerner, R., Easterbrooks, M., Mistry, J., & Weiner, I. (2013). Developmental psychology. *Handbook of psychology* (6th ed.). John Wiley & Sons.

LeVine, R., & LeVine, S. (2016). *Do parents matter?* Public Affairs.

Lindon, J. (2012). *Supporting children's social development positive relationships in the early years.* Andrews Publications.

Lippard, C., La Paro, K., Rouse, H., & Crosby, D. (2018). A closer look at teacher–child relationships and classroom emotional context in preschool. *Child Youth Care Forum, 47*, 1–21.

Liu, L., & Wang, M. (2015). Parenting stress and children's problem behavior in China: The mediating role of parental psychological aggression. *Journal of Family Psychology, 29*(1), 20.

Louis, J., Ortiz, V., Barlas, J., Lee, J., Lockwood, G., Chong, W., Louis, K., & Sim, P. (2021). The good enough parenting early intervention schema therapy based program: Participant experience. *PLOS ONE, 16*(1), e0243508.

Low, Y., & Tsang, A. (2019). *A comparison of eastern and western parenting: Programmes, policies and approaches.* Routledge.

Lynch, J. (2018). Navigating gender and social influences on early literacy development. In B. Guzzetti, T. Bean, & J. Dunkerly-Bean (Eds.), *Exploring gender through multicultural literature*. Routledge.

Ma, H. (2013). The moral development of the child: An integrated model. *Frontiers in Public Health, 1*, 57.

Macintosh, T., Desai, M., Lewis, T., Jones, B., & Nunez-Smith, M. (2013). Socially-assigned race, healthcare discrimination and preventive healthcare services. *PLOS ONE, 8*(5), e64522.

Manning, B., Roberts, M., Estabrook, R., Petitclerc, A., Burns, J., Briggs-Gowan, M., Wakschlag, L., & Norton, E. (2019). Relations between toddler expressive language and temper tantrums in a community sample. *Journal of Applied Developmental Psychology, 65*, 101070.

Maree, J. (2021). The psychosocial development theory of Erik Erikson: Critical overview. *Early Child Development and Care, 191*(5).

Mascolo, M., & Fischer, K. (2007). The co-development of self and sociomoral emotions. In C. Brownell & C. Kopp (Eds.), *Socioemotional development in the toddler years: Transitions and transformations*. Guilford.

Mata-McMahon, J., Haslip, M., & Schein, D. (2018). Early childhood educators' perceptions of nurturing spirituality in secular settings. *Early Child Development and Care, 48(5).*

Mata-McMahon, J., Haslip, M., & Schein, D. (2020). Connections, virtues, and meaning-making: How early childhood educators describe children's spirituality. *Early Childhood Education Journal, 48*(5), 657–669.

McClelland, M., Tominey, S., Schmitt, S., & Duncan, R. (2017). *The future of children: Social and emotional learning*. The Wallace Foundation, *27* (1). https://www.wallacefoundation.org/knowledge-center/Documents/FOC-Spring-Vol27-No1-Compiled-Future-of-Children-spring-2017.pdf

McHale, S., Kim, J., & Whiteman, S. (2006). Sibling relationships in childhood and adolescence. In P. Noller & J. Feeney (Eds.), *Close relationships: Functions, forms and processes*. Psychology Press.

McHale, S., Updegraff, K., Shanahan, L., Crouter, A., & Killoren, S. (2005). Siblings' differential treatment in Mexican American families. *Journal of Marriage and Family, 67*, 1259–1274.

McHale, S., Updegraff, K., & Whiteman, S. (2012). Sibling relationships and influences in childhood and adolescence. *Journal of Marriage and the Family, 74*(5), 913–930.

Mcluckie, A., Landers, A., Curran, J., Cann, R., Carrese, D., Nolan, A., Corrigan, K., & Carrey, N. (2019). A scoping review of mental health prevention and intervention initiatives for infants and preschoolers at risk for socio-emotional difficulties. *Systematic Reviews, 8.*

Milica, J. (2014). Developing a sense of identity in preschoolers. *Mediterranean Journal of Social Sciences, 5*, 225–234.

Miller, S., Smith-Bonahue, T., & Kemple, K. (2017). Preschool teachers' responses to challenging behavior: The role of organizational climate in referrals and expulsions. *International Research in Early Childhood Education, 8*(1), 38–57.

Mooney, C. (2013). *Theories of childhood: An introduction to Dewey, Montessori, Erikson, Piaget & Vygotsky*. Redleaf Press.

Moore, C., Paulus, M., & Williams, A. (2015). *Sugar and spice, and everything nice: Exploring prosocial development through infancy and early childhood*. Frontiers Media.

Moore, E., Michael, A., Penick-Parks, M., Singleton, G., & Hackman, H. (2018). *The guide for White women who teach Black boys: Understanding, connecting, respecting*. Corwin.

Moran, K., Turiano, N., & Gentzler, A. (2018). Parental warmth during childhood predicts coping and well-being in adulthood. *Journal of Family Psychology, 32*(5), 610–621.

Mottweiler, C., & Taylor, M. (2014). Elaborated role play and creativity in preschool age children. *Psychology of Aesthetics, Creativity, and the Arts, 8*(3), 277–286.

Murano, D., Sawyer, J., & Lipnevich, A. (2020). A meta-analytic review of preschool social and emotional learning interventions. *Review of Educational Research, 90*(2), 227–263.

Ng, Y. (2012). Spiritual development in the classroom: Pupils' and educators' learning reflections. *International Journal of Children's Spirituality, 17*(2), 167–185.

Novoa, C., & Malik, R. (2018). *Suspensions are not support: The disciplining of preschoolers with disabilities*. Center for American Progress.

Obradovic, J., Sulik, M., & Shaffer, A. (2021). Learning to let go: Parental over-engagement predicts poorer self-regulation in kindergartners. *Journal of Family Psychology, 35*(8), 1160–1170.

O'Brien, I., Duffy, A., & Nicholl, H. (2009). Impact of childhood chronic illnesses on siblings: A literature review. *British Journal of Nursing, 8*(22), 1358–1365.

Ostrov, J., & Keating, C. (2004). Gender differences in preschool aggression during free play and structured interactions: An observational study. *Social Development, 13*(2), 255–277.

Painter, K., & Scannapieco, M. (2021). *Understanding the mental health problems of children and adolescents: A guide for social workers*. Oxford University Press.

Parker, E. (2018). *How states fund pre-k: A primer for policymakers*. Education Commission of the States. https://www.ecs.org/wp-content/uploads/How-States-Fund-Pre-K_A-Primer-for-Policymakers.pdf

Parten, M. (1933). Leadership among preschool children. *Journal of Abnormal and Social Psychology, 27*(4), 430–440.

Paulus, M. (2014). The emergence of prosocial behavior: Why do infants and toddlers help, comfort, and share? *Child Development Perspectives, 8*, 77–81.

Paulus, M., Worle, M., & Christner, N. (2020). The emergence of human altruism: Preschool children develop a norm for empathy-based comforting. *Journal of Cognition and Development, 21*(1), 104–124.

Pellis, S., Pellis, V., & Bell, H. (2010). The function of play in the development of the social brain. *American Journal of Play, 2*, 278–296.

Perry, D., Pauletti, R., & Cooper, P. (2019). Gender identity in childhood: A review of the literature. *International Journal of Behavioral Development, 43*(4), 289–304.

Perszyk, D., Lei, R., Bodenhausen, G., Richeson, J., & Waxman, S. (2019). Bias at the intersection of race and gender: Evidence from preschool-aged children. *Developmental Science, 22*, e12788.

Piaget, J. (1932). *The moral judgment of the child*. Routledge and Kegan Paul.

Pinquart, M., & Gerke, D. (2019). Associations of parenting styles with self-esteem in children and adolescents: A meta-analysis. *Journal of Child and Family Studies, 28*, 2017–2035.

Piper, R. (2018). Preschool-aged children's gender identity development. In B. Guzzetti, T. Bean, & J. Dunkerly-Bean (Eds.), *Exploring gender through multicultural literature*. Routledge.

Posthumus, J., Raaijmakers, M., Maassen, G., Van Engeland, H., & Matthys, W. (2012). Sustained effects of incredible years as a preventive intervention in preschool children with conduct problems. *Journal of Abnormal Child Psychology, 40*(4), 487–500.

Potegal, M., Kosorok, M., & Davidson, R. (2003). Temper tantrums in young children: Tantrum duration and temporal organization. *Developmental and Behavioral Pediatrics, 24*(3), 148–154.

Poushter, J., & Fetterolf, J. (2019). *A changing world: Global views on diversity, gender equality, family life and the importance of religion*, PEW Research Center. https://www.pewresearch.org/global/2019/04/22/a-changing-world-global-views-on-diversity-gender-equality-family-life-and-the-importance-of-religion/

Price, C., & Steed, E. (2016). Culturally responsive strategies to support young children with challenging behavior. *Young Children, 71*(5).

Qu, L., Shen, P., Chee, Y., & Chen, L. (2015). Teachers' theory-of-mind coaching and children's executive function predict the training effect of sociodramatic play on children's theory of mind. *Social Development, 24*(4), 716–733.

Quintana, S. (2007). Racial and ethnic identity: Developmental perspectives and research. *Journal of Counseling Psychology, 54*, 259–270.

Raikes, H., & Edwards, C. (2009*). Extending the dance in infant and toddler caregiving: Enhancing attachment and relationships*. Brookes Publishing.

Ramani, G. B. (2012). Influence of a playful, child directed context on preschool children's peer cooperation. *Merrill-Palmer Quarterly, 58*(2), 159–190.

Rambura, P. (2015). The self—Who am I? Children's identity and development through early childhood education. *Journal of Educational and Social Research, 5*(1), 95.

Rivers, S., Tominey, S., O' Bryon, E., & Brackett, M. (2013). Introduction to the special issue on social and emotional learning in early education. *Early Education and Development, 24*, 953–959.

Robinson, M. (2008). *Child development 0–8: A journey through the early years*. McGraw-Hill.

Rogoff, B. (2003). *The cultural nature of human development*. Oxford University Press.

Rollin, A. (2019). Racial socialization: A developmental perspective. In R. Nazarinia & A. Rollins (Eds.), *Biracial families: Crossing boundaries, blending cultures, and challenging racial ideologies*. Springer.

Ross, J. (2017). You and me: Investigating the role of self-evaluative emotion in preschool prosociality. *Journal of Experimental Child Psychology, 155*, 67–83.

Rubin, K., Burgess, K., Dwyer, K., & Hastings, P. (2003). Predicting preschoolers' externalizing behaviors from toddler temperament, conflict, and maternal negativity. *Developmental Psychology, 39*(1), 164–176.

Ruble, D., Martin, C., & Berenbaum, S. (2006). Gender development. In W. Damon, R. M. Lerner, & N. Eisenberg, (Eds.), *Handbook of child psychology: Social, emotional, and personality development*. John Wiley.

Russo-Netzer, P. (2018). Spiritual development. In M. Bornstein, M. Arterberry, K. Fingerman & J. Lansford (Eds.) *The SAGE encyclopedia of lifespan human development*. Sage.

Sanders, M., & Morawska, A. (2018). *Handbook of parenting and child development across the lifespan*. Springer.

Sangrigoli, S., & De Schonen, S. (2004). Recognition of own-race and other-race faces by three-month-old infants. *Journal of Child Psychology and Psychiatry, 45*(7), 1219–1227.

Scheier, L., Hansen, W., & Botzet, A. (2014). *Parenting and teen drug use: The most recent findings from research, prevention, and treatment*. Oxford University Press.

Schein, D. (2017). *Inspiring wonder, awe, and empathy: Spiritual development for children*. Redleaf Press.

Schore, A. (2015). *Affect regulation and the origin of the self*. Routledge.

Schoon, I., Parsons, S., Rush, R., & Law, J. (2010). Children's language ability and psychosocial development: A 29-year follow-up study. *Pediatrics, 126*(1), e73–e80.

Sclafani, J. (2012). *The educated parent 2: Child rearing in the 21st century*. Praeger.

Sette, S., Baldwin, D., Zava, F., Baumgartner, E., & Coplan, R. (2019). Shame on me? Shyness, social experiences at preschool, and young children's self-conscious emotions. *Early Childhood Research Quarterly, 47*, 229–238.

Shanahan, L, McHale, S., Crouter, A., & Osgood, D. (2008). Linkages between parents' differential treatment, youth depressive symptoms, and sibling relationships. *Journal of Marriage and Family, 70*, 480–494.

Shek, D. (2012). Spirituality as a positive youth development construct: A conceptual review. *The Scientific World Journal*, 458953.

Sherman, L., Rice, K., & Cassidy, J. (2015). Infant capacities related to building internal working models of attachment figures: A theoretical and empirical review. *Developmental Review, 37*, 109–141.

Sisterhen, L., & Wy, P. (2021). *Temper tantrums*. StatPearls Publishing. https://www.ncbi.nlm.nih.gov/books/NBK544286/

Sklad, M., Diekstra, R., De Ritter, M., Ben, J., & Gravesteijn, C. (2012). Effectiveness of school-based universal social, emotional, and behavioral programs: Do they enhance students' development in the area of skill, behavior, and adjustment? *Psychology in the Schools, 49*(9), 892–909.

Smetana, J. (2013). Moral development: The social domain theory view. In P. Zelazo (Ed.), *The Oxford handbook of developmental psychology: Body and mind (Vol. 1)*, pp. 832–863. Oxford Library of Psychology.

Solomon, J. (2016). Gender identity and expression in the early childhood classroom: Influences on development within sociocultural contexts (voices). *Young Children, 71*(3).

Solter, A. (1992). Understanding tears and tantrums. *Young Children, 47*(4), 64–68.

Sommerville, J., Schmidt, M., Yun, J., & Burns, M. (2012). The development of fairness expectations and prosocial development in the second year of life. *Infancy, 18*, 40–66.

Sorkhabi, N., & Mandara, J. (2013). Are the effects of Baumrind's parenting styles culturally specific or culturally equivalent? In R. Larzelere, A. Morris, & A. Harrist (Eds.), *Authoritative parenting: Synthesizing nurturance and discipline for optimal child development*. American Psychological Association.

Spinrad, T., & Gal, D. (2018). Fostering prosocial behavior and empathy in young children. *Current Opinion in Psychology, 20*, 40–44.

Stern, J., & Cassidy, J. (2018). Empathy from infancy to adolescence: An attachment perspective on the development of individual differences. *Developmental Review, 47*, 1–22.

Stipek, D. (1995). The development of pride and shame in toddlers. In J. Tangney & K. Fischer (Eds.), *The self-conscious emotions: The psychology of shame, guilt, embarrassment, and pride*. Guilford.

Stocker, C., & Youngblade, L. (1999). Marital conflict and parental hostility: Links with children's sibling and peer relationships. *Journal of Family Psychology, 13*, 598–609.

Swanson, D., Cunningham, M., Youngblood, J., & Spencer, M. (2009). *Racial identity development during childhood*. University of Pennsylvania Scholarly Commons. http://repository.upenn.edu/gse_pubs/198

Tamis-LeMonda, C., Shannon, J., Cabrera, N., & Lamb, M. (2004). Fathers and mothers at play with their 2- and 3-year-olds: Contributions to language and cognitive development. *Child Development, 75*, 1806–1820.

Thibodeau, R., Gilpin, A., Brown, M., & Meyer, B. (2016). The effects of fantastical pretend-play on the development of executive functions: An intervention study. *Journal of Experimental Child Psychology, 145*, 120–138.

Thomas, E. (2019). Empowerment through Disney? Third wave feminist discourse in the "dream big, princess" campaign. In K. Foss (Ed.), *Beyond princess culture: Gender and children's marketing*. Peter Lang.

Thompson, R. (2012). Whither the preconventional child? Toward a life-span moral development theory. *Child Development Perspectives, 6*(4), 423–429.

Tobin, J. (2019). *The UN Convention on the rights of the child: A commentary*. Oxford University Press.

Trent, M., Dooley, D., & Dougé, J. (2019). The impact of racism on child and adolescent health. *Pediatrics, 144*(2), e20191765.

Ubani, M. (2013). Existentially sensitive education. In J. Arthur & T. Lovat (Eds.), *The Routledge international handbook on education, religion and values*. Routledge.

Ubani, M., & Murtonen, S. (2018). Issues in spiritual formation in early lifespan contexts. *International Journal of Children's Spirituality, 23*(2), 103–108.

Updegraff, K., McHale, S., & Crouter, A. (2002). Adolescents' sibling relationships and friendships: Developmental patterns and relationship associations. *Social Development, 1*, 182–211.

Updegraff, K., McHale, S., Killoren, S., & Rodriguez, S. (2010). Cultural variations in sibling relationships. In J. Caspi (Ed.), *Sibling development: Implications for mental health practitioners*. Springer.

Umami, D., & Sari, L. (2020). Confirmation of five factors that affect temper tantrums in preschool children: A literature review. *Journal of Global Research in Public Health, 5*(2), 151–157.

UNICEF (2020). https://www.unicef.org

Vaish, A. (2018). Sophisticated concern in early childhood. In N. Roughley & T. Schramme (Eds.) *Forms of fellow feeling: Empathy, sympathy, concern and moral agency*. Cambridge University Press.

Vaishali, V., & Walker, B. (2019). Unpacking "culture": Caregiver socialization of emotion and child functioning in diverse families. *Developmental Review, 51*, 146–174.

Vitiello, V., & Williford, A. (2020). Context influences on task orientation among preschoolers who display disruptive behavior problems. *Early Childhood Research Quarterly, 51*, 256–266.

Vogel, M., Monesson, A., & Scott, L. (2012). Building biases in infancy: The influence of race on face and voice emotion matching. *Developmental Science, 5*(3), 359–372, 375.

Wakschlag, L., Choi, S., Carter, A., Hullsiek, H., Burns, J., McCarthy, K., Leibenluft, E., & Briggs-Gowan, M. (2012). Defining the developmental parameters of temper loss in early childhood: Implications for developmental psychopathology. *Journal of Child Psychology and Psychiatry, 53*, 1099–1108.

Warin, J., & Adriany, V. (2017). Gender flexible pedagogy in early childhood education. *Journal of Gender Studies, 26*(4), 375–386.

Watson, J., De Souza, M., & Trousdale, A. (2014). Global perspectives and contexts for spirituality in education. In J. Watson, M. De Souza, & A. Trousdale (Eds.), *Global perspectives on spirituality and education*. Routledge.

Webster-Stratton, C., Reid, M., & Stoolmiller, M. (2008). Preventing conduct problems and improving school readiness: Evaluation of the incredible years teacher and child training programs in high-risk schools. *Journal of Child Psychology and Psychiatry, 49*(5), 471–488.

Weiner, I., Lerner, R., & Easterbrooks, M. (2012). *Handbook of psychology, developmental psychology*. John Wiley & Sons.

Williams, A., & Moore, C. (2014). Exploring disadvantageous inequality aversion in children: How cost and discrepancy influence decision-making. *Frontiers in Psychology, 5*.

Williams, P., & Lerner, M. (2019). School readiness. *Pediatrics, 144*(2).

Wojciak, A., & Gamboni, C. (2020). Prevention and treatment of problems with sibling relationships. *The handbook of systemic family therapy: Systemic family therapy with children and adolescents* (Vol. 2). Wiley-Blackwell.

Xiao, N., Quinn, P., Liu, S., Ge, L., Pascalis, O., & Lee, K. (2018). Older but not younger infants associate own-race faces with happy music and other-race faces with sad music. *Developmental Science, 21*(2).

Xing, X., Liu, X., & Wang, M. (2019). Parental warmth and harsh discipline as mediators of the relations between family SES and Chinese preschooler's inhibitory control. *Early Childhood Research Quarterly, 48*, 237–245.

Yates, T., Ostrosky, M., Cheatham, G., Fettig, A., Shaffer, L., & Santos, R. (2008). *Research synthesis on screening and assessing social–emotional competence*. Center on the Social Emotional Foundations for Early Learning. http://csefel.vanderbilt.edu/documents/rs_screening_assessment.pdf

Yogman, M., Garner, A., Hutchinson, J., Hirsh-Pasek, K., & Golinkoff, R. (2018). The power of play: A pediatric role in enhancing development in young children. Committee on the Psychological Aspects of Child and Family Health, Council on Communications and Media. *Pediatrics, 142*(3), e20182058.

Youngblade, L., & Dunn, J. (1995). Individual differences in young children's pretend play with mother and sibling: Links to relationships and understanding of other people's feelings and beliefs. *Child Development, 66*, 1472–1492.

Zeng, S., Corr, C., O'Grady, C., & Guan, Y. (2019). Adverse childhood experiences and preschool suspension expulsion: A population study. *Child Abuse & Neglect, 97.*

Zosuls, K., Andrews, N., Martin, C., England, D., & Field, R. (2016). Developmental changes in the link between gender typicality and peer victimization and exclusion. *Sex Roles, 75,* 243–256.

Chapter 10

Abramson, A. (2020). How COVID-19 may increase domestic violence and child abuse. *American Psychological Association, 8.*

Agathão, B., Lopes, C., Cunha, D., & Sichieri, R. (2020). Gender differences in the impact of sleep duration on common mental disorders in school students. *BMC Public Health, 20,* 148.

Alderman, H., Behrman, J. R., Glewwe, P., Fernald, L., & Walker, S. (2017). Evidence of impact of interventions on growth and development during early and middle childhood. *Child and Adolescent Health and Development, 8,* 1790.

Alonge, O., & Hyder, A. (2014). Reducing the global burden of childhood unintentional injuries. *Archives of Disease in Childhood, 99*(1), 62.

Al-Yateem, N., & Rossiter, R. (2017). Unstructured play for anxiety in pediatric inpatient care. *Journal for Specialists in Pediatric Nursing, 22*(1), e12166.

American Academy of Pediatrics (2013). The crucial role of recess in school. *Pediatrics, 131*(1), 183–188.

American Academy of Pediatrics (2016). *American Academy of Pediatrics supports childhood sleep guidelines.* https://www.aap.org/en-us/about-the-aap/aap-press-room/Pages/American-Academy-of-Pediatrics-Supports-Childhood-Sleep-Guidelines.aspx

American Academy of Pediatrics (2016). Media use in school-aged children and adolescents. *Pediatrics, 138*(5), e20162592.

American Academy of Pediatrics (2019). *Brushing up on oral health: Never too early to start.* https://www.healthychildren.org/English/healthy-living/oral-health/Pages/Brushing-Up-on-Oral-Health-Never-Too-Early-to-Start.aspx

An, R., Yang, Y., Hoschke, A., Xue, H., & Wang, Y. (2017). Influence of neighbourhood safety on childhood obesity: A systematic review and meta-analysis of longitudinal studies. *Obesity Reviews, 18*(11), 1289–1309.

Anderson, S., & Caseman, K. (2020). School-based health centers can deliver care to vulnerable populations during COVID-19 pandemic. *Childtrends.* https://www.childtrends.org/blog/school-based-health-centers-can-deliver-care-to-vulnerable-populations-during-the-covid-19-pandemic

Anderson-Steeves, E., Jones-Smith, J., Hopkins, L., & Gittelsohn, J. (2016). Perceived social support from friends and parents for eating behavior and diet quality among low-income, urban, minority youth. *Journal of Nutrition Education and Behavior, 48*(5), 304–310.

Arnold, K., Umanath, S., Thio, K., Reilly, W., McDaniel, M., & Marsh, E. J. (2017). Understanding the cognitive processes involved in writing to learn. *Journal of Experimental Psychology: Applied, 23*(2), 115.

Babic, M., Morgan, P., Plotnikoff, R., Lonsdale, C., White, R., & Lubans, D. (2014). Physical activity and physical self-concept in youth: Systematic review and meta-analysis. *Sports Medicine, 44*(11), 1589–1601.

Bagley, E., Kelly, R., Buckhalt, J., & El-Sheik, M. (2015). What keeps low-SES children from sleeping well: The role of presleep worries and sleep environment. *Sleep Medicine, 16*(4), 496–502.

Balantekin, K., Anzman-Frasca, S., Francis, L., Ventura, A., Fisher, J., & Johnson, S. (2020). Positive parenting approaches and their association with child eating and weight: A narrative review from infancy to adolescence. *Pediatric Obesity, 15,* e12722.

Banfield, E., Liu, Y., Davis, J., Chang, S., & Frazier-Wood, A. (2016). Poor adherence to US dietary guidelines for children and adolescents in the National Health and Nutrition Examination Survey population. *Journal of the Academy of Nutrition and Dietetics, 116*(1), 21–27.

Barkovich, A., & Raybaud, C. (2019). *Pediatric neuroimaging.* Wolters Kluwer.

Barlow, S. (2007). Expert committee recommendations regarding the prevention, assessment, and treatment of child and adolescent overweight and obesity: Summary report. *Pediatrics, 120,* S164–S192.

Barnett, T., Kelly, A., Young, D., Perry, C., Pratt, C., Edwards, N., Rao, G., Vos, M., & American Heart Association Obesity Committee of the Council on Lifestyle and Cardiometabolic Health, Council on Cardiovascular Disease in the Young, and Stroke Council (2018). Sedentary behaviors in today's youth: Approaches to the prevention and management of childhood obesity: A scientific statement from the American Heart Association. *Circulation, 138*(11), e142–e159.

Ben-Joseph, E. (2020). *Growth charts.* Kid's Health from Nemours. https://kidshealth.org/en/parents/growth-charts.html

Berberoglu, M. (2009). Precocious puberty and normal variant puberty: Definition, etiology, diagnosis and current management. *Journal of Clinical Research in Pediatric Endocrinology, 1*(4), 164–174.

Berk, L. E. (2013). *Child development.* Pearson Education.

Berman, E. (2021). *Gray and white matter of the human brain.* MedlinePlus. US Library of Health. https://medlineplus.gov/ency/imagepages/18117.htm

Biehl, M., Park, M., Brindis, C., Pantell, R., & Irwin, C. (2002). *The health of America's middle childhood population.* University of California, San Francisco, Public Policy Analysis and Education Center for Middle Childhood and Adolescent Health.

Birch, L., Savage, J., & Ventura, A. (2007). Influences on the development of children's eating behaviors: From infancy to adolescence. *Canadian Journal of Dietetic Practice and Research, 68*(1), s1–s56.

Blanche, E., Bodison, S., Chang, M., & Reinoso, G. (2012). Development of the comprehensive observations of proprioception (COP): Validity, reliability, and factor analysis. *The American Journal of Occupational Therapy, 66,* 691–698.

Bonomo, V. (2010). Gender matters in elementary education: Research-based strategies to meet the distinctive learning needs of boys and girls. *Educational Horizons, 88*(4), 257–264.

Boswell, N., Byrne, R., & Davies, P. (2019). Family food environment factors associated with obesity outcomes in early childhood. *BMC Obesity, 6*(1), 1–11.

Brown, S., Nobiling, B., Teufel, J., & Birch, D. (2011). Are kids too busy? Early adolescents' perceptions of discretionary activities, overscheduling, and stress. *The Journal of School Health, 81*(9), 574–580.

Cadoret, G., Bigras, N., Duval, S., Lemay, L., Tremblay, T., & Lemire, J. (2017). The mediating role of cognitive ability on the relationship between motor proficiency and early academic achievement in children. *Human Movement Science, 57*, 149–157.

Cameron, C., Cottone, E., Murrah, W., & Grissmer, D. (2016). How are motor skills linked to children's school performance and academic achievement? *Child Development Perspectives, 10*(2), 93–98.

Carbonaro, W., & Maloney, E. (2019). Extracurricular activities and student outcomes in elementary and middle school: Causal effects or self-selection? *Socius, 5*.

Carson, V., Hunter, S., Kuzik, N., Gray, C., Poitras, V., Chaput, J., Saunders, T., Katzmarzyk, P., Okely, A., Connor Gorber, S., Kho, M., Sampson, M., Lee, H., & Tremblay, M. (2016). Systematic review of sedentary behaviour and health indicators in school-aged children and youth: An update. *Applied Physiology, Nutrition, and Metabolism, 41*(6 Suppl 3), S240–S265.

Center on the Developing Child, Harvard University. (2021). *Lifelong health.* https://developingchild.harvard.edu/science/deep-dives/lifelong-health/

Cheuiche, A., da Silveira, L., de Paula, L., Lucena, I., & Silveiro, S. (2021). Diagnosis and management of precocious sexual maturation: An updated review. *European Journal of Pediatrics, 180*(10), 3073–3087.

Chu, V. (2017). Assessing proprioception in children: A review. *Journal of Motor Behavior, 49*(4), 458–466.

Cleland, V., Dwyer, T., & Venn, A. (2012). Which domains of childhood physical activity predict physical activity in adulthood? A 20-year prospective tracking study. *British Journal of Sports Medicine, 46*, 595–602.

Dahlgren, A., Sjoblom, L., Eke, H., Bonn, S., & Trolle Lagerros, Y. (2021). Screen time and physical activity in children and adolescents aged 10–15 years. *PLOS ONE, 15*(7), 1–14.

David-Ferdon, C., Vivolo-Kantor, A., Dahlberg, L., Marshall, K., Rainford, N., & Hall, J. (2016). *A comprehensive technical package for the prevention of youth violence and associated risk behaviors.* National Center for Injury Prevention and Control, Centers for Disease Control and Prevention.

Davies, D., & Troy, M. (2020). *Child development: A practitioner's guide.* Guilford.

Del Giudice, M. (2014). Middle childhood: An evolutionary-developmental synthesis. *Child Development Perspectives, 8*, 193–200.

de Souza, M., de Chaves, R., Lopes, V., Malina, R., Garganta, R., Seabra, A., & Maia, J. (2014). Motor coordination, activity, and fitness at 6 years of age relative to activity and fitness at 10 years of age. *Journal of Physical Activity and Health, 11*, 1239–1247.

Development Services Group, Inc. (2016). *Child labor trafficking: Literature review.* Office of Juvenile Justice and Delinquency Prevention. https://www.ojjdp.gov/mpg/litreviews/child-labor-trafficking.pdf

Dhanuka, S., & Vasthare, R. (2019). The association of secondhand smoke exposure and dental caries in children and adolescents: A literature review. *General Dentistry, 67*(6), 20–24.

Dinehart, L. H. (2015). Handwriting in early childhood education: Current research and future implications. *Journal of Early Childhood Literacy, 15*(1), 97–118.

Doane, L., Breitenstein, R., Beekman, C., Clifford, S., Smith, T., & Lemery-Chalfant, K. (2019). Early life socioeconomic disparities in children's sleep: The mediating role of the current home environment. *Journal of Youth and Adolescence, 48*(1), 56–70.

Dowshen, S. (2014). *Braces.* Kid's Health from Nemours. https://kidshealth.org/en/kids/braces.html

Draper, N., & Stratton, G. (2019). *Physical activity: A multi-disciplinary introduction.* Routledge.

Drewnowski, A., Dwyer, J., King, J., & Weaver, C. (2019). A proposed nutrient density score that includes food groups and nutrients to better align with dietary guidance. *Nutrition Reviews, 77*(6), 404–416.

Dubois, L., Ohm Kyvik, K., Girard, M., Tatone-Tokuda, F., Pérusse, D., Hjelmborg, J., Skytthe, A., Rasmussen, F., Wright, M., Lichtenstein, P., & Martin, N. (2012). Genetic and environmental contributions to weight, height, and BMI from birth to 19 years of age: An international study of over 12,000 twin pairs. *PLOS ONE, 7*(2), e30153.

Dufford, A., & Kim, P. (2017). Family income, cumulative risk exposure, and white matter structure in middle childhood. *Frontiers in Human Neuroscience, 11*, 547.

Dufford, A., Kim, P., & Evans, G. (2020). The impact of childhood poverty on brain health: Emerging evidence from neuroimaging across the lifespan. *International Review of Neurobiology, 150*, 77–105.

Eales, L., Gillespie, S., Alstat, R., Ferguson, G., & Carlson, S. (2021). Children's screen and problematic media use in the United States before and during the COVID-19 pandemic. *Child Development, 92*, O866–O882.

Edmonds, C., & Jeffes, B. (2009). Does having a drink help you think? 6- to 7-year-old children show improvements in cognitive performance from baseline to test after having a drink of water. *Appetite, 53*, 469–472.

Evans, A., & Scutter, S. (2004). Prevalence of "growing pains" in young children. *Journal of Pediatrics, 145*, 255–258.

Evans, A. (2008). Growing pains: Contemporary knowledge and recommended practice. *Journal of Foot and Ankle Research, 1*(1), 4.

Faigenbaum, A., Lloyd, R., Oliver, J., & American College of Sports Medicine (2020). *Essentials of youth fitness.* Human Kinetics.

Farah, M. (2017). The neuroscience of socioeconomic status: Correlates, causes, and consequences. *Neuron, 96*, 56–71.

Fedina, L., Williamson, C., & Perdue, T. (2019). Risk factors for domestic child sex trafficking in the United States. *Journal of Interpersonal Violence, 34*(13), 2653–2673.

Field, A. (2017). Epidemiology of childhood obesity and associated risk factors: An overview. In M. Goran (Ed.), *Childhood obesity.* CRC Press.

Flais, S. (2019). *Caring for your school-age child: Ages 5–12.* American Academy of Pediatrics. Random House.

Flores, D., & Barroso, J. (2017). 21st century parent-child sex communication in the United States: A process review. *Journal of Sex Research, 54*(4–5), 532–548.

Fortin, C., Barlaam, F., Vaugoyeau, M., & Assaiante, C. (2021). Neurodevelopment of posture-movement coordination from late childhood to adulthood as assessed from bimanual load-lifting task: An event-related potential study. *Neuroscience, 457,* 125–138.

Fuqua, J. (2013). Treatment and outcomes of precocious puberty: An update. *The Journal of Clinical Endocrinology & Metabolism, 98*(6), 2198–2207.

Gaul, D., & Issartel, J. (2016). Fine motor skill proficiency in typically developing children: On or off the maturation track? *Human Movement Science, 46,* 78–85.

Ghassabian, A., Sundaram, R., Bell, E., Bello, S., Kus, C., & Yeung, E. (2016). Gross motor milestones and subsequent development. *Pediatrics, 138*(1), e20154372.

Giedd, J. N., & Rapoport, J. L. (2010). Structural MRI of pediatric brain development: What have we learned and where are we going? *Neuron, 67,* 728–734.

Ginsburg, K. (2007). The importance of play in promoting healthy child development and maintaining strong parent-child bonds. *Pediatrics, 119*(1), 182–191.

Gluckman, P., & Hanson, M. (2006). Changing times: The evolution of puberty. *Molecular and Cellular Endocrinology, 254–255,* 26–31.

Gong, T., Wu, Q., Vogtmann, E., Lin, B., & Wang, Y. (2013). Age at menarche and risk of ovarian cancer: A meta-analysis of epidemiological studies. *International Journal of Cancer, 132*(12), 2894–2900.

Grayson, D., & Fair, D. (2017). Development of large-scale functional networks from birth to adulthood: A guide to the neuroimaging literature. *NeuroImage, 160,* 15–31.

Gunter, K., Almstedt, H., & Janz, K. (2012). Physical activity in childhood may be the key to optimizing lifespan skeletal health. *Exercise and Sport Sciences Reviews, 40*(1), 13–21.

Guttmacher Institute (2020). *General requirements for sex education and HIV education.* https://www.guttmacher.org/state-policy/explore/sex-and-hiv-education

Haddad, J., Ullah, S., Bell, L., Leslie, E., & Magarey, A. (2018). The influence of home and school environments on children's diet and physical activity, and body mass index: A structural equation modelling approach. *Maternal and Child Health Journal, 22*(3), 364–375.

Hair, N., Hanson, J., Wolfe, B., & Pollak, S. (2015). Association of child poverty, brain development, and academic achievement. *JAMA Pediatrics, 169,* 822.

Hales, C., Fryar, C., Carroll, M., Freedman, D., & Ogden, C. (2018). Trends in obesity and severe obesity prevalence in US youth and adults by sex and age, 2007–2008 to 2015–2016. *JAMA, 319*(16), 1723–1725.

Hamilton, S. (2002). Evaluation of clumsiness in children. *American Family Physician, 66*(8), 1435–1441.

Hamlon, H., Thatcher, R., & Cline, M. (1999). Gender differences in the development of EEG coherence in normal children. *Developmental Neuropsychology, 16*(3), 479–506.

Harvey, A., Towner, E., Peden, M., Soori, H., & Bartolomeos, K. (2009). Injury prevention and the attainment of child and adolescent health. *Bulletin of the World Health Organization, 87,* 390–394.

Haugen, T., & Johansen, B. (2018). Difference in physical fitness in children with initially high and low gross motor competence: A ten-year follow-up study. *Human Movement Science, 62,* 143–149.

Hayiou-Thomas, M. E., Dale, P. S., & Plomin, R. (2012). The etiology of variation in language skills changes with development: A longitudinal twin study of language from 2 to 12 years. *Developmental Science, 15,* 233–249.

Haywood, K., & Getchell, N. (2020). *Life span motor development.* Human Kinetics.

Helsel, B., Liang, J., Williams, J., Griffin, S., & Spitler, H. (2019). Family and friend influences on fruit and vegetable intake in elementary aged children. *Journal of Community Health, 44*(5), 932–940.

Hochberg, Z. (2010). Evo-devo of child growth III: Premature juvenility as an evolutionary trade-off. *Hormone Research in Pediatrics, 73,* 430–437.

Hoffman, J., & Miller, E. (2020). Addressing the consequences of school closure due to COVID-19 on children's physical and mental well-being. *World Medical & Health Policy, 12,* 300–310.

Howley, N., & Rosales, J. (2017). *Good health key to student learning.* National Education Association. https://www.nea.org/advocating-for-change/new-from-nea/good-health-key-to-student-learning

Hoyland, A., Dye, L., & Lawton, C. (2009). A systematic review of the effect of breakfast on the cognitive performance of children and adolescents. *Nutrition Research Reviews, 22,* 220–243.

Hoyt, L., Niu, L., Pachucki, M., & Chaku, N. (2020). Timing of puberty in boys and girls: Implications for population health. *Social Science and Medicine—Population Health, 10,* 100549.

Hsieh, C., Trichopoulos, D., Katsouyanni, K., & Yuasa, S. (1990). Age at menarche, age at menopause, height and obesity as risk factors for breast cancer: Associations and interactions in an international case-control study. *International Journal of Cancer, 46,* 796–800.

Humphrey, J. (2003). *Child development through sports.* Haworth Press.

Hurwitz, L., & Schmitt, K. (2020). Can children benefit from early internet exposure? Short- and long-term links between internet use, digital skill, and academic performance. *Computers & Education, 46,* 103750.

Igras, S., Macieira, M., Murphy, E., & Lundgren, R. (2014). Investing in very young adolescents' sexual and reproductive health. *Global Public Health: An International Journal for Research, Policy and Practice, 9*(5), 555–556.

International Justice Mission (2020). *Sex trafficking.* https://www.ijm.org/our-work/sex-trafficking

Jahic, I., DeLisi, M., & Vaughn, M. (2021). Psychopathy and violent video game playing: Multiple associations in a juvenile justice system involved sample. *Aggressive Behavior, 47*(4), 385–393.

James, K., & Berninger, V. (2019). Brain research shows why handwriting should be taught in the computer age. *Learning Difficulties Australia Bulletin, 51*(1), 25–30.

Janz, K., Medema-Johnson, H., Letuchy, E., Burns, T., Eichenberger Gilmore, J., Torner, J., Willing, M., & Levy, S. (2008). Subjective and objective measures of physical activity in relationship to bone mineral content during late childhood: The Iowa bone development study. *British Journal of Sports Medicine, 42,* 658–663.

Jelenkovic, A., Sund, R., Hur, Y., Yokoyama, Y., Hjelmborg, J., Moller, S., Honda, C., Magnusson, P., Pedersen, N., Ooki, S., & Aaltonen, S. (2016). Genetic and environmental influences on height from infancy to early adulthood: An individual-based pooled analysis of 45 twin cohorts. *Scientific Reports, 6*(1), 1–13.

Jones, P., Pendergast, L., Schaefer, B., Rasheed, M., Svensen, E., Scharf, R., Shrestha, R., Maphula, A., Roshan, R., Rasmussen, Z., Seidman, J., Murray-Kolb, L., & MAL-ED Network Investigators (2017). Measuring home environments across cultures: Invariance of the HOME scale across eight international sites from the MAL-ED study. *Journal of School Psychology, 64*, 109–127.

Kaplowitz, P., Bloch, C., & Section on Endocrinology, American Academy of Pediatrics (2016). Evaluation and referral of children with signs of early puberty. *Pediatrics, 137*(1).

Katagiri, M., Ito, H., Murayama, Y., Hamada, M., Nakajima, S., Takayanagi, N., Uemiya, A., Myogan, M., Nakai, A., & Tsujii, M. (2021). Fine and gross motor skills predict later psychosocial maladaptation and academic achievement. *Brain and Development, 43*(5), 605–615.

Kaufmann, C., & Elbel, G. (2001). Frequency dependence and gender effects in visual cortical regions involved in temporal frequency dependent pattern processing. *Human Brain Mapping, 14*(1), 28–38.

Kaviraja, K. (2021). Proprioception impairment and treatment approaches in pediatrics. In *Proprioception*. IntechOpen. https://www.intechopen.com/chapters/75427

Kim, K., & Smith, P. (1999). Family relations in early childhood and reproductive development. *Journal of Reproductive & Infant Psychology, 17*(2), 133.

Kim, Y., Cubbin, C., & Oh, S. (2019). A systematic review of neighbourhood economic context on child obesity and obesity-related behaviours. *Obesity Reviews, 20*(3), 420–431.

Klopack, E., Simons, R., & Leslie, G. (2020). Puberty and girls' delinquency: A test of competing models explaining the relationship between pubertal development and delinquent behavior. *Justice Quarterly, 37*(1), 25–52.

Knell, G., Durand, C., Kohl, H., Wu, I., & Pettee, G. (2019). Prevalence and likelihood of meeting sleep, physical activity, and screen-time guidelines among US youth. *JAMA Pediatrics, 173*(4), 387–389.

Konnikova, M. (2014). What's lost as handwriting fades. *The New York Times.* https://www.nytimes.com/2014/06/03/science/whats-lost-as-handwriting-fades.html

Korhonen, L. (2021). The good, the bad and the ugly of children's screen time during the COVID-19 pandemic. *Acta Paediatrica, 110*, 2671–2672.

Kota, A., & Ejaz, S. (2021). *Precocious puberty.* StatPearls Publishing. https://www.ncbi.nlm.nih.gov/books/NBK544313/

Larsen, J., Sleddens, E., Vink, J., Fisher, J., & Kremers, S. (2018). General parenting styles and children's obesity risk: Changing focus. *Frontiers in Psychology, 9*, 2119.

Lassi, Z., Moin, A., & Bhutta, Z. (2017). Nutrition in middle childhood and adolescence. In D. Bundy, N. Silva, & S. Horton (Eds.), *Child and adolescent health and development.* The International Bank for Reconstruction and Development/The World Bank.

Labe, C., & Fuhrmann, D. (2020). Is early good or bad? Early puberty onset and its consequences for learning. *Current Opinion in Behavioral Sciences, 36,* 150–156.

Laube, C., van den Bos, W., & Fandakova, Y. (2020). The relationship between pubertal hormones and brain plasticity: Implications for cognitive training in adolescence. *Developmental Cognitive Neuroscience, 42.*

Lee, R., Lane, S., Brown, G., Leung, C., Kwok, S., & Chan, S. (2020a). Systematic review of the impact of unstructured play interventions to improve young children's physical, social, and emotional wellbeing. *Nursing & Health Sciences, 22*(2), 184–196.

Lee, R., Lane, S., Tang, A., Leung, C., Louie, L., Browne, G., & Chan, S. (2020b). Effects of an unstructured free play and mindfulness intervention on wellbeing in kindergarten students. *International Journal of Environmental Research and Public Health, 17*(15), 5382.

Lee, S., Hale, L., Chang, A., Nahmod, N., Master, L., Berger, L., & Buxton, O. (2019). Longitudinal associations of childhood bedtime and sleep routines with adolescent body mass index. *Sleep, 42*(1), zsy202.

Lenroot, R., Gogtay, N., Greenstein, D., Wells, E., Wallace, G., Clasen, L., Blumental, J., Lerch, J., Zijdenbos, A., Evans, A., Thompson, P., & Giedd, J. (2007). Sexual dimorphism of brain developmental trajectories during childhood and adolescence. *NeuroImage, 36*, 1065–1073.

Leversen, J., Haga, M., & Sigmundsson, H. (2012). From children to adults: Motor performance across the life-span. *PLOS ONE, 7*(6), e38830.

Levi, J., Vinter, S., St. Laurent, R., & Segal, L. (2010). *F as in fat: How obesity threatens America's future.* Robert Wood Johnson Foundation. http://www.rwjf.org/files/research/20100629fasinfatmainreport.pdf

Limony, Y., Kozieł, S., & Friger, M. (2015). Age of onset of a normally timed pubertal growth spurt affects the final height of children. *Pediatric Research, 78*(3), 351–355.

Lindberg, L., Santelli, J., & Singh, S. (2006). Changes in formal sex education: 1995–2002. *Perspectives on Sexual and Reproductive Health, 38*(4), 182–189.

Liu, W., Zeng, N., McDonough, D., & Gao, Z. (2020). Effect of active video games on healthy children's fundamental motor skills and physical fitness: A systematic review. *International Journal of Environmental Research and Public Health, 17*(21), 8264.

Mackey, A., Finn, A., Leonard, J., Jacoby-Senghor, D., West, M., Gabrieli, C., & Gabrieli, J. (2015). Neuroanatomical correlates of the income-achievement gap. *Psychological Science, 26*(6), 925–933.

MacKenzie, B. (2019). *How to teach handwriting—and why it matters.* George Lucas Educational Foundation. https://www.edutopia.org/article/how-to-teach-handwriting-and-why-it-matters

Maiano, C., Hue, O., & April, J. (2019). Effects of motor skill interventions on fundamental movement skills in children and adolescents with intellectual disabilities: A systematic review. *Journal of Intellectual Disability Research, 63*(9), 1163–1179.

Mayo Clinic (2021). *Precocious puberty.* https://www.mayoclinic.org/diseases-conditions/precocious-puberty/symptoms-causes/syc-20351811

McArthur, B., Racine, N., Browne, D., McDonald, S., Tough, S., & Madigan, S. (2021). Recreational screen time before and during COVID-19 in school-aged children. *Acta Paediatrica, 110*, 2805–2807.

McCoy, D., Peet, E., Ezzati, M., Danaei, G., Black, M., Sudfeld, C., Fawzi, W., & Fink, G. (2016). Early childhood developmental status in low- and middle-income countries: National, regional, and global prevalence estimates using predictive modeling. *PLOS Medicine, 13*(6), e1002034.

McDermott, C., Seidlitz, J., Nadig, A., Liu, S, Clasen, L., Blumenthal, J., Reardon, P., Lalonde, F., Greenstein, D., Patel, R., Chakravarty, M., Lerch, J., & Raznahan, A. (2019). Longitudinally mapping childhood socioeconomic status associations with cortical and subcortical morphology. *The Journal of Neuroscience, 39*(8), 1365–1373.

Melman, S., Little, S., & Akin-Little, A. (2007). Adolescent overscheduling: The relationship between levels of participation in scheduled activities and self-reported clinical symptomology. *The High School Journal, 90*, 18–30.

Mercadante, A., & Tadi, P. (2021). *Neuroanatomy, gray matter.* StatPearls. https://www.ncbi.nlm.nih.gov/books/NBK553239/

Micha, R., Karageorgou, D., Bakogianni, I., Trichia, E., Whitsel, L., Story, M., Penalvo, J., & Mozaffarian D. (2018). Effectiveness of school food environment policies on children's dietary behaviors: A systematic review and meta-analysis. *PLOS ONE, 13*(3), e0194555.

Milteer, R., & Ginsburg, K. (2012). The importance of play in promoting healthy child development and maintaining strong parent-child bond: Focus on children in poverty. *Pediatrics, 129*(1), e204–e213.

Minh, A., Muhajarine, N., Janus, M., Brownell, M., & Guhn, M. (2017). A review of neighborhood effects and early child development: How, where, and for whom, do neighborhoods matter? *Health & Place, 46,* 155–174,

Mishra, A., Pandey, R., Minz, A., & Arora, V. (2017). Sleeping habits among school children and their effects on sleep pattern. *Journal of Caring Sciences, 6*(4), 315.

Movassagh, E., Baxter-Jones, A., Kontulainen, S., Whiting, S., & Vatanparast, H. (2017). Tracking dietary patterns over 20 years from childhood through adolescence into young adulthood: The Saskatchewan pediatric bone mineral accrual study. *Nutrients, 9*(9), 990.

National Association for Sport and Physical Education/American Heart Association (2012). *Shape of the nation report: Status of physical education in the USA.* http://www.shapeamerica.org/advocacy/son/2012/upload/2012-Shape-of-Nation-full-report-web.pdf

National Center for Missing and Exploited Children (2020). *Child sex trafficking.* https://www.missingkids.org/theissues/traffickinglbs.riskfactors

Oberer, N., Gashaj, V, & Roebers, C. (2017). Motor skills in kindergarten: Internal structure, cognitive correlates and relationships to background variables. *Human Movement Science, 52*, 170–180.

Ogden, C., Carroll, M., Kit, B., & Flegal, K. (2014). Prevalence of childhood and adult obesity in the United States. *JAMA, 311*(8), 806–814.

Ose Askvik, E., van der Weel, F., & van der Meer, A. (2020). The importance of cursive handwriting over typewriting for learning in the classroom: A high-density EEG study of 12-year-old children and young adults. *Frontiers in Psychology, 11*, 1810.

Paciorek, C., Stevens, G., Finucane, M., Ezzati, M., & The Nutrition Impact Model Study Group (2013). Children's height and weight in rural and urban populations in low-income and middle-income countries: A systematic analysis of population-representative data. *The Lancet Global Health, 1*(5), e300–e309.

Palines, P., Rabbitt, A., Pan, A., Nugent, M., & Ehrman, W. (2020). Comparing mental health disorders among sex trafficked children and three groups of youth at high-risk for trafficking: A dual retrospective cohort and scoping review. *Child Abuse & Neglect, 100.*

Parasuraman, S., Ghandour, R., & Kogan, M. (2020). Epidemiological profile of health and behaviors in middle childhood. *Pediatrics, 145*(6), e20192244.

Pate, C., Zahran, H., Qin, X., Johnson, C., Hummelman, E., & Malilay, J. (2021). Asthma surveillance—United States, 2006–2018. *MMWR Surveillance Summary, 70*(SS-5), 1–32.

Pierce, M., & Hardy, R. (2012). Commentary: The decreasing age of puberty—As much a psychosocial as biological problem? *International Journal of Epidemiology, 41*(1), 300–302.

Pierce, M., Kuh, D., & Hardy, R. (2011). The tole of BMI across the life course in the relationship between age at menarche and diabetes. *Diabetic Medicine, 29*(5), 600–603.

Pierce, M., & Leon, D. (2005). Age at menarche and adult BMI in the Aberdeen children of the 1950s cohort study. *American Journal of Clinical Nutrition, 82*, 733–798.

Pierret, J., Beyaert, C., Paysant, J., & Caudron, S. (2020). How do children aged 6 to 11 stabilize themselves on an unstable sitting device? The progressive development of axial segment control. *Human Movement Science, 71*, 102624.

Planned Parenthood (2020). *Parents and teens talk about sexuality: A national survey.* https://www.plannedparenthood.org/uploads/filer_public/ac/50/ac50c2f7-cbc9-46b7-8531-ad3e92712016/nationalpoll_09–14_v2_1.pdf

Prabhakar, R., Saravanan, R., Karthikeyan, M., Vishnuchandran, C., & Sudeepthi (2014). Prevalence of malocclusion and need for early orthodontic treatment in children. *Journal of Clinical and Diagnostic Research, 8*, ZC60–1.

Proia, P., Amato, A., Drid, P., Korovljev, D., Vasto, S., & Baldassano, S. (2021). The impact of diet and physical activity on bone health in children and adolescents. *Frontiers in Endocrinology, 12*, 704647.

Rampersaud, C., Pereira, M. Girard, B., Adams, J., & Metzl, J. (2005). Breakfast habits, nutritional status, body weight, and academic performance in children and adolescents. *Journal of the American Dietetic Association, 105*, 743–760.

Reedy, J., & Krebs-Smith, S. (2010). Dietary sources of energy, solid fats, and added sugars among children and adolescents in the United States. *Journal of the American Dietetic Association, 110*, 1477–1484.

Rollins, B., Loken, E., Savage, J., & Birch, L. (2014). Effects of restriction on children's intake differ by child temperament, food reinforcement, and parent's chronic use of restriction. *Appetite, 73*, 31–39.

Rule, A., & Stewart, R. (2002). Effects of practical life materials on kindergartners' fine motor skills. *Early Childhood Education Journal, 30*(1), 9–13.

Sanders, T., Feng, X., Fahey, P., Lonsdale, C., & Astell-Burt, T. (2015). The influence of neighbourhood green space on children's physical activity and screen time: Findings from the longitudinal study of Australian children. *The International Journal of Behavioral Nutrition and Physical Activity, 12,* 126.

Saunders, T., & Vallance, J. (2017). Screen time and health indicators among children and youth: Current evidence, limitations and future directions. *Applied Health Economics and Health Policy, 15*(3), 323–331.

Sawyer, S. (2020). Global growth trends in school-aged cand adolescents. *The Lancet, 396*(10261), 1465–1467.

Scaglioni, S., De Cosmi, V., Ciappolino, V., Parazzini, F., Brambilla, P., & Agostoni, C. (2018). Factors influencing children's eating behaviours. *Nutrients, 10*(6), 706.

Schmeer, K., & Piperata, B. (2017). Household food insecurity and child health. *Maternal & Child Nutrition, 13*(2).

Schmeer, K., & Yoon, A. (2016). Home sweet home? Home physical environment and inflammation in children. *Social Science Research, 60*, 236–248.

Schreier, H., & Chen, E. (2013). Socioeconomic status and the health of youth: A multilevel, multidomain approach to conceptualizing pathways. *Psychological Bulletin, 139*(3), 606.

Semeraro, C., Coppola, G., Cassibba, R., & Lucangeli, D. (2019). Teaching of cursive writing in the first year of primary school: Effect on reading and writing skills. *PLOS ONE, 14*(2), e0209978.

Sex Ed for Social Change (2020). *The future of sex education initiative.* National Sex Education Standards: Core Content and Skills, K–12. https://siecus.org/wp-content/uploads/2020/03/NSES-2020-2.pdf

SHAPE America (2016). *Guide for recess policy.* SHAPE America.

Skinner, A., & Skelton, J. (2014). Prevalence and trends in obesity and severe obesity among children in the United States, 1999–2012. *JAMA Pediatrics, 168*(6), 561–566.

Smith, S., Zhang, X., Basile, K., Merrick, M., Wang, J., Kresnow, M., & Chen, J. (2018). *The national intimate partner and sexual violence survey (NISVS): 2015 data brief—Updated release.* National Center for Injury Prevention and Control, Centers for Disease Control and Prevention. https://www.cdc.gov/violenceprevention/pdf/2015data-brief508.pdf

Soliman, A., Sanctis, V., & Elalaily, R. (2014). Nutrition and pubertal development. *Indian Journal of Endocrinology and Metabolism, 18*, S39–S47.

Sowell, E., Thompson, P., Leonard, C., Welcome, S., Kan, E., & Toga, A. (2004). Longitudinal mapping of cortical thickness and brain growth in normal children. *The Journal of Neuroscience, 24*(38), 8223–8231.

Stiles, J., & Jernigan, T. (2010). The basics of brain development. *Neuropsychological Review, 20*, 327–348.

Stricker, P. (2009). *Hand-eye coordination in school age children.* American Academy of Pediatrics. https://www.healthychildren.org/English/ages-stages/gradeschool/fitness/Pages/Hand-Eye-Coordination-in-School-Age-Children.aspx

Suchert, V., Hanewinkel, R., & Isensee, B. (2015). Sedentary behavior and indicators of mental health in school-aged children and adolescents: A systematic review. *Preventive Medicine, 76*, 48–57.

Sun, Y., Mensah, F., Azzopardi, P., Patton, G., & Wake, M. (2017). Childhood social disadvantage and pubertal timing: A national birth cohort from Australia. *Pediatrics, 139*(6).

Sween, J., Wallington, S., Sheppard, V., Taylor, T., Llanos, A., & Adams-Campbell, L. (2014). The role of exergaming in improving physical activity: A review. *Journal of Physical Activity & Health, 11*(4), 864–870.

Taras, H. (2005). Nutrition and student performance at school. *Journal of School Health, 75*, 199–213.

Tremblay, M., LeBlanc, A., Kho, M., Saunders, T., Larouche, R., Colley, R., Goldfield, G., & Connor Gorber, S. (2011). Systematic review of sedentary behaviour and health indicators in school-aged children and youth. *The International Journal of Behavioral Nutrition and Physical Activity, 8*, 98.

True, L., Martin, E., Pfeiffer, K., Siegel, S., Branta, C., Haubenstricker, J., & Seefeldt, V. (2021). Tracking of physical fitness components from childhood to adolescence: A longitudinal study. *Measurement in Physical Education and Exercise Science, 25*(1), 22–34.

Tsuda, E., Goodway, J., Famelia, R., & Brian, A. (2020). Relationship between fundamental motor skill competence, perceived physical competence and free-play physical activity in children. *Research Quarterly for Exercise & Sport, 91*(1), 55–63.

Tupetz, A., Friedman, K., Zhao, D., Liao, H., Von Isenburg, M., Keating, E., Nickenig Vissoci, J., & Staton, C. (2020). Prevention of childhood unintentional injuries in low- and middle-income countries: A systematic review. *PLOS ONE, 15*(12), 1–46.

UNICEF (2020). *UNICEF is the custodian or co-custodian for 17 SDG indicators.* https://data.unicef.org/children-sustainable-development-goals/

United Nations on Drugs and Crime (2021). *Human trafficking.* https://www.unodc.org/toc/en/crimes/human-trafficking.html

US Centers for Disease Control and Prevention (2017). *Technical packages for violence prevention: Using evidence-based strategies in your violence prevention efforts.* https://www.cdc.gov/violenceprevention/pub/technical-packages.html

US Centers for Disease Control and Prevention (2018). *Defining childhood obesity.* https://www.cdc.gov/obesity/childhood/defining.html

US Centers for Disease Control and Prevention (2019). *Recess.* https://www.cdc.gov/healthyschools/physicalactivity/recess.htm

US Centers for Disease Control and Prevention (2020a). *Clinical growth charts.* https://www.cdc.gov/growthcharts/clinical_charts.htm

US Centers for Disease Control and Prevention (2020b). *Children's oral health.* https://www.cdc.gov/oralhealth/basics/childrens-oral-health/index.html

US Centers for Disease Control and Prevention (2020c). *Sexual violence is preventable.* https://www.cdc.gov/injury/features/sexual-violence/index.html

US Centers for Disease Control and Prevention (2021). *Childhood obesity causes & consequences.* https://www.cdc.gov/obesity/childhood/causes.html

US Department of Agriculture (2020a). *Choose my plate.* https://www.choosemyplate.gov/browse-by-audience/view-all-audiences/children/health-and-nutrition-information/preschoolers-food-groups

US Department of Agriculture (2020b). *Free lunch program.* https://www.ers.usda.gov/topics/food-nutrition-assistance/child-nutrition-programs/national-school-lunch-program.aspx

US Department of Health and Human Services (2020a). *Healthy people 2020.* http://www.healthypeople.gov/2020/default.aspx

US Department of Health and Human Services (2020b). *President's council on sports, fitness & nutrition: Facts and statistics.* https://www.hhs.gov/fitness/resource-center/facts-and-statistics/index.html

US Department of Health and Human Services (2020c). *BMI percentile calculator for children.* https://www.cdc.gov/healthyweight/bmi/calculator.html

US Department of Health and Human Services, and US Department of Agriculture (2015). *2015–2020 Dietary guidelines for Americans.* https://health.gov/our-work/food-and-nutrition/2015-2020-dietary-guidelines

US Department of Justice (2017). *Sex trafficking*. https://www. justice.gov/criminal-ceos/child-sex-trafficking

Van Deursen, A., Courtois, C., & van Dijk, J. (2014). Internet skills, sources of support, and benefiting from internet use. *International Journal of Human-computer Interaction*, 30(4), 278–290.

Walts, K. (2017). Child labor trafficking in the United States: A hidden crime. *Social Inclusion, 5*(2), 59–68.

Wang, Y., & Lim, H. (2012). The global childhood obesity epidemic and the association between socio-economic status and childhood obesity. *International Review of Psychiatry, 24*(3), 176–188.

Wang, Y., & Lobstein, T. (2006). Worldwide trends in childhood overweight and obesity. *International Journal of Pediatric Obesity, 1*(1), 11–25.

Wang, Y., & Zhang, Q. (2006). Are American children and adolescents of low socioeconomic status at increased risk of obesity? Changes in the association between overweight and family income between 1971 and 2002. *American Journal of Clinical Nutrition, 84*(4), 707–716.

Watchman, T., & Spencer-Cavaliere, N. (2017). Times have changed: Parent perspectives on children's free play and sport, *Psychology of Sport and Exercise, 32*, 102–112.

Watts, A., Miller, J., Larson, N., Eisenberg, M., Story, M., & Neumark-Sztainer, D. (2018). Multicontextual correlates of adolescent sugar-sweetened beverage intake. *Eating Behaviors, 30*, 42–48.

Weisenberger, J. (2020). How sleep habits affect healthy weight. *Academy of Nutrition and Dietetics*. https://www.eatright.org/health/weight-loss/overweight-and-obesity/how-sleep-habits-affect-healthy-weight

World Health Organization (2016). *State of inequality: Childhood immunization*.

World Health Organization (2020). *Noncommunicable diseases: Childhood overweight and obesity*.

Yang, H.-W., Meadan, H., & Ostrosky, M. (2021). A parent-implemented gross motor intervention for young children with disabilities. *Journal of Early Intervention, 1*.

Chapter 11

Alanis, I., Arreguín-Anderson, M., & Salinas-Gonzalez, I. (2021). *The essentials: Supporting dual language learners in diverse environments in preschool & kindergarten*. National Association for the Education of Young Children.

Allen, C., Diamond-Myrsten, S., & Rollins, L. (2018). School absenteeism in children and adolescents. *American Family Physician, 98*, 738–744.

Allen, K., Giofre, D., Higgins, S., & Adams, J. (2020). Working memory predictors of written mathematics in 7- to 8-year-old children. *Quarterly Journal of Experimental Psychology, 73*(2), 239–248.

American Academy of Child and Adolescent Psychiatry (2019). *Learning disabilities*. https://www.aacap.org/AACAP/Families_and_Youth/Facts_for_Families/FFF-Guide/Children-With-Learning-Disorders-016.aspx

Andre, Q., Geeraert, B., & Lebel, C. (2020). Brain structure and internalizing and externalizing behavior in typically developing children and adolescents. *Brain Structure and Function, 225*, 1369–1378.

Annie E. Casey Foundation (2008). *Closing the achievement gap: School, community, family connections*. https://www.aecf.org/resources/closing-the-achievement-gap/

Annie E. Casey Foundation (2013). *Reading proficiency in early grades key to closing achievement gap*. https://www.aecf.org/blog/reading-proficiency-in-early-grades-key-to-closing-achievement-gap/

Annie E. Casey Foundation (2020). *2020 Kids Count Data book: 2020 state trends in child well-being*. https://www.aecf.org/resources/2020-kids-count-data-book/

Bakken, J., Obiakor, F., & Rotatori, A. (2012). Behavioral disorders identification, assessment, and instruction of students with EBD. *Advances in Special Education, 22*.

Bandura, A. (2001). Social cognitive theory: An agentic perspective. *Annual Review of Psychology, 52*, 1–26.

Barkovich, A., & Raybaud, C. (2019). *Pediatric neuroimaging*. Wolters-Kluwer.

Barrouillet, P. (2015). Theories of cognitive development: From Piaget to today. *Developmental Review, 38*(C), 1–12.

Bates, B. (2019). *Learning theories simplified*. Sage.

Bates, J., & Munday, S. (2005). *Able, gifted and talented*. Continuum.

Bauer, P., & Pathman, T. (2020). Memory and early brain development. *Encyclopedia of Early Childhood Development*. http://www.child-encyclopedia.com/brain/according-experts/memory-and-early-brain-development

Berman, R. (2007). Developing linguistic knowledge and language use across adolescence. In E. Hoff & M. Schatz (Eds). *Blackwell handbook of language development*. Blackwell.

Biotteau, M., Albaret, J., Lelong, S., & Chaix, Y. (2017). Neuropsychological status of French children with developmental dyslexia and/or developmental coordination disorder: Are both necessarily worse than one? *Child Neuropsychology, 23*(4), 422–441.

Bishop, D., & Rutter, M. (2008). Neurodevelopmental disorders: Conceptual issues. In M. Rutter, D. Bishop, S. Pine, S. Scott, J. Stevenson, E. Taylor, & A. Thapar, (Eds), *Rutter's child and adolescent psychiatry*. Blackwell.

Bjorklund, D. (2004). *Children's thinking: Cognitive development and individual differences*. Wadsworth.

Blair, C., & Raver, C. (2016). Poverty, stress, and brain development: New directions for prevention and intervention. *Academic Pediatrics, 16*(3 Suppl), S30–S36.

Bock, A., Cartwright, K., McKnight, P., Patterson, A., Shriver, A., Leaf, B., Mohtasham, M., Vennergrund, K., & Pasnak, R. (2018). Patterning, reading, and executive functions. *Frontiers in Psychology, 9*, 1802.

Bonomo, V. (2010). Gender matters in elementary education: Research-based strategies to meet the distinctive learning needs of boys and girls. *Educational Horizons, 88*(4), 257–264.

Bowyer-Crane, C., Snowling, M., Duff, F., Fieldsend, E., Carroll, J., Miles, J., Gotz, K., & Hulme, C. (2008). Improving early language and literacy skills: Differential effects of an oral language versus a phonology with reading intervention. *Journal of Child Psychology and Psychiatry, 49*, 422–432.

Bronfenbrenner, U. (1996). *The ecology of human development experiments by nature and design*. Harvard University Press.

Bruner, J. (1973). *The relevance of education*. Norton.

Burgoyne, K., Witteveen, K., Tolan, A., Malone, S., & Hulme, C. (2017). Pattern understanding: Relationships with arithmetic and reading development. *Child Development Perspectives, 11*(4), 239–244.

Buttelmann, F., & Karbach, J. (2017). Development and plasticity of cognitive flexibility in early and middle childhood. *Front Psychol*ogy, *8*, 1040.

Buyanova, I., & Arsalidou, M. (2021). Cerebral white matter myelination and relations to age, gender, and cognition: A selective review. *Frontiers in Human Neuroscience*, *15*, 356.

Byrne, B., & Fielding-Barnsley, R. (1989). Phonemic awareness and letter knowledge in the child's acquisitions of the alphabetic principle. *Journal of Educational Psychology*, *80*, 313–321.

Cain, K., & Oakhill, J. (2006). Profiles of children with specific reading comprehension difficulties. *British Journal of Educational Psychology*, *76*, 683–696.

Calzada, E., Barajas-Gonzalez, R., Dawson-McClure, S., Huang, K., Palamar, J., Kamboukos, D., & Miller-Brotman, L. (2015). Early academic achievement among American low-income Black students from immigrant and non-immigrant families. *Prevention Science*, *16*(8), 1159–1168.

Catts, H., Adlof, S., & Ellis, W. (2006). Language deficits in poor comprehenders: A case for the simple view of reading. *Journal of Speech, Language, and Hearing Research*, *49*, 293–298.

Che, J., Malgieri, P., Ramos, V., Page, H., & Holt, A. (2015). *Early elementary on-track indicators leading to third-grade reading proficiency.* Fellowship Capstone Report, Strategic Data Project. Center for Education Policy Research at Harvard University.

Claessens, A., Engel, M., & Curran, F. (2015). The effects of maternal depression on child outcomes during the first years of formal schooling. *Early Childhood Research Quarterly*, *32*, 80–93.

Clearman, J., Klinger, V., & Szucs, D. (2017). Visuospatial and verbal memory in mental arithmetic. *Quarterly Journal of Experimental Psychology*, *70*(9), 1837–1855.

Cohen, D. (2018). *How the child's mind develops.* Routledge.

Conti-Ramsden, G., Durkin, K., Simkin, Z., & Knox, E. (2009). Specific language impairment and school outcomes: Identifying and explaining variability at the end of compulsory education. *International Journal of Language & Communication Disorders*, *44*, 15–35.

Corbetta, M., & Shulman, G. (2002). Control of goal-directed and stimulus-driven attention in the brain. *Nature Reviews Neuroscience*, *3*, 201–215.

Cortiella, C., & Horowitz, S. (2015). *The state of learning disabilities: Facts, trends, and emerging issues.* National Center for Learning Disabilities. http://www.ncld.org/wp-content/uploads/2014/11/2014-State-of-LD.pdf.

Cowan, N. (2014). Working memory underpins cognitive development, learning, and education. *Educational Psychology Review*, *26*(2), 197–223.

Crosby, D., & Dunbar, A. (2012). *Patterns and predictors of school readiness and early childhood success among young children in black immigrant families.* Migration Policy Institute. https://www.migrationpolicy.org/research/CBI-book-ChildrenofBlackImmigrants

Dahhan, N., Kirby, J., & Munoz, D. (2016). Understanding reading and reading difficulties through naming speed tasks: Bridging the gaps among neuroscience, cognition, and education. *AERA Open.* https://journals.sagepub.com/doi/10.1177/2332858416675346

Davies, D., & Troy, M. (2020). *Child development: A practitioner's guide.* Guilford.

Davis, T. (2018). The individualized education program (IEP): A powerful, often overlooked solution to behavioral problems at school. *Psych Central.* https://psychcentral.com/lib/the-individualized-education-program-iep-a-powerful-often-overlooked-solution-to-behavioral-problems-at-school/

Del Giudice, M. (2014). Middle childhood: An evolutionary-developmental synthesis. *Child Development Perspectives*, *8*, 193–200.

Devine, R., & Apperly, I. (2021). Willing and able? Theory of mind, social motivation, and social competence in middle childhood and early adolescence. *Developmental Science*, e13137.

Devine, R., & Hughes, C. (2016). Measuring theory of mind across middle childhood: Reliability and validity of the silent films and strange stories tasks. *Journal of Experimental Child Psychology*, *149*, 23–40.

Devine, R., White, N., Ensor, R., & Hughes, C. (2016). Theory of mind in middle childhood: Longitudinal associations with executive function and social competence. *Developmental Psychology*, *52*(5), 758–771.

Diamond, A., & Lee, K. (2011). Interventions shown to aid executive function development in children 4 to 12 years old. *Science*, *333*(6045), 959–964.

Doebel, S. (2020). Rethinking executive function and its development. *Perspectives on Psychological Science*, *15*(4), 942–956.

Eckert, R., & Robins, J. (2016). *Designing services and programs for high-ability learners: A guidebook for gifted education.* Sage.

Elkind, D., & Weiner, I. (1978). *Development of the child.* Wiley.

Estes, D., & Bartsch, K. (2017). Theory of mind: A foundational component of human general intelligence. *Behavioral Brain Science*, *40*, e201.

Fandakova, Y., & Hartley, C. (2020). Mechanisms of learning and plasticity in childhood and adolescence. *Developmental Cognitive Neuroscience*, *42*, 100764.

Fisher, D., Frey, N., & Almarode, J. (2021). *Student learning communities: A springboard for academic and social-emotional development.* ASCD.

Flouri, E., Francesconi, M., Midouhas, E., & Lewis, G. (2020). Prenatal and childhood adverse life events, inflammation and depressive symptoms across adolescence. *Journal of Affective Disorders*, *260*, 577–582.

Flouri, E., Francesconi, M., Papachristou, E., Midouhas, E., & Lewis, G. (2019). Stressful life events, inflammation and emotional and behavioural problems in children: A population-based study. *Brain, Behavior, and Immunity*, *80*, 66–72.

Ford, D., & Moore, J. (2013). Understanding and reversing underachievement, low achievement, and achievement gaps among high-ability African American males in urban school contexts. *The Urban Review*, *45*, 399–415.

Fosco, W., Kofler, M., Groves, N., Chan, E., & Raiker, J. (2020). Which 'working' components of working memory aren't working in youth with ADHD? *Journal of Abnormal Child Psychology*, *48*(5), 647–660.

Garcia, E., & Weiss, E. (2017). *Education inequalities at the school starting gate: Gaps, trends, and strategies to address them.* Economic Policy Institute. https://www.epi.org/publication/education-inequalities-at-the-school-starting-gate

Garcia, E., & Weiss, E. (2018). *Student absenteeism: Who misses school and how missing school matters for performance.* Public Policy Institute. https://www.epi.org/publication/student-absenteeism-who-misses-school-and-how-missing-school-matters-for-performance/

Gargiulo, R., & Kilgo, J.L. (2020). *An introduction to young children with special needs: Birth through age eight*. Sage.

Gazzaniga, M., & Mangun, G. R. (2014). *Cognitive neuroscience*. MIT Press.

Goswami, U. (2010). *The Wiley-Blackwell handbook of childhood cognitive development*. Wiley-Blackwell.

Gottfried, M. (2019). Chronic absenteeism in the classroom context: Effects on achievement. *Urban Education, 54*(1), 3–34.

Gray, C., & MacBlain, S. (2015). *Learning theories in childhood*. Sage.

Gueldner, B., Feuerborn, L., & Merrell, K. (2020). *Social and emotional learning in the classroom: Promoting mental health and academic success*. Guilford.

Hahn, R., Knopf, J., Wilson, S., Truman, B., Milstein, B., Johnson, L., Feilding, J., Muntaner, C., Jones, C., Fullilove, M., Davis-Moss, R., Ueffing, E., & Hunt, P. (2014). Programs to increase high school completion: A community guide systematic health equity review. *American Journal of Preventative Medicine, 48*(5), 599–608.

Hahn, R., Rammohan, V., Truman, B., Milstein, B., Johnson, R., Muntaner, C., Jones, C., Fullilove, M., Chattopadhyay , S., Hunt, P., & Abraido-Lanza, A. (2015). Effects of full-day kindergarten on the long-term health prospects of children in low-income and racial/ethnic-minority populations: A community guide systematic review. *American Journal of Preventative Medicine, 46*(3), 312–323.

Hair, N., Hanson, J., Wolfe, B., & Pollak, S. (2015). Association of child poverty, brain development, and academic achievement. *JAMA Pediatrics, 169*(9), 822–829.

Hall, K. (2013). *International handbook of research on children's literacy, learning and culture*. Wiley-Blackwell.

Hayiou-Thomas, M., Dale, P., & Plomin, R. (2014). Language impairment from 4 to 12 years: Prediction and etiology. *Journal of Speech, Language, and Hearing Research, 57*(3), 850–864.

Hernandez, D. (2011). Double jeopardy: How third grade reading skills and poverty influence school graduation (Special Report). *Annie E. Casey Family Foundation*. http://fcd-us.org/sites/default/files/DoubleJeopardyReport.pdf.

Hetherington, E., Parke, R., Gauvain, M., & Locke, V. (2006). *Child psychology: A contemporary view*. McGraw-Hill.

Hopkins, J. (2011). The enduring influence of Jean Piaget. *Psychological Science*. psychologicalscience.org/observer/jean-piaget

Houston, S., Herting, M., & Sowell, E. (2014). The neurobiology of childhood structural brain development: Conception through adulthood. *Current Topics in Behavioral Neurosciences, 16*, 3–17.

Hulme, C., & Snowling, M. (2015). Learning to read: What we know and what we need to understand better. *Child Development Perspectives, 7*(1), 1–5.

Imuta, K., Henry, J., Slaughter, V., Selcuk, B., & Ruffman, T. (2016). Theory of mind and prosocial behavior in childhood: A meta-analytic review. *Developmental Psychology, 52*(8), 1192–1205.

Isbell, E., Stevens, C., Pakulak, E., Wray, A., Bell, T., & Neville, H. (2017). Neuroplasticity of selective attention: Research foundations and preliminary evidence for a gene by intervention interaction. *PNAS Proceedings of the National Academy of Sciences of the United States of America, 114*(35), 9247–9254.

Jacobson, L., Ryan, M., Martin, R., Ewen, J., Mostofsky, S., Denckla, M., & Mahone, E. (2011). Working memory influences processing speed and reading fluency in ADHD. *Child Neuropsychology, 17*(3), 209–224.

Kaufman, S. (2018). *Twice exceptional: Supporting and educating bright and creative students with learning difficulties*. Oxford University Press.

Kearney, C., Gonzálvez, C., Graczyk, P., & Fornander, M. (2019). Reconciling contemporary approaches to school attendance and school absenteeism: Toward promotion and nimble response, global policy review and implementation, and future adaptability (Part 1). *Frontiers in Psychology, 10*, 2222.

Khan, M., & Ahmed, J. (2021). Child education in the time of pandemic: Learning loss and dropout. *Children and Youth Services Review, 127*, 106065.

Kim, K., Kaufman, J., Baer, J., & Sriraman, B. (2013). *Creatively gifted students are not like other gifted students: Research, theory, and practice*. Brill/Sense.

Klee, T., & Stokes, S. (2011). Language development. In D. Skuse, H. Bruce, L. Dowdney, & D. Mrazek (Eds.), *Child psychology and psychiatry: Frameworks for practice*. John Wiley.

Knudsen, E. (2004). Sensitive periods in the development of the brain and behavior. *Journal of Cognitive Neuroscience, 16*(8), 1412–1425.

Kokosi, T., Flouri, E., & Midouhas, E. (2020). Do upsetting life events explain the relationship between low socioeconomic status and systemic inflammation in childhood? Results from a longitudinal study. *Brain, Behavior, and Immunity, 84*, 90–96.

Kokosi, T., Flouri, E., & Midouhas, E. (2021). The role of inflammation in the association between poverty and working memory in childhood. *Psychoneuroendocrinology, 123*, 105040.

Ladefoged, P. (2001). *Vowels and consonants: An introduction to the sounds of language*. Blackwell.

Lave, J. (1991). Situating learning in communities of practice. *Perspectives on Socially Shared Cognition, 2*, 63–82.

Lave, J., & Wenger, E. (1998). *Communities of practice: Learning, meaning, and identity*. Cambridge University Press.

Lecce, S., Bianco, F., Devine, R., & Hughes, C. (2017). Relations between theory of mind and executive function in middle childhood: A short-term longitudinal study. *Journal of Experimental Child Psychology, 163*, 69–86.

Lecce, S., Bianco, F., Devine, R., Hughes, C., & Banerjee, R. (2014). Promoting theory of mind during middle childhood: A training study. *Journal of Experiential Child Psychology, 126*, 52–67.

Lenneberg, E. (1967). *Biological foundations of language*. John Wiley.

Lenroot, R., Gogtay, N., Greenstein, D., Wells, E., Wallace, G., Clasen, L., Blumenthal, J., & Leonard, D. (2007). *Learning theories, A to Z*. Greenwood Press.

Madden-Dent, T., & Oliver, D. (2021). *Leading schools with social, emotional, and academic development (SEAD)*. IGI Global, Information Science Reference.

Magalhaes, S., Carneiro, L., Limpo, T., & Filipe, M. (2020). Executive functions predict literacy and mathematics achievements: The unique contribution of cognitive flexibility in grades 2, 4, and 6. *Child Neuropsychology, 26*.

Malanchini, M., Rimfeld, K., Allegrini, A., Ritchie, S., & Plomin, R. (2020). Cognitive ability and education: How behavioural genetic research has advanced our knowledge and understanding of their association. *Neuroscience & Biobehavioral Reviews, 111*, 229–245.

Margolis, A. (2020). Zone of proximal development, scaffolding and teaching practice. *Cultural-Historical Psychology, 16*(3), 15–26.

Marti, E., & Rodríguez, C. (2012). *After Piaget*. Transaction.

Maziero, S., Tallet, J., Bellocchi, S., Jover, M., Chaix Y., & Jucla, M. (2020). Influence of comorbidity on working memory profile in dyslexia and developmental coordination disorder. *Journal of Clinical and Experimental Neuropsychology, 42*(7), 660–674.

McGill, R., Styck, K., & Dombrowski, S. (2020). Learning disabilities. In E. Youngstrom, M. Prinstein, E. Mash, & R. Barkley, (Eds.), *Assessment of disorders in childhood and adolescence*. Guilford.

McLeod, S. (2018). Jean Piaget's theory and stages of cognitive development. *Simply Psychology*. simplypsychology.org/piaget.html

Melby-Lervag, M., Lyster, S., & Hulme, C. (2012). Phonological skills and their role in learning to read: A meta-analytic review. *Psychological Bulletin, 138*, 322–352.

Meltzer, L. (2011). *Executive function in education: From theory to practice*. Guilford.

Miller, B., McCardle, P., & Connelly, V. (2018). *Writing development in struggling learners: Understanding the needs of writers across the lifecourse*. Brill.

Miller, P. (2010). Piaget's theory: Past, present, and future. In U. Goswami (Ed.), *The Wiley-Blackwell handbook of childhood cognitive development*. https://onlinelibrary.wiley.com/doi/book/10.1002/9781444325485

Moen, P., Elder, G., Lüscher, K., & Bronfenbrenner, U. (1995). *Examining lives in context: Perspectives on the ecology of human development*. American Psychological Association.

Mohades, S., Van Schuerbeek, P., Rosseel, Y., Van De Craen, P., Luypaert, R., & Baeken, C. (2015). White-matter development is different in bilingual and monolingual children: A longitudinal DTI study. *PLOS ONE, 10*(2), 1–16.

Moldovan, M., & Visu-Petra, L. (2021). Theory of mind, anxiety, and interpretive bias during middle childhood. *Journal of Child and Family Studies*. doi:10.1007/s10826-021-02023-0

Monsell, S. (2003). Task switching. *Trends in Cognitive Science, 7*, 134–140.

Morin, A. (2012). Inner speech: Vygotsky's position. In V. Ramachandran (Ed.) *Encyclopedia of human behavior*. Academic Press.

Morsy, L., & Rothstein, R. (2019). Toxic stress and children's outcomes: African American children growing up poor are at greater risk of disrupted physiological functioning and depressed academic achievement. *Economic Policy Institute*. www.pi.org/publication/toxic-stress-and-childrens-outcomes-african-american-children-growing-up-poor-are-at-greater-risk-of-disrupted-physiological-functioning-and-depressed-academic-achievement/

Muter, V., Hulme, C., Snowling, M., & Stevenson, J. (2004). Phonemes, rhymes and language skills as foundations of early reading development: Evidence from a longitudinal study. *Developmental Psychology, 40*, 663–681.

Myers, C., Vandermosten, M., Farris, E., Hancock, R., Gimenez, P., Black, J., Casto, B., Drahos, M., Tumber, M., Hendren, R., & Hulme, C. (2014). White matter morphometric changes uniquely predict children's reading acquisition. *Psychological Science, 25*(10), 1870–1883.

Narimani, M., Taghizadeh, S., Sadeghi, G., & Basharpoor, S. (2020). Effectiveness of visual perception training in the improvement of the working memory of students with attention deficit/hyperactivity disorder. *Journal of Research in Psychopathology, 1*(2), 4–11.

National Assessment of Educational Progress (2019). *NAEP Report Card: Reading*. National achievement-level results. https://www.nationsreportcard.gov/reading/nation/achievement/?grade=4

National Association for Gifted Children (2020). *What is giftedness?* https://www.nagc.org/resources-publications/resources/what-giftedness

Ng, C., & Bartlett, B. J. (2017). *Improving reading and reading engagement in the 21st century: International research and innovation*. Springer.

Oliver, R., & Azkarai, A. (2017). Review of child second language acquisition (SLA): Examining theories and research. *Annual Review of Applied Linguistics, 37*, 62–76.

Osterhaus, C., & Koerber, S. (2021). The development of advanced theory of mind in middle childhood: A longitudinal study from age 5 to 10 years. *Child Development, 92*(5), 1872–1888.

Ostroff, W. (2012). *Understanding how young children learn: Bringing the science of child development to the classroom*. Association for Supervision & Curriculum Development.

Owens, R. (2020). *Language development: An introduction*. Pearson Education.

Pennington, B., & Olson, R. (2005). Genetics of dyslexia. In M. Snowling & C. Hulme (Eds.), *The science of reading: A handbook*. Blackwell.

Pfeiffer, S. (2015). *Essentials of gifted assessment*. Wiley.

Plomin, R., & Kovas, Y. (2005). Generalist genes and learning disabilities. *Psychological Bulletin, 131*, 592–617.

Poll, G., & Miller, C. (2013). Late talking, typical talking, and weak language skills at middle childhood. *Learning and Individual Differences, 26*, 177–184.

Posner, M., & Rothbart, M. (2007). *Educating the human brain*. American Psychological Association.

Pritchard, A. (2008). *Ways of learning: Learning theories and learning styles in the classroom*. Routledge.

Ramos, A., Hamdan, A., & Machado, L. (2020). A meta-analysis on verbal working memory in children and adolescents with ADHD. *The Clinical Neuropsychologist, 34*(5), 873–898.

Ravid, D. (2004). Derivational morphology revisited: Later lexical development in Hebrew. In R. Berman (Ed.), *Language development across childhood and adolescence*. Benjamins.

Ready, D. (2010). Socioeconomic disadvantage, school attendance, and early cognitive development: The differential effects of school exposure. *Sociology of Education, 83*, 271–286.

Reuter, E., Vieluf, S., Koutsandreou, F., Hubner, L., Budde, H., Godde, B., & Voelcker-Rehage, C. (2019). A non-linear relationship between selective attention and associated ERP markers across the lifespan. *Frontiers in Psychology, 10*.

Reyes, S., Kleyn, T., Garcia, O., & Atta Scott, S. (2010). *Teaching in 2 languages: A guide for k–12 bilingual educators*. Corwin, A Sage Company.

Rinaldi, L., & Karmiloff-Smith, A. (2017). Intelligence as a developing function: A neuroconstructivist approach. *Journal of Intelligence, 5*(2), 18.

Schmitt, J., Raznahan, A., Clasen, L., Wallace, G., Pritikin, J. Lee, N., Giedd, J., & Neale, M. (2019). The dynamic associations between cortical thickness and general intelligence are genetically mediated. *Cerebral Cortex, 29*(11), 4743–4752.

Schunk, D. (2012). *Learning theories an educational perspective.* Pearson.

Schunk, D., & Usher, E. (2019). Social cognitive theory and motivation. In R. Ryan (Ed.), *The Oxford handbook of human motivation.* Oxford University Press.

Semrud-Clikeman, M. (2010). *Research in brain function and learning.* American Psychological Association. http://www.apa.org/education/k12/brain-function

Singleton, N., & Shulman, B. (2020). *Language development: Foundations, processes, and clinical applications.* Jones & Bartlett Learning.

Simonton, Dean. (2005). Giftedness and genetics: The emergenic-epigenetic model and its implications. *Journal for the Education of the Gifted, 28,* 270–286.

Smith, D. (2018). At what age does our ability to learn a new language like a native speaker disappear? *Scientific American Mind, 29*(4), 5–8.

Smogorzewska, J., Szumski, G., & Grygiel, P. (2020). Theory of mind goes to school: Does educational environment influence the development of theory of mind in middle childhood? *PLOS ONE, 15*(8), e0237524.

Smolucha, L., & Smolucha, F. (2021). Vygotsky's theory in-play: Early childhood education. *Early Child Development and Care, 32.*

Snowling, M., & Hulme, C. (2005). *The science of reading: A handbook.* Blackwell.

Sowell, E., Thompson, P., Leonard, C., Welcome, S., Kan, E., & Toga, A. (2004). Longitudinal mapping of cortical thickness and brain growth in normal children. *Journal of Neuroscience, 24*(38), 8223–8231.

Teimouri, Y., Goetze, J., & Plonsky, L. (2019). Second language anxiety and achievement: A meta-analysis. *Studies in Second Language Acquisition, 41*(2), 363–387.

Titz, C., & Karbach, J. (2014). Working memory and executive functions: Effects of training on academic achievement. *Psychological Research, 78,* 852–868.

Tomson, A., Oberle, E., Gadermann, A., Guhn, M., Rowcliffe, P., & Schonert-Reichl, K. (2018). Measuring social-emotional development in middle childhood: The middle years development instrument. *Journal of Applied Developmental Psychology, 55,* 107–118.

Twachtman-Cullen, D., & Twachtman-Bassett, J. (2011). *The IEP from A to Z: How to create meaningful and measurable goals and objectives.* John Wiley.

UNESCO (2015). *Education for All 2000–2015: Achievements and challenges.* http://unesdoc.unesco.org/images/0023/002322/232205e.pdf

UNESCO (2021). *Barriers to school attendance.* https://policytoolbox.iiep.unesco.org/policy-option/barriers-to-school-attendance/

UNICEF (2019). *The state of the world's children—Nutrition.* https://features.unicef.org/state-of-the-worlds-children-2019-nutrition/

UNICEF (2020). *Huge inequality in educational achievement in every rich nation.* https://www.unicef.org/media/media_19241.html

United Nations (2019). *17 goals to transform our world.* https://www.un.org/sustainabledevelopment/

United Nations (2015). *Toward a world free from violence on children.* https://www.unicef.org/sites/default/files/2020-04/Toward-a-world-free-from-violence-global-survey.pdf

US Centers for Disease Control and Prevention (2020). *Developmental disabilities.* https://www.cdc.gov/ncbddd/developmentaldisabilities/index.html

Vidergor, H., & Harris, C. (2015). *Applied practice for educators of gifted and able learners.* Brill/Sense.

Vygotsky, L. (1978). *Mind and society: The development of higher mental processes.* Harvard University Press.

Wang, M., & Singer, George H. S. (2016). *Supporting families of children with developmental disabilities: Evidence-based and emerging practices.* Oxford University Press.

Wang, X. (2014). *Understanding language and literacy development: Diverse learners in the classroom.* John Wiley.

Wendelken, C., Ferrer, E., Ghetti, S., Bailey, S., Cutting, L., & Bunge, S. (2017). Frontoparietal structural connectivity in childhood predicts development of functional connectivity and reasoning ability: A large-scale longitudinal investigation. *Journal of Neuroscience, 37*(35), 8549–8558.

Wenger, E. (2018). A social theory of learning. In K. Illeris (Ed.), *Contemporary theories of learning: Learning theorists in their own words.* Routledge.

Wertsch, J., & Sohmer, R. (1995). Vygotsky on learning and development. *Human Development, 38,* 332–337.

Wessel, I., Schweig, T., & Huntjens, R. (2019). Manipulating the reported age in earliest memories. *Memory, 27*(1), 6–18.

Wexler, N. (2019). *The knowledge gap: The hidden cause of America's broken education system—And how to fix it.* Avery.

Whitehead, M. (2010). *Language and literacy in the early years 0–7.* Sage Publications.

Whitehouse, A., Line, E., Watt, H., & Bishop, D. (2009). Adult psychosocial outcomes of children with specific language impairment, pragmatic language impairment, and autism. *International Journal of Language & Communication Disorders, 44,* 511–528.

Wilmshurst, L. (2012). *Clinical and educational child psychology: An ecological-transactional approach to understanding child problems and interventions.* Wiley.

Wood, S., & Peterson, J. (2018). *Counseling gifted students: A guide for school counselors.* Springer.

Yeniad, N., Malda, M., Mesman, J., van Ijzendoorn, M., & Pieper, S. (2013). Shifting ability predicts math and reading performance in children: A meta-analytical study. *Learning and Individual Differences, 23,* 1–9.

Visu-Petraa, L., Cheiea, L, Bengaab, O., & Micleab, M. (2011). Cognitive control goes to school: The impact of executive functions on academic performance. *Procedia-Social and Behavioral Sciences, 11,* 240–244.

Zablotsky, B., Black, L., Maenner, M., Schieve, L, Danielson, M., Bitsko, R., Blumberg, S., Kogan, M., & Boyle, C. (2019). Prevalence and trends of developmental disabilities among children in the United States: 2009–2017. *Pediatrics, 144*(4), e20190811.

Zatorre R., Fields R., & Johansen-Berg, H. (2012). Plasticity in gray and white: Neuroimaging changes in brain structure during learning. *Nature Neuroscience, 15*(4), 528–536.

Chapter 12

Abuhatoum, S., & Howe, N. (2013). Power in sibling conflict during early and middle childhood. *Social Development, 22*, 738–754.

Ager, A. (2013). Resilience and child well-being: Public policy implications. Annual research review. *Journal of Child Psychology and Psychiatry, 54*(4), 488–500.

Albright, M., Weissberg, R., & Dusenbury, L. (2011). *School-family Partnership Strategies to Enhance Children's Social, Emotional, and Academic Growth.* National Center for Mental Health Promotion and Youth Violence Prevention, Education Development Center.

Allen, J. (2008). The attachment system in adolescence. In J. Cassidy & P. Shaver (Eds.), *Handbook of attachment: Theory, research, and clinical applications.* Guilford.

Amodio, D., & Ratner, K. (2013). The neuroscience of social cognition. In M. Anderson & S.

Della Sala (Eds.), *Neuroscience in education: The good, the bad, and the ugly.* Oxford University Press.

Anschutz, D., Engels, R., & Van Strien, T. (2012). Increased body satisfaction after exposure to thin ideal children's television in young girls showing thin ideal internalization. *Psychology & Health, 27*(5), 603–617.

Bagwell, C., & Schmidt, M. (2011). *Friendships in childhood and adolescence.* Guilford.

Baker, J. (2006). Contributions of teacher-child relationships to positive school adjustment during elementary school. *Journal of School Psychology, 44*, 211–229.

Balaghi, D., Hierl, K., & Snyder, E. (2021). Self-monitoring for students with obsessive-compulsive disorder and autism spectrum disorder. *Intervention in School and Clinic,* 10534512211047585.

Baldry, A. (2003). Bullying in schools and exposure to domestic violence. *Child Abuse & Neglect, 27*, 713–732.

Bailey, R. (2011). *Letting children be children: Report of an independent review of the commercialisation and sexualisation of childhood.* https://www.gov.uk/government/publications/letting-children-be-children-report-of-an-independent-review-of-the-commercialisation-and-sexualisation-of-childhood.

Barreto-Zarza, F., Sancghez de Miguel, M., Ibarluzea, J., González-Safont, L., Rebagliato, M., & Arranz-Freijo, E. (2021). Family context assessment in middle childhood: A tool supporting social, educational, and public health interventions. *International Journal of Environmental Research and Public Health, 18*(3), 1094.

Basu, K., Das, S., & Dutta, B. (2010). Child labor and household wealth: Theory and empirical evidence of an inverted-U. *Journal of Development Economics, 91*, 8–14.

Baumeister, R., & Leary, M. (1995). The need to belong: Desire for interpersonal attachments as a fundamental human motivation. *Psychological Bulletin, 117*, 497–529.

Becht, A., Wierenga, L., Mills, K., Meuwese, R., van Duijvenvoorde, A., Blakemore, S., & Crone, E. (2021). Beyond the average brain: Individual differences in social brain development are associated with friendship quality. *Social Cognitive and Affective Neuroscience, 16*(3), 292–301.

Beegle, K., Dehejia, R., & Gatti, R. (2004). Why should we care about child labor? The education, labor market, and health consequences of child labor. *Journal of Human Resources, 44*, 871–889.

Best, J., & Miller, P. (2010). A developmental perspective on executive function. *Child Development, 81*, 1641–1660.

Betts, L., Rotenberg, K., Trueman, M., & Stiller, J. (2012). Examining the components of children's peer liking as antecedents of school adjustment. *British Journal of Developmental Psychology, 30*, 303–325.

Bhandari, S. (2018). Mental health and conduct disorder. *WebMD Medical Reference.* https://www.webmd.com/mental-health/mental-health-conduct-disorder#1

Bitsko, R., Holbrook, J., Ghandour, R., Blumberg, S., Visser, S., Perou, R., & Walkup, J. (2018). Epidemiology and impact of healthcare provider diagnosed anxiety and depression among US children. *Journal of Developmental and Behavioral Pediatrics. 39*(5), 395–403.

Blair, C., & Raver, C. (2015). School readiness and self-regulation: A developmental psychobiological approach. *Annual Review of Psychology, 66*, 711–731. https://doi.org/10.1146/annurev-psych-010814-015221

Bosacki, S. (2016). *Social cognition in middle childhood and adolescence: Integrating the personal, social, and educational lives of young people.* John Wiley.

Bosmans, G., Braet, C., Koster, E., & De Raedt, R. (2009). Attachment security and attentional breadth toward the attachment figure in middle childhood. *Journal of Clinical Child & Adolescent Psychology, 38*(6), 872–882.

Bosmans, G., De Raedt, R., & Braet, C. (2007). The invisible bonds: Does the secure base script of attachment influence children's attention towards their mother? *Journal of Clinical Child and Adolescent Psychology, 36*, 557–567.

Bosmans, G., & Kerns, K. A. (2015). Attachment in middle childhood: Progress and prospects. New directions for child and adolescent development. (148), 1–14.

Boulton, M., Don, J., & Boulton, L. (2011). Predicting children's liking of school from their peer relationships. *Social Psychology of Education, 14*, 489–501.

Bowes, L., Wolke, D., Joinson, C., Lereya, S., & Lewis, G. (2014). Sibling bullying and risk of depression, anxiety, and self-harm: A prospective cohort study. *Pediatrics, 134*(4), E1032–E1039.

Boyle, C. (2017). What is the impact of birth family contact on children in adoption and long-term foster care? A systematic review. *Child & Family Social Work, 22*, 22–33.

Briesch, A., Daniels, B., & Beneville, M. (2019). Unpacking the term "self-management": Understanding intervention applications within the school-based literature. *Journal of Behavioral Education, 28*, 54–57.

Brock, L., Nishida, T., Chiong, C., Grimm, K., & Rimm-Kaufman, S. (2008). Children's perceptions of the classroom environment and social and academic performance: A longitudinal analysis of the contribution of the responsive classroom approach (abstract). *Journal of School Psychology, 46*, 129–149.

Brody, G., & Stoneman, Z. (1987). Sibling conflict: Contributions of the siblings themselves, the parent-sibling relationship, and the broader family system. *Journal of Children in Contemporary Society, 19*, 39–53.

Broussard, S., & Garrison, M. (2004). The relationship between classroom motivation and academic achievement in elementary school-aged children. *Family and Consumer Sciences Research Journal, 33*(2), 106–120.

Brown, S., Manning, W., & Stykes, J. (2015). Family structure and child well-being: Integrating family complexity. *Journal of Marriage and the Family, 77*(1), 177–190.

Buist, K., Dekovic, M., & Prinzie, P. (2013). Sibling relationship quality and psychopathology of children and adolescents: A meta-analysis. *Clinical Psychology Review, 33*(1), 97–106.

Burke, J., Pardini, D., & Loeber, R. (2008). Reciprocal relationships between parenting behavior and disruptive psychopathology from childhood through adolescence. *Journal of Abnormal Child Psychology, 36*(5), 679–692.

Busacca, M., Anderson, A., & Moore, D. (2015). Self-management for primary school students demonstrating problem behavior in regular classrooms: Evidence review of single-case design research. *Journal of Behavioral Education, 24*, 373–401.

Caliendo, M., Lanzara, V., Vetri, L., Roccella, M., Marotta, R., Carotenuto, M., Russo, D., Cerroni, F., & Precenzano, F. (2020). Emotional–behavioral disorders in healthy siblings of children with neurodevelopmental disorders. *Medicina, 56*(10), 491.

Campione-Barr, N., & Killoren, S. (2015). Sibling relationships and development. In R. Scott & S. Kosslyn (Eds.), *Emerging trends in the social and behavioral sciences*. John Wiley.

Cantrell, S., & Kane, T. (2013). *Ensuring fair and reliable measures of effective teaching: Culminating findings from the MET project's three-year study*. Bill & Melinda Gates Foundation, Policy and Practice Brief, Measures of Effective Teaching Project.

Carl, T., & Bussey, K. (2019). Contextual and age-related determinants of children's lie telling conceal a transgression. *Infant & Child Development, 28*(3).

Carpendale, J., & Lewis, C. (2004). Constructing an understanding of mind: The development of children's social understanding within social interaction. *Behavioral and Brain Sciences, 27*(1), 79–96.

Cherlin, A. (2009). *The marriage-go-round: The state of marriage and the American family today*. Knopf.

Chetty, R., Friedman, J., & Rockoff, J. (2014). Measuring the impacts of teachers II: Teacher value-added and student outcomes in adulthood. *American Economic Review, 104*(9), 2633–2679.

Cicchetti, D. (2016). *Developmental psychopathology: Risk, resilience, and intervention* (Vol 4). John Wiley.

Coie, J., & Miller-Johnson, S. (2001). Peer factors and interventions. In R. Loeber & D. Farrington (Eds.), *Child delinquents: Development, intervention, and service needs*. Sage.

Collins, R., Strasburger, V., Brown, J., Donnerstein, E., Lenhart, A., & Ward, L. (2017). Sexual media and childhood well-being and health. *Pediatrics, 140*, S162–S166.

Collins, W., & Madsen, S. (2019. Parenting during middle childhood. In M. Bornstein (Ed.) *Handbook of parenting*. Routledge.

Cook, C., Williams, K., Guerra, N., Kim, T., & Sadek, S. (2010). Predictors of bullying and victimization in childhood and adolescence: A meta-analytic investigation. *School Psychology Quarterly, 25*, 65–83.

Copeland, W., Wolke, D., Angold, A., & Costello, E. (2013). Adult psychiatric outcomes of bullying and being bullied by peers in childhood and adolescence. *Journal of the American Medical Association Psychiatry, 70*, 419–426.

Cowie, H. (2012). *From birth to sixteen: Children's health, social, emotional and linguistic development*. Routledge.

Cree, R., Bitsko, R., Robinson, L., Holbrook, J., Danielson, M., Smith, D., Kaminski, J., Kenney, M., & Peacock, G. (2018). Health care, family, and community factors associated with mental, behavioral, and developmental disorders and poverty among children aged 2–8 years: United States. *Morbidity and Mortality Weekly Report, 67*(5), 1377–1383. https://www.cdc.gov/mmwr/index.html

Crocetti, E., Jahromi, P., & Meeus, W. (2012). Identity and civic engagement in adolescence. *Journal of Adolescence, 35*, 521–532.

Curby, T., Rimm-Kaufman, S., & Ponitz, C. (2009). Teacher-child interactions and children's achievement trajectories across kindergarten and first grade. *Journal of Educational Psychology, 101*(4), 912–925.

Danese, A., & Lewis, S. (2017). Psychoneuroimmunology of early-life stress: The hidden wounds of childhood trauma? *Neuropsychopharmacology, 42*(1), 99–114.

Darling-Churchill, K., & Lippman, L. (2016). Early childhood social and emotional development: Advancing the field of measurement. *Journal of Applied Developmental Psychology, 45*, 1–7.

Darwich, L., Hymel, S., & Waterhouse, T. (2012). School avoidance and substance use among lesbian, gay, bisexual, and questioning youths: The impact of peer victimization and adult support. *Journal of Educational Psychology, 104*, 381–392.

Decety, J., & Cowell, J. (2018). Why developmental neuroscience is critical for the study of morality. In K. Gray & J. Graham (Eds.), *Atlas of moral psychology*. Guilford.

Decker, S., & Van Winkle, B. (1996). *Life in the gang: Family, friends, and violence*. Cambridge University Press.

Deighton, J., Humphrey, N., Belsky, J., Boehnke, J., Vostanis, P., & Patalay, P. (2018). Longitudinal pathways between mental health difficulties and academic performance during middle childhood and early adolescence. *British Journal of Developmental Psychology, 36*(1), 110–126.

Denny, B., Kober, H., Wager, T., & Ochsner, K. (2012). A meta-analysis of functional neuroimaging studies of self- and other judgments reveals a spatial gradient for mentalizing in medial prefrontal cortex. *Journal of Cognitive Neuroscience, 24*(8), 1742–1752.

Derlan, C., Umaña-Taylor, A., Toomey, R., Jahromi, L., & Updegraff, K. (2016). Measuring cultural socialization attitudes and behaviors of Mexican-origin mothers with young children: A longitudinal investigation. *Family Relations, 65*(3), 477–489.

De Souza, M. (2014). The empathetic mind: The essence of human spirituality. *International Journal of Children's Spirituality, 19*, 45–54.

Devine, R., & Apperly, I. (2021). Willing and able? Theory of mind, social motivation, and social competence in middle childhood and early adolescence. *Developmental Science*, e13137.

Devine, R., White, N., Ensor, R., & Hughes, C. (2016). Theory of mind in middle childhood: Longitudinal associations with executive function and social competence. *Developmental Psychology, 52*, 758–771.

de Wilde, A., Koot, H., & van Lier, P. (2016). Developmental links between children's working memory and their social relations with teachers and peers in the early school years. *Journal of Abnormal Child Psychology, 44,* 19–30.

Ding, X., Omrin, D., Evans, A., Fu, G., Chen, G., & Lee, K. (2014). Elementary school children's cheating behavior and its cognitive correlates. *Journal of Experimental Child Psychology, 121,* 85–95.

Dixon, L., Perkins, D., Hamilton-Giachritsis, C., & Craig, L. (2017). *The Wiley handbook of what works in child maltreatment: An evidence-based approach to assessment and intervention in child protection.* Wiley-Blackwell.

Dodge, K., Coie, J., & Lynam, D. (2006). Aggression and antisocial behavior in youth. In W. Damon & N. Eisenberg (Eds.), *Handbook of child psychology: Social, emotional, and personality development.* Wiley.

Domitrovich, C., Durlak, J., Staley, K., & Weissberg, R. (2017). Social-emotional competence: An essential factor for promoting positive adjustment and reducing risk and school children. *Child Development, 88,* 408–416.

Dowling, M. (2014). *Young children's personal, social and emotional development.* Sage.

Downey, D., & Condron, D. (2004). Playing well with others in kindergarten: The benefit of siblings at home. *Journal of Marriage and Family, 66*(2), 333–350.

Duckworth, A., & Yeager, D. (2015). Measurement matters: Assessing personal qualities other than cognitive ability for educational purposes. *Educational Researcher, 44*(4), 237–251.

Dweck, C. (2008). *Mindset: The new psychology of success.* Ballantine Books.

Dweck, C. (2016). *Self-theories: Their role in motivation, personality, and development.* Routledge.

Dweck, C., Walton, G., & Cohen, G. (2014). *Academic tenacity: Mindsets and skills that promote long-term learning.* Bill & Melinda Gates Foundation.

Erdley, C., & Day, H. (2017). Friendship in childhood and adolescence. In M. Hojjat & A. Moyer (Eds.), *The psychology of friendship.* Oxford.

Erikson, E. (1950). *Childhood and society.* Norton & Company.

Eriksen, S., & Jensen, V. (2009). A push or a punch: Distinguishing the severity of sibling violence. *Journal of Interpersonal Violence, 24*(21), 183–208.

Erwin, P. (2013). *Friendship in childhood and adolescence.* Routledge.

Espelage, D., Rose, C., & Polanin, J. (2015). Social-emotional learning program to reduce bullying, fighting, and victimization among middle school students with disabilities. *Remedial & Special Education, 36*(5), 299–311.

Fawley-King, K., Trask, E., Zhang, J., Gregory A., & Aarons, G. (2017). The impact of changing neighborhoods, switching schools, and experiencing relationship disruption on children's adjustment to a new placement in foster care. *Child Abuse & Neglect, 63,* 141–150.

Fink, E., Begeer, S., Peterson, C., Slaughter, V., & de Rosnay, M. (2015). Friendlessness and theory of mind: A prospective longitudinal study. *British Journal of Developmental Psychology, 33,* 1–17.

Flett, G., & Hewitt, I. (2014). A proposed framework for preventing perfectionism and promoting resilience and mental health among vulnerable children and adolescents. *Psychology in the Schools, 51,* 899–912.

Furman, W., & Buhrmester, D. (1985). Children's perceptions of the personal relationships in their social networks. *Developmental Psychology, 21,* 1016–1024.

Gamble, W., & Yu, J. (2014). Young children's sibling relationship interactional types: Associations with family characteristics, parenting, and child characteristics. *Education and Development, 25,* 223–239.

Garrett-Peters, P., Mokrova, I., Vernon-Feagans, L., Willoughby, M., & Pan, Y. (2016). The role of household chaos in understanding relations between early poverty and children's academic achievement. *Early Child Research Quarterly, 37,* 16–25.

Ghandour, R. M., Sherman, L. J., Vladutiu, C. J., Ali, M. M., Lynch, S. E., Bitsko, R. H., & Blumberg, S. J. (2019). Prevalence and treatment of depression, anxiety, and conduct problems in US children. *The Journal of Pediatrics, 206,* 256–267.

Gibbs, J. (2014). *Moral development and reality: Beyond the theories of Kohlberg, Hoffman, and Haidt.* Oxford University Press.

Gilligan, C. (1982). *In a different voice: Psychological theory and women's development.* Harvard University Press.

Gilligan, C. (1988). *Mapping the moral domain: A contribution of women's thinking to psychological theory and education.* Center for the Study of Gender, Education, and Human Development, Harvard U Graduate School of Education. Harvard University Press.

Glowiak, M., & Mayfield, M. A. (2016). Middle childhood: Emotional and social development. *Human growth and development across the lifespan: Applications for counselors,* 277.

Gonzalez-DeHass, A., & Willems, P. (2012). *Theories in educational psychology: Concise guide to meaning and practice.* Rowman & Littlefield Education.

Greenbaum, J., & Bodrick, N. (2017). Global human trafficking and child victimization. *Pediatrics, 140*(6).

Greene, S., Anderson, E., Forgatch, M., DeGarmo, D., & Hetherington, E. (2012). *Risk and resilience after divorce.* In F. Walsh (Ed.), *Normal family processes: Growing diversity and complexity.* Guilford.

Guerra, N., Williams, K., & Sadek, S. (2011). Understanding bullying and victimization during childhood and adolescence: A mixed methods study. *Child Development, 82,* 295–310.

Gueldner, B., Feuerborn, L., Merrell, K., & Weissberg, R. (2020). *Social and emotional learning in the classroom: Promoting mental health and academic success.* Guilford.

Gypen, L., Vanderfaeillie, J., De Maeyer, S., Belenger, L., & Van Holen, F. (2017). Outcomes of children who grew up in foster care: Systematic review. *Children and Youth Services Review, 76,* 74–83.

Hansen, C. (2018). *The heart and science of teaching: Transformative applications that integrate academic and social-emotional learning.* Teachers College Press.

Hart, L., Cornell, C., Damiano, S., & Paxton, S. (2014). Parents and prevention: A systematic review of interventions involving parents that aim to prevent body dissatisfaction or eating disorders. *International Journal of Eating Disorders, 48*(2), 157–169.

Harvard University's Center on the Developing Child (2020). *Resilience.* https://developingchild.harvard.edu/science/key-concepts/resilience/

Hay, D., Payne, A., & Chadwick, A. (2004). Peer relations in childhood. *Journal of Child Psychology and Psychiatry, 45,* 84–108.

Helton, L., & Smith, M. (2013). *Mental health practice with children and youth: A strengths and well-being model.* Taylor and Francis.

Heyman, G., Fu, G., Lin, J., Qian, M., & Lee, K. (2015). Eliciting promises from children reduces cheating. *Journal of Experimental Child Psychology, 139,* 242–248.

Hipwell, A., Keenan, K., Kasza, K., Loeber, R., Stouthamer-Loeber, M., & Bean, T. (2008). Reciprocal influences between girls' conduct problems and depression, and parental punishment and warmth: A six year prospective analysis. *Journal of Abnormal Child Psychology, 36,* 663–677.

Hoerr, T. (2020). *Taking social emotional learning schoolwide: The formative five success skills for students and staff.* ASCD.

Holbrook, J., Bitsko, R., Danielson, M., & Visser, S. (2017). Interpreting the prevalence of mental disorders in children: Tribulation and triangulation. *Health Promotion Practice, 18*(1), 5–7.

Holder, M., & Coleman, B. (2015). Children's friendships and positive well-being. In M. Demir (Ed.), *Friendship and happiness: Across the lifespan and cultures.* Springer.

Hong, Y., McCormick, S., Deater-Deckard, K., Calkins, S., & Bell, M. (2021). Household chaos, parental responses to emotion, and child emotion regulation in middle childhood. *Social Development, 30*(3), 786–805.

Housman, D. (2017). The importance of emotional competence and self-regulation from birth: A case for the evidence-based emotional cognitive social early learning approach. *International Journal of Child Care and Education Policy, 11,* 13.

Howe, N., & Bruno, A. (2010). Sibling pretend play in middle childhood: The role of creativity and maternal context. *Early Education and Development, 21,* 1–23.

Howe, N., Fiorentino, L., & Gariepy, N. (2003). Sibling conflict in middle childhood: Influence of maternal context and mother-sibling interaction over four years. *Merrill Palmer Quarterly 49*(2), 183–208.

Howe, N., & Recchia, (H. 2014). Introduction to special issue on the sibling relationship as a context for learning and development. *Early Education and Development, 25,* 155–159.

Hruschka, D. (2010). *Friendship development, ecology, and evolution of a relationship.* University of California

Huesmann, L., & Taylor, L. (2011). Media effects in middle childhood. In C. Huston & M. Ripke (Eds.), *Developmental contexts in middle childhood: Bridges to adolescence and adulthood.* Cambridge.

Hughes, J., Cavell, T., & Wilson, V. (2001). Further support for the developmental significance of the quality of the teacher-student relationship. *Journal of School Psychology, 39*(4), 289–301.

Hyde, J. (2014). Gender similarities and differences. *Annual Review of Psychology, 65,* 373–398.

Jambon, M., Madigan, S., Plamondon, A., Daniel, E., & Jenkins, J. (2018). The development of empathic concern in siblings: A reciprocal influence model. *Child Development, 90*(5), 1598–1613.

Jambon, M., & Smetana, J. (2014). Moral complexity in middle childhood: Children's evaluations of necessary harm. *Developmental Psychology, 50,* 22–33.

Jan, C., Zhoub, X., & Stafford, R. (2017). Improving the health and well-being of children of migrant workers. *Bulletin of the World Health Organization, 95,* 850–852. https://www.ncbi.nlm.nih.gov/pmc/articles/PMC5710085/pdf/BLT.17.196329.pdf

Jensen, L. (2015). *Moral development in a global world research from a cultural-developmental perspective.* Cambridge University Press.

Jiang, J., Zhang, Y., Ke, Y., Hawk, S., & Qui, H. (2015). Can't buy me friendship? Peer rejection and adolescent materialism: Implicit self-esteem as a mediator. *Journal of Experimental Social Psychology, 58,* 48–55.

Johnson-Smith, G. (2021). "Potato recess" in Aroostook County, Maine. *New England Living.* https://newengland.com/today/living/new-england-history/potato-recess/

Jones, S., Brush, K., Bailey, R., Brion-Meisels, G., McIntyre, J., Kahn, J., Nelson, B., & Stickle L. (2017a). *Navigating SEL from the inside out: Looking inside & across 25 leading SEL programs: A practical resource for schools and cost providers.* Harvard Graduate School of Education. https://www.wallacefoundation.org/knowledge-center/Documents/Navigating-Social-and-Emotional-Learning-from-the-Inside-Out.pdf

Jones, S., Barnes, S., Bailey, R., & Doolittle, E. (2017b). Promoting social and emotional competencies in elementary school. *Future of Children. 27,* 49–72.

Julien, G., Gaudreau, H., Melançon, A., Mena, D., Gagnon-Trudeau, C., Bouvette-Turcot, A., & Meaney, M. (2017). Intergenerational risk transmission and toxic stress: Impact on child development in a community social pediatrics context. *Paediatric Child Health, 22,* e32–e33.

Kann, L., Olsen, E., McManus, T., Harris, W., Shanklin, S., Flint, K., & Zaza, S. (2016). *Sexual identity, sex of sexual contacts, and health-related behaviors among students in grades 9–12 — United States and selected sites.* https://www.cdc.gov/mmwr/volumes/65/ss/ss6509a1.htm

Keelan, K. (2020). Return to schools: Bully prevention, SEL, and more. *Delta Kappa Gamma Bulletin, 87*(2), 25–27.

Kendrick, K., Jutengren, G., & Stattin, H. (2012). The protective role of supportive friends against bullying perpetration and victimization. *Journal of Adolescence, 35,* 1069–1080.

Khaleque, A. (2013). Perceived parental warmth, and children's psychological adjustment, and personality dispositions: A meta-analysis. *Journal of Child and Family Studies, 22,* 297–306.

Khaleque, A., & Rohner, R. (2011). Pancultural associations between perceived parental acceptance and psychological adjustment of children and adults: A meta-analytic review of worldwide research. *Journal of Cross-Cultural Psychology, 43*(5), 784–800.

Killen, M., Rutland, A., Abrams, D., Mulvey, K., & Hitti, A. (2013). Development of intra- and intergroup judgments in the context of moral and social-conventional norms. *Child Development, 84,* 1063–1080.

Kirby G., & Hodges, J. (2018). Parenting of preschool and school-aged children. In M. Sanders & A. Morawska (Eds.), *Handbook of parenting and child development across the lifespan.* Springer.

Knop, B. (2020). *One in six children live with a half sibling under 18.* US Census Bureau. https://www.census.gov/library/stories/2020/01/more-children-live-with-half-siblings-than-previously-thought.html

Kohlberg, L. (1981). *Essays on moral development: The philosophy of moral development* (Vol. 1). Harper & Row.

Kostelnik, M., Soderman, A., Whiren, A., Rupiper, M., & Gregory, K. (2015). *Guiding children's social development and learning: Theory and skills.* Cengage.

Kramer, L. (2014). Learning emotional understanding and emotion regulation through sibling interaction. *Early Education and Development, 25,* 160–184.

Kramer, S. (2021). *US has world's highest rate of children living in single-parent households.* PEW Research Center. https://www.pewresearch.org/fact-tank/2019/12/12/u-s-children-more-likely-than-children-in-other-countries-to-live-with-just-one-parent/

Lafko, N., Murray-Close, D., & Shoulberg, E. (2015). Negative peer status and relational victimization in children and adolescents: The role of stress physiology. *Journal of Clinical Child & Adolescent Psychology, 44,* 405–416.

Lam, C., McHale, S., & Crouter, A. (2014). Time with peers from middle childhood to late adolescence: Developmental course and adjustment correlates. *Child Development, 85,* 1677–1693.

Lamb, S., & Koven, J. (2019). *Sexualization of girls: Addressing criticism of the APA report, presenting new evidence.* SAGE Open.

Lansford, J., French, D., & Gauvain, M. (2021a). *Child and adolescent development in cultural context.* American Psychological Association.

Lansford, J., Rothenberg, W., & Bornstein, M. (2021b). *Parenting across cultures from childhood to adolescence: Development in nine countries.* Routledge.

Laursen, B., Bukowski, W., Aunola, K., & Nurmi, J. (2007). Friendship moderates prospective associations between social isolation and adjustment problems in young children. *Child Development, 78*(4), 1395–1404.

Laursen, B., Hartl, A., Vitaro, F., Brendgen, M., Dionne, G., & Boivin, M. (2016). The spread of substance use and delinquency between adolescent twins. *Developmental Psychology, 53*(2), 329–339.

Lecce, S., Bianco, F., & Ronchi, L. (2020). Executive function in the school context: The role of peer relationships. *Infant & Child Development, 29*(1), 1–23.

Lee, K. (2013). Little liars: Development of verbal deception in children. *Child Development Perspectives, 7,* 91–96.

Lee, J. (2020). Mental health effects of school closures during COVID-19. *Lancet Child and Adolescent Health, 4*(6), 421.

Lerner, R., Easterbrooks, M., Mistry, J., & Weiner, I. (2013). Developmental psychology. *Handbook of psychology.* John Wiley & Sons.

Madden-Dent, T., & Oliver, D. (2021). *Leading schools with social, emotional, and academic development (SEAD).* IGI Global, Information Science Reference.

Marcone, R., Caputo, A., & della Monica, C. (2015). Friendship competence in kindergarten and primary school children. *European Journal of Developmental Psychology, 12*(4), 412–428.

Marsh, S., Dobson, R., & Maddison, R. (2020). The relationship between household chaos and child, parent, and family outcomes: A systematic scoping review. *BMC Public Health, 20,* 513.

Maunder, R., & Monks, C. (2019). Friendships in middle childhood: Links to peer and school identification, and general self-worth. *British Journal of Developmental Psychology, 37,* 211–229.

McClelland, M., Morrison, F., Gestsdóttir, S., Cameron, C., Bowers, E., Duckworth, A., Little, T., & Grammer, J. (2017). Self-regulation. In N. Halfon, C. B. Forrest, R. M. Lerner, & E. Faustman (Eds.), *Handbook of life course health-development science.* Springer.

McCormick, C., & Scherer, D. (2018). *Child and adolescent development for educators.* Guilford.

McCrory, E., Palmer, A., & Puetz, V. (2017). The neurobiology and genetics of childhood maltreatment. In L. Dixon, D. Perkins, C. Hamilton-Giachritsis, & L. Craig (Eds.), *The Wiley handbook of what works in child maltreatment: An evidence-based approach to assessment and intervention in child protection.* Wiley-Blackwell.

McHale, S., Dariotis, J., & Kauh, T. (2003). Social development and social relationships in middle childhood. In I. Weiner (Ed.). *Handbook of psychology.* John Wiley.

Medina, John (2014). *Brain rules for babies.* Pear Press.

Meier, M., Slutske, W., Heath, A., & Martin, N. (2011). Sex differences in the genetic and environmental influences on childhood conduct disorder and adult antisocial behavior. *Journal of Abnormal Psychology, 120*(2), 377–388.

Mermelshtine, R. (2017). Parent–child learning interactions: A review of the literature on scaffolding. *British Journal of Educational Psychology, 87*(2), 241–254.

Meunier, J., Roskam, I., Stievenart, M., Van, D., Browne, D., & Wade, M. (2012). Parental differential treatment, child's externalizing behavior and sibling relationships: Bridging links with child's perception of favoritism and personality, and parents' self-efficacy. *Journal of Social and Personal Relationships, 29,* 612–638.

Milica, J. (2014). Developing a sense of identity in preschoolers. *Mediterranean Journal of Social Sciences, 5,* 225–234.

Miller, M. (2010). Child labor and protecting young workers around the world: An introduction to this issue. *International Journal of Occupational and Environmental Health, 16*(2), 103–112.

Modry-Mandell, K., Gamble, W., & Taylor, A. (2007). Family emotional climate and sibling relationship quality: Influences on behavioral problems and adaptation in preschool-aged children. *Journal of Child and Family Studies, 16,* 61–73.

Morawska, A., Dittman, C., & Rusby, J. (2019). Promoting self-regulation in young children: The role of parenting interventions. *Clinical Child and Family Psychology Review, 22*(1), 43–51.

National Alliance on Mental Illness (2020). *Mental health by the numbers.* https://www.nami.org/About-Mental-Illness

Nucci, L. (2013). It's a part of life to do what you want. The role of personal choice in social development. In B. Sokol, M. Grouzet, & U. Muller (Eds.), *Self-regulation and autonomy: Social and developmental dimensions of human conduct.* Cambridge University Press.

O'Brien, I., Duffy, A., & Nicholl, H. (2009). Impact of childhood chronic illnesses on siblings: A literature review. *British Journal of Nursing, 18*(22), 1358–1365.

O'Connor, E., Collins, B., & Supplee, L. (2012). Behavior problems in late childhood: The roles of early maternal attachment and teacher-child relationship trajectories. *Attachment & Human Development, 14*(3), 265–288.

Orth, U., & Robins, R. (2019). Development of self-esteem across the lifespan. In D. McAdams, R. Shiner, & J. Tackett (Eds.), *Handbook of personality development.* Guilford.

Pacilli, M., Spaccatini, F., Barresi, C., & Tomasetto, C. (2019). Less human and help-worthy: Sexualization affects children's perceptions of and intentions toward bullied peers. *International Journal of Behavioral Development, 43*(6), 481–491.

Panayiotou, M., & Humphrey, N. (2017). Mental health difficulties and academic attainment: Evidence for gender-specific developmental cascades in middle childhood. *Development and Psychopathology*, 1–17.

Parker, K., Horowitz, M., & Roha, M. (2015). *Parenting in America: Outlook, worries, aspirations are strongly linked to financial situation*. Pew Research. https://www.pewresearch.org/wp-content/uploads/sites/3/2015/12/2015-12–17_parenting-in-america_FINAL.pdf

Pascoe, E., & Smart Richman, L. (2009). Perceived discrimination and health: A meta-analytic review. *Psychological Bulletin*, *135*, 531–554.

Perou, R., Bitsko, R., Blumberg, S., Pastor, P., Ghandour, R., Gfroerer, J., Hedden, S., Crosby, A., Visser, S., Schieve, L., Parks, S., Hall, J., Brody, D., Simile, C., Thompson, W., Baio, J., Avenevoli, S., Kogan, M., & Huang, L. (2013). Mental health surveillance among children—United States, 2005–2011. *Morbidity and Mortality Weekly Report*, *62*, 1–35. https://pubmed.ncbi.nlm.nih.gov/23677130/

Pew Research Center (2015). *Parenting in America: Outlook, worries, aspirations are strongly linked to financial situation*. www.pewresearch.org

Pew Research Center (2018.) *The changing profile of unmarried parents*. www.pewresearch.org

Piaget, J. (1932). *The moral judgment of the child*. Routledge and Kegan Paul.

Pianta, R., Hamre, B., & Stuhlman, M. (2003). Relationships between teachers and children. In W. Reynolds, G. Miller, & I. Weiner (Eds.), *Handbook of psychology*. Wiley.

Pinquart, M. (2016). Associations of parenting styles and with academic achievement in children and adolescents: A meta-analysis. *Educational Psychology Review*, 28, 475–493.

Pinquart, M. (2017). Associations of parenting dimensions and styles with internalizing symptoms in children and adolescents: A meta-analysis. *Marriage and Family Review*, *53*, 613–640.

Pollard, E., & Lee, P. (2003). Child well-being: A systematic review of the literature. *Social Indicators Research*, *61*, 59–78.

Racine, N., McArthur, B., Cooke, J., Eirich, R., Zhu, J., & Madigan, S. (2021). Global prevalence of depressive and anxiety symptoms in children and adolescents during COVID-19: A meta-analysis. *JAMA Pediatrics*, *175*(11), 1142–1150.

Radfar, A., Asgharzadeh, S., Quesada, F., & Filip, I. (2018). Challenges and perspectives of child labor. *Industrial Psychiatry Journal*, *27*(1), 17–20.

Rambura, P. (2015). The self: Who am I? Children's identity and development through early childhood education. *Journal of Educational and Social Research*, *5*(1), 95.

Ramos, A. (2018). Child labor in global tobacco production: A human rights approach to an enduring dilemma. *Health and Human Rights*, *20*(2), 235–248.

Rawlins, W. (1992). *Friendship matters: Communication, dialectics, and the life course*. Aldine De Gruyter.

Rice, K., Prichard, I., Tiggemann, M., & Slater, A. (2016). Exposure to Barbie: Effects on thin-ideal internalization, body esteem and body dissatisfaction among young girls. *Body Image*, 9, 142–149.

Richmond, M., Stocker, C., & Rienks, S. (2005). Longitudinal associations between sibling relationship quality, parental differential treatment, and children's adjustment. *Journal of Family Psychology*, *19*, 550–559.

Rimm-Kaufman, S. (2010). *Improving students' relationships with teachers*. American Psychological Association. http://www.apa.org/education/k12/relationships

Rimm-Kaufman, S., & Chiu, Y. J. (2007). Promoting social and academic competence in the classroom: An intervention study examining the contribution of the responsive classroom approach (abstract). *Psychology in the Schools*, *44*(4), 397–413.

Rimm-Kaufman, S., Fan, X., Chiu, Y. J., & You, W. (2007). The contribution of the responsive classroom approach on children's academic achievement: Results from a three-year longitudinal study. *Journal of School Psychology*, *45*, 401–421.

Rivers, I., Poteat, V., Noret, N., & Ashurst, N. (2009). Observing bullying at school: The mental health implications of witness status. *School Psychology Quarterly*, *24*(4), 211–223.

Rizzolatti, G., & Fabbri-Destro, M. (2008). The mirror system and its role in social cognition. *Current Opinion in Neurobiology*, *28*, 179–184.

Rodkin, P., & Espelage, D. (2015). A relational framework for understanding bullying developmental antecedents and outcomes. *American Psychologist*, *70*(94), 311–321.

Rosenthal, L., Earnshaw, V., Carroll-Scott, A., Henderson, K., Peters, S., McCaslin, C., & Ickovics, J. (2015). Weight and race-based bullying: Health associations among urban adolescents. *Journal of Health Psychology*, *20*(4), 401–412.

Rogoff, B. (2003). *The cultural nature of human development*. Oxford University Press.

Rohner, R. (2004). The parental acceptance–rejection syndrome: Universal correlates of perceived rejection. *American Psychologist*, *59*, 827–840.

Ross, H., & Lazinski, M. (2014). Parent mediation empowers sibling conflict resolution. *Education and Development*, *25*, 259–275.

Rowell, L. (2021). Social and emotional learning: 3 SEL practices teachers use every day. *Edutopia*. https://www.edutopia.org/article/3-sel-practices-teachers-can-use-every-day

Rubin, K., Bukowski, W., & Parker, J. (2006). Peer interactions, relationships, and groups. In N. Eisenberg, W. Damon, & R. Lerner (Eds.), *Handbook of child psychology*. Wiley.

Rudolph, K., Hammen, C., & Burge, D. (1995). Cognitive representations of self, family, and peers in school-age children: Links with social competence and sociometric status. *Child Development*, *66*, 1385–1402.

Sakyi, K., Surkan, P., Fombonne, E., Chollet, A., & Melchior, M. (2015). childhood friendships and psychological difficulties in young adulthood: An 18-year follow-up study. *European Child and Adolescent Psychiatry*, *24*, 815–826.

Sanchez, H. (2021). *The poverty problem: How education can promote resilience and counter poverty's impact on brain development and functioning*. Corwin.

Sanders, M., & Morawska, A. (2018). *Handbook of parenting and child development across the lifespan*. Springer.

Sarkar, J., & Sarkar, D. (2016). Why does child labor persist with declining poverty? *Economic Inquiry*, *54*(1),139–158.

Scales, P., Sesma, A., & Bolstrom, B. (2004). Coming into their own: How developmental assets promote positive growth in middle childhood. *Journal of Adolescence*, *29*(5), 691–708.

Scherrer, V., & Preckel, F. (2019). Development of motivational variables and self-esteem during the school career: A meta-analysis of longitudinal studies. *Review of Educational Research*, *89*(2), 211–258.

Schore, A. (2015). *Affect regulation and the origin of the self.* Routledge.

Schul, R., Townsend, J., & Stiles, J. (2003). The development of attentional orienting during the school-age years. *Developmental Science, 6,* 262–272.

Schwartz, D., Lansford, J., Dodge, K., Petit, G., & Bates, J. (2015). Peer victimization during middle childhood as a lead indicator of internalizing problems and diagnostic outcomes in late adolescence. *Journal of Clinical Child and Adolescent Psychology, 44,* 393–404.

Seibert, A., & Kerns, K. (2009). Attachment figures in middle childhood. *International Journal of Behavioral Development, 33,* 347–355.

Singh, S., Roy, D., Sinha, K., Parveen, S., Sharma, G., & Joshi, G. (2020). Impact of COVID-19 and lockdown on mental health of children and adolescents: A narrative review with recommendations. *Psychiatry Research, 293,* 113429.

Skinner, J., & Kowalski, R. M. (2013). Profiles of sibling bullying. *Journal of Interpersonal Violence, 28*(8), 1726–1736.

Skuse, D., Bruce, H., & Dowdney, L. (2017). *Child psychology and psychiatry: Frameworks for clinical training and practice.* John Wiley.

Slater, A., Halliwell, E., Jarman, H., & Gaskin, E. (2017). More than just child's play? An experimental investigation of the impact of an appearance-focused internet game on body image and career aspirations of young girls. *Journal of Youth and Adolescence, 46*(9), 2047–2059.

Slater, A., & Tiggemann, M. (2016a). Little girls in a grown-up world: Exposure to sexualized media, internalization of sexualization messages, and body image in 6–9 year-old girls. *Body Image, 18,* 19–22.

Slater, A., & Tiggemann, M. (2016b). The influence of maternal self-objectification, materialism and parenting style on potentially sexualized 'grown up' behaviors and appearance concerns in 5–8-year-old girls. *Eat Behaviors, 22,* 113–118.

Smith, B., & Low, S. (2013). The role of social-emotional learning in bullying prevention efforts. *Theory into Practice, 52*(4), 280–287.

Smith, P., & Hart, C. (2011). *The Wiley-Blackwell handbook of childhood social development.* Wiley-Blackwell.

Smolak, L., & Murnen, S. (2011). The sexualization of girls and women as a primary antecedent of self-objectification. In R. Calogero, S. Tantleff-Dunn, & J. Thompson (Eds.), *Self-objectification in women: Causes, consequences, and counteractions.* American Psychological Association.

Solomon, B., Klein, S., Hintze, J., Cressey, J., & Peller, S. (2012). A meta-analysis of school-wide positive behavior support: An exploratory study using single-case synthesis. *Psychology in the Schools, 49*(2).

Solomon, J. (2016). Gender identity and expression in the early childhood classroom: Influences on development within sociocultural contexts (Voices). *Young Children, 71*(3). https://www.naeyc.org/resources/pubs/yc/jul2016/gender-identity

Southwick, S., Litz, B., Charney, D., & Friedman, M. (2011). *Resilience and mental health: Challenges across the lifespan.* Cambridge University Press.

Stalker, K., Wu, Q., Evans, C., & Smokowski, P. (2018). The impact of the positive action program on substance use, aggression, and psychological functioning: Is school climate a mechanism of change? *Children & Youth Services Review, 84,* 143–151.

Statman-Weil, K. (2020). *Trauma-responsive strategies for early childhood.* Redleaf.

Stiglic, N., & Viner, R. (2019). Effects of screentime on the health and well-being of children and adolescents: A systematic review of reviews. *British Medical Journal, 9*(1), e023191.

Sun, X., McHale, S., & Updegraff, K. (2019). Sibling experiences in middle childhood predict sibling differences in college graduation. *Child Development, 90,* 25–34.

Swartz, M. (2016). A comprehensive plan to prevent bullying. *Journal of Pediatric Health Care: Official Publication of National Association of Pediatric Nurse Associates & Practitioners, 30*(6), 515–516.

Talwar, V., & Lee, K. (2011). A punitive environment fosters children's dishonesty: A natural experiment. *Child Development, 82,* 1751–1758.

Taylor, R., Oberle, E., Durlak, J., & Weissberg, R. (2017). Promoting positive youth development through school-based social and emotional learning interventions: A meta-analysis of follow-up effects. *Child Development, 88*(4), 1156–1171.

Telzer, E. H., van Hoorn, J., Rogers, C. R., & Do, K. T. (2018). Social influence on positive youth development: A developmental neuroscience perspective. *Advances in child development and behavior, 54,* 215–258.

Thomson, K., Oberle, E., Gadermann, A., Guhn, M., Rowcliffe, P., & Schonert-Reichl, K. (2018). Measuring social-emotional development in middle childhood: The middle years development instrument. *Journal of Applied Developmental Psychology, 55,* 107–118.

Toseeb, U., McChesney, G., & Wolke, D. (2018). The prevalence and psychopathological correlates of sibling bullying in children with and without autism spectrum disorder. *Journal of Autism and Developmental Disorders, 48,* 2308–2318.

Trang, D., & Tuppett, M. (2020). (In)congruent parent–child reports of parental behaviors and later child outcomes. *Journal of Child and Family Studies, 29*(7), 1845–1860.

Tucker, C., Finkelhor, D., & Turner, H. (2017). Victimization by siblings in children with disability or weight problems. *Journal of Developmental and Behavioral Pediatrics, 38*(6), 378–384.

Tzampazi, F., Kyridis, A., & Christodoulou, A. (2013). 'What will I be when I grow up?' Children's preferred future occupations and their stereotypical views. *International Journal of Social Science Research, 1*(1), 19–38.

United Nations, Office of the Special Representative of the Secretary-General on Violence against Children (2016). *Ending the torment: Tackling bullying from the schoolyard to cyberspace.* https://shop.un.org/sources/srsgvac

Urhahne, D. (2019). Teacher influences and parental involvement. *Educational Psychology, 39*(7), 859–861.

Ursache, A., & Noble, K. (2016). Neurocognitive development in socioeconomic context: Multiple mechanisms and implications for measuring socioeconomic status. *Psychophysiology, 53*(1), 71–82.

US Centers for Disease Control (2020). *Data and statistics on children's mental health.* https://www.cdc.gov/childrensmentalhealth/data.html

US Department of Health and Human Services (2017). *What is bullying?* https://www.stopbullying.gov/what-is-bullying/index.html

Van den Berg, Y., Deutz, M., Smeekens, S., & Cillessen, A. (2017). Developmental pathways to preference and popularity in middle childhood. *Child Development, 88,* 1629–1641.

Vandevivere, E., Braet, C., & Bosmans, G. (2015). Under which conditions do early adolescents need maternal support? *The Journal of Early Adolescence, 35*(2).

van Drunen, L., Dobbelaar, S., van der Cruijsen, R., van der Meulen, M., Achterberg, M., Wierenga, L., & Crone, E. (2021). The nature of the self: Neural analyses and heritability estimates of self-evaluations in middle childhood. *Human Brain Mapping, 42*(17), 5609–5625.

Van Lier, P., & Koot, H. (2010). Developmental cascades of peer relations and symptoms of externalizing and internalizing problems from kindergarten to fourth-grade elementary school. *Development and Psychopathology, 22*, 569–582.

Verschelden, C., & Lomotey, K. (2021). *Bandwidth recovery for schools: Helping pre-k–12 students regain cognitive resources lost to poverty, trauma, racism, and social marginalization.* Stylus.

Verschueren, K. (2015). Middle childhood teacher-child relationships: Insights from an attachment perspective and remaining challenges. *New Directions for Child and Adolescent Development,* (148), 77–91.

Vozzola, E. (2014). *Moral development: Theory and applications.* Routledge.

Waid, J., Tanana, M., Vanderloo, M., Voit, R., & Kothari, B. (2020). The role of siblings in the development of externalizing behaviors during childhood and adolescence: A scoping review. *Journal of Family Social Work, 23*(4), 318–337.

Walsh, F. (2016). *Foundations of a family resilience approach: Strengthening family resilience.* Guilford.

Wang, C., Williams, K., Shahaeian, A., & Harrison, L. (2018). Early predictors of escalating internalizing problems across middle childhood. *School Psychology Quarterly, 33*(2), 200–212.

Wang, D., & Fletcher, A. (2017). The role of interactions with teachers and conflict with friends in shaping school adjustment. *Social Development, 26*, 545–559.

Warin, J., & Adriany, V. (2017). Gender flexible pedagogy in early childhood education. *Journal of Gender Studies, 26*(4), 375–386.

Waters, A., & Tucker, D. (2013). Social regulation of neural development. In B. Sokol, M. Grouzet, & U. Muller (Eds.), *Self-regulation and autonomy: Social and developmental dimensions of human conduct.* Cambridge University Press.

Watson, R., & Vaughn, L. (2006). Limiting the effects of the media on body image: Does the length of a media literacy intervention make a difference? *Eating Disorders: The Journal of Treatment & Prevention, 14*, 385–400.

Wellman, H. (2014). *Making minds: How theory of mind develops.* Oxford University Press.

Whiteman, S., McHale, S., & Soli, A. (2011). Theoretical perspectives on sibling relationships. *Journal of Family Theory & Review, 3*(2), 124–139.

Wildeboer, A., Thijssen, S., Muetzel, R., Bakermans-Kranenburg, M., Tiemeier, H., White, T., Marinus, H., & van IJzendoorn, H. (2018). Neuroanatomical correlates of donating behavior in middle childhood. *Social Neuroscience, 13*(5), 541–552.

Wilder, S. (2014). Effects of parental involvement on academic achievement: A meta-synthesis. *Educational Review, 66*, 377–397.

Wigfield, A., & Eccles, J. (2002). *Development of achievement motivation.* Academic Press.

Williams, D., & Mohammed, S. (2009). Discrimination and racial disparities in health: Evidence and needed research. *Journal of Behavioral Medicine, 32*, 20–47.

Williams, P., & Lerner, M. (2019). School readiness. *Pediatrics, 144*(2).

Williford, A., Maier, M., Downer, J., Pianta, R., & Howes, C. (2013). Understanding how children's engagement and teachers' interactions combine to predict school readiness. *Journal of Applied Developmental Psychology, 34*(6), 299–309.

Wolke, D., Copeland, W., Angold, A., & Costello, E. (2013). Impact of bullying in childhood on adult health, wealth, crime, and social outcomes. *Psychological Science, 24*(10), 1958–1970.

Wolke, D., Tippett, N., & Dantchev, S. (2015). Bullying in the family: Sibling bullying. *Lancet Psychiatry, 2*(10), 917–929.

Yates, T., Ostrosky, M., Cheatham, G., Fettig, A., Shaffer, L., & Santos, R. (2008). *Research synthesis on screening and assessing social–emotional competence.* Center on the Social Emotional Foundations for Early Learning. http://csefel.vanderbilt.edu/documents/rs_screening_assessment.pdf

Yu, Y., Liew, Z., Cnattingius, S., Olsen, J., Vestergaard, M., Fu, B., Parner, E., Qin, G., Zhao, N., & Li, J. (2017). Association of mortality with the death of a sibling in childhood. *JAMA Pediatrics, 171*(6), 538–545.

Yuill, N., & Carr, A. (2018). Scaffolding: Integrating social and cognitive perspectives on children's learning at home. *British Journal of Educational Psychology, 88*(2), 171–173.

Zimmer-Gembeck, M., Waters, A., & Kindermann, T. (2010). A social relations analysis of liking for and by peers: Associations with gender, depression, peer perception, and worry. *Journal of Adolescence, 33*, 69–81.

Chapter 13

Abma, J., & Martinez, G. (2017). Sexual activity and contraceptive use among teenagers in the United States 2011–2015. *National Health Statistics Reports, 104.*

Adhia, A., Kernic, M., Hemenway, D., Vavilala, M., & Rivara, F. (2019). Intimate partner homicide of adolescents. *JAMA Pediatrics, 173*(6), 571–577.

Akseer, N., Al-Gashm, S., Mehta, S., Mokdad, A., & Bhutta, Z. (2017). Global and regional trends in the nutritional status of young people: A critical and neglected age group. *Annals of the New York Academy of Sciences, 1393*(1), 3–20.

Alghadir, A., Gabr, S., & Al-Eisa, E. (2015). Physical activity and lifestyle effects on bone mineral density among young adults: Sociodemographic and biochemical analysis. *Journal of Physical Therapy Science, 27*(7), 2261–2270.

American Academy of Child and Adolescent Psychiatry (2021). *Eating disorders in teens.* https://www.aacap.org/AACAP/Families_and_Youth/Facts_for_Families/FFF-Guide/Teenagers-With-Eating-Disorders-002.aspx

American Academy of Pediatric Dentistry (2020). *Adolescent health care.* https://www.aapd.org

American Academy of Pediatrics (2014) Physical changes during puberty. https://www.healthychildren.org/English/ages-stages/gradeschool/puberty/Pages/Physical-Development-of-School-Age-Children.aspx

American Academy of Pediatrics (2016). Confidentiality protections for adolescents and young adults in the health care delivery and insurance claims process. *Journal of Adolescent Health, 58*, 374–377.

American Association of Orthodontists (2013). *The right time for an orthodontic check-up: No later than age 7*. https://www.aaoinfo.org/system/files/media/documents/Right_Time_for_Ortho-MLMS-hl.pdf

American College of Obstetricians and Gynecologists (2017). *Adolescent pregnancy, contraception, and sexual activity*. Committee on Adolescent Health Care. https://www.acog.org/clinical/clinical-guidance/committee-opinion/articles/2017/05/adolescent-pregnancy-contraception-and-sexual-activity

Amialchuk, A., & Gerhardinger, L. (2015). Contraceptive use and pregnancies in adolescents' romantic relationships: Role of relationship activities and parental attitudes and communication. *Journal of Developmental and Behavioral Pediatrics, 36*(2), 86–97.

Argyriou, E., Um, M., Carron, C., & Cyders, M. (2018). Age and impulsive behavior in drug addiction: A review of past research and future directions. *Pharmacology Biochemistry and Behavior, 164,* 106–117.

Armstrong, S., Wong, C., Perrin, E., Page, S., Sibley, L., & Skinner, A. (2018). Association of physical activity with income, race/ethnicity, and sex among adolescents and young adults in the United States: Findings from the national health and nutrition examination survey, 2007–2016. *JAMA Pediatrics, 72*(8), 732–740.

Asato, M., Terwilliger, R., Woo, J., & Luna, B. (2010). White matter development in adolescence: A DTI study. *Cerebral Cortex, 20*(9), 2122–2131.

Bann, D., Scholes, S., Fluharty, M., & Shure, N. (2019). Adolescents' physical activity: Cross-national comparisons of levels, distributions and disparities across 52 countries. *The International Journal of Behavioral Nutrition and Physical Activity, 16*(1), 141.

Banspach, S., Zaza, S., Dittus, P., Michael, S., Brindis, C., & Thorpe, P. (2016). CDC grand rounds: Adolescence: Preparing for lifelong health and wellness. *Morbidity and Mortality Weekly Report, 65*(30), 759–762.

Banyard, V. (2011). Who will help prevent sexual violence? Creating an ecological model of bystander intervention. *Psychological Violence, 1*(3), 216–229.

Banyard, V., Weber, M., Grych, J., & Hamby, S. (2016). Where are the helpful bystanders? Ecological niche and victims' perceptions of bystander intervention. *Journal of Community Psychology, 44*(2), 214–231.

Barlow, S., & the Expert Committee (2007). Expert committee recommendations regarding the prevention, assessment, and treatment of child and adolescent overweight and obesity: Summary report. *Pediatrics, 120*, S164–S192.

Behringer, M., Vom Heede, A., Yue, Z., & Mester, J. (2010). Effects of resistance training in children and adolescents: A meta-analysis. *Pediatrics, 126*(5), e1199–e1210.

Belcher, B., Berrigan, D., Dodd, K., Emken, B., Chou, C., & Spruijt-Metz, D. (2010). Physical activity in US youth: Effect of race/ethnicity, age, gender, and weight status. *Medicine and Science in Sports and Exercise, 42*(12), 2211–2221.

Ben-Joseph, E. (2020). *Growth charts*. Kid's Health from Nemours. https://kidshealth.org/en/parents/growth-charts.html

Best, O., & Ban, S. (2021). Adolescence: Physical changes and neurological development. *British Journal of Nursing, 30*(5), 272–275.

Biddle, S., & Asare, M. (2011). Physical activity and mental health in children and adolescents: A review of reviews. *British Journal of Sports Medicine, 45*, 886–895.

Biro, F., Pajak, A., Wolff, M., Pinney, S., Windham, G., Galvez, M., Greenspan, L., Kushi, L., & Teitelbaum, S. (2018). Age of menarche in a longitudinal US cohort. *Journal of Pediatric and Adolescent Gynecology, 31*(4), 339–345.

Blanc, A. (2014). Excess risk of maternal mortality in adolescent mothers. *Lancet Global Health, 2*, e201.

Bonanno, L., Metro, D., Papa, M., Finzi, G., Maviglia, A., Sottile, F., Corallo, F., & Manasseri, L. (2019). Assessment of sleep and obesity in adults and children: Observational study. *Medicine, 98*(46), e17642.

Bordini, B., & Rosenfield, R. (2011). Normal pubertal development: Part I: The endocrine basis of puberty. *Pediatrics in Review, 32*(6), 223–229.

Brand, S., & Kirov, R. (2011). Sleep and its importance in adolescence and in common adolescent somatic and psychiatric conditions. *International Journal of General Medicine, 4*, 425–442.

Brusie, C. (2019). *When do boys stop growing?* Healthline. https://www.healthline.com/health/when-do-boys-stop-growing

Buehler, J. (2017). Racial/ethnic disparities in the use of lethal force by US police, 2010–2014. *American Journal of Public Health, 107*, 295–297.

Burrows, T., Goldman, S., Pursey, K., & Lim, R. (2017). Is there an association between dietary intake and academic achievement: A systematic review. *Journal of Human Nutrition and Dietetics, 30*(2), 117–140.

Chaput, J., & Dutil, C. (2016). Lack of sleep as a contributor to obesity in adolescents: Impacts on eating and activity behaviors. *The International Journal of Behavioral Nutrition and Physical Activity, 13*(1), 103.

Chehal, P., Shafer, L., & Cunningham, S. (2021). Examination of sleep and obesity in children and adolescents in the United States. *American Journal of Health Promotion, 36*(1), 46–54. https://doi.org/10.1177/08901171211029189,

Chelsey, R., Canavan, W., & Fawzi, W. (2019). Addressing knowledge gaps in adolescent nutrition: Toward advancing public health and sustainable development, *Current Developments in Nutrition, 3*(7).

Cheng, G., Gerlach, S., Libuda, L., Kranz, S., Gunther, A., Karaolis-Danckert, N., Kroke, A., & Buyken, A. (2010). Diet quality in childhood is prospectively associated with the timing of puberty but not with body composition at puberty onset. *Journal of Nutrition, 140*, 95–102.

Cirelli, C., & Tononi, G. (2008). Is sleep essential? *PLOS Biology, 6*, e216.

Cla, T. (2018). Time to tackle the physical activity gender gap. *Health, 6*, e1077–86.

Corder, K., Sharp, S., Atkin, A., Griffin, S., Jones, A., Ekelund, U., & van Sluijs, E. (2015). Change in objectively measured physical activity during the transition to adolescence. *British Journal of Sports Medicine, 49*, 730–736.

Cunningham, R., Walton, M., & Carter, P. (2018). The major causes of death in children and adolescents in the United States. *The New England Journal of Medicine, 379*(25), 2468–2475.

Curtin, S., Hedegaard, H., & Ahmad, F. (2021). *Provisional numbers and rates of suicide by month and demographic characteristics: United States, 2020.* Vital Statistics Rapid Release Report (16). US Department of Health and Human Services. https://www.cdc.gov/nchs/data/vsrr/VSRR016.pdf

Curtin, S., Heron, M., Miniño, A., & Warner, M. (2018). Recent increases in injury mortality among children and adolescents aged 10–19 years in the United States: 1999–2016. *National Vital Statistics Reports, 67*(4). https://www.cdc.gov/nchs/data/nvsr/nvsr67/nvsr67_04.pdf

Dahab, K., & McCambridge, T. (2009). Strength training in children and adolescents: Raising the bar for young athletes? *Sports Health, 1*(3), 223–226.

Darroch, J., Woog, V., Bankole, A., & Ashford, L. (2016). *Adding it up: Costs and benefits of meeting the contraceptive needs of adolescents.* Guttmacher Institute.

Deardorff, J., Abrams, B., Ekwaru, J., & Rehkopf, D. (2014). Socioeconomic status and age at menarche: An examination of multiple indicators in an ethnically diverse cohort. *Annals of Epidemiology, 24*(10), 727–733.

Dellar, R., Dlamini, S., & Karim, Q. (2015). Adolescent girls and young women: Key populations for HIV epidemic control. *Journal of the International AIDS Society, 18*(2), 19408.

De Leonibus, C., Marcovecchio, M., Chiavaroli, V., de Giorgis, T., Chiarelli, F., & Mohn, A. (2014). Timing of puberty and physical growth in obese children: A longitudinal study in boys and girls. *Pediatric Obesity, 9*, 292–299.

Demerath, E., Towne, B., Chumlea, W., Sun, S., Czerwinski, S., Remsberg, K., & Siervogel, R. (2004). Recent decline in age at menarche: The Fels longitudinal study. *American Journal of Human Biology, 16*, 453–457.

Dietary Guidelines Advisory Committee (2020). *Scientific report of the 2020 dietary guidelines advisory committee: Advisory report to the secretary of agriculture and the secretary of health and human services.* US Department of Agriculture, Agricultural Research Service.

Doane, L., Breitenstein, R., Beekman, C., Clifford, S., Smith, T., & Lemery-Chalfant, K. (2019). Early life socioeconomic disparities in children's sleep: The mediating role of the current home environment. *Journal of Youth and Adolescence, 48*(1), 56–70.

Dowshen, S. (2014). *Braces.* Kid's Health from Nemours. https://kidshealth.org/en/kids/braces.html

Duncan, S., Seeley, J., Gau, J., Strycker, L., & Farmer, R. (2012). A latent growth model of adolescent physical activity as a function of depressive symptoms. *Mental Health and Physical Activity, 5*(1), 57–65

Edwards, F., Lee, H., & Esposito, M. (2019). Risk of being killed by police use of force in the United States by age, race, ethnicity, and sex. *Proceedings of the National Academy of Sciences, 116*(34), 16793–16798.

Edwards, K., Neal, A., & Rodenhizer-Stämpfli, K. (2017). Domestic violence prevention. In B. Teasdale & M. Bradley (Eds.), *Preventing crime and violence.* Springer.

Edwards, K., Sessarego, S., Banyard, V., Rizzo, A., & Mitchell, K. (2019). School personnel's bystander action in situations of teen relationship abuse and sexual assault: Prevalence and correlates. *Journal of School Health, 89*, 345–353.

Edwardson, C., Gorely, T., Pearson, N., & Atkin, A. (2013). Sources of activity-related social support and adolescents' objectively measured after-school and weekend physical activity: Gender and age differences. *Journal of Physical Activity & Health, 10*, 1153–1158.

Ekelund, U., Luan, J., Sherar, L., Esliger, D. Griew, P., & Cooper, A. (2012). Moderate to vigorous physical activity and sedentary time and cardiometabolic risk factors in children and adolescents. *JAMA, 307*, 704–712.

Ersig, A., Brown, R., & Malecki, K. (2021). Clinical measures of allostatic load in children and adolescents with food allergy, depression, or anxiety. *Journal of Pediatric Nursing, 61*, 346–354.

Fitzgerald, C., Messias, E., & Buysse, D. (2009). Teen sleep and suicidality: Results from the youth risk behavior surveys of 2007 and 2009. *Journal of Clinical Sleep Medicine, 7*, 351–356.

Fonseca, R., de França, N., & Van Praagh, E. (2008). Relationship between indicators of fitness and bone density in adolescent Brazilian children. *Pediatric Exercise Science, 20*, 40–49.

Forsyth, S., & Rogstad, K. (2015). Sexual health issues in adolescents and young adults. *Clinical Medicine, 15*(5), 447–451.

Fowler, P., Henry, D., & Marcal, K. (2015). Family and housing instability: Longitudinal impact on adolescent emotional and behavioral well-being. *Social Science Research, 53*, 364–374.

Freeman, R., & Sheiham, A. (1997). Understanding decision-making process for sugar consumption in adolescents. *Community Dental Oral Epidemiology, 25*(3), 228–232.

Frost, J., & Lindberg, L. (2019). Trends in receipt of contraceptive services: Young women in the United States, 2002–2015. *American Journal of Preventive Medicine, 56*(3), 343–351.

Fuhrmann, D., Knoll, L., & Blakemore, S. (2015). Adolescence as a sensitive period of brain development. *Trends in Cognitive Sciences, 19*(10), 558–566.

Galovski, T., Peterson, Z., Beagley, M., Strasshofer, D., Held, P., & Fletcher, T. (2016). Exposure to violence during Ferguson protests: Mental health effects for law enforcement and community members. *Journal of Traumatic Stress, 29*, 283–292.

Galvan, A. (2018). *The neuroscience of adolescence.* Cambridge University Press.

Gaudreault, P., Brunet, J., Godin, R., Michaud, F., Green-Demers, I., & Forest, G. (2019). Changes in sleep habits as a function of age in late adolescence. *Sleep, 42*, A321–A322.

Gavin, M. (2018). *Your child's weight.* Kid's Health from Nemours. https://kidshealth.org/en/parents/childs-weight.html#catgrowth

Gentile, S. (2017). Untreated depression during pregnancy: Short- and long-term effects in offspring. A systematic review. *Neuroscience, 342*, 154–166.

Gentzke, A., Creamer, M., Cullen, K., Ambrose, B., Willis, G., Jamal, A., & King, B. (2019). Vital signs: Tobacco product use among middle and high school students—United States, 2011–2018. *Morbidity and Mortality Weekly Report, 68*(6), 157–164.

Gidding, S., Dennison, B., Birch, L., Daniels, S., Gilman, M., Lichtenstein, A., Rattay, K., Steinberger, J., Stettler, N., Van Horn, L., & the American Heart Association, (2006). Dietary recommendations for children and adolescents: A guide for practitioners. *Pediatrics, 117*, (2).

Guthold, R., Stevens, G., Riley, L., & Bull, F. (2020). Global trends in insufficient physical activity among adolescents: A pooled analysis of 298 population-based surveys with 1.6 million participants. *The Lancet Child & Adolescent Health, 4*(1), 23–35.

Hadland, S., Bagley, S., Rodean, J., Silverstein, M., Levy, S., Larochelle, M., Samet, J., & Zima, B. (2018). Receipt of timely addiction treatment and association of early medication treatment with retention in care among youths with opioid use disorder. *JAMA Pediatrics, 172*(11), 1029–1037.

Hagan, J., Shaw, J., & Duncan, P. (2017). *Bright futures: Guidelines for health supervision of infants, children and adolescents* (4th ed.). American Academy of Pediatrics.

Haltom, C. (2018.) *Understanding teen eating disorders: Warning signs, treatment options, and stories of courage.* Routledge.

Hamilton, K., Warner, L., & Schwarzer, R. (2017). The role of self-efficacy and friend support on adolescent vigorous physical activity. *Health Education & Behavior, 44*(1), 175–181.

Harding, S., Page, A., Falconer, C., & Cooper, A. (2015). Longitudinal changes in sedentary time and physical activity during adolescence. *International Journal of Behavioral Nutrition and Physical Activity, 12*(1), 1–7.

Hargreaves, D., Elliott, M., Viner, R., Richmond, T., & Schuster, M. (2015). Unmet health care need in US adolescents and adult health outcomes. *Pediatrics, 136*(3), 513–520.

Harrell, J., Hall, S., & Taliaferro, J. (2003). Physiological responses to racism and discrimination: An assessment of the evidence. *American Journal of Public Health, 93*, 243–248.

Hasstedt, K. (2018). Ensuring adolescents' ability to obtain confidential family planning services in title X. *Guttmacher Policy Review, 21*, 48–54.

Heath, G., Parra, D., Sarmiento, O., Andersen, L., Owen, N., Goenka, S., Montes, F., Brownson, R., & Lancet Physical Activity Series Working Group (2012). Evidence-based intervention in physical activity: Lessons from around the world. *The Lancet, 380*(9838), 272–281.

Hedegaard, H., Miniño, A.M., & Warner, M. (2020) Drug overdose deaths in the United States, 1999–2019. *NCHS Data Brief*, no 394. https://www.cdc.gov/nchs/products/databriefs/db394.htm

Hennequin-Hoenderdos, N., Slot, D., & Van der Weijden, G. (2016). The incidence of complications associated with lip and/or tongue piercings: A systematic review. *International Journal of Dental Hygiene, 14*(1), 62–73.

Herpertz-Dahlmann, B. (2015). Adolescent eating disorders: Update on definitions, symptomatology, epidemiology, and comorbidity. *Child and Adolescent Psychiatric Clinics of North America, 24*(1), 177–196.

Herting, M., Maxwell, E., Irvine, C., & Nagel, B. (2012). The impact of sex, puberty and hormones on white matter microstructure in adolescents. *Cerebral Cortex. 22*(9), 1979–1992.

Hindin, M., Kalamar, A., Thompson, T., & Upadhyay, U. (2016). Interventions to prevent unintended and repeat pregnancy among young people in low- and middle-income countries: A systematic review of the published and gray literature. *Journal of Adolescent Health, 59*(3), S8–S15.

Holland, K., Vivolo-Kantor, A., Logan, J., & Leemis, R. (2017). Antecedents of suicide among youth aged 11–15: A multistate mixed methods analysis. *Journal of Youth and Adolescence, 46*(7), 1598–1610.

Holt, M., Vivolo-Kantor, A., Polanin, J., Holland, K., DeGue, S., Matjasko, J., Wolfe, M., & Reid, G. (2015). Bullying and suicidal ideation and behaviors: A meta-analysis. *Pediatrics, 135*(2), e496–e509.

Hornberger, L., & Lane, M. (2020). Identification and management of eating disorders in children and adolescents. *American Academy of Pediatrics*. https://pediatrics.aappublications.org/content/pediatrics/early/2020/12/17/peds.2020–040279.full.pdf

Hwang, L. (2019). Analyze this: Most teen girls don't meet guidelines for daily exercise, African-American boys tend to be the most active. *Science News for Students*. https://www.sciencenewsforstudents.org/article/analyze-most-teen-girls-dont-meet-guidelines-daily-exercise

Jackson, F., James, S., Owens, T., & Bryan, A. (2017). Anticipated negative police-youth encounters and depressive symptoms among pregnant African American women: A brief report. *Journal of Urban Health, 94*, 259–265

Jamieson, D,, Beaudequin, D., McLoughlin, L., Parker, M., Lagopoulos, J., & Hermens, D. (2020). Associations between sleep quality and psychological distress in early adolescence. *Journal of Child & Adolescent Mental Health, 32*(2–3), 77–86.

Jefferson, I., Robinson, S., Tung-Hahn, E., Schumann, R., Marrero-Conti, S., Walton, J. M., Golden, E., Poon, E., Alam, M., & Tung, R. (2021). Assessing and improving the knowledge of sexually transmitted infections among high school adolescents. *Dermatology Research and Practice*. https://doi.org/10.1155/2021/6696316

Jensen, F., & Nutt, A. (2015). *The teenage brain: A neuroscientist's survival guide to raising adolescents and young adults.* HarperCollins.

Kalamar, A., Bayer, A., & Hindin, M. (2016). Interventions to prevent sexually transmitted infections, including HIV, among young people in low- and middle-income countries: A systematic review of the published and gray literature. *Journal of Adolescent Health, 59*(3), S22–S31.

Kann, L., McManus, T., Harris, W., Shanklin, S., Flint, K., Hawkins, J., Queen, B., Lowry, R., Olsen, E., Chyen, D., Whittle, L, Thornton, J., Lim, C., Yamakawa, Y., Brener, N., & Zaza, S. (2018). Youth risk behavior surveillance—United States, 2017. *Morbidity and Mortality Weekly Report Surveillance Summary, 65*(6), 1–174.

Kerr, Z., Register-Mihalik, J., Marshall, S., Evenson, K., Mihalik, J., & Guskiewicz, K. (2014). Disclosure and non-disclosure of concussion and concussion symptoms in athletes: Review and application of the socio-ecological framework. *Brain Injury, 28*(8), 1009–1021.

Kesten, J., Griffiths, P., & Cameron, N. (2011). A systematic review to determine the effectiveness of interventions designed to prevent overweight and obesity in pre-adolescent girls. *Obesity Review, 12*, 997–1021.

Khalid, A., & Quiñonez, C. (2015). Straight, white teeth as a social prerogative. *Sociology of Health and Illness, 37*(5), 782–796.

Kipke, M. (1999). *Adolescent development and the biology of puberty: Summary of a workshop on new research.* National Academy Press.

Klopack, E., Simons, R., & Leslie, G. (2020). Puberty and girls' delinquency: A test of competing models explaining the relationship between pubertal development and delinquent behavior. *Justice Quarterly, 37*(1), 25–52.

Kowal-Connelly, S., & American Academy of Pediatrics (2019.) *Parenting through puberty: Mood swings, acne, and growing pains.* American Academy of Pediatrics.

Kowal-Connelly, S. (2019) *Parenting through puberty: Mood swings, acne, and growing pains.* American Academy of Pediatrics.

Labe, C., & Fuhrmann, D. (2020). Is early good or bad? Early puberty onset and its consequences for learning. *Current Opinion in Behavioral Sciences, 36*, 150–156.

Lenroot, R., & Giedd, J. (2009). Sex differences in the adolescent brain. *Brain and Cognition.* 72(1), 46.

Lindberg, L., Santelli, J., & Desai, S. (2018). Changing patterns of contraceptive use and the decline in rates of pregnancy and birth among US adolescents, 2007–2014. *Journal of Adolescent Health, 63*, 253–256.

Liu, J., Tu, Y., Lai, Y., Lee, H., Tsai, P., Chen, T., Huang, H., Chen, Y., & Chiu, H. (2019). Associations between sleep disturbances and suicidal ideation, plans, and attempts in adolescents: A systematic review and meta-analysis. *Sleep, 42*(6), zsz054.

Logan, R., Hasler, B., Forbes, E., Franzen, P., Torregrossa, M., Huang, Y., Buysse, D., Clark, D. &, McClung, C. (2018). Impact of sleep and circadian rhythms on addiction vulnerability in adolescents. *Biological Psychiatry, 83*(12), 987–996.

Lowry, R., Eaton, D., Foti, K., McKnight-Eily, L., & Galuska, D. (2012). Association of sleep duration with obesity among US high school students. *Journal of Obesity, 2012*, 476914.

Lucas, A., Salsman, J., Levine, B., Stoner, L., Skelton, J., & Moore, J. (2021). The role of motivation on physical activity and screen time behaviors among parent-adolescent dyads: The FLASHE study. *Preventive Medicine, 153*, 106725.

Maas, M., Bray, B., & Noll, J. (2019). Online sexual experiences predict subsequent sexual health and victimization outcomes among female adolescents: A latent class analysis. *Journal of Youth and Adolescence, 48*(5), 837–849.

Maharaja, S. (2018). *Adolescent health sourcebook: Basic consumer health information about adolescent growth and development, puberty, sexuality, reproductive health, and physical, emotional, social, and mental health concerns of teens and their parents, including facts about nutrition, physical activity, weight management, acne, allergies, cancer, diabetes, growth disorders, juvenile arthritis, infections, substance abuse, and more, along with information about adolescent safety concerns, youth violence, a glossary of related terms, and a directory of resources.* Omnigraphics.

Marcin, A. (2019). *Height in girls: When do they stop growing, what's the median height, and more.* Healthline. https://www.healthline.com/health/when-do-girls-stop-growing

Marzilli, E., Cerniglia, L., & Cimino, S. (2018). A narrative review of binge eating disorder in adolescence: Prevalence, impact, and psychological treatment strategies. *Adolescent Health, Medicine and Therapeutics, 9*, 17–30.

Matkins, P. (2013). Sexually transmitted infections in adolescents. *North Carolina Medical Journal, 74*(1), 48–52.

McCormick, C., & Scherer, D. (2018). *Child development for educators.* Guilford.

McMakin, D., & Alfano, C. (2015). Sleep and anxiety in late childhood and early adolescence. *Current Opinion in Psychiatry, 28*(6), 483.

Middeldorp, C. (2020). Editorial: Childhood stress and psychopathology: It's not too early to look at biological aging. *Journal of the American Academy of Child and Adolescent Psychiatry, 59*(1), 38–39.

Miller, M., Cheatham, C., & Patel, N. (2011). Resistance training for adolescents. *Pediatric Clinics of North America, 57*(3), 671–682.

Montemayor, R. (2019). *Sexuality in adolescence and emerging adulthood.* Guilford.

Monterrosa, E., Frongillo, E., Drewnowski, A., de Pee, S., & Vandevijvere, S. (2020). Sociocultural influences on food choices and implications for sustainable healthy diets. *Food and Nutrition Bulletin, 41*(2), 59S–73S.

Morris, D., Jones, M., Schoemaker, M., Ashworth, A., & Swerdlow, A. (2011). Familial concordance for age at menarche: Analyses from the breakthrough generations study. *Pediatric Perinatal Epidemiology, 25*, 306–311.

Morton, K., Atkin, A., Corder, K., Suhrcke, M., & van Sluijs, E. (2016). The school environment and adolescent physical activity and sedentary behaviour: A mixed-studies systematic review. *Obesity Reviews, 17*(2), 142–158.

Nankinga, O., Misinde, C., & Kwagala, B. (2016). Gender relations, sexual behaviour, and risk of contracting sexually transmitted infections among women in union in Uganda. *BMC Public Health, 16*, 440.

National Institute on Drug Abuse (2020). *Drugs and the brain.* https://www.drugabuse.gov/publications/drugs-brains-behavior-science-addiction/drugs-brain

Navarro, R. (2011). Protective equipment and the prevention of concussion: What is the evidence? *Current Sports Medicine Reports, 10*(1), 27–31.

Nguyen, H., Frongillo, E., Fram, M., & Bernal, J. (2017). Prevalence of food insecurity of adolescent students from 83 countries. *FASEB Journal, 31*(Suppl. 1), Abstract No. 791.5.

Nittle, N. (2020). *African American men and the criminal justice system.* https://www.thoughtco.com/african-american-men-criminal-justice-system-2834814

Nokoff, N., Thurston, J., Hilkin, A., Pyle, L., Zeitler, P., Nadeau, K., Santoro, N., & Kelsey, M. (2019). Sex differences in effects of obesity on reproductive hormones and glucose metabolism in early puberty. *The Journal of Clinical Endocrinology and Metabolism, 104*(10), 4390–4397.

O'Leary, N., Jairaj, C., Molloy, E., McAuliffe, F., Nixon, E., & O'Keane, V. (2019). Antenatal depression and the impact on infant cognitive, language and motor development at six and twelve months postpartum. *Early Human Development, 134*, 41–46.

Owens, J. (2014). Adolescent sleep working group, committee on adolescence. insufficient sleep in adolescents and young adults: An update on causes and consequences. *Pediatrics, 134*, e921–e932.

Park-Lee, E., Ren, C., Sawdey, M., Gentzke, A., Cornelius, M., Jamal, A., & Cullen, K. (2021). Notes from the field: E-cigarette use among middle and high school students—National youth tobacco survey, United States, 2021. *Morbidity and Mortality Weekly Report, 70*(39), 1387–1389.

Paruthi, S., Brooks, L., D'Ambrosio, C., Hall, W., Kotagal, S., Lloyd, R., Malow, B., Maski, K., Nichols, C., Quan, S., Rosen, C., Troester, M., & Wise, M. (2016). Consensus statement of the American Academy of Sleep Medicine on the recommended amount of sleep for healthy children: Methodology and discussion. *Journal of Clinical Sleep Medicine, 12*, 1549–1561.

Patel, V., Petroni, S., Reavley, N., Taiwo, K., Waldfogel, J., Wickremarathne, D., Barroso, C., Bhutta, Z., Fatusi, A., Mattoo, A., Diers, J., Fang, J., Ferguson, J., Ssewamala, F., & Viner, R. (2016). Our future: A Lancet commission on adolescent health and wellbeing. *Lancet, 387*(10036), 2423–2478.

Patton, C., Sawyer, S., Santelli, J., Ross, D., Afifi, R., Allen, N., Arora, M., Azzopardi, P., Baldwin, W., Bonell, C., Kakuma, R., Kennedy, E., Mahon, J., McGovern, T., Mokdad, A., Paus, T., Keshavan, M., & Giedd, J. (2016). Why do many psychiatric disorders emerge during adolescence? *National Review of Neuroscience, 9*, 947–957.

Perrin, J., Hervé, P., Leonard G, Perron, M., Pike, G., Pitiot, A., Richer, L., Veillette, S., Pausova, Z., & Paus, T. (2008). Growth of white matter in the adolescent brain: Role of testosterone and androgen receptor. *Journal of Neuroscience, 28*(38), 9519–9524.

Potenza, M. (2013). Biological contributions to addictions in adolescents and adults: Prevention, treatment, and policy implications. *The Journal of Adolescent Health, 52*(2), S22–S32.

Prabhakar, R., Saravanan, R., Karthikeyan, M., Vishnuchandran, C., & Sudeepthi, (2014). Prevalence of malocclusion and need for early orthodontic treatment in children. *Journal of Clinical and Diagnostic Research, 8*, ZC60–ZC61.

Pradhan, R., Wynter K., & Fisher, J. (2015). Factors associated with pregnancy among adolescents in low-income and lower middle-income countries: A systematic review. *Journal of Epidemiology and Community Health, 69*, 918–924.

Pringle, J., Mills, K., McAteer, J., Jepson, R., Hogg, E., Anand, N., & Blakemore, S. (2017). The physiology of adolescent sexual behaviour: A systematic review. *Cogent Social Sciences, 3*(1), 1368858.

Raj, A., & Boehmer, U. (2013). Girl child marriage and its association with national rates of HIV, maternal health, and infant mortality across 97 countries. *Violence Against Women, 19*(4), 536–551.

Ramchand, R., Gordon, J., & Pearson, J. (2021). Trends in suicide rates by race and ethnicity in the United States. *JAMA, 4*(5), e2111563.

Rape, Abuse & Incest National Network (2021). *Child sexual abuse is a widespread problem.* https://www.rainn.org/statistics/children-and-teens

Reilly, J., & Kelly, J. (2011). Long-term impact of overweight and obesity in childhood and adolescence on morbidity and premature mortality in adulthood: Systematic review. *International Journal of Obesity, 35*(7), 891–898.

Reinehr, T. (2018). Long-term effects of adolescent obesity: Time to act. *Nature Reviews Endocrinology, 14*(3), 183–188.

Rivara, F., Schiff, M., Chrisman, S., Chung, S., Ellenbogen, R., & Herring, S. (2014). The effect of coach education on reporting of concussions among high school athletes after passage of a concussion law. *American Journal of Sports Medicine, 42*(5), 1197–1203.

Rutherford, H., Mayes, L., & Potenza, M. (2010). Neurobiology of adolescent substance use disorders: Implications for prevention and treatment. *Child and Adolescent Psychiatric Clinics of North America, 19*(3), 479–492.

Salam, R., Das, J., Lassi, Z., & Bhutta, Z. (2016a). Adolescent health and well-being: Background and methodology for review of potential interventions. *Journal of Adolescent Health, 59*(Suppl. 4), S4–S10.

Salam, R., Das, J., Lassi, Z., & Bhutta, Z. (2016b). Adolescent health interventions: Conclusions, evidence gaps, and research priorities. *Journal of Adolescent Health, 59*(Suppl. 4), S88–S92

Salmanzadeh, H., Ahmadi-Soleimani, S., Pachenari, N., Azadi, M., Halliwell, R., Rubino, T., & Azizi, H. (2020). Adolescent drug exposure: A review of evidence for the development of persistent changes in brain function. *Brain Research Bulletin, 156*, 105–117.

Saloner, B., Feder, K., & Krawczyk, N. (2017). Closing the medication-assisted treatment gap for youth with opioid use disorder. *JAMA Pediatrics, 171*(8), 729–731.

Sanderson, J., & Weathers, M. (2020). Snapchat and child sexual abuse in sport: Protecting child athletes in the social media age. *Sport Management Review, 23*(1), 81–94.

Sanyaolu, A., Okorie, C., Qi, X., Locke, J., & Rehman, S. (2019). Childhood and adolescent obesity in the United States: A public health concern. *Global Pediatric Health, 6*, 2333794X19891305. https://doi.org/10.1177/2333794X19891305

Sedgh, G., Finer, L., Bankole, A., Eilers, M., & Singh, S. (2015). Adolescent pregnancy, birth, and abortion rates across countries: Levels and recent trends. *Journal of Adolescent Health, 56*(2), 223–230.

Shannon, C., & Klausner, J. (2018). The growing epidemic of sexually transmitted infections in adolescents: A neglected population. *Current Opinion in Pediatrics, 30*(1), 137–143.

Sharma, V., Coleman, S., Nixon, J., Sharples, L., Hamilton-Shield, J., Rutter, H., & Bryant, M. (2019). A systematic review and meta-analysis estimating the population prevalence of comorbidities in children and adolescents aged 5 to 18 years. *Obesity Reviews, 20*(10), 1341–1349.

Singh, A., Uijtdewilligen, L., Twisk, J., van Mechelen, W., & Chinapaw, M. (2012). Physical activity and performance at school: A systematic review of the literature including a methodological quality assessment. *Archives of Pediatrics and Adolescent Medicine, 166*, 49– 55.

Singh, J., & Gupta, P. (2017). Drug addiction: Current trends and management. *The International Journal of Indian Psychology, 5*(1), 186–201.

Sivertsen, B., Hysing, M., Elgen, I., Stormark, K., & Lundervold, A. (2009). Chronicity of sleep problems in children with chronic illness: A longitudinal population-based study. *Child and Adolescent Psychiatry and Mental Health, 3*(1), 1–7.

Sisk, C., & Romeo, R. (2020). *Coming of age: The neurobiology and psychobiology of puberty and adolescence.* Oxford University Press.

Sisk, C., & Zehr, J. (2005). Pubertal hormones organize the adolescent brain and behavior. *Frontiers of Neuroendocrinology, 26*(3–4), 163–174.

Slopen, N., Shonkoff, J., & Albert, M. (2016). Racial disparities in child adversity in the United States: Interactions with family immigration history and income. *American Journal of Preventive Medicine, 50*(1), 47–56.

Steele, I., Thrower, N., Noroian, P., & Saleh, F. (2018). Understanding suicide across the lifespan: A United States perspective of suicide risk factors, assessment & management. *Journal of Forensic Science, 63*, 162–171.

Steinberg, L. (2014). *Age of opportunity: Lessons from the new science of adolescence.* Houghton Mifflin, Harcourt.

Strathearn, L., Mertens, C., Mayes, L., Rutherford, H., Rajhans, P., Xu, G., Potenza, M., & Kim, S. (2019). Pathways relating the neurobiology of attachment to drug addiction. *Frontiers in Psychiatry, 10*, 737.

Straatmann, V., Oliveira, A., Rostila, M., & Lopes, C. (2016). Changes in physical activity and screen time related to psychological well-being in early adolescence: Findings from longitudinal study ELANA. *BMC Public Health, 16*(1), 1–11.

Studen-Pavlovich, D., Pinkham, J., & Adair, S. (2012). The dynamics of change. In P. Casamassimo, H. Fields, D. McTigue, & A. Nowak (Eds.), *Pediatric dentistry: Infancy through adolescence.* Elsevier Saunders.

Sturman, D., & Moghaddam, B. (2011). The neurobiology of adolescence: Changes in brain architecture, functional dynamics, and behavioral tendencies. *Neuroscience and Biobehavioral Reviews*, 35(8), 1704–1712.

Suleiman, A., Galvan, A., Harden, K., & Dahl, R. (2017). Becoming a sexual being: The 'elephant in the room' of adolescent brain development. *Developmental Cognitive Neuroscience*, 25, 209–220.

Suleiman, B., Johnson, M., Shirtcliff, E., & Galván, A. (2015). School-based sex education and neuroscience: What we know about sex, romance, marriage, and adolescent brain development. *The Journal of School Health*, 85(8), 567–574.

Sun, R., Mendez, D., & Warner, K. E. (2021). Trends in nicotine product use among US adolescents, 1999–2020. *JAMA, 4*(8), e2118788.

Szucs, L., Lowry, R., Fasula, A., Pampati, S., Copen, C., Hussaini, K., Kachur, R., Koumans, E., & Steiner, R. (2020). Condom and contraceptive use among sexually active high school students—Youth risk behavior survey, United States, 2019. *Morbidity and Mortality Weekly Report*, 69(Suppl-1), 11–18.

Trent, M., Dooley, D., & Douge, J. (2019). The impact of racism on child and adolescent health. *Pediatrics*, 144(2), e20191765.

Tulloch, T., & Kaufman, M. (2013). Adolescent sexuality. *Pediatrics in Review*, 34(1), 29–38.

UNICEF (2020). *Adolescent health risks and solutions.* https://www.who.int/news-room/fact-sheets/detail/adolescents-health-risks-and-solutions#.XxpkMKA3Swg.email

US Census Bureau (2019). *Age and sex composition in the United States: 2019.* https://www.census.gov/data/tables/2019/demo/age-and-sex/2019-age-sex-composition.html

US Centers for Disease Control and Prevention (2019). *Youth risk behavior survey data.* www.cdc.gov/yrbs.

US Centers for Disease Control and Prevention (2020). *Opioid overdose.* https://www.cdc.gov/drugoverdose/index.html

US Department of Health and Human Services (2018). *Physical activity guidelines for Americans* (2nd ed.). US Department of Health and Human Services.

US Office of Disease Prevention and Health Promotion (2019). *Physical activity.* https://www.healthypeople.gov/2020/topics-objectives/topic/physical-activity

Verloigne, M., Veitch, J., Carver, A., Salmon, J., Cardon, G., De Bourdeaudhuij, I., & Timperio, A. (2014). Exploring associations between parental and peer variables, personal variables and physical activity among adolescents: A mediation analysis. *BMC Public Health*, 14, 966.

Weston, A., Petosa, R., & Pate, R. (1997). Validation of an instrument for measurement of physical activity in youth. *Medicine & Science in Sports & Exercise*, 29, 138–143.

Witwer, E., Jones, R., & Lindberg, L. (2018). Sexual behavior and contraceptive and condom use among US high school students, 2013–2017. Guttmacher Institute.

Wheaton, A., Everett Jones, S., & Cooper Croft, J. (2018). Short sleep duration among middle school and high school students: United States, 2015. *Morbidity and Mortality Weekly Report*, 67, 85–90.

Whelan, E., O'Shea, J., Hunt, E., & Dockray, S. (2021). Evaluating measures of allostatic load in adolescents: A systematic review. *Psychoneuroendocrinology*, 105324.

Wildeman, C., & Wang, E. (2017). Mass incarceration, public health, and widening inequality in the United States. *Lancet*, 389, 1464–1474.

Winters, K., & Arria, A. (2011). Adolescent brain development and drugs. *The Prevention Researcher*, 18(2), 21–24.

World Health Organization (2016). *Global health estimates 2015: Deaths by cause, age, sex, by country and by region, 2000–2015.* https://www.who.int/healthinfo/global_burden_disease/estimates_regional_2000_2015/en/

World Health Organization (2018). *Adolescents: Health risks and solutions.* https://www.who.int/en/news-room/fact-sheets/detail/adolescents-health-risks-and-solutions

World Health Organization (2020). *Adolescent health.* https://www.who.int/health-topics/adolescent-health#tab=tab_2

World Health Organization (2020). *Adolescent pregnancy.* https://www.who.int/news-room/fact-sheets/detail/adolescent-pregnancy

Xu, J., Murphy, S., Kochanek, K., Bastian, B., & Arias, E. (2018). Deaths: Final data for 2016. *National Vital Statistics Reports*, 67(5). https://www.cdc.gov/nchs/data/nvsr/nvsr67/nvsr67_05.pdf

Yearwood, E., Pearson, G., & Newland, J. (2021.) *Child and adolescent behavioral health: A resource for advanced practice psychiatric and primary care practitioners in nursing.* John Wiley & Sons.

Zajacova, A., & Lawrence, E. (2018). The relationship between education and health: Reducing disparities through a contextual approach. *Annual Review of Public Health*, 39, 273–289.

Zhang, J., Paksarian, D., Lamers, F., Hickie, I., He, J., & Merikangas, K. (2017). Sleep patterns and mental health correlates in US adolescents. *The Journal of Pediatrics*, 182, 137–143.

Ziegler, A., Kasprzak, C., Mansouri, T., Gregory, A., Barich, R., Hatzinger, L., Leone, L., & Temple, J. (2021). An ecological perspective of food choice and eating autonomy among adolescents. *Frontiers in Psychology*, 12, 654139.

Zulfarina, M. S., Sharkawi, A. M., Aqilah, Z., Mokhtar, S., Nazrun, S., & Naina-Mohamed, I. (2016). Influence of adolescents' physical activity on bone mineral acquisition: A systematic review article. *Iranian Journal of Public Health*, 45(12), 1545–1557.

Chapter 14

Alvarado, N., Rodríguez Ontiveros, M. & Gaytan, E. (2019) Do mindsets shape students' well-being and performance? *The Journal of Psychology*, 153(8), 843–859,

American Academy of Child and Adolescent Psychiatry (2016). *Teen brain: Behavior, problem solving, and decision making.* https://www.aacap.org/AACAP/Families_and_Youth/Facts_for_Families/FFF-Guide/The-Teen-Brain-Behavior-Problem-Solving-and-Decision-Making-095.aspx

Amsel, E., & Smetana, J. (2011). *Adolescent vulnerabilities and opportunities: Constructivist developmental perspectives.* Cambridge.

Armstrong, T. (2016). *The power of the adolescent brain: Strategies for teaching middle and high school students.* ASCD.

Arain, M., Haque, M., Johal, L., Mathur, P., Nel, W., Rais, A., Sandhu, R., & Sharma, S. (2013). Maturation of the adolescent brain. *Neuropsychiatric Disease and Treatment*, 9, 449–461.

Arsenio, W., & Willems, C. (2017). Adolescents' conceptions of national wealth distribution: Connections with perceived societal fairness and academic plans. *Developmental Psychology, 53*(3), 463–474.

Asato, M., Terwilliger, R., Woo, J., & Luna, B. (2010). White matter development in adolescence: A DTI study. *Cerebral Cortex, 20*(9), 2122–2131.

Bandura, A. (1977). *Social learning theory.* Prentice Hall.

Barrouillet, P. (2015). Theories of cognitive development: From Piaget to today. *Developmental Review, 38*(C), 1–12.

Bates, B. (2019). *Learning theories simplified.* Sage.

Beland, L., & Murphy, R. (2015). *Communication: Technology, distraction & student performance.* CEP Discussion Paper No 1350. Centre for Economic Performance. London School of Economics and Political Science. http://cep.lse.ac.uk/pubs/download/dp1350.pdf

Bialystok, E., & Craik, F. (2006). *Lifespan cognition: Mechanisms of change.* Oxford University Press.

Blakemore, S., & Mills, K. (2014). Is adolescence a sensitive period for sociocultural processing? *Annual Review of Psychology, 65,* 187–207.

Blakemore, S., & Robbins, T. (2012). Decision-making in the adolescent brain. *Nature Neuroscience, 15,* 1184–1191.

Bodrova, E., & Leong, D. (1996). *Tools of the mind: The Vygotskian approach to early childhood education.* Merrill.

Bottiani, H., Bradshawm, P., & Gregory, A. (2018). Nudging the gap: Introduction to the special issue closing in on discipline disproportionality. *School Psychology Review, 47*(2), 109–117.

Boyer, S., & Bishop, P. (2004). Young adolescent voices: Students' perceptions of interdisciplinary teaming, *RMLE Online, 28*(1), 1–19.

Bronfenbrenner, U. (1996). *The ecology of human development experiments by nature and design.* Harvard University Press.

Brown, D., & Knowles, T. (2007). *What every middle school teacher knows.* Heinemann.

Brown, P., Concannon, J., Marx, D., Donaldson, C., & Black, A. (2016). An examination of middle school students' STEM self-efficacy with relation to interest and perceptions of STEM. *Journal of STEM Education, 17*(3), 27–38.

Bruner, J. (1973). *The relevance of education.* Norton.

Caissy, G. (2002). *Early adolescents: Understanding the 10 to 15 year olds.* Da Capo Press.

Capuzzi, D., & Stauffer, M. (2016). *Human growth and development across the lifespan: Applications for counselors.* Wiley.

Casey, B., & Caudle, K. (2013). The teenage brain: Self-control. *Current Directions in Psychological Science, 22*(2), 82–87. https://journals.sagepub.com/doi/full/10.1177/0963721413480170

Casey, B., Getz, S., & Galvan, A. (2008). The adolescent brain. *Developmental Review, 28*(1), 62–77.

Chandler, A. (2018). *The 3 S's of the middle school mind.* Association for Middle Level Education. http://www.amle.org/BrowsebyTopic/WhatsNew/WNDet/TabId/270/ArtMID/888/ArticleID/962/The-3-Ss-of-the-Middle-School-Mind.aspx

Chatterji, P., & Li, Y. (2021). Effects of COVID-19 on school enrollment. *Economics of Education Review, 83.* 102128. https://doi.org/10.1016/j.econedurev.2021.102128

Chemers, M., Zurbriggen, E., Syed, M., Goza, B., & Bearman, S. (2011). The Role of efficacy and identity in science career commitment among underrepresented minority students. *Journal of Social Issues, 67,* 469–491.

Cheryan, S., Master, A., & Meltzoff, A. N. (2015). Cultural stereotypes as gatekeepers: Increasing girls' interest in computer science and engineering by diversifying stereotypes. *Frontiers in Psychology, 6,* 49.

Cheryan, S., Plaut, V., Davies, P., & Steele, C. (2009). Ambient belonging: How stereotypical cues impact gender participation in computer science. *Journal of Personality and Social Psychology, 97,* 1045–1060.

Choe, D. (2021). Longitudinal relationships amongst child neglect, social relationships, and school dropout risk for culturally and linguistically diverse adolescents. *Child Abuse & Neglect, 112,* 104891.

Choudhury, S. (2010). Culturing the adolescent brain: What can neuroscience learn from anthropology. *Social Cognitive Affective Neuroscience, 5,* 159–167.

Choudhury, S., & Wannyn, W. (2022). Politics of plasticity: Implications of the new science of the "teen brain" for education. *Culture, Medicine, and Psychiatry, 46*(1), 31–58.

Colizzi, M., Lasalvia, A., & Ruggeri, M. (2020). Prevention and early intervention in youth mental health: Is it time for a multidisciplinary and trans-diagnostic model for care? *International Journal of Mental Health Systems, 14,* 23.

Copeland, W., Wolke, D., Angold, A., & Costello, E. (2013). Adult psychiatric outcomes of bullying and being bullied by peers in childhood and adolescence. *Journal of the American Medical Association Psychiatry, 70,* 419–426.

Crone, E. (2016). *The adolescent brain: Changes in learning, decision-making and social relations.* Routledge.

Crone, E., & Dahl, R. (2012). Understanding adolescence as a period of social-affective engagement and goal flexibility. *Nature Reviews Neuroscience, 13,* 636–650.

Cyr, B., Berman, S., & Smith, M. (2015). The role of communication technology in adolescent relationships and identity development. *Child & Youth Care Forum, 44*(1), 79–92.

Dahl, R. (2004). Adolescent brain development: A period of vulnerabilities and opportunities. *Annals of the New York Academy of Sciences, 1021,* 251–279.

Davidow, J., Insel, C., & Somerville, L. (2018). Adolescent development of value-guided goal pursuit. *Trends in Cognitive Sciences, 22*(8), 725–736.

Dawes, N., & Larson, R. (2011). How youth get engaged: Grounded-theory research on motivational development in organized youth programs. *Developmental Psychology, 47,* 259–269.

Delgado, M., Henderson, D., & Parmeter, C. (2014). Does education matter for economic growth? *Oxford Bulletin of Economics and Statistics, 76*(3), 334–359.

Del Giudice, M. (2014). Middle childhood: An evolutionary-developmental synthesis. *Child Development Perspectives, 8,* 193–200.

Demetriou, A., Christou, C., Spanoudis, G., & Platsidou, M. (2002). The development of mental processing: Efficiency, working memory, and thinking. *Monographs of the Society for Research in Child Development, 67*), 1–155.

De Wit, D., Karioja, K., & Rye, B. (2010). Student perceptions of diminished teacher and classmate support following the transition to high school: Are they related to declining attendance? *School Effectiveness and School Improvement, 21*(4), 451–472.

Dubuc, M., Aubertin-Leheudre, M., & Karelis, A. (2020). Lifestyle habits predict academic performance in high school students: The adolescent student academic performance longitudinal study (ASAP). *International Journal of Environmental Research and Public Health, 17*(1), 243.

Dupere, V., Dion, E., Nault-Briere, F., Archambault, I., Leventhal, T., & Lesage, A. (2018). Revisiting the link between depression symptoms and high school dropout: Timing of exposure matters. *The Journal of Adolescent Health, 62*(2), 205–211.

Dweck, C. (2006). *Mindset: The new psychology of success.* Penguin Random House.

Elkind, D. (1967). Piaget's theory of perceptual development: It's application to reading and special education. *The Journal of Special Education, 1*(4), 357–361.

Elkind, D. (1978). Understanding the young adolescent. *Adolescence, 13*(49), 127–134.

Else-Quest, N., Mineo, C., & Higgins, A. (2013). Math and science attitudes and achievement at the intersection of gender and ethnicity. *Psychology of Women Quarterly, 37*, 293–309.

Ernst, M. (2014). The triadic model perspective for the study of adolescent motivated behavior. *Brain Cognition, 89*, 104–111.

Espelage, D., Rose, C., & Polanin, J. (2015). Social-emotional learning program to reduce bullying, fighting, and victimization among middle school students with disabilities. *Remedial & Special Education, 36*(5), 299–311.

Fandakova, Y., & Bunge, S. (2016). What connections can we draw between research on long-term memory and student learning? *Mind, Brain, and Education, 10*(3).

Fandakova, Y., & Gruber, M. (2020). States of curiosity and interest enhance memory differently in adolescents and in children. *Developmental Science*, e13005.

Feiler, J., & Stabio, M. (2018). Three pillars of educational neuroscience from three decades of literature. *Trends in Neuroscience and Education, 13*, 17–25.

Flowers, A., & Banda, R. (2016). Cultivating science identity through sources of self-efficacy. *Journal for Multicultural Education, 10*, 405–417.

Fore, H. (2021). *UNICEF welcomes reopening of secondary schools in Afghanistan, stresses that girls must not be left out.* https://www.unicef.org/afghanistan/press-releases/unicef-welcomes-reopening-secondary-schools-afghanistan-stresses-girls-must-not-be

Foulkes, L., & Blakemore, S. (2018). Studying individual differences in human adolescent brain development. *Nature Neuroscience, 21*, 315–323.

Fuchs, E., & Flugge, G. (2014). Adult neuroplasticity: More than 40 years of research. *Neural Plasticity, 2014*, 541870.

Funk, C., & Parker, K. (2018). *Most Americans believe STEM jobs pay better, but few see them as offering more flexibility for family time.* PEW Research Center. https://www.pewsocialtrends.org/2018/01/09/most-americans-believe-stem-jobs-pay-better-but-few-see-them-as-offering-more-flexibility-for-family-time/

García-Hermoso, A., & Marina, R. (2017). Relationship of weight status, physical activity and screen time with academic achievement in adolescents. *Obese Research and Clinical Practice, 11*, 44–50.

Geier, R., Blumenfeld, P., Marx, R., Krajcik, J., Fishman, B., & Soloway, E. (2008). Standardized test outcomes of urban students participating in standards and project based science curricula. *Journal of Research in Science Teaching, 45*(8), 922–939.

Gestsdottir, S., & Lerner, R. (2008). Positive development in adolescence: The development and role of intentional self-regulation. *Human Development, 51*(3), 202–224.

Giedd, J. (2004). Structural magnetic resonance imaging of the adolescent brain. *Annals of the New York Academy of Sciences, 1021*, 77–85.

Glewwe, P., & Muralidharan, K. (2016). Improving education outcomes in developing countries: evidence, knowledge gaps, and policy implications. In E.A. Hanushek et al. (Eds.), *Handbook of the economics of education* (Vol. 5, 653–743). Elsevier. https://doi.org/10.1016/B978-0-444-63459-7.00010-5

Gogtay, N., Giedd, J. N., Lusk, L., Hayashi, K. M., Greenstein, D., Vaituzis, A. C., Nugent, T. F., Herman, D. H., Clasen, L. S., Toga, A. W., Rapoport, J. L., & Thompson P. M. Dynamic mapping of human cortical development during childhood through early adulthood. (May 2004) *Proceedings of the National Academy of Sciences, 101*(21), 8174–8179. https://doi.org/10.1073/pnas.0402680101

Gray, C., & MacBlain, S. (2015). *Learning theories in childhood.* Sage.

Grøntved, A., Singhammer, J., Froberg, K., Møller, N., Pan, A., Pfeiffer, K., & Kristensen, P. (2015). A prospective study of screen time in adolescence and depression symptoms in young adulthood. *Preventive Medicine, 81*, 108–113.

Gwathney, A. (2021). Offsetting racial divides: Adolescent African American males & restorative justice practices. *Clinical Social Work Journal, 49*(3), 346–355.

Halpern, R. (2009). *The means to grow up: Reinventing apprenticeship as a developmental support in adolescence.* Routledge.

Hansen, C. (2018). *The heart and science of teaching: Transformative applications that integrate academic and social-emotional learning.* Teachers College Press.

Heddy, B., & Sinatra, G. (2017). Transformative parents: Facilitating transformative experiences and interest with a parent involvement intervention. *Science Education, 101*, 765–786.

Herting, M., Maxwell, E., Irvine, C., & Nagel, B. (2012). The impact of sex, puberty and hormones on white matter microstructure in adolescents. *Cerebral Cortex, 22*(9), 1979–1992.

Hochanadel, A., & Finamore, D. (2015). Fixed and growth mindset in education and how grit helps students persist in the face of adversity. *Journal of International Education Research, 11*(1), 47–50.

Hopkins, J. (2011). *The enduring influence of Jean Piaget.* Psychological Science. psychologicalscience.org/observer/jean-piaget

Houston, S., Herting, M., & Sowell, E. (2014). The neurobiology of childhood structural brain development: Conception through adulthood. *Current Topics in Behavioral Neurosciences, 16*, 3–17.

Hughes, R., Nzekwe, B., & Molyneaux, K. (2013). The single sex debate for girls in science: A comparison between two informal science programs on middle school students' STEM identity formation. *Research in Science Education, 43*, 1979–2007.

Jensen, F., & Nutt, A. (2015). *The teenage brain: A neuroscientist's survival guide to raising adolescents and young adults.* Harper.

Johnson, A., & Proctor, R. (2004). *Attention theory and practice.* Sage.

Keating, D. (1990). Adolescent thinking. In S. Feldman & G. Elliott (Eds.), *At the threshold: The developing adolescent*. Harvard University Press.

Keelan, K. (2020). Return to schools: Bully prevention, SEL, and more. *Delta Kappa Gamma Bulletin, 87*(2), 25–27.

Kessels, U. (2015). Bridging the gap by enhancing the fit: How stereotypes about STEM clash with stereotypes about girls. *International Journal of Gender, Science, and Technology, 7*, 280–296.

Kihlstrom, J., & Harackiewicz, M. (1990). An evolutionary milestone in the psychology of personality. *Psychological Inquiry, 1*(1), 86–92.

Kim, Y., Sanders, J., Makubuya, T., & Yu, M. (2020). Risk factors of academic performance: Experiences of school violence, school safety concerns, and depression by gender. *Child & Youth Care Forum, 49*(5), 725–742.

Kleibeuker, S., De Dreu, C., & Crone, E. (2013a). The development of creative cognition across adolescence: Distinct trajectories for insight and divergent thinking. *Developmental Science, 16*(1), 2–12. https://onlinelibrary.wiley.com/doi/abs/10.1111/j.1467-7687.2012.01176.x

Kleibeuker, S., Koolschijn, P., Jolles, D., De Dreu, C., & Crone, E. (2013b). The neural coding of creative idea generation across adolescence and early adulthood. *Frontiers in Human Neuroscience, 7*, 905. https://www.ncbi.nlm.nih.gov/pmc/articles/PMC3874541/

Knoll, L., Fuhrmann, D., Sakhardande, A., Stamp, F., Speekenbrink, M., & Blakemore, S. (2016). A window of opportunity for cognitive training in adolescence. *Psychological Science, 27*(12), 1620–1631.

Krajcik, J., & Shin, N. (2014). Project-based learning. In R. Sawyer (Ed.), *The Cambridge handbook of the learning sciences*. Cambridge University Press.

Kuhn, D. (2009). Adolescent thinking. In R. Lerner & L. Steinberg (Eds.), *Handbook of adolescent psychology* (Vol. 1), 152–186. Wiley.

Kuznekoff, J., & Titsworth, S. (2013). The impact of mobile phone usage on student learning. *Communication Education, 62*(3), 233–252.

Kwak, Y., Payne, J., Cohen, A., & Huettel, S. (2015). The rational adolescent: Strategic information processing during decision making revealed by eye tracking. *Cognitive Development, 36*, 20–30.

Langley, Liz (2019). *Changing America. Should cell phones be banned from classrooms?* The Hill. https://thehill.com/changing-america/enrichment/education/471957-should-cellphones-be-banned-from-classrooms

Lebel, C., & Beaulieu, C. (2011). Longitudinal development of human brain wiring continues from childhood into adulthood. *Journal of Neuroscience, 31*(30), 10937–10947.

Lebel, C., Walker, L., Leemans, A., Phillips, L., & Beaulieu, C. (2008). Microstructural maturation of the human brain from childhood to adulthood. *NeuroImage, 40*(3), 1044–1055.

Lee, J., & Lee, H. (2016). Human capital in the long run. *Journal of Development Economics, 122*, 147–169.

Lu, J., Bridges, S., & Hmelo-Silver, C. (2014). Problem-based learning. In R. Sawyer (Ed.), *The Cambridge handbook of the learning sciences*. Cambridge University Press.

Luna, B., Garver, K., Urban, T., Lazar, N., & Sweeney, J. (2004). Maturation of cognitive processes from late childhood to adulthood. *Child Development, 75*, 1357–1372.

Mah, V., & Ford-Jones, E. (2012). Spotlight on middle childhood: Rejuvenating the 'forgotten years.' *Paediatrics & Child Health, 17*(2), 81–83.

McLeod, S. (2010). *Formal operational stage*. Simply Psychology. http://www.simplypsychology.org/formal-operational.html

McLeod S. (2018). *Jean Piaget's theory and stages of cognitive development*. Simply Psychology. simplypsychology.org/piaget.html

Meruelo, A., Jacobus, J., Idy, E., Nguyen-Louie, T., Brown, G., & Tapert, S. (2019). Early adolescent brain markers of late adolescent academic functioning. *Brain Imaging Behavior, 13*, 945–952.

Miller, P. (2010). Piaget's theory: Past, present, and future. In U. Goswami (Ed.), *The Wiley-Blackwell handbook of childhood cognitive development*. https://onlinelibrary.wiley.com/doi/book/10.1002/9781444325485

Morrow, A., & Villodas, M. (2018). Direct and indirect pathways from adverse childhood experiences to high school dropout among high-risk adolescents. *Journal of Research on Adolescence, 28*(2), 327–341.

Moustafa, A. (2018). *Computational models of brain and behavior*. John Wiley & Sons.

Murphy, T., Laible, D. M., & Augustine, M. (2017). The influences of parent and peer attachment on bullying. *Journal of Child and Family Studies, 26*, 1388–1397. https://doi.org/10.1007/s10826-017-0663-2

Murty, V., Calabro, F., & Luna, B. (2016). The role of experience in adolescent cognitive development: Integration of executive, memory, and mesolimbic systems. *Neuroscience and Biobehavioral Reviews, 70*, 46–58. https://www.ncbi.nlm.nih.gov/pmc/articles/PMC5605811

National Institutes of Health (2020). *The teen brain: 7 things to know*. US Department of Health and Human Services, NIH Publication No. 20-MH-8078. https://www.nimh.nih.gov/health/publications/the-teen-brain-7-things-to-know/index.shtml

Ng, B. (2018). The neuroscience of growth mindset and intrinsic motivation. *Brain Sciences, 8*(2), 20.

Ostroff, W. (2012). *Understanding how young children learn: Bringing the science of child development to the classroom*. Association for Supervision & Curriculum Development.

Patrick, A. (2020). *The memory and processing guide for neurodiverse learners: Strategies for success*. Jessica Kingsley.

Paus, T., Keshavan, M., & Giedd, J. (2008). Why do many psychiatric disorders emerge during adolescence? *Nature Reviews Neuroscience, 9*, 947–957.

Payne, A., & Welch, K. (2015). Restorative justice in schools: The influence of race on restorative discipline. *Youth and Society, 47*(4), 539–564.

PEW Research (2018). *Teens, social media & technology, 2018*. https://www.pewresearch.org/internet/2018/05/31/teens-social-media-technology-2018/

Piaget, J. (1950). *The psychology of intelligence*. International Universities Press.

Program for International Student Assessment (2019). http://www.oecd.org/pisa/

Raghubar, K., Barnes, M., & Hecht, S. (2010). Working memory and mathematics: A review of developmental, individual difference, and cognitive approaches. *Learning and Individual Differences, 20*(2), 110–122.

Rice, L., Barth, J., Guadagno, R., Smith, G., McCallum, D., & ASERT (2013). The role of social support in students' perceived abilities and attitudes toward math and science. *Journal of Youth and Adolescence, 42*, 1028–1040.

Riegle-Crumb, C., Farkas, G., & Muller, C. (2006). The role of gender and friendship in advanced course taking. *Sociology of Education, 79*, 206–228.

Riegle-Crumb, C., & Morton, K. (2017). Gendered expectations: Examining how peers shape female students' intent to pursue STEM fields. *Frontiers in Psychology, 8*, 329–340.

Robnett, R., & Leaper, C. (2013). Friendship groups, personal motivation, and gender in relation to high school students' STEM career interest. *Journal of Research on Adolescence, 23*, 652–664.

Rolls, E. (2016). *Cerebral cortex: Principles of operation*. Oxford.

Romer, D., Reyna, V., & Satterthwaite, T. (2017). Beyond stereotypes of adolescent risk taking: Placing the adolescent brain in developmental context. *Developmental Cognitive Neuroscience, 27*, 19–34.

Rozek, C., Hyde, J., Svoboda, R., Hulleman, C., & Harackiewicz, J. (2015). Gender differences in the effects of a utility-value intervention to help parents motivate adolescents in mathematics and science. *Journal of Educational Psychology, 107*, 195–206.

Rumberger, R. (2020). The economics of high school dropouts. In S. Bradley & C. Green (Eds.), *The economics of education*. Academic Press.

US Department of Education, National Center for Education Statistics (2021). *The Condition of Education 2021* (NCES 2021–144). https://nces.ed.gov/fastfacts/display.asp?id=16#

Sanchez, H. (2021). *The poverty problem: How education can promote resilience and counter poverty's impact on brain development and functioning*. Corwin.

Sawyer, R. (2014). *The Cambridge handbook of the learning sciences*. Cambridge University Press.

Schacter, D., Addis, D., & Buckner, R. (2007). Remembering the past to imagine the future: The prospective brain. *Nature Reviews Neuroscience, 8*, 657–661.

Schaeffer, K. (2019). *Most US teens who use cellphones do it to pass time, connect with others, learn new things*. PEW Research. https://www.pewresearch.org/fact-tank/2019/08/23/most-u-s-*teens*-who-use-cellphones-do-it-to-pass-time-connect-with-others-learn-new-things/

Siegel, D. (2015). *Brainstorm: The power and purpose of the teenage brain*. Penguin Random House.

Smith, T., Brumskill, R., Johnson, A., & Zimmer, T. (2018). The impact of teacher language on students' mindsets and statistics performance. *Social Psychology of Education: An International Journal, 21*, 775–786.

Spear, L., & Silveri, M. (2016). Special issue on the adolescent brain. *Neuroscience and Biobehavioral Reviews, 70*, 1–3.

Stalker, K., Wu, Q., Evans, C., & Smokowski, P. (2018). The impact of the positive action program on substance use, aggression, and psychological functioning: Is school climate a mechanism of change? *Children & Youth Services Review, 84*, 143–151.

Steinberg, L. (2008). A neurobehavioral perspective on adolescent risk-taking. *Developmental Review, 28*(1), 78–106.

Steinke, J. (2017). Adolescent girls' STEM identity formation and media images of STEM professionals: Considering the influence of contextual cues. *Frontiers in Psychology, 8*, 716.

Stevenson, C., Kleibeuker, S., de Dreu, C., & Crone, E. (2014). Training creative cognition: Adolescence as a flexible period for improving creativity. *Frontiers in Human Neuroscience, 8*, 827.

Sturman, D., & Moghaddam, B. (2011). The neurobiology of adolescence: Changes in brain architecture, functional dynamics, and behavioral tendencies. *Neuroscience and Biobehavioral Reviews, 35*(8), 1704–1712.

Sun, X., Nancekivell, S., Gelman, S., & Shah, P. (2021). Growth mindset and academic outcomes: A comparison of US and Chinese students. *Science of Learning, 6*, 21.

Szostak, R. (2007). How and why to teach interdisciplinary research practice. *Journal of Research Practice, 3*(2), M17. https://files.eric.ed.gov/fulltext/EJ800362.pdf

Thapar, A. (2015). *Rutter's child and adolescent psychiatry*. Wiley.

The National Center for Learning Disabilities (2020). https://www.ncld.org

UNESCO, 2017. *Cracking the code: Girls' and women's education in science technology, engineering, and mathematics (STEM)*. A Report Commissioned by the United Nations Educational, Scientific and Cultural Organization. https://unesdoc.unesco.org/ark:/48223/pf0000253479

UNICEF (2017). *The adolescent brain: A second window of opportunity*. https://www.unicef-irc.org/publications/pdf/adolescent_brain_a_second_window_of_opportunity_a_compendium.pdf

UNICEF (2019). *Secondary education*. https://data.unicef.org/topic/education/secondary-education/

United Nations (2016). *Sustainable development goals*. https://www.carbonfootprint.com/un_sus_dev_goals.html

US Department of Health and Human Services (2019). *Dyscalculia*. Eunice Kennedy Shriver National Institute of Child Health and Human Development, National Institutes of Health. https://www.nichd.nih.gov/newsroom/digital-media/infographics/MathLearningDisability-txtalt

US Department of Health and Human Services (2019). *The teen brain: 6 things to know*. National Institutes of Health, NIH Publication No. 19-MH-8078. https://www.nimh.nih.gov/health/publications/the-teen-brain-6-things-to-know/index.shtml

Vedder-Weis, D., & Fortuc, D. (2011). Adolescents' declining motivation to learn science: Inevitable or not? *Journal of Research in Science Teaching, 48*(2), 199–216.

Vygotsky, L. (1978). *Mind and society: The development of higher mental processes*. Harvard University Press.

Vygotsky, L. (1993). *The collected works of L. S. Vygotsky* (Vols. 1 and 2). Plenum Press.

Ward, A., Duke, K., Gneezy, A.,, & Bos, M. (2017). Brain drain: The mere presence of one's own smartphone reduces available cognitive capacity. *Journal of the Association for Consumer Research, 2*(2). https://www.journals.uchicago.edu/doi/10.1086/691462

Wendelken, C., Munakata, Y., Baym, C., Souza, M., & Bunge, S. (2012). Flexible rule use: Common neural substrates in children and adults. *Developmental Cognitive Neuroscience, 2*, 329–339.

Wertsch, J., & Sohmer, R. (1995). Vygotsky on learning and development. *Human Development, 38*, 332–337.

Westwood, P. (2014). *Learning and learning difficulties: A handbook for teachers*. Routledge.

Wils, A., Sheehan, P., & Shi, H. (2019). Better secondary schooling outcomes for adolescents in low- and middle-income countries: Projections of cost-effective approaches. *Journal of Adolescent Health, 65*(1), S25–S33.

Youngblood, D. (2007). Interdisciplinary studies and the bridging disciplines: A matter of process. *Journal of Research Practice, 3*(2). https://files.eric.ed.gov/fulltext/EJ800366.pdf

Chapter 15

Ackard, D., & Peterson, C. (2001). Association between puberty and disordered eating, body image, and other psychological variables. *International Journal of Eating Disorders, 29*(2), 187–194.

Adams, G., Montemayor, R., & Gullotta, T. (1989). *Advances in adolescent development: Biology of adolescent behavior and development*. Sage.

Allemand, M., Steiger, A., & Fend, H. (2015). Empathy development in adolescence predicts social competencies in adulthood. *Journal of Personality, 83*(2), 229–241.

Allison, B. (2000). Adolescent conflict in early adolescence: Research and implications for middle school programs. *Journal of Family and Consumer Sciences Education, 18*(2).

Allison, R., & Risman, B. (2013). A double standard for "hooking up": How far have we come toward gender equality? *Social Science Research, 42*, 1191–1206.

Alto, M., Handley, E., Rogosch, F., Cicchetti, D., & Toth, S. (2018). Maternal relationship quality and peer social acceptance as mediators between child maltreatment and adolescent depressive symptoms: Gender differences. *Journal of Adolescence, 63*, 19–28.

American Academy of Child and Adolescent Psychiatry (2016). *Children and gangs*. https://www.aacap.org/AACAP/Families_and_Youth/Facts_for_Families/FFF-Guide/Children-and-Gangs-098.aspx

American Academy of Child and Adolescent Psychiatry (2016). *Teen brain: Behavior, problem solving, and decision making*. https://www.aacap.org/AACAP/Families_and_Youth/Facts_for_Families/FFF-Guide/The-Teen-Brain-Behavior-Problem-Solving-and-Decision-Making-095.aspx

Anderson, J., & Jiang, J. (2018). *Teens, social media & technology 2018*. PEW Research Center. https://www.pewresearch.org/internet/2018/05/31/teens-social-media-technology-2018/

Andrew, R., Tiggemann, M., & Clark, L. (2016). Predictors and health-related outcomes of positive body image in adolescent girls: A prospective study. *Developmental Psychology, 52*(3), 463–474.

Archibald, A., Graber, J., & Brooks-Gunn, J. (2003). Pubertal processes and physiological growth in adolescence. In G. Adams & M. Berzonsky (Eds.), *Blackwell handbook of adolescence*. Blackwell Publishing.

Arnett, J. (2001). Conceptions of the transition to adulthood: Perspectives from adolescence through midlife. *Journal of Adult Development, 8*(2), 133–143.

Arnett, J. (2006). G. Stanley Hall's *Adolescence*: Brilliance and nonsense. *History of Psychology, 9*(3), 186–197.

Arnett, J. (2007). Emerging adulthood: What is it, and what is it good for? *Child Development Perspectives, 1*(2), 68–73.

Arnett, J., McLean, K., & Syed, M. (2014). Identity development from adolescence to emerging adulthood: What we know and (especially) what we don't know. *The Oxford handbook of identity development*. Oxford University Press.

Atkin, A., Yoo, H., & Yeh, C. (2019). What types of racial messages protect Asian American adolescents from discrimination? A latent interaction model. *Journal of Counseling Psychology, 66*(2), 247.

Bailey, J., Vasey, P., Diamond, L., Breedlove, S., Vilain, E., & Epprecht, M. (2016). Sexual orientation, controversy, and science. *Psychological Science in the Public Interest, 17*, 45–101.

Bao, A., & Swaab, D. (2011). Sexual differentiation of the human brain: Relation to gender identity, sexual orientation and neuropsychiatric disorders. *Frontiers in Neuroendocrinology, 32*, 214–226.

Batanova, M., & Loukas, A. (2016). Empathy and effortful control effects on early adolescents' aggression: When do students' perceptions of their school climate matter? *Applied Developmental Science, 20*(2), 79–93.

Becht, A., Nelemans, S., Branje, S., Volleberg, W., & Meeus, W. (2021). Daily identity dynamics in adolescence shaping identity in emerging adulthood: An 11-year longitudinal study on continuity in development. *Journal of Youth & Adolescence, 50*(8), 1616–1633.

Berns, G., Moore, S., & Capra, M. (2009). Adolescent engagement in dangerous behaviors is associated with increased white matter maturity of frontal cortex. *PLOS ONE, 4*(8), 1–12.

Berzonsky, M. (2011). A social-cognitive perspective on identity construction. In S. Schwartz, K. Luyckx, & V. Vignoles (Eds.), *Handbook of identity theory and research: Structures and processes*, 55–75. Springer.

Beyens, I., Pouwels, J., van Driel, I., Keijsers, L., & Valkenburg, P. (2020). The effect of eocial media on well-being differs from adolescent to adolescent. *Scientific Reports, 10*, 10763.

Bialik, K. (2018). *Americans unhappy with family, social or financial life are more likely to say they feel lonely*. PEW Research Center. https://www.pewresearch.org/fact-tank/2018/12/03/americans-unhappy-with-family-social-or-financial-life-are-more-likely-to-say-they-feel-lonely/

Blakemore, S. (2012). Development of the social brain in adolescence. *Journal of the Royal Society of Medicine, 105*, 111–116.

Blondeel, K., de Vasconcelos, S., García-Moreno, C., Stephenson, R., Temmerman, M., & Toskin, I. (2018). Violence motivated by perception of sexual orientation and gender identity: A systematic review. *Bulletin of the World Health Organization, 96*(1), 29–41.

Boele, S., Denissen, J., Moopen, N., & Keijsers, L. (2019a). Over-time fluctuations in parenting and adolescent adaptation within families: A systematic review. *Adolescent Research Review*, 1–23.

Boele, S., Van der Graaff, J., de Wied, M., Van der Valk, I., Crocetti, E., & Branje, S. (2019b). Linking parent–child and peer relationship quality to empathy in adolescence: A multilevel meta-analysis. *Journal of Youth Adolescence, 48*, 1033–1055.

Bogaerts, A., Claes, L., Buelens, T., Verschueren, M., Palmeroni, N., Bastiaens, T., & Luyckx, K. (2021). Identity synthesis and confusion in early to late adolescents: Age trends, gender differences, and associations with depressive symptoms. *Journal of Adolescence, 87*, 106–116.

Bornstein, M., & Lamb, M. (2011). *Developmental science: An advanced textbook*. Psychology Press.

Brand, M., Labudda, K., & Markowitsch, H. (2006). Neuropsychological correlates of decision-making in ambiguous and risky situations. *Neural Network, 19*, 1266–1276.

Breiner, K., Li, A., Cohen, A., Steinberg, L., Bonnie, R., Scott, E., Taylor-Thompson, K., Rudolph, M., Chein, J., Richeson, J., & Dellarco, D. (2018). Combined effects of peer presence, social cues, and rewards on cognitive control in adolescents. *Developmental Psychobiology, 60*(3), 292–302.

Buccieri, K. (2019). My brother was his little angel, I was the problem child: Perceived sibling favoritism in the narratives of youth who become homeless. *Journal of Family Issues, 40*(11), 1419–1437.

Buckner, J., & Bassuk, E. (2001). Predictors of academic achievement among homeless and low-income housed children. *Journal of School Psychology, 39*(1).

Butterfield, R., Siegle, G., Lee, K., Ladouceur, C., Forbes, E., Dahl, R., Ryan, N., Sheeber, L., & Silk, J. (2019). Parental coping socialization is associated with healthy and anxious early–adolescents' neural and real-world response to threat. *Developmental Science, 22*(6), e12812.

Butterfield, R., Silk, J., Lee, K., Siegle, G., Dahl, R., Forbes, E., Ryan, N., Hooley, J., & Ladouceur, C. (2021). Parents still matter! Parental warmth predicts adolescent brain function and anxiety and depressive symptoms 2 years later. *Development and Psychopathology, 33*(1), 226–239.

Cama, S., & Sehgal, P. (2021). Racial and ethnic considerations across child and adolescent development. *Academic Psychiatry, 45*(1), 106–109.

Carlsson, J., Wangqvist, M., & Frisen, A. (2016). Life on hold: Staying in identity diffusion in the late twenties. *Journal of Adolescence, 47*, 220–229.

Cash, T. (2011). Cognitive-behavioral perspectives on body image. In T. Cash & L. Smolak (Eds.), *Body image: A handbook of science, practice and prevention*. Guilford.

Caspi, A., Roberts, B., & Shiner, R. (2005). Personality development: Stability and change. *Annual Review of Psychology, 56*, 453–484.

Cech, E. A. (2017). What fosters concern for inequality among American adolescents? *Social science research*, 61, 160–180.

Chandler, A. (2018). *The 3 S's of the middle school mind*. Association for Middle Level Education. http://www.amle.org/BrowsebyTopic/WhatsNew/WNDet/TabId/270/ArtMID/888/ArticleID/962/The-3-Ss-of-the-Middle-School-Mind.aspx

Chavez, R. (2016). Psychosocial development factors associated with occupational and vocational identity between infancy and adolescence. *Adolescent Research Review, 1*, 307–327.

Chen, P., & Harris, K. (2019). Association of positive family relationships with mental health trajectories from adolescence to midlife. *JAMA Pediatrics, 173*(12), e193336.

Chiang, L., Howard, A., & Butchart, A. (2021). Taking action to prevent violence against adolescents in the time of COVID-19. *Journal of Adolescent Health, 68*(1), 11–12.

Chopik, W., O'Brien, E., & Konrath, S. (2017). Differences in empathic concern and perspective taking across 63 countries. *Journal of Cross-Cultural Psychology, 48*(1), 23–38.

Cicchetti, D., & Toth, S. (2016). Child maltreatment and developmental psychopathology: A multilevel perspective. In D. Cicchetti (Ed.), *Developmental psychology, maladaptation, and psychopathology* (Vol. 3). Wiley.

Cillessen, A., & Mayeux, L. (2004). From censure to reinforcement: Developmental changes in the association between aggression and social status. *Child Development, 75*(1), 147–163.

Cillessen, A., Schwartz, D., & Mayeux, L. (2011). *Popularity in the peer system*. Guilford.

Claveirole, A., & Gaughan, M. (2011). *Understanding children and young people's mental health*. Wiley-Blackwell.

Cohen, P., Cosgrove, K., DeVille, D., Akeman, E., Singh, M., White, E., Stewart, J., Aupperle, R., Paulus, M., & Namik, K. (2021). The impact of COVID-19 on adolescent mental health: Preliminary findings from a longitudinal sample of healthy and at-risk adolescents. *Frontiers in Pediatrics, 9*, 440.

Collibee, C., & Furman, W. (2015). Quality counts: Developmental shifts in associations between romantic relationship qualities and psychosocial adjustment. *Child Development, 86*(5), 1639–1652.

Collins, W. (2003). More than myth: The developmental significance of romantic relationships during adolescence. *Journal of Research on Adolescence, 13*, 1–24.

Cooley, E., Toray, T., Wang, M., & Valdez, N. (2008). Maternal effects on daughters' eating pathology and body image. *Eating Behaviors, 9*, 52–61.

Crespo, C., Kielpikowski, M., Jose, P., & Pryor, J. (2010). Relationships between family connectedness and body satisfaction: A longitudinal study of adolescent boys and girls. *Journal of Youth and Adolescence, 39*, 1392–1401.

Crocetti, E., Branje, S., Rubini, M., Koot, H., & Meeus, W. (2017). Identity processes and parent–child and sibling relationships in adolescence: A five-wave multi-informant longitudinal study. *Child Development, 88*, 210–228.

Crocetti, E., Jahromi, P., & Meeus, W. (2012). Identity and civic engagement in adolescence. *Journal of Adolescence, 35*, 521–532.

Crocetti, E., Klimstra, T., Keijsers, L., Hale, W., & Meeus, W. (2009). Anxiety trajectories and identity development in adolescence: A five-wave longitudinal study. *Journal of Youth and Adolescence, 38*, 839–849.

Crone, E. (2016). *The adolescent brain: Changes in learning, decision-making and social relations*. Routledge.

Dalhoff, A., Frausto, H., Romer, G., & Wessing, I. (2019). Perceptive body image distortion in adolescent anorexia nervosa: Changes after treatment. *Frontiers in Psychiatry, 15*. https://www.frontiersin.org/articles/10.3389/fpsyt.2019.00748/full

Daniels, E., & Sherman, A. (2016). Model versus military pilot: A mixed-methods study of adolescents' attitudes toward women in varied occupations. *Journal of Adolescent Research, 31*(2), 176–201.

da Silva Pinho, A., Molleman, L., Braams, B., & van den Bos, W. (2021). Majority and popularity effects on norm formation in adolescence. *Scientific Reports, 11*(1), 1–10.

Davis, M. (2018). *Empathy: A social psychological approach*. Routledge.

de Figueiredo, C., Sandre, P., Portugal, L., Mázala-de-Oliveira, T., da Silva Chagas, L., Raony, I., Ferreira, E., Giestal-de-Araujo, E., Dos Santos, A., & Bomfim, P. (2021). COVID-19 pandemic impact on children and adolescents' mental health: Biological, environmental, and social factors. *Progress in Neuro-psychopharmacology & Biological Psychiatry, 106*, 110171.

de Graaf, N., & Carmichael, P. (2019). Reflections on emerging trends in clinical work with gender diverse children and adolescents. *Clinical Child Psychology and Psychiatry, 24*(2), 353–364.

Devine, R., & Apperly, I. (2021). Willing and able? Theory of mind, social motivation, and social competence in middle childhood and early adolescence. *Developmental Science,* e13137.

Dunkel, C., & Anthis, K. (2001). The role of possible selves in identity formation: A short-term longitudinal study. *Journal of Adolescence, 24*, 765–776.

Eisenberg, N., Eggum, N., & Di Giunta, L. (2010). Empathy-related responding: Associations with prosocial behavior, aggression, and intergroup relations. *Social Issues and Policy Review, 4*, 143–180.

Elkind, D. (1967). Piaget's theory of perceptual development: It's application to reading and special education. *The Journal of Special Education, 1*(4), 357–361.

Ellis, W., Dumas, T., & Forbes, L. (2020). Physically isolated but socially connected: Psychological adjustment and stress among adolescents during the initial COVID-19 crisis. *Canadian Journal of Behavioural Science, 52*(3), 177.

Embleton, L., Lee, H., Gunn, J., Ayuku, D., & Braitstein, P. (2016). Causes of child and youth homelessness in developed and developing countries: A systematic review and meta-analysis. *JAMA Pediatrics, 170*(5), 435–444.

Erikson, E. (1950). *Childhood and society.* Norton & Company.

Espelage, D., Ingram, K., Hong, J., & Merrin, G. (2021). Bullying as a developmental precursor to sexual and dating violence across adolescence: Decade in review. *Trauma, Violence, & Abuse.* https://journals.sagepub.com/doi/10.1177/15248380211043811

Fardouly, J., & Vartanian, L. (2015). Negative comparisons about one's appearance mediate the relationship between Facebook usage and body image concerns. *Body Image, 12*, 82–88.

Ferguson, K. (2009). Exploring family environment characteristics and multiple abuse experiences among homeless youth. *Journal of Interpersonal Violence, 24*, 1875–1891.

Fett, A., Shergill, S., Gromann, P., Dumontheil, I., Blakemore, S., Yakub, F., & Krabbendam, L. (2014). Trust and social reciprocity in adolescence—A matter of perspective-taking. *Journal of Adolescence, 37*(2), 175–184.

Fisher, A, Ristori, J., Morelli, G., & Maggi, M. (2017). The molecular mechanisms of sexual orientation and gender identity. *Molecular and Cellular Endocrinology, 467*, 3–13.

Flannery, D., Modzeleski, W., & Kretschmar, J. (2013). Violence and school shootings. *Current Psychiatry Reports, 15*(1), 331.

Forney, K., Keel, P., O'Connor, S., Sisk, C., Burt, S., & Klump, K. (2019). Interaction of hormonal and social environments in understanding body image concerns in adolescent girls. *Journal of Psychiatric Research, 109*, 178–184.

Frank, K., Muller, C., & Mueller, A. (2013). The embeddedness of adolescent friendship nominations: The formation of social capital in emergent network structures. *American Journal of Sociology, 119*(1), 216.

Galliher, R., McLean, K., & Syed, M. (2017). An integrated developmental model for studying identity content in context. *Developmental Psychology, 53*(11), 2011–2022.

Galvan, A. (2018). *The neuroscience of adolescence.* Cambridge University Press.

Giano, Z., Williams, A., Hankey, C., Merrill, R., Lisnic, R., & Herring, A. (2020). Forty years of research on predictors of homelessness. *Community Mental Health Journal, 56*(4), 692–709.

Gibbs, J. (2014). *Moral development and reality: Beyond the theories of Kohlberg, Hoffman, and Haidt.* Oxford University Press.

Gilligan, C. (1982). *In a different voice: Psychological theory and women's development.* Harvard University Press.

Gilligan, C. (1988). *Mapping the moral domain: A contribution of women's thinking to psychological theory and education.* Center for the Study of Gender, Education, and Human Development, Harvard U Graduate School of Education. Harvard University Press.

Graham, S., & Echols, L. (2018). Race and ethnicity in peer relations research. In W. Bukowski, B. Laursen, & K. Rubin (Eds.), *Handbook of peer interactions, relationships, and groups.* Guilford.

Gregory, A., Allen, J., Mikami, A., Hafen, C., & Pianta, R. (2014). Effects of a professional development program on behavioral engagement of students in middle and high school. *Psychology in the Schools, 51*(2), 143–163.

Grogan, S. (2017). *Body image: Understanding body dissatisfaction in men, women and children.* Routledge.

Grych, J., Hamby, S., & Banyard, V. (2015). The resilience portfolio model: Understanding healthy adaptation in victims of violence. *Psychology of Violence, 5*(4), 343.

Guzman, N., & Nishina, A. (2014). A longitudinal study of body dissatisfaction and pubertal timing in an ethnically diverse adolescent sample. *Body Image, 111*(1), 68–71.

Hair, E., Moore, K., Garrett, S., Ling, T., & Cleveland, K. (2008). The continued importance of quality parent–adolescent relationships during late adolescence. *Journal of Research on Adolescence, 18*, 187–200.

Hankin, B. (2005). Childhood maltreatment and psychopathology: Prospective tests of attachment, cognitive vulnerability, and stress as mediating processes. *Cognitive Therapy and Research, 29*(6), 645–671.

Hardy, S., Francis, S., Zamboanga, B., Kim, S., Anderson, S., & Forthun, L. (2013a). the roles of identity formation and moral identity in college student mental health, health risk behaviors, and psychological well-being. *Journal of Clinical Psychology, 69*, 364–382.

Hardy, S., Steelman, M., Coyne, S., & Ridge, R. (2013b). Adolescent religiousness as a protective factor against adolescent pornography use. *Journal of Applied Developmental Psychology, 34*, 131–139.

Hardy, S., Walker, L., Olsen, J., Woodbury, R., & Hickman, J. (2014). Moral identity as moral ideal self: Links to adolescent outcomes. *Developmental Psychology, 50*(1), 45–57.

Hart, D., & Carlo, G. (2005). Moral development in adolescence. *Journal of Research on Adolescence, 15*(3), 223–233.

Harter, S. (2012). *The construction of the self: Developmental and sociocultural foundations.* Guilford.

Heinze, H., Hernandez Jozefowicz, D., Toro, P., & Blue, L. (2012). Reasons for homelessness: An empirical typology. *Vulnerable Children and Youth Studies, 7*, 88–101.

Hoffmann, S., & Warschburger, P. (2017). Weight, shape, and muscularity concerns in male and female adolescents: Predictors of change and influences on eating concern. *International Journal of Eating Disorders, 50*, 139–147.

Horowitz, J., & Graf, N. (2019). *Most US teens see anxiety and depression as a major problem among their peers*. PEW Research Center. https://www.pewsocialtrends.org/2019/02/20/most-u-s-teens-see-anxiety-and-depression-as-a-major-problem-among-their-peers/

Hufer, A., Kornadt, A., Kandler, C., & Riemann, R. (2020). Genetic and environmental variation in political orientation in adolescence and early adulthood: A nuclear twin family analysis. *Journal of Personality & Social Psychology, 118*(4), 762–776.

Hughes, J., Clark, S., Wood, W., Cakmak, S., Cox, A., Macinnis, M., Warren, B., Handrahan, E., & Broom, B. (2010). Youth homelessness: The relationships among mental health, hope, and service satisfaction. *Journal of the Canadian Academy of Child and Adolescent Psychiatry, 19*(4), 274–283.

Hyde, J. (2005). From home to street: Understanding young people's transitions into homelessness. *Journal of Adolescence, 28*, 171–183.

Jones, D. (2001). Social comparison and body image: Attractiveness comparisons to models and peers among adolescent girls and boys. *Sex Roles, 45*, 645–664.

Jones, R., Vaterlaus, J., Jackson, M., & Morrill, T. (2014). Friendship characteristics, psychosocial development, and adolescent identity formation. *Personal Relationship, 21*, 51–67.

Kansky, J., & Allen, J. (2018). Long-term risks and possible benefits associated with late adolescent romantic relationship quality. *Journal of Youth and Adolescence, 47*(7), 1531–1544.

Kaplan, A., & Garner, J. (2017). A complex dynamic systems perspective on identity and its development: The dynamic systems model of role identity. *Developmental Psychology, 53*, 11.

Kellner, D. (2018). School shootings, societal violence and gun culture. In H. Shapiro (Ed.), *The Wiley handbook on violence in education*. Wiley.

Kelly, D. (2018). Parents' influence on youths' civic behaviors: The civic context of the caregiving environment, families in society. *The Journal of Contemporary Social Services, 87*(3), 447–455.

Kim, J., McHale, S., Osgood D., & Crouter, A. (2006). Longitudinal course and family correlates of sibling relationships from childhood through adolescence. *Child Development, 77*, 1746–1761.

Kipke, M. (1999). *Adolescent development and the biology of puberty summary of a workshop on new research*. National Academy Press.

Kleemans, M., Daalmans, S., Carbaat, I., & Anschütz, D. (2018). Picture perfect: The direct effect of manipulated Instagram photos on body image in adolescent girls. *Media Psychology, 21*(1), 93–110.

Klimstra, T. (2013). Adolescent personality development and identity formation. *Child Development Perspectives, 7*, 80–84.

Kloep, M. (2015). *Development from adolescence to early adulthood: A dynamic systemic approach to transitions and transformations*. Psychology Press.

Knopf, A. (2020). During and after COVID-19, anxiety and depression will increase: Study. *Brown University Child & Adolescent Behavior Letter, 36*(9), 6–7.

Koepke, S., Jaap, J., & Denissen, A. (2012). Dynamics of identity development and separation–individuation in parent–child relationships during adolescence and emerging adulthood—A conceptual integration. *Developmental Review, 32*(1), 67–88.

Kohlberg, L. (1981). *Essays on moral development: The philosophy of moral development* (Vol. 1). Harper & Row.

Kong, F., & You, X. (2013). Loneliness and self-esteem as mediators between social support and life satisfaction in late adolescence. *Social Indicators Research, 110*(1), 271–279.

Kreager, D., Staff, J., Gauthier, R., Lefkowitz, E., & Feinberg, M. (2016). The double standard at sexual debut: Gender, sexual behavior and adolescent peer acceptance. *Sex Roles, 75*, 377–392.

Lafko, N., Murray-Close, D., & Shoulberg, E. (2015). Negative peer status and relational victimization in children and adolescents: The role of stress physiology. *Journal of Clinical Child & Adolescent Psychology, 44*, 405–416.

LaFontana, K., & Cillessen, A. (2010). Developmental changes in the priority of perceived status in childhood and adolescence. *Social Development, 19*(1), 130–147.

Laible, D. (2007). Attachment with parents and peers in late adolescence: Links with emotional competence and social behavior. *Personality & Individual Differences, 43*(5), 1185–1197.

Laible, D., Carlo, G., & Roesch, S. (2004). Pathways to self-esteem in late adolescence: The role of parent and peer attachment, empathy, and social behaviours. *Journal of Adolescence, 27*(6), 703–716.

Lansford, J., Rothenberg, W., & Bornstein, M. (2021). *Parenting across cultures from childhood to adolescence: Development in nine countries*. Routledge.

Lapsley, D. (2008). Moral self-identity as the aim of education. In L. Nucci & D. Narvaez (Eds.), *Handbook of moral and character education*. Routledge.

Laursen, B., & Mooney, (2007). Individual differences in adolescent dating and adjustment. In R. Engels, K. M. Kerr, & H. Stattin (Eds.), *Friends, lovers and groups: Key relationships in adolescence*. Wiley.

Lee, C., Padilla-Walker, L., & Memmott-Elison, M. (2016). The role of parents and peers on adolescents' prosocial behavior and substance use. *Journal of Social & Personal Relationships, 34*(7), 1053–1069.

Lerner, J., Phelps, E., Forman, Y., & Bowers, E. (2009). Positive youth development. In R. Lerner & L. Steinberg (Eds.), *Handbook of adolescent psychology: Individual bases of adolescent development*. Wiley.

Lima, M., Marques, S., Muinos, G., & Camilo, C. (2017). All you need is Facebook friends? Associations between online and face-to-face friendships and health. *Frontiers in Psychology, 8*, 1–12.

Lin, J., Chan, M., Kwong, K., & Au, L. (2018). Promoting positive youth development for Asian American youth in a teen resource center: Key components, outcomes, and lessons learned. *Children & Youth Services Review, 91*, 413–423.

Loades, M., Chatburn, E., Higson-Sweeney, N., Reynolds, S., Shafran, R., Brigden, A., Linney, C., McManus, M., Borwick, C., & Crawley, E. (2020). Rapid systematic review: The impact of social isolation and loneliness on the mental health of children and adolescents in the context of COVID-19. *Journal of the American Academy of Child & Adolescent Psychiatry*. https://jaacap.org/article/S0890-8567(20)30337-3/fulltext

Lopez, E., Perez, S., Ochoa, G., & Ruiz, D. (2008). Adolescent aggression: Effects of gender and family and school environments. *Journal of Adolescence, 31*, 433–450.

Lui, C. K., Sterling, S. A., Chi, F. W., Lu, Y., & Campbell, C. I. (2017). Socioeconomic differences in adolescent substance abuse treatment participation and long-term outcomes. *Addictive Behaviors, 68*, 45–51.

Mahon, N., Yarcheski, A., Yarcheski, T., Cannella, B., & Hanks, M. (2006). A meta-analytic study of predictors for loneliness during adolescence. *Nursing Research, 55*, 308–315.

Marcia, J. (1980). Identity in adolescence. In J. Adelson (Ed.), *Handbook of adolescent psychology*, 159–187. Wiley.

Marcia, J. (2010). Life transitions and stress in the context of psychosocial development. In T. Miller (Ed.), *Handbook of stressful transitions across the lifespan*, 19–34. Springer.

Markey, C. (2010). Invited commentary: Why body image is important to adolescent development. *Journal of Youth Adolescence, 39*, 1387–1391.

McAdams, D., & Pals, J. (2006). A new big five: Fundamental principles for an integrative science of personality. *American Psychologist, 6*, 204–217.

McCormick, C., & Scherer, D. (2018). *Child and adolescent development for educators.* Guilford.

McCrae, N., Gettings, S., & Purssell, E. (2017). Social media and depressive symptoms in childhood and adolescence: A systematic review. *Adolescent Research Review, 2*, 315–330.

McCrae, R., & John, O. (1992). An introduction to the five-factor model and its applications. *Journal of Personality, 60*, 175–215.

McHale, S., Kim, J., & Whiteman, S. D. (2006). Sibling relationships in childhood and adolescence. In P. Noller & J. Feeney (Eds.) *Close relationships: Functions, forms and processes.* Psychology Press/Taylor & Francis.

McIntosh-Dalmedo, S., Devonport, T., Nicholls, W., Friesen, & Andrew, P. (2018). Examining the effects of sport and exercise interventions on body image among adolescent girls: A systematic review. *Journal of Sport Behavior, 41*(3), 245–269.

McLean, K., & Pasupathi, M. (2012). Processes of identity development: Where I am and how I got there. *Identity: An International Journal of Theory and Research, 12*, 8–28.

McLean, K., & Syed, M. (2015). *The Oxford handbook of identity development.* Oxford University Press.

Meca, A., Rodil, J., Paulson, J., Kelley, M., Schwartz, S., Unger, J., Lorenzo-Blanco, E., Des Rosiers, S., Gonzales-Backen, M., Baezconde-Garbanati, L., & Zamboanga, B. (2019). Examining the directionality between identity development and depressive symptoms among recently immigrated Hispanic adolescents. *Journal of Youth & Adolescence, 48*(11), 2114–2124.

Menesini, E., & Salmivalli, C. (2017). Bullying in school: The state of knowledge and effective interventions. *Psychology, Health & Medicine, 22*(S1), 240–253.

Mestre, M., Carlo, G., Samper, P., Malonda, E., & Ana Llorca, M. (2018). Bidirectional relations among empathy-related traits, prosocial moral reasoning, and prosocial behaviors. *Social Development, 28*(3), 514–528.

Meuwese, R., Cillessen, A., & Güroğlu, B. (2017). Friends in high places: A dyadic perspective on peer status as predictor of friendship quality and the mediating role of empathy and prosocial behavior. *Social Development, 26*(3), 503–519.

Mikami, A., Gregory, A., Allen, J., Pianta, R., & Lun, J. (2011). Effects of a teacher professional development intervention on peer relationships in secondary classrooms. *School Psychology Review, 40*(3), 367–385.

Milevsky, A. (2015). *Understanding adolescents for helping professionals.* Springer.

Miller, P., Fung, H., Lin, S., Chen, E., & Boldt, B. (2012). How socialization happens on the ground: Narrative practices as alternate socializing pathways in Taiwanese and European-American families. *Monographs of the Society for Research in Child Development, 77*, 1–140.

Mills, K., Goddings, A., Clasen, J., Giedd, S., & Blakemore, J. (2014). The developmental mismatch in structural brain maturation during adolescence. *Developmental Neuroscience, 36*, 147–160.

Montgomery, M. (2021). Identity development theories. In S. Hupp & J. Jewell (Eds.), *The encyclopedia of child and adolescent development.* Wiley.

Moses, J., & Villodas, M. (2017). The potential protective role of peer relationships on school engagement in at-risk adolescents. *Journal of Youth and Adolescence, 46*(11), 2255–2272.

Moshman, D. (2011). *Adolescent rationality and development: Cognition, morality, and identity.* Psychology Press.

Mund, M., Freuding, M., Möbius, K., Horn, N., & Neyer, F. (2020). The stability and change of loneliness across the life span: A meta-analysis of longitudinal studies. *Personality & Social Psychology Review, 24*(1), 24–52.

Namy, S., Carlson, C., O'Hara, K., Nakuti, J., Bukuluki, P., Lwanyaaga, J., Namakula, S., Nanyunja, B., Wainberg, M., Naker, D., & Michau, L. (2017). Towards a feminist understanding of intersecting violence against women and children in the family. *Social Science & Medicine, 184*, 40–48.

National Conference of State Legislatures (2019). *Youth homelessness overview.* https://www.ncsl.org/research/human-services/homeless-and-runaway-youth.aspx

Nowland, R., Necka, E., & Cacioppo, J. (2018). Loneliness and social internet use: Pathways to reconnection in a digital world? *Perspectives on Psychological Science, 13*, 70–87.

Nucci, L. (2013). It's a part of life to do what you want. The role of personal choice in social development. In B. Sokol, M. Grouzet, & U. Muller (Eds.), *Self-regulation and autonomy: Social and developmental dimensions of human conduct.* Cambridge University Press.

Oberle, E., Schonert-Reichl, K., & Thomson, K. (2010). Understanding the link between social and emotional well-being and peer relations in early adolescence: Gender-specific predictors of peer acceptance. *Journal of Youth and Adolescence, 39*(11), 1330–1342.

Odudu, C., Williams, M., & Campione, B. (2020). Associations between domain differentiated sibling conflict and adolescent problem behavior. *Journal of Marriage & Family, 82*(3), 1015–1025.

Olson-Kennedy, J., Cohen-Kettenis, P., Kreukels, B., Meyer-Bahlburg, H., Garofalo, R., Meyer, W., & Rosenthal, S. (2016). Research priorities for gender nonconforming/transgender youth: Gender identity development and biopsychosocial outcomes. *Current Opinion in Endocrinology, Diabetes, and Obesity, 23*(2), 172–179.

Oyserman, D., & James, L. (2011). Possible identities. In S. Schwartz, K. Luyckx, & V. Vignoles (Eds.), *Handbook of identity theory and research.* Springer.

Pasupathi, M., Mansour, E., & Brubaker, J. R. (2007). Developing a life story: Constructing relations between self and experience in autobiographical narratives. *Human Development, 50*, 85–110.

Patterson, G., Dishion, T., & Yoerger, K. (2000). Adolescent growth in new forms of problem behavior: Macro- and micro-peer dynamics. *Prevention Science, 1,* 3–13.

Paxton, S., Neumark-Sztainer, D, Hannan, P., & Eisenberg, M. (2006). Body dissatisfaction prospectively predicts depressive mood and low self-esteem in adolescent girls and boys. *Journal of Clinical Child and Adolescent Psychology, 35*(4), 539–49.

Piaget, J. (1932). *The moral judgment of the child.* Routledge and Kegan Paul.

Pinquart, M. (2017a). Associations of parenting dimensions and styles with internalizing symptoms in children and adolescents: A meta-analysis. *Marriage and Family Review, 53,* 613–640.

Pinquart, M. (2017b). Associations of parenting dimensions and styles with internalizing symptoms in children and adolescents: An updated meta-analysis. *Developmental Psychology, 53,* 873–932.

Porter, T. (2013). Moral and political identity and civic involvement in adolescents. *Journal of Moral Education, 42*(2), 239–255.

Portt, E., Person, S., Person, B., Rawana, E., & Brownlee, K. (2020). Empathy and positive aspects of adolescent peer relationships: A scoping review. *Journal of Child and Family Studies, 29,* 2416–2433.

Qualter, P., Brown, S., Rotenberg, K., Vanhalst, J., Harris, R., Goossens, L., Bangee, M., & Munn, P. (2013). Trajectories of loneliness during childhood and adolescence: Predictors and health outcomes. *Journal of Adolescence, 36*(6), 1283–1293.

Ragelienė, T. (2016). Links of adolescents identity development and relationship with peers: A systematic literature review. *Journal of the Canadian Academy of Child and Adolescent Psychiatry, 25*(2), 97–105.

Recchia, H., Wainryb, C., Bourne, S., & Pasupathi, M. (2014). The construction of moral agency in mother-child conversations about helping and hurting across childhood and adolescence. *Developmental Psychology, 50*(1), 34–44.

Reid, G., & Boyer, W. (2013). Social network sites and young adolescent identity development. *Childhood Education, 89*(4), 243–253.

Reijntjes, A., Vermande, M., Thomaes, S., Goossens, F., Olthof, T., Aleva, L., & Van der Meulen, M. (2016). Narcissism, bullying, and social dominance in youth: A longitudinal analysis. *Journal of Abnormal Child Psychology, 44,* 63–74.

Reinders, H., & Youniss, J. (2006). School-based required community service and civic development in adolescents. *Applied Developmental Science, 10,* 2–12.

Rice, K., & Mulkeen, P. (1995). Relationships with parents and peers: A longitudinal study of adolescent intimacy. *Journal of Adolescent Research, 10*(3), 338–357.

Richmond, M., & Stocker, C. (2006). Associations between family cohesion and adolescent siblings' externalizing behavior. *Journal of Family Psychology, 20*(4), 663–669.

Rodkin, P., Espelage, D., & Hanish, D. (2015). A relational framework for understanding bullying: Developmental antecedents and outcomes. *American Psychologist, 70*(4), 311–321.

Roelofs, J., Meesters, C., Ter Huurne, M., Bamelis, L., & Muris, P. (2006). On the links between attachment style, parental rearing behavior, and internalizing and externalizing problems in nonclinical children. *Journal of Child and Family Studies, 15,* 331–344.

Rogers, A., Ha, T., & Ockey, S. (2021). Adolescents' perceived socio-emotional impact of COVID-19 and implications for mental health: Results from a US-based mixed-methods study. *The Journal of Adolescent Health, 68*(1), 43–52.

Rohde, P., Stice, E., & Marti, C. (2015). Development and predictive effects of eating disorder risk factors during adolescence: Implications for prevention efforts. *International Journal of Eating Disorders, 48*(2), 187–198.

Romund, L., Raufelder, D., Flemming, E., Lorenz, R., Pelz, P., Gleich, T., Heinz, A., & Beck, A. (2016). Maternal parenting behavior and emotion processing in adolescents—An fMRI study. *Biological Psychology, 120,* 120–125.

Rose, R. (2008). Peers, parents, and processes of adolescent socialization: A twin–study perspective. In R. Engels, M. Kerr, & H. Statin (Eds.), *Friends, lovers and groups.* Wiley.

Roselli, C. (2018). Neurobiology of gender identity and sexual orientation. *Journal of Neuroendocrinology, 30*(7), e12562.

Rosenthal, N., & Kobak, R. (2010). Assessing adolescents' attachment hierarchies: Differences across developmental periods and associations with individual adaptation. *Journal of Research on Adolescence, 20*(3), 678–706.

Rothbart, M., & Bates, J. (2006). Temperament. In W. Damon & R. Lerner (Series Eds.), & N. Eisenberg (Vol. Ed.), *Handbook of child psychology* (Vol. 3), 99–166. Wiley.

Rowhani-Rahbar, A., & Moe, C. (2019). School shootings in the US: What is the state of evidence? *The Journal of Adolescent Health, 64*(6), 683–684.

Rubin, K., Bukowski, W., & Parker, J. (2006). Peer interactions, relationships, and groups. In N. Eisenberg, W. Damon, & R. Lerner (Eds.) *Handbook of child psychology.* Wiley.

Rudolph, K., Miernicki, M., Troop-Gordon, W., Davis, M., & Telzer, E. (2016). Adding insult to injury: Neural sensitivity to social exclusion is associated with internalizing symptoms in chronically peer-victimized girls. *Social Cognitive and Affective Neuroscience, 11,* 829–842.

Saewyc, E. (2011). Research on adolescent sexual orientation: Development, health disparities, stigma, and resilience. *Journal of Research on Adolescence, 21*(1), 256–272.

Schulenberg, J., Maggs, J., & O'Malley, P. (2003). How and why the understanding of developmental continuity and discontinuity is important: The sample case of long-term consequences of adolescent substance use. In J. Mortimer & M. Shanahan (Eds.), *Handbook of the life course.* Plenum Press.

Schmitz, R., & Tyler, K. (2016). Growing up before their time: The early adultification experiences of homeless young people. *Children and Youth Services Review, 64,* 15–22.

Schwartz, S., Luyckx, K., & Vignoles, L. (Eds.) (2011). *Handbook of identity theory and research,* 1–2. Springer.

Sequeira, S., Butterfield, R., Silk, J., Forbes, E., & Ladouceur, C. (2019). Neural activation to parental praise interacts with social context to predict adolescent depressive symptoms. *Frontiers in Behavioral Neuroscience, 13,* 222.

Shulman, S., & Collins, W. (1998). New directions for child development. *Romantic relationships in adolescence: Developmental Perspectives.* Jossey-Bass.

Skrzypiec, G., Wyra, M., & Didaskalou, E. (2020). *A global perspective of young adolescents` peer aggression and well-being: Beyond bullying.* Routledge.

Skuse, D., Bruce, H., & Dowdney, L. (2017). *Child psychology and psychiatry: Frameworks for clinical training and practice.* John Wiley.

Smith, H. (2008). Searching for kinship: The creation of street families among homeless youth. *American Behavioral Scientist, 51,* 756–771.

Smith, P., Kwak, K., & Toda, Y. (2016). *School bullying in different cultures: Eastern and Western perspectives.* Cambridge University Press.

Smith, R. (2015). Adolescents' emotional engagement in friends' problems and joys: Associations of empathetic distress and empathetic joy with friendship quality, depression, and anxiety. *Journal of Adolescence, 45,* 103–111.

Smith, R., & Rose, A. (2011). The "cost of caring" in youths' friendships: Considering associations among social perspective taking, co-rumination, and empathetic distress. *Developmental Psychology, 47*(6), 1792–1803.

Snarey, J., & Keljo, K. (1991). The cross-cultural expansion of moral development theory. *Handbook of moral behavior and development.* Lawrence Erlbaum.

Spear, L. (2010). *The behavioral neuroscience of adolescence.* Norton.

Spear, L. (2013). Adolescent neurodevelopment. *Journal of Adolescent Health, 52,* S7–S13.

Spear, L., & Silveri, M. (2016). Special issue on the adolescent brain. *Neuroscience and Biobehavioral Reviews, 70,* 1–3.

Spencer, C., Toews, M., Anders, K., & Emanuels, S. (2021). Risk markers for physical teen dating violence perpetration: A meta-analysis. *Trauma, Violence & Abuse, 22*(3), 619–631.

Stephenson, J. (2021). Children and teens struggling with mental health during COVID-19 pandemic. *JAMA Health Forum, 2*(6), e211701.

Stice, E., & Shaw, H. (2002). Role of body dissatisfaction in the onset and maintenance of eating pathology: A synthesis of research findings. *Journal of Psychosomatic Research, 53,* 985–993.

Strahan, E., Wilson, A., Cressman, K., & Buote, V. (2006). Comparing to perfection: How cultural norms for appearance affect social comparisons and self-image. *Body Image, 3*(3), 211–227.

Stynes, H., Lane, C., Pearson, B., Wright, T., Ranieri, V., Masic, U., & Kennedy, E. (2021). Gender identity development in children and young people: A systematic review of longitudinal studies. *Clinical Child Psychology & Psychiatry, 26*(3), 706–719.

Sumner, R., Burrow, A., & Hill, P. (2018). The development of purpose in life among adolescents who experience marginalization: Potential opportunities and obstacles. *American Psychologist, 73*(6), 740–752.

Thoma, S., Walker, D., Chen, Y., Frichand, A., Moulin-Stożek, D., & Kristjánsson, K. (2019). Adolescents' application of the virtues across five cultural contexts. *Developmental Psychology, 55*(10), 2181–2192.

Thomas, A., & Chess, S. (1977). *Temperament and development.* Brunner/Mazel.

Tiggemann, M. (2011). Sociocultural perspectives on human appearance and body image. In T. Cash & L. Smolak (Eds.), *Body image: A handbook of science, practice and prevention.* Guilford.

Tiggemann, M., & Slater, A. (2013). NetGirls: The internet, Facebook, and body image concern in adolescent girls. *International Journal of Eating Disorders, 46,* 630–634.

Turiel, E. (2002). *The culture of morality: Social development, context, and conflict.* Cambridge University Press.

Twenge, J., Spitzberg, B., & Campbell, W. (2019). Less in-person social interaction with peers among US adolescents in the 21st century and links to loneliness. *Journal of Social & Personal Relationships, 36*(6), 1892–1913.

Tylka, T., & Wood-Barcalow, N. (2015). A positive complement. *Body Image, 14,* 115–117.

United Nations Children's Fund (2014). *Hidden in plain sight: A statistical analysis of violence against children.* UNICEF.

van den Berg, Y., Burk, W., & Cillessen, A. (2015). Identifying subtypes of peer status by combining popularity and preference: A cohort-sequential approach. *Journal of Early Adolescence, 35*(8), 1108–1137.

Van der Graaff, J., Branje, S., De Wied, M., Hawk, S., Van Lier, P., & Meeus, W. (2014). Perspective taking and empathic concern in adolescence: Gender differences in developmental changes. *Developmental Psychology, 50*(3), 881–888.

Van Doeselaar, L., Becht, A., Klimstra, T., & Meeus, W. (2018). A review and integration of three key components of identity development. *European Psychologist, 23,* 278–288.

Van Holland De Graaf, J., Hoogenboom, M., De Roos, S., & Bucx, F. (2018). Socio-demographic correlates of fathers' and mothers' parenting behaviors. *Journal of Child and Family Studies, 27,* 2315–2327.

Vaquera, E., & Kao, G. (2008). Do you like me as much as I like you? Friendship reciprocity and its effects on school outcomes among adolescents. *Social Science Research, 37*(1), 55–72.

Voelker, D., Reel, J., & Greenleaf, C. (2015). Weight status and body image perceptions in adolescents: Current perspectives. *Adolescent Health, Medicine and Therapeutics, 6,* 149–158.

Waid, J., Tanana, M., Vanderloo, M., Voit, R., & Kothari, B. (2020). The role of siblings in the development of externalizing behaviors during childhood and adolescence: A scoping review. *Journal of Family Social Work, 23*(4), 318–337.

Waldrip, A., Malcolm, K., & Jensen-Campbell, L. (2008). With a little help from your friends: The importance of high-quality friendships on early adolescent adjustment. *Social Development, 17*(4), 832–852.

Walker, L. (2004). Gus in the gap: Bridging the judgment–action gap in moral functioning. In D. Lapsley & D. Narvaez (Eds.), *Moral development, self, and identity.* Erlbaum.

Wang, K., Chen, Y., Zhang, J., & Oudekerk, B. (2020). *Indicators of school crime and safety: 2019 (NCES 2020–063/ NCJ 254485).* National Center for Education Statistics, US Department of Education, and Bureau of Justice Statistics, Office of Justice Programs, US Department of Justice.

Wang, M., & Eccles, J. (2012). Social support matters: Longitudinal effects of social support on three dimensions of school engagement from middle to high school. *Child Development, 83*(3), 877–895.

Webb, H., & Zimmer-Gembeck, M. (2014). The role of friends and peers in adolescent body dissatisfaction: A review and critique of 15 years of research. *Journal of Research on Adolescence, 24*(4), 564–590.

Wentzel, K., Barry, C., & Caldwell, K. (2004). Friendships in middle school: Influences on motivation and school adjustment. *Journal of Educational Psychology, 96*(2), 195–203.

Whitbourne, S. (2002). Identity processes in adulthood: Theoretical and methodological challenges. *Identity: An International Journal of Theory and Research, 2,* 29–45.

White, R., & Renk, K. (2012). Externalizing behavior problems during adolescence: An ecological perspective. *Journal of Child and Family Studies, 21*(1), 158–171.

Whiteman, S., McHale, S., & Crouter, A. (2011). Family relationships from adolescence to early adulthood: Changes in the family system following firstborns' leaving home. *Journal of Research on Adolescence, 21*(2), 461–474.

Wiltz, T. (2017). *A hidden population: Youth homelessness is on the rise.* Pew Trust Research Center. https://www.pewtrusts.org/en/research-and-analysis/blogs/stateline/2017/07/07/a-hidden-population-youth-homelessness-is-on-the-rise

Wiseman, R. (2021). *Owning up: Empowering adolescents to create cultures of dignity and confront social cruelty and injustice.* Corwin.

Wolak, J., & Stapleton, C. (2020). Self-esteem and the development of partisan identity. *Political Research Quarterly, 73*(3), 609–622.

World Health Organization (2020). *Youth violence.* https://www.who.int/news-room/fact-sheets/detail/youth-violence

Xia, M., Fosco, G. M., Lippold, M. A., & Feinberg, M. E. (2018). A developmental perspective on young adult romantic relationships: Examining family and individual factors in adolescence. *Journal of Youth and Adolescence, 47*(7), 1499–1516.

Xie, M., Fowle, J., Ip, P., Haskin, M., & Yip, T. (2021). Profiles of ethnic-racial identity, socialization, and model minority experiences: Associations with well-being among Asian American adolescents. *Journal of Youth and Adolescence, 50*(6), 1173–1188.

Yang, C., Chan, M., & Ma, T. (2020). School-wide social emotional learning (SEL) and bullying victimization: Moderating role of school climate in elementary, middle, and high schools. *Journal of School Psychology, 82,* 49–69.

Yates, M., & Youniss, J. (1998). Community service and political identity development in adolescence. *Journal of Social Issues, 54*(3), 495–512.

Zarrett, N., & Eccles, J. (2006). The passage to adulthood: Challenges of late adolescence. *New Directions for Youth Development,* (111), 13–28.

Zimmer-Gembeck, M., Siebenbruner, J., & Collins, W. (2001). The divergent influence of romantic involvement on individual and social functioning from early to middle adolescence. *Journal of Adolescence, 24,* 313–336.

Index

Note: Page numbers followed by *f* indicate figures.